$m\angle ABC = 45°$; $12\% \times n = 75$; 1,

$c + 2.8 = 4.1$; $y = 2x + 4$; $A = \pi r^2$

$7^3 = 343$; $7x + 2x + 5 = 9x + 5$

$-1.2 + -3.45$; $\frac{n}{100}$

$c + 2.8 = 4.1$; $12\% \times n = 75$; 1, 1, 2, 3, 5, 8, . . .

$+2x + 5 = 9x + 5$; $-1.2 + -3.45$; $\frac{n}{100} = \frac{81}{300}$

$c + 2.8 = 4.1$; $12\% \times n = 75$; 1, 1, 2, 3, 5, 8,

$m\angle ABC = 45°$; $y = 2x + 4$; A

$c + 2.8 = 4.1$; $12\% \times n =$

PREPARATION FOR ALGEBRA

Math

ADVANTAGE

Orlando • Atlanta • Austin • Boston • San Francisco • Chicago • Dallas • New York • Toronto • London

http://www.hbschool.com

Printed in the United States of America

ISBN 0-15-311440-1

11 12 13 14 15 032 07 06 05 04 03

Senior Authors

Grace M. Burton
Chair, Department of Curricular Studies
Professor, School of Education
University of North Carolina at Wilmington
Wilmington, North Carolina

Evan M. Maletsky
Professor of Mathematics
Montclair State University
Upper Montclair, New Jersey

Authors

George W. Bright
Professor of Mathematics Education
The University of North Carolina at Greensboro
Greensboro, North Carolina

Sonia M. Helton
Professor of Childhood Education
Coordinator, College of Education
University of South Florida
St. Petersburg, Florida

Loye Y. (Mickey) Hollis
Professor of Mathematics Education
Director of Teacher Education and Undergraduate Programs
University of Houston
Houston, Texas

Howard C. Johnson
Dean of the Graduate School
Associate Vice Chancellor for Academic Affairs
Professor, Mathematics and Mathematics Education
Syracuse University
Syracuse, New York

Joyce C. McLeod
Visiting Professor
Rollins College
Winter Park, Florida

Evelyn M. Neufeld
Professor, College of Education
San Jose State University
San Jose, California

Vicki Newman
Classroom Teacher
McGaugh Elementary School
Los Alamitos Unified School District
Seal Beach, California

Terence H. Perciante
Professor of Mathematics
Wheaton College
Wheaton, Illinois

Karen A. Schultz
Associate Dean and Director of Graduate Studies and Research
Research Professor, Mathematics Education
College of Education
Georgia State University
Atlanta, Georgia

Muriel Burger Thatcher
Independent Mathematics Consultant
Mathematical Encounters
Pine Knoll Shores, North Carolina

Advisors

Anne R. Biggins
Speech-Language Pathologist
Fairfax County Public Schools
Fairfax, Virginia

Carolyn Gambrel
Learning Disabilities Teacher
Fairfax County Public Schools
Fairfax, Virginia

Lois Harrison-Jones
Education Consultant
Dallas, Texas

Asa G. Hilliard, III
Fuller E. Callaway Professor of Urban Education
Georgia State University
Atlanta, Georgia

Marsha W. Lilly
Secondary Mathematics Coordinator
Alief Independent School District
Alief, Texas

Judith Mayne Wallis
Elementary Language Arts/ Social Studies/Gifted Coordinator
Alief Independent School District
Houston, Texas

Focus on Problem Solving

NUMBER SENSE — CHAPTERS 1–2

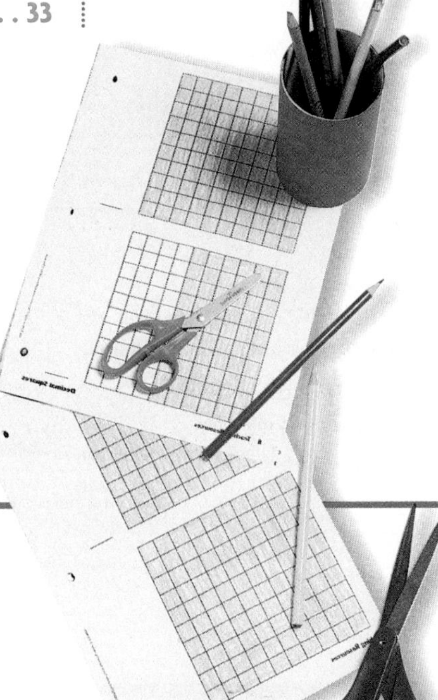

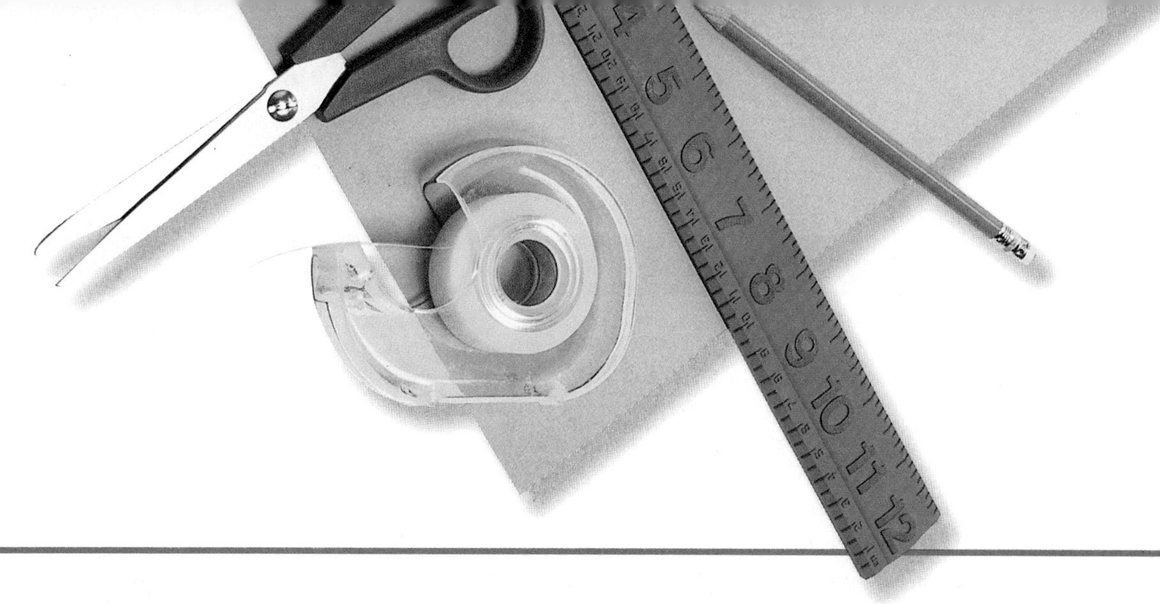

Assessment Checkpoint ✓ Chapters 1–2

OPERATIONS CHAPTERS 3–5

Key Skills

Key Skills

CHAPTER 5 • Operations with Integers and Rational Numbers

Key Skills

Assessment Checkpoint ✓ Chapters 3–5

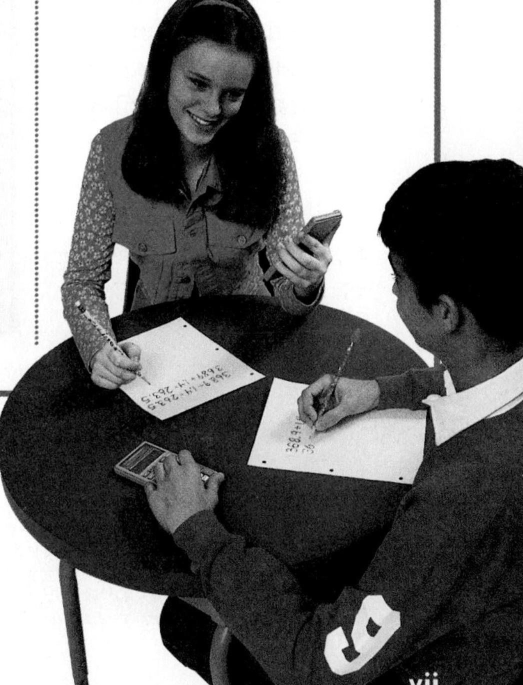

ALGEBRA CHAPTERS 6–9

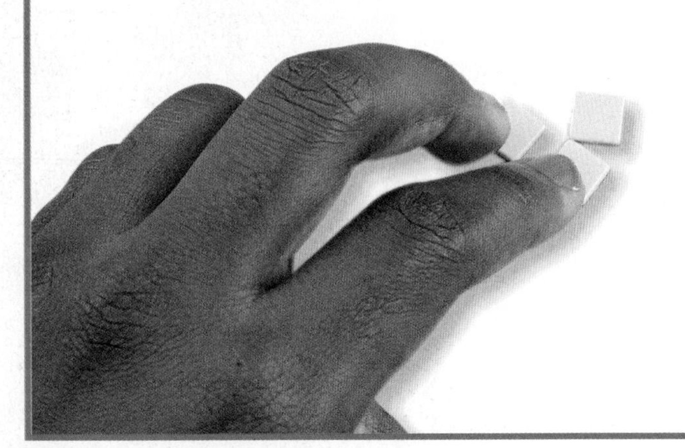

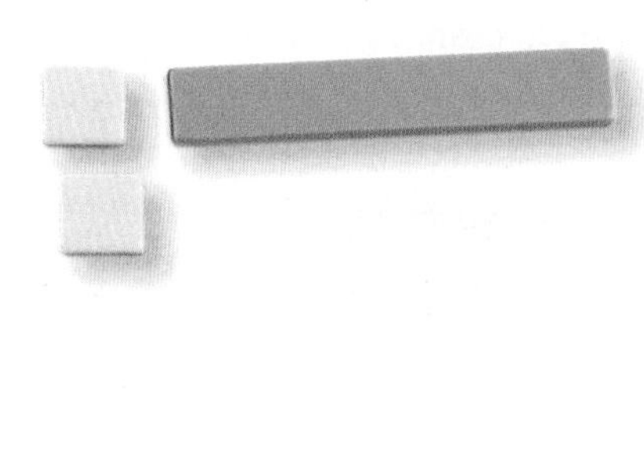

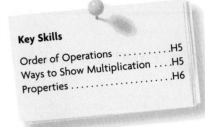

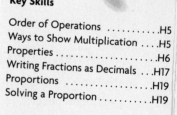

CHAPTER 8 • Algebra: Solving Two-Step Equations and Inequalities 158

CHAPTER 9 • Algebra: Exploring Linear Equations .. 174

Assessment Checkpoint ✓ Chapters 6–9

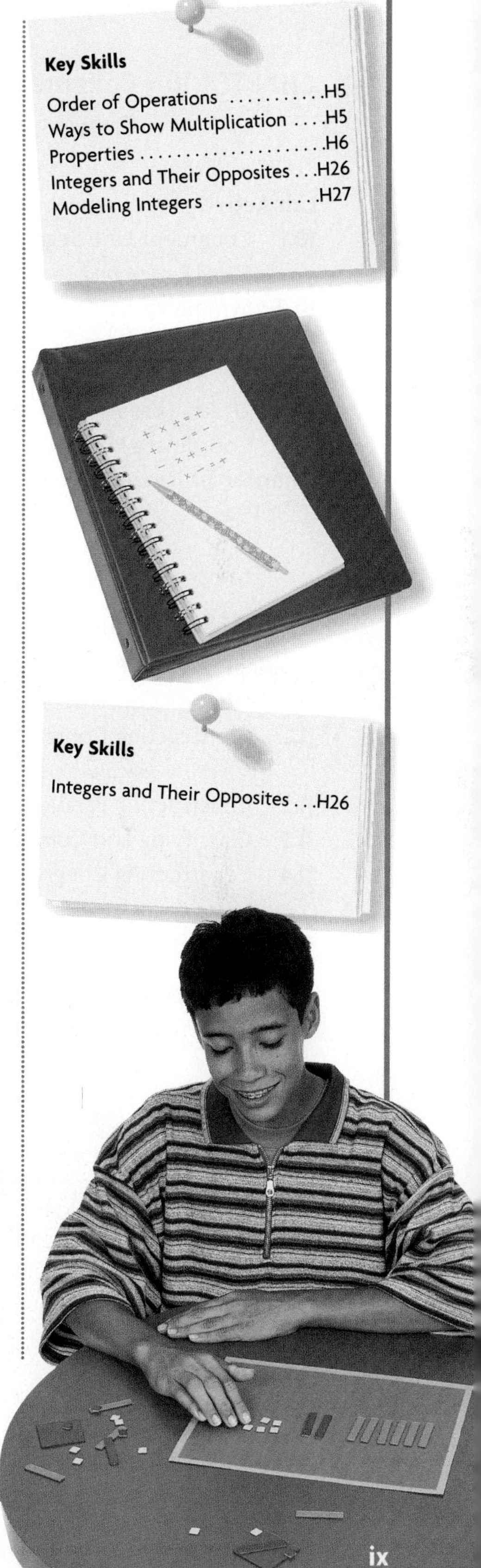

CHAPTER 10 • Congruence, Symmetry, and Transformations

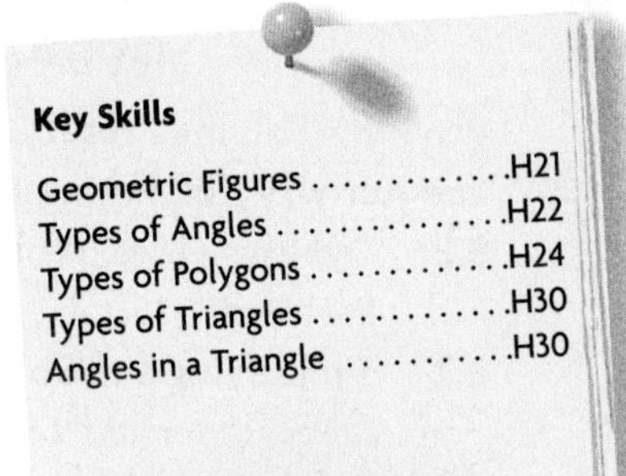

CHAPTER 11 • Constructing and Drawing

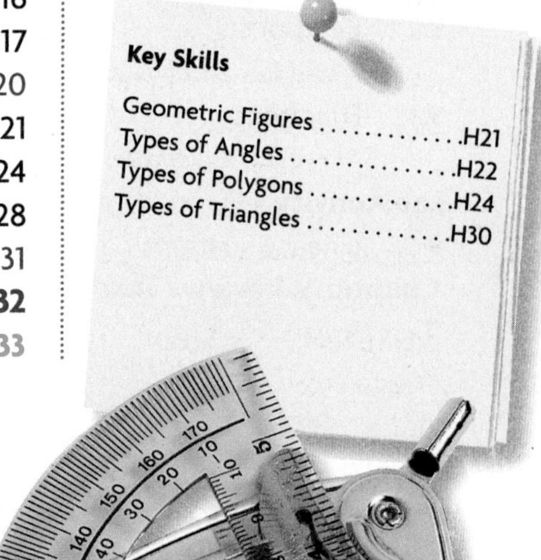

CHAPTER 12 • Picturing and Modeling Solid Figures

Key Skills

CHAPTER 13 • Changing Geometric Shapes

Key Skills

Assessment Checkpoint ✓ Chapters 10–13

PROPORTIONAL REASONING CHAPTERS 14–17

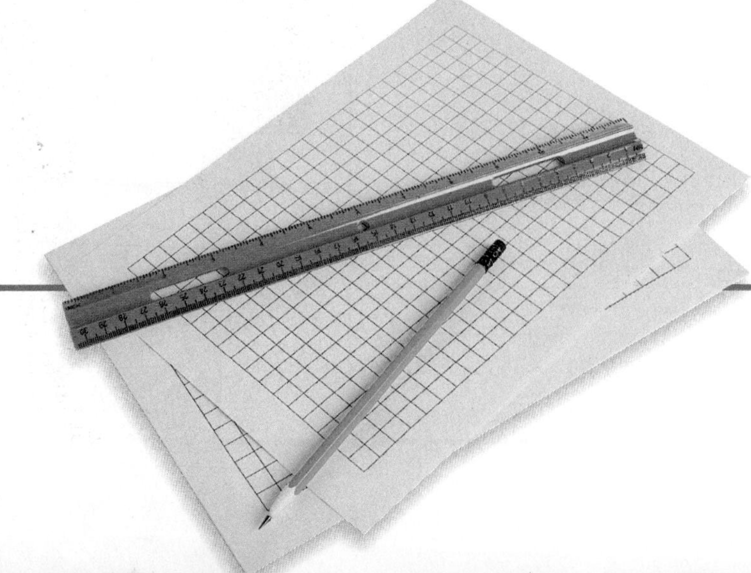

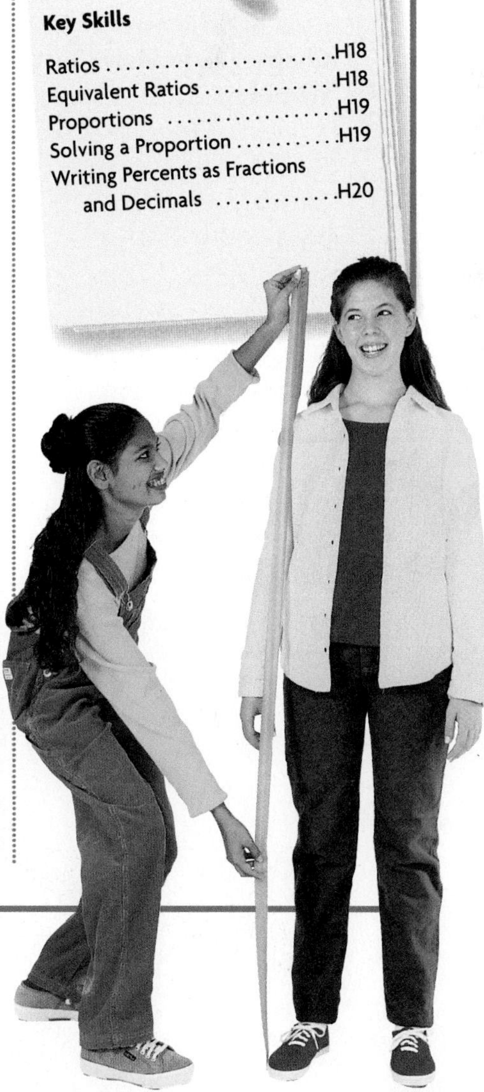

Key Skills

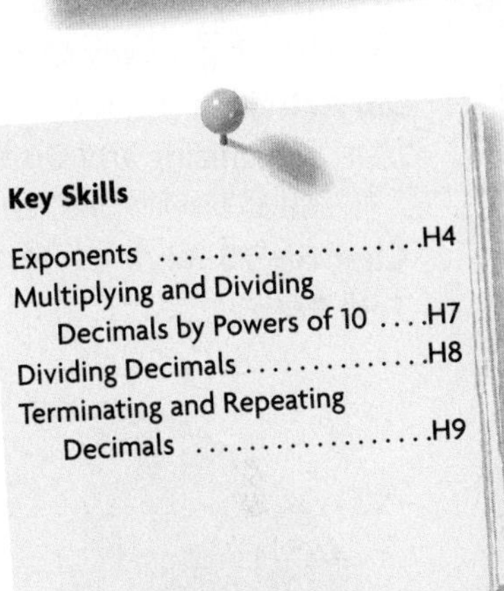

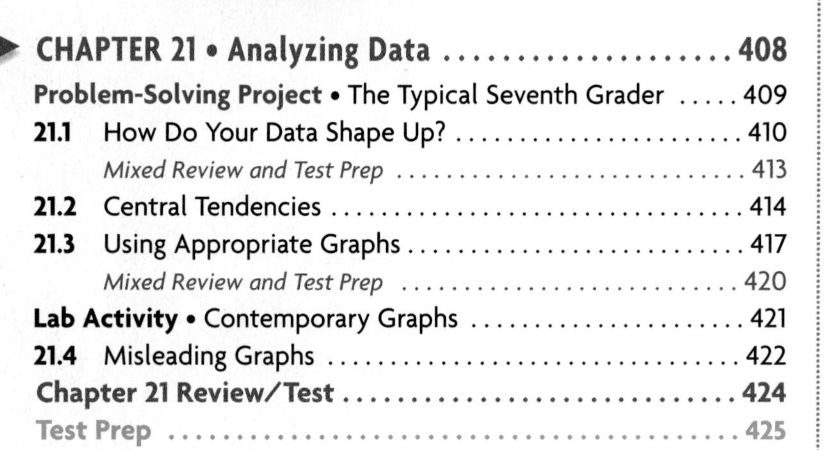

Key Skills

CHAPTER 22 • Data and Probability 426

Key Skills

CHAPTER 23 • Experiments with Probability 442

Key Skills

Assessment Checkpoint ✓ Chapters 20–23

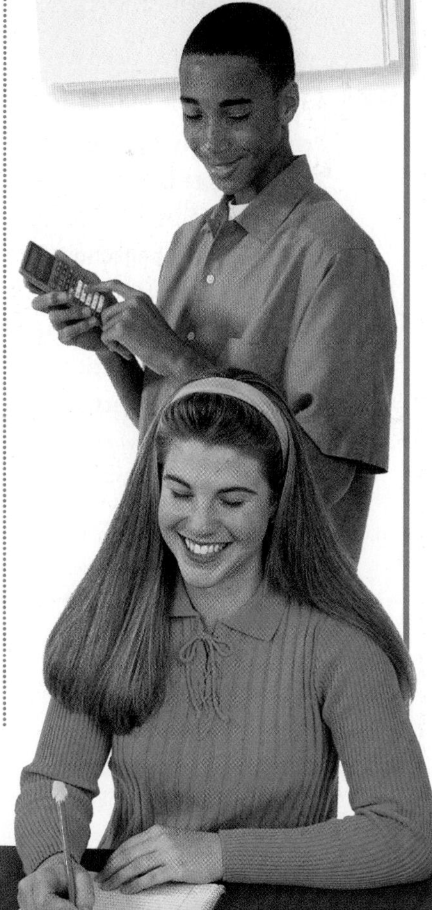

Key Skills

Key Skills

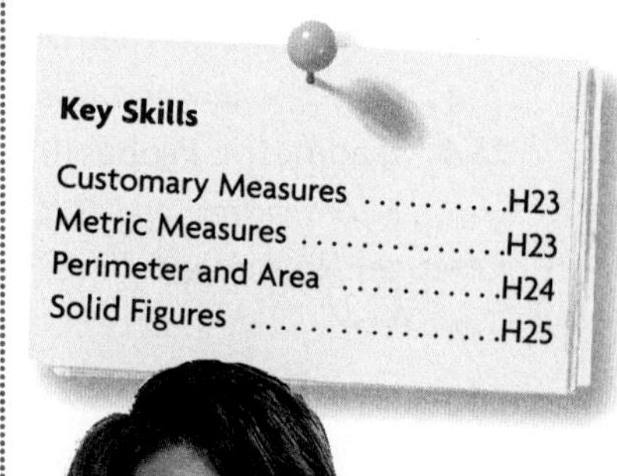

Key Skills

Assessment Checkpoint ✓ Chapters 24–26

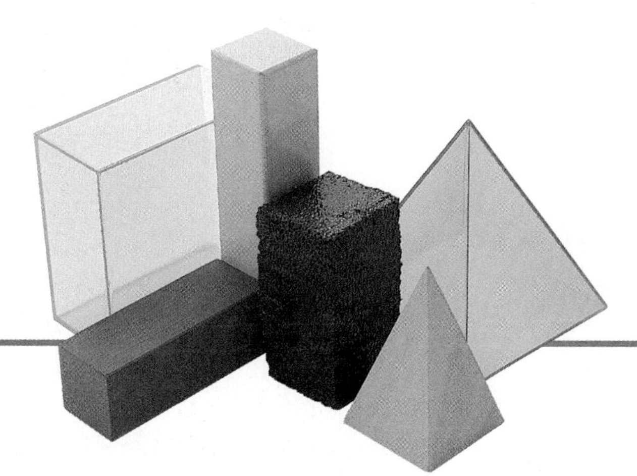

Key Skills

Assessment Checkpoint ✓Chapters 27–28

STUDENT HANDBOOK

FOCUS ON PROBLEM SOLVING

Good problem solvers need to be good thinkers. They also need to know these strategies.

- Draw a Diagram
- Act It Out
- Make a Model
- Use a Formula
- Work Backward
- Find a Pattern
- Guess and Check
- Solve a Simpler Problem
- Make a Table or Graph
- Write an Equation
- Account for All Possibilities

After a strategy has been chosen, a good problem solver then decides how to solve the problem. They think about whether using paper or pencil, a calculator, manipulatives, or mental math is the best way to get the answer.

CHOOSE a strategy and a tool.

- **Draw a Diagram**
- **Make a Model**
- **Use a Formula**
- **Write an Equation**

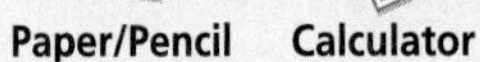

Paper/Pencil | Calculator | Hands-On | Mental Math

A good problem solver thinks through a problem carefully before trying to solve it. This plan can help you learn how to think through a problem.

UNDERSTAND the problem

Ask yourself...	Then try this.
What is the problem about?	Retell the problem in your own words.
What is the question?	Say the question as a fill-in-the-blank sentence.
What information is given?	List the information given in the problem.

PLAN how to solve it

Ask yourself...	Then try this.
What strategies might I use?	List some strategies you can use.
About what will the answer be?	Predict what your answer will be. Make an estimate if it will help.

SOLVE the problem

Ask yourself...	Then try this.
How can I solve the problem?	Follow your plan and show your solution.
How can I write my answer?	Write your answer in a complete sentence.

LOOK BACK and check your answer

Ask yourself...	Then try this.
How can I tell if my answer is reasonable?	Compare your answer to your estimate. Check your answer by redoing your work. Match your answer to the question.
How else might I have solved the problem?	Try using another strategy to solve the problem.

On the following pages, you can practice being a good problem solver. Each page reviews a different strategy that you can use throughout the year. These pages will help you recognize the kinds of problems that can be solved with each strategy. Think through each problem you work on and ask yourself questions as you **Understand**, **Plan**, **Solve**, and **Look Back**. Then be proud of your success!

PROBLEM SOLVING

- **Understand**
- **Plan**
- **Solve**
- **Look Back**

Draw a Diagram

Katelynn has two sheets of paper $8\frac{1}{2}$ in. by 11 in. She cuts out a 3 in. square from the center top edge of one of the sheets. Which has the greater perimeter, the sheet with the square cut out or the uncut sheet? How much greater?

UNDERSTAND You must find the dimensions of the cut sheet of paper. You know the dimensions of the uncut sheet.

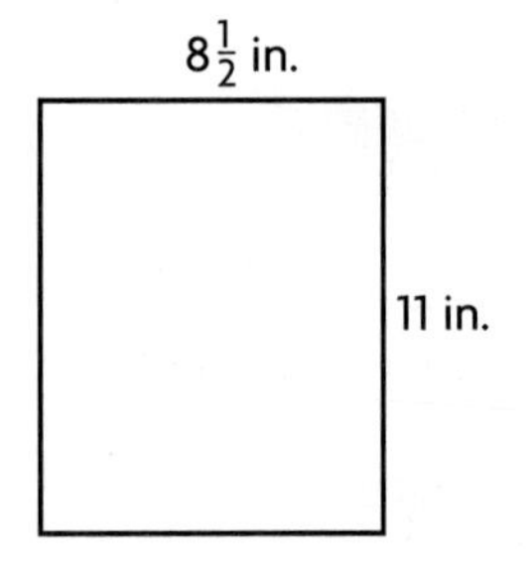

PLAN Draw a diagram of both sheets of paper. Label all the sides of the uncut sheet. Picture and sketch the other sheet with the 3-in. square removed from the center of the top.

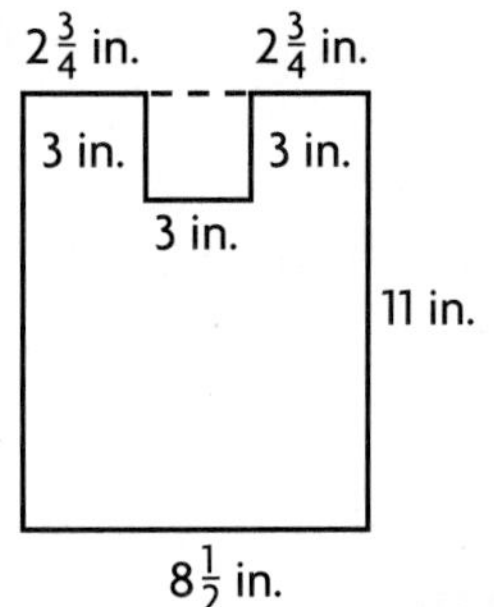

SOLVE Use the diagrams to find the perimeters.

The perimeter of the uncut sheet is the sum of the four sides:
$8\frac{1}{2}$ in. + 11 in. + $8\frac{1}{2}$ in. + 11 in. = 39 in.

The cut sheet has two additional edges that should be added to its perimeter.

So, the perimeter of the cut sheet is greater. It has 3 in. + 3 in., or 6 additional inches.

LOOK BACK The sum of the lengths of the uncut sheet is 39 in. The sum of the lengths of the cut sheet is 39 in. + 6 in. = 45 in. ✓

Try These

1. A refreshment table at the school carnival is 10 ft long and 4 ft wide. Sarah is putting balloons 1 ft apart on three sides with a balloon at each corner. How many balloons will she need?
2. Amid hammered nails into a board to make a circular pegboard. The nails were the same distance apart, and the 6th nail was directly opposite the 18th nail. How many nails formed the circle?
3. The sign post shows the distance to four places along a trail. How far is Sugar Creek from the campsite?

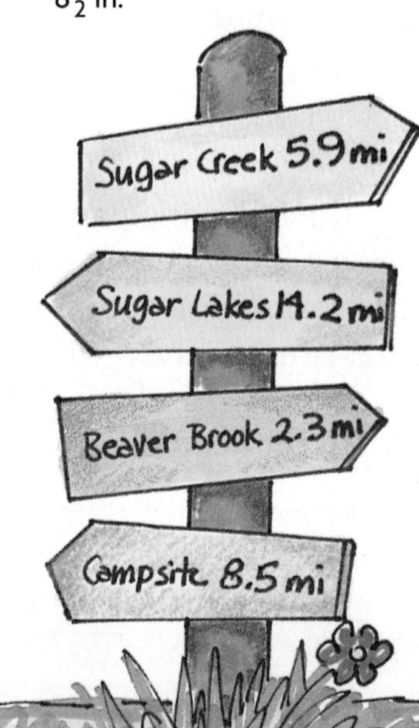

Act It Out

Todd bought a baseball card for $15, sold it to a friend for $20, bought it back for $22, and then sold it for $30. How much money did Todd make or lose?

UNDERSTAND You need to find the amount of money Todd gained or lost.

PLAN You can act out the purchases and sales using slips of paper for the cards and for the money. Set up 2 places: one for Todd and one for the buyer. Let Todd begin with $100. His friend begins with the baseball card.

Todd's Account	Friend
$100	card

SOLVE

Todd buys the card from his friend for $15. $\$100 - \$15 = \$85 +$ card
Todd sells the card for $20. $\$85 + \$20 = \$105$
Todd buys the card back for $22. $\$105 - \$22 = \$83 +$ card
Finally, Todd sells the card for $30. $\$83 + \$30 = \$113$

So, Todd now has $13 more than the $100 he began with.

LOOK BACK Is it reasonable that Todd made a $13 profit?

Tally the amount: he spent buying $\$15 + \$22 = \$37$
he received selling $\$20 + \$30 = \$50$

The difference is $13. ✓

Try These

1. A teacher has to select 1 of her 20 students to represent their homeroom on the student council. She places the students in a circle and gives each a number, from 1 through 20. Then starting with student 2, she sends every other student back to his or her seat. She sends student 2 back, student 4 back, student 6 back, and so on, until she goes completely around the circle. She continues skipping every other student until only 1 person is left. In which position should a student stand in order to be selected to represent the homeroom on the student council?

2. A shipper has packed 3 large boxes. Inside each large box there are 4 medium boxes. Inside each medium box are 5 separate small boxes. How many boxes are there altogether?

PROBLEM SOLVING

- **Understand**
- **Plan**
- **Solve**
- **Look Back**

Make a Model

A game company packages 6 mini-puzzles in a decorated 4-in. cube. They are shipped to the toy stores in cartons. Twenty cubes fit in the carton. What are the dimensions of the carton?

UNDERSTAND You must find the dimensions of the carton.

You know the size of each cube and how many fit in the carton.

PLAN Use 20 cubes and arrange them so that they can be packed. Record the dimensions.
Do you think there could be more than one way to pack the 20 cubes?

SOLVE Find the length, width, and height of 20 cubes ready for shipping. Sketch your model and record the dimensions. In this model, the length is 20 in., the width is 8 in., and the height is 8 in. So the dimensions of this carton are 20 in. × 8 in. × 8 in. Other possible solutions are 40 in. × 8 in. × 4 in. and 80 in. × 4 in. × 4 in.

LOOK BACK The volume of each carton should equal the volume of the 20 cubes.

volume of cartons: 8 in. × 20 in. × 8 in. = 1,280 in.^{3}
40 in. × 8 in. × 4 in. = 1,280 in.^{3}
80 in. × 4 in. × 4 in. = 1,280 in.^{3}

volume of 1 cube: 4 in. × 4 in. × 4 in. = 64 in.^{3}
volume of 20 cubes: 20 × 64 = 1,280 in.^{3}

1,280 in.^{3} = 1,280 in.^{3} ✓

Try These

1. Glenda has a plan for building triangle tessellations from toothpicks. Her plan looks like this:

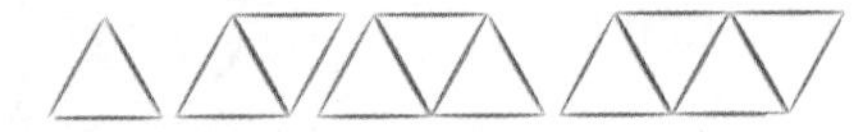

If she has a box of 100 toothpicks, how many triangles would be in the largest shape she could make?

2. John used exactly 8 cubes to form a rectangular prism. Find the length, width, and height of the prism.

Guess and Check

PROBLEM SOLVING

- Understand
- Plan
- Solve
- Look Back

Riding the bus to work costs $0.75. Taking a taxi to work costs $3.25. During the week, Judy took 10 rides and spent $12.50. How many times did Judy take a taxi to work that week?

UNDERSTAND You must find the number of taxi rides Judy took to work. You know the cost of each type of ride, the number of rides, and the total amount Judy spent for the week.

PLAN Guess a number of taxi and bus rides totaling 10. Check to see if the cost of both totals $12.50.

SOLVE Record your first guess and total the cost of both rides.

	Rides	Cost	
Taxi	1 ×	$3.25 =	$3.25
Bus	9 ×	$0.75 =	$6.75
	10		= $10.00

$10.00 is too low. Increase the number of taxi rides to 2:

	Rides	Cost	
Taxi	2 ×	$3.25 =	$6.50
Bus	8 ×	$0.75 =	$6.00
	10		= $12.50

So, the number of taxi rides is 2.

LOOK BACK The cost of the taxi rides and the cost of the bus rides should equal $12.50.

$6.50 + $6.00 = $12.50 ✓

Try These

1. How many triangles, rectangles, and pentagons would you need to have a total of 38 vertices?
2. Louise was playing darts. She threw 6 darts and all 6 hit the target. Which of the following could be her scores?
   4, 17, 18, 28, 29, 31, 57

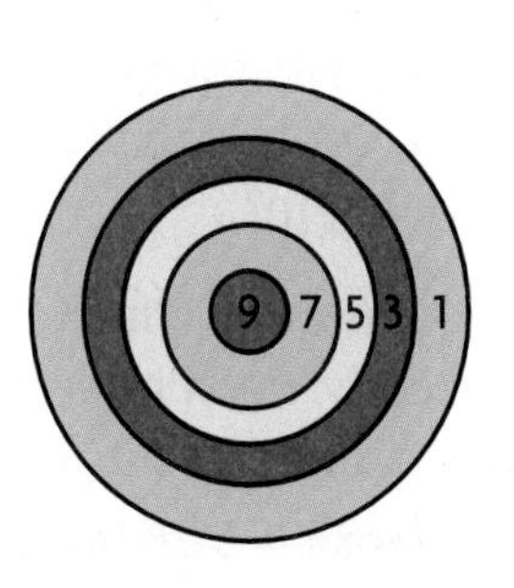

3. Cassettes cost $12. Compact discs cost $15. Your total cost is $120 before sales tax. How many different combinations of cassettes and CDs could you have purchased?

PROBLEM SOLVING

- Understand
- Plan
- Solve
- Look Back

Work Backward

Michael started with a number, and performed the operations shown below. His final number was 6. What was the starting number?

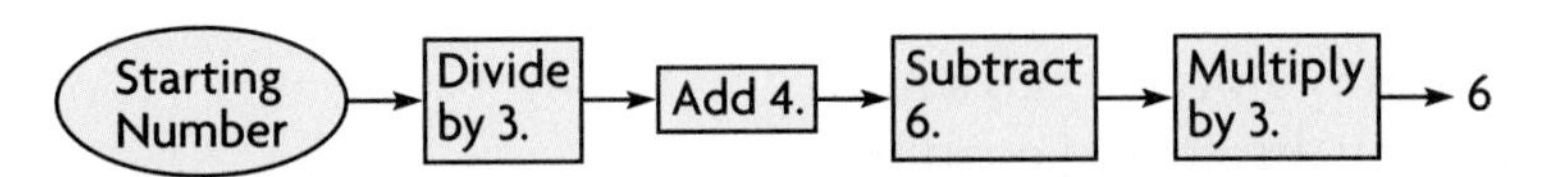

UNDERSTAND You must find the starting number. You know the ending number.

PLAN Start from the end and work backward. Draw the arrow in the opposite direction and do the opposite, or inverse operation.

SOLVE Work from the ending number of 6. Do the inverse of each operation. Move from right to left.

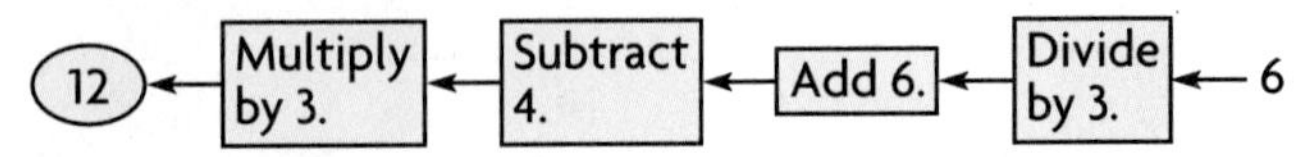

So, 12 is the starting number.

LOOK BACK Check the original problem using 12 as the starting number.

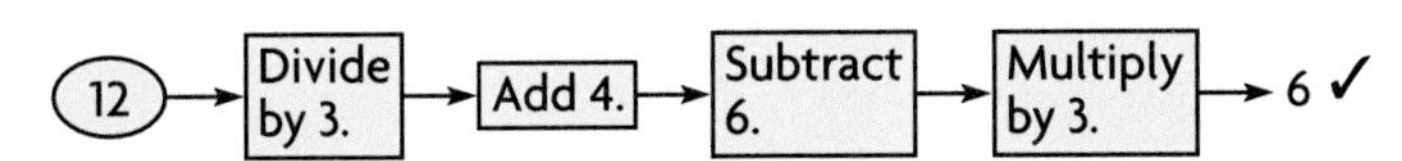

Try These

1. Missouri City's streets are numbered and the avenues are lettered. To get to school on the corner of 9th Street and Avenue E, Philip walks 2 blocks north, 4 blocks east, 1 block north, and 3 blocks east. On what corner does Philip live?

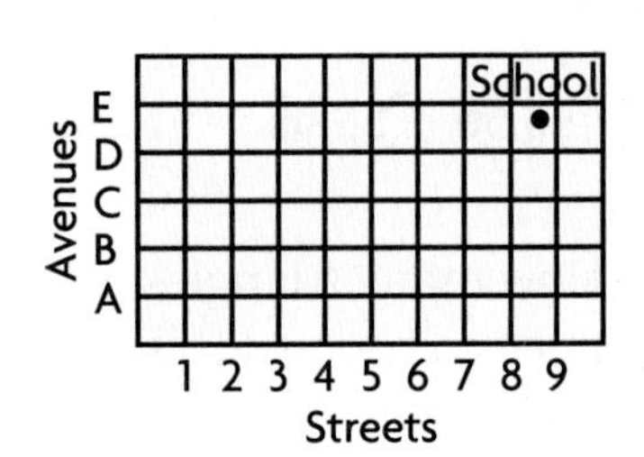

2. The Craft Show is after school on Friday, October 19. Each school day, the seventh-grade class can make 9 items for the show. Their goal is to submit 100 items. On what day should work begin?

3. In the math trivia bowl, each finalist must answer 4 questions correctly. Each question is worth twice as much as the question before it. The fourth question is worth $1,000. How much is the first question worth?

PROBLEM SOLVING

- **Understand**
- **Plan**
- **Solve**
- **Look Back**

Account for All Possibilities

Sarah made a pair of identical number cubes. She wrote the numbers from 5 through 10 on each cube. If she rolls the two cubes, how many different sums can she get?

UNDERSTAND You must find all the possible sums that can be rolled. You know the numbers on the face of each cube.

PLAN Make a list to account for all possible sums of pairs of numbers you can get when rolling the two number cubes.

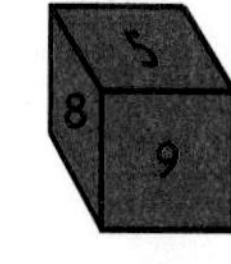

SOLVE List all the possible sums. Since pairs like 5-6 and 6-5 give the same sum, list only one of them.

Pairs	Sum
5-5	10
5-6	11
5-7	12
5-8	13
5-9	14
5-10	15

Pairs	Sum
6-6	12
6-7	13
6-8	14
6-9	15
6-10	16

Pairs	Sum
7-7	14
7-8	15
7-9	16
7-10	17

Pairs	Sum
8-8	16
8-9	17
8-10	18

Pairs	Sum
9-9	18
9-10	19

Pairs	Sum
10-10	20

There are 21 possible pairs. Several of the sums repeat. For example, $5 + 7 = 12$ and $6 + 6 = 12$. List each sum only once.

10, 11, 12, 13, 14, 15, 16, 17, 18, 19, 20 ← 11 different sums

LOOK BACK The sums range from 10 through 20. Listing each sum once, there are 11 different sums. ✓

Try These

1. How many times would the digit, 7, be written if you wrote down all the numbers from 1 to 100?
2. There are 4 runners in a race. In how many different ways can the runners finish first, second, third, or fourth?
3. Clem has this ballot for the seventh-grade election. How many different election outcomes are possible for president, secretary, and treasurer?

BALLOT

PRESIDENT: Tina ❑, Tom ❑
SECRETARY: John ❑, Jake ❑, Ginger ❑
TREASURER: Maxine ❑, Seth ❑, Phillip ❑, Larry ❑, Eby ❑

PROBLEM SOLVING

- Understand
- Plan
- Solve
- Look Back

Find a Pattern

Kari is helping her father design a border for their pond in the shape of a regular octagon. How can they find the measure of each angle of the regular octagon?

UNDERSTAND You must determine the measure of each interior angle of a regular octagon.

PLAN Look for a pattern in the sums of the measures of the angles of other polygons. Use the pattern to find the sum for the angles of an octagon. Divide the sum by 8.

SOLVE Recall that the sum of the angles of a triangle is 180°. Draw a triangle, quadrilateral, pentagon, and hexagon. Separate each into triangles.

triangle

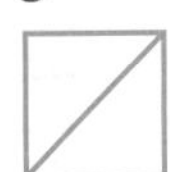
quadrilateral

pentagon

hexagon

Make a table to record and analyze your data.

Polygon	Sides	Triangles	Sum of Angle Measures
triangle	3	1	$(1 \times 180°)$ or $180°$
quadrilateral	4	2	$(2 \times 180°)$ or $360°$
pentagon	5	3	$(3 \times 180°)$ or $540°$
hexagon	6	4	$(4 \times 180°)$ or $720°$
n-gon	n	$n - 2$	$(n - 2) \times 180°$

Use the pattern to find the sum of the angles of an octagon.

$$(8 - 2) \times 180° = 6 \times 180° = 1{,}080°$$

Each angle of a regular octagon measures $1{,}080° \div 8$ or $135°$.

LOOK BACK You can check your answer by using a protractor to measure one angle of a regular octagon. ✓

Try These

Find the measure of each angle of the regular polygon.

1. hexagon **2.** nonagon **3.** decagon **4.** 18-gon **5.** 25-gon

Make a Table or Graph

PROBLEM SOLVING

- **Understand**
- **Plan**
- **Solve**
- **Look Back**

Wendy and Macalia both bought a half gallon of milk today. Wendy buys milk every 4 days and Macalia buys milk every 5 days. If today's date is November 1, when will Wendy and Macalia again buy milk on the same day?

UNDERSTAND You need to know on which day both will buy milk. You know they both bought milk on November 1. You know when each returns to buy milk.

PLAN Make a table showing the days each person returns to the store.

SOLVE Identify each person's trip to the store in the table with an X. For Wendy, add an X on every fourth day after November 1 and so on. For Macalia, add an X every fifth day after November 1.

The table shows that they will again buy milk on the same day on November 21.

	Wendy	Macalia
Nov 1	X	X
2		
3		
4		
5	X	
6		X
7		
8		
9	X	
10		
11		X
12		
13	X	
14		
15		
16		X
17	X	
18		
19		
20		
21	X	X
22		
23		

LOOK BACK The sum of 1 and five 4s should equal the sum of 1 and four 5s.

$1 + 4 + 4 + 4 + 4 + 4 = 21$ $\quad$ $1 + 5 + 5 + 5 + 5 = 21$ ✓

Try These

1. The machines in the exact change lane of a tollway accept any combination of coins that total exactly 75¢, but they do not accept pennies or half dollars. In how many different ways can a driver pay the toll in an exact change lane?

2. Oblong rectangular numbers can be made by a rectangular array with the length one unit more than the width. The first three oblong rectangular numbers are shown below. Find the 10th oblong rectangular number.

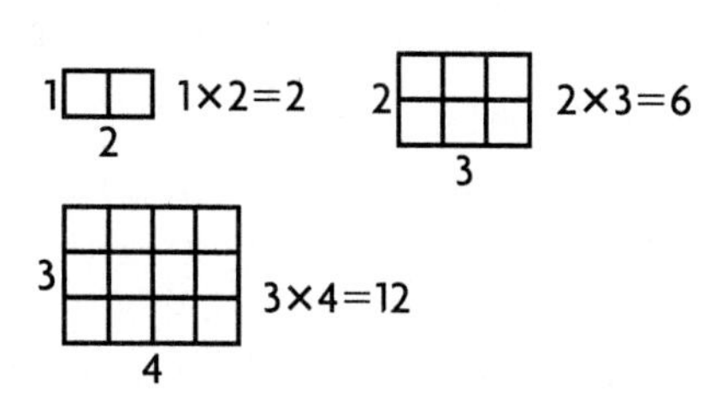

3. Jess, Kathy, and Linda work on the newpaper for the math club. One is the editor, one is a reporter, and one is a word processor. Linda's only exercise is swimming. Jess and the editor play tennis together. Linda and the reporter are cousins. Find each person's job.

PROBLEM SOLVING

- **Understand**
- **Plan**
- **Solve**
- **Look Back**

Solve a Simpler Problem

How many squares are contained in this 7-stair figure? Include squares of all sizes.

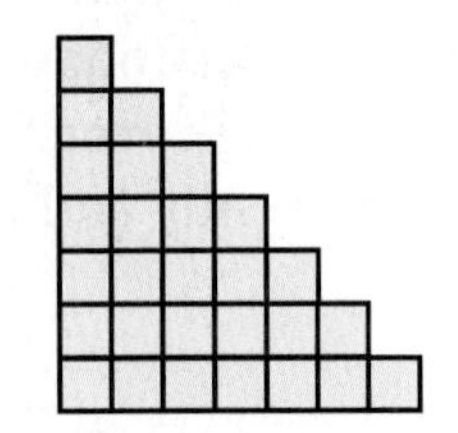

UNDERSTAND You know that there are 1×1 squares in the figure. You need to know what other size squares there are and choose a procedure for counting them.

PLAN Make simpler stair figures. Collect and record the data on a table. Look for a pattern.

SOLVE Sketch each stair figure and count the 1×1, 2×2, 3×3, and 4×4 squares in each. Analyze the number patterns in each of the simpler figures as the data is collected.

Squares	1-stair	2-stair	3-stair	4-stair	5-stair	6-stair	7-stair
1×1	1	3	6	10	15	21	28
2×2	0	0	1	3	6	10	15
3×3	0	0	0	0	1	3	6
4×4	0	0	0	0	0	0	1
Total	1	3	7	13	22	34	50

So, there are 50 squares in the 7-stair figure.

LOOK BACK You can check your answer by drawing the 7-stair figure and systematically counting all of the squares.

Try These

1. The numbers 11; 444; and 8,888 all contain repeated, single digits. How many numbers between 10 and 1,000,000 contain repeated, single digits?

2. How many diagonals are there in a dodecagon (a 12-sided polygon)?

Use a Formula

Michael is putting a border around his rectangular garden. The garden is 12.5 ft wide and 22 ft long. How many feet of border will he need for his garden?

UNDERSTAND You are asked to find the amount of border Michael will need to go around his garden. You know the width and length of the garden.

PLAN The distance around the garden is the perimeter. You can use the formula for the perimeter of a rectangle, $P = 2w + 2l$, where P is the perimeter, w is the width, and l is the length.

SOLVE Use the formula to find the perimeter. The width is 12.5 ft and the length is 22 ft.

$P = 2w + 2l$

$P = 2 \times 12.5 + 2 \times 22$ *Replace w with 12.5 and l with 22.*

$P = 25 + 44$

$P = 69$

So, Michael will need 69 ft of border for his garden.

LOOK BACK The sum of all the lengths of the sides of the garden should equal 69 ft.

12.5 ft + 22 ft + 12.5 ft + 22 ft = 69 ft ✓

Try These

1. A taxi charges $3.75 for the first mile plus $2.50 for each additional mile. How much would a 12-mi trip cost? Use the formula, $C = \$3.75 + \$2.50m$ where m is each additional mile.

2. If the diameter of a music CD is 4.5 in., what is its circumference? Use $C = \pi d$ and use 3.14 for π.

3. The floor of a room is 6 yd long and $4\frac{1}{2}$ ft wide. How many square yards of carpet will be needed to completely cover the floor? The formula for the area of a rectangle is $A = l \times w$.

PROBLEM SOLVING

- **Understand**
- **Plan**
- **Solve**
- **Look Back**

Write an Equation

A solid cube is 1 in. × 1 in. × 1 in. and weighs 1 pound. What would the weight of a cube made of the same material be if each of the sides were doubled?

UNDERSTAND In the smaller cube, volume and weight are compared. You know the volume of the larger cube but the weight is unknown.

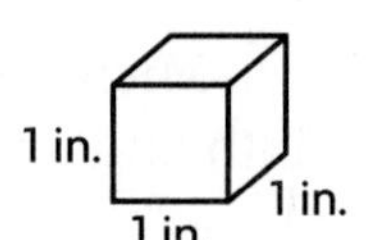

PLAN The same two things are compared in both cases. Compare the volume and weight of each cube.

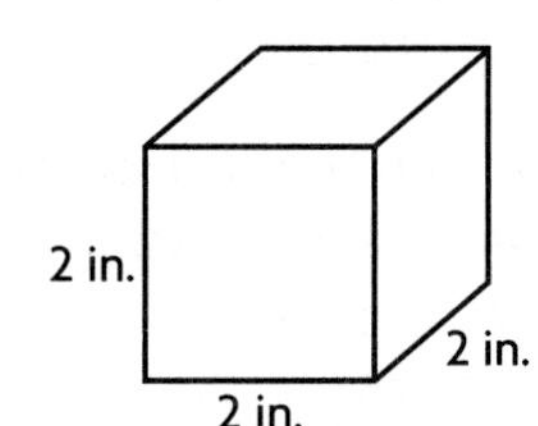

SOLVE Use a proportion to compare the cubes. Then solve the proportion.

	1-in. Cube		**2-in. Cube**
Volume (in.^{3})→ / Weight (lb)→	$\frac{1 \times 1 \times 1}{1}$	$=$	$\frac{2 \times 2 \times 2}{w}$

$\frac{1}{1} = \frac{8}{w}$ *Find the cross products.*

$1 \times 8 = 1 \times w$ *Solve for w.*

$8 = w$

So, the weight of the larger cube is 8 lb.

LOOK BACK The large cube can be thought of as 8 small cubes. If each small cube weighs 1 lb, then the large cube weighs 8 × 1, or 8 lb.

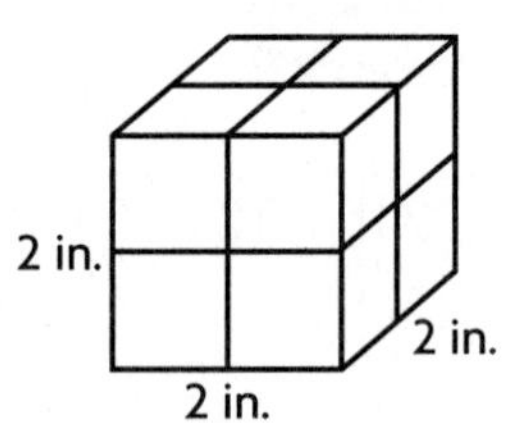

Try These

1. A rectangle 27 cm long and 15 cm wide was reduced on the copy machine. The reduced rectangle is 9 cm long. What is its width?

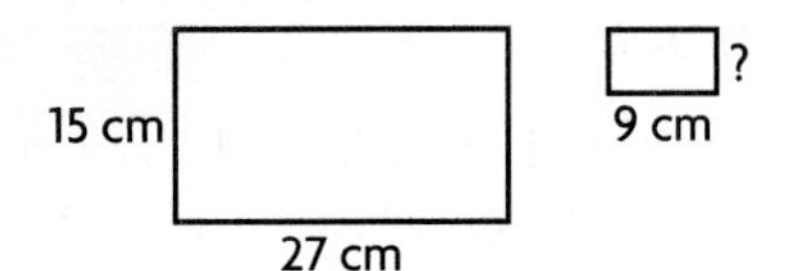

2. If 5 peaches cost $0.85, what would be the cost of 16 peaches at the same rate?

MIXED APPLICATONS

Use the strategy of your choice to solve.

1. On Saturday afternoon, six friends agreed to call each other. Each friend talked to every other friend once. How many phone calls were made?

2. How many people can be seated at 12 square tables lined up end-to-end if each table individually holds four persons?

3. At a banquet the caterer allows 3 desserts for every 2 people. How many desserts must she prepare for 50 people?

4. A rectangular field has a perimeter of 220 meters and an area of 2,976 m^2. What are the dimensions of the field?

5. You are at a phone booth with $1.60 in your pocket and you need to make a long distance call. The call costs $0.25 for the first minute and $0.15 for each additional minute. How long can you talk?

6. Jackita bought 20 lb of dog food. The dog food is packaged in 2, 4, and 8 lb bags. How many bags of each size could Jackita have bought?

7. Look for a pattern in the sums of the first 6 rows of Pascal's Triangle. Then, find the sum of the numbers of the tenth row.

1
1 1
1 2 1
1 3 3 1
1 4 6 4 1
1 5 10 10 5 1

8. How many different ways are there to get from A to Z? The only allowable moves are right (R) and up (U).

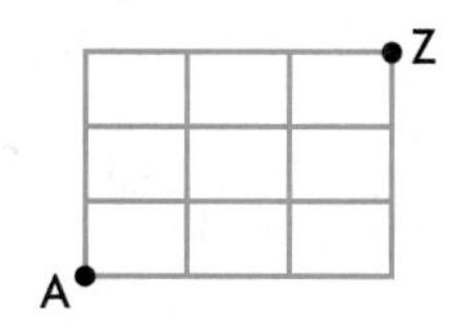

9. The standard size for business cards is 2 in. × 3.5 in. What is the maximum number of business cards that could fit on a page 8.5 in. × 11 in.?

10. The printer used 2,989 digits in numbering the pages of a telephone book. How many pages did the telephone book have?

11. There are 7 dots on a piece of paper. No 3 dots are in a straight line. How many line segments are needed to connect each dot to every other dot?

12. Ken Griffey, Jr. hit 28 home runs in 72 games. At this rate, how many home runs would Griffey hit over a 162-game season?

13. John enlarged a 5-in. × 7-in. photo so that the short side was 12.5 in. long. If the ratio of the length to the width stayed the same, how long was the longer side of the enlargement?

14. Stan can wash a car in 12 min. It takes Jill 9 min to wash a car. They begin at the same time. How much time will they spend washing cars if they finished at the same time?

15. An example of five consecutive numbers is 32, 33, 34, 35, 36. The sum of the five consecutive numbers is 620. What is the greatest of these five numbers?

16. The numbers 123, 235, and 347 use the first two digits to find the third. What number follows the same pattern and has 9 as the digit in the ones place?

CHAPTER

1 MAKING NUMBER CONNECTIONS

LOOK AHEAD

In this chapter you will solve problems that involve

- classifying numbers
- modeling percents and writing equivalent fractions, decimals, and percents
- making circle graphs

HEALTH LINK

Now that school is in session, you will see lots of students getting there on bikes, skates, and skateboards. Will you also see them wearing bicycle helmets?

Doctors know that wearing a helmet can reduce serious head injuries in about 9 out of 10 cases. However, nationally only 1 out of 5 bike riders wears a helmet. The news is even worse for skateboarders (1 out of 10) and in-line skaters (1 out of 12). These statistics are alarming. Doctors treat more than a half million bikers and almost 100 thousand skaters every year in emergency rooms. Most are under the age of 15.

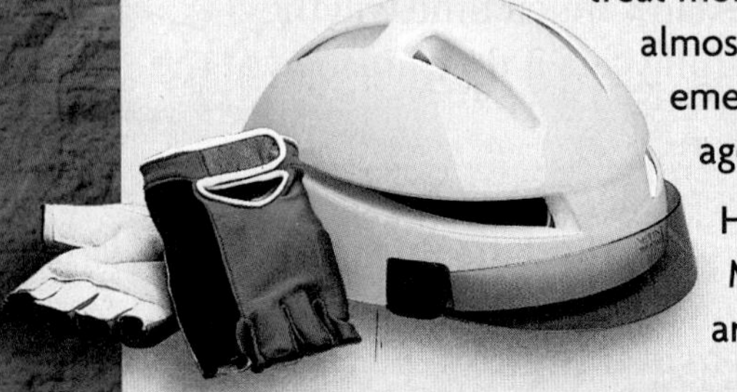

Helmets are relatively inexpensive. Most cost from $30.00 to $80.00 and are comfortable, colorful, and stylish.

Problem-Solving Project

In the News

How important are numbers in what you read?

Predict the types of numbers you will find when reading magazine and newspaper articles. Read some articles and look for different types of numbers (whole numbers, decimals, fractions, percents, amounts of money, measurements). Make a poster that summarizes the data you collect.

PROJECT CHECKLIST

- ✓ Did you predict the types of numbers you would find?
- ✓ Did you read articles and look for numbers?
- ✓ Did you make a poster to summarize your data?

LESSON 1.1

ALGEBRA CONNECTION

Sets of Numbers

What You'll Learn
How to classify and compare sets of numbers

Why Learn This?
To solve real-life problems requiring logical reasoning skills

VOCABULARY

Venn diagram
integers
rational number

A **prime number** is a whole number greater than 1 that has exactly two factors, itself and 1. A **composite number** is a whole number greater than 1 with more than two whole-number factors. **See page H11.**

prime 2, 3, 5, 7
composite 4, 6, 8, 9

Since you started studying mathematics, you've used many different sets, or groups, of numbers.

- Identify these sets of numbers.

{1, 2, 3, 4, 5, 6, . . .} {0, 1, 2, 3, 4, 5, . . .}

{2, 4, 6, 8, 10, 12, . . .} {1, 3, 5, 7, 9, 11, . . .}

{2, 3, 5, 7, 11, 13, . . .} {4, 6, 8, 9, 10, 12, . . .}

You can use **Venn diagrams** to describe the relationships among sets of numbers.

EXAMPLE 1 Start with the whole numbers that are 20 or less. Use a Venn diagram to show which are odd and which are prime.

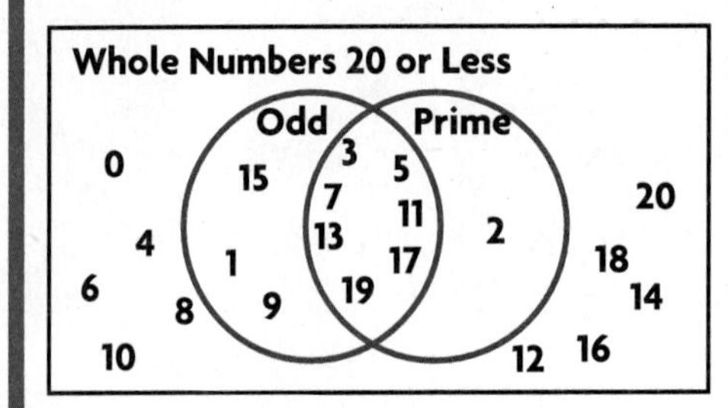

Use a rectangle for the set of whole numbers 20 or less.

Use overlapping circles for the sets of odd numbers and prime numbers 20 or less.

Then sort the numbers into the diagram.

So, the odd numbers are 1, 3, 5, 7, 9, 11, 13, 15, 17, and 19. The prime numbers are 2, 3, 5, 7, 11, 13, 17, and 19.

CRITICAL THINKING

- Look at the Venn diagram in Example 1. Which numbers are both odd and prime? What part of the diagram shows these numbers?
- How many whole numbers 20 or less are neither odd nor prime? What are the numbers?

Most sets of numbers are parts of other sets of numbers. This Venn diagram shows that all prime numbers and all composite numbers are counting numbers and that all counting numbers are whole numbers.

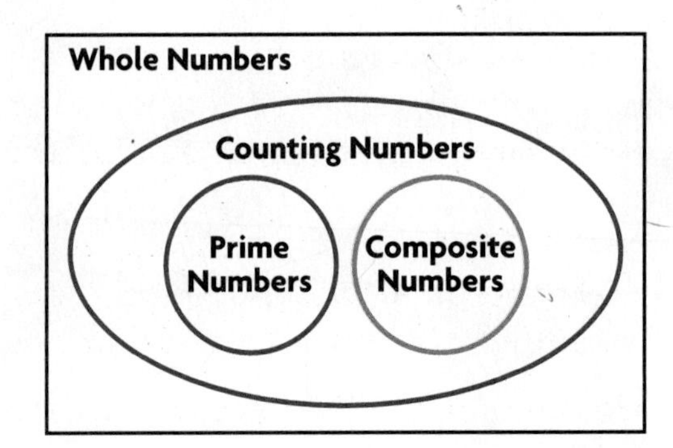

GUIDED PRACTICE

For Exercises 1–2, use the Venn diagram at the right.

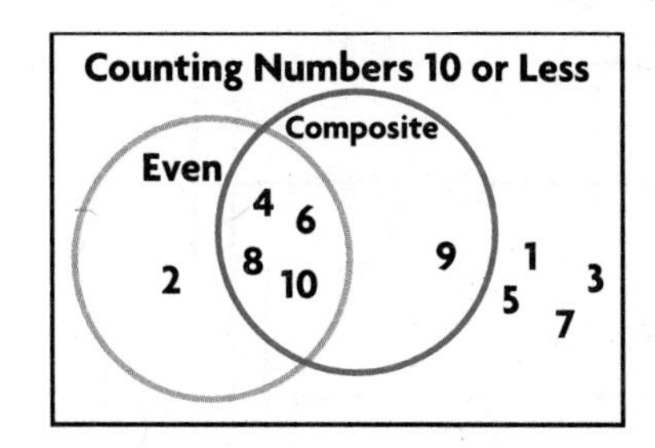

1. Which counting numbers 10 or less are even? Which are composite? Which are both even and composite?

2. Which counting numbers 10 or less are both odd and composite?

3. Copy and complete the Venn diagram at the right. Sort the whole numbers 20 or less into the diagram.

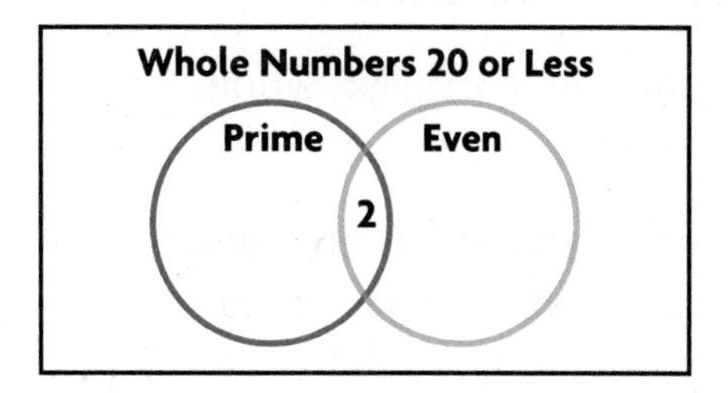

4. In Exercise 3, which numbers are both prime and even?

5. In Exercise 3, which numbers are neither prime nor even?

6. In a Venn diagram, what does it mean when a number is in the area where two circles overlap? when it is outside both circles?

HISTORY LINK

Since about 300 B.C., mathematicians have been interested in prime numbers. Today over 600,000 prime numbers are known, but there is only one that is even. What is it, and why is it the only one?

Rational Numbers

Other sets of numbers used in mathematics include decimals, fractions, integers, and rational numbers. The set of **integers** is made up of whole numbers and their opposites. Examples of integers are shown on the number line.

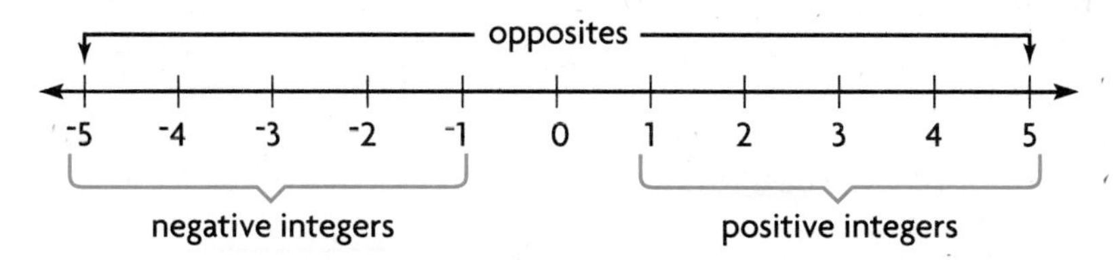

A **rational number** is any number that can be expressed as a ratio in the fraction form $\frac{a}{b}$, where a and b are integers and $b \neq 0$. These are examples of rational numbers:

$$6 \quad 0 \quad \frac{1}{2} \quad \frac{^{-}3}{4} \quad 7.9 \quad ^{-}4.25 \quad ^{-}2$$

- Are integers rational numbers? Are whole numbers rational numbers? Are decimals and fractions rational numbers?
- Write a ratio to show that $^{-}3.8$ is a rational number.

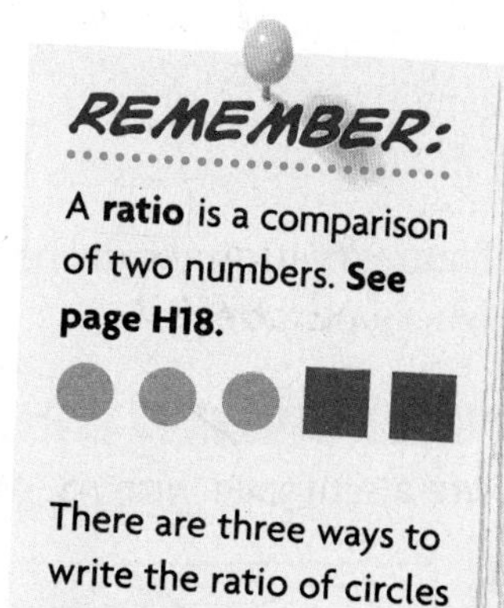

REMEMBER:
A ratio is a comparison of two numbers. See page H18.
There are three ways to write the ratio of circles to squares.
3 to 2 3:2 3/2

The Venn diagram below shows how counting numbers, whole numbers, integers, and rational numbers are related.

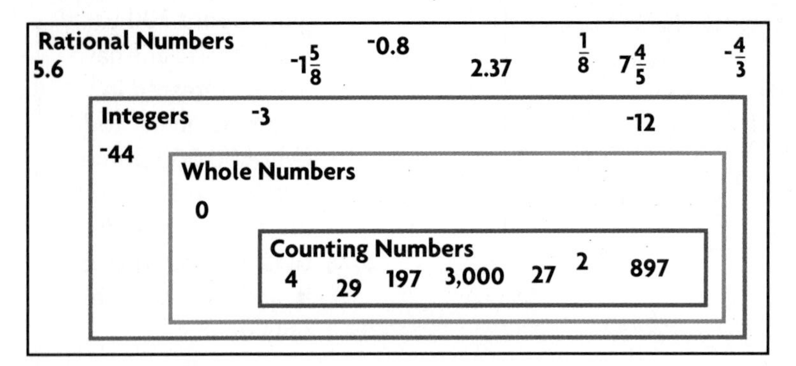

You can classify a number as a counting number, a whole number, an integer, or a rational number.

EXAMPLE 2 Classify the following numbers as counting numbers, whole numbers, integers, or rational numbers: 2, 0, $^-3$, $2\frac{3}{4}$, 1.5. Make a table to show your results.

	Counting Number	Whole Number	Integer	Rational Number
2	✓	✓	✓	✓
0		✓	✓	✓
$^-3$			✓	✓
$2\frac{3}{4}$				✓
1.5				✓

• Name a rational number that is an integer but is not a whole number.

Rational numbers were used in a *Sports Illustrated for Kids* article about a female football player. Crystle Velez, a seventh grader, practiced $2\frac{1}{2}$ hr per day five days per week as the second-string quarterback. She played in two games.

INDEPENDENT PRACTICE

Write a sentence with *no, some,* or *all* to describe the relationship.

1.

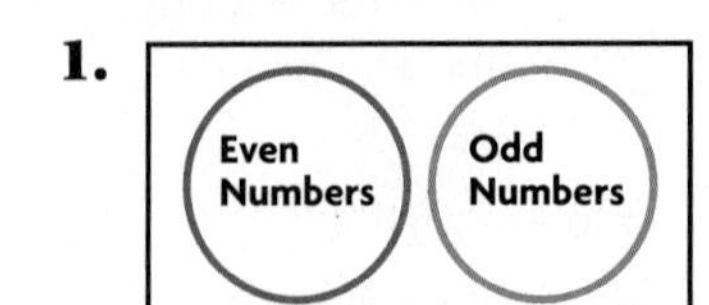

2.

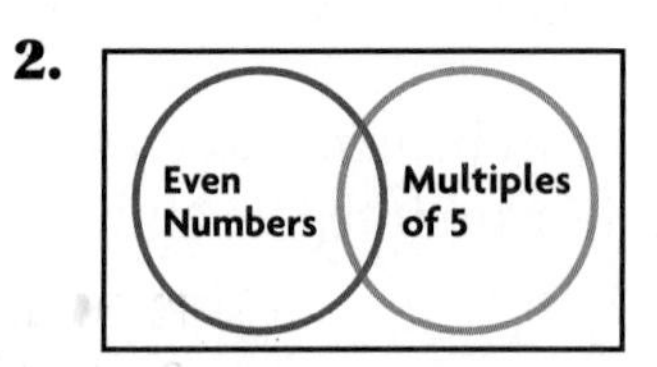

3.

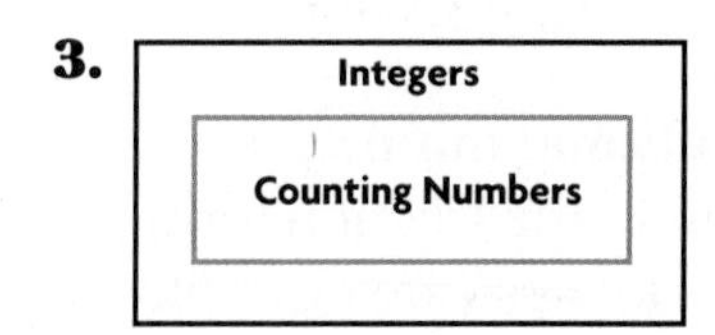

Make a Venn diagram using the categories and numbers.

4. multiples of five; multiples of ten

5, 10, 15, 20, 23, 25, 30, 34, 35, 40, 45, 47

5. counting numbers; whole numbers; integers; rational numbers

1.3, 22, 0, $^-4$, 7, $^-12$, $^-13$, $\frac{^-3}{5}$, $^-9$, $\frac{1}{2}$, $^-32$

Classify the numbers as counting numbers, whole numbers, integers, or rational numbers. Make a table to show your work.

6. $^-0.4, 60, \frac{^-3}{4}, 5.6, 3\frac{1}{3}$

7. $^-4\frac{5}{8}, ^-12, 1, 14.5, 250$

8. $0, 18, ^-0.45, 6\frac{2}{3}, ^-1.7$

Tell whether each statement is *true* or *false*. If it is true, draw a Venn diagram to show the relationship.

9. Some birds are insects.

10. No birds are insects.

11. Some vegetables are not green.

12. Some students play both soccer and baseball.

Problem-Solving Applications

For Problems 13–15, use the Venn diagram.

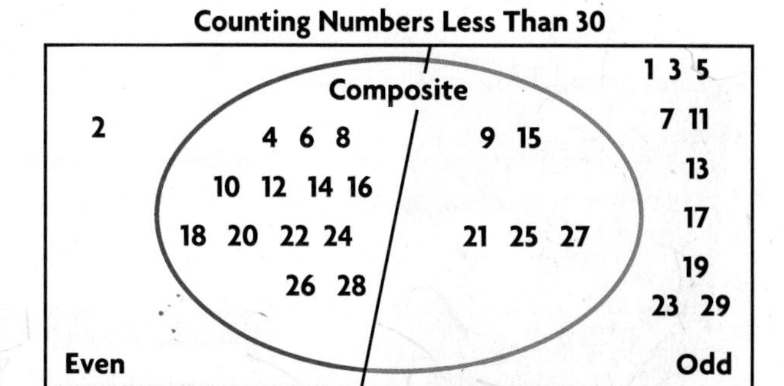

13. How many counting numbers less than 30 are composite but neither odd nor even?

14. How many counting numbers less than 30 are either odd or even, but not both?

15. Which counting numbers less than 30 are both odd and composite?

16. **NUMBER SENSE** How many counting numbers less than 50 are even and not composite? Name them.

17. **CRITICAL THINKING** How many counting numbers less than 50 are both even and composite?

18.  **WRITE ABOUT IT** How can a number belong to more than one set of numbers? Name such a number and the sets it belongs to.

Mixed Review and Test Prep

Name the numbers graphed on the number line.

19. 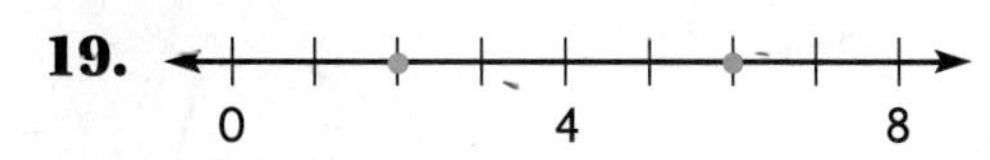

20. 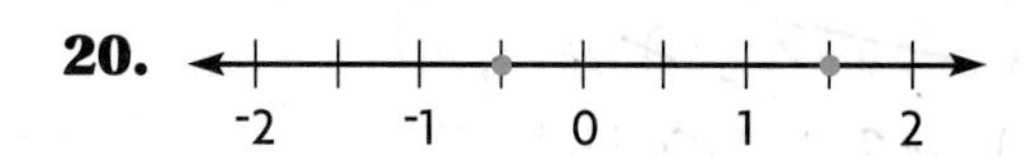

Write an integer to describe the situation.

21. 45 ft under ground

22. loss of $50

23. up 3 flights of stairs

24. **PERCENT** Which shows 0.87 written as a percent?

A 0.87%
B 8.7%
C 87%
D 870%

25. **NUMBER SENSE** Which is the value of $3^2 + 12 \times 2$?

F 33
G 42
H 30
J 36

LESSON 1.2

ALGEBRA CONNECTION

Understanding Rational Numbers

What You'll Learn
How to write different names for a rational number and how to graph rational numbers on a number line

Why Learn This?
To describe athletes' performances

During a recent NBA basketball game, Shaquille O'Neal completed 5 of 10 free throws. The media reported his performance by using these equivalent rational numbers: $\frac{5}{10}$, $\frac{1}{2}$, 0.5, and 0.50.

The number line and Example 1 below show that you can write rational numbers in many different ways.

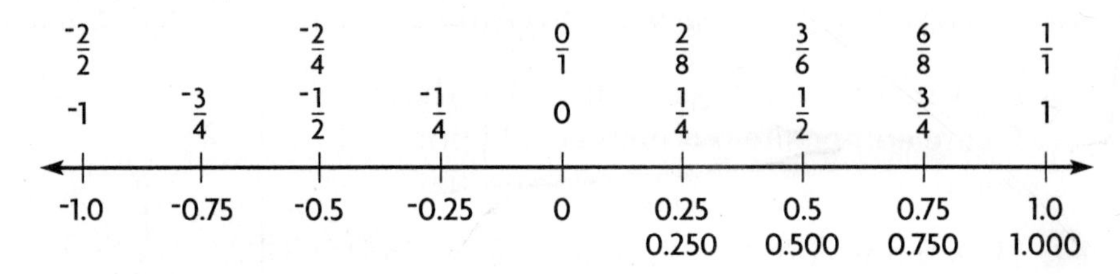

EXAMPLE 1 Give at least three other names for the rational numbers 3 and $^-4.7$.

$3 = \frac{3}{1}, \frac{6}{2}$, 3.0, and 3.000

$^-4.7 = {^-4.70}, {^-4.700}, {^-4\frac{7}{10}}$, and $\frac{^-47}{10}$

Write decimals and fractions that are equivalent to the numbers.

You can graph rational numbers on a number line.

EXAMPLE 2 Graph 1.5, $\frac{1}{4}$, and $^-2.00$ on the same number line.

Place a dot on the number line to represent each rational number.

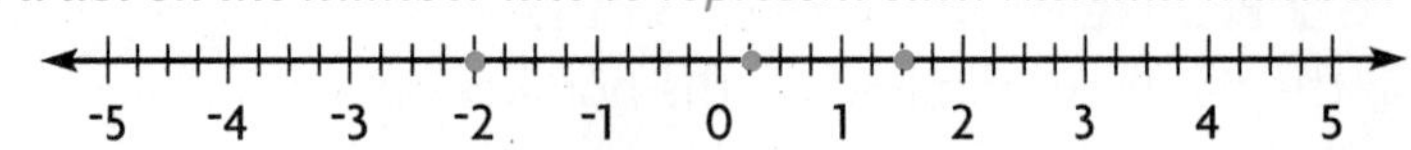

REMEMBER:

You can use place value to write a decimal as a fraction. See page H8.

$0.25 = \frac{25}{100}$

You can use a number line to help you compare rational numbers. Use < or > to compare and order rational numbers.

EXAMPLE 3 Use a number line to compare and order $^-2$, $1\frac{1}{4}$, and $^-4$. Order them from least to greatest.

$^-4$ is to the left of $^-2$, and $^-2$ is to the left of $1\frac{1}{4}$.

So, $^-4 < {^-2} < 1\frac{1}{4}$.

GUIDED PRACTICE

Give three other names for each rational number.

1. 4 **2.** $^{-}3$ **3.** 1.5 **4.** $\frac{3}{10}$ **5.** $^{-}2.5$

Graph the rational numbers on the same number line.

6. 2.5 **7.** $^{-}0.5$ **8.** $2\frac{3}{4}$ **9.** $^{-}3.0$ **10.** $^{-}2\frac{1}{4}$

INDEPENDENT PRACTICE

Name a rational number for the given point on the number line.

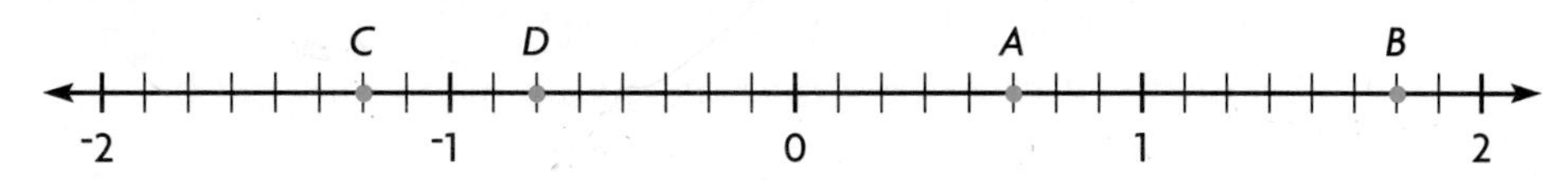

1. point A **2.** point B **3.** point C **4.** point D

Give at least three other names for each rational number.

5. $^{-}12$ **6.** $8\frac{3}{4}$ **7.** $\frac{9}{10}$ **8.** 9.7 **9.** $^{-}2.1$

10. 0.084 **11.** 15 **12.** $^{-}4.5$ **13.** $^{-}3\frac{2}{5}$ **14.** 8

Graph the rational numbers. Use one number line for each exercise.

15. 0.25, $\frac{3}{4}$, 1.50 **16.** 2.5, 2.000, $\frac{3}{2}$ **17.** $\frac{5}{8}$, 1.875, $\frac{^{-}1}{2}$ **18.** 2.25, $2\frac{1}{4}$, $\frac{9}{4}$

19. 0.7, $1\frac{3}{10}$, $\frac{^{-}3}{4}$ **20.** $-2\frac{1}{2}$, $^{-}0.5$, $\frac{^{-}5}{2}$ **21.** $\frac{4}{5}$, $\frac{^{-}4}{5}$, $^{-}1.8$ **22.** $^{-}1.5$, $^{-}1.50$, $\frac{^{-}6}{4}$

Compare the rational numbers and order them from least to greatest.

23. $^{-}3$, $2\frac{3}{4}$, $^{-}1$ **24.** $\frac{1}{3}$, $^{-}2$, $\frac{1}{2}$ **25.** $6\frac{2}{7}$, $^{-}5$, $^{-}8$ **26.** $^{-}5$, $8\frac{1}{3}$, 0

Problem-Solving Applications

27. **SPORTS** A sports reporter described Cal Ripken's batting average as $\frac{29}{100}$. A batting average is usually given as a decimal to the thousandths place. What is Ripken's batting average as a decimal?

28. **RATIOS** During an Arena League football game, quarterback Pat O'Hara completed 18 out of 30 passes. How else could the media report his performance, using two equivalent rational numbers?

29. **RATIOS** In a basketball game, Yolanda Jackson made 4 of 5 free throws. Suppose Jill Black throws a total of 10 free throws and wants to make a higher ratio of her free hrows than Yolanda Jackson. How many ee throws must Jill Black make?

30. **WRITE ABOUT IT** Suppose you wanted to find a number between 0.45 and 0.46. Would you write a decimal, a fraction, or neither? Explain.

ACTIVITY

Rational Numbers: Modeling Percents

What You'll Explore
How to use decimal squares to model percents

What You'll Need
decimal squares, markers or colored pencils

VOCABULARY
percent

You have seen that ratios can be expressed as integers, decimals, and fractions. Ratios can also be expressed as percents. A **percent** is a ratio that compares a number to 100. *Percent* means "per hundred."

Explore

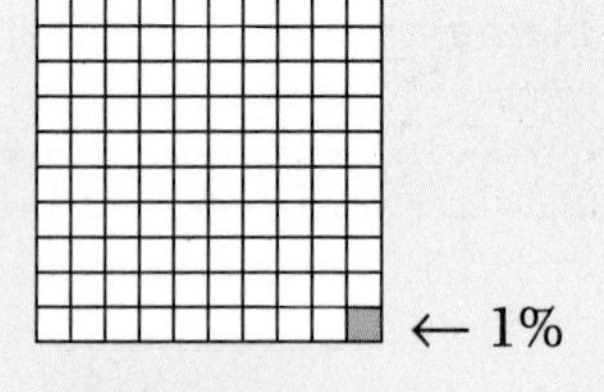

Work with a partner. Use decimal squares. A decimal square contains 100 small squares, and each small square represents 1%.

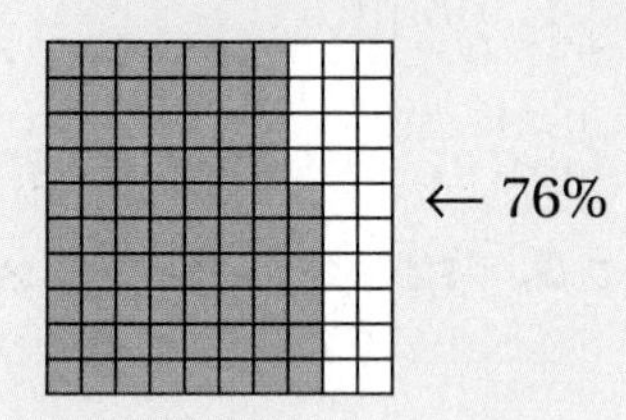

- This decimal square represents the 100 points on a science test. The shaded small squares represent a score of 76%. Now shade two different decimal squares to model 76% in two other ways.
- On a different decimal square, model 100%.
- Model 50%. On a different decimal square, model 5%.

Technology Link

You can make geometric models of percents by using E-Lab, Activity 1. Available on CD-ROM and on the Internet at **www.hbschool.com/elab**

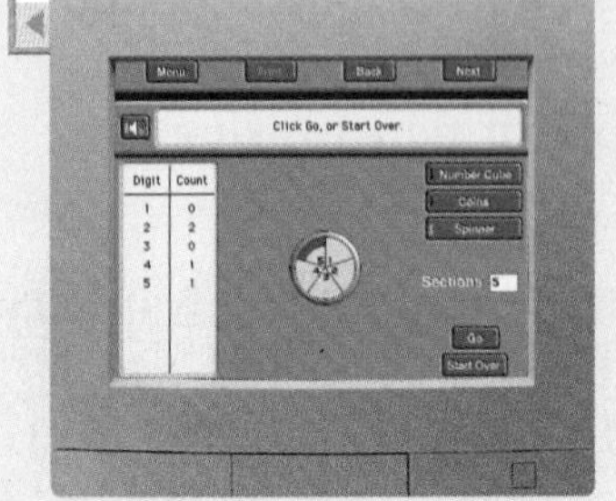

Think and Discuss CRITICAL THINKING

- Look at your models for 76%. Does it matter which squares you shade to model a percent? Explain.
- How many small squares did you shade to model 76%? 100%? How many small squares would you shade to model 150%? 200%?
- How many small squares did you shade to model 50%? 5%? How many would you shade to model 0.5%, or $\frac{1}{2}$%?

Try This

- Use decimal squares to model these percents:

  37% 150% 200% 0.5% 45.5%

- Suppose a decimal square represents $200. Model $100. What percent did you model?

GEOMETRY CONNECTION

Parts as Percents

What You'll Learn
How to use percents to compare parts of two- and three-dimensional figures with the whole

Why Learn This?
To find the remaining part of a pizza, a cake, or a gallon of ice cream

Appleton Middle School is selling team T-shirts. So far, they have sold 75 of 100, $\frac{3}{4}$, or 75% of the T-shirts.

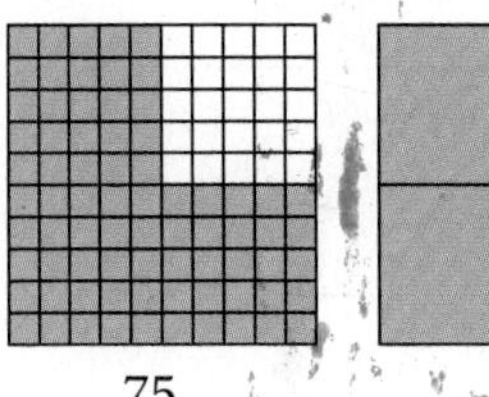

$\frac{75}{100} = \frac{3}{4} = 75\%$

When a fractional part such as $\frac{3}{4}$ can be seen easily, it can be modeled using geometric figures other than 10 by 10 grids. Each whole figure shown below represents 100 T-shirts. The shaded portions of each of these figures represent $\frac{3}{4}$, or 75%, of the T-shirts. They all represent an equal number of T-shirts.

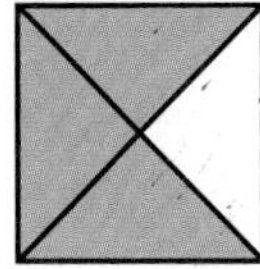

$\frac{3}{4} = 75\%$

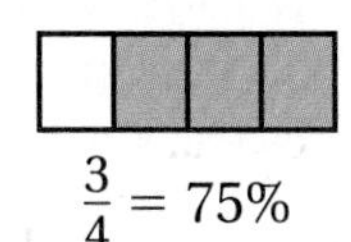

$\frac{3}{4} = 75\%$

$\frac{3}{4} = 75\%$

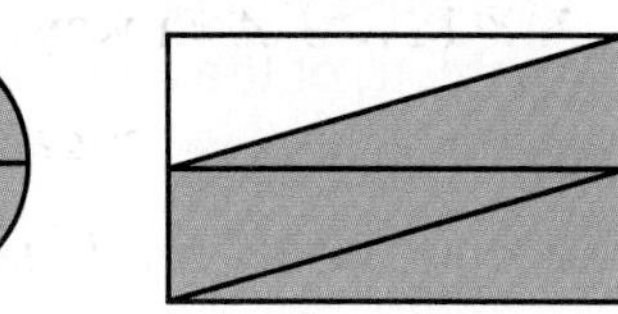

$\frac{3}{4} = 75\%$

EXAMPLE 1 Write percents for the area covered by the small unshaded squares and for the area covered by the small shaded ones.

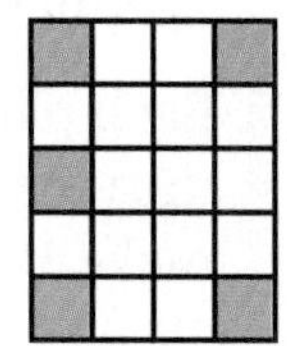

unshaded: $\frac{15}{20} = \frac{3}{4} = 75\%$ *Write the ratio of unshaded squares to the total. Write the ratio as a percent.*

shaded: $\frac{5}{20} = \frac{1}{4} = 25\%$ *Write the ratio of shaded squares to the total. Write the ratio as a percent.*

So, 75% of the area is unshaded and 25% is shaded.

- **CRITICAL THINKING** Suppose you draw a 5 × 4 grid like the one in Example 1. How many rows would you shade if the unshaded rows are to represent 40%?

CAREER LINK

Every day your local meteorologist uses percents to report relative humidity. This is the amount of moisture in the air divided by the largest amount the air could hold. At 60°F, is there more moisture in the air when the relative humidity is 50% or 75%?

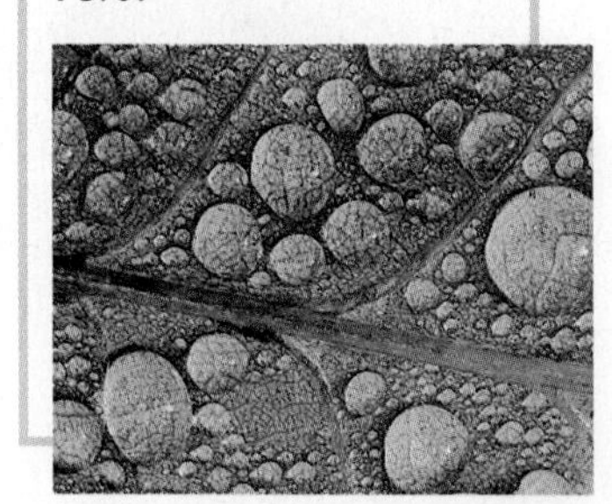

You can visualize a part of a whole and describe it by using a percent.

ACTIVITY **WHAT YOU'LL NEED:** a sheet of paper

- Cut out a square piece of paper.
- Fold it in half horizontally and vertically.
- Hold the folded paper in your hand.

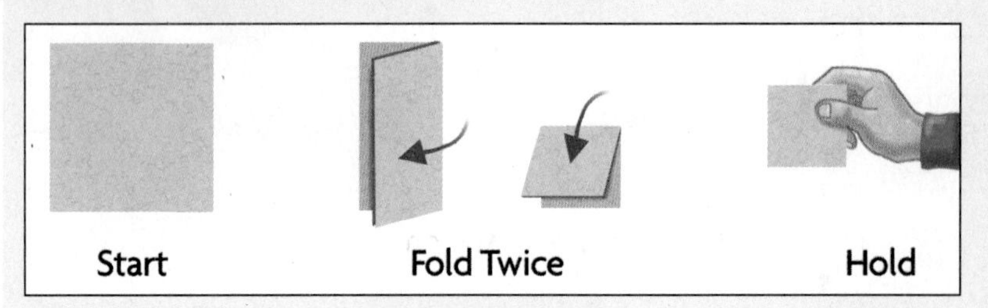

Visualize the paper unfolded.

- How many small squares do you see?
- What percent of the area of the whole is each square?
- Suppose you fold the paper in half one more time. What percent of the area of the whole is each rectangle?

SOCIAL STUDIES LINK

Young people 14 to 19 years old make up about 8% of the total United States population. Do you think this percent will be higher, lower, or the same in the year 2010?

You can also use percents to describe parts of solid figures.

EXAMPLE 2 Suppose a cube is cut in half vertically as shown. What percent of the volume of the whole cube is each piece?

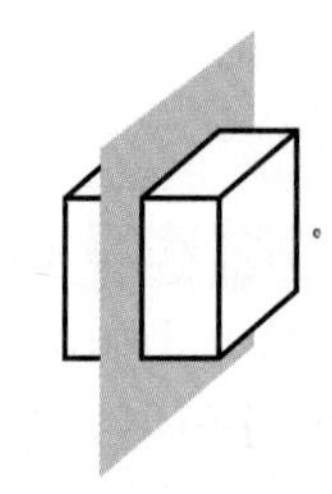

Each piece is $\frac{1}{2}$, or 50%, of the volume of the whole cube. Together, the two pieces make 100% of the original cube.

GUIDED PRACTICE

What percent of the figure is shaded?

1. 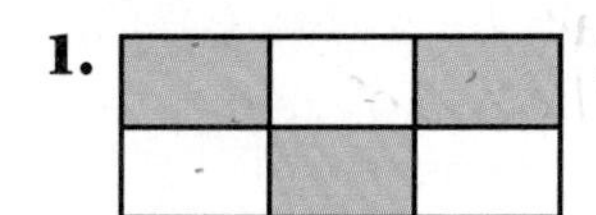

2. 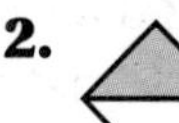 

3. 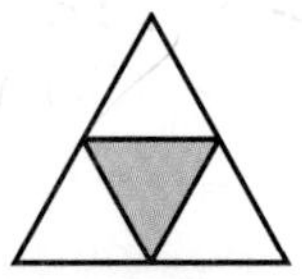

4. 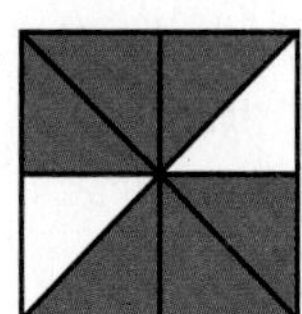

5. 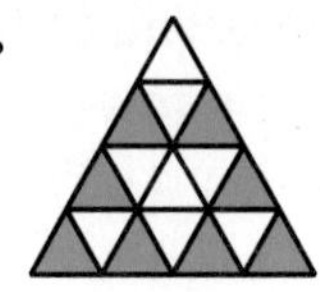

6. 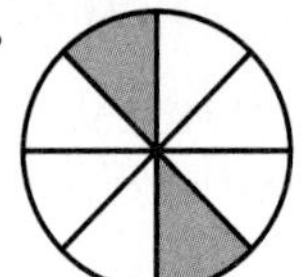

INDEPENDENT PRACTICE

Write percents for the area covered by the small unshaded parts and for the area covered by the small shaded parts.

1.

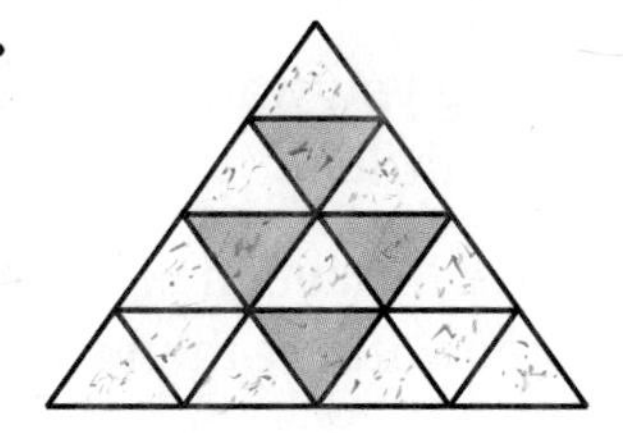

2.

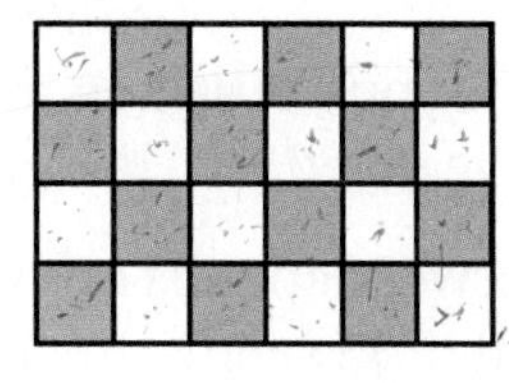

3.

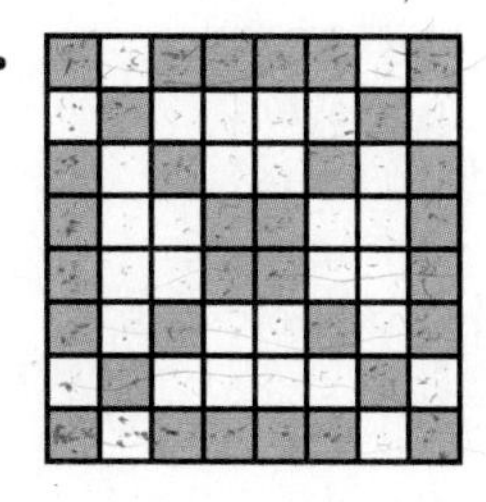

Suppose a 2-in. × 5-in. rectangular piece of paper is folded and then unfolded as shown.

2 in.

5 in.

4. How many 1-in. × 1-in. squares are formed?

5. How many 1-in. × 2-in. rectangles are formed? 1-in. × 3-in. rectangles?

6. Make a table listing all the different sizes of rectangles (and squares) that can be found. Give the number of each size. What percent of the whole does each of their areas represent?

Suppose a cube is cut 3 ways to form smaller cubes with equal volumes as shown.

7. How many 1 × 1 × 1 cubes are formed?

8. What percent of the volume of the whole cube are two small cubes? four small cubes? six small cubes? eight small cubes?

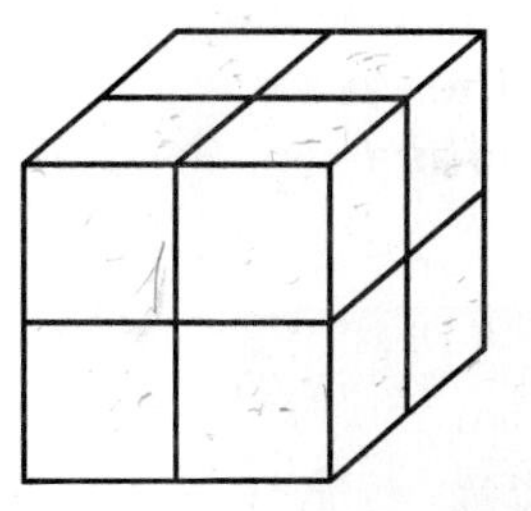

Problem-Solving Applications

9. **CRITICAL THINKING** At her party, Lavona served 2 identical pizzas, each cut into 12 equal slices. The guests ate 10 slices of one pizza and 8 slices of the other. What percent of the pizzas remains?

10. **PERCENTS** Five friends contributed equally for a gift for Lavona. What percent of the gift's cost did two of them pay for in all?

11. **CRITICAL THINKING** Into how many pieces would you cut a cake to make each piece of cake 5% of the whole?

12. **WRITE ABOUT IT** Look at the figures. Use percents to describe how the square in Step 1 was folded in Steps 2 and 3.

Step 1 Step 2 Step 3

MORE PRACTICE Lesson 1.3, page H43

LESSON 1.4

Connecting Fractions, Decimals, and Percents

What You'll Learn
How to use several methods to write equivalent fractions, decimals, and percents

How You'll Use It
To understand the meaning of percents in advertisements or sports statistics

Suppose you are saving money for something you want to buy. You have saved \$3. Have you saved a lot or a little?

The answer depends on how much you have to save in all. The amount of \$3 seems greater when compared with \$1 than when compared with \$1,000.

You can show comparisons by writing ratios, fractions, decimals, or percents.

Ratio	Fraction	Decimal	Percent
3 to 1	$\frac{3}{1}$	3.0	300%
3 to 10	$\frac{3}{10}$	0.3	30%
3 to 100	$\frac{3}{100}$	0.03	3%
3 to 1,000	$\frac{3}{1,000}$	0.003	0.3%

- Suppose Susan has saved \$3 toward her goal of \$10 and Jeff has saved \$3 toward his goal of \$100. How can you find out who has saved a greater percent of the goal?

SCIENCE LINK

Did you know that about $\frac{4}{5}$ of your brain is water? How would that be written as a decimal and as a percent?

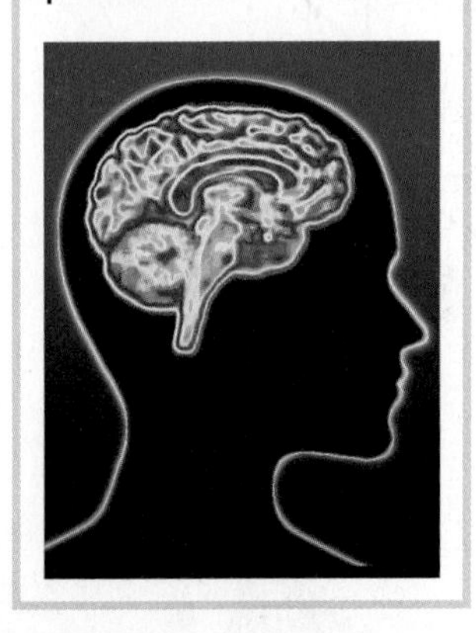

Writing Fractions and Decimals as Percents

You can use several methods to write fractions and decimals as percents.

EXAMPLE 1 Miguel won $\frac{9}{10}$ of his tennis games. What percent of his games did he win?

$\frac{9}{10} = \frac{9 \times 10}{10 \times 10} = \frac{90}{100}$ *Write an equivalent fraction with a denominator of 100.*

$\frac{90}{100} = 90\%$ *Write the fraction as a percent.*

So, Miguel won 90% of his games.

- CRITICAL THINKING Which gives Miguel a better record, winning $\frac{7}{10}$ of his games or $\frac{9}{15}$ of his games? Explain.

Calculator Activities, page H33

EXAMPLE 2 Write the decimal 0.076 as a percent.

$0.076 = \frac{76}{1{,}000}$ *Write the decimal as a fraction.*

$= \frac{7.6}{100}$ *Write an equivalent fraction with a denominator of 100.*

$= 7.6\%$ *Write the fraction as a percent.*

- What is 0.089 expressed as a fraction? as a percent?

Some fractions are easier to express as percents by using decimals.

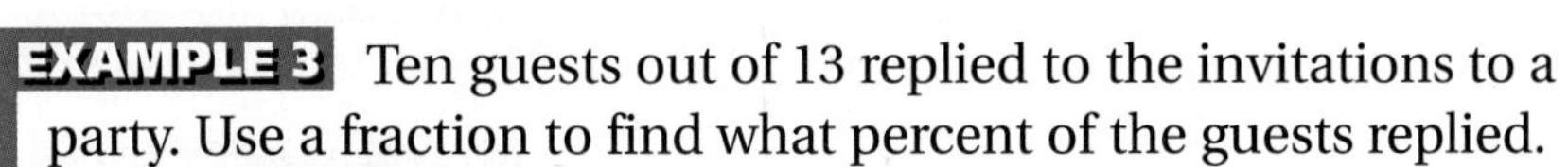

EXAMPLE 3 Ten guests out of 13 replied to the invitations to a party. Use a fraction to find what percent of the guests replied.

10 out of 13: $\frac{10}{13}$ *Write the ratio in fraction form.*

$\frac{10}{13} = 10 \div 13 \approx 0.769230769$ *Use division to write the fraction as a decimal.*

$\frac{10}{13} \approx 0.77$ *Round to the nearest hundredth.*

$0.77 = 0.77 = 77\%$ *Multiply by 100 and write a percent symbol.*

So, about 77% of the guests replied.

- What would you do to write $\frac{5}{8}$ as a decimal? as a percent?

GUIDED PRACTICE

Write the fraction as a percent.

1. $\frac{1}{4}$ **2.** $\frac{3}{50}$ **3.** $\frac{5}{2}$ **4.** $\frac{8}{1}$

Write the decimal as a percent.

5. 0.66 **6.** 0.93 **7.** 0.04 **8.** 4.6

Write the ratio as a fraction. Then write the fraction as a percent.

9. 48 of 100 **10.** 1 out of 10 **11.** 2 to 1

12. How can you use division to express the ratio 5 out of 12 as a percent?

13. Moving the decimal point two places to the right is a shortcut for what operation?

REMEMBER:

When multiplying decimal numbers by powers of 10, move the decimal point one place to the right for each power of 10.

When dividing by powers of 10, move the decimal point one place to the left for each power of 10. **See page H7.**

$1.86 \times 10 = 18.6$
$1.86 \times 100 = 186$
$1.86 \times 1{,}000 = 1{,}860$

$225 \div 10 = 22.5$
$225 \div 100 = 2.25$
$225 \div 1{,}000 = 0.225$

Writing Percents as Fractions and Decimals

You can write a percent as an equivalent fraction.

EXAMPLE 4 The manager of a music store describes a 40%-off sale by marking a sign with a fraction. What fraction does she use for the percent?

$40\% = \frac{40}{100}$ *Express the percent as a fraction with a denominator of 100.*

$\frac{40}{100} = \frac{4}{10} = \frac{2}{5}$ *Write the fraction in simplest form.*

So, she would use $\frac{2}{5}$.

- Suppose the price of a CD decreases by 25%. What would you do to write the percent as a fraction in simplest form?

REMEMBER:

A fraction is in **simplest form** if the numerator and the denominator have no common factors other than 1. **See page H14.**

$\frac{6}{8} = \frac{3}{4} \leftarrow$ simplest form

You can write any percent as an equivalent decimal.

EXAMPLE 5 Write 250% as a decimal.

$250\% = \frac{250}{100}$ *Write the percent as a fraction with a denominator of 100.*

$\frac{250}{100} = 2.50$ *Write the fraction as a decimal.*

So, you can write 250% as 2.50.

ANOTHER METHOD To change a percent to a decimal, divide by 100 and remove the percent symbol.

95% = 0.95

- Moving the decimal point two places to the left is a shortcut for what operation?
- Write 0.5% as a decimal.

SPORTS LINK

Calvin Murphy, while playing for the Houston Rockets in 1980–1981, set the NBA record for free-throw shooting in a single season by completing 95.8% of his free throws. What are some other ways to express his record?

INDEPENDENT PRACTICE

Write as a percent.

1. $\frac{9}{10}$ **2.** $\frac{5}{1}$ **3.** $\frac{18}{24}$ **4.** $3\frac{7}{50}$ **5.** 0.98

6. 0.03 **7.** 2.50 **8.** 0.002 **9.** 6 of 150 **10.** 5 of 8

Write each percent as a fraction in simplest form.

11. 8% **12.** 70% **13.** 16% **14.** 35% **15.** 1%

16. 75% **17.** 45% **18.** 28% **19.** 50% **20.** 100%

Write each percent as a decimal.

21. 2% **22.** 5.0% **23.** 10% **24.** 60% **25.** 800%

26. 119% **27.** 4% **28.** 6.5% **29.** 48% **30.** 1%

Copy and complete the table.

	Fraction	Decimal	Percent
31.	$\frac{1}{4}$	?	?
33.	?	0.39	?

	Fraction	Decimal	Percent
32.	?	?	48%
34.	$\frac{5}{4}$	?	?

Problem-Solving Applications

35. RATIOS During a recent NBA season, the Chicago Bulls won 87 of 100 games. Write this ratio as a fraction. Then express it as a percent.

36. PERCENTS Mark sold $\frac{8}{10}$ of his pep ribbons. What percent of his pep ribbons did he sell?

37. CONSUMER MATH A skirt is marked down 15% for a store sale. What fraction would you use to compute the amount of the discount?

38. WRITE ABOUT IT Tell how to move the decimal point when changing decimals to percents and percents to decimals.

Mixed Review and Test Prep

Complete to find the equivalent fraction.

39. $\frac{1}{10} = \frac{■}{100}$ **40.** $\frac{1}{2} = \frac{■}{100}$ **41.** $\frac{2}{5} = \frac{■}{100}$

Use mental math to evaluate the expression.

42. $5 \times 11 \times 2$ **43.** $0.5 + 3.5 + 22$

44. $7.6 - (4.3 + 1.3)$ **45.** $4.08 \div 8$

46. $\frac{9}{8} \times \frac{4}{9}$ **47.** $\frac{21}{4} \div \frac{3}{4}$

48. COMPARING During the school year, Tai grew $\frac{7}{9}$ in. taller, Maria, $\frac{5}{6}$ in., and Kerri, $\frac{2}{3}$ in. What is the order from greatest to least according to how much they grew?

A Tai, Maria, Kerri **B** Maria, Tai, Kerri

C Maria, Kerri, Tai **D** Kerri, Maria, Tai

49. CHOOSE A STRATEGY Ian has 4 CDs that he wants to play. In how many different orders can he play them?

F 6 **G** 12

H 18 **J** 24

Technology Link

In **Mighty Math Astro Algebra,** you can practice finding equivalent rational numbers in the missions *Fuel for the Glop I* and *II.* Use Grow Slide Level Red D and I.

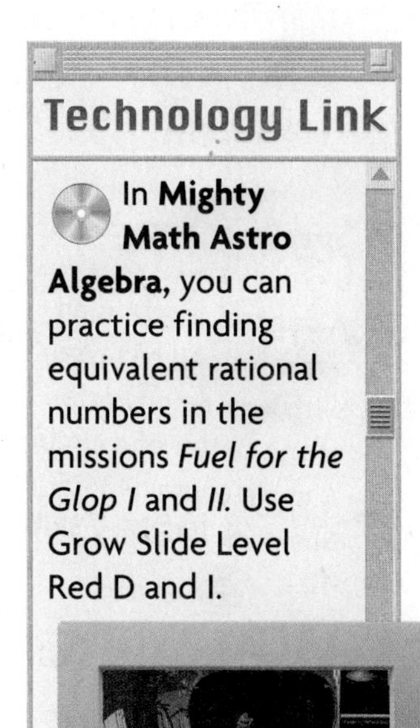

MORE PRACTICE Lesson 1.4, page H44

LESSON 1.5

Making Circle Graphs

What You'll Learn
How to make a circle graph by using equivalent percents, decimals, and fractions

Why Learn This?
To interpret circle graphs you see and to organize and display data you gather about money or time

VOCABULARY
circle graph

What sports do teens like? Keisha and Todd want to organize and display the results of a survey of 1,000 teens about their favorite sports.

Favorite Sports	
Soccer	30%
Track	25%
Baseball	20%
Basketball	20%
Gymnastics	5%

Keisha and Todd will draw a circle graph. A **circle graph** shows a whole, or 100% of the data, and it can be used to compare the parts with the whole.

Keisha and Todd follow these steps to make a circle graph.

Step 1: Calculate the measure of each central angle.

To calculate the measure of each central angle, multiply 360° by the equivalent decimal or fraction.

Keisha's Method		Todd's Method
30%: $0.30 \times 360° = 108°$	Soccer	30%: $\frac{3}{10} \times 360° = 108°$
25%: $0.25 \times 360° = 90°$	Track	25%: $\frac{1}{4} \times 360° = 90°$
20%: $0.20 \times 360° = 72°$	Baseball	20%: $\frac{1}{5} \times 360° = 72°$
20%: $0.20 \times 360° = 72°$	Basketball	20%: $\frac{1}{5} \times 360° = 72°$
5%: $0.05 \times 360° = 18°$	Gymnastics	5%: $\frac{1}{20} \times 360° = 18°$

Step 2: Use a compass to draw a circle. Draw a radius.

Step 3: Draw the first central angle.

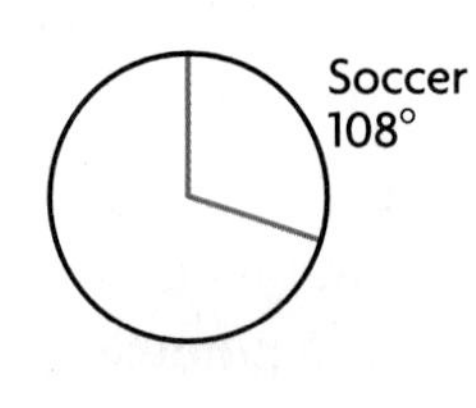

Step 4: Draw the second central angle.

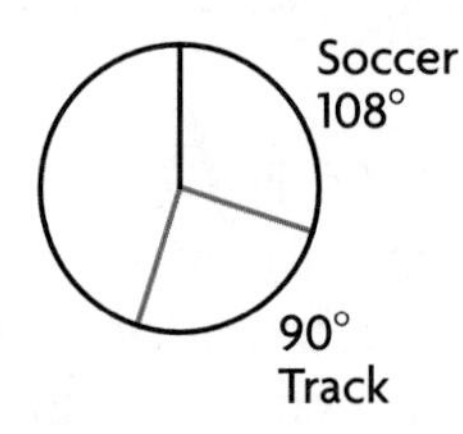

Step 5: Continue until graph is complete.

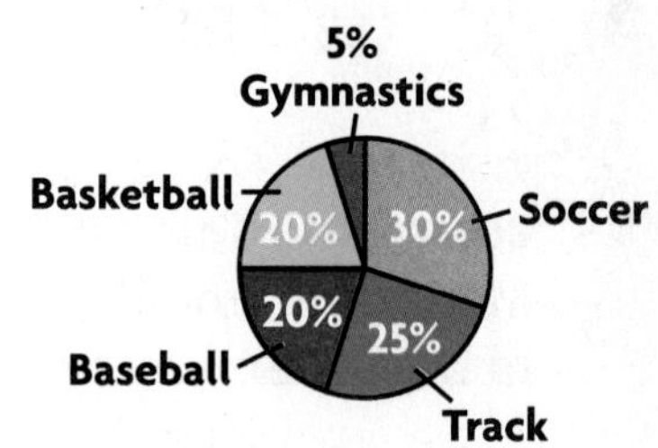

REMEMBER:
A **central angle** is an angle formed by rays with a common vertex at the center of a circle. A circle contains 360°. **See page H22, Key Skill 40.**
central angle

Talk About It

- Which method do you prefer for finding the central angles?
- How do you determine the number of sections in a circle graph?
- Why do you multiply the percents by 360?

GUIDED PRACTICE

Copy and complete the tables to find the central angle measures for a circle graph of the survey results.

	Food	Percent	Angle Measure
1.	Pizza	35%	?
3.	Fries	15%	?
5.	Salad	10%	?

	Food	Percent	Angle Measure
2.	Burger	20%	?
4.	Taco	15%	?
6.	Other	5%	?

Technology Link

In ***Data ToolKit*** you can practice making circle graphs.

INDEPENDENT PRACTICE

For Exercises 1–8, use the given percents for the O'Malley family's monthly budget to calculate the central angles for a circle graph. Round your answers to the nearest degree.

1. rent, 40%
2. food, 16%
3. savings, 9%
4. clothing, 18%
5. recreation, 3%
6. vehicle, 7%
7. insurance, 5%
8. other, 2%

9. Use a protractor to draw the central angles for the circle graph. Write the title, the categories, and the percents on your graph.

Problem-Solving Applications

For Problems 10–13, use the information and your circle graph from Exercises 1–9.

10. **CONSUMER MATH** If the O'Malley family has a monthly income of $1,500, how much do they spend for rent each month? for food?

11. **BUDGET** If the O'Malley family decides to save 20% of their income, how must they adjust their budget?

12. **CRITICAL THINKING** If the O'Malley family's monthly income increases to $2,000 per month, will the amount of money saved increase? Will the area of the savings section in the circle graph increase?

13. **CRITICAL THINKING** How are the areas of the sections of the circle graph related to the percents for each section? Give an example.

14. Make a circle graph to show how Dennis spends his day: sleep, 38%; school, 31%; meals, 6%; exercise, 9%; computer programs, 8%; and homework, 8%.

15. **WRITE ABOUT IT** Conduct a survey of your classmates on a topic of your choice. Organize your data in a table. Then display the data with a circle graph. Present the results of your survey to the class.

MORE PRACTICE Lesson 1.5, page H44

CHAPTER 1 Review/Test

1. **VOCABULARY** The set of numbers made up of whole numbers and their opposites is the __?__. (page 17)

2. **VOCABULARY** Any number that can be expressed as a ratio in the fraction form $\frac{a}{b}$, where a and b are integers with $b \neq 0$, is a __?__. (page 17)

Classify the numbers as counting, whole, rational, or integers. Make a table to show your results. (pages 16–19)

3. 17, 0, $\frac{^-5}{6}$, $^-9.1$ 4. $^-1$, 35, $\frac{^-15}{3}$, 0.28 5. $^-4\frac{3}{5}$, 0.06, 51, $\frac{7}{8}$ 6. $^-0.2$, $\frac{7}{12}$, 6.5, 14

Give at least three other names for each rational number. (pages 20–21)

7. 0.45 8. 8 9. $\frac{^-3}{4}$ 10. $2\frac{4}{5}$

Graph the numbers on a number line. (pages 20–21)

11. 3.5 12. $\frac{2}{4}$ 13. $^-5$ 14. $^-2.00$

15. **VOCABULARY** A ratio that compares a number to 100 is a __?__. (page 22)

Write percents for the unshaded and shaded areas. (pages 22–25)

16. 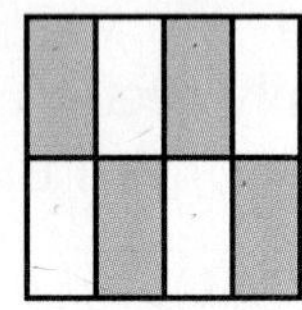

17. 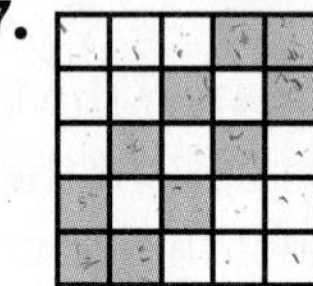

18. 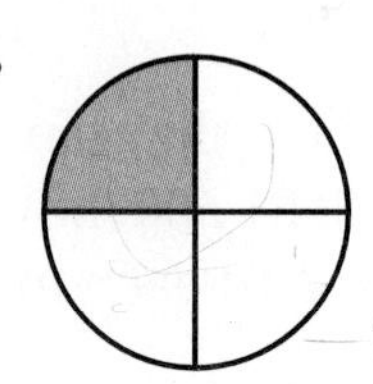

19. 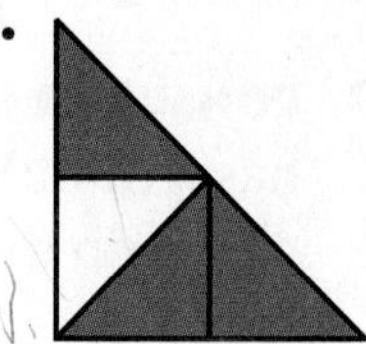

Write as a percent. (pages 26–29)

20. 0.35 21. 0.7 22. $\frac{6}{8}$ 23. $\frac{3}{10}$

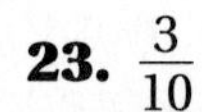

Write each percent as a decimal. (pages 26–29)

24. 3% 25. 111% 26. 56% 27. 32.7%

Find the measure of each central angle of a circle graph that shows the results of a music survey. (pages 30–31)

28. rock, 25% 29. pop, 45% 30. country, 10% 31. jazz, 5% 32. rap, 15%

Test Prep

1. Compare and order 2, $^{-}3$, and 5.7.

A 2, $^{-}3$, 5.7
B $^{-}3$, 5.7, 2
C $^{-}3$, 2, 5.7
D 5.7, $^{-}3$, 2

2. Which is equivalent to 0.36?

F $\frac{18}{100}$

G $\frac{9}{25}$

H $\frac{3}{6}$

J $\frac{36}{10}$

3. Which decimal is equivalent to the percent that represents the shaded area?

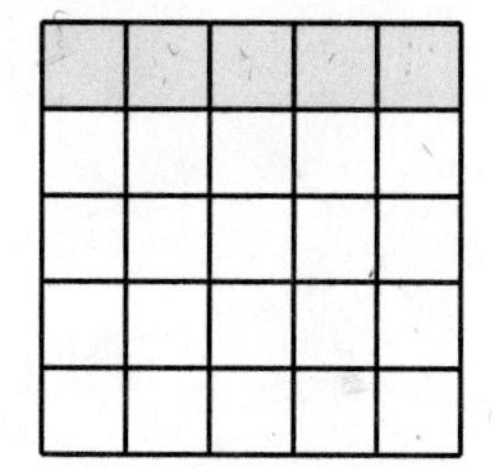

A 0.25
B 0.20
C 0.10
D 0.05

4. Which letter best represents $4\frac{3}{4}$ on the number line?

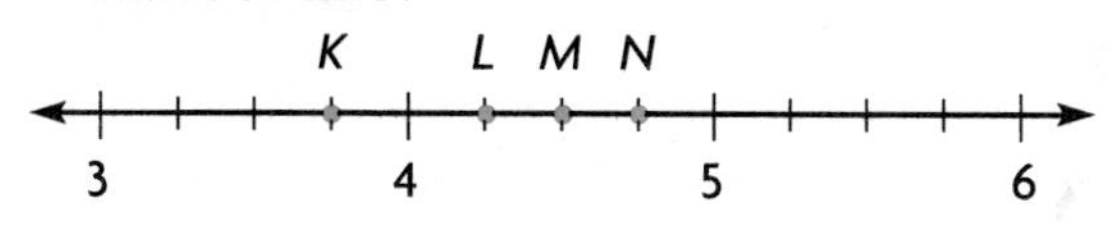

F *K* **G** *L*
H *M* **J** *N*

5. Which percent is equivalent to 0.4?

A 0.4%
B 4%
C 40%
D 400%

6. Which decimal is equivalent to $\frac{2}{5}$?

F 0.2
G 0.4
H 0.35
J 0.52

7. The Venn diagram shows how whole numbers, integers, and rational numbers are related.

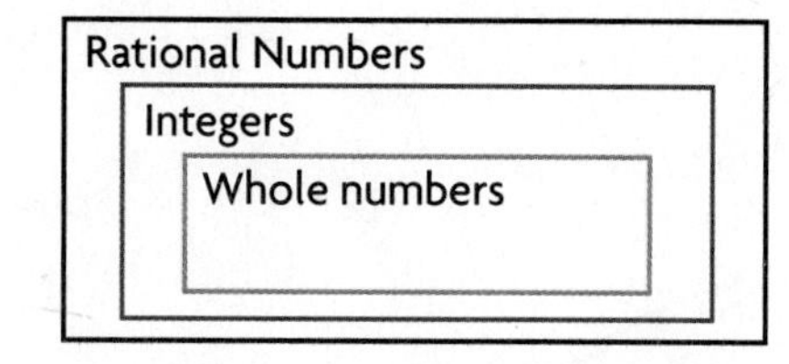

Which is a reasonable conclusion?

A All rational numbers are whole numbers.
B No whole number is an integer.
C All integers are rational numbers.
D Some whole numbers are not integers.

8. Which is not equivalent to the ratio 5 to 1?

F 500%
G 5
H 0.5
J $\frac{5}{1}$

9. Which percent best represents the shaded part of the circle?

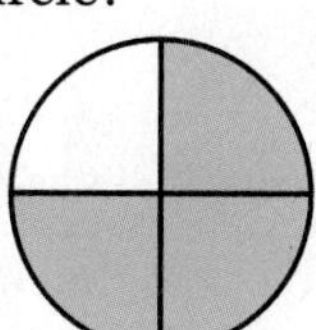

A 80% **B** 75%
C 50% **D** 25%

10. Which percent is equivalent to 1?

F 0.1% **G** 1%
H 10% **J** 100%

CHAPTER

2

EXPRESSING NUMBERS

LOOK AHEAD

In this chapter you will solve problems that involve

- writing and evaluating numbers with exponents
- writing binary numbers as decimal numbers
- modeling squares, square roots, and repeated calculations

SCIENCE LINK

Computer programmers represent data by using coding systems that are numbers in bases other than base 10. One coding system uses 7-digit binary numbers, which are combinations of 0's and 1's. Another coding system uses hexadecimal numbers, which are combinations of the digits 0 through 9 and the letters A through F. For example, the binary number for 183 is 10110111 and the hexadecimal number is B7.

Identify each number as binary or hexadecimal.

- 1011111
- F2
- A5
- 1010001

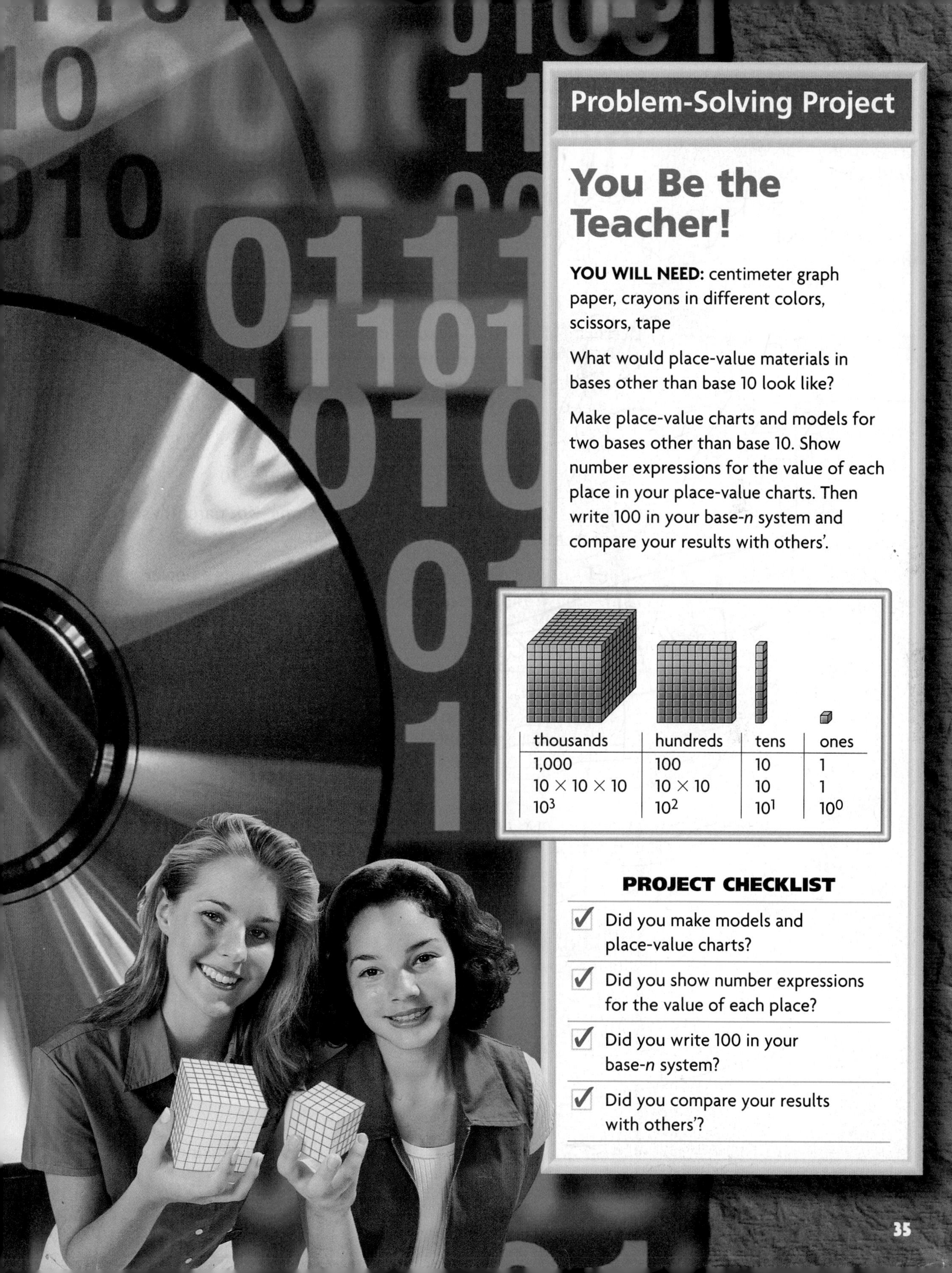

Problem-Solving Project

You Be the Teacher!

YOU WILL NEED: centimeter graph paper, crayons in different colors, scissors, tape

What would place-value materials in bases other than base 10 look like?

Make place-value charts and models for two bases other than base 10. Show number expressions for the value of each place in your place-value charts. Then write 100 in your base-*n* system and compare your results with others'.

thousands	hundreds	tens	ones
1,000	100	10	1
$10 \times 10 \times 10$	10×10	10	1
10^3	10^2	10^1	10^0

PROJECT CHECKLIST

- ✓ Did you make models and place-value charts?
- ✓ Did you show number expressions for the value of each place?
- ✓ Did you write 100 in your base-*n* system?
- ✓ Did you compare your results with others'?

LESSON 2.1

ALGEBRA CONNECTION

Using Exponents

What You'll Learn
How to use exponents and scientific notation

Why Learn This?
To evaluate large numbers or expressions in a science class or a science occupation

VOCABULARY

power
base
exponent
scientific notation

There are many ways to represent numbers. You can use words, numerals, and pictures, like these:

five **5** **V** **101_{two}**

⁘ 卌 **cinco**

There are also many arithmetic expressions you can use to represent a number. Although different in form, the following expressions are equivalent, since they all represent the same number, 5.

$2 + 3$ $\sqrt{25}$ $12 - 7$

$1 + 8 \div 2$ $(1 + 49) \div 10$

- Write at least three arithmetic expressions with parentheses to represent the number 6.

Another way to represent a number is to write it as a **power**, using a **base** and an **exponent**.

base $\rightarrow 3^4 \leftarrow$ exponent

Read the expression 3^4 as "the fourth power of 3."

REMEMBER:

The **prime factorization** of a number is a product of prime numbers.
$20 = 2 \times 2 \times 5 = 2^2 \cdot 5$
See page H12.

EXAMPLE 1 Show two ways to represent the number 16, using a power of 2 and a power of 4.

Power of 2	**Power of 4**
$2^4 \rightarrow 2 \times 2 \times 2 \times 2 = 16$	$4^2 \rightarrow 4 \times 4 = 16$

- CRITICAL THINKING Find another number that can be written as a power of 2 and a power of 4.

EXAMPLE 2 Show three ways to represent the number 625, using powers.

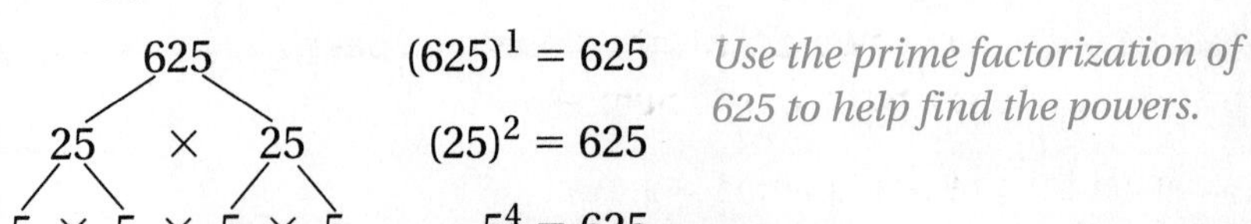

$(625)^1 = 625$

$(25)^2 = 625$

$5^4 = 625$

Use the prime factorization of 625 to help find the powers.

So, the powers are $(625)^1$, $(25)^2$, and 5^4.

- Show three ways to represent the number 81, using powers.

These charts show what happens when a counting-number base is fixed and the exponent takes on increasing values. Recall that a nonzero number with a 0 exponent has a value of 1.

$9^0 = 1$	$= 1$
$9^1 = 9$	$= 9$
$9^2 = 9 \times 9$	$= 81$
$9^3 = 9 \times 9 \times 9$	$= 729$
$9^4 = 9 \times 9 \times 9 \times 9$	$= 6{,}561$

$4^0 = 1$	$= 1$
$4^1 = 4$	$= 4$
$4^2 = 4 \times 4$	$= 16$
$4^3 = 4 \times 4 \times 4$	$= 64$
$4^4 = 4 \times 4 \times 4 \times 4$	$= 256$

Talk About It

- Suppose a base is greater than 1. As the value of the exponent increases, what happens to the value of the expression?
- Which has a greater value, 3^5 or 3^6? Explain.
- Which power of 8 is equal to 2^6?

EXAMPLE 3 Find the values of $(256)^2$ and $(1.5)^4$.

$(256)^2 = 256 \times 256$ 256 

$= 65{,}536$

$(1.5)^4 = 1.5 \times 1.5 \times 1.5 \times 1.5$ 1.5 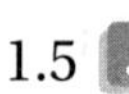  

$= 5.0625$

- Find the values of $(198)^2$ and $(\frac{1}{4})^2$.

CULTURAL LINK

The ancient Egyptians used reeds and papyrus to write numerals for computation, accounting, and record keeping. Which Egyptian numeral do you think represents 1? 4?

GUIDED PRACTICE

Find the value.

1. 2^9 **2.** 3^5 **3.** 7^3 **4.** $(15)^2$ **5.** $(2.2)^3$

Write as a power of 2.

6. 32 **7.** 64 **8.** 1,024 **9.** 512 **10.** 16

From the list, select two different numbers—a base and an exponent—to form the number

2
3
5
9

11. with the greatest possible value.

12. with the least possible value.

13. with the value nearest to 100.

14. with the value nearest to 10.

Scientific Notation

Scientific notation is a convenient way to represent large numbers by using exponents. To express a number in this way, write it as a product. The first factor is a number from 1 up to but not including 10. The second factor is a power of 10.

Divide to change a large number from standard form to scientific notation.

EXAMPLE 4 A drop of water contains about 33,000,000,000,000,000,000 molecules. Change this number from standard form to scientific notation.

33,000,000,000,000,000,000 — *Move the decimal point 19 places to the left. Use the exponent 19 on the base 10.*

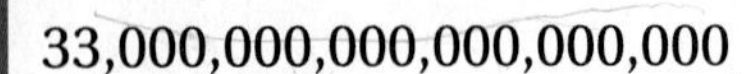

3.3×10^{19}

So, a drop of water contains about 3.3×10^{19} molecules.

- Change 32,000,000 to scientific notation.

REMEMBER:

When multiplying or dividing decimal numbers by powers of 10, move the decimal point one place for each power of 10.

See page H7.

$1.86 \times 10 = 18.6$
$1.86 \times 100 = 186$
$1.86 \times 1{,}000 = 1{,}860$

$245.3 \div 10 = 24.53$
$245.3 \div 100 = 2.453$
$245.3 \div 1{,}000 = 0.2453$

Multiply to change a large number from scientific notation to standard form.

EXAMPLE 5 Neptune is about 2.8×10^9 miles from Earth. Express this distance in standard form.

$2.8 \times 10^9 = 2.8 \times 1{,}000{,}000{,}000$
$= 2{,}800{,}000{,}000$

Move the decimal point 9 places to the right.

So, Neptune is about 2,800,000,000 miles from Earth.

- The star cluster Theta Carina is about 7.4×10^{15} miles from Earth. What would you do to write the number in standard form?

INDEPENDENT PRACTICE

Complete the powers to show two ways to represent the number.

1. $2^{\blacksquare} = 64$
$8^{\blacksquare} = 64$

2. $2^{\blacksquare} = 256$
$4^{\blacksquare} = 256$

3. $3^{\blacksquare} = 729$
$9^{\blacksquare} = 729$

4. $2^{\blacksquare} = 1{,}024$
$4^{\blacksquare} = 1{,}024$

Show three ways to represent the number by using powers.

5. 512

6. 1,296

7. 2,401

8. 10,000

Calculator Activities, page H36

Find the value. You may want to use a calculator.

9. 8^3 **10.** 98^2 **11.** 5^6 **12.** 2^{10} **13.** 10^7

14. 125^1 **15.** 4^8 **16.** 225^2 **17.** 3^0 **18.** $(0.6)^2$

19. $(3.2)^3$ **20.** 81^3 **21.** 128^2 **22.** $(\frac{1}{3})^4$ **23.** $(\frac{2}{5})^2$

Write in scientific notation.

24. 8,200 **25.** 45,300 **26.** 907,000,000 **27.** 1,802,000,000

Write in standard form.

28. 6.4×10^4 **29.** 1.76×10^5 **30.** 8.56×10^6 **31.** 6.7×10^{10}

Problem-Solving Applications

32. A 17-in. monitor displays 1,024 pixels on each of 768 lines. Write the total number of pixels in scientific notation.

33. **SCIENCE** Astronomers predict that in about 10^8 years one of Neptune's moons will pass near the planet and be torn apart. In about how many years will this happen?

34. **CRITICAL THINKING** A laser printer prints 300 dots to the square inch. How many dots can it print on one side of a single sheet of $8\frac{1}{2}$-in. $\times$ 11-in. paper if it leaves a $\frac{1}{2}$-in. border around all sides? Express the answer in standard form and in scientific notation.

35. **WRITE ABOUT IT** Your lungs take in about 0.47 L of air with each breath. How much air might you breathe if you live to be 100 years old? Write the amount in standard form and in scientific notation.

Technology Link

In ***Mighty Math Astro Algebra*** you can complete the mission *The Strange Cloud of Machine Parts III* to sort exponential expressions. Use Grow Slide Level Red S.

Mixed Review and Test Prep

Evaluate.

36. $10^0 + 10^2$ **37.** $10^1 + 10^3$ **38.** $2^1 + 2^2 + 2^4$

Find a rational number between the two given numbers.

39. 0.75, 0.8 **40.** $\frac{2}{5}, \frac{3}{5}$ **41.** $^-10, ^-11$

42. **GEOMETRY** A light is to be placed every 25 feet on the walls of a 350-ft $\times$ 400-ft room. How many lights are needed?

A 30 **B** 56
C 60 **D** 64

43. **ESTIMATION** Vic spends an average of \$19.85 a month on fast food. About how much does Vic spend on fast food in 1 year?

F \$200 **G** \$240
H \$280 **J** \$320

MORE PRACTICE Lesson 2.1, page H44

LESSON 2.2

ALGEBRA CONNECTION

Exploring Decimal and Binary Numbers

What You'll Learn
How to write binary numbers as decimal numbers

Why Learn This?
To explore the language of computers

VOCABULARY

binary number system

REAL-LIFE LINK

Computers, tapes, compact discs, laser discs, and many other technologies use the binary system. The two digits, 0 and 1, are represented by having electrical current on or off. Combinations of the two digits transmit data such as numbers. What decimal number would be transmitted by 111_{two}?

Ten is a very special number. It is the base for our decimal, or base-ten, number system. Each place is a power of 10. The decimal number system uses these ten digits: 0, 1, 2, 3, 4, 5, 6, 7, 8, and 9.

The **binary number system** uses only two digits, 0 and 1. The binary number system has a base of two. So, each place is a power of 2.

The binary number system is the language of computers. A computer works with only the digits 0 and 1. When you type a number, letter, or symbol on a computer keyboard, the computer changes it into a pattern of 0's and 1's.

The value of a number depends on the number system in which the number is written. The table below shows the values of the decimal number 1,010 and the binary number 1010.

Decimal Number	1	0	1	0
Powers of 10	(1×10^3) +	(0×10^2) +	(1×10^1) +	(0×10^0)
Decimal Value	1,000	+ 0	+ 10	+ 0 = 1,010

Binary Number	1	0	1	0
Powers of 2	(1×2^3) +	(0×2^2) +	(1×2^1) +	(0×2^0)
Decimal Value	8	+ 0	+ 2	+ 0 = 10

The table shows that the binary number 1010 has the same value as the decimal number 10.

$1010_{two} = 10$

↑ Use the subscript *two* when writing a binary number.

- Look at the table above. For the decimal number, what powers of 10 were used to find the value of 1010? For the binary number, what powers of 2 were used to find the value?

This table shows the first ten counting numbers written in both decimal and binary form.

	NUMBER SYSTEMS Decimal	Binary		PLACE VALUES 2^3 2^2 2^1 2^0
one	1	1_{two}	=	$(1 \times 1) = 1$
two	2	10_{two}	=	$(1 \times 2) + (0 \times 1) = 2$
three	3	11_{two}	=	$(1 \times 2) + (1 \times 1) = 3$
four	4	100_{two}	=	$(1 \times 4) + (0 \times 2) + (0 \times 1) = 4$
five	5	101_{two}	=	$(1 \times 4) + (0 \times 2) + (1 \times 1) = 5$
six	6	110_{two}	=	$(1 \times 4) + (1 \times 2) + (0 \times 1) = 6$
seven	7	111_{two}	=	$(1 \times 4) + (1 \times 2) + (1 \times 1) = 7$
eight	8	1000_{two}	=	$(1 \times 8) + (0 \times 4) + (0 \times 2) + (0 \times 1) = 8$
nine	9	1001_{two}	=	$(1 \times 8) + (0 \times 4) + (0 \times 2) + (1 \times 1) = 9$
ten	10	1010_{two}	=	$(1 \times 8) + (0 \times 4) + (1 \times 2) + (0 \times 1) = 10$

You can use powers of 2 to find the value of a binary number.

EXAMPLE 1 Use expanded form to find the value of 1001_{two}.

$1001_{two} = (1 \times 2^3) + (0 \times 2^2) + (0 \times 2^1) + (1 \times 2^0)$ *Multiply each*
$= (1 \times 8) + (0 \times 4) + (0 \times 2) + (1 \times 1)$ *digit by its*
$= 8 + 0 + 0 + 1$ *power of 2.*
$= 9$ *Find the sum.*

You can write any binary number as a decimal number.

EXAMPLE 2 Use expanded form to find the decimal number for 101011_{two}.

Count from the right to find the power of 2 for the first binary digit on the left.

Start with 2^0.
Move to the left to 2^5.

101011_{two}

$(1 \times 2^5) + (0 \times 2^4) + (1 \times 2^3) + (0 \times 2^2) + (1 \times 2^1) + (1 \times 2^0)$

$= (1 \times 32) + (0 \times 16) + (1 \times 8) + (0 \times 4) + (1 \times 2) + (1 \times 1)$

$= 32 + 0 + 8 + 0 + 2 + 1 = 43$

So, the decimal number for 101011_{two} is 43.

- Find the decimal number for 101100_{two}. How did you use addition to find the value?

HISTORY LINK

The binary number system has been used since ancient times. The numbers 0 and 1 were given the names of common objects. Only 1 sun and 1 moon existed. So, *sun* and *moon* were names for 1. A person had 2 eyes and 2 ears. So, *eyes* and *ears* were names for 2. Other numbers could be expressed by repeating the words for 1 and 2. *Eyes sun* was a name for 3. What might have been a name for 4?

GUIDED PRACTICE

Find the value of the binary number.

1. $110_{two} = 1 \times 2^2 + 1 \times 2^1 + 0 \times 2^0$

2. $1011_{two} = 1 \times 2^3 + 0 \times 2^2 + 1 \times 2^1 + 1 \times 2^0$

3. $111_{two} = 1 \times 2^2 + 1 \times 2^1 + 1 \times 2^0$

4. $1101_{two} = 1 \times 2^3 + 1 \times 2^2 + 0 \times 2^1 + 1 \times 2^0$

INDEPENDENT PRACTICE

Use expanded form to write each binary number as a decimal number.

1. 110_{two} **2.** 1000_{two} **3.** 100_{two} **4.** 101_{two}

5. 1011_{two} **6.** 1100_{two} **7.** 100001_{two} **8.** 101010_{two}

9. 1000000_{two} **10.** 11100_{two} **11.** 1001011_{two} **12.** 1100100_{two}

Problem-Solving Applications

A computer may use a conversion code, such as the ASCII code, to change each letter, number, or symbol you type into a block of 8 binary digits. A partial table of the ASCII code is shown below. The code numbers are given as decimal numbers.

Example

01010011 equals the decimal number 83. In the ASCII code, 83 represents the letter *S*.

ASCII Character Code (partial list)

Code	Char	Code	Char	Code	Char	Code	Char	Code	Char	Code	Char	Code	Char	Code	Char
32	(space)	46	.	57	9	69	E	79	O	89	Y	105	i	115	s
33	!	48	0	58	:	70	F	80	P	90	Z	106	j	116	t
34	“	49	1	59	;	71	G	81	Q	97	a	107	k	117	u
35	#	50	2	61	=	72	H	82	R	98	b	108	l	118	v
36	$	51	3	62	>	73	I	83	S	99	c	109	m	119	w
37	%	52	4	63	?	74	J	84	T	100	d	110	n	120	x
40	(	53	5	65	A	75	K	85	U	101	e	111	o	121	y
41	)	54	6	66	B	76	L	86	V	102	f	112	p	122	z
43	+	55	7	67	C	77	M	87	W	103	g	113	q	246	÷
44	,	56	8	68	D	78	N	88	X	104	h	114	r	251	1√

In Problems 13–16, each item appears as the computer reads it, as a block of 8 binary digits. Find the decimal numbers for the binary numbers, and then use the ASCII code to write what was typed.

13. 
00110010

14. 00110111

15. 00100101

16. 01101101

17. LOGICAL REASONING The computer read Mr. Meyer's age as 101010 and Mrs. Meyer's age as 101001. What are the decimal numbers for their ages?

18. WRITE ABOUT IT What is the difference between decimal numbers and binary numbers?

MORE PRACTICE Lesson 2.2, page H45

Modeling Squares and Square Roots

What You'll Learn
How to model squares and square roots

Why Learn This?
To understand squares and square roots that you see and use in math and science

VOCABULARY
- **square number**
- **figurate number**
- **perfect square**

You can build a square array with squares, with circles, or with many other shapes.

ACTIVITY **WHAT YOU'LL NEED:** 50 pennies or counters

- Work in a small group to build as many square arrays as you can, using up to 50 pennies or counters.
- What is the largest square array you can build from a roll of 50 pennies?

  from $1 in pennies?

  from $10 in pennies?

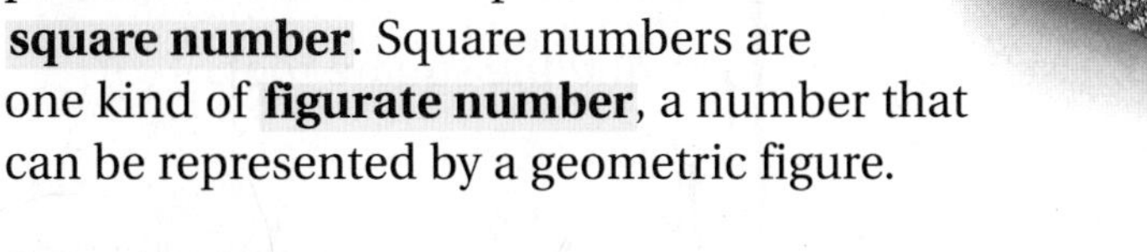

Each square array you made with pennies or counters represents a **square number**. Square numbers are one kind of **figurate number**, a number that can be represented by a geometric figure.

EXAMPLE 1 Use square arrays to represent 1, 4, and 9.

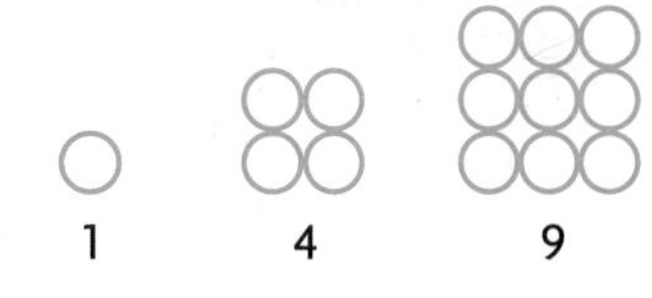

- Build or draw square arrays for 25 and 36.

REMEMBER:
The **square** of a number is the product of a number and itself.
See page H4.

Since $4 \times 4 = 16$, 16 is the square of 4.

The first five square numbers are 1, 4, 9, 16, and 25. Square numbers are also called perfect squares. A **perfect square** is a number that is the square of an integer.

$1^2 = 1$ $\quad 2^2 = 4$ $\quad 3^2 = 9$ $\quad 4^2 = 16$ $\quad 5^2 = 25$

The numbers 1, 4, 9, 16, and 25 are examples of perfect squares.

GUIDED PRACTICE

In Exercises 1–5, try to build or draw a square array to determine if the number is a square number. Write *yes* or *no*.

1. 36 **2.** 24 **3.** 49 **4.** 60 **5.** 100

6. Explain why 64 is a perfect square.

7. What is the square of 64?

8. Find the first perfect square before the square number 64.

9. Find the first perfect square after the square number 64.

REMEMBER:

The **square root** of a number is one of its two equal factors.

See page H4.

Since $36 = 6 \times 6$, 6 is the square root of 36.

Square Roots

You can draw squares to model the square roots of numbers.

EXAMPLE 2 Find the square root of 16.

Draw a square and divide it into 16 congruent squares. The length of each side is 4 units.

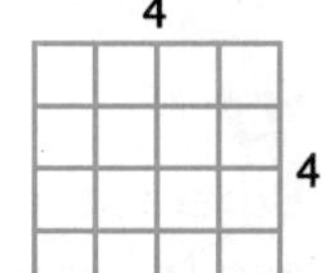

$4 \times 4 = 16$, so the square root of 16 is 4.

- Draw a square and use it to show the square root of 25.

Every positive rational number has a square root. The radical symbol, $\sqrt{\ }$, is used to represent the square root.

$\sqrt{81} = 9$, since $9 \times 9 = 81$ $\sqrt{2{,}500} = 50$, since $50 \times 50 = 2{,}500$

EXAMPLE 3 Use mental math to find the square root.

a. $\sqrt{0.81}$

Think:

$0.9 \times 0.9 = 0.81$

So, $\sqrt{0.81} = 0.9$.

b. $\sqrt{0.0025}$

Think:

$0.05 \times 0.05 = 0.0025$

So, $\sqrt{0.0025} = 0.05$.

TEEN TIMES

Although it doesn't take a rocket scientist to find a square root, square roots are important to rocket scientists. Scientists determine a rocket's escape velocity, or the speed it must have to escape Earth's gravity, by calculating square roots.

Talk About It CRITICAL THINKING

- Suppose a square has an area of 144 in.^{2} What is the length of a side?
- Suppose a square has a side with a length of $\sqrt{25}$ units. What is the area?
- Between which two integers is $\sqrt{60}$? Explain.
- Between which two integers is $\sqrt{32}$? Explain.

INDEPENDENT PRACTICE

Tell how many counters you need to make a square array with the given number of counters on one side.

1. 7 **2.** 9 **3.** 11 **4.** 15 **5.** 20

For Exercises 6–8, suppose a square array is made up of 900 pennies.

6. How many pennies are on each side?

7. How many pennies are on all the sides combined?

8. How many pennies are not on a side? Explain.

9. Suppose a square array has n pennies on each side. How many pennies are in the entire array?

10. Suppose a square array has n pennies on each side. How many pennies are not on any side?

11. How can you use square root to find the length of a side of a square with an area of 144 square units?

Find the square.

12. 8^2 **13.** $(10)^2$ **14.** $(21)^2$ **15.** $(1.2)^2$ **16.** $(0.8)^2$

Find the square root.

17. $\sqrt{100}$ **18.** $\sqrt{169}$ **19.** $\sqrt{1,600}$ **20.** $\sqrt{576}$ **21.** $\sqrt{3,600}$

22. $\sqrt{361}$ **23.** $\sqrt{1.69}$ **24.** $\sqrt{2.56}$ **25.** $\sqrt{20.25}$ **26.** $\sqrt{0.0289}$

Use mental math to find the square root.

27. $\sqrt{0.36}$ **28.** $\sqrt{400}$ **29.** $\sqrt{0.09}$ **30.** $\sqrt{0.64}$ **31.** $\sqrt{6,400}$

32. $\sqrt{0.01}$ **33.** $\sqrt{10,000}$ **34.** $\sqrt{8,100}$ **35.** $\sqrt{810,000}$ **36.** $\sqrt{0.0121}$

Locate each square root between two integers.

37. $\sqrt{14}$ **38.** $\sqrt{85}$ **39.** $\sqrt{77}$ **40.** $\sqrt{24}$ **41.** $\sqrt{42}$

42. $\sqrt{29}$ **43.** $\sqrt{115}$ **44.** $\sqrt{159}$ **45.** $\sqrt{140}$ **46.** $\sqrt{55}$

Problem-Solving Applications

47. **NUMBER SENSE** The square of a given number is the same as twice the number. What is the number?

48. **AREA** A square afghan has a side with a length of $\sqrt{36}$ ft. What is the area?

49. **CRITICAL THINKING** The Coast Guard is searching for a ship lost at sea. The square search pattern has an area of 10,000 mi^2. How long is each side of the search pattern?

50. **WRITE ABOUT IT** A square array is made up of 400 pennies. How many pennies are not on any side? Explain why the answer must be a perfect square.

MORE PRACTICE Lesson 2.3, page H45

LESSON 2.4

What You'll Learn
How to use the strategy *guess and check* to solve problems involving square root

Why Learn This?
To find the length of a side of a square

- Understand
- Plan
- Solve
- Look Back

PROBLEM-SOLVING STRATEGY

Using Guess and Check to Find Square Roots

To solve certain problems, you need to find the square root of a number that is not a perfect square. When you do not have a calculator available, you can use the strategy *guess and check.*

Joella needs 44 yd^2 of wall-to-wall carpeting to cover the floor of a square room. What is the length of each side of the room, to the nearest tenth of a yard?

UNDERSTAND What are you asked to find?

What facts are given?

PLAN What strategy will you use?

You can *guess and check* to solve the problem. Make some guesses. Check each guess. Keep a record of your guesses and checks, and try to improve each guess.

SOLVE How will you solve the problem?

Think: Area = 44 yd^2 length of side = $\sqrt{44}$ yd

Make guesses, and organize them in a table. Check each guess.

Guess 1	Guess 2	Guess 3	Guess 4
7 yd	6 yd	6.5 yd	6.6 yd
Check 1	**Check 2**	**Check 3**	**Check 4**
$7^2 = 49$ *Too high; use a lower value.*	$6^2 = 36$ *Too low; use a greater value.*	$6.5^2 = 42.25$ *Too low; use a greater value.*	$6.6^2 = 43.56$; 43.56 to the nearest yard is 44. *Correct.*

So, the length of each side of the room is approximately 6.6 yd.

LOOK BACK Why is 6 yd a good second guess?

What if . . . Joella needs 56 yd^2 of wall-to-wall carpeting for a square room? What is the length of a side of the room, to the nearest tenth of a yard?

PRACTICE

Use the *guess and check* strategy to solve.

1. Dionne needs 74 m^2 of wall-to-wall carpeting to cover the floor of her square living room. What is the length of a side of the living room, to the nearest tenth of a meter?

2. The area of Velma's square vegetable garden is 38 yd^2. What is the length of a side of the garden to the nearest tenth of a yard?

3. Kurt's square patio is paved with square ceramic blocks. The area of each ceramic block is 6.25 ft^2. The patio contains 64 blocks. What is the length of each side of the patio?

4. Wayne has two square animal cages. One has a perimeter of 12 ft. The other has an area of 16 ft^2. Which cage has longer sides?

MIXED APPLICATIONS

Solve.

CHOOSE a strategy and a tool.

- Guess and Check
- Use a Formula
- Make a Table
- Solve a Simpler Problem
- Write an Equation
- Draw a Diagram

Paper/Pencil

Calculator

Hands-On

Mental Math

5. A square microchip has an area of 0.1225 cm^2. What is the length of a side of the microchip?

6. Latonya jogged in the park at a rate of 6 miles per hr for 1 hr 15 min. How far did she jog?

7. Amy, Bill, Juan, and Molly are sitting at the corners of a rectangular mat. Boys and girls alternate around the mat. Write all possible seating orders.

8. Pedro is putting a fence around a rectangular garden. The garden is 8.5 m long and 6 m wide. How much fencing does he need for the garden?

9. The formula $D = 3.56 \bullet \sqrt{A}$ gives the distance, D, in kilometers to the horizon from an airplane at an altitude, A, in meters. Suppose you are flying at an altitude of 2,000 m. About how far away is the horizon?

10. The area of square parking lot A is 422,500 ft^2. This is 4 times the area of square parking lot B, 105,625 ft^2. How many times as long is a side of parking lot A than a side of parking lot B?

11. Samantha is 7 years older than David, who is twice as old as Marta. Samantha is 25. How old is Marta?

12. Classify the first 16 counting numbers as square numbers, even numbers, or odd numbers.

13. Timothy is fencing in a rectangular area that is 24 ft wide and 36 ft long. The fence posts will be 3 ft apart. How many fence posts will he need?

14. **WRITE ABOUT IT** Write a problem about finding the length of a side of a square. Show how the problem can be solved by using guess and check.

MORE PRACTICE Lesson 2.4, page H45

LESSON 2.5

ALGEBRA CONNECTION

Repeated Calculations

What You'll Learn
How to model repeated calculations or procedures

Why Learn This?
To understand how repeating a calculation affects the result

VOCABULARY

iteration

iteration diagram

Many things repeat. The Earth rotates once every 24 hr to produce alternating days and nights over and over again. You also do some things over and over. For example, every school day you get up, go to school, come home, and go to sleep.

An **iteration** is a step in the process of repeating something over and over again.

- Think about the four seasons of the year. Why is the sequence of seasons an iteration?
- Think of another example of an iteration. Explain why it is an iteration.

REMEMBER:

Counting numbers are positive whole numbers. The first counting number is 1. **See page 16.**

You can show the steps of an iterating process in an **iteration diagram**.

ACTIVITY **WHAT YOU'LL NEED:** calculator

The following iteration diagram models the rules of a game. Playing this game will help you understand the meaning of iteration.

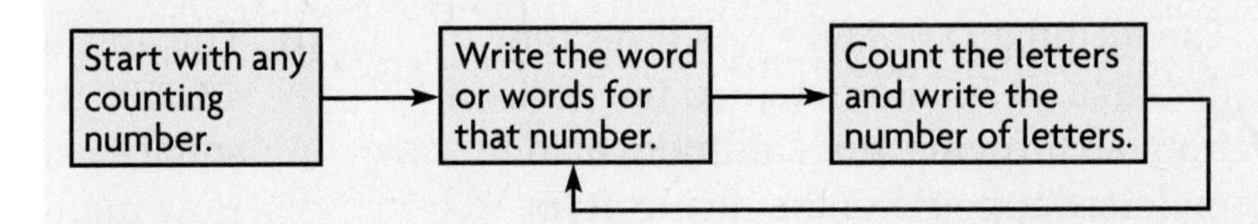
Start with any counting number.
Write the word or words for that number.
Count the letters and write the number of letters.

- Play the iteration game with a partner, repeating the steps over and over. Partners take turns choosing the counting number.
- Keep iterating until something special occurs. Write down what happens and why.
- Play the game several times. Look for a starting number that will keep you in the game as long as possible before that something special happens.

7
56
81
23
15

The iteration diagram below shows a numerical iteration.

Start with a number.
Find the square.

EXAMPLE 1 Start with 2. Use the iteration diagram above and complete the process three times. What is the square at stage 3?

2	→	4	→	16	→	256
Start		Stage 1		Stage 2		Stage 3

16 x^2 256.

So, the square is 256 at stage 3.

- Now start with 0.5, using the same iteration. Write the results of the first 3 stages. How are the squares different from those above?

EXAMPLE 2 Start with 2. Use the iteration diagram at the right, and complete the process three times. Round each square root to the nearest hundredth.

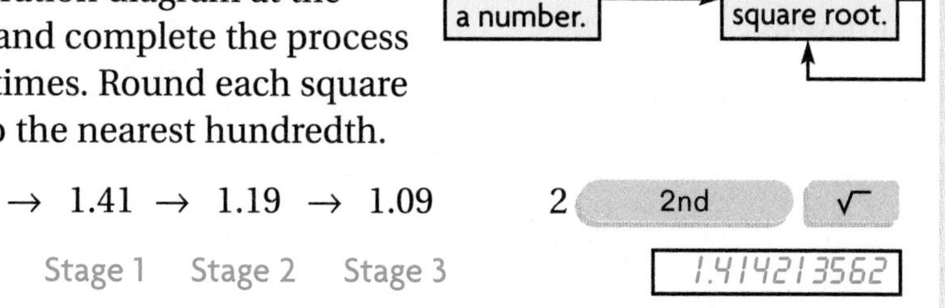

Start with a number.
Find the square root.

2	→	1.41	→	1.19	→	1.09
Start		Stage 1		Stage 2		Stage 3

2 2nd √ 1.414213562

So, the square root is approximately 1.09 at stage 3.

Talk About It

- Look back at the squares in Example 1 and the square roots in Example 2. How do the squares of numbers greater than 1 compare with the square roots of numbers greater than 1?

You can see the results of a numerical iteration on a number line. This number line shows the results from Example 2.

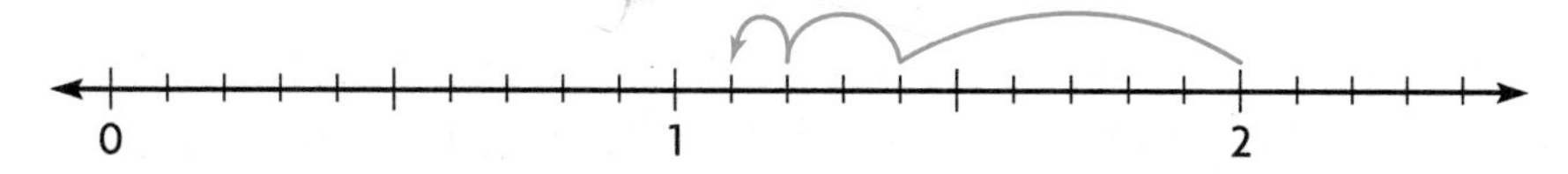

0
1
2

- Use the iteration diagram for Example 2. Start with 4. Record your results on a number line.
- CRITICAL THINKING Suppose you started with 0.5 in the iteration diagram for Example 2 and completed the process three times. How would the results be different from the results shown on the number line above?

TEEN TIMES

Every time you turn on a computer, it completes an iteration of a start-up procedure for checking components and loading software. After this start-up procedure, the computer is ready to run applications.

Calculator Activities page H31

GUIDED PRACTICE

For Exercises 1–6, use the iteration process shown at right. Start with the given number and write the results of the first six iterations.

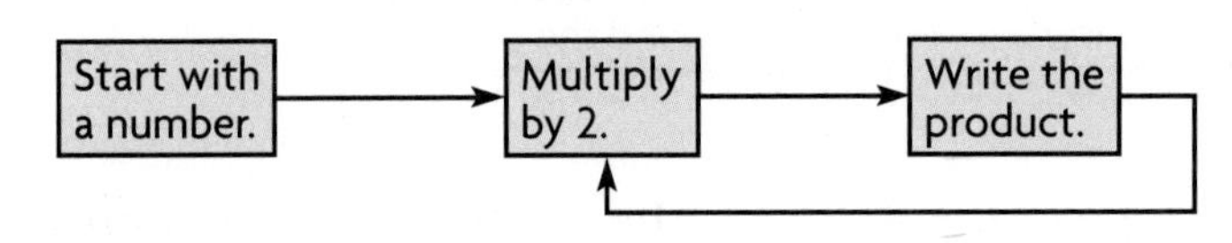

1. 10 **2.** 0.5 **3.** $1\frac{1}{4}$ **4.** 3.5 **5.** 6 **6.** $\frac{1}{4}$

INDEPENDENT PRACTICE

For Exercises 1–6, use the iteration process shown at right. Start with the given number and write the results of the first six iterations.

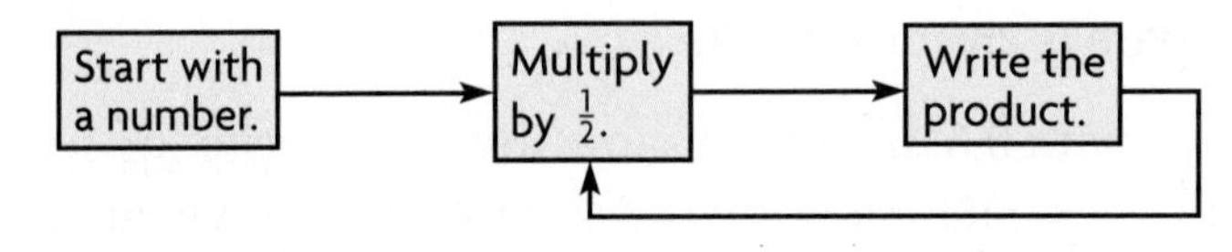

1. 20 **2.** 1.6 **3.** $1\frac{1}{2}$ **4.** 8 **5.** 12.4 **6.** $\frac{1}{5}$

For Exercises 7–8, use the iteration process shown above.

7. Start with 36. At what stage is the result nearest to 1?

8. Start with 1,000. What is the first stage with a result less than 100?

Problem-Solving Applications

9. **NUMBER SENSE** Amy completed the square-root iteration process 4 times. Her number after stage 4 was 3. What was her starting number? Explain how you found it.

10. **SPORTS** Jim jogged for 3 min on Sunday. He doubled the time he spent jogging on each of the next 5 days. How long did Jim jog on Friday?

11. **WRITE ABOUT IT** Describe an iteration that you perform each day.

Mixed Review and Test Prep

Round each of the following to the nearest one, ten, and hundred.

12. 235.6 **13.** 862.4 **14.** 790.3 **15.** 955.4 **16.** 555.4

Write each percent as a decimal.

17. 54% **18.** 119% **19.** 0.05% **20.** 3% **21.** 7.4%

22. **NUMBER SENSE** A car can travel 32 miles on 1 gallon of gasoline. If the gas tank holds 14 gallons, what is a reasonable maximum number of miles to travel on 1 tank of gas?

A 5 mi **B** 30 mi
C 100 mi **D** 400 mi

23. **PATTERNS** Each night a worm climbs $2\frac{1}{2}$ ft up a 20-ft wall. The next day the worm falls back $1\frac{3}{4}$ ft. How many nights will it take the worm to reach the top?

F 23 **G** 24
H 25 **J** 26

MORE PRACTICE Lesson 2.5, page H46

GEOMETRY CONNECTION

Geometric Iteration

What You'll Explore
How to model repeated procedures geometrically

What You'll Need
rectangular pieces of paper

You can also perform geometric iterations.

Explore

- Start with a rectangular piece of paper. Complete the process shown in the iteration diagram below three times.

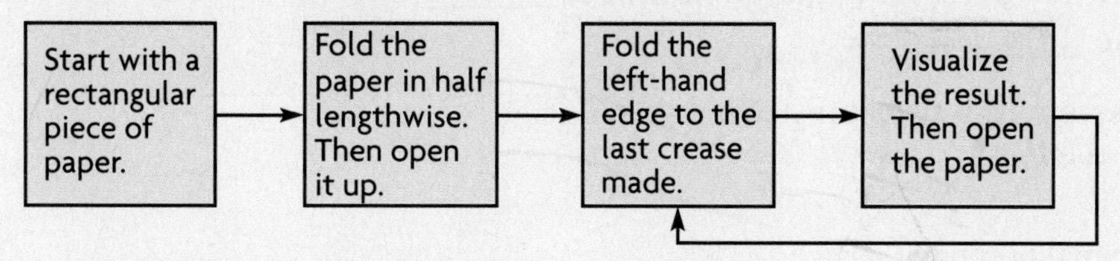

Think and Discuss

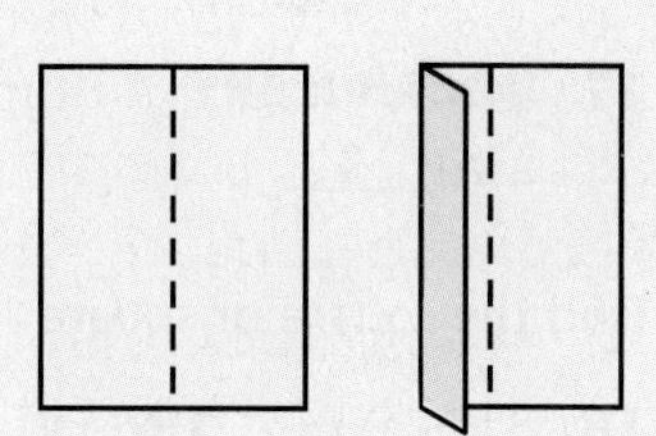

- What part of the area of the initial rectangle is the folded flap after you complete the process the first time, at stage 1?
- Express the areas of the folded flaps at stages 2 and 3 as parts of the initial rectangle.
- How is the geometric iteration similar to the numerical iteration below?

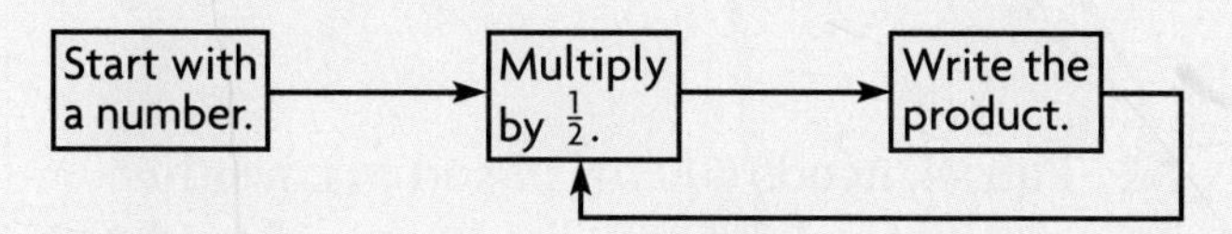

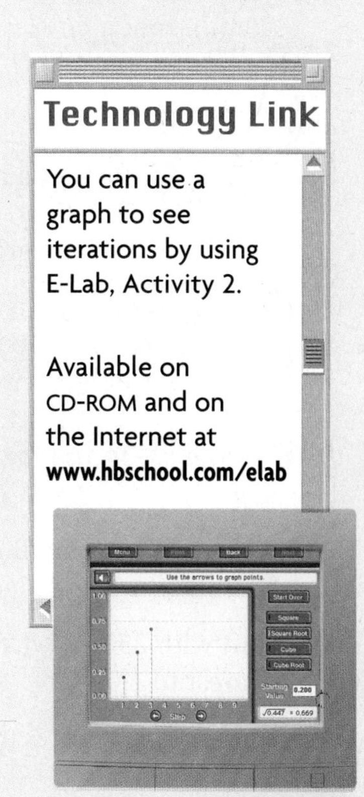

Technology Link
You can use a graph to see iterations by using E-Lab, Activity 2.
Available on CD-ROM and on the Internet at www.hbschool.com/elab

Try This

- Perform the iteration process one time. Draw a diagram to show the unfolded result of stage 1. What is the area of the stage-1 rectangle if the area of the starting rectangle is 1 square unit?

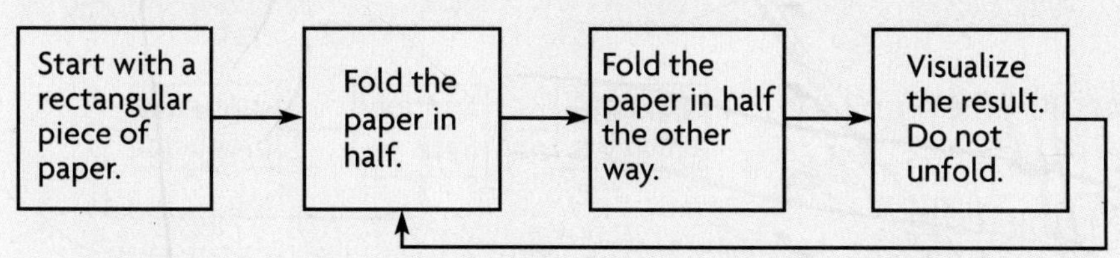

- Complete the iteration process two more times. At each stage, express the area of the folded rectangle as a part of the initial rectangle.

CHAPTER 2 Review/Test

Find the value. (pages 36–39)

1. 7^5 **2.** 15^4 **3.** 10^9 **4.** 121^3 **5.** 343^1 **6.** 4^0

Write in scientific notation. (pages 36–39)

7. 6,700 **8.** 34,100 **9.** 850,000,000 **10.** 29,030,000,000

11. VOCABULARY A convenient way to represent large numbers by using exponents is to use __?__. (page 38)

12. VOCABULARY A number system that uses only two digits, 0 and 1, is the __?__ number system. (page 40)

Write the binary number as a decimal number. (pages 40–42)

13. 110001_{two} **14.** 111101_{two} **15.** 1010101_{two} **16.** 10001_{two}

17. VOCABULARY A number that is the square of an integer is a(n) __?__. (page 43)

Find the square or square root. (pages 43–45)

18. 3^2 **19.** 11^2 **20.** 14^2 **21.** $(2.4)^2$ **22.** $(0.7)^2$ **23.** 4.2^2

24. $\sqrt{196}$ **25.** $\sqrt{4,900}$ **26.** $\sqrt{1,225}$ **27.** $\sqrt{441}$ **28.** $\sqrt{17.64}$ **29.** $\sqrt{0.0324}$

Solve. (pages 46–47)

30. A square foyer contains 36 tiles. The area of each tile is 2.25 ft^2. What is the length of each side of the foyer? What is the total area of the foyer?

31. Patrick needs 600 m^2 of sod to cover his square yard. What is the length of a side of the yard, to the nearest tenth of a meter?

32. VOCABULARY A step in the process of repeating something over and over again is a(n) __?__. (page 48)

For Exercises 33–34, use the iteration diagram at the right. (pages 48–50)

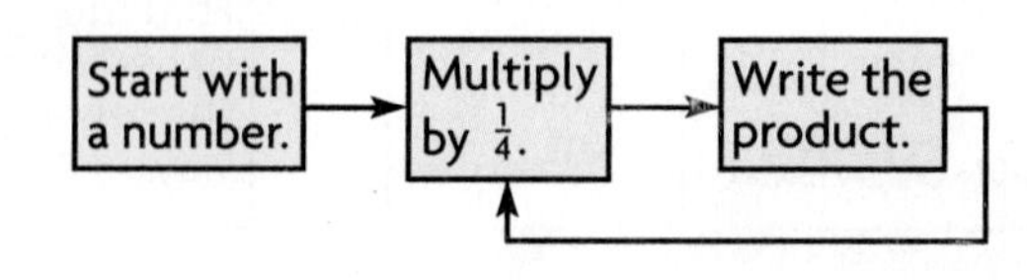

33. Start with 12. Find the results of the first four stages.

34. Start with 250. At what stage is the result nearest to 1?

35. Start with 1. What is the result at stage 3?

Test Prep

CUMULATIVE
CHAPTERS 1–2

1. Which best represents the geometric model?

A 3^2
B 6^2
C 8^2
D 9^2

2. Use the model to find the square root of 36.

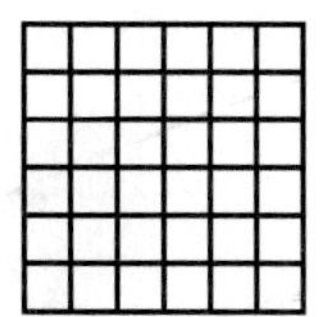

F 3
G 6
H 8
J 9

3. Which fraction best represents 0.8?

A $\frac{8}{100}$
B $\frac{1}{8}$
C $\frac{4}{5}$
D $\frac{8}{5}$

4. Carla needs 800 square inches of fabric to cover the square top of a box. Use a model to find the length of a side of the box top.

F about 24 in.
G about 28 in.
H about 30 in.
J about 90 in.

5. A square tablecloth has a side with length $\sqrt{25}$ feet. Use a model to find the area.

A 5 ft^2
B 25 ft^2
C 50 ft^2
D 100 ft^2
E Not Here

6. Which percent best represents the part of the figure that is shaded?

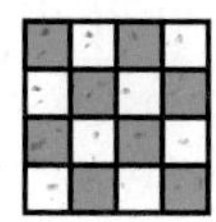

F 100%
G 60%
H 50%
J 25%

7. Into how many pieces could you cut a cake to make each piece 5% of the entire cake?

A 5
B 10
C 20
D 50
E Not Here

8. Jennifer has two square pieces of wrapping paper. The first piece of wrapping paper has a perimeter of 28 inches. The second piece of wrapping paper has an area of 64 square inches. Find the length of the sides of the piece of wrapping paper that has longer sides.

F 6 in.
G 7 in.
H 8 in.
J 9 in.
K Not Here

PARTS OF A WHOLE

PURPOSE To practice relating fractions, decimals, and percents to each other (pages 23–25)
YOU WILL NEED tangram pattern, scissors

One of the most popular puzzles of the 19th century was a Chinese puzzle called a tangram. Work with a partner. Cut out and label the tangram pieces as shown. Express each piece as a fraction, a decimal, and a percent of the whole pattern. Make a table like the one shown to keep a record.

Piece	Fraction	Decimal	Percent
A	$\frac{1}{4}$	0.25	25%

Have your family perform this activity. See if they get the same results.

ESTIMATION GAME

PURPOSE To practice estimating the value of exponents, the standard form of scientific notation, and square roots (pages 36–45)
YOU WILL NEED calculator, timepiece with second hand

Each player has 5 seconds to write down an estimate to Problem 1. Then use a calculator to find the answer. The player who is closest to the answer gets 1 point. Repeat for each problem.

Make up your own game to play with classmates.

1. $\sqrt{79}$
2. $\sqrt{183}$
3. 4.2×10^5
4. $\sqrt{124}$
5. $\sqrt{220}$
6. 9^3
7. 97^2
8. $\sqrt{398}$
9. 7.05×10^7
10. $\sqrt{0.50}$

THE TRICK

PURPOSE To practice using an iteration process (pages 48–50)

A king rewarded one of his subjects with anything he wanted. His subject asked for just one penny the first day, and to receive double the last amount each day for the rest of his life. How many pennies would his subject receive on the tenth day? on the fifteenth day? on the thirtieth day?

Write a story similar to this using an iteration process.

Summing Data and Making Circle Graphs

In this activity you will use a spreadsheet to sum data and make a circle graph.

The results of a survey about favorite milkshake flavors appear in the table. Enter the data in the spreadsheet. To find the total number surveyed, enter the formula "=sum(B3:B8)" in cell B9.

Favorite Milkshake Flavors	
Strawberry	219
Chocolate	553
Vanilla	301
Banana	188
Malted	193
Other	46

To make a circle graph, highlight the flavors and numbers and click the circle graph icon. Use the graph menu to label the graph.

A11	A	B
1	Flavors	Number
2		
3	Strawberry	219
4	Chocolate	553
5	Vanilla	301
6	Banana	188
7	Malted	193
8	Other	46
9	Total	1500
10		

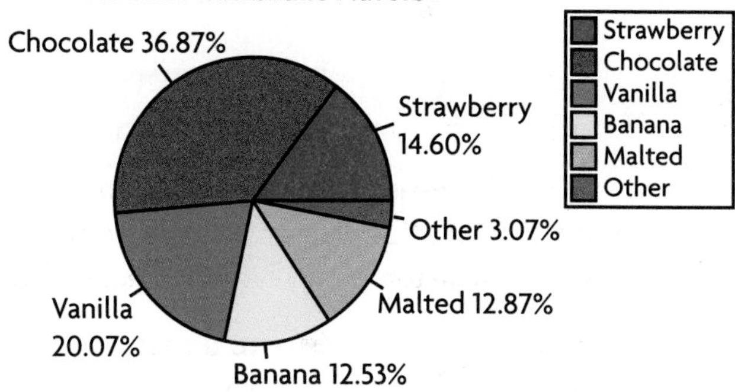

1. What percent of the people surveyed preferred chocolate milkshakes?
2. Which flavor of milkshake did most of the people surveyed prefer?
3. Describe how to make a circle graph comparing strawberry, chocolate, and vanilla only.
4. How would you find the sum of data if the data were in cells B5 through B20?

USING A SPREADSHEET

5. Enter the data on a spreadsheet and use it to make a circle graph.
6. Use a spreadsheet formula to find the total number of people surveyed. What spreadsheet formula did you use?

Favorite Subject	
Science	184
English	179
Math	242
History	234
Health	108

CHAPTERS 1–2

Study Guide and Review

Vocabulary Check

1. The set of whole numbers and their opposites are __?__ . (page 17)
2. Any number that can be expressed as a ratio in the fraction form, $\frac{a}{b}$, where a and b are integers with $b \neq 0$ is a __?__ . (page 17)
3. The number system that uses only two digits, 0 and 1 is __?__ . (page 40)
4. A step in the process of repeating something over and over is an __?__ . (page 48)

EXAMPLES

- **Write other names for a rational number and graph rational numbers on a number line.** (pages 20–21)

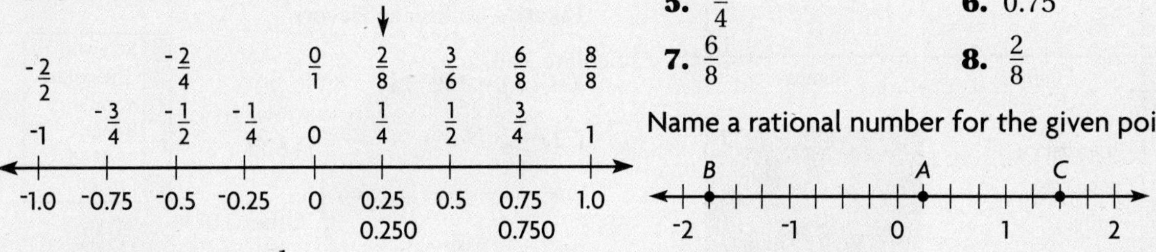

Find other names for $\frac{1}{4}$.

0.25, 0.250, $\frac{2}{8}$

- **Use percents to compare parts with the whole.** (pages 23–25)

Write percents for the unshaded and shaded areas.

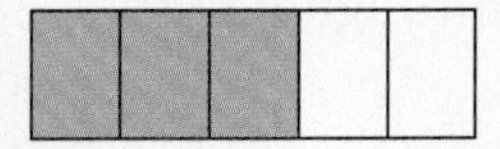

unshaded: $\frac{2}{5} = \frac{40}{100} = 40\%$

shaded: $\frac{3}{5} = \frac{60}{100} = 60\%$

- **Write equivalent fractions, decimals, and percents.** (pages 26–29)

Write $\frac{1}{5}$ as a decimal and as a percent.

$\frac{1}{5} = \frac{2}{10} = 0.2$; $\frac{1}{5} = \frac{20}{100} = 20\%$

EXERCISES

Write two other names for the rational number.

5. $\frac{^-1}{4}$
6. 0.75
7. $\frac{6}{8}$
8. $\frac{2}{8}$

Name a rational number for the given point.

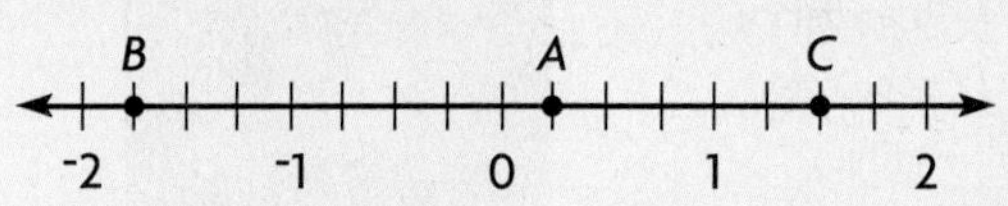

9. point A
10. point B

Write percents for the unshaded and shaded areas.

11. 
12. 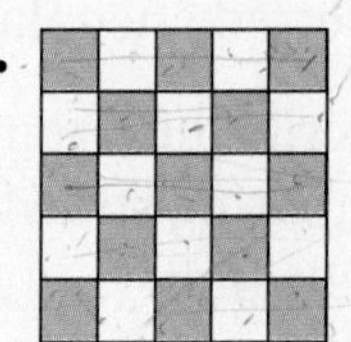

Write each percent as a decimal.

13. 5%
14. 125%
15. 64%

Write as a percent.

16. $\frac{4}{5}$
17. 0.6
18. $\frac{3}{10}$

- **Make a circle graph.** (pages 30–31)

Find the central angle measure for 30% of a circle graph.

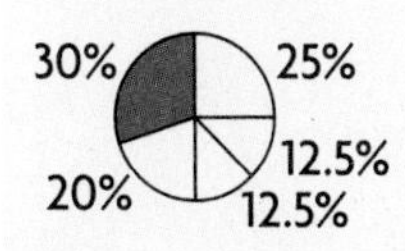

30% = $0.30 \times 360° = 108°$

Find the measure for each central angle of a circle graph of the given data.

	Favorite Lunch Choices		
19.	Pizza	60%	?
20.	Salad	20%	?
21.	Hot dogs	15%	?
22.	Peanut butter	5%	?

- **Write and evaluate expressions with exponents and numbers in scientific notation.** (pages 36–39)

Find the value of 3^7 and write the answer in scientific notation.

$3^7 = 3 \times 3 \times 3 \times 3 \times 3 \times 3 \times 3 = 2{,}187$

$2{,}187 = 2.187 \times 10^3$

Find the value.

23. 7^3 **24.** 10^6

25. 8^2 **26.** 4^4

Write in scientific notation.

27. 55,200 **28.** 4,300

Write in standard form.

29. 1.56×10^5 **30.** 8.9×10^6

- **Model squares and square roots.** (pages 43–45)

Find the square root of 25.

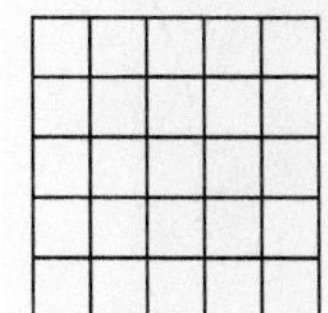

The area is 25 square units. The length of each side is 5 units.

$5 \times 5 = 25$

So, the square root of 25 is 5.

Find the square.

31. 9^2 **32.** 11^2

33. 20^2 **34.** 50^2

Find the square root.

35. $\sqrt{49}$ **36.** $\sqrt{100}$

37. $\sqrt{81}$ **38.** $\sqrt{196}$

Problem-Solving Applications

Solve. Explain your method.

39. Ty Cobb had a lifetime batting average in the major leagues of 0.367. Express this as a fraction and another decimal. (pages 20–21)

40. Into how many pieces would you cut a loaf of bread to make each piece 20% of the loaf? (pages 23–25)

41. The 1996 World Almanac estimates the population of China for the 1995 census at 1,000,000,000. How is this written in scientific notation? (pages 36–39)

42. Andre's square kitchen is covered with 74 ft^2 of vinyl. About how long is each side of the kitchen? (pages 46–47)

CHAPTERS 1–2

Performance Assessment

Tasks: Show What You Know

1. Give three other names for each rational number 0.4 and $\frac{1}{2}$. Then name a rational number between 0.4 and $\frac{1}{2}$. Explain your method for finding the number.
(pages 20–21)

2. Show two ways to represent 10,000 using exponents. Then write 62,000,000 in scientific notation. Explain your methods.
(pages 36–39)

Problem Solving

Solve. Explain your method.

CHOOSE a strategy and a tool.

- Make a Table
- Write an Equation
- Guess and Check
- Make a Model
- Act it Out

Paper/Pencil

Calculator

Hands-On

Mental Math

3. Alana plays basketball on Monday and Wednesday afternoons and Tuesday and Thursday nights. She wants to know whether she scores more points more often in day or night games. Alana scored 7 and 11 points on Mondays, 15 and 18 points on Tuesdays, 9 and 6 points on Wednesdays, and 10 and 13 points on Thursdays. Organize this information to show when Alana scores more than 10 points.
(pages 16–17)

4. The art class plans to paint a border on the ceiling of the student center. A group of students will be responsible for painting each side. The ceiling of the square room is 97 yd^2. What is the length of one side to the nearest tenth of a yard? (pages 46–47)

Cumulative Review

CHAPTERS 1–2

Solve the problem. Then write the letter of the correct answer.

1. 0.60 is a(n) __?__ number. (pages 16–19)

A. counting **B.** whole
C. rational **D.** integer

2. Which of the following is a rational number between $^-4.2$ and $^-4.21$? (pages 20–21)

A. $^-4.22$ **B.** $^-4.205$
C. $^-4.1$ **D.** not here

3. What percent of this figure is shaded? (pages 23–25)

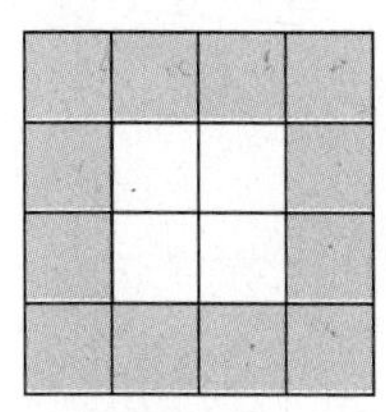

A. 0.5% **B.** 3%
C. 25% **D.** 75%

4. Which percent is equivalent to 0.3? (pages 26–29)

A. 0.3% **B.** 30%
C. 3% **D.** 300%

5. Which decimal is equivalent to $\frac{3}{5}$? (pages 26–29)

A. 0.060 **B.** 0.16
C. 0.60 **D.** not here

6. What is the central angle measure for 20% of a circle graph? (pages 30–31)

A. 20° **B.** 36°
C. 72° **D.** 720°

7. What is the value of 20^3? (pages 36–39)

A. 200 **B.** 400
C. 2,000 **D.** 8,000

8. What is 750,000,000 written in scientific notation? (pages 36–39)

A. 7.5×10^8 **B.** 7.5×10^7
C. 7.50×10^6 **D.** 7.5×0^7

9. What is the value of 1100100_{two}? (pages 40–42)

A. 6 **B.** 100
C. 110 **D.** not here

10. What is the square root of 900? (pages 43–45)

A. 30 **B.** 300
C. 450 **D.** 810,000

11. Marta needs 484 yd^2 of sod to cover her square-shaped yard. What is the length of each side of the yard? (pages 46–47)

A. 968 yd **B.** 242 yd
C. 22 yd **D.** 21 yd

12. Use the iteration diagram below. (pages 48–50)

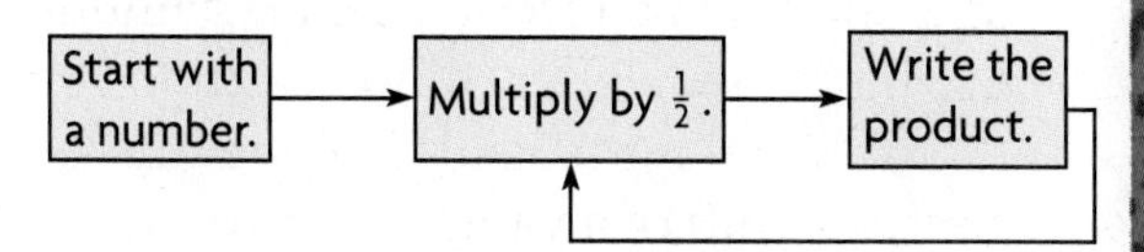

Start with 100. At what stage is the result nearest to 1?

A. Stage 0 **B.** Stage 1
C. Stage 4 **D.** Stage 6

CHAPTER

3

USING WHOLE NUMBERS AND DECIMALS

LOOK AHEAD

In this chapter you will solve problems that involve

- estimating and operating with whole numbers and decimals
- using the order of operations

CONSUMER **LINK**

The table below shows the percent of recorded music sold in 1996 for some categories of music.

RECORDED MUSIC SOLD IN 1996	
Category	**Percent**
Classical	3.4
Contemporary	12.1
Country	14.7
Pop	9.3
Rap	8.9
Rock	32.6

- Which category had the greatest sales?
- Which category had the least amount of sales?

Problem-Solving Project

Stocking Up on CDs

At Magnificent Music, an average of 107 CDs per day are sold from the Top Ten charts. With a monthly budget of $20,000, decide how many CDs to order in each category for a month. Calculate the wholesale cost of the CDs. Then calculate the profit if all the CDs you order are sold. Prepare a recommendation for the store manager.

Magnificent Music Mall
TOP 10 CD SALES OF THE WEEK

Number Sold	Category	Wholesale Price (Cost to Store)	Retail Price
115	Alternative Rock	$7.88	$11.99
42	Reggae/ Male Vocal	$9.20	$13.99
78	Rap	$9.20	$13.99
101	Country/ Female Vocal	$9.20	$13.99
125	Metal/Rock	$7.88	$11.99
31	Blues	$7.88	$11.99
70	Latin/ Female Vocal	$7.88	$11.99
54	Movie Soundtrack	$8.44	$12.99
60	R&B	$7.88	$11.99
74	Folk/Pop	$9.20	$13.99

PROJECT CHECKLIST

- ✓ Did you decide how many CDs to order?
- ✓ Did you calculate the wholesale cost?
- ✓ Did you calculate the profit?
- ✓ Did you prepare a recommendation for the store manager?

LESSON 3.1

Estimating Sums and Differences

What You'll Learn
How to estimate the sum or difference of whole numbers and decimals

Why Learn This?
To decide whether you have enough money to buy something

Do you think William Henry (Bill) Gates III has exactly $23,900,000,000, or is this amount an estimate?

Sometimes you need to know an exact sum or difference. When you don't need an exact answer, you can estimate. You can also estimate to check the reasonableness of an answer.

BILL GATES NAMED AMERICA'S RICHEST PERSON
William Henry Gates III, of Microsoft Corporation, is Worth $23,900,000,000

BUSINESS LINK

The $100 bill is the largest bill currently printed by the United States Treasury. A 1-in. stack of $100 bills contains about $15,000. Suppose Bill Gates' $23,900,000,000 is counted out in a stack of $100 bills. How tall would the stack be?

You can estimate sums by rounding.

EXAMPLE 1 Ana saved the following amounts from her last five paychecks: $5.38, $3.79, $3.63, $9.41, $4.89. Estimate to find whether Ana has enough money to buy jeans that cost $35.99.

$5.38 →	$5	*Round to the nearest dollar.*
3.79 →	4	
3.63 →	4	
9.41 →	9	
+ 4.89	+ 5	
	$27	← estimated savings

$\$27 < \$35.99$ *Compare the estimated savings with the cost of the jeans.*

So, Ana does not have enough money to buy the jeans.

You can find a range for an estimated sum.

EXAMPLE 2 Find a range for an estimate of the sum of the following amounts of silver: 3.42 g, 2.11 g, and 4.79 g.

Find an underestimate.

3.42 →	3
2.11 →	2
+4.79 →	+4
	9

Find an overestimate.

3.42 →	4
2.11 →	3
+4.79 →	+5
	12

So, the range is 9 g to 12 g.

You can use clustering to estimate a sum when all the addends are about the same.

EXAMPLE 3 Janine is buying three CDs. How can she use clustering to estimate the sum?

$$\begin{array}{r} \$10.29 \\ 9.79 \\ +\ 10.29 \\ \hline \end{array}$$

$\$10.29 \rightarrow \$10$ *All the numbers are close to 10.*
$\$\ 9.79 \rightarrow \$10$
$\$10.29 \rightarrow \$10$

$3 \times \$10 = \$30$ *Multiply.*

So, Janine's estimated sum is $30.

- Estimate the sum $8.59 + 8.31 + 7.82 + 8.05$ by clustering.
- Why is clustering not appropriate when estimating the sum $8.59 + 83.1 + 782 + 0.85$?

TEEN TIMES

Altogether, American teenagers earn about $102 billion a year from part-time jobs, allowances, gifts, and savings bonds and other investments. Of that $102 billion, teens spend about $67 billion on clothes and food and on CDs, movies, and other forms of entertainment. They save the remaining $35 billion for schooling or for a large purchase, such as a car.

GUIDED PRACTICE

1. Which method of estimating sums can you use to find the range for a sum?

2. Use an underestimate and an overestimate to find the range for an estimate of the sum $5.67 + 9.32 + 3.48$.

3. Which method of estimating sums can you use when all the addends are about the same?

Choose rounding or clustering to estimate the sum. Name the method used.

4. $98 + 46 + 78 + 9$ **5.** $9.8 + 10.1 + 9.5$ **6.** $41 + 39.7 + 40.9$

7. $61 + 31 + 52 + 8$ **8.** $26.78 + 49.31$ **9.** $2.9 + 3.3 + 3.5$

Give a range for an estimate of the sum.

10. $255 + 652$ **11.** $3.6 + 8.5 + 3.7$ **12.** $34.2 + 28.9 + 26$

Use an estimation strategy of your choice to determine whether the estimate is reasonable. Write *yes* or *no*.

13. $9.78 + 19.42 \approx 20$ **14.** $0.2 + 9.7 + 1.4 \approx 11$

15. $1.8 + 2.3 + 2.1 \approx 6$ **16.** $5.024 + 7.48 \approx 12$

17. $8.7 + 9.1 + 9.3 \approx 32$ **18.** $0.4 + 0.7 + 0.5 \approx 4$

19. $9.4 + 3.9 + 5.2 \approx 18$ **20.** $29.4 + 13.8 \approx 30$

You can use rounding to estimate differences.

EXAMPLE 4 Mateo's sister is paying her monthly cellular phone bill. Since the bill for this month seems high, she decides to compare it with last month's bill. About how much more did she pay for the cellular phone this month than last month?

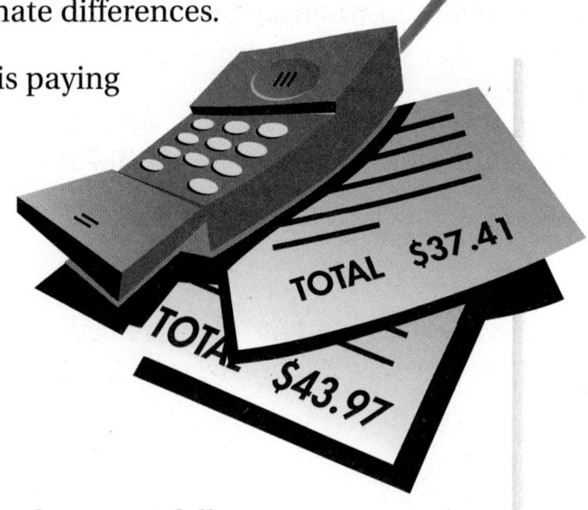

$$\begin{array}{rcr} \$43.97 & \rightarrow & \$44 \\ -\ 37.41 & \rightarrow & -\ 37 \\ \hline & & \$\ 7 \end{array}$$ *Round to the nearest dollar.*

$$\begin{array}{rcr} \$43.97 & \rightarrow & \$40 \\ -\ 37.41 & \rightarrow & -\ 40 \\ \hline & & \$\ 0 \end{array}$$ *Round to the nearest ten dollars.*

For this problem, it makes more sense to round to the nearest dollar.

So, the cellular phone bill is about \$7 more this month.

SCIENCE LINK

Today cellular phones and computer connections to the Internet are common. Soon the two will be combined to form cyber-cell phones. You will be able to use cyber-cell phones to send and receive e-mail, faxes, and voice communications and to access the Internet. A cyber-cell phone costs about \$1,500. A cellular phone costs about \$50. What is the difference in cost?

Talk About It

- Describe a method of estimation that would give you an estimate close to the exact difference for 651.2 − 248.9.
- **CRITICAL THINKING** Why is it important to estimate before using a calculator or paper and pencil to find an exact answer?

INDEPENDENT PRACTICE

During a science experiment, the masses of rocks are measured. Estimate the sum of the masses of each group of rocks by clustering.

1. 21.8 g, 19.8 g, 19.6 g, 21.3 g, 19.4 g

2. 174.3 g, 168 g, 167.8 g, 173.5 g

3. 34 g, 36 g, 28.9 g, 27.5 g, 34 g, 31.7 g

4. 256 g, 268 g, 267.4 g, 259.1 g, 260.3 g

Choose rounding or clustering to estimate each sum. Name the method you used.

5. \$2.39 + \$5.67 + \$7.96 + \$9.98

6. 6.7 m + 7.2 m + 7.3 m + 6.75 m + 7.4 m

7. 57 + 61.3 + 58.8 + 63.5

8. 36.7 + 109.3 + 51.5 + 23.02

Each group of numbers gives the average points scored per game by five basketball players. Find a range for an estimate of the total points scored by these players in a game.

9. Team 1: 23.4, 19.6, 12.7, 3.8, 8.6

10. Team 2: 14.8, 15.4, 19.3, 2.6, 6.7

11. Team 3: 29.8, 17.5, 8.2, 10.1, 3.3

12. Team 4: 31.7, 22.5, 18.9, 5.7, 6.5

Lee has $25.00 to purchase groceries. The prices of grocery items are given. Use any method of estimation to decide whether Lee can buy the group of groceries. Write *yes* or *no*, give the estimated total, and name the method you used.

13. $3.98, $2.43, $2.89, $5.56, $3.76, $9.99

14. $3.18, $2.88, $2.95, $3.69, $2.77, $3.49

15. $2.25, $4.76, $6.32, $1.05, $0.79, $7.32

16. $4.98, $4.43, $2.89, $9.56, $3.35, $1.98

Estimate the difference by rounding.

17. 23.94 − 17.44

18. 25.67 − 12.44

19. 178.09 − 24.45

20. 365.78 − 239.63

21. 8,541.6 − 889.3

22. 57,934 − 8,297

23. 5.794 − 3.428

24. 4,786.6 − 3,267.2

Problem-Solving Applications

25. ESTIMATION Mr. Griffin has a budget of $100.00 for math supplies. He wants to buy items that cost $19.95, $23.47, $11.25, $7.99, $32.67, and $19.23. Estimate to see if he can buy all of the supplies.

26. MEASUREMENT Wanda's pickup truck can carry 1,200 kg. Building materials with masses of 179 kg, 317 kg, 253 kg, and 217 kg are loaded into the truck. About how much more can Wanda's truck hold?

27. CRITICAL THINKING Miguel must earn a total of 27 points to advance in the ice-skating competition. He earns scores of 6.0, 6.0, 5.8, 5.9, and 5.9. Miguel estimates that he will advance. Is his estimate reasonable? Explain.

28. WRITE ABOUT IT Explain how an estimate helps you decide whether an answer is reasonable.

Mixed Review and Test Prep

Tell the number of decimal places in each.

29. 17.5

30. 0.43

31. 239.0675

32. 1.00072

Find the value.

33. 2^4

34. 3^4

35. 5^3

36. 11^2

37. 6^3

38. 17^2

39. NUMBER SENSE Simplify $6 + 5 \times 2 + 3^2$.

A 22 **B** 25
C 28 **D** 31

40. EXPONENTS How is $4 \times 4 \times 4 \times 5 \times 5$ expressed in exponential notation?

F $3^2 \times 2^2$ **G** 20^5
H $4^3 \times 5^2$ **J** 4×5^4

LESSON 3.2 Multiplying Whole Numbers and Decimals

What You'll Learn
How to multiply whole numbers and decimals

Why Learn This?
To solve problems such as finding the total amount of money you will earn for working a number of hours

You can use decimal squares to model the product of a decimal and a whole number.

Model 4×0.3 by shading 0.3 four times.

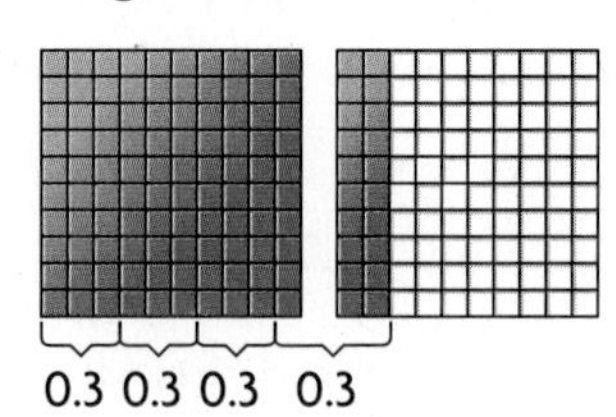

$4 \times 0.3 = \blacksquare$

- How many decimal squares are shaded? What is the product?

You can also multiply decimals and whole numbers by using pencil and paper.

REMEMBER:
The number of decimal places in the product equals the sum of the decimal places in the factors. **See page H7.**

EXAMPLE 1 Amy walks at a speed of 3.8 mph for 7 hr. How far does she walk?

Multiply as with whole numbers.

$$\begin{array}{r} 3.8 \\ \times\ \ 7 \\ \hline 266 \end{array}$$

Place the decimal point by counting decimal places.

$$\begin{array}{rl} 3.8 & \leftarrow \text{1 decimal place} \\ \times\ \ 7 & \\ \hline 26.6 & \leftarrow \text{1 decimal place} \end{array}$$

So, Amy walks 26.6 mi.

You can use decimal squares to find the product of a decimal and a decimal.

ACTIVITY **WHAT YOU'LL NEED:** decimal squares, markers or colored pencils

- To find 0.3×0.4, first model the factor 0.3 by shading three rows.
- Model the factor 0.4 by shading four columns with a different color.
- How many squares are shaded with both colors? What part of the whole is this? What is the product?

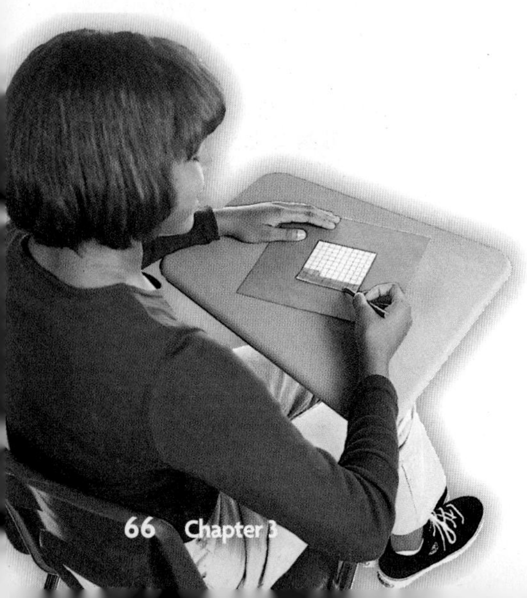

You can also multiply to find decimal products.

EXAMPLE 2 Nina worked 37.5 hr and earned \$6.80 per hour. How much did she earn?

\$6.80 ← 2 decimal places	*Multiply as with whole numbers.*
× 37.5 ← 1 decimal place	
3400	
4760	*Place the decimal point by counting decimal places.*
2040	
\$255.000 ← 3 decimal places	

So, Nina earned \$255.00.

- Suppose Nina worked 31.25 hr. How much would she earn?

Sometimes you have to use zeros as placeholders.

EXAMPLE 3 Find the product 0.75×0.036.

0.036 ← 3 decimal places	*Multiply as with whole numbers.*
× 0.75 ← 2 decimal places	
180	
252	*Place the decimal point. Write a zero to hold the correct number of places.*
0.02700 ← 5 decimal places	

So, the product is 0.027.

- How many decimal places are there in the product of 0.56 and 3.26?

TEEN TIMES

Most states limit the number of hours a teenager can work each week, particularly during the school year. For example, in Florida a 16-year-old can legally work only 3 hr on school nights and only 24 hr in a week.

GUIDED PRACTICE

Use decimal squares to find the product.

1. 2×0.8 **2.** 3×0.7 **3.** 0.6×0.6 **4.** 0.8×0.5

Copy the problem. Place the decimal point in each product. Add zeros where necessary.

5. $\begin{array}{r} 0.002 \\ \times \quad 4 \\ \hline 8 \end{array}$ **6.** $\begin{array}{r} 0.076 \\ \times\ 0.08 \\ \hline 608 \end{array}$ **7.** $\begin{array}{r} 5.027 \\ \times 0.010 \\ \hline 5027 \end{array}$

Find the product.

8. 7×0.9 **9.** 3.7×63 **10.** 0.6×0.8 **11.** 0.76×0.06

12. 2.3×0.006 **13.** 0.048×0.04 **14.** 2.28×4.83

INDEPENDENT PRACTICE

Use decimal squares to find the product.

1. 5×0.6 **2.** 9×0.3 **3.** 0.7×0.4 **4.** 0.5×0.9

5. 0.2×0.3 **6.** 0.4×0.2 **7.** 0.5×0.4 **8.** 3×0.7

Copy the problem. Place the decimal point in the product. Add zeros as needed.

9. $\begin{array}{r} 17.9 \\ \times \quad 6 \\ \hline 1074 \end{array}$ **10.** $\begin{array}{r} 57.8 \\ \times 0.13 \\ \hline 7514 \end{array}$ **11.** $\begin{array}{r} 0.003 \\ \times \ 0.02 \\ \hline 6 \end{array}$ **12.** $\begin{array}{r} 0.001 \\ \times \quad 9 \\ \hline 9 \end{array}$

13. $\begin{array}{r} 1.29 \\ \times \quad 8 \\ \hline 1032 \end{array}$ **14.** $\begin{array}{r} 6.96 \\ \times 0.21 \\ \hline 14616 \end{array}$ **15.** $\begin{array}{r} 0.037 \\ \times \ 0.12 \\ \hline 444 \end{array}$ **16.** $\begin{array}{r} 0.008 \\ \times \quad 12 \\ \hline 96 \end{array}$

Find the product.

17. 5.9×8 **18.** 9.3×7 **19.** 12×2.2 **20.** 6×4.7

21. 2.58×33.4 **22.** 8.7×6.32 **23.** 15.42×7.28 **24.** 6.45×14.07

25. 7.6×9.2 **26.** 0.006×2.3 **27.** 25×0.09 **28.** 235.2×6.81

29. 0.048×0.92 **30.** 57.8×0.13 **31.** 59.96×1.42 **32.** 0.0007×8.9

33. 35.6×0.008 **34.** 98.45×9.6 **35.** 0.68×10.45 **36.** 0.34×876.2

37. 0.75×0.054 **38.** 0.038×0.25 **39.** 1.75×0.024 **40.** 2.48×0.017

Problem-Solving Applications

41. ESTIMATION On Wednesday the movie theater sold 351 tickets for $3.00 each. The manager of the theater estimated the day's earnings to be $10,000. Is this a reasonable estimate? Explain your answer.

42. ALGEBRA The seventh graders of Eastside Middle School held a car wash. They charged $3.50 to wash a car and $4.75 to wash a van. They washed 157 cars and 43 vans. How much did they earn?

43. WRITE A PROBLEM Write a word problem that can be solved by writing a multiplication expression with decimals. Exchange with a classmate and solve.

44. ALGEBRA Last week Shawanda worked 21 hr at Tom's Tacos, where she earns $5.25 per hour. Last week she also baby-sat for 12 hr and earned $3.50 per hour. How much did she earn last week?

45. CRITICAL THINKING Which has the greater product, 2.5×0.32 or 0.25×3.2? Explain.

46. WRITE ABOUT IT Explain how you would place the decimal point in the product $2.4 \times 36.02 = 86448$.

MORE PRACTICE Lesson 3.2, page H46

ALGEBRA CONNECTION

Decimal Patterns on a Calculator

What You'll Explore
How to use patterns in whole-number and decimal division problems to predict quotients

What You'll Need
calculator

You can use patterns to predict quotients.

Explore

Find patterns in the sets of problems below.

- Use a calculator to find the first two quotients in each set. Then try to predict the other quotients.

Set A	Set B
368.9 ÷ 1.4 = ■	169.7625 ÷ 0.0135 = ■
3,689 ÷ 14 = ■	1,697.625 ÷ 0.135 = ■
36,890 ÷ 140 = ■	16,976.25 ÷ 1.35 = ■
368,900 ÷ 1,400 = ■	169,762.5 ÷ 13.5 = ■

- Record your predictions in a table. Also record the quotients obtained when you verify your predictions with a calculator.

Think and Discuss

CRITICAL THINKING

- What is the same about the division problems in each set? What is different?
- Describe the pattern that helped you to predict the quotients.
- For each set, name one other problem that fits the pattern.
- Name a related division problem with the same quotient as 126.9 ÷ 2.35 = 54.

Technology Link

You can model multiplication of decimals by using E-Lab, Activity 3. Available on CD-ROM and on the Internet at **www.hbschool.com/elab**

Try This

- Write at least four division problems the same as the one at the right but with decimal points placed differently. Predict the quotients of the new problems. Record the results you obtain when you verify the quotients with a calculator.

Given:

76.8 ÷ 1.6 = 48

LESSON 3.3

Dividing Whole Numbers and Decimals

What You'll Learn
How to divide decimals by whole numbers or decimals and how to estimate quotients

Why Learn This?
To solve measurement problems, such as finding average speed

VOCABULARY
compatible numbers

You can use decimal squares to model division of whole numbers and decimals.

ACTIVITY **WHAT YOU'LL NEED:** decimal squares, markers or colored pencils, scissors

- Shade 1.5 decimal squares. Divide the shaded squares into 3 equal groups. What part of a decimal square is in each group? What is the quotient $1.5 \div 3$?
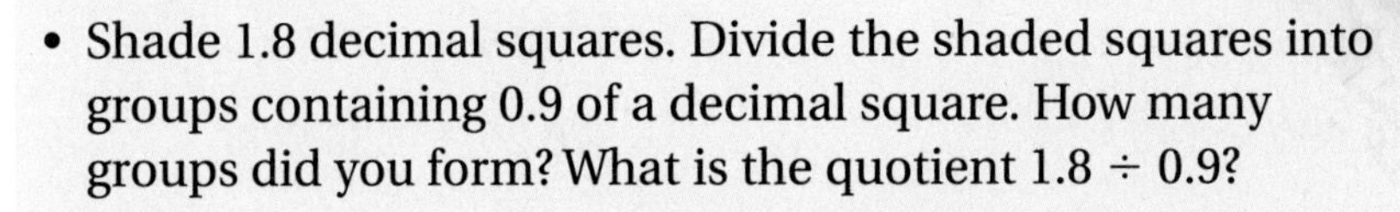
- Shade 1.8 decimal squares. Divide the shaded squares into groups containing 0.9 of a decimal square. How many groups did you form? What is the quotient $1.8 \div 0.9$?
- Shade 0.42 of a decimal square. Divide the shaded squares into 6 equal groups. What part of a decimal square is in each group? What is the quotient $0.42 \div 6$?

You can also divide whole numbers and decimals with paper and pencil. Sometimes you need to use zeros as placeholders.

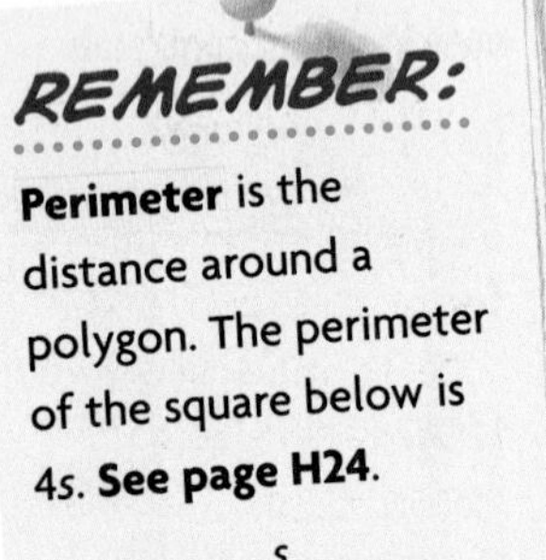
REMEMBER:
Perimeter is the distance around a polygon. The perimeter of the square below is 4*s*. **See page H24.**

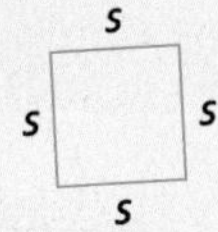

EXAMPLE 1 The perimeter of a square is 12.12 m. What is the length of a side?

Think: To find the length of a side of a square, divide the perimeter by 4.

Place the decimal point above the one in the dividend.	*Since the first digit will be in the ones place, divide the 12 ones.*	*Divide the 1 tenth. Since 4 > 1, write 0 in the quotient.*	*Divide the 12 hundredths.*
$\begin{array}{r} . \\ 4\overline{)12.12} \end{array}$	$\begin{array}{r} 3. \\ 4\overline{)12.12} \\ -12 \\ \hline 0 \end{array}$	$\begin{array}{r} 3.0 \\ 4\overline{)12.12} \\ -12\downarrow \\ \hline 0\,1 \end{array}$	$\begin{array}{r} 3.03 \\ 4\overline{)12.12} \\ -12\downarrow\downarrow \\ \hline 0\,12 \\ -12 \\ \hline 0 \end{array}$

So, the length of a side is 3.03 m.

Recall that when you multiply a divisor and a dividend by the same power of 10, the quotient does not change.

$$15\overline{)75} = 5 \qquad \text{divisor: } 15 \times 10 = 150 \quad \text{dividend: } 75 \times 10 = 750 \qquad 150\overline{)750} = 5$$

To divide a decimal by a decimal, multiply the divisor and the dividend by the same power of 10.

EXAMPLE 2 Emil traveled 28.5 mi in 1.25 hr. Find his speed in miles per hour by dividing the distance by the time.

Multiply the divisor and the dividend by the same power of 10.

$1.25\overline{)28.50}$ ← Write a zero.

$1.25 \times 100 = 125$
$28.5 \times 100 = 2{,}850$

Divide as with whole numbers. Continue dividing until the remainder is zero.

$$\begin{array}{r} 22.8 \\ 125\overline{)2850.0} \\ -250 \\ \hline 350 \\ -250 \\ \hline 100\,0 \\ -100\,0 \\ \hline 0 \end{array}$$
← Write a zero.

So, his speed was 22.8 mph.

- By what power of 10 would you multiply to find the quotient $74 \div 0.037$? $6.9 \div 0.0003$?

You can use compatible numbers to estimate quotients of whole numbers and decimals. **Compatible numbers** are close to the dividend and divisor, divide with a remainder of zero, and are easy to compute.

$9\overline{)7{,}418} \rightarrow 9\overline{)7{,}200}$ (quotient 800) **Think:** $72 \div 9 = 8$, or $9 \times \blacksquare = 72$

EXAMPLE 3 Estimate the quotient $786.4 \div 4.2$ by using compatible numbers.

$4.2\overline{)786.4}$ *Use compatible numbers.* $4\overline{)800}$ (quotient 200)

So, $786.4 \div 4.2$ is about 200.

- How would you use compatible numbers to estimate the quotient $31.04 \div 0.82$?

When multiplying decimal numbers by powers of 10, move the decimal point one place to the right for each power of 10. **See page H7.**

HISTORY LINK

In the mid-1970's, the United States set a national speed limit of 55 mph. The national speed limit remained at 55 mph until the mid-1990's, when individual states could set their own speed limits. Some states raised their speed limits to 60, 65, or 70 mph. Suppose a state's fine is $10.50 for every mile per hour over the speed limit and a driver is fined a total of $84.00 for speeding in a 55-mph area. What was the driver's speed?

GUIDED PRACTICE

Use decimal squares to find the quotient.

1. 2.0 ÷ 5 **2.** 2.7 ÷ 3 **3.** 0.14 ÷ 2 **4.** 0.24 ÷ 4

Find the quotient.

5. 1,029 ÷ 4.9 **6.** 92.6 ÷ 5 **7.** 24.18 ÷ 4 **8.** 76.34 ÷ 8

INDEPENDENT PRACTICE

Find the quotient.

1. 67.5 ÷ 5.4 **2.** 9.85 ÷ 0.05 **3.** 18.6 ÷ 3 **4.** 158.4 ÷ 0.12

5. 9.632 ÷ 1.6 **6.** 15.12 ÷ 4.2 **7.** 1.14 ÷ 0.19 **8.** 12.505 ÷ 3.05

9. 8.128 ÷ 0.32 **10.** 32.144 ÷ 1.6 **11.** 0.104 ÷ 0.32 **12.** 274.89 ÷ 1.5

A regular polygon and its perimeter are given. Find the length of a side.

13. equilateral triangle, 240.3 m **14.** square, 27.9 cm **15.** hexagon, 34.71 m **16.** octagon, 65.2 cm

Find the speed in miles per hour by dividing the distance (d) by the time (t).

17. $d = 24.6$ mi, $t = 1.5$ hr **18.** $d = 78.05$ mi, $t = 1.75$ hr **19.** $d = 298.2$ mi, $t = 3.5$ hr **20.** $d = 75.33$ mi, $t = 18.6$ hr

Estimate the quotient by using compatible numbers.

21. 8.17 ÷ 1.9 **22.** 36.15 ÷ 7.2 **23.** 23.2 ÷ 6.4 **24.** 55.9 ÷ 8.1

Problem-Solving Applications

25. **TIME** Fabrina is trying out for the school swim team. To make the team, she must average no more than 24.75 sec per lap. She swims 4.5 laps in 110.25 sec. What is her average time per lap? Does she make the team?

26. **CONSUMER MATH** Eight identical dresses were purchased for the school play, at a cost of $189.92. The budget allows only $24.50 to be spent for each dress. What was the cost of each dress? Was the cost within the budget?

27. **CRITICAL THINKING** A car loan totaling $13,456.44 is to be paid off in 36 equal monthly payments. Jon can afford no more than $350 per month. Can he afford the loan? Explain.

28. **WRITE ABOUT IT** Write two word problems that can be solved by writing division expressions with decimals. Exchange with a classmate and solve.

MORE PRACTICE Lesson 3.3, page H47

Order of Operations

What You'll Learn
How to use the order of operations

Why Learn This?
To solve a problem that requires more than one operation

VOCABULARY
order of operations
algebraic operating system (AOS)

For many everyday actions, you must complete steps in a certain order. For example, when using a phone, you first pick up the receiver, then dial, and then listen for a connection or ringing.

In mathematics, you follow rules called **order of operations** when a problem contains more than one operation.

Order of Operations

1. Operate inside parentheses.
2. Clear exponents.
3. Multiply and divide from left to right.
4. Add and subtract from left to right.

EXAMPLE 1 Give the operations used to find the value.

$65 \div 5 \times 3 - 2^3$

$65 \div 5 \times 3 - 2^3$	*Clear exponent.*
$65 \div 5 \times 3 - 8$	*Divide.*
$13 \times 3 - 8$	*Multiply.*
$39 - 8$	*Subtract.*
31	

The order of operations applies to decimals as well as to whole numbers.

EXAMPLE 2 Give the operations used to find the value.

$4.9 + 4.5 \div 1.5 - (0.5 \times 3)^2$

$4.9 + 4.5 \div 1.5 - (0.5 \times 3)^2$	*Multiply in parentheses.*
$4.9 + 4.5 \div 1.5 - (1.5)^2$	*Clear exponent.*
$4.9 + 4.5 \div 1.5 - 2.25$	*Divide.*
$4.9 + 3 - 2.25$	*Add.*
$7.9 - 2.25$	*Subtract.*
5.65	

- What if there were no parentheses in Example 2? What would the value be?

LANGUAGE LINK

A mnemonic (nih • MAH • nik) is a pattern or technique for aiding memory. How can you use the first letters of these words to help you remember the order of operations?

Please **E**xcuse **M**y **D**ear **A**unt **S**ally

Algebraic Operating Systems

When using a calculator, you need to know whether or not it uses the algebraic order of operations.

Many calculators simply operate from left to right unless parentheses are inserted. However, scientific calculators use an **algebraic operating system (AOS)**, which automatically follows the order of operations.

Test your calculator to see whether it uses an AOS.

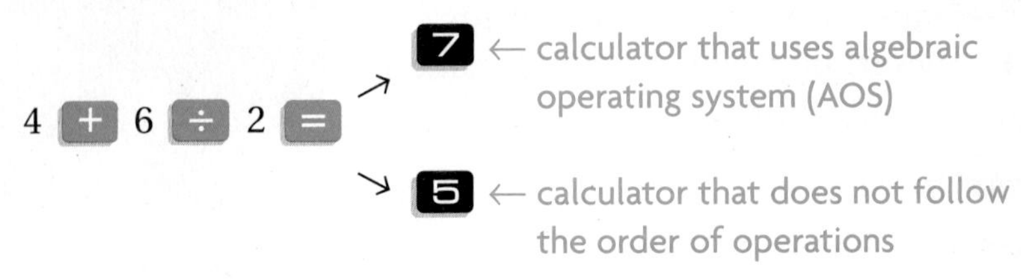

If you do not have an AOS calculator, you can follow the order of operations by using the memory keys.

EXAMPLE 3 Find the value of $6.2 + 4.9 \times 3.1$ by using an AOS calculator and by using a calculator without AOS.

AOS calculator:

6.2 [+] 4.9 [×] 3.1 [=] 21.39 *Enter operations from left to right.*

calculator without AOS:

6.2 [M+] 4.9 [×] 3.1 [M+] [MRC] 21.39 *Use the memory keys.*

SOCIAL STUDIES LINK

Demography is the study of human populations. School demographics are tracked to balance resources, faculty, and staff. Suppose in October your school has 82 students in the seventh-grade class. A month later, there are 13 more seventh graders. Then the class is divided into 5 teams. Find the number of students on each team by finding the value of $(82 + 13) \div 5$.

GUIDED PRACTICE

1. Follow this sequence of operations to find the value.
cube → divide → multiply → add → subtract
$4 + 4^3 \div 4 \times 4 - 4$

Give the correct order of operations for finding the value.

2. $4 \times 12 - 3 + 8$ **3.** $2^5 - (4.5 \times 2 + 5)$ **4.** $20 - 5 \times 3 + 16$

Find the value.

5. $3 \times 6 + 8$ **6.** $9 - 4 \div 2 + 5$ **7.** $3^2 + 4 - (2 + 1)$

8. $7 + 3 \times 4$ **9.** $12 + 8 \times 2 - 6$ **10.** $3^3 \div (13 - 4) + 8$

INDEPENDENT PRACTICE

Give the correct order of operations for finding the value.

1. $(18 - 6) \div 2$

2. $(12 - 1.30) \times 6.6$

3. $2^5 - (3 + 8.98 \div 2)$

4. $5 \times (9.4 - 3.6)$

5. $5 \times 9.4 - 3.6$

6. $2.1 - 2 + 1.5 \times 2^2$

7. Follow this sequence of operations to find the value.
cube → divide → multiply → add → subtract
$3 \div 3 + 3 \times 3^3 - 3$

Give the correct order of operations for finding the value, and find the value.

8. $(3 \times 3 + 3)^3 \div 3 - 3$

9. $(3 \div 3) + 3 \times 3^3 - 3$

10. $3 \div 3 + 3 \times (3^3 - 3)$

11. $(6.75 - 0.48) \div (0.5)^3 + 4$

12. $(36 - 3) \div 3 + 45 \div 9$

13. $(1.4 + 2.6)^2 - (10.2 - 2.2)$

Find the value by using a calculator.

14. $3 + 7 \times 5 - 1$

15. $2^5 - (4 \times 5 + 3)$

16. $42 \div (2 + 5) \times 3$

17. $(18 - 2 \times 3 + 6) \div 3$

18. $(3.6 + 6.4) \times (5 - 1)^3$

19. $56.25 - 4.2 \times 8.35$

Problem-Solving Applications

20. CONSUMER MATH Tremayne bought 6 stamps at $0.20 each and 8 at $0.32 each. How much did he spend on stamps?

21. ALGEBRAIC THINKING Marissa has nickels and dimes in her purse. The 10 coins have a value of $0.80. How many of each does she have?

22. WRITE ABOUT IT A calculator shows 9 as the value of $24 + 32 \div 8 + 2$. Does the calculator use an AOS system? Explain.

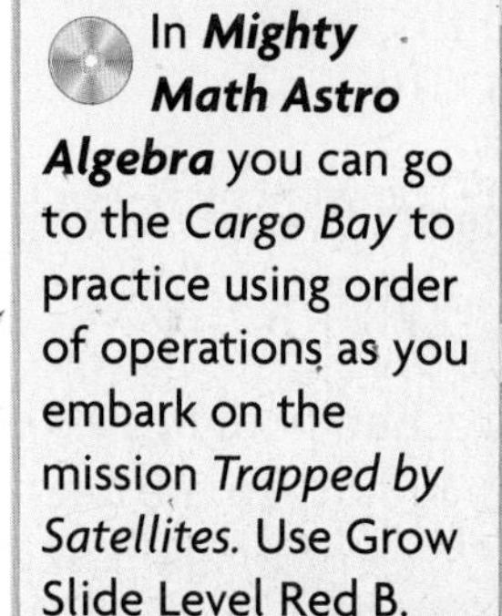

In *Mighty Math Astro Algebra* you can go to the *Cargo Bay* to practice using order of operations as you embark on the mission *Trapped by Satellites.* Use Grow Slide Level Red B.

Mixed Review and Test Prep

Find the least common multiple.

23. 3, 15

24. 8, 12

25. 3, 4, 6

26. 2, 3, 5

Find the square root.

27. $\sqrt{16}$

28. $\sqrt{64}$

29. $\sqrt{361}$

30. $\sqrt{1.44}$

31. PERCENTS Convert $\frac{13}{25}$ to a percent.

A 0.52% **B** 52%
C 0.13% **D** 13%

32. DECIMALS Convert 136% to a decimal.

F 0.136 **G** 1.36
H 13.6 **J** 136

MORE PRACTICE Lesson 3.4, page H47

CHAPTER 3 Review/Test

Find a range for an estimate of the sum. (pages 62–65)

1. $8.4 + 9.6 + 1.2$ **2.** $18.6 + 8.4 + 6.8$ **3.** $23.6 + 1.5 + 17.2$ **4.** $94.5 + 87.2 + 6.7$

Estimate the sum or difference. (pages 62–65)

5. $38 + 74.8 + 9.8$ **6.** $85.68 - 24.25$ **7.** $1{,}219.7 - 843.2$ **8.** $23.6 + 17.2$

Find the product. (pages 66–68)

9. 18.7×9 **10.** 1.7×3.35 **11.** 12.76×2.94 **12.** 0.247×0.72

13. 8.3×14.2 **14.** 17×0.009 **15.** 0.067×8.2 **16.** 78.39×0.54

17. Jan worked 9.5 hr and earned $5.84 per hour. How much did she earn?

18. Tim's Tamales sold 2,194 tamales for $1.25 each. What were the earnings?

19. Fred bought 8 pencils for $0.29 and 6 pens for $1.21 each. How much did he spend in all?

20. Shelly drove 2.5 hr at 50 mi per hr and 1.25 hr at 62 mi per hr. How far did Shelly drive?

Find the quotient. (pages 70–72)

21. $24.6 \div 3$ **22.** $16.56 \div 8$ **23.** $171.19 \div 8.5$ **24.** $6.3 \div 0.28$

25. $216 \div 2.7$ **26.** $14.16 \div 4.8$ **27.** $253.5 \div 32.5$ **28.** $66.98 \div 19.7$

Estimate the quotient by using compatible numbers. (pages 70–72)

29. $24.6 \div 5.2$ **30.** $1{,}209.6 \div 19.548$ **31.** $541.2 \div 90.7$ **32.** $2{,}104.3 \div 68.9$

33. Chen bought 10.8 gallons of gasoline for $13.81. To the nearest cent, what is the cost of 1 gallon of gasoline?

34. Julio ran 6 laps around his back yard in 97.2 sec. What was his average time per lap?

35. **VOCABULARY** Numbers that are used to estimate quotients, are close to the dividend and divisor, and divide with a remainder of zero are __?__ numbers. (page 71)

36. **VOCABULARY** A calculator that automatically follows the order of operations uses a(n) __?__ operating system. (page 74)

Find the value. (pages 73–75)

37. $18.2 \div 3.2 + 2.5 \times 1.8$ **38.** $95 - 2^3 \times 5 \div (24 - 4)$ **39.** $(12 + 2)^2 \times (18 - 15)^3$

40. $3 \times (8 + 2)^2 - 5 \times (4 - 3)^3$ **41.** $(3^2 + 9) - 2 \times 6$ **42.** $3 \times (8 + 2)^2 - 5 \times 3^3$

Test Prep

1. Which is a reasonable estimate of the sum $25.2 + 4.9 + 11.4$?

A 60
B 50
C 40
D 35

2. Which is a reasonable estimate of the product 19.2×4?

F 20
G 40
H 60
J 80

3. Which is a reasonable estimate of the quotient $913 \div 33$?

A 300
B 40
C 30
D 3

4. If 5 packages of hot dogs cost $9.25, what is the cost of 1 package?

F $0.92
G $1.15
H $1.85
J $2.10
K Not Here

5. Jacques' square bedroom is covered with 80 square feet of carpet. About how long is each side of the bedroom?

A 8 ft
B 9 ft
C 10 ft
D 20 ft

6. What is $2 \times 2 \times 2 \times 2 \times 2 \times 2 \times 2$ expressed in exponential notation?

F 2^2 **G** 2^7
H 7^2 **J** 2^6

7. The graph shows the favorite seasons of 100 students.

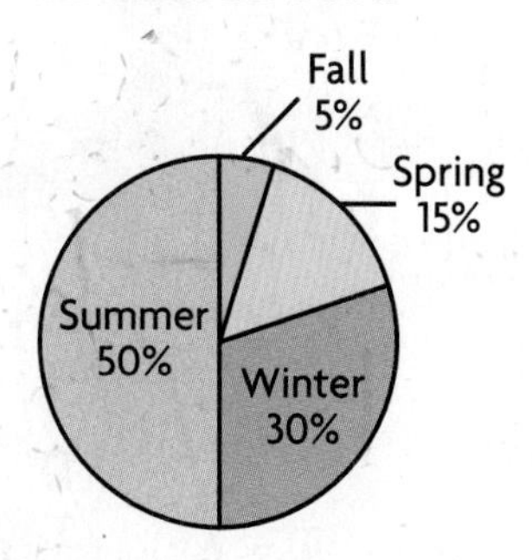

Which is a reasonable conclusion?

A Fall is favored over spring.
B Winter is the favorite season.
C More students prefer summer than spring or fall.
D Most students go on vacation in the summer.

8. A baker makes 90 cookies per hour, of which 5 are broken. How many broken cookies would you expect the baker to make in 6 hours?

F 30 **G** 510
H 540 **J** 570

9. Mr. Rodriguez pays $3.25 a week for a newspaper subscription. Which is the best estimate of the cost of the newspaper for 1 year?

A $36 **B** $150
C $200 **D** $250

10. The value of a stock is $15\frac{3}{8}$. Which is the value of the stock written as a decimal?

F 15.125
G 15.375
H 15.38
J 15.875

CHAPTER

4 OPERATIONS WITH FRACTIONS

LOOK AHEAD

In this chapter you will solve problems that involve

- adding and subtracting fractions and mixed numbers
- estimating sums and differences
- multiplying and dividing fractions and mixed numbers

HEALTH LINK

A typical slice of cheese pizza contains 248 calories, 11 grams of protein, 24 grams of carbohydrates, and 12 grams of fat.

1 gram of protein	4 calories
1 gram of carbohydrates	4 calories
1 gram of fat	9 calories

- How many of the calories in the pizza slice come from protein? carbohydrates? fat?
- How many calories are in an eight-slice pizza?

Problem-Solving Project

Shopping for Pizza Ingredients

You are in charge of making personal pizzas for yourself and seven friends. Decide how many servings eight hungry students will eat. Make a list of ingredients and a shopping list showing what you need to buy and how much you will spend. Present your decisions to the class.

SHOPPING LIST

Tomato sauce - 35¢/can

English muffins - 6/$1.79

Mozzarella cheese - $3.99/lb

Pepperoni in slices - $4.99/lb

Parmesan cheese - $2.99/box

PROJECT CHECKLIST

- ✓ Did you decide how many servings to make?
- ✓ Did you make a list of ingredients?
- ✓ Did you make a detailed shopping list?
- ✓ Did you present your decisions to the class?

Pizza

A recipe for: **8 Personal Pizzas**

Ingredients:

- 4 English muffins, split
- 1 8-oz can tomato sauce
- $\frac{1}{4}$ pound mozzarella cheese
- $\frac{1}{3}$ pound pepperoni (16 slices)
- $\frac{1}{2}$ teaspoon oregano
- $\frac{1}{2}$ teaspoon basil
- Parmesan cheese (optional)

Directions: Preheat oven to 400 degrees. Split English muffins. Combine tomato sauce, basil, and oregano in small bowl. Grate mozzarella cheese. Spread 2 tablespoons of tomato mixture on each muffin half. Put 2 pepperoni slices on each. Sprinkle mozzarella then Parmesan cheese on each. Bake 15–20 minutes. Cool before eating.

Serving size: 2 pizzas

LESSON 4.1

Adding and Subtracting Fractions

What You'll Learn
How to add and subtract fractions

Why Learn This?
To solve everyday money problems, such as comparing savings and spending

How do you spend the money you earn?

Aletha has a part-time job at a video store. She spends $\frac{1}{4}$ of her earnings on clothes and $\frac{1}{6}$ on entertainment. She saves the rest. What fraction of her earnings does she spend?

You can use fraction bars to find $\frac{1}{4} + \frac{1}{6}$.

- Which fraction bars can make exactly the same length as $\frac{1}{4}$ and $\frac{1}{6}$?
- What fractions in the model are equivalent to $\frac{1}{4}$? to $\frac{1}{6}$?
- How many $\frac{1}{12}$'s equal $\frac{1}{4} + \frac{1}{6}$?

$\frac{1}{4}$			$\frac{1}{6}$	
$\frac{1}{12}$	$\frac{1}{12}$	$\frac{1}{12}$	$\frac{1}{12}$	$\frac{1}{12}$

So, Aletha spends $\frac{5}{12}$ of her earnings.

REMEMBER:

The **least common denominator (LCD)** is the smallest common multiple of two or more denominators. **See page H15.**

The LCD for $\frac{2}{3}$ and $\frac{4}{5}$ is fifteenths.

You can find the **simplest form** of a fraction by dividing the numerator and denominator by their greatest common factor (GCF). **See page H14.**

The GCF of 10 and 15 is 5.

$\frac{10}{15} = \frac{10 \div 5}{15 \div 5} = \frac{2}{3}$

ANOTHER METHOD To add, you can find equivalent fractions by using the LCD.

EXAMPLE 1 Find $\frac{2}{3} + \frac{5}{6}$.

Write equivalent fractions using the LCD, sixths.

$$\frac{2}{3} = \frac{4}{6}$$
$$+\frac{5}{6} = \frac{5}{6}$$

Add. Use the GCF to write the answer in simplest form.

$$\frac{2}{3} = \frac{4}{6}$$
$$+\frac{5}{6} = \frac{5}{6}$$
$$\frac{9}{6} = \frac{9 \div 3}{6 \div 3} = \frac{3}{2}, \text{ or } 1\frac{1}{2}$$

You can use the same method to subtract fractions.

EXAMPLE 2 Aletha spends $\frac{1}{4}$ of her earnings on clothes and $\frac{1}{6}$ on entertainment. How much more does she spend on clothes than on entertainment?

$$\frac{1}{4} = \frac{3}{12}$$ *Write equivalent fractions using the LCD, twelfths.*

$$-\frac{1}{6} = \frac{2}{12}$$ *Subtract.*

$$\frac{1}{12}$$

Aletha spends $\frac{1}{12}$ more of her earnings on clothes.

GUIDED PRACTICE

Tell what addition problem and sum are modeled.

1.

$\frac{1}{3}$	$\frac{1}{3}$	$\frac{1}{4}$

$\frac{1}{12}$ $\frac{1}{12}$ $\frac{1}{12}$ $\frac{1}{12}$ $\frac{1}{12}$ $\frac{1}{12}$ $\frac{1}{12}$ $\frac{1}{12}$ $\frac{1}{12}$ $\frac{1}{12}$ $\frac{1}{12}$

2.

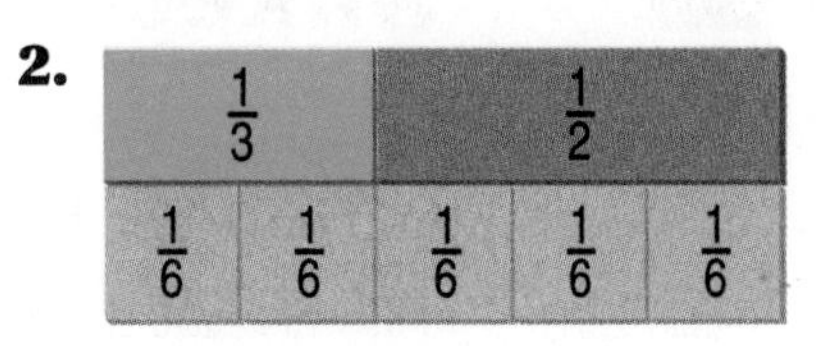

Write equivalent fractions using the LCD.

3. $\frac{1}{2}, \frac{3}{4}$ **4.** $\frac{5}{6}, \frac{1}{9}$ **5.** $\frac{3}{4}, \frac{2}{5}$ **6.** $\frac{1}{3}, \frac{3}{4}$ **7.** $\frac{4}{5}, \frac{6}{7}$

Write the GCF of each pair of numbers.

8. 9 and 15 **9.** 24 and 32 **10.** 12 and 16 **11.** 10 and 15 **12.** 7 and 9

INDEPENDENT PRACTICE

Add. Write the answer in simplest form.

1. $\frac{1}{6} + \frac{1}{12}$ **2.** $\frac{1}{5} + \frac{2}{3}$ **3.** $\frac{5}{6} + \frac{3}{4}$ **4.** $\frac{2}{7} + \frac{3}{4}$ **5.** $\frac{3}{8} + \frac{2}{5}$

6. $\frac{7}{8} + \frac{2}{3} + \frac{5}{6}$ **7.** $\frac{3}{10} + \frac{5}{8} + \frac{1}{5}$ **8.** $\frac{1}{3} + \frac{1}{2} + \frac{1}{6} + \frac{5}{12}$

Subtract. Write the answer in simplest form.

9. $\frac{7}{9} - \frac{4}{9}$ **10.** $\frac{4}{5} - \frac{3}{10}$ **11.** $\frac{7}{8} - \frac{5}{6}$

12. $\frac{4}{5} - \frac{3}{5}$ **13.** $\frac{17}{18} - \frac{5}{12}$ **14.** $\frac{3}{5} - \frac{2}{6}$

15. $\frac{2}{3} - \frac{1}{2}$ **16.** $\frac{1}{2} - \frac{2}{7}$ **17.** $\frac{8}{9} - \frac{6}{7}$

18. $\frac{2}{3} - \frac{3}{8}$ **19.** $\frac{2}{5} - \frac{11}{30}$ **20.** $\frac{21}{24} - \frac{1}{2}$

21. $\frac{3}{4} - \frac{2}{7}$ **22.** $\frac{11}{12} - \frac{4}{9}$ **23.** $\frac{11}{12} - \frac{3}{4}$

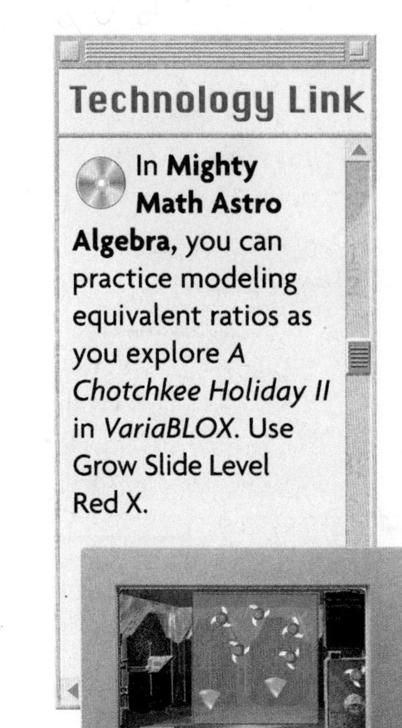

Technology Link
In **Mighty Math Astro Algebra,** you can practice modeling equivalent ratios as you explore *A Chotchkee Holiday II* in *VariaBLOX*. Use Grow Slide Level Red X.

Problem-Solving Applications

24. **BUDGET** Each week, Jennifer saves $\frac{1}{5}$ of her allowance and spends $\frac{2}{3}$ of it on school lunches. What fraction of her allowance is left?

25. **CRITICAL THINKING** To make $\frac{3}{4}$ lb of mixed nuts, what part of a pound of cashews would you add to $\frac{1}{8}$ lb of almonds?

26. **WRITE ABOUT IT** Explain the steps you use to add or subtract fractions that have different denominators.

MORE PRACTICE Lesson 4.1, page H47

LESSON 4.2

Adding and Subtracting Mixed Numbers

What You'll Learn
How to add and subtract mixed numbers

Why Learn This?
To solve everyday measurement problems, as in cooking

A fraction with the same numerator and denominator can be used to rename the whole number 1.
See page H15.

$1 = \frac{2}{2} = \frac{13}{13} = \frac{125}{125}$

You have decided to make a dessert for your family. You have $1\frac{3}{4}$ c of flour, but that is not enough. A neighbor says that he has $1\frac{2}{3}$ c of flour you can borrow. How much flour will you have if you borrow $1\frac{2}{3}$ c from your neighbor?

To solve the problem, find $1\frac{3}{4} + 1\frac{2}{3}$.

$$1\frac{3}{4} = 1\frac{9}{12}$$ *Write equivalent fractions with the LCD.*

$$+1\frac{2}{3} = 1\frac{8}{12}$$

$$2\frac{17}{12} = 2 + \frac{12}{12} + \frac{5}{12}$$ *Add the fractions. Add the whole numbers.*

$$= 3\frac{5}{12}$$ *Rewrite the sum if necessary.*

So, you will have $3\frac{5}{12}$ c of flour.

When subtracting mixed numbers, you may have to rename the greater mixed number so that you can subtract.

EXAMPLE 1 Your recipe requires $2\frac{2}{3}$ c of flour. Since you have $3\frac{5}{12}$ c, you will have some left. How much will be left?

$$3\frac{5}{12} = 3\frac{5}{12} = 2\frac{17}{12} \quad \leftarrow 3\frac{5}{12} = 2\frac{12}{12} + \frac{5}{12}$$

$$-2\frac{2}{3} = 2\frac{8}{12} = 2\frac{8}{12}$$

Write equivalent fractions with the LCD. Rename if necessary.

$$\frac{9}{12} = \frac{3}{4}$$ *Subtract. Write the answer in simplest form.*

So, there will be $\frac{3}{4}$ c of flour left.

ANOTHER METHOD Some calculators operate with fractions.

EXAMPLE 2 Find the sum. $2\frac{1}{2} + 1\frac{5}{8} + 6\frac{1}{3}$

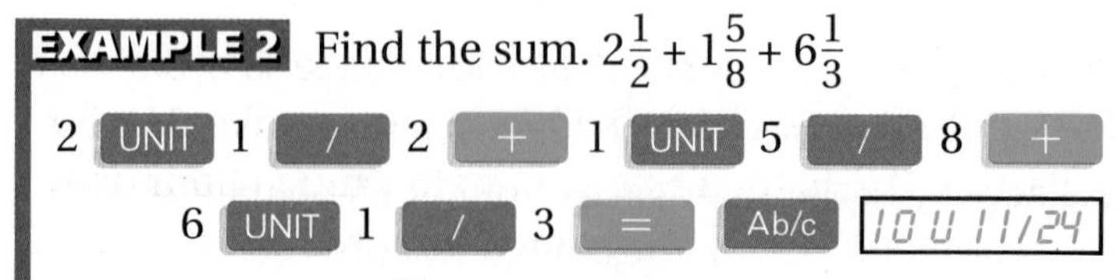

So, the sum is $10\frac{11}{24}$.

- What display would you expect to see if you used this sequence of calculator keys?

4 UNIT 1 / 2 − 3 UNIT 7 / 8 =

TEEN TIMES

Do you cook for yourself? Many young people do. In fact, 71% of U.S. teenagers cook for themselves.

Calculator Activities, page H33

GUIDED PRACTICE

Rewrite the problem using equivalent fractions with the LCD.

1. $2\frac{1}{2} + 3\frac{1}{3}$ **2.** $6\frac{1}{8} + 1\frac{1}{2}$ **3.** $9\frac{5}{12} - 3\frac{3}{8}$ **4.** $5\frac{1}{3} - 1\frac{3}{4}$

Rename the greater number.

5. $2\frac{1}{14} - 1\frac{3}{14}$ **6.** $4\frac{5}{12} - 1\frac{7}{12}$ **7.** $8 - 2\frac{3}{4}$ **8.** $4\frac{2}{5} - 3\frac{1}{2}$

INDEPENDENT PRACTICE

Add. Write the answer in simplest form.

1. $2\frac{3}{10} + 4\frac{1}{2}$ **2.** $2\frac{7}{8} + 5\frac{2}{3}$ **3.** $9\frac{1}{6} + 4\frac{6}{9}$ **4.** $5\frac{1}{12} + 2\frac{3}{4}$

5. $7\frac{1}{3} + 8\frac{2}{10}$ **6.** $11\frac{3}{7} + 9\frac{1}{2}$ **7.** $6\frac{1}{8} + 8\frac{9}{10}$ **8.** $6\frac{1}{6} + 5\frac{3}{10}$

9. $4\frac{2}{3} + 1\frac{7}{8} + 3\frac{1}{2}$ **10.** $2\frac{3}{5} + 1\frac{11}{12} + 5\frac{1}{4}$ **11.** $7\frac{5}{8} + 6\frac{3}{4} + 2\frac{5}{12}$

Subtract. Write the answer in simplest form.

12. $2\frac{1}{4} - 1\frac{5}{6}$ **13.** $7\frac{2}{3} - 3\frac{2}{7}$ **14.** $6\frac{1}{4} - 3\frac{5}{12}$ **15.** $10\frac{3}{8} - 7\frac{3}{4}$

16. $2\frac{1}{3} - 1\frac{5}{9}$ **17.** $9\frac{1}{3} - 1\frac{1}{12}$ **18.** $8\frac{1}{4} - 3\frac{1}{3}$ **19.** $3 - 2\frac{3}{10}$

Problem-Solving Applications

20. TRAVEL Jonathan is going to his aunt's house. One route is $1\frac{2}{3}$ mi long; another is $1\frac{5}{6}$ mi long. Which route is shorter? How much shorter is it?

21. MUSIC Pamela practiced the violin $2\frac{1}{2}$ hr on Monday and $1\frac{3}{4}$ hr on Wednesday. How much time has she spent practicing?

22. MENTAL MATH Miguel has $2\frac{1}{2}$ cans of juice, and Wilbur has $2\frac{2}{3}$ cans of juice. What do you know about fractions that lets you know who has more juice?

23. MEASUREMENT Sandy is making cakes for a bake sale. She has 15 c of flour. She needs $4\frac{1}{4}$ c of flour for a lemon cake, $3\frac{2}{3}$ c for a carrot cake, and $2\frac{1}{2}$ c for a spice cake. How much flour does she use to make the cakes? How much flour will she have left?

24. CRITICAL THINKING Three friends share a pizza that has 8 slices. There are $1\frac{1}{2}$ slices left. Diantha had $2\frac{1}{2}$ slices, and Alana had $1\frac{1}{2}$ slices. How many slices did George have?

25. WRITE ABOUT IT Give an example of a subtraction problem in which you need to rename a mixed number.

MORE PRACTICE Lesson 4.2, page H48

LESSON 4.3

Estimating Sums and Differences

What You'll Learn
How to estimate sums and differences of fractions

Why Learn This?
To estimate answers to everyday problems when exact answers are not needed

Look at the number line below. Is $\frac{1}{6}$ closest to 0, to $\frac{1}{2}$, or to 1?

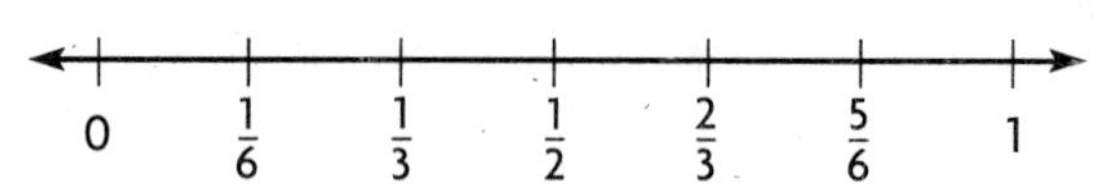

One way to estimate with fractions less than 1 is to round them to 0, $\frac{1}{2}$, or 1.

Round $\frac{1}{6}$ to 0. The numerator is much less than the denominator.

Round $\frac{3}{8}$ to $\frac{1}{2}$. The numerator is about half the denominator.

Round $\frac{3}{4}$ to 1. The numerator is about the same as the denominator.

EXAMPLE 1 Estimate $\frac{1}{6} + \frac{3}{8} + \frac{3}{4}$.

Round each fraction.

$$\frac{1}{6} + \frac{3}{8} + \frac{3}{4}$$
$$\downarrow \quad \downarrow \quad \downarrow$$
$$0 + \frac{1}{2} + 1$$

Add.

$$0 + \frac{1}{2} + 1 = 1\frac{1}{2}$$

So, $\frac{1}{6} + \frac{3}{8} + \frac{3}{4}$ is about $1\frac{1}{2}$.

- What is a reasonable estimate of $\frac{7}{8} - \frac{1}{3}$?

MUSIC LINK

In music, the time signature is a fraction that tells how many beats there are per measure and which note gets 1 beat. For example, in a time signature of $\frac{3}{4}$, there are 3 beats per measure, and a quarter note gets 1 beat. How many beats are in a measure with a time signature of $\frac{4}{4}$?

You estimate the sums and differences of mixed numbers by rounding the fractions to 0, $\frac{1}{2}$, or 1.

EXAMPLE 2 Barry jogs $8\frac{6}{10}$ mi daily. Kerry jogs $5\frac{3}{4}$ mi daily. What is a reasonable estimate for how many more miles Barry jogs than Kerry?

Round each fraction.

$$8\frac{6}{10} - 5\frac{3}{4}$$
$$\downarrow \quad \downarrow$$
$$8\frac{1}{2} - 6$$

Subtract.

$$8\frac{1}{2} - 6 = 2\frac{1}{2}$$

So, the difference is about $2\frac{1}{2}$ mi.

- What is a reasonable estimate of $2\frac{3}{4} + 5\frac{1}{8} + 9\frac{1}{2}$?

GUIDED PRACTICE

Round each fraction to 0, $\frac{1}{2}$, or 1. Explain your reasoning.

1. $\frac{6}{7}$ **2.** $\frac{3}{7}$ **3.** $\frac{1}{5}$ **4.** $\frac{4}{10}$ **5.** $\frac{7}{9}$ **6.** $\frac{2}{9}$

Estimate the sum or difference.

7. $\frac{4}{5} + \frac{1}{6}$ **8.** $\frac{7}{8} - \frac{5}{9}$ **9.** $3\frac{4}{10} - 1\frac{1}{7}$ **10.** $2\frac{2}{9} + 3\frac{3}{5}$ **11.** $6\frac{4}{7} - 2\frac{2}{3}$

INDEPENDENT PRACTICE

Estimate the sum or difference.

1. $\frac{1}{3} + \frac{5}{9}$ **2.** $\frac{3}{4} + \frac{1}{8} + \frac{2}{3}$ **3.** $1\frac{7}{8} + 2\frac{1}{4}$ **4.** $8\frac{1}{3} - \frac{9}{10}$

5. $3\frac{5}{6} + 4\frac{1}{5} + 1\frac{7}{10}$ **6.** $\frac{15}{16} - \frac{4}{9}$ **7.** $\frac{3}{8} - \frac{1}{7}$ **8.** $\frac{7}{8} + \frac{15}{16}$

9. $3\frac{1}{3} - 2\frac{5}{8}$ **10.** $8\frac{3}{4} - 6\frac{2}{5}$ **11.** $\frac{4}{9} + \frac{3}{10}$ **12.** $5\frac{5}{8} - 4\frac{1}{6}$

Problem-Solving Applications

13. **ESTIMATION** Mark mailed packages weighing $\frac{3}{8}$ lb, $5\frac{1}{2}$ lb, and $3\frac{1}{16}$ lb. What is a reasonable estimate of the total weight of the packages?

14. **MEASUREMENT** Joy's cat weighs $8\frac{3}{4}$ lb. Her puppy weighs $6\frac{1}{10}$ lb. What is a reasonable estimate of the difference in weights?

15. **NUMBER SENSE** Steve's goal is to work $23\frac{1}{2}$ hr a week. So far he has worked $4\frac{1}{4}$ hr, $3\frac{3}{4}$ hr, $1\frac{1}{2}$ hr, and $7\frac{3}{4}$ hr. About how many hours has he worked so far?

16. **WRITE ABOUT IT** Is an estimate of 5 for $3\frac{1}{5} + 2\frac{1}{6}$ greater than or less than the actual sum? Explain.

Mixed Review and Test Prep

Write as a fraction or mixed number.

17. $2\frac{1}{2}$ **18.** $4\frac{2}{5}$ **19.** $3\frac{4}{7}$ **20.** $\frac{14}{4}$ **21.** $\frac{4}{3}$ **22.** $\frac{11}{3}$

Estimate the product.

23. 28×11 **24.** 56×42 **25.** 485×91 **26.** 390×110

27. **ESTIMATION** Jim saved \$7.92, \$8.04, \$3.76, and \$12.32. What is a reasonable estimate for the total amount he saved?

A \$20.00 **B** \$24.00
C \$26.00 **D** \$32.00

28. **CONSUMER MATH** Bill buys yams that cost \$1.29 per pound. He has \$3.70 with him. How many pounds can he buy?

F 4 lb **G** 3 lb
H 2 lb **J** 1 lb

LAB ACTIVITY

Multiplying and Dividing Fractions

What You'll Explore
How to use fraction bars to multiply and divide fractions

What You'll Need
fraction bars

One way to multiply or divide fractions is to use fraction bars.

ACTIVITY 1

Explore

Find $\frac{2}{3} \times \frac{3}{8}$. **Think:** What is $\frac{2}{3}$ of $\frac{3}{8}$?

- Use fraction bars to show the second fraction, $\frac{3}{8}$.

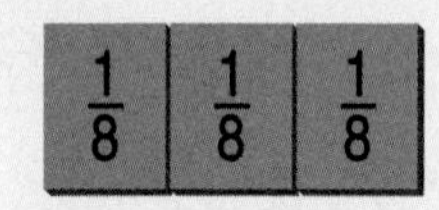

- Multiplying by $\frac{2}{3}$ means finding 2 of 3 equal parts. The denominator of $\frac{2}{3}$ tells you to separate $\frac{3}{8}$ into 3 equal parts.

- The numerator of $\frac{2}{3}$ tells you to take 2 of the 3 equal parts.

Since 2 of the 3 parts are $\frac{2}{8}$, then $\frac{2}{3} \times \frac{3}{8} = \frac{2}{8}$, or $\frac{1}{4}$.

Think and Discuss

- Which factor of the multiplication problem do you model first?
- Why is the product, $\frac{1}{4}$, less than the factor, $\frac{3}{8}$?
- Which fraction bars would you need to model $\frac{2}{3} \times \frac{3}{10}$?
- Explain how to model $\frac{4}{5} \times \frac{5}{12}$.

Try This

Use fraction bars to model each problem and find each product.

1. $\frac{1}{2} \times \frac{4}{5}$ **2.** $\frac{3}{4} \times \frac{4}{8}$ **3.** $\frac{1}{3} \times \frac{3}{4}$

4. $\frac{2}{3} \times \frac{9}{10}$ **5.** $\frac{3}{4} \times \frac{8}{12}$ **6.** $\frac{2}{3} \times \frac{6}{10}$

7. Kim played $\frac{1}{2}$ of a basketball game that lasted $\frac{3}{4}$ hr. Use fraction bars to help find how long Kim played in the game.

ACTIVITY 2

Explore

Work with a partner to find $\frac{6}{12} \div \frac{2}{12}$.

Think: How many groups of $\frac{2}{12}$ are there in $\frac{6}{12}$?

- Use fraction bars to model the dividend, $\frac{6}{12}$.

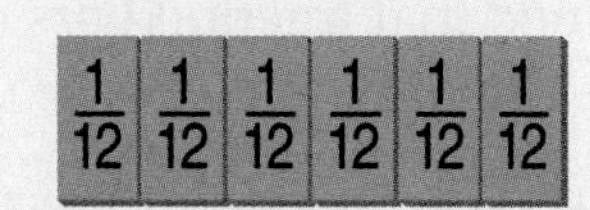

- Separate $\frac{6}{12}$ into groups of $\frac{2}{12}$.

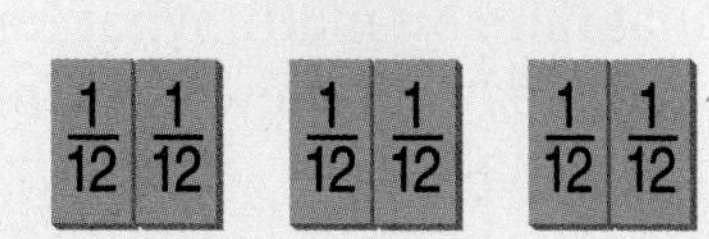

Since there are 3 groups of $\frac{2}{12}$, $\frac{6}{12} \div \frac{2}{12} = 3$.

You can also use fraction bars to divide fractions with unlike denominators.

- Find $\frac{8}{10} \div \frac{2}{5}$. **Think:** How many groups of $\frac{2}{5}$ are in $\frac{8}{10}$?
- Use fraction bars to show the dividend, $\frac{8}{10}$.
- To find how many $\frac{2}{5}$ are in $\frac{8}{10}$, place $\frac{1}{5}$ bars under the bars for $\frac{8}{10}$.
- Separate the $\frac{1}{5}$ bars into groups of $\frac{2}{5}$.

  There are 2 groups of $\frac{2}{5}$ in $\frac{8}{10}$.

  So, $\frac{8}{10} \div \frac{2}{5} = 2$.

Think and Discuss

- CRITICAL THINKING Why is the quotient, 2, greater than the dividend, $\frac{8}{10}$?

Try This

Use fraction bars to model each problem and find each quotient.

1. $\frac{5}{6} \div \frac{1}{6}$ **2.** $\frac{1}{3} \div \frac{4}{12}$ **3.** $\frac{6}{8} \div \frac{1}{4}$

4. Steve mows $\frac{2}{5}$ of his lawn in $\frac{4}{5}$ hr. Use fraction bars to help find how long it takes Steve to mow the whole lawn.

Technology Link

You can model division of fractions and decimals by using E-Lab, Activity 4. Available on CD-ROM and on the Internet at **www.hbschool.com/elab**

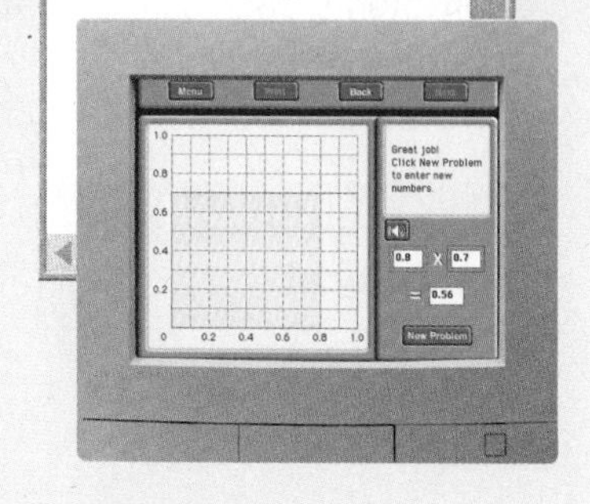

LESSON 4.4

Multiplying and Dividing Fractions and Mixed Numbers

What You'll Learn
How to multiply and divide fractions and mixed numbers

Why Learn This?
To solve everyday problems, such as finding distances traveled

VOCABULARY
reciprocal

You learned that fraction bars can be used to multiply fractions. You can also draw pictures or use multiplication.

EXAMPLE 1 You spent $\frac{2}{3}$ hr doing your homework. You spent $\frac{1}{4}$ of that time on math. What fraction of an hour did you spend on math homework? Find $\frac{1}{4} \times \frac{2}{3}$.

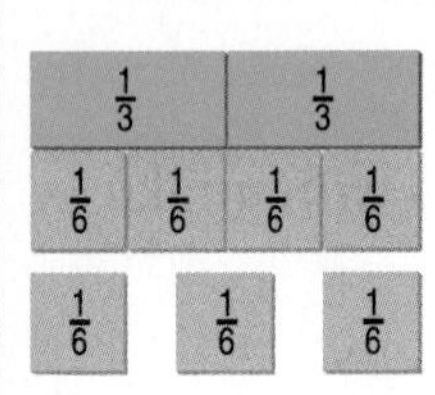

Draw $\frac{2}{3}$. Since $\frac{2}{3}$ cannot be put into 4 groups, draw enough sixths to equal $\frac{2}{3}$.

Separate $\frac{4}{6}$ into 4 groups. The product is the number of sixths in one group.

$\frac{1}{4} \times \frac{2}{3} = \frac{1}{6}$

ANOTHER METHOD You can use multiplication to find products of fractions or mixed numbers.

Multiply the numerators. Multiply the denominators.

$\frac{1}{4} \times \frac{2}{3} = \frac{1 \times 2}{4 \times 3} = \frac{2}{12}$

Use the GCF to write in simplest form.

$\frac{2}{12} = \frac{2 \div 2}{12 \div 2} = \frac{1}{6}$

So, you spent $\frac{1}{6}$ of the time on math homework.

When you multiply fractions or mixed numbers, you can simplify the factors before you multiply.

EXAMPLE 2 You and your family travel $2\frac{1}{2}$ mi to school for open house. The route you take home is $1\frac{3}{5}$ times as long. How far do you travel to get home? Find $1\frac{3}{5} \times 2\frac{1}{2}$.

Write the mixed numbers as fractions.

$1\frac{3}{5} \times 2\frac{1}{2} = \frac{8}{5} \times \frac{5}{2}$

Divide any numerator and denominator by their GCF. Multiply.

$\frac{\overset{4}{\cancel{8}}}{\underset{1}{\cancel{5}}} \times \frac{\overset{1}{\cancel{5}}}{\underset{1}{\cancel{2}}} = \frac{4}{1}$, or 4

So, you travel 4 mi to get home.

TEEN TIMES

Middle-school students do an average of $1\frac{1}{2}$ hr of homework a night. Middle-school teachers assign homework an average of four nights a week.

Calculator Activities, page H34

GUIDED PRACTICE

Simplify the factors.

1. $\frac{3}{8} \times \frac{4}{5}$ **2.** $\frac{5}{3} \times \frac{2}{5}$ **3.** $\frac{3}{4} \times \frac{8}{9}$

Rewrite the problem by changing each mixed number to a fraction.

4. $7\frac{1}{2} \times 1\frac{1}{3}$ **5.** $2\frac{1}{4} \times 1\frac{1}{9}$ **6.** $4\frac{2}{7} \times 2\frac{1}{2}$

Find the product by drawing a picture and by multiplying. Write the product in simplest form.

7. $\frac{1}{2} \times \frac{2}{3}$ **8.** $\frac{1}{3} \times \frac{3}{4}$ **9.** $\frac{3}{5} \times \frac{1}{2}$

Dividing Fractions and Mixed Numbers

Look at these related multiplication and division problems.

$6 \div 2 = 3$ $\frac{1}{5} \div \frac{1}{5} = 1$ $\frac{3}{7} \div \frac{1}{7} = 3$

$6 \times \frac{1}{2} = 3$ $\frac{1}{5} \times 5 = 1$ $\frac{3}{7} \times 7 = 3$

- What related multiplication problem can you write for $\frac{4}{5} \div \frac{1}{2}$?

REMEMBER:

The product of a number and its reciprocal is 1. **See page H16.**

$\frac{2}{3} \times \frac{3}{2} = \frac{6}{6} = 1$

You can rewrite any division problem as a multiplication problem by using the reciprocal of the divisor. The **reciprocal** is the number you get when you exchange the numerator and the denominator of a fraction.

$\frac{4}{7} \div \frac{3}{5} = \frac{4}{7} \times \frac{5}{3} \leftarrow \frac{5}{3}$ is the reciprocal of $\frac{3}{5}$.

EXAMPLE 3 Jason has $\frac{3}{4}$ gal of orange drink. He pours it into glasses that hold $\frac{1}{8}$ gal each. How many glasses of orange drink can he fill?

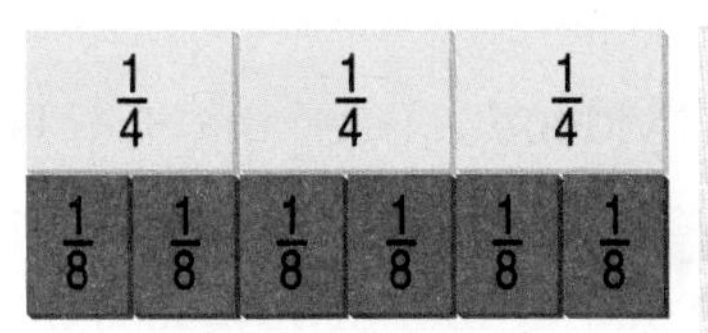

Think: How many $\frac{1}{8}$s in $\frac{3}{4}$? Find $\frac{3}{4} \div \frac{1}{8}$.

Rewrite the problem, using the reciprocal of the divisor.

$\frac{3}{4} \div \frac{1}{8} = \frac{3}{4} \times \frac{8}{1}$

Use the GCF to simplify the factors.

$\frac{3}{4} \div \frac{1}{8} = \frac{3}{\cancel{4}_1} \times \frac{\cancel{8}^2}{1}$

Multiply.

$\frac{3}{\cancel{4}_1} \times \frac{\cancel{8}^2}{1} = \frac{6}{1}$, or 6

So, Jason can fill 6 glasses of orange drink.

- Draw a picture to find how many glasses he could fill if each glass held $\frac{3}{8}$ gal.
- **CRITICAL THINKING** In $\frac{3}{4} \div \frac{7}{8}$, is the quotient less than, equal to, or greater than 1? Explain.

EXAMPLE 4 A bicycle team is training for a relay race. Each member rides $2\frac{1}{3}$ mi. Together they will ride $9\frac{1}{3}$ mi. How many people will they need for their team?

Find $9\frac{1}{3} \div 2\frac{1}{3}$.

$9\frac{1}{3} \div 2\frac{1}{3} = \frac{28}{3} \div \frac{7}{3}$ *Write the mixed numbers as fractions.*

$= \frac{28}{3} \times \frac{3}{7}$ *Rewrite using the reciprocal of the divisor.*

$= \frac{\overset{4}{\cancel{28}}}{\underset{1}{\cancel{3}}} \times \frac{\overset{1}{\cancel{3}}}{\underset{1}{\cancel{7}}}$ *Use the GCFs to simplify.*

$= \frac{4}{1}$, or 4 *Multiply. Write in simplest form.*

So, they will need 4 people for the team.

- How many people would they need if they covered $5\frac{1}{2}$ mi and each rider cycled $2\frac{3}{4}$ mi?
- If each person rides no more than $2\frac{1}{2}$ mi, how many people are needed on a team to ride $9\frac{1}{3}$ mi?

HEALTH LINK

Fitness experts say you should exercise moderately for about $\frac{1}{2}$ hr four or five times a week. If you run for $\frac{1}{2}$ of the time and lift weights for $\frac{1}{3}$ of the time, how many minutes will you have left to warm up and cool down during $\frac{1}{2}$ hr?

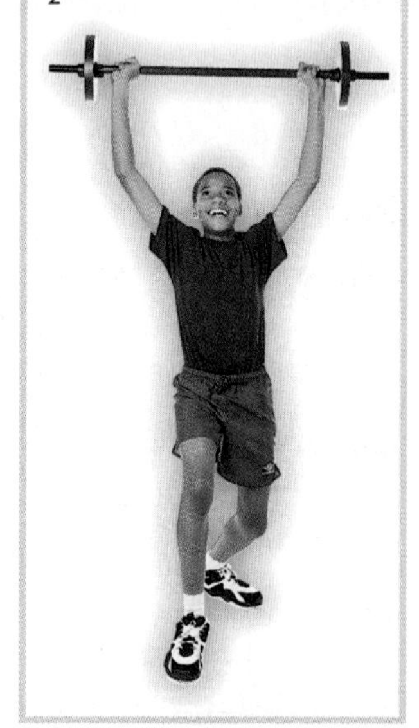

Talk About It

- Explain how to write the reciprocal of a fraction.
- How are the divisor and the dividend related in $\frac{2}{3} \div \frac{4}{9}$? Is the quotient less than, equal to, or greater than 1?
- Why is the reciprocal of a mixed number always less than 1?

INDEPENDENT PRACTICE

Multiply. Write the product in simplest form.

1. $\frac{2}{5} \times \frac{3}{4}$ **2.** $\frac{1}{8} \times \frac{4}{9}$ **3.** $\frac{17}{18} \times \frac{3}{5}$ **4.** $\frac{9}{16} \times \frac{8}{15}$

5. $\frac{6}{7} \times \frac{8}{9}$ **6.** $2\frac{1}{5} \times 4\frac{1}{6}$ **7.** $\frac{3}{7} \times 1\frac{2}{3}$ **8.** $\frac{3}{7} \times 4$

9. $2\frac{3}{7} \times 1\frac{2}{3}$ **10.** $3\frac{1}{8} \times 2\frac{2}{5}$ **11.** $\frac{3}{8} \times \frac{2}{7}$ **12.** $\frac{4}{9} \times \frac{3}{16}$

13. $1\frac{1}{2} \times 7\frac{1}{9}$ **14.** $3 \times 2\frac{1}{2}$ **15.** $2\frac{2}{5} \times 1\frac{4}{7}$ **16.** $1\frac{1}{2} \times 2\frac{1}{3}$

17. $2\frac{1}{2} \times 3\frac{1}{3}$ **18.** $4\frac{2}{5} \times 5$ **19.** $4\frac{3}{8} \times 1\frac{4}{5}$ **20.** $5\frac{3}{7} \times 3\frac{1}{2}$

Write the reciprocal of the divisor. Then write the related multiplication problem.

21. $15 \div 5 = 3$ **22.** $\frac{1}{5} \div 7 = \frac{1}{35}$ **23.** $\frac{2}{3} \div \frac{3}{5} = 1\frac{1}{9}$ **24.** $6 \div \frac{3}{7} = 14$

Draw a picture to find the quotient.

25. $\frac{3}{4} \div \frac{1}{4}$ **26.** $\frac{2}{3} \div \frac{1}{6}$ **27.** $\frac{3}{5} \div \frac{2}{10}$ **28.** $3 \div \frac{1}{2}$ **29.** $2 \div \frac{2}{3}$

Divide. Write the quotient in simplest form.

30. $\frac{1}{2} \div \frac{3}{4}$ **31.** $\frac{2}{3} \div \frac{3}{5}$ **32.** $4 \div \frac{3}{5}$ **33.** $\frac{3}{8} \div \frac{1}{4}$

34. $1\frac{4}{5} \div 2\frac{3}{5}$ **35.** $11 \div \frac{1}{2}$ **36.** $\frac{9}{10} \div \frac{2}{3}$ **37.** $\frac{2}{7} \div 2$

38. $\frac{2}{7} \div \frac{4}{5}$ **39.** $\frac{3}{4} \div \frac{1}{6}$ **40.** $2\frac{1}{8} \div \frac{3}{4}$ **41.** $5\frac{2}{3} \div 2\frac{3}{4}$

42. $2\frac{1}{6} \div 7\frac{4}{5}$ **43.** $1\frac{2}{3} \div 1\frac{1}{4}$ **44.** $3\frac{1}{5} \div 4$ **45.** $1\frac{5}{6} \div 2\frac{1}{3}$

Problem-Solving Applications

46. **MEASUREMENT** Beth has $4\frac{1}{2}$ yd of fabric for making costumes. Each costume takes $2\frac{1}{8}$ yd. How many costumes can she make?

47. **MEASUREMENT** Marlon has 36 paper clips lying end to end. Each clip is $1\frac{1}{4}$ in. long. What is the total length of the 36 clips?

48. **INEQUALITIES** Write three problems to show that the product of two fractions can be less than, equal to, or greater than 1.

49. **CRITICAL THINKING** Is the reciprocal of a whole number always less than 1? Explain.

50. Write a multiplication word problem that can be solved using $\frac{3}{4} \times \frac{1}{4}$ and a division word problem for $\frac{3}{4} \div \frac{1}{4}$. Then solve both problems.

51. **WRITE ABOUT IT** Write a word problem that can be solved by multiplying or dividing fractions. Draw a picture to show the solution.

Mixed Review and Test Prep

Find the product.

52. 25×100 **53.** 30×100 **54.** $8.7 \times 1{,}000$ **55.** $0.001 \times 6{,}000$

Find the product or quotient.

56. 12.6×0.8 **57.** 2.95×0.03 **58.** $662.4 \div 0.828$ **59.** $4.8 \div 2.4$

60. **ESTIMATION** The line segment is the length of a large paper clip.

____

Estimate the length of the paper clip.

A 25 centimeters **B** 45 centimeters
C 25 millimeters **D** 45 millimeters

61. **ESTIMATION** Tim's mother asked him to go to the grocery store to get a can of tomatoes. Which can of tomatoes has the lowest price per ounce?

F 8 oz for \$0.89 **G** 12 oz for \$1.49
H 16 oz for \$2.29 **J** 32 oz for \$3.79

MORE PRACTICE Lesson 4.4, page H48

LESSON 4.5

Solve a Simpler Problem

What You'll Learn
How to solve a problem by solving a simpler problem

Why Learn This?
To solve everyday problems, such as finding the number of items sold

Sometimes a problem involves large numbers that make it difficult to solve. You can use a simpler problem to help you solve the difficult one.

Marvin had 6,500 cassette tapes at the grand opening of his music store. He gave away $\frac{1}{5}$ of them as door prizes, and $\frac{1}{2}$ of the remaining tapes were sold. How many tapes were sold?

- Understand
- Plan
- Solve
- Look Back

UNDERSTAND What are you asked to find?

What facts are given?

PLAN What strategy will you use?

You can *solve a simpler problem* by using small numbers.

SOLVE How will you solve the problem?

Use a smaller number instead of 6,500. Since 100 times 65 equals 6,500, let 65 stand for the number of tapes Marvin started with.

a. $\frac{1}{5}$ of 65 = number of tapes given away

$\frac{1}{5} \times 65 = 13$

b. 65 − number of tapes given away = number of tapes left

$65 - 13 = 52$

c. $\frac{1}{2}$ of number of tapes left = number of tapes sold

$\frac{1}{2} \times 52 = 26$

d. Multiply 26 by 100 to get the actual number of tapes sold.

$26 \times 100 = 2{,}600$

So, 2,600 tapes were sold.

LOOK BACK How can you check your answer?

What if . . . Marvin had 5,400 tapes, gave away $\frac{1}{3}$ of them, and sold $\frac{3}{4}$ of the remaining tapes? How many would he have sold?

PRACTICE

Solve a simpler problem.

1. Howie's store had 3,500 CDs at the beginning of the month. He put aside $\frac{1}{7}$ of them and sold $\frac{1}{2}$ of the remaining CDs. How many did he sell?

2. Shelley earns $1,500 a month. Her car payments are $\frac{1}{5}$ of her monthly earnings. How much are her car payments?

3. Keith and Scott drove 2,000 mi during their family's vacation. Keith drove $\frac{1}{2}$ of the distance, and Scott drove $\frac{2}{5}$ of the remaining distance. How far did Scott drive?

4. Amanda owns 6,300 paperback books. She read $\frac{1}{3}$ of them before she was 12 years old and $\frac{1}{5}$ of the remaining ones before she was 18 years old. How many books did she read between the ages of 12 and 18?

MIXED APPLICATIONS

Solve.

CHOOSE **a strategy and a tool.**

- **Find a Pattern**
- **Make a Table**
- **Write an Equation**
- **Work Backward**
- **Use a Formula**
- **Act It Out**

Paper/Pencil

Calculator

Hands-On

Mental Math

5. Amy is 7 years older than her younger sister, who is $\frac{3}{4}$ the age of her 12-year-old brother. How old is Amy?

6. Elena's rectangular garden is $4\frac{1}{2}$ ft long and $3\frac{1}{4}$ ft wide. What is the perimeter of her garden?

7. Greg took his dog to the park on April 11, April 17, and April 23. If he continues this pattern, when will he take his dog to the park again?

8. Hector paints $2\frac{1}{2}$ walls. Each gallon of paint covers $\frac{1}{2}$ wall. How many gallons of paint does Hector use?

9. Victor's class collected 1,500 magazines. Victor gave away $\frac{1}{5}$ of the magazines, and then Cinar gave away $\frac{7}{10}$ of what was left. How many magazines did Cinar give away?

10. Gasoline costs $1.20 a gallon. Naveen's father puts $9\frac{1}{2}$ gal in his car's gasoline tank. He receives $8.60 in change. How much money did he give the cashier?

11. The hobby shop purchased 4,500 model kits. They sold $\frac{1}{3}$ of them in October and the remainder in November. How many kits were sold in November?

12. Suppose the hobby shop can make a profit of $6.75 for every spaceship model kit they sell. About how many kits would they have to sell to make a $1,000 profit?

13. **WRITE ABOUT IT** Write a problem that can be solved by solving a simpler problem.

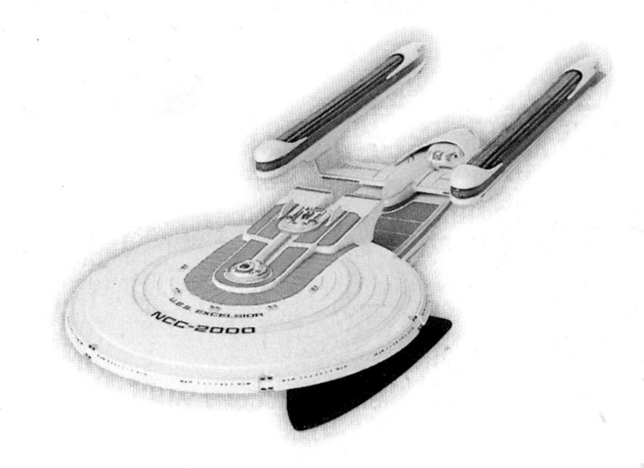

MORE PRACTICE Lesson 4.5, page H49

CHAPTER 4 Review/Test

Add or subtract. Write in simplest form. (pages 80–81)

1. $\frac{2}{3} - \frac{1}{6}$ **2.** $\frac{1}{2} + \frac{4}{5}$ **3.** $\frac{7}{12} - \frac{1}{3}$ **4.** $\frac{3}{4} + \frac{5}{6}$

5. $\frac{2}{9} + \frac{3}{4}$ **6.** $\frac{2}{7} - \frac{1}{4}$ **7.** $\frac{2}{3} - \frac{5}{8}$ **8.** $\frac{6}{7} + \frac{3}{4}$

9. Joan needs $\frac{3}{4}$ c of flour. She has $\frac{1}{3}$ c of flour. How much more flour does she need?

Add or subtract. Write in simplest form. (pages 82–83)

10. $2\frac{3}{8} + 5\frac{1}{4}$ **11.** $8\frac{11}{12} - 6\frac{1}{4}$ **12.** $3\frac{3}{4} - 2\frac{1}{8}$ **13.** $2\frac{1}{2} + 7\frac{5}{6}$

14. $9\frac{2}{3} - 4\frac{1}{5}$ **15.** $1\frac{2}{9} + 3\frac{1}{2}$ **16.** $9\frac{4}{7} + 5\frac{8}{9}$ **17.** $8\frac{2}{5} - 7\frac{2}{3}$

18. Nigel had swimming practice for $2\frac{1}{2}$ hr on Thursday and $2\frac{2}{3}$ hr on Saturday. How much time did he spend at practice?

Estimate the sum or difference. (pages 84–85)

19. $\frac{7}{8} + \frac{15}{16}$ **20.** $\frac{8}{9} - \frac{1}{8}$ **21.** $6\frac{1}{8} + 1\frac{2}{5}$ **22.** $5\frac{5}{8} - 4\frac{1}{6}$

23. It rained $3\frac{1}{5}$ in. Monday, $2\frac{3}{4}$ in. Tuesday, and $4\frac{1}{3}$ in. Wednesday. Estimate the total amount of rainfall.

Multiply or divide. Write in simplest form. (pages 88–91)

24. $\frac{1}{8} \times \frac{4}{5}$ **25.** $\frac{5}{8} \div \frac{3}{4}$ **26.** $1\frac{1}{5} \times 7\frac{2}{3}$ **27.** $3 \times 2\frac{4}{7}$

28. $1\frac{3}{7} \div 6$ **29.** $1\frac{1}{3} \times \frac{1}{4}$ **30.** $1\frac{2}{5} \times 2\frac{1}{4}$ **31.** $4\frac{2}{5} \div 2\frac{1}{2}$

32. Marsha spent $2\frac{1}{2}$ hr doing chores. She spent $\frac{1}{3}$ of that time washing the car. How much time did she spend washing the car?

33. **VOCABULARY** The number you get when you exchange the numerator and denominator of a fraction is the __?__. (page 89)

Solve. (pages 92–93)

34. Paige started with 4,800 plastic name tags. She used $\frac{1}{2}$ of them and kept $\frac{1}{3}$ of the remaining ones for a show. How many name tags did Paige keep for the show?

35. Paul earned $3,600 working on weekends. He put $\frac{1}{4}$ of his earnings in savings and spent $\frac{1}{9}$ of the remaining money. How much money did he spend?

Test Prep

CUMULATIVE CHAPTERS 1–4

1. Each week Jan spends $\frac{1}{3}$ of her earnings on rent, and $\frac{1}{5}$ of her earnings on groceries. What fraction is left?

A $\frac{1}{2}$

B $\frac{7}{15}$

C $\frac{8}{15}$

D $\frac{3}{5}$

2. For five days, the high temperatures in Anchorage were ⁻8°F, ⁻12°F, 2°F, ⁻7°F, and 4°F. Arrange the temperatures from least to greatest.

F ⁻8°F, ⁻12°F, 2°F, ⁻7°F, 4°F
G 4°F, 2°F, ⁻7°F, ⁻8°F, ⁻12°F
H ⁻12°F, ⁻8°F, 4°F, 2°F, ⁻7°F
J ⁻12°F, ⁻8°F, ⁻7°F, 2°F, 4°F

3. Helen has a stack of cards $1\frac{3}{4}$ inches tall. Jimmy has a stack of cards $1\frac{2}{3}$ inches tall. How much taller is Helen's stack of cards than Jimmy's?

A $\frac{1}{12}$ in.

B $\frac{1}{4}$ in.

C $\frac{1}{3}$ in.

D $\frac{5}{12}$ in.

4. Which is the best estimate for the difference?

$$25.4 - 11.9$$

F 10
G 13
H 20
J 35

5. Abby saved 2,400 pennies. She used $\frac{1}{2}$ of them to buy a CD, and $\frac{1}{3}$ of the remaining pennies to buy lunch. How many pennies does she have left?

A 8
B 400
C 800
D 1,200
E Not Here

6. Which is not equivalent to 0.6?

F $\frac{3}{5}$

G $\frac{6}{10}$

H 6%
J 60%

7. Which best represents the geometric model?

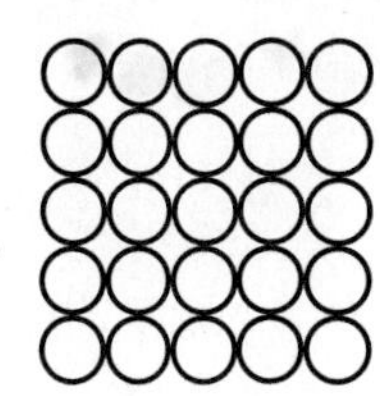

A 2^2
B 3^2
C 4^2
D 5^2

8. The dry ingredients of a recipe are $2\frac{1}{8}$ cups of sugar and $4\frac{3}{4}$ cups of flour. What is the total amount of dry ingredients in the recipe?

F $6\frac{3}{32}$ c

G $6\frac{1}{3}$ c

H $6\frac{1}{2}$ c

J $6\frac{7}{8}$ c

CHAPTER

5

OPERATIONS WITH INTEGERS AND RATIONAL NUMBERS

LOOK AHEAD

In this chapter you will solve problems that involve

- modeling addition and subtraction of integers
- adding, subtracting, multiplying, and dividing integers and rational numbers

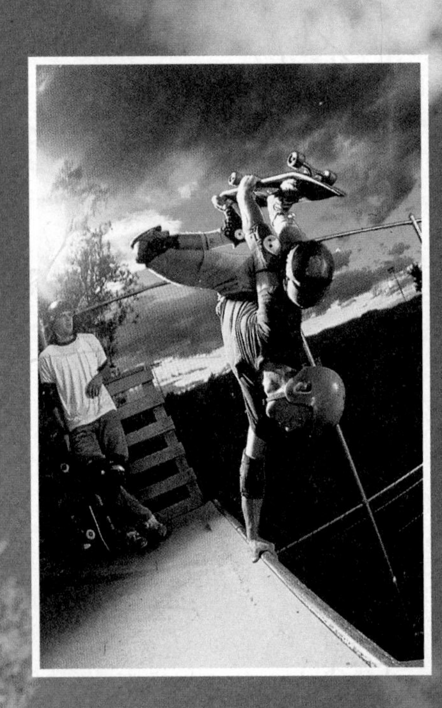

SPORTS LINK

In 1997, Eleftherios Argiropoulos still held the record for riding a skateboard the farthest. He skateboarded 271.3 miles in 36 hours 33 minutes 17 seconds in Ekali, Greece, on November 4–5, 1993.

- The Boston marathon is 26 miles long. About how many "Boston marathons" did Eleftherios skate?
- Describe how to find Eleftherios's average speed in miles per hour.

Problem-Solving Project

Profiting from a Concession Stand

You are in charge of running the taqueria stand at the school carnival to raise money for the skateboarding club. Suppose you buy 500 tacos for $75 and 240 sodas for $60. Decide how much profit you want to make. Then, decide on prices for each item or combinations of items. Make a pricing-profit chart showing at least two pricing strategies, your calculations, and recommendation. Present your plans to the class.

COST PRICE PROFIT

	Suggested Price #1		Suggested Price #2	
	Price	Profit	Price	Profit
Taco -15¢	25¢	+10¢	30¢	+15¢
Soda -25¢	35¢	+10¢	40¢	+15¢

PROJECT CHECKLIST

- ✓ Did you decide on a profit?
- ✓ Did you decide on prices?
- ✓ Did you make a pricing-profit chart?
- ✓ Did you present your plans to the class?

ACTIVITY

What You'll Explore
How to model addition of integers

What You'll Need
two-color counters

ALGEBRA CONNECTION

Modeling Addition of Integers

You can model integers by using methods and tools that emphasize opposites. One way is with two-color counters. Use the yellow side of the counter to represent 1, and the red side to represent $^{-}1$.

 ← represents $1 + {}^{-}1 = 0$

The sum of opposite integers is always 0.

Explore

Explore this procedure.

- Model each addend with the appropriate number of counters of the designated color.

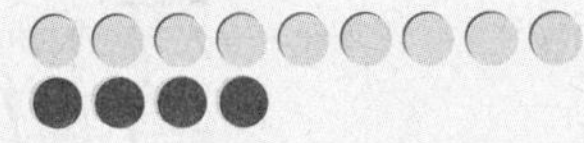

$9 + {}^{-}4 = ?$

- Form pairs of counters, which represent 0.

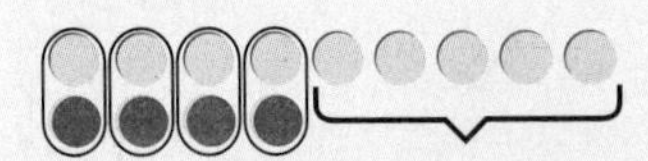

$9 + {}^{-}4 = 5$

- To find the sum, count the unpaired counters.
- Use two-color counters to find each sum.

$^{-}2 + {}^{-}7$ $\quad$ $2 + 7$ $\quad$ $2 + {}^{-}7$ $\quad$ $^{-}2 + 7$

Think and Discuss CRITICAL THINKING

- How does the model for $^{-}2 + {}^{-}7$ compare with the model for $2 + 7$?
- How does the model for $^{-}2 + 7$ compare with the model for $2 + {}^{-}7$?
- Without using counters, how can you find the sum of integers with the same sign? with different signs?

Try This

Find each sum.

$4 + 6$ $\quad$ $^{-}4 + {}^{-}6$ $\quad$ $4 + {}^{-}6$ $\quad$ $^{-}4 + 6$

Adding Integers

What You'll Learn
How to add integers

Why Learn This?
To find changes in temperature or in amount of money owed

You can relate integer addition to changes in temperatures.

During the harsh winter of 1996, temperatures as low as 40° below zero on the Fahrenheit scale, ⁻40°F, were recorded. In one cold spell, the temperature changed drastically—as much as 100° in 24 hours!

EXAMPLE 1 Suppose the temperature drops from 45°F to ⁻23°F. What is the temperature change?

Step 1: Draw a diagram of a thermometer to show the given temperatures.

Step 2: Find the number of degrees from 45°F to 0°F and the number of degrees from 0°F to ⁻23°F.

Step 3: Find the sum of the two changes. Since both changes are drops in temperature, use negative values.

$$\begin{array}{r} ^{-}45^\circ \\ +\,^{-}23^\circ \\ \hline ^{-}68^\circ \end{array}$$

So, the temperature change is ⁻68°F, or a drop of 68° on the Fahrenheit thermometer.

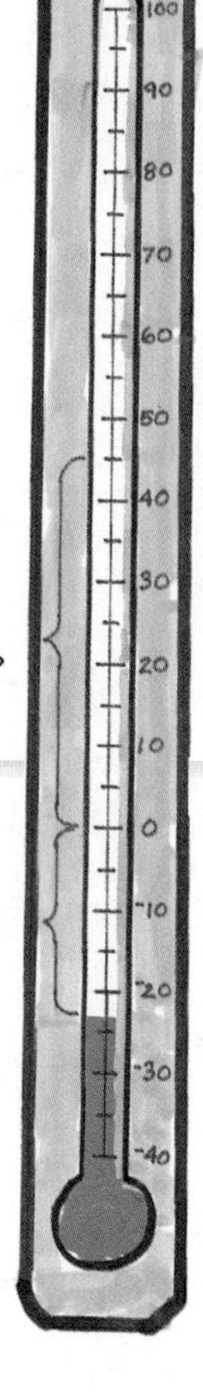

Talk About It

- What is the temperature change if the temperature rises from ⁻20°F to 32°F?
- Suppose the temperature is 68°F and then drops 80° on the Fahrenheit thermometer. What is the temperature?
- What other strategy can you use to solve the problem?

CULTURAL LINK

Several countries, such as Canada, use the Celsius temperature scale, on which the freezing point of water is 0°C. The people of Edmonton, a large city in Canada, enjoy mild summers with temperatures that can reach 21°C (70°F). However, they also must endure temperatures that drop to ⁻18°C (0°F) during the winter. What is the temperature change between 21°C and ⁻18°C?

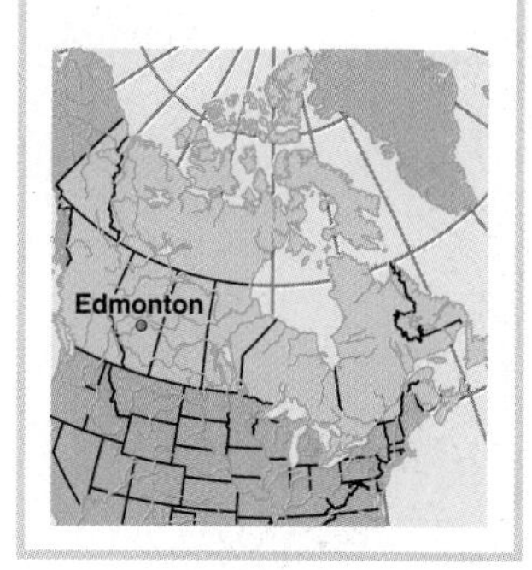

SOCIAL STUDIES LINK

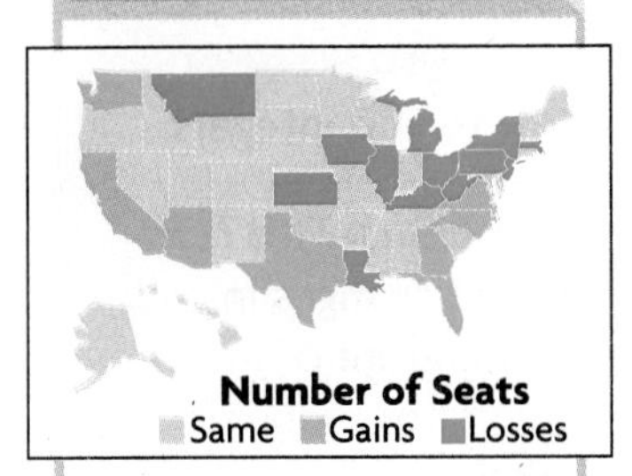

The number of congressional representatives for many states changes after a census. This map shows changes after the 1990 census. Where were most of the losses? most of the gains?

REMEMBER:

The **absolute value** of a number is its distance from 0 on the number line. **See page H27.**

$|{}^{-}12| = 12$

Read: The absolute value of negative twelve is twelve.

$|12| = 12$

Read: The absolute value of positive twelve is twelve.

You can use a number line to show the addition of integers.

EXAMPLE 2

A. Find the sum. $9 + {}^{-}4$

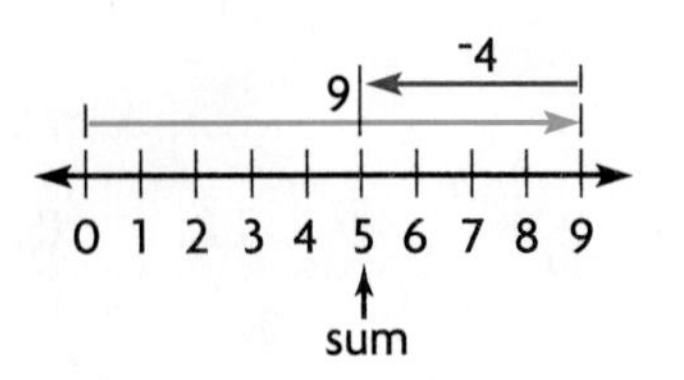

Start at 0. Move 9 spaces to the right. Then move 4 spaces to the left.

You finish at 5, so $9 + {}^{-}4 = 5$.

B. Find the sum. ${}^{-}8 + 3$

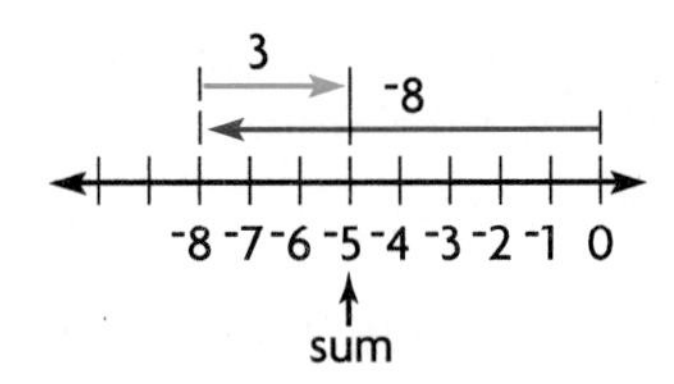

Start at 0. Move 8 spaces to the left. Then move 3 spaces to the right.

You finish at ${}^{-}5$, so ${}^{-}8 + 3 = {}^{-}5$.

ANOTHER METHOD When adding integers, you can use their absolute values to find the sum.

EXAMPLE 3

A. Find the sum. ${}^{-}4 + {}^{-}1$

When adding integers with the same sign, add the absolute values of the integers.

$|{}^{-}4| + |{}^{-}1| = 4 + 1 = 5$

Then use the sign of the addends.

So, ${}^{-}4 + {}^{-}1 = {}^{-}5$.

B. Find the sum. ${}^{-}7 + 3$

When the addends have unlike signs, find the difference of their absolute values.

$|{}^{-}7| - |3| = 7 - 3 = 4$

Then use the sign of the addend with the greater absolute value.

Think: $|{}^{-}7| > |3|$

So, ${}^{-}7 + 3 = {}^{-}4$.

GUIDED PRACTICE

Write the addition equation modeled on the number line.

1.

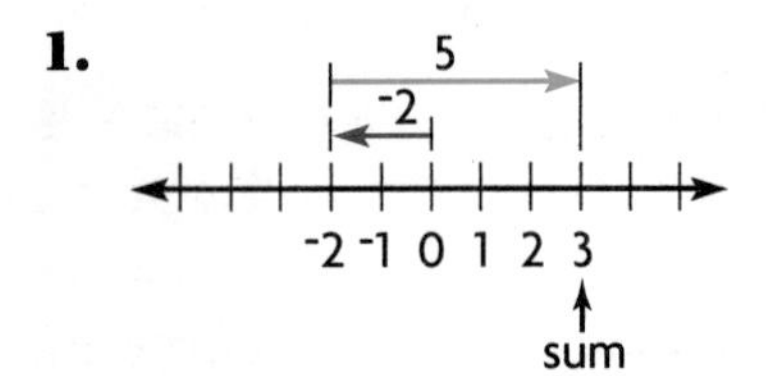

2.

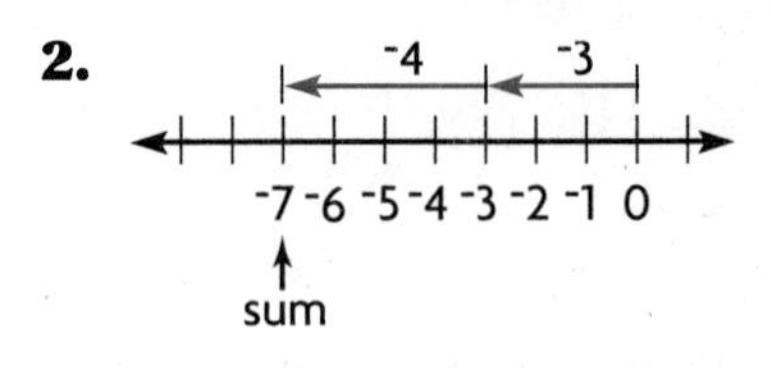

Find the sum.

3. ${}^{-}5 + 3$ **4.** $9 + {}^{-}4$ **5.** ${}^{-}7 + {}^{-}8$ **6.** ${}^{-}56 + 37$

INDEPENDENT PRACTICE

Draw a number line to find the sum.

1. $^{-}8 + 6$ **2.** $9 + {}^{-}11$ **3.** $^{-}5 + {}^{-}3$ **4.** $6 + {}^{-}3$

5. $^{-}5 + {}^{-}6$ **6.** $^{-}8 + 4$ **7.** $10 + {}^{-}10$ **8.** $^{-}10 + 10$

Give the value of each.

9. $|^{-}8|$ **10.** $|14|$ **11.** $|^{-}100|$ **12.** $|^{-}63|$

Find the sum by using absolute values.

13. $^{-}9 + {}^{-}12$ **14.** $13 + {}^{-}3$ **15.** $22 + 38$ **16.** $^{-}24 + 25$

17. $57 + 13$ **18.** $^{-}11 + {}^{-}11$ **19.** $^{-}5 + {}^{-}3 + 1$ **20.** $3 + {}^{-}1 + {}^{-}3$

Problem-Solving Applications

21. TEMPERATURE Suppose the temperature drops from 35°F to $^{-}$12°F. What is the temperature change?

22. BUSINESS Rachel's profits and losses selling tacos for 4 weeks were $^{-}$\$380, \$420, $^{-}$\$145, \$620. How much was her profit or loss for the 4 weeks?

23. Mark borrowed \$53 from his parents for graduation expenses. He paid back \$29. How much does Mark still owe? Use this calculator key sequence to solve the problem: 53 [+/-] [+] 29 [=]

24. WRITE ABOUT IT Which method do you prefer to use to find sums of integers: counters, a number line, or absolute values? Explain.

Mixed Review and Test Prep

Select two models that represent the given integer.
Let [R] represent $^{-}1$ and [Y] represent 1.

25. $^{-}3$ **a.** [R][R][R] **b.** [R][R][R][R][Y] **c.** [Y][Y][Y][Y][R]

26. $^{-}1$ **a.** [R][Y] **b.** [R][Y][R][Y][R] **c.** [R][R][R][Y][Y]

27. 2 **a.** [Y][Y][Y][R] **b.** [R][R] **c.** [R][R][Y][Y][Y][Y]

Find the sum or difference.

28. $\frac{2}{3} + \frac{3}{4}$ **29.** $11\frac{1}{5} - 9\frac{1}{2}$ **30.** $5\frac{3}{8} + 1\frac{1}{4}$ **31.** $13\frac{3}{4} - 7\frac{1}{3}$

32. NUMBER LINE Which number does point A best represent?

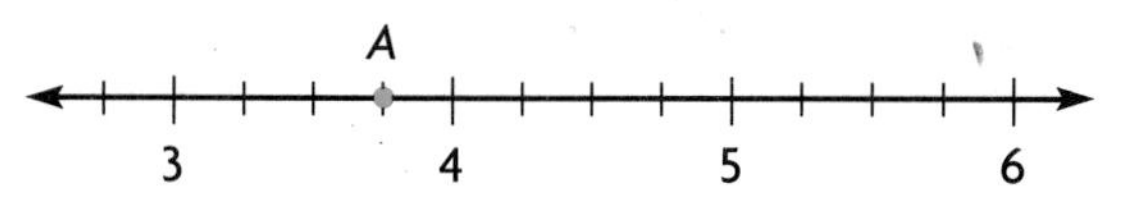

A $4\frac{3}{4}$ **B** $4\frac{1}{4}$ **C** $3\frac{1}{3}$ **D** $3\frac{3}{4}$

33. TIME Jean ran for 31 min 20 sec today. What is a reasonable estimate of the time she will run in 7 days if her daily time is about the same?

F 140 min **G** 210 min
H 250 min **J** 300 min

MORE PRACTICE Lesson 5.1, page H49

ACTIVITY

What You'll Explore
How to model subtraction of integers

What You'll Need
two-color counters

REMEMBER:

There are many different models for a given integer. **See page H28.**

Here are models of $^{-}2$.

1. ●●
2. ○ ●●●
3. ○○ ●●●●

Technology Link

You can subtract integers while solving magic circles by using E-Lab, Activity 5. Available on CD-ROM and on the Internet at **www.hbschool.com/elab**

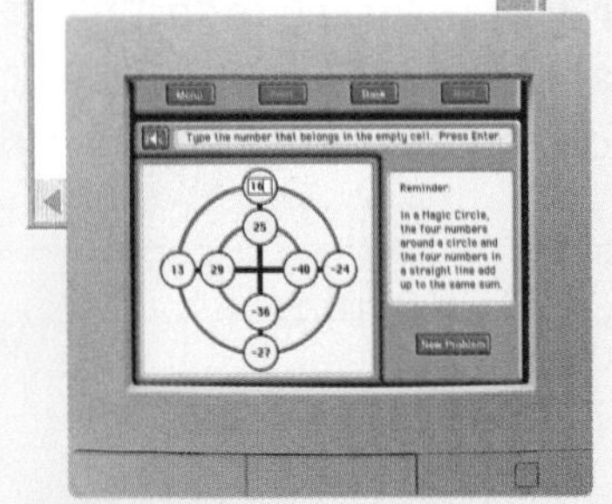

ALGEBRA CONNECTION

Modeling Subtraction of Integers

In this activity you will discover how to subtract integers by building an appropriate model and then taking away the designated number of counters.

Explore

Use a red counter to represent $^{-}1$ and a yellow counter to represent 1. Find the difference: $3 - 5$.

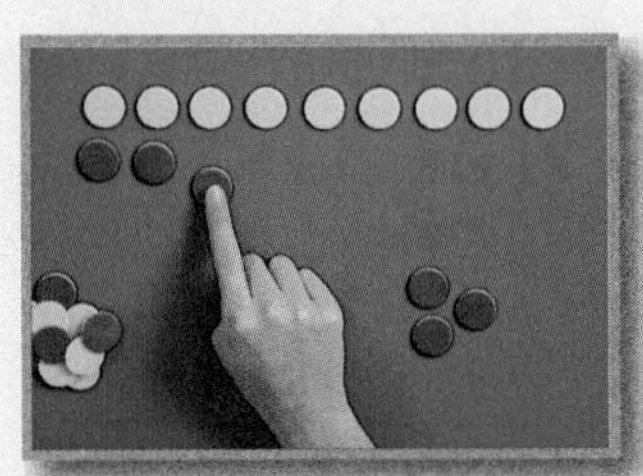

- Use red and yellow counters to make a model of 3. Put at least 5 yellow counters in your model so you can take away 5.
- From your model for 3, take away 5 yellow counters.
- Make as many pairs of red and yellow counters as possible. Count the unpaired counters.

Think and Discuss

- Tell how many unpaired counters remain and what color they are. What number do these represent?
- What is $3 - 5$?
- What do the pairs of red and yellow counters in your model represent?
- What if your problem is $3 - 8$? Your model of 3 should include at least how many yellow counters?
- What if your problem is $3 - {}^{-}5$? Your model of 3 should include at least how many red counters?

Try This

Make a model to find each difference.

$4 - 6$	$^{-}4 - {}^{-}6$	$4 - {}^{-}6$	$^{-}4 - 6$
$7 - 5$	$^{-}7 - {}^{-}5$	$7 - {}^{-}5$	$^{-}7 - 5$

Subtracting Integers

What You'll Learn
How to solve integer subtraction problems by changing them to addition problems

Why Learn This?
To solve everyday problems, as in sporting events

You know that addition and subtraction are inverse operations for whole numbers, fractions, and decimals. Now let's see how the operations of integer subtraction and addition are related.

How are the problems $^-2 - 3$ and $^-2 + {}^-3$ related?

Subtraction

$^-2 - 3$ *Model $^-2$ using at least 3 yellow counters.*

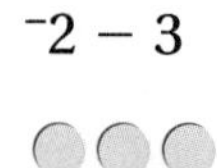

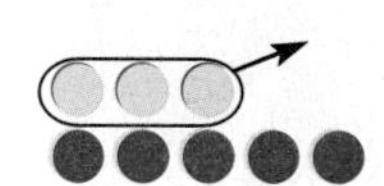

Take away 3 yellow counters.

Since 5 red counters remain, $^-2 - 3 = {}^-5$.

Addition

$^-2 + {}^-3$ *Model $^-2$ using 2 red counters and $^-3$ using 3 red counters.*

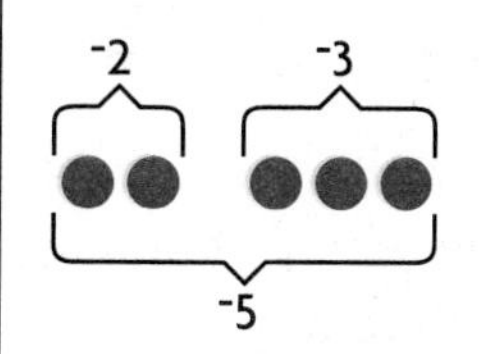

Since there are 5 red counters, $^-2 + {}^-3 = {}^-5$.

The models show that $^-2 - 3 = {}^-5$ and $^-2 + {}^-3 = {}^-5$, so $^-2 - 3 = {}^-2 + {}^-3$. The problems are equivalent.

- Write a pair of problems similar to those above. Show how the two problems are equivalent to each other.

If you compare several other sets of similar subtraction and addition problems for integers, you will discover that you can always **subtract an integer by adding its opposite.**

EXAMPLE 1

A. Find the difference.

$5 - {}^-6$

$5 + 6$ *To subtract $^-6$, add 6, its opposite.*

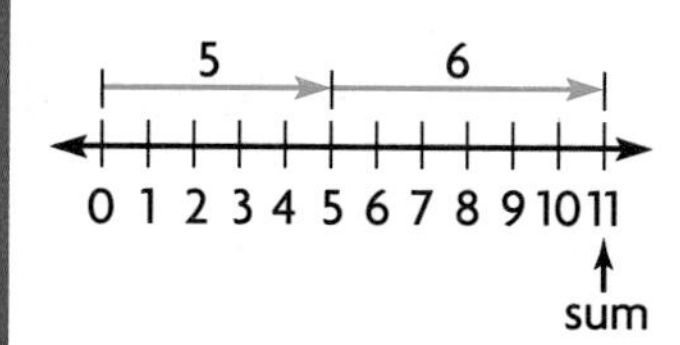

$5 + 6 = 11$

So, $5 - {}^-6 = 11$.

B. Find the difference.

$^-4 - {}^-12$

$^-4 + 12$ *To subtract $^-12$, add 12, its opposite.*

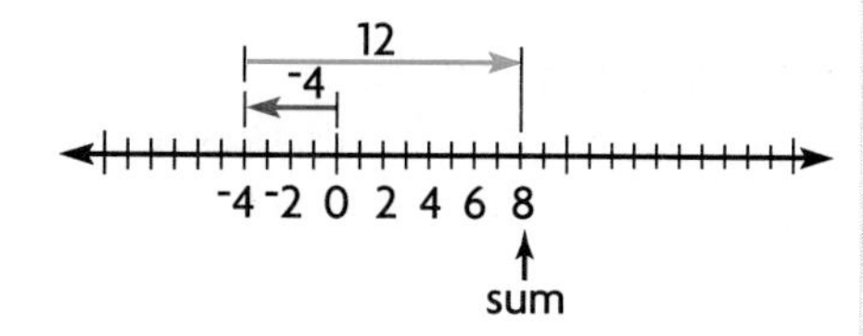

$^-4 + 12 = 8$

So, $^-4 - {}^-12 = 8$.

- What addition problem is equivalent to $^-7 - 3$?

CONSUMER LINK

When you reduce a debt, you are subtracting a negative amount. Suppose you owe a store \$50. Your account balance is $^-$\$50. When you return a sweater you purchased for \$22, the store subtracts part of the debt from your account. It is like making a payment of \$22. What is your new balance?

Calculator Activities, page H37

SPORTS LINK

In golf you try to complete each of the 18 holes in as few shots as possible. Par is the target number of shots for each hole. When you take 1 shot more than par to complete a hole, your score is 1 over par, or $^{+}1$. When you take 1 shot less than par, your score is 1 under par, or $^{-}1$.

Suppose you finish the first hole with a $^{-}2$ and the second hole with a $^{-}1$. How far under par are you at the end of two holes?

EXAMPLE 2 Gerri is on the high school golf team. On the first hole in today's match, she had a $^{-}1$, or 1 shot under par. On the second hole, she had 3 shots over par, or 3. What is the difference between her scores on the two holes?

Find the difference. $3 - {}^{-}1$

$3 - {}^{-}1 = 3 + 1$ *To subtract, add 1, the opposite of $^{-}1$.*
$= 4$

So, $3 - {}^{-}1 = 4$. The difference in her scores is 4 shots.

- What if you solve the problem $^{-}1 - 3$? Is the difference still 4 shots? Explain.
- Suppose Gerri's score is $^{-}2$ on the first hole and $^{-}1$ on the second hole. What is the difference between her scores on the two holes?

You can use a calculator to subtract integers.

EXAMPLE 3 Show that $2 - 8 = 2 + {}^{-}8 = {}^{-}6$.

Use a calculator.

2 [−] 8 [=] [$^{-}6$] and

2 [+] 8 [+/−] [=] [$^{-}6$]

So, $2 - 8 = 2 + {}^{-}8 = {}^{-}6$.

GUIDED PRACTICE

Write an addition problem for each. Then find the difference.

1. $^{-}2 - {}^{-}5$ **2.** $2 - {}^{-}5$ **3.** $^{-}2 - 5$

4. $2 - 5$ **5.** $^{-}5 - 2$ **6.** $^{-}5 - {}^{-}2$

Use a calculator to find the difference.

7. $20 - {}^{-}5$ **8.** $^{-}20 - {}^{-}5$ **9.** $^{-}5 - 20$

INDEPENDENT PRACTICE

Write an addition equation and a solution for each of the following.

1. $3 - {}^-9 = n$ **2.** $5 - {}^-3 = n$ **3.** ${}^-3 - {}^-4 = n$ **4.** ${}^-6 - 5 = n$

Find the difference.

5. ${}^-2 - 1$ **6.** $8 - {}^-4$ **7.** ${}^-3 - 5$ **8.** $5 - {}^-4$ **9.** ${}^-9 - {}^-3$

10. ${}^-5 - 3$ **11.** ${}^-2 - {}^-6$ **12.** ${}^-12 - 8$ **13.** $11 - {}^-11$ **14.** $13 - 13$

15. ${}^-10 - {}^-10$ **16.** ${}^-20 - 20$ **17.** $6 - {}^-4$ **18.** ${}^-9 - 3$ **19.** ${}^-5 - 12$

Find the difference. Use a calculator.

20. ${}^-8 - {}^-15$ **21.** $12 - 67$ **22.** $37 - {}^-55$ **23.** ${}^-125 - 63$ **24.** ${}^-248 - {}^-572$

Problem-Solving Applications

25. SPORTS Bert's football team needs to gain 10 yd for a first down. On the first play, Bert is tackled for a 9-yd loss. What is the distance from his team's position on the field to the position the team needs to reach for the first down?

26. SPORTS At a high school golf tournament, a par score for 18 holes is 72 strokes. Kimiko completes the 18 holes in 67 strokes. What is the difference between her score and a par score?

27. MEASUREMENT In a free-diving contest, Sue reaches a depth of 16 feet and Rani reaches a depth of 23 feet below the surface of the water. What is the difference between the depths reached by Sue and Rani?

28. WRITE ABOUT IT Make up a problem that can be solved by finding the difference between a positive integer and a negative integer.

Mixed Review and Test Prep

Find the sum.

29. ${}^-6 + {}^-6 + {}^-6$ **30.** ${}^-3 + {}^-3 + {}^-3 + {}^-3$ **31.** ${}^-2 + {}^-2 + {}^-2 + {}^-2 + {}^-2$

Solve. Write your answer in simplest form.

32. $\frac{2}{5} \times 3\frac{1}{2}$ **33.** $\frac{3}{7} \div \frac{2}{3}$ **34.** $2\frac{4}{7} \times 1\frac{1}{2}$ **35.** $1\frac{3}{4} \div 3$

36. TIME Coach Johnson allows $1\frac{1}{2}$ hours for baseball practice every Monday and Wednesday. Her team spends $\frac{1}{3}$ of that time on batting practice. How much time does the team practice batting each week?

A $\frac{1}{2}$ hr **B** 1 hr
C $1\frac{1}{2}$ hr **D** 2 hr

37. BUSINESS A radio manufacturer produces 150 radios per hour, of which 12 are damaged. How many radios ***without*** damage would the manufacturer expect to produce in 6 hours?

F 72 radios **G** 138 radios
H 432 radios **J** 828 radios

MORE PRACTICE Lesson 5.2, page H49

LESSON 5.3

What You'll Learn
How to multiply and divide integers

Why Learn This?
To solve problems related to gains and losses in games

ALGEBRA CONNECTION

Multiplying and Dividing Integers

In some everyday settings, it is helpful to know how to multiply integers. Examples include

- football games in which the same number of yards is lost repeatedly
- payments of the same amount of money to repay a loan
- monthly deductions of the same amount of money from a paycheck for a savings account

EXAMPLE 1 Suzanne and Kevin are keeping statistics for their little brother's football team. In one possession the offensive squad lost 4 yards on each of 3 consecutive plays. How far did the ball move from the starting line of scrimmage in this series of plays?

To solve the problem, find the product $3 \times {}^{-}4$.

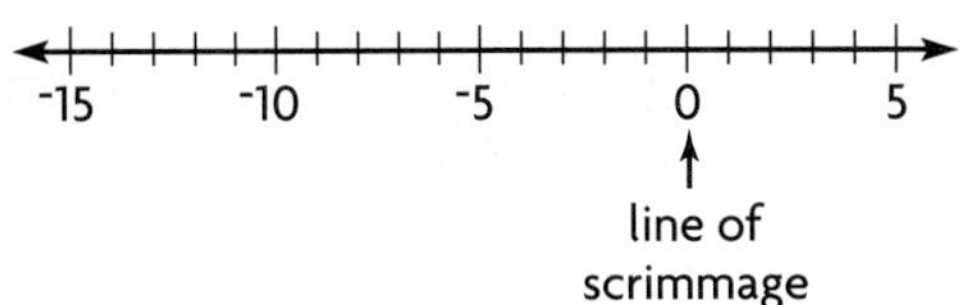

Draw a number line. Let 0 represent the starting line of scrimmage.

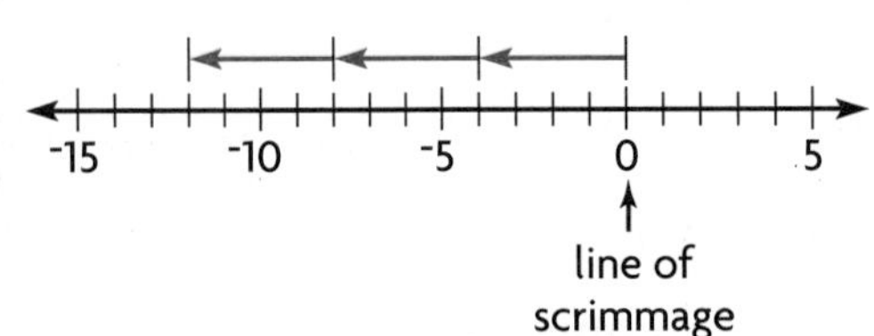

Show 3 lengths of $^{-}4$.

The number line shows that $3 \times {}^{-}4 = {}^{-}4 + {}^{-}4 + {}^{-}4 = {}^{-}12$.

So, the ball moved $^{-}12$ yd, or 12 yd behind the starting line of scrimmage.

Talk About It

- What if the team loses 8 yd on 2 consecutive plays? How far would the ball move from the starting line of scrimmage?
- What number would you expect to see in the display of a calculator following this sequence of keys?

2.5   4 

Calculator Activities, page H37

Dividing Integers

You can use counters to model division of integers.

EXAMPLE 2 Robert owes his father \$10. You can say that he has a balance of $^{-}\$10$. He is going to repay his father the same amount each week for 5 weeks. By how much will his balance change each week as he repays his father?

To solve the problem, find the quotient $^{-}10 \div 5$.

Use red counters to model $^{-}10$.

Separate the counters into 5 equal groups.

The counters show that $^{-}10 \div 5 = {}^{-}2$. So, his balance will change by $^{-}\$2$ each week as he repays his father.

GUIDED PRACTICE

Use a number line to find each product.

1. $4 \times {}^{-}3$ **2.** $2 \times {}^{-}6$ **3.** $6 \times {}^{-}2$

Use counters to find each quotient.

4. $^{-}15 \div 5$ **5.** $^{-}9 \div 3$ **6.** $^{-}20 \div 4$

For Exercises 7–8, use the patterns shown below.

Column 1	Column 2	Column 3	Column 4
$4 \times {}^{-}5 = {}^{-}20$	$^{-}1 \times {}^{-}5 = ■$	$^{-}20 \div 5 = {}^{-}4$	$20 \div {}^{-}5 = {}^{-}4$
$3 \times {}^{-}5 = {}^{-}15$	$^{-}2 \times {}^{-}5 = ■$	$^{-}15 \div 5 = {}^{-}3$	$15 \div {}^{-}5 = {}^{-}3$
$2 \times {}^{-}5 = {}^{-}10$	$^{-}3 \times {}^{-}5 = ■$	$^{-}10 \div 5 = {}^{-}2$	$10 \div {}^{-}5 = {}^{-}2$
$1 \times {}^{-}5 = {}^{-}5$	$^{-}4 \times {}^{-}5 = ■$	$^{-}5 \div 5 = {}^{-}1$	$5 \div {}^{-}5 = {}^{-}1$
$0 \times {}^{-}5 = 0$	$^{-}5 \times {}^{-}5 = ■$	$0 \div 5 = 0$	$0 \div {}^{-}5 = 0$
		$5 \div 5 = ■$	$^{-}5 \div {}^{-}5 = ■$

7. Complete the pattern in Column 2. Then look at the related division problems in Columns 3 and 4. Complete those patterns.

8. What is the sign of the product or quotient of two integers with unlike signs? What is the sign of the product or quotient of two integers with like signs?

9. Use the patterns in Columns 1–4 to write rules for multiplying and dividing integers.

INDEPENDENT PRACTICE

Copy the number line and show the product.

1. $4 \times {}^{-}2$

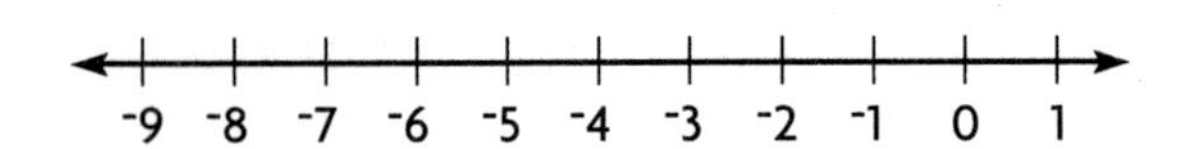

2. $3 \times {}^{-}3$

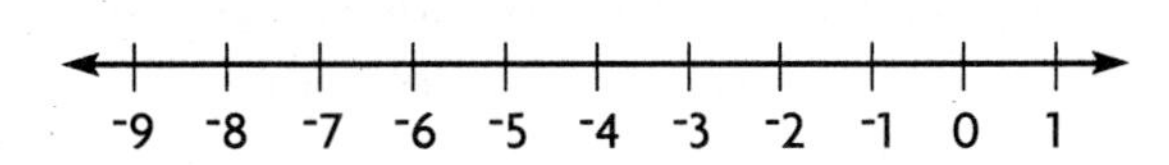

Find the product.

3. ${}^{-}6 \times {}^{-}4$ **4.** ${}^{-}6 \times 4$ **5.** $6 \times {}^{-}4$ **6.** 60×4 **7.** ${}^{-}6 \times {}^{-}40$

8. ${}^{-}3 \times {}^{-}15$ **9.** $15 \times {}^{-}3$ **10.** $3 \times {}^{-}15$ **11.** ${}^{-}3 \times 150$ **12.** $30 \times {}^{-}15$

13. $4 \times {}^{-}12$ **14.** ${}^{-}8 \times {}^{-}12$ **15.** $30 \times {}^{-}12$ **16.** ${}^{-}60 \times {}^{-}120$ **17.** $500 \times {}^{-}12$

18. $3 \times {}^{-}91$ **19.** $5 \times {}^{-}55$ **20.** ${}^{-}84 \times {}^{-}7$ **21.** $0 \times {}^{-}300$ **22.** $100 \times {}^{-}100$

23. $17 \times {}^{-}25$ **24.** ${}^{-}32 \times 26$ **25.** ${}^{-}55 \times {}^{-}75$ **26.** ${}^{-}1 \times {}^{-}17 \times {}^{-}42$ **27.** ${}^{-}2 \times {}^{-}34 \times {}^{-}42$

Use counters to find the quotients. Then complete the related multiplication problem.

28. ${}^{-}32 \div 4 = ■$ $4 \times ■ = {}^{-}32$

29. ${}^{-}28 \div 7 = ■$ $7 \times ■ = {}^{-}28$

30. ${}^{-}35 \div 5 = ■$ $5 \times ■ = {}^{-}35$

Find the quotient.

31. $81 \div {}^{-}3$ **32.** ${}^{-}72 \div {}^{-}6$ **33.** $0 \div {}^{-}5$ **34.** ${}^{-}92 \div 4$

35. $24 \div {}^{-}4$ **36.** ${}^{-}57 \div {}^{-}3$ **37.** ${}^{-}125 \div 5$ **38.** ${}^{-}250 \div 25$

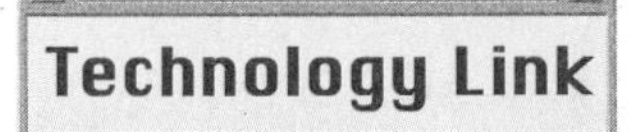

Technology Link

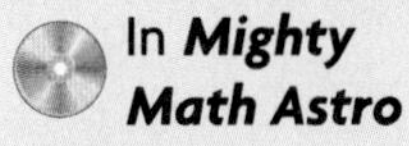

In ***Mighty Math Astro Algebra*** you can go to the *Calculator* to practice writing products of integers as you explore *The Expired Warranty.* Use Grow Slide Level Red G.

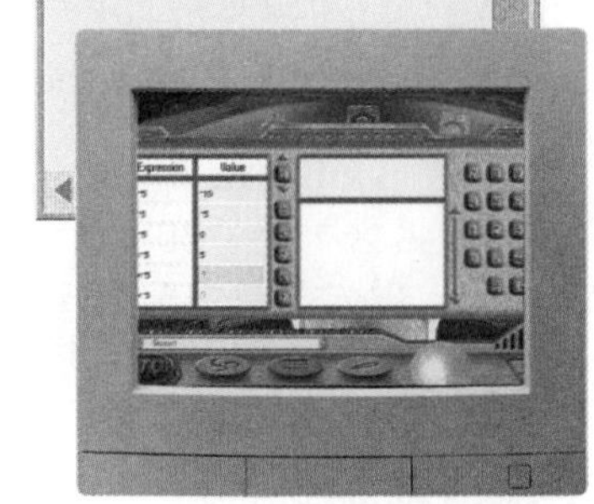

Problem-Solving Applications

39. **CRITICAL THINKING** If an integer is divided by an integer with the opposite sign, will the quotient be positive or negative? Give three examples.

40. **CALCULATOR** The low temperatures for four days at a winter sports festival were ${}^{-}15°C$, $2°C$, ${}^{-}5°C$, and $8°C$. Find the average low temperature for the four-day period using a calculator, and show the key sequence used.

41. **WRITE ABOUT IT** Explain in your own words how writing a related multiplication problem helps you determine the sign of a quotient.

MORE PRACTICE Lesson 5.3, page H50

Adding and Subtracting Rational Numbers

What You'll Learn
How to add and subtract positive and negative fractions and decimals

Why Learn This?
To solve real-world problems, such as problems related to the stock market

You can use number lines, calculators, or rules for adding and subtracting positive and negative fractions and decimals, just as you do for integers.

EXAMPLE 1 Andy bought Microsoft Corporation stock at $91\frac{7}{8}$ per share. When he sold the stock, it was at $89\frac{1}{4}$. How much did he earn or lose per share?

To solve the problem, find the difference between the selling price and the buying price, $89\frac{1}{4} - 91\frac{7}{8}$.

$89\frac{1}{4} - 91\frac{7}{8} = 89\frac{2}{8} + {}^{-}91\frac{7}{8}$ *To subtract, write the corresponding addition problem, changing to a common denominator.*

$\left|{}^{-}91\frac{7}{8}\right| = 91\frac{7}{8}$ $\quad 91\frac{7}{8}$

$\left|89\frac{2}{8}\right| = 89\frac{2}{8}$ $\quad -89\frac{2}{8}$

$\quad 2\frac{5}{8}$

Since the signs are different, subtract the absolute values of the addends.

$2\frac{5}{8}$ represents \$2.625 per share. Since he sold the stock for less than when he bought it, Andy lost almost \$2.63 per share.

REMEMBER:

The sum of two negative numbers is always negative, and the sum of two positive numbers is always positive.

${}^{-}11 + {}^{-}5 = {}^{-}16$

$11 + 5 = 16$

When the signs are different, subtract the absolute values of the addends and use the sign of the addend that has the greater absolute value. **See page H28.**

$2 + {}^{-}3 = {}^{-}1$

Talk About It

- What if Andy had sold the stock at 92? Would he have earned or lost money? How much per share?
- What would the price of the stock have been if Andy had sold his stock and earned $2\frac{1}{2}$ per share?
- Find the sum. ${}^{-}7\frac{1}{2} + {}^{-}3\frac{3}{4}$
- Why is the sum negative for $4 + {}^{-}6.5$?

LANGUAGE LINK

A common meaning of the word *rational* is "sensible or reasonable." When *rational* refers to numbers, its meaning is related to the word *ratio*. A rational number is a ratio. How can you express the rational number 0.143 as a ratio?

rating; a TV show's *rating*.
ra·tio [rā'shō *or* rā'shē·ō] *n., pl.* **ra·tios** The way in which one quantity is related to another; proportion. It is expressed as the quotient of the first divided by the second: In a group of 10 juniors and 5 seniors, the *ratio* of juniors to seniors is 2 to 1, or 2/1.
ra·ti·o·ci·nate [rash'ē·os'ə·nāt'] *v.* **ra·ti·o·ci·nat·ed, ra·ti·o·ci·nat·ing** To think logically; reason. **—ra'ti·o'ci·na'tion** *n.*
ra·tion [rash'ən *or* rā'shən] **1** *v.* To limit the amount of (something scarce) that a person can have or use: to *ration* meat in wartime. **2** *n.* A portion; share. **3** *n.* Food for one person for one day. **4** *v.* To issue rations to, as an army.
ra·tion·al [rash'ən·əl] *adj.* **1** Able to reason: A porpoise is a *rational* animal. **2** Based on or guided by reason: a *rational* argument. **3** Sane, sensible, or reasonable. **—ra·tion·al·i·ty** [rash'ən·al'ə·tē] *n.* **—ra'tion·al·ly** *adv.*
ra·tion·ale [rash'ə·nal'] *n.* A reason that justifies

EXAMPLE 2 Find the difference. $^{-}27.75 - {}^{-}45.25$

$^{-}27.75 - {}^{-}45.25 = {}^{-}27.75 + 45.25$ *Write the corresponding addition problem.*

$$\begin{array}{r} 45.25 \\ -27.75 \\ \hline 17.50 \end{array}$$

Subtract the absolute values of the addends.

Think: Since $|45.25| > |{}^{-}27.75|$, the sum will be positive.

So, $^{-}27.75 - {}^{-}45.25 = 17.50$.

You can use the Commutative and Associative Properties when operating with any rational numbers.

EXAMPLE 3 The Miller family has a family "bank" from which the children can take out and repay loans. Last month there was \$200.00 in the bank. Then Pat borrowed \$26.50, Cheryl paid back \$14.25, and Bill borrowed \$68.75. What is a reasonable estimate of how much is in the bank now?

$\$200.00 + {}^{-}\$26.50 + \$14.25 + {}^{-}\$68.75$ *Estimate each addend.*

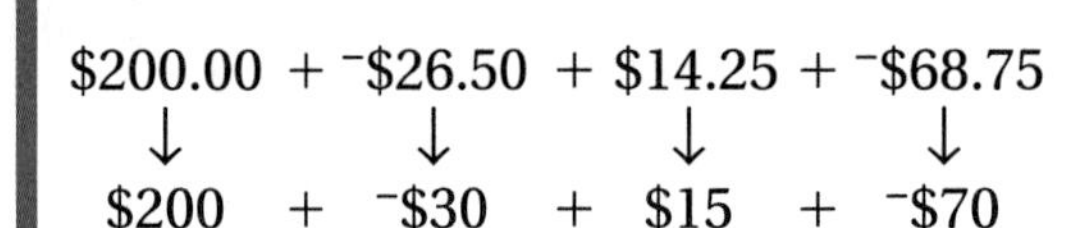

$\$200 + {}^{-}\$30 + \$15 + {}^{-}\$70$

$\$200 + \$15 + {}^{-}\$30 + {}^{-}\$70 =$ *Commutative Property*

$(\$200 + \$15) + ({}^{-}\$30 + {}^{-}\$70) =$ *Associative Property*

$\$215 + {}^{-}\$100 = \$115$

So, there is about \$115 left in the family bank.

REMEMBER:

The **Commutative** and **Associative Properties** can make mental math easier. **See page H6.**

To find $8 + 7 + 12 + 23$, first use the Commutative Property:
$8 + 7 + 12 + 23 =$
$8 + 12 + 7 + 23$

Then use the Associative Property:
$8 + 12 + 7 + 23 =$
$(8 + 12) + (7 + 23) =$
$20 + 30 = 50$

Talk About It

- Suppose this month Bill pays back \$37.00, Mason borrows \$73.60, and Vanessa borrows \$58.00. About how much will be in the bank?
- Show how you would use the Commutative and Associative Properties to find the sum $44 + {}^{-}39 + {}^{-}27 + {}^{-}161 + 56$.
- Make up a new rational number addition problem that can be solved with mental math using the Commutative and Associative Properties.

GUIDED PRACTICE

Use the rules for adding rational numbers to tell whether the sum is positive or negative. Do not add.

1. ${}^-12.6 + {}^-3.25$ **2.** $57.5 + {}^-67.9$ **3.** $98.1 + 245.7$ **4.** ${}^-3.036 + 3.36$ **5.** ${}^-14\frac{2}{3} + 14\frac{1}{5}$

6. ${}^-19 + 32$ **7.** ${}^-524 + {}^-832$ **8.** $4.55 + {}^-45.6$ **9.** $5 + {}^-50$ **10.** $124 + {}^-109$

INDEPENDENT PRACTICE

Find the sum.

1. ${}^-4.2 + {}^-7.8$ **2.** $1\frac{1}{2} + 2\frac{1}{3}$ **3.** ${}^-24.8 + 5.5$ **4.** $0 + {}^-5\frac{5}{6}$ **5.** $8.4 + {}^-2.4$

Find the difference.

6. $45.4 - 24.6$ **7.** $24\frac{1}{4} - 32\frac{1}{2}$ **8.** $23.8 - 54.3$ **9.** ${}^-15.7 - 5.9$ **10.** ${}^-18\frac{3}{4} - 7\frac{2}{3}$

Find the sum or difference.

11. ${}^-8\frac{3}{8} + 6\frac{1}{2}$ **12.** $65.4 - 56.4$ **13.** ${}^-35.6 + {}^-21.1$ **14.** $25\frac{3}{4} - 30\frac{1}{8}$ **15.** $13\frac{5}{8} + 12\frac{1}{4}$

Solve.

16. Show the key sequence you would use to find $22\frac{1}{2} - {}^-12\frac{3}{4}$ with a calculator.

17. Show the key sequence you would use to find ${}^-78.8 + 46.9$ with a calculator.

Problem-Solving Applications

18. **BUSINESS** Amanda and John bought one share of Toys Я Us stock at $27\frac{3}{8}$ per share. During the day the stock fell $\frac{1}{2}$ point and then rose, closing at $28\frac{1}{4}$. How much money could they have lost, and how much did they make?

19. **ESTIMATION** Georgio Rinaldi bought 4 shares of stock at $63\frac{7}{8}$ per share and sold them for $72\frac{1}{2}$ per share. Estimate his gain.

20. **CRITICAL THINKING** Suppose you buy stock in a soft-drink company. On Tuesday the stock sells for \$10 per share. This is a change of $\frac{-3}{8}$ from the previous day. What was the closing price of the stock on Monday? During the last 12 months the high was $14\frac{1}{4}$ and the low was $8\frac{1}{2}$. How much did the price of the stock change?

21. **WRITE ABOUT IT** Compare the rules for adding and subtracting rational numbers with the rules for adding and subtracting integers. What is your conclusion? How can you explain your conclusion?

BUSINESS LINK

Private companies sell shares of stock to investors. The prices of stocks are listed daily in newspapers, on television, and on computer networks. A stock listed at $28\frac{3}{4}$ sells for \$28.75 per share. What would 100 shares of this stock cost?

MORE PRACTICE Lesson 5.4, page H50

LESSON 5.5 **ALGEBRA CONNECTION**

Multiplying and Dividing Rational Numbers

What You'll Learn
How to multiply and divide rational numbers

Why Learn This?
To solve real-world problems, such as how to plan budgets and compute daily costs

To multiply and divide rational numbers, use the rules for integer multiplication.

- Is the product positive or negative when the signs of the two factors are alike? when the signs of the two factors are different?

EXAMPLE 1 Jenny is making a budget. Over the last month she has spent an average of $12.75 per week on gasoline. Using this amount, how much should she budget for gasoline for 6 months?

Let $^{-}12.75$ represent the amount Jenny spends per week and 26 the number of weeks in 6 months.

Find the product. $26 \times {}^{-}12.75$

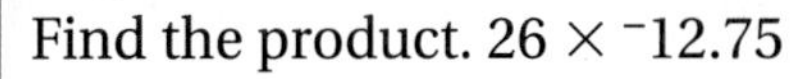  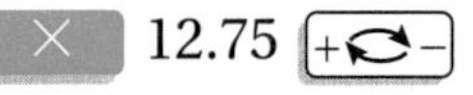  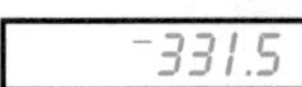

For a 6-month period, Jenny should budget expenses of $331.50 for gasoline.

- What if Jenny spent an average of $52.60 per month for gasoline? How much should she budget for 6 months?

EXAMPLE 2 Find the quotient.

A. $\frac{^{-}4}{7} \div \frac{^{-}2}{7} = \frac{^{-}4}{7} \times \frac{^{-}7}{2} = \frac{28}{14} = 2$

B. $178.5 \div {}^{-}10.5$

$178.5 \div {}^{-}10.5 = {}^{-}17$

- CRITICAL THINKING What is the sign of the product of two negative rational numbers? a negative and a positive rational number? three negative rational numbers? four negative rational numbers? five negative rational numbers?

GUIDED PRACTICE

Find the product or quotient.

1. $4 \times {}^-0.25$
2. ${}^-3 \times {}^-1\frac{1}{2}$
3. ${}^-28 \div 0.7$
4. $125 \div {}^-50$
5. ${}^-6.5 \times 2$
6. 1.75×4
7. ${}^-8 \div \frac{{}^-1}{2}$
8. $12.5 \div 0.25$
9. $18 \div {}^-3.75$
10. $20.5 \div 10$
11. $12 \times \frac{{}^-3}{4}$
12. 37.6×1.5

INDEPENDENT PRACTICE

Show the key sequence you would use to solve the problem with a calculator.

1. ${}^-9.4 \times 5.2$
2. ${}^-2.1 \div {}^-0.4$
3. $4\frac{1}{2} \times {}^-4\frac{3}{8}$
4. ${}^-3.75 \times {}^-4.2$

Find the product or quotient.

5. 15×9
6. ${}^-128 \div 8$
7. ${}^-156 \div 12$
8. ${}^-28 \times {}^-12$
9. 15.25×12
10. ${}^-12.4 \div 2.5$
11. $5\frac{1}{3} \times {}^-2\frac{1}{2}$
12. ${}^-2{,}450 \div 125$
13. ${}^-52.8 \div {}^-4.5$
14. $4\frac{1}{6} \div {}^-2\frac{1}{3}$
15. ${}^-4.34 \times 0.75$
16. $\frac{7}{8} \div \frac{{}^-1}{2}$
17. ${}^-17.4 \times {}^-2.7$
18. $3\frac{1}{2} \times {}^-4\frac{3}{4}$
19. $\frac{5}{9} \times \frac{{}^-3}{7}$
20. ${}^-18.75 \div 0.75$

Find the quotient, and tell what two integers the quotient is between.

21. $1{,}375 \div 150$
22. ${}^-24{,}650 \div {}^-320$
23. ${}^-50{,}525 \div 250$
24. ${}^-165{,}278 \div {}^-2{,}500$
25. $215.75 \div {}^-25$
26. ${}^-998.4 \div {}^-39$
27. ${}^-2{,}332.9 \div 82$
28. ${}^-140{,}515 \div {}^-1{,}570$

Problem-Solving Applications

29. **BUDGET** Lamont is making a budget. Over the last 6 months he has spent an average of $105.50 per month on utilities. Using this amount, how much should he budget for utilities for the next 6 months?

30. Felipe gained $15\frac{3}{4}$ lb over the past 5 months. If he gained the same amount each month, how many pounds did he gain in one month?

31. **MEASUREMENT** At the local grocery store, pears come in $12\frac{1}{4}$-oz cans. Jennifer bought 7 cans of pears. How many ounces of pears did Jennifer buy?

32. Brian and Sonya invested in 12 shares of stock. The value of the stock has decreased $6\frac{3}{8}$ per share. How much has the value of the 12 shares of stock decreased?

33. **WRITE ABOUT IT** Explain under what conditions a product or quotient is positive or negative.

MORE PRACTICE Lesson 5.5, page H50

CHAPTER 5

Review/Test

Find the sum. (pages 99–101)

1. $2 + {}^-13$

2. ${}^-31 + {}^-19$

3. ${}^-16 + 21$

4. ${}^-8 + {}^-3 + {}^-2$

5. ${}^-87 + {}^-23 + {}^-25 + 45$

6. $87 + {}^-23 + 25 + {}^-45$

7. Nate's team must gain 10 yd on four plays. On the first three plays, they lose 12 yd, gain 9 yd, and lose 7 yd. How many yards must they gain to achieve their goal?

8. Amy plays golf. On the first 4 holes, she shot 1 under par, 2 over par, even par, and 3 over par. What is her score, under or over par, after 4 holes?

Find the difference. (pages 103–105)

9. $4 - 9$

10. ${}^-12 - {}^-8$

11. $34 - {}^-16$

12. ${}^-7 - 13$

13. $65 - {}^-17$

14. ${}^-131 - 24$

15. ${}^-403 - 167$

16. $76 - 135$

17. Raul has passed his scuba diving tests at the ${}^-20$-ft level. Beatrice has passed her diving tests at the ${}^-12$-ft level. How much deeper is Raul's level than Beatrice's level?

18. Scott is visiting his aunt in Vermont. When he left Florida, it was 71°F. In Vermont, it is ${}^-6$°F. What kind of temperature change did Scott experience?

Find the product or quotient. (pages 106–108)

19. ${}^-12 \times {}^-3$

20. ${}^-13 \times 5$

21. ${}^-41 \times {}^-10$

22. $157 \times {}^-3$

23. ${}^-24 \div 8$

24. ${}^-210 \div {}^-7$

25. ${}^-3{,}060 \div {}^-15$

26. $10{,}200 \div {}^-30$

27. During a dry spell, the depth of a river decreased 3 in. every day for 7 days. How many inches did the depth decrease during that time?

28. Eileen is \$3,240 in debt and wants to repay her debt in 24 equal payments. How much is each payment?

Find the sum or difference. (pages 109–111)

29. ${}^-8\frac{1}{10} + {}^-3\frac{4}{5}$

30. $6\frac{1}{2} - {}^-1\frac{3}{4}$

31. ${}^-30.24 + 19.76$

32. ${}^-0.14 - 1.38$

Find the product or quotient. (pages 112–113)

33. $2.25 \div {}^-0.25$

34. ${}^-14.7 \times {}^-4$

35. ${}^-7\frac{3}{4} \div \frac{1}{2}$

36. $4 \times {}^-1\frac{1}{8}$

37. $1\frac{2}{3} \times {}^-2\frac{1}{5}$

38. $\frac{{}^-7}{4} \div {}^-5$

39. $1.42 \times {}^-0.4$

40. ${}^-2.45 \times {}^-0.07$

Test Prep

1. $^-34 + 25 + {}^-18 =$

A $^-27$
B $^-11$
C $^-9$
D 41

2. Which is not equivalent to 512?

F 2^9
G 4^5
H 8^3
J 512^1

3. $^-51 \div {}^-3 =$

A $^-19$
B $^-17$
C 17
D 19

4. Mark played basketball for $2\frac{3}{4}$ hours each day for 5 days. How many hours did he practice in all?

F $13\frac{3}{4}$ hr
G $10\frac{3}{4}$ hr
H $7\frac{3}{4}$ hr
J $5\frac{3}{4}$ hr

5. During a basketball game, Wendy made 60% of her shots. Which fraction is equivalent to 60%?

A $\frac{1}{8}$
B $\frac{2}{5}$
C $\frac{3}{4}$
D $\frac{7}{8}$
E Not Here

6. Tabitha buys a video recorder for $399.96 to be paid in 4 equal payments. How much is each payment?

F $96.98
G $98.88
H $99.99
J $104.98

7. $^-21 \times 5 =$

A $^-100$
B $^-105$
C 100
D 105

8. There were 18,000 people attending a concert. Of the people attending, $\frac{1}{3}$ were over 25 years old. Of the remaining people attending, $\frac{1}{2}$ were under 20 years old. How many people attending the concert were 20 to 25 years old?

F 3,000
G 4,500
H 6,000
J 9,000
K Not Here

9. Which is the best estimate of the difference $7\frac{5}{8} - 2\frac{1}{5}$?

A 7
B $5\frac{1}{2}$
C $4\frac{1}{2}$
D 4

10. $^-128 - {}^-47 =$

F $^-175$
G $^-81$
H 81
J 175

ZERO OR TEN

PURPOSE To practice estimating sums and differences of decimals (pages 62–65)
YOU WILL NEED 24 index cards

Make two sets of cards numbered 1 through 12. Work with a partner and challenge another team. Players take turns drawing cards until all have two. Each player forms a decimal with the number cards. Teams decide whether to go for zero or ten and form an addition or subtraction problem. The team closest to its target number, zero or ten, wins.

EXAMPLE: Partner 1 draws 2 and 5 and makes 5.2. Partner 2 draws 1 and 4 and makes 4.1. They go for zero and find $5.2 - 4.1 = 1.1$. They are 1.1 from zero.

READING FRACTIONS

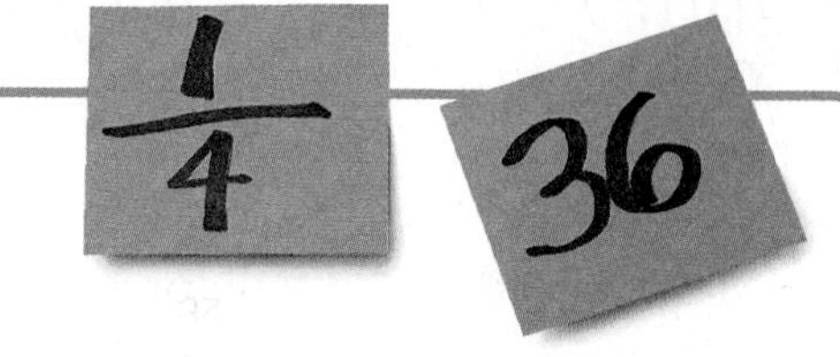

PURPOSE To practice multiplying and dividing with fractions (pages 88–91)
YOU WILL NEED 10 index cards, scissors

Write one of these numbers on each card: $\frac{1}{4}$, $\frac{1}{2}$, $\frac{2}{3}$, $\frac{3}{4}$, $\frac{5}{6}$, 36, 12, 24, 48, 60. Make a fraction stack and a whole-number stack. Shuffle. Place the stacks face down. Each player in turn takes a card from each stack. Then each player answers the following questions:

How many ■ can you take out of ■ ?

What is ■ of ■ ?

Add the two answers for your total. The player with the highest total wins a point. The first player to win five points is the winner.

INTEGER MAGIC

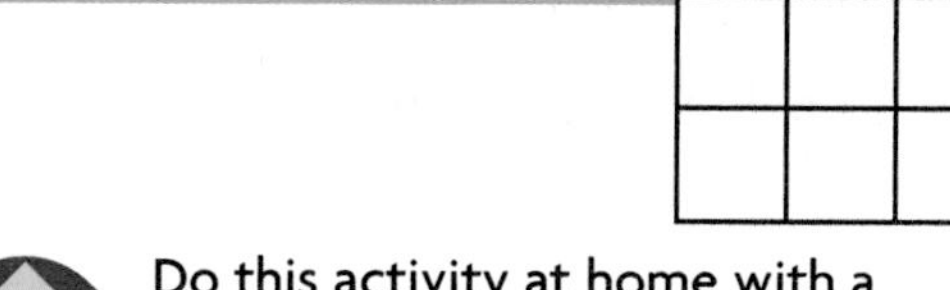

PURPOSE To practice adding integers (pages 99–101)
YOU WILL NEED scissors, paper

A magic square is a square array of numbers in which the rows, columns, and diagonals have the same sums. Cut nine pieces of paper. Write the integers from $^-1$ to $^-9$ on the pieces of paper. Arrange them to make a magic square.

HINT: The magic sum is $^-15$.

Do this activity at home with a family member. See if he or she can make a magic square.

Converting Temperatures by Using a Spreadsheet

To convert degrees Fahrenheit to degrees Celsius you can use the formula $C = \frac{F - 32}{1.8}$. You can enter this formula on a spreadsheet and easily convert the temperatures in the table from degrees Fahrenheit to degrees Celsius.

Enter the data and conversion formula. Then use the Fill Down feature to copy the formula in column C.

RECORD LOW TEMPERATURES THROUGH 1995 (IN °F)			
State	**Low**	**State**	**Low**
Alaska	⁻80	Ohio	⁻39
Florida	⁻2	Oklahoma	⁻27
Hawaii	12	Texas	⁻23
Minnesota	⁻59	Vermont	⁻50
New York	⁻52	Wyoming	⁻66

A11	A	B	C
1	State	Low(°F)	Low(°C)
2	Alaska	-80	=(B2-32)/1.8
3	Florida	-2	
4	Hawaii	12	
5	Minnesota	-59	
6	New York	-52	
7	Ohio	-39	
8	Oklahoma	-27	
9	Texas	-23	
10	Vermont	-50	
11	Wyoming	-66	
12			

A11	A	B	C
1	State	Low(°F)	Low(°C)
2	Alaska	-80	-62.22
3	Florida	-2	-18.89
4	Hawaii	12	-11.11
5	Minnesota	-59	-50.56
6	New York	-52	-46.67
7	Ohio	-39	-39.44
8	Oklahoma	-27	-32.78
9	Texas	-23	-30.56
10	Vermont	-50	-45.56
11	Wyoming	-66	-54.44
12			

1. What symbol was used to represent division in cell C2?

2. In cell C2 what does B2 represent in the formula?

3. What do you notice about the temperatures for Hawaii?

USING THE SPREADSHEET

The formula to convert degrees Celsius to degrees Fahrenheit is $F = 1.8C + 32$. Use a spreadsheet to convert the temperatures to degrees Fahrenheit.

4. 20°C **5.** 10°C **6.** 0°C **7.** ⁻10°C **8.** ⁻20°C **9.** ⁻30°C

CHAPTERS 3–5

Study Guide and Review

EXAMPLES

EXERCISES

- **Estimate the sum or difference of whole numbers and decimals.** (pages 62–65)

Estimate the sum. Use clustering.

$$\begin{array}{ccccccccc} 14.33 & + & 15.24 & + & 14.88 & + & 15.63 & + & 15.19 \\ \downarrow & & \downarrow & & \downarrow & & \downarrow & & \downarrow \\ 15 & + & 15 & + & 15 & + & 15 & + & 15 \end{array}$$

$5 \times 15 = 75 \leftarrow$ *estimated sum*

Find a range for an estimate of the sum.

1. $4.6 + 7.5 + 4.7$ **2.** $45.6 + 55.01 + 49.09$

Estimate the sum or difference.

3. $24.7 + 15.2$ **4.** $67.75 + 13.5$
5. $54.62 - 25.13$ **6.** $83.72 - 22.23$
7. $17.83 - 9.94$ **8.** $36.58 + 24.3$
9. $29.09 + 31.82$ **10.** $62.17 - 14.95$

- **Multiply and divide whole numbers and decimals.** (pages 66–72)

$2.5\overline{)17.55} \rightarrow$

$$\begin{array}{r} 7.02 \\ 25\overline{)175.5} \\ -175 \\ \hline 050 \\ -\ 50 \\ \hline 0 \end{array}$$

$\leftarrow$ *Write a zero.*

$2.5 \times 10 = 25$
$17.55 \times 10 = 175.5$

Find the product or quotient.

11. 17.86×5 **12.** 0.045×0.72
13. $42.7 \div 7$ **14.** $4.29 \div 0.26$
15. 5.6×0.82 **16.** 3.91×2.5
17. $9.554 \div 0.34$ **18.** $354.9 \div 4.2$
19. 6.87×0.9 **20.** $9.87 \div 1.75$
21. $8.342 \div 0.97$ **22.** 76.8×8.9
23. 3.84×0.96 **24.** $97.2 \div 1.8$

- **Use the order of operations.** (pages 73–75)

Find the value.

$95 - 2^3 \times 5 \div (24 - 4)$ *Parentheses first.*
$95 - 2^3 \times 5 \div 20$ *Clear exponent.*
$95 - 8 \times 5 \div 20$ *Multiply.*
$95 - 40 \div 20$ *Divide.*
$95 - 2$ *Subtract.*
93

Find the value.

25. $54 \div (3 + 6) \times 4$
26. $4 + 3^3 \times (6.3 - 2.25)$
27. $(5 \times 5 + 5)^2 \div 5 - 5$
28. $(10 + 2)^2 \times 3 - 8.5$
29. $4 \times 5 \div 2 + (8 - 5)^2$
30. $24 - 16 \div (9 - 7)^3$

- **Add and subtract fractions and mixed numbers.** (pages 80–83)

Subtract. Write the answer in simplest form.

$$5\tfrac{1}{6} = 5\tfrac{1}{6} = 4\tfrac{7}{6} \leftarrow 5\tfrac{1}{6} = 4\tfrac{6}{6} + \tfrac{1}{6} = 4\tfrac{7}{6}$$

$$-2\tfrac{2}{3} = 2\tfrac{4}{6} = 2\tfrac{4}{6}$$

$$2\tfrac{3}{6} = 2\tfrac{1}{2}$$

Add or subtract. Write the answer in simplest form.

31. $\frac{5}{6} - \frac{3}{4}$ **32.** $\frac{2}{3} + \frac{5}{6}$
33. $2\frac{7}{8} + 8\frac{2}{3}$ **34.** $10\frac{1}{6} + 4\frac{3}{10}$
35. $8 - 5\frac{6}{9}$ **36.** $10\frac{1}{4} - 4\frac{5}{12}$
37. $9\frac{1}{9} - 6\frac{1}{3}$ **38.** $16\frac{3}{8} + 7\frac{5}{6}$
39. $8\frac{3}{8} + 7\frac{3}{10}$ **40.** $28\frac{1}{6} - 19\frac{4}{15}$
41. $15\frac{3}{4} + 6\frac{1}{12}$ **42.** $31\frac{1}{12} - 18\frac{1}{8}$

- **Multiply and divide fractions and mixed numbers.** (pages 88–91)

Multiply or divide. Write the answer in simplest form.

Invert the divisor and multiply.

$3\frac{1}{4} \times 1\frac{2}{3} = \frac{13}{4} \times \frac{5}{3}$

$= \frac{65}{12}$, or $5\frac{5}{12}$

$1\frac{1}{2} \div 4\frac{1}{2} = \frac{3}{2} \div \frac{9}{2}$

$= \frac{\overset{1}{\cancel{3}}}{\underset{1}{\cancel{2}}} \times \frac{\overset{1}{\cancel{2}}}{\underset{3}{\cancel{9}}} = \frac{1}{3}$

Multiply or divide. Write the answer in simplest form.

43. $\frac{1}{4} \times \frac{1}{9}$ **44.** $\frac{9}{10} \div \frac{2}{3}$

45. $4 \times 2\frac{4}{5}$ **46.** $3\frac{2}{3} \div 2$

47. $3\frac{3}{5} \times \frac{4}{9}$ **48.** $4\frac{1}{4} \div 2\frac{1}{8}$

49. $2\frac{2}{3} \times 4\frac{1}{2}$ **50.** $5\frac{1}{2} \div 2\frac{3}{4}$

51. $9\frac{3}{8} \times 3\frac{3}{7}$ **52.** $7\frac{2}{7} \div 4\frac{1}{4}$

- **Add, subtract, multiply, and divide integers.** (pages 99–108)

$38 + {}^-42 = {}^-4$ $\quad {}^-50 - {}^-23 = {}^-27$

${}^-10 \times {}^-5 = 50$ $\quad {}^-640 \div 80 = {}^-8$

Find the sum or difference.

53. ${}^-8 + {}^-6$ **54.** ${}^-16 - {}^-9$

Find the product or quotient.

55. ${}^-11 \times {}^-5$ **56.** ${}^-720 \div 9$

57. ${}^-216 \div {}^-8$ **58.** ${}^-86 \times 2$

- **Add, subtract, multiply, and divide rational numbers.** (pages 109–113)

$4\frac{3}{5} \times {}^-1\frac{1}{2} = \frac{23}{5} \times \frac{-3}{2}$

$= \frac{-69}{10}$

$= {}^-6\frac{9}{10}$

Find the sum or difference.

59. $16.5 - {}^-10.6$ **60.** ${}^-14.46 + {}^-7.32$

61. ${}^-5\frac{1}{2} + 6\frac{2}{3}$ **62.** $6\frac{3}{5} - {}^-3$

Find the product or quotient.

63. ${}^-2\frac{2}{3} \times {}^-2\frac{5}{8}$ **64.** $4.25 \times {}^-8$

65. ${}^-6\frac{1}{2} \div 3$ **66.** ${}^-63.36 \div {}^-3$

Problem-Solving Applications

Solve. Explain your method.

67. A game at the carnival had 2,400 prizes to give away. On Friday, $\frac{1}{2}$ of the prizes were given out. On Saturday, $\frac{1}{4}$ of the remaining prizes were given out. How many prizes were given away on Saturday? (pages 92–93)

68. In the Alaskan Arctic, the temperature ranges from an average of ${}^-24$°C in January to 8°C in July. What is the difference between these temperatures? (pages 103–105)

69. Kaitlin had 6,300 baseball cards. She sold $\frac{1}{3}$ of them, and then she traded $\frac{1}{2}$ of the remaining ones. How many did she trade? (pages 92–93)

70. Samantha earned $237.25 for working 36.5 hr. How much did she make per hour? (pages 70–72)

Performance Assessment

Tasks: Show What You Know

1. Explain how you would use the order of operations to evaluate $75 - 5^2 \times 2 \div (8 - 6)$. (pages 73–75)

2. Explain how you could use the strategy *solve a simpler problem* to solve this problem. Then solve the problem. Ali Davidson earned $4,500 last year. She put $\frac{1}{5}$ of her earnings in a savings account and spent $\frac{1}{3}$ of the remaining money on a used car. How much money did she spend on the car? (pages 92–93)

3. Find the quotient: $^{-}\frac{3}{4} \div \frac{1}{2}$. Explain your method. (pages 112–113)

Problem Solving

Solve. Explain your method.

CHOOSE a strategy and a tool.

- Find a Pattern
- Write an Equation
- Draw a Diagram
- Make a Model
- Act It Out

Paper/Pencil

Calculator

Hands-On

Mental Math

4. Melanie is baking some bread for the school bake sale. She has 9.5 lb of flour. Each pound is 16 oz. She needs 25 oz of flour for each loaf. How many loaves of bread can she bake? (pages 70–72)

5. Sound travels at about 4,800 m per sec through nickel. It travels about $\frac{3}{4}$ as fast through brick. Through lead it travels at only about $\frac{1}{3}$ of its speed through brick. About how fast does it travel through brick and through lead? (pages 92–93)

6. The high temperatures for 1 week in January were recorded as:

Monday	2°
Tuesday	11°
Wednesday	⁻3°
Thursday	5°
Friday	⁻8°

What was the greatest one-day change in high temperatures? What was the greatest difference in high temperatures between any two days? (pages 103–105)

Cumulative Review

CHAPTERS 1–5

Solve the problem. Then write the letter of the correct answer.

1. Which of the following is an integer? (pages 16–19)

A. $^-0.23$ **B.** $^-3$
C. 0.03 **D.** $1\frac{1}{4}$

2. What percent of the figure is shaded? (pages 23–25)

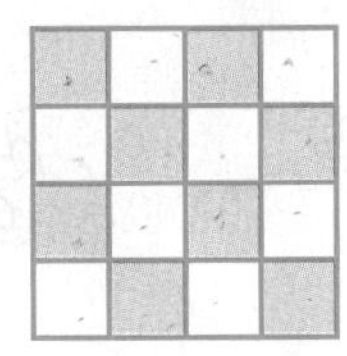

A. 25% **B.** 50%
C. 60% **D.** 75%

3. Which percent is equivalent to $\frac{1}{4}$? (pages 26–29)

A. 0.25% **B.** 4%
C. 25% **D.** not here

4. Which decimal is equivalent to 5%? (pages 26–29)

A. 0.05 **B.** 0.2
C. 0.5 **D.** 20

5. What is the value of 10^5? (pages 36–39)

A. 50 **B.** 105
C. 10,000 **D.** 100,000

6. What is 42,300 written in scientific notation? (pages 36–39)

A. 4.23×10^4 **B.** 4.23×10^3
C. 4.23×10^2 **D.** 4.23×10^5

7. What is $\sqrt{1{,}764}$? (pages 43–45)

A. 42 **B.** 882
C. 3,528 **D.** 3,111,696

8. 12.84×0.65 (pages 66–68)

A. 6.7840 **B.** 8.3460
C. 834.60 **D.** not here

9. $201.45 \div 8.5$ (pages 70–72)

A. 0.237 **B.** 2.37
C. 2.51 **D.** not here

10. $(5 + 7)^2 - 3 \times 4$ (pages 73–75)

A. 7 **B.** 42
C. 132 **D.** 204

11. Add. Write the answer in simplest form. (pages 82–83)

$5\frac{11}{12} + 6\frac{1}{4}$

A. $11\frac{7}{12}$ **B.** $11\frac{3}{4}$
C. $11\frac{1}{6}$ **D.** $12\frac{1}{6}$

12. Multiply. Write the answer in simplest form. (pages 88–91)

$1\frac{2}{3} \times 6\frac{2}{5}$

A. $4\frac{1}{3}$ **B.** $6\frac{4}{15}$
C. $10\frac{2}{3}$ **D.** $10\frac{1}{5}$

13. $15 + {}^-6$ (pages 99–101)

A. 21 **B.** 9
C. $^-9$ **D.** $^-21$

14. $^-40 \times {}^-4$ (pages 106–108)

A. 160 **B.** 10
C. $^-160$ **D.** not here

15. Subtract. Write the answer in simplest form. (pages 109–111)

$25\frac{1}{2} - 32\frac{3}{4}$

A. $7\frac{1}{4}$ **B.** $^-7\frac{1}{4}$
C. $8\frac{1}{4}$ **D.** $^-8\frac{1}{4}$

CHAPTER

6 WRITING AND SIMPLIFYING EXPRESSIONS

LOOK AHEAD

In this chapter you will solve problems that involve

- writing and evaluating numerical and algebraic expressions
- combining like terms to simplify an expression
- writing rules and expressions for sequences

Recycling in the United States has been increasing. Since the early 1970's, Americans have earned $6.4 billion from recycling aluminum cans. In some areas, you can earn $0.44 per pound of recyclable aluminum.

- Suppose your school has a goal of raising $100 by recycling aluminum. How many pounds would you have to collect if you were paid $0.44 per pound?

Problem-Solving Project

Reduce, Reuse, Recycle

Suppose your school is raising money by collecting items to recycle. Estimate how much money you could raise by collecting cans, bottles, and paper. Use the data in the chart to write algebraic expressions to predict how much money you could raise. Calculate the total amount you could raise, and share your results with the class.

Profiting from Recycling

Recyclable Item	Price
Aluminum Cans	$0.25 per pound
No. 1 Plastic Bottles	$0.05 each
White Paper	$0.08 per pound

PROJECT CHECKLIST

- ✓ Did you estimate how much money you could raise?
- ✓ Did you write algebraic expressions to predict how much money you could raise?
- ✓ Did you calculate the total amount you could raise?
- ✓ Did you share your results with the class?

LESSON 6.1

Numerical and Algebraic Expressions

What You'll Learn
How to identify, write, and read numerical and algebraic expressions

Why Learn This?
To translate mathematical expressions into everyday language and vice versa

VOCABULARY
numerical expression
algebraic expression
variable

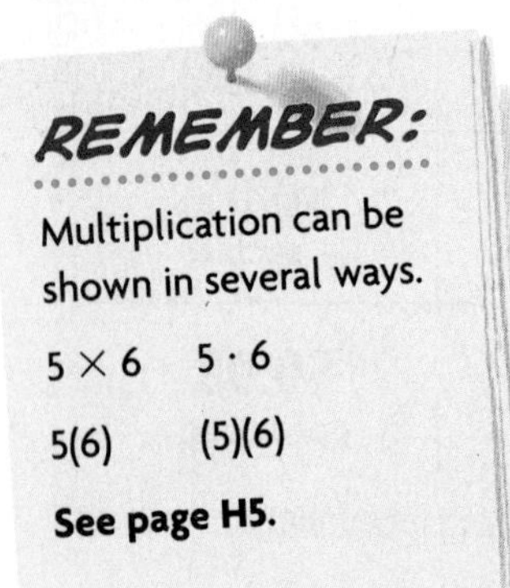

REMEMBER:
Multiplication can be shown in several ways.
5 × 6   5 · 6
5(6)   (5)(6)
See page H5.

In the 1960's, a popular expression with teens was "See you later, alligator." What are some expressions that you use?

There are many different types of expressions. Some are simple phrases, such as *nice work* and *good job.* In mathematics, expressions include numbers, operation symbols, and sometimes variables.

A **numerical expression** is a phrase that has only numbers and operation symbols. These are examples of numerical expressions:

$35 - 15.5$ $\quad 1\frac{1}{2} \times \frac{3}{4}$ $\quad 3^2 + 2^3$ $\quad {}^-12 \div (3 \div 0.75)$

An **algebraic expression** includes variables. Recall that a **variable** is a letter or symbol that represents one or more numbers.

$7n - 4$ $\quad 3^2 \cdot a$ $\quad \frac{c}{4}$ $\quad 2n + 4$

Sometimes expressions are shown in words.

Word Expression	Numerical or Algebraic Expression
7 times 70, the number of people at the festival the previous year	7×70
The cost, \$128, increased by \$5	\$128 + \$5
The quotient of 24 and *n*	$\frac{24}{n}$
Three times the difference of 12 and a number, *d*	$3(12 - d)$

You can write word expressions for numerical and algebraic expressions.

EXAMPLE Write the expressions in words in two different ways.

$1\frac{1}{2} + {}^-2$: the sum of $1\frac{1}{2}$ and $^-2$ or $1\frac{1}{2}$ increased by $^-2$

$5n - 3$: 3 less than the product of 5 and a number, *n*, or 3 subtracted from the product 5 times *n*

- Write two word expressions that can be represented by the algebraic expression $8t$.

GUIDED PRACTICE

Tell whether the expression is numerical, algebraic or a word expression.

1. 8 multiplied by 4 **2.** $12.5 \div 4$ **3.** $3x - 5$

4. $7 + 10k + 23$ **5.** 7 less than 19 **6.** $14 \times 72 + 32$

7. $(325 - 91) \times 7.6$ **8.** $17x + 32y - 14z$ **9.** 1 increased by 9

Technology Link

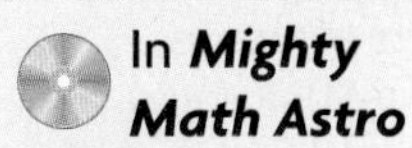

In ***Mighty Math Astro Algebra*** you can have fun writing equivalent numerical expressions by entering the *Cargo Bay* and engaging *The Abandoned Satellites I, II,* and *III.* Use Grow Slide Levels Red E, O, and Y.

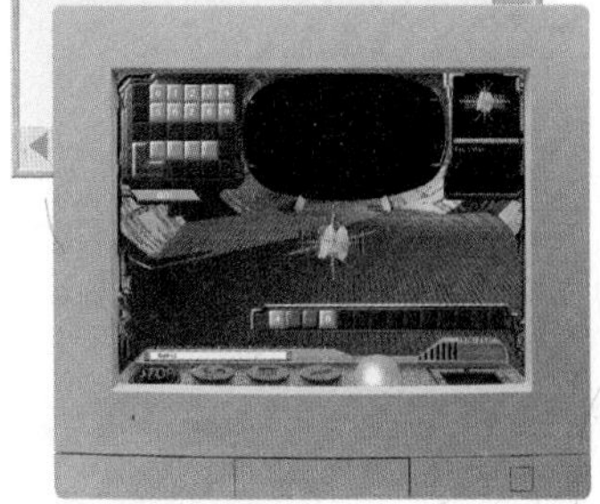

INDEPENDENT PRACTICE

Match the correct algebraic expression to the words.

1. 7 increased by a number, n

2. the product of 7 and n

3. the sum of a number, n, and 7 cubed

$7n$
$7 + n$
$n + 7^3$

Write a numerical expression for each word expression.

4. the number of bicycles, 32, decreased by 15

5. 6 more than the quotient of 20 and 4

Write a word expression for each expression.

6. $25 \div 5$ **7.** $78 + {}^{-}7$ **8.** $1.3 - 0.7$ **9.** $59 + 4^2$

10. $5 + n$ **11.** $t - 19$ **12.** $3(6 + s)$ **13.** $4^2 + (w \cdot 8)$

Write an algebraic expression for each word expression.

14. the sum of 11.2 and a number, t

15. the product of 100 and a number, x

16. twice the distance, d

17. the difference of 6 and a number, r

18. The quotient of $45 and the number of students, s

19. 2.5 times a number, y

Problem-Solving Applications

20. **ALGEBRA** Bryce paid $1.50 more for a CD than he had expected. Write an algebraic expression that represents how much Bryce paid. Let c represent the amount he had expected to pay for the disc.

21. **ALGEBRA** Kyle bought a book on sale at $3.25 off the regular price, r. Write an algebraic expression that represents the sale price of the book.

22. **CRITICAL THINKING** If the value of $x + 12$ is 21, what is the value of $x + 16$ and the value of $x - 16$?

23. **WRITE ABOUT IT** How are numerical and algebraic expressions different?

MORE PRACTICE Lesson 6.1, page H51

LESSON 6.2 Evaluating Expressions

What You'll Learn
How to evaluate numerical and algebraic expressions

Why Learn This?
To write an expression as a single number so that it is easier to describe or understand

VOCABULARY
evaluate

When you **evaluate** a numerical expression, you put it in its simplest numerical form, as a single number.

Suppose you have the numerical expression that is the product of four $^-5$'s. To evaluate the expression, you multiply.

Write the expression.	Evaluate.
$(^-5)\ (^-5)\ (^-5)\ (^-5)$	$(^-5 \cdot {^-5})\ (^-5 \cdot {^-5}) = (25)\ (25)$
	$= 625$

Evaluating gives the positive value of 625.

- Explain why the value of $(^-5)\ (^-5)\ (^-5)\ (^-5)$ is positive.
- Name a multiplication expression using only $^-5$'s that has a negative value.

Remember that when you evaluate an expression, you have to follow the order of operations.

EXAMPLE 1 Evaluate the expression $\frac{3}{2} \div 3 + \frac{1}{4} \times 2^3$, using the order of operations.

$\frac{3}{2} \div 3 + \frac{1}{4} \times 2^3 = \frac{3}{2} \div 3 + \frac{1}{4} \times 8$ *Clear the exponent.*

$= \frac{3}{2} \div 3 + \frac{1}{4} \times 8$ *Divide.*

$= \frac{1}{2} + \frac{1}{4} \times 8$ *Multiply.*

$= \frac{1}{2} + 2$ *Add.*

$= 2\frac{1}{2}$

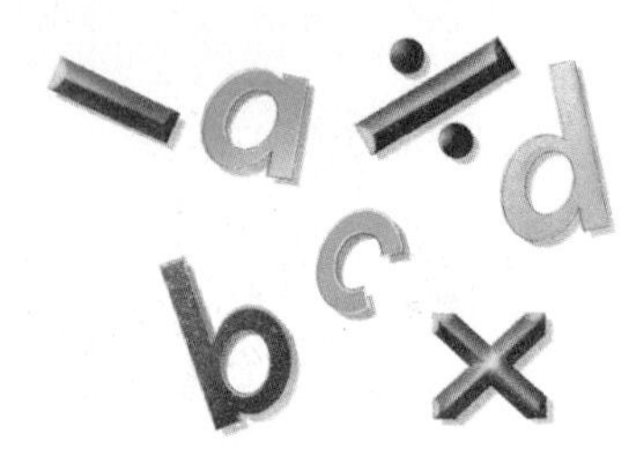

REMEMBER:

Order of Operations

1. Operate inside parentheses.
2. Clear exponents.
3. Multiply and divide from left to right.
4. Add and subtract from left to right.

See page H5.

Talk About It CRITICAL THINKING

- Evaluate the expression $\frac{3}{2} \div (3 + \frac{1}{4} \times 2^3)$, using the order of operations. How is this expression different from the expression evaluated in Example 1?
- The following sequences of keys are for a calculator that follows the order of operations.

a. 3 [×] 24 [÷] 8 [−] 2 [=]

b. 3 [×] [(] 24 [÷] 8 [−] 2 [)] [=]

Why do the sequences result in different displays?

Algebraic Expressions

Algebraic expressions are evaluated by replacing the variables with numbers and then performing the indicated operations.

EXAMPLE 2 Evaluate the algebraic expressions.

A. $\frac{1}{2}n$ for $n = 6$

$\frac{1}{2}(6)$ *Replace n with 6 and multiply.*

3

B. $3x - \frac{1}{2}$ for $x = 5$

$3(5) - \frac{1}{2}$ *Replace x with 5 and multiply.*

$15 - \frac{1}{2}$ *Subtract.*

$14\frac{1}{2}$

- Evaluate $3n + 5$ for $n = 3$.

ACTIVITY

n | 3 | $\frac{1}{2}$ | $-$

Cut small pieces of paper, and label them as shown. Use one or more of your papers to write algebraic expressions. These are examples of some of the algebraic expressions that are possible:

$\frac{1}{2}n$ $\quad n - 3 \quad$ $3n - \frac{1}{2}$

- See how many more expressions you can make. Then evaluate each one for $n = {}^-2$.

CAREER LINK

When building a road, civil engineers use the expression $\frac{D}{L}$ to find the steepness, or slope, of the road. Suppose that D, the difference in elevation of two points, is 4 ft, and that L, the horizontal distance between the points, is 50 ft. Find the slope of the road.

GUIDED PRACTICE

Use the order of operations to evaluate the expression.

1. $3 \div 3 + 3 \times 3^3 - 3$ **2.** $3 - 3 \div 3 + 3^3 \times 3$ **3.** $3 + 3 \div 3 - 3^3 \times 3$

Evaluate each expression for $b = 14$.

4. $b + 12$ **5.** $b - 4$ **6.** b^2 **7.** $b + 2.3$

8. $18 - b$ **9.** $2b - b$ **10.** $\frac{1}{2}b + \frac{2}{3}$ **11.** $53 - b$

Evaluate the expression $1.5n + 2.5$ for each value of n.

12. $n = 3$ **13.** $n = {}^-3$ **14.** $n = {}^-0.3$ **15.** $n = 2$

16. $n = 0.5$ **17.** $n = {}^-0.5$ **18.** $n = 10$ **19.** $n = {}^-10$

More Than One Variable

Sometimes the same variable occurs more than once in an expression. When you evaluate the expression, you must replace the variable each time with the same value.

EXAMPLE 3 Evaluate $3x + 2x + 4$ for $x = {}^-1.5$.

$3(x) + 2(x) + 4$	*Replace x with ⁻1.5.*
$3({}^-1.5) + 2({}^-1.5) + 4$	*Evaluate.*
${}^-4.5 + {}^-3 + 4 = {}^-3.5$	

- Evaluate $3x + 2x + 4$ for $x = 1.5$.

An expression can have more than one variable.

EXAMPLE 4 Evaluate $3b - 2c + 5$ for $b = 6$ and $c = \frac{1}{2}$.

$3(b) - 2(c) + 5$	*Replace b with 6 and c with $\frac{1}{2}$.*
$3(6) - 2\left(\frac{1}{2}\right) + 5$	*Evaluate.*
$18 - 1 + 5 = 22$	

- Evaluate $5b + 2c - 3$ for $b = 3$ and $c = \frac{1}{2}$.
- Is the expression $5b - 3 + 2c$ equivalent to $5b + 2c - 3$ for $b = 3$ and $c = \frac{1}{2}$? Explain.
- Evaluate $5b + 2c - 3$ for $b = \frac{1}{2}$ and $c = 3$.

CULTURAL LINK

Some of the earliest known symbols for addition and subtraction were used by the ancient Egyptians. The symbol [symbol] was used to show addition and the symbol [symbol] was used to show subtraction. To subtract 4 they might have written IIII [symbol]. How do you think they might have shown adding 4?

INDEPENDENT PRACTICE

Tell what operation you would perform first.

1. $18 + 6 \div 2$ **2.** $4 \times 12 - 3 + 8$ **3.** $(2 + 5) \times 3$ **4.** $8 - 2 + 3$

Evaluate each expression.

5. $\frac{1}{3} \times 12 + 8 \div 4$ **6.** $2^3 - 4 \times 2$ **7.** $({}^-5)(4) \div 5$ **8.** $9 + \frac{6}{3}$

9. $4 \times (9 \div 3)$ **10.** $10.5 + 4.5 - 2$ **11.** $3 + (4 \times 6)$ **12.** $12 \div 3 \times 5 - 2$

Evaluate the expression $5 - \frac{n}{3}$ for each value of n.

13. $n = 6$ **14.** $n = 1.5$ **15.** $n = 3$ **16.** $n = {}^-3$

Evaluate the expression ${}^-3n + 1$ for each value of n.

17. $n = 4$ **18.** $n = {}^-2$ **19.** $n = \frac{1}{2}$ **20.** $n = \frac{{}^-1}{2}$

Evaluate each expression for $y = 30$.

21. $6y + 2y + 8$

22. $\frac{1}{2}y + 3y - 0.5$

23. $^-8y + 81$

24. $5 + 8y$

25. $y^2 + 100$

26. $\frac{y}{1.5} - y$

Evaluate the expression for the given values of the variables.

27. $4a + 3b + 88$ for $a = 12$ and $b = {}^-9$

28. $17f - g$ for $f = 0.1$ and $g = 0.25$

29. $\frac{x}{4} + z^2$ for $x = 12$ and $z = {}^-10$

Problem-Solving Applications

30. ALGEBRA Sarah bought b bags of ice that cost \$0.99 each. Write an expression that represents the total cost of the bags of ice. Then find the total cost if $b = 4$.

31. MONEY Use the expression $n(0.05) + d(0.10) + q(0.25)$ where n = nickels, d = dimes, and q = quarters to find the total amount, in dollars, if $n = 10$, $d = 12$, and $q = 15$.

32. FORMULA Airline personnel use the formula $D = \frac{LWH}{194}$ to determine the cost of shipping a live animal. In the formula, D is the dimensional weight of the kennel, in pounds, and L, W, and H are the dimensions of the kennel in inches. What is the dimensional weight of a kennel 36 in. × 26 in. × 20 in.? Round your answer to the nearest hundredth.

33. WRITE ABOUT IT What is the difference between the value of the expression $3 + 2$ and the value of the expression $x + 2$?

Mixed Review and Test Prep

Find the missing number. Name the property used.

34. $26 + 37 = p + 26$

35. $p \times 6 = (4 \times 6) + (3 \times 6)$

36. $3 + (4 + p) = (3 + 4) + 6$

Find each sum.

37. $5 + {}^-7$

38. $^-12 + 8$

39. $^-20 + {}^-6$

40. $^-11 + 5$

41. $^-25 + {}^-8$

42. $53 + {}^-8$

43. $^-101 + 60$

44. $^-60 + 101$

45. MEASUREMENT Danny is planning to make some cookies for a few friends. The original recipe calls for $3\frac{3}{4}$ cups of flour. How much flour should Danny use if he makes half of the recipe?

A $7\frac{1}{2}$ c **B** $3\frac{3}{8}$ c **C** $2\frac{1}{4}$ c **D** $1\frac{7}{8}$ c

46. ESTIMATION Philip made three trips to move a display of cans. He moved 383 cans, 521 cans, and 415 cans. What is a reasonable estimate of the total number of cans he moved?

F 2,500 **G** 2,000
H 1,300 **J** 800

MORE PRACTICE Lesson 6.2, page H51

LAB ACTIVITY

What You'll Explore
How to model combining like terms

What You'll Need
Algebra tiles, or paper rectangles and squares

VOCABULARY
term
like terms

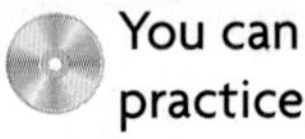

Technology Link
You can practice combining expressions by using E-Lab, Activity 6. Available on CD-ROM and on the Internet at **www.hbschool.com/elab**

Models and Like Terms

The parts of an algebraic expression that are separated by an addition or subtraction sign are called **terms**. The terms in the algebraic expression $2x + 6$ are $2x$ and 6. Sometimes expressions have terms that are alike. When two or more terms have the same variable raised to the same power, they are called **like terms**.

Explore

Use rectangles to represent variables, and use squares to represent whole numbers.

- Make the model below. Use the variable x to write the expression the model represents. Then change the model by combining the rectangles (like terms). What expression can you write now?

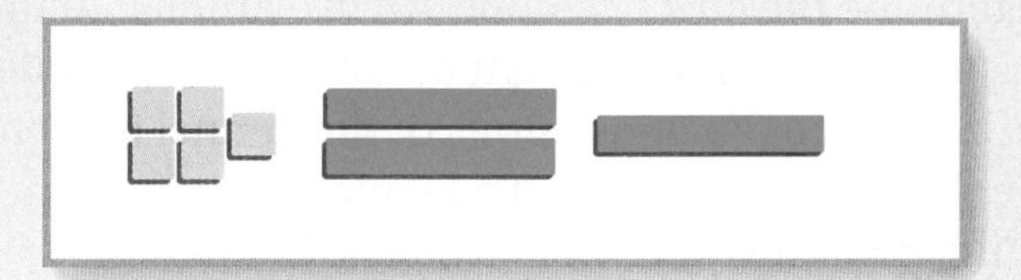

- Use rectangles and squares to model this expression:

  $3x + 3 + 2x$

Combine like terms to make one group that represents the x's. What expression can you write now?

Think and Discuss

- Replace the variable in $5 + 2x + x$ with 2. What is the value of the expression? Then replace the variable in $5 + 3x$ with 2. What is the value of the expression?
- Are the two expressions you wrote for the first model equivalent? Explain.

Try This

- Model these expressions. Then change the model by combining like terms. Write the new expressions.

  $3x + x$ $\quad$ $4a + a + 2$ $\quad$ $3b + 2 + 2b$

Combining Like Terms

LESSON 6.3

What You'll Learn
How to combine like terms in expressions

Why Learn This?
To simplify expressions so they are easier to evaluate

VOCABULARY
simplest form

When you combine like terms in an expression, you are writing the expression in **simplest form**. The original expression and the simplified expression are equivalent.

To combine like terms, add or subtract the numerical parts of the terms.

EXAMPLE 1 Combine like terms: $7x + 2x + 5$.

$7x + 2x + 5$ — *Identify the like terms.*

$7x + 2x + 5 = 9x + 5$ — *Perform the operation on the numerical parts of the like terms.*

So, $7x + 2x + 5$ is equivalent to $9x + 5$.

- Combine like terms: $4x - x + 5$.

Sometimes the like terms in an expression are not grouped together. In such an expression, you can use what you know about properties to combine like terms.

EXAMPLE 2 Combine like terms: $3p - 2p + 6 - 2 + p$.

$3p - 2p + 6 - 2 + p$ — *Use the Commutative and Associative Properties to group like terms.*

$3p - 2p + p + 6 - 2$ ← Commutative Property

$(3p - 2p + p) + (6 - 2)$ ← Associative Property

$(3p - 2p + p) + (6 - 2)$ — *Perform the operations on the like terms. Remember that $p = 1p$. So, $3p - 2p + 1p = 2p$.*

$2p \quad + \quad 4$

So, $3p - 2p + 6 - 2 + p$ equals $2p + 4$.

Talk About It

- Suppose you had the expression $m + 2y + x + 3y$. What are the terms? Which terms are like terms?
- Explain why the expression $11.3m - 6$ is not equal to $5.3m$.
- Combine like terms: $7n^2 + 18 - 2 + n^2$.

LANGUAGE LINK

Poems are written using patterns of sounds, syllables, and lines. One way to observe the pattern of a poem is to write an algebraic expression using the number of syllables in each line of a poem. Write an algebraic expression that includes the number of syllables in each line of the poem below. Let s equal one syllable.

A cold cold night
Can make you quiver.
I'll need a blanket
So I won't shiver.

In some expressions, you have to use the Distributive Property before you can combine like terms.

EXAMPLE 3 Combine like terms: $3(s - 4) + 6s$.

$3(s - 4) + 6s$	*Use the Distributive Property.*
$(3 \cdot s) - (3 \cdot 4) + 6s$	*Multiply.*
$3s - 12 + 6s$	*Group like terms.*
$3s + 6s - 12$	*Add the like terms.*
$9s - 12$	

- Use the Distributive Property and then combine like terms: $5(t + 2) + t$.

Sometimes an expression has more than one variable. You can use the Commutative and Associative Properties to group the like terms.

EXAMPLE 4 Combine like terms: $2x + 3y + 7x + 2y$.

$2x + 3y + 7x + 2y$

$2x + 7x + 3y + 2y$ ← Commutative Property

$(2x + 7x) + (3y + 2y)$ ← Associative Property

$9x + 5y$

REMEMBER:

Properties can help you make a problem simpler.

Commutative Property

$3 + 9 + 7 = 3 + 7 + 9$

$= 10 + 9$

Associative Property

$5 + 2 + 8$

$= 5 + (2 + 8)$

$= 5 + 10$

Distributive Property

$6 \cdot 52 = 6(50 + 2)$

$= 300 + 12$

See page H6.

GUIDED PRACTICE

Identify the like terms in each list of terms.

1. $7x, 2x^2, 3x, 5, 1$ **2.** $4m, 3n, 4, n$ **3.** $2l, w, 4h$

Combine like terms.

4. $8x + 2x + 7$ **5.** $19p - 11 + 6p$ **6.** $12y - 3y + 4$

7. $20a - 7 - 6a + a$ **8.** $15t + 6t - 9t$ **9.** $3.2n - 1.9n - 8$

INDEPENDENT PRACTICE

Use the Commutative and Associative Properties to combine like terms.

1. $20r + 30s + 3r + 2s$ **2.** $18y + 6z - 15y - 3z$ **3.** $5c - d - 8c - d$

4. $3.7f - 9.1g - 0.3f$ **5.** $17a - 12b + 9.5a + 20b$ **6.** $^{-}10g + 5.3g - 12g + h$

Use the Distributive Property to combine like terms.

7. $5(x + 4) - 2x$

8. $3a + 2(a - 3)$

9. $7 - 3t + 2(2t + 4)$

10. $5n + 3(n - 2) - 7$

11. $^-3(r + 4) + 4(r - 3)$

12. $8(0.5 + 2x) - 6x$

13. $\frac{1}{2}(6c + 10) - 2c$

14. $1.5y + 3(0.5y - 2.5)$

15. $^-2x - 8 + 2(x + 4)$

Combine like terms.

16. $5(7 + 4x) + x$

17. $2a + 2b - a$

18. $7c + 4d - 5d - 9c$

19. $5(0.8x + 1.1)$

20. $18(2q - 14) - q$

21. $^-5m - 6m + 19n - 20n$

22. $\frac{2}{3}(\frac{1}{3}a + 9) + 2$

23. $^-0.3r + 1.6s + 0.16r + 8s$

24. $\frac{1}{2}x + \frac{1}{3}y - 1\frac{1}{2}x + 2\frac{2}{3}y$

Problem-Solving Applications

25. **ALGEBRA** Cheryl baby-sat for 2 hours Wednesday, 3 hours Thursday, and 2.5 hours Friday. She makes n dollars per hour. Write an expression for the total amount she earned that week. Then evaluate the expression for $n = \$3.80$.

26. **GEOMETRY** The angles of a triangle measure $3t$, $8t$, and t. Write the sum of the three angles as an expression. Then give the measures of the three angles if $t = 15$.

27. Write a new problem like Problem 25 that can be solved by writing and evaluating an expression.

28. **WRITE ABOUT IT** Explain how you know which terms to combine when combining like terms.

Mixed Review and Test Prep

Look for a pattern. Use the pattern to write the next three numbers in each sequence.

29. $\frac{1}{3}, \frac{2}{3}, 1, 1\frac{1}{3}, \ldots$

30. $\frac{1}{6}, \frac{1}{3}, \frac{1}{2}, \frac{2}{3}, \ldots$

31. $\frac{1}{2}, 1, 1\frac{1}{2}, 2, \ldots$

Find the sum or difference.

32. $21 + {}^-13$

33. $19 - {}^-3$

34. $12 + {}^-9$

35. $^-12 - 6$

36. $^-15 + {}^-3$

37. $^-14 - {}^-7$

38. **LOGICAL THINKING** Bill enters a fun house and walks 4.5 meters along a ground-level passage. The passage rises 3 meters and then is horizontal for 5.5 meters. Suddenly, the passage drops 1 meter and opens into a room. How far above ground is the room?

A 1 m **B** 2 m
C 3 m **D** 4 m

39. **NUMBER SENSE** Usually only 2% of the apples in a market are bruised. About how many apples are bruised if the market has 200 apples?

F 2 **G** 4
H 20 **J** 40

MORE PRACTICE Lesson 6.3, page H51

LESSON 6.4

Sequences and Expressions

What You'll Learn
How to use the common difference to extend a sequence

Why Learn This?
To recognize patterns or trends

VOCABULARY

sequence
term
arithmetic sequence
common difference

A **sequence** is an ordered set of numbers. A **term** is an element, or a number, in the sequence.

An **arithmetic sequence** is a sequence in which the difference of any term and the one after it is always the same. You can describe the patterns of an arithmetic sequence by finding the common difference between terms. The **common difference** is the difference between any two successive terms.

EXAMPLE 1 Find the common difference in this sequence:

4, 8, 12, 16, 20, . . .

Find the differences between terms.

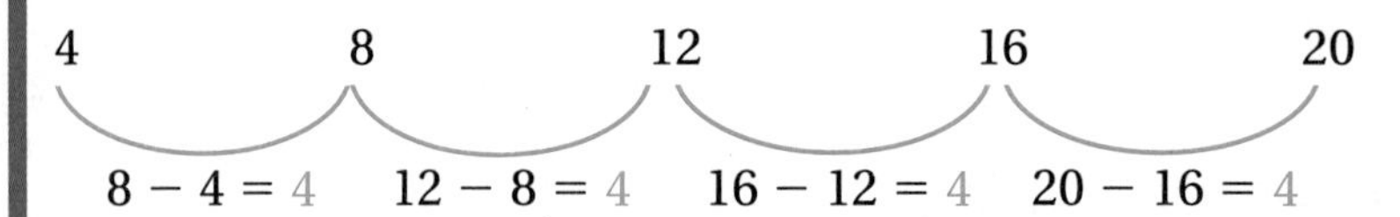

All of the differences are 4. So, the common difference is 4.

- Find the common difference in this sequence:

  3, 6, 9, 12, 15, . . .

MUSIC LINK

One of the most famous sequences is the Fibonacci sequence, 1, 1, 2, 3, 5, 8, 13, ... It can be found in many natural and manufactured objects. Where do you find this sequence on a piano keyboard?

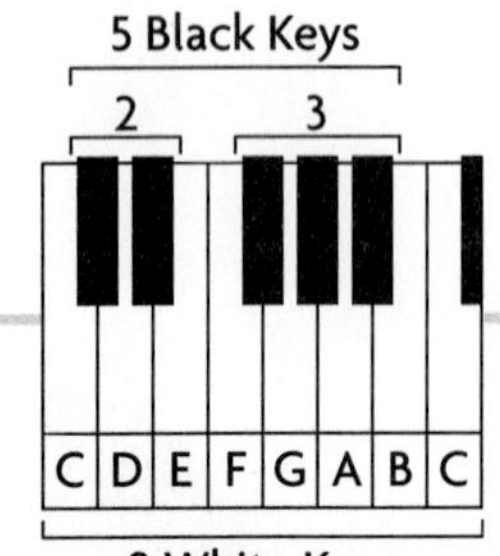

Sometimes the common difference is a negative number.

EXAMPLE 2 Find the common difference in this sequence:

21, 14, 7, 0, $^{-}7$, . . .

Find the differences between terms.

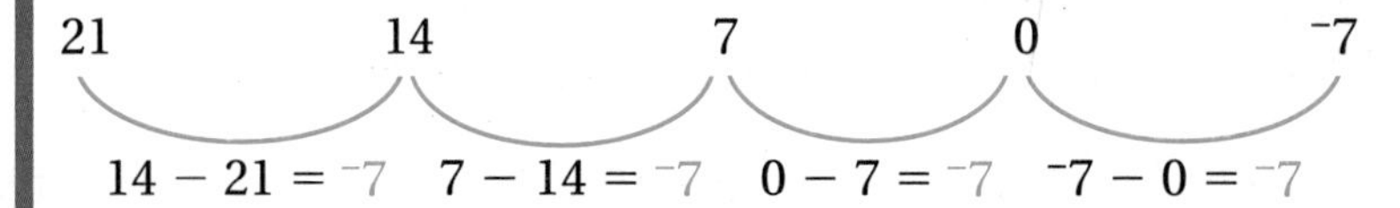

The common difference is $^{-}7$.

- Find the common difference in this sequence:

  11, 7, 3, $^{-}1$, $^{-}5$, . . .

CRITICAL THINKING Write an arithmetic sequence that starts with 100 and has a common difference of 50. Then write one that has a common difference of $^{-}20$.

You can use the common difference to extend a sequence.

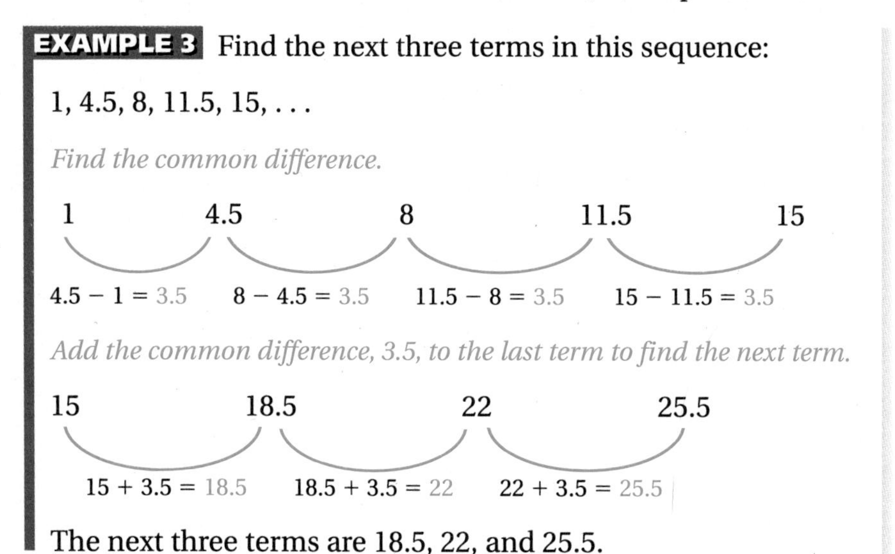

EXAMPLE 3 Find the next three terms in this sequence:

1, 4.5, 8, 11.5, 15, . . .

Find the common difference.

1   4.5   8   11.5   15

$4.5 - 1 = 3.5$ $8 - 4.5 = 3.5$ $11.5 - 8 = 3.5$ $15 - 11.5 = 3.5$

Add the common difference, 3.5, to the last term to find the next term.

15   18.5   22   25.5

$15 + 3.5 = 18.5$ $18.5 + 3.5 = 22$ $22 + 3.5 = 25.5$

The next three terms are 18.5, 22, and 25.5.

HISTORY LINK

There is no known pattern for the sequence of prime numbers. A priest and mathematician who lived in the 17th century, Marin Mersenne, used the expression $2^n - 1$ to produce prime numbers, but it does not always work. Does it work if $n = 2$? if $n = 3$? if $n = 4$?

GUIDED PRACTICE

Find the common difference.

1. 2, 4, 6, 8, 10, . . .   **2.** 9, 3, $^-3$, $^-9$, . . .   **3.** 2, 2.5, 3, 3.5, . . .

Find the common difference. Then find the next three terms in each sequence.

4. 0, 5, 10, 15, . . .   **5.** 1, 5, 9, 13, . . .   **6.** 30, 20, 10, 0, . . .

Writing an Expression

What if you wanted to find the fiftieth term in a sequence? It would take a long time to find the fiftieth term by repeatedly adding the common difference. However, you can find any term by writing an expression that describes the sequence.

Tammy made a table to show this sequence: 1, 4, 7, 10, ...

1st Term	2nd Term	3rd Term	4th Term	5th Term
1	4	7	10	13
	1 + 3(1)	1 + 3(2)	1 + 3(3)	1 + 3(4)

- Look at the table. What do the expressions for all of the terms have in common?
- What do you think the expression would be for the sixth term? the seventh term? the *n*th term?

You can find any term, n, of an arithmetic sequence by using this expression:

first term + common difference × $(n - 1)$

EXAMPLE 4 Use an expression to find the tenth term of this sequence:

26, 38, 50, 62, ...

Find the common difference.

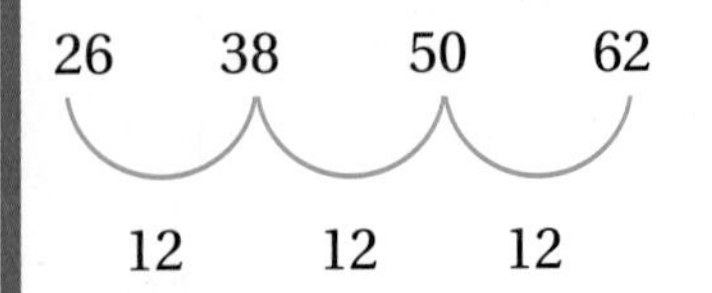

Write an expression. The first term is 26, and the common difference is 12.

$26 + 12 \times (n - 1)$

Replace n with 10, since you want to find the tenth term.

$26 + 12 \times (n - 1) =$

$26 + 12 \times (10 - 1)$

Evaluate the expression.

$26 + 12 \times (10 - 1)$

$26 + 12 \times 9$

$26 + 108$

134 ← tenth term

- In the sequence 10, 8, 6, 4, . . . the common difference is $^-2$. The expression you could use to find any term is $10 + {}^-2 \times (n - 1)$. Use the expression to find the twentieth term.

INDEPENDENT PRACTICE

Tell whether the sequence is an arithmetic sequence. Explain your reasoning.

1. 2, 4, 8, 16, 32, . . .

2. 58, 69, 80, 91, 102, . . .

Find the common difference for each arithmetic sequence.

3. 27, 32, 37, 42, 47, . . .

4. 19, 23, 27, 31, 35, . . .

5. 20, 18, 16, 14, 12, . . .

6. 8, 17, 26, 35, 44, . . .

Write the next three terms in each sequence.

7. 35, 70, 105, 140, . . .

8. 15, 12, 9, 6, . . .

9. $^-11, {}^-8, {}^-5, {}^-2$, . . .

10. 1.44, 1.74, 2.04, 2.34, . . .

11. Use the expression $9 + 4 \times (n - 1)$ to find the thirteenth term in this sequence.

$$9, 13, 17, 21, \ldots$$

Write an expression to find any term in the sequence. Then use the expression to find the twelfth term.

12. 3, 8, 13, 18, . . .

13. 12, 15, 18, 21, . . .

14. 10, 7, 4, 1, $^{-}2$, . . .

15. 0.5, 1.5, 2.5, 3.5, . . .

Use the given expression to write the first three terms of a sequence.

16. $0 + 3 \times (n - 1)$

17. $4 + {}^{-}2 \times (n - 1)$

18. $10 + 8 \times (n - 1)$

Problem-Solving Applications

19. **PATTERNS** Leslie is going to run in a 4-mile fun race. She uses an increasing arithmetic pattern to decide how far to run each day of practice. The first day of practice she will run $\frac{1}{4}$ mile, the second day $\frac{1}{2}$ mile, the third day $\frac{3}{4}$ mile, the fourth day 1 mile, and so on. Write an expression to find any term in her running pattern. Then tell what day Leslie will run the same distance as she is going to run in the race.

20. **NUMBER SENSE** Generate several arithmetic sequences. Then exchange with a partner and write an expression for each pattern.

21. **CRITICAL THINKING** Is the sequence 1, 3, 9, 27, . . . an arithmetic sequence? Explain.

22. **WRITE ABOUT IT** Write a problem that can be solved by extending an arithmetic sequence. Show your solution.

Mixed Review and Test Prep

Replace the ■ with 1, 2, 3, 4, or 5 to make the number sentence true.

23. $■ + 1 = 6$

24. $3(■ - 2) = 3$

25. $^{-}1 + ■ = 0$

Find the product or quotient.

26. $^{-}6 \times 4.5$

27. $^{-}0.24 \div {}^{-}0.06$

28. $16.2 \times {}^{-}2$

29. **PATTERNS** A recipe uses 2 eggs to make 24 cookies. At this rate, how many eggs are needed for 96 cookies?

A 6 **B** 8
C 10 **D** 12

30. **GEOMETRY** A certain pyramid has 9 faces, including its base. What is the shape of the pyramid's base?

F square **G** pentagon
H octagon **J** decagon

MORE PRACTICE Lesson 6.4, page H52

CHAPTER 6 Review/Test

Write an algebraic expression for each word expression. (pages 124–125)

1. a number, b, increased by 10

2. a number, y, divided by 8

3. two times the difference of 15 and m

4. the product of 7 and s, decreased by 2

5. **VOCABULARY** A letter or symbol that represents one or more numbers is a(n) __?__. (page 124)

6. **VOCABULARY** A mathematical phrase that has numbers, operation symbols, and variables is called a(n) __?__. (page 124)

Write a word expression for each algebraic expression. (pages 124–125)

7. $\frac{1}{2} \times n$

8. $t + 7$

9. $d - 18$

10. $3(m - 4)$

Evaluate each expression. (pages 126–129)

11. $3 + 2 \times 6$

12. $(^-1)(^-4)(3)$

13. $(9 + 3) \times 5 - (12 \div 3)$

14. $4x - 7x + 9$, for $x = 7$

15. $1.2s \div 2 + s$, for $s = 3$

16. The cost, d, of a dress was \$5.50 more than the amount Kappa had. Write an expression for how much money Kappa had.

17. Posters are on sale for $\frac{1}{4}$ of the regular price. If the regular price is p, what expression represents the sale price?

Combine like terms. (pages 131–133)

18. $5y + 3 - 2y + y$

19. $^-2x - 5 + 6x$

20. $c + 3c + 8 - c + 4$

21. $w - 2 + 2w + x - x$

22. **VOCABULARY** Two or more terms with the same variable raised to the same power are called __?__. (page 130)

Find the common difference. (pages 134–137)

23. 1, 4, 7, 10, 13, . . .

24. 9, 2, $^-5$, $^-12$, . . .

25. 12, 25, 38, 51, . . .

26. **VOCABULARY** An ordered set of numbers is called a(n) __?__. (page 134)

Write an expression to find any term. Use the expression to find the seventh term. (pages 134–137)

27. 5, 7, 9, 11, . . .

28. 8, 13, 18, 23, . . .

29. 8, 0, $^-8$, $^-16$, . . .

30. 0, 3, 6, 9, . . .

Test Prep

CUMULATIVE
CHAPTERS 1–6

1. Margo bought 8 pounds of bananas for \$0.29 per pound. How much did she pay for the bananas?

A \$2.32
B \$2.24
C \$1.56
D \$1.42
E Not Here

2. Which is a correct algebraic expression for the phrase 8 times a number, *b*?

F $\frac{b-8}{4}$
G $b + 8$
H $8b$
J $b \div 8$

3. $9\frac{4}{5} - 2\frac{3}{8} =$

A $12\frac{7}{40}$ **B** $11\frac{7}{40}$
C $7\frac{17}{40}$ **D** $7\frac{7}{40}$

4. In a survey of 100 people, 40% responded *yes* and 25% responded *no.* Which of the following is not a reasonable conclusion?

F 35% of the people did not respond with *yes* or *no.*
G More people responded *yes* than responded *no.*
H More people responded *no* than responded *yes.*
J The most popular response was *yes.*

5. Evaluate $1.4t \div 7 + t$, for $t = 4$.

A 3.2
B 4.2
C 4.8
D 7.2
E Not Here

6. $8\frac{1}{8} + 5\frac{3}{10} =$

F $13\frac{17}{40}$
G $13\frac{3}{40}$
H $14\frac{7}{10}$
J $13\frac{4}{18}$

7. Lawrence bought a CD for \$15.95, including tax. He paid the clerk with a \$50-bill. Which is a good estimate of the amount of change he should receive from the clerk?

A a little more than \$40
B a little more than \$35
C a little less than \$35
D a little less than \$30
E a little more than \$25

8. Paula mowed a square lawn. She estimated that she mowed 225 square feet. What is the length of the side of the lawn?

F 12 ft
G 13 ft
H 14 ft
J 15 ft

9. What is the common difference of the sequence 11, 8, 5, 2, $^{-}1$, . . . ?

A 4
B $\frac{1}{2}$
C 3
D $^{-}3$

CHAPTER

7

SOLVING ONE-STEP EQUATIONS

LOOK AHEAD

In this chapter you will solve problems that involve

- writing equations for word problems
- solving one-step equations
- using the strategy *work backward*
- solving proportions

SOCIAL STUDIES LINK

Many modern board games have been played for thousands of years. The game *Go* can be traced back to 546 B.C. and chess can be traced back to A.D. 600. Currently, the world's largest game board is for the game *Galaxion*. It has the dimensions 33 in. × 33 in. It was created in Hong Kong by Cerebe Design International.

- What two possible shapes could the game board for *Galaxion* be?
- What is the length of each side of the game board in feet?

Problem-Solving Project

World Games

Suppose you can help your school spend $400 on games from around the world. Make a list of games you think your class would enjoy. Include at least one game from a country your class will study this year. Decide how many of each game to buy. Write and solve an equation for each purchase.

Games from Around the World

Title	Cost
Board Games from Around The World	$16.95
Board & Table Games from Many Civilizations	$9.95
World Globe Jigsaw Puzzle	$25.95
Mancala (an ancient Egyptian game)	$14.95
Pente (an ancient Oriental game)	$29.95
Games of Africa	$17.95
Where in the World is Carmen Sandiego?	$23.95
Take Off (world geography game)	$29.95
Yote (an African game)	$11.95

PROJECT CHECKLIST

- ✓ Did you make a list of games your class would enjoy?
- ✓ Did you decide how many of each game to buy?
- ✓ Did you write and solve equations to show your spending?
- ✓ Did you spend no more than $400?

LESSON 7.1

Connecting Equations and Words

What You'll Learn
How to write equations for problems

Why Learn This?
To write an equation to represent a problem situation such as finding the amount for 3 movie tickets

VOCABULARY
equation

An **equation** is a sentence that shows two expressions are equivalent. The expressions can be numerical or algebraic.

$10 = 3 + 7$ $\quad\quad$ $x = 3 + 7$

Sometimes you have to translate words into mathematical expressions or equations to solve a problem. The table below shows some problems and their equations.

Problem	Equation
Shadom has 32 baseball cards. This is 7 more than his friend Bill has. How many cards does Bill have?	$32 = b + 7$
Kim paid 2 times as much as her friend for a new game. If Kim paid $42, how much did her friend pay for the game?	$2x = 42$

Sometimes words or phrases in a problem help you determine the operations to write in your equation.

TEEN TIMES

The National Baseball Hall of Fame, in Cooperstown, New York, has 6,000 baseball treasures. The museum covers an area of 60,000 square feet.

Talk About It

- What words or phrases in the problems above describe the operations used in the equations?
- Suppose the first problem said that Shadom has 7 fewer cards than Bill. What equation could you write?

EXAMPLE 1 James purchased a box of detergent with a coupon. He paid $5.45, which was $0.45 less than what he would have paid without the coupon. How much would James have paid without the coupon? Write an equation for the problem.

Let p equal the amount James would have paid.

price − amount of coupon = amount he paid

$$\begin{array}{ccccc} \downarrow & & \downarrow & & \downarrow \\ p & - & 0.45 & = & 5.45 \end{array}$$

So, an equation for the problem is $p - 0.45 = 5.45$.

- What would the equation be if the amount of the coupon was $0.75?

GUIDED PRACTICE

Choose the equation that best represents the problem.

$m + 6 = 18$ $6m = 18$ $m - 6 = 18$ $18m = 6$

1. Sam spent $6 for a book. He has $18 left. How much did he have before he bought the book?
2. Sam spent a total of $18. If he spent $6 for a book, how much did his other purchases cost?
3. Sam spent $18 on books. If each book costs $6, how many books did he buy?
4. Sam bought 18 pens for $6. What was the cost of each pen?

INDEPENDENT PRACTICE

First, choose a variable and tell what it represents. Then, write an equation for each word sentence.

1. Six hours more than the number of hours worked is 45 hours.
2. Three times the cost of a concert ticket is $24.
3. The total number of cars decreased by 39 cars sold today equals 29 cars.
4. The cost of a bat increased by $24.45 for a glove equals $37.95.
5. The quotient of $570.00 and the number of payments is $47.50.
6. Thirty-five degrees less than the average daily temperature in June equals 30°F.

Write a word problem for each equation.

7. $x + 7 = 12$
8. $5x = 34$
9. $x - 4 = 16$
10. $\frac{x}{4} = 28$

Problem-Solving Applications

For Problems 11–15, write the equation you would use to solve the problem. Do not solve.

11. **CONSUMER MATH** Anna sold her surfboard for $13 more than she paid for it. She sold her surfboard for $62. How much did she pay for the surfboard?
12. **GEOGRAPHY** Derek paid $24 for a computer geography game. This was $8 less than the regular price of the game. What was the regular price of the game?
13. **ENTERTAINMENT** Chad and three of his friends went out to dinner. The total cost of the dinner was divided equally among all of them. Each person paid $5.25. What was the total cost of the dinner?
14. Mrs. Parker traveled 2,175 miles on business trips this year. She traveled twice as many miles last year. How many miles did she travel last year?
15. Marcus sold 63 fewer tickets than Christi sold. Marcus sold 312 tickets. How many tickets did Christi sell?
16. **WRITE ABOUT IT** Write a list of key words and the symbols you use with them when writing equations to solve problems.

MORE PRACTICE Lesson 7.1, page H52

LAB ACTIVITY

Modeling Equations

What You'll Explore
How to model the solutions to equations

What You'll Need
algebra tiles, or paper rectangles and squares

VOCABULARY
solve
solution

Technology Link

You can practice solving equations by using E-Lab, Activity 7. Available on CD-ROM and on the Internet at **www.hbschool.com/elab**

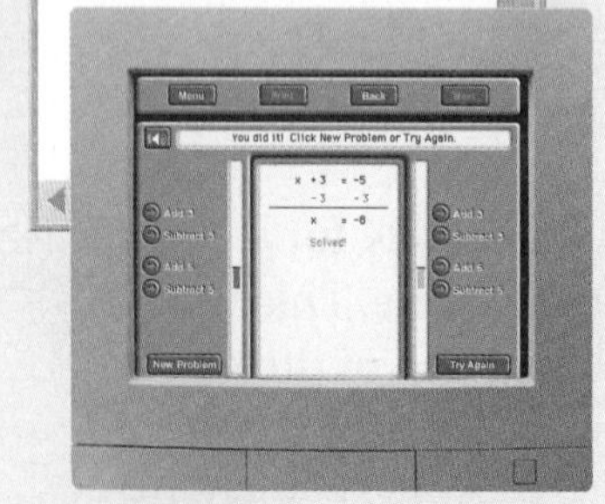

After you have written an algebraic equation for a problem, you need to find the correct value of the variable, or **solve** the equation. The value that makes the two sides of the equation equal is the **solution** of that equation.

$x + 3 = 10$ $\mathbf{7} + 3 = 10$ ← 7 is the solution.

$12 = x + 9$ $12 = \mathbf{3} + 9$ ← 3 is the solution.

Explore

- You can use a model to solve an addition equation. Use a rectangle to represent a variable, such as x, and use a square to represent 1. Copy this model and find the solution of $x + 2 = 3$. Remember that the two sides of the equation must always be equal.

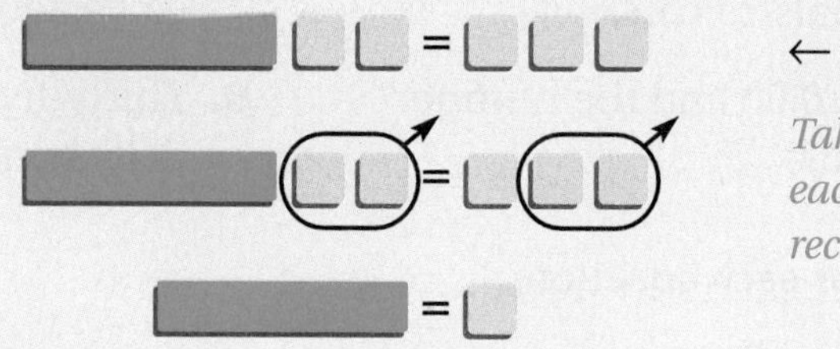

← $x + 2 = 3$

Take away 2 squares from each side so that the rectangle is by itself.

Think and Discuss

- What is the solution of $x + 2 = 3$?
- Why did you have to take the same number of squares from each side of the equation?
- What operation does taking the squares away represent?
- What operation is used in the equation? What operation did you use to solve the equation?
- What operation would you use to solve the equation $x - 5 = 12$?

Try This

- Solve each equation by using a model.

$x + 5 = 11$ $8 = x + 1$ $x + 6 = 9$ $x + 4 = 6$

Solving Addition and Subtraction Equations

LESSON 7.2

What You'll Learn
How to solve addition and subtraction equations

Why Learn This?
To solve problems with increased or decreased values such as the amount of money saved or owed

Addition and subtraction are inverse operations. You can solve an addition or subtraction equation by using the inverse operation so that the variable is by itself on one side of the equation. You use subtraction to undo addition and addition to undo subtraction.

The two sides of an equation must always be equal. When you add or subtract a number on one side of an equation, you must add or subtract the same number on the other side.

EXAMPLE 1 Katy borrowed $12 from Will. Now he has only $32. How much money did Will have before Katy borrowed money from him?

Choose a variable.

Let w = the amount Will had. Then $w - 12$ = the amount he has now.

Write an equation.

$w - 12 = 32$

To solve a subtraction equation, add the same number to both sides of the equation.

Solve the equation. Add 12 to each side of the equation so that w is by itself.

$$w - 12 = 32$$
$$w - 12 + 12 = 32 + 12$$
$$w = 44$$

Check the solution. Replace w with 44.

$$w - 12 = 32$$
$$44 - 12 = 32$$
$$32 = 32 \checkmark$$

So, Will had $44.

- Solve the equation. $x - 8.4 = 15.5$

HISTORY LINK

Women who have been shown on U.S. bills and coins include Pocahontas, Susan B. Anthony, and Lucy Pickens. Pocahontas appeared on the back of the 1875 $20 bill. Susan B. Anthony appeared on $1 coins from 1979 to 1981. Lucy Pickens, wife of the governor of South Carolina, was on the $100 bill of the Confederate States of America (1861–1865). Write and solve a problem involving $100 bills.

Talk About It CRITICAL THINKING

- Tell how you choose a variable when solving a problem.
- In Example 1, why was a subtraction equation used to solve the problem?
- Why do you use addition to solve a subtraction equation?
- Why is it important to check a solution?

Use subtraction when solving an addition equation.

EXAMPLE 2 Cosmo jogged $1\frac{1}{2}$ more miles on Wednesday than Tuesday. He jogged $3\frac{1}{4}$ miles on Wednesday. How many miles did he jog on Tuesday?

Let t = miles on Tuesday. Then $t + 1\frac{1}{2}$ = miles on Wednesday. *Choose a variable.*

$$t + 1\frac{1}{2} = 3\frac{1}{4}$$ *Write an equation.*

$$t + 1\frac{1}{2} - 1\frac{1}{2} = 3\frac{1}{4} - 1\frac{1}{2}$$ *Solve the equation.*

$$t = 1\frac{3}{4}$$ *Subtract $1\frac{1}{2}$ from each side.*

$$t + 1\frac{1}{2} = 3\frac{1}{4}$$ *Check the solution.*

$$1\frac{3}{4} + 1\frac{1}{2} = 3\frac{1}{4}$$ *Replace t with $1\frac{3}{4}$.*

$$3\frac{1}{4} = 3\frac{1}{4} \checkmark$$

- Solve and check. $x + 7.7 = 20.2$

CULTURAL LINK

In the ninth century, an Arab mathematician, al-Khwârizmî, wrote *Kitâb al-jabr wa al-muqâbalah* (*The Science of Reduction and Cancellation*). Our word *algebra* comes from the title of this work. Which word do you think it is?

EXAMPLE 3 Solve and check. $c + 12 = {}^-7$

$$c + 12 = {}^-7$$ *Subtract 12 from each side of the equation.*

$$c + 12 - 12 = {}^-7 - 12$$

$$c = {}^-19 \leftarrow \text{solution}$$

$$c + 12 = {}^-7$$ *Check the solution. Replace c with ⁻19.*

$${}^-19 + 12 = {}^-7$$

$${}^-7 = {}^-7 \checkmark$$

- Solve and check. ${}^-1 = x - 9$

GUIDED PRACTICE

Tell whether the given value is the solution to the equation. Answer *yes* or *no*.

1. $t - 7 = 35, t = 28$ **2.** $p + 3 = 21, p = 18$ **3.** $m - 3 = 26, m = 29$

4. $n + 4 = 6, n = 2$ **5.** $b - 4 = 92, b = 108$ **6.** $19 = h + 33, h = {}^-14$

Tell whether you would add or subtract to solve.

7. $x + 3.5 = 72.5$ **8.** $z - 1\frac{3}{4} = 2\frac{1}{2}$ **9.** $y - 0.6 = 3$ **10.** $2.45 + c = 24.5$

Calculator Activities, page H33

INDEPENDENT PRACTICE

Solve and check.

1. $x - 32 = 26$ **2.** $k + 9 = 13$ **3.** $25 = n + 3$ **4.** $t - 4 = 15$

5. $c - 18 = 6$ **6.** $75 = n - 128$ **7.** $0.42 = r + 0.23$ **8.** $n + 1.2 = 5.4$

9. $3.2 = x - 1.8$ **10.** $t - 20 = 0$ **11.** $n - 4 = {}^{-}2$ **12.** $b + 5 = 1$

13. $r + \frac{1}{6} = \frac{2}{3}$ **14.** $22\frac{1}{2} = p + 6\frac{1}{2}$ **15.** $2 + n = {}^{-}3$ **16.** $1.7 + k = {}^{-}7$

For each word sentence, choose a variable and write an equation. Then find the value of the variable.

17. 15 points more than the number of points scored is 82 points.

18. The difference of John's age and Phil's age, 16, is 8.

19. The number of pounds decreased by 35.6 pounds is 125.6 pounds.

20. The cost of a portable stereo increased by \$24.45 for a video game equals \$37.95.

Problem-Solving Applications

Solve.

21. **GEOMETRY** The measure of one angle is 46° more than the measure of another. Their sum is 180°. What are the measures of the angles?

22. **ALGEBRA** The cost of a double-scoop ice-cream cone is \$3.25. This is \$0.85 more than the cost of a single-scoop cone. How much is a single-scoop cone?

23. Bill sold his car for \$2,300 less than he paid for it. He sold his car for \$6,500. How much did he pay for the car?

24. **WRITE ABOUT IT** Explain how to solve the equation $x + 3 = 5$.

Mixed Review and Test Prep

Mentally find the value of r.

25. $6 \times r = 36$ **26.** $r \div 5 = 6$ **27.** $r \div 2 = 12$ **28.** $4 \times r = 48$

Evaluate the expression for $x = 12$.

29. $x - 4.3$ **30.** $x + 6\frac{2}{3}$ **31.** $3x + 4 \div 2$ **32.** ${}^{-}x \div 3 - {}^{-}2$

33. **AREA** Outdoor carpeting costs \$9.73 a square yard. What will it cost to carpet a patio that is 14 yards × 7 yards?

A \$408.66 **B** \$471.87 **C** \$953.54 **D** \$1,887.48

34. **CONSUMER MATH** Bill put linoleum on his kitchen floor for \$328.32. The area of the kitchen is 48 square yards. What was the cost per square yard for the linoleum?

F \$6.23 **G** \$6.84 **H** \$6.98 **J** \$12.45

Technology Link

In ***Mighty Math Astro Algebra*** you can practice solving addition and subtraction equations in *Burning Out*. Use Grow Slide Level Green L.

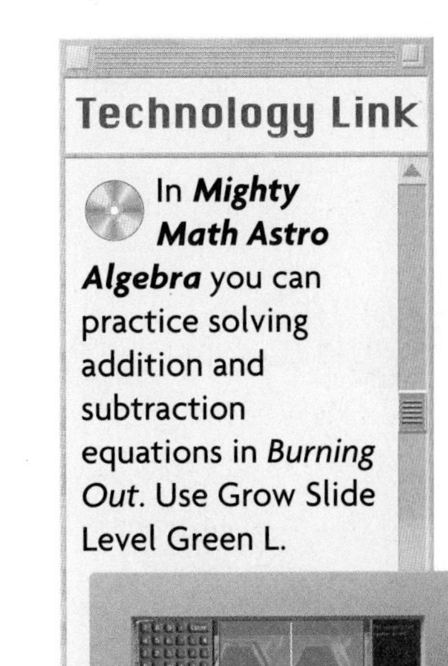

LESSON 7.3

Multiplication and Division Equations

What You'll Learn
How to solve multiplication and division equations

Why Learn This?
To solve problems such as finding the amount of equal payments

REMEMBER:

A division problem can be written as a fraction. **See page H17, Key Skill 29.**

$4 \div 5 = \frac{4}{5}$

$t \div 4 = \frac{t}{4}$

Division and multiplication are inverse operations. To solve equations, you can use multiplication to undo division and you can use division to undo multiplication.

EXAMPLE 1 Tasha has saved \$120. This is $\frac{1}{4}$ of what she needs to save to buy a new snowboard. What is the total amount Tasha needs to save?

Choose a variable.

Let t = the amount Tasha needs.
Then $\frac{t}{4}$ = the amount she has saved.

Write an equation.

$$\frac{t}{4} = 120$$

Solve the equation. Multiply each side of the equation by 4.

$$\frac{t}{4} = 120$$
$$4 \cdot \frac{t}{4} = 120 \cdot 4$$
$$t = 480$$

Check the solution. Replace t with 480.

$$\frac{t}{4} = 120$$
$$\frac{480}{4} = 120$$
$$120 = 120 \checkmark$$

So, Tasha needs to save a total of \$480.

- Solve and check. $\frac{a}{3} = 6$
- **CRITICAL THINKING** Explain how to get the variable alone on one side of a division equation.

EXAMPLE 2 Solve and check. $4.25h = 85$

$$4.25h = 85$$
$$\frac{4.25h}{4.25} = \frac{85}{4.25}$$
$$h = 20 \leftarrow \text{solution}$$

The equation shows multiplication. So, divide each side of the equation by 4.25.

$$4.25h = 85$$
$$4.25(20) = 85$$
$$85 = 85 \checkmark$$

Check the solution. Replace h with 20.

- Solve and check. $8a = 296$

GUIDED PRACTICE

Tell whether the given value is the solution of the equation. Write *yes* or *no*. If the value is not the solution, solve the equation.

1. $6x = 18$
$x = 3$

2. $9t = 72$
$t = 4$

3. $\frac{w}{16} = 8$
$w = 2$

4. $\frac{z}{7} = 5$
$z = 35$

INDEPENDENT PRACTICE

Solve and check.

1. $4t = 12$

2. $\frac{n}{7} = 20$

3. $9n = 27$

4. $8a = 288$

5. $6y = 54$

6. $9x = 81$

7. $\frac{t}{3} = 21$

8. $7 = \frac{s}{7}$

9. $41 = \frac{w}{2}$

10. $\frac{z}{3} = 7.3$

11. $1.8 = 0.6n$

12. $\frac{b}{^-0.3} = 30$

13. $\frac{x}{2.3} = 12$

14. $^-75 = {^-5}h$

15. $9h = 3.6$

16. $24 = \frac{h}{31}$

17. $81 = \frac{k}{3}$

18. $\frac{t}{5} = 13$

19. $7n = {^-56}$

20. $9.4 = 0.4a$

For each word sentence, choose a variable and write an equation. Then find the value of the variable.

21. The total cost of a dinner is shared equally by 6 people, with each person paying $7.80.

22. A monthly payment times 20 months equals a balance of $320.

23. A table's cost divided into 4 equal payments equals $36.00 for each payment.

24. A group of people rent a boat for $30.00 each, or $120.00 in all.

Problem-Solving Applications

The formula $d = rt$ relates distance (d), rate (r), and time (t). Use this formula to solve Problems 25–26.

25. **TIME** A 747 jumbo jet flew 1,100 miles at an average rate of 440 miles per hour. How long did the plane fly?

26. **TRAVEL** The fastest passenger train in France can travel 690 miles in 3 hours. What is its average rate in miles per hour?

27. **CONSUMER MATH** Dax ordered slices of pizza. He divided them equally among 8 people. Each person got $3\frac{1}{2}$ slices. How many slices of pizza did Dax order?

28. **WRITE ABOUT IT** Explain how to solve a multiplication or division equation.

MORE PRACTICE Lesson 7.3, page H53

LESSON 7.4

PROBLEM-SOLVING STRATEGY

Working Backward to Solve Problems

What You'll Learn
How to use the strategy *work backward* to solve one-step problems

Why Learn This?
To solve problems such as finding the amount you have spent shopping

PROBLEM SOLVING

- **Understand**
- **Plan**
- **Solve**
- **Look Back**

In the previous lessons, you saw how you can use the strategy *write an equation* to solve problems. In this lesson you will look at a similar strategy called *work backward.*

Tina buys an issue of *Seventeen* once a month at a newsstand. Kay told her she could save $18.45 a year by buying a subscription. Kay pays $16.95 a year for a subscription. How much does Tina pay in a year for *Seventeen* at the newsstand?

UNDERSTAND What are you asked to find?

What facts are given?

PLAN What strategy will you use?

You can use inverse operations and the strategy *work backward* to solve the problem.

SOLVE How will you solve the problem?

newsstand price for the year	−	amount of subscription	=	amount Tina could save
■	−	$16.95	=	$18.45

Work backward by using the inverse operation, addition.

$18.45	+	$16.95	=	■
$18.45	+	$16.95	=	$35.40

So, Tina pays $35.40 for 12 issues of *Seventeen* at a newsstand.

LOOK BACK Explain how you can check your answer.

What if . . . the subscription price is $19.99 and the amount Tina could save is $8.45. What would Tina pay in a year at a newsstand?

PRACTICE

Use the *work backward* strategy to solve each problem.

1. Ms. Iseminger has 9 shelves in her classroom to display books. She has added 2 shelves every school year for the past 3 years. How many shelves did Ms. Iseminger have originally?
2. Diane spent $3.45 more than Joanne on a recent field trip to the Space Center. Diane spent $8.20. How much did Joanne spend?
3. Karen turned in her science exam at 2:15 P.M. It took her $2\frac{1}{2}$ hours to complete it. When did Karen start her science exam?
4. Bill received his weekly paycheck from his part-time job. He deposited $\frac{1}{2}$ in a savings account. Bill then bought lunch for $4.36. He had $20.50 left. How much money did Bill get in his weekly paycheck?

MIXED APPLICATIONS

Solve.

CHOOSE a strategy and a tool.

- **Make/Use a Table**
- **Use a Formula**
- **Guess and Check**
- **Write an Equation**
- **Account for All Possibilities**
- **Work Backward**

Paper/Pencil

Calculator
Hands-On
Mental Math

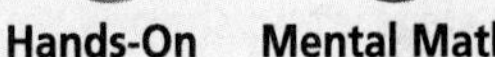

5. A mail truck delivers two boxes of mail to the post office. The total weight of the boxes is 24 pounds. One box is 6 pounds heavier than the other box. How much does each box weigh?
6. Jacob rides his bike to school every day. He travels $1\frac{1}{2}$ miles in 6 minutes. What is Jacob's average rate of speed?
7. A dance group has 316 members. There are 30 more women than men. How many members of the group are women?
8. Leon has as many dimes as quarters. The total value of these coins is $2.10. How many quarters does he have?
9. The table at the right gives postage rates for first-class mail. Use the table to determine the cost of mailing a first-class letter weighing 10 ounces.

First Class	
First ounce	$0.32
Each additional ounce	$0.23

10. Bob jogs along a rectangular path. He jogs east, then south, then west, then north. If he jogs 2 miles east and then 3 miles south, how far does he jog?
11. **WRITE ABOUT IT** Write a problem that could be solved by using the *work backward* strategy.

MORE PRACTICE Lesson 7.4, page H53

LESSON 7.5

Proportions

What You'll Learn
How to identify, write, and solve proportions

Why Learn This?
To compare values such as distance and time

VOCABULARY
proportion

A **proportion** is a special kind of equation that states that two ratios are equivalent. A proportion can be numerical or algebraic.

Here are some examples of proportions.

Write:		**Read:**
$\frac{3}{6} = \frac{1}{2}$	$3:6 = 1:2$	3 is to 6 as 1 is to 2.
$\frac{n}{10} = \frac{3}{5}$	$n:10 = 3:5$	n is to 10 as 3 is to 5.

- What is the difference between a numerical proportion and an algebraic proportion? Which of the proportions above is algebraic?

The solution of an algebraic proportion is the value that makes the two ratios equivalent. Algebraic proportions can often be solved by making a model.

CULTURAL LINK

Paper folding using geometric shapes to make objects such as hats, cups, birds, and other animals is a popular activity in many countries. **Origami** is the Japanese art of folding paper to form figures. Look in your library for a book on origami and choose a figure to make.

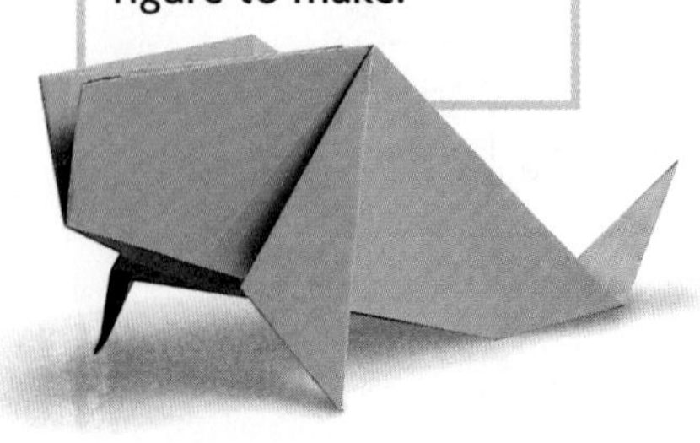

ACTIVITY

WHAT YOU'LL NEED: paper

Solve the proportion $\frac{3}{4} = \frac{n}{64}$ by finding the value of n.

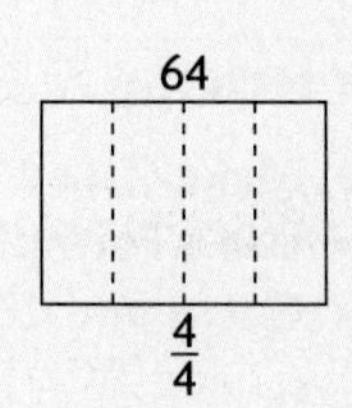

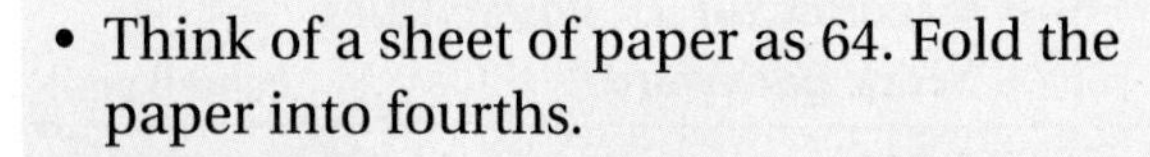

- Think of a sheet of paper as 64. Fold the paper into fourths.
- If 4 fourths represent 64, what does each fourth represent?
- What do 3 fourths represent?
- What is the value of n?

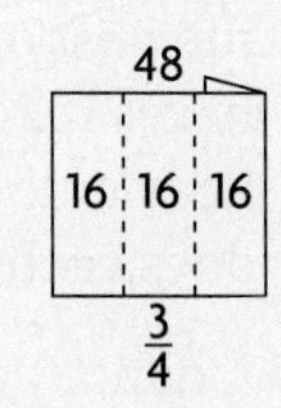

Since each fourth represents 16, 3 fourths represent 48.

- Use a model to solve this proportion.

$$\frac{2}{3} = \frac{m}{18}$$

CRITICAL THINKING How can you verify, or check, your solution by writing a fraction in simplest form?

You can also solve proportions without a model.

EXAMPLE 1 Solve the proportion. $\frac{3}{7} = \frac{w}{9.1}$

Write the cross products.	*Multiply.*	*Divide to solve the equation.*
$\frac{3}{7} = \frac{w}{9.1}$	$7w = 9.1 \cdot 3$	$\frac{7w}{7} = \frac{27.3}{7}$
$7w = 9.1 \cdot 3$	$7w = 27.3$	$w = 3.9$

EXAMPLE 2 Solve the proportion. $45:n = 135:10$

$\frac{45}{n} = \frac{135}{10}$

$135n = 45 \cdot 10$ — *Write the cross products.*

$\frac{135n}{135} = \frac{45 \cdot 10}{135}$ — *Divide.*

$n = \frac{\overset{1}{\cancel{45}} \cdot 10}{\underset{3}{\cancel{135}}}$ — *Simplify.*

$n = \frac{10}{3}$, or $3\frac{1}{3}$ — *Write the solution.*

REAL-LIFE LINK

The average life expectancy of a dog is 12 to 14 years. One dog year is said to equal 7 human years. If Ted 's dog is 3 years old in human years, what proportion can you write to find his dog's age in dog years?

ANOTHER METHOD You can use a calculator to solve proportions.

EXAMPLE 3 Solve the proportion. $\frac{2.3}{2} = \frac{e}{1.1}$

$\frac{2.3}{2} = \frac{e}{1.1}$ — *Write the cross products.*

$2e = 1.1 \cdot 2.3$ — *Using the calculator, multiply, and then divide to solve the equation.*

$\frac{2e}{2} = \frac{1.1 \cdot 2.3}{2}$ — 1.1 × 2.3  2 

$e = 1.265$ — 

1.265

GUIDED PRACTICE

Tell whether the ratio is equivalent to $\frac{3}{4}$. Write *yes* or *no*.

1. 15:20 **2.** 8:12 **3.** $\frac{12}{16}$ **4.** $\frac{30}{20}$

5. What proportion can you write using the ratios from Exercises 1–4?

Use a model to solve each proportion.

6. $\frac{1}{2} = \frac{x}{84}$ **7.** $\frac{2}{5} = \frac{a}{90}$ **8.** $\frac{3}{4} = \frac{w}{68}$ **9.** $\frac{1}{3} = \frac{c}{33}$

Using Proportions

Proportions can be used in solving problems. Let a variable represent an unknown value.

EXAMPLE 4 A marathon runner completes the 42.2 km of the race in 160 minutes. At the same rate, how far would you expect to run in 120 minutes?

Let d = the distance traveled in 120 minutes. *Write a proportion.*

Use ratios to compare distance and time.

$\frac{\text{distance}}{\text{time}} \longrightarrow \frac{42.2}{160} = \frac{d}{120}$ *Solve the proportion.*

$\frac{42.2}{160} = \frac{d}{120}$ *Write the cross products.*

$160d = 42.2 \cdot 120$ *Multiply.*

$160d = 5{,}064$

$\frac{160d}{160} = \frac{5{,}064}{160}$ *Divide.*

$d = 31.65$

So, in 120 minutes, you would expect to complete about 32 km.

TEEN TIMES

One of the most famous and largest marathons is the Boston Marathon, which has been an annual event since 1897. On its hundredth anniversary, more than 37,500 people participated. Since the race has so many runners, the last runner does not cross the starting line until about 40 minutes after the race has officially started.

Talk About It

- How can you check your solution?
- CRITICAL THINKING Is the solution of the proportion $\frac{2}{3} = \frac{n}{18}$ the same as the solution of the proportion $\frac{3}{2} = \frac{18}{n}$? Explain.

INDEPENDENT PRACTICE

Use a model to solve each proportion. Draw a diagram of your model and solution.

1. $\frac{3}{4} = \frac{n}{16}$ **2.** $\frac{2}{3} = \frac{n}{30}$ **3.** $\frac{7}{8} = \frac{n}{24}$

4. $\frac{2}{5} = \frac{n}{45}$ **5.** $\frac{5}{8} = \frac{n}{56}$ **6.** $\frac{5}{6} = \frac{n}{24}$

Write the cross products for each proportion.

7. $\frac{8}{5} = \frac{40}{x}$ **8.** $\frac{m}{12.5} = \frac{8}{100}$ **9.** $\frac{3}{t} = \frac{25}{50}$

10. $\frac{2.5}{10} = \frac{x}{4}$ **11.** $\frac{a}{0.75} = \frac{1.25}{5}$ **12.** $\frac{17}{200} = \frac{c}{800}$

Solve each proportion.

13. $4:5 = 8:n$

14. $b:8 = 3:2$

15. $9:p = 5:10$

16. $\frac{3}{2} = \frac{m}{5}$

17. $\frac{c}{4} = \frac{9}{4}$

18. $\frac{16}{e} = \frac{8}{3}$

19. $\frac{6}{5} = \frac{90}{x}$

20. $\frac{3}{5} = \frac{a}{6.5}$

21. $\frac{1.5}{z} = \frac{30}{5}$

22. $\frac{2.7}{8.1} = \frac{n}{15}$

23. $\frac{1.4}{1.5} = \frac{1.75}{t}$

24. $\frac{17}{k} = \frac{6.8}{2}$

25. $\frac{1.2}{1.5} = \frac{n}{2.5}$

26. $\frac{4.2}{2} = \frac{m}{6.25}$

27. $\frac{10.3}{8} = \frac{a}{4.4}$

Solve each proportion for d. Let $a = 6$, $b = 9$, and $c = 15$.

28. $\frac{a}{b} = \frac{c}{d}$

29. $\frac{2a}{3b} = \frac{d}{3c}$

30. $\frac{a + b}{b + c} = \frac{d}{bc}$

Problem-Solving Applications

31. **SPORTS** A student on the track team takes 67 sec to run the 400-m dash. At the same rate, how long would it take to run 300 m?

32. **SPORTS** A recent Olympic world record for the four-man 400-m relay was 37.40 sec. At this average speed, how far could one runner travel in 10 sec?

33. **ALGEBRA** Judy works at Biff's Big Burger as a cook. She can cook 12 hamburgers in 4 min. At this rate, how many hamburgers can she cook in 60 min?

34. **WRITE ABOUT IT** How do you know that the two ratios $\frac{1}{2}$ and $\frac{4}{8}$ can make a proportion?

Mixed Review and Test Prep

Combine like terms. Then find the value when $c = 3.5$ and $a = 2.03$.

35. $3c + 4a + 5c - 2a$

36. $9a + 2c + 3c - 5a$

37. $5a + 3c - 4a + 3c$

Write a rule to describe the pattern. Find the next three terms in the sequence.

38. 2.62, 2.6, 2.58, 2.56, . . .

39. 39, 46, 53, 60, . . .

40. 79, 75, 71, 67, . . .

41. **LOGICAL REASONING** Sarah has some dogs and birds as pets. They have a total of 22 legs. Which equation can be used to represent this situation?

A $4d + 2b = 22$ **B** $2b + 2d = 22$
C $4d + 4b = 22$ **D** $b + d = 22$

42. **PERIMETER** Janice doubles the dimensions of a rectangular garden 8 feet × 12 feet. What is the perimeter of the new garden?

F 40 ft **G** 80 ft
H 96 ft **J** 192 ft

MORE PRACTICE Lesson 7.5, page H53

CHAPTER 7 Review/Test

Write an equation for each problem. (pages 142–143)

1. Jan owes her brother \$120. She is making \$10 payments to him every month for x months. How many payments will she make?

2. The price of a basketball goal, decreased by a coupon for \$12.50, equals \$48.49. What is the price of the goal?

3. The chef increased the number of recipe ingredients by 7 to equal 22 ingredients. How many ingredients did she originally have?

4. An auditorium has 14 seats in each row. There are 322 seats in all. How many rows are there?

5. **VOCABULARY** A sentence that shows two expressions are equivalent is a(n) __?__. (page 142)

Solve. (pages 145–147)

6. $m + 2.3 = 4.1$

7. $23 = s - 12.5$

8. $x - 7 = 9$

9. $d + 12 = 6$

10. $c + 2.4 = 18$

11. $p - 18.5 = 31.3$

12. $n + 2 = {}^{-}5$

13. $14 = b - 5.2$

14. $k + 5.4 = 17.2$

15. $g - 9.1 = 3.5$

16. $w - 4 = {}^{-}7$

17. $t + {}^{-}2 = 5$

Solve. (pages 148–149)

18. $2x = {}^{-}32$

19. $\frac{n}{3} = {}^{-}8$

20. $5y = 3$

21. $\frac{m}{1.2} = 98$

22. $12d = 144$

23. $\frac{s}{0.8} = 0.1$

24. $8w = {}^{-}12$

25. $6z = 0.6$

26. $15e = 225$

27. $\frac{b}{7} = {}^{-}63$

28. $\frac{c}{0.5} = 12$

29. $\frac{x}{{}^{-}5} = {}^{-}25$

Solve. (pages 150–151)

30. A newspaper stopped publication in 1985. It was printed daily for 88 years. In what year did the newspaper start publication?

31. Tony gave 3 cookies to Sarah, 4 cookies to Marcus, and 2 cookies to Joan. He has 7 cookies left. How many cookies did he start with?

Solve each proportion. (pages 152–155)

32. $\frac{6}{8} = \frac{n}{12}$

33. $\frac{1.8}{n} = \frac{12}{17}$

34. $\frac{n}{55} = \frac{5}{11}$

35. $\frac{5}{28} = \frac{45}{n}$

36. $\frac{n}{100} = \frac{81}{300}$

37. $\frac{16}{n} = \frac{1,600}{400}$

38. $\frac{5}{n} = \frac{30}{48}$

39. $\frac{9}{14} = \frac{n}{7}$

40. **VOCABULARY** An equation that states that two ratios are equivalent is called a(n) __?__. (page 152)

Test Prep

CUMULATIVE
CHAPTERS 1–7

1. For what value of y is $8y = {}^{-}2$ a true statement?

A $^{-}16$
B $^{-}4$
C $\frac{-1}{4}$
D $\frac{1}{4}$

2. Which best describes $\sqrt{27}$?

F a little less than 4
G a little more than 5
H a little more than 6
J about 9

3. $^{-}34 \times {}^{-}18 =$

A $^{-}532$
B $^{-}52$
C 384
D 612

4. Juan took 8 pieces of candy from a jar, 5 of which were lemon flavored. If he takes 120 out of the jar, how many can he expect to be lemon flavored?

F 75
G 70
H 65
J 60

5. A sweatshirt you want to buy is on sale for 25% off. What fraction of the price is this?

A $\frac{1}{25}$
B $\frac{1}{4}$
C $\frac{1}{2}$
D $\frac{3}{4}$

6. Which expression could you use to find the next term in the sequence 4, 9, 14, 19, . . . ?

F $5 + 4 \times (n - 1)$
G $4 + 5 \times (n - 1)$
H $19 + 5 \times (n - 1)$
J $4 \times 5 + (n - 1)$

7. Denise and her two sisters need to deliver 48 newspapers. Denise decides to deliver $\frac{1}{2}$ of the papers. One of her sisters decides to deliver $\frac{1}{3}$ of the papers. Based on the information given, which is a reasonable conclusion?

A Denise delivers fewer papers than either of her sisters.
B Denise's other sister delivers 8 papers.
C Denise can read papers faster than her sisters.
D Denise is older than her two sisters.

8. Sean is saving part of his allowance to buy a skateboard that costs \$60. So far he has saved \$28. Which equation could be used to find m, the amount of money that Sean still needs so he can buy the skateboard?

F $28 \times m = 60$
G $28 + m = 60$
H $28 - m = 60$
J $\frac{m}{60} = 28$

9. $5^2 - 2 \times 4 + 8 =$

A 100
B 25
C 9
D 1

CHAPTER

8

SOLVING TWO-STEP EQUATIONS AND INEQUALITIES

LOOK AHEAD

In this chapter you will solve problems that involve

- solving two-step equations
- using the strategy *write an equation*
- solving inequalities

SPORTS LINK

Basketball is considered to be the world's most popular indoor sport. In 1997, the Women's National Basketball Association (WNBA) was established. The table below shows the win and loss records for each of the eight teams in the league.

1997 WNBA FINAL STANDINGS		
Team	Wins	Losses
Houston Comets	18	10
New York Liberty	17	11
Phoenix Mercury	16	12
Charlotte Sting	15	13
Cleveland Rockers	15	13
Los Angeles Sparks	14	14
Sacramento Monarchs	10	18
Utah Starzz	7	21

- Write the ratio of wins to losses for each team.
- For which teams is the ratio of wins to losses greater than 1?

Problem-Solving Project

Class Trip to a Basketball Game

Your class is going to attend a basketball game. Decide how many students and chaperones will attend. Use the pricing chart to choose seats. Write a two-step equation to calculate the total cost for student tickets, adult tickets, and transportation. Present your plan to the class.

TICKET PRICING	
Section I	$24.00
Section II	$17.50
Section III	$9.50

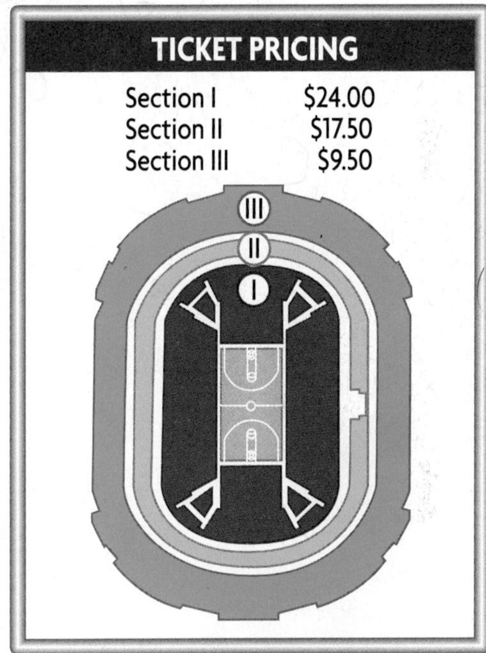

PROJECT CHECKLIST

- ✓ Did you decide how many people will attend the game?
- ✓ Did you write a two-step equation to calculate the total cost?
- ✓ Did you present your plan to the class?

LAB ACTIVITY

What You'll Explore
Modeling two-step equations

What You'll Need
algebra tiles or paper squares and rectangles

Exploring Two-Step Equations

You have solved equations that have one step. In this activity you will model equations that have two steps.

Explore

- Use algebra tiles or paper squares and rectangles to model $2x + 3 = 7$. Use a rectangle to represent the variable, x, and use a square to represent 1.

$2x \quad + \quad 3 \quad = \quad 7$

- Remember, to solve an equation, you need to have the rectangles (variables) alone on one side of the equation. Take away 3 squares from each side of the equation.

$2x \quad + 3 - 3 \quad = \quad 7 - 3$

- Now the model shows $2x = 4$.

- Divide the model into 2 equal groups, each with one rectangle and the same number of squares.

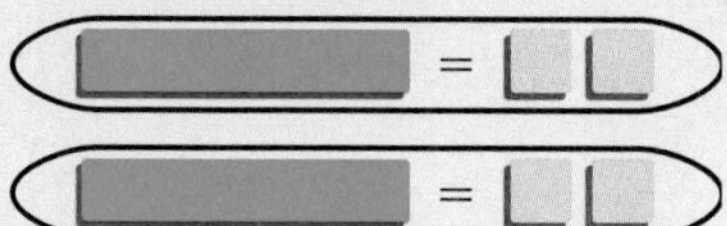

- What does each group show?

- What is the solution?

Think and Discuss

- Explain what you did to the model to undo the addition so that the variables were alone on one side.
- Explain what you did to the model to undo the multiplication so that the variable was alone on one side.
- CRITICAL THINKING How could you use a model to check your solution?
(**Think:** A rectangle equals how many squares?)
- Look at this model. What equation does it represent?

- Use the model to solve the equation. Then make a drawing to explain how you found the solution.

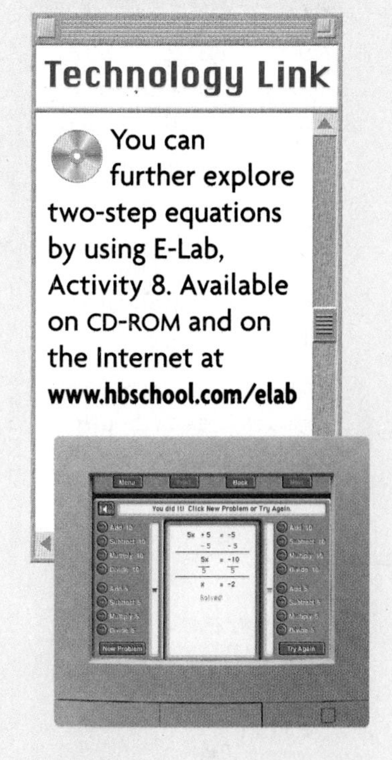

Technology Link
You can further explore two-step equations by using E-Lab, Activity 8. Available on CD-ROM and on the Internet at www.hbschool.com/elab

Try This

- Use a model to solve each equation.

$5x + 4 = 14$ $\quad$ $4x + 3 = 7$ $\quad$ $3x + 6 = 12$

- Look at this model.

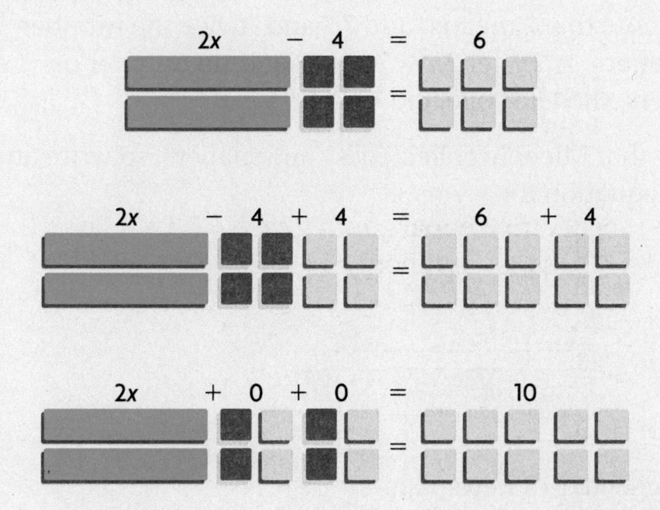

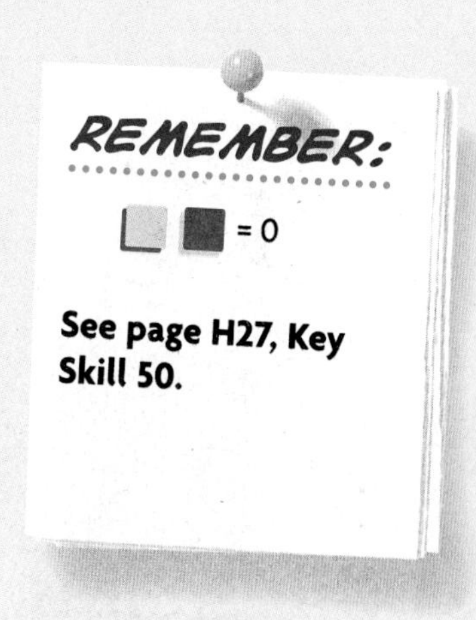

See page H27, Key Skill 50.

- What would you do to this model to find the solution?
- How is this model different from the model for $2x + 4 = 8$?

LESSON 8.1

PROBLEM-SOLVING STRATEGY

Write an Equation to Solve Two-Step Problems

What You'll Learn
How to use the strategy *write an equation* to solve problems

Why Learn This?
To make complicated problems easier

When you need to solve a problem that involves two operations, you can write a two-step equation.

Michele collected 7 more than twice the number of newspapers David collected. Michele collected 33 newspapers. How many did David collect?

PROBLEM SOLVING

- **Understand**
- **Plan**
- **Solve**
- **Look Back**

UNDERSTAND What are you asked to find?

What facts are given?

PLAN What strategy will you use?

You can *write an equation* to solve the problem.

SOLVE How will you solve the problem?

- Let n represent the number of newspapers David collected.
- Since "7 more than" means "add 7," and "twice the number of newspapers" is $2n$, let $2n + 7$ represent the number of newspapers Michele collected.
- You know that Michele collected 33 newspapers, so write and solve the equation $2n + 7 = 33$.

$$2n + 7 = 33$$
$$2n + 7 - 7 = 33 - 7 \quad \textit{Subtract 7 from each side.}$$
$$2n = 26$$
$$\frac{2n}{2} = \frac{26}{2} \quad \textit{Divide each side by 2.}$$
$$n = 13$$

So, David collected 13 newspapers.

LOOK BACK How can you check your answer?

What if . . . Michele collected 6 more than $\frac{1}{2}$ the number of newspapers David collected? If Michele collected 33 newspapers, how many did David collect?

PRACTICE

Write an equation and solve.

1. The length of a community swimming pool is 10 ft shorter than 2 times the width. The length of the pool is 35 ft. What is the width?
2. This week Jason scored 5 less than twice as many goals as he did last week. He scored 11 goals this week. How many goals did he score last week?
3. On Saturday, Megan earned $1.75 more than 3 times the amount she earned on Friday. She earned $22.75 on Saturday. How much did she earn on Friday?
4. The number of tapes Leslie has is 4 fewer than twice the number of tapes Michele has. If Leslie has 8 tapes, how many does Michele have?

MIXED APPLICATIONS

Solve.

CHOOSE a strategy and a tool.

- **Write an Equation**
- **Make a Table**
- **Draw a Diagram**
- **Guess and Check**
- **Work Backward**
- **Use a Formula**

Paper/Pencil

Calculator

Hands-On

Mental Math

5. A 5-gal can of asphalt sealant contains enough to cover about 265 sq ft. About how many cans of sealant are needed to cover a tennis court 78 ft $\times$ 27 ft?
6. There are 32 students in Dominic's math class. There are 3 times as many boys as girls. How many girls are in the class?
7. Seth, Bill, Ed, and Ashley are in different activities. One sings, one runs, one plays soccer, and one swims. Seth and Bill are taller than the swimmer. Ed and Ashley do not sing or play soccer. Seth and the soccer player are cousins. What is Bill's activity?
8. The Music Club is buying tickets for the concert. Front-row tickets cost $7.95 more than 3 times the price of balcony tickets. Front-row tickets cost $94.95. How much do balcony tickets cost?
9. After the game, half the Pep Band went out for pizza. Of the remaining members, half went to the school dance, and 3 went home. The 4 that were left went to a party. How many members had been at the game?
10. **WRITE ABOUT IT** Write a problem that you could solve by writing a two-step equation. Then show how to solve your problem.

MORE PRACTICE Lesson 8.1, page H54

LESSON 8.2 Simplifying and Solving

What You'll Learn
How to simplify an equation before solving

Why Learn This?
To combine like terms of an equation to make it a simpler problem

Most equations you will use to solve problems are one- or two-step equations. Sometimes these equations need to be simplified before you solve them. You can simplify by combining like terms.

EXAMPLE 1 Solve and check. $x + 2x + 5x - 6 = 10$

$$x + 2x + 5x - 6 = 10 \quad \textit{Combine like terms.}$$
$$8x - 6 = 10$$
$$8x - 6 + 6 = 10 + 6 \quad \textit{Solve.}$$
$$8x = 16$$
$$\frac{8x}{8} = \frac{16}{8}$$
$$x = 2$$

$$x + 2x + 5x - 6 = 10 \quad \textit{Check the solution. Use the original equation.}$$
$$2 + 2(2) + 5(2) - 6 = 10$$
$$2 + 4 + 10 - 6 = 10$$
$$10 = 10 \checkmark$$

- Solve and check. $m + 3m - 3^2 + 12 = 19$

REMEMBER:

You can combine like terms to simplify an expression.

$3x + 4x + 7x + 5 = 14x + 5$

See pages 131–133.

To simplify some problems before solving, you need to use the Distributive Property.

EXAMPLE 2 Solve. $3(x - 3) + 4x = 33$

$$3(x - 3) + 4x = 33 \quad \textit{Multiply, using the Distributive Property.}$$
$$3x - 9 + 4x = 33$$
$$3x - 9 + 4x = 33 \quad \textit{Simplify.}$$
$$7x - 9 = 33$$
$$7x - 9 + 9 = 33 + 9 \quad \textit{Solve.}$$
$$7x = 42$$
$$\frac{7x}{7} = \frac{42}{7}$$
$$x = 6$$

Talk About It

- In the equation $x + 2x + 5x - 6 = 10$ in Example 1, explain why you cannot simplify the left side of the equation as $2x$.
- Solve. $4.1(1 + 2m) + 10 = 108.4$

Sometimes the equation you write for a problem has to be simplified before you can solve it.

EXAMPLE 3 You and a friend want to go to a concert. There are only two seats left. One of the seats is in the upper level of the arena, and the other is in the lower level. The ticket for the lower level costs \$12 more than the other ticket. The total cost for both tickets is \$42. What is the price of each ticket?

Choose a variable.

Let t = the price of a ticket for the upper level, and
$t + 12$ = the price of a ticket for the lower level.

Write an equation.

$t + t + 12 = 42$

Simplify and solve the equation.

$$t + t + 12 = 42$$
$$2t + 12 = 42$$
$$2t + 12 - 12 = 42 - 12$$
$$2t = 30$$
$$\frac{2t}{2} = \frac{30}{2}$$
$$t = 15$$

Find the value of $t + 12$ for $t = 15$.

$$t + 12$$
$$15 + 12 = 27$$

So, the ticket for the upper level costs \$15, and the ticket for the lower level costs \$27.

- **CRITICAL THINKING** A 38-ft rope is cut into three pieces. One piece is 2 ft longer than each of the other two pieces. What is the length of each piece of rope?

Concert tickets can be very expensive, but concerts are expensive to produce. The cost of a concert ticket includes many things, such as stage and sound systems, transportation, and stagehands. Before the show begins, part of your ticket cost also goes to insurance, security, rent, performers, and a promoter.

GUIDED PRACTICE

Tell whether the given value is a solution of the equation. Write *yes* or *no*.

1. $3m = 15, m = 5$
2. $6x + x - 7 = 9, x = 7$
3. $7c - 4 + c = 14, c = 2$
4. $2x = 41, x = 20.5$
5. $18 - 3n = 0, n = {}^{-}6$
6. $0.75 + t = 1, t = 0.5$

Solve and check.

7. $3x + x + 4 = 8$
8. $5a + {}^{-}4 + {}^{-}4a = 6$
9. ${}^{-}6 + 12t - 8t = 6$
10. $5.1 + 3w = {}^{-}1.2$
11. $4m + 3.8 + m = 7$
12. $1.2y + 1.3y = 0.64$

INDEPENDENT PRACTICE

Tell whether the given value is a solution of the equation. Write *yes* or *no*.

1. $2p + 4 = 14, p = 5$

2. $3y - 9 = 9, y = 3$

3. $4r - 3 + 3r = 16, r = 4$

4. $10q + 5(15 - q) = 135, q = 12$

5. $15b - 2b - 12 = 14, b = 3$

6. $2a + 32a + 7 = {}^{-}27, a = {}^{-}1$

Solve and check.

7. $12m - 14 + 7m = 81$

8. $9c - 9 - 8c = 23$

9. $3(x - 4) - x + 3 = 16$

10. $12.7d - 4.7d + 8 = 6$

11. $3^2 + 3.8f - 1.8f = 5.4$

12. $21 = 4(q - 6) + 11q$

13. $3(2p - 4) = {}^{-}24$

14. $8z + 4z - 5z = 63$

15. $2(x + 9) + 8x = 24$

16. $6r + 2^3 - 5 = 51$

17. $4(2d - 4) + 6 = 6$

18. $2.8b - 1.4b - 6 = 1$

Problem-Solving Applications

19. **INTEREST** The interest on Jody's savings account is $10.11 less this year than last year. The total interest for the past two years is $58.33. How much interest did she earn this year?

20. **NUMBER SENSE** Minh can type 19 words per min faster than Juan. Their combined typing speed is 97 words per minute. What is Minh's typing speed?

21. **MEASUREMENT** Kathleen is going to cut a 44-ft rope into four pieces for a school project. One piece of the rope will be 2 ft longer than the other three pieces. What will be the length of each piece of rope?

22. Crystal earns $5 a week more than her brother Dustin. Together, Crystal's and Dustin's salaries total $365 a week. How much per week does each of them earn?

23. **WRITE ABOUT IT** How can you check your solution of an equation?

Mixed Review and Test Prep

Tell whether each statement is *true* or *false*.

24. $4 + 3 < 2 + 3$

25. $7 - {}^{-}2 > 7 + {}^{-}2$

26. $8 = 4^2$

27. $6 + 3 = 2^2 + 5$

Solve and check.

28. $8n = {}^{-}32$

29. $4 + n = 1$

30. $24 = n + 7$

31. $3 = \frac{n}{8}$

32. **ESTIMATION** José is taking a 1,200-mile trip. After 9 hr he has traveled 873 miles. Which is the best estimate of the number of miles he has left to travel?

A 200 mi **B** 300 mi
C 500 mi **D** 2,100 mi

33. **CONSUMER MATH** Latosha bought a stereo for $248.50 and an entertainment center for $78.40. How much did she spend on the two items?

F $170.10 **G** $330.00
H $326.90 **J** $1,033.00

MORE PRACTICE Lesson 8.2, page H54

Comparing Equations and Inequalities

LESSON 8.3

What You'll Learn
To identify and find solutions of inequalities

Why Learn This?
To determine the relationship in a problem

VOCABULARY
inequality

The recommended number of grams of fat for a teenager is less than 80 grams per day. You could write the inequality $g < 80$ to express this amount.

An equation is a number sentence that shows two quantities are equivalent. An **inequality** is a number sentence that shows the relationship between two quantities that are not equivalent.

An inequality uses one of these five symbols: $<$, $>$, $\leq$, $\geq$, or $\neq$. Inequalities can be used to relate both numerical and algebraic expressions.

- Tell how to read each of these inequalities.

$8 - 6 < 5$ $2x \leq 9$ $5t \neq 10$ $18 > 7$ $4p \geq 4$

To determine when an algebraic sentence is an inequality and when it is an equation, replace the variable with different values and then simplify to see whether an inequality symbol or the equals symbol makes the sentence true.

EXAMPLE Replace the variable in $12y \bullet 100 - 4^3$ with each given value. Simplify, and replace the $\bullet$ with an inequality or equals symbol to make a true sentence.

$y = 2$	$y = 3$	$y = 4$
$12y \bullet 100 - 4^3$	$12y \bullet 100 - 4^3$	$12y \bullet 100 - 4^3$
$12(2) \bullet 100 - 4^3$	$12(3) \bullet 100 - 4^3$	$12(4) \bullet 100 - 4^3$
$24 \bullet 100 - 64$	$36 \bullet 100 - 64$	$48 \bullet 100 - 64$
$24 \bullet 36$	$36 \bullet 36$	$48 \bullet 36$
$24 < 36$	$36 = 36$	$48 > 36$
inequality	equation	inequality

So, for $y = 3$, the algebraic sentence is an equation, but for $y = 2$ or $y = 4$, the algebraic sentence is an inequality.

- Is $7p \bullet 84$ an equation or an inequality for $p = 10$? $p = 11$? $p = 12$?
- In $3n + 6 \bullet 15$, which inequality symbols can replace the $\bullet$ to make a true sentence for $n = 4$?

HEALTH LINK

Today many people are concerned about the amount of fat in their diets. Some terms commonly used on products are *light, reduced-fat, low-fat*, and *fat-free*. But what do these terms really tell you about the amount of fat? Use inequality symbols to put these terms in order of fat content, from greatest to least.

An inequality can have several solutions. Any number that produces a true statement is a solution of an inequality. For example, for $x + 4 < 7$, the solution $x < 3$ means that any number less than 3 makes the statement true.

Inequality:	$x + 4 < 7$	$x + 4 \leq 7$	$x + 4 \geq 7$
Solution:	$x < 3$	$x \leq 3$	$x \geq 3$

These inequalities are all associated with the equation $x + 4 = 7$, which has the solution $x = 3$.

The solutions of equations and inequalities can be shown on a number line. On a number line an open circle (○) means that the value it is on is not a solution. A closed circle (●) means that the value it is on is a solution.

Equality	Solution	Number Line
$x + 4 = 7$	$x = 3$	-2 0 2 4 6 8

Inequality	Solution	Number Line
$x + 4 < 7$	$x < 3$	-2 0 2 4 6 8
$x + 4 \leq 7$	$x \leq 3$	-2 0 2 4 6 8
$x + 4 > 7$	$x > 3$	-2 0 2 4 6 8
$x + 4 \geq 7$	$x \geq 3$	-2 0 2 4 6 8
$x + 4 \neq 7$	$x \neq 3$	-2 0 2 4 6 8

Talk About It

- In which direction on the number line do you draw the graph of an inequality whose solution uses the symbol $>$? whose solution uses the symbol $<$?
- Does the graph of $x < 3$ include the 3? Why or why not?
- What numbers does the graph of $x \leq 3$ include?

GUIDED PRACTICE

Replace the variable with each given value. Tell whether the algebraic sentence is an *equation* or an *inequality*.

$s + 9 \bullet 12$	**1.** $s = 3$	**2.** $s = 7$	**3.** $s = 8$
$4n - 2 \bullet 12$	**4.** $n = 2$	**5.** $n = 2.5$	**6.** $n = 3.5$

INDEPENDENT PRACTICE

Tell whether the given value of x is a solution of the inequality. Write *yes* or *no*.

1. $x + 3 \leq 5; x = 2$

2. $3x > 12; x = 4.5$

3. $x - 9 < 0; x = 10$

4. $2x \geq 4^2; x = {}^-8$

5. $x - 3 \neq 7; x = {}^-3$

6. $x < \frac{3}{2} + \frac{3}{2}; x = 2$

7. $2x + 8 < 2^3; x = 0$

8. $x + 0.8 \leq 1.5; x = 0.75$

9. $x + 7.2 \geq 0.5; x = 5.2$

Write an inequality or an equation for each graph.

10. ⁻6 ⁻4 ⁻2 0 2

11.

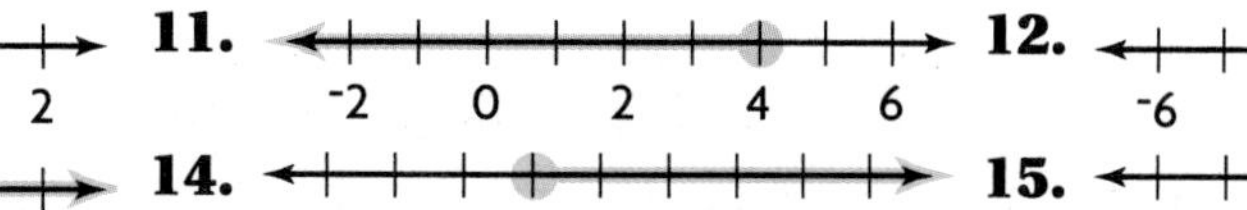

12.

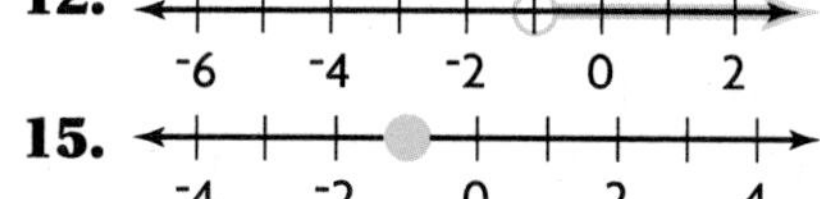

13. ⁻4 ⁻2 0 2 4

14.

15.

Problem-Solving Applications

16. VISUAL THINKING Describe the solution shown by the graph. What numbers are not among the solutions?

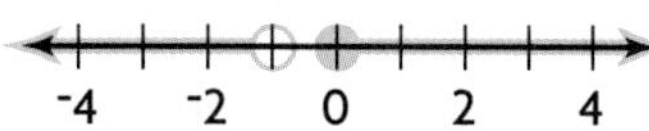

17. SPORTS Marty's baseball glove cost $30 more than his bat. The glove cost less than $52. Write an inequality for these word sentences. Let b represent the cost of the bat.

18. WRITE ABOUT IT How is an equation different from an inequality?

Mixed Review and Test Prep

Graph each set of numbers on a number line.

19. negative integers greater than ⁻3

20. integers less than 3 and greater than ⁻4

Write an equation for each word sentence.

21. Twelve tickets less than the total number of tickets equals 5 tickets.

22. The quotient of 54 pencils and a number of students equals 6 pencils.

23. NUMBER SENSE Fernando chose a number, subtracted 2, added 3 to the difference, and multiplied the sum by 6. His final answer was 48. What number did he choose?

A 7 **B** 14 **C** 28 **D** 64

24. LOGICAL THINKING Thai has 8 pencils. Sean has 4 times as many as Melvin. LaToya has 3 more than Melvin. Melvin has $\frac{1}{2}$ as many as Thai. How many pencils does Sean have?

F 4 **G** 7 **H** 16 **J** 32

Technology Link

In ***Mighty Math Astro Algebra*** you can explore inequalities in *The Trouble with Temperatures.* Use Grow Slide Level Green U.

MORE PRACTICE Lesson 8.3, page H54

LESSON 8.4

Solving Inequalities

What You'll Learn
How to solve inequalities

Why Learn This?
To determine the grade you must get to reach an average you have set as a goal

Solving an inequality is similar to solving an equation. When you add, subtract, multiply by, or divide by the same number on both sides of an inequality, you form an equivalent inequality.

EXAMPLE 1 Solve the inequality. Graph the solution. $3n < 15$

$3n < 15$

$\frac{3n}{3} < \frac{15}{3}$ *Divide each side by 3.*

$n < 5$ *Graph the solution.*

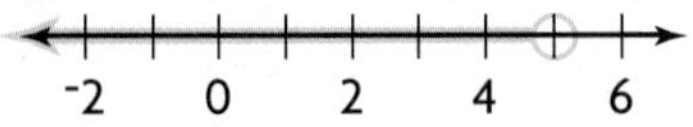

[Number line from -2 to 6 with an open circle at 5 and arrow pointing left]

-2 0 2 4 6

So, n is equal to all numbers less than 5.

- Solve the inequality $\frac{t}{4} \geq 2$. Graph the solution.

CONSUMER LINK

Insurance rates make teen driving very expensive. A teen may pay $1,900 to $2,300 a year. A teen can get a lower rate if he or she has good grades or has taken driver education. A discounted rate for a teen can be $1,500 to $1,750 a year. If a teen pays $160 a month for insurance, what is the cost for a year?

Sometimes you have to write an inequality to solve a problem.

EXAMPLE 2 Angela is averaging her grades. On 4 tests she scored 92, 87, 90, and 85. She wants her average score for 5 tests to be at least 90. Find the lowest score Angela can get on her fifth test.

Let x = Angela's score on the fifth test. *Choose a variable.*

Think: The average score for 5 tests must be greater than or equal to 90.

$\frac{92 + 87 + 90 + 85 + x}{5} \geq 90$ *Write an inequality.*

$\frac{92 + 87 + 90 + 85 + x}{5} \geq 90$ *Combine like terms.*

$\frac{354 + x}{5} \geq 90$

$5\left(\frac{354 + x}{5}\right) \geq 90(5)$ *Multiply each side by 5.*

$354 + x \geq 450$

$354 - 354 + x \geq 450 - 354$ *Subtract 354 from each side.*

$x \geq 96$

So, the lowest score Angela can get is 96.

- **CRITICAL THINKING** On 3 tests your scores are 75, 80, and 85. You want an average score for 4 tests to be at least 80. What is the lowest score you can get on your fourth test?

GUIDED PRACTICE

Tell what operation and number you would use to solve each inequality.

1. $x - 12 > 71$

2. $0.6y \geq 0.06$

3. $z + 1\frac{3}{4} \neq 3$

4. $\frac{a}{99} \leq 100$

5. $b + 8 \neq 9$

6. $10^5 < 10c$

7. $a - 6 \leq 8$

8. $\frac{1}{2}r > 12$

9. $t + \frac{1}{2} \neq \frac{2}{3}$

INDEPENDENT PRACTICE

Solve. Write the whole numbers that make the inequality true.

1. $n + 6 < 10$

2. $b + 2 \geq 115$

3. $4n - 1 > 15$

Solve the equation or inequality.

4. $x + 3 < 8$

5. $6 + c \leq 1$

6. $\frac{t}{4} \geq {}^{-}1$

7. $6z + 3 \neq 21$

8. $w + 12 = 100$

9. $c - 3 > 2$

10. ${}^{-}3b = 12$

11. $6n + 3 \geq 21$

12. $\frac{r}{2} \geq \frac{{}^{-}1}{2}$

Solve the equation or inequality. Graph the solution.

13. $x + 5 = 6$

14. $8y = 28$

15. $e - 2 = 5$

16. $4x < 8$

17. $y - 5 \neq 2$

18. $\frac{n}{2} \geq 1$

19. $p + 2 \leq 1$

20. $0.4q > 0.8$

21. $r - 1\frac{1}{2} \neq 2$

Problem-Solving Applications

22. ALGEBRAIC THINKING The Brody family bought a new radio and a new television. The television cost 4 times as much as the radio. The television cost less than $300. Is it possible that the radio cost $70?

23. SPORTS At Mac's Sports the number of bicycles sold in May was 40 fewer than the number sold in April. The total number sold in both months was fewer than the 120 bicycles sold in March. How many were sold in April and May?

24. CONSUMER MATH At Camp America a tent costs $20 more than a sleeping bag. Darryl wants to buy both items for less than $100. What is the greatest amount Darryl can spend for a sleeping bag?

25. Logan scored 85, 87, 89, 92, and 94 on 5 of the 6 math tests for the semester. He wants his average score for the 6 tests to be greater than 90. What is the lowest score Logan can get on his sixth test?

26. WRITE ABOUT IT Write a real-life problem with $x < 5$ as a solution.

MORE PRACTICE Lesson 8.4, page H55

CHAPTER 8 Review/Test

Write an equation and solve. (pages 162–163)

1. Josh collected 12 more than 4 times the number of baseball cards Sarah collected. If Josh collected 72 baseball cards, how many did Sarah collect?

2. Jenny wants a CD player that costs \$165.00. She baby-sits 10 hr a week for \$4.50 an hour. How many weeks will it take to save for the CD player?

3. Carla threw the javelin 10 ft less than twice the distance Lakisha threw it. Carla threw the javelin 80 ft. How far did Lakisha throw it?

4. The length of the school auditorium is 20 ft more than twice the width. If the length is 140 ft, what is the width?

Solve. (pages 164–166)

5. $x + 2x + {}^{-}5 = 16$

6. $7 + 3.2n - n = 51$

7. $s + 5(s - 2) = 2$

8. $2c + 3(2c + 3) = 8$

9. $m + 3m + 2(m - 3) = 12$

10. $2(y - 5) + 5y - 8 = 17$

11. $q - 5.2q + 7 = 9.1$

12. $3n + 8 - 7n = 11$

13. $5g - 2(g + 3) = 12$

Write an equation and solve. (pages 164–166)

14. Jamar rides his bike 41 mi a week more than Micah. Together, Jamar and Micah ride a total of 93 mi a week. How many miles does each ride in a week?

15. Brendan scored 6 points less than Ricky scored. Together they scored 32 points. How many points did each score?

Tell whether x is a solution of the given inequality. Write *yes* or *no*. (pages 167–169)

16. $x + 4 \leq 7; x = {}^{-}3$

17. $2x \geq 3^2; x = 5$

18. $4x - 6 < 29; x = 9$

19. $8 \neq 4x + 1; x = {}^{-}2$

20. $x + 2^3 > 12; x = 4$

21. $7 - 5x \geq 4; x = 1$

22. $y + 7 \leq {}^{-}13; y = {}^{-}22$

23. $4g < 5^2; g = 7$

24. $r - 7 \neq 13; r = {}^{-}6$

25. **VOCABULARY** A number sentence that shows the relationship between two quantities that are not equivalent is a(n) __?__. (page 167)

Solve the equation or inequality. Graph the solution. (pages 170–171)

26. $t - 4 = 9$

27. $3g + 5 \leq 32$

28. $5n \neq {}^{-}75$

29. $x + 3 = 8$

30. $3s - 4 \leq 11$

31. $2 + 6c < 38$

32. $y + 0.65 \geq 2$

33. $5n - 6 \neq 19$

34. $4z > {}^{-}16$

Test Prep

CUMULATIVE
CHAPTERS 1–8

1. Eloise has 3 more than twice as many comic books as Vincent. Eloise has 32 comic books. Which equation could you use to find the number of comic books, n, that Vincent has?

A $2n - 3 = 32$
B $2n + 3 = 32$
C $3n + 2 = 32$
D $3n - 2 = 32$

2. A square is divided into 4 equal parts and one of the parts is shaded. What percent of the square is shaded?

F 12.5%
G 15%
H 20%
J 25%

3. $^-7\frac{1}{10} + {^-4}\frac{3}{4} =$

A $^-11\frac{17}{20}$

B $^-11\frac{13}{20}$

C $^-11\frac{4}{14}$

D $^-11\frac{3}{40}$

4. For what value of b is the equation $2b + 3(b - 5) = 60$ a true statement?

F 15
G 13
H 11
J 9
K Not Here

5. What is the eighth term in the sequence 13, 20, 27, 34, . . . ?

A 69
B 62
C 55
D 41

6. Which situation could be represented by the equation $b + 8 = 17$?

F 8 more than 17 is b.
G 8 less than b is 17.
H 8 times b is 17.
J 8 more than b is 17.

7. Jackie buys a notebook for $2.69, a pen for $0.89, and a calculator for $12.25. Which is the best estimate of how much she spent?

A $20
B $19
C $16
D $12

8. $(^-3)(^-7)(^-5) =$

F 105
G 55
H $^-38$
J $^-105$

9. Solve. $2x + 5 + 3x = 30$

A $x = 5$
B $x = 7$
C $x = 9$
D $x = 11$

10. Mr. Tomkins borrowed $1,200 to buy a computer. He wants to repay the loan in 8 equal payments. How much will each payment be?

F $200
G $150
H $100
J $80

CHAPTER

9

EXPLORING LINEAR EQUATIONS

LOOK AHEAD

In this chapter you will solve problems that involve

- finding and graphing ordered pairs on a coordinate plane
- identifying and describing relations and functions
- solving and graphing linear equations

HEALTH LINK

When you do an activity such as walking, running, bicycling, or swimming, you want your pulse rate to be within a certain range.

Use the process below to find your target pulse rate range.

TARGET PULSE RATE RANGE	
Age	Range per Minute
20	140–170
30	133–162
40	126–153
50	119–145

Calculating Target Pulse Rate Range

1. Subtract your age from 220.
2. Multiply the difference by 0.7. This is the minimum beats per minute.
3. Multiply the difference by 0.85. This is the maximum beats per minute.
4. Write the range, showing the minimum and maximum.

Problem-Solving Project

Exercise and Good Health

What effect do sit-ups have on your pulse rate?

Study the results of Tim's pulse rate experiment. Then conduct your own experiment. Make a table and graph to summarize your results, and draw a conclusion about the effect of sit-ups on your pulse rate.

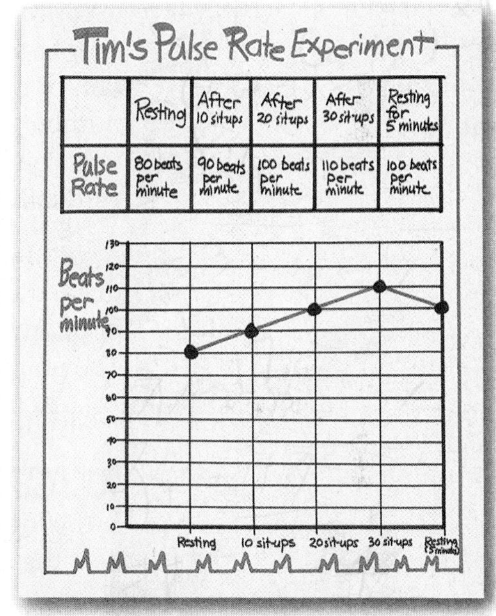

Tim's Pulse Rate Experiment

	Resting	After 10 sit-ups	After 20 sit-ups	After 30 sit-ups	Resting for 5 minutes
Pulse Rate	80 beats per minute	90 beats per minute	100 beats per minute	110 beats per minute	100 beats per minute

PROJECT CHECKLIST

- ✓ Did you record the results of your own experiment?
- ✓ Did you choose an appropriate graph?
- ✓ Did you summarize your data and identify a conclusion?

LESSON 9.1

Graphing Ordered Pairs

What You'll Learn
How to identify and graph ordered pairs on a coordinate plane

Why Learn This?
To find locations, such as those shown on a map

VOCABULARY
- **coordinate plane**
- ***x*-axis**
- ***y*-axis**
- **origin**
- **ordered pairs**
- ***x*-coordinate**
- ***y*-coordinate**
- **quadrant**

When you look up a city in a map index, you find its location given by a letter and a number. How do you use the city location A-2 to find it on the map?

A coordinate plane is similar to a map. Ordered pairs of numbers (x,y) name the positions of points on the plane.

A **coordinate plane** is formed by two perpendicular lines, the ***x*-axis** and the ***y*-axis**. Their point of intersection is the **origin**, (0,0).

Ordered pairs (x,y) tell how far to move from the origin and in what direction. The order is important!

The first number in an ordered pair is the ***x*-coordinate**. It tells you how to move horizontally (left or right). The second number, the ***y*-coordinate**, tells you how to move vertically (up or down).

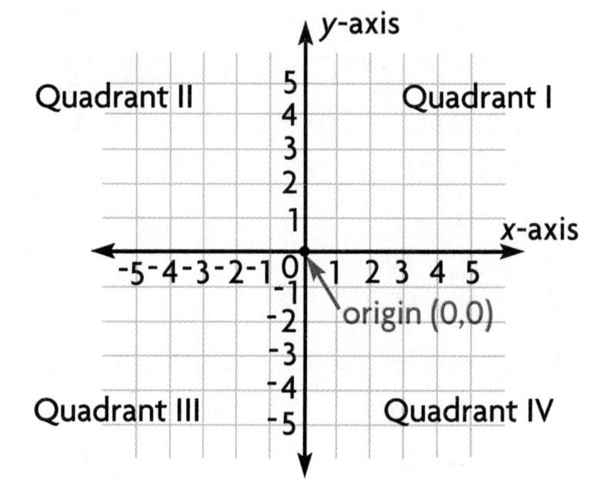

A coordinate plane is divided into four regions, or **quadrants**, as shown. The point $A\ (^-3,2)$ is in Quadrant II.

- Give the quadrant for each point: (3,2), $(^-3,2)$, $(^-3,^-2)$, $(3,^-2)$.

EXAMPLE John marked a dot on a coordinate plane to show the location of his house in relation to his school. His school is at the origin. Write an ordered pair to tell where his house is located. What quadrant is it in?

*Identify the **x-coordinate** by counting along the x-axis: 3.*

*Identify the **y-coordinate** by counting up: 2.*

So, John's house is at (3,2), in Quadrant I.

- On graph paper, draw a coordinate plane. Then graph the following points: $(^-2,4)$, $(^-1,^-1)$, $(3,^-4)$. Name the quadrant where each point is located.

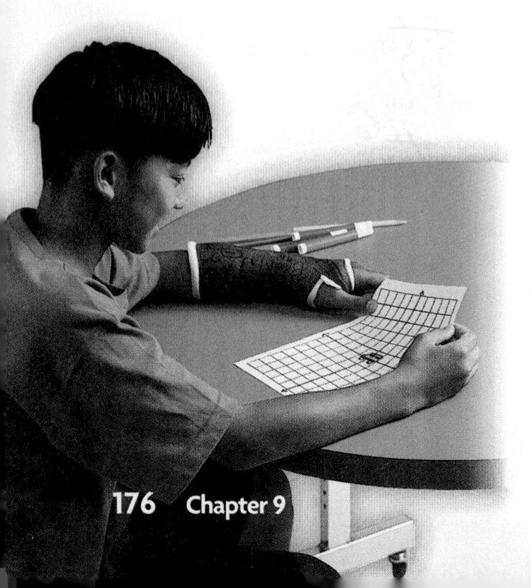

GUIDED PRACTICE

Write the ordered pair for each point.

1. *A* **2.** *B* **3.** *C*

4. *D* **5.** *E* **6.** *F*

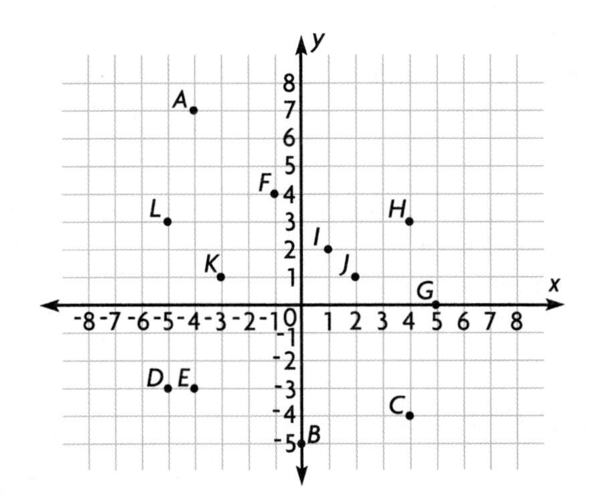

Write the letter for each ordered pair.

7. (4,3) **8.** (5,0) **9.** (1,2)

10. $(^-3,1)$ **11.** (2,1) **12.** $(^-5,3)$

13. Are $(3,^-4)$ and $(4,^-3)$ located in the same quadrant? Explain.

14. Name all points in Quadrant II.

INDEPENDENT PRACTICE

For Exercises 1–4, use graph paper to graph the ordered pairs. Use a different coordinate plane for each exercise.

1. (2,4), $(^-1,5)$, (0,6), $(^-3,^-4)$

2. (0,0), $(5,^-2)$, $(^-4,0)$, (7,6)

3. $(2,^-3)$, $(3,^-5)$, (8,1)

4. (4,3), $(0,^-4)$, $(^-5,^-1)$, $(^-1,6)$

5. Connect the points on the graph paper for Exercise 3. Name the figure and the quadrants in which the figure is located.

6. Connect the points on graph paper for Exercise 4 in the order given. Connect the first and last points. Name the figure.

7. When both the *x*-coordinate and the *y*-coordinate are negative, in which quadrant is the point located? What if both coordinates are positive?

8. When a point lies on the *x*-axis, what can be said about the *y*-coordinate? What is the *x*-coordinate when a point lies on the *y*-axis?

Problem-Solving Applications

9. **SPORTS** Tim is sitting in row P, seat 34. Write an ordered pair that could be used to identify his location.

10. Amanda and Sean started at the same point. Amanda walked 4 miles east and then 3 miles north. Sean walked 4 miles west and then 3 miles north. How far apart were they when they stopped?

11. **GEOMETRY** Parallelogram *EFGH* has vertex *E* $(^-3,2)$, vertex *F* $(^-5,0)$, and vertex *G* (2,0). What is the ordered pair for vertex *H* if the points are connected in the order of the letters?

12. **WRITE ABOUT IT** Why is order important when graphing an ordered pair on a coordinate plane?

MORE PRACTICE Lesson 9.1, page H55

LESSON 9.2

Relations

What You'll Learn
How to identify and describe relations

Why Learn This?
To describe how things are related, such as the number of hours worked as well as the amount earned

VOCABULARY

elements
relation
domain
range

Sometimes there is a relationship between two sets of things.

- The diagram below is called a mapping diagram. What relationship does it show?

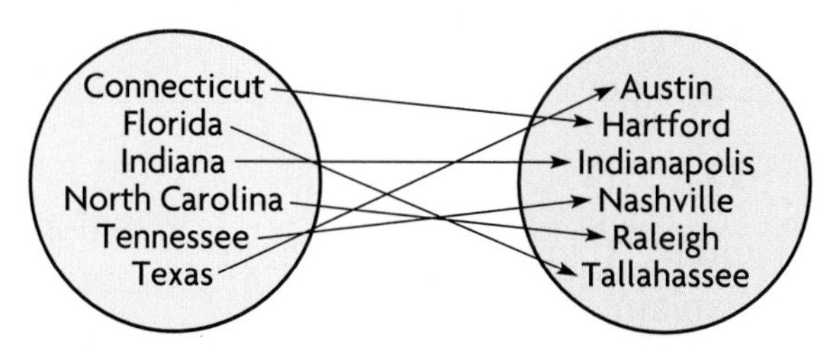

The numbers, words, or objects in a set are called the members, or **elements**, of the set. When you match the elements of one set to the elements of another set, you form a **relation**. You can express relations through words, mapping diagrams, tables, ordered pairs, equations, or graphs.

EXAMPLE 1 Josh works as a cashier at a local grocery store for $5 an hour. The table of ordered pairs shows the relationship between the number of hours worked, h, and his wages, w. Express the relation in words, as an equation, and as a graph.

Hours, h	1	2	3	4
Wages, w	$5	$10	$15	$20

As a sentence: Wages are equal to the number of hours worked multiplied by $5.

As ordered pairs:
{(1,5), (2,10), (3,15), (4,20)}

As an equation:
$w = h \cdot 5$ or $w = 5h$

As a graph:

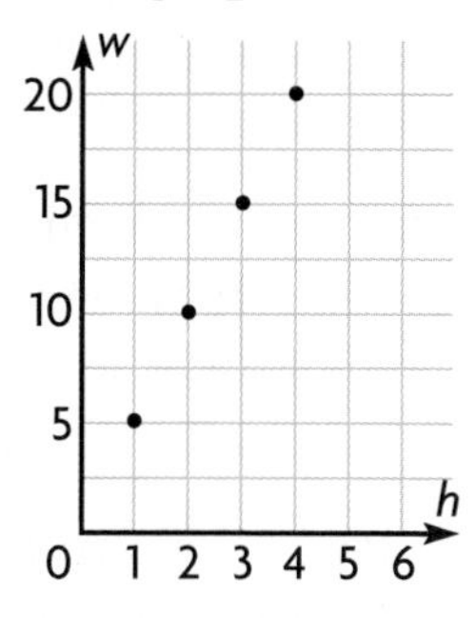

- **CRITICAL THINKING** Express the relation as a mapping diagram.
- What if Josh earned $6 an hour? Write an equation to describe that relation.

TEEN TIMES

Many teens earn money by doing jobs. Some of the jobs teens enjoy are baby-sitting, coaching younger children, and working in grocery or retail stores.

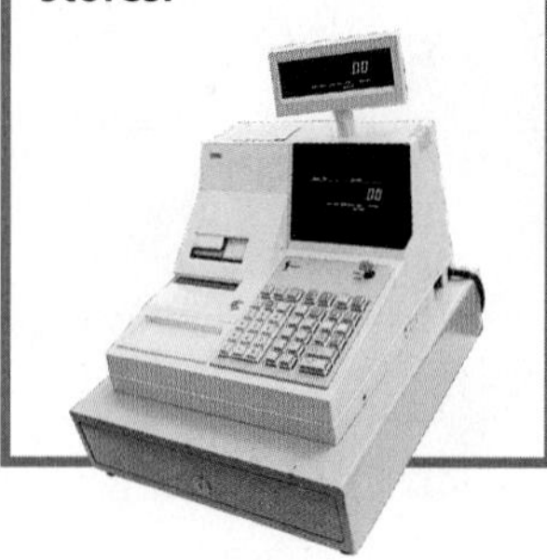

In a relation, the first set of elements, or coordinates, is the **domain** and the second set of elements, or coordinates, is the **range**.

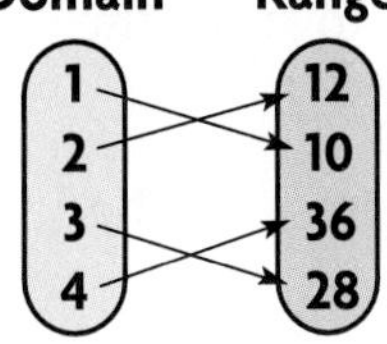

Domain	Range
1	10
2	12
3	28
4	36

domain = {1, 2, 3, 4}
range = {10, 12, 28, 36}

EXAMPLE 2 Write the ordered pairs for the relation shown in the graph. Then identify the domain and the range of the relation.

Write an ordered pair for each point.

$(^-4,0)$, $(^-6,2)$, $(^-8,4)$, $(^-10,6)$, $(^-12,8)$

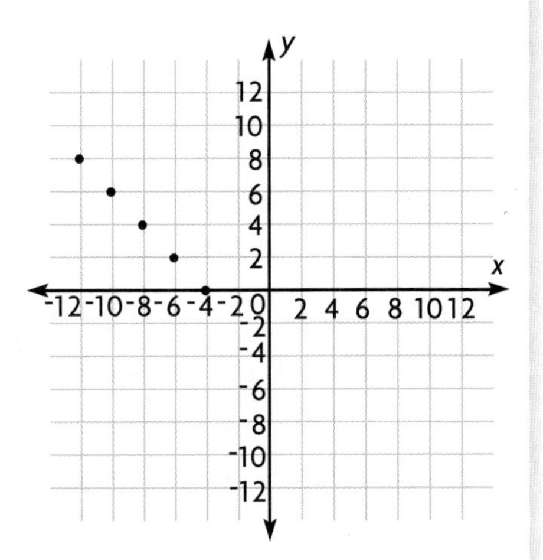

Write the x-coordinates as the domain and the y-coordinates as the range.

domain = $\{^-4, {}^-6, {}^-8, {}^-10, {}^-12\}$
range = {0, 2, 4, 6, 8}

- Which do you think is the best way to show the relationship of the domain and range—a table, a mapping diagram, an equation, or a graph? Explain.

CULTURAL LINK

A coordinate plane is also called a Cartesian plane, after René Descartes, a famous French mathematician (1596–1650). The *x*- and *y*-coordinates are also called the abscissa (ab•SIH•suh) and the ordinate. What is the abscissa in $(^-3,^-5)$?

GUIDED PRACTICE

Write the ordered pairs for each relation.

1.

Bob's age, *b*	1	2	3	4	5
Diane's age, *d*	12	13	14	15	16

2.

Original price, *x*	$10	$14	$20	$24	$27
Sale price, *y*	$6	$10	$16	$20	$23

Write an equation for each relation.

3.

Map distance (in inches), *m*	1	3	6	9
Actual distance (in miles), *a*	125	375	750	1,125

4.

Hours, *x*	1	2	3	4	5
Distance (in miles), *y*	65	130	195	260	325

INDEPENDENT PRACTICE

Use the relation $\{(^-2,^-4), (^-1,^-2), (0,0), (1,2), (2,4), (3,6)\}$ for Exercises 1–4.

1. What is the domain of the relation? What is the range of the relation?

2. Make a mapping diagram to show the relation.

3. Make a table to show the relation. Label the domain and range.

4. Write an equation that represents the relation.

5. Write the ordered pairs for the relation in this mapping diagram.

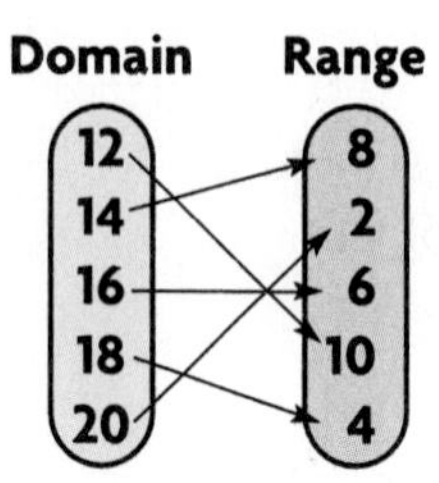

6. Use the graph to identify the domain and range of the relation.

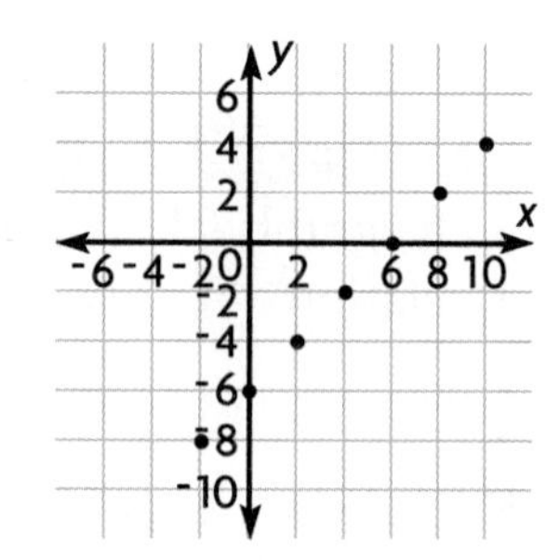

For each of Exercises 7–9, copy the table at the right. Complete the table for each relation. Then graph the relation.

x	$^-4$	0	1	3
y	■	■	■	■

7. y equals x multiplied by 2.

8. y equals x multiplied by $^-3$.

9. y equals x plus $^-1$.

Problem-Solving Applications

10. **TIME/DISTANCE** David is traveling in his car at an average speed of 45 miles per hour. Write an equation for the relation between the number of hours, x, and the distance in miles, y, that he travels.

11. **MAPS** Kathy will move to a city 250 miles away. On her map the distance is 2 inches. Write an equation for the relation of the map distance in inches, x, to the actual distance in miles, y.

12. **WRITE ABOUT IT** How can you express a relationship?

Mixed Review and Test Prep

Tell which ordered pairs have the same x-coordinates.

13. (3,4), (4,5), (2,6), (3,2)

14. (5,0), (1,7), (3,7), (1,3)

Solve and check.

15. $3m - 14 = 1$

16. $2x + 5 = 11$

17. $8z - 3 = {}^-19$

18. $^-4t + 8 = 0$

19. **ESTIMATION** Teri had \$100.00. She spent \$68.95 for a camera and \$14.70 for film. Which is the best estimate of the amount of money she had left?

A \$5 **B** \$10 **C** \$15 **D** \$20

20. **MEASUREMENT** A marathon race is approximately 42 kilometers long. What is this distance in meters?

F 420,000 m **G** 42,000 m
H 420 m **J** 0.042 m

MORE PRACTICE Lesson 9.2, page H55

Functions

What You'll Learn
How to identify functions

Why Learn This?
To decide if a relation, such as one between hours worked and pay received, is a function

VOCABULARY
function
vertical line test

There are many types of relations. A **function** is a relation in which each element of the domain corresponds to one and only one element of the range.

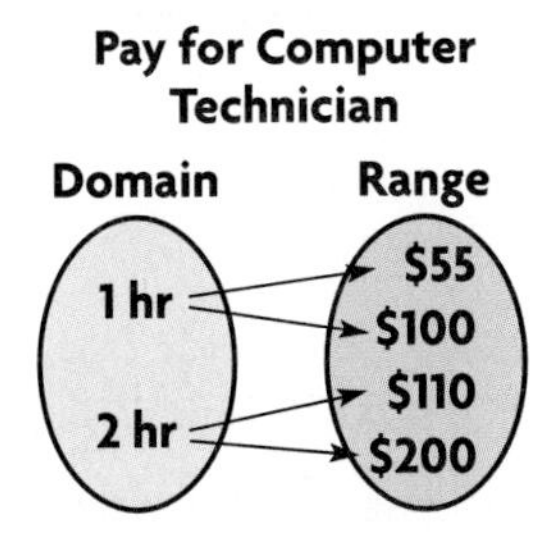

Since each element of the domain is mapped to more than one element of the range, this relation **is not a function.**

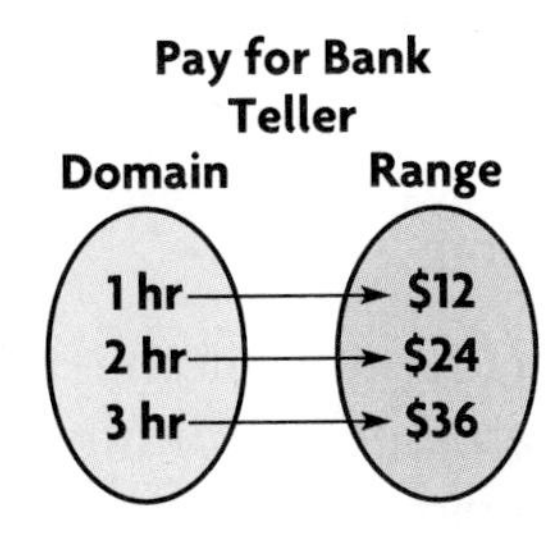

Since each element of the domain is mapped to only one element of the range, this relation **is a function.**

- The computer technician makes $55 an hour during regular business hours and $100 an hour during other hours. How is the bank teller's rate of pay different?

You can look at ordered pairs to identify whether a relation is a function. If none of the elements of the domain are repeated, then the relation is a function.

EXAMPLE 1 Identify each relation as a function or not a function.

Relation	Repeated Elements of the Domain	Is This Relation a Function?
{($^{-}2$,3), ($^{-}1$,3), (1,6), (2,6)}	None	Yes
{(3,4), (3,5), (4,4), (5,5)}	(3,4), (3,5)	No
{(0,5), (1,15), (2,25), (3,35)}	None	Yes
{(8,4), (8,8), (8,12), (8,16)}	(8,4), (8,8), (8,12), (8,16)	No

- CRITICAL THINKING Write two sets of ordered pairs with four members in each set. Make one set a function and the other set not a function.

CAREER LINK

People get paid in different ways, such as a fixed amount for completing a project, an hourly rate, or a monthly salary. How much more would a factory worker make for 3 hours of the night shift if the day shift paid $10 an hour and the night shift paid $12 an hour?

You can graph relations and functions.

relation | function | relation

By using the **vertical line test**, you can identify whether a relation is a function. If a vertical line crosses two or more points on the graph, the relation is not a function.

EXAMPLE 2 Use the vertical line test to determine whether the relations are functions.

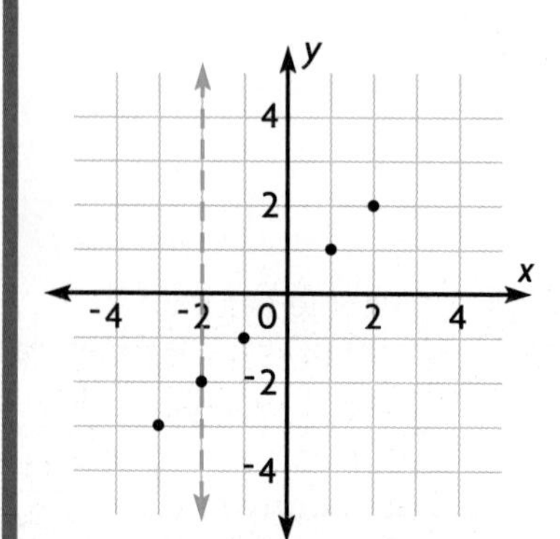

Every vertical line like the blue vertical line crosses only one point on the graph, so this relation **is a function.**

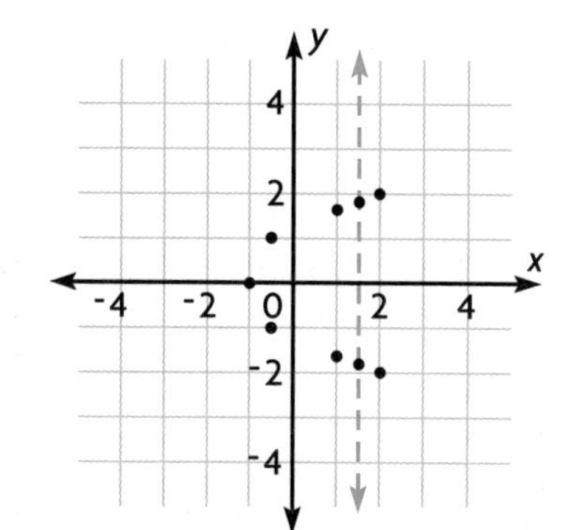

There is at least one vertical line like the blue vertical line that crosses two points on the graph, so this relation **is not a function.**

LANGUAGE LINK

The graph below shows that the number of words the average child knows is a function of the child's age. About how many words does the average 30-month-old child know?

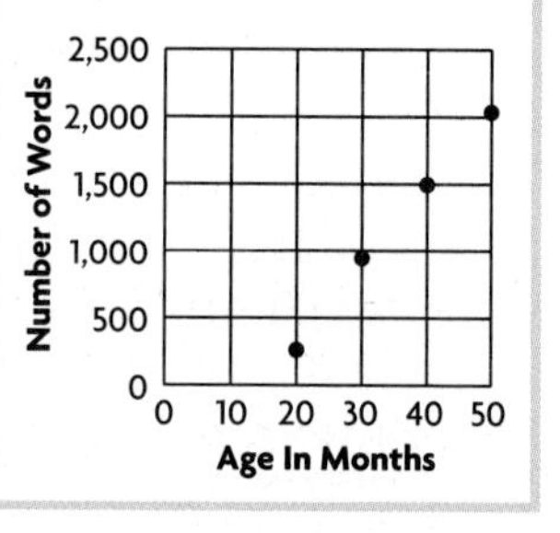

GUIDED PRACTICE

Is the relation a function? Write *yes* or *no*. If you write *no*, explain.

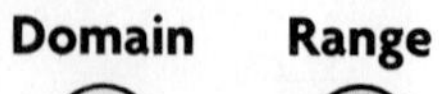

1. Domain Range

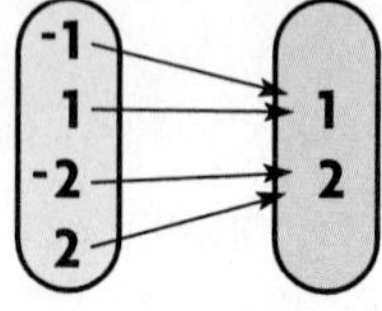

2. Domain Range

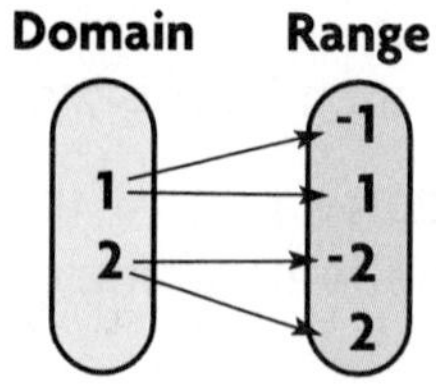

3. Domain Range

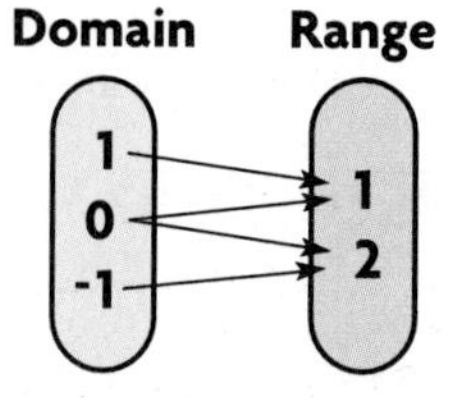

4. {(1,4), (3,6), (4,7), (6,9)}

5. {(0,1), (1,2), (1,1), (2,2)}

6. {(1,1), (2,2), (3,3), (4,4)}

7. {(3,⁻3), (2,2), (5,5), (3,3), (2,⁻2)}

INDEPENDENT PRACTICE

Use the vertical line test to determine if the relation is a function.

1.

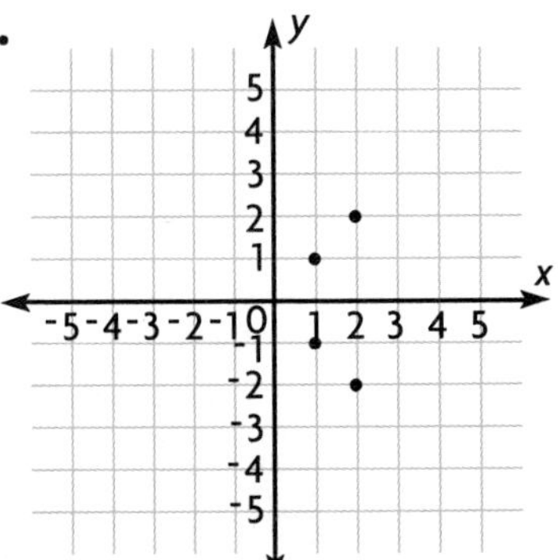

2.

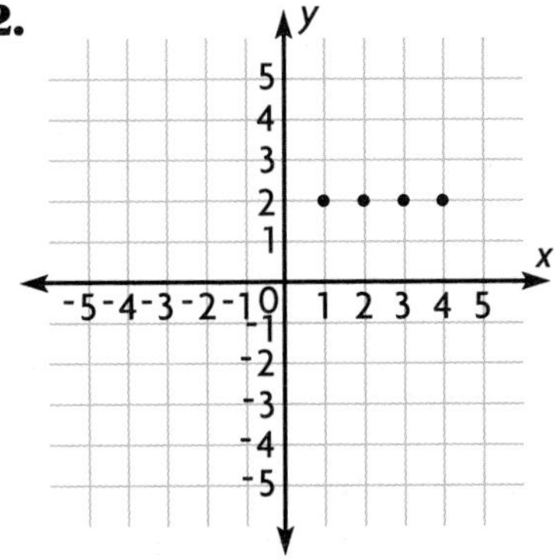

3.

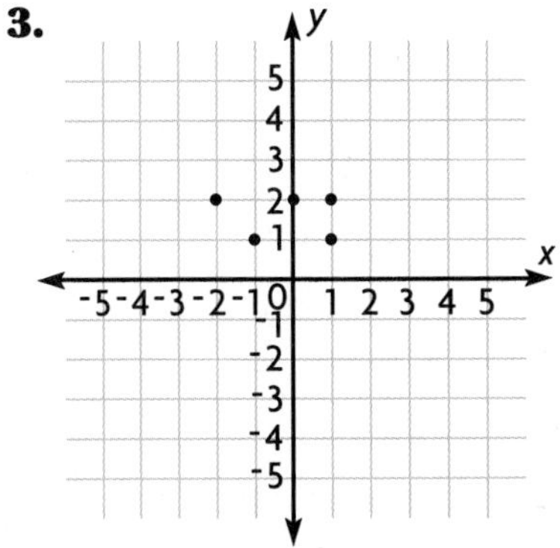

Write the ordered pairs for the relation. Then graph the set of ordered pairs. Tell whether the relation is a function or not.

4.

x	3	2	1	0
y	9	4	1	0

5.

x	1	1	1	1	1
y	$^{-}1$	0	1	2	3

Problem-Solving Applications

6. **CRITICAL THINKING** Which describes a function?

a. {movies, show times}

b. {temperature in degrees Celsius, temperature in degrees Fahrenheit}

7. **SCIENCE** The equation $F = 1.8C + 32$ can be used to change degrees Celsius to degrees Fahrenheit. Does the equation represent a function? Show 3 ordered pairs.

8. **WRITE ABOUT IT** How can you tell whether the graph of a relation represents a function?

Mixed Review and Test Prep

On a coordinate plane, graph the point for each ordered pair.

9. $B\,(3,2)$ **10.** $D\,(5,8)$ **11.** $L\,(3,5)$ **12.** $A\,(7,0)$ **13.** $C\,(0,6)$

For the value, tell if the sentence is an *equation* or an *inequality*.

14. Let $s = 7$. $s + 9$ ● 12 **15.** Let $r = {}^{-}4$. $8r$ ● $^{-}32$ **16.** Let $n = 3.5$. $4n - 2$ ● 12

17. **ALGEBRA** April earned \$20. Tom earned twice that amount. Which equation can be used to find how much Tom earned?

A $2t = 20$ **B** $t = 20 - 2$

C $t = 2 \times 20$ **D** $t = 20 \div 2$

18. **NUMBER SENSE** How is 3,400,000 expressed in scientific notation?

F 3.4×10^6 **G** 34×10^5

H 34×10^6 **J** 3.4×10^5

MORE PRACTICE Lesson 9.3, page H56

LAB ACTIVITY

What You'll Explore
How to look for patterns in the graphs of functions

What You'll Need
unit cubes or paper squares, graph paper

GEOMETRY CONNECTION

Patterns in Functions

You can learn about special functions by looking at patterns.

Explore

The model at the right shows Stage 1 to Stage 3 of a pattern.

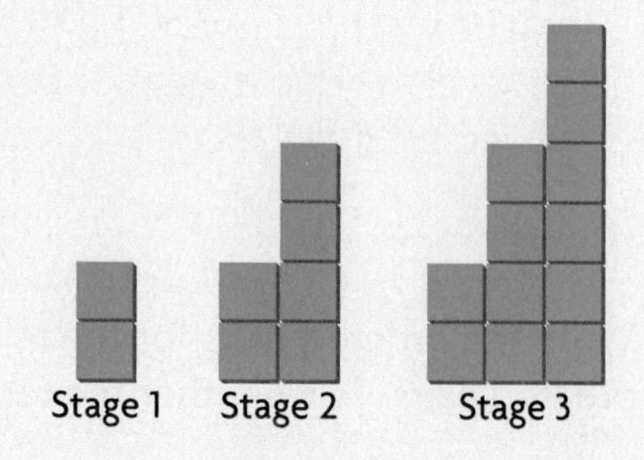

- Use unit cubes or paper squares to build Stages 4, 5, and 6 of the pattern.
- Record each stage and the perimeter of each figure in a table.
- Write the ordered pairs (x,y) from the table. Draw a coordinate plane on your graph paper. Then graph points for the pairs.

Stage, x	Perimeter, y
1	6
2	12
3	?

Technology Link

You can practice finding patterns in functions by using E-Lab, Activity 9.

Available on CD-ROM and on the Internet at **www.hbschool.com/elab**

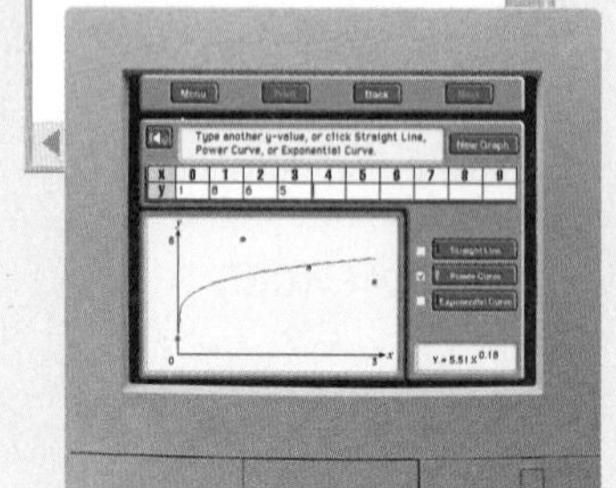

Think and Discuss

- What pattern do you see in the y-values of the ordered pairs?
- What pattern do you see in the points you graphed?
- Write a formula to show the relationship between each stage and the perimeter.
- Name the ordered pair for Stage 8.

Try This

- Make a table that shows the stage, x, and the perimeter, y, of each figure.
- Write a formula to find the perimeter. Graph the ordered pairs (x, y).
- What pattern do you see in the graph? How is this pattern similar to the one in Explore?

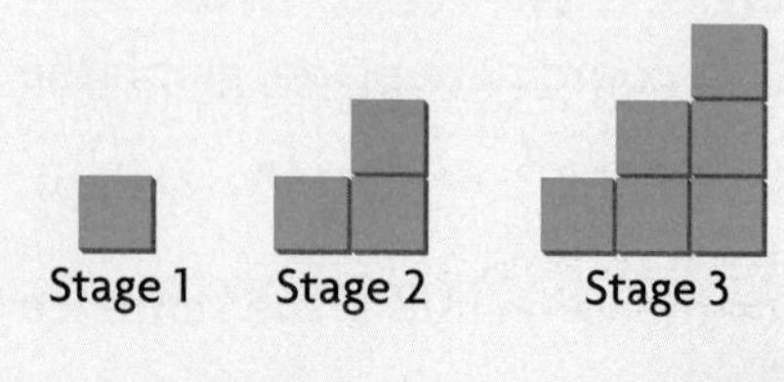

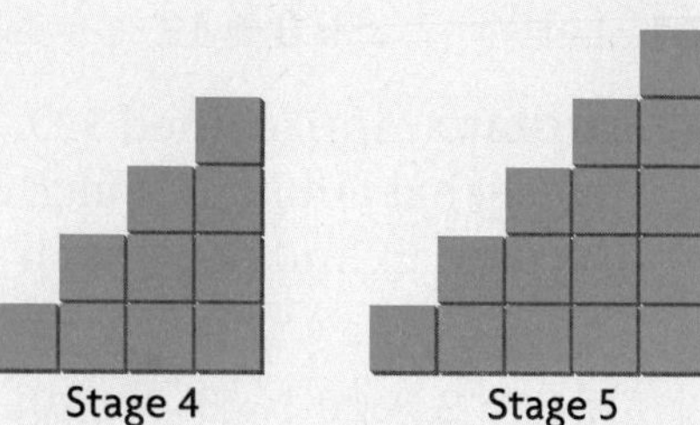

Linear Equations

LESSON 9.4

What You'll Learn
To solve and graph linear equations

Why Learn This?
To identify linear relationships between things such as distance traveled and traveling time

VOCABULARY
linear equation

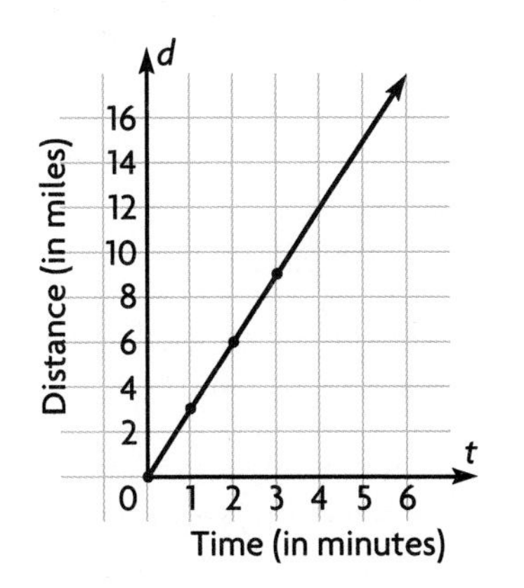

When you graph the ordered pairs of some functions, they form a straight line. The equations that express these functions are called **linear equations**. The linear equation for the graph at the right is $d = 3t$. Since the time can be any value greater than or equal to 0, the domain is $t \geq 0$.

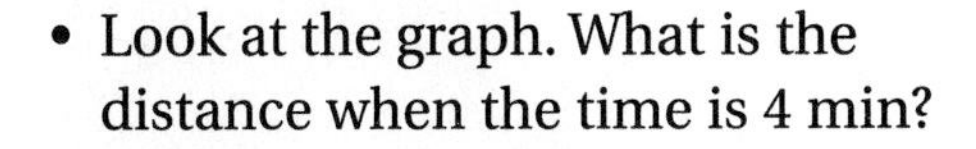

- Look at the graph. What is the distance when the time is 4 min?

Notice that the equation $d = 3t$ has two variables, d and t. You can use any two variables in a linear equation. In algebra, you often use x and y.

To find solutions to an equation with two variables, you first choose a replacement value for one variable and then find the value of the other variable.

EXAMPLE 1 Find solutions of the equation $d = 3t$.

Make a table of values. Choose values for t, and then find values for d.

Write these solutions as ordered pairs.

t	$3t$	d	(t,d)
1	$3 \cdot 1$	3	(1,3)
2	$3 \cdot 2$	6	(2,6)
3	$3 \cdot 3$	9	(3,9)
4.5	$3 \cdot 4.5$	13.5	(4.5,13.5)

- Find two other ordered pairs that are solutions of $d = 3t$.

You can test an ordered pair to determine whether it is a solution of a given equation.

EXAMPLE 2 Determine whether (8,16) is a solution of $y = 2x$.

$y = 2x$ *Replace x with 8 and y with 16.*

$16 \stackrel{?}{=} 2 \cdot 8$

$16 = 16$ ✓ So, (8,16) is a solution.

REMEMBER:

To check the **solution** of an equation, replace each variable with a value and perform the operations.

See page 146.

$x + 3 = 9,\ x = 6$

$6 + 3 = 9$

$9 = 9$ ✓

Most linear equations have an infinite number of solutions. You can use a graph to show some of the solutions.

EXAMPLE 3 Graph the equation $y = 2x + 1$.

Make a table of values.

x	$2x + 1$	y
$^{-}3$	$(2 \cdot {}^{-}3) + 1$	$^{-}5$
$^{-}1$	$(2 \cdot {}^{-}1) + 1$	$^{-}1$
0	$(2 \cdot 0) + 1$	1
1	$(2 \cdot 1) + 1$	3
3	$(2 \cdot 3) + 1$	7

Write your solutions as ordered pairs.

$(^{-}3,{}^{-}5)$, $(^{-}1,{}^{-}1)$, $(0,1)$, $(1,3)$, $(3,7)$

Graph points for these ordered pairs. When there are no restrictions on the variable x, you can show all solutions by drawing a line through these points.

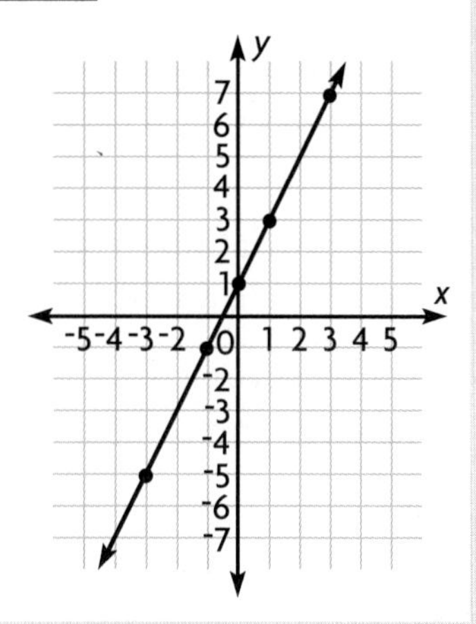

- Look at the graph. Name two other ordered pairs that are solutions to $y = 2x + 1$.

GUIDED PRACTICE

Copy and complete each table of values.

1. $y = {}^{-}4x$

x	$^{-}4x$	y
$^{-}2$	$^{-}4 \cdot {}^{-}2$	?
$^{-}1$	$^{-}4 \cdot {}^{-}1$	?
0	$^{-}4 \cdot 0$	?
1	?	?

2. $y = 2x - 1$

x	$2x - 1$	y
0	$(2 \cdot 0) - 1$	?
0.5	$(2 \cdot 0.5) - 1$	?
?	?	1
?	$(2 \cdot 1.5) - 1$	?
?	$(2 \cdot 2) - 1$	?

Determine whether the ordered pair is a solution of $y = 3x - 6$. Write *yes* or *no*.

3. $(^{-}1,{}^{-}9)$ **4.** $(2,5)$ **5.** $(2,0)$ **6.** $(0,{}^{-}6)$

7. $(4,6)$ **8.** $(^{-}2,12)$ **9.** $(1,1)$ **10.** $(1,{}^{-}3)$

Technology Link

In ***Data ToolKit*** you can practice making a coordinate plane graph by using a table of values.

TEEN TIMES

NASCAR racing is a rapidly growing spectator sport in the United States. But its growth probably can't compare with the speed of the race cars themselves. The average 500-mile race takes about 3 hours and 20 minutes. That means the race cars are traveling at approximately 150 mph and are going 2.5 miles a minute.

Calculator Activities, page H41

INDEPENDENT PRACTICE

For each equation, replace *x* with 4. Write the solution as an ordered pair.

1. $y = x - 1$ **2.** $x + 4 = y$ **3.** $y = 6x$ **4.** $\frac{1}{4}x = y$

5. $y = x + 2$ **6.** $y = x + 12$ **7.** $y = {}^{-}3x$ **8.** $y = {}^{-}x$

Make a table of values for each equation. Write the ordered pairs.

9. $y = x + 6$ **10.** $y = x - 4$ **11.** $y = 3x$ **12.** $y = x - 3$

13. $y = 2x + 5$ **14.** $y = {}^{-}3x - 2$ **15.** $y = 4x + 3$ **16.** $y = {}^{-}4x$

Write the equation for each table of values.

17.

x	*y*
1	3
2	6
5	15

18.

x	*y*
⁻2	0
1	3
4	6

19.

x	*y*
⁻4	⁻2
2	1
10	5

Graph each equation by making a table of values. Use at least three ordered pairs.

20. $y = 2x + 3$ **21.** $y = x$ **22.** $y = 3x + 6$ **23.** $y = {}^{-}2x - 1$

24. $y = {}^{-}2x$ **25.** $y = x + 2$ **26.** $y = x - 1$ **27.** $y = 4x + 2$

Problem-Solving Applications

28. The amount of time Nina spends on her homework is 2 hours more than the amount of time she spends on her paper route. Write an equation to show the relationship of the two activities. Show three possible solutions to the equation.

29. **SCIENCE** At the beginning of an experiment, the temperature of a liquid is 20°C. The temperature increases 2° each minute.

a. Make a table of values to show minutes and temperature for 0 to 5 minutes.

b. Write a linear equation for the function.

c. Graph the equation.

30. **CRITICAL THINKING** Write a problem that involves the linear relationship between time and distance.

31. **WRITE ABOUT IT** How many solutions (ordered pairs) does any linear equation have?

In ***Mighty Math, Astro Algebra*** you can graph more linear equations in the mission *Sparky Takes Off* in the *Grapher.* Use Grow Slide Level Blue G.

CHAPTER 9 Review/Test

1. **VOCABULARY** Two perpendicular lines known as the x-axis and y-axis form a(n) __?__. (page 176)

2. **VOCABULARY** A coordinate plane is divided into four __?__. (page 176)

Write the ordered pair or letter for each point. (pages 176–177)

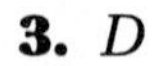

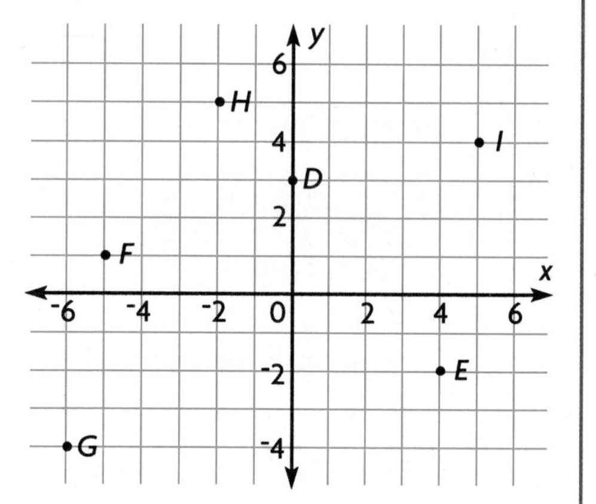

3. D
4. E
5. F
6. (5,4)
7. $(^-2,5)$
8. $(^-6,^-4)$

9. **VOCABULARY** A(n) __?__ is formed when you match the elements of one set to the elements of another set. (page 178)

10. **VOCABULARY** A(n) __?__ is a relation in which each element of the domain corresponds to one and only one element of the range. (page 181)

For Exercises 11–14, use this relation. (pages 178–180)

$\{(^-1,^-3), (0,0), (1,3), (2,6), (3,9), (4,12)\}$

11. Name the domain.
12. Name the range.
13. Make a mapping diagram.
14. Write an equation for the relation.

Is the relation a function? Write *yes* or *no*. If you write *no*, explain. (pages 181–183)

15. $\{(2,5), (3,6), (4,7), (5,8)\}$
16. $\{(0,0), (0,1), (1,0), (1,1)\}$
17. $\{(1,2), (2,3), (3,4), (4,5)\}$
18. $\{(4,^-1), (2,^-1), (3,3), (5,5)\}$

Make a table of values for each equation. Use at least three ordered pairs. (pages 185–187)

19. $y = 2x$
20. $y = x - 4$
21. $y = x + {}^-3$
22. $y = 3x + 1$

Graph each equation. (pages 185–187)

23. $y = x + 4$
24. $y = x - 5$
25. $y = 4x$

Test Prep

CUMULATIVE
CHAPTERS 1–9

1. Which percent is equivalent to 0.6?

A 0.6%
B 6%
C 60%
D 600%

2. Which can be expressed as 2^5?

F 5×5
G $2 \times 2 \times 2 \times 2$
H 2×2
J $2 \times 2 \times 2 \times 2 \times 2$

3. The Coast Guard is searching for a ship lost in the Gulf of Mexico. The area of the square search pattern is 6,400 square miles. What is the length of a side of the search pattern?

A 8 mi
B 80 mi
C 240 mi
D 800 mi

4. What is the value of $3^2 + 6 \times 8$?

F 21
G 54
H 57
J 120
K 432

5. A recipe for pumpkin cookies requires $1\frac{3}{4}$ cups of pumpkin. Shana wants to triple the recipe. How much pumpkin does she need?

A $5\frac{1}{4}$ c

B $4\frac{3}{4}$ c

C $1\frac{5}{7}$ c

D $1\frac{1}{4}$ c

E Not Here

6. Mario earns $5.75 per hour. Last week he worked 19.5 hrs. Which is the best estimate of his earnings?

F $1,100 **G** $190
H $120 **J** $30

7. Tyrone bought 8 cans of tuna for $7.12. What equation can be used to find t, the cost of one can of tuna?

A $t = \frac{8}{7.12}$

B $t = 12 \times 8$
C $t = 7.12 - 8$
D $t = 8 + 7.12$
E Not Here

8. Laura wants to purchase a TV that costs $1,050. She has $600. Which equation could she use to find m, the amount of money she needs to save during each of the next 6 months?

F $6m - 600 = 1{,}050$
G $6m = 1{,}050$
H $6m + 600 = 1{,}050$
J $\frac{1{,}050}{600} = m$

9.

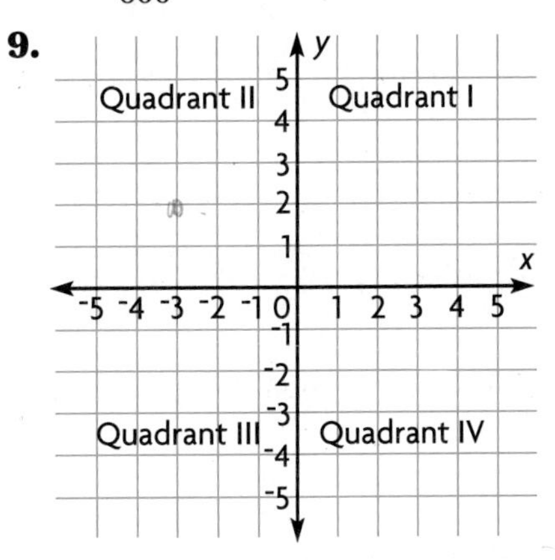

In which quadrant is (⁻3,2) located?

A Quadrant I **B** Quadrant II
C Quadrant III **D** Quadrant IV

CHAPTERS 6–9

MATH FUN!

What an Expression!

PURPOSE To practice writing expressions (pages 124–125)

Numbers are a big part of our daily lives. Below are some examples of numbers used in phrases or in movie and television titles. Find ten other common phrases or titles that use numbers.

Share your list of phrases or titles with your family. Then have members of your family share others that they know.

Phrases	Movies and Television Programs
nine lives	*Apollo 13*
three-dimensional	*Beverly Hills 90210*
911	*Star Trek: Deep Space Nine*

SIMPLY SOLVE IT

PURPOSE To practice writing equations to solve one-step problems (pages 145–149)

YOU WILL NEED paper, pencil, scissors, newspaper, glue or tape

Cut out five to ten examples of percents, decimals, and integers from the newspaper. Tape or glue them to a sheet of paper. Use the information to write your own problem that can be represented by an addition, subtraction, multiplication, or division equation. Next to each problem, write the equation needed to solve it.

USING COMPARISONS

PURPOSE To practice solving inequalities (pages 170–171)

YOU WILL NEED number cubes

Play with a partner, alternating turns. Roll two number cubes. Use the sum and product of the numbers showing to form this inequality:

$$x + \text{sum} < \text{product}$$

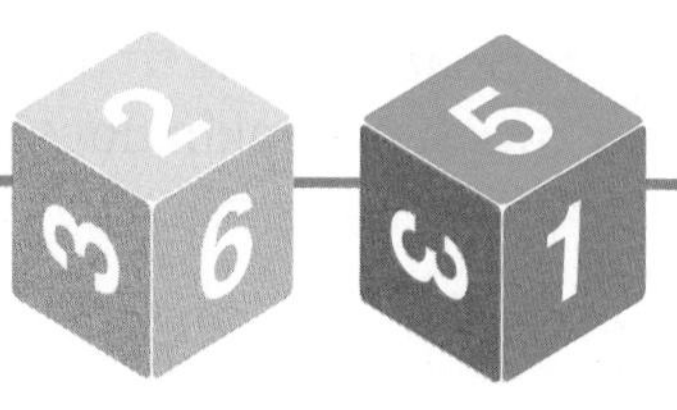

$$x + 7 < 10$$

Test each of the numbers in the inequality. If a number makes the inequality true, you score a point. The first player to reach 15 points is the winner.

Graphing More Than One Equation

Graphing calculators are powerful handheld tools that allow students, business people, and engineers to look at a set of data in a graph. You could use graph paper to graph an equation. But in this activity you will see how much easier and quicker it is to use a graphing calculator.

Look at the *TI-82* graphing calculator displays below. The first display shows the graph of the equation $y = x$. The second display shows the graph of the equations $y = x + 2$, $y = x$, and $y = x - 2$.

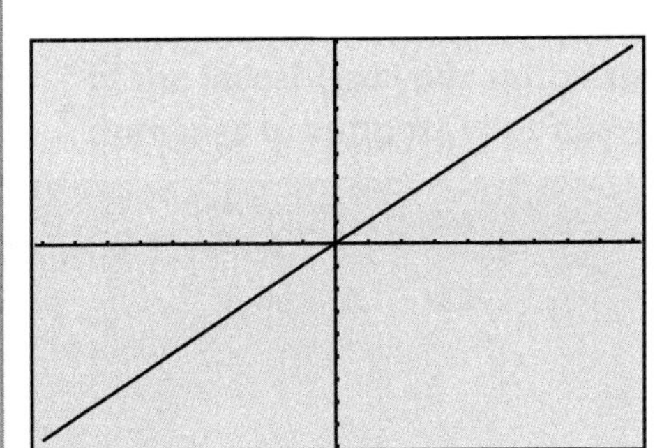

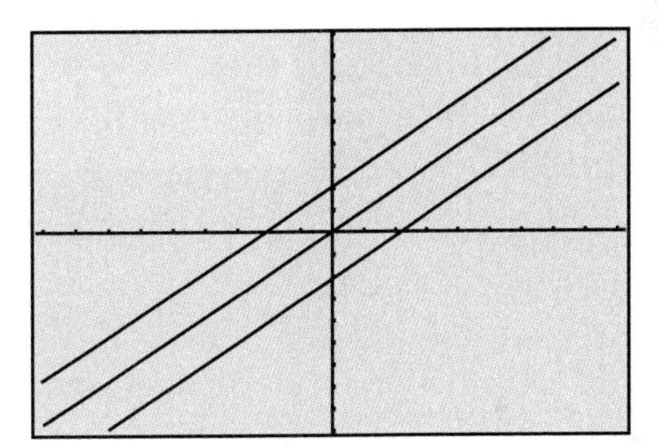

1. At what point does the first graph cross the y-axis?

2. At what points do the two new graphs cross the y-axis?

3. How are the graphs similar? How are they different?

4. What is the purpose of the X,T,Θ key on the calculator?

USING THE CALCULATOR

Graph the following equations on one screen.

$y = 2x \qquad y = 2x + 5 \qquad y = 2x - 7$

5. How are these graphs similar?

6. How are these graphs different?

7. Write an equation that is similar to the equations above. Then graph the equation on your calculator.

CHAPTERS 6–9

Study Guide and Review

Vocabulary Check

1. Two or more terms with the same variable raised to the same power are called __?__. (page 130)
2. An equation that states that two ratios are equivalent is called a(n) __?__. (page 152)
3. A number sentence that shows the relationship between two quantities that are not equal is a(n) __?__. (page 167)
4. When you match the elements of one set to the elements of another set, you form a(n) __?__. (page 178)

EXAMPLES

- **Write expressions to describe sequences.** (pages 134–137)

Write an expression to describe the sequence. Then use the expression to find the tenth term. 9, 12, 15, 18, . . .

common difference: 3
expression: $3n + 6$
tenth term: 36

EXERCISES

Write an expression to find any term. Use the expression to find the seventh term.

5. 15, 19, 23, 27, . . .
6. 0, 5, 10, 15, . . .
7. 8, 10, 12, 14, . . .
8. 11, 17, 23, 29, . . .
9. 8, 6, 4, 2, . . .
10. 1, 2.5, 4, 5.5, . . .
11. 7.5, 5, 2.5, 0, . . .
12. $^-12, ^-10, ^-8, ^-6, \ldots$

EXAMPLES

- **Solve addition, subtraction, multiplication, and division equations.** (pages 145–149)

$\frac{x}{8} = {}^-3$

$8 \times \frac{x}{8} = {}^-3 \times 8$ *Multiply each side by 8.*

$x = {}^-24$

EXERCISES

Solve.

13. $z - 0.6 = 3$
14. $22\frac{1}{2} = n + 6\frac{1}{2}$
15. $9.8 = 0.4a$
16. $\frac{b}{^-40} = 8$

EXAMPLES

- **Write and solve proportions.** (pages 152–155)

$\frac{c}{6} = \frac{5}{10}$

$6 \times 5 = 10 \times c$ *Write the cross products.*

$30 = 10c$ *Multiply.*

$\frac{30}{10} = \frac{10c}{10}$ *Divide to solve the equation.*

$3 = c$

EXERCISES

Solve each proportion.

17. $\frac{9.1}{y} = \frac{7}{3}$
18. $\frac{3}{4} = \frac{z}{20}$
19. $\frac{x}{4.5} = \frac{4}{6}$
20. $\frac{2}{3} = \frac{5}{w}$
21. $\frac{1.8}{e} = \frac{6}{5}$
22. $\frac{n}{10} = \frac{7}{8}$

- **Solve inequalities.** (pages 170–171)

Solve the inequality. Graph the solution.

$3x - 1 < {}^-7$

$3x - 1 + 1 < {}^-7 + 1$ *Add 1 to each side.*

$3x < {}^-6$

$\frac{3x}{3} < \frac{{}^-6}{3}$ *Divide each side by 3.*

$x < {}^-2$

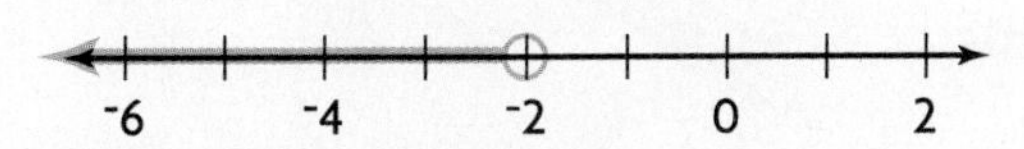

Solve the equation or inequality. Graph the solution.

23. $x + 4 \leq 12$

24. $2y > 8^2$

25. $3z - 4 \neq 11$

26. $a - 5.45 = 4.55$

27. $\frac{m}{3} \geq {}^-1$

28. $4a < 2^4$

- **Solve and graph linear equations.** (pages 185–187)

Graph the equation $y = x - 2$.

x	$x - 2$	y
$^-2$	$^-2 - 2$	$^-4$
2	$2 - 2$	0
4	$4 - 2$	2

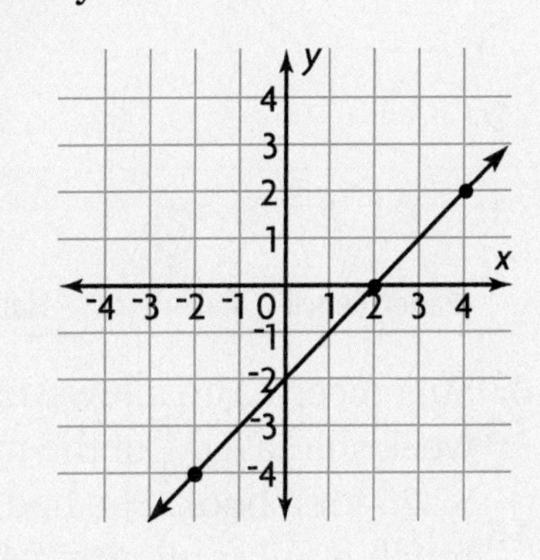

Make a table of values for each equation. Write three ordered pairs.

29. $y = 2x + 4$

30. $y = {}^-3x + 1$

Graph each equation.

31. $y = {}^-2x - 1$

32. $y = x + 2$

Problem-Solving Applications

Solve. Explain your method.

33. Thomas has 5 less than 3 times the number of books Sarah has. If Thomas has 25 books, how many does Sarah have? (pages 162–163)

34. The total cost of a dinner is shared equally by 4 people. Each person pays \$8.65. What is the total cost of the dinner? (pages 148–149)

35. It takes Abe 60 min to drive 45 mi to work. At the same rate, how long would it take Abe to drive 30 mi? (pages 152–155)

36. Marie has \$125 to spend on shoes and a jacket. She plans to spend \$35 more on the jacket than on shoes. What is the most Marie plans to spend on shoes? (pages 170–171)

CHAPTERS 6–9

Performance Assessment

Tasks: Show What You Know

1. Combine like terms $2(3n - 6) + 4$. Then explain how to evaluate the expression for $n = 3$ and give the value. (pages 131–133)

2. Write an equation for this word sentence: $12 less than the price of the CD player equals $195. Then tell what the variable represents. (pages 142–143)

3. Solve and graph the inequality $n - 2 < 3$. Explain each step. (pages 170–171)

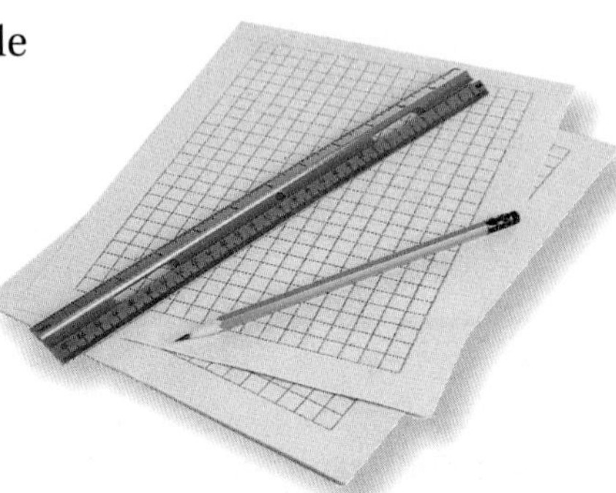

4. Make a mapping diagram and write an equation for this relation. Explain each step of your work.
$\{(2,^-4), (1,^-2), (0,0), (^-1,2), (^-2,4)\}$
(pages 178–180)

Problem Solving

Solve. Explain your method.

CHOOSE a strategy and a tool.

- Find a Pattern
- Write an Equation
- Draw a Picture
- Act It Out
- Make a Model
- Work Backward

Paper/Pencil

Calculator

Hands-On

Mental Math

5. Joe is training for a 100-mi bike race. He rode 20 mi the first day, 36 mi the second day, 52 mi the third day, and 68 mi the fourth day. Write an expression that describes Joe's pattern. On what day will he ride 100 mi? (pages 134–137)

6. Suki receives an allowance each week. Last week she saved $\frac{1}{4}$ of the money and spent $2.25 for a book. She had $0.75 left. How much is Suki's allowance? (pages 150–151)

7. This week Alma earned $3.40 less than twice the amount she earned last week. This week she earned $33.50. How much did she earn last week? (pages 162–163)

8. Each school night, Leon spends twice as much time doing homework as watching television. Write an equation for the relationship between the activities. How many hours does Leon spend watching television on a school night if he spends 3 hr doing homework? (pages 178–180)

Cumulative Review

CHAPTERS 1–9

Solve the problem. Then write the letter of the correct answer.

1. A(n) __?__ is any number that can be expressed as a ratio in the fraction form $\frac{a}{b}$, where a and b are integers and $b \neq 0$. (pages 16–19)

A. counting number **B.** integer
C. rational number **D.** whole number

2. What is the central angle measure for 40% of a circle graph? (pages 30–31)

A. 40° **B.** 72°
C. 144° **D.** 14,400°

3. What is the value of 10101_{two}? (pages 40–42)

A. 6 **B.** 10
C. 13 **D.** not here

4. Sid needs 196 ft^2 of carpet to cover his square bedroom floor. What is the length of one of the sides of the bedroom? (pages 46–47)

A. 14 ft **B.** 49 ft
C. 98 ft **D.** 38,416 ft

5. Find the value. (pages 73–75)
$5 + 4^2 \times (4.6 - 2.5)$

A. 21.8 **B.** 38.6
C. 44.1 **D.** not here

6. Subtract. Write the answer in simplest form. (pages 82–83)

$4\frac{1}{6} - 2\frac{2}{3}$

A. $1\frac{1}{6}$ **B.** $1\frac{1}{2}$

C. $2\frac{1}{3}$ **D.** $2\frac{3}{6}$

7. Find the sum. (pages 99–101)

$^-3 + 7$

A. $^-4$ **B.** 4
C. 10 **D.** 21

8. Find the difference. (pages 103–105)

$31 - {}^-21$

A. $^-52$ **B.** $^-10$
C. 10 **D.** 52

9. Find the quotient. (pages 106–108)

$366 \div {}^-6$

A. $^-61$ **B.** 61
C. 360 **D.** 2,196

10. Evaluate the expression for $x = 5$. (pages 126–129)
$4x - 7x + 9$

A. $^-24$ **B.** $^-6$
C. 6 **D.** not here

11. Solve. $\frac{x}{^-60} = 5$ (pages 148–149)

A. $x = {}^-300$ **B.** $x = {}^-12$
C. $x = 12$ **D.** $x = 300$

12. Solve. $x + 2x - 6 = {}^-24$ (pages 164–166)

A. $x = {}^-6$ **B.** $x = 6$
C. $x = 10$ **D.** not here

13. Which equation describes the relation? (pages 178–180)
$\{(^-3,^-9), (^-2,^-6), (^-1,^-3), (0,0), (1,3), (2,6)\}$

A. $x = {}^-3y$ **B.** $y = {}^-3x$
C. $x = 3y$ **D.** $y = 3x$

14. Which is a solution of $y = x - 4$? (pages 185–187)

A. (2, 2) **B.** $(3, {}^-1)$
C. (0, 4) **D.** $(^-1, 3)$

CHAPTER

10

CONGRUENCE, SYMMETRY, AND TRANSFORMATIONS

LOOK AHEAD

In this chapter you will solve problems that involve

- congruent plane figures
- congruent line segments and angles
- line and rotational symmetry
- translations, reflections, and rotations

Jigsaw puzzles come in many shapes and forms, ranging from simple 5-piece puzzles to more complex two-sided and three-dimensional puzzles. The world's largest jigsaw puzzle was assembled on July 8, 1992, in France. It was 51,484 ft² and contained 43,924 pieces.

- How many square inches was the largest puzzle?
- What was the average size of a puzzle piece?

Problem-Solving Project

It's Puzzling!

The jigsaw puzzle below is made up of two different shapes. Using these two shapes, design a new puzzle. Draw your puzzle on paper, with no gaps or overlaps. Using the paper patterns, draw your puzzle on poster board. Color it, add a design, and then carefully cut so that each piece still fits. Put all the pieces in an envelope. Exchange puzzles and solve.

PROJECT CHECKLIST

- ✓ Did you design a puzzle and draw it on paper?
- ✓ Did you draw the puzzle on poster board and color it?
- ✓ Did you add a design and cut it out?
- ✓ Did you solve another person's puzzle?

ACTIVITY

What You'll Explore
How to divide a shape into congruent parts

What You'll Need
graph paper, scissors

VOCABULARY
congruent

Congruent Plane Figures

Geometric figures are **congruent** when they have the same size and shape. To see whether figures are congruent, just move them to see if they match or coincide.

Explore

Use 4×4 square grids.

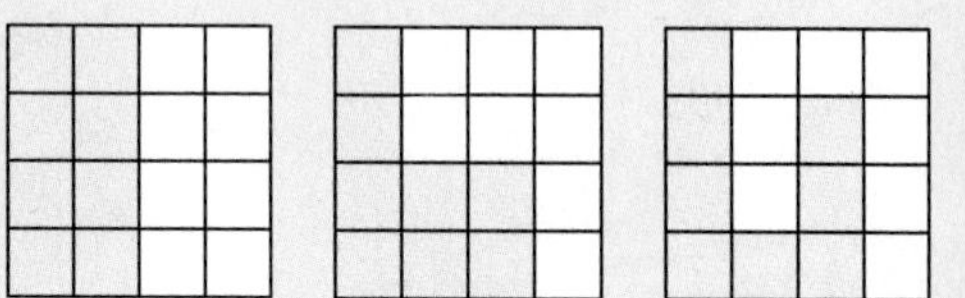

- Shade three grids as shown.
- Cut each square into two pieces, the shaded and unshaded parts.
- What fractional part of the square does each piece represent?

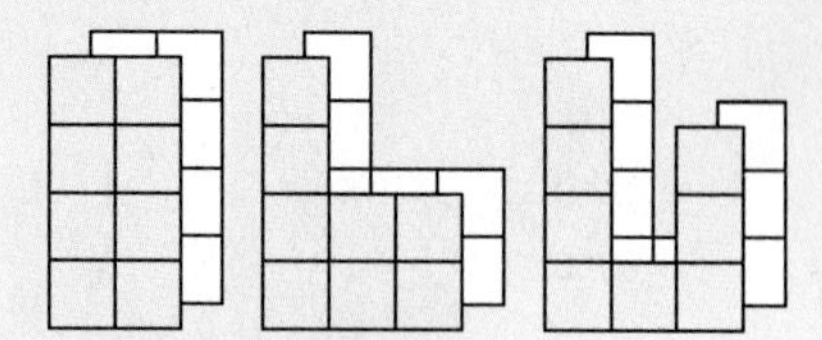

- Move the two pieces of each square so that they match or coincide.
- Are the two pieces of each square congruent?
- There are three more ways that the 4×4 squares can be cut into congruent halves by cutting on the grid lines. See if you can find them all. Remember to look for different shapes.

Think and Discuss

- Why are the figures you cut from each grid congruent?
- How can you tell whether any two figures are congruent? Explain.
- Does the position of a figure affect whether it is congruent to another figure? Explain.

Technology Link

You can make congruent shapes by using E-Lab, Activity 10. Available on CD-ROM and on the Internet at **www.hbschool.com/elab**

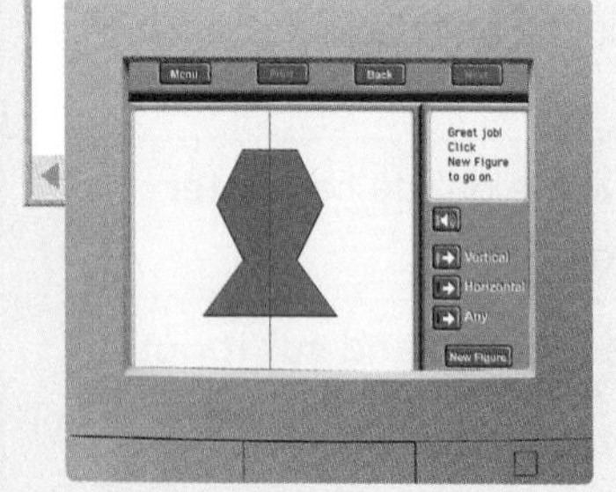

Try This

Study the figures carefully. Visualize whether a figure could be moved to match another figure. Identify the congruent figures.

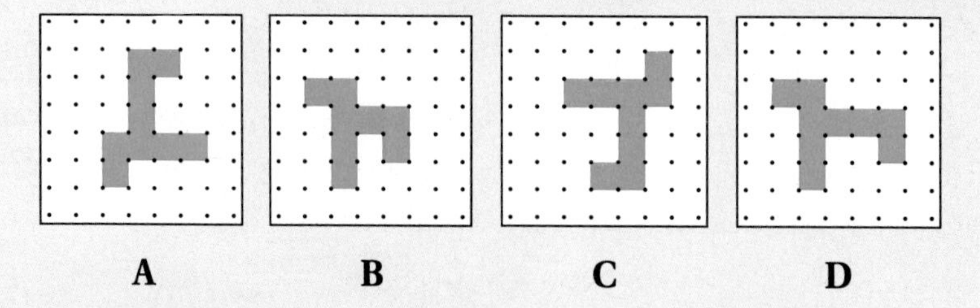

Congruent Line Segments and Angles

LESSON 10.1

What You'll Learn
How to identify congruent line segments and angles

Why Learn This?
To match lengths of segments and measures of angles when sawing a board or making a design such as a quilt or a scale drawing

VOCABULARY

complementary angles
supplementary angles
adjacent angles
vertical angles
equilateral triangle
equiangular triangle

Look at the photo of the Olympic stadium. Where did the builders use congruent line segments and angles?

Two line segments are congruent when they have the same length. Lengths can be measured by using a ruler.

Two angles that contain the same number of degrees are congruent. Angles can be measured by using a protractor.

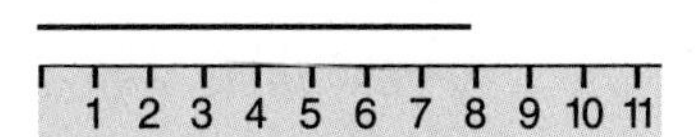

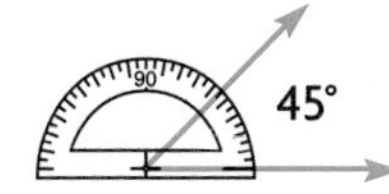

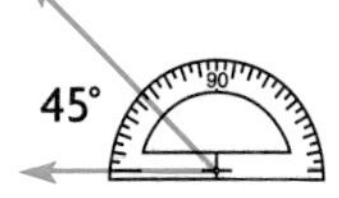

You can use dot paper to compare the measures of line segments and angles.

ACTIVITY **WHAT YOU'LL NEED:** dot paper, protractor, ruler

- Copy the line segments and angles on dot paper.
- Explain how you can show that segments *AB* and *CD* are congruent without using a ruler to measure. (HINT: Try counting spaces.)

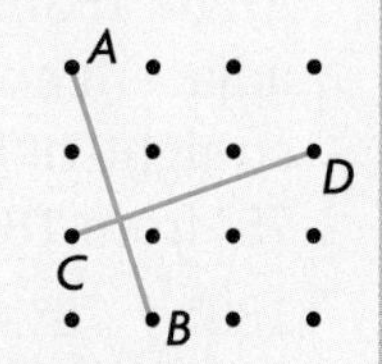

- Explain how you can use dot paper to determine whether the angles are congruent without using a protractor. (HINT: Compare the places where the rays intersect the dots.)

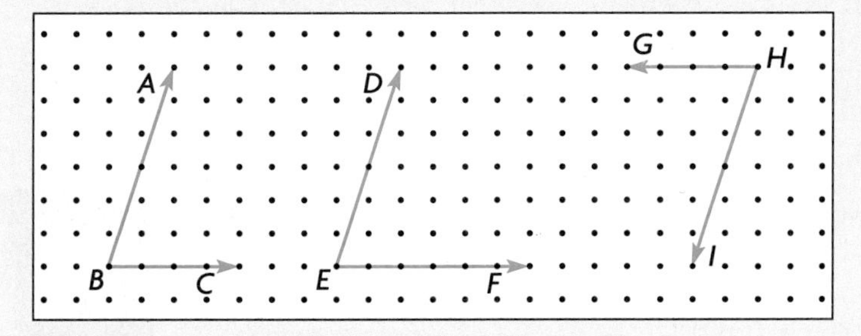

- Describe to a classmate how you compared the line segments and the angles on dot paper. Did you compare the line segments and angles differently? Explain.

Angle pairs that occur in geometry are given special names.

Complementary angles are two angles whose sum equals 90°.

complementary angles: $\angle EBC$ and $\angle DBE$

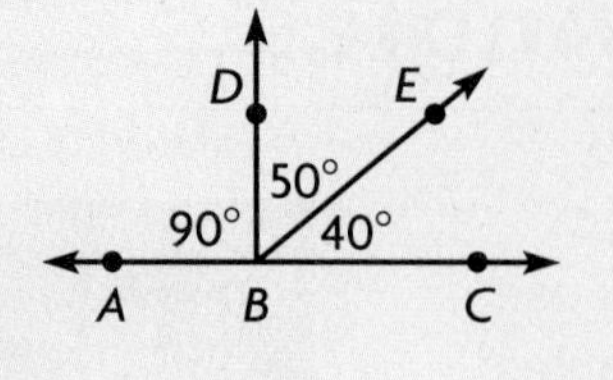

Supplementary angles are two angles whose sum equals 180°.

supplementary angles: $\angle EBC$ and $\angle ABE$ or $\angle ABD$ and $\angle DBC$

Adjacent angles have the same vertex and are side-by-side.

adjacent angles: $\angle 1$ and $\angle 2$, $\angle 2$ and $\angle 3$, $\angle 3$ and $\angle 4$, $\angle 4$ and $\angle 1$

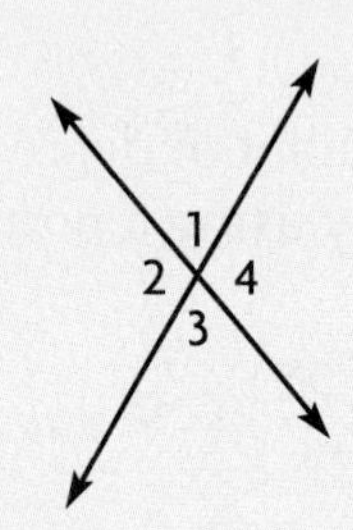

Vertical angles are opposite angles formed when two lines intersect. Vertical angles are always congruent.

vertical angles: $\angle 1$ and $\angle 3$, $\angle 2$ and $\angle 4$

REMEMBER:

The measure of a straight angle is equal to 180°. Adjacent angles have a common vertex and a common side. Adjacent angles that form a straight angle have a total measure of 180°. **See page H22.**

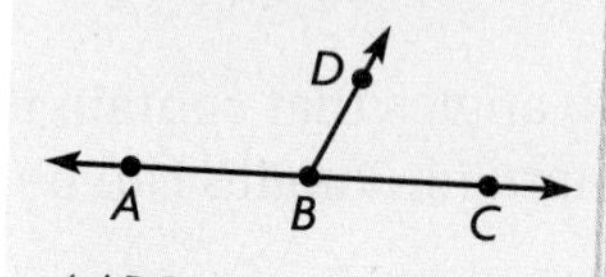

$\angle ABC$ is a **straight angle**. You can write $m\angle ABC = 180°$.
See page H22.

EXAMPLE 1 In the figure above, suppose $m\angle 2 = 75°$. What is $m\angle 4$? What is $m\angle 1$?

Angle 4: Since $\angle 2$ and $\angle 4$ are vertical angles, they are congruent.

$m\angle 2 = m\angle 4$
$m\angle 2 = 75°$

So, $m\angle 4 = 75°$.

Angle 1: Since $\angle 1$ and $\angle 2$ are adjacent angles and form a straight 180° angle, subtract 75° from 180°.

$180° - 75° = 105°$

So, $m\angle 1 = 105°$.

- Suppose $m\angle 4 = 100°$. What is $m\angle 2$? $m\angle 3$?

TEEN TIMES

Pinball machines are tilted at an angle called a *pitch*. The pitch is usually 6° to 7°. The pitch determines the speed of the ball. If the pitch is too great, the ball will roll too fast. If the pitch is too small, the ball will roll too slowly, making the game too easy.

GUIDED PRACTICE

Use the figure at the right for Exercises 1–3.

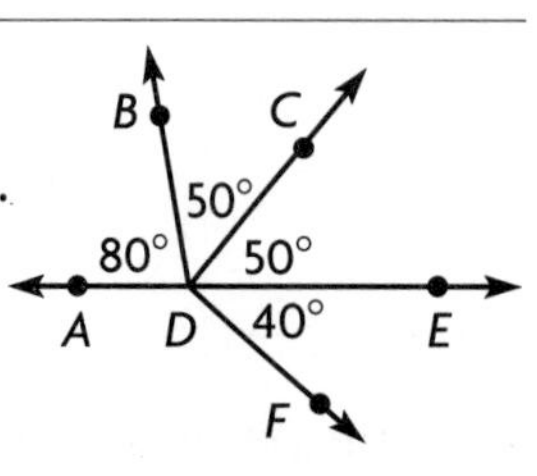

1. Name two pairs of complementary angles.
2. Complete: $\angle ADF$ and $\angle FDE$ are adjacent angles and __?__ angles.
3. Name two pairs of adjacent angles.
4. Sketch intersecting lines that form one pair of vertical angles that are about 60° each.

Using Congruent Segments and Angles

Congruent line segments and congruent angles occur in many geometric figures. One example is the equilateral triangle. When a triangle has three congruent sides, it is an **equilateral triangle**. When a triangle has three congruent 60° angles, it is an **equiangular triangle**.

- Why is triangle *ABC* an equilateral triangle? Why is triangle *DEF* equiangular?

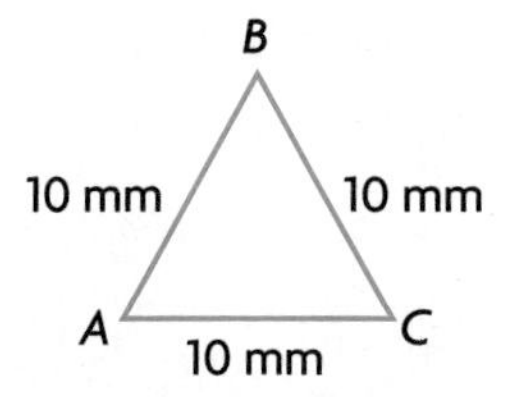

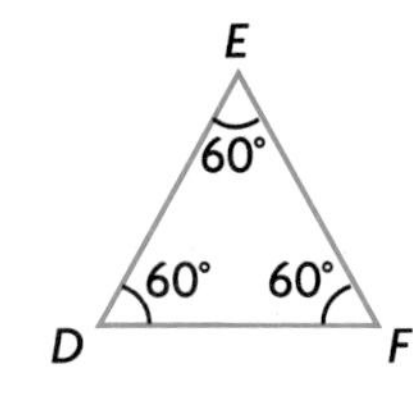

Equilateral triangles are also equiangular.

The legs and the base angles of isosceles triangles are congruent. In the triangle at the right, the legs each measure 1.5 cm and the base angles each measure 45°.

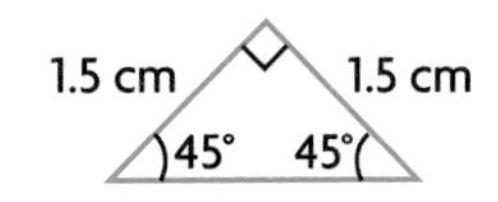

You can use what you know about congruence to solve problems with isosceles triangles.

EXAMPLE 2 Triangle *ABC* is an isosceles triangle. $m\angle CAB = 65°$. Find $m\angle ABC$ and $m\angle ACB$.

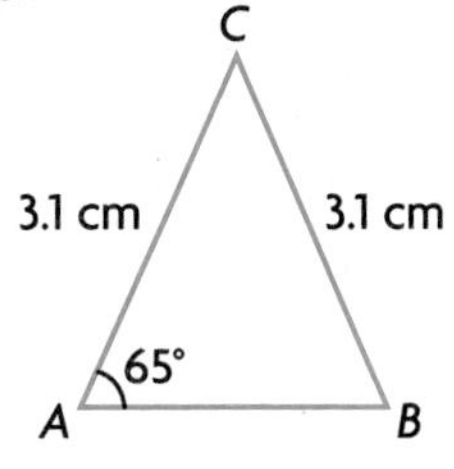

Solve the problem by *working backward* from something you know to find what you do not know. The measure of $\angle ABC$ is 65°, since the base angles of an isosceles triangle are congruent.

To find the measure of ∠ACB, subtract the sum of the measures of the two base angles from 180°.

$$180° - (65° + 65°) = 180° - 130°$$
$$= 50°$$

So, $m\angle ABC = 65°$, and $m\angle ACB = 50°$.

REMEMBER:

The sum of the measures of the three angles in a triangle is 180°. **See page H30.**
An **isosceles triangle** has two congruent sides. **See page H30.**

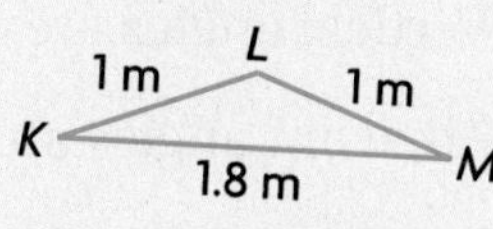

Triangle *KLM* is an isosceles triangle.

INDEPENDENT PRACTICE

$\angle APB$ is congruent to $\angle CPD$. Find the measure of each angle.

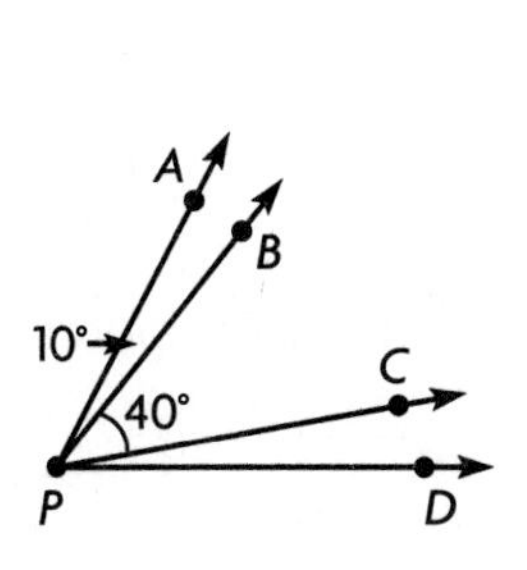

1. $\angle CPD$ **2.** $\angle APC$ **3.** $\angle BPD$ **4.** $\angle APD$

5. Are $\angle APC$ and $\angle BPD$ congruent? Explain.

Use the figure at the right.

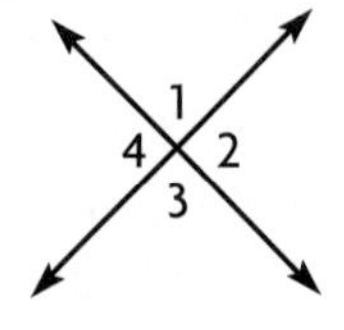

6. Which are vertical angles? adjacent angles?

7. Which angles are congruent?

Triangle *CAR* is an isosceles triangle. Find each measure.

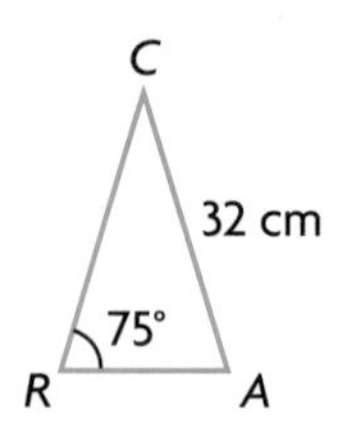

8. $\angle RAC$ **9.** $\angle ACR$ **10.** side *CR*

Write *always, sometimes,* or *never*.

11. Vertical angles are congruent.

12. Adjacent angles are congruent.

13. Every isosceles triangle has two sides that are congruent.

14. Equilateral triangles have no congruent sides.

15. Every equilateral triangle has three angles that measure 50°.

CAREER LINK

A draftsperson makes two-dimensional drawings of solids by using a tool called a triangle. One type of triangle has two 45° angles and one 90° angle. What kind of triangle is this?

Problem-Solving Applications

16. ART LaShonda is making a poster in the shape of an equilateral triangle. The length of one side is 22 in. What are the lengths of the other sides? the measures of the angles?

17. CRITICAL THINKING Can the measures of the angles of an isosceles triangle be 60°, 50°, and 70°? Explain.

18. WRITE ABOUT IT How can you tell whether line segments or angles are congruent?

Mixed Review and Test Prep

Name each triangle. Write *equilateral, isosceles,* or *scalene*.

19.

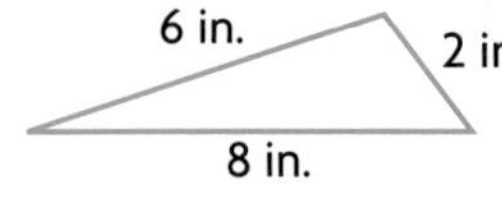

20.

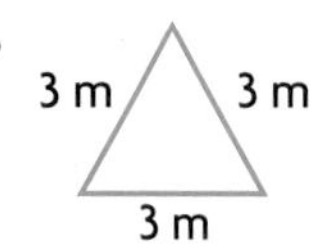

21.

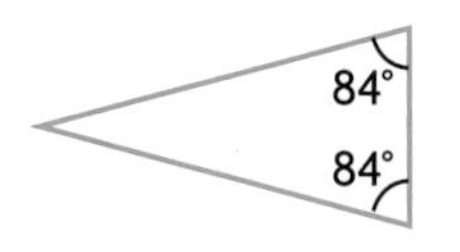

22.

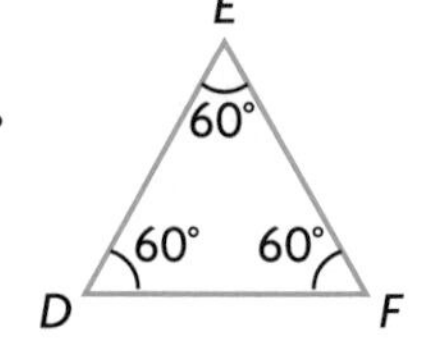

Name three ordered pairs that are solutions to each linear equation.

23. $y = x - 1$ **24.** $y = 3x$ **25.** $y = x + 5$ **26.** $y = 2x$

27. MUSIC Of 600 people surveyed about rock music and country music, 150 prefer rock to country. What percent of the people prefer rock music?

A 15% **B** 25% **C** 40% **D** 60%

28. ESTIMATION Leanne practiced her batting for 65 days in a row. For about how many weeks did Leanne practice her batting?

F 9 **G** 11 **H** 13 **J** 15

MORE PRACTICE Lesson 10.1, page H56

Symmetry

What You'll Learn
How to identify line symmetry and rotational symmetry

Why Learn This?
To create symmetric designs like those you see on clothing, wallpaper, and wrapping paper

VOCABULARY
- line symmetry
- rotational symmetry
- point of rotation

Symmetry is a fascinating geometric property that is all around you. It appears widely in nature and in many decorative designs.

Line symmetry exists when two halves of a figure can be made to match by folding on a line.

Lines of Symmetry

Vertical

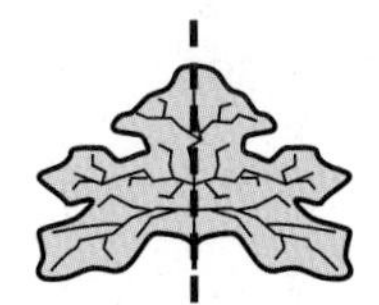

Horizontal

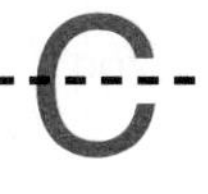

ACTIVITY **WHAT YOU'LL NEED:** star pattern, scissors, ruler

- Copy and cut out the star. Fold it in half in different ways. Use a ruler to draw lines to show each fold.
- How many lines of symmetry does the star have?

Rotational symmetry exists when a figure can be rotated less than 360° about a central point, called the **point of rotation**, and be made to match, or coincide with, the original figure.

Rotational Symmetry

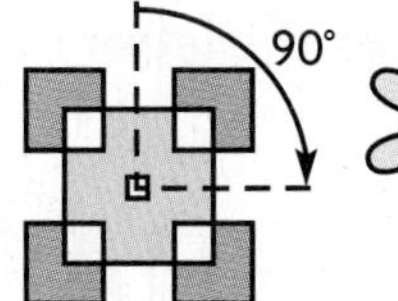

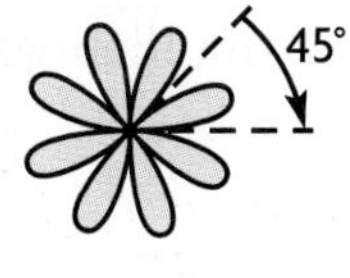

EXAMPLE The flower at the right has rotational symmetry. Identify the fraction and the angle measure of each turn.

Trace the flower and rotate it about the point of rotation so that it coincides with the original figure.

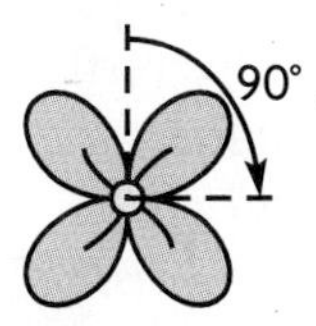

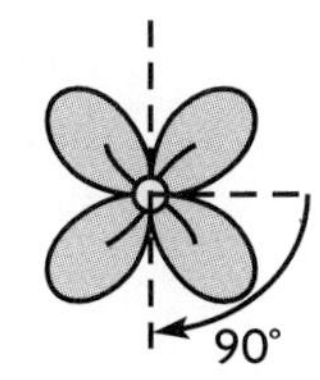

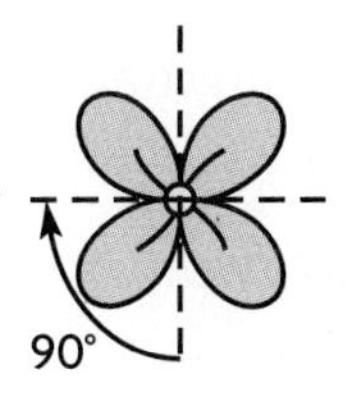

So, the flower has $\frac{1}{4}$-turn, or 90°, symmetry.

- Does the flower have line symmetry? Trace it and draw a diagram to support your answer.

GUIDED PRACTICE

Regular polygons have symmetry properties.

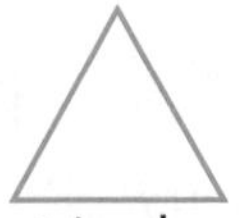
triangle

square

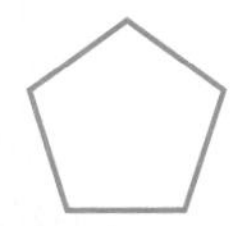
pentagon

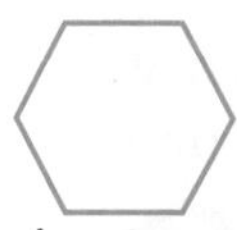
hexagon

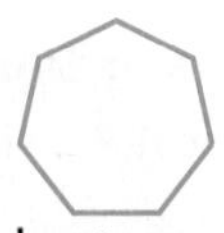
heptagon

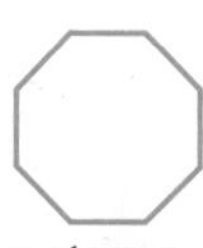
octagon

1. Trace each of the polygons. Then draw all the lines of symmetry for each polygon.

2. Look at your answers to Exercise 1. Compare the number of lines of symmetry to the number of sides for each polygon. If you have a regular polygon with n sides, how many lines of symmetry does it have?

The center of each regular polygon is a point of rotation. Since the regular pentagon has 5 sides, the figure has $\frac{1}{5}$-turn, or 72°, symmetry (360° ÷ 5 = 72°).

3. Describe the turn symmetry for each of the other regular polygons shown above.

4. If a regular polygon has n sides, what is its rotational symmetry?

Trace the letters in the word shown below. Identify the letter or letters with each given property.

5. line but not rotational symmetry

6. rotational but not line symmetry

7. both line and rotational symmetry

8. neither line nor rotational symmetry

INDEPENDENT PRACTICE

Write *always, sometimes,* or *never.*

1. Every figure with line symmetry has at least two congruent parts.

2. Every figure with rotational symmetry has at least two congruent parts.

3. A figure with a vertical line of symmetry also has a horizontal line of symmetry.

4. A figure with rotational symmetry coincides with the original after a 360° turn about a central point.

John Langdon, a graphic designer and the author of *Wordplay,* uses symmetry to create designs with names and other words. Look at the design below; then turn your book 180° and look again. What do you notice?

Symmetry

SCIENCE LINK

Biologists classify animals by using symmetry. Insects have bilateral symmetry: each can be divided into two symmetric halves. Does this butterfly have bilateral symmetry?

Write *line, rotational,* or *none* to describe the symmetry.

5. 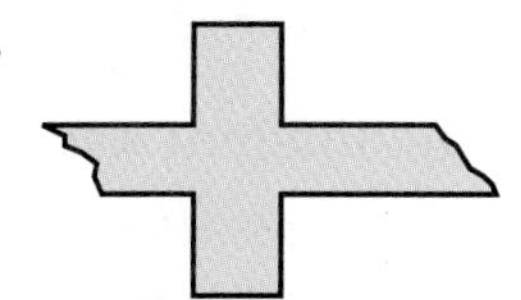

6. 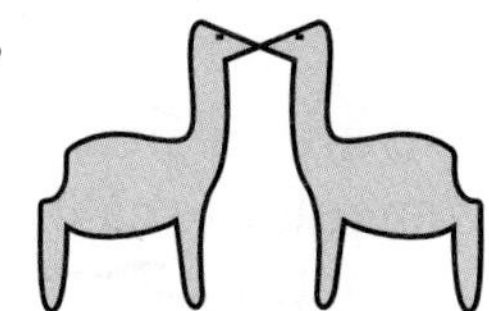

7. 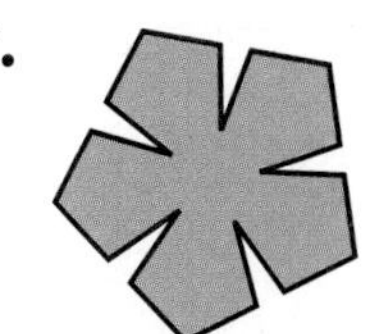

8. 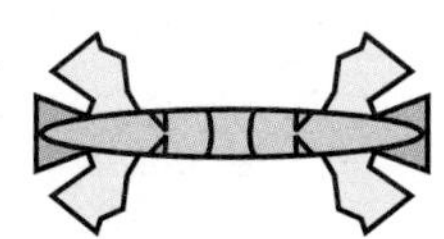

9. 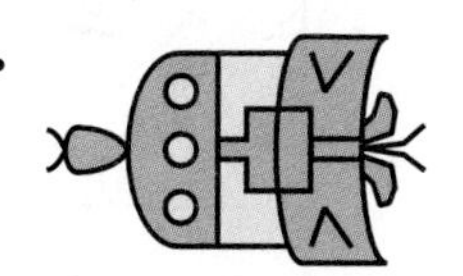

10. 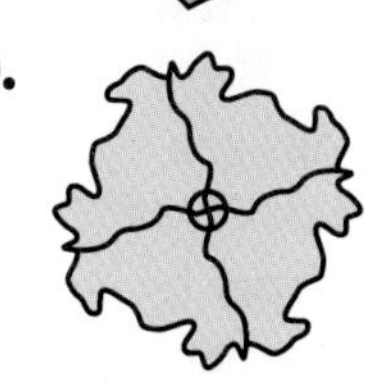

Identify the turn symmetry as a fraction of a turn and in degrees.

11. 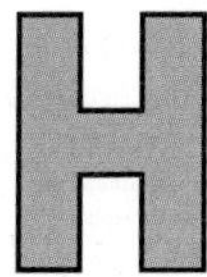

12. 

13. 

14. 

Identify the regular polygon that has the given measure of turn symmetry.

15. $\frac{1}{4}$ turn, or 90°

16. $\frac{1}{3}$ turn, or 120°

17. $\frac{1}{6}$ turn, or 60°

18. $\frac{1}{5}$ turn, or 72°

Print your first and last names in capital letters. Identify the letters with each given property.

19. a vertical line of symmetry

20. a horizontal line of symmetry

21. both a horizontal line of symmetry and a vertical line of symmetry

22. rotational symmetry

23. both line symmetry and rotational symmetry

24. neither line symmetry nor rotational symmetry

Problem-Solving Applications

25. **GEOMETRY** Draw a figure with at least two lines of symmetry.

26. **CRITICAL THINKING** Print a word in capitals, using only letters with line symmetry.

27. **ART** Fold a rectangular piece of paper in half horizontally and then in half vertically. Cut or tear a design into one of the folded edges. Open the sheet of paper. Does the design have a vertical line of symmetry? a horizontal line of symmetry? rotational symmetry? Why or why not?

28. **WRITE ABOUT IT** How would you explain line symmetry to a younger sister or brother? How would you explain rotational symmetry? Write a paragraph describing each of these so a younger sister or brother would be able to understand.

MORE PRACTICE Lesson 10.2, page H57

LESSON 10.3

Transformations

What You'll Learn
How to identify and draw transformations of figures

Why Learn This?
To create designs for a book cover or wrapping paper by moving congruent figures

VOCABULARY
- **transformation**
- **rotation**
- **translation**
- **reflection**
- **image**

Many designs are created by moving a figure in different ways. These movements are called **transformations**.

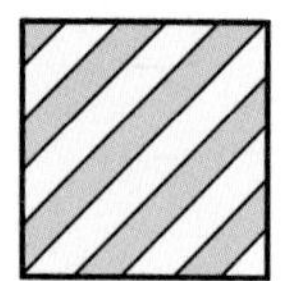
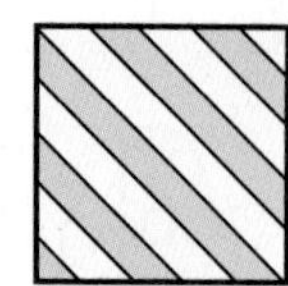
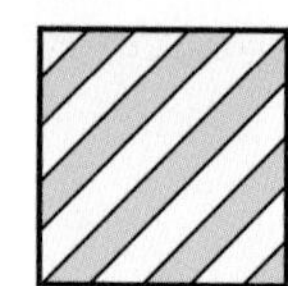
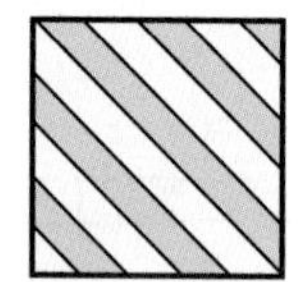

Rotations, or turns, **translations**, or slides, and **reflections**, or flips, are transformations that can change the orientation and location of a figure but not its size or shape.

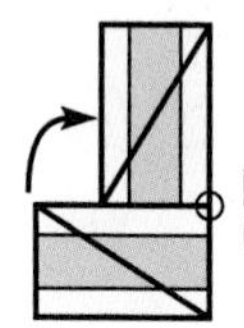
point of rotation

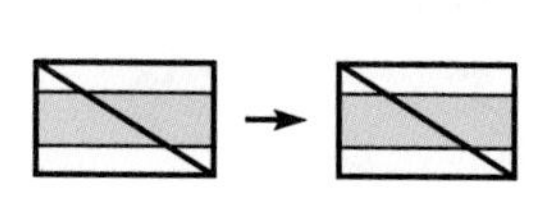

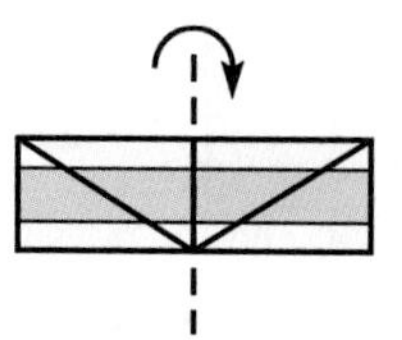

rotation
The rectangle can be turned clockwise or counterclockwise about a point. Both the orientation and the location can change.

translation
The rectangle can be slid in any direction. The orientation remains the same, but the location changes.

reflection
The rectangle can be flipped over a line. Both the orientation and the location change.

EXAMPLE 1 How will the grid appear after the letter *F* is translated onto each of the other three squares?

Trace the letter *F* in its original orientation and location.

Begin each translation from the initial location. Slide the letter onto each square, and copy the letter in the new location.

- Show how the letter *F* will appear in the other three squares after reflecting it about the grid lines.
- Show how the letter *F* will appear in the other three squares after rotating it about the vertex shared by all four squares.

When a geometric figure is moved on a plane, the figure in its final orientation and location is called the **image**. A reflection or rotation transforms a figure into an image that can be more difficult to recognize as an image of the original.

You can use a map of Texas to show transformations.

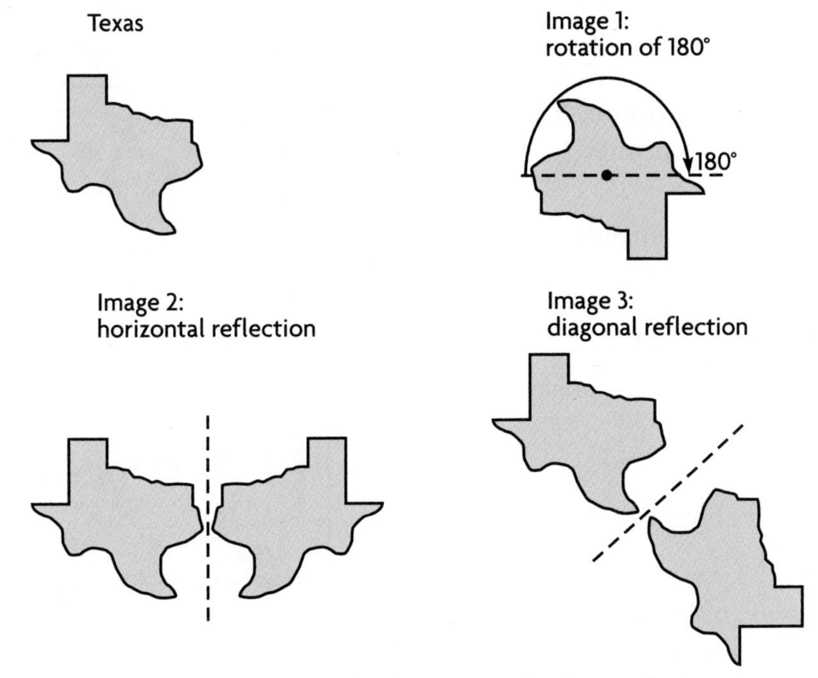

- Trace the map of Texas, and show a vertical translation.

CULTURAL LINK

Transformations are often used to design images in art. African art has many examples of the use of transformations. Kente cloths and stoles often have designs that are transformations of geometric shapes. What type of transformations do you see in the Kente stoles pictured below?

GUIDED PRACTICE

Print your name on a square piece of paper. Move the paper as indicated, and draw a picture to show the original and the image.

1. a horizontal translation

2. a clockwise rotation of 90°

3. a vertical reflection

4. a diagonal reflection

5. a counterclockwise rotation of 90°

6. a horizontal reflection

Identify the transformation that moves the original figure into the position and location shown. Write *translation, reflection,* or *rotation.*

7.

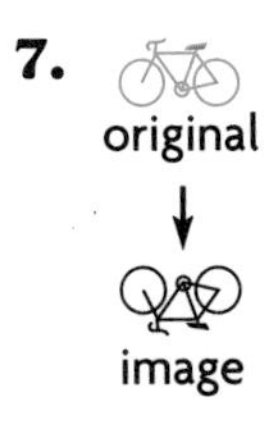

8.

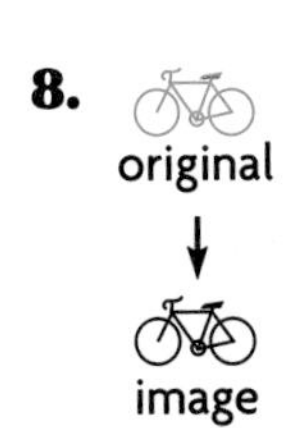

9.

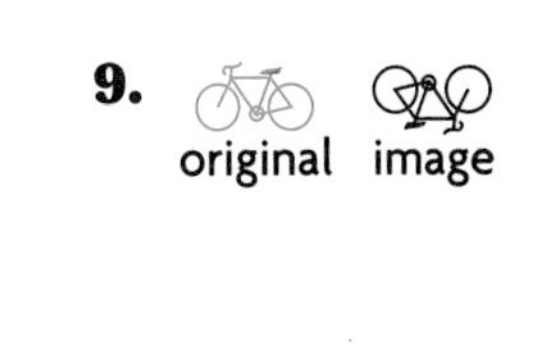

Geometric Transformations

You can use the vertices of a geometric figure to help you describe a transformation more precisely.

When you do a transformation such as a horizontal translation of quadrilateral *PQRS*, the new figure can be named quadrilateral *P′Q′R′S′*.

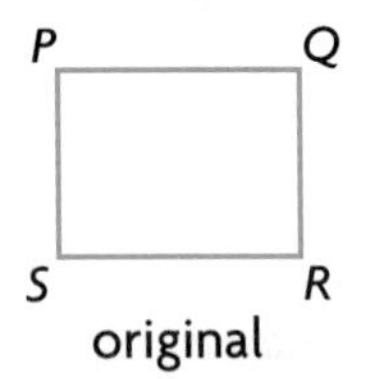

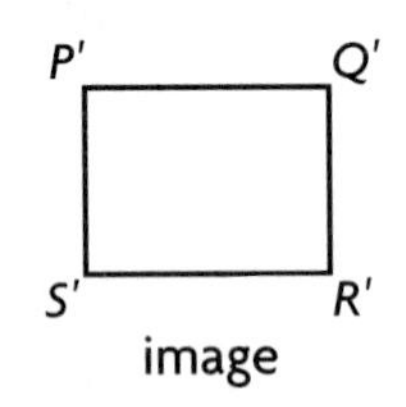

You read *P′Q′R′S′* as "*P* prime, *Q* prime, *R* prime, *S* prime."

EXAMPLE 2 Reflect quadrilateral *ABCD* about side *AD*.

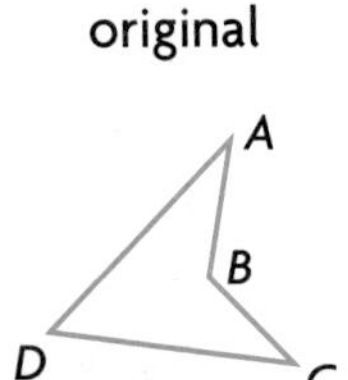

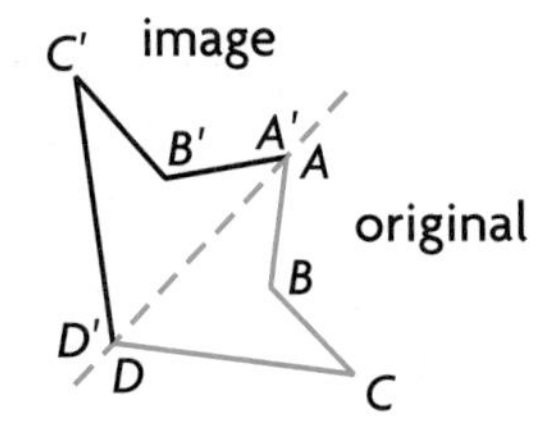

- Trace quadrilateral *ABCD*. Reflect it about side *CD*. Draw *ABCD* and *A′B′C′D′*.
- Trace quadrilateral *ABCD*. Rotate it 180° about point *D*. Draw *ABCD* and *A′B′C′D′*.

HISTORY LINK

Look at this Persian drawing done in the seventeenth century. Can you find the four horses? What type of transformation is used in this picture?

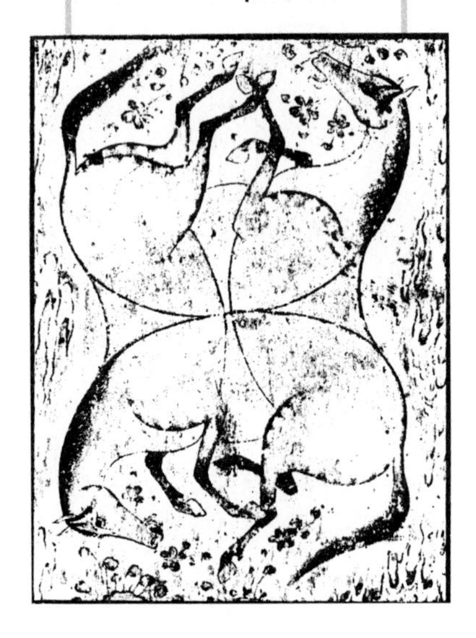

INDEPENDENT PRACTICE

For Exercises 1–6, use the word shown at the right. Draw the image that is described.

1. Reflect the first letter horizontally.
2. Reflect the second letter vertically.
3. Rotate the fifth letter 180°.
4. Rotate the fourth letter 90° counterclockwise.
5. Rotate the fifth letter 270° clockwise.
6. Reflect the third letter diagonally.

Describe the transformation that changes the original into the image.

7. original: MATH — image: MATH (reflected)
8. original: MATH — image: MATH
9. original: MATH — image: MATH (rotated)

Print the word MATH, and use it as the original figure. Then draw the image of each transformation.

10. 180° rotation
11. 90° counterclockwise rotation
12. horizontal reflection

Identify the type of reflection. Write *vertical, horizontal,* or *diagonal.*

13. original image

14. original image

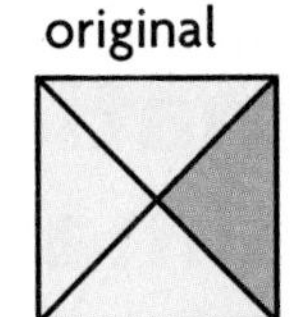

15. original image

Draw and label the image of each transformation of figure *ABCDE.*

16. Reflect about side *AE.*

17. Rotate 90° clockwise about *C.*

18. Reflect about side *DE.*

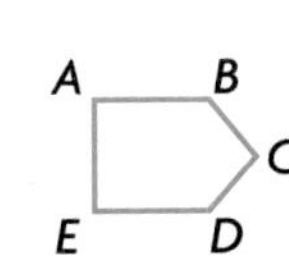

Problem-Solving Applications

19. Maria Elena starts a mathematics test with her paper face down. What type of transformation can she use so that her paper is face up?

20. **CRITICAL THINKING** Abdul looks at his test paper and realizes that it is upside down. What type of transformation can he use so that his paper is right side up?

21. **GEOMETRY** Alicia writes her name and looks at the image in a mirror. What type of transformation is the image?

22. **ART** From the given puzzle piece, create a wallpaper design that uses only reflections or rotations.

23. **WRITE ABOUT IT** What type of transformation produces an image that is in the same orientation as the original? an image that is in a different orientation?

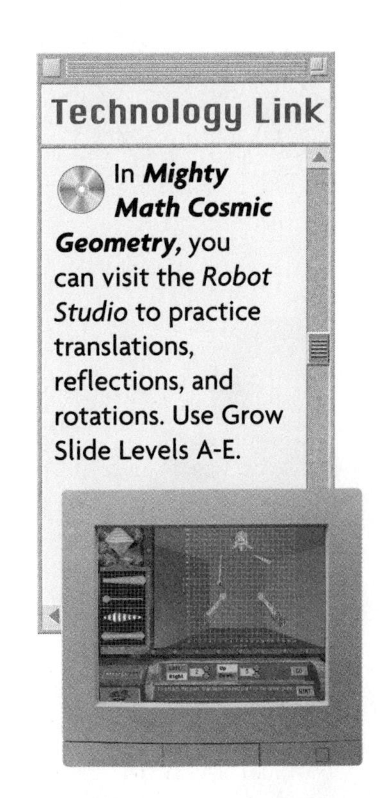

Technology Link
In *Mighty Math Cosmic Geometry,* you can visit the *Robot Studio* to practice translations, reflections, and rotations. Use Grow Slide Levels A-E.

Mixed Review and Test Prep

Write the number of sides and number of angles for each polygon.

24. triangle **25.** quadrilateral **26.** hexagon

Locate the point for each ordered pair on a coordinate plane.

27. $A(5,7)$ **28.** $W(^-5,^-4)$ **29.** $M(0,1)$

30. **PATTERNS** Linda made 2 dolls the first week, 5 dolls the second week, and 9 dolls the third week. If the pattern continues, how many dolls will she make the fourth week?

A 12 **B** 13 **C** 14 **D** 15

31. **SMART SHOPPING** Tom bought 5 pieces of poster board for $3.95. At this rate, how much would 45 pieces of poster board cost?

F $7.11 **G** $19.75 **H** $35.55 **J** $43.45

MORE PRACTICE Lesson 10.3, page H57

What You'll Learn
How to identify and graph translations, reflections, and rotations of figures on the coordinate plane

Why Learn This?
To make designs such as tessellations on the coordinate plane

ART LINK

This design shows several of the concepts and ideas described in this chapter. Which ones do you see?

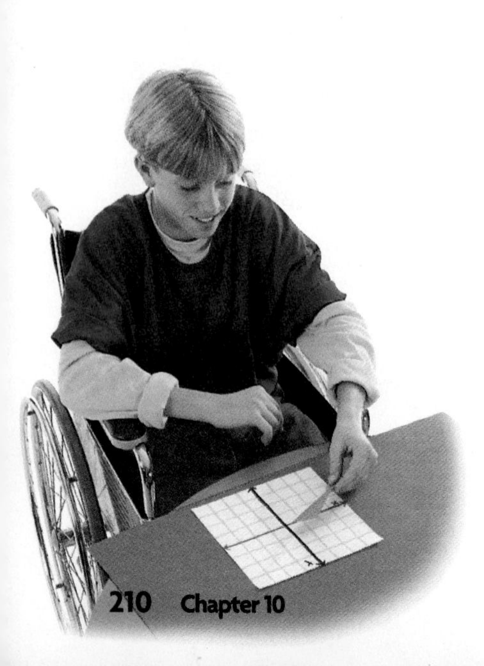

ALGEBRA CONNECTION

Transformations on the Coordinate Plane

You can move geometric figures from one location to another on the coordinate plane by using transformations.

ACTIVITY **WHAT YOU'LL NEED:** coordinate plane, scissors, paper, protractor

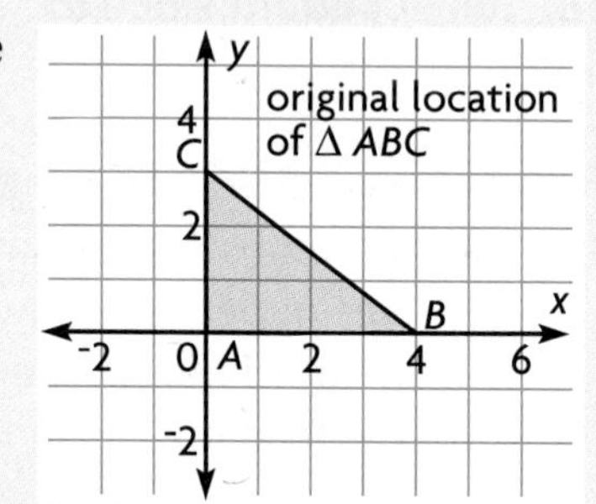

- Copy and cut out $\triangle ABC$, and place it on a coordinate plane as shown.
- Trace the triangle. Label the vertices A, B, and C and the triangle *original.*
- Rotate the triangle 180° clockwise about point (0,0).
- Trace the image. Label the vertices A', B', and C'. Label $\triangle A'B'C'$ with the word *image.*
- Compare the sizes, shapes, orientations, and locations of the triangles.
- Record the coordinates of the vertices of $\triangle ABC$ and $\triangle A'B'C'$. In which quadrant is the image?

You can describe any transformation by naming the coordinates of the vertices of an original figure and an image.

EXAMPLE Reflect $\triangle ABC$ about the x-axis. Compare the triangles.

$\triangle ABC \qquad \triangle A'B'C'$

$A(0,0) \rightarrow A'(0,0)$
$B(4,0) \rightarrow B'(4,0)$
$C(0,3) \rightarrow C'(0,^-3)$

The orientations, locations, and coordinates may change, but the sizes and shapes do not. The y-coordinate of vertex C' is opposite the one for vertex C.

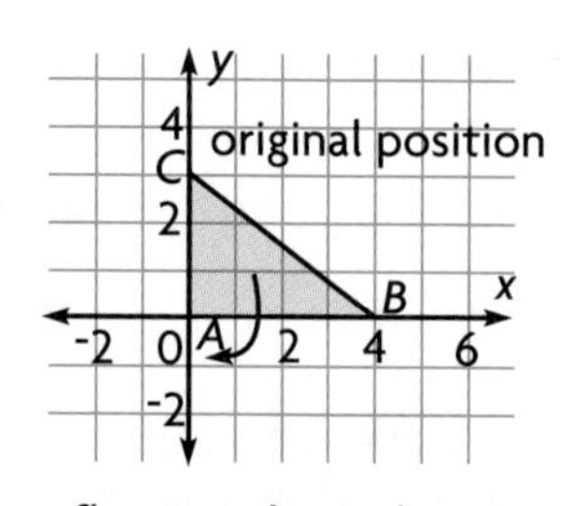

reflection about the x-axis

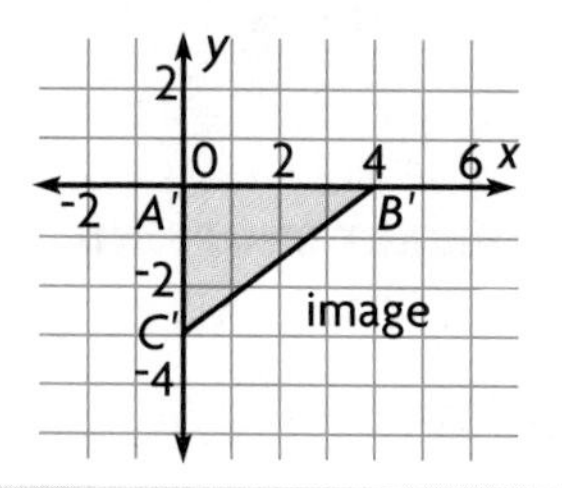

Calculator Activities, page H42

GUIDED PRACTICE

Use $\triangle CDE$ as the original figure. For each transformation, graph the image and record the coordinates of its vertices.

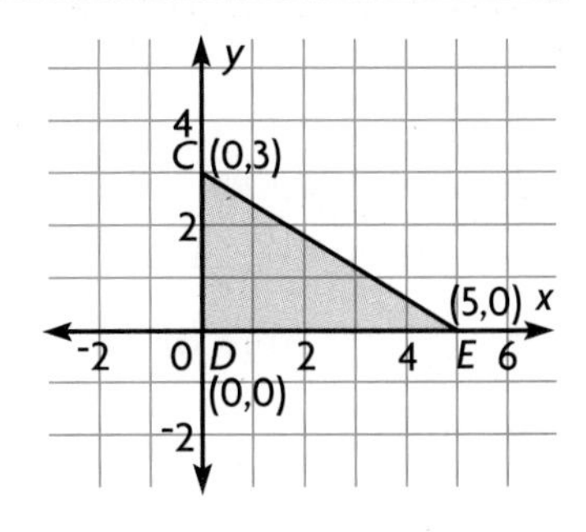

1. Translate 3 units up.

2. Reflect about the y-axis.

3. Rotate 90° clockwise about vertex D.

4. Reflect about the x-axis.

INDEPENDENT PRACTICE

Identify the type of transformation. Write *translation, reflection*, or *rotation.*

1. original 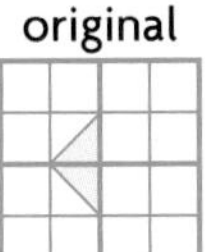 image

2. original 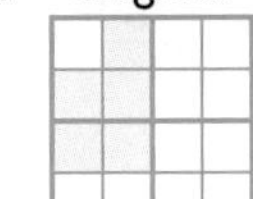 image 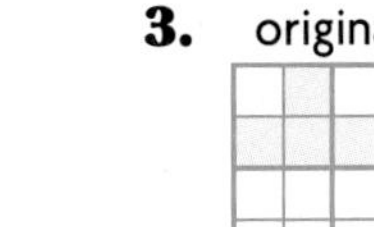

3. original image 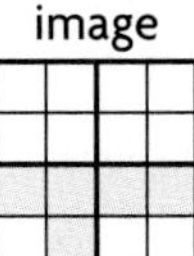

Draw figure *ABCDE* on a coordinate plane. Graph each image, and give the coordinates of its vertices.

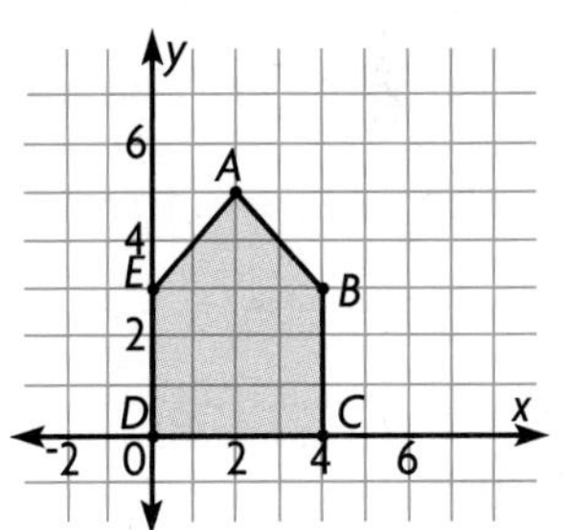

4. Reflect about the x-axis.

5. Translate 5 units left.

6. Rotate 90° clockwise about (0,0).

Draw figure *ABCD* on a coordinate plane. Graph each image, and give the coordinates of its vertices.

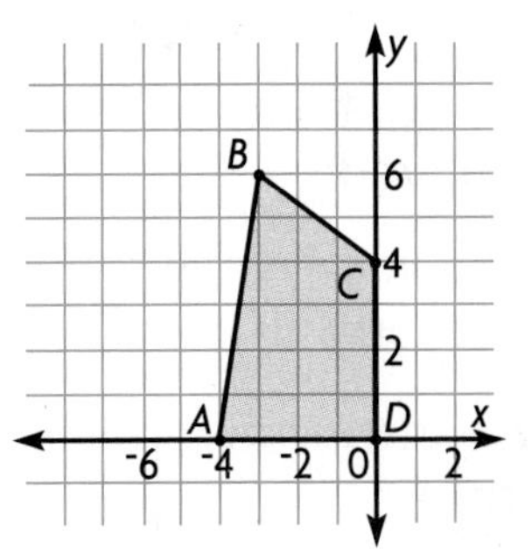

7. Translate 3 units down and 2 units right.

8. Reflect about side AD.

9. Rotate 180° about D.

Problem-Solving Applications

10. **GEOMETRY** Draw a trapezoid on a coordinate plane so that one vertex is at (0,0) and another is at (⁻6,4). Rotate the trapezoid 180° about (0,0), and draw the image.

11. **CAREER** A graphic designer created a fabric design by reflecting this figure over the x-axis, translating the reflection 5 units to the right, and rotating the translation 90° counterclockwise about P. Draw the design on a piece of graph paper.

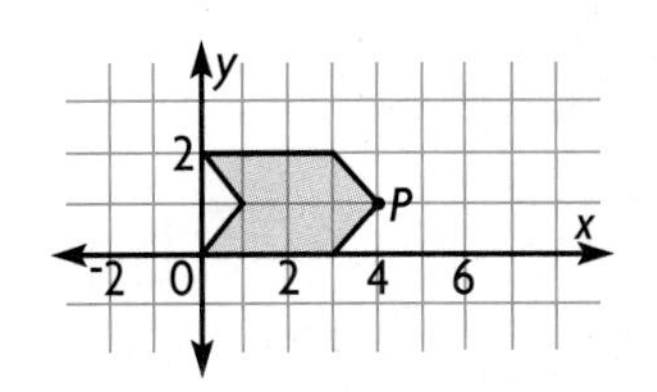

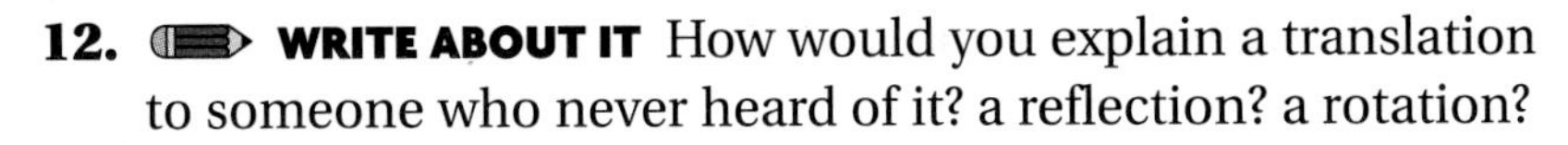

12. **WRITE ABOUT IT** How would you explain a translation to someone who never heard of it? a reflection? a rotation?

MORE PRACTICE Lesson 10.4, page H57

CHAPTER 10 Review/Test

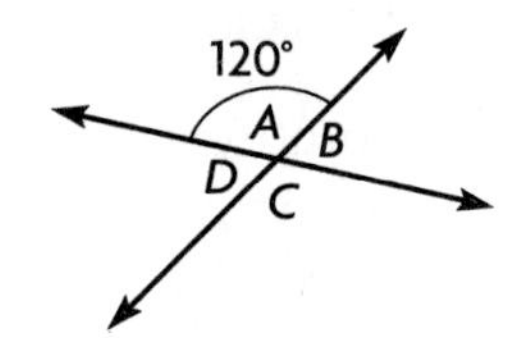

1. VOCABULARY When two lines intersect, the opposite angles are called ___?___. (page 200)

Find the measure of each angle. (pages 199–202)

2. $m\angle C$ **3.** $m\angle B$ **4.** $m\angle D$ **5.** $m\angle C + m\angle D$

Write *always*, *sometimes*, or *never*. (pages 199–202)

6. Equilateral triangles have exactly two sides that are congruent.

7. The base angles of an isosceles triangle are congruent.

$\angle XYW$ is congruent to $\angle WYZ$. Find the measure of each angle. (pages 199–202)

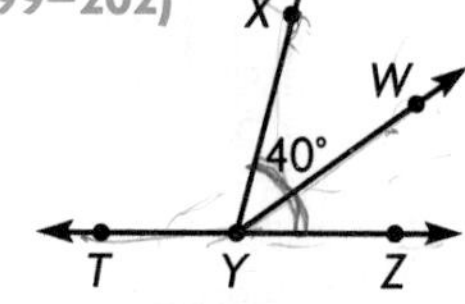

8. $m\angle WYZ$ **9.** $m\angle XYZ$

10. $m\angle TYX$ **11.** $m\angle TYW$

12. A base angle of an isosceles triangle measures 30°. What are the measures of the other two angles of the triangle?

Identify the letters in the word SPAIN with each property. (pages 203–205)

13. line symmetry

14. rotational symmetry

15. both line symmetry and rotational symmetry

16. neither line symmetry nor rotational symmetry

Identify the letters in the word HORSE with each property. (pages 203–205)

17. line symmetry but not rotational symmetry

18. rotational symmetry but not line symmetry

19. both line symmetry and rotational symmetry

20. neither line symmetry nor rotational symmetry

Describe the transformation that changes the original figure into the given image. (pages 206–209)

21. **22.** **23.** **24.**

original

25. Name three kinds of transformations.

Write *translation*, *reflection*, or *rotation* for each transformation. (pages 210–211)

26. **27.** **28.** **29.**

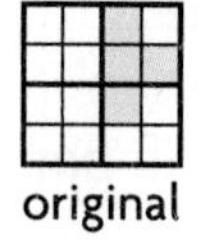
original

30. Draw a triangle on a coordinate plane. Reflect it over the x-axis and draw the image.

Test Prep

1. $\angle$CED is complementary to —

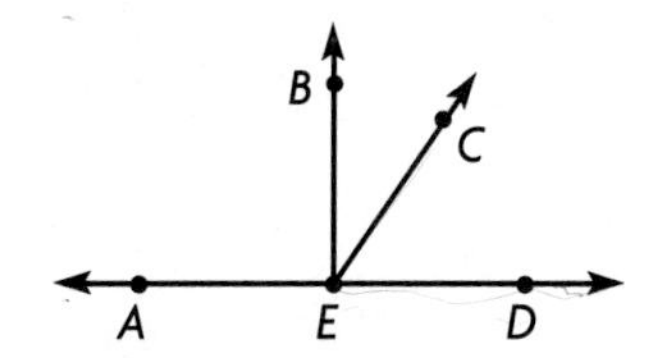

A $\angle AEB$
B $\angle BEC$
C $\angle AEC$
D $\angle AED$

2. A chocolate chip cookie recipe uses 2 cups of chocolate chips to make 36 cookies. How many cups of chocolate chips would be used to make 90 cookies?

F 4 c
G 6 c
H 9 c
J 5 c
K Not Here

3. For what value of b is the equation $2.3 + b = {}^{-}5$ a true statement?

A $^{-}7.3$
B $^{-}2.7$
C 2.7
D 2.8

4. $42\frac{3}{4} - 50\frac{1}{8} =$

F $^{-}8\frac{5}{8}$

G $^{-}7\frac{5}{8}$

H $^{-}7\frac{3}{8}$

J $7\frac{3}{8}$

5. $48 \div (3 + 5) \times 2 =$

A 3
B 8
C 12
D 42

6. Owen spent $1\frac{1}{2}$ hours doing chores, $2\frac{1}{2}$ hours doing homework, and $2\frac{3}{4}$ hours playing outside. Which is the best estimate of the amount of time Owen spent doing those 3 activities?

F $6\frac{1}{2}$ hr　　**G** $7\frac{1}{2}$ hr

H 8 hr　　**J** $8\frac{1}{2}$ hr

7. Figure *MNOP* is a rectangle with coordinates $M(^{-}3,2)$, $N(^{-}3,5)$, and $O(2,5)$. What are the coordinates of point P?

A $(2,^{-}2)$　　**B** $(^{-}3,^{-}5)$
C $(3,^{-}5)$　　**D** $(2,2)$

8. Timothy and Bart mowed lawns last Saturday. Timothy earned \$2 less than twice the amount Bart earned. Timothy earned \$32. Which equation could you use to find b, the amount Bart earned?

F $b + 2 = 32$
G $2b - 2 = 32$
H $2b + 2 = 32$
J $b + 32 = 2b$

9. Figure *ABCD* is translated 3 units up and 2 units right. What are the coordinates of the image?

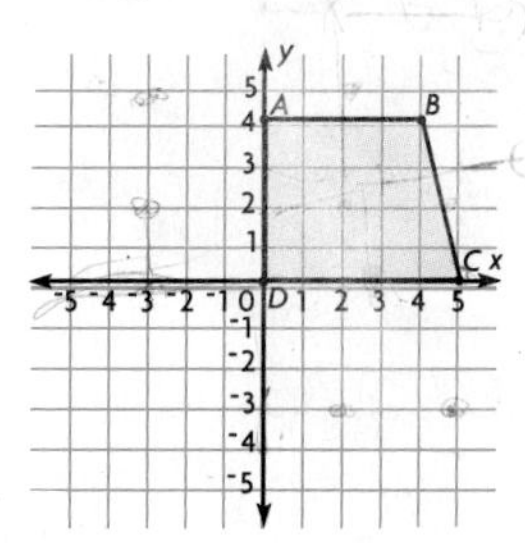

A $A'(2,7)$, $B'(6,7)$, $C'(7,3)$, $D'(2,3)$
B $A'(3,6)$, $B'(7,6)$, $C'(8,2)$, $D'(3,2)$
C $A'(2,1)$, $B'(6,1)$, $C'(7,^{-}2)$, $D'(2,^{-}3)$
D $A'(^{-}2,7)$, $B'(2,7)$, $C'(3,3)$, $D'(^{-}2,3)$

CHAPTER 11

CONSTRUCTING AND DRAWING

LOOK AHEAD

In this chapter you will solve problems that involve

- constructing regular polygons, congruent angles, parallel and perpendicular lines, and congruent triangles
- bisecting angles and line segments
- classifying and comparing triangles

SOCIAL STUDIES LINK

The bar graph below shows the five cities in the world that have the most skyscrapers.

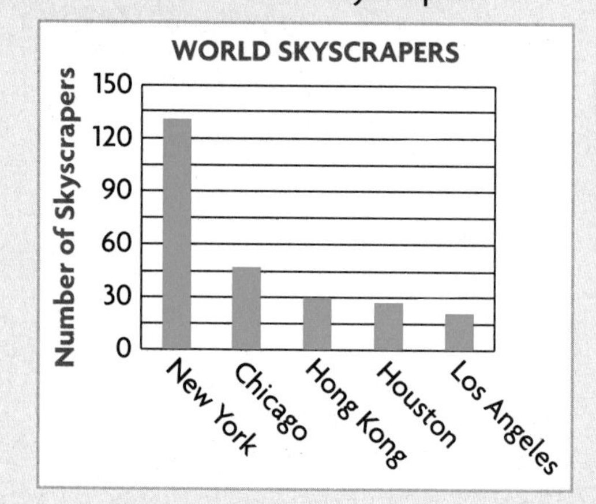

- Which city has the most skyscrapers?
- About how many more skyscrapers are there in Chicago than in Hong Kong?

Problem-Solving Project

Skyscraper Survey

Buildings are made up of different shapes. What shapes make the tallest towers or the best windows?

YOU WILL NEED: poster board, markers

Choose a building and describe it in geometric terms naming at least four geometric shapes that are in its design. Then design your own building. Use poster board to present your design to the class, identifying the different geometric shapes you used.

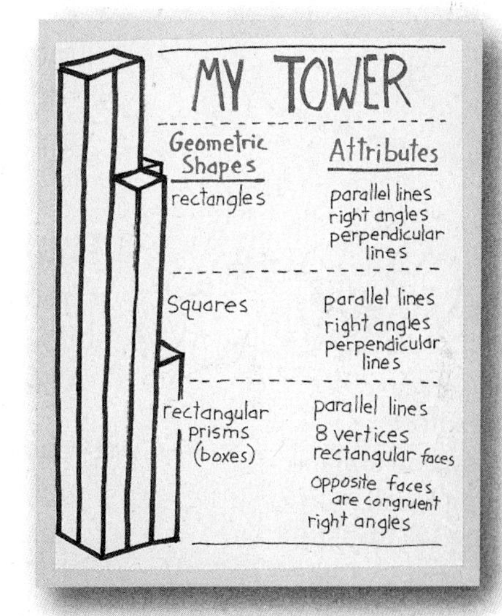

MY TOWER
Geometric Shapes
Attributes
rectangles
parallel lines
right angles
perpendicular lines
squares
parallel lines
right angles
perpendicular lines
rectangular prisms (boxes)
parallel lines
8 vertices
rectangular faces
opposite faces are congruent
right angles

PROJECT CHECKLIST

- ✓ Did you choose a building?
- ✓ Did you name four geometric shapes in the building?
- ✓ Did you design your own building?
- ✓ Did you present your design to the class?

ACTIVITY

What You'll Explore
Constructing a regular polygon from a circle

What You'll Need
paper, compass, straightedge

Technology Link

You can explore polygons on a plane by using E-Lab, Activity 11. Available on CD-ROM and on the Internet at **www.hbschool.com/elab**

Constructing Regular Polygons from Circles

A circle is a special geometric figure. You can use it to form many regular polygons. For example, you can construct a regular hexagon from a circle, with a compass and a straightedge.

Explore

Construct a regular hexagon using only a compass and a straightedge. The first three steps are given below.

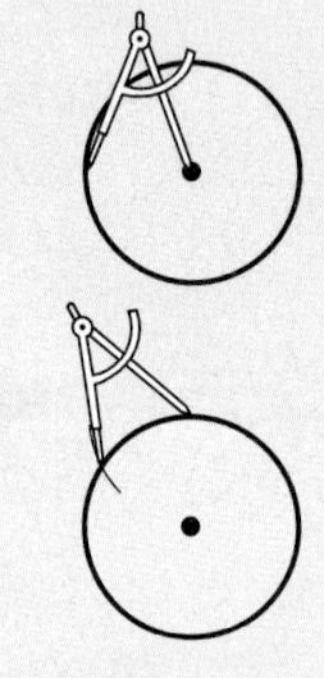

- Use the compass to draw a circle. Mark the center of the circle.
- Using the same compass opening, place the point on the circle and draw an arc that intersects the circle.
- Keeping the same compass opening, move the point to the intersection of the arc and the circle. Draw another arc that intersects the circle.

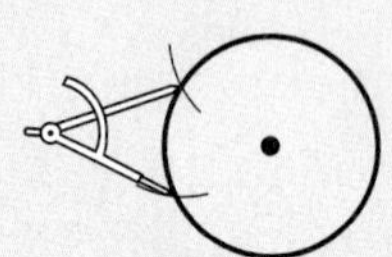

Think and Discuss CRITICAL THINKING

- You have drawn two arcs. These arcs are for two vertices of your hexagon. How many more arcs do you need to draw until you are back at your original position?
- Look at the points where the arcs intersect the circle. How can you use these points and your straightedge to form a regular hexagon? Does the order matter? Explain.
- How is the compass opening related to the radius of the circle?

Try This

- Draw $\overline{OG}$. With O as the center and $\overline{OG}$ as the radius, draw a circle. Construct a regular hexagon in the circle. Label it *GHIJKL*.
- Mark off six equal arcs on a circle, and construct an equilateral triangle.

Constructing Congruent Angles and Line Segments

LESSON 11.1

Look at $\angle RST$ and $\angle XYZ$. They are congruent angles. You can write $\angle RST \cong \angle XYZ$. The symbol $\cong$ means "is congruent to."

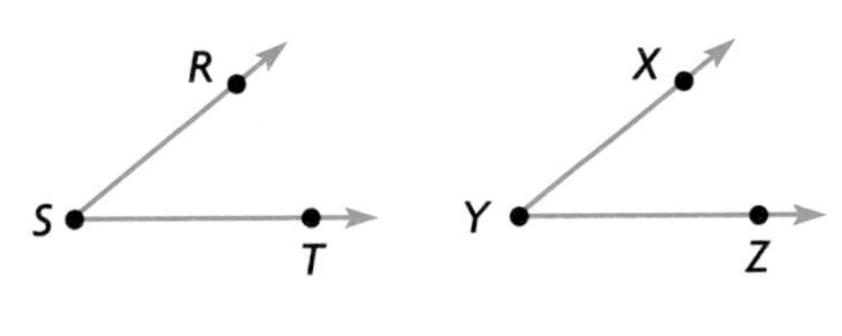

- How can you show that $\angle RST$ and $\angle XYZ$ are congruent?

You can construct an angle that is congruent to a given angle. Constructing angles is different from drawing angles. To construct an angle, you use a compass and a straightedge.

ACTIVITY **WHAT YOU'LL NEED:** tracing paper, straightedge, compass, protractor, ruler

Construct an angle congruent to $\angle B$. The first two steps are given below.

- Trace $\angle B$. Use a straightedge to draw ray DE below $\angle B$.
- Place the compass point on B. Draw an arc through $\angle B$. Place the point of the compass on D. Use the same compass opening to draw an arc on $\overrightarrow{DE}$.
- You have constructed one ray of the angle. What other part of the angle do you need to construct?
- To find the position of the second ray, you need to measure $\angle B$. How can you do that, using only a compass? How can you duplicate that measure for your new angle?
- What is the last step in your construction?

Talk About It CRITICAL THINKING

- Are $\angle B$ and $\angle D$ congruent? How can you verify your answer?
- How are constructing and drawing different?

What You'll Learn

How to construct a congruent angle, the bisector of an angle, and the bisector of a line segment

Why Learn This?

To make angles and line segments in diagrams and drawings

VOCABULARY

bisect

midpoint

REMEMBER:

If two angles have the same measure, they are **congruent**.

See page 199.

$m\angle J = m\angle M$

So, $\angle J$ is congruent to $\angle M$.

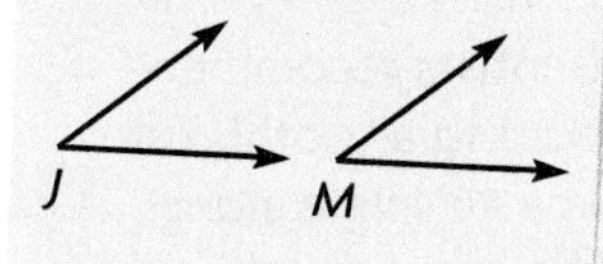

LANGUAGE LINK

Bi is a prefix that means "two." A *bicycle* is a vehicle with two wheels. A *biathlon* is an athletic contest with two events. *Binoculars* are two small telescopes joined side by side. They make distant objects seem closer by magnifying them. Suppose Paco earns $10 biweekly. How often does he earn $10?

HEALTH LINK

Dentists recommend holding a toothbrush at a 45° angle along the gum line while brushing. Draw a diagram to show the proper position of the toothbrush.

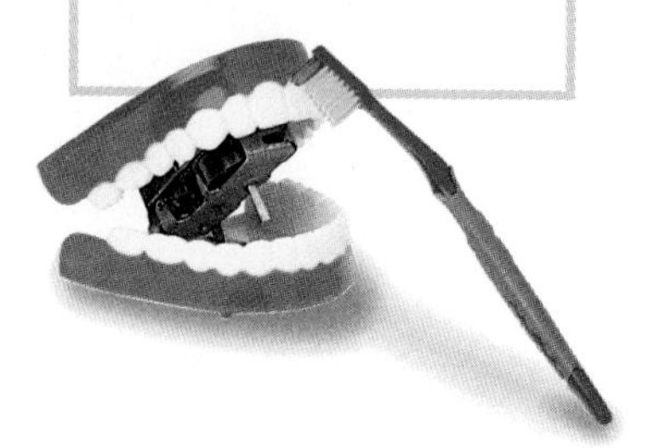

GUIDED PRACTICE

Trace the angle. Use your tracing to construct a congruent angle.

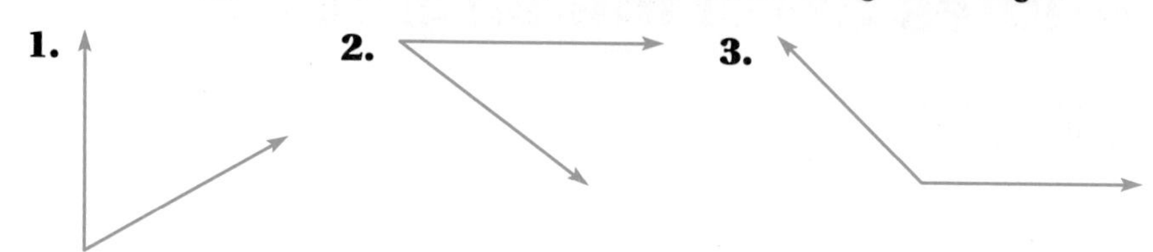

Bisecting Angles and Segments

Lighting engineers design special lighting effects. Sometimes they position lights so that they divide, or bisect, an object into two parts.

To **bisect** means to divide into two congruent parts.

You can bisect angles and line segments by using a compass and a straightedge.

- When you bisect an angle, how many congruent angles do you form?

EXAMPLE 1 Construct the bisector of an angle.

Step 1

Draw $\angle K$. Place the point of the compass at vertex K and draw an arc through the two rays. Label the intersection points G and H.

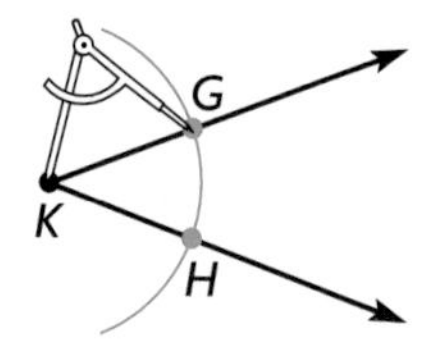

Step 2

With the same compass opening, draw intersecting arcs from points G and H. Label the intersection point F.

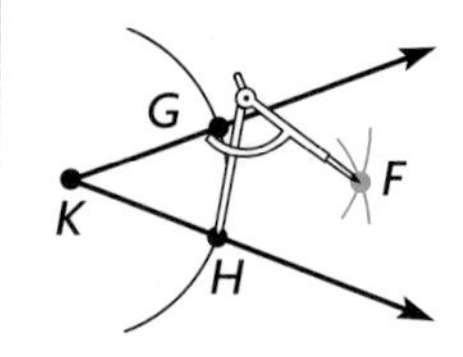

Step 3

Draw $\overrightarrow{KF}$, the bisector of $\angle K$. $\angle GKF \cong \angle FKH$

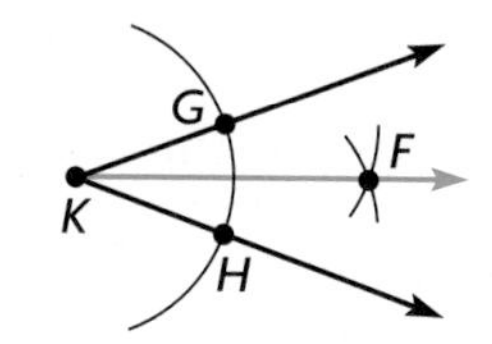

- Measure $\angle GKH$, $\angle GKF$, and $\angle FKH$ with a protractor. How do the measures of $\angle GKF$ and $\angle FKH$ compare? How are the measures of $\angle GKF$ and $\angle FKH$ related to the measure of $\angle GKH$?

You can measure with a ruler to find the point in the middle, or the **midpoint**, of a line segment. A more accurate way to find the midpoint of a line segment is by constructing a bisector.

EXAMPLE 2 Construct a bisector of a line segment.

Step 1

Draw $\overline{RS}$. Place the point of the compass on R. Open the compass more than halfway to S. Draw an arc that intersects $\overline{RS}$.

Step 2

With the same compass opening, draw a similar arc from S. Label the intersection points T and U.

Step 3

Draw $\overleftrightarrow{TU}$. Label the intersection of $\overline{RS}$ and $\overleftrightarrow{TU}$ point X.

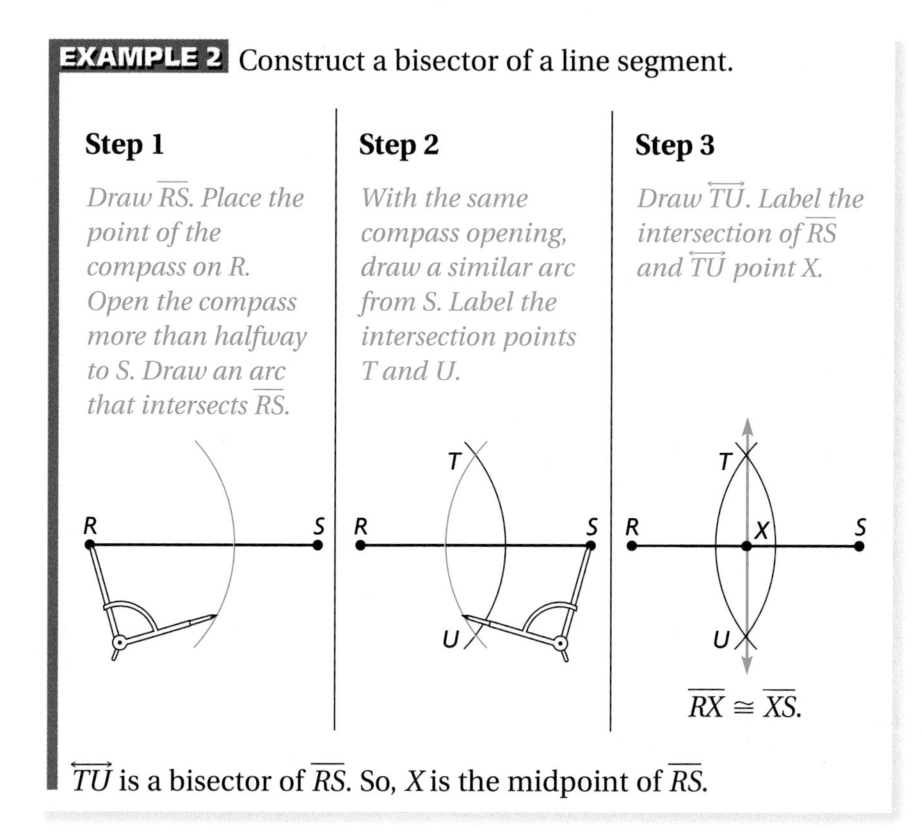

$\overline{RX} \cong \overline{XS}$.

$\overleftrightarrow{TU}$ is a bisector of $\overline{RS}$. So, X is the midpoint of $\overline{RS}$.

CULTURAL LINK

Euclid, an early Greek mathematician, distinguished between a *drawing* and a *construction*. About 300 B.C. Euclid explained that only an unmarked straightedge and a compass are used for a construction. Why do you think a straightedge was used instead of a ruler?

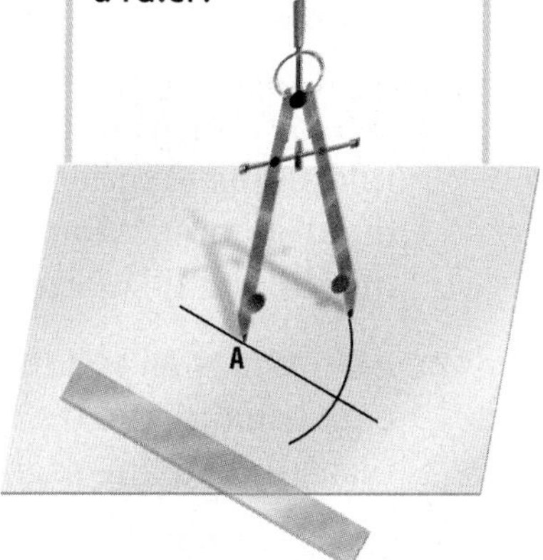

Talk About It

- How many midpoints can a line segment have? How many bisectors can a line segment have?
- How is bisecting a line segment like bisecting an angle?
- Which construction seems easier to you, bisecting an angle or bisecting a segment?

INDEPENDENT PRACTICE

Trace the angle. Then use your tracing to construct a congruent angle.

1.

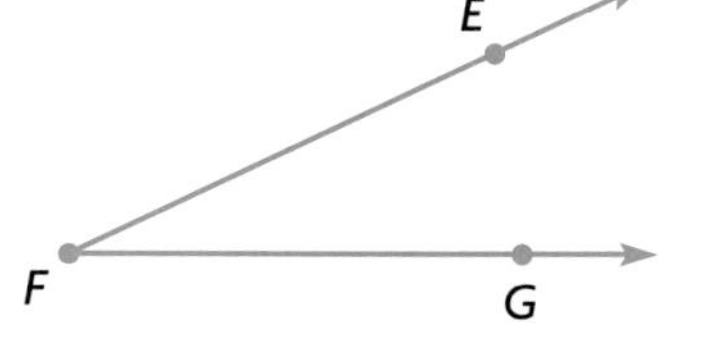

2.

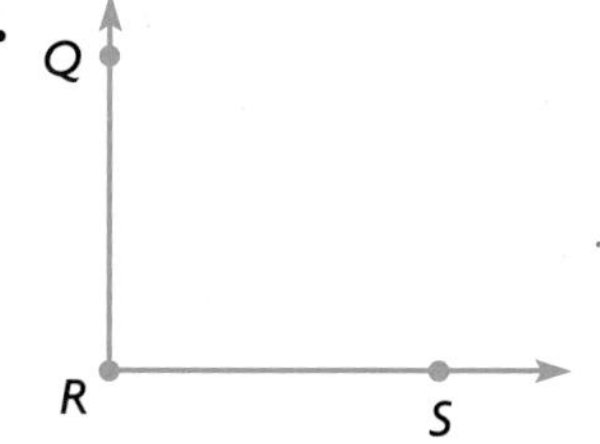

3.

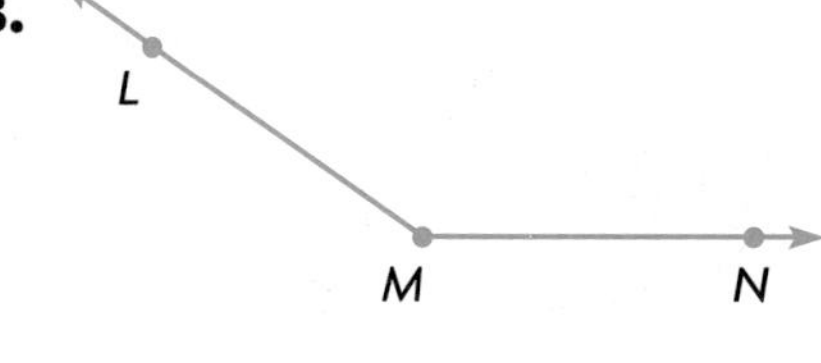

Trace the figure. Then bisect it.

4.

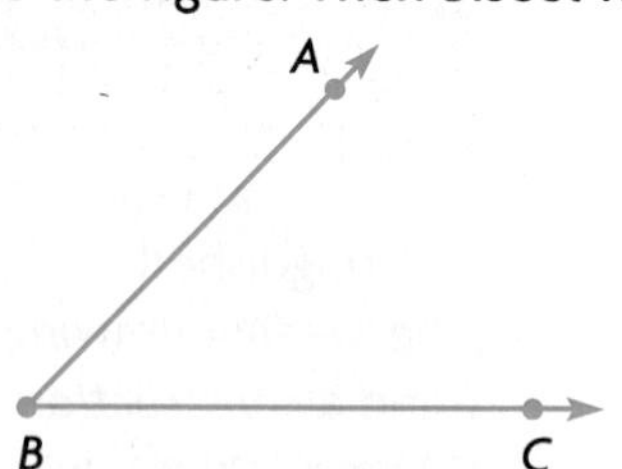

5.

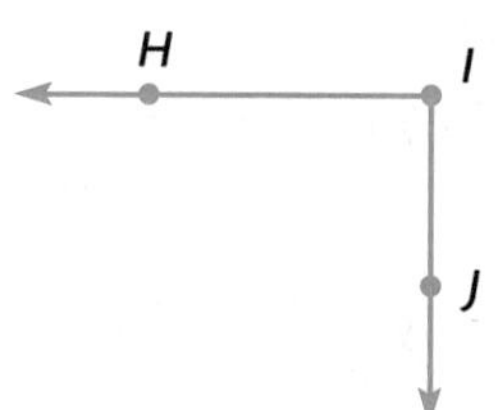

6.

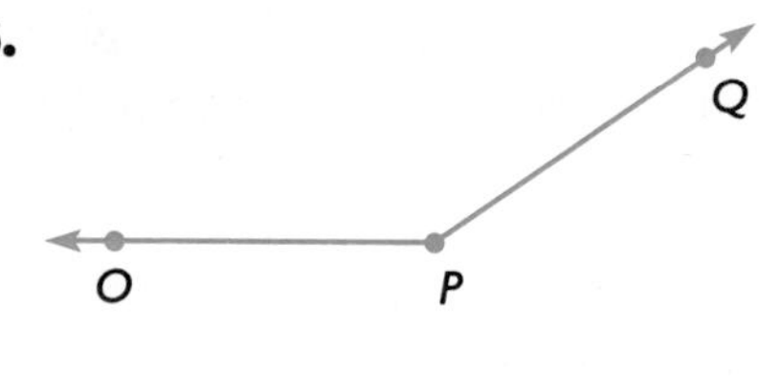

7. U ——— Y

8. J ——— K

Problem-Solving Applications

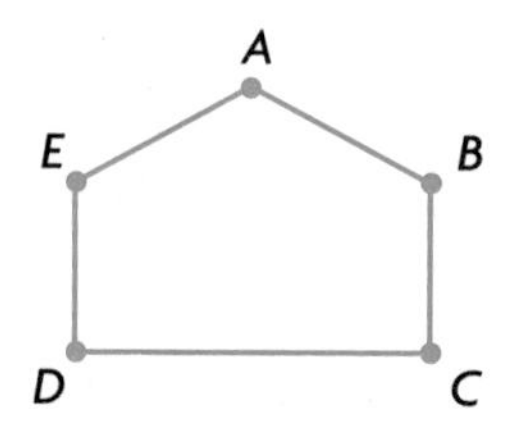

9. Copy figure *ABCDE* using a compass and a straightedge. HINT: Start at a vertex and copy successive sides and angles.

10. **DESIGN** Use a straightedge to draw any quadrilateral. Find the midpoint of each side by construction. Connect the midpoints in order to form a new quadrilateral. What type of new quadrilateral is formed?

11. **CRITICAL THINKING** Suppose you bisect a 90° angle. Next, you bisect one of the smaller angles formed. Then, you bisect one of the still smaller angles formed. What is the measure of the smallest angle formed by the three repeated bisections?

12. **WRITE ABOUT IT** What is the difference between constructing the bisector of an angle and constructing the bisector of a line segment?

Mixed Review and Test Prep

Use *perpendicular, parallel,* or *neither* to descibe the lines in the figure.

13.

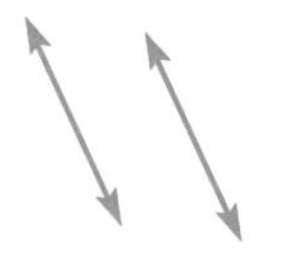

14.

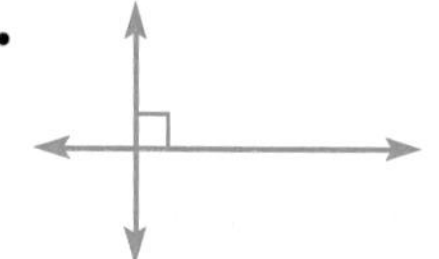

15.

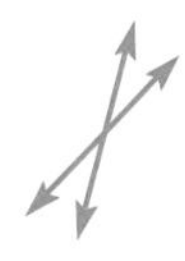

16.

Identify the number of lines of symmetry for each polygon.

17.

18.

19.

20.

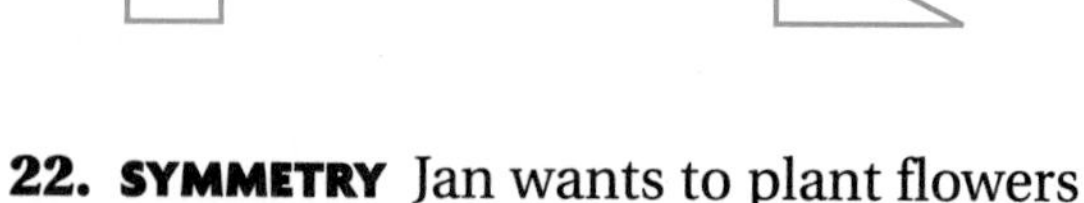

21. **ART** Erika is drawing a variety of polygons to make a mosaic. She can draw 13 every $\frac{1}{2}$ hour. How many can she draw in $4\frac{1}{2}$ hours?

A 52   **B** 58

C 65   **D** 117

22. **SYMMETRY** Jan wants to plant flowers symmetrically in her square garden. How many lines of symmetry does a square have?

F 0   **G** 2

H 4   **J** 8

MORE PRACTICE Lesson 11.1, page H58

Constructing Parallel and Perpendicular Lines

LESSON 11.2

What You'll Learn
How to construct parallel and perpendicular lines

Why Learn This?
To draw polygons and to model solids in arts and crafts

VOCABULARY
- parallel lines
- perpendicular lines
- perpendicular bisector

Parallel lines are in the same plane and do not intersect. **Perpendicular lines** intersect to form right angles.

ACTIVITY **WHAT YOU'LL NEED:** rectangular paper, straightedge, compass

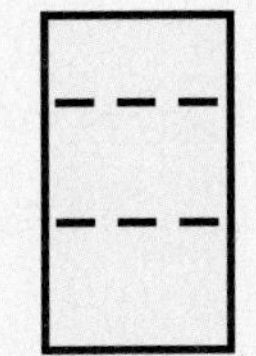

Start with a rectangular piece of paper. Fold the paper as shown to form a line. Then fold the paper again to form a line parallel to the first line.

- Why do you think the lines are parallel?
- How many folds are needed to form five parallel lines?

Start with another rectangular piece of paper, and fold the paper one time to form a line. Then fold the paper again to form a line perpendicular to the first one.

- Describe how you can fold the paper a third time to form a second line perpendicular to the first line.
- What is the relationship between the two lines that are perpendicular to the first line?

You can also use a compass and a straightedge to construct parallel and perpendicular lines.

EXAMPLE 1 Construct a line parallel to a given line.

Step 1

Draw $\overleftrightarrow{YZ}$. Choose any point P above $\overleftrightarrow{YZ}$. Draw a line through point P that intersects $\overleftrightarrow{YZ}$. Label the point of intersection W.

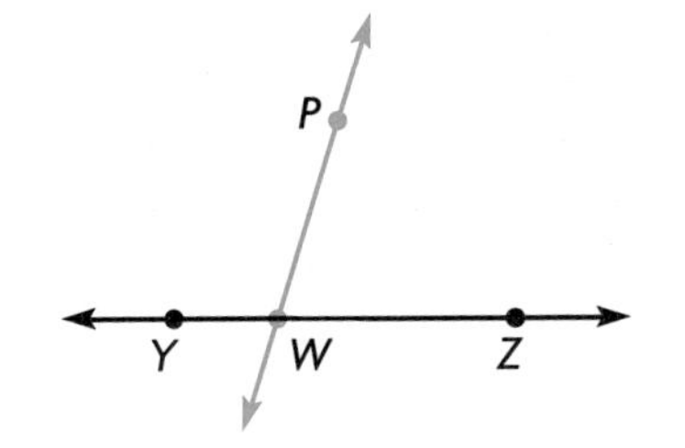

Step 2

Construct an angle congruent to $\angle PWZ$ at point P. Label the point Q.

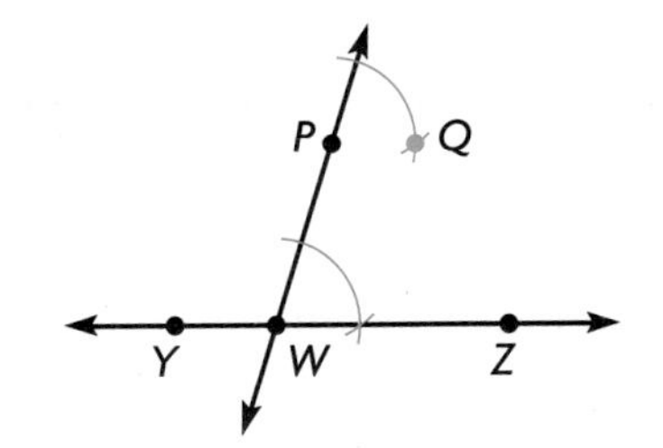

Step 3

Draw $\overleftrightarrow{PQ}$. $\overleftrightarrow{PQ}$ is a line parallel to $\overleftrightarrow{YZ}$. $\overleftrightarrow{PQ} \parallel \overleftrightarrow{YZ}$

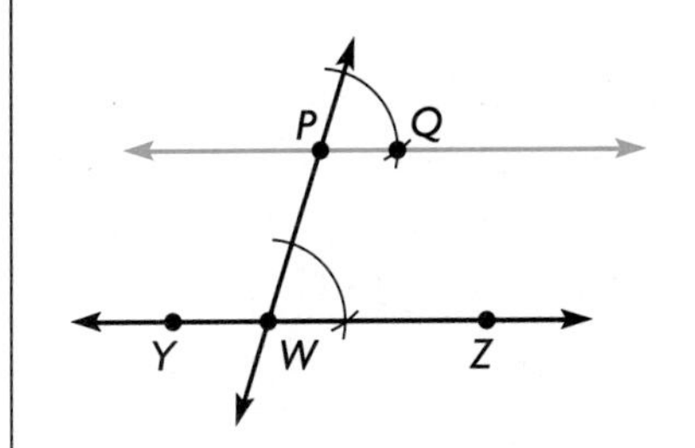

Constructing Perpendicular Lines

You can construct a line perpendicular to another line by using some of the same methods you used to construct parallel lines.

EXAMPLE 2 Construct a line perpendicular to a given line.

Step 1

Draw a line. Place the compass point on any point P on the line. Draw two arcs the same distance from P that intersect the line. Label the intersection points C and D.

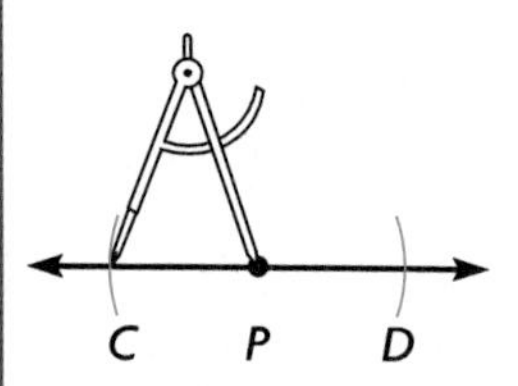

Step 2

Open the compass to a wider radius. From C and D, draw two arcs that intersect at point E.

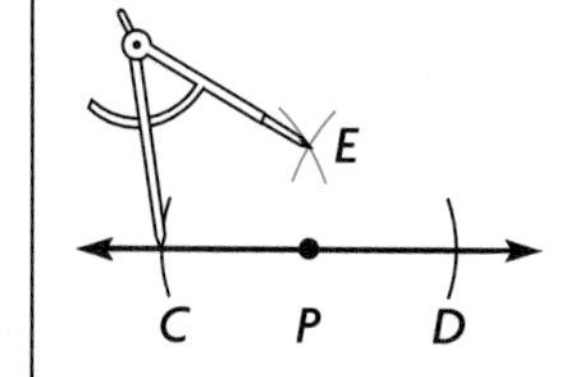

Step 3

Draw $\overleftrightarrow{PE}$. $\overleftrightarrow{PE}$ is a line perpendicular to $\overleftrightarrow{CD}$ at point P. $\overleftrightarrow{PE} \perp \overleftrightarrow{CD}$.

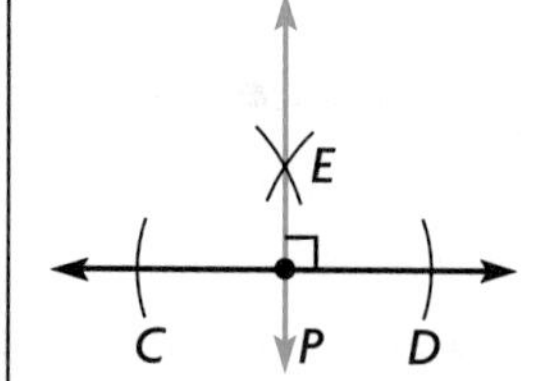

- Draw line JK. Construct $\overleftrightarrow{GH}$ perpendicular to $\overleftrightarrow{JK}$ at point G.

If a perpendicular line intersects a line segment at its midpoint, the line is called a **perpendicular bisector**.

GUIDED PRACTICE

Use a compass and a straightedge only.

1. Draw a line. Construct another line parallel to it.
2. Write down the steps to follow in constructing a right angle.
3. Draw a line segment. Construct the perpendicular bisector of the segment.
4. Draw line k. Construct two lines l and m parallel to line k. Then construct line n perpendicular to it. How are lines l and m related to line n?
5. Draw line a. Construct lines b and c perpendicular to line a and line d parallel to line a. How are lines b and c related? lines c and d?

TEEN TIMES

Real-life examples of parallel lines include wires strung on telephone poles, lines on notebook paper, lines separating sections of sidewalk, rows of crops in a field, and gymnastics parallel bars. The world's record for parallel bar dips is held by Kim Yang-ki of South Korea, who did 3,726 dips in 1 hour.

INDEPENDENT PRACTICE

Draw the lines and points shown.

1. Copy the figure. Then construct a line through point Q parallel to $\overleftrightarrow{JM}$.

2. Copy the figure. Then construct a line through point P perpendicular to $\overleftrightarrow{RS}$.

3. Use a straightedge to draw line m on a sheet of paper. Using a compass and a straightedge, construct line l perpendicular to line m.

4. Look at your construction in Exercise 3. Construct line n parallel to line m. What is the relationship between line n and line l? How do you know?

5. Describe at least three examples of perpendicular lines that you see in your classroom, community, or home.

Problem-Solving Applications

6. **GEOMETRY** Construct two perpendicular lines. Label their intersection point P. Draw a circle, using P as the center. Label the points of intersection A, B, C, and D. Construct a polygon by connecting in order the four points A, B, C, and D. What figure do they form? Explain.

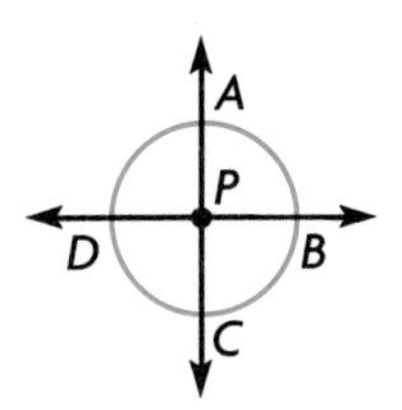

7. **CRITICAL THINKING** Can you construct the perpendicular bisector of a line? Explain.

8. **MUSIC** Brian has a square room with a stereo speaker in each corner. The speakers face the center of the room. Brian wants to place his chair at the center so he will be equally distant from each speaker. Trace the floor plan shown at the right. Use a compass and a straightedge to find the center of the room. Explain your method.

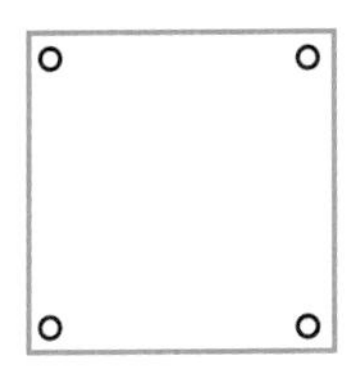

9. Construct a square and bisect each side to find the midpoint. Connect the adjacent midpoints with line segments. What polygon did you form?

10. Trace the equilateral triangle at the right. Construct the perpendicular bisector of each side. What do you notice?

11. **WRITE ABOUT IT** Explain how to verify that lines constructed as perpendicular intersect at right angles.

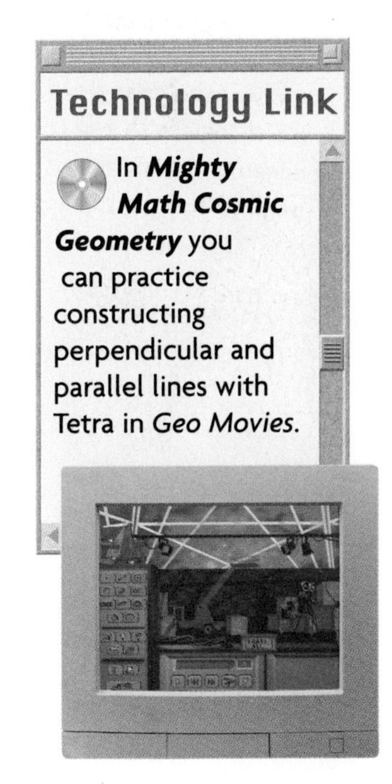

LESSON 11.3

Classifying and Comparing Triangles

What You'll Learn
How to classify triangles by sides and angles and how to identify corresponding parts of congruent triangles

Why Learn This?
To describe triangles around you

VOCABULARY

Side-Side-Side (SSS)

Side-Angle-Side (SAS)

Angle-Side-Angle (ASA)

Many architects and artists use triangles in their blueprints and designs. What type of triangle do you see in the Eiffel Tower?

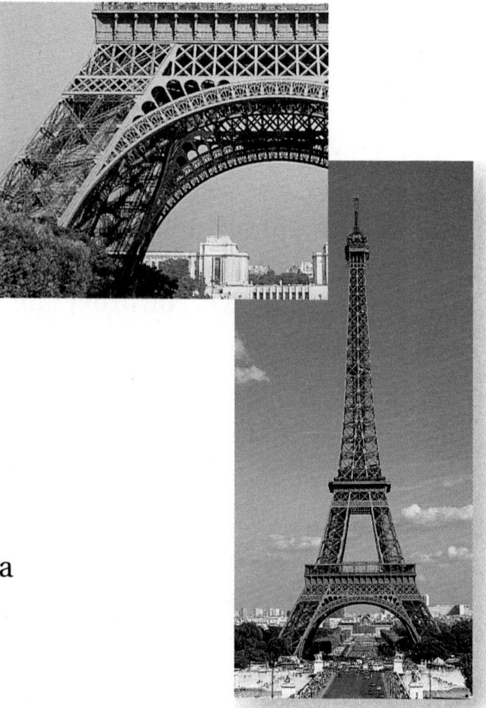

Triangles can be classified by the lengths of their sides as equilateral, isosceles, and scalene triangles. Triangles can also be classified by the measures of their angles as acute, right, and obtuse triangles.

Suppose you move one vertex of a triangle while keeping the other two fixed. Does the classification of the triangle change?

REMEMBER:

An **isosceles triangle** is a triangle with two congruent sides. **See page H30.**

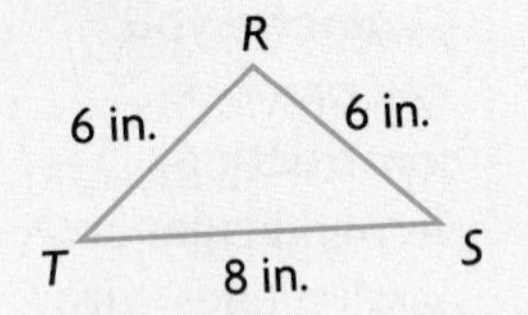

ACTIVITY

WHAT YOU'LL NEED: geoboard, geoband

- Form the sides of isosceles triangle *ABC* by wrapping a geoband around three pegs of a geoboard as shown. **Think:** $\overline{AB}$ and $\overline{BC}$ are congruent sides.

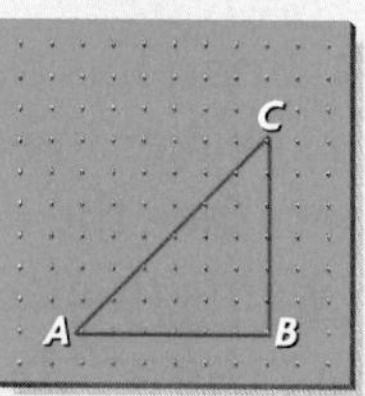

- Keep vertices *A* and *B* in place, but move vertex *C* around to form other isosceles triangles that also have $\overline{AB}$ as a side.

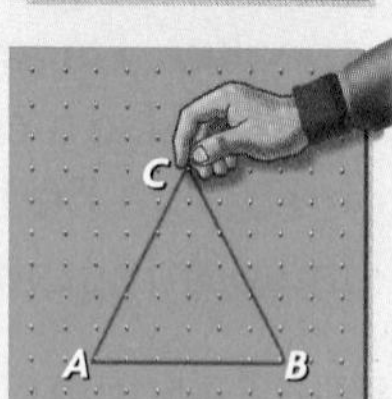

- Find as many locations as you can for vertex *C* that still make $\triangle ABC$ an isosceles triangle.
- Find locations of vertex *C* that make $\triangle ABC$ both right and isosceles.
- Record your results by sketching the triangles.

A triangle may be classified both by its sides and by its angles. Triangle PQR is both scalene and obtuse.

P Q R 2.6 cm 1.3 cm 2 cm 100°

You can use Venn diagrams to classify triangles.

EXAMPLE 1 Draw a Venn diagram to show the relationship between right triangles and isosceles triangles. Where in the diagram does $\triangle DEF$ belong?

D E F 38 mm 24 mm 20 mm 120°

Triangles can be right, isosceles, both right and isosceles, or neither right nor isosceles. Draw two overlapping circles, one circle for right triangles and the other for isosceles triangles.

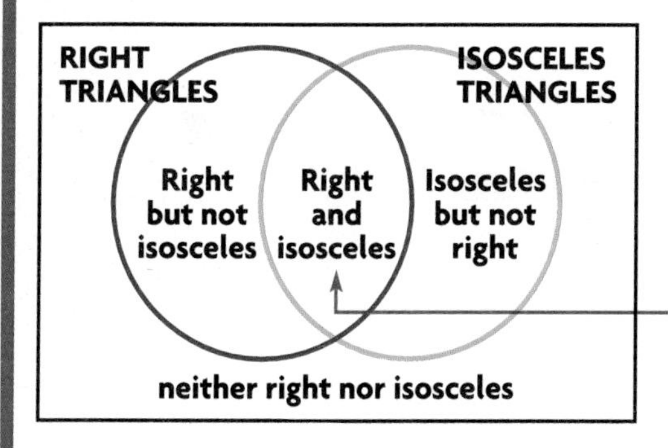

The overlapping part represents triangles that are both right and isosceles.

Triangle DEF is neither right nor isosceles. So, it belongs outside both circles.

Draw a triangle that belongs inside both circles.

REMEMBER:

A **Venn diagram** is used to show relationships between sets.

See page 16.

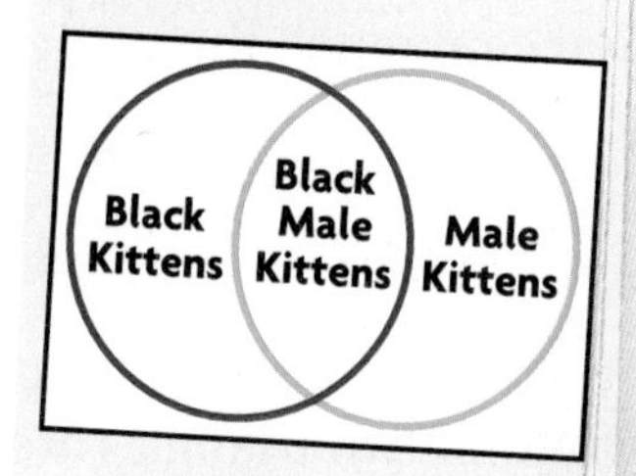

GUIDED PRACTICE

1. Classify this triangle by the lengths of its sides: 8 cm, 12 cm, and 8 cm.
2. Classify this triangle by the measures of its angles: 30°, 45°, and 105°.
3. Draw a triangle that is acute and isosceles.
4. Can a triangle be right and scalene? Support your answer by drawing a triangle.
5. **CRITICAL THINKING** Are all acute triangles also equilateral triangles? Are all equilateral triangles also acute triangles? Draw a Venn diagram to show the relationship between equilateral triangles and acute triangles.

ENVIRONMENT LINK

Poachers illegally sell elephant tusk ivory, passing it off as mammoth tusk ivory, which is legal to sell. Scientists distinguish between elephant and mammoth tusk ivory by angle-shaped tusk markings. Angles on elephant tusks are obtuse; those on mammoth tusks are right or acute. Can a piece of ivory with markings forming 127° angles be sold legally?

Congruent Triangles

Two triangles are congruent when they have the same size and shape. $\triangle ABC \cong \triangle DEF$

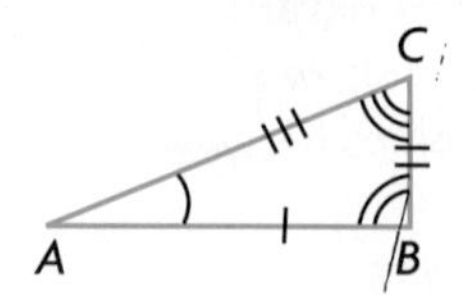

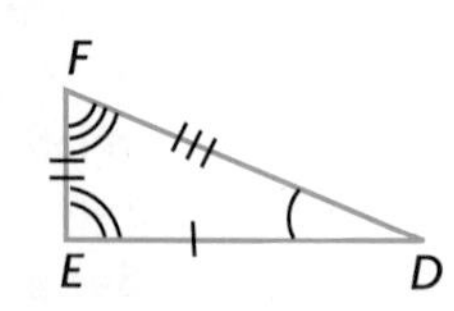

Corresponding sides and angles are congruent. The same marking on two sides or angles indicates they are congruent.

You can match the vertices and sides of congruent triangles.

$\angle A \cong \angle D$ $\angle B \cong \angle E$ $\angle C \cong \angle F$

$\overline{AB} \cong \overline{DE}$ $\overline{BC} \cong \overline{EF}$ $\overline{CA} \cong \overline{FD}$

You do not need to compare all sides and all angles to determine whether two triangles are congruent. You need only three corresponding congruent parts and the following rules.

MATHEMATICS LINK

A *golden triangle* is an isosceles triangle with base angles that measure 72° and a third angle that measures 36°. Draw a golden triangle, and then bisect both base angles. Did you form two new golden triangles?

If this is true, triangles are congruent.	Name of Rule	Example
Three sides of one triangle match three sides of another triangle.	**Side-Side-Side** (SSS)	
Two sides and the included angle of one triangle match two sides and the included angle of another triangle.	**Side-Angle-Side** (SAS)	
Two angles and the included side of one triangle match two angles and the included side of another triangle.	**Angle-Side-Angle** (ASA)	

EXAMPLE 2 Compare the markings on the triangles. Are the triangles congruent by SSS, SAS, or ASA?

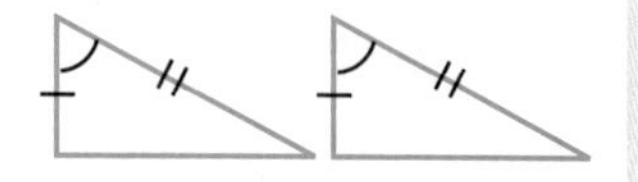

Since a side, an included angle, and a side are shown as congruent, the triangles are congruent by SAS.

INDEPENDENT PRACTICE

Classify each triangle according to the lengths of its sides.

1. 30 m, 20 m, 15 m **2.** 3 cm, 5 cm, 3 cm **3.** 16 in., 16 in., 16 in.

Classify each triangle according to the measures of its angles.

4. 40°, 60°, 80° **5.** 15°, 75°, 90° **6.** 10°, 20°, 150°

Use the congruent triangles *UQM* and *VZR*.

7. Name three pairs of congruent sides and three pairs of congruent angles for the triangles.

8. Use symbols to say that the triangles are congruent.

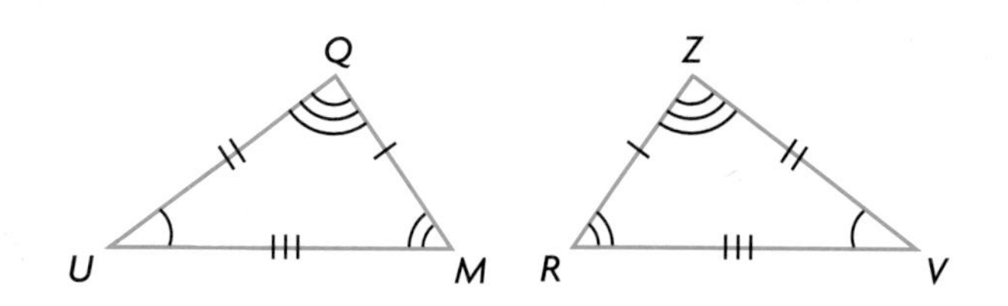

Determine whether the triangles are congruent by SSS, SAS, or ASA.

9.

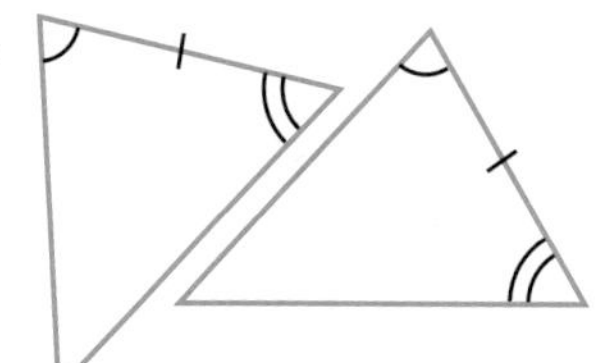

10.

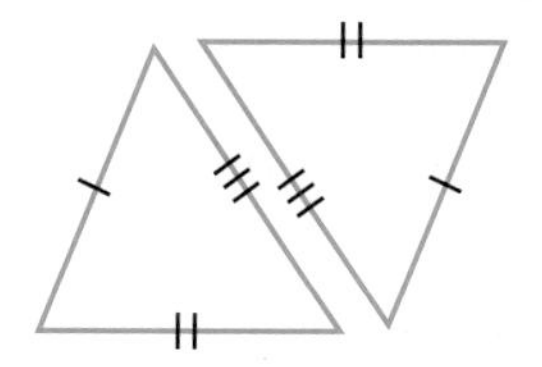

11.

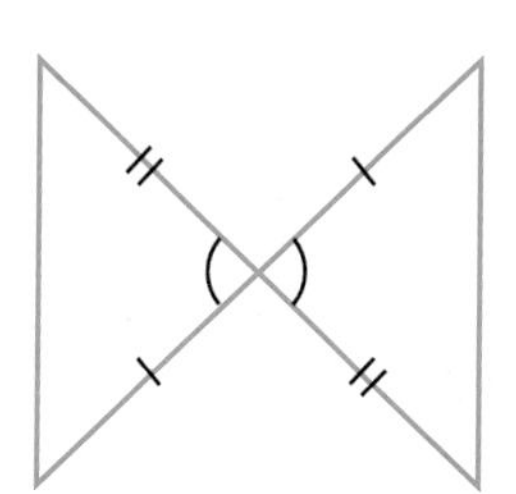

Determine whether the triangles are congruent. Write *yes, no,* or *not enough information.* If you write *yes,* explain how you know.

12.

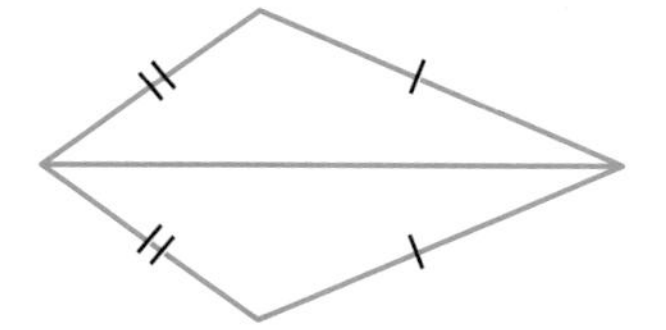

13.

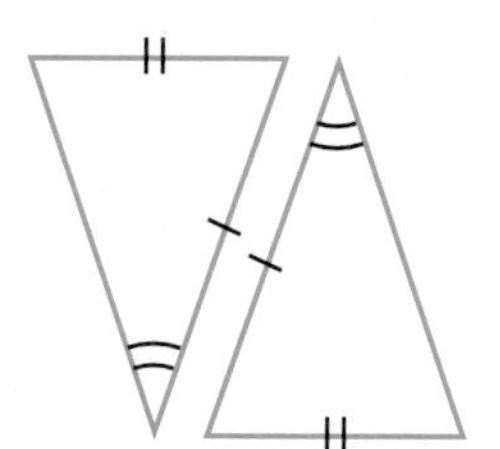

14.

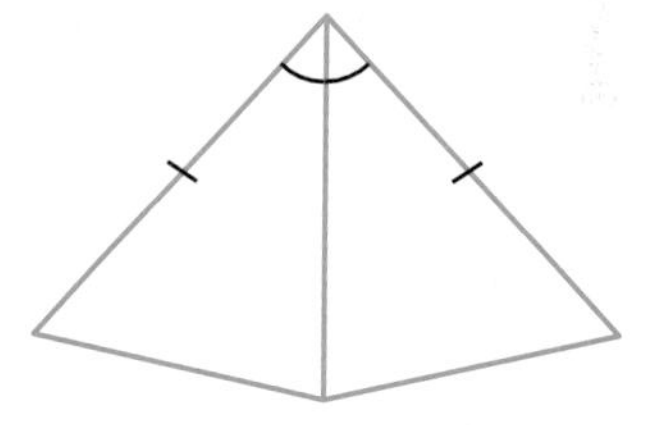

Problem-Solving Applications

15. Are all acute triangles also scalene triangles? Draw a Venn diagram and a triangle to support your answer.

16. **CRITICAL THINKING** Does an obtuse equilateral triangle exist? Explain.

In the figure, trees *A* and *B* are on opposite sides of a stream. Sally wants to string a rope between them. She needs to know the distance between the trees to be sure she has enough rope. Distances *AC, DC,* and *DE* and angle *BCA* are measured.

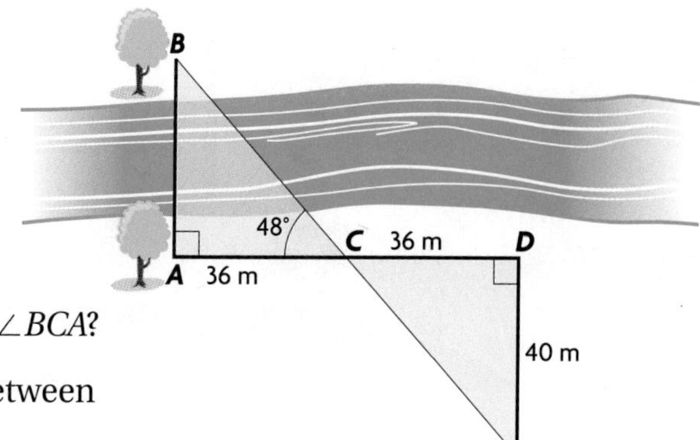

17. **CRITICAL THINKING** Why is $\angle ECD$ congruent to $\angle BCA$?

18. **DISTANCE** Find the length of $\overline{AB}$, the distance between the trees. Give a reason for your answer.

19. **WRITE ABOUT IT** Explain the rules that you can use to decide whether two triangles are congruent.

LESSON 11.4

Constructing Congruent Triangles

What You'll Learn
How to construct congruent triangles

Why Learn This?
To make exact copies of triangles

You can use the rules for congruence of two triangles, along with a straightedge and a compass, to construct congruent triangles.

EXAMPLE 1 Using the Side-Side-Side (SSS) rule, construct a triangle congruent to $\triangle JKL$.

Think: The corresponding sides must have the same length.

Step 1

Draw $\overrightarrow{MN}$. Construct $\overline{MO} \cong \overline{JK}$.

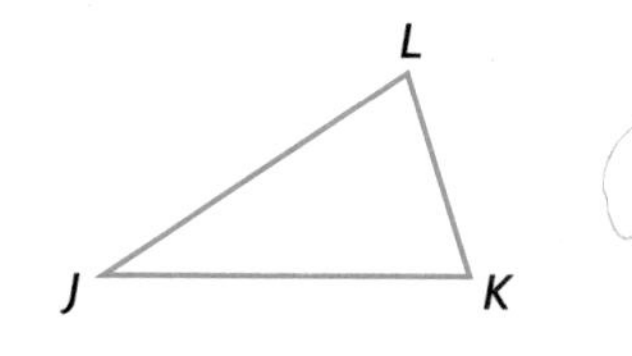

Step 2

Use the compass to measure $\overline{JL}$. With the same compass opening, place the compass point on M and draw an arc as shown.

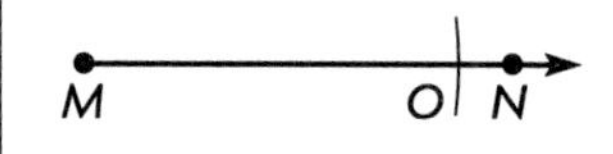

Step 3

Use the compass to measure $\overline{KL}$. With the same compass opening, place the compass point on O and draw an arc that intersects the arc drawn in Step 2. Label the point P.

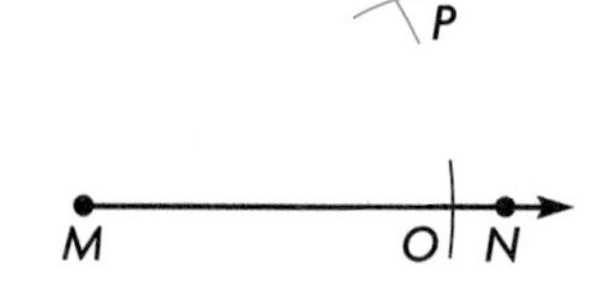

Step 4

Draw $\overline{MP}$ and $\overline{OP}$.
$\triangle MOP \cong \triangle JKL$

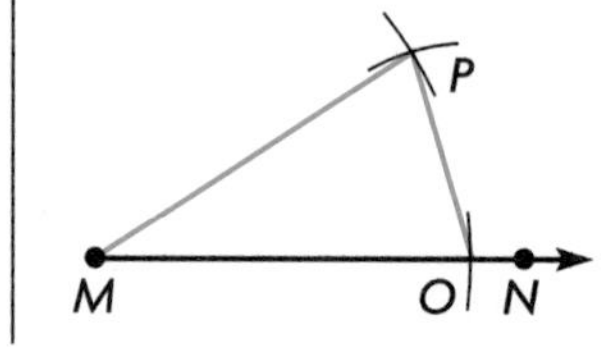

Talk About It

- Look at Example 1. Why must the compass opening remain the same in Step 2? in Step 3?
- Suppose the two triangles are congruent by the SSS rule. Are the corresponding angles congruent? Explain.

CAREER LINK

Navigators direct the movement of airplanes, ships, and spacecraft. A navigator uses a straightedge and a compass to plot a vehicle's course and position on a chart that shows natural and constructed landmarks. Name other professions where the use of a straightedge and compass is necessary.

You can also use the Side-Angle-Side (SAS) rule to construct congruent triangles.

EXAMPLE 2 Using the SAS rule, construct a triangle congruent to $\triangle ABC$.

Think: Use these parts: $\overline{AB}$, $\angle A$, and $\overline{AC}$.

Step 1

Construct $\overline{PR} \cong \overline{AB}$.

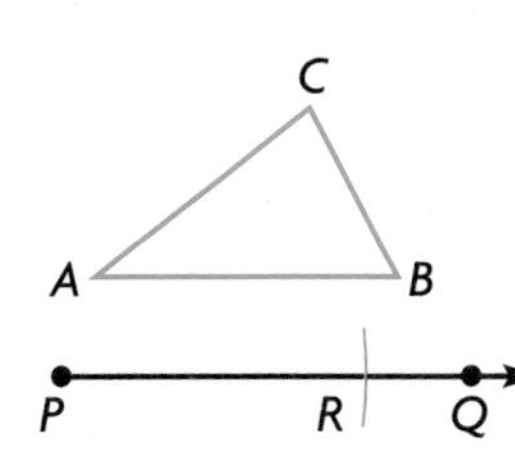

Step 2

Construct $\angle P \cong \angle A$.

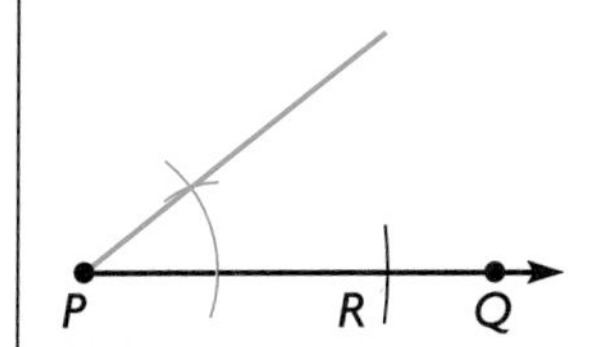

Step 3

Construct $\overline{PT} \cong \overline{AC}$.

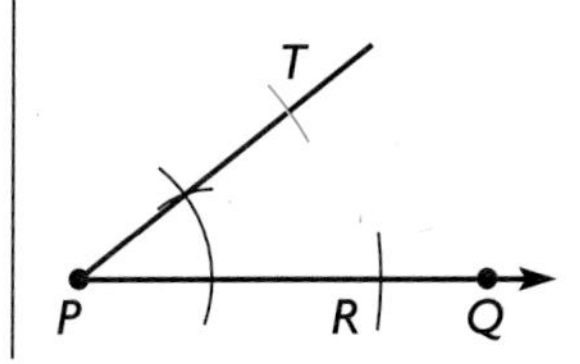

Step 4

Draw $\overline{TR}$.
$\triangle PRT \cong \triangle ABC$

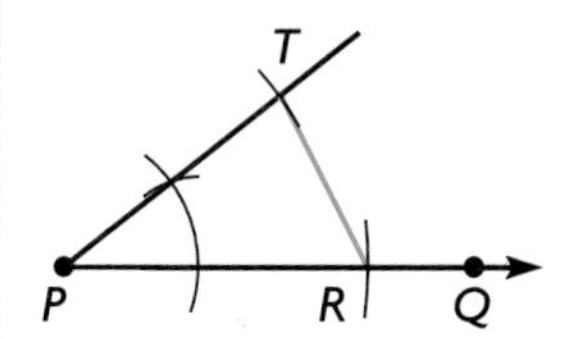

- Using the SAS rule, which other parts could you use to construct a triangle congruent to $\triangle ABC$?
- Why is the choice of parts important when using the SAS rule?

GUIDED PRACTICE

Trace the triangle. Use the SSS rule to construct a congruent triangle.

1. 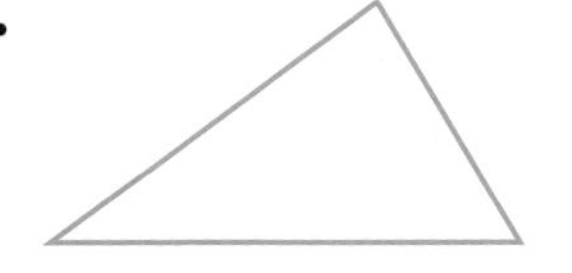

2. 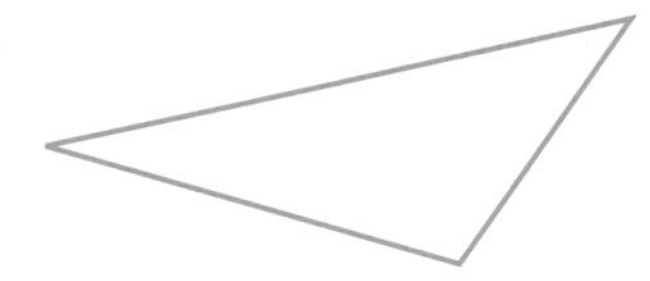

3. 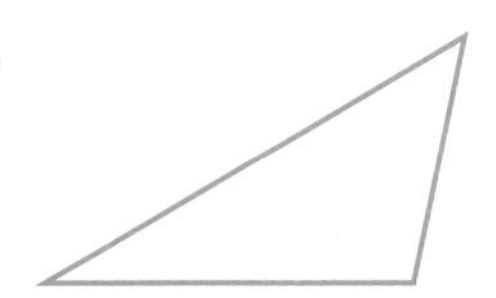

4. 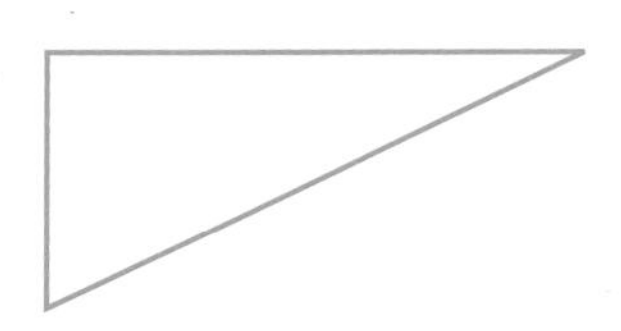

Trace the triangle. Use the SAS rule to construct a congruent triangle.

5. 

6. 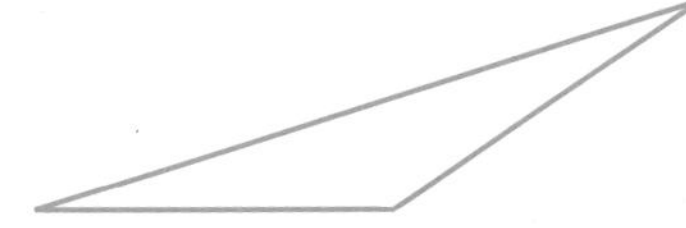

7. 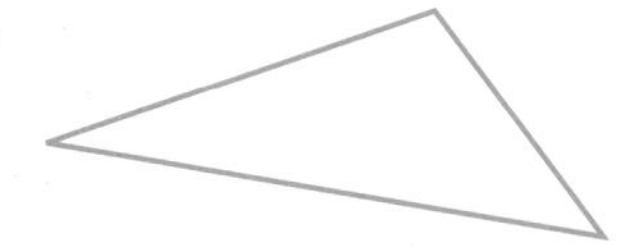

8. 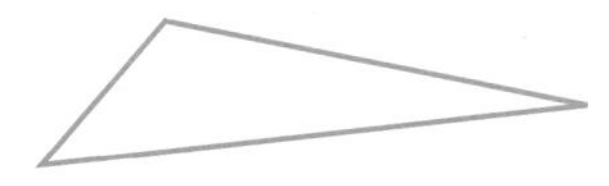

GEOGRAPHY LINK

The Global Positioning System is a navigation system that uses satellites to determine latitude, longitude, and altitude for any location very accurately. A receiver on Earth determines position by using data from three satellites, along with triangles whose sides represent distances. What are the latitude, longitude, and altitude of your hometown?

You can also construct congruent triangles by using the Angle-Side-Angle (ASA) rule.

EXAMPLE 3 Using the ASA rule, construct a triangle congruent to $\triangle DEF$.

Think: Use these parts: $\angle D$, $\overline{DE}$, and $\angle E$.

Step 1

Construct $\overline{AB} \cong \overline{DE}$.

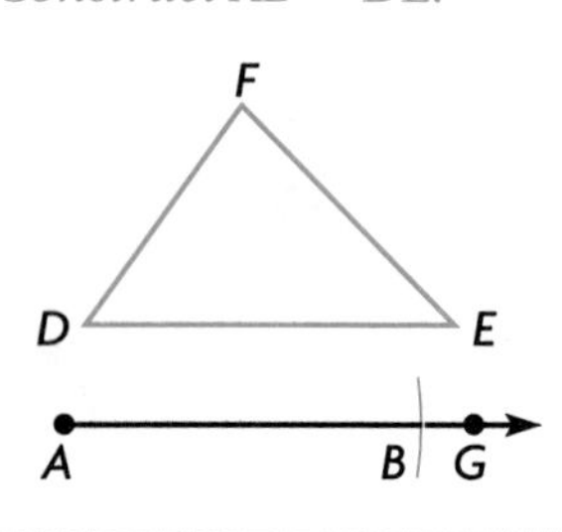

Step 2

Construct $\angle A \cong \angle D$.

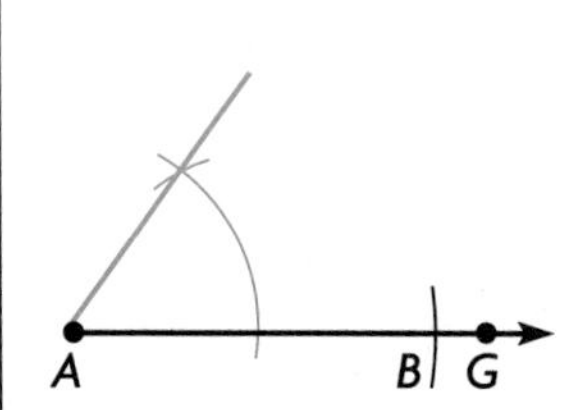

Step 3

Construct $\angle B \cong \angle E$.

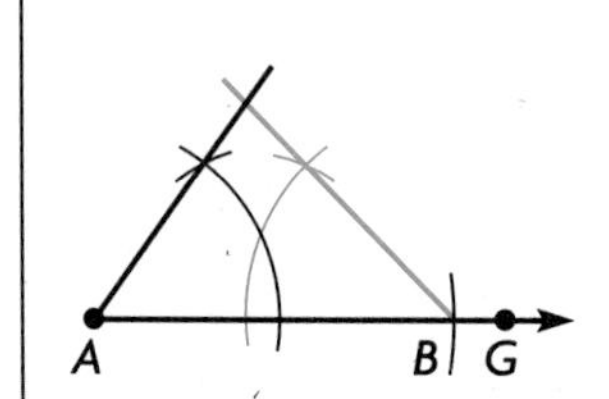

Step 4

Label C.
$\triangle ABC \cong \triangle DEF$

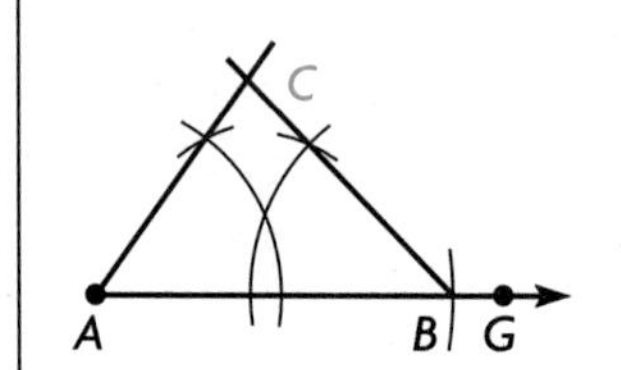

Talk About It CRITICAL THINKING

- In Example 3, what other parts could you use to construct a triangle congruent to $\triangle DEF$ by using the ASA rule?
- Why is the choice of angles and side important when using the ASA rule?
- Can you always construct congruent triangles by using an angle-angle-angle rule? Why or why not?

INDEPENDENT PRACTICE

Trace the triangle. Use the indicated rule to construct a congruent triangle.

1. SSS

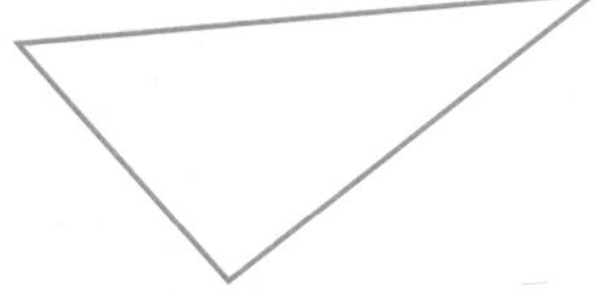
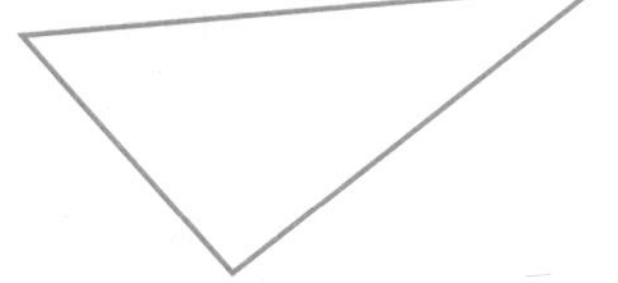

2. SAS

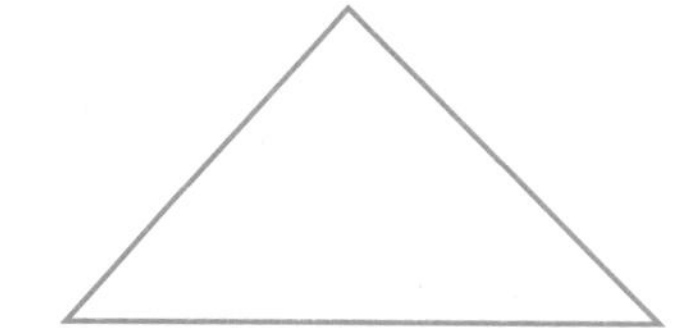

3. ASA

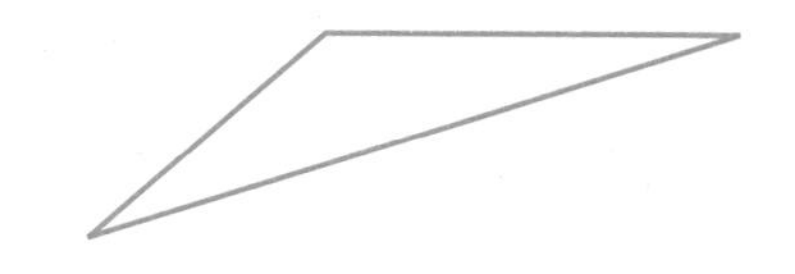

4. SAS

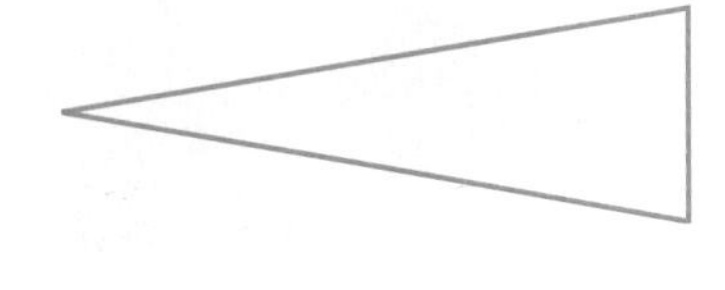

5. ASA

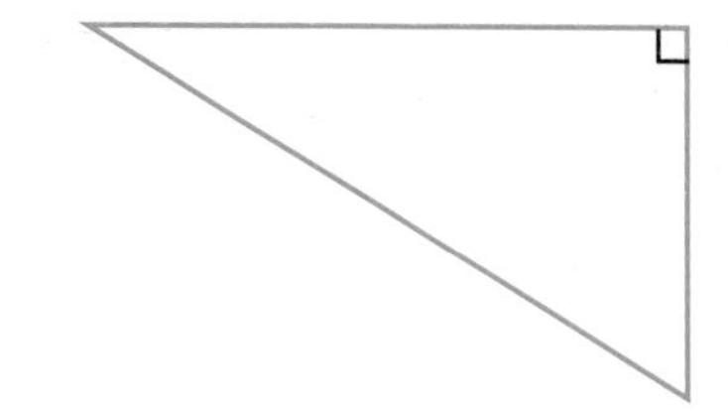

6. SSS

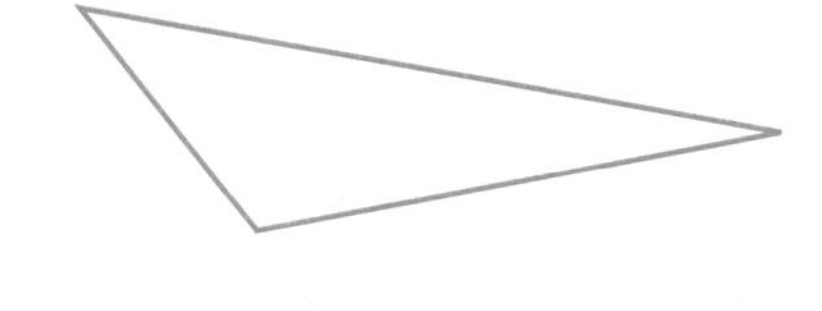

Use the SSS rule and the three given segments to try to construct a triangle.

7.

8.

9.

10.

Problem-Solving Applications

11. CRITICAL THINKING In which of Exercises 7–10 was the construction not possible? Explain.

12. COMPARE Study your constructions in Exercises 7–10. How are the lengths of the sides of a triangle related? Could a triangle be formed with line segments of length 4 cm, 5 cm, and 7cm? Explain.

13. WRITE ABOUT IT Explain how you can use the rules for congruence of triangles to construct congruent triangles.

Mixed Review and Test Prep

Describe the solid figure formed by each pattern. Write *prism* or *pyramid.*

14.

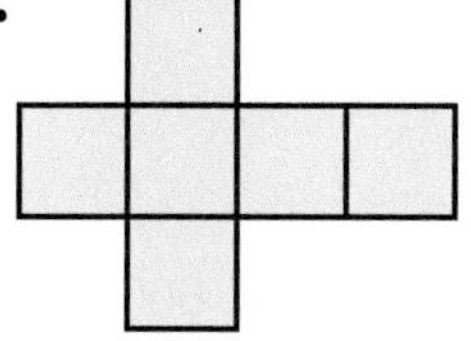

15.

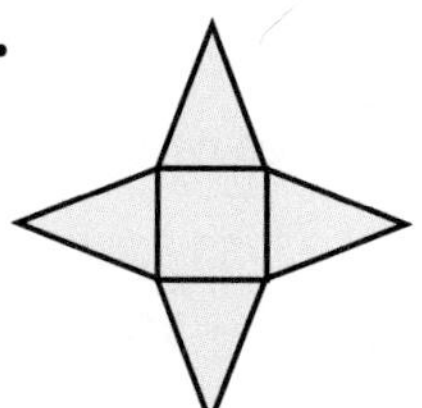

16.

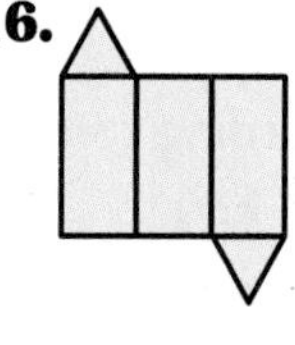

Identify the transformation that forms the second figure. Write *translation, rotation,* or *reflection.*

17.

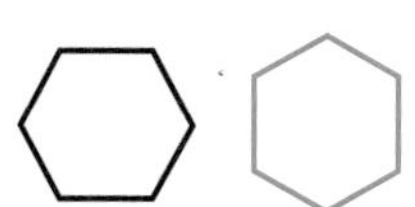

18.

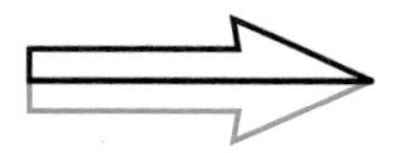

19.

20. TRANSFORMATIONS Point *A* with coordinates (4,3) is reflected about the *y*-axis. What are the coordinates of the image?

A (3,4) **B** $(^-4,3)$

C $(4,^-3)$ **D** $(^-4,^-3)$

21. ART Jacob drew 55 pictures. Three-fifths of them were tessellations. How many were not tessellations?

F 11 **G** 22

H 33 **J** 44

MORE PRACTICE Lesson 11.4, page H59

CHAPTER 11 Review/Test

1. **VOCABULARY** When you divide an angle or line segment into two congruent parts, you __?__ it. (page 218)

2. **VOCABULARY** The point in the middle of a line segment is called the __?__. (page 219)

Trace the angle and construct an angle congruent to it. (pages 217–220)

3.

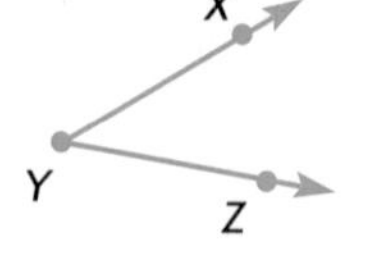

4.

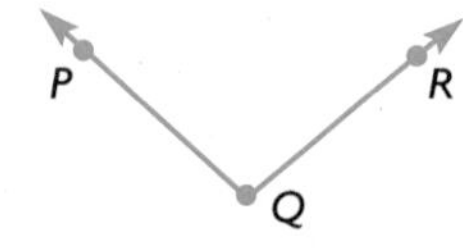

5.

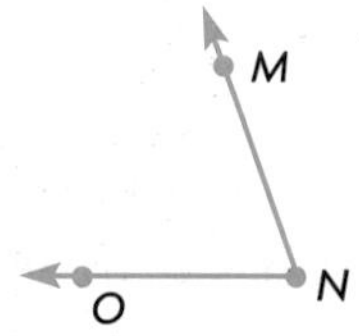

Trace the figure. Then bisect it. (pages 217–220)

6.

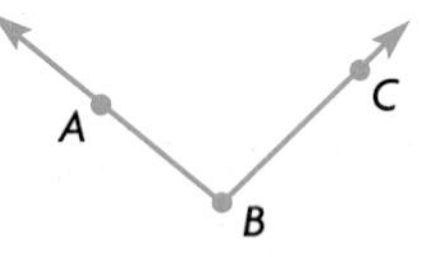

7.

8.

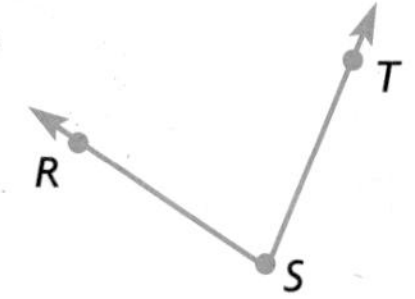

9. **VOCABULARY** A perpendicular line that intersects a line segment at its midpoint is called a(n) __?__. (page 222)

10. Trace $\overrightarrow{PQ}$ two times. Then construct the following. (pages 221–223)

a. $\overleftrightarrow{AB} \perp \overleftrightarrow{PQ}$

b. $\overleftrightarrow{CD} \parallel \overleftrightarrow{PQ}$

Classify each triangle according to the lengths of its sides or to its angle measures. (pages 224–227)

11. 10 in., 10 in., 10 in. **12.** 7 in., 7 in., 12 in. **13.** 45°, 65°, 70° **14.** 30°, 60°, 90°

Determine whether the triangles are congruent by SSS, SAS, or ASA. (pages 224–227)

15.

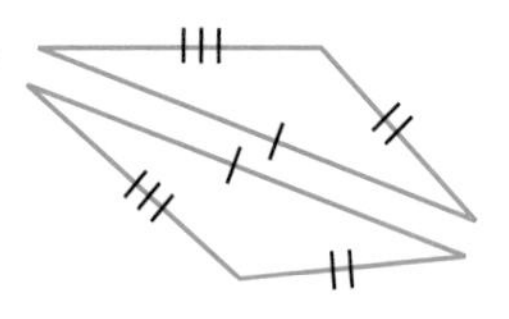

16.

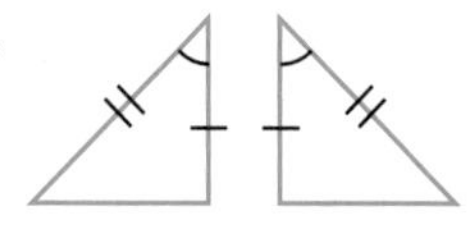

17.

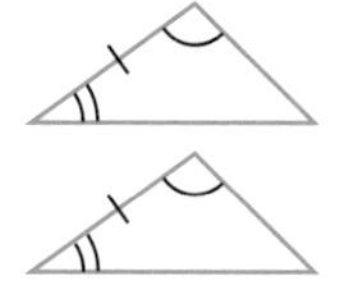

Trace the triangle. Use the indicated rule to construct a congruent triangle. (pages 228–231)

18. ASA

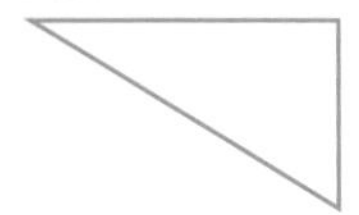

19. SSS

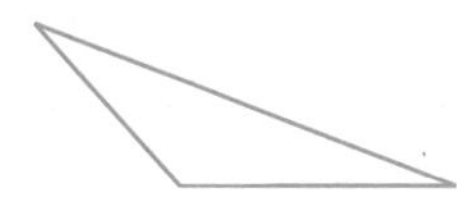

20. SAS

Test Prep

CUMULATIVE
CHAPTERS 1–11

1. Which are the angle measures of an acute triangle?

A 40°, 40°, 100°
B 30°, 60°, 90°
C 40°, 55°, 85°
D 25°, 50°, 105°

2. Jerry worked 4 fewer hours than Natalie did. Jerry worked 26 hours. Which equation can be used to find the number of hours, h, Natalie worked?

F $4 - h = 26$
G $h + 4 = 26$
H $\frac{h}{4} = 26$
J $h - 4 = 26$

3. For what value of t is the equation $5t + {}^{-}2 + {}^{-}2t = 7$ a true statement?

A $^{-}3$
B $\frac{1}{3}$
C $\frac{7}{9}$
D $\frac{5}{3}$
E Not Here

4. $^{-}2.57 + {}^{-}1.49 =$

F $^{-}4.06$
G $^{-}3.06$
H $^{-}1.08$
J 4.06

5. Compare and order $^{-}5$, $\sqrt{49}$, and 3.9 from least to greatest.

A $^{-}5, \sqrt{49}, 3.9$
B $^{-}5, 3.9, \sqrt{49}$
C $\sqrt{49}, 3.9, {}^{-}5$
D $3.9, {}^{-}5, \sqrt{49}$

6. $4 + 3(5 - 2) \div 6 =$

F 5.5
G 11.5
H 16
J 17.5

7. Which is equivalent to $\frac{1}{8}$?

A 0.0125
B 12.5%
C 0.18
D 18%

8. For what value of b is the equation $\frac{b}{7.2} = 5$ a true statement?

F 1.44
G 12.2
H 35.7
J 36
K Not Here

9. A book store received a shipment of 4,500 books, $\frac{3}{5}$ of which were adult fiction. Of the remaining books, $\frac{1}{2}$ were non-fiction. The rest were children's books. How many books were children's books?

A 500
B 900
C 1,800
D 2,700

10. $3\frac{1}{2} \div 1\frac{7}{8} =$

F $1\frac{5}{12}$
G $1\frac{13}{15}$
H $3\frac{1}{3}$
J $6\frac{9}{16}$

CHAPTER

12

PICTURING AND MODELING SOLID FIGURES

LOOK AHEAD

In this chapter you will solve problems that involve

- drawing solid figures
- making nets for polyhedrons
- cutting solid figures into new figures

TECHNOLOGY LINK

The number of U.S. households with home computers has increased dramatically since the early 1980's. The line graph below shows the percent of U.S. households with computers, from 1983 to 1996.

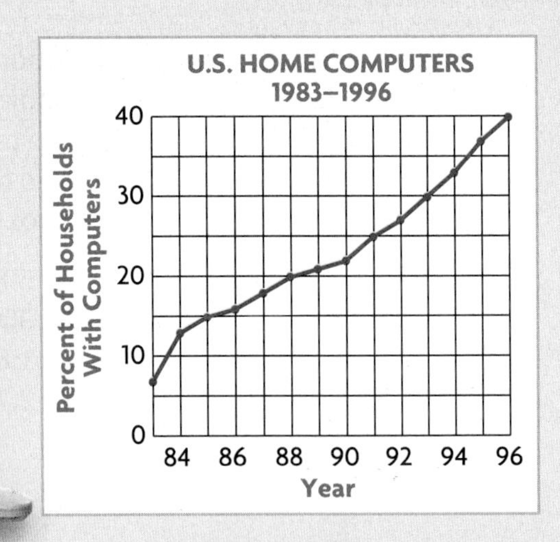

- Between which two years was the greatest increase in percent of households with home computers?
- About what was the gain in the percent of households with home computers, between 1983 and 1996?

Problem-Solving Project

Building Solids for Plato

The Greek philosopher Plato, who lived about 386 B.C., called the solid figures below *regular solids*.

YOU WILL NEED: paper or tagboard; patterns for equilateral triangle, square, and regular pentagon; scissors, tape

Select two of the regular solids to construct. Cut out the polygons that you will need for the faces of your solid figures. Tape the faces together. Write about what the solids have in common and why Plato called them regular solids. Present your analysis to the class.

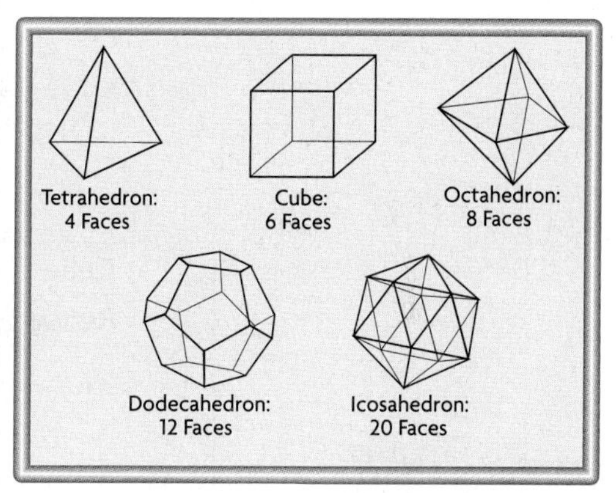

PROJECT CHECKLIST

- ✓ Did you select two regular solids?
- ✓ Did you make them?
- ✓ Did you write about why Plato called them regular solids?
- ✓ Did you present your analysis to the class?

LESSON 12.1

Solid Figures

What You'll Learn
How to identify solid figures

Why Learn This?
To describe the shapes of real-life objects such as buildings and food containers

VOCABULARY
solid figures
polyhedron

If you look at the shapes of the buildings in any town or city, you will see a variety of three-dimensional figures. These are often called **solid figures**, or space figures.

ACTIVITY

- Look at the solid figures below. Make a table that lists the name of each figure, the number of faces, and the name of its base.

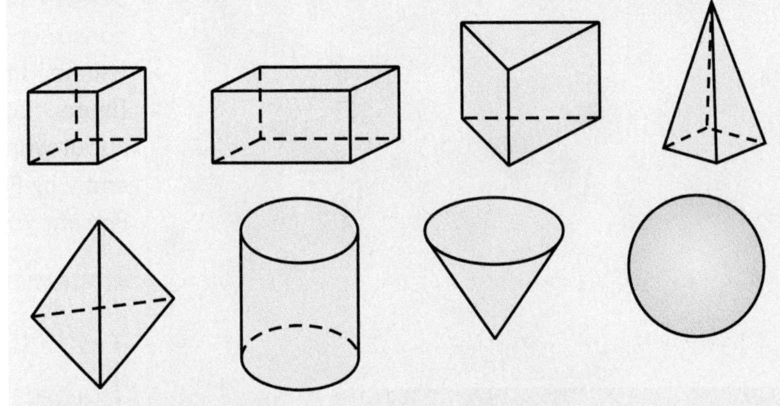

Solid Figure	Number of Faces	Base
Cube	6	square
Rectangular prism	?	?

- Choose two of the solid figures. How are they alike? How are they different?

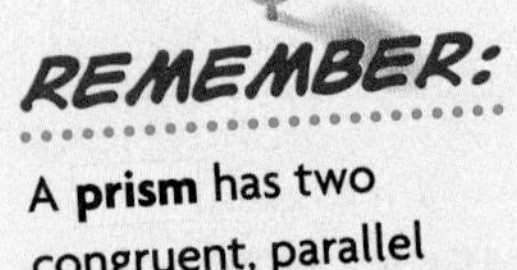

REMEMBER:
A **prism** has two congruent, parallel bases, and a **pyramid** has one base. **See page H25.**

If all the faces of a solid figure are polygons, the figure is a **polyhedron**. A cube is a polyhedron. Figures that have curved surfaces, such as a cylinder, are not polyhedrons.

Talk About It

- Look at the solid figures. How many are prisms? How many are pyramids? How many are not polyhedrons?
- Can a polyhedron have a base that is a circle? Explain.

GUIDED PRACTICE

Write *polyhedron* or *not polyhedron* for each solid figure.

1. 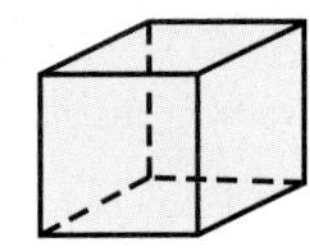

2. 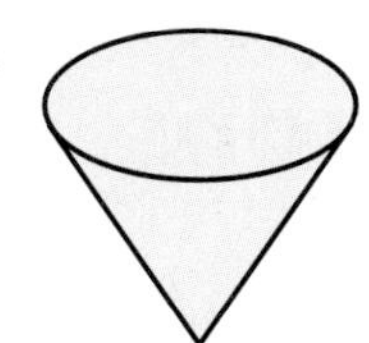

3. 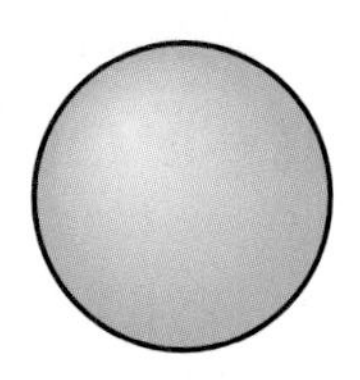

4. 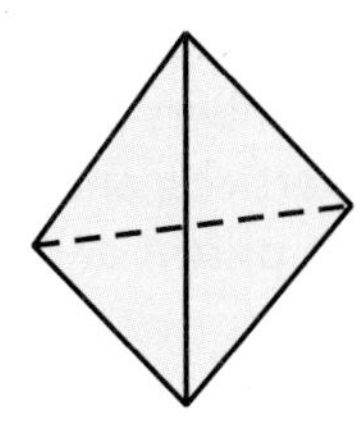

5. Write the names of the solid figures in Exercises 1–4.

INDEPENDENT PRACTICE

Name the figure that is the base of each solid figure.

1. 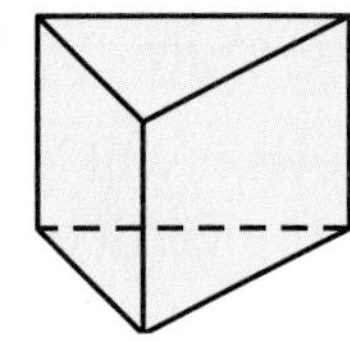

2. 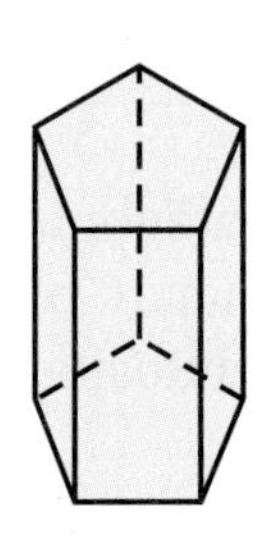

3. 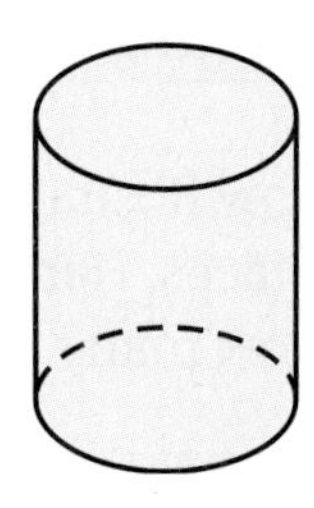

4. 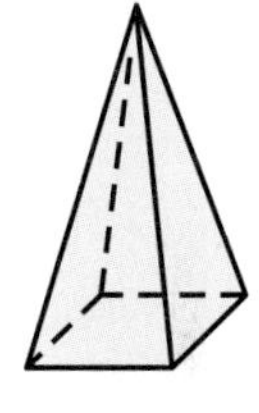

Write *true* or *false.* Write a true statement from any false statement.

5. All prisms are polyhedrons.

6. No pyramid is a prism.

7. Some cylinders are polyhedrons.

8. All cones have a circle as a base.

9. Some polygons are polyhedrons.

10. All faces of a pyramid are triangles.

Problem-Solving Applications

11. Jason made the Venn diagram below to show how pyramids and prisms are related to other polyhedrons. However, he made a mistake. What was his mistake?

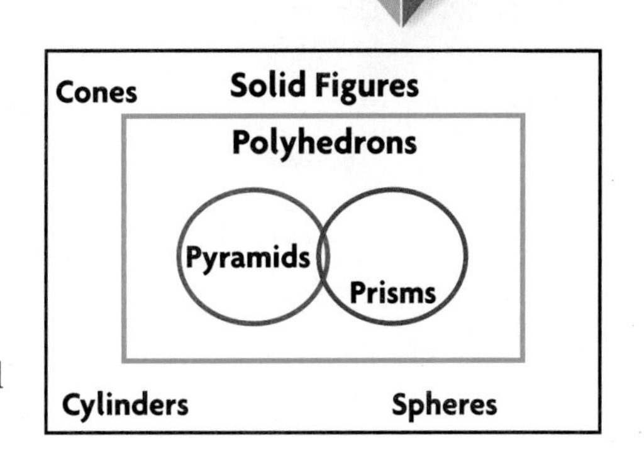

12. **ART** Marta has a piece of clay shaped like a rectangular prism. She wants to make one cut to change the rectangular prism into two triangular prisms. Draw a picture to show how she should cut the clay.

13. **CRITICAL THINKING** Karen made two square pyramids and glued the congruent bases together. Is the new figure a polyhedron? Explain.

14. **WRITE ABOUT IT** Explain why cylinders, cones, and spheres are not polyhedrons.

MORE PRACTICE Lesson 12.1, page H59

LESSON 12.2

PROBLEM-SOLVING STRATEGY

Finding Patterns in Polyhedrons

What You'll Learn
How to find patterns in the numbers of faces, vertices, and edges in prisms and pyramids

Why Learn This?
To build prisms and pyramids

PROBLEM SOLVING
- Understand
- Plan
- Solve
- Look Back

Rosita is building polyhedrons by using pieces of clay for the vertices and toothpicks for the edges. She recorded the numbers of faces, vertices, and edges for three models she has built.

Name of Figure	Number of Faces (*F*)	Number of Vertices (*V*)	Number of Edges (*E*)
Triangular prism	5	6	9
Triangular pyramid	4	4	6
Rectangular prism	6	8	12

Now Rosita will build a pentagonal prism. She knows it will have 7 faces. Her teacher gives her 10 pieces of clay for the vertices. How many toothpicks does Rosita need for the edges?

UNDERSTAND What are you asked to find?

What facts are given?

PLAN What strategy will you use?

You can *find a pattern* among the numbers of faces, vertices, and edges shown in the table. Then you can use the pattern to make a prediction for the pentagonal prism.

SOLVE How will you carry out your plan?

The pattern in the table shows that the number of edges is 2 less than the sum of the numbers of faces and vertices.

$E = F + V - 2$ *Write an equation.*

$E = 7 + 10 - 2$ *Replace F with 7 and V with 10 in the equation to find E.*

$E = 15$

There will be 15 edges. So, Rosita needs 15 toothpicks.

LOOK BACK How can you check your answer?

What if . . . you build a pyramid from 16 toothpicks and 9 pieces of clay? How many faces will it have?

PRACTICE

For Problems 1–2, use a pattern. For Problem 3, find a pattern.

1. A hexagonal prism has 8 faces and 12 vertices. How many edges does it have?

2. Thomas is building a square pyramid. He knows it will have 5 vertices and 8 edges. How many faces will it have?

3. As she is building her polyhedrons, Rosita notices that the triangular pyramid has 4 faces, the rectangular pyramid has 5 faces, and the pentagonal pyramid has 6 faces. How many faces will she find on the hexagonal pyramid? Sketch a hexagonal pyramid to check your prediction.

CULTURAL LINK

Leonhard Euler (OY • ler) (1707–1783) was a Swiss mathematician who wrote about many topics. He discovered the relationships among the numbers of vertices, faces, and edges of polyhedrons. Find out some of Euler's other contributions to mathematics.

ACTIVITY

- Look at these prisms.

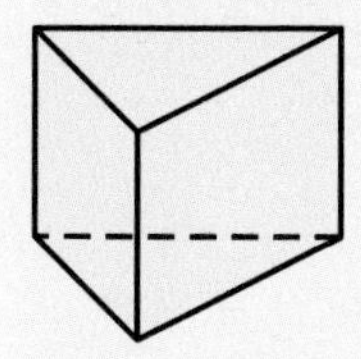

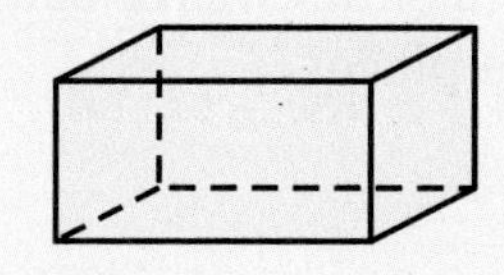

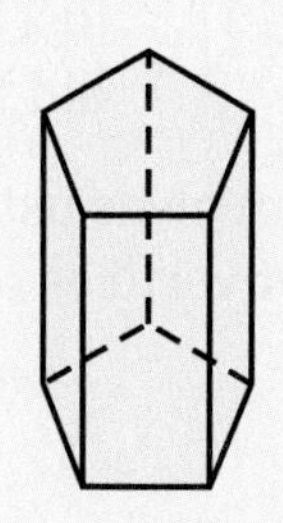

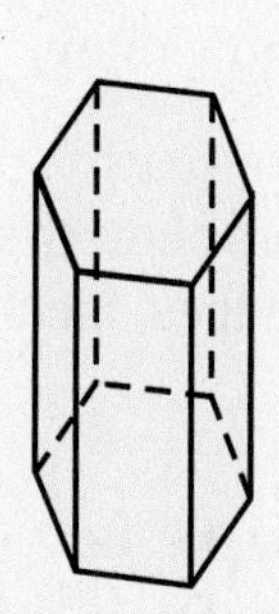

- Copy and complete this table.

Prism	Number of Sides in Each Base (S)	Number of Faces (F)	Number of Vertices (V)	Number of Edges (E)
Triangular	3	5	?	?
Rectangular	?	?	?	?
Pentagonal	?	?	?	?
Hexagonal	?	?	?	?

- Find a pattern in the relationship of the number of sides in each base to the number of faces in each solid.
- Find a pattern in the relationship of the number of sides in each base to the number of vertices in each solid.
- Find a pattern in the relationship of the number of sides in each base to the number of edges in each solid.
- Suppose each base of a prism has 10 sides. How many faces, vertices, and edges does the prism have?

MIXED APPLICATIONS

Solve.

CHOOSE a strategy and a tool.

- **Find a Pattern**
- **Write an Equation**
- **Draw a Diagram**
- **Guess and Check**
- **Use a Formula**
- **Make a Table**

Paper/Pencil

Calculator

Hands-On

Mental Math

1. Julie and her family took a walking tour of Philadelphia from 1:00 P.M. until 5:00 P.M. They walked at a rate of 3 km per hour. How far did they walk?

2. Ted is building a prism that has 9 faces. Use the pattern from the table on page 239 to find the number of sides there will be in each base.

3. Mr. Walton sold 20 more red shirts than blue shirts. He sold a total of 66 shirts. How many red shirts did he sell?

4. Pencils cost \$0.25 and pens cost \$0.60. Stuart spent \$3.15 on pencils and pens. How many of each did he buy?

5. There are 8 players in the chess tournament. If each player plays one game with every other player, how many games will be played in all?

6. In the 3-km race, Sarah placed ahead of Mike but behind Jose. Doug was behind Jose, and Sarah was ahead of Amy. Where did Jose place?

7. **WRITE ABOUT IT** Write a problem that involves using a pattern to find the number of edges, faces, or vertices of a polyhedron.

Mixed Review and Test Prep

Name the polygons that are the faces of each figure.

8. 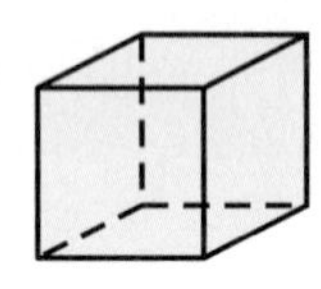

9. 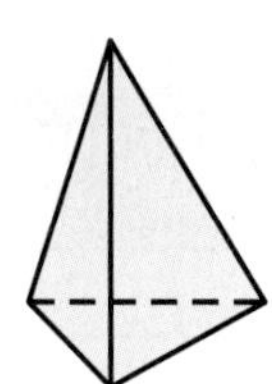

10. 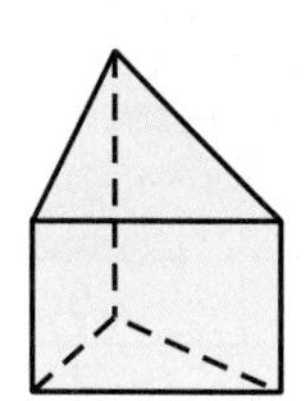

11. 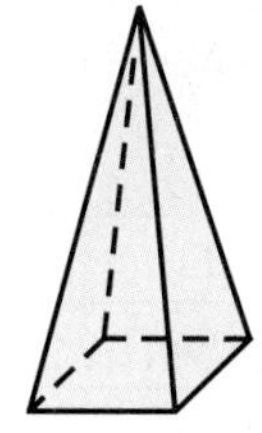

Tell whether each angle is *acute, obtuse,* or *right.*

12. 

13. 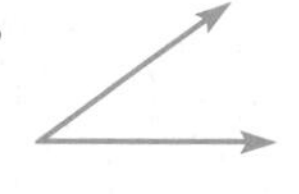

14. 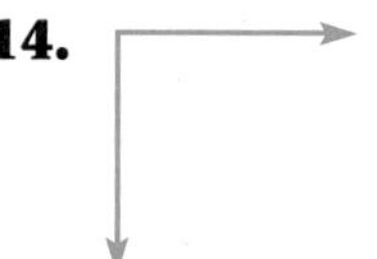

15. 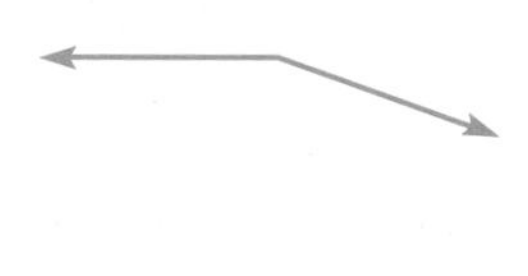

16. **NUMBER SENSE** Which expression has a value of $^-8$?

A $6 + 13 - 4 - 5$
B $6 - 13 + 4 + 5$
C $6 + 13 - 4 \times 5$
D $6 - 13 + 4 - 5$

17. **REASONABLENESS** The weights of 6 packages range from 2 pounds to 7 pounds. Which is a reasonable total weight for the 6 packages?

F 9 lb
G 11 lb
H 27 lb
J 45 lb

MORE PRACTICE Lesson 12.2, page H59

Building Prisms

What You'll Explore
Using pattern blocks to build prisms

What You'll Need
10 of each kind of pattern block

Pattern blocks come in a variety of shapes. Four of them are shown at the right.

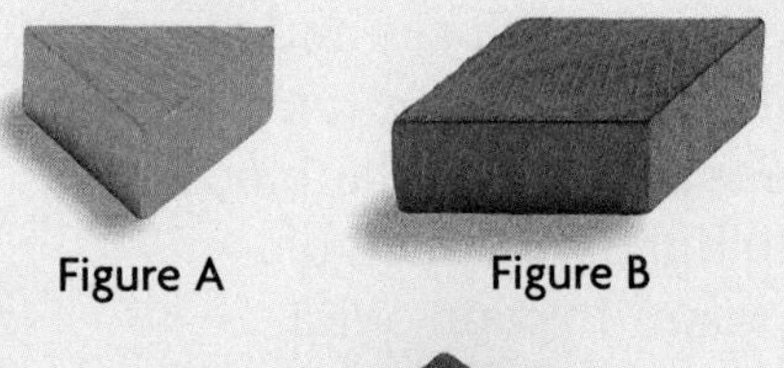

Figure A Figure B

Each of these pattern blocks is a prism. You can build other prisms by combining pattern block pieces.

Figure C

Explore

Use pattern blocks, diagrams, and your visualization skills to build different kinds of prisms.

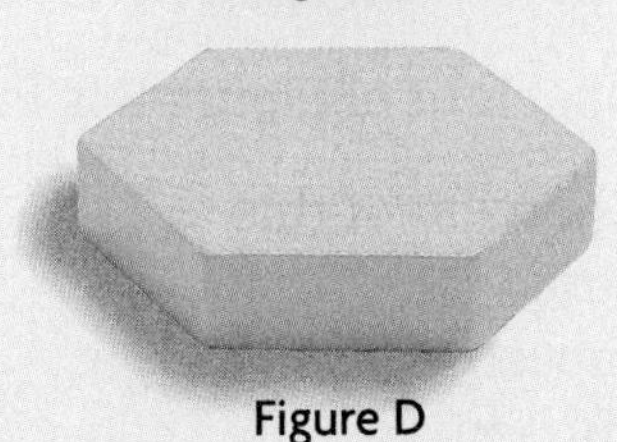

Figure D

- Build each of these hexagonal prisms from blocks shaped like each other.

Figure E

Figure F

Figure G

- For Figures E, F, and G, count the number of blocks and describe the shape of their bases.
- A hexagonal prism can also be built from blocks of different shapes. Find as many ways as you can to build a hexagonal prism by using any number of the other shapes.
- CRITICAL THINKING Find as many ways as you can to build a hexagonal prism by using only two different shapes.

Think and Discuss CRITICAL THINKING

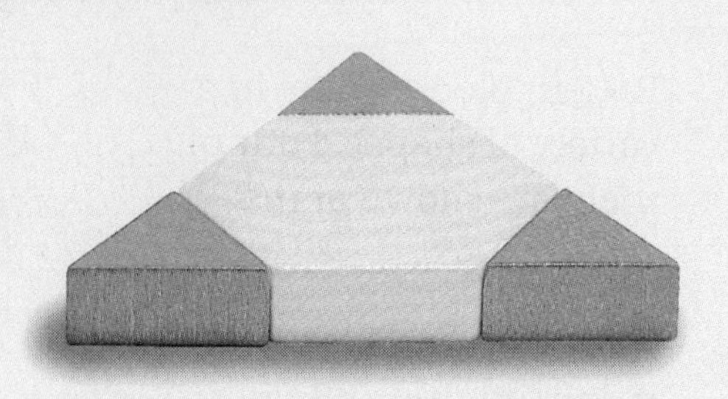

- A large triangular prism can be built from three triangular blocks and one hexagonal block. Can you use only triangular blocks to build this triangular prism? Explain. What fraction of the large triangular prism would one triangular block be?
- Look back at Figures A–G on page 241. What percent of Figure F is Figure B?
- What percent of Figure E is Figure C?

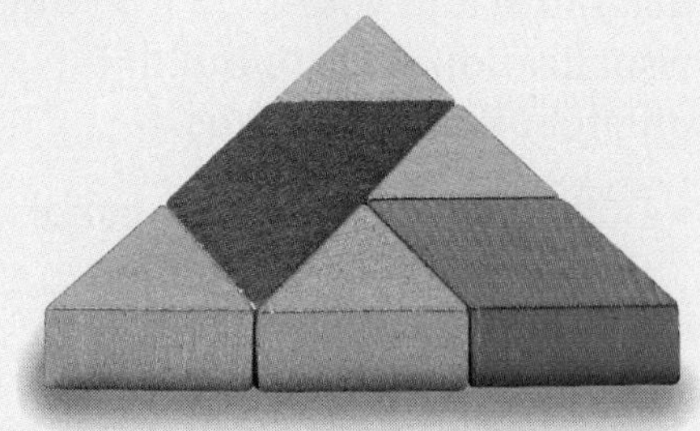

- What percent of this large triangular prism is the trapezoid block? Explain how you determined your answer.

Try This

- If you use three congruent blocks to build a large triangular prism, which shape will they be?

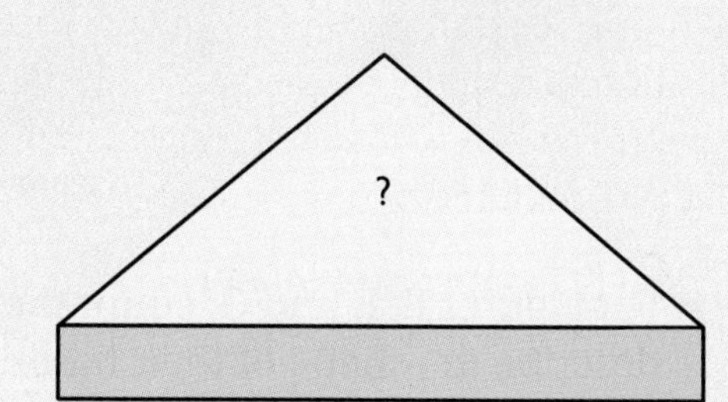

- Draw at least three different ways to build this large triangular prism using the pattern blocks in Figures A–D on page 241.
- Make a different prism using at least two different pattern blocks.

Nets for Solid Figures

LESSON 12.3

What You'll Learn
How to make nets for solid figures

Why Learn This?
To build patterns for containers such as boxes or cans

VOCABULARY
net

Models for solid figures can be cut from a solid material, such as wood, or they can be built using toothpicks for edges and clay for vertices. Another method is to cut the faces from paper, tape them together, and fold them up to form the solids.

ACTIVITY

WHAT YOU'LL NEED: 12 congruent, equilateral paper triangles; tape

- Arrange your triangles in the three ways shown.

Figure A

Figure B

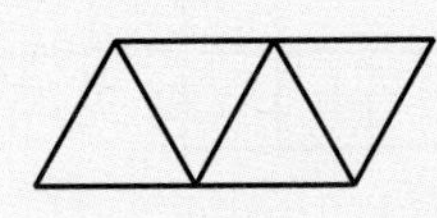

Figure C

- Predict which patterns will form triangular pyramids when folded up.
- Tape together each pattern of triangles. Check your predictions by folding your patterns. Which are nets for a triangular pyramid?

A polyhedron is three-dimensional, but it is made up of flat, two-dimensional faces that are polygons. A connected arrangement of these polygons in a plane is called a **net** if the arrangement can be folded up to form the polyhedron.

The nets shown below form a cube, a rectangular prism, a square pyramid, and a triangular prism.

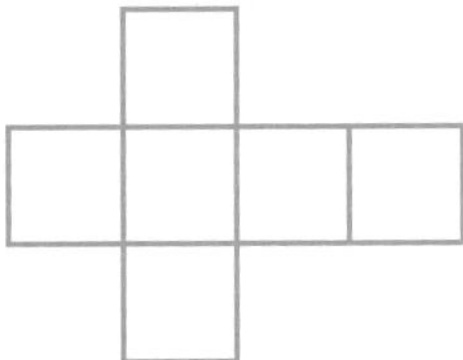

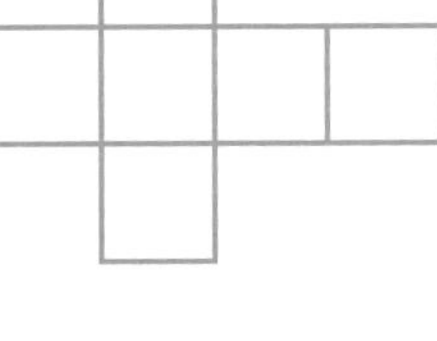

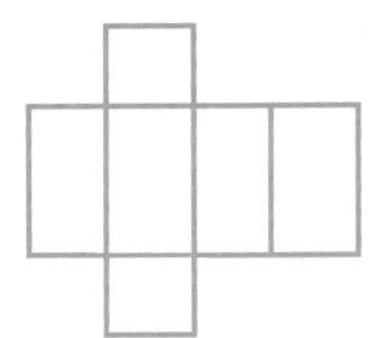

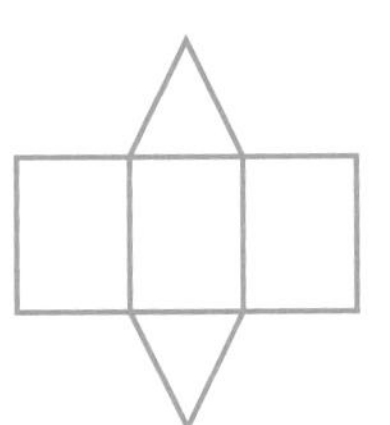

GUIDED PRACTICE

Draw each net, using six 1-in. squares. Cut out each net. Fold and tape it together to make a cube.

1. 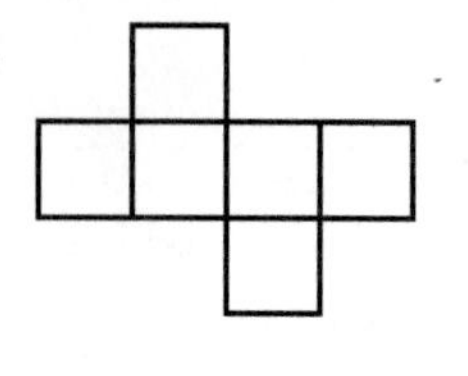

2. 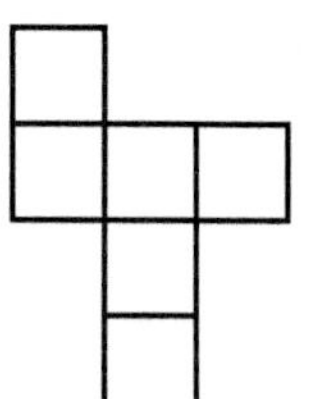

3. 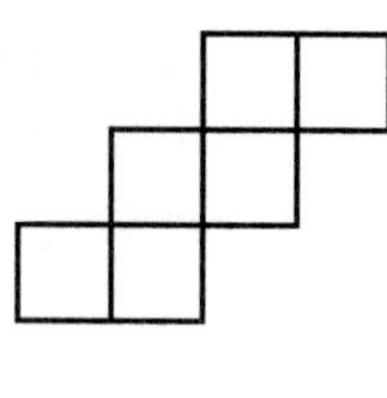

Tell whether each arrangement of squares is a net for a cube. If it is not, explain why.

4. 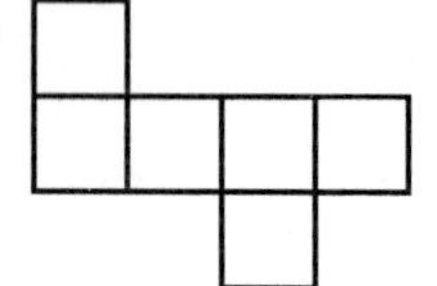

5. 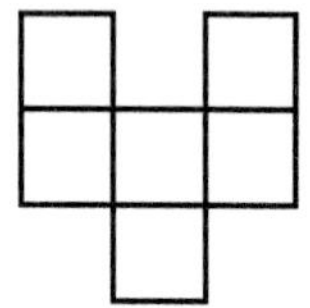

6. 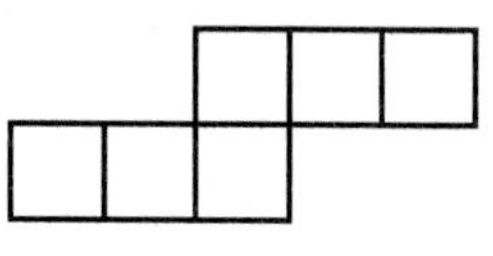

Making Nets

Suppose you wanted to make this rectangular prism. You could draw and cut out six rectangles. Then you could tape them together in an arrangement that folds up to make the prism.

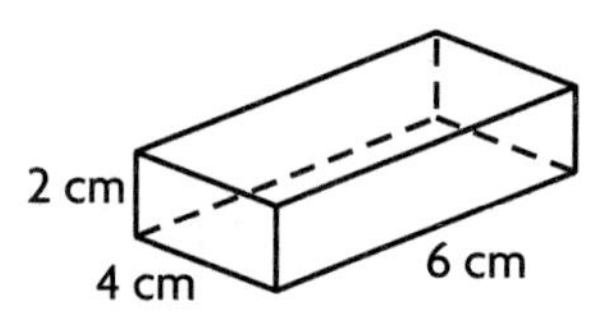

two rectangles, 2 cm × 4 cm

two rectangles, 2 cm × 6 cm

two rectangles, 4 cm × 6 cm

The net at the right shows one way to arrange the rectangles.

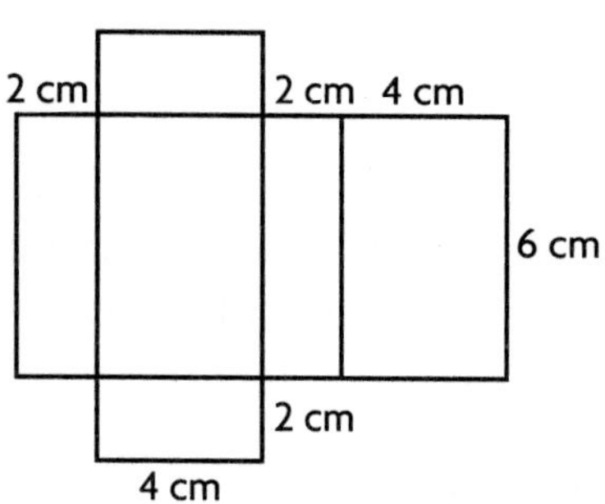

- **CRITICAL THINKING** Decide on two other ways to arrange the rectangles into a net for the prism. Draw your nets on graph paper.

INDEPENDENT PRACTICE

Name the prism or pyramid that can be formed from the net.

1. 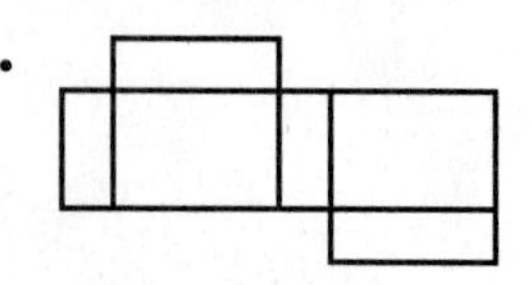

2. 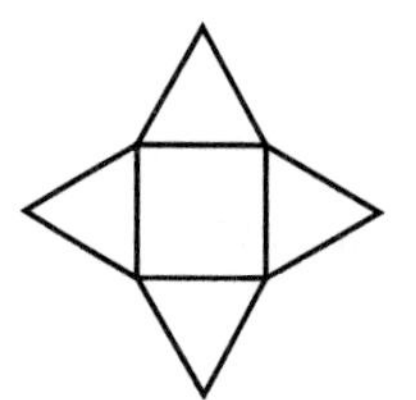

3. 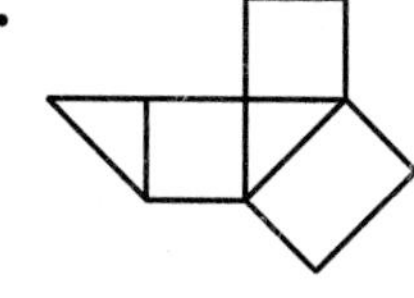

Tell whether each arrangement of squares will make a cube.

4. 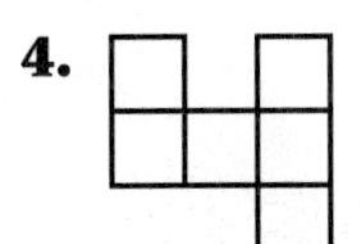

5. 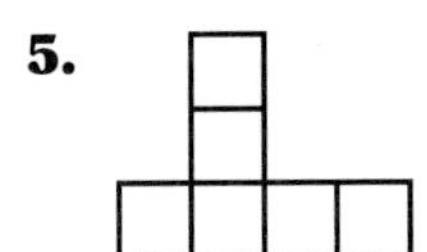

6. 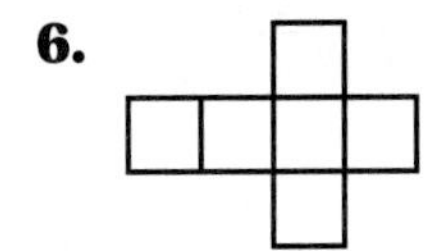

7. 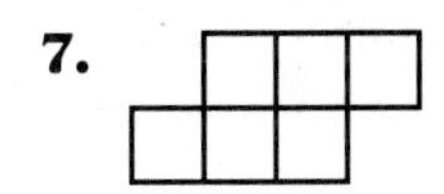

For Exercises 8–9, look at the rectangular prism at the right.

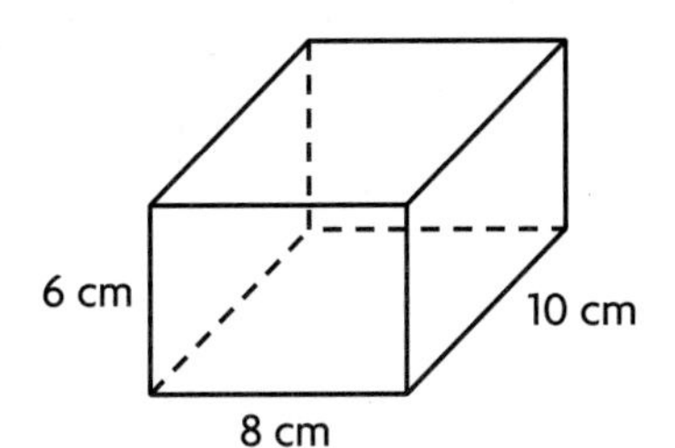

8. Draw a net for the prism.

9. Draw a second, different net for the prism.

10. What shapes did you use to draw the nets?

For Exercises 11–12, look at the triangular prism at the right. The prism has right triangles as its bases.

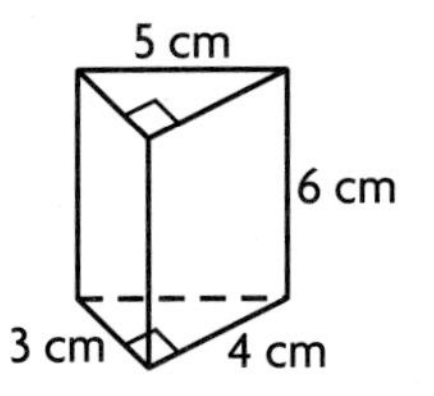

11. How many faces does the prism have? What types of polygons are the faces?

12. Draw a net for the prism.

For Exercises 13–15, visualize the net at the right folded into a square prism with the letters on the outside.

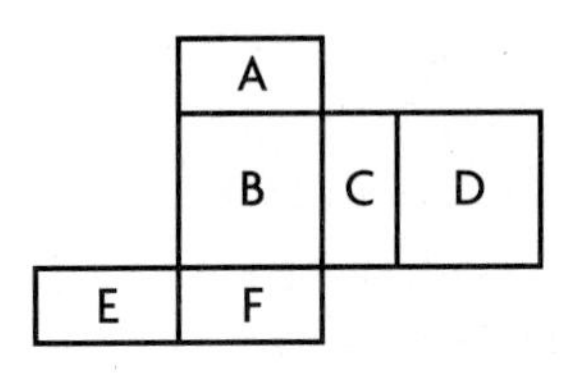

13. **CRITICAL THINKING** Which face will be on top if face A is on the bottom?

14. **CRITICAL THINKING** Which face will be on the top if face F is in the front and face B is on the left?

15. **CRITICAL THINKING** Which face will be on the top if face C is on the right and face D is in the back?

Problem-Solving Applications

Darrell drew this pentagonal pyramid to show the birdhouse that he wants to build. Each side of the base is 5 in. long.

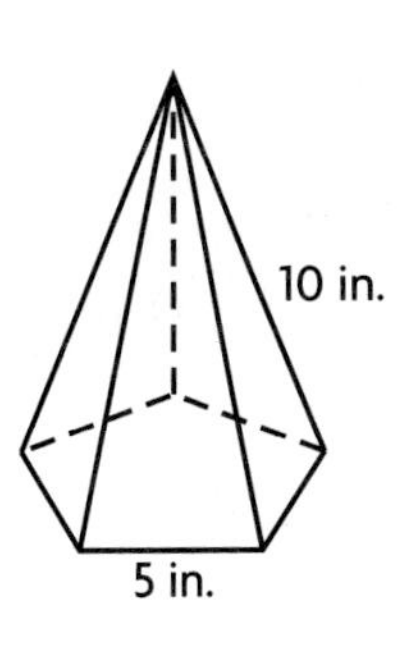

16. Draw a net for the pentagonal pyramid. Mark all edges with the correct length.

17. **LOGICAL REASONING** Darrell is going to paint the faces of the pyramid. What is the least number of colors he needs if no two adjacent faces are to be the same color?

18. **WRITE ABOUT IT** In your own words, explain what a net is and when you might want to make one.

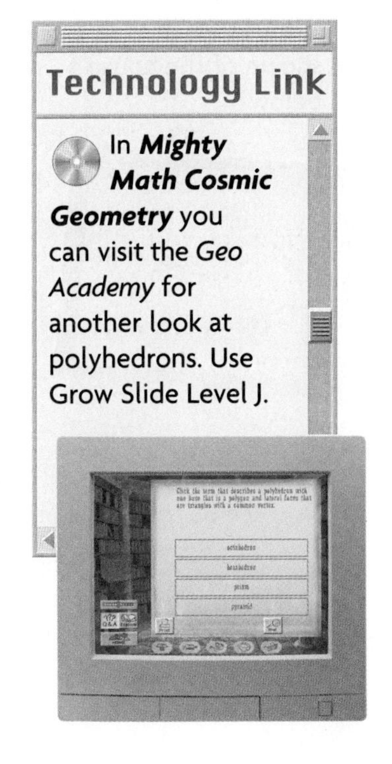

Technology Link
In *Mighty Math Cosmic Geometry* you can visit the *Geo Academy* for another look at polyhedrons. Use Grow Slide Level J.

MORE PRACTICE Lesson 12.3, page H60

LESSON 12.4

Drawing Three-Dimensional Figures

What You'll Learn
How to identify and draw a solid figure

Why Learn This?
To draw real-life solid figures such as food containers, buildings, or models

VOCABULARY

lateral face

Katie built a scale model of the space shuttle. She drew the top view, front view, and side view of her model.

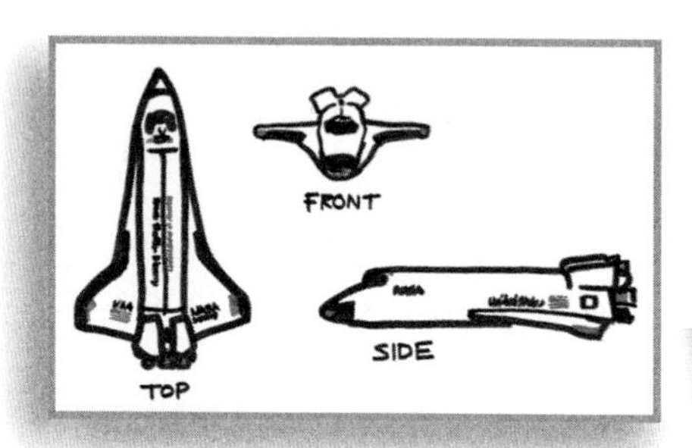

One of the simplest solid figures is a cube. Its top, front, and side views are all squares of the same size. Sometimes, you may want to show a simple three-dimensional view of a solid figure.

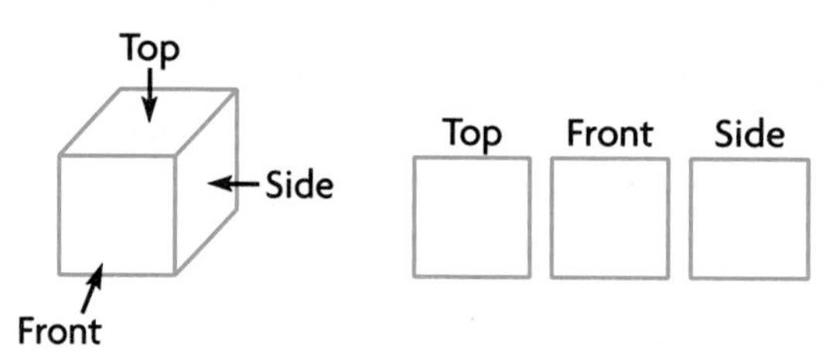

- Suppose you looked at the cube from the bottom. What would the view be?

The views of other solids show plane figures such as rectangles, circles, and triangles.

CAREER LINK

Architects, designers, and engineers draw front, top, and side views when designing a house. What view is shown of the house below?

EXAMPLE 1 Draw the top, front, and side views of the cylinder.

The soda can is a cylinder. Its top view is a circle, and its front and side views are rectangles.

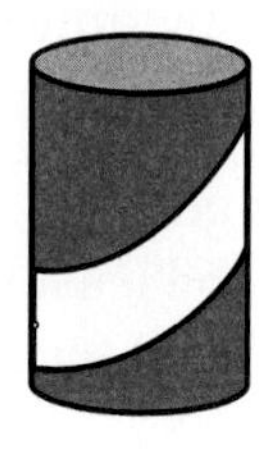

Top

Front Side

- Draw the top and front views of a cone.

One way to draw a three-dimensional view of a cube is to start with a square. Then draw the top and right faces.

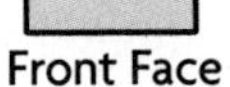
Front Face

Top Face

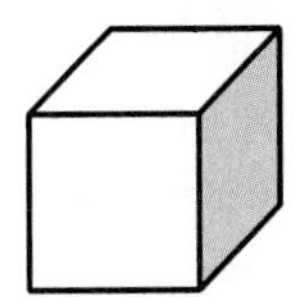
Right Face

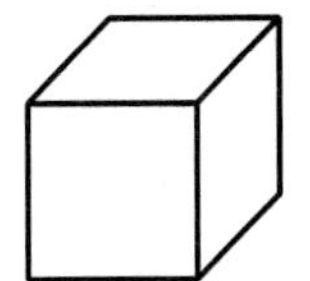
3 Visible Faces

Dashed lines show the three faces which are not visible.

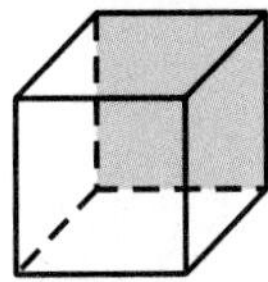
Back Face

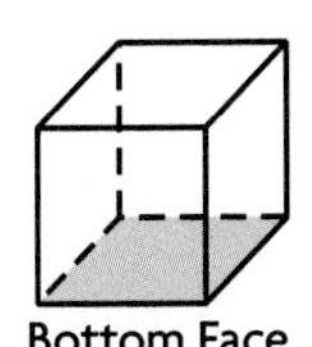
Bottom Face

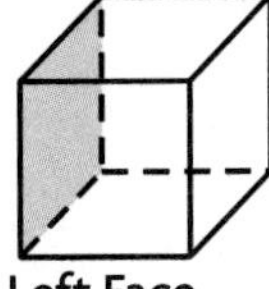
Left Face

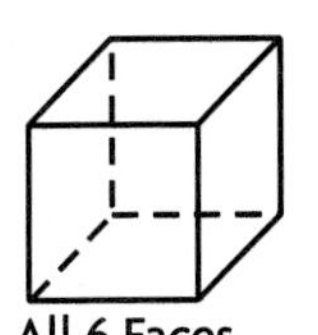
All 6 Faces

People in the United States buy about 2.7 billion boxes of breakfast cereal each year. If you placed this many cereal boxes end to end, they would reach to the moon and back.

ACTIVITY **WHAT YOU'LL NEED:** paper, ruler

- Think about a three-dimensional view of a rectangular prism such as a cereal box. Draw the front face of the prism.
- Draw the top and right faces.
- Draw dashed lines to show the faces that are not visible.

Remember that the bases of a polyhedron are used to name it. For example, the bases of a rectangular prism are rectangles. The other faces of a polyhedron are called **lateral faces**.

GUIDED PRACTICE

These are three views of a solid figure. Name the figure.

1. Top

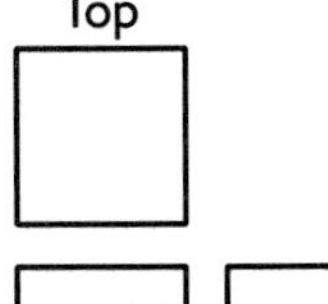

Front Side

2. Top

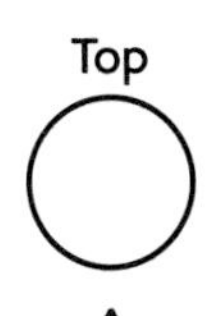

Front Side

3. Top

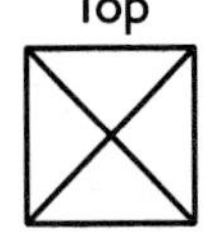

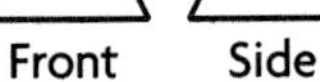

Front Side

Copy the polyhedrons. Use dashed lines to show the hidden edges.

4.

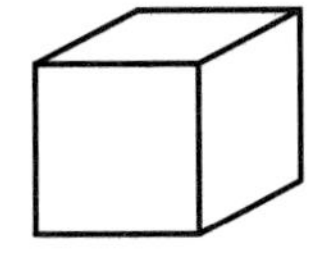

5.

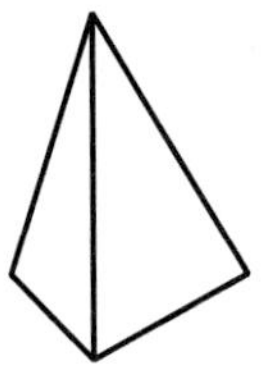

6.

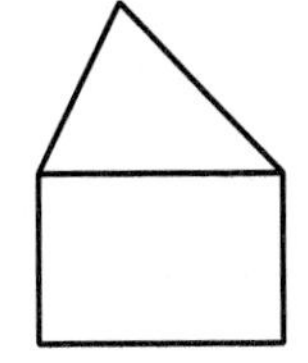

Another Way to Draw Solid Figures

If you are given the front, top, and side views of a three-dimensional figure, you can draw the figure on a flat, two-dimensional plane using graph paper or dot paper and a straightedge. You can use dashed lines to show locations of hidden edges.

EXAMPLE 2 Draw a pentagonal prism.

Draw two identical bases, one above the other.

Draw the lateral faces.

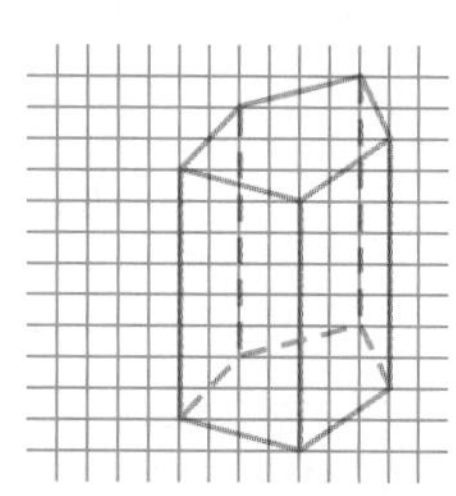

- Use graph paper or dot paper to draw a triangular prism.

INDEPENDENT PRACTICE

For Exercises 1–3, look at the rectangular prism at the right.

1. How many faces are visible in this view?

2. How many edges and vertices are visible?

3. Copy the figure. Use a straightedge to draw the hidden edges.

For Exercises 4–5, look at the triangular prism at the right.

4. How many faces are visible in this view? are hidden?

5. How many edges and vertices are visible? are hidden?

For Exercises 6–9, use the figures shown below.

a. 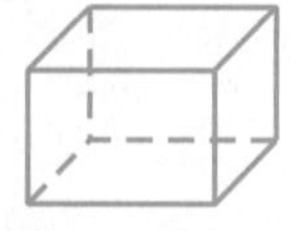

b. 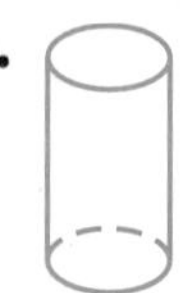

c. 

d. 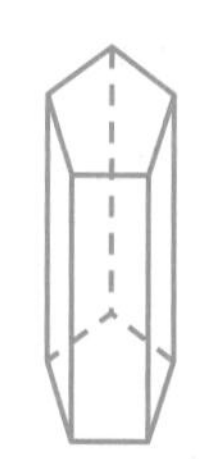

e. 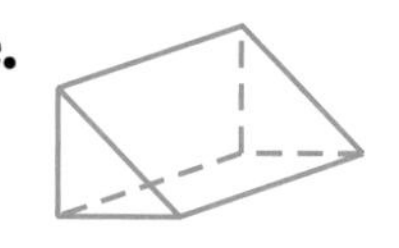

6. For which figure(s) is a rectangle in one of the three views?

7. For which figure(s) is a triangle in one of the three views?

8. For which figure(s) is a circle in one of the three views?

9. For which figure(s) is a pentagon in one of the three views?

Draw and name the plane figure you would see in each view.

10. Front View

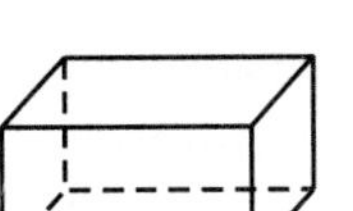

11. Top View

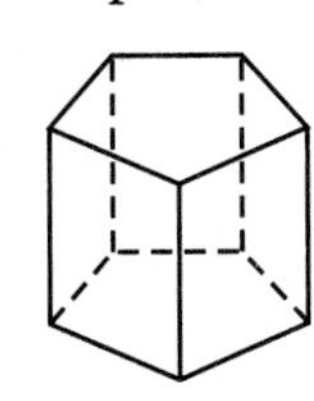

12. Bottom View

13. Side View

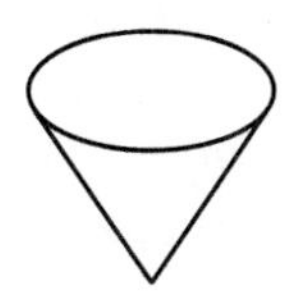

Copy the polyhedrons. Use dashed lines to show the hidden edges.

14. Rectangular Prism

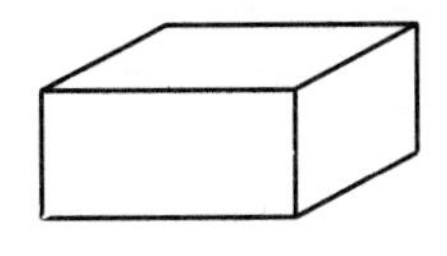

15. Pentagonal Prism

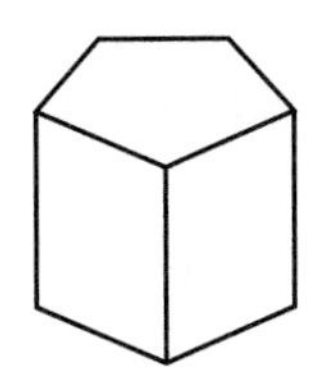

16. Rectangular Pyramid

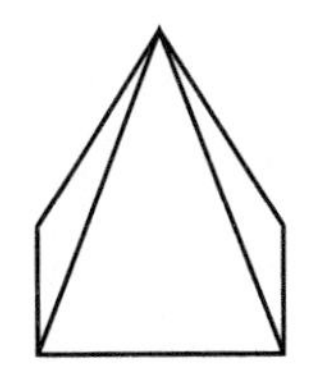

17. Hexagonal Prism

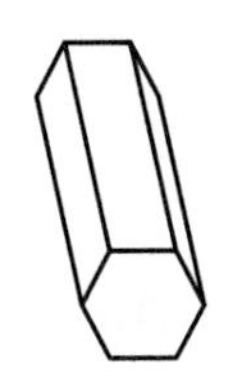

Problem-Solving Applications

For Problems 18–19, make two copies of this view of a pentagon on graph or dot paper.

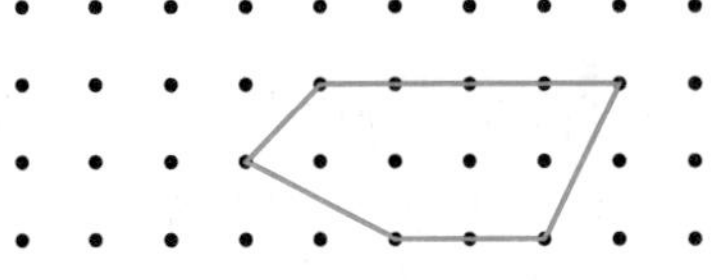

18. **ART** Draw a prism with the pentagon as a base.

19. **ART** Draw a pyramid with the pentagon as a base.

20. **WRITE ABOUT IT** Jasmine drew a solid figure that has five sides. Three of the sides are rectangles, and two of the sides are triangles. What solid figure did she draw? Draw it.

Mixed Review and Test Prep

Name each plane figure.

21. 

22. 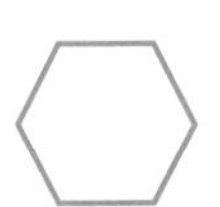

23. 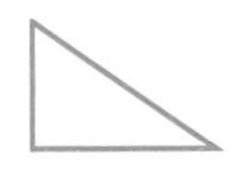

24. 

Determine whether the triangles are congruent by SSS, SAS, or ASA.

25. 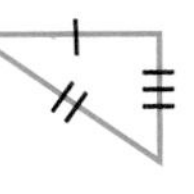 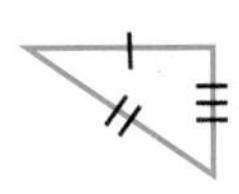

26. 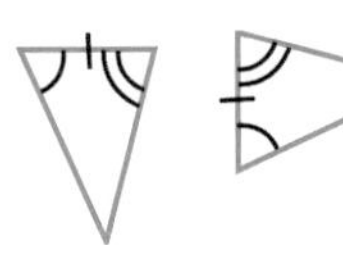

27. 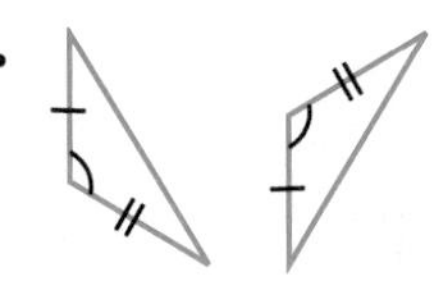

28. **ESTIMATION** Travis spent 25% of his money. He had $45.30. About how much did he spend?

A $10 **B** $11
C $20 **D** $25

29. **MENTAL MATH** If 3 oranges cost $2, how much will 2 dozen oranges cost?

F $6 **G** $8
H $12 **J** $16

ACTIVITY

What You'll Explore
How cutting a polyhedron can create different polyhedrons

What You'll Need
modeling clay and thin string

Technology Link

You can slice cylinders, cones, and pyramids by using E-Lab, Activity 12.

Available on CD-ROM and on the Internet at **www.hbschool.com/elab**

Cutting Solid Figures

When a solid three-dimensional polyhedron is cut straight through by a plane, the pieces formed are also polyhedrons.

ACTIVITY 1

Explore

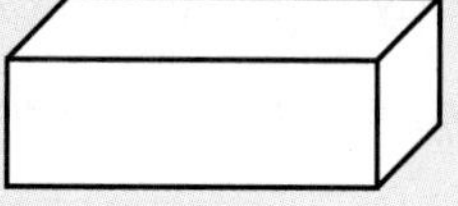

- Mold your clay so that it has the shape of a rectangular prism.

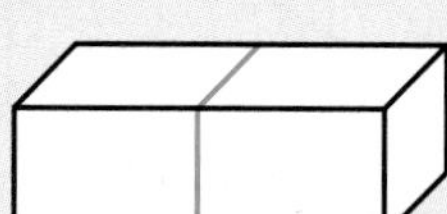

- Use your string to cut the prism in half as shown.
- The prism is cut into two polyhedrons. Name them.
- Now take one of the new polyhedrons and cut it diagonally as shown. What two new polyhedrons are formed?

Think and Discuss

- After the first cut, how did the faces of each of the new polyhedrons compare to the faces of the original prism?

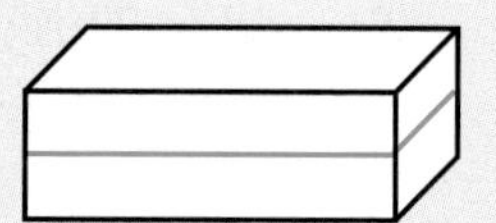

- Suppose you had cut the prism lengthwise as shown. What two new polyhedrons would have been formed? How would their faces compare to the faces of the original prism?

Try This

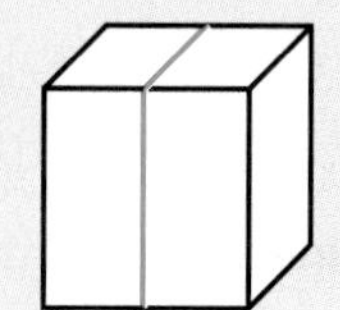

- Mold your clay so that it has the shape of a cube. Cut the cube as shown.
- Tell what types of polyhedrons are formed by the cut. Then decide how you can cut one of the new figures to form a cube.

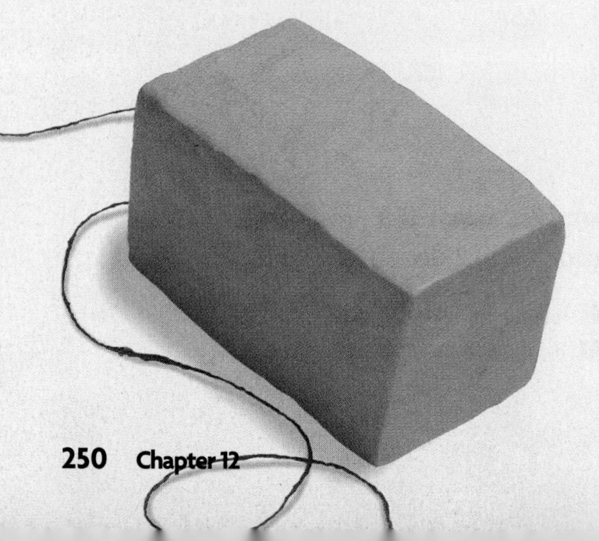

ACTIVITY 2

Explore

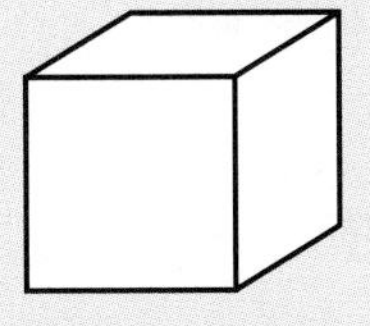

- Look at the cube at the right. Then visualize the cube being cut diagonally by a plane.

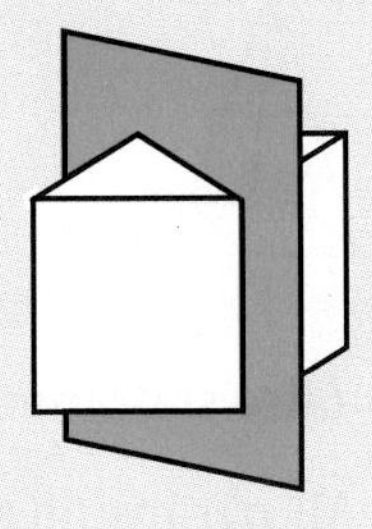

- Name the two polyhedrons formed by the cut.
- Visualize one of the new polyhedrons. What are the shapes of its faces?

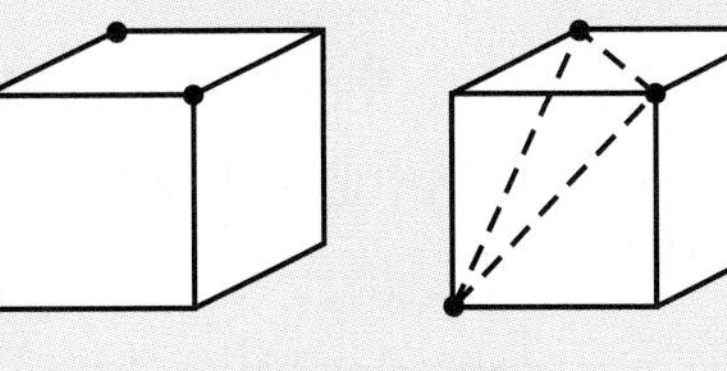

- Now visualize the original cube being cut through the three vertices shown.
- A triangular pyramid and a seven-faced polyhedron are formed. Name the shapes of the faces of each.

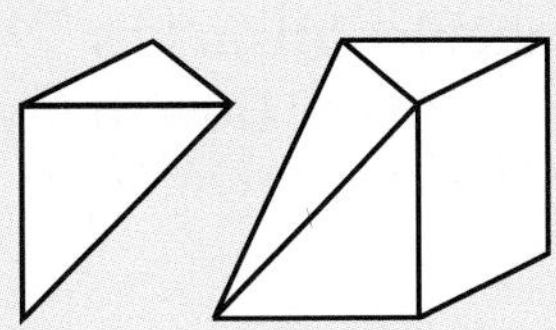

REMEMBER:

In geometry, a **plane** is a flat surface that continues forever in all directions. However, a plane is usually represented by a four-sided figure. **See page H21.**

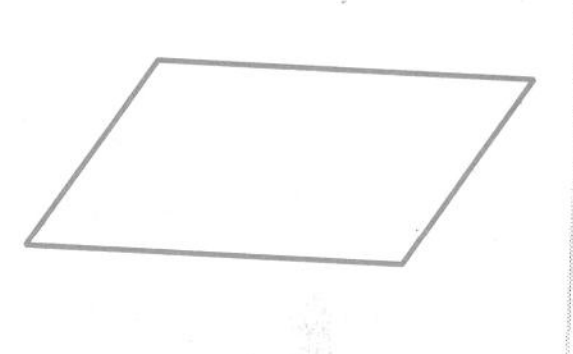

Think and Discuss

- How were the two cuts through the cube the same?
- How were the cuts different?

Try This

- Visualize a cube cut as shown. Name the two polyhedrons formed by the cut.
- Name the faces of each prism.

CHAPTER 12 Review/Test

Name the figure. Write *polyhedron* or *not polyhedron*. (pages 236–237)

1. 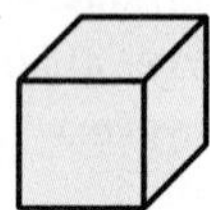

2. 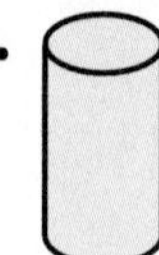

3. 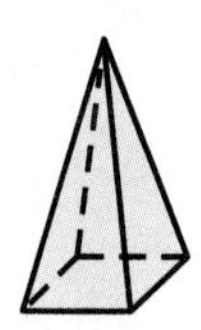

4. 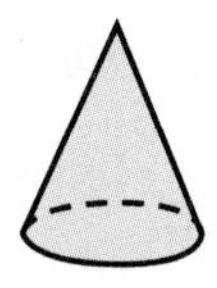

Write *true* or *false*. Write a true statement from any false statement. (pages 236–237)

5. Some cones are polyhedrons.

6. All pyramids are polyhedrons.

7. Cylinders are never polyhedrons.

8. Some prisms are not polyhedrons.

9. A pentagonal prism has 7 faces and 10 vertices. How many edges does it have? (pages 238–240)

10. A triangular prism has 9 edges, a rectangular prism has 12 edges, and a pentagonal prism has 15 edges. How many edges does a hexagonal prism have? (pages 238–240)

Name the figure that can be formed from the net. (pages 243–245)

11. 

12. 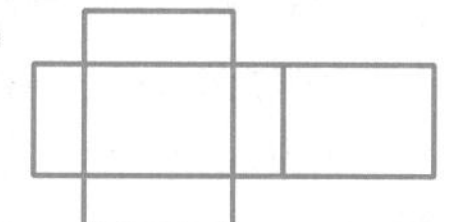

13. 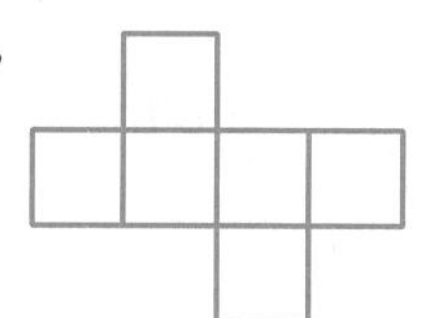

14. 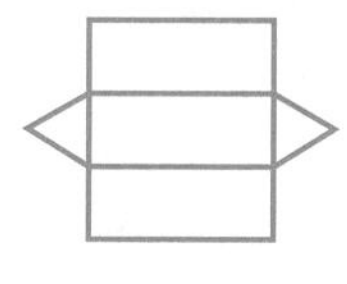

Draw a net for the figure. (pages 243–245)

15. 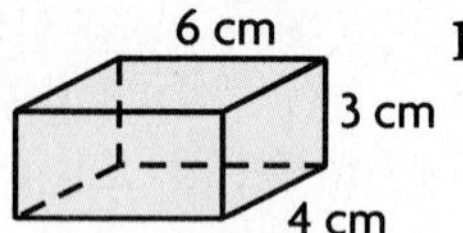

16. 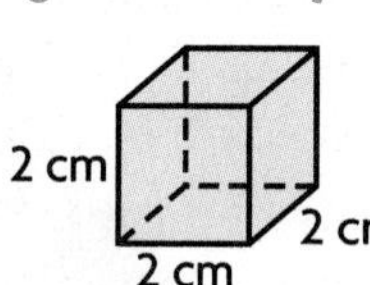

17. 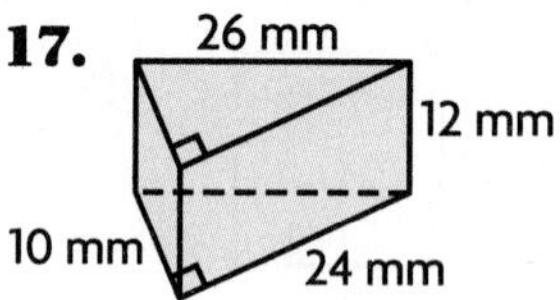

18. 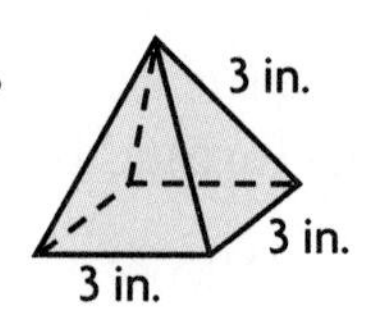

Name the plane figure you would see in a top view. (pages 246–249)

19. 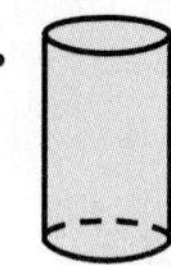

20. 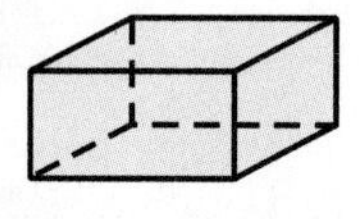

21. 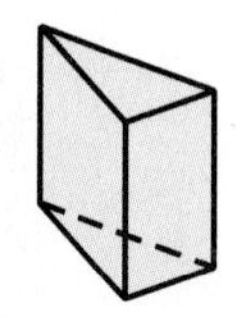

22. 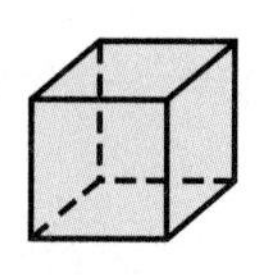

23. Draw the top view of the cylinder in Exercise 19. (pages 246–249)

24. Draw the bottom view of the prism in Exercise 20. (pages 246–249)

25. Draw the side view of the cube in Exercise 22. (pages 246–249)

Test Prep

1. What are the coordinates of *A*, *B*, *C*, and *D*?

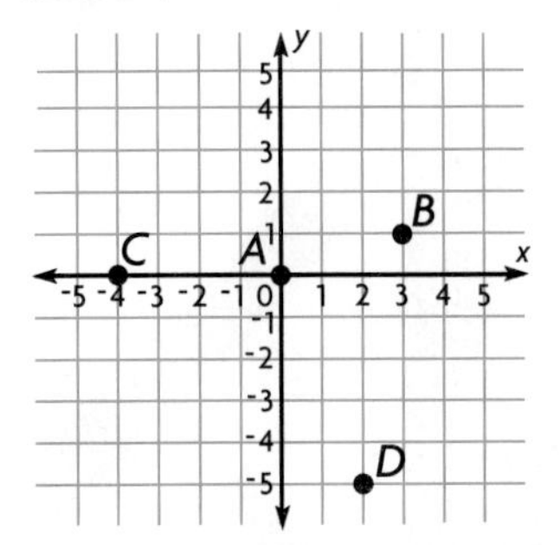

A $A(0,0)$, $B(1,3)$, $C(0,^-4)$, $D(^-5,2)$
B $A(0,0)$, $B(3,1)$, $C(0,^-4)$, $D(2,^-5)$
C $A(0,0)$, $B(3,1)$, $C(^-4,0)$, $D(2,^-5)$
D $A(0,0)$, $B(3,1)$, $C(^-4,0)$, $D(^-2,^-5)$

2. Which is the best name for the figure shown below?

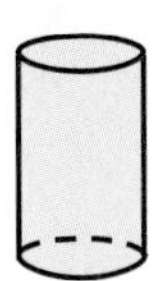

F solid
G cone
H polyhedron
J cylinder

3. Two angles of a triangle measure 45° and 45°. Which is a reasonable conclusion?

A The triangle is a scalene triangle.
B The triangle is a right triangle.
C The triangle is an obtuse triangle.
D The triangle is an equilateral triangle.

4. Which is not equivalent to $\frac{3}{5}$?

F 0.35
G 60%
H 0.6
J $\frac{6}{10}$

5. Which sequence is an arithmetic sequence?

A 2, 4, 8, 16, . . .
B 1, 3, 5, 7, . . .
C $\frac{1}{3}, \frac{1}{9}, \frac{1}{81}, \ldots$
D 1; 12; 123; 1,234; . . .

6. $\angle M$ and $\angle N$ are supplementary. $\angle M$ measures 72°. What is the measure of $\angle N$?

F 8°
G 27°
H 72°
J 108°

7. Which figure can be formed from the net shown below?

A square pyramid
B triangular prism
C rectangular prism
D triangular pyramid
E Not Here

8. The highest temperature ever recorded in the U.S. is 134°F. The lowest temperature ever recorded in the U.S. is $^-79.8$°F. Which is the best estimate of the difference in these temperatures?

F 50°F
G 70°F
H 210°F
J 230°F

9. A rectangular prism has 6 faces and 8 vertices. How many edges does it have?

A 6
B 8
C 12
D 10

CHAPTER

13

CHANGING GEOMETRIC SHAPES

LOOK AHEAD

In this chapter you will solve problems that involve

- making tessellation patterns
- using iteration rules to change geometric figures
- making figures that are self-similar
- building the repeating patterns that are called fractals

Different art styles throughout history have incorporated properties of mathematics. Artists and the types of art they are known for are listed below.

M. C. Escher (1898–1972)	graphic arts
Roy Lichtenstein (1923–1997)	pop art
Claude Monet (1840–1926)	impressionism
Pablo Picasso (1881–1973)	cubism
George Catlin (1796–1872)	portraits

- Make a time line showing the years the artists lived.

Stuart Davis

Roy Lichtenstein

Pablo Picasso

Problem-Solving Project

Letter Art

The artist Stuart Davis used letters and whole words in some of his paintings. You can design a sheet of wrapping paper using only one letter of the alphabet with no gaps or overlaps.

YOU WILL NEED: graph paper or dot paper, markers, scissors, tape, gift box

List the possible letters you could use. Then choose one letter. Make your design on graph or dot paper, and color it. Make a large version of your design, and use it to wrap a gift box. Present your design and wrapped gift box to the class.

PROJECT CHECKLIST

- ✓ Did you choose a letter?
- ✓ Did you make and color your design?
- ✓ Did you make a larger version of your design?
- ✓ Did you present your design and wrapped box to the class?

LESSON 13.1

Tessellations

What You'll Learn
How to make and predict tessellation patterns

Why Learn This?
To use tessellations to design wallpaper, wrapping paper, quilts, or tile patterns

VOCABULARY
tessellation
basic unit

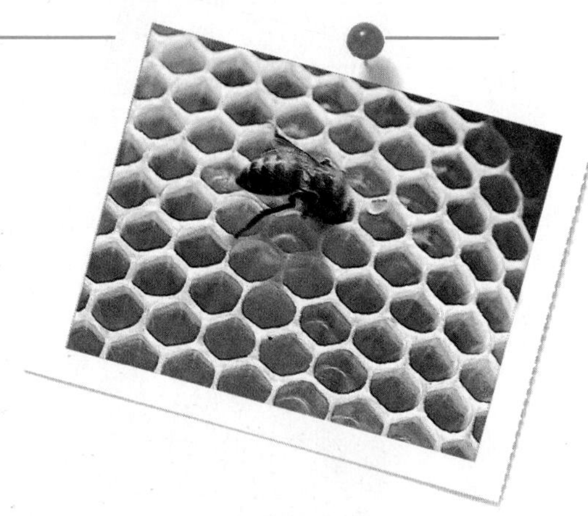

A **tessellation** is a repeating pattern of congruent plane figures that completely cover a plane, with no gaps or overlapping.

Tessellations appear in nature and have been used by artists, builders, and designers for more than 2,000 years.

- Think about the tessellations that appear in your home, school, or community. What types of polygons are used?

You can make a tessellation by using one type or several types of regular polygons.

EXAMPLE 1 Name the polygons used to make this tessellation.

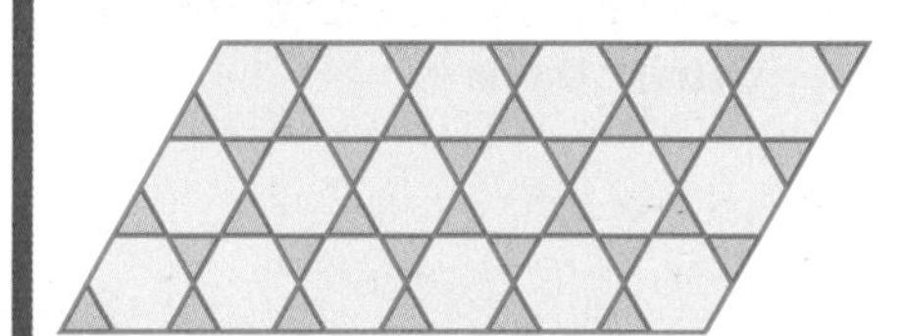

Regular hexagons and equilateral triangles were used.

- How many hexagons and triangles do you need to have four rows in this pattern?

You can make a tessellation by using polygons that are not regular and by performing translations, reflections, or rotations.

REMEMBER:

A **transformation** is a movement of a figure. **Translations**, **reflections**, and **rotations** are types of transformations.
See page 206.

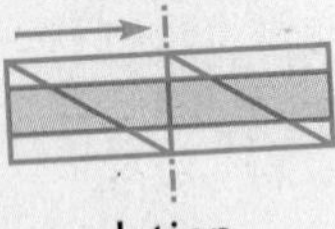

translation

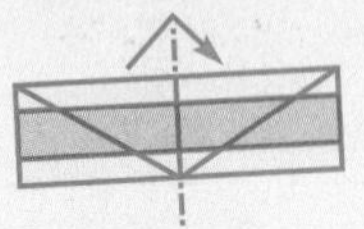

reflection

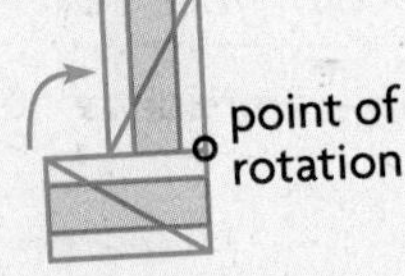

rotation

ACTIVITY **WHAT YOU'LL NEED:** drawing paper, scissors, straightedge

Make a tessellation using a scalene triangle.

- Draw a scalene triangle. Cut out your figure.
- Use your triangle as a pattern. Place it on a sheet of drawing paper, trace it a few times, and cut out the congruent triangles.
- Use translations, reflections, or rotations of the triangles to make at least three rows of a tessellation. What transformations did you use?

GUIDED PRACTICE

Use the figure(s) to make at least two rows of a tessellation.

1. square

2. equilateral triangle

3. trapezoid

4. isosceles triangle

5. rectangle and right triangle

6. hexagon and equilateral triangle

The Dutch artist M. C. Escher (1898–1972) made many artistic tessellations by using basic units in the shapes of animals. A **basic unit** is a figure that is repeated to make a pattern.

You can make an Escher-like tessellation by starting with a polygon and changing its shape with a translation.

EXAMPLE 2 Use a translation to change the shape of the square shown at the right. Use the new shape to make at least two rows of a tessellation.

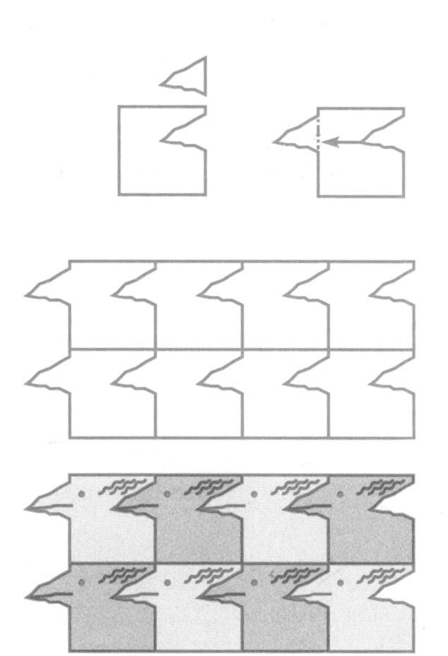

Change one of the sides by cutting out an irregular shape.

Translate the cutout shape to the opposite side of the square. Tape.

Trace the basic unit. Use transformations to place the basic unit next to the traced shape, without gaps or overlapping. Repeat until you have two rows.

Add detail and color to each basic unit.

- Start with a square. Use a translation to make a different basic unit. Then use your basic unit to make at least two rows of a tessellation.

CULTURAL LINK

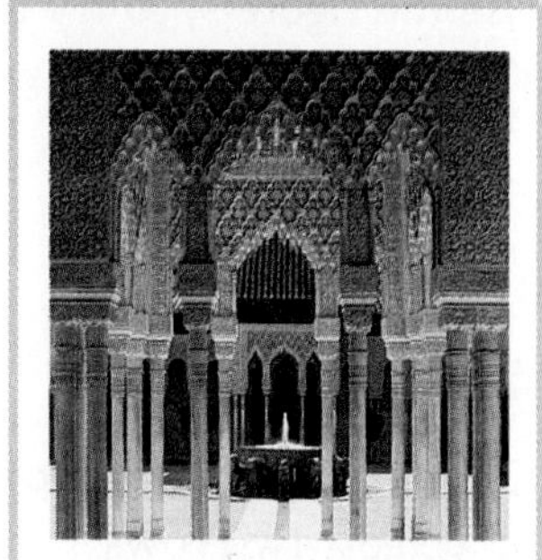

Moorish architecture in Spain is decorated with tessellations. The beauty of the designs can be seen in the Alhambra. This is a fortress, a palace, and a royal city all in one. What geometric patterns do you see?

ART LINK

M. C. Escher was a graphic artist who blended the worlds of mathematics and art. Escher is known for his use of optical illusions as well as repeating geometric patterns. What geometric shape did Escher use to form a bird?

INDEPENDENT PRACTICE

Use the figure(s) to try to make at least two rows of a tessellation. Write *yes* or *no* to tell whether a tessellation can be made.

1. rectangle

2. right triangle

3. regular pentagon

4. parallelogram

5. regular hexagon and square

6. square and equilateral triangle

Cut the basic unit out of graph paper. Use it to make a tessellation of at least two rows.

7. 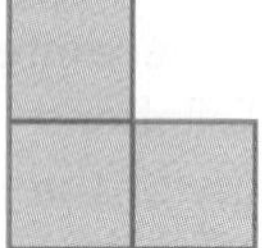

8. 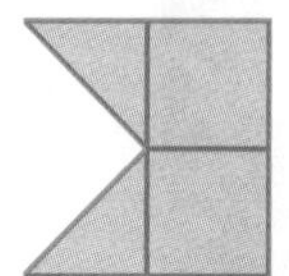

9. 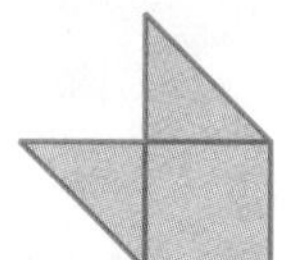

10. 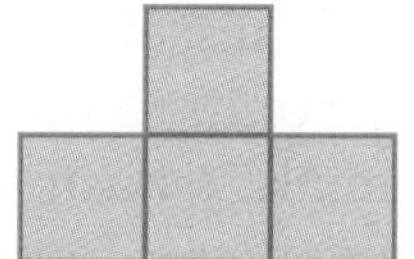

Problem-Solving Applications

11. **MEASUREMENT** Choose one of the tessellations that you made in Exercises 7–10. Find a vertex where two or more figures meet. Measure each angle at the vertex. What is the sum of the measures?

12. **ART** Draw an equilateral triangle. Use translations to change the shape of the triangle. Use the new shape to make at least two rows of a tessellation. Add detail and color to your pattern.

13. Draw two different triangles and two different quadrilaterals. Can the individual figures form tessellations?

14. **WRITE ABOUT IT** Trace the letter to make a tessellation.

W

Mixed Review and Test Prep

Trace line segment AB, and rotate it about point A as described.

A ——— B

15. 90° clockwise

16. 45° clockwise

Find the number of edges.

17. rectangular pyramid

18. pentagonal pyramid

19. octagonal prism

20. **LOGIC** Jane can run around the track in 4 minutes. It takes Jon 6 minutes. They start at the same place. When will they next reach the starting point at the same time?

A 12 min
B 24 min
C 30 min
D 48 min

21. **COMPARISON SHOPPING** Which is a better buy?

F 2 lb for \$2.39
G 3 lb for \$3.49
H 4 lb for \$4.99
J 5 lb for \$6.19

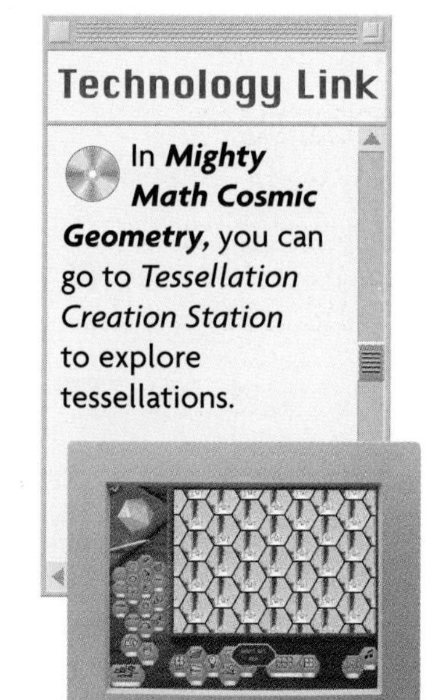

Technology Link
In Mighty Math Cosmic Geometry, you can go to Tessellation Creation Station to explore tessellations.

MORE PRACTICE Lesson 13.1, page H60

Geometric Iterations

LESSON 13.2

What You'll Learn
How to make visual patterns by changing positions or sizes of geometric figures

Why Learn This?
To see some of the ways that engineers, architects, dentists, and surveyors change geometric figures

You can make visual patterns by applying iteration rules that change the positions or sizes of geometric figures.

You can change the position of a geometric figure by using an iteration rule. The following iteration rule describes a repeated reflection or rotation.

Start with the figure shown as Stage 0.
Reflect it vertically or rotate it 180°.
Continue the iteration process three times.

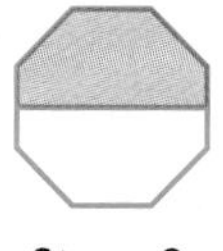
Stage 0

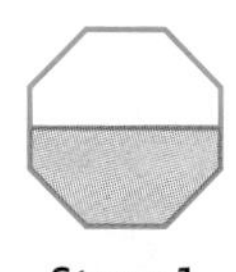
Stage 1

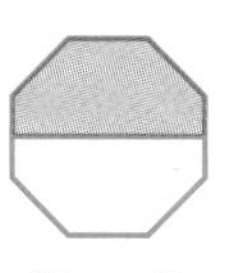
Stage 2

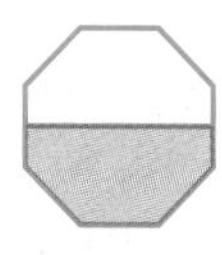
Stage 3

Talk About It

- Why can you reflect the figure vertically or rotate it 180°?
- Which part of the figure would be shaded at Stage 4? at Stage 9? at Stage 26? What is the pattern?

You can also change the size of a geometric figure by using an iteration rule.

EXAMPLE Use the following iteration rule, and complete the process four times.

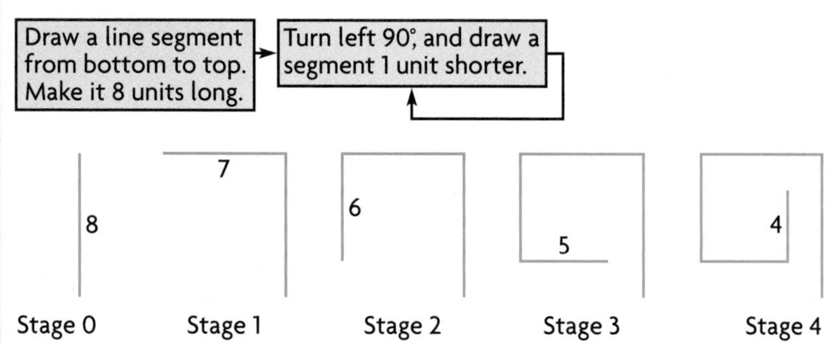

- How long will the new line segment be at Stage 5? at Stage 6?
- Can you perform this iteration process forever? Explain.

HISTORY LINK

A beautiful use of repeating patterns is the sewing of quilts. Quilts tell important stories about the lives and times of their creators. The Amish, who came to the United States from Germany and Switzerland in the early 1700's, named quilts for important events, such as weddings. How are transformations and tessellations used in this quilt pattern?

GUIDED PRACTICE

For Exercises 1–5, rotate the trapezoid 90° clockwise. Complete this iteration process five times. Draw the figure at each stage.

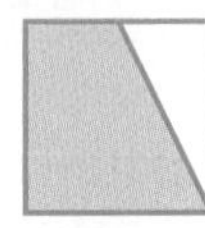
Stage 0

1. Stage 1 **2.** Stage 2 **3.** Stage 3 **4.** Stage 4 **5.** Stage 5

6. When do the positions repeat themselves?

INDEPENDENT PRACTICE

Using the figure above, reflect the trapezoid vertically. Complete the iteration process five times. Draw the figure at each stage.

1. Stage 1 **2.** Stage 2 **3.** Stage 3 **4.** Stage 4 **5.** Stage 5

6. Predict the position of the trapezoid at every stage.

Trace the octagon. Rotate it 45° clockwise and complete this iteration process four times. For Exercises 7–10, write the number where red stops and the number where blue stops.

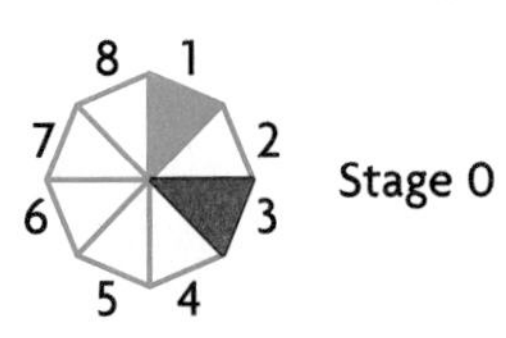

Stage 0

7.
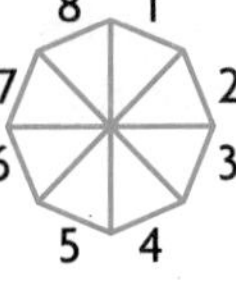

Stage 1

8.
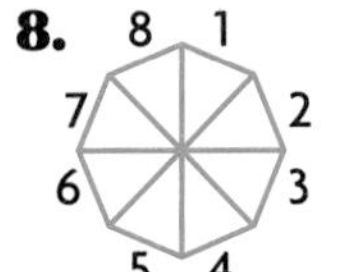

Stage 2

9.

Stage 3

10.

Stage 4

Give the number of the part of the octagon where red stops for the given stage of iteration.

11. Stage 5 **12.** Stage 8 **13.** Stage 7 **14.** Stage 6

Give the number of the part of the octagon where blue stops for the given stage of iteration.

15. Stage 5 **16.** Stage 8 **17.** Stage 7 **18.** Stage 6

Problem-Solving Applications

19. **ROTATIONS** Draw *CD*, a segment with a length of 12 cm. Rotate the segment 60° clockwise about its midpoint. How many times do you have to complete the process to reach the original segment?

20. **MEASUREMENT** Draw a segment left to right 12 units long. Turn right 90°, and draw a segment with half the length. Continue this process and record the figure at Stages 0 through 3.

21. Draw a square. Shade the left half. Repeatedly reflect the figure horizontally. Record the results of the first four stages of this iteration process.

22. **WRITE ABOUT IT** Design a visual pattern, and describe it using an iteration rule. Record the results of four stages of your iteration process.

MORE PRACTICE Lesson 13.2, page H61

Self-Similarity

Many natural objects such as trees are self-similar because they contain reduced images of the whole figure.

You can make a self-similar figure with an equilateral triangle.

LESSON 13.3

What You'll Learn
How to identify self-similarity in patterns of changing geometric figures

Why Learn This?
To understand the geometry of patterns of nature

VOCABULARY

self-similarity

ACTIVITY **WHAT YOU'LL NEED:** yellow and green construction paper, metric ruler, scissors

- Draw an equilateral triangle measuring 8 cm on each side on green construction paper.

Stage 0

- **Stage 0** Cut out a yellow paper triangle the same size and place it on the green triangle.

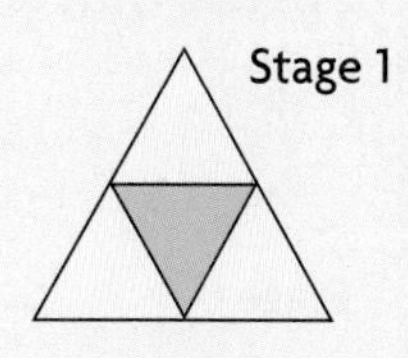

- **Stage 1** Cut through the midpoints of the yellow triangle. Place 3 small yellow triangles in the corners of the green triangle as shown.

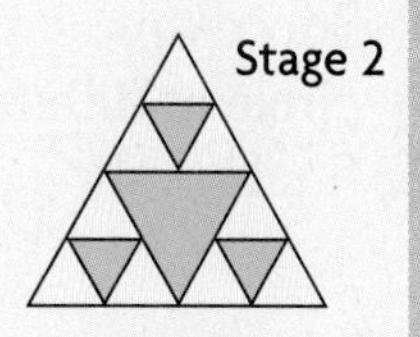

- **Stage 2** Cut through the midpoints of the 3 small yellow triangles as above. Replace each of them with 3 of the smaller yellow triangles as shown.

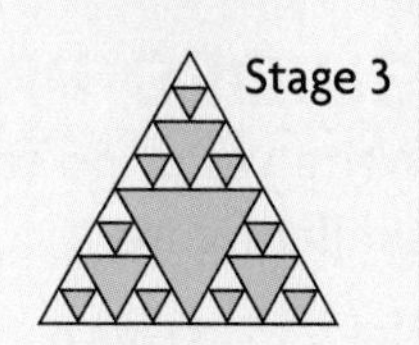

- **Stage 3** Repeat the process a third time on the 9 yellow triangles that remain.
- Compare your figures in Stage 1 and Stage 2. How are they alike? How are they different?
- Compare your figures in Stage 2 and Stage 3. How are they alike? How are they different?

An equilateral triangle is also equiangular. Each angle measures 60°. **See page 201.**

Think of this as an iterative process that continues on and on. Stage 1 contains 3 reduced copies of Stage 0. Stage 2 contains 3 reduced copies of Stage 1. Stage 3 contains 3 reduced copies of Stage 2, and so on. This process is leading to a self-similar figure.

A figure has **self-similarity** if it contains a repeating pattern of smaller and smaller parts that are like the whole but different in size.

You can determine self-similarity by comparing, from stage to stage, the shape of the parts with the shape of the whole.

REAL-LIFE LINK

What is your favorite vegetable? Some vegetables, such as broccoli and cauliflower, are self-similar. Is your favorite vegetable self-similar?

EXAMPLE 1 Look at the results of repeating an iteration process over and over. Is the process leading to self-similarity?

 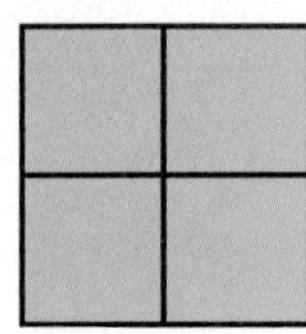 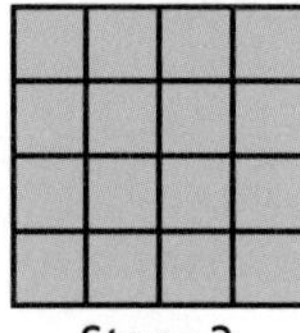 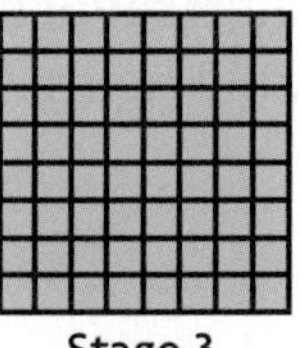

Stage 0 Stage 1 Stage 2 Stage 3

Stage 1 contains 4 reduced copies of Stage 0, Stage 2 contains 4 reduced copies of Stage 1, and Stage 3 contains 4 reduced copies of Stage 2. The process is generating a self-similar figure.

- How do the figures change from stage to stage?

EXAMPLE 2 Look at the results of completing an iteration process three times. Does the process appear to be generating a figure that is self-similar?

 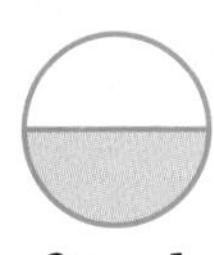 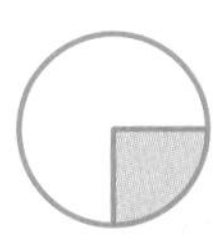 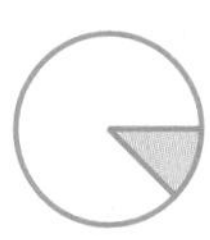

Stage 0 Stage 1 Stage 2 Stage 3

Successive stages do not contain reduced copies of the whole circle at different scales. There will be no self-similarity in the final result.

GUIDED PRACTICE

Write *yes* or *no* to tell whether the process is leading to a self-similar figure.

Stage 0 Stage 1 Stage 2 Stage 3

1. 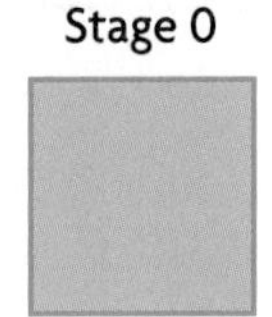 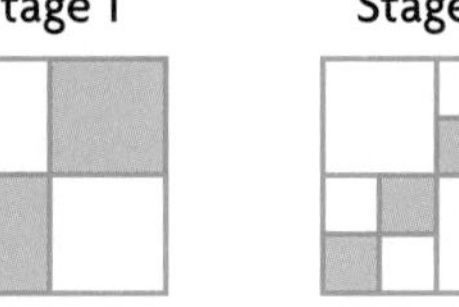 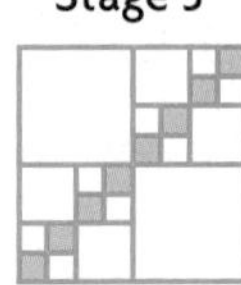

2. 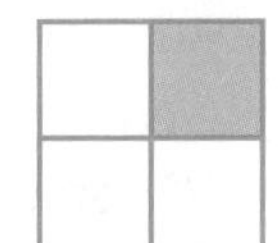  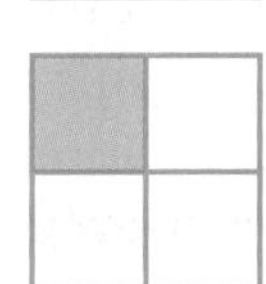

3. 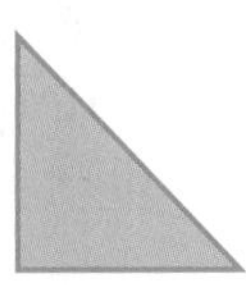  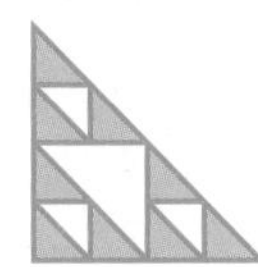 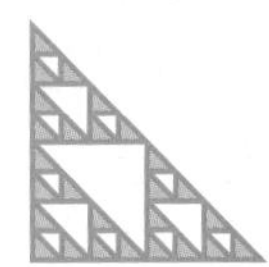

INDEPENDENT PRACTICE

These drawings show successive stages in an iterative process. For Exercises 1–4, refer to these drawings.

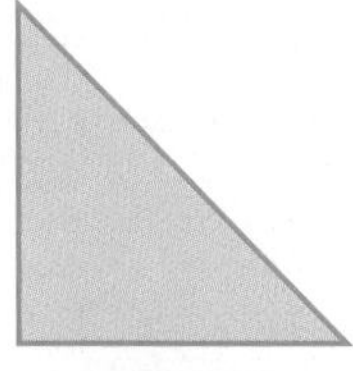
Stage 0

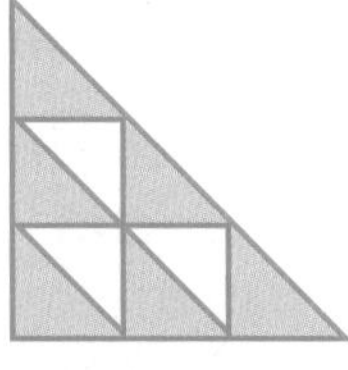
Stage 1

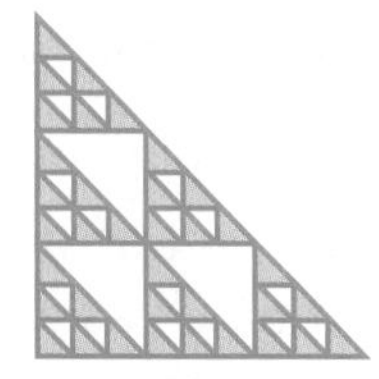
Stage 2

1. What geometric figure is being used repeatedly?
2. Are 6 reduced copies of Stage 0 in Stage 1? of Stage 1 in Stage 2?
3. How many small shaded triangles will be in Stage 3 of the process?
4. Does it appear the process is leading to a self-similar figure?

Problem-Solving Applications

Stage 0

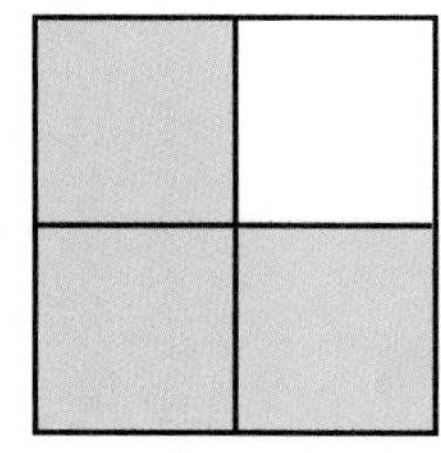
Stage 1

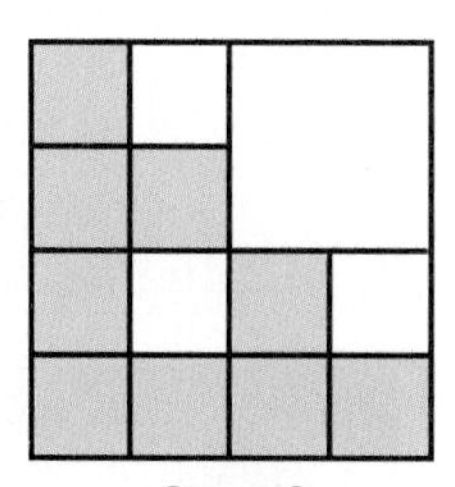
Stage 2

5. **CRITICAL THINKING** Describe the iteration process at the right.
6. **ART** Draw the next stage. Is the process leading to a self-similar figure?
7. Write your own iteration rule, using one or more geometric figures. Complete the iteration process several times. Record the stages. Will the resulting figure have self-similarity?
8. **WRITE ABOUT IT** How can you tell whether a process is generating a self-similar figure?

Mixed Review and Test Prep

Start with the given number and find half of it. Complete the iteration process four times.

9. 100
10. 18
11. 50
12. $\frac{1}{2}$

Draw a net for the figure.

13. cube
14. square pyramid
15. rectangular prism
16. **GEOMETRY** A board is 4 inches wide and 6 feet long. What is the area of the board in square feet?

    A 2 ft^2 **B** 24 ft^2
    C 128 ft^2 **D** 288 ft^2

17. **FRACTIONS** Which sum is the greatest?

    F $\frac{5}{2} + \frac{4}{3}$ **G** $\frac{2}{5} + \frac{3}{4}$
    H $\frac{5}{3} + \frac{4}{2}$ **J** $\frac{5}{4} + \frac{3}{2}$

MORE PRACTICE Lesson 13.3, page H61

LESSON 13.4 Fractals

What You'll Learn
How to build fractals by repeatedly changing geometric figures

Why Learn This?
To see how computer graphic artists create fractal images that look like trees, clouds, mountains, and planets

VOCABULARY
fractal

What do trees, clouds, ferns, frost on a window, and popcorn have in common?

They all illustrate self-similarity. Also, each can be described as a **fractal**. A fractal has a repeating pattern containing shapes that are like the whole but of different sizes throughout.

You can build fractals by iterating line segments.

ACTIVITY

WHAT YOU'LL NEED: drawing paper, ruler

Follow the steps to create a fractal.

- Draw a vertical line segment with a length of 12 cm. This is Stage 0.
- Find the endpoint that is closer to the top of the page. Draw three line segments from the endpoint, half the length of the previous line segment. This is Stage 1.
- Repeat the iteration process for Stage 2. Build similar structures on the 3 branches. How many new branches did you draw?

(dimensions in cm)

12
Stage 0
6
Stage 1
3
Stage 2

LANGUAGE LINK

The word *fractal* comes from the Latin word *fractus* and describes a very irregular line or surface formed from an endless number of self-similar parts. Many natural objects, such as clouds, frost, and stream patterns, are fractals. Why do you think these clouds are called fractus clouds?

You can build fractals from two-dimensional figures.

EXAMPLE 1 Repeat the iteration process two times.

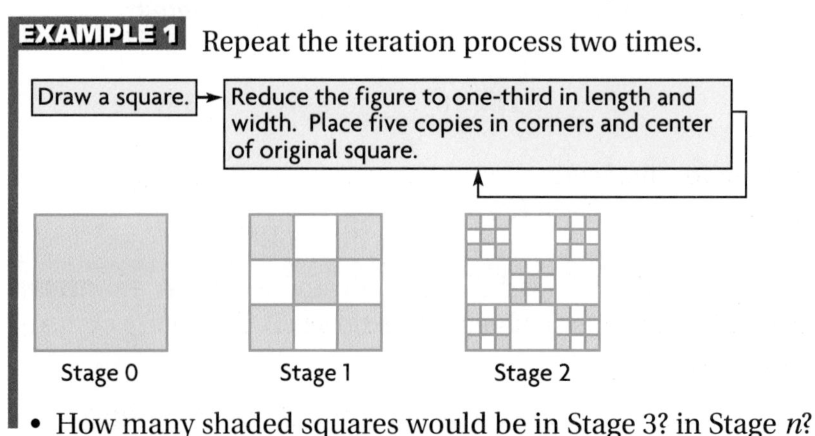
Draw a square.
Reduce the figure to one-third in length and width. Place five copies in corners and center of original square.
Stage 0
Stage 1
Stage 2

- How many shaded squares would be in Stage 3? in Stage n?

You can build fractals from geometric figures using iteration rules that reduce, copy, and rebuild. When you reduce the size of a geometric figure, you decrease all the dimensions by the same amount.

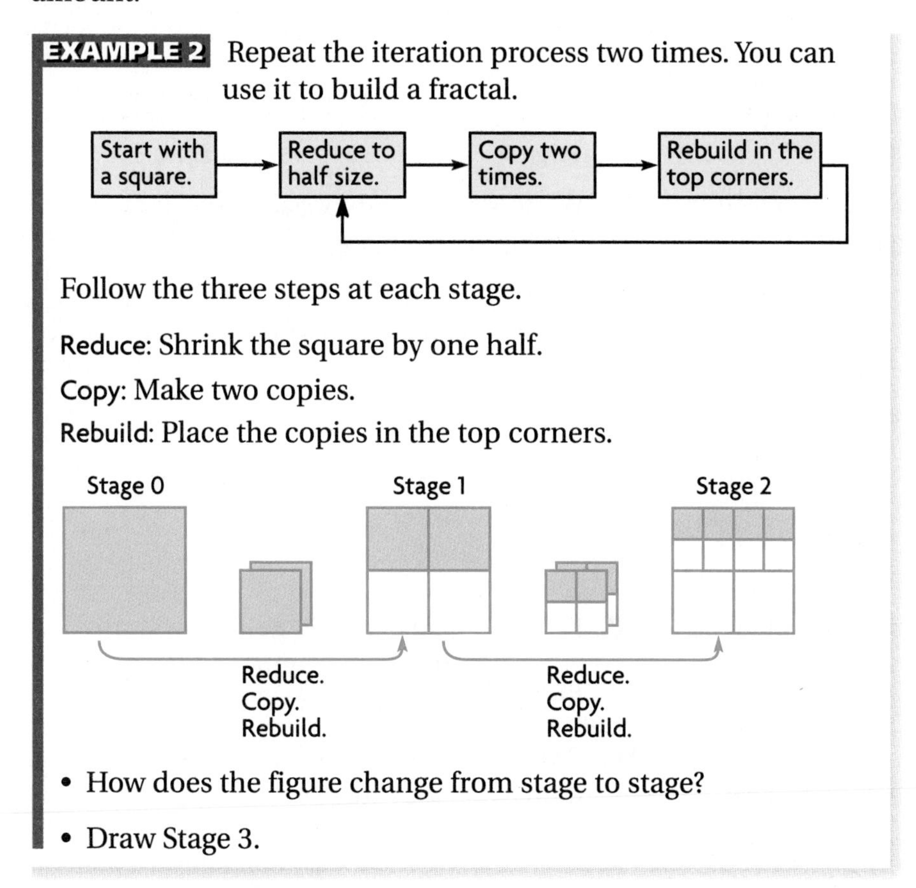

EXAMPLE 2 Repeat the iteration process two times. You can use it to build a fractal.

Follow the three steps at each stage.

Reduce: Shrink the square by one half.

Copy: Make two copies.

Rebuild: Place the copies in the top corners.

- How does the figure change from stage to stage?
- Draw Stage 3.

TEEN TIMES

Can you always believe your eyes? One of the more recent uses of fractals is in the field of computer graphics—especially in the creation of landscapes. Designers can build fractal-based scenes showing the ground, forests, water surfaces, and cloud layers. And they look almost real!

GUIDED PRACTICE

Use the following diagram for Exercises 1–4.

Stage 0

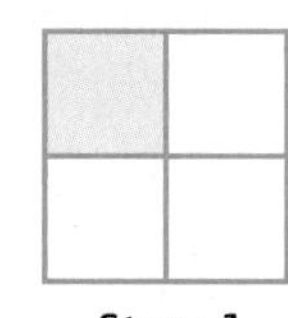

Stage 1

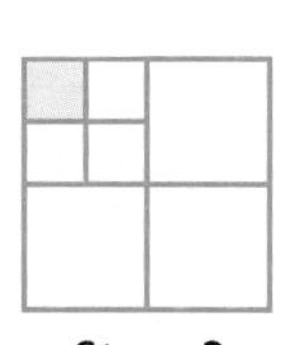

Stage 2

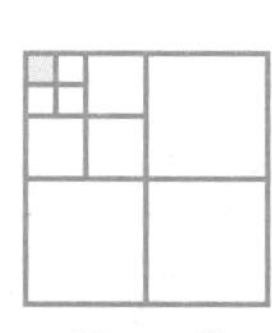

Stage 3

1. How many shaded squares appear at Stage 0? at Stage 1? at Stage 2? at Stage 3? at Stage *n*?

2. How does the shaded figure change from stage to stage?

3. How does the length of each side of the shaded figure change from stage to stage?

4. How does the area of the shaded figure change from stage to stage?

INDEPENDENT PRACTICE

For Exercises 1–6, study the iteration process shown in the figures at the right.

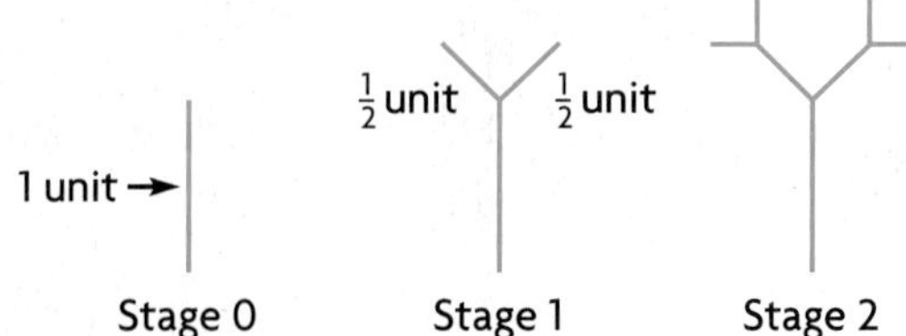

1. How many new branches do you see at Stage 1? at Stage 2?

2. How does the number of new branches change from Stage 1 to Stage 2?

3. How many new branches would you see at Stage 3? at Stage 4? at Stage *n*?

4. What is the length of each new branch that appears at Stage 2?

5. How does the length of each new branch change from stage to stage?

6. What would be the length of each new branch at Stage 3? at Stage 4?

For Exercises 7–11, use the figures below.

Stage 0

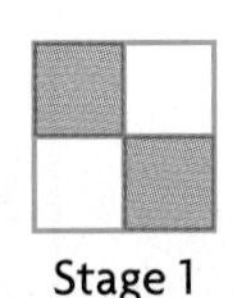
Stage 1

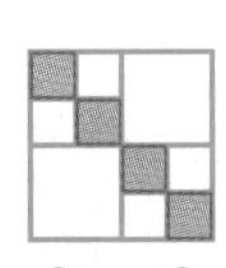
Stage 2

7. How does the length of a side of a shaded square change from stage to stage?

8. Look at Stage 0 and Stage 1. How many copies of the Stage 0 figure are used to build Stage 1? Stage 2?

9. Draw Stage 3 of the iteration process. How many shaded squares do you see at Stage 3?

10. Predict the number of shaded squares there will be at Stage 4.

11. Describe the pattern for the number of shaded squares at each successive stage.

Technology Link

In ***Mighty Math Cosmic Geometry,*** go to *Amazing Angles* to explore fractal relationships. Use Grow Slide Level R.

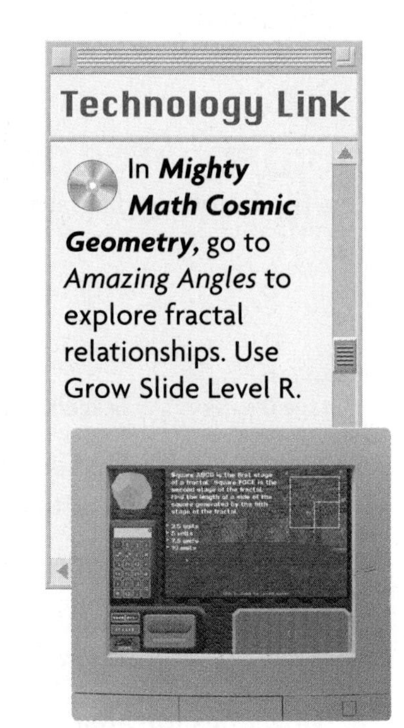

Problem-Solving Applications

12. **PATTERNS** Create a fractal spiral. Draw a line segment. Turn right 90°, and draw a segment with a length reduced by half. Repeat the process four times.

13. **NATURE** Think about fractals that occur in nature. Choose one, and draw it by using an iteration process.

14. Suppose you draw a circle, insert a square in the circle, and then insert a smaller circle in the square. After completing the process, have you built a fractal?

15. **WRITE ABOUT IT** Make your own fractal by using an iteration rule to repeatedly change a geometric figure. How do your figures change from stage to stage?

MORE PRACTICE Lesson 13.4, page H61

GEOMETRY CONNECTION

Building Snowflake Fractals

LAB ACTIVITY

What You'll Explore
How to change a polygon into a snowflake fractal by using an iteration rule

What You'll Need
square and isometric dot paper, straightedge

You can change the shape of an equilateral triangle by using an iteration rule. With each iteration, the figure looks more and more like a snowflake.

Explore

This is how you build a snowflake fractal.

- Draw a large equilateral triangle on isometric dot paper. Call this Stage 0.
- Divide each side into thirds. Replace the middle third of each side with two segments equal in length to the removed segment. Place the two segments to form two sides of a smaller equilateral triangle pointing outward. This is Stage 1.
- Repeat the process on each new line segment to form Stage 2.

18 → 6, 6, 6

Stage 0

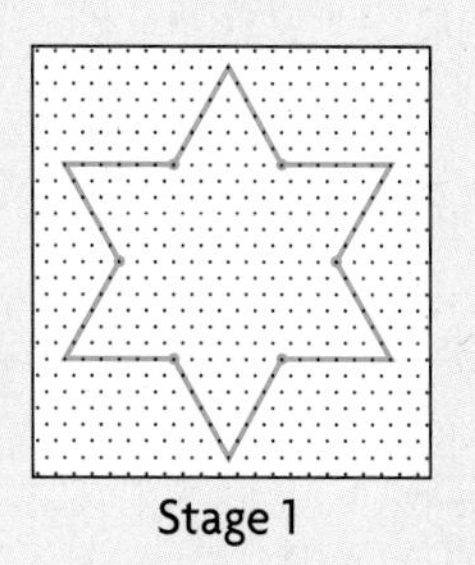

Stage 1

Think and Discuss

- How does the length of each segment change from stage to stage?
- How does the perimeter of the figure change from stage to stage? How does the area change?
- How did the snowflake change from Stage 1 to Stage 2? Do the edges of the snowflake show self-similarity?

Try This

- Using square dot paper, draw Stage 2 of the snowflake iteration, using squares instead of equilateral triangles. Record your results.

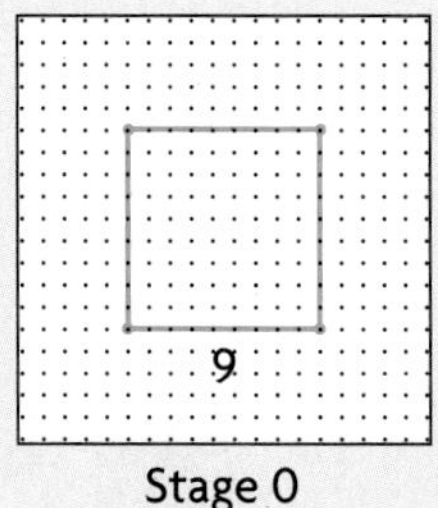

Stage 0

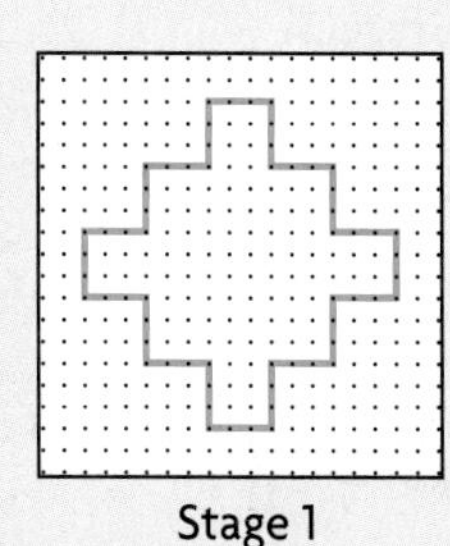

Stage 1

Technology Link

You can work with fractal patterns by using E-Lab, Activity 13. Available on CD-ROM and on the Internet at **www.hbschool.com/elab**

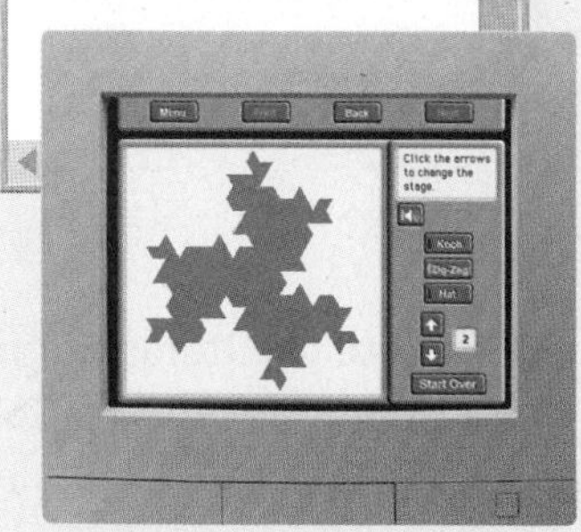

CHAPTER 13 Review/Test

1. **VOCABULARY** A repeating pattern of congruent plane figures that completely cover a plane, with no gaps or overlapping, is a(n) __?__. (page 256)

Use the figure to make at least two rows of a tessellation. (pages 256–258)

2. 

3. 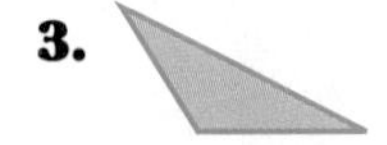

4. 

5. 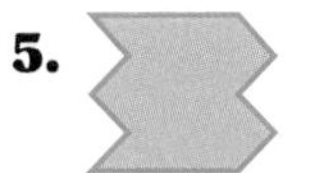

6. Draw a line segment 12 units long. Turn right 90°, and draw a segment with a length decreased by 2 units. Complete the process three times. (pages 259–260)

7. Draw a line segment 4 units long. Turn left 90°, and draw a segment 1 unit longer. Complete this process three times. (pages 259–260)

Start with the given figure. Reduce to half size. Complete the process two times. (pages 259–260)

8. 

9.

10. 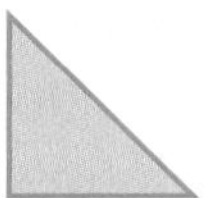

11. 

12. **VOCABULARY** A figure that has a repeating pattern of smaller and smaller parts that are like the whole, but different in size, has __?__. (page 261)

Write *yes* or *no* to tell whether the process is leading to self-similarity. (pages 261–263)

13. 
Stage 0
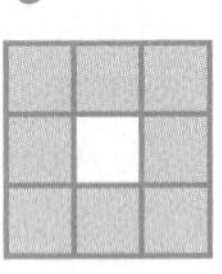
Stage 1
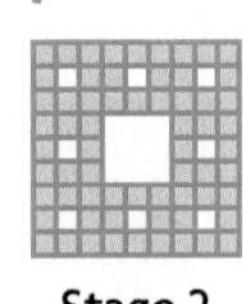
Stage 2

14. 
Stage 0

Stage 1
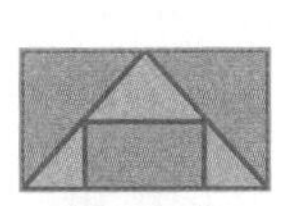
Stage 2

15. 
Stage 0
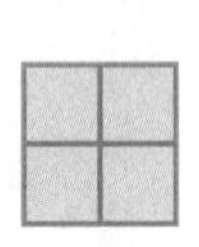
Stage 1
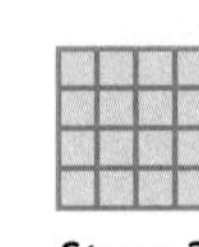
Stage 2

16. 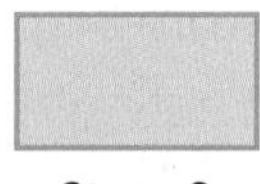
Stage 0
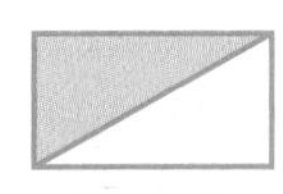
Stage 1

Stage 2

Complete the iteration process at the right two times. (pages 264–266)

Draw the given figure. → Reduce to half size. → Make one copy. → Rebuild in top right corner. (→ back to Reduce to half size.)

17. 

18. 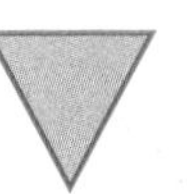

19. 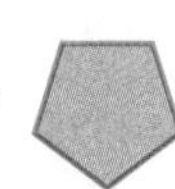

20. 

Test Prep

1. For what value of y is $8y = {}^{-}4$ a true statement?

A $^{-}16$
B $^{-}4$
C $\frac{^{-}1}{2}$
D $\frac{1}{2}$

2. Which expression could you use to find the number of inches in x yards?

F $3x$ **G** $12x$
H $16x$ **J** $36x$

3. You and 4 of your friends order pizza. The bill is $27.25. If you split the bill equally, how much will each person pay?

A $5.00
B $5.55
C $6.92
D $7.00
E Not Here

4. Which process is leading to self-similarity?

F

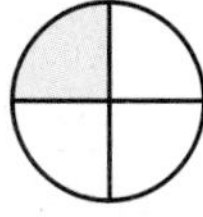
Stage 0

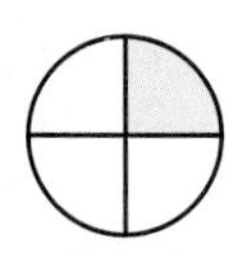
Stage 1

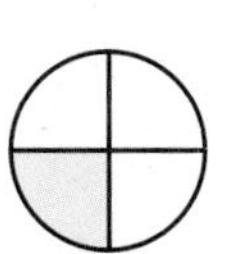
Stage 2

G

Stage 0

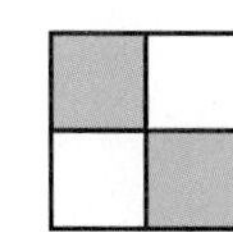
Stage 1

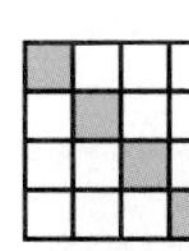
Stage 2

H

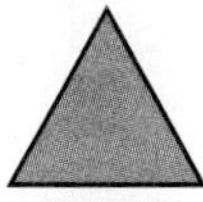
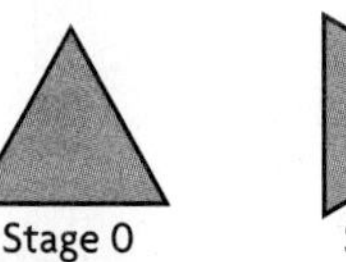
Stage 0

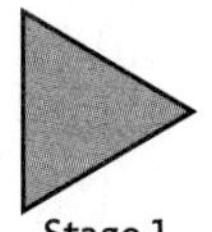
Stage 1

Stage 2

J

Stage 0

Stage 1

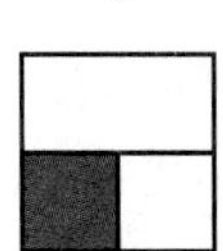
Stage 2

5. What solid can be formed from the net?

A triangular prism
B cube
C triangular pyramid
D cone

6. Which statement is **NOT** true?

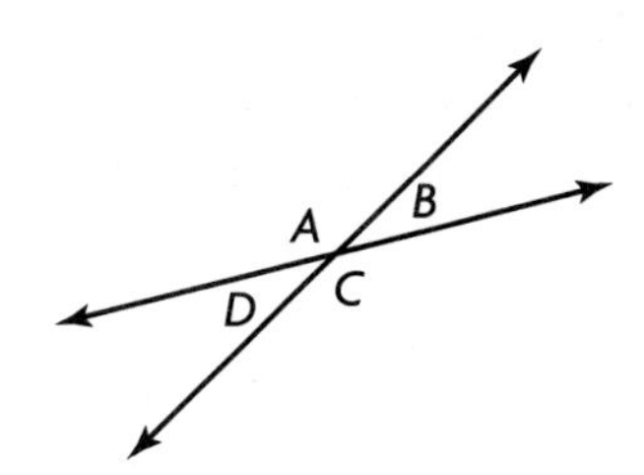

F $\angle A$ and $\angle B$ are supplementary.
G $\angle A$ and $\angle C$ are vertical angles.
H $\angle A$ and $\angle B$ are congruent.
J $\angle A$ and $\angle C$ are congruent.

7. At the local video store, you receive a $2 coupon for every 5 videos you rent. What is the total value of your coupons if you rent 30 videos?

A $10
B $12
C $25
D $60

8. By which rule are the triangles congruent?

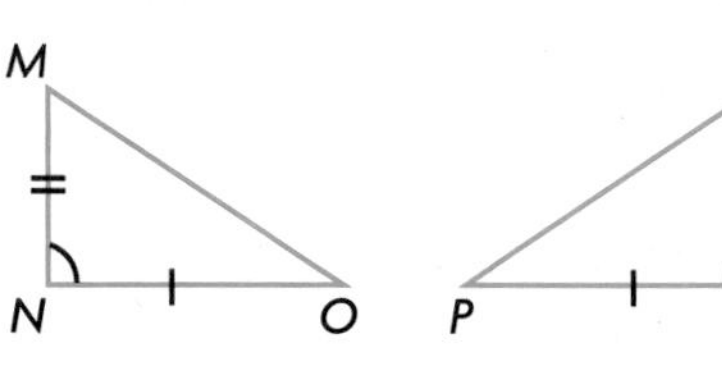

F SSS
G SAS
H ASA
J AAA

CHAPTERS 10–13

CUTTING CONGRUENT QUILTS

PURPOSE To practice identifying congruent plane figures (pages 198–202)

YOU WILL NEED tracing paper, scissors

Twin sisters, Diane and Cindy, made congruent halves of a patchwork quilt and then sewed the two parts together to form the square quilt.

- Trace the quilt, including all sections.
- Find the possible line segments that connect the two congruent parts.
- Make your own quilt design that can be divided into two congruent pieces.

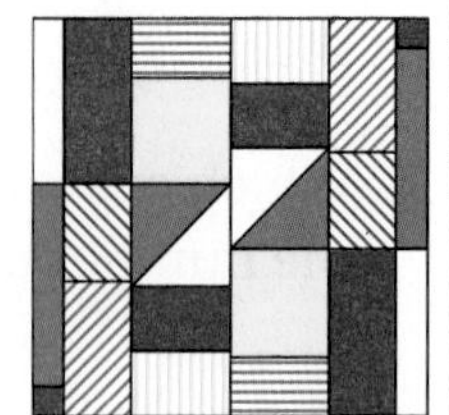

FLAGS, INCORPORATED

PURPOSE To practice making symmetrical designs (pages 221–223, 228–231)

Flags have been used for thousands of years to represent nations, government leaders, organizations, or ideas such as peace or unity.

Suppose you are a designer for Flags, Incorporated, a company that manufactures flags for a variety of clients. Design a flag with parallel and perpendicular lines and congruent triangles for your school, community, or club.

3-D DAYS!

PURPOSE To practice recognizing three-dimensional figures given the top, front, and side views (pages 246–249)

YOU WILL NEED centimeter cubes

Using the views shown at the right, build a solid figure with centimeter cubes. Next, draw the top, front, and side views of three different figures. Exchange your drawings with a classmate and build models of all three figures. The first person to build a model of all three figures is the winner.

Play this game with your family.

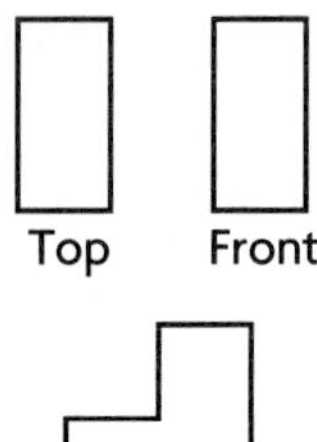

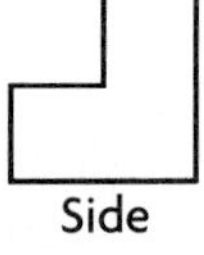

Side

Reflecting and Rotating Triangles

In this activity you will see how to reflect and rotate a triangle by using a drawing program.

To reflect a triangle, first use the drawing program to draw and label a triangle and line as shown below.

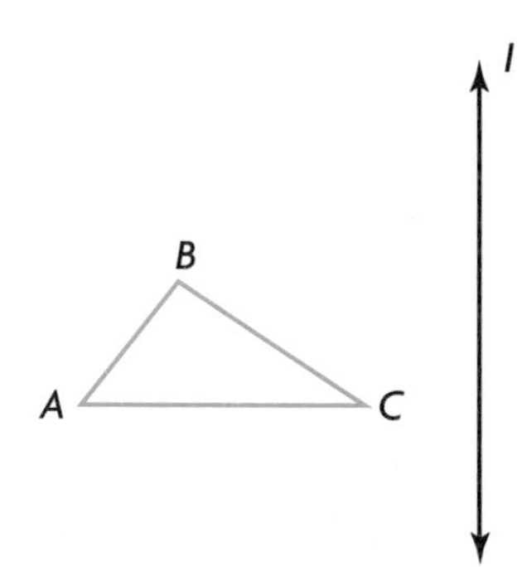

Select line l as the line of reflection. Then select $\triangle ABC$. Use the Reflect command to reflect $\triangle ABC$ over line l.

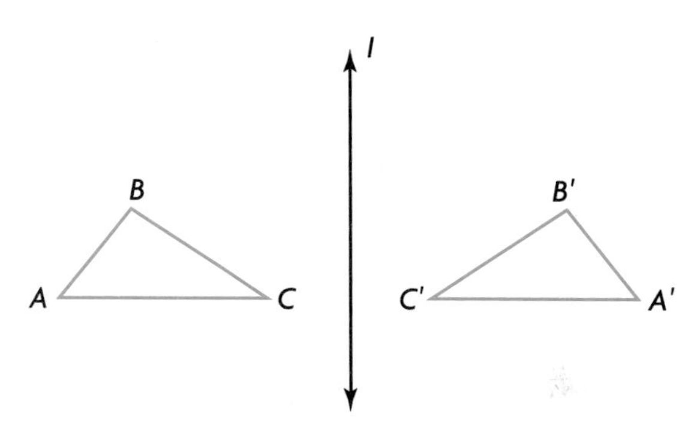

To rotate a triangle, first use the drawing program to draw and label a triangle as shown here.

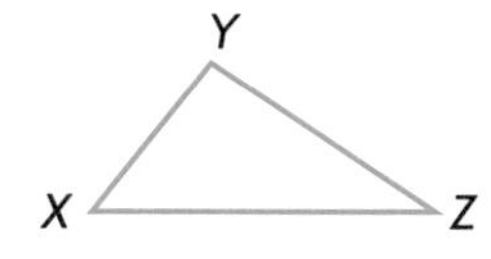

Select point Z as the point of rotation. Then select $\triangle XYZ$. Use the Rotate command to rotate $\triangle XYZ$ 90° about point Z.

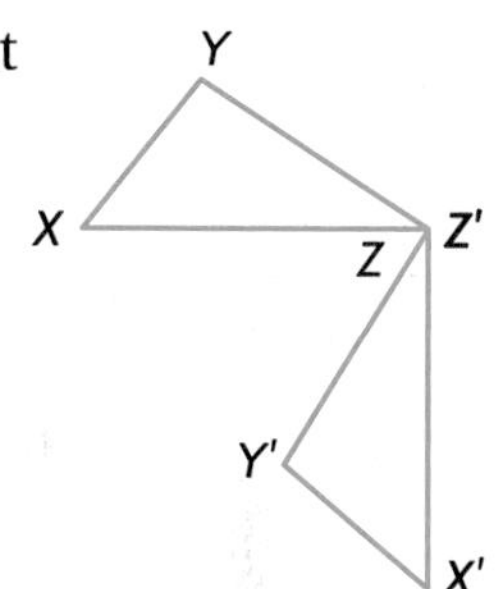

1. In the reflection, which angle corresponds to $\angle B$?

2. Describe how you could reflect $\angle ABC$ over another line.

3. In the rotation, which angle corresponds to $\angle X$?

4. Describe how you could rotate $\triangle XYZ$ about another point.

USING THE DRAWING TOOL

5. Draw a triangle different in size and shape from $\triangle ABC$. Draw a line and reflect it over the line.

6. Draw an irregular shape. Draw a line and reflect the irregular shape over the line.

7. Draw a triangle different in size and shape from $\triangle XYZ$. Select a vertex as the point of rotation. Rotate the triangle 120°.

8. Draw an irregular shape. Select a point on the shape as the point of rotation. Rotate the shape 120°.

CHAPTERS 10–13

Study Guide and Review

Vocabulary Check

1. When two lines intersect, the opposite angles are called ? . (page 200)
2. Movements that change the position and location of a figure but not its size or shape are called ? . (page 206)
3. A perpendicular line that intersects a line segment at its midpoint is called a(n) ? . (page 222)
4. A figure has ? if smaller and smaller parts of it are like the whole but different in size. (page 261)

EXAMPLES

- **Identify congruent line segments and angles.** (pages 199–202)

Name two pairs of congruent angles.

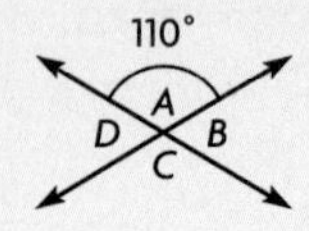

$\angle A$ is congruent to $\angle C$.
$\angle B$ is congruent to $\angle D$.

EXERCISES

Use the figure to the left to find the measure.

5. $\angle C$
6. $\angle B$
7. $\angle D$
8. Name two adjacent angles.
9. Name two vertical angles.

EXAMPLES

- **Identify and graph transformations on the coordinate plane.** (pages 210–211)

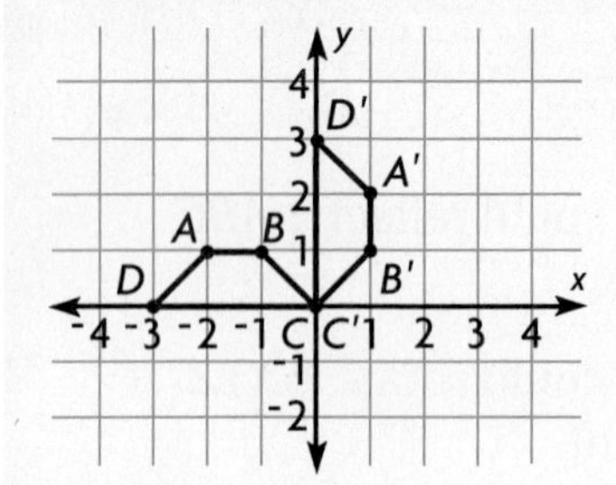

Trapezoid ABCD is rotated clockwise 90° about the origin.

ABCD coordinates: (⁻2,1), (⁻1,1), (0,0), (⁻3,0)
A'B'C'D' coordinates: (1,2), (1,1), (0,0), (0,3)

EXERCISES

10. Graph triangle *ABC* with coordinates (1,2), (1,0), and (3,0), and translate it 4 units left. What are the new coordinates?
11. Use the new triangle in Exercise 10, and reflect it across the *x*-axis. What are the new coordinates?

Copy *ABCD* onto a coordinate grid. Transform the figure according to the directions given.

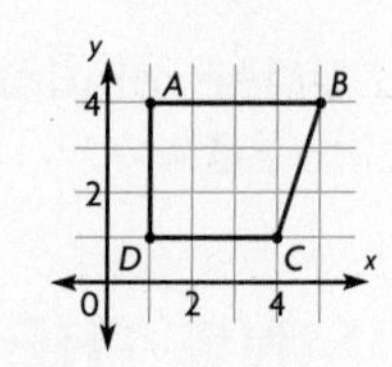

12. reflect across the *y*-axis
13. translate 3 units right
14. rotate 180° about point *A*
15. reflect across the *x*-axis

- **Classify and construct triangles and identify corresponding parts of congruent triangles.** **(pages 224–231)**

Determine whether the triangles are congruent by SSS, SAS, or ASA.

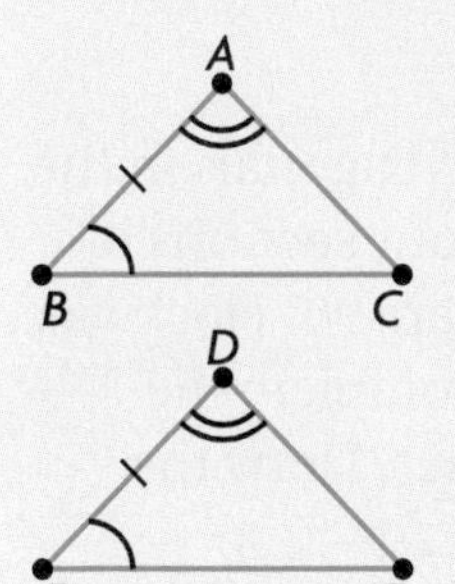

Two angles and the included side of △ABC match two angles and the included side of △DEF.

The triangles are congruent by ASA.

Determine whether the triangles are congruent by SSS, SAS, or ASA.

16.

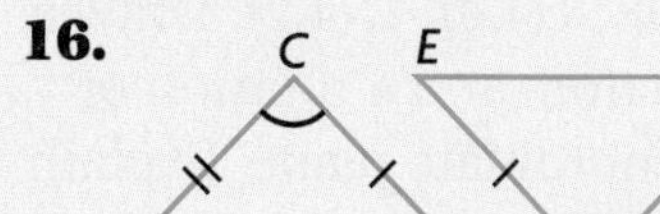

17.

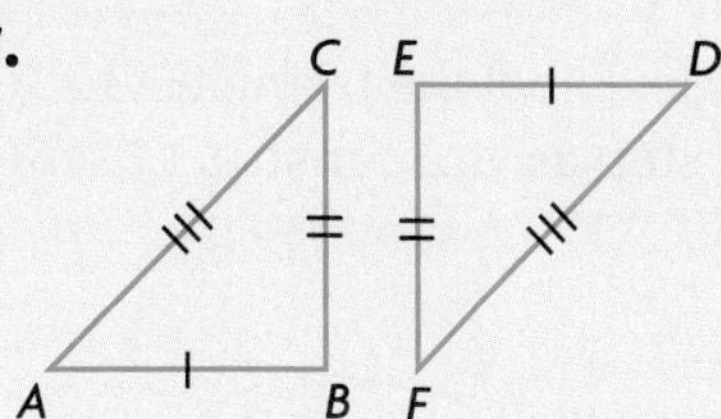

- **Create visual patterns by changing geometric figures.** **(pages 259–260)**

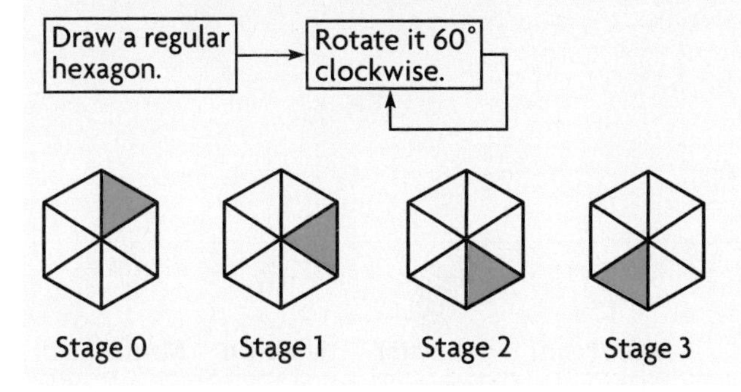

18. Draw a line segment 14 units long. Turn right 90°, and draw a segment with a length decreased by 2 units. Complete the process five more times.

19. Draw a square. Divide the square into four congruent squares. Shade the top left section, rotate clockwise 90°, and draw Stage 3.

Problem Solving

Solve. Explain your method. **(pages 238–240)**

20. A triangular pyramid has 4 vertices, a rectangular pyramid has 5 vertices, and a hexagonal pyramid has 7 vertices. How many vertices does a pentagonal pyramid have?

21. An octagonal prism has 10 faces and 16 vertices. How many edges does it have?

22. A rectangular prism has 8 vertices and 12 edges. How many faces does it have?

23. A square pyramid has 5 vertices and 8 edges. How many faces does it have?

CHAPTERS 10–13

Performance Assessment

Tasks: Show What You Know

1. On a coordinate plane, graph a triangle with vertices A (0,0), B (4,0), C (4,2). Draw a translation, a reflection, and a rotation of this figure on the coordinate plane. Explain how you drew each transformation. (pages 210–211)

2. Draw a triangle. Label the triangle XYZ. Explain each step as you construct $\triangle ABC$ congruent to $\triangle XYZ$. (pages 228–231)

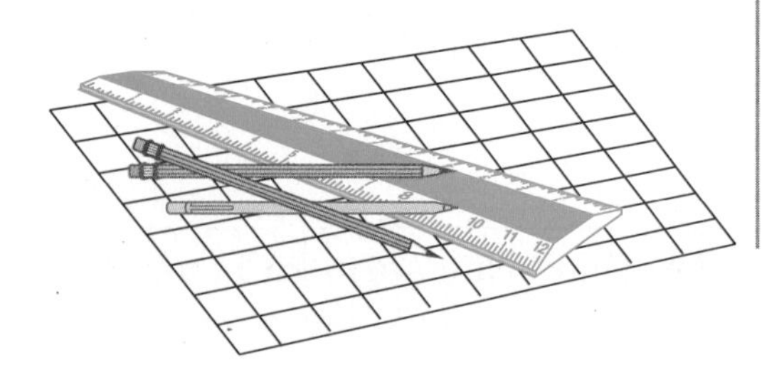

3. Draw an arrangement of 6 squares that form a net for a cube. Explain how you know the arrangement is a net for a cube. (pages 243–245)

4. Draw a square. Draw both diagonals in the square. Shade one of the four sections of the square. Rotate the square 90° clockwise. Explain each step as you complete the iteration process three times. Draw the figure at each stage. (pages 259–260)

Problem Solving

Solve. Explain your method.

CHOOSE a strategy and a tool.

- Find a Pattern
- Make a Model
- Write an Equation
- Act It Out
- Draw a Picture

Paper/Pencil

Calculator

Hands-On

Mental Math

5. $\triangle ABC$ is an isosceles triangle. The measure of $\angle ABC$ is 80°. Find the measures of $\angle BAC$ and $\angle BCA$. Could there be more than one answer? Explain. (pages 199–202)

6. Mia was wondering if a triangle could be both obtuse and isosceles. Draw a Venn diagram to answer her question and to show the relationship between obtuse and isosceles triangles. (pages 224–227)

7. For prisms, the relationship $F + V - 2 = E$ shows a pattern among the numbers of faces, F, vertices, V, and edges, E. Find the relationship that describes the number of faces, F, in terms of V and E. (pages 238–240)

8. Mrs. Chen wants to cover a 3-ft by 3-ft bulletin board with repeating geometric shapes. She wants to use triangles to cover the entire board with no gaps. Show three rows of one pattern that she could use. If possible, write an iteration rule for making the pattern. (pages 256–260)

Cumulative Review

Solve the problem. Then write the letter of the correct answer.

1. What is another name for $\frac{^{-}6}{8}$? (pages 20–21)

A. $^{-}0.75$ **B.** $^{-}0.34$
C. 0.75 **D.** $\frac{3}{4}$

2. What percent of the figure is shaded? (pages 23–25)

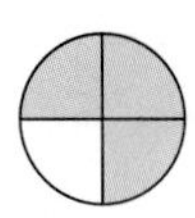

A. $\frac{3}{4}\%$ **B.** 25%
C. 34% **D.** not here

3. Use compatible numbers to estimate the quotient $47.7 \div 8.1$. (pages 70–72)

A. 4 **B.** 6
C. 7 **D.** 8

4. Add. Write the answer in simplest form. (pages 82–83)

$8\frac{1}{2} + 6\frac{5}{6}$

A. $14\frac{6}{8}$ **B.** $14\frac{8}{6}$
C. $15\frac{1}{3}$ **D.** not here

5. Find the difference. (pages 103–105)

$^{-}50 - 45$

A. $^{-}95$ **B.** $^{-}5$
C. 5 **D.** 95

6. Find the product. (pages 106–108)

$^{-}21 \times 7$

A. 147 **B.** 3
C. $^{-}3$ **D.** $^{-}147$

7. Find the difference. (pages 109–111)

$^{-}0.36 - 1.64$

A. $^{-}2$ **B.** $^{-}1.28$
C. 1.28 **D.** not here

8. Write an algebraic expression for the following. (pages 124–125)

6 less than the product of x and 5

A. $6 - x(5)$ **B.** $6 - x + 5$
C. $5x - 6$ **D.** $6 < x5$

9. Solve $x + 0.75 > 3.25$. (pages 170–171)

A. $x > 4$ **B.** $x > 2.5$
C. $x = 2.5$ **D.** $x < 2.5$

10. Which is a reflection of this figure? (pages 206–209)

original

A. 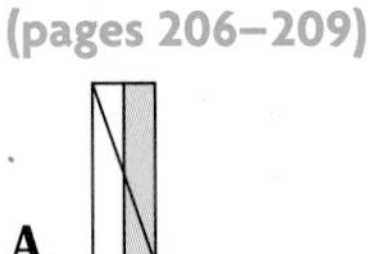
B. 
C.
D.

11. How many faces does a rectangular prism have? (pages 238–240)

A. 6 **B.** 8
C. 10 **D.** 12

12. Name the figure that can be formed from the net. (pages 243–245)

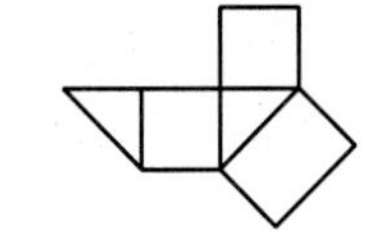

A. rectangular prism **B.** square pyramid
C. triangular prism **D.** cylinder

13. A(n) __?__ is a repeating pattern of congruent plane figures that completely covers a plane with no gaps or overlapping. (pages 256–258)

A. fractal **B.** iteration
C. self-similarity **D.** tessellation

CHAPTER 14

RATIOS AND RATES

LOOK AHEAD

In this chapter you will solve problems that involve

- unit rates and unit prices
- using tables and graphs to see rates
- the Golden Ratio
- pi

Listed below are the names, dates, and inventors of some telecommunication equipment.

ADVANCES IN TELECOMMUNICATIONS		
Invention	Year	Inventor
Electric Telegraph	1774	George Louis Lesage
Transatlantic Telegraph	1866	Lord Kelvin
Telephone	1876	Alexander Graham Bell
Fax Machine	1907	Arthur Korn
Pocket Telephone	1986	

- Use the data above to make a time line showing advances in telecommunications.
- How many years passed between the inventions of the electric telegraph and the fax machine?

Problem-Solving Project

7th Graders on the Phone

YOU WILL NEED: poster board, markers

Estimate how much time you spend on the telephone each week. Be sure you include time on the Internet. Use the phone rates at the left to calculate how much you would be charged. On a sheet of poster board, make your own chart of telephone rates. Then present your proposed rates to the class.

General Telephone Company Rates

Weekdays		
daytime	7 A.M. – 5:59 P.M.	28¢/min
evening	6 P.M. – 10:59 P.M.	18¢/min
late night	11 P.M. – 6:59 A.M.	15¢/min
Weekends/Holidays		
anytime		15¢/min

TELEPHONE RATES

School Days		Weekends/Holidays	
Time	Rate	Time	Rate
3 P.M.-5 P.M.	15¢/min	10 A.M.-6 P.M.	30¢/min
5 P.M.-10 P.M.	50¢/min	6 P.M.-10 P.M.	35¢/min
After 10 P.M.	75¢/min	After 10 P.M.	60¢/min

PROJECT CHECKLIST

- ✓ Did you estimate the time you spend on the phone?
- ✓ Did you calculate your phone charges?
- ✓ Did you make your own chart of phone rates?
- ✓ Did you present your proposal to the class?

PROBLEM-SOLVING STRATEGY

Drawing a Diagram to Show Ratios

What You'll Learn
How to draw a diagram to show ratios

Why Learn This?
To solve problems about everyday activities such as running

Some problems are much easier to understand and solve when you draw a diagram.

Anne runs faster than Desmond. When they run laps together, Anne runs a lap in 3 min, and Desmond runs it in 4 min. The ratio of Anne's time to Desmond's time is 3 to 4. If they start at the same time and place and run 25 min, when will Anne and Desmond meet at the starting line?

PROBLEM SOLVING
- Understand
- Plan
- Solve
- Look Back

UNDERSTAND What are you asked to do?

What facts are given?

PLAN What strategy will you use?

You can *draw a diagram* to find when they will meet.

SOLVE What kind of diagram can you draw to show the 3-to-4 ratio for 25 min?

You can use a number line to show when each runner crosses the starting line.

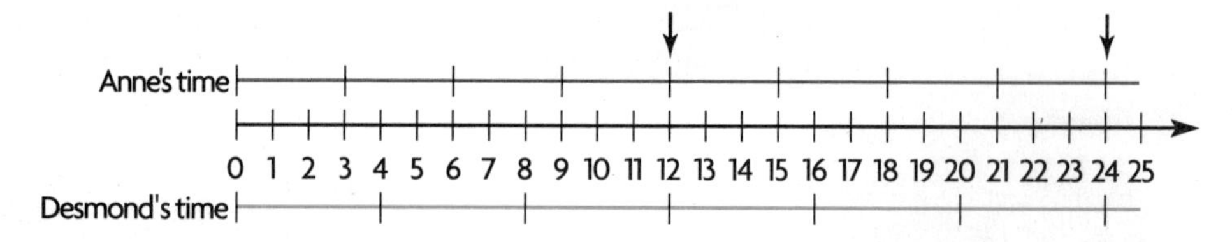

The diagram shows that they will meet at 12 min and 24 min.

LOOK BACK How are 12 and 24 related to 3 and 4?

What if . . . the ratio of Desmond's time to Anne's time is 5 to 3? If they start at the same time and place and run 25 minutes, when will they meet at the starting line?

PRACTICE

Draw a diagram and solve.

1. José skates faster than Jim. When they skate laps together, the ratio of José's time to Jim's time is 2 min to 3 min. If they start at the same time and skate 25 minutes, when will they meet at the starting line?

2. Tina is in charge of drinks for a picnic and she plans to serve lemonade. The ratio of concentrate to water is 1:3. How many cans of water will she combine with 9 cans of concentrate?

3. Leroy has 10 dimes in his pocket. Marcie has 20 nickels in her pocket. If Leroy takes one coin from his pocket at the same time Marcie takes one from hers until they have removed all the coins, how many times will they have the same amount of money showing?

4. Samantha travels 105 miles by going to work, coming home, and going to work again. She travels the same route to and from work every weekday. How far does Samantha travel in one round-trip to work and back home?

MIXED APPLICATIONS

Solve.

CHOOSE a strategy and a tool.

- **Make a Table**
- **Guess and Check**
- **Look for a Pattern**
- **Use a Formula**
- **Draw a Diagram**
- **Account for All Possibilities**

Paper/Pencil

Calculator

Hands-On

Mental Math

5. Tom backpacked 32 mi in 3 days. He traveled $4\frac{1}{2}$ fewer miles on the second day than on the first. He traveled $3\frac{1}{2}$ more miles on the third day than on the second. How many miles did he travel each day?

6. Thelma decides to go to the mall to buy postcards and a book. After spending $\frac{1}{6}$ of her weekly allowance on postcards and $\frac{1}{3}$ on a book, Thelma has $7.50 left. What is her weekly allowance?

7. In the past four months, Stella has earned $125, $120, $110, and $95. If the pattern continues, how much will Stella earn in the sixth month?

8. There are 15 students in a classroom. Each student shakes hands one time with every other student in the room. Find the total number of handshakes.

9. Sue and Lisa are swimming laps at swim practice. The ratio of Sue's laps to Lisa's laps is 3 to 4. If the girls start at the same time and swim 30 laps, how many times will they meet at the starting point?

10. Reggie's recipe says to cool the sauce to about 43°C, but he has a Fahrenheit thermometer. At about what reading on his thermometer should the temperature of the sauce be?

11. **WRITE ABOUT IT** Look back at Problem 1. Explain how you solved the problem by drawing a diagram.

MORE PRACTICE Lesson 14.1, page H62

LESSON 14.2

What You'll Learn
How to identify rates, unit rates, and unit prices

Why Learn This?
To solve problems such as finding the best price when shopping

VOCABULARY
rate
unit rate
unit price

ALGEBRA CONNECTION

Ratios and Rates

You can compare two numbers by writing a ratio. A **rate** is a special ratio that compares one quantity with another quantity. There are many types of rates:

55 miles per hour ← rate of speed

$5.00 per hour ← pay rate

450 students per year ← graduation rate

There are different ways to solve rate problems. You can use mental math to solve some everyday problems.

EXAMPLE 1 Jill agrees to baby-sit from 4:30 P.M. to 6:00 P.M. Friday and from 9:30 A.M. to noon Saturday. At a rate of $4.25 per hour, how much will she earn?

4:30–6:00 → $1\frac{1}{2}$ hr

9:30–12:00 → $2\frac{1}{2}$ hr

4 hr

First, add to find the total amount of time she will baby-sit.

Think: $4 \times \$4 = \$16$ *Then, multiply to find how much she'll earn.*

$4 \times \$0.25 = \$1$

$\$16 + \$1 = \$17$ So, Jill will earn $17.

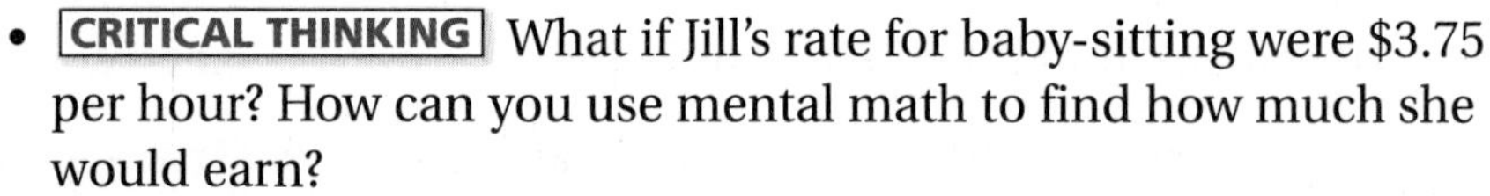

• CRITICAL THINKING What if Jill's rate for baby-sitting were $3.75 per hour? How can you use mental math to find how much she would earn?

EXAMPLE 2 Hilary charges $3.50 per bag for raking and bagging leaves. On Saturday she worked 8 hours and bagged 22 bags of leaves. About how much per hour did she earn?

$20 \times \$3.50 + 2 \times \$3.50 =$

$\$70 + \$7.00 = \$77.00$

Find the amount earned.

$\$9$ per hour: $8\overline{)\$72}$ and $\$10$ per hour: $8\overline{)\$80}$

Use compatible numbers to estimate the hourly rate.

Since $77 is between $72 and $80, Hilary earned about $9.50 per hour.

You can also use proportions to solve rate problems.

EXAMPLE 3 Tommy put together 63 pieces of his puzzle in $1\frac{1}{2}$ hr. At this rate, what is a reasonable estimate of the time it will take him to finish his 750-piece puzzle?

$\frac{60}{1.5} = \frac{750}{e}$

$60e = 750 \times 1.5$

$\frac{60e}{60} = \frac{1,125}{60}$

$e = 18.75 \leftarrow$ estimate

Round 63 to 60. Then estimate the time by using a proportion. Let e represent the estimate of hours to finish the puzzle.

So, at this rate, Tommy will finish the puzzle in about 19 hr.

GUIDED PRACTICE

1. If your rate of pay is \$4.25 per hour, how much will you earn if you work 10 hr? 20 hr? 15 hr?

2. Suppose your rate of reading is about 18 pages in 30 min. What is a reasonable estimate of the time it will take you to read 200 pages?

3. What if Tommy puts together 49 pieces of his puzzle in $1\frac{1}{4}$ hr? How can you use the table below to estimate how long Tommy will take to finish his 750-piece puzzle?

Number of Pieces	50	100	200	400	800
Time (in hours)	1.25	2.5	5	10	20

4. Suppose your cellular phone rate is \$0.27 per minute. About how much does a $3\frac{1}{2}$-minute call cost?

Unit Rates

You are probably familiar with such expressions as *per pound, per minute,* and *per gallon.* When you describe a rate in terms of one unit of measure or one item, you are using a **unit rate**. When you can write a rate as a fraction with the denominator 1, the rate is a unit rate.

\$50 for 10 hr work $\rightarrow \frac{\$50}{10 \text{ hr}} \rightarrow \frac{\$50 \div 10}{10 \text{ hr} \div 10} = \frac{\$5}{1 \text{ hr}} \leftarrow$ unit rate

You can write the unit rate as \$5 per hour.

124 mi in 8 hr $\rightarrow \frac{124 \text{ mi}}{8 \text{ hr}} \rightarrow \frac{124 \text{ mi} \div 8}{8 \text{ hr} \div 8} = \frac{15.5 \text{ mi}}{1 \text{ hr}} \leftarrow$ unit rate

You can write the unit rate as 15.5 mi per hr.

Consumers can make better decisions about what to buy when they compare prices. A good way to do this is to find the unit rates of the items or services you are comparing. Such a unit rate is called the **unit price**.

Dave's Dude Ranch

EXAMPLE 4 The weekly rate at Dave's Dude Ranch is \$504. Is this a better price for 7 days than the \$68 per night charged at Tex's Dude Ranch?

$$\frac{\$504}{7\text{ days}} = \frac{\$504 \div 7}{7\text{ days} \div 7}$$ *Find the unit price at Dave's Dude Ranch.*

$$= \frac{\$72}{1\text{ day}} \leftarrow \text{unit price}$$

The price at Dave's is not a better price, because it is more than the price at Tex's.

- What if the rate were \$472.50 per week at Dave's? Which ranch would be less expensive?

EXAMPLE 5 The grocery store sells notebook paper in packs of 150 sheets for \$1.19. The discount store sells it in packs of 250 sheets for \$1.80. Which is the better buy?

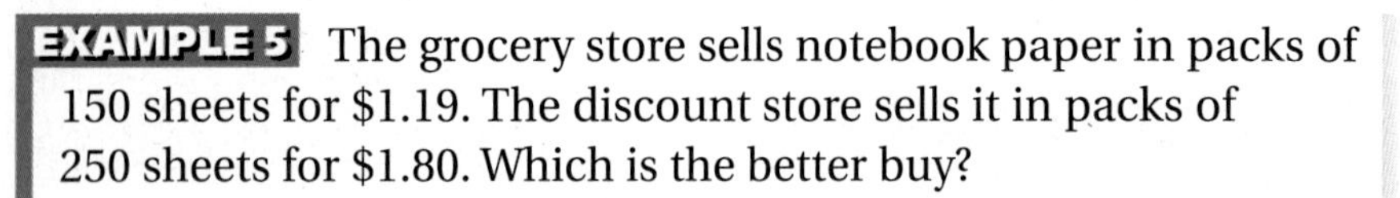

Find each unit price.

1.19 ÷ 150 = 0.007933333 ← unit price at grocery store

1.80 ÷ 250 = 0.0072 ← unit price at discount store

Since \$0.0079 per sheet is more than \$0.0072 per sheet, the better buy is 250 sheets for \$1.80 from the discount store.

- CRITICAL THINKING Is \$0.0072 per sheet more than, less than, or the same price as 1¢ per sheet?

TEEN TIMES

Baby-sitters and pet-sitters usually charge hourly rates for their services. For example, you might charge Ms. Perez \$2.00 per hour to walk her dog and Mr. Jones \$2.50 per hour to walk both of his dogs. Your reason is that walking two dogs together is not much more work.

INDEPENDENT PRACTICE

Use the given rate of pay and the time worked to find how much is earned.

1. \$5.50 per hour for 24 hr

2. \$6.75 per hour for 40 hr

3. \$12.00 per hour for $9\frac{1}{2}$ hr

Find the unit rate.

4. 132 mi in 4 hr, or _?_ mi per hr

5. 228 students in 6 buses, or _?_ in each bus

6. 6 for \$16.50, or _?_ each

Find each unit price. Round to the next cent when necessary. Then tell which choice has the lower unit price.

7. a 5-lb box of soap powder for $4.95 or a 10-lb box for $8.50

8. a 2.2-kg bag of apples for $5.06 or a 4.0-kg bag of apples for $9.16

Technology Link
In *Mighty Math Astro Algebra* you can go to *VariaBLOX* for more challenges with ratios, as you explore *A Chotchkee Holiday.* Use Grow Slide Level Red Q.

Problem-Solving Applications

9. **COMPARE** Ed is shopping for ski gloves. The Ski Fanatic's price is $21.95 a pair. The Slope Store sells 2 pairs of the same gloves for $43.00. Which is the better buy?

10. **CONSUMER MATH** Lamar and Sarah can buy 1 L of soda for $1.09 or 2 L for $1.99. Or, they can buy a 6-pack of soda for $2.99 or a 12-pack for $3.59. Each can in the pack contains 355 mL. Which packaging of soda has the best price?

11. **WRITE ABOUT IT** Write and solve a problem about finding a unit rate.

Mixed Review and Test Prep

For Exercises 12–15, use the graph at the right.

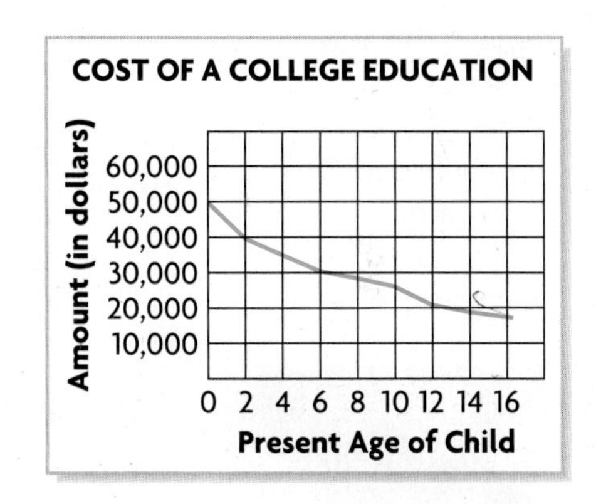

12. How much will a college education cost for a baby born today?

13. How much will a college education cost for a child who is 8 years old now?

14. How much more will a college education cost for a 2-year-old than for a 14-year-old?

15. How much will your college education cost?

For Exercises 16–19, make a tessellation that uses the figure as the basic unit.

16. 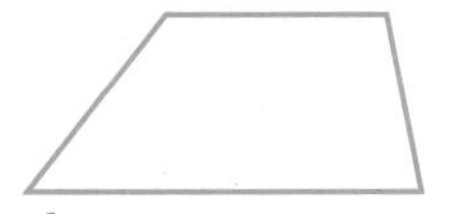

17. 

18. 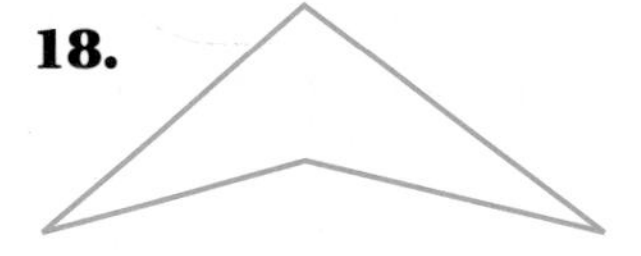

19. 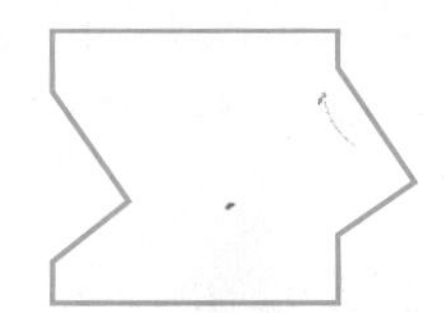

20. **GEOMETRY** $\angle A$ and $\angle B$ are supplementary. The measure of $\angle A = 46°$. What is the measure of $\angle B$?

A 44° **B** 46°
C 134° **D** 144°

21. **PATTERNS** What is the common difference in this sequence? 8, 5, 2, ⁻1, . . .

F ⁻1 **G** ⁻3
H 2 **J** 3

MORE PRACTICE Lesson 14.2, page H62

LESSON 14.3

ALGEBRA CONNECTION

Rates in Tables and Graphs

What You'll Learn
How to use tables and graphs to show rates

Why Learn This?
To solve problems about rates, such as parking fees

At the 1996 Olympic Games, Michael Johnson set a world record of 19.32 sec for the 200-m race. Johnson became the fastest human in recorded history.

You can use a table to organize data about rates. The table below shows that Michael Johnson ran at a rate of 19.32 sec for 200 m in the 1996 Olympics. The table also shows what the times for 25 m, 50 m, and 100 m would be if he ran at the same rate.

- What pattern do you see in the table?

200 m	19.32 sec
100 m	9.66 sec
50 m	4.83 sec
25 m	2.415 sec

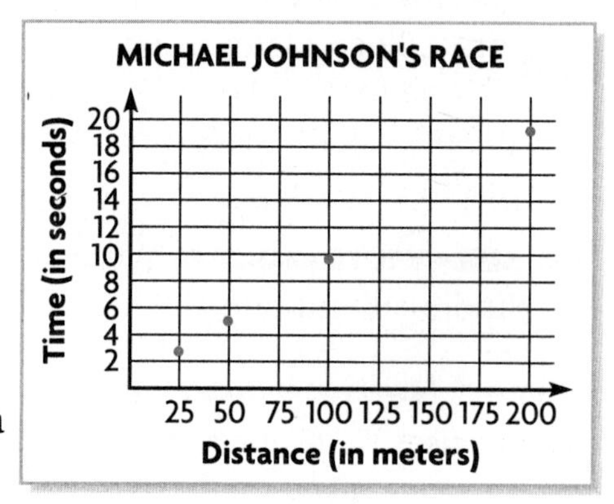

Graphs can help you see patterns or relationships in data. This graph is of the data given in the table.

- What pattern or relationship do you see in the graph?

SPORTS LINK

Michael Johnson was the first man to win gold medals in the 200-m race and the 400-m race in the same Olympics. His time in the 400-m race was 43.49 sec. What was his unit rate for each race? That is, how far did Johnson run per second in each race?

EXAMPLE

Mrs. Diaz parks in a parking garage that charges \$2.50 for the first hour or any part of the hour, and \$1.50 for each additional hour or part of an hour. Use the graph to find how much Mrs. Diaz pays to park in the garage for $4\frac{1}{2}$ hr.

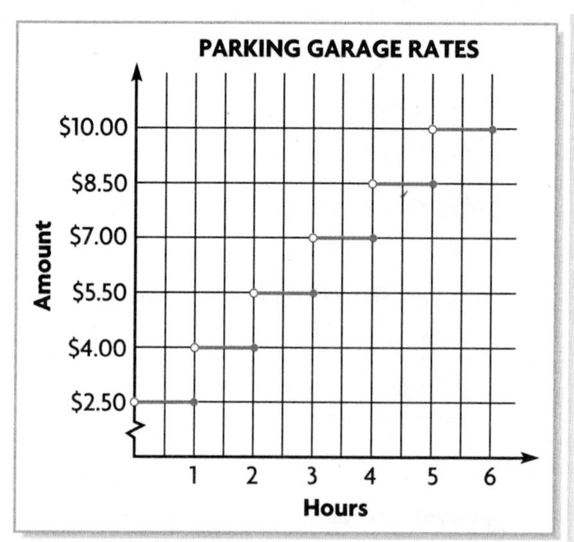

The graph shows Mrs. Diaz pays \$8.50 for $4\frac{1}{2}$ hr.

- What does the open circle mean on each step of the graph?

GUIDED PRACTICE

1. The table shows how long it took stock cars at a 250-mi race to travel certain distances. If the cars continued at the same average speed, about how long did it take to complete the race?

Distance	Time
50 mi	33 min
100 mi	66 min
150 mi	99 min

2. Ellie collected data to explore relationships among metric measurements of water. Look for patterns in her data. Then copy the table, and use the patterns to complete it.

Capacity	5 L	4.5 L	4 L	3.5 L
Volume	5,000 cm^3	4,500 cm^3	?	?
Mass	5 kg	4.5 kg	?	?

INDEPENDENT PRACTICE

1. The table at the right shows increases in the price of a breakfast cereal for the last three years. Compare the prices for any two consecutive years by making a ratio. Use the ratio to find the pattern in the table. Describe the pattern.

CRUNCHY FLAKES				
Year	0	1	2	3
Price	$3.20	$3.52	$3.87	$4.26

2. If the pattern continues, what will the cost of a box of Crunchy Flakes be in year four? in year five?

Problem-Solving Applications

For Problems 3–7, use the graph of taxicab rates.

3. What does the taxi service charge for the first $\frac{1}{8}$ mi? for each $\frac{1}{8}$ mi after the first?
4. How much is a 1-mi ride?
5. **CRITICAL THINKING** Does a 2-mile taxicab ride cost $6.00? Explain.
6. **TRAVEL** Mary Jo takes a taxi to see her grandparents, who live 4 mi away. How much will Mary Jo owe the driver?
7. **LOGICAL REASONING** Mr. West lives 10 mi from the airport. How much will he pay for a ride from his home to the airport?
8. **WRITE ABOUT IT** Write and solve a problem about ratios, using one of the tables or the graph on this page.

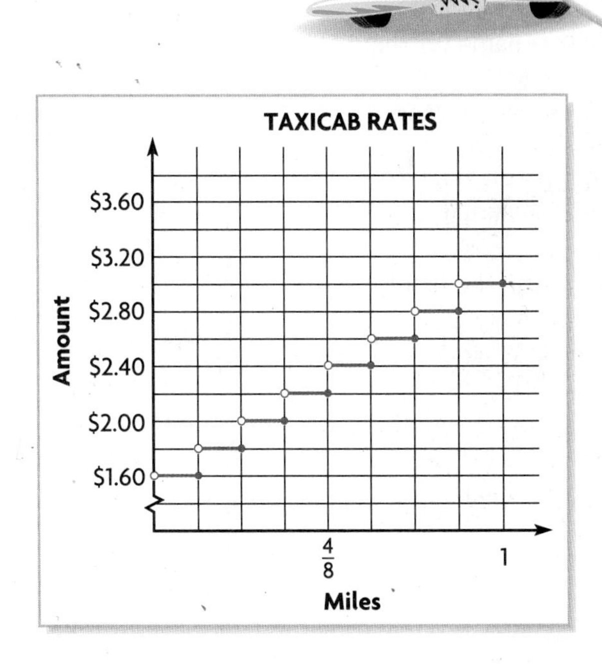

MORE PRACTICE Lesson 14.3, page H62

LESSON 14.4

Finding Golden Ratios

What You'll Learn
How to identify the Golden Ratio

Why Learn This?
To see how artists and photographers use the Golden Ratio

VOCABULARY

Golden Ratio

Golden Cut

Golden Section

ART LINK

Another name for the Golden Ratio is *phi* (fy). The symbol for *phi* is the Greek letter ø. It is the first letter of Phidias, the name of a Greek sculptor in the fifth century B.C. Much of Phidias's work included the Golden Ratio. Why do you think the Golden Ratio has been used in art and architecture?

How do you think artists use mathematics?

Artists commonly use a ratio that is shown in this diagram. The line segment is divided at a very special place.

Point B divides $\overline{AC}$ to form these equivalent ratios.

$$\frac{\text{longer segment}}{\text{shorter segment}} \rightarrow \frac{BC}{AB} = \frac{AC}{BC} \leftarrow \frac{\text{total segment}}{\text{longer segment}}$$

Each of these ratios is approximately equal to 1.61. This ratio is called the **Golden Ratio**. The division of the segment into parts that form the Golden Ratio is called a **Golden Cut** or a **Golden Section**. The Golden Ratio occurs in nature and in the works of such famous artists as Albrecht Dürer and Leonardo da Vinci.

EXAMPLE Segment PR is 34 cm long. Where should a point, Q, be placed on $\overline{PR}$ to make the Golden Cut?

34 cm

P —————————————— R

To make the Golden Cut, point Q can divide $\overline{PR}$ into a shorter segment, $\overline{PQ}$, and a longer segment, $\overline{QR}$.

The ratio $\frac{PR}{QR}$ must be 1.61.

To locate point Q, you must find the lengths of $\overline{PQ}$ and $\overline{QR}$.

You can use a proportion and the Golden Ratio, $\frac{1.61}{1}$.

$\frac{PR}{x} = \frac{1.61}{1}$ *Let x represent the length of $\overline{QR}$.*

$\frac{34}{x} = \frac{1.61}{1}$ *Replace PR with 34.*

$1.61x = 34 \times 1$ *Find the cross products and solve.*

$\frac{1.61x}{1.61} = \frac{34}{1.61}$

$x \approx 21$

So, the length of $\overline{QR}$ is about 21 cm.

- What is the distance from point P to point Q? from point Q to point R?

ACTIVITY **WHAT YOU'LL NEED:** string, ruler marked in millimeters

In this activity, you will look for the Golden Ratio in famous faces.

- Work with a partner and trace the diagram shown.
- Measure and record in a table the lengths of the segments marked *a*–*g*.
- Use the measurements to find ratios such as:

  $\frac{a}{b}$ $\frac{c}{d}$ $\frac{c}{e}$ $\frac{b}{g}$

- Trace the famous faces shown below. Draw sets of parallel line segments that match the segments *a*–*g*, and measure the lengths of the segments.
- Can you find the Golden Ratio in either of the faces? Use your ratios and drawings to support your answers.

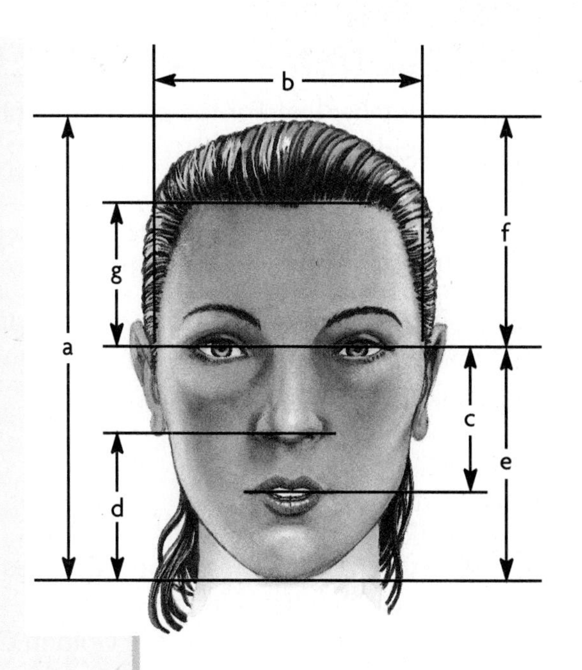

GUIDED PRACTICE

Segment *EG* is 21 cm long. Point *F* on this segment makes a Golden Cut.

1. Write and solve a proportion to find the length of the longer segment, $\overline{EF}$.
2. What is the distance from point *F* to point *G*? from point *E* to point *F*?
3. How can you be sure that point *F* makes a Golden Cut?
4. If segment *EG* is 42 cm long, find the length of the longer segment, $\overline{EF}$.

INDEPENDENT PRACTICE

Copy the number line. For the given segment, mark a point, C, that makes a Golden Cut.

1.

2.

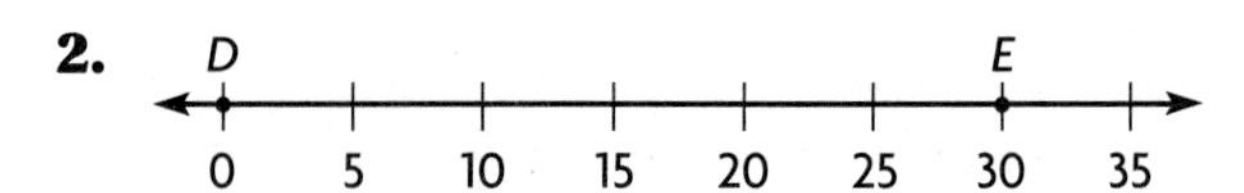

3. Point T divides $\overline{MN}$ so that $MT = 24$ in. and $TN = 15$ in. Does T come close to making a Golden Cut? Support your answer.

4. Segment RT is 40 cm long. Where should point S be placed on $\overline{RT}$ to make $\frac{RT}{ST}$ a Golden Ratio?

Problem-Solving Applications

5. **MEASURE** Use a ruler to find examples of the Golden Ratio in this regular pentagon. Describe how the Golden Cuts are formed.

6. **RATIOS** Measure the lengths of the different parts of the man at the far right to find as many ratios as you can that approximate the Golden Ratio.

7. **WRITE ABOUT IT** Trace a picture of a face or figure from a book or newspaper. Measure the different parts to find as many ratios as you can that approximate the Golden Ratio.

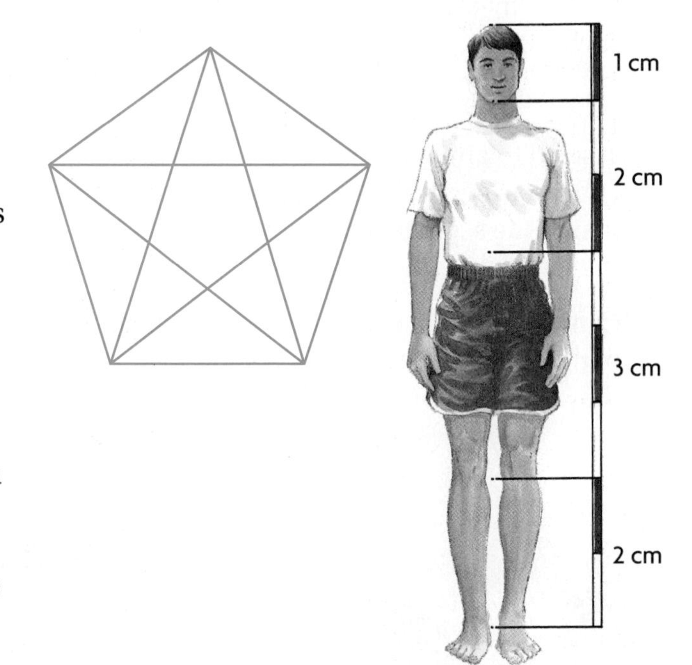

Mixed Review and Test Prep

For Exercises 8–15, rename the fraction with a denominator of 100.

8. $\frac{4}{10}$ **9.** $\frac{2}{5}$ **10.** $\frac{17}{25}$ **11.** $\frac{18}{30}$

12. $\frac{7}{5}$ **13.** $\frac{9}{2}$ **14.** $\frac{3}{20}$ **15.** $\frac{17}{4}$

For Exercises 16–19, tell whether the given figure will form a tessellation.

16. equilateral triangle **17.** square **18.** regular pentagon **19.** regular hexagon

20. **LOGICAL REASONING** If $\frac{1}{2}$ of a number is $\frac{1}{4}$, what is $\frac{1}{3}$ of the number?

A $\frac{1}{12}$ B $\frac{1}{9}$
C $\frac{1}{6}$ D $\frac{1}{5}$

21. **STATISTICS** How many buses are needed for 897 students if one bus holds 42 students?

F 20 G 21
H 22 J 25

MORE PRACTICE Lesson 14.4, page H63

GEOMETRY CONNECTION

Finding Pi

In this activity, you will find one of the best-known ratios, pi. The symbol for pi is π.

What You'll Explore
How pi, diameter, and circumference are related

What You'll Need
compass, scissors, ruler, calculator

Explore

- Using a compass, draw four circles, each with a different radius. Be sure to mark the centers of your circles.

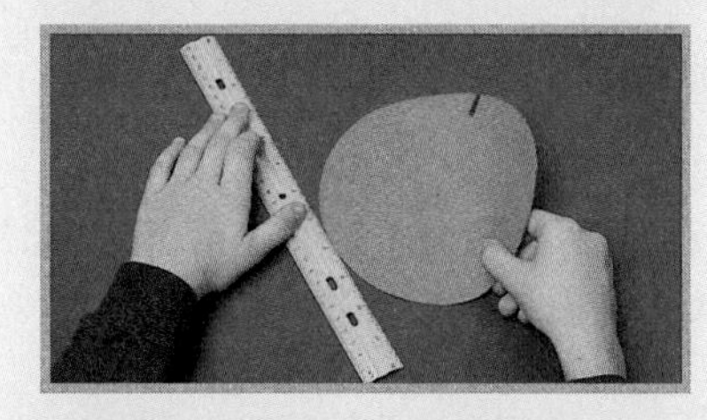

- After you cut out each circle, mark a point on the edge, and roll the circle along the ruler to measure the circumference. Then measure the diameter of each circle. Record all data in a table.

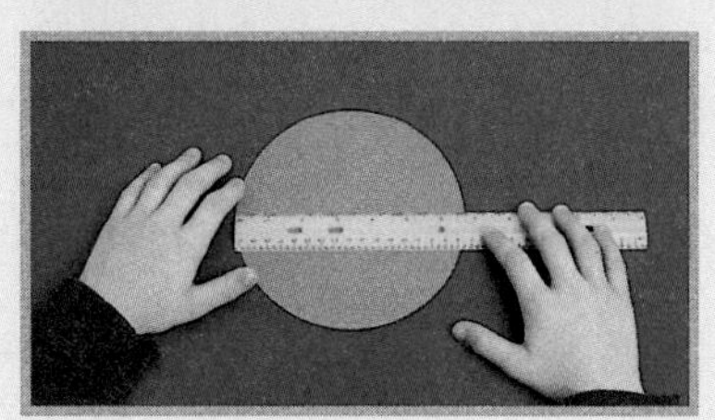

- In the table, record for each circle the ratio of the circumference to the diameter. Write each ratio as a decimal.

Think and Discuss

- Look at the ratios for your circles. How are the ratios related?
- In your table, look at the ratios of circumference to diameter. What is the mean of the decimal values for these ratios?
- Compare this mean with the means from other students. What relationship do you see?
- What conclusions can you draw from the class data?

Try This

- Push the π key on your calculator. What number is in the display?
- How is this related to the mean of the ratios computed by your class?
- Using π for the ratio, write a formula to show the relationship between circumference and diameter of a circle.

Technology Link

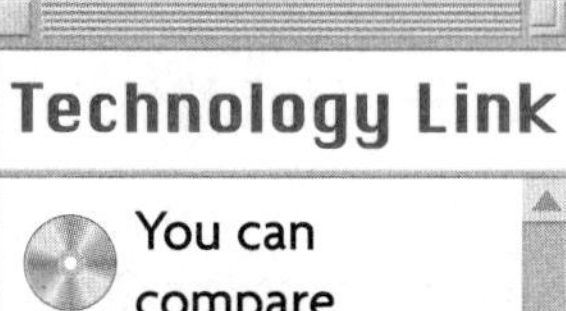

You can compare circumference and diameter by using E-Lab, Activity 14. Available on CD-ROM and on the Internet at **www.hbschool.com/elab**

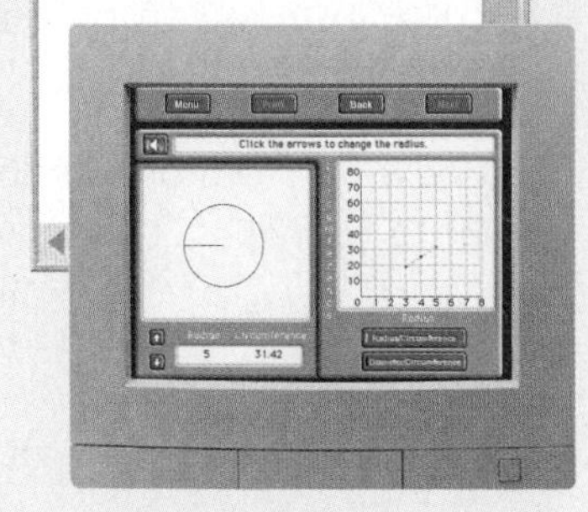

CHAPTER 14 Review/Test

1. Mike can type an order in 4 min and Julie can type one in 5 min. They each have 45 orders, and they start at the same time. How many more times will they start an order at the same time? (pages 278–279)

2. Caryn made a design using 4 trapezoids and 12 triangles. If she uses the same ratio and extends the design to include 48 triangles, how many trapezoids should be included? (pages 278–279)

3. Bettina walks around a track in 5 min. Derrick walks around the same track in 4 min. If they start at the same time and walk for 60 min, when will they meet at the starting line? (pages 278–279)

4. Jeremy is making punch for a party. The ratio of fruit juice to ginger ale is 2:1. How many quarts of ginger ale will he mix with 6 quarts of fruit juice? (pages 278–279)

5. **VOCABULARY** A ratio that compares one quantity with another quantity is a(n) __?__. (page 280)

6. **VOCABULARY** When you can write a rate as a fraction with the denominator 1, the rate is a(n) __?__. (page 281)

Find the unit rate. (pages 280–283)

7. 2,880 ft in 12 min
8. 876 mi in 6 days
9. $120.75 for 23 hr
10. 156 cookies in 13 boxes

Find the unit price. (pages 280–283)

11. 3 CDs for $29.95
12. 20 pencils for $1.80
13. 12 bananas for $1.92
14. 6 pairs of socks for $15.00

Use the table of after-school child-care rates. (pages 284–285)

Children	Number of Days Per Week		
	2	3	5
1	$22.00	$29.00	$39.00
2	$41.80	$55.10	$74.10

15. How much does Mr. Huggins pay each day for 3 days for 2 children?

16. How much does Mr. Huggins pay for each child per week and per day for the 3 days?

17. How much would Mr. Huggins pay for each child per week and per day for 5 days of care?

18. Mrs. Buckridge has 1 child in after-school care for 5 days each week. What does she pay per day?

19. **VOCABULARY** A ratio approximately equal to $\frac{1.61}{1}$ is a(n) __?__. (page 286)

Tell how far from one endpoint of the segment you would place point Q to make a Golden Cut. (pages 286–288)

20. $\overline{RS}$ is 25 cm long.
21. $\overline{GH}$ is 2.6 m long.
22. $\overline{XY}$ is 260 cm long.
23. $\overline{BD}$ is 4 m long.
24. $\overline{AB}$ is 16 in. long.
25. $\overline{JK}$ is 48 cm long.

Test Prep

1. Bus A makes a round-trip from the terminal in 45 minutes. Bus B makes a round-trip in 60 minutes. How long will it be before the buses meet again if they leave the terminal at the same time?

A 90 min
B 180 min
C 210 min
D 360 min

2. Which figure has the following top, front, and side views?

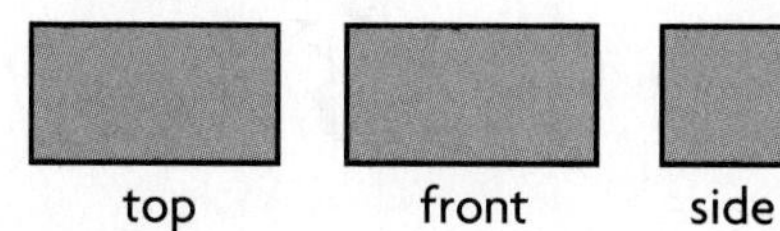

F cube
G rectangular pyramid
H square pyramid
J rectangular prism
K Not Here

3. A package of 12 computer disks costs \$5.49. A package of 24 computer disks costs \$12.99. Which is **NOT** a reasonable conclusion?

A The unit cost of a disk from the 12-disk package is about \$0.46.
B The unit cost of a disk from the 24-disk package is about \$0.54.
C The 24-disk package is a better buy.
D The 12-disk package is a better buy.

4. $4\frac{1}{2} \times 3\frac{3}{8} =$

F $7\frac{3}{16}$

G $12\frac{3}{10}$

H $12\frac{3}{16}$

J $15\frac{3}{16}$

5. A theater charges \$12.50 more for orchestra seats than for balcony seats. The cost of an orchestra seat is \$47.50. Which equation could you use to find *b*, the cost of a balcony ticket?

A $b + 12.50 = 47.50$
B $b - 12.50 = 47.50$
C $b = 47.50 + 12.50$
D $b + 47.50 = 12.50$

6. The ratio of length to width of a Golden Rectangle is about 1.61. Which are the dimensions of a Golden Rectangle?

F 50 in. by 35 in.
G 35 in. by 18 in.
H 21 in. by 13 in.
J 15 in. by 8 in.

7. Mrs. Reardon drives $47\frac{3}{4}$ miles every day. Which is the best estimate of the number of miles she drives in 1 week?

A 220 mi
B 250 mi
C 350 mi
D 500 mi

8. Which figure will **NOT** tessellate the plane?

F square
G triangle
H regular pentagon
J rectangle

9. Triangle *BCD* has coordinates $B(0,0)$, $C(5,0)$, and $D(0,4)$. What is the image of triangle *BCD* translated 5 units left?

A $B'(0,{}^-5)$, $C'(5,{}^-5)$, $D'(0,{}^-1)$
B $B'({}^-5,0)$, $C'(0,0)$, $D'({}^-5,4)$
C $B'({}^-5,{}^-5)$, $C'(0,{}^-5)$, $D'({}^-5,4)$
D $B'(0,0)$, $C'(0,{}^-5)$, $D'(0,4)$

CHAPTER

15

RATIO, PROPORTION, AND PERCENT

LOOK AHEAD

In this chapter you will solve problems that involve

- changing ratios to percents
- using ratios, proportions, and equations to find percents
- finding the percent one number is of another
- finding a number when a percent of it is known

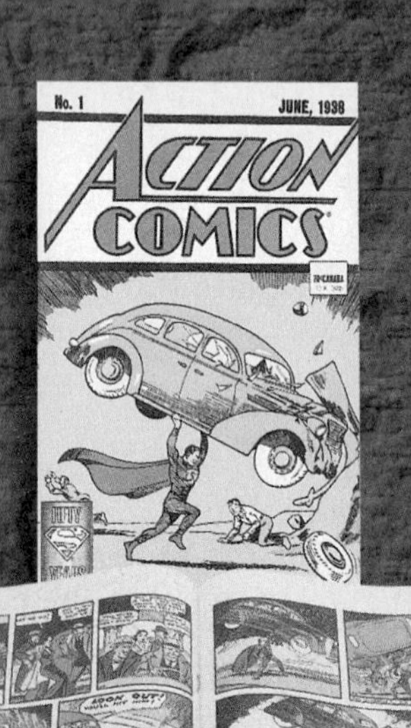

ART LINK

Collectable items such as baseball cards, stamps, and comic books can be worth thousands of dollars. Listed below are some of the most valuable comic books in the United States.

Comic Book	Special Feature	Value
Action Comics No. 1 (1938)	First appearance of Superman	\$105,000
Detective Comics No. 27 (1939)	First to feature Batman	\$96,000
Whiz Comics No. 1 (1940)	First to feature Captain Marvel	\$44,000
Superman No. 1 (1939)	First devoted to Superman	\$72,000
Captain America Comics (1941)	First appearance of Captain America	\$38,000

- Make a bar graph to display the values of the comic books.

Problem-Solving Project

Bodily Proportions

Artists learn to draw the human body by recognizing the proportional relationships between body parts.

YOU WILL NEED: tape measure or yardstick

Copy the chart. Estimate the percent each body part is of the other. Measure the body parts to the nearest half inch. Then record your actual ratios, write them as percents, and use them to make a sketch of a person.

BODY PROPORTIONS

	Estimated Percent	Actual Ratio	Actual Percent
Length of leg to height	50%	29:63	46%
Length of hand to length of arm			
Length of hand to total arm span			
Length of foot to height			
Head circumference to height			

PROJECT CHECKLIST

- ✓ Did you copy the chart?
- ✓ Did you make estimates?
- ✓ Did you measure the body parts?
- ✓ Did you write the ratios and percents?
- ✓ Did you sketch a person?

LESSON 15.1

What You'll Learn
How to change ratios to percents

Why Learn This?
To compare ratios, such as sports statistics, more easily

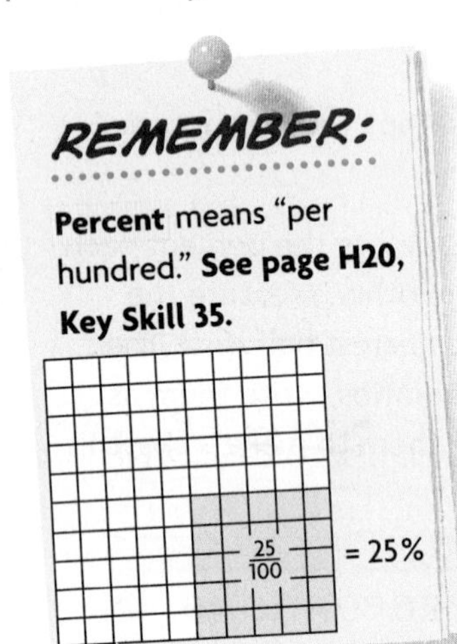

REMEMBER:
Percent means "per hundred." **See page H20, Key Skill 35.**
25/100 = 25%

ALGEBRA CONNECTION

Changing Ratios to Percents

To write a ratio as a percent, write an equivalent ratio that has 100 as the denominator.

EXAMPLE 1 In their last few basketball games, Andrea made 13 of 25 free throws and Bert made 6 of 10. Who made a greater percent of free throws?

Write the ratios of free throws made to free throws shot. Change each ratio to an equivalent fraction with 100 as the denominator, and then write the ratio as a percent.

Andrea

$$\frac{13}{25} = \frac{13 \times ?}{25 \times ?} = \frac{?}{100}$$

25 times what is 100?

$$\frac{13}{25} = \frac{13 \times 4}{25 \times 4} = \frac{52}{100} = 52\%$$

Bert

$$\frac{6}{10} = \frac{6 \times ?}{10 \times ?} = \frac{?}{100}$$

10 times what is 100?

$$\frac{6}{10} = \frac{6 \times 10}{10 \times 10} = \frac{60}{100} = 60\%$$

Bert made a greater percent of his free throws.

EXAMPLE 2

A. Write the ratio 3 : 2 as a percent.

$$\frac{3}{2} = \frac{3 \times 50}{2 \times 50} = \frac{150}{100} = 150\%$$

B. Write the ratio 5 : 1,000 as a percent.

$$\frac{5}{1{,}000} = \frac{5 \div 10}{1{,}000 \div 10} = \frac{0.5}{100}$$

$$= 0.5\%$$

- CRITICAL THINKING If a ratio has a denominator less than the numerator, will the equivalent percent be less than, equal to, or greater than 100%?
- If a ratio has a denominator greater than 100 and greater than the numerator, will the equivalent percent be less than, equal to, or greater than 100%?

TEEN TIMES

Have you ever heard sports announcers say a basketball player is "in the zone"? This expression means the player is making most of his or her shots. It seems as if defenders cannot stop a player who is "in the zone."

IN THE ZONE

When the denominator of a ratio is not a factor of 100, you can use more than one operation to find an equivalent ratio with 100 as the denominator.

EXAMPLE 3 Write the ratio $\frac{12}{30}$ as a percent.

Since 30 is not a factor of 100, divide the numerator and denominator by 6 to get a factor of 100.

Then, multiply the new numerator and denominator by 20.

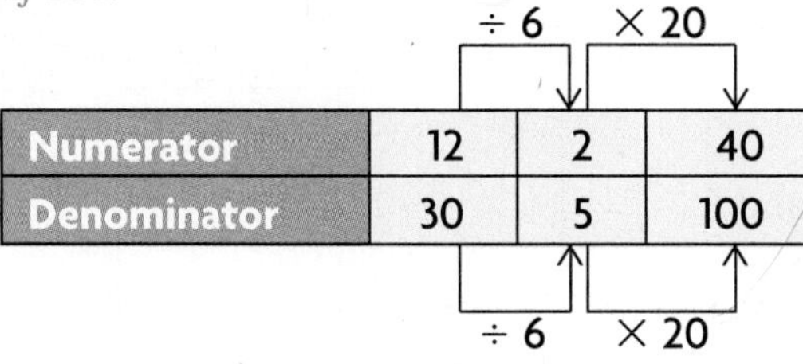

	÷ 6		× 20
Numerator	12	2	40
Denominator	30	5	100
	÷ 6		× 20

Since $\frac{12}{30} = \frac{40}{100}$, you can write $\frac{12}{30}$ as 40%.

- Write $\frac{66}{60}$ as a percent.

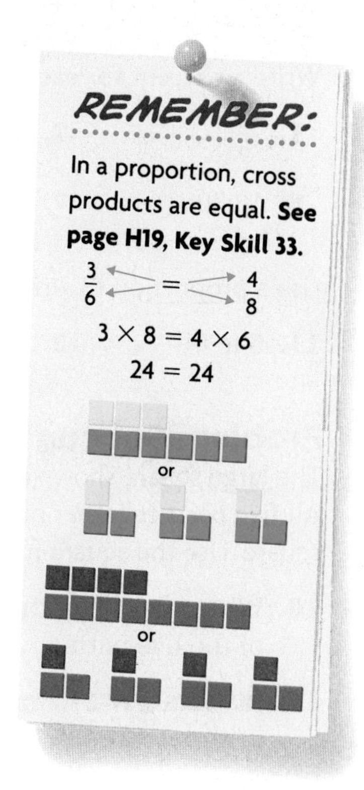

ANOTHER METHOD It is not always obvious how to multiply or divide to make the denominator 100 when changing a ratio to a percent. However, you can always use proportions to change ratios to percents.

EXAMPLE 4

A. Use a proportion to write the ratio 1:8 as a percent.

$$\frac{1}{8} = \frac{n}{100}$$

$$8n = 100 \times 1$$

$$8n = 100$$

$$\frac{8n}{8} = \frac{100}{8}$$

$$n = 12.5$$

Since $\frac{1}{8} = \frac{12.5}{100}$,

1:8 = 12.5%.

B. Use a proportion to write the ratio 4 to 500 as a percent.

$$\frac{4}{500} = \frac{n}{100}$$

$$500n = 100 \times 4$$

$$500n = 400$$

$$\frac{500n}{500} = \frac{400}{500}$$

$$n = 0.8$$

Since $\frac{4}{500} = \frac{0.8}{100}$,

4 to 500 = 0.8%.

GUIDED PRACTICE

Write each ratio as a percent.

1. $\frac{4}{5}$ **2.** 13 to 20 **3.** 18:25 **4.** $\frac{18}{24}$ **5.** 24 to 40

INDEPENDENT PRACTICE

Write a percent for each ratio.

1. $\frac{15}{75}$ **2.** 5:4 **3.** 8 to 1,000 **4.** $\frac{7}{2}$ **5.** 12:10,000

6. 18:30 **7.** $\frac{19}{50}$ **8.** 6 to 5 **9.** 150:1,000 **10.** $\frac{18}{20}$

Use a proportion to write each ratio as a percent.

11. 5 to 8 **12.** $\frac{2}{3}$ **13.** 6:200 **14.** $\frac{34}{102}$ **15.** 28 to 400

Problem-Solving Applications

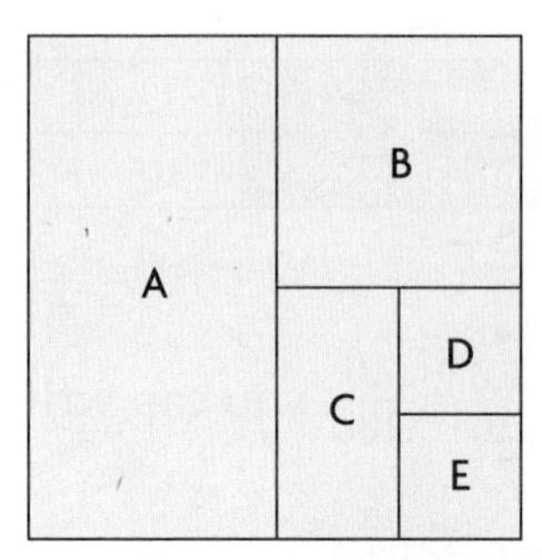

The large square shown is divided into five parts: A, B, C, D, and E. All five parts together make up 100% of the area of the original square. Use the square for Problems 16–18.

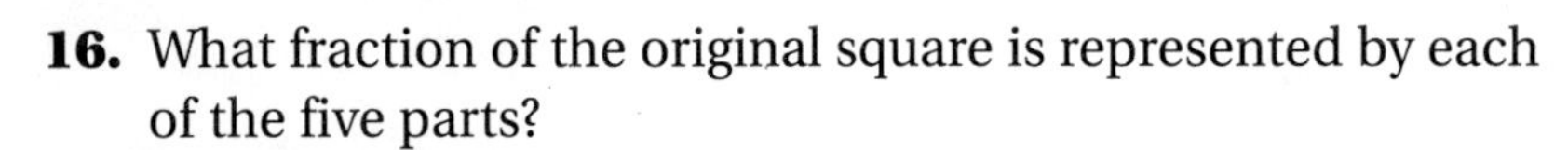

16. What fraction of the original square is represented by each of the five parts?

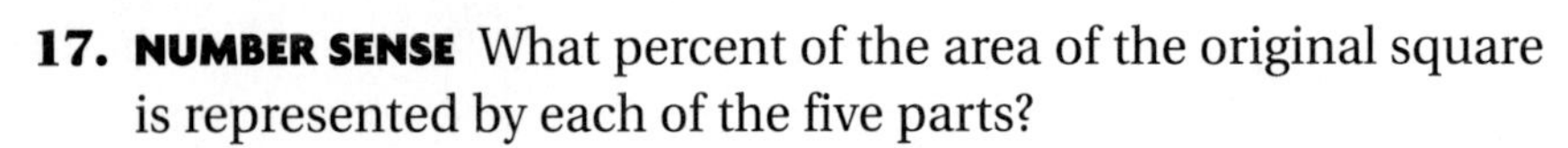

17. **NUMBER SENSE** What percent of the area of the original square is represented by each of the five parts?

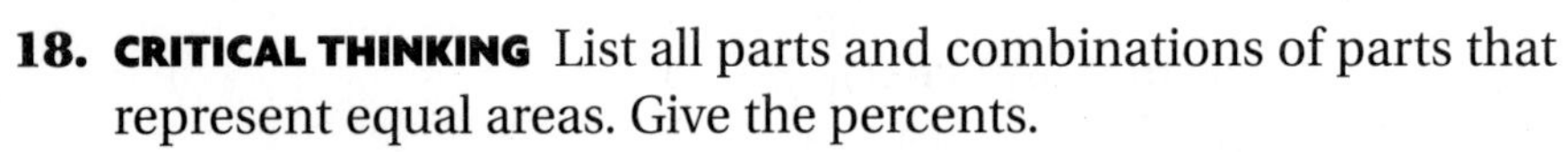

18. **CRITICAL THINKING** List all parts and combinations of parts that represent equal areas. Give the percents.

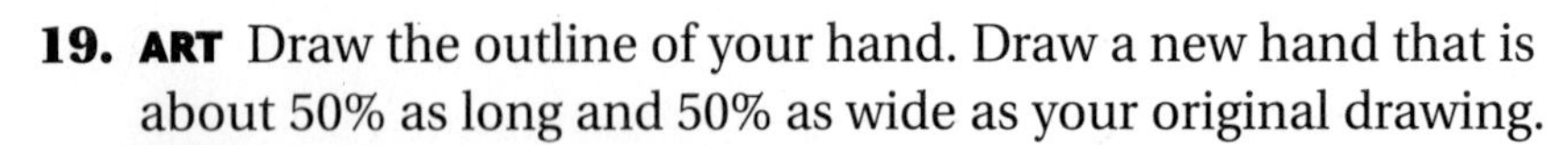

19. **ART** Draw the outline of your hand. Draw a new hand that is about 50% as long and 50% as wide as your original drawing.

20. **WRITE ABOUT IT** How would you decide whether to write an equivalent ratio or use a proportion to change a ratio to a percent?

Mixed Review and Test Prep

Multiply.

21. 0.3×20 **22.** $\frac{1}{2} \times 28$ **23.** 1.8×65 **24.** $\frac{1}{4} \times 35$

Can the shapes tessellate? Write *yes* or *no*.

25. regular hexagons **26.** regular pentagons

27. squares **28.** equilateral triangles

29. **MEASUREMENT** Jim had a rope that was 9 feet 7 inches long. He used $3\frac{1}{2}$ feet for a project and the rest for a swing. How much rope did Jim use for the swing?

A 5 ft 11 in. **B** 6 ft 1 in.
C 6 ft 2 in. **D** 6 ft 5 in.

30. **GUESS AND CHECK** The difference of two numbers is 3.7. The sum of the same two is 21.5. What are the numbers?

F 8.6, 12.9 **G** 8.9, 12.6
H 9.9, 11.6 **J** 10.7, 14.4

MORE PRACTICE Lesson 15.1, page H63

Percent of a Number

LAB ACTIVITY

What You'll Explore
How to model a percent of a number

What You'll Need
paper, ruler

Explore

Start with a piece of paper.

- Fold the piece of paper in half. Fold it in quarters.

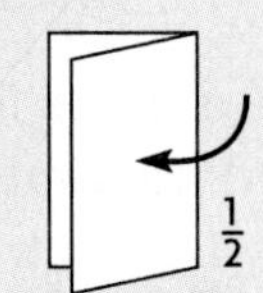

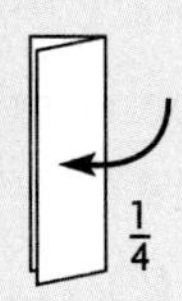

- If the whole paper represents 100%, what percent does each half represent? each quarter?
- If the whole paper represents 12, what number does each half represent? each quarter?

THINK	DO			SEE
Percent	100%	50%	25%	75% (3 | 3 | 3)
Number	12	6	3	9

Think and Discuss

- You can think of the paper in two ways: as 100% and also as 12. What are two ways of thinking of half the paper? of one quarter? three quarters?
- What if you let your paper represent 100% and 48? Explain how you can use this model to find 25% of 48 and 75% of 48.

Try This

- Use one of the models below to solve each problem.

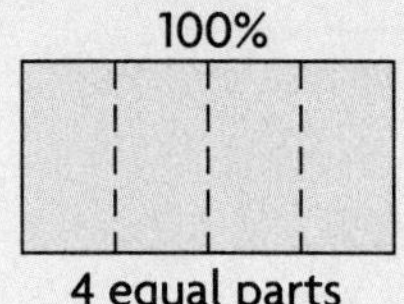

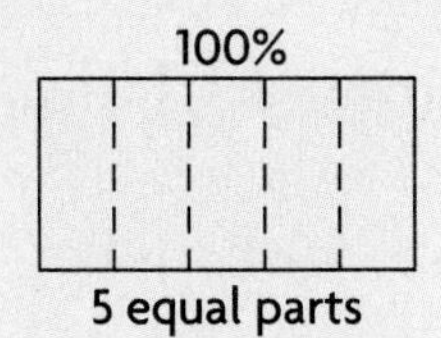

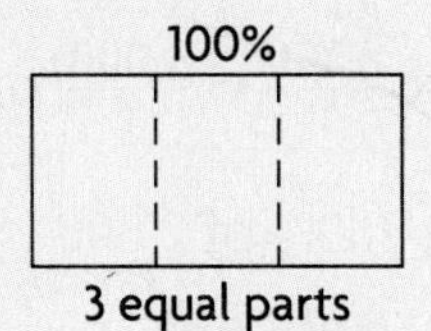

a. 50% of 380 **b.** 75% of 400 **c.** $33\frac{1}{3}$% of 900

d. 20% of 5,000 **e.** $66\frac{2}{3}$% of 360 **f.** 60% of 200

You can model percent of a number by using E-Lab, Activity 15. Available on CD-ROM and on the Internet at **www.hbschool.com/elab**

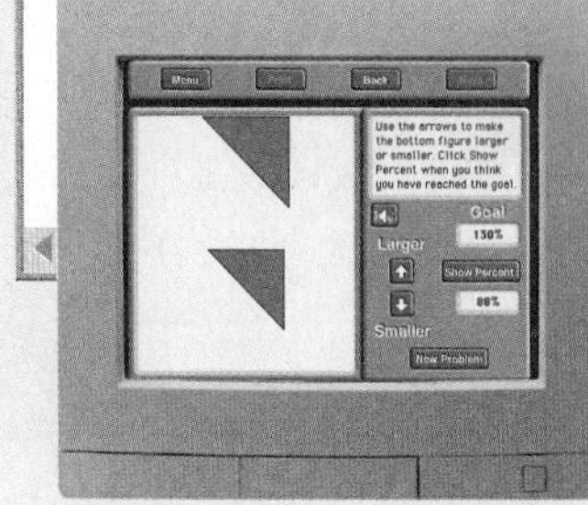

LESSON 15.2

What You'll Learn
How to find a percent of a number

Why Learn This?
To solve problems such as making circle graphs or finding how much your pay raise is

CULTURAL LINK

The systems of money in many countries are based on 100 equal parts. For example, in Mexico 1 peso is equivalent to 100 centavos. How many centavos are in 4.5 pesos?

Technology Link

In *Data ToolKit* you can practice making circle graphs to find percents.

ALGEBRA CONNECTION

Finding a Percent of a Number

The paper-folding method used to find a percent of a number in the lab activity works for problems that use friendly percents.

- What does the phrase *friendly percents* mean to you?

Another way to find a percent of a number is to change the percent to a fraction or a decimal and then multiply.

EXAMPLE 1 Scotty plans to save 75% of his earnings for college. This month he has earned $80. How much should he save?

To find 75% of $80, change the percent to a fraction.

$75\% = \frac{75}{100} = \frac{3}{4}$

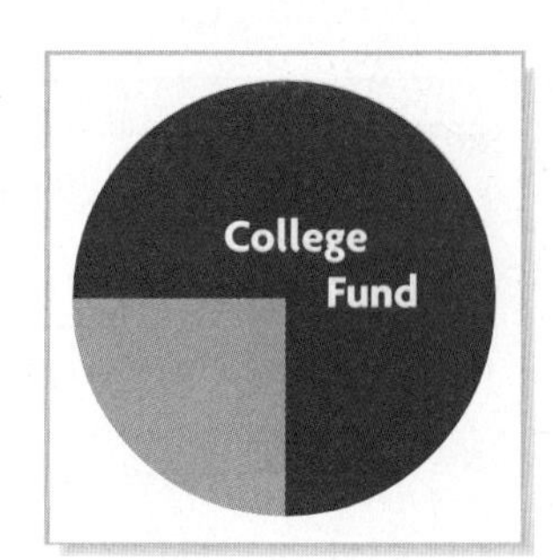

Then multiply.

$\frac{3}{\not{4}_1} \times \frac{\not{80}^{20}}{1} = \frac{60}{1}$, or 60

So, Scotty should save $60.

- What if Scotty earns $120? How much should he save?

EXAMPLE 2 Find 160% of 2,500.

Fraction

Change the percent to a fraction.

$160\% = \frac{160}{100} = \frac{16}{10} = \frac{8}{5}$

Then multiply.

$\frac{8}{5} \times 2{,}500 =$

$\frac{8}{\not{5}_1} \times \frac{\not{2{,}500}^{500}}{1} = \frac{4{,}000}{1}$, or 4,000

So, 160% of 2,500 is 4,000.

Decimal

Change the percent to a decimal.

$160\% = 1.6$

Then multiply.

$1.6 \times 2{,}500$

1.6 [×] 2500 [=] 4000.

- **CRITICAL THINKING** What is 160% of 250? 160% of 25? 160% of 2.5?

EXAMPLE 3 Justin's starting pay was \$4.85 per hour. After his three-month trial period, he received a 3% raise. How much per hour was Justin's raise (rounded to the nearest cent), and how much does he earn with the raise?

$3\% \times 4.85 = 0.03 \times 4.85$
$= 0.1455$

Find 3% of \$4.85 by changing 3% to a decimal and multiplying.

So, Justin's raise was \$0.15 per hour.

$\$0.15 + \$4.85 = \$5.00$

Add the raise to his hourly pay.

So, Justin earns \$5.00 per hour with the raise.

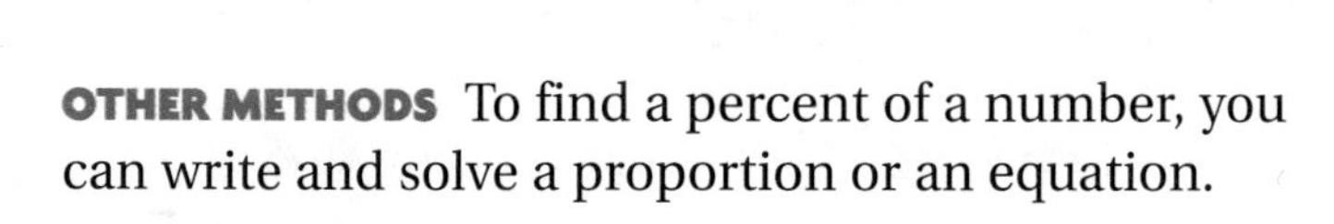

OTHER METHODS To find a percent of a number, you can write and solve a proportion or an equation.

EXAMPLE 4 Camille wants to make a circle graph to show the following survey results: 40% said *yes,* 45% said *no,* 15% said *no opinion.* How large should Camille make the central angle for *yes* in her circle graph?

Let $x =$ the number of degrees for the *yes* vote.

Proportion

40 is to 100 as what number is to 360?

$$\frac{40}{100} = \frac{x}{360}$$
$$100x = 360 \times 40$$
$$100x = 14{,}400$$
$$x = 14{,}400 \div 100$$
$$x = 144$$

Equation

What is 40% of 360°?

$$x = 40\% \times 360$$
$$x = 0.40 \times 360$$
$$x = 144$$

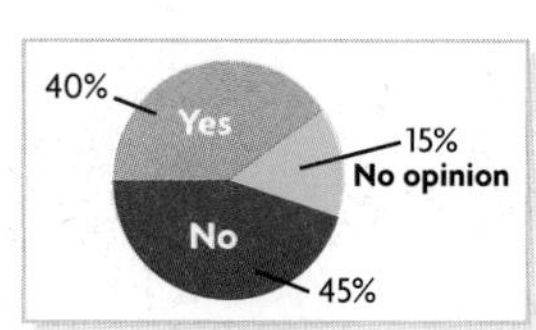

So, the central angle for *yes* should be 144°.

- Use each method to show that the central angle for *no* should be 162° and the central angle for *no opinion* should be 54°.

REMEMBER:
Central angles are angles formed by rays with a common vertex at the center of a circle. A circle contains 360°.
See page H22, Key Skill 40.

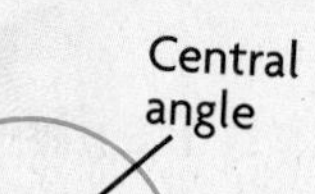

GUIDED PRACTICE

Find the percent of each number.

1. 30% of 20 **2.** 50% of 108 **3.** 1% of 72 **4.** 8% of 20

5. 0.2% of 130 **6.** 12% of 400 **7.** 37% of 200 **8.** 100% of 3,600

INDEPENDENT PRACTICE

Find the percent of each number.

1. 60% of 10 **2.** 25% of 160 **3.** 15% of 30 **4.** 10% of 84

5. 25% of 47 **6.** 59% of 20 **7.** 125% of 4,100 **8.** 150% of 150

Study the example below. Then use mental math to find the percent of each number.

12% of 50 = $0.12 \times 50 = 6$, and 50% of 12 = $0.50 \times 12 = 6$.
So, 12% of 50 is equivalent to 50% of 12.

9. 16% of 50 **10.** 35% of 20 **11.** 48% of 25 **12.** 115% of 200

Problem-Solving Applications

13. Quan's pay was $5.25 per hour. He received a 5% raise. How much per hour was Quan's raise (rounded to the nearest cent), and how much does he earn with the raise?

14. **PERCENT** Wilma plans to keep 40% of the amount of her paycheck and deposit the rest in her savings account. This week her paycheck is $220. How much will she keep?

15. **BUDGET** Copy and complete the table for Stephen's weekly budget.

Expenses	Percent	Central Angle Measure
College savings	55%	$0.55 \times 360 = ?$
Books and supplies	20%	$0.2 \times 360 = ?$
Lunches	15%	$0.15 \times 360 = ?$
Transportation	10%	$0.1 \times 360 = ?$

16. **DATA** Use the table you completed in Problem 15 to draw a circle graph showing Stephen's weekly budget.

17. **WRITE ABOUT IT** Write and solve a problem in which a percent of a given number is less than the number.

Technology Link

In ***Mighty Math Astro Algebra*** you can work with percents in *The Great Galactic Garage Sale.* Use Grow Slide Level Green Q.

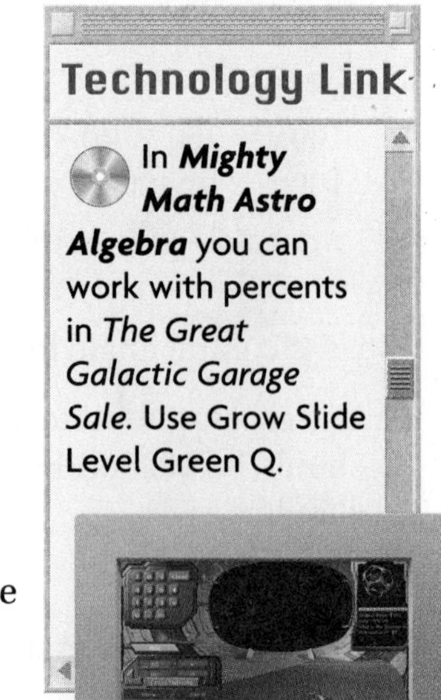

Mixed Review and Test Prep

Use mental math to find the value of y.

18. $y \times 16 = 32$ **19.** $y \times 20 = 80$ **20.** $y \times 12 = 84$

Write each ratio as a fraction in simplest form.

21. 6 to 8 **22.** 5 to 10 **23.** 25 to 75

24. **GEOMETRY** A quadrilateral has 4 equal sides. What can you conclude?

A It is a square.
B The sides are 4 cm long.
C It is a rhombus.
D It is a rectangle.

25. **CONSUMER MATH** Find the lowest unit cost.

F 8 ounces for $0.96
G 12 ounces for $1.32
H 16 ounces for $1.44
J 32 ounces for $2.24

MORE PRACTICE Lesson 15.2, page H63

ALGEBRA CONNECTION

LESSON 15.3

Finding What Percent One Number Is of Another

What You'll Learn
How to find what percent one number is of another

Why Learn This?
To solve problems such as finding how much of an assignment you have completed

There are different ways to find what percent one number is of another. When the numbers are friendly, you can often solve the problem mentally.

EXAMPLE 1 Jason answered 9 of 12 questions correctly on the quiz he took today. To maintain his grade, he needed to score at least 70%. Did Jason score high enough to maintain his grade? Explain.

9 out of 12 is what percent?

Think of the ratio as a percent. $\frac{9}{12} = \frac{3}{4} = \frac{75}{100} = 75\%$

Since 9 is 75% of 12 and 75% > 70%, Jason did score high enough to maintain his grade.

ANOTHER METHOD You can draw proportional diagrams to find the percent.

EXAMPLE 2 What percent of 15 is 6?

Since both 15 and 6 are divisible by 3, you can use small regions, each representing 3.

— 6 —	
3	3

		— 15 —		
3	3	3	3	3

Use a common factor to sketch proportional diagrams of 15 and 6.

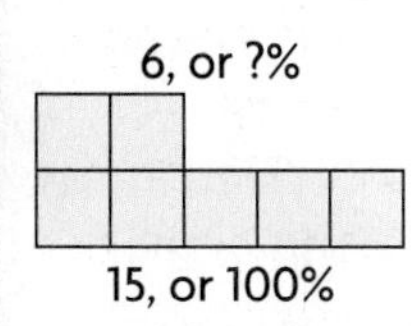

Compare the two diagrams.

$\frac{2 \text{ regions}}{5 \text{ regions}}$, or $\frac{2}{5}$

$\frac{2}{5} \times 100\% = 40\%$ *Use the ratio to find the percent.*

So, 6 is 40% of 15.

- What percent of 15 is 12?

MUSIC LINK

Garth Brooks is a popular musician. As of 1994, more than 35 million of his albums had been sold. The population of the United States is about 265 million. If each album was sold to a different person in the United States, about what percent would own Garth Brooks albums?

Using Equations and Proportions

When you compare numbers that do not seem friendly, it may be easier to use equations or proportions to find the percent one number is of another.

EXAMPLE 3 Arilla's parents say she may watch a video concert on TV when she has read at least 80% of her assigned book. Arilla has read 198 of the 350 pages. Has she read enough?

Equation

What percent of 350 is 198?

$$p \times 350 = 198$$

$$350p = 198$$

$$p = \frac{198}{350}$$

$p \approx 0.566$, or about 57%

Proportion

What number is to 100 as 198 is to 350?

$$\frac{n}{100} = \frac{198}{350}$$

$$350n = 100 \times 198$$

$$350n = 19{,}800$$

$$n = \frac{19{,}800}{350}$$

$n \approx 56.6$, or about 57

$$\frac{57}{100} = 57\%$$

Since Arilla has read only about 57% of the assigned book, she hasn't read enough.

- About how many more pages does Arilla need to read?

EXAMPLE 4 What percent of 25 is 28?

Equation

What percent of 25 is 28?

$$p \times 25 = 28$$

$$25p = 28$$

$$p = \frac{28}{25}$$

$p = 1.12$, or 112%

Proportion

What number is to 100 as 28 is to 25?

$$\frac{n}{100} = \frac{28}{25}$$

$$25n = 100 \times 28$$

$$25n = 2{,}800$$

$$n = \frac{2{,}800}{25}$$

$$n = 112$$

$$\frac{112}{100} = 112\%$$

So, 28 is 112% of 25.

- What percent of 20 is 15?

GUIDED PRACTICE

Use the diagrams to find the percent.

1. What percent of 50 is 30?

30

10	10	10		
10	10	10	10	10

50

2. What percent of 60 is 45?

45

15	15	15	
15	15	15	15

60

3. What percent of 50 is 10?

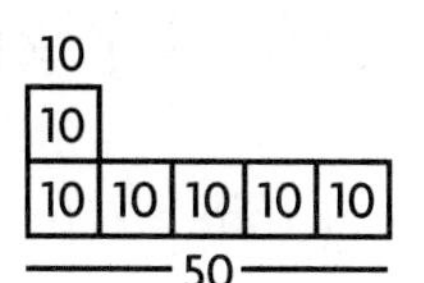

4. What percent of 60 is 30?

30

15	15		
15	15	15	15

60

INDEPENDENT PRACTICE

Draw a diagram. Then solve.

1. What percent of 20 is 4?

2. What percent of 20 is 16?

Write an equation. Then solve.

3. What percent of 36 is 9?

4. What percent of 80 is 60?

Write a proportion. Then solve.

5. What percent of 36 is 18?

6. 27 is what percent of 30?

Solve. Use any of the methods you have studied.

7. What percent of 100 is 25?

8. What percent of 32 is 32?

9. What percent of 5 is 4?

10. What percent of 120 is 60?

11. What percent of 4 is 5?

12. What percent of 60 is 120?

Problem-Solving Applications

13. **CRITICAL THINKING** Vicki answered 10 of 15 questions correctly in her computer math lesson. To advance to the next level of challenge, she needs to score at least 75%. Did Vicki score high enough to advance to the next level? Explain.

14. **ESTIMATION** Use the circle graph to estimate the percent of students who voted *yes* on the constitutional amendment.

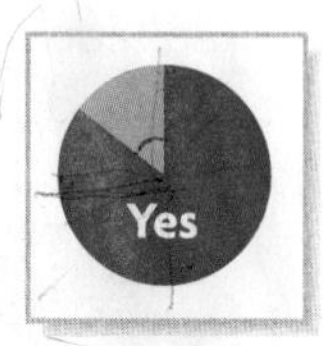

Each night, Eric reads 12 pages of a 286-page novel for his history class. Use this information to answer Problems 15 and 16.

15. **NUMBER SENSE** What percent of the book does Eric read each night?

16. About how many nights of reading will it take Eric to complete the book?

17. **WRITE ABOUT IT** Tell why the proportion $\frac{2}{5} = \frac{n}{100}$ can be used to solve the following problem: What percent of 5 is 2?

MORE PRACTICE Lesson 15.3, page H64

LESSON 15.4

What You'll Learn
How to find a number when a percent of it is known

Why Learn This?
To solve problems such as finding the total distance you must travel

ALGEBRA CONNECTION

Finding a Number When the Percent Is Known

Sometimes you know an amount and the percent of the whole that it represents. However, you don't know how much the whole amount is. As with other percent problems, there are several ways to find a number when a percent of it is known.

USING MODELS When the numbers are friendly, you can often solve the problem mentally by thinking of a model.

EXAMPLE 1 Tory and Courtney baked 3 dozen cookies. They baked 25% of the cookies in the bake sale. How many dozen cookies are in the bake sale?

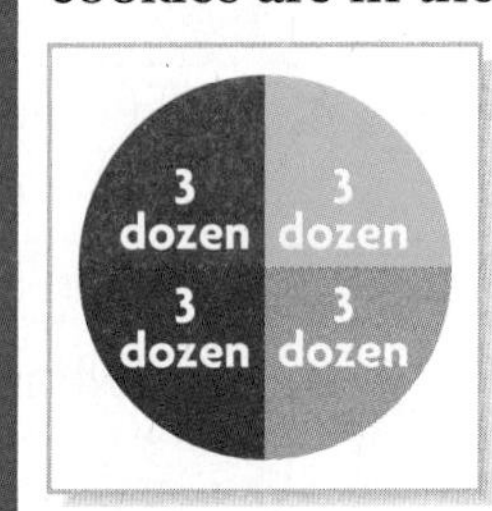

← 25% is 3 dozen.

If 25% is 3 dozen, then 50% is 6 dozen, and 100% is 12 dozen. So, there are 12 dozen cookies in the bake sale.

CONSUMER LINK

Every month about 625 million Oreo® cookies are consumed. This number is about 8.3% of the yearly total. About how many Oreo® cookies are consumed yearly?

EXAMPLE 2 As the cross-country team passes a marker, its members see that they have run 1,500 m. If this distance is 20% of their course, how long is their course?

↑ 20% ↑ 20% ↑ 20% ↑ 20% ↑ 20%

$20\% = 1{,}500$ m
$40\% = 3{,}000$ m
$60\% = 4{,}500$ m
$80\% = 6{,}000$ m
$100\% = 7{,}500$ m

So, their course is 7,500 m.

GUIDED PRACTICE

Tell how to use a model to mentally solve each problem.

1. Victoria received her monthly allowance and decided to pay back her sister \$7.50, 50% of what she had borrowed. How much had Victoria borrowed?

2. Chris has walked 12 mi this month. This distance is 25% of the amount he usually walks in a month. How far does he usually walk?

SPORTS LINK

Soccer is probably the most popular sport in the world. More than 100 million people participate in the game, but they still represent less than 2% of the population of the world. About how large is the world population?

Use the given model to answer the questions.

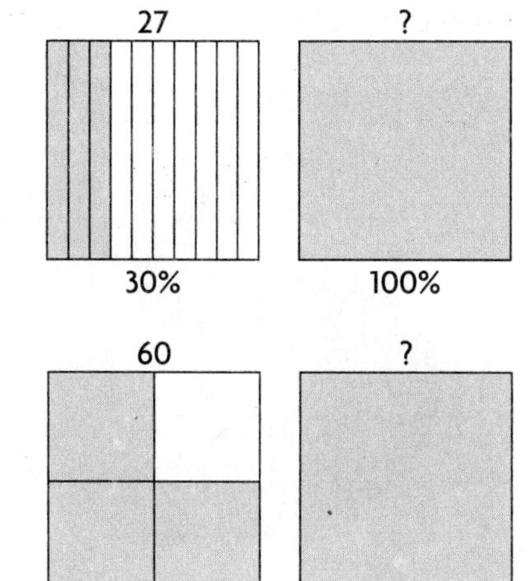

3. If 30% is 27, what is 10%?

4. What is 100%?

5. 30% of what number is 27?

6. If 75% is 60, what is 25%?

7. What is 100%?

8. 75% of what number is 60?

This model shows fifths. Explain how it can be used to find each of these numbers.

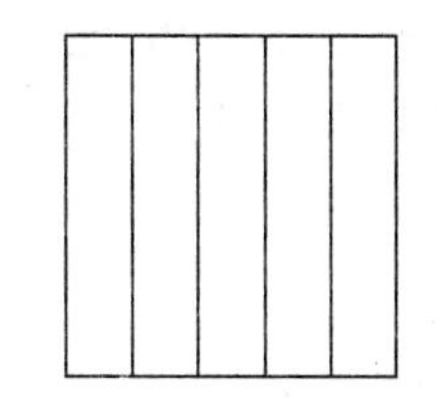

9. 6 is 20% of what number?

10. 16 is 80% of what number?

11. 1.5 is 20% of what number?

12. 4.5 is 60% of what number?

Talk About it

- In the left-most model, how many of the 100 little squares are shaded?
- If $\frac{6}{100} = 120$, then $\frac{1}{100} = ?$
- What number does the right-most model, or 100% represent?
- How could you use the model to find 94% of 2,000?

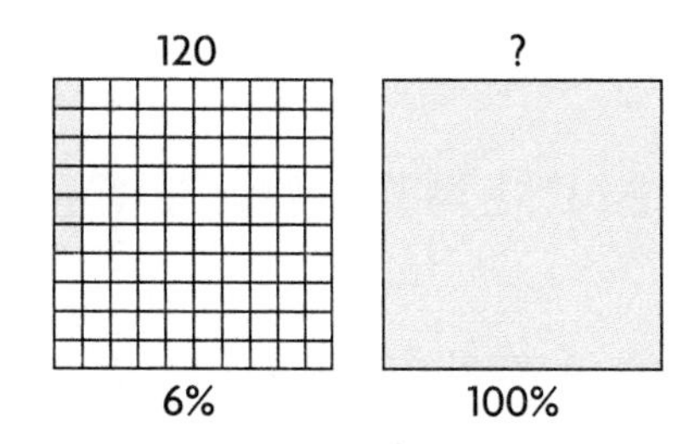

Using Proportions and Equations

You can also use proportions or equations to solve percent problems where you need to find the total amount.

EXAMPLE 3 Mrs. Edwards bought a truck for her landscaping business. She made a 15% down payment of $2,700. What was the total price of her truck?

Proportion

15 is to 100 as 2,700 is to what number?

$$\frac{15}{100} = \frac{2,700}{n}$$

$$15n = 2,700 \times 100$$

$$n = 270,000 \div 15$$

$$n = 18,000$$

Equation

15% of n is 2,700.

↓ ↓ ↓

$$0.15n = 2,700$$

$$n = \frac{2,700}{0.15}$$

$$n = 18,000$$

So, the total price of Mrs. Edwards' truck was $18,000.

- A family makes a 5% down payment of $800 on a car. What is the total price of the car?

EXAMPLE 4 4.06 is 28% of what number?

Proportion

28 is to 100 as 4.06 is to what number?

$$\frac{28}{100} = \frac{4.06}{n}$$

$$28n = 4.06 \times 100$$

$$n = \frac{406}{28} = 14.5$$

Equation

28% of n is 4.06.

$$0.28n = 4.06$$

$$n = \frac{4.06}{0.28}$$

$$n = 14.5$$

So, 4.06 is 28% of 14.5.

CAREER LINK

In landscape architecture, the elevation, or the grade, can be expressed as a ratio of vertical change to horizontal change, or as a percent. A 10% grade has a ratio of 1 unit of vertical change to 10 units of horizontal change. What is a 25% grade?

INDEPENDENT PRACTICE

Solve.

1. 6 is 10% of what number?

2. 18 is 20% of what number?

3. 75% of what number is 27?

4. 81 is 3% of what number?

Solve.

5. 3.36 is 32% of what number?

6. 85% of what number is 20.74?

7. 21 is 5% of what number?

8. 30% of what number is 120?

9. 105 is 150% of what number?

10. 54 is 300% of what number?

11. 26 is 130% of what number?

12. 125% of what number is 30?

13. 210% of what number is 210?

14. 19.6 is 35% of what number?

15. 18.6 is 93% of what number?

16. 46% of what number is 13.8?

17. 175% of what number is 59.5?

18. 50 is 500% of what number?

19. 121 is 22% of what number?

20. 15% of what number is 45?

Problem-Solving Applications

21. **SURVEY** Juan's survey showed that 45 students, or 75% of those surveyed, preferred Air Jordan™ or Air Penny™ basketball shoes. How many students did Juan survey?

22. **SPORTS** The first lap of the auto race is 2,500 m. This is 10% of the total race distance. How many laps is the race, and how long is the race?

23. Washington Middle School is expecting a total of 376 seventh graders next year. This is 40% of the expected school enrollment. How many students are expected to enroll in the school?

24. **CAREER** Dr. Kelsey will earn $62,850 this year. This year's salary is 114% of last year's salary. About how much did she earn last year? About how much did her salary increase?

25. **WRITE ABOUT IT** Write a percent problem that can be represented by the equation $0.2n = 35$.

Mixed Review and Test Prep

Are the fractions equivalent? Write *yes* or *no*.

26. $\frac{1}{2}, \frac{3}{4}$

27. $\frac{8}{12}, \frac{2}{3}$

28. $\frac{3}{12}, \frac{1}{4}$

29. $\frac{6}{18}, \frac{1}{6}$

Make a drawing to show the ratio.

30. The ratio of blue boxes to red boxes is 4:6.

31. The ratio of yellow squares to green squares is $\frac{7}{2}$.

32. **MUSIC** A CD club offers 6 free CDs to new members. Each CD costs $8.50. The club gives a free CD for every 5 CDs purchased. How many CDs could a new member receive for $100.00?

A 11 **B** 15 **C** 19 **D** 21

33. **PATTERNS** Tamika arranged numbers in this pattern: 6, 3, 1.5, 0.75, . . . If she continued the pattern, what would be the next number?

F 0.5 **G** 0.375
H 0.25 **J** 0.15

MORE PRACTICE Lesson 15.4, page H64

CHAPTER 15 Review/Test

Write each ratio as a percent. (pages 294–296)

1. $\frac{3}{4}$ **2.** $\frac{15}{40}$ **3.** 14 to 20 **4.** 12:25 **5.** 9:4

6. 5 to 8 **7.** 3:16 **8.** $\frac{9}{50}$ **9.** 17:20 **10.** 1 to 10

11. Maura got 16 correct answers out of 20 questions on her first science quiz and 21 correct answers out of 25 questions on her second science quiz. On which quiz did Maura have a better percentage of correct answers? Explain. (pages 294–296)

12. In his last football game, Josh completed 11 of 20 passes in the first half and 9 of 15 passes in the second half. In which half did Josh have a better completion percentage? Explain. (pages 294–296)

Find the percent of each number. (pages 298–300)

13. 35% of 60 **14.** 75% of 120 **15.** 1% of 44 **16.** 16% of 300

17. 50% of 224 **18.** 125% of 88 **19.** 40% of 1,500 **20.** 15% of 750

21. Dominique budgets 45% for food, 30% for clothes, 20% for entertainment, and 5% for other items. In a circle graph, what central angle will represent each percent?

22. Alex is saving to buy a video game for $39.50. He has saved 60% of the cost of the game. How much more does he have to save?

Find the percent. (pages 301–303)

23. What percent of 120 is 45?

24. What percent of 34 is 102?

25. What percent of 8 is 5?

26. 66 is what percent of 150?

27. What percent of 40 is 8?

28. What percent of 60 is 24?

29. 12 is what percent of 4?

30. What percent of 48 is 42?

Solve. (pages 304–307)

31. 13 is 10% of what number?

32. 3 is 25% of what number?

33. 56% of what number is 44.8?

34. 22 is 8% of what number?

35. 85% of what number is 34?

36. 14 is 70% of what number?

37. 200% of what number is 75?

38. 18% of what number is 45?

39. 36 is 45% of what number?

40. 87 is 25% of what number?

Test Prep

CUMULATIVE
CHAPTERS 1–15

1. A car traveled 258 miles in 6 hours. What was the car's average speed?

A 34 mi per hr
B 40 mi per hr
C 43 mi per hr
D 55 mi per hr

2. The perimeter of the figure is 35 ft. Which equation could you use to find x?

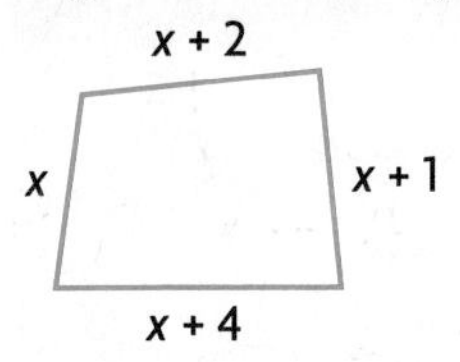

F $x(x + 4) = 35$
G $x + x + 4 = 35$
H $4x + 7 = 35$
J $2x + 2(x + 4) = 35$

3. Which point is located in Quadrant II?

A $(^-4,^-5)$
B $(4,^-3)$
C $(2,4)$
D $(^-2,5)$

4. Raul is 7 inches shorter than Alex. Raul is 63 inches tall. How tall is Alex?

F 54 in.
G 56 in.
H 70 in.
J 72 in.
K Not Here

5. What is the best name for the figure below?

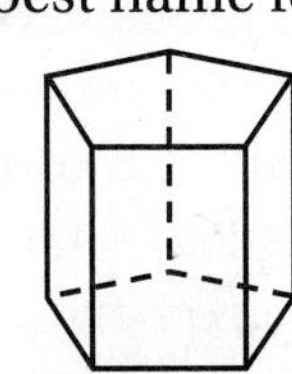

A Hexagonal prism
B Pentagonal pyramid
C Triangular prism
D Pentagonal prism

6. Figure $RSTV$ has coordinates $R(0,0)$, $S(0,5)$, $T(4,5)$, and $V(4,0)$. What best describes the figure?

F Square
G Rectangle
H Rhombus
J Trapezoid

7. Enrique is collecting a set of trading cards. So far, he has collected 70% of the set. There are 500 cards in the entire set. How many cards has Enrique collected so far?

A 350
B 250
C 200
D 150

8. For what value of h is $\frac{h}{6.3} = 45$ a true statement?

F 7.14
G 38.7
H 51.3
J 283.5

9. $5^2 + 3 \times 7 - 4 =$

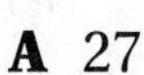

A 27
B 34
C 42
D 192

10. Which figure has the following views?

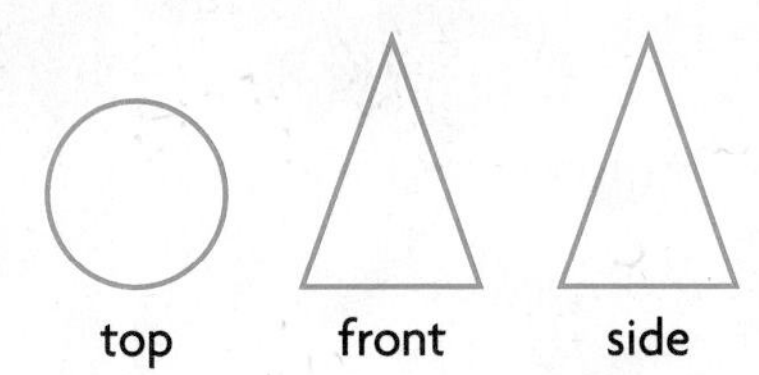

F Cone
G Triangular pyramid
H Cylinder
J Triangular prism

CHAPTER

16

RATIOS, PROPORTIONS, AND SIMILARITY

LOOK AHEAD

In this chapter you will solve problems that involve

- identifying and making similar figures
- using scale factors
- comparing areas and volumes of similar figures

ART LINK

Spaceship Earth is a geodesic dome in Florida's Epcot Center. Spaceship Earth resembles a sphere, and it is covered with 954 triangular panels. It is 165 feet in diameter and weighs about 16 million pounds.

- Use the formula for the volume of a sphere, $V = \frac{4}{3}\pi r^3$, to approximate the volume of Spaceship Earth.

Problem-Solving Project

Out of Africa

YOU WILL NEED: graph paper

The cloth shown below was made in Nigeria by the Yoruba people. Copy the design on graph paper. Record the total number of triangles in a chart or table. Look for relationships between angles and relationships between sides. Compare the areas of triangles. Find and write about the similarities of all the triangles.

PROJECT CHECKLIST

- ✓ Did you copy the design on graph paper?
- ✓ Did you record the total number of triangles?
- ✓ Did you write about the similarities of the triangles?

LESSON 16.1

What You'll Learn
How to identify similar figures and how scale factors are related to similar figures

Why Learn This?
To make similar figures such as enlargements or reductions of posters

VOCABULARY
similar figures
proportional
scale factor

ALGEBRA CONNECTION

Similar Figures and Scale Factors

What do magnifying glasses, telescopes, binoculars, microscopes, and projectors have in common? Each device shows an enlarged view of an original object. In all respects other than size, the enlargement and the original object look identical.

ACTIVITY

- Aim an overhead projector at a chalkboard. Using a ruler, draw any polygon on a transparency, and project it onto the chalkboard. Label the vertices with uppercase letters, starting with *A*.
- Measure the polygon on the transparency and the polygon on the chalkboard. Record the sizes of the angles and the lengths of the sides.
- How do the two polygons compare?
- What is the relationship between corresponding angles of the two polygons?
- Do the corresponding sides have the same relationship as the corresponding angles? Explain.
- Write a ratio for the lengths of each pair of corresponding sides.
- Compare all of the ratios by finding a decimal value for each with a calculator.
- What pattern or relationship do you notice in the ratios of corresponding sides?

REMEMBER:

Corresponding parts of polygons are matching parts.

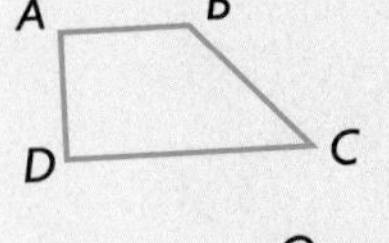

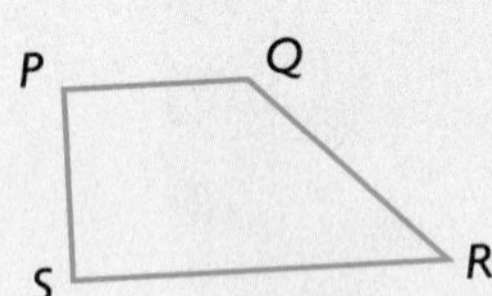

$\angle A$ corresponds to $\angle P$.
$\angle B$ corresponds to $\angle Q$.
$\angle C$ corresponds to $\angle R$.
$\angle D$ corresponds to $\angle S$.
$\overline{AB}$ corresponds to $\overline{PQ}$.
$\overline{BC}$ corresponds to $\overline{QR}$.
$\overline{CD}$ corresponds to $\overline{RS}$.
$\overline{DA}$ corresponds to $\overline{SP}$.

Similar Figures

When figures are the same shape but not necessarily the same size, they are called **similar figures**.

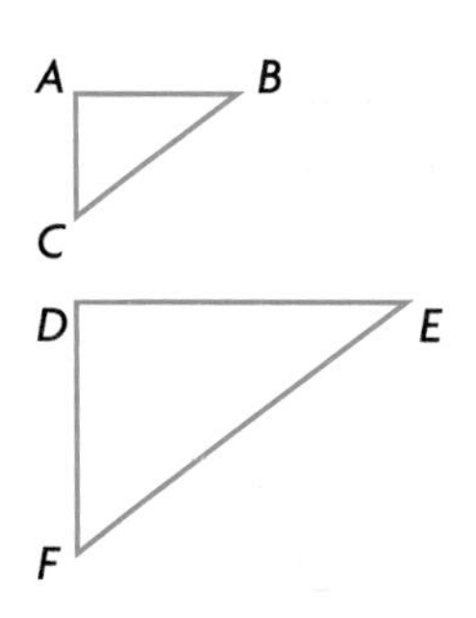

- In the Activity, what relationship did you find between corresponding angles? among corresponding sides?

Similar figures always have congruent corresponding angles, and the pairs of corresponding sides have lengths that form equivalent ratios. You can say the sides are **proportional** or the sides are in proportion.

To decide whether or not geometric figures with the same shape are similar, check for congruent corresponding angles and equivalent ratios of the lengths of corresponding sides.

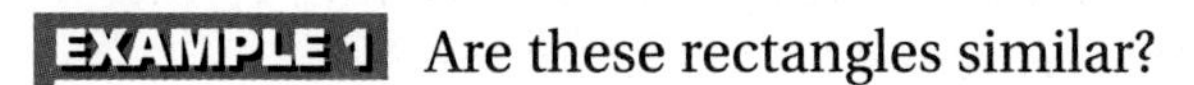

Are these rectangles similar?

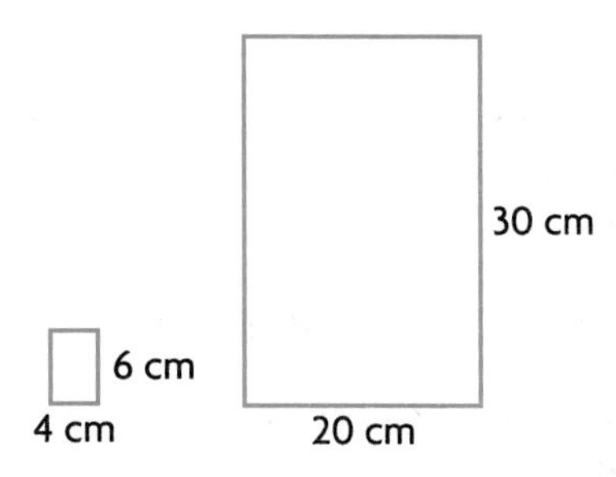

Check to see whether corresponding angles are congruent.

In rectangles, all angles are right angles.
So, all corresponding angles are congruent.

Check to see whether corresponding sides are proportional.

$$\frac{\text{width of small rectangle}}{\text{width of large rectangle}} \rightarrow \frac{4}{20} \stackrel{?}{=} \frac{6}{30} \leftarrow \frac{\text{length of small rectangle}}{\text{length of large rectangle}}$$

$$20 \times 6 \stackrel{?}{=} 30 \times 4$$ *Show the cross products.*

$$120 = 120$$

The cross products are equal, so the ratios are equivalent.

Since the corresponding angles are congruent and the corresponding sides are proportional, the rectangles are similar.

- What if you use the ratios $\frac{20}{4}$ and $\frac{30}{6}$? Can you still show equivalent ratios? Explain.
- What if you use the ratios $\frac{20}{4}$ and $\frac{6}{30}$? Can you still show equivalent ratios? Explain.

A **proportion** is an equation stating that two ratios are equivalent.

Proportions have equal cross products. **See page H19.**

$$\frac{3}{4} = \frac{9}{12}$$

$$4 \times 9 = 12 \times 3$$

$$36 = 36$$

GUIDED PRACTICE

Are the figures similar? Explain your reasoning.

1. all squares

2. all rectangles

3. all parallelograms

4. all right triangles

5. Each prism in the diagram at the right is made up of 8 cubes. Are the prisms similar? Explain your reasoning.

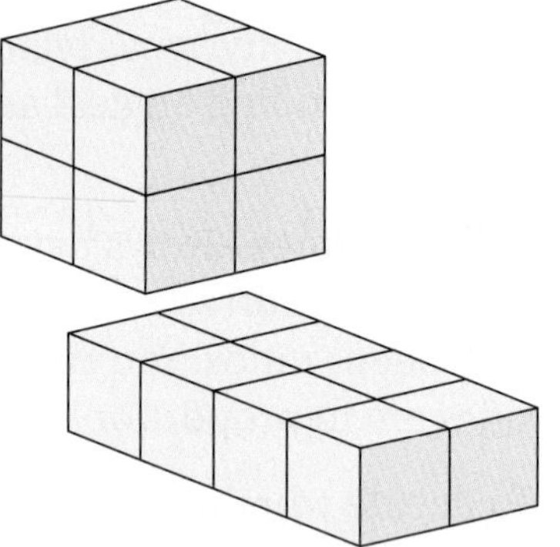

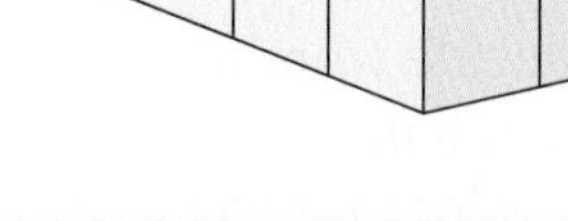

6. A parallelogram measures 27 cm on the short sides and 60 cm on the long sides. The short sides of another parallelogram are 18 cm, and the long sides are 27 cm. The corresponding angles of the parallelograms are congruent. Are the parallelograms similar? Explain.

Scale Factors

The common ratio for pairs of corresponding sides of similar figures is called the **scale factor**. You can use a scale factor to make a larger or smaller similar figure.

EXAMPLE 2 The sides of $\triangle ABC$ are 3 in., 4 in., and 5 in. Lucyanne needs to draw a larger, similar triangle, $\triangle DEF$, using a scale factor of $\frac{3}{2}$. How long should the sides of $\triangle DEF$ be?

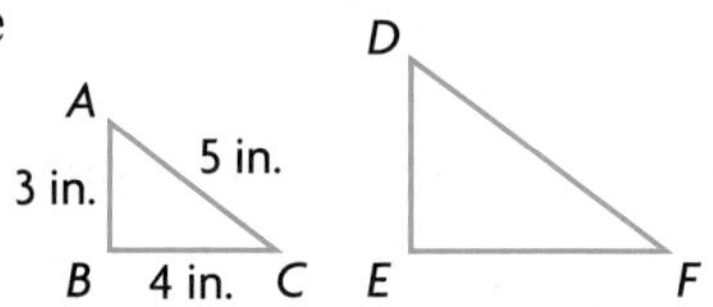

$\frac{3}{2} \times 3 = \frac{9}{2} = 4\frac{1}{2}$ *Multiply the measure of each side of $\triangle ABC$ by the scale factor.*

$\frac{3}{2} \times 4 = \frac{12}{2} = 6$

$\frac{3}{2} \times 5 = \frac{15}{2} = 7\frac{1}{2}$

So, the sides of $\triangle DEF$ should be $4\frac{1}{2}$ in., 6 in., and $7\frac{1}{2}$ in.

- CRITICAL THINKING Suppose Lucyanne makes a new similar triangle that is a reduction of $\triangle DEF$. How long will the sides of her new triangle be if she uses a scale factor of $\frac{3}{4}$?

CONSUMER LINK

You can have different-size prints made from photographic negatives. Are 4-in. × 6-in. and 5-in. × 7-in. prints similar? Explain.

INDEPENDENT PRACTICE

Determine whether the polygons are similar. Write *yes* or *no*, and support your answer.

1.

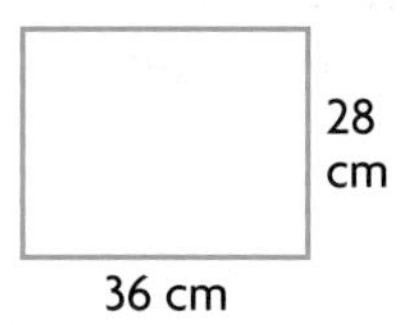

2.

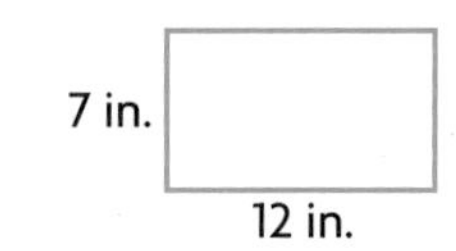

3. angles: 60°
sides: 4.5 cm

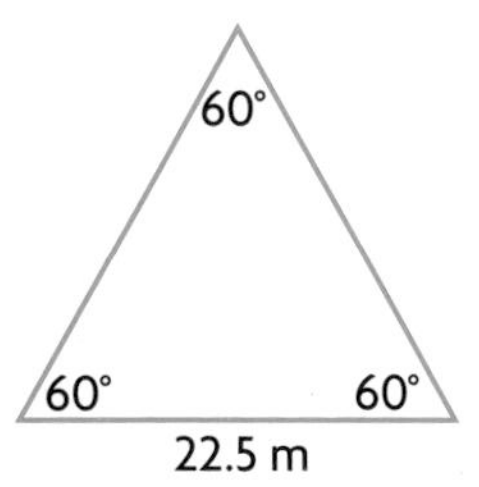

4.

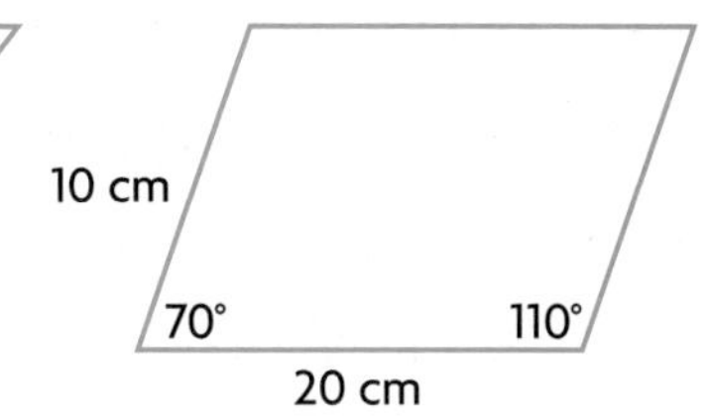

The sides of triangle *MNO* are 16 cm, 30 cm, and 34 cm long. Draw a similar triangle, using the given scale factor. Give the length of each side.

5. scale factor: $\frac{5}{4}$

6. scale factor: $\frac{4}{5}$

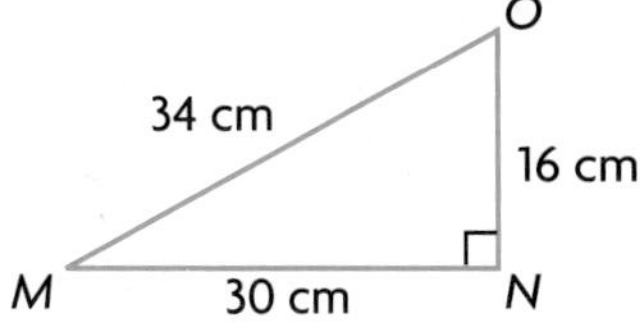

Problem-Solving Applications

7. **HOBBIES** Michelle wants similar prints made in various sizes, both small and large. The photo lab offers prints in these sizes: 3 in. × 5 in., 4 in. × 6 in., 8 in. × 18 in., 9 in. × 20 in., 16 in. × 24 in., and 20 in. × 30 in. Which could she order to get similar prints?

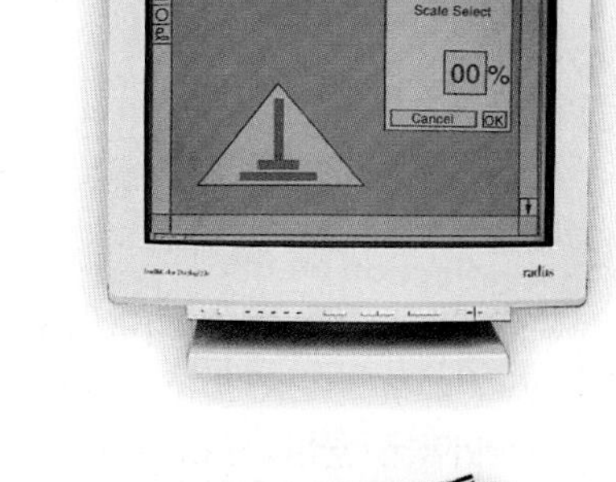

8. **ART** Pedro has drawn a triangular logo on his computer screen. He wants to reduce the dimensions of the logo by $\frac{1}{4}$. What percent should he enter for the scale selection?

9. **CRITICAL THINKING** Write a challenge problem where you decide whether a polygon has been enlarged or reduced.

10. **WRITE ABOUT IT** Tell how to decide whether or not two given triangles are similar.

Mixed Review and Test Prep

Solve the proportion.

11. $\frac{3}{9} = \frac{4}{n}$ **12.** $\frac{4}{6} = \frac{x}{12}$ **13.** $\frac{y}{7} = \frac{9}{21}$ **14.** $\frac{2}{a} = \frac{4}{8}$

Find the number.

15. 8% of 20 **16.** 30% of 25 **17.** 50% of 83 **18.** 45% of 20

19. **BUDGETS** You have a monthly budget of \$128.00. You save \$55.36 and spend \$61.76 on food and clothes. How much do you have left?

A \$6.40 **B** \$10.88
C \$66.24 **D** \$72.64

20. **SPORTS** Thai bought a baseball and a bat for \$76.25. The bat cost \$56.25 more than the baseball. How much did the baseball cost?

F \$66.25 **G** \$26.25
H \$20.00 **J** \$10.00

MORE PRACTICE Lesson 16.1, page H64

LAB ACTIVITY

What You'll Explore
How to create similar figures on a coordinate plane

What You'll Need
ruler, graph paper

REMEMBER:

A **reflection** on the coordinate plane is the figure formed by flipping a figure about a line to obtain a mirror image. **See page 206.**

Technology Link

You can make similar figures by slicing solids using E-Lab, Activity 16. Available on CD-ROM and on the Internet at **www.hbschool.com/elab**

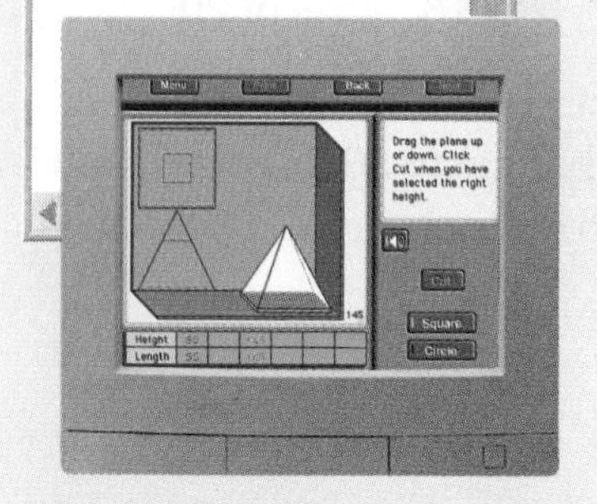

ALGEBRA CONNECTION

Similar Figures on the Coordinate Plane

Explore

- Use graph paper to make a coordinate plane. Label the x- and y-axes. Plot these points.

  (0,0)   ($^-5$,0)   ($^-10$,5)   ($^-10$,10)   ($^-5$,10)   (0,5)

- With a ruler, draw line segments connecting the points in the order shown above. Close the polygon by connecting the first and last points.

- In the table below, find a pattern that relates the given coordinates to the new coordinates and find the missing values.

Given Coordinates	New Coordinates
(0,0)	(0,0)
($^-5$,0)	($^-1$,0)
($^-10$,5)	($^-2$,1)
($^-10$,10)	($^-2$,?)
($^-5$,10)	(?,?)
(0,5)	(?,?)

- Plot points for the new coordinates, and make a new polygon by connecting these points as you did before.

Think and Discuss

- What pattern did you find that relates the given coordinates to the new coordinates?
- Do the two polygons look similar? Are the two polygons related by a scale factor? Support your answers.

Try This

- Draw two polygons in the first quadrant that are reflections of the polygons you just drew in the second quadrant. Label each vertex with its coordinates. What relationship do you see between the coordinates?

ALGEBRA CONNECTION

LESSON 16.2

Proportions and Similar Figures

What You'll Learn
How to find unknown lengths of sides of similar figures

Why Learn This?
To make similar enlargements or reductions of signs, posters, or models

You can use proportions to find unknown lengths of sides of similar figures.

EXAMPLE 1 $\triangle ABC$ is similar to $\triangle DEF$. Use a proportion to find the length of $\overline{FE}$. Let n = the length of $\overline{FE}$.

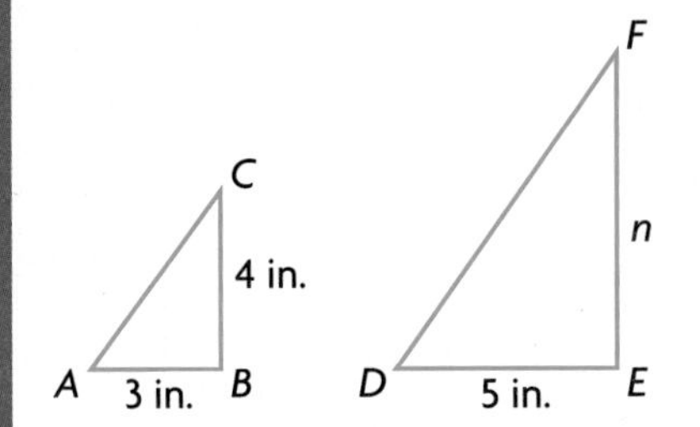

$\triangle ABC \sim \triangle DEF$
↑ *means "is similar to"*

Since corresponding sides of similar figures are proportional, you can start with this proportion and then substitute the appropriate values.

$$\frac{AB}{DE} = \frac{CB}{FE}$$

$$\frac{3}{5} = \frac{4}{n}$$ *Find the cross products.*

$$3n = 4 \times 5$$

$$3n = 20$$

$$n = \frac{20}{3}$$

So, the length of $\overline{FE}$ is $\frac{20}{3}$ in., or $6\frac{2}{3}$ in.

Talk About It

- Suppose you also know that the length of $\overline{AC}$ is 5 in. What proportion can you write to find the length of $\overline{DF}$? Solve your proportion.
- Suppose the sides of a triangle measure 8 cm, 5 cm, and 5 cm. A similar triangle has two sides each measuring 12.5 cm. What is the length of the third side?
- Make up a problem like Example 1 which can be solved by using proportions. Share your problems with the rest of the class.

MUSIC LINK

A triangle is not only a geometric figure. It is also a percussion instrument that consists of a steel bar bent into a triangular shape with one open corner. The smaller the triangle, the higher its pitch. How could you determine if two musical triangles of different sizes are similar?

Proportions and Similar Solid Figures

You can use scale factors and proportions to find the measures of sides of similar solid figures.

Suppose your math class is designing the props for a school play. The actors, who are about 5 ft tall, must appear to be about 1 ft tall. To accomplish this, you need to make enlarged props that are similar to but 5 times as large as real objects.

- To be similar, the large props and the real objects must be the same shape and have congruent corresponding angles. What must be true about the measures of corresponding sides?

EXAMPLE 2 Using a 5:1 scale factor, how large should you make a prop of an actual cereal box that is 7 in. long, 10 in. high, and 3 in. wide?

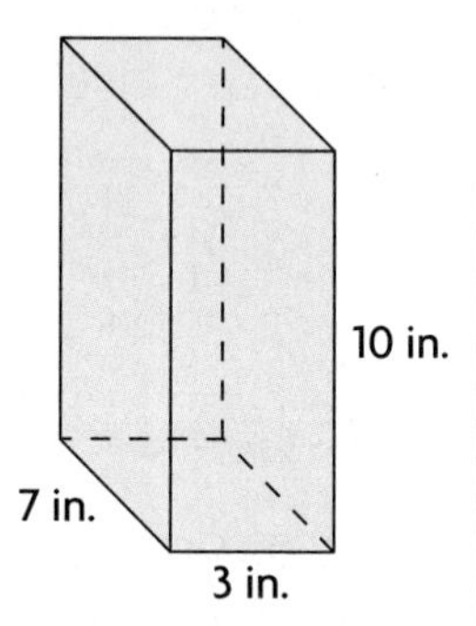

To find each dimension of the enlarged cereal box prop, you can solve a proportion for the unknown measurement, using the scale factor $\frac{5}{1}$.

Let h represent the height of the cereal box prop.

$$\text{scale factor} \rightarrow \frac{5}{1} = \frac{h}{10} \leftarrow \frac{\text{prop's height}}{\text{actual height}}$$

$$1h = 10 \times 5$$

$$h = 50$$

So, the height of the cereal box prop should be 50 in.

- Write and solve proportions to verify that the cereal box prop should be 35 in. long and 15 in. wide.

GUIDED PRACTICE

Use a proportion to find the unknown length in the pair of similar figures.

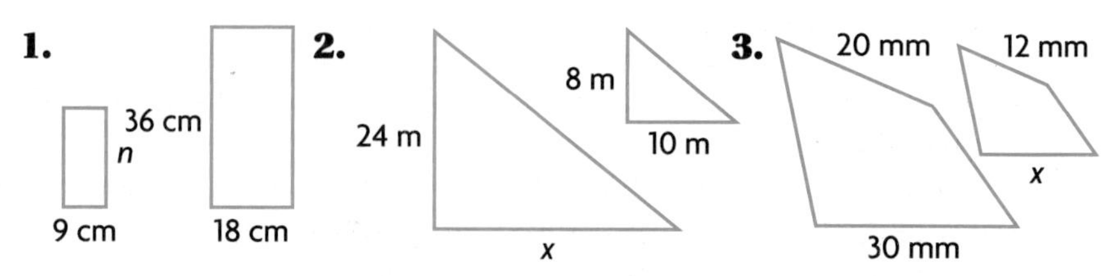

4. What are the scale factors for the figures in Exercises 1–3?

INDEPENDENT PRACTICE

The figures in each pair are similar. Use a proportion to find the unknown length.

1.

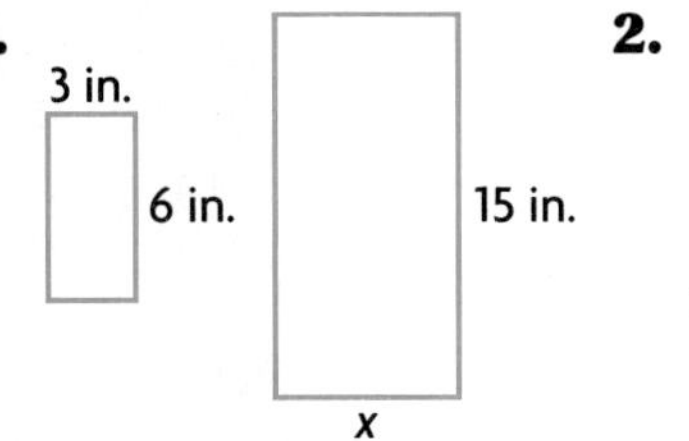

2.

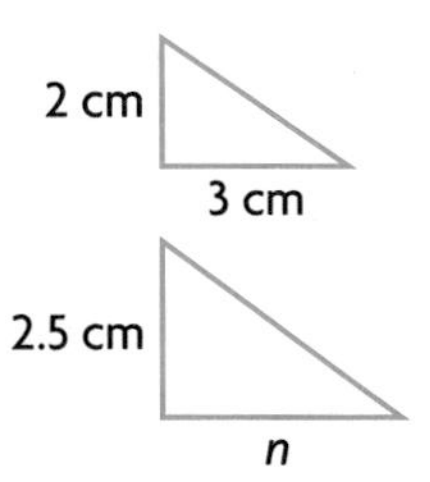

3.

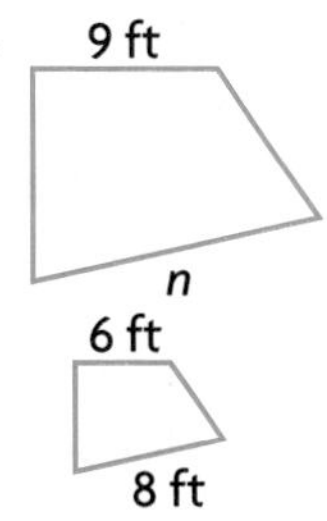

4.

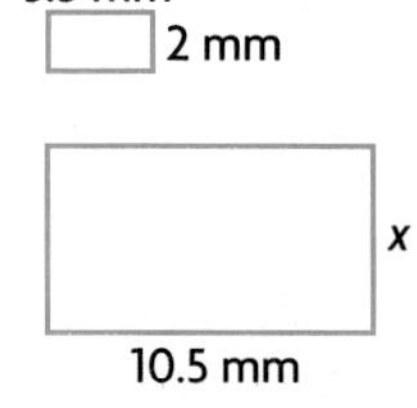

Copy and complete the tables, using a scale factor of 4 for the enlarged model.

		Real Object	Model
5.	Length	?	60 in.
6.	Width	?	24 in.
7.	Height	?	16 in.

		Real Object	Model
8.	Length	12.7 cm	?
9.	Width	5.8 cm	?
10.	Height	7.3 cm	?

Using a 3 : 1 scale factor, tell how large you would make an enlarged model.

11.

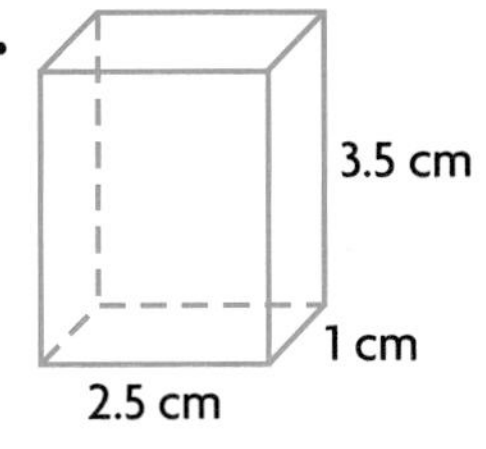

12.

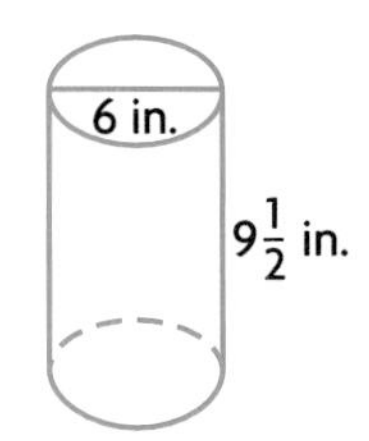

13.

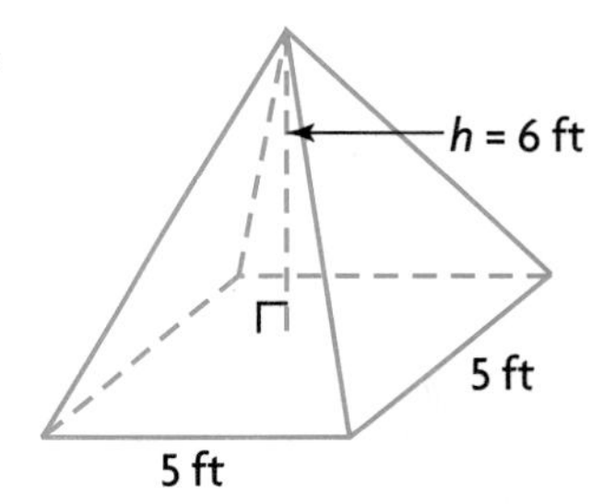

Problem-Solving Applications

14. **DRAMA** Suppose your math class is designing props for the school play *Teacher, You Shrunk the Students.* The props need to be 14 times as large as the real objects. How large should you make props for a cup and pencil if the real ones have the measurements that are shown?

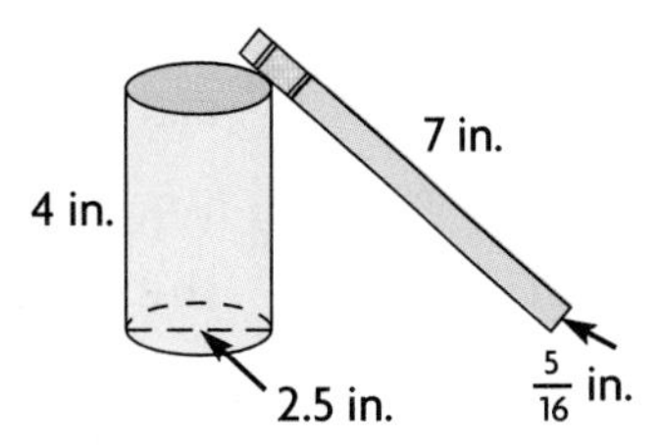

15. **CAREER** Cedric builds models for movies' special effects. He will build a reduced model and film its collapse. Using $\frac{1}{50}$ as the scale factor, give the dimensions of the model for a real building that has a 75-ft square base and a 50-ft height.

16. **WRITE ABOUT IT** Describe the models that result when you multiply by a scale factor less than 1, and by a scale factor greater than 1.

MORE PRACTICE Lesson 16.2, page H65

LESSON 16.3

ALGEBRA CONNECTION

Areas of Similar Figures

What You'll Learn
How areas of similar figures are related

Why Learn This?
To decide whether you have enough material to make an enlarged poster or quilt

You can have photo enlargements made that are similar to the original, smaller photos.

- Suppose two rectangular photos are similar. How are the corresponding sides related?

In this lesson you will compare the areas of similar figures and find the scale factor that relates the areas.

CAREER LINK

Are you interested in photography? Some possible careers to choose from are commercial photography, portraiture, photojournalism, and scientific photography. How are similar figures related to photography?

EXAMPLE 1 A rectangular wallet-size photo is 8 cm × 5.5 cm. An enlargement made with a scale factor of 3 is 24 cm × 16.5 cm. How is the area of the enlargement related to the area of the wallet-size photo?

Use the formula $A = lw$ to find the area of each photo.

Area of Wallet-size Photo
$A = lw$
$A = 8 \times 5.5$
$A = 44$, or 44 cm^2

Area of Enlarged Photo
$A = lw$
$A = 24 \times 16.5$
$A = 396$, or 396 cm^2

You can write a ratio and use division to compare the areas:

$\frac{396}{44}$ 396 [÷] 44 [=] [9]

So, the area of the enlargement is 9 times the area of the wallet-size photo. The scale factor for the area is 9, or 9 to 1.

When the measures of the sides are tripled, the scale factor for the area is not 3—it is 9, or 3^2. The scale factor for the area of the enlargement is the square of the scale factor for the lengths of the sides.

- What if the sides of a 5-in. × 8-in. rectangular photo are enlarged with a scale factor of 4? What is the scale factor that relates the areas?
- **CRITICAL THINKING** If the scale factor relating the lengths of the sides of similar rectangular photos is x, what is the scale factor that relates the areas?

EXAMPLE 2 Bill and Marcia have a total of 8 yd of 36-in.-wide fabric, or a little more than 10,000 in.^{2} of fabric, for their quilt. They select a quilt pattern that has 42 blocks, each measuring 12 in. $\times$ 12 in. Bill suggests they enlarge the quilt by using a scale factor of $\frac{5}{4}$ for the sides. How can they make sure they have enough fabric?

Marcia solves the problem by using these steps.

area of block $\rightarrow$ $12 \times 12 = 144$

area of quilt $\rightarrow$ 42×144

Find the area of each block and the area of the original quilt.

42  144  

So, the area of the original quilt is 6,048 in.^{2}

$\left(\frac{5}{4}\right)^2 = \frac{5}{4} \times \frac{5}{4} = \frac{25}{16}$ *Find the scale factor for the area by squaring the scale factor for the lengths of the sides.*

$6{,}048 \times \frac{25}{16}$ *Multiply the area of the original quilt by the scale factor for the area.*

6048  25  16 

The new area would be 9,450 in.^{2}

9,450 in.^{2} < 10,000 in.^{2} *Compare the area of the enlarged quilt with their 10,000 in.^{2} of material.*

Marcia concludes that they do have enough fabric.

- **CRITICAL THINKING** Suppose Bill wants to check the solution by solving in another way. How else can he solve the problem?

HISTORY LINK

The Amish came to the United States from Germany and Switzerland in the early 1700s. Their quilts are made from solid-color fabrics only, in both bright and dark colors. The patterns are usually geometric. Look at the quilt below. Do you see examples of similar geometric figures?

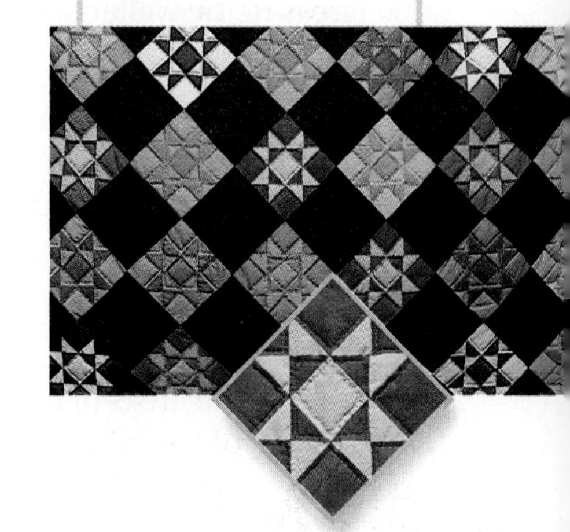

GUIDED PRACTICE

Write a ratio to relate the area of the similar enlargement to the area of the original rectangle. The widths (w) and lengths (l) are given.

1. original rectangle: $w = 6$ cm, $l = 8$ cm
enlargement: $w = 12$ cm, $l = 16$ cm

2. original rectangle: $w = 1.2$ m, $l = 4.8$ m
enlargement: $w = 3$ m, $l = 12$ m

The scale factor for the lengths of the sides of two similar polygons is given. Find the scale factor for their areas.

3. 5:1 **4.** $\frac{3}{2}$ **5.** 5:3 **6.** $\frac{8}{7}$

INDEPENDENT PRACTICE

Find the areas of the similar polygons. Then find the scale factor for the areas. HINT: For triangles, $A = \frac{1}{2}bh$; for trapezoids, $A = \frac{1}{2}(b_1 + b_2)h$.

1.

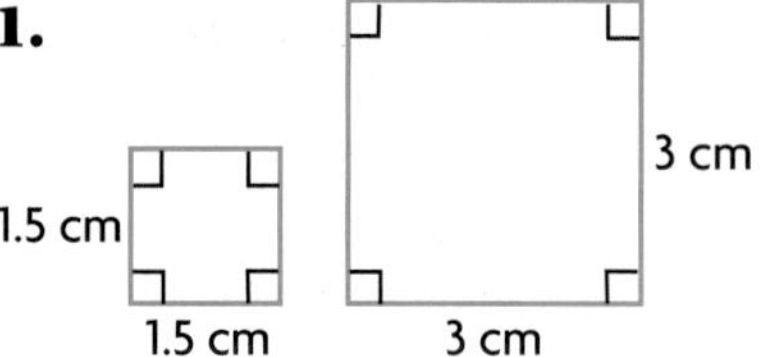

2.

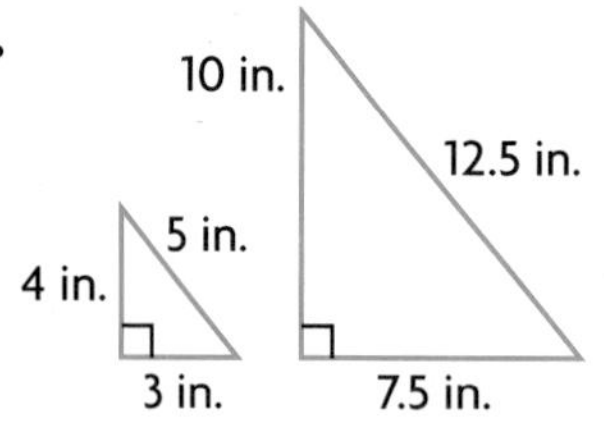

3.

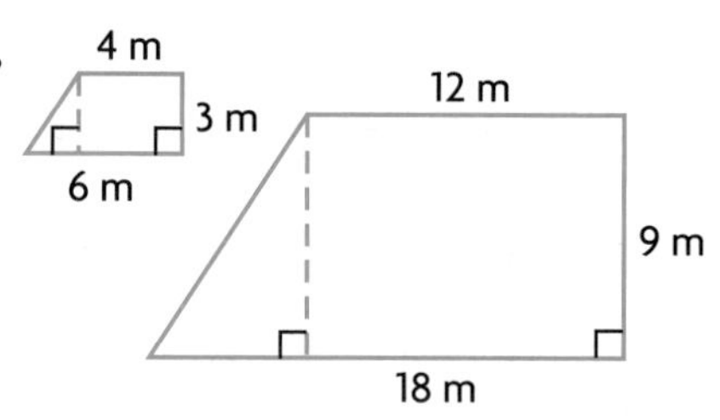

Problem-Solving Applications

4. **RATIOS** Debra wants a similar, wallet-size print made from a rectangular photograph that measures 32 cm × 22 cm. If the wallet-size print is to be 8 cm × 5.5 cm, what scale factor must be used for the sides? What scale factor relates the areas of the wallet-size photo and the original?

5. **CRAFTS** Tim and Lana have a total of 11 yd of 36-in.-wide fabric, or a little more than 14,000 in.^{2} of fabric for their quilt. They select a quilt pattern with 48 blocks, each measuring 12 in. × 12 in. Do they have enough fabric to enlarge the quilt by a scale factor of $\frac{3}{2}$ for the lengths of the sides? Explain.

6. **WRITE ABOUT IT** Describe the relationship between the ratio of the areas of two similar polygons and the ratio of the lengths of any two corresponding sides.

Technology Link

In ***Mighty Math Cosmic Geometry***, you can find more problems about scale factors in *Amazing Angles*. Use Grow Slide Level Q.

Mixed Review and Test Prep

Find the volume.

7.

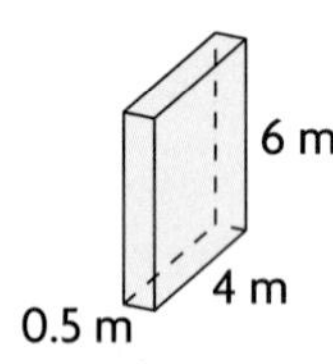

8.

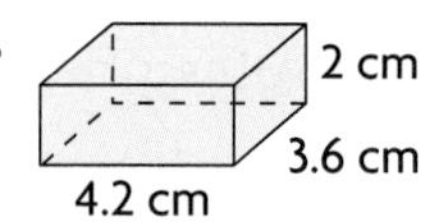

9.

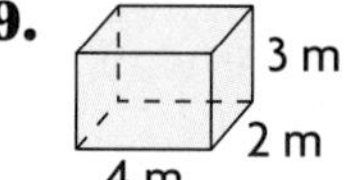

Find the percent.

10. What percent of 20 is 7?

11. What percent of 32 is 16?

12. **ESTIMATION** Kim's monthly expenses for 3 months were \$4,269, \$8,035, and \$6,438. Which is the best estimate of her expenses for the next 3 months?

   A \$15,000 **B** \$18,000
   C \$22,000 **D** \$25,000

13. **WORK BACKWARD** The Panama Canal took 36 years to build. It opened in 1917. Determine when work first began on the Panama Canal.

   F 1821 **G** 1881
   H 1921 **J** 1953

MORE PRACTICE Lesson 16.3, page H65

ALGEBRA CONNECTION

LESSON 16.4

Volumes of Similar Figures

What You'll Learn
How volumes of similar prisms are related

Why Learn This?
To compare sizes of similar containers, such as popcorn or cereal boxes

Suppose you are selling boxes of popcorn for your club's fund-raising project. The boxes are similar rectangular prisms in two sizes. You must decide how much to charge for each size.

The length, width, and height of the large box are twice those of the small box. Does this mean that there is twice as much popcorn in the large box? Should the price be twice as much?

EXAMPLE 1 The dimensions of the small box are 3.5 in. × 1.5 in. × 5 in. If the small box sells for $0.25, how much should you charge for the large box with twice the length, width, and height?

Small Box

Find the volume of each box. Use the formula $V = lwh$.

$V = lwh$

$= 3.5 \times 1.5 \times 5$

$= 26.25$ The volume of the small box is 26.25 in.^{3}

Large Box

$V = lwh$

$= 7 \times 3 \times 10 \leftarrow$ Each dimension is doubled.

$= 210$ The volume of the large box is 210 in.^{3}

$\frac{\text{volume of large box}}{\text{volume of small box}} \rightarrow \frac{210}{26.25}$

$\frac{210}{26.25} = \frac{8}{1}$, or $8 \leftarrow$ scale factor

Find the scale factor that relates the volume of the large box to the volume of the small box. Write a ratio.

There is 8 times as much popcorn in the large box as in the small box. Assuming price is determined by volume, the price should be 8 times the price of the small box.

$8 \times \$0.25 = \$2.00$ *Use the scale factor to find the price of the large box.*

So, the price of the large box should be $2.00.

When the measures of the length, width, and height are all doubled, the scale factor for the volumes is not 2—it is 8, or 2^3. The scale factor relating the volumes of the boxes is the cube of the scale factor for the lengths of the edges.

- **CRITICAL THINKING** Suppose the scale factor relating the lengths of the edges of similar rectangular prisms is n. What is the scale factor that relates the volumes of the prisms?

Did you know that unpopped popcorn, which buyers prepare at home, now outsells the ready-popped varieties? The Orville Redenbacher brand made approximately $243,700,000 in sales during the first four months of 1994.

You can use a calculator to compute volumes and scale factors.

EXAMPLE 2 Suppose you triple the lengths of the edges of this small cube to make a large cube. What is the scale factor that relates the volume of the large cube to that of the small cube?

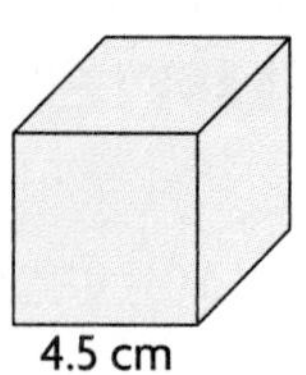

Small Cube *Find the volume of each cube. Use the formula $V = s^3$.*

$V = s^3$

$= (4.5)^3$ 4.5  3 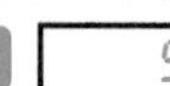 91.125

The volume of the small cube is 91.125 cm^3.

Large Cube

$V = s^3$

$= (13.5)^3$ 13.5  3  2460.375

The volume of the large cube is 2,460.375 cm^3.

$\frac{2{,}460.375}{91.125} = \frac{27}{1}$ *Write a ratio to relate the volume of the large cube to the volume of the small cube.*

2460.375  91.125  27

So, the scale factor relating the volume of the large cube to the volume of the small cube is $\frac{27}{1}$, or 27.

- Suppose you enlarge the lengths of the edges of the small cube by a scale factor of 5. What is the scale factor that relates the volume of the large cube to the volume of the small cube?

GUIDED PRACTICE

Find the volume of each box. Then tell the scale factor that relates the volume of the large box to the volume of the small box.

1.

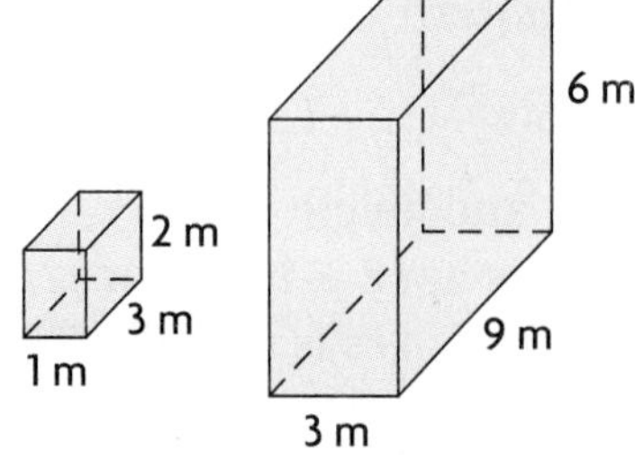

2.

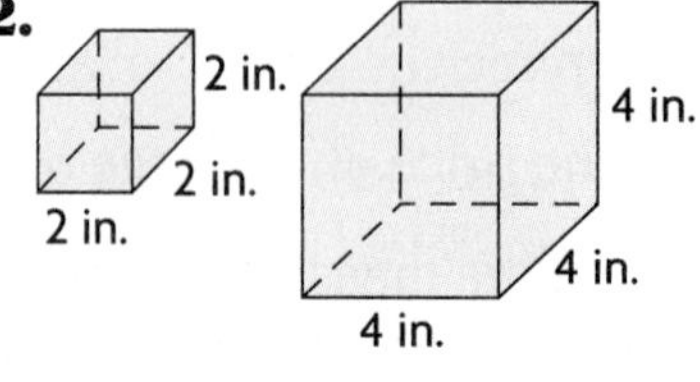

Tell the scale factor that relates the larger volume to the smaller volume.

3. $V_1 = 225\ m^3$ $V_2 = 9\ m^3$

4. $V_1 = 68\ ft^3$ $V_2 = 34\ ft^3$

Calculator Activities, page H31

INDEPENDENT PRACTICE

Tell the dimensions of a similar enlarged figure, made with a scale factor of 2.5 for the lengths of the edges.

1.

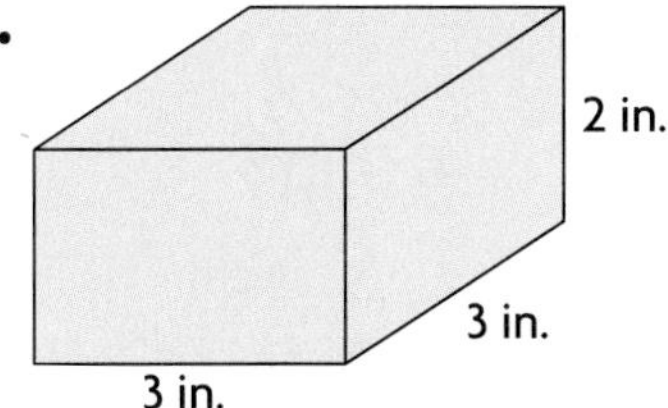

2.

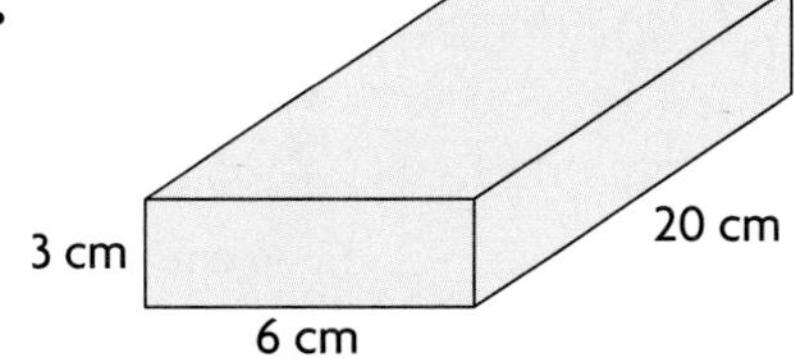

3.

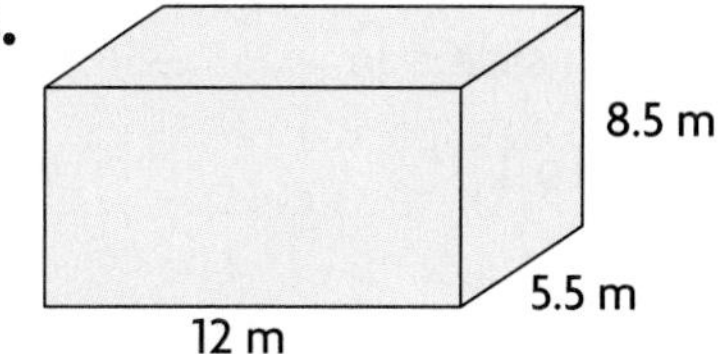

Find the volumes of the similar prisms. Then find the scale factor for the volumes, relating the larger prism to the smaller prism.

4.

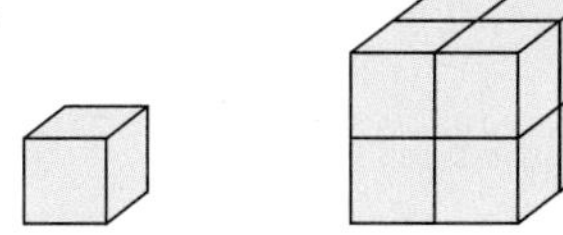

5.

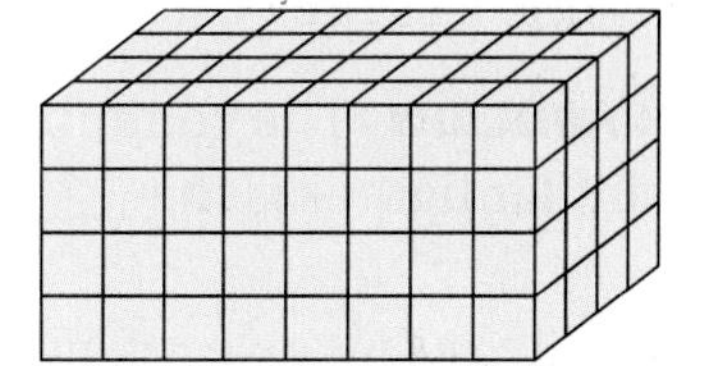

Write a scale factor for the volumes, relating the larger cube to the smaller cube.

6.

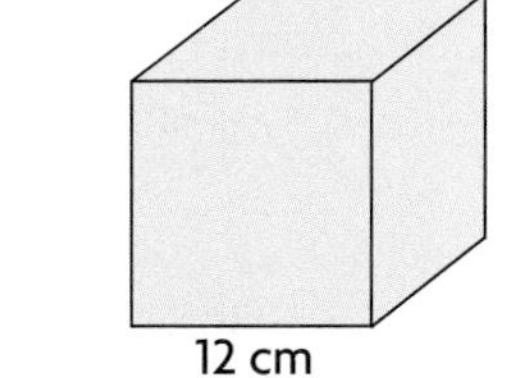

7.

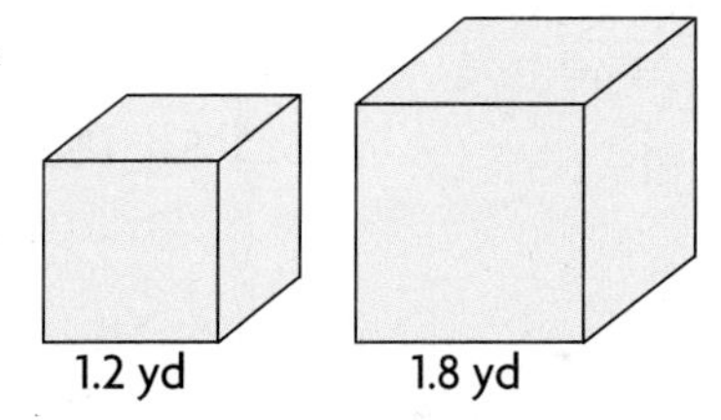

Problem-Solving Applications

8. **CONSUMER MATH** The dimensions of a small box of cereal are 2 in. × 6.5 in. × 8 in. The small box sells for $3.20. The length, width, and height of a large box of the cereal are 1.5 times those of the small box. What is a reasonable estimate of how much the large box of cereal should cost?

9. **COMPARE** Yolanda decides that she wants to buy a soft drink at the movie theater. The theater charges $1.25 for the 8-oz size, $3.00 for the 16-oz size, and $5.50 for the 32-oz size. If Yolanda wants to get the best value, which size should she buy? Explain.

10. **ESTIMATION** The dimensions of a small box of raisins are 5 cm × 2 cm × 7 cm. The small box sells for $0.39. The dimensions of a large box of raisins are 10 cm × 4 cm × 14 cm. What is a reasonable estimate of how much the large box of raisins should cost?

11. **NUMBER SENSE** Suppose the lengths of the edges of a prism are enlarged by a scale factor of 2.5. What scale factor relates the volumes of the original prism and the enlarged prism?

12. **WRITE ABOUT IT** Write a problem involving volumes of similar figures.

MORE PRACTICE Lesson 16.4, page H65

CHAPTER 16 Review/Test

Draw a similar figure, using the given scale factor. Give the length of each side. (pages 312–316)

1. 3 to 1

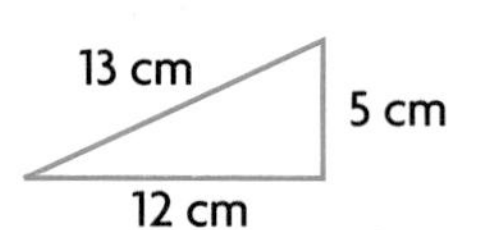

2. 1 to 4

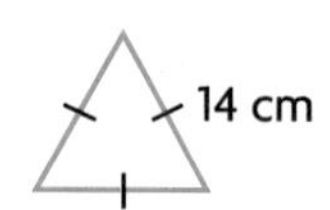

3. 2 to 1

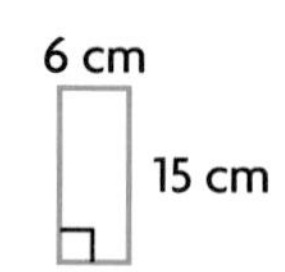

4. 1 to 5

4 cm

2 cm

5. VOCABULARY Figures that are the same shape but not necessarily the same size are called __?__. (page 313)

6. VOCABULARY The common ratio for pairs of corresponding sides of similar figures is the __?__. (page 314)

The figures in each pair are similar. Use a proportion to find the unknown length. (pages 317–319)

7.

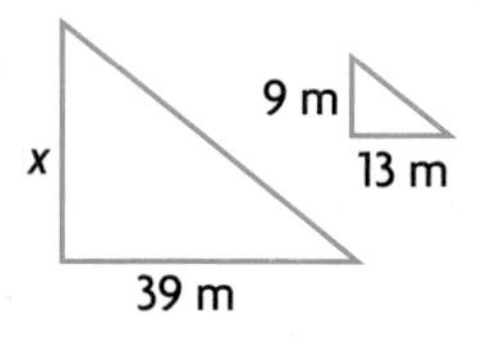

8.

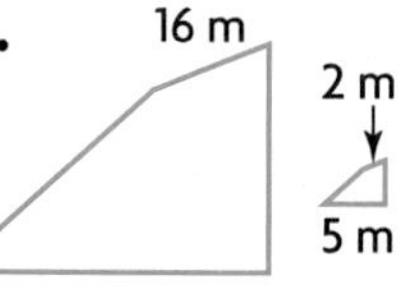

9.

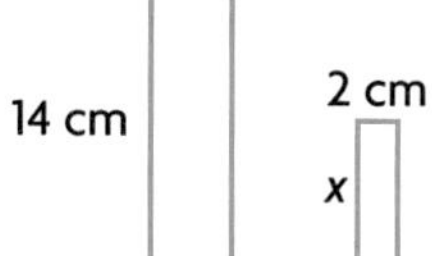

10.

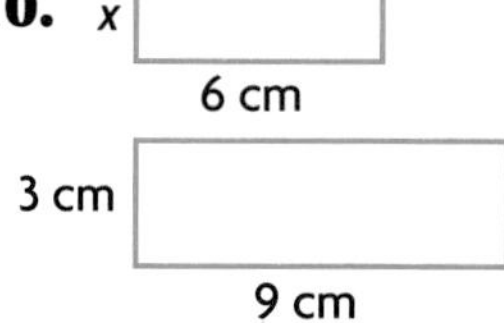

Copy and complete the table. (pages 320–322)

Scale Factor for Sides	Scale Factor for Areas	Original Area	New Area
2 to 1	**11.** ?	12 m^2	**12.** ?
3 to 2	**13.** ?	164 cm^2	**14.** ?
15. ?	16:1	25 $in.^2$	**16.** ?
17. ?	9:16	64 ft^2	**18.** ?
4:5	**19.** ?	100 mm^2	**20.** ?

Find each volume. (pages 323–325)

21.

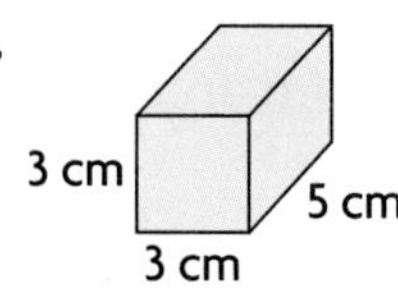

22.

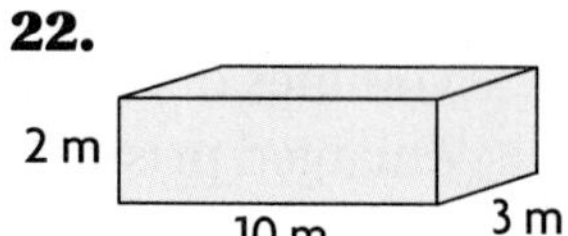

23.

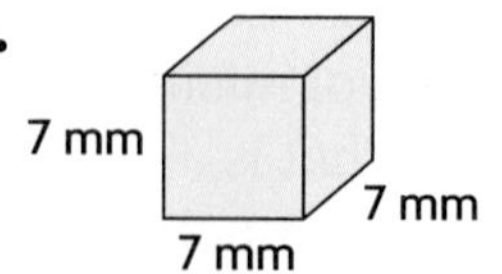

24.

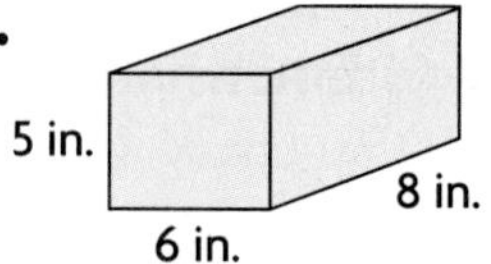

25. Use a scale factor of 4 to enlarge the figures in Exercises 21–24. Find the new volumes.

Test Prep

1. Which is greater than 2^5?

A 2×15
B $2 \times 2 \times 2 \times 2$
C 5^2
D 4^3

2. A pentagonal prism has 7 faces and 10 vertices. How many edges does it have?

F 7
G 10
H 15
J 19

3. This week Patricia watched television for $4\frac{1}{6}$ hours. Marcia watched television for $2\frac{7}{8}$ hours. About how much longer did Patricia watch television?

A $\frac{1}{2}$ hr

B 1 hr

C $1\frac{3}{4}$ hr

D 2 hr

4. The triangles shown below are similar. What is the value of x?

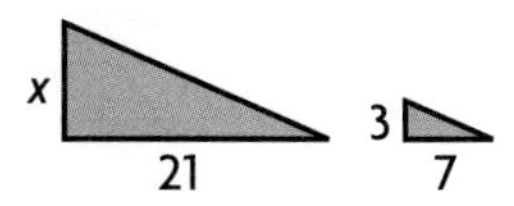

F 9
G 14
H 17
J 63

5. 27% of what number is 54?

A 15
B 50
C 81
D 200
E Not Here

6. A 72-inch piece of ribbon is cut into 3 pieces. One piece is 4 inches longer than the other 2 pieces. Which equation could be used to find the length of the shorter two pieces?

F $r + r + r - 4 = 72$
G $r + 4 + r = 64$
H $r + r + r + 4 = 72$
J $r + 4 + r + 4 + r = 72$

7. The sides of a triangle measure 4 inches, 5 inches, and 5 inches. Which is a reasonable conclusion?

A The triangle is isosceles.
B The triangle is scalene.
C The triangle is obtuse.
D The triangle is right.

8. What is the volume of the figure?

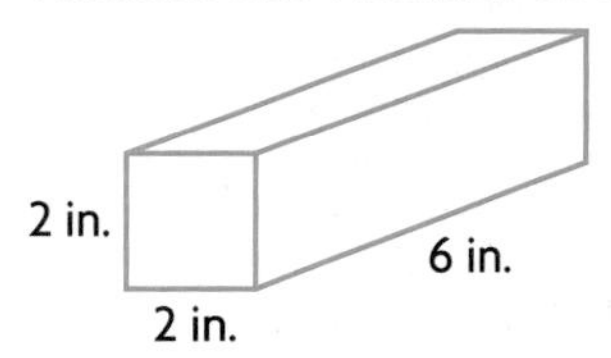

F 216 in.^{3}
G 72 in.^{3}
H 56 in.^{3}
J 24 in.^{3}
K Not Here

9. Which statement is false?

A All prisms are polyhedrons.
B All cylinders are not polyhedrons.
C All pyramids are polyhedrons.
D No cone is a polyhedron.
E Not Here

10. Which is the best buy?

F 10 for \$1.89
G 6 for \$1.08
H 4 for \$0.88
J 1 for \$0.21

CHAPTER

17 APPLICATIONS OF SIMILAR FIGURES

LOOK AHEAD

In this chapter you will solve problems that involve

- similar figures and dilations
- scale drawings and maps
- indirect measurement
- Golden Rectangles

NATURE LINK

The pictograph below shows the 5 most visited national parks in 1996.

MOST VISITED NATIONAL PARKS IN THE U.S.

National Parks	Number of Visitors
Great Smoky Mountains	
Grand Canyon	
Yosemite	
Olympic	
Yellowstone	

Each [tree] = 1 million visitors

- About how many more people visited Great Smoky Mountains National Park than Grand Canyon National Park?
- The number of visitors to Great Smoky Mountains National Park was about how many times the number of visitors to Yellowstone National Park?

Problem-Solving Project

Navigating the National Parks

YOU WILL NEED: metric ruler

Choose a vacation route through seven national parks, starting at the Grand Canyon and ending at Zion National Park. Arches and Canyonlands National Parks are 40 km apart. Use this distance to find the distances between the other parks. Calculate the total distance for the trip. Write a daily travel plan. Be sure that you drive no more than 300 km per day.

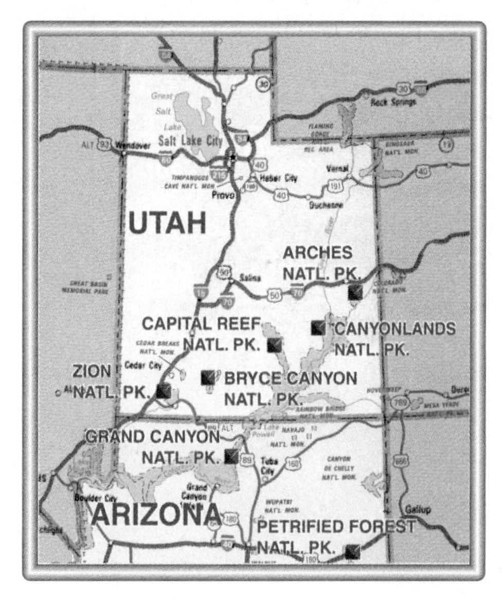

PROJECT CHECKLIST

- ✓ Did you choose a route?
- ✓ Did you find the distances between parks?
- ✓ Did you calculate the total distance for the trip?
- ✓ Did you write a daily travel plan?

LESSON 17.1 Drawing Similar Figures

What You'll Learn
How to use measurements and scale factors to draw similar figures

Why Learn This?
To reduce or enlarge drawings

What You'll Need
ruler, protractor

One way to reduce or enlarge a drawing is to use a scale factor to draw a similar figure.

- Does multiplying by a scale factor less than 1 increase or decrease a measurement?

EXAMPLE Using a scale factor of $\frac{1}{3}$ for the lengths, draw a new trapezoid *DEFG* that is similar to but smaller than trapezoid *PQRS*.

P 15 cm Q
127°
24 cm
30 cm
53°
S 33 cm R

Measure the angles and sides of the given figure. Use the same measures for the angles in the new figure, but multiply each side's length by the scale factor to find the length of the new side.

GIVEN TRAPEZOID *PQRS*		NEW TRAPEZOID *DEFG*	
Angle Measure	**Side Length**	**Angle Measure**	**Side Length**
P: 90°	*PQ*: 15 cm	*D*: 90°	*DE*: $\frac{1}{3} \times 15$ cm $= 5$ cm
Q: 127°	*QR*: 30 cm	*E*: 127°	*EF*: $\frac{1}{3} \times 30$ cm $= 10$ cm
R: 53°	*RS*: 33 cm	*F*: 53°	*FG*: $\frac{1}{3} \times 33$ cm $= 11$ cm
S: 90°	*SP*: 24 cm	*G*: 90°	*GD*: $\frac{1}{3} \times 24$ cm $= 8$ cm

Use a ruler and a protractor to draw the sides and angles of the new figure.

For *DEFG*, start with the longest side, *FG*. Then use the data in the table to draw the angles and the other sides in order.

G 11 cm F

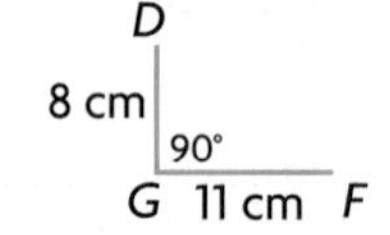

D 5 cm
90° E
8 cm
90°
G 11 cm F

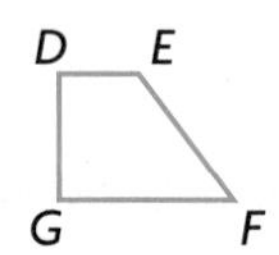

HINT: Notice that for this trapezoid, if you draw the 90° angles first, you form the other angles as you draw side *EF*.

- Using a scale factor of 2.5, find the lengths of the sides of a new trapezoid *WXYZ* that is similar to *PQRS*.

Similar figures are the same shape but not necessarily the same size. Corresponding sides are proportional, and corresponding angles are congruent.
See page 313.

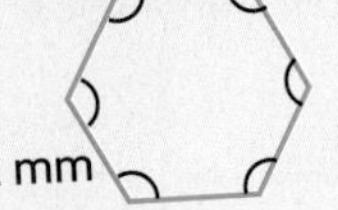

GUIDED PRACTICE

Use the scale factor to draw a triangle that is similar to the triangle at the right.

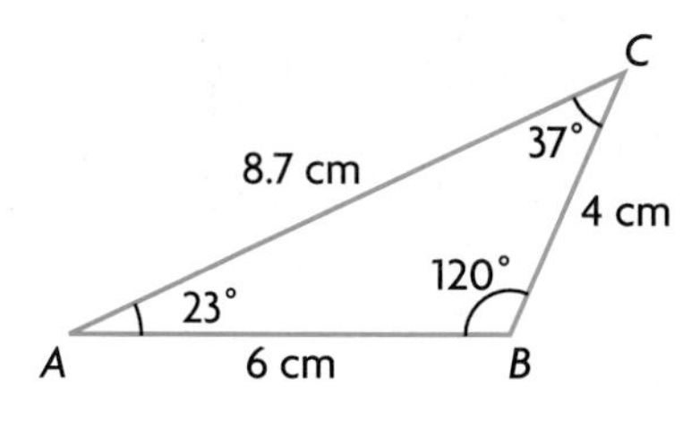

1. scale factor: $\frac{1}{2}$
2. scale factor: $\frac{1}{8}$
3. scale factor: 1.5
4. scale factor: 2.5
5. scale factor: $\frac{1}{4}$
6. scale factor: 2

INDEPENDENT PRACTICE

Use the scale factor to find the lengths of the sides of a parallelogram that is similar to the parallelogram at the right.

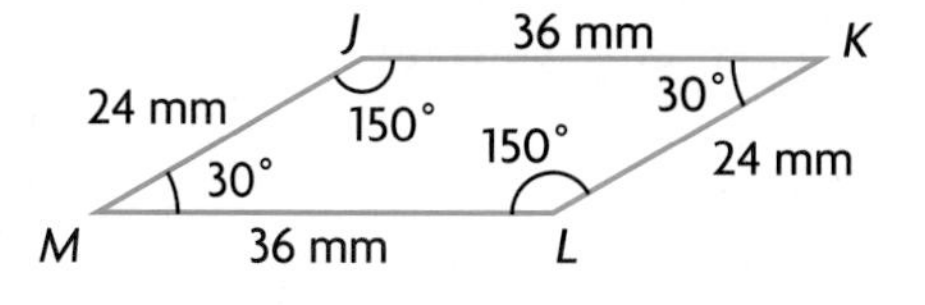

1. scale factor: $\frac{1}{3}$
2. scale factor: $\frac{1}{4}$
3. scale factor: 1.25
4. scale factor: 3

Use the scale factor to draw a pentagon that is similar to the pentagon at the right.

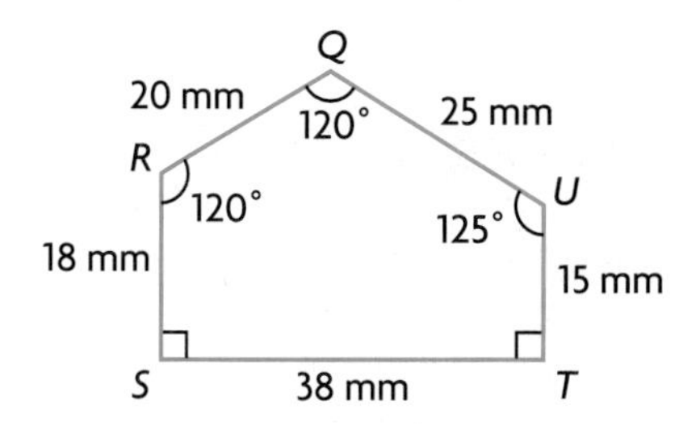

5. scale factor: $\frac{1}{2}$
6. scale factor: $\frac{1}{5}$
7. scale factor: 2
8. scale factor: 3.5

Problem-Solving Applications

9. **ART** Janice used computer software to draw the design shown below on her computer screen. She began by drawing the two figures at the left. Draw the design by tracing the two figures, cutting them out, and making similar figures as needed.

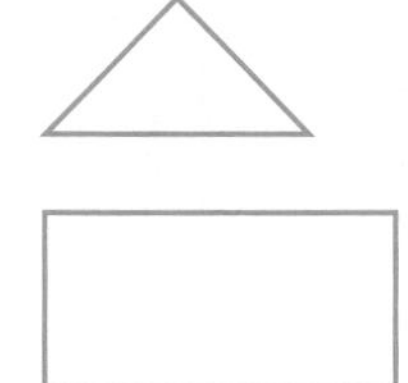

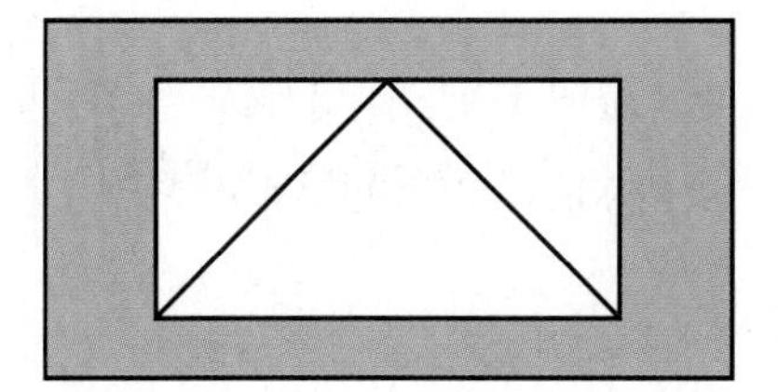

10. **COMPARE** Tell what scale factors you used in Exercise 9.

11. Kevin is taking a drafting course. He has been asked to reduce the size of a 6 in. × 4 in. rectangle using a scale factor of $\frac{3}{4}$. Make a drawing of the new rectangle.

12. **WRITE ABOUT IT** How do you know that a new drawing is similar to the original figure?

Technology Link
In *Mighty Math Astro Algebra*, go to the *Cargo Bay* to explore scale factors in *The Ruler of the Chotchkees.* Use Grow Slide Level Green S.

MORE PRACTICE Lesson 17.1, page H66

LAB ACTIVITY

What You'll Explore
Another method of drawing similar figures

What You'll Need
paper, protractor, straightedge or ruler

VOCABULARY
dilation

Similar Figures by Dilation

What if you want to draw similar figures, but you don't have a ruler or protractor? You can draw them by using a geometric transformation called a **dilation**. To dilate means to change the scale. The procedure is easy. From a point, you draw rays through the vertices of the figure, applying a given scale factor.

Explore

Make a triangle similar to $\triangle XYZ$ using a scale factor of 2 for the lengths of the sides.

- Use a straightedge, or fold a piece of paper. Use the straightedge to trace or copy $\triangle XYZ$.

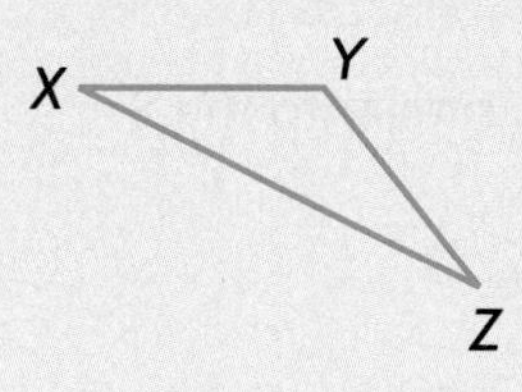

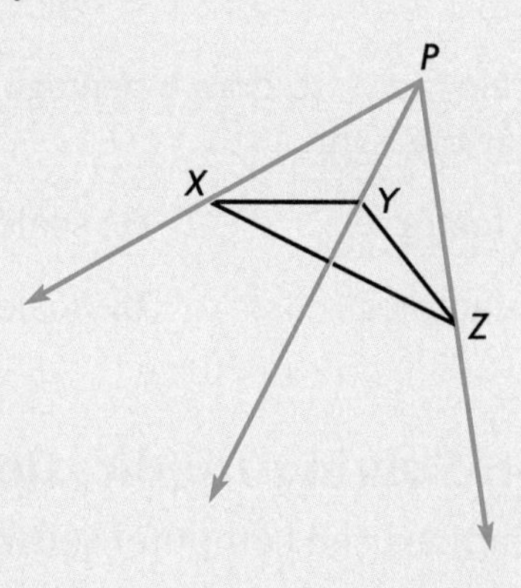

- Use your straightedge to draw rays from some point *P*, not on the triangle, through each of the points *X*, *Y*, and *Z*.

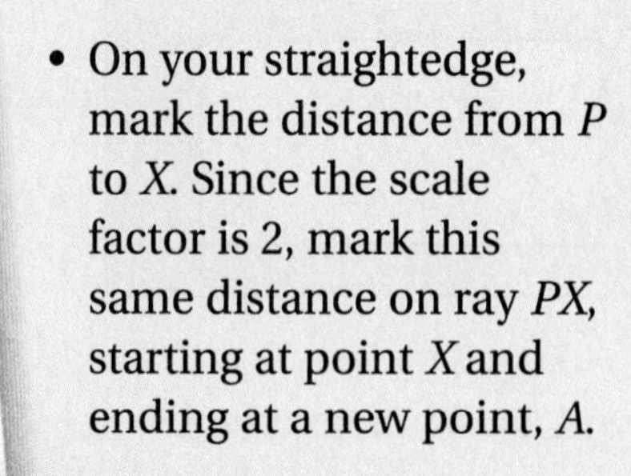

- On your straightedge, mark the distance from *P* to *X*. Since the scale factor is 2, mark this same distance on ray *PX*, starting at point *X* and ending at a new point, *A*.

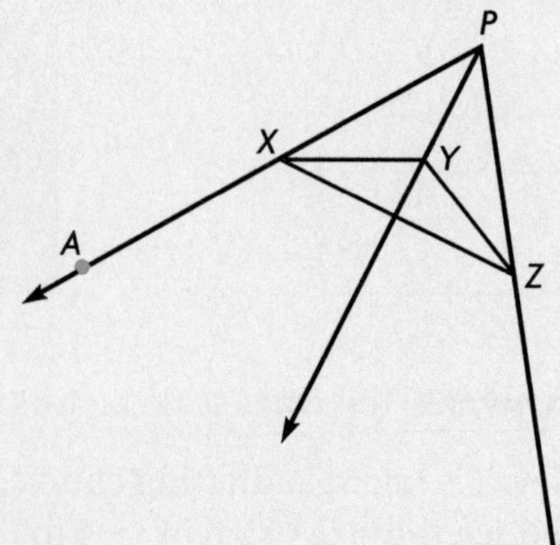

- Repeat this procedure on ray PY and on ray PZ, using the distances from P to Y and from P to Z. Name the new points on these rays B and C.

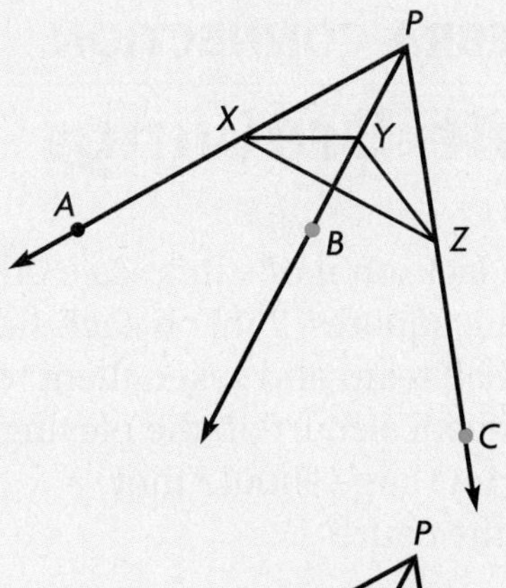

- Use your straightedge to connect A, B, and C. $\triangle ABC$ is similar to $\triangle XYZ$.

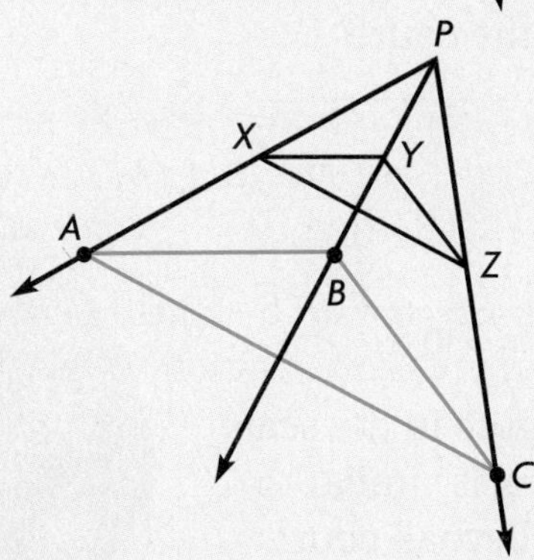

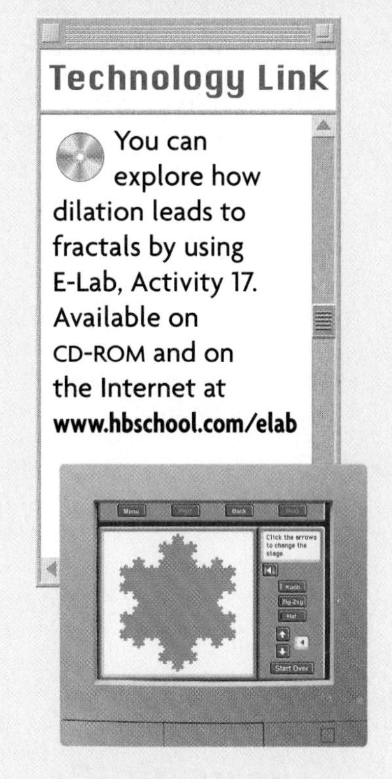

Technology Link
You can explore how dilation leads to fractals by using E-Lab, Activity 17. Available on CD-ROM and on the Internet at www.hbschool.com/elab

Think and Discuss CRITICAL THINKING

- Predict what you will find if you measure and compare the angles of the two triangles. Use a protractor to check your prediction.
- Predict what you will find if you measure and compare the sides of the two triangles. Use a ruler to check your prediction.

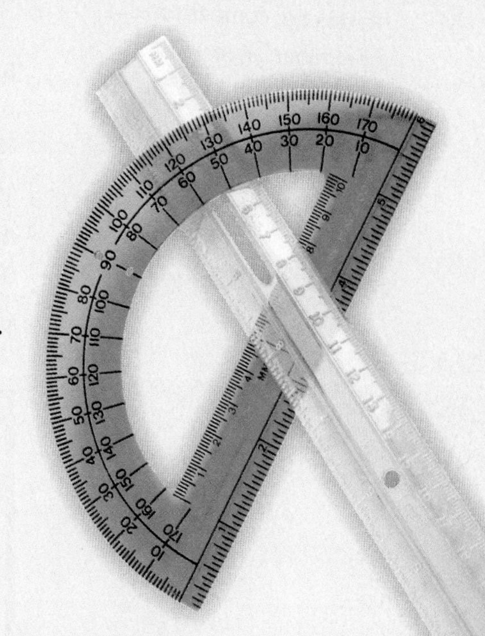

Try This

- Trace $MNOP$, and mark a point Q outside, inside, or on $MNOP$. Using a scale factor of 2 and the dilation method, draw a quadrilateral similar to $MNOP$.

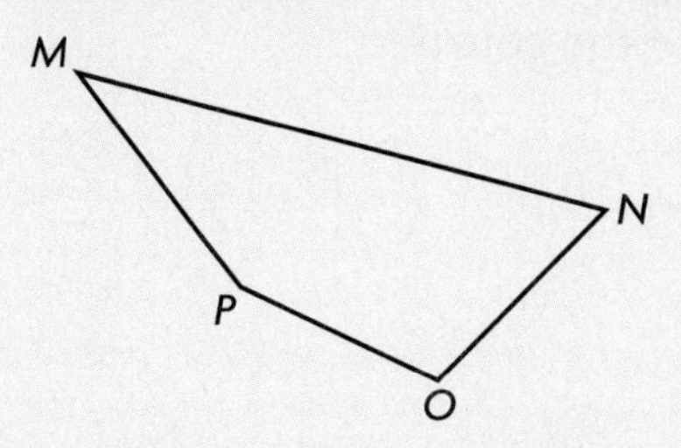

- Extend your drawing and make a similar quadrilateral, using a scale factor of 3 for the lengths of the sides.
- Are there other similar figures between the two figures? If yes, describe their scale factors.

LESSON 17.2

What You'll Learn
How to read and make scale drawings

Why Learn This?
To read and interpret diagrams or floor plans

VOCABULARY
scale drawing

ALGEBRA CONNECTION

Scale Drawings

Coach Jackson made this scale drawing with two adjacent squares, 3 in. on each side, for the volleyball team and asked them to mark off a practice court on the playing field. How large should they make the court?

Scale: 1 in. = 10 ft

The figure in the scale drawing is similar to the volleyball court. Every **scale drawing** has the same shape as the object it represents, and its dimensions are related by a ratio, or scale, to the dimensions of the object. You can make a scale drawing that is larger, smaller, or the same size as the original object.

REMEMBER:
Ratios are comparisons of numbers. **See page H18, Key Skill 31.**

Write: $\frac{4}{5}$, 4:5, or 4 to 5
Read: four to five

The scale given in the drawing may be written in different ways. All of the following say that 1 in. on the drawing represents 10 ft on the actual volleyball court.

1 in. = 10 ft   1 in.:10 ft   1 in. to 10 ft $\frac{1 \text{ in.}}{10 \text{ ft}}$

EXAMPLE 1 On the scale drawing, the total length of the court is 6 in. What is the actual length of the court?

Let m represent the actual length.

scale $\rightarrow \frac{1}{10} = \frac{6}{m} \leftarrow \frac{\text{drawing length}}{\text{actual length}}$ *Use the scale and the length on the drawing to write a proportion.*

$\frac{1}{10} = \frac{6}{m}$ *Solve the proportion.*

$1 \cdot m = 6 \cdot 10$

$m = 60$

So, the actual length of the court is 60 ft.

- What is the actual width of the volleyball court?

Scale drawings are also used to make enlarged drawings of small objects.

EXAMPLE 2 For his science fair display, John made a scale drawing of a certain kind of ant. Use the scale to find a reasonable estimate of the actual length of the ant.

The given scale is 20 cm:1 cm. This means that 20 cm on the drawing represents 1 cm on the ant. Since the drawing is 36 cm long, the length of the ant must be more than 1 cm but less than 2 cm.

$$\text{scale} \rightarrow \frac{20}{1} = \frac{36}{n} \leftarrow \frac{\text{drawing length}}{\text{actual length}}$$

To find the actual length, you can write and solve a proportion. Let n represent the actual length.

$$20 \cdot n = 36 \times 1$$
$$20n = 36$$
$$\frac{20n}{20} = \frac{36}{20}$$
$$n = 1.8$$

So, the actual length is 1.8 cm.

- If the head of the ant measures 6 cm long on the drawing, what is the actual length of the head?

GUIDED PRACTICE

Find the missing dimension.

1. drawing length: 3 in.
actual length: _?_ ft
scale: 1 in.:15 ft

2. drawing length: 5,000 mm
actual length: _?_ mm
scale: 1,000 mm:1 mm

Write *larger* or *smaller* to indicate whether the dimensions in the scale drawing are larger or smaller than those of the object. The first measure is for the scale drawing, and the second measure is for the actual object.

3. 1 cm:10 cm **4.** 1 in.:50 ft **5.** 1 cm:1 mm

6. 100 mm:1 mm **7.** 10 in.:3 ft **8.** 1 mm:0.01 mm

9. 2 in.:10 in. **10.** 1 in.:1 mi **11.** 1 cm:5 mm

SCIENCE LINK

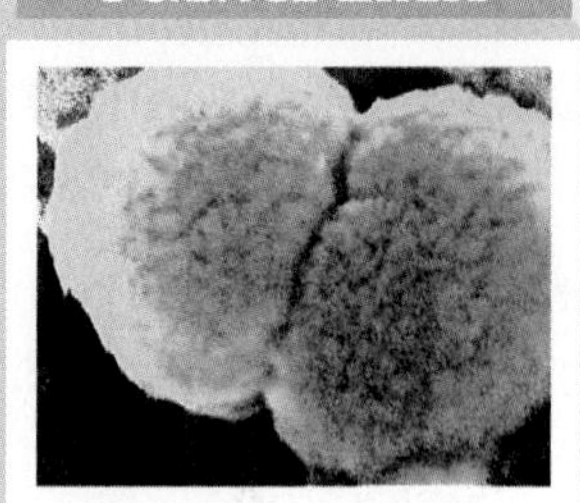

Scale drawings of microorganisms often indicate the magnification. The magnification is the factor by which the actual size has been multiplied. For example, a drawing with a magnification of 100X is 100 times as large as the actual organism. If a drawing of a certain virus is 2 cm long and the magnification is 100,000X, how long is the actual virus?

ACTIVITY **WHAT YOU'LL NEED:** ruler, paper

Make a scale drawing of the floor of your classroom on an $8\frac{1}{2}$-in. × 11-in. sheet of paper. Follow this procedure.

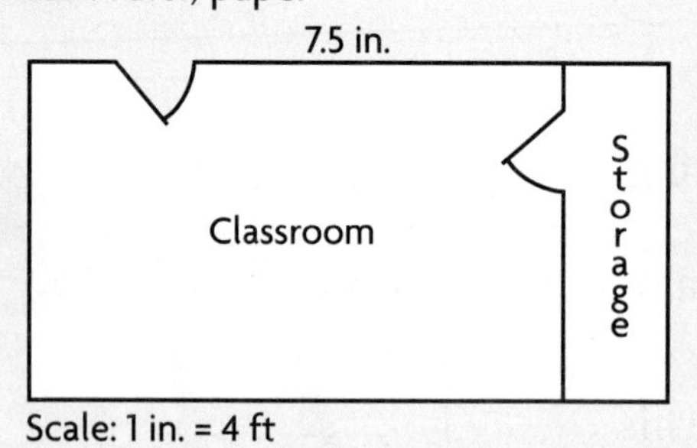

- Sketch the general shape of the room. What shape is it?
- Measure the length of each wall. Round the measurements to the nearest foot, and record them in a table.
- Choose an appropriate scale for your drawing by writing the ratio of the length of your paper to the longest measurement in the room. For example, if your room is 49 ft long, the ratio could be $\frac{10 \text{ in.}}{49 \text{ ft}}$. For your scale, use compatible numbers close to the value of your ratio, such as $\frac{10 \text{ in.}}{50 \text{ ft}}$, or $\frac{1 \text{ in.}}{5 \text{ ft}}$.
- Use your scale to find the lengths for your drawing. Record these computed measures in your table. Check that the length and width of the room will fit on the paper. Adjust your scale if necessary.
- Use a ruler and your measures to make your scale drawing.

SOCIAL STUDIES LINK

There is a full-scale model, or replica, of a famous Greek temple, the Parthenon, in Nashville, Tennessee. Splendid China, near Orlando, Florida, is a theme park with small-scale models of famous Chinese landmarks, such as the Great Wall. Like scale drawings, scale models have the same shapes as the actual objects. They are usually reduced in size. Make a scale drawing of the front of your school.

Talk About It

- Would a scale of 1 in.:2 ft be appropriate for your drawing on the $8\frac{1}{2}$-in. × 11-in. sheet of paper? Explain.
- What if you make the scale drawing on a piece of poster paper that is 22 in. × 27 in.? What scale would you choose? Explain your reasoning.

INDEPENDENT PRACTICE

Use the scale of 1 cm:15 cm to find the missing dimension. The first measure is from the scale drawing and the second measure is from the actual object.

1. drawing: 3 cm
actual: __?__ cm

2. drawing: 10 cm
actual: __?__ cm

3. drawing: __?__ cm
actual: 60 cm

4. drawing: __?__ cm
actual: 90 cm

5. drawing: __?__ cm
actual: 21 cm

6. drawing: 12.5 cm
actual: __?__ cm

Use the scale of 15 cm:1 cm to find the missing dimension. The first measure in the scale is for the scale drawing and the second measure is for the actual object.

7. drawing: 36 cm
actual: _?_ cm

8. drawing: _?_ cm
actual: 7 cm

9. drawing: 48 cm
actual: _?_ cm

10. drawing: _?_ cm
actual: 9 cm

11. drawing: 225 cm
actual: _?_ cm

12. drawing: _?_ cm
actual: 0.5 cm

Write an appropriate scale for a scale drawing of each item. Each scale drawing should fill most of the page on an $8\frac{1}{2}$-in. × 11-in. sheet of paper.

13. truck: 19 ft long

14. space shuttle orbiter: 37.2 m long

15. Empire State Building: 1,250 ft tall

16. flea: 0.08 cm long

Problem-Solving Applications

Measure this drawing of a killer-whale exhibit tank. Then use the dimensions of the drawing and the scale 1 in.:40 ft to find the actual dimensions. Write the drawing dimensions and the actual dimensions.

Holding area
Gate
Show area
Trainer platform

17. Show area

18. Holding area

19. Trainer platform

20. **WRITE ABOUT IT** Which would be better for an enlarged scale drawing of a microscopic marine animal, the scale 1 cm:500 cm or 1 cm:$\frac{1}{500}$ cm? Explain.

Mixed Review and Test Prep

Solve the proportion.

21. $\frac{3}{x} = \frac{6}{4}$

22. $\frac{18}{4} = \frac{b}{10}$

23. $\frac{2.5}{11} = \frac{4}{n}$

24. $\frac{a}{20} = \frac{12.6}{30}$

The figures in each pair are similar. Find the missing length.

25.

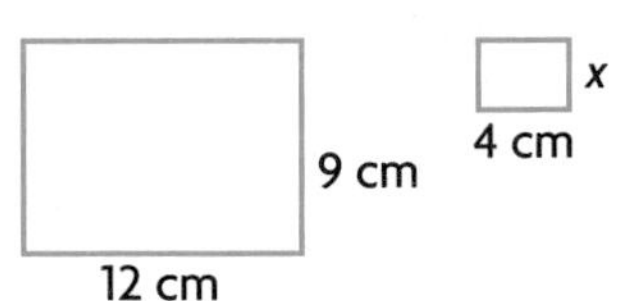

26.

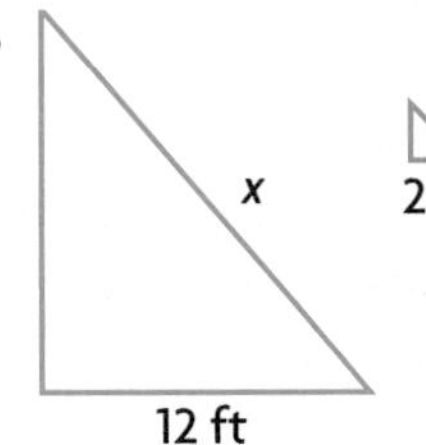

27.

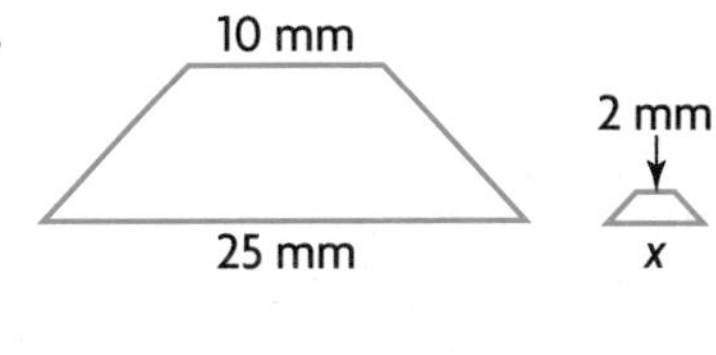

28. **CIRCUMFERENCE** Mary jogged 4 times around a circular garden with a radius of 24 ft. About how many yards did she jog?

A 140 yd **B** 200 yd
C 600 yd **D** 1,800 yd

29. **STATISTICS** Nasir scored 84, 92, 98, 75, and 80 on five tests. What must he score on his sixth test to have an 85 average?

F 78 **G** 81 **H** 88 **J** 90

MORE PRACTICE Lesson 17.2, page H66

LESSON 17.3

What You'll Learn
How to use different types of map scales

Why Learn This?
To find your way in unfamiliar places

ALGEBRA CONNECTION

Using Maps

Maps are drawings of such areas as continents, countries, states, districts, counties, cities, towns, and neighborhoods.

- What other places have you seen maps of?

There are different types of maps. Some show the relative positions of locations but are not drawn to scale. When maps are drawn to scale, distances on the map are in proportion to the real-life figures. To find distances between locations, you need a map with a scale.

Scales on maps are often shown with line segments that are labeled with the number of miles they represent. You can measure the segment in customary or metric units—it is your choice.

Study the map of Washington, D.C., shown below. Look at the scale and the famous landmarks on the map. You can use the map to find the straight-line distance between the Lincoln Memorial and the Capitol.

HISTORY LINK

Benjamin Banneker assisted in the survey and layout of Washington, D.C. His tools were probably a chain, a compass, and a transit (for measuring angles). What would you use to measure an angle?

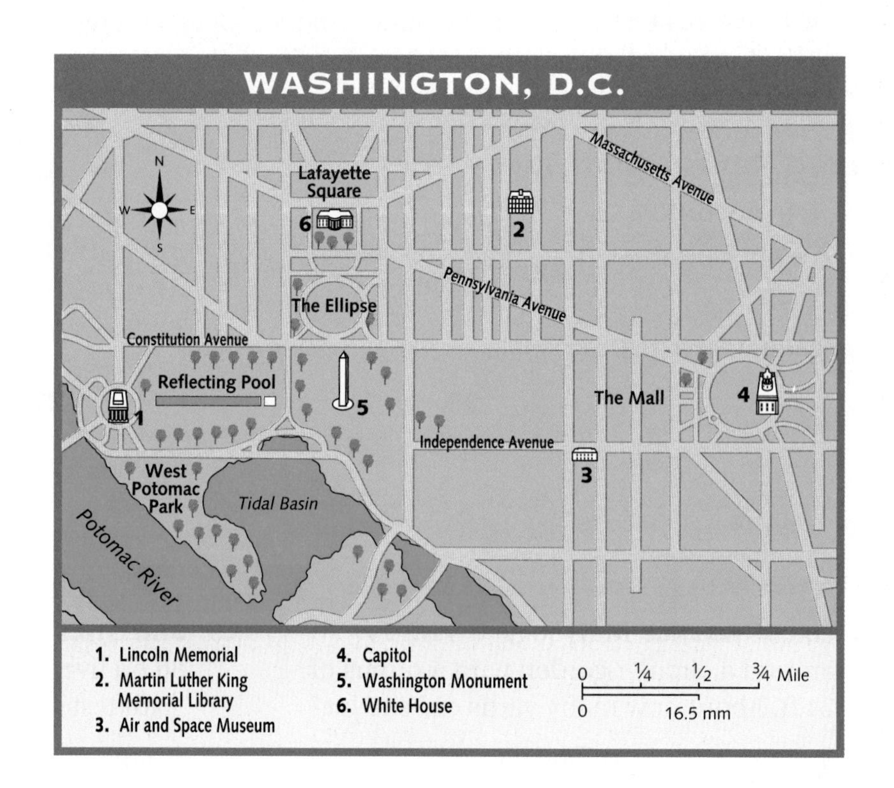

The Lincoln Memorial and the Capitol are about 85 mm apart on the map.

Measure the distance between the two locations on the map.

scale → $16.5 \text{ mm}:\frac{1}{2}\text{ mi}$ or $\frac{33 \text{ mm}}{1 \text{ mi}}$

Write the given scale as a ratio of the map distance to the actual distance.

scale → $\frac{33}{1} = \frac{85}{d}$ ← ratio of map distance to actual distance

Write and solve a proportion. Let d = the actual distance.

$$33d = 85 \times 1$$

$$33d = 85$$

$$\frac{33d}{33} = \frac{85}{33}$$

$$d \approx 2.58$$

So, the actual straight-line distance between the Lincoln Memorial and the Capitol is a little more than 2.5 mi, or $2\frac{1}{2}$ mi.

EXAMPLE Samantha and Andy are at the Washington Monument and want to walk to the Lincoln Memorial. On the map on page 338, they measure a distance of about $1\frac{1}{4}$ in., or 1.25 in. What is the actual distance?

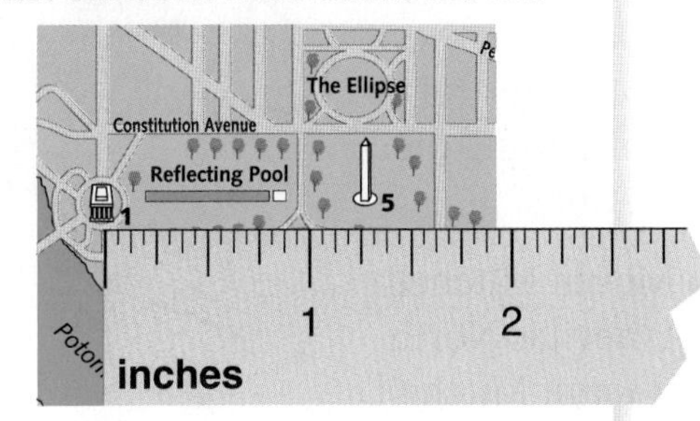

Use the scale, written as a ratio of inches to miles, to write and solve a proportion.

scale → 1 in.:0.75 mi

scale → $\frac{1}{0.75} = \frac{1.25}{d}$ ← $\frac{\text{map distance}}{\text{actual distance}}$

$$1d = 1.25 \times 0.75$$

$$d = 0.9375$$

So, the actual distance is a little less than 1 mi.

Use the map on page 338.

- Suppose you are at the Washington Monument. About how far are you from the White House?
- What is the actual distance between the Capitol and the White House?

SOCIAL STUDIES LINK

The map scales in this lesson are called *verbal scales.* Map scales can also be written as ratios called *fractional scales*, which do not use units of distance. A fractional scale of 1:10,000, for example, means that any distance on the map is 10,000 times longer on the earth's surface. How would the verbal scale of 1 in. = 10 mi be written as a fractional scale?

(HINT: 10 mi = __?__ in.)

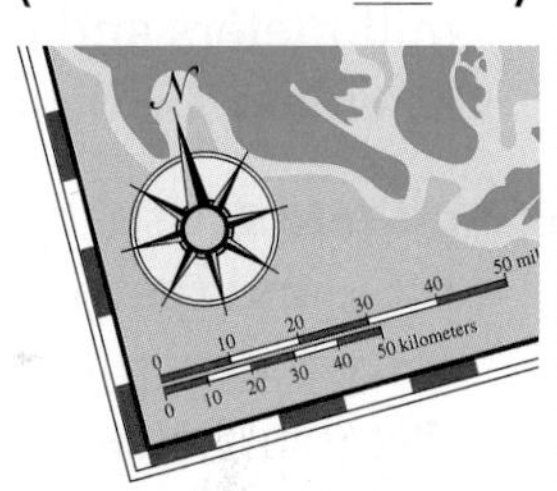

INDEPENDENT PRACTICE

Write and solve a proportion to find the actual distance using a map scale of 1 in.:4 mi.

1. map distance: 12 in.
2. map distance: 15 in.
3. map distance: $\frac{1}{2}$ in.
4. map distance: $1\frac{1}{2}$ in.
5. map distance: $2\frac{3}{4}$ in.
6. map distance: $5\frac{1}{4}$ in.

Write and solve a proportion to find the actual distance using a map scale of 1 in.:12 mi.

7. map distance: 3 in.
8. map distance: 7 in.
9. map distance: $\frac{1}{4}$ in.
10. map distance: $1\frac{1}{4}$ in.
11. map distance: $3\frac{3}{4}$ in.
12. map distance: $6\frac{1}{2}$ in.

Problem-Solving Applications

13. DISTANCE Mr. and Mrs. Menendez plan to arrive at Washington National Airport and drive to nearby Georgetown University to visit their daughter. Use the map to find the straight-line distance in miles from the airport to the university. Use both millimeters and inches to measure and calculate the distance.

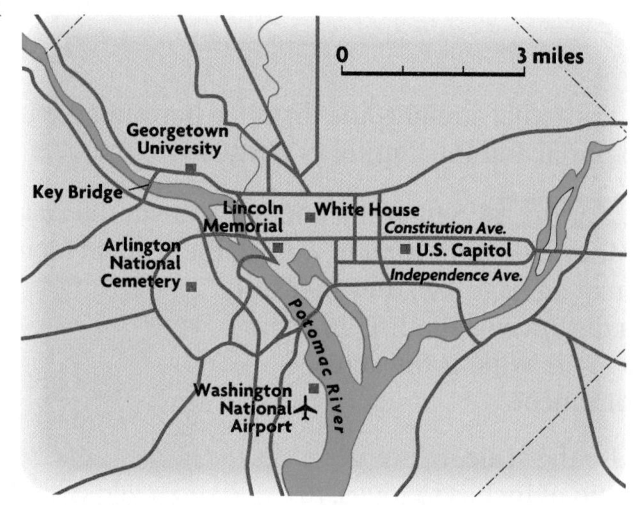

14. DISTANCE Use the map of Washington, D.C., and the given scale to write and solve a new problem about finding the distance between two locations.

15. SPORTS The Assault on Mount Mitchell bicycle race runs from Asheville, North Carolina, to the peak of Mount Mitchell, the highest mountain in the eastern United States. On a map, the distance is about $1\frac{3}{4}$ in. If the scale is $\frac{3}{4}$ in.:15 mi, what is the actual distance of the race?

16. An Explorer troop is rafting down the Colorado River through Grand Canyon National Park from the Little Colorado River to Lava Point Rapids. About how far will they travel in miles and in kilometers?

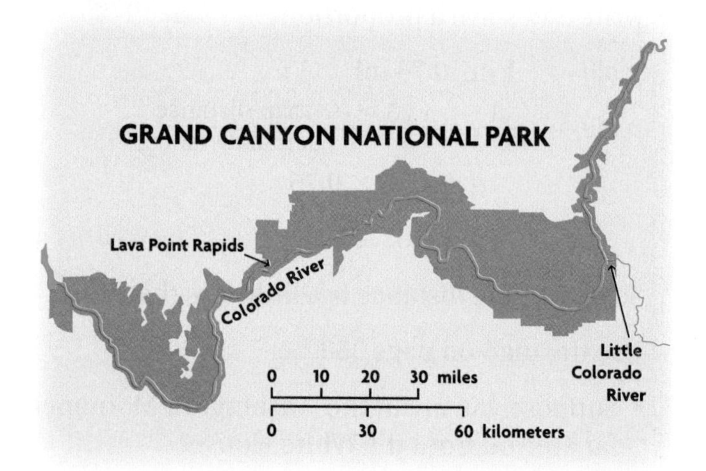

17. WRITE ABOUT IT Describe how to use a map scale to estimate a distance.

MORE PRACTICE Lesson 17.3, page H66

ALGEBRA CONNECTION

LESSON 17.4

Indirect Measurement

What You'll Learn
How to use similar figures to measure lengths and distances indirectly

Why Learn This?
To measure distances that are difficult or impossible to measure directly

VOCABULARY
indirect measurement

Did you know that you can measure the heights of tall buildings, towers, and trees without leaving the ground? You can use **indirect measurement**. To use this method, you draw and label similar figures, measure distances that are convenient, and set up and solve a proportion.

EXAMPLE 1 A tree casts a 32-ft shadow at the time of day when a yardstick casts an 8-ft shadow. How tall is the tree?

Since the tree is taller than the man, it is probably taller than 6 ft. It is shorter than the house, so it is probably less than 20 ft. A possible estimate is 10 ft.

Estimate the height of the tree by comparing its height with familiar heights.

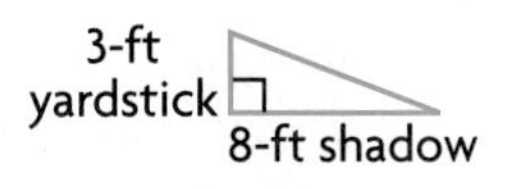

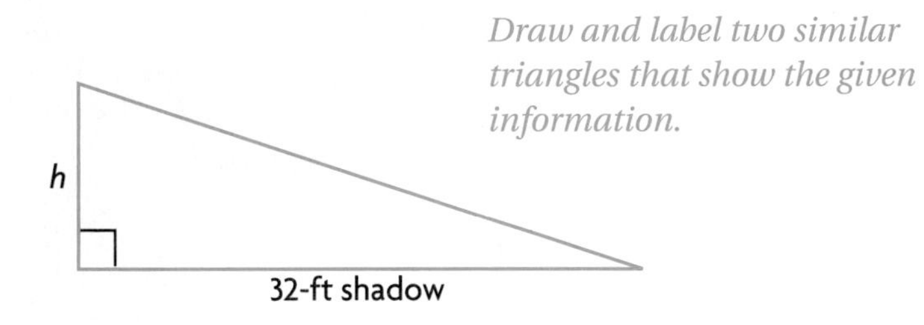

Draw and label two similar triangles that show the given information.

$$\frac{3}{h} = \frac{8}{32}$$
$$8h = 3 \times 32$$
$$8h = 96$$
$$h = 12$$

Since the triangles are similar, you can write and solve a proportion, using the ratios of the corresponding sides.

So, the height of the tree is 12 feet.

- Compare this solution with the estimate. Does it seem reasonable? Explain.

To find a distance that you can't measure directly, you can include it as one side of a right triangle. Then draw a similar triangle whose corresponding side is easier to measure directly.

EXAMPLE 2 Cedric needs to know the distance across the river. How can he find it without measuring it directly?

To find the distance, x, across the river, Cedric draws a diagram of similar right triangles. Then he measures two sides of the small triangle, and the side of the large triangle that is on land.

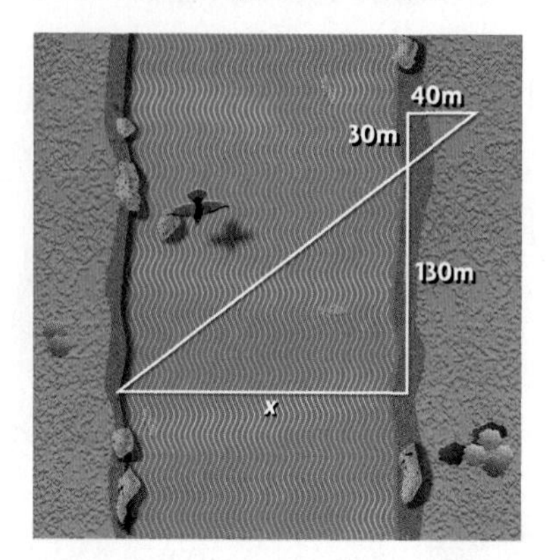

Draw a diagram of two similar figures.

Since the triangles are similar, Cedric uses the ratios of the corresponding sides to write a proportion.

$$\frac{30}{130} = \frac{40}{x}$$

Write and solve a proportion to find x.

$$30x = 40 \times 130$$

$$30x = 5{,}200$$

$$\frac{30x}{30} = \frac{5{,}200}{30}$$

5200  30  173.3333333

$$x = 173.\overline{3}$$

So, the distance across the river is about 173 m.

TEEN TIMES

Small handheld devices called GPS receivers are used by hikers, boaters, and even golfers to find their location and to find distances between locations. These receivers pick up signals from a system of 24 Global Positioning System satellites launched by NASA.

GUIDED PRACTICE

The triangles in each pair are similar. Find x.

1.

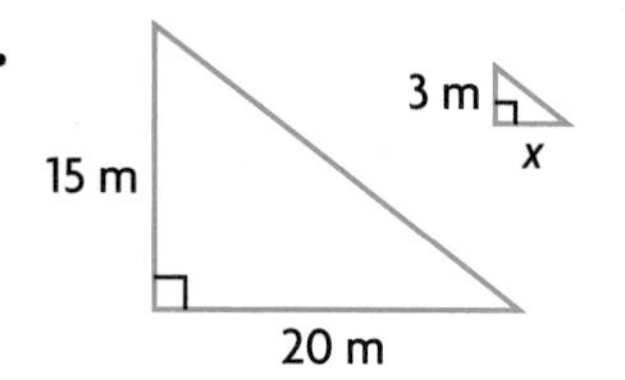

2.

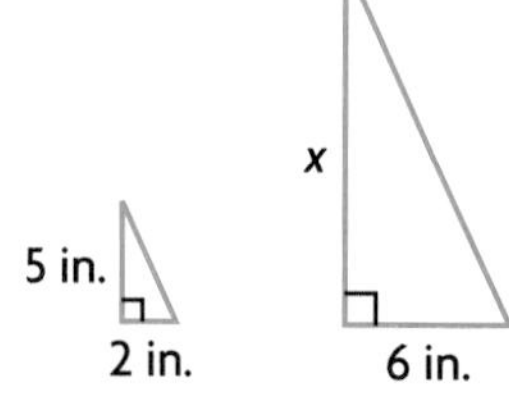

3.

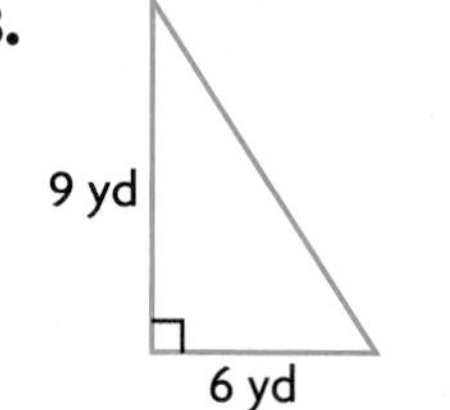

INDEPENDENT PRACTICE

The triangles in each pair are similar. Find *x*.

1.

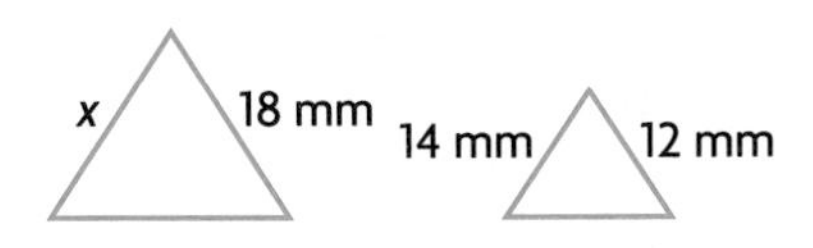

2.

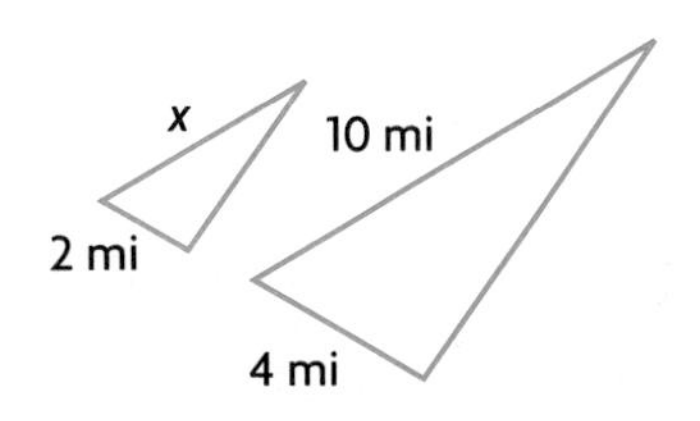

3.

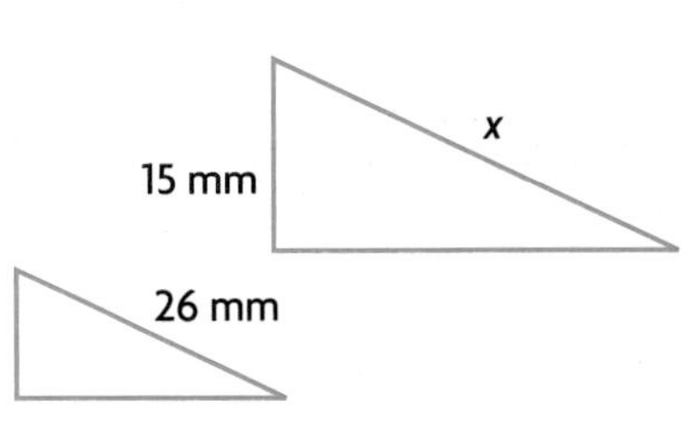

4.

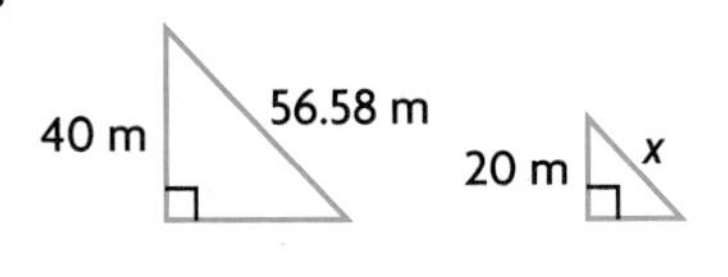

5.

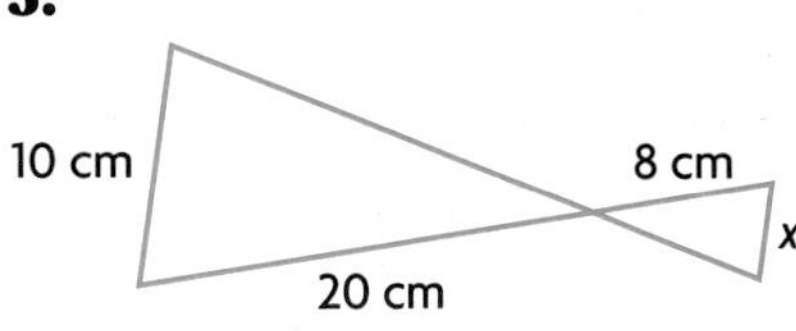

6.

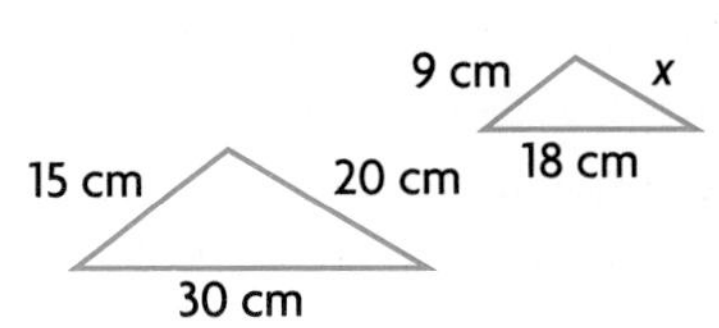

Problem-Solving Applications

7. **PROPORTION** A flagpole casts a shadow 8 m long at the same time a neighboring pole, 4 m high, casts a 2-m shadow. How tall is the flagpole?

4 m
2 m
8 m

8. **COMPARE** Brigit and her father stand next to each other. Brigit is 130 cm tall and her father is 200 cm tall. Brigit's shadow is 100 cm long. About how long is her father's shadow?

9. **WRITE ABOUT IT** Write a problem like Example 2 on page 342. Use a diagram to show the solution.

Mixed Review and Test Prep

Write the ratio as a decimal.

10. 4:5 **11.** $\frac{5}{4}$ **12.** $\frac{16}{10}$ **13.** 10:16 **14.** 6:5

The scale factor for the lengths of the sides of two similar polygons is given. Find the scale factor for their areas.

15. 3:1 **16.** $\frac{2}{5}$ **17.** 7:4 **18.** $\frac{6}{7}$ **19.** 9:4

20. **TRANSFORMATIONS** A triangle has vertices at $(^-2,5)$, $(^-2,^-3)$, and $(^-5,8)$. Where will the vertices of the triangle be if it is reflected across the *y*-axis?

A $(^-2,^-5)$, $(^-2,3)$, $(^-5,^-8)$
B $(5,^-2)$, $(^-3,^-2)$, $(8,^-5)$
C $(2,5)$, $(2,^-3)$, $(5,8)$
D $(2,^-5)$, $(2,3)$, $(5,^-8)$

21. **PATTERNS** Randall has 100 jelly beans. He offers some to his friends. The first friend takes 1, the next takes 4, the next takes 9, and the next takes 16. At that rate, how many friends will be able to take jelly beans before they are all gone?

F 7 **G** 6
H 5 **J** 4

MORE PRACTICE Lesson 17.4, page H67

LESSON 17.5

Golden Rectangles

What You'll Learn
How similarity is related to Golden Ratios and Golden Rectangles

Why Learn This?
To recognize a common pattern in the world

VOCABULARY

Golden Rectangle

Golden Ratio

A rectangle with a length-to-width ratio of $\frac{1 + \sqrt{5}}{2}$, or approximately 1.61 to 1 is called a **Golden Rectangle**. Any ratio that has a decimal value of approximately 1.61 is commonly called a **Golden Ratio**. The Golden Rectangle is pleasing to the eye and has been described as the perfect rectangle.

There are many examples of the Golden Ratio in nature, art, and architecture. The Parthenon, shown below, is one of the most famous examples of Greek architecture in which you can see the Golden Rectangle.

Because all Golden Rectangles have the same length-to-width ratio of approximately 1.61 to 1, all Golden Rectangles appear to be similar.

- Do you see any rectangles in your classroom that appear to be Golden Rectangles?

HISTORY LINK

The Parthenon is a temple that was built during the fifth century B.C. in Athens, Greece. Find another example in architecture of the use of the Golden Ratio or the Golden Rectangle.

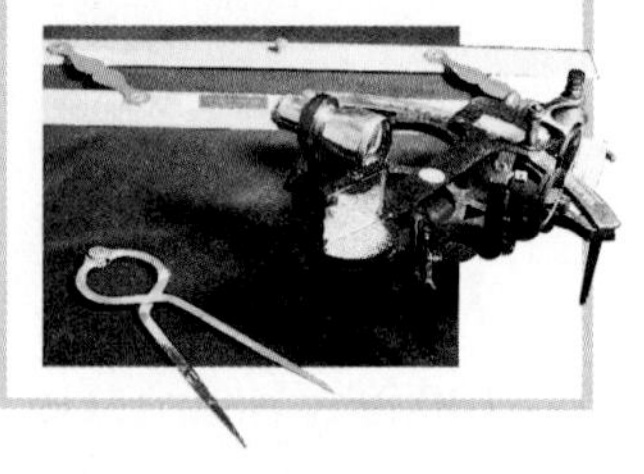

GUIDED PRACTICE

1. Draw a rectangle that is 5 in. × 8 in. Does it appear to be a Golden Rectangle? Explain.
2. Draw three new rectangles that are similar to your first rectangle. Do they appear to be Golden Rectangles? Explain.
3. Use a calculator to find a decimal value for $\frac{1 + \sqrt{5}}{2}$, the Golden Ratio.
4. How can you determine whether the rectangle outlined in the photograph is a Golden Rectangle?

Calculator Activities, page H31

INDEPENDENT PRACTICE

Is the rectangle a Golden Rectangle? Explain.

1. $l = 13$, $w = 8$

2.

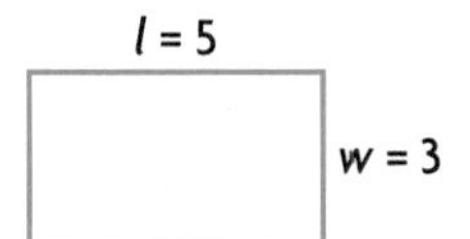

3.

8 in.

10 in.

4.

Math Advantage **USA**
V Gold
5436 756 000 444
01/97 12/98
V
John Q. Public

$w = 2.6$ cm

$l = 4.2$ cm

Draw rectangles with the following dimensions. Do the rectangles appear to be Golden Rectangles? Support your answers.

5.

Length	Width
4.0 cm	2.5 cm

6.

Length	Width
6.8 cm	4.2 cm

7.

Length	Width
12.5 cm	6.5 cm

8.

Length	Width
18 mm	10 mm

9.

Length	Width
1.5 in.	0.75 in.

10.

Length	Width
20.4 mm	12.6 mm

Problem-Solving Applications

For Exercises 11–16, use a compass and a straightedge to construct a Golden Rectangle without any measuring or computation.

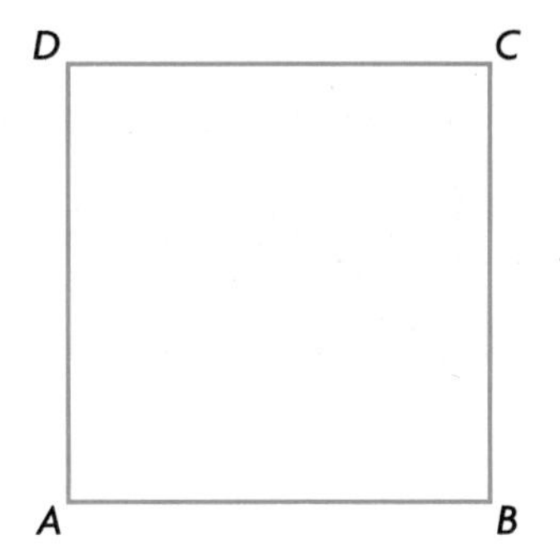

11. CONSTRUCTION Construct any square *ABCD*.

12. CONSTRUCTION Bisect segment *AB* at point *N*.

13. With the point of the compass at *N* and the pencil at *C*, draw an arc from *C* to a point below segment *AB*.

14. GEOMETRY Extend ray *AB* to intersect the arc at *E*.

15. Extend ray *DC*.

16. CONSTRUCTION Construct segment *EF* perpendicular to segment *AE* so that ray *DC* intersects ray *EF* at *F*. Rectangle *ADFE* is a Golden Rectangle.

17. WRITE ABOUT IT A rectangle has length 7 cm and width 3 cm. Is it a Golden Rectangle? Explain.

MORE PRACTICE Lesson 17.5, page H67

CHAPTER 17 Review/Test

Use the scale factor to draw a similar figure. (pages 330–331)

1. scale factor: $\frac{1}{3}$

2. scale factor: $\frac{1}{2}$

3. scale factor: 1.5

36 mm
24 mm
18 mm

4. scale factor: $\frac{1}{4}$

5. scale factor: $\frac{1}{3}$

6. scale factor: $\frac{1}{2}$

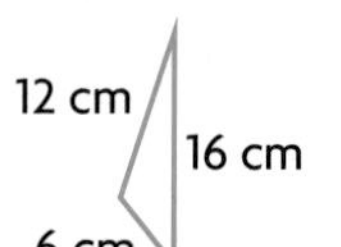

7. VOCABULARY A drawing that has the same shape as the object it represents and whose dimensions are related by a ratio, or scale, to the dimensions of the object is a(n) __?__ . (page 334)

Use the scale 1 cm:8 cm to find the missing dimension. (pages 334–337)

8. drawing: 2 cm actual: __?__ cm

9. drawing: 8.5 cm actual: __?__ cm

10. drawing __?__ cm actual: 84 cm

11. drawing: __?__ cm actual: 112 cm

12. drawing: 30 cm actual: __?__ cm

13. drawing: __?__ cm actual: 96 cm

Write and solve a proportion to find the actual distance by using a map scale of 1 in.:6 mi. (pages 338–340)

14. map distance: 7.5 in.

15. map distance: $3\frac{3}{4}$ in.

16. map distance: 18 in.

17. map distance: 9.25 in.

18. map distance: 1.5 in.

19. map distance: $8\frac{1}{2}$ in.

20. A building casts a 75-ft shadow at the same time of day a 20-ft pole casts a 15-ft shadow. How tall is the building? (pages 341–343)

21. A 25-foot-tall street lamp casts a 20-foot shadow at the same time a 6-foot-tall man casts a shadow. How long is the man's shadow? (pages 341–343)

The triangles of each pair are similar. Find *x*. (pages 341–343)

22.

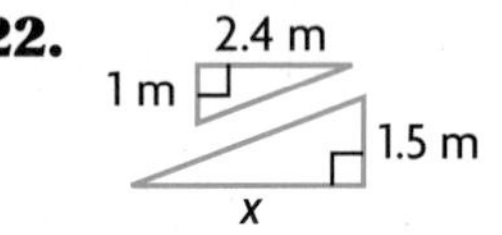

23.

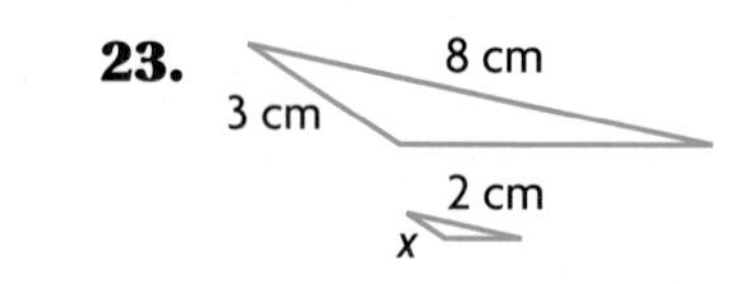

24.

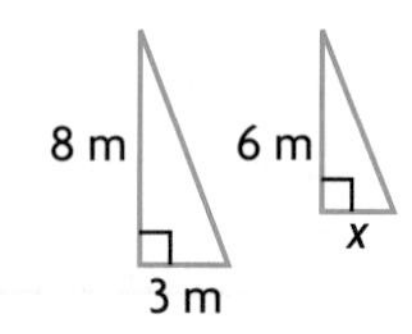

Draw a rectangle with the given dimensions. Does it appear to be a Golden Rectangle? Explain. (pages 344–345)

25. length: 16 cm, width: 10 cm

26. length: 36 m, width: 24 m

27. length: 14.5 mm, width: 9 mm

28. length: 66 cm, width: 41 cm

29. length: 9.7 in., width: 6 in.

30. length: 12 cm, width: 8 cm

Test Prep

CUMULATIVE
CHAPTERS 1–17

1. A building casts a 60-foot shadow at the same time of day a 15-foot pole casts a 12-foot shadow. How tall is the building?

A 48 ft
B 55 ft
C 57 ft
D 75 ft

2. The pep club sold program books at a football game. They sold 84 books out of 120 books. What percent of the books did they sell?

F 84%
G 75%
H 70%
J 30%

3. What are the coordinates of point *P*?

A $(4,{}^-3)$
B $({}^-3,{}^-4)$
C $(3,{}^-4)$
D $({}^-3,4)$

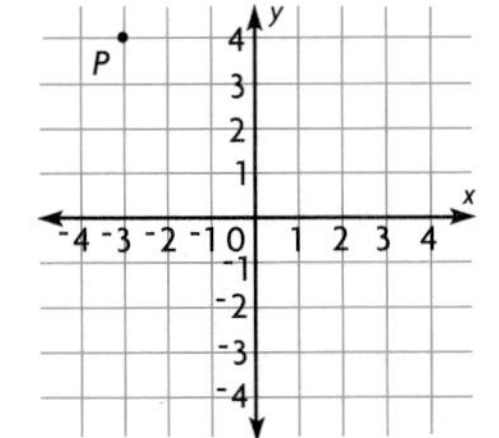

4. The scale factor for the sides of 2 similar figures is 3 to 4. What is the scale factor for their areas?

F 3 to 4
G 6 to 8
H 9 to 16
J 27 to 64

5. The scale on a map is 1 inch:150 miles. If the distance between two cities on the map is 4.5 inches, what is the actual distance?

A 750 mi
B 675 mi
C 600 mi
D 450 mi

6. A rectangle has length 9 millimeters and width 6 millimeters. What are the dimensions of a similar rectangle with scale factor $\frac{3}{4}$?

F $l = 12$ mm, $w = 8$ mm
G $l = 12$ mm, $w = 9$ mm
H $l = 6\frac{3}{4}$ mm, $w = 4\frac{1}{2}$ mm
J $l = 6$ mm, $w = 4$ mm

7. What is the solution of the equation $25x = 2{,}500$?

A $x = {}^-21$
B $x = 0.16$
C $x = 6.25$
D $x = 100$

8. Harry can run 4 laps in 12 minutes. At this rate, how many laps can he run in 45 minutes?

F 8
G 12
H 15
J 18

9. $37 - {}^-85 =$

A $^-122$
B $^-48$
C 48
D 122

10. M & C Records sold 20,000 CDs last year. The store sold $\frac{1}{2}$ of them between January and June. Of the remaining CDs, $\frac{3}{5}$ were sold in December. How many CDs did the store sell in December?

F 10,000
G 8,000
H 6,000
J 4,000
K Not Here

CHAPTERS 14–17

MATH FUN!

ALL THAT GLITTERS IS NOT GOLD

PURPOSE To practice finding Golden Ratios (pages 286–288)

YOU WILL NEED old magazines or newspapers

Find pictures of your favorite celebrities in sports or entertainment. Then mark and measure their faces as you did in the activity on page 287. Show in which of your celebrities' faces you are able to find Golden Ratios.

Time for Tessellations

PURPOSE To practice drawing similar figures (pages 317–319)

YOU WILL NEED paper, ruler, scissors, pencil, glue or tape

Designs on tile walls and floors are often tessellations. You can use any quadrilateral or triangle in a tessellation. Use a ruler to draw five triangles and five quadrilaterals, each having at least one side that is 4 cm long. Use the scale factor $\frac{3}{2}$ to make a similar figure for each of your figures. Cut out your figures, and tape or glue them onto a piece of paper to make your own tessellation. Color your design, and display your finished project for your classmates to enjoy.

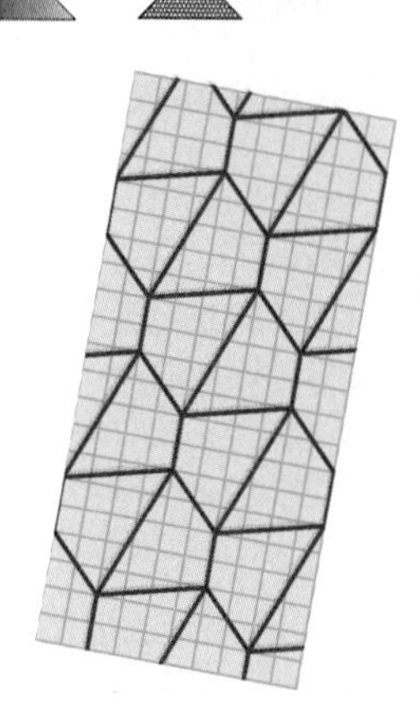

NESTING BLOCKS

PURPOSE To practice using scale factors to draw similar figures (pages 330–331)

YOU WILL NEED 5 sheets of paper, pencil, ruler, tape, a copy of the rectangular prism net

Cut out the net. Cut off one face so that, after assembly, you will have an open box. Measure and record the length, width, and height.

Using a scale factor of 0.8, draw a net similar to the one you cut out. Use the scale factor to draw three more nets that are similar, each one smaller than the previous one. Cut out each net and assemble into a box. After assembly, the boxes will fit inside one another, giving you a set of nesting blocks.

HOME NOTE Make a list of similar-looking figures, such as cereal boxes or pizza boxes. Write proportions to see if the sides are proportional. Add to your list as you notice more figures.

CHAPTERS 14–17

Similar Triangles

A spreadsheet has many uses. In this activity you will see how to use a spreadsheet to solve for missing lengths of similar triangles.

The triangles below are similar. Find the missing length.

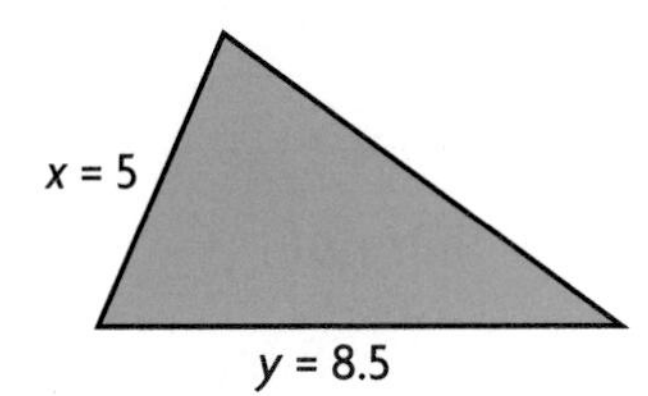

$x' = 3.2$

$y' = ?$

To solve for y', you can use a spreadsheet to solve the proportion $\frac{5}{3.2} = \frac{8.5}{y'}$.

Label the columns as shown below. Enter the values for x, x', and y. Then enter the formula shown to find the value of y'.

The spreadsheet will then calculate the value of y'.

untitled 3

All	A	B	C	D
1	x	x'	y	y'
2	5	3.2	8.5	=(B2*C2)/A2
3				
4				
5				
6				

untitled 3

All	A	B	C	D
1	x	x'	y	y'
2	5	3.2	8.5	5.44
3				
4				
5				
6				

1. What do A2, B2, and C2 represent in the formula in cell D2?

2. The formula in cell D2 gives the solution of what proportion?

3. How could you copy the formula to other cells in column D?

4. What is the value of y'?

USING THE SPREADSHEET

The triangles are similar. Use a spreadsheet to find the missing length.

5. $x = 3$, $y = 4.5$; $x' = 2.5$, $y' = ?$

6. $x = 10$, $y = 14.75$; $x' = 9.2$, $y' = ?$

CHAPTERS 14–17

Study Guide and Review

Vocabulary Check

1. A rate that is described in terms of one unit of measure is a(n) _?_ rate. (page 281)

2. A ratio that is approximately equal to 1.61 is the _?_. (page 286)

3. Similar figures have sides that are _?_. (page 313)

EXAMPLES

- **Find unit rates and unit prices.** (pages 280–283)

Caryn is paid $183.75 for 35 hr of work. What is her rate of pay per hour, or unit rate?

$183.75 ÷ 35 = $5.25 ← unit rate

So, Caryn's rate is $5.25 per hour.

EXERCISES

Find the unit rate.

4. 520 mi in 8 hr, or _?_ mi per hr
5. 4,980 m in 12 hr, or _?_ m per hr

Find the unit price.

6. 5 lb of detergent for $5.25
7. 10 lb of detergent for $9.75

EXAMPLES

- **Change ratios to percents by using proportions.** (pages 294–296)

$\frac{3}{12} = \frac{n}{100}$ *Find cross products.*

$12n = 300$ *Solve for n.*

$n = 25$ ← So, $\frac{3}{12} = 25\%$.

EXERCISES

Write each ratio as a percent.

8. $\frac{4}{5}$
9. 3:2
10. $\frac{7}{8}$
11. $\frac{6}{25}$
12. 9 to 10
13. 5 to 1

EXAMPLES

- **Find the percent one number is of another.** (pages 301–303)

What percent of 40 is 4?

↓ ↓ ↓↓

$p \times 40 = 4$ *Write an equation.*

$40p = 4$ *Solve for p.*

$p = \frac{1}{10}$, or 10%

EXERCISES

Find the percent.

14. What percent of 80 is 24?
15. 40 is what percent of 160?
16. What percent of 23 is 69?

EXAMPLES

- **Find a number when a percent of it is known.** (pages 304–307)

21 is 70% of what number?

$70\% \text{ of } n = 21$ *Write an equation.*

$0.7n = 21$ *Change to a decimal.*

$n = 30$ *Solve for n.*

EXERCISES

Solve.

17. 74 is 10% of what number?
18. 60% of what number is 90?
19. 18 is 80% of what number?

- **Use proportions to find unknown lengths of sides of similar figures.** (pages 317–319)

The figures are similar. Find n.

$\frac{4}{12} = \frac{3}{n}$ *Write a proportion.*

$4n = 36$ *Find cross products.*

$n = 9$ *Solve for n.*

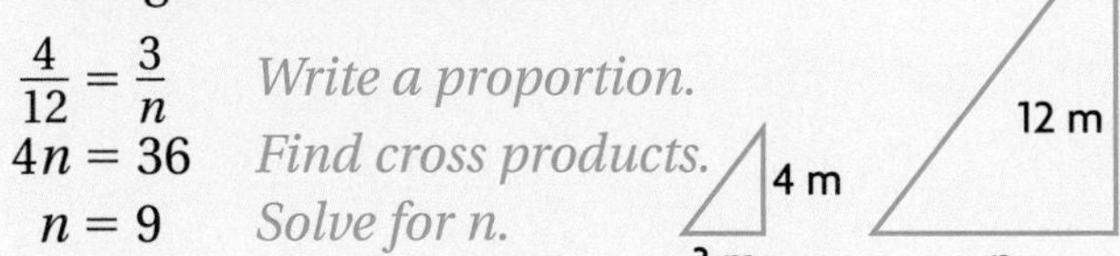

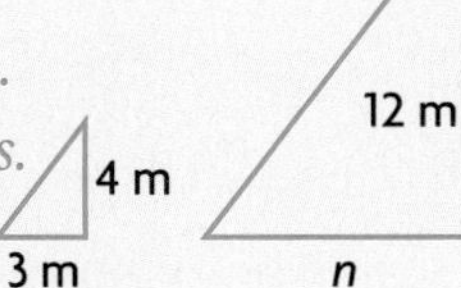

The figures in each pair are similar. Use a proportion to find the unknown length.

20.

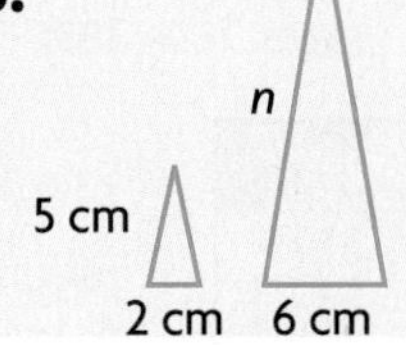

21.

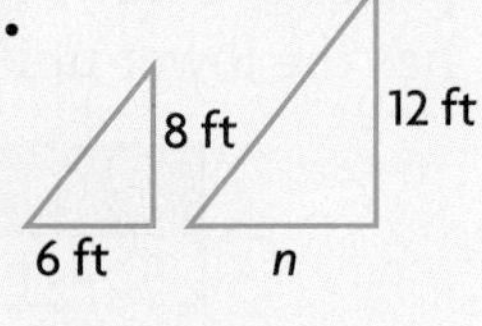

- **Find the scale factor that relates areas or volumes of similar figures.** (pages 320–325)

original *enlargement*

$A = 3 \times 4 \rightarrow$scale factor: $3 \rightarrow A = 9 \times 12$

$A = 12$ $A = 108$

$\frac{\text{area or volume of enlargement}}{\text{area or volume of original}} = \frac{108}{12} = \frac{9}{1}$

So, the scale factor relating the areas is 9.

22. A picture is 2 in. $\times$ 3 in. It is enlarged by a scale factor of 3. What is the scale factor relating the areas?

23. A rectangular prism has the dimensions 4 cm $\times$ 4 cm $\times$ 8 cm. It is enlarged by a scale factor of 2. What is the volume of the first prism? the second? What is the scale factor relating the volumes?

- **Read and interpret scale drawings and map scales.** (pages 334–340)

Use a drawing length of 30 cm and the scale 10 cm:1 cm to find the actual length.

scale $\rightarrow \frac{10}{1} = \frac{30}{n} \leftarrow \frac{\text{drawing length}}{\text{actual length}}$

$10n = 30$ *Find cross products.*

$n = 3$ cm *Solve for n.*

Use the scale 1 cm:5 cm.

24. drawing: 5 cm
actual: _?_ cm

25. drawing: _?_ cm
actual: 15.5 cm

The map scale is 1 in.:25 mi. Find the miles.

26. map distance: 7.5 in.; actual miles: _?_

27. map distance: $3\frac{3}{4}$ in.; actual miles: _?_

Problem-Solving Applications

Solve. Explain your method.

28. Leroy takes 3 min to play a video game from start to finish. Peter takes 4 min. If they start at the same time and play continuously, how many minutes will pass before both start at the same time again? (pages 278–279)

29. Margo's starting pay was \$6.50 an hour. After her 6-month evaluation, she received a 2% pay raise. How much per hour was the raise? What is her new hourly rate? (pages 298–300)

30. Tony bought 2 lb of nectarines for \$2.24. Robyn bought 3 lb of nectarines for \$3.45. Who got the better buy? Explain. (pages 280–283)

31. A building casts a 96-ft shadow at the same time of day a 12-ft pole casts a 32-ft shadow. How tall is the building? (pages 341–343)

CHAPTERS 14–17

Performance Assessment

Tasks: Show What You Know

1. Explain each step as you find the unit prices of these items. Tell which package has the lower unit price. (pages 280–283)

Cheese	
10-oz package	$1.79
16-oz package	$2.99

2. Explain each step as you find 30% of 55. (pages 298–300)

3. Draw a rectangle with a length of 7.5 cm and a width of 4.5 cm. Explain how you would find the dimensions of a smaller rectangle, using the scale factor $\frac{2}{3}$. Draw the similar rectangle. (pages 312–315)

4. The map distance is 6.5 in. and the map scale is 1 in. : 6 mi. Explain each step as you write and solve a proportion to find the actual distance. (pages 338–340)

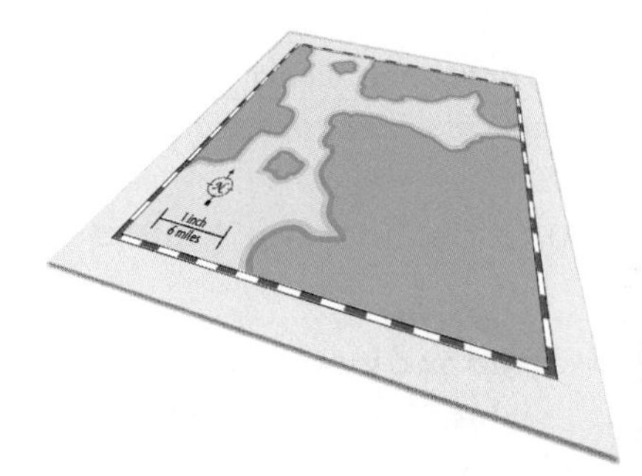

Problem Solving

Solve. Explain your method.

CHOOSE a strategy and a tool.

- Find a Pattern
- Make a Model
- Write an Equation
- Act It Out
- Draw a Picture

Paper/Pencil
Calculator

Hands-On

Mental Math

5. Wanda plays the piano and has a weekly schedule for her practice. She practices 20 min every Monday, 28 min on Tuesdays, and 36 min on Wednesdays. If she continues this pattern, on what day does Wanda practice for an hour? (pages 278–279)

6. Dwayne spends 25% of his allowance on entertainment, 20% on savings, and 55% on clothing. Draw a circle graph to show this information, and give the measure of each central angle. (pages 298–300)

7. The dimensions of a small cereal box are 5 in. × 4 in. × 1.25 in. The small cereal box sells for $0.50. The dimensions of a large cereal box are greater by a scale factor of 2. What are the dimensions and volume of the larger box? What is a reasonable estimate of its cost, based on its volume? Use the formula $V = l \times w \times h$. (pages 323–325)

8. Kim and his father, who is 6 ft tall, visited the Washington Monument in Washington, D.C. The monument cast a 1,110-ft shadow at the same time that Kim's father cast a 12-ft shadow. How tall is the Washington Monument? (pages 341–343)

Cumulative Review

CHAPTERS 1–17

Solve the problem. Then write the letter of the correct answer.

1. Which decimal is equivalent to $\frac{2}{5}$? (pages 26–29)

A. 0.25 **B.** 0.40
C. 2.5 **D.** not here

2. Choose the best estimate. (pages 62–65)

$24.5 + 81.2 + 33.9$

A. 100 **B.** 120
C. 135 **D.** 200

3. Divide. Write the answer in simplest form. (pages 88–91)

$\frac{9}{10} \div \frac{4}{5}$

A. $\frac{18}{25}$ **B.** $\frac{8}{9}$
C. $\frac{9}{8}$, or $1\frac{1}{8}$ **D.** not here

4. Find the sum. (pages 109–111)

$^-5\frac{2}{5} + {}^-3\frac{3}{10}$

A. $^-8\frac{7}{10}$ **B.** $^-8\frac{5}{15}$
C. $^-2\frac{1}{10}$ **D.** $8\frac{7}{10}$

5. Solve. $x + 3x - x + 6 = 36$ (pages 164–166)

A. $x = {}^-10$ **B.** $x = 10$
C. $x = 14$ **D.** $x = 30$

6. Solve. $12x + 14 - 3x = 41$ (pages 164–166)

A. $x = 3$ **B.** $x = 9$
C. $x = 15$ **D.** $x = 27$

7. Solve. $\frac{x}{3} \leq {}^-1$ (pages 170–171)

A. $x \leq 3$
B. $x \geq 3$
C. $x \leq {}^-3$
D. $x \geq {}^-3$

8. What is the location of point *A*? (pages 176–177)

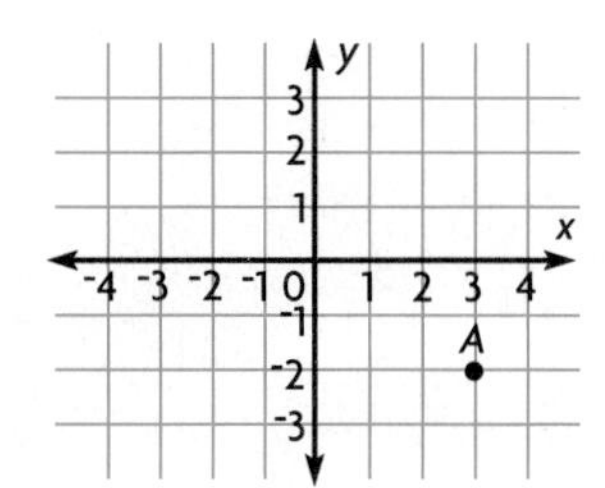

A. $(^-2,0)$ **B.** $(^-2,3)$
C. $(3,^-2)$ **D.** not here

9. How are the following triangles shown to be congruent? (pages 224–227)

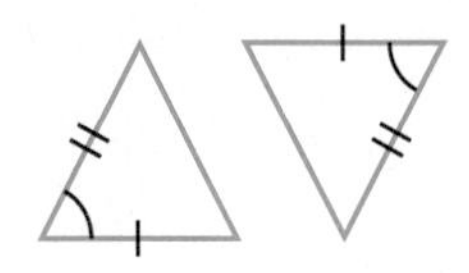

A. SSS **B.** SAS
C. ASA **D.** AAA

10. What is the unit rate if \$230.00 is paid for 40 hr of work? (pages 280–283)

A. \$5.75 **B.** \$57.50
C. \$575 **D.** \$9,200

11. What is 25% of 150? (pages 298–300)

A. 6 **B.** 25
C. 37.5 **D.** not here

12. Use a map distance of 5.5 in. and a scale of 1 in.:22 mi to find the actual distance. (pages 338–340)

A. 4 mi
B. 27.5 mi
C. 110 mi
D. 121 mi

CHAPTER

18 GROWING AND SHRINKING PATTERNS

LOOK AHEAD

In this chapter you will solve problems that involve

- triangular numbers
- Pascal's triangle
- geometry
- exponents and powers

Companies spend billions of dollars a year advertising their products. The table below shows the amount of money spent advertising some products in 1996.

1996 ADVERTISING DOLLARS	
Category	**Amount**
Automotive	$11.6 billion
Food	$4.0 billion
Computers	$1.6 billion
Sporting goods/toys	$1.3 billion
Pets and pet foods	$0.2 billion

- What was the total amount of money spent on advertising for the five categories?
- Make a circle graph to compare the advertising dollars spent on the five categories in the table.

Problem-Solving Project

Cracker Box Pyramids

Plan a grocery display of cracker boxes. Use the pattern of squares shown below. How many boxes are needed to stack 4 layers? 5 layers? 15 layers? Make a chart and generalize the pattern. Using the pattern of cubes below, find how many boxes are needed for 6 layers. Make a chart and generalize the pattern.

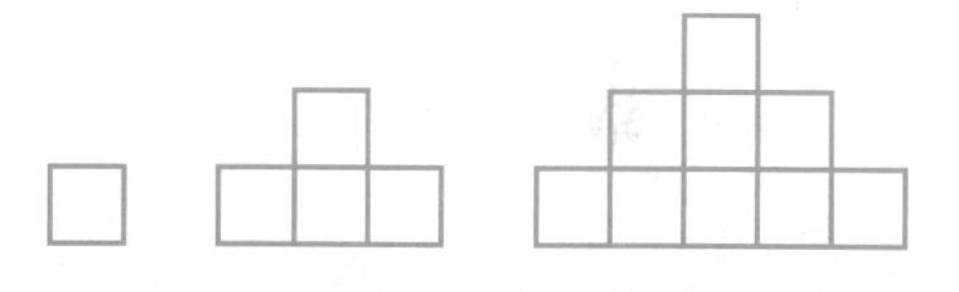

number of layers	1	2	3		
number of boxes					

PROJECT CHECKLIST

- ✓ Did you find a pattern for the squares?
- ✓ Did you make a chart and generalize the pattern?
- ✓ Did you find the pattern for the cubes?
- ✓ Did you make a chart and generalize the pattern?

LESSON 18.1

ALGEBRA CONNECTION

Triangular Arrays

What You'll Learn
How to use patterns to describe and extend triangular arrays

Why Learn This?
To recognize patterns that occur all around you

VOCABULARY
triangular numbers

Growth and change occur in many ways. They can be gradual and take many years, as when a large oak tree develops from a small acorn. Or, they can occur in days, as when a blade of grass sprouts from a tiny seed.

In mathematics you can see growth and change in triangular arrays and numbers. **Triangular numbers** are a special sequence of numbers that can be shown geometrically with triangular arrays. As you build the numbers in the sequence, the arrays become larger and larger.

Bowling pins are arranged in a triangular array. The ten pins are arranged in four rows, with one, two, three, and four pins.

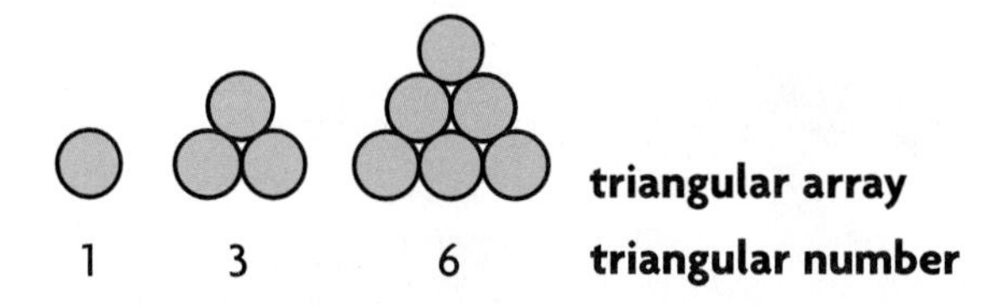

ACTIVITY **WHAT YOU'LL NEED:** counters and a calculator

- Use counters to build the triangular arrays above. Then build arrays to find the next four triangular numbers.
- Make a table like the one started for you to record the number of counters and the first seven triangular numbers.

	First	Second	Third
Number of Counters	1	1 + 2	1 + 2 + 3
Triangular Number	1	3	6

- Describe the pattern you see in the number of counters used in the rows of each array.
- What numbers would you add to find the eighth triangular number?

The first triangular number is 1. From the table you can see that the pattern grows from one triangular number to the next by the addition of the next counting number.

To find the eighth triangular number, for example, you can find the sum of the first eight counting numbers.

$1 + 2 + 3 + 4 + 5 + 6 + 7 + 8 = 36$ ← *eighth triangular number*

You can also use a pattern of adding pairs of numbers. Write the sum both forward and backward in two rows.

$1 + 2 + 3 + 4 + 5 + 6 + 7 + 8$

$8 + 7 + 6 + 5 + 4 + 3 + 2 + 1$

The numbers in each vertical pair—such as 1 and 8, 2 and 7, and 3 and 6—add up to 9. There are 8 pairs, so the sum for the two rows is 8×9, or 72. You want the sum for only one row, so divide by 2 to get 36.

$$\frac{8 \times 9}{2} = 36$$

The nth triangular number is the sum of the first n counting numbers. You can use this formula to find the nth triangular number.

$$1 + 2 + 3 + 4 + \ldots + n = \frac{n(n + 1)}{2}$$

EXAMPLE 1 Use the formula to find the one-hundredth triangular number.

Replace n with 100, and solve.

$$n^{th} \text{ triangular number} = \frac{n(n + 1)}{2}$$

$$100^{th} \text{ triangular number} = \frac{100(100 + 1)}{2} = \frac{100(101)}{2} = \frac{10{,}100}{2} = 5{,}050$$

So, the one-hundredth triangular number is 5,050.

HISTORY LINK

The German mathematician Carl Friedrich Gauss (1777–1855) showed his mathematical ability at an early age. His teacher was amazed when Gauss found the sum of the counting numbers 1–100 right away, without writing anything. Gauss added pairs of numbers that summed 101. Name at least five of those pairs.

GUIDED PRACTICE

1. Use an array to show the sixth triangular number.

2. Find the first triangular number greater than 100.

Use patterns to find the triangular number.

3. tenth **4.** eighteenth **5.** thirteenth

Use the formula to find the triangular number.

6. fiftieth **7.** forty-third **8.** ninety-eighth

Triangular Number Arrays

Many interesting number patterns appear within triangular arrays. The array at the right can be extended by adding rows of counting numbers at the bottom. It can grow and grow without end.

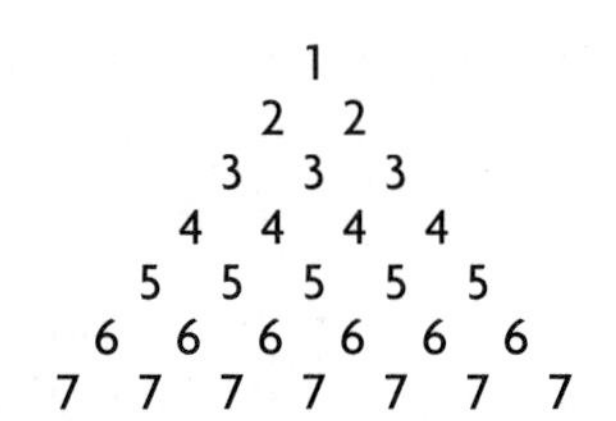

EXAMPLE 2 Add the entries in each row. What pattern do you see in the sums?

1
2 + 2
3 + 3 + 3
4 + 4 + 4 + 4
5 + 5 + 5 + 5 + 5
6 + 6 + 6 + 6 + 6 + 6
7 + 7 + 7 + 7 + 7 + 7 + 7

Row	Sum
1	1
2	4
3	9
4	16
5	25
6	36
7	49

The pattern shows that the sum for each row is equal to the row number squared.

Row 2: sum = 2^2, or 4 Row 5: sum = 5^2, or 25

SPORTS LINK

Billiard balls are also arranged in a triangular array for the start of several popular games. How many rows do 15 billiard balls form in such an array?

Talk About It

- What number will be repeated in Row 12? How many numbers will be in that row? What will be their sum?
- What number will be repeated in Row *n*? How many numbers will be in that row? What will be their sum?

INDEPENDENT PRACTICE

Find the triangular number.

1. ninth **2.** twenty-fifth **3.** fortieth **4.** seventy-fifth

For Exercises 5–6, use the triangular array at the right.

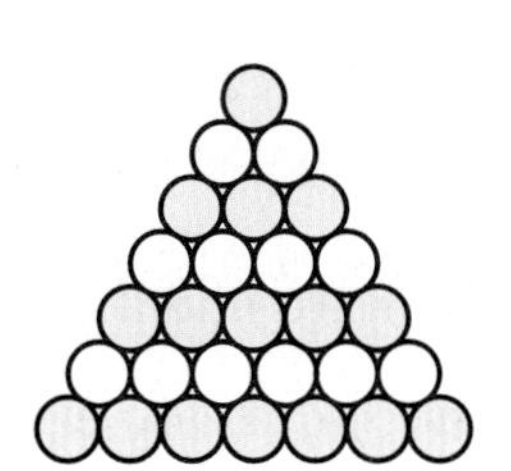

5. How is this triangular array similar to and different from the triangular array in Example 2?

6. What rule was used to determine which circles are shaded and which remain white?

7. Suppose you work in a grocery. Draw a diagram to show how you would make a display of cereal boxes that form a triangular array.

For Exercises 8–10, use the array at the right.

```
            1
          1   2
        1   2   3
      1   2   3   4
    1   2   3   4   5
  1   2   3   4   5   6
1   2   3   4   5   6   7
```

8. What will be the next row in the array? What pattern did you use to find the next row?

9. How many numbers are in each of the rows? How many numbers will be in Row 15? in Row *n*?

10. What is the sum for each of the first seven rows? What will be the sum for Row 8? Explain how to find it.

For Exercises 11–14, use the array at the right.

```
          1
        1 2 1
      1 2 3 2 1
    1 2 3 4 3 2 1
  1 2 3 4 5 4 3 2 1
1 2 3 4 5 6 5 4 3 2 1
```

11. What will be the next row in the array? What pattern did you use?

12. Find the sum for each row shown in the array. Look for a pattern. Use an exponent to express the sum for the *n*th row.

13. How many numbers are in Row 1? Row 2? Row 3? How many will there be in Row 12? Row *n*?

14. Make a new array by replacing the numbers with circles. Shade the odd entries and leave the even ones blank.

Problem-Solving Applications

15. **NUMBER SENSE** Some students want to make a triangular array for a school project. They plan to stack empty boxes 4 levels high. How many boxes will they need?

16. The world record for a triangular array formed by a human pyramid is 9 levels. How many people were used to build an array 9 levels high?

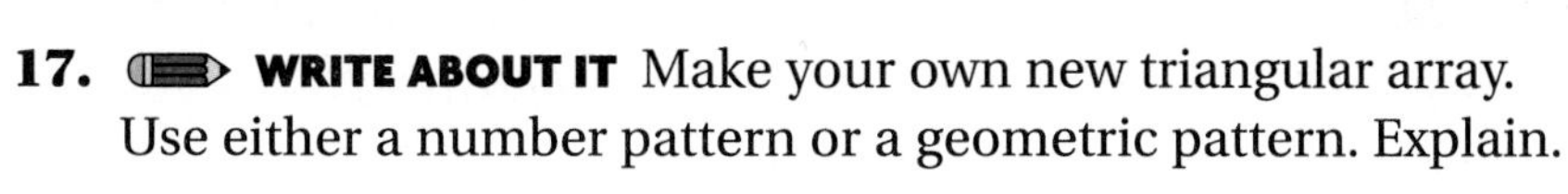

17. **WRITE ABOUT IT** Make your own new triangular array. Use either a number pattern or a geometric pattern. Explain.

Mixed Review and Test Prep

Find the next term in the pattern.

18. 1, 3, 5, 7, . . .

19. 14, 10, 6, 2, . . .

20. 2, 6, 18, 54, . . .

21. 7, 3, $^{-}1$, $^{-}5$, . . .

Write ratios to determine whether the rectangles are similar. Write *yes* or *no*.

22. width 6 cm, length 8 cm
width 10 cm, length 15 cm

23. width 2.5 mm, length 5 mm
width 3 mm, length 6 mm

24. **LOGICAL REASONING** Manuel has two numbers. Their sum is 80. Their difference is 48. One number is 4 times the other. What are the two numbers?

A 32 and 8 **B** 48 and 32
C 48 and 12 **D** 64 and 16

25. **MEASUREMENT** It took Sanya 1 minute to fill her aquarium $\frac{1}{3}$ full. How long will it take her to fill the aquarium $\frac{3}{4}$ full?

F 2 min **G** $2\frac{1}{4}$ min
H $2\frac{1}{2}$ min **J** 3 min

MORE PRACTICE Lesson 18.1, page H67

LESSON 18.2

Pascal's Triangle

What You'll Learn
How to use patterns to extend Pascal's triangle and how to use Pascal's triangle to solve problems

Why Learn This?
To find the number of possible arrangements of beads on bracelets and selections of toppings on pizza

VOCABULARY
Pascal's triangle

Pascal's triangle is a special triangular array of counting numbers. It was developed by a French mathematician named Blaise Pascal in 1653.

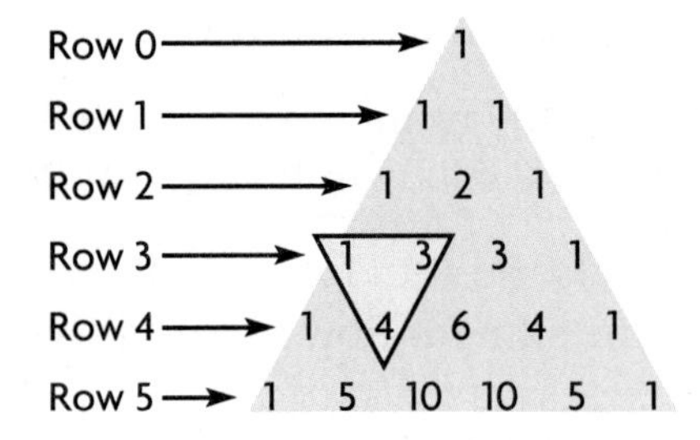

Each row of **Pascal's triangle** starts and ends with a 1.
Each of the other numbers is the sum of the two closest numbers above it. Notice that the 4 in Row 4 is the sum of the 1 and the 3 above it in Row 3.

EXAMPLE 1 Write Row 6 of Pascal's triangle.
Use the numbers from Row 5.

Row 5 → 1 + 5 + 10 + 10 + 5 + 1
Row 6 → 1 6 15 20 15 6 1

- Extend the array to complete Rows 7 and 8.

TEEN TIMES

Jewelry fads, such as wearing friendship bracelets, have long been a part of teen culture. Teens in the 1950's wore long strings of "pop beads," little plastic beads that snapped together to make bracelets and necklaces.

You can use Pascal's triangle to solve problems.

EXAMPLE 2 Lauren has 2 colors of beads, red and white. She wants to string 4 of them in a row. How many ways can she use just 2 red beads in a row of 4 beads?

Look at Row 4, since she has 4 beads.

Row 4 → 1 4 6 4 1
0 1 2 3 4

Each number in Row 4 shows the number of ways she could string the 4 beads with 0, 1, 2, 3, or 4 red beads.

The center column shows there are 6 ways to string 2 red beads in a row of 4 beads.

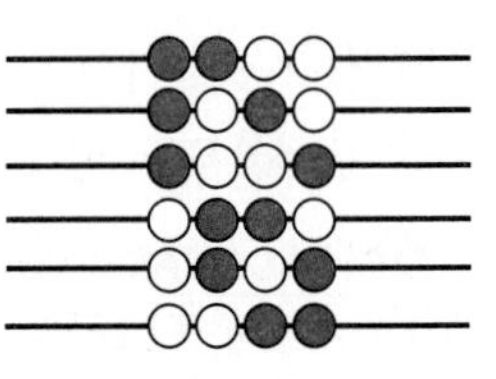

- How many ways are there to string 3 red beads in a row of 4 beads?
- What if you wanted to string 5 beads in a row? What row of Pascal's triangle would you use to find the number of ways to string the red beads?

GUIDED PRACTICE

For Exercises 1–2, use the Pascal's triangle at the right.

Row 0 → 1
1 1
1 2 1
1 3 3 1
1 4 6 4 1
1 5 10 10 5 1
1 6 15 20 15 6 1

1. Find Row 6. The 20 in it is the sum of what two numbers above it in Row 5? Each 15 in this row is the sum of what two numbers above it?

2. What number in Row 7 will be below and between the 6 and 15 in Row 6? Will the same number also be below the 15 and 6?

INDEPENDENT PRACTICE

For Exercises 1–10, use the Pascal's triangle above.

1. Copy Rows 0–6. Then extend the triangle by writing the numbers in Rows 7, 8, and 9.

2. One number above 1,716 in Pascal's triangle is 924. What is the other number above 1,716?

3. Find the sum of the numbers in each of Rows 0–5. What is the pattern of the sums? Use the pattern to find the sum of the numbers in Row 6.

4. The sums for Rows 0–5 can be written as these powers of 2: 2^0, 2^1, 2^2, 2^3, 2^4, 2^5. What power of 2 would you write for the sum of the numbers in Row 12? in Row *n*?

5. Look at Rows 0–8 of your triangle. How many entries are in each row? How many entries will be in Row 50? How many will be in Row *n*?

6. Identify two diagonals of Pascal's triangle that contain triangular numbers.

7. The pattern to the right shows Rows 0–7 of Pascal's triangle when some entries are shaded in and others are not. Describe and extend the pattern you see.

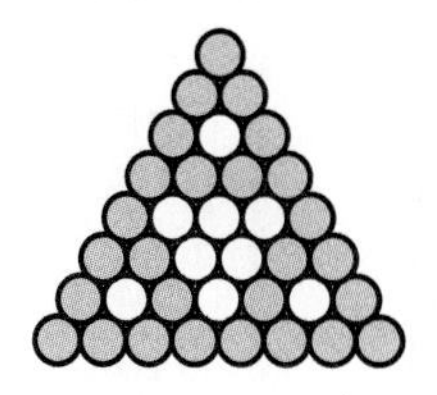

Problem-Solving Applications

8. **CRAFTS** Suppose you have red and white beads. How many different ways can you make a string of 5 beads where 2 of the beads are red? HINT: Look at Row 5 of Pascal's triangle.

9. **PATTERNS** A pizza parlor advertises a special where you can choose 3 of 5 toppings for its pizzas. It has pepperoni, sausage, peppers, black olives, and mushrooms. Use Row 5 of Pascal's triangle to find how many different ways you could select 3 toppings.

10. **WRITE ABOUT IT** Write a rule for generating additional rows of Pascal's triangle.

MORE PRACTICE Lesson 18.2, page H68

LESSON 18.3

What You'll Learn
How repeated doubling or halving affects positive numbers

Why Learn This?
To identify patterns, such as population growth, as convergent or divergent

VOCABULARY

diverge

converge

ALGEBRA CONNECTION

Repeated Doubling and Halving

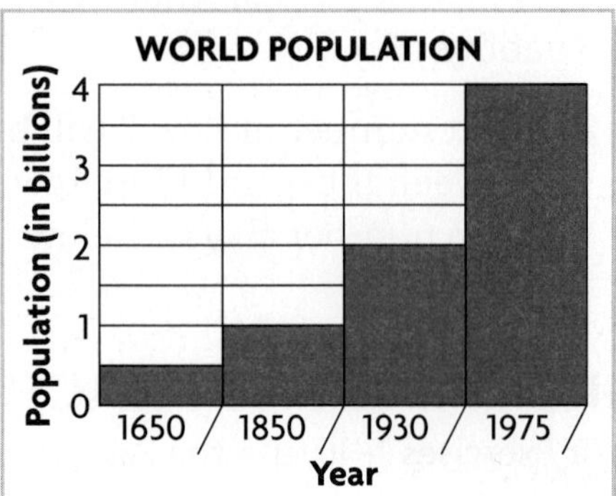

The population of the world is growing faster and faster. It doubled from 1850 to 1930, doubled again from 1930 to 1975, and will probably double again by 2015.

- What will the world population be in 2015 if it doubles the number for 1975?

EXAMPLE Suppose the world population continued to double. How many times would 4 billion have to double to reach a number equal to or greater than 100 billion?

$4 \times 2 = 8$ *Start with the number 4, and double it.*

$8 \times 2 = 16$ *Continue to double the result until you reach a number equal to or greater than 100.*
$16 \times 2 = 32$
$32 \times 2 = 64$
$64 \times 2 = 128$

So, the population would have to double 5 times.

- What if the world population began to shrink by half? How many times would the population in 1975 have to be halved to be less than 0.5 billion?

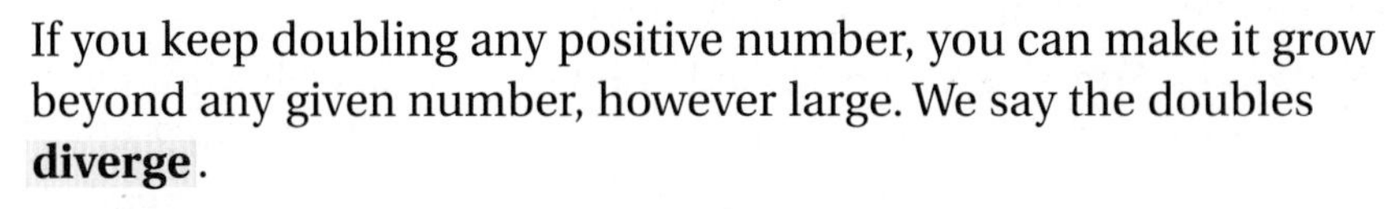

If you keep doubling any positive number, you can make it grow beyond any given number, however large. We say the doubles **diverge**.

1, 2, 4, 8, 16, . . .
5, 10, 20, 40, . . . ← The doubles diverge.

If you keep halving any positive number, you can make it shrink below any given number, however small. We say the halves **converge**.

$1, \frac{1}{2}, \frac{1}{4}, \frac{1}{8}, \ldots$
48, 24, 12, 6, . . . ← The halves converge.

GUIDED PRACTICE

Determine how many times 4 must be doubled to reach or exceed the given number.

1. 64 **2.** 8,192 **3.** 444,444 **4.** four million

Determine how many times 10,000 must be halved to reach or be less than the given number.

5. 2,500 **6.** 20 **7.** 2 **8.** two tenths

INDEPENDENT PRACTICE

As the pattern continues, tell whether the numbers converge or diverge.

1. 3, 6, 12, 24, . . . **2.** 36, 18, 9, 4.5, . . . **3.** $3, 1\frac{1}{2}, \frac{3}{4}, \frac{3}{8}, \ldots$ **4.** $\frac{1}{200}, \frac{1}{100}, \frac{1}{50}, \frac{1}{25}, \ldots$

For Exercises 5–7, use the graph.

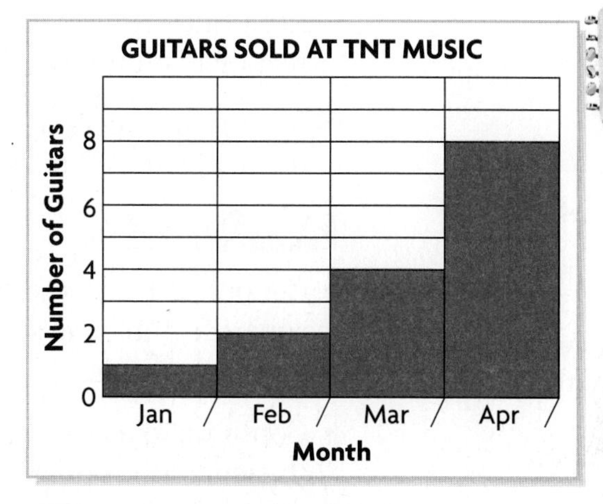

5. Does the data displayed in the graph appear to converge or diverge?

6. Suppose the number of guitars sold continues to double. How many guitars will be sold in June?

7. If the doubling continues, in what month will the number of guitars sold at TNT Music be greater than or equal to 100?

8. Write an equation for the doubling pattern in the table.

x	5	10	20	40	80
y	10	20	40	80	160

Problem-Solving Applications

9. **PATTERNS** Daniel's class is collecting old newspapers to raise money. The first day they collected 15 lb of papers. The second day they collected 30 lb, and the third day they collected 60 lb. If this pattern continues, how many pounds of newspaper will Daniel's class have collected at the end of 7 days?

10. **SPORTS** Meisha is training to run in a marathon, which is 26 mi long. She wants to double her daily running distance every 2 weeks. If she starts the first week running 1 mi a day, how long will it take her to be running at least the marathon distance?

11. **WRITE ABOUT IT** Take $\frac{1}{1,000}$ and halve it 4 times. Do you get zero? Explain why you can never reach zero by halving.

MORE PRACTICE Lesson 18.3, page H68

ACTIVITY

What You'll Explore
How halving and doubling the length of a figure affects area

What You'll Need
paper and a ruler

Technology Link

You can find symmetry lines by halving figures by using E-Lab, Activity 18. Available on CD-ROM and on the Internet at **www.hbschool.com/elab**

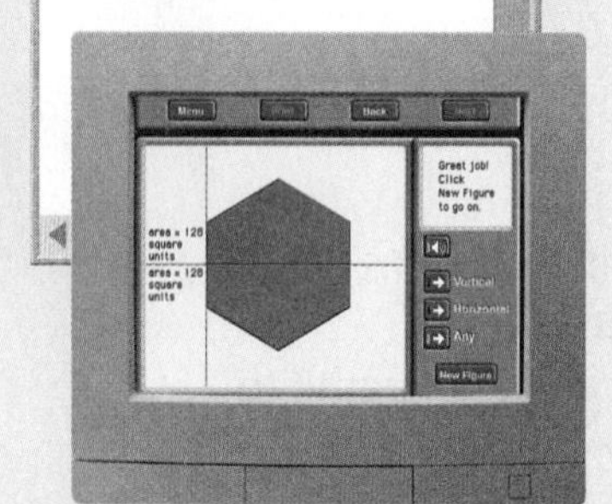

GEOMETRY CONNECTION

Doubling and Halving Lengths

You can look at patterns of doubling and halving of geometric figures to see how the figures can grow or shrink.

Explore

10 cm

1 cm

ACTIVITY 1

- Cut out a 10-cm × 1-cm rectangle. Cut the rectangle in half.
- Cut one of the new rectangles in half. Continue until you have halved the first rectangle four times.
- Record the length and area of each rectangle in a table like this one.

Stage	0	1	2
Length (cm)	10	5	2.5
Area (cm^2)	10	5	2.5

ACTIVITY 2

- Cut out 32 1-cm squares. Start with one 1-cm square. Double the length by adding a square to form a rectangle.
- Continue to add squares until you have doubled the length four times.
- In a table, record the length and area of each figure.

Think and Discuss

- What effect does halving the length of a rectangle have on the area of the rectangle?
- What effect does doubling the length of a rectangle have on the area of the rectangle?

Try This

- Start with a 1-cm square, and double the length and the width three times. Record the lengths, widths, and areas in a table.
- How does doubling the length and the width affect the area of the square?

Exponents and Powers

What You'll Learn
How to see patterns in powers of numbers

Why Learn This?
To understand very large numbers and very small numbers

To find powers of a number, start with 1 and repeatedly multiply by the number. Remember that the repetition of a process is called iteration.

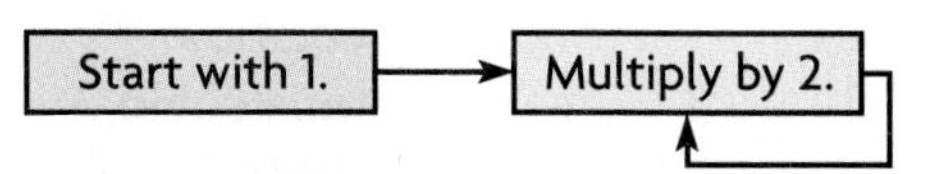

EXAMPLE 1 Use the iteration diagram above to find the first five powers of 2. How do successive powers of 2 change?

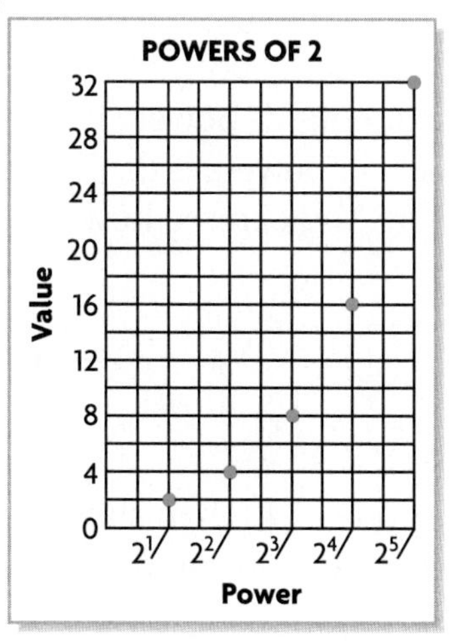

$2^1 = 2$
$2^2 = 2 \times 2 = 4$
$2^3 = 2 \times 2 \times 2 = 8$
$2^4 = 2 \times 2 \times 2 \times 2 = 16$
$2^5 = 2 \times 2 \times 2 \times 2 \times 2 = 32$

The powers of 2 diverge, growing larger without bound.

- Find the first five powers of 3. How do successive powers of 3 change?

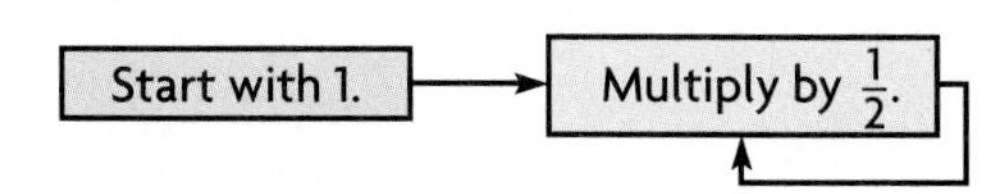

EXAMPLE 2 Use the iteration diagram to find the first five powers of $\frac{1}{2}$. How do the successive powers change?

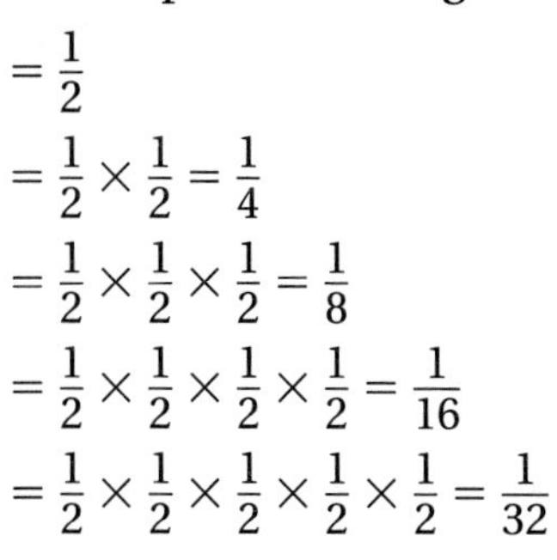

$(\frac{1}{2})^1 = \frac{1}{2}$
$(\frac{1}{2})^2 = \frac{1}{2} \times \frac{1}{2} = \frac{1}{4}$
$(\frac{1}{2})^3 = \frac{1}{2} \times \frac{1}{2} \times \frac{1}{2} = \frac{1}{8}$
$(\frac{1}{2})^4 = \frac{1}{2} \times \frac{1}{2} \times \frac{1}{2} \times \frac{1}{2} = \frac{1}{16}$
$(\frac{1}{2})^5 = \frac{1}{2} \times \frac{1}{2} \times \frac{1}{2} \times \frac{1}{2} \times \frac{1}{2} = \frac{1}{32}$

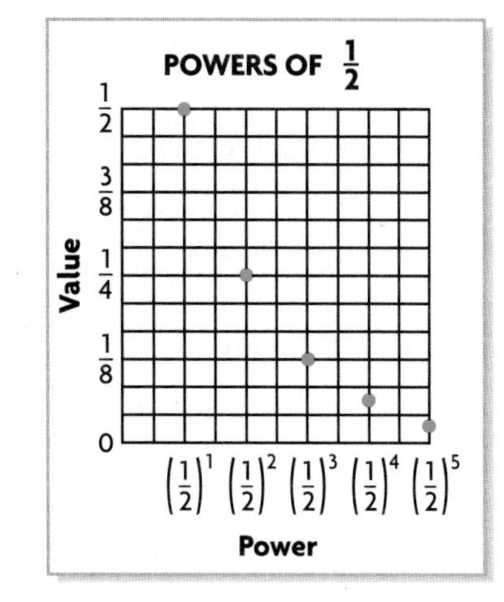

The powers of $\frac{1}{2}$ converge, shrinking toward 0.

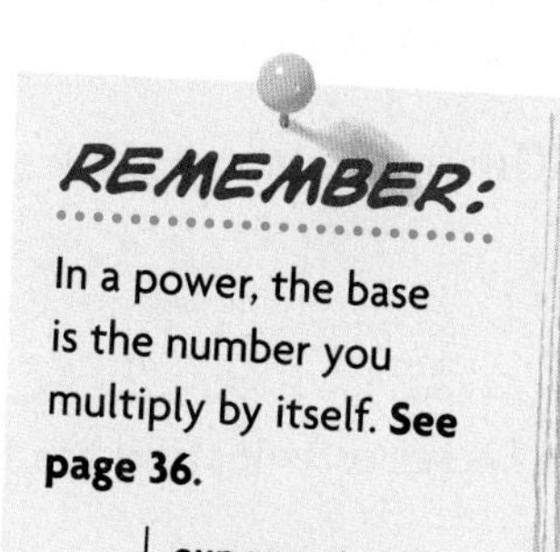

REMEMBER:
In a power, the base is the number you multiply by itself. See page 36.
↓ exponent
$2^3 = 8$ ← power
↑ base

You can view the growth and change in a sequence of powers by drawing a geometric model or making a number line.

Area is used in this geometric model to show the first four stages of a convergent sequence.

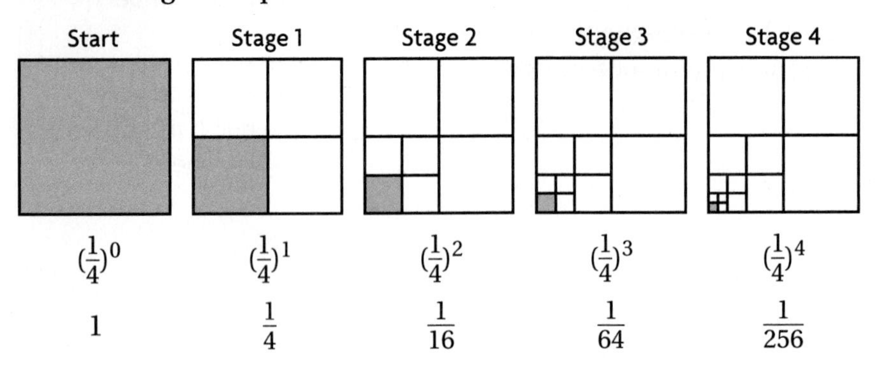

$(\frac{1}{4})^0$	$(\frac{1}{4})^1$	$(\frac{1}{4})^2$	$(\frac{1}{4})^3$	$(\frac{1}{4})^4$
1	$\frac{1}{4}$	$\frac{1}{16}$	$\frac{1}{64}$	$\frac{1}{256}$

Another way to show change in a sequence of powers is to use a number line. Here the same sequence of powers is displayed as an orbit of a point on the number line. You can see how quickly the sequence converges toward 0.

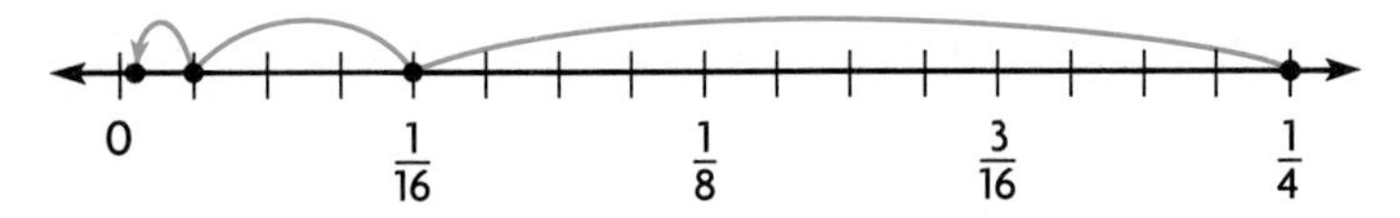

EXAMPLE 3 Find the first four powers of 4. Then show the sequence as an orbit of a point. Identify how the powers change.

$$4^1 = 4$$
$$4^2 = 16$$
$$4^3 = 64$$
$$4^4 = 256$$

Find the successive powers of 4.

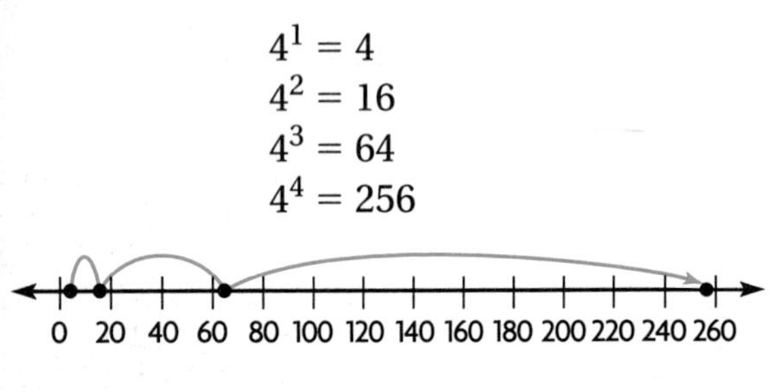

Graph the powers on a number line, and show the orbit of one point to another.

The number line shows that the sequence is divergent.

SCIENCE LINK

Bacteria reproduce by splitting into two cells. Under ideal conditions, reproduction can occur every 20 minutes. If conditions were perfect, how many bacteria could be produced from one original cell in 2 hours? in 4 hours?

GUIDED PRACTICE

For Exercises 1–16, find the first four powers of the given number.

1. 1 **2.** 5 **3.** 12 **4.** $\frac{1}{3}$

5. $\frac{1}{7}$ **6.** 40 **7.** 10 **8.** $\frac{1}{4}$

9. 6 **10.** 11 **11.** 15 **12.** 7

13. 20 **14.** 25 **15.** $\frac{1}{6}$ **16.** 8

INDEPENDENT PRACTICE

1. In Exercise 12 on page 366, how do the successive powers of 7 change?

2. In Exercise 4 on page 366, how do the successive powers of $\frac{1}{3}$ change?

3. Determine the power shown in each stage of this geometric model of a convergent sequence.

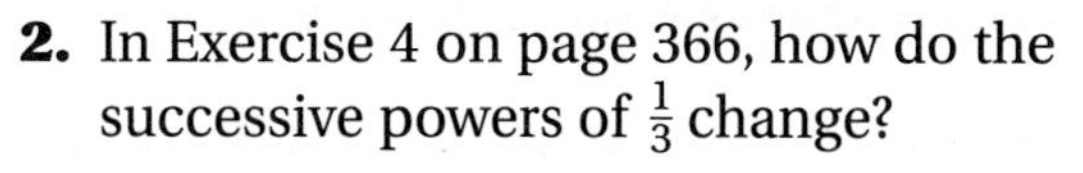

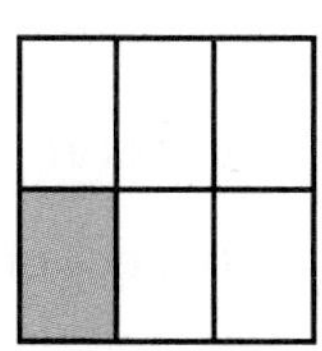
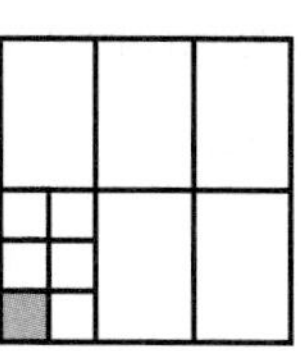
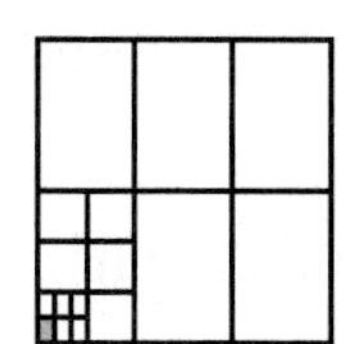

Find the values. Then show the sequence as an orbit of a point on a number line.

4. $4^0, 4^1, 4^2, 4^3$

5. $(\frac{1}{12})^0, (\frac{1}{12})^1, (\frac{1}{12})^2$

6. $1^0, 1^1, 1^2, 1^3, 1^4$

7. $11^0, 11^1, 11^2, 11^3$

Find the exponent n that will make the equation true.

8. $2^n = 64$

9. $4^n = 64$

10. $8^n = 64$

11. $7^n = 1$

Problem-Solving Applications

12. **SCIENCE** A certain colony of bacteria is tripling in length every 15 min. Its length now is 1 mm. How long will it be in 1 hr?

13. Ron won a prize of $2,000 in an essay contest. He gave $\frac{1}{3}$ of his prize money to a friend, Maurice. Maurice gave $\frac{1}{3}$ of his money to Bob, and Bob gave $\frac{1}{3}$ of his money to Shelly. What fraction of Ron's prize did Shelly get?

14. **WRITE ABOUT IT** Explain the difference between successive powers converging and diverging.

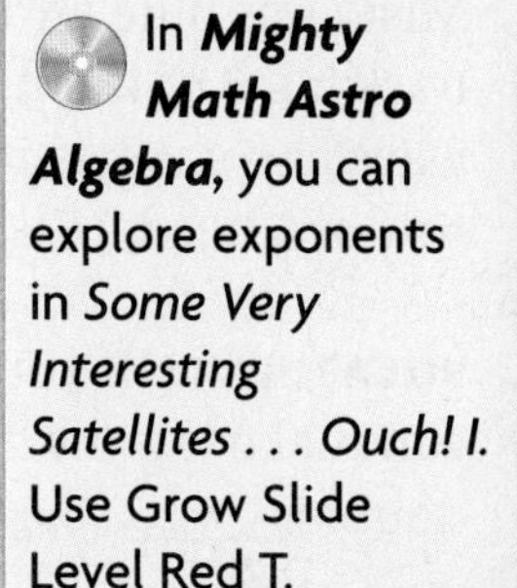

Technology Link

In ***Mighty Math Astro Algebra***, you can explore exponents in *Some Very Interesting Satellites . . . Ouch! I.* Use Grow Slide Level Red T.

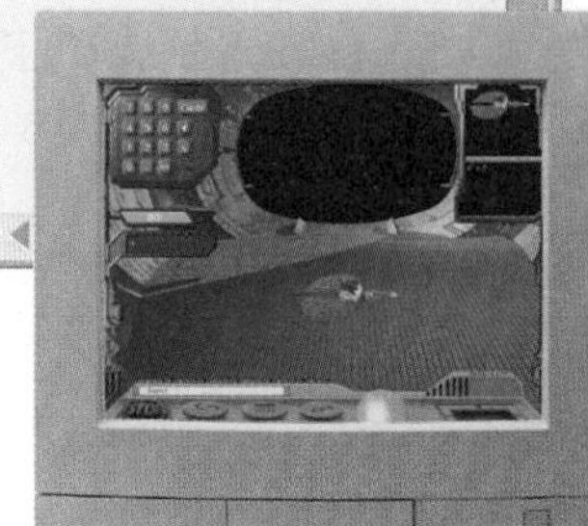

Mixed Review and Test Prep

Rename the fraction as a decimal.

15. $\frac{1}{4}$

16. $\frac{1}{2}$

17. $\frac{1}{10}$

18. $\frac{2}{5}$

19. $\frac{3}{8}$

The figures of each pair are similar. Find x.

20.

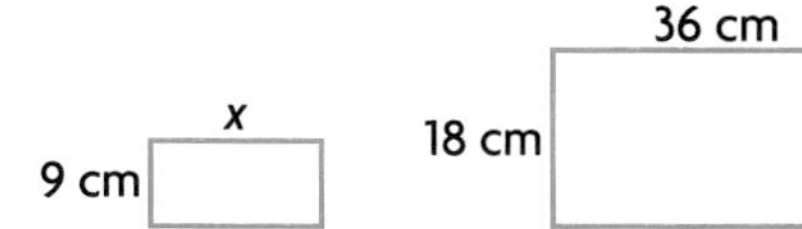

21.

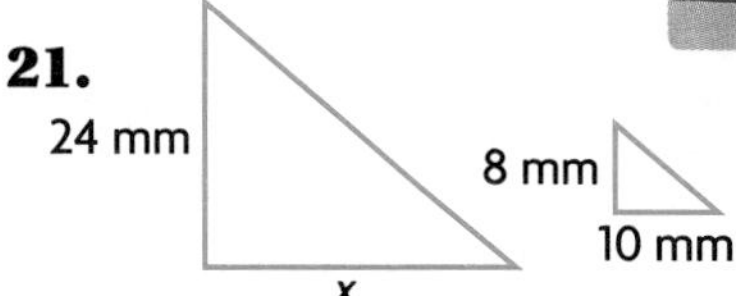

22. **AVERAGE** Don sailed on a ship for 11 days. It averaged 365.75 miles a day. What was the total distance the ship sailed?

A 403.33 mi
B 4,023.25 mi
C 40,232.5 mi
D 402,325 mi

23. **NUMBER SENSE** Which expression has a value of 100?

F $\frac{44}{4} - \frac{4}{4}$
G $\frac{444}{4} - \frac{44}{4}$
H $\frac{440}{44} - \frac{44}{4}$
J $\frac{44}{4}$

MORE PRACTICE Lesson 18.4, page H68

CHAPTER 18 Review/Test

Find the triangular number. (pages 356–359)

1. seventh **2.** nineteenth **3.** thirty-fifth **4.** eightieth

5. fiftieth **6.** forty-second **7.** twenty-fifth **8.** sixty-fifth

For Exercises 9–12, use the array at the right. (pages 356–359)

Row 0 ⟶ 1
Row 1 ⟶ 1 2 1
1 2 3 2 1
1 2 3 4 3 2 1

9. What will be the seventh row in the array?

10. What will be the eleventh row in the array?

11. What are the sums for the first four rows?

12. What do the sums for the first four rows have in common?

13. Row 6 of Pascal's triangle is 1 6 15 20 15 6 1. Write Row 7. (pages 360–361)

14. Write Row 8 of Pascal's triangle. (pages 360–361)

15. Misty has blue and black beads. She wants to string 6 of them in a row. How many ways can she use just 3 blue beads in a row of 6 beads? (pages 360–361)

16. Misty's friend also has blue and black beads. She wants to string 8 in a row. How many ways can she use just 3 blue beads in a row of 8 beads? (pages 360–361)

17. **VOCABULARY** If you keep doubling any positive number, you can make it grow beyond any given number. We say the doubles __?__. (page 362)

18. **VOCABULARY** If you keep halving any positive number, you can make it shrink below any given number. We say the halves __?__. (page 362)

Determine how many times 6 must be doubled to reach or exceed the given number. (pages 362–363)

19. 36 **20.** 6,144 **21.** 180,000 **22.** 10 million

Determine how many times 10,000 must be halved to reach or be less than the given number. (pages 362–363)

23. 2,000 **24.** 100 **25.** 5 **26.** $\frac{3}{10}$

Find the first four powers of the given number. (pages 365–367)

27. 5 **28.** 11 **29.** $\frac{1}{10}$ **30.** $\frac{2}{3}$

Test Prep

1. What is the fourth power of $\frac{2}{5}$?

A $\frac{32}{3,125}$

B $\frac{16}{625}$

C $\frac{8}{125}$

D $\frac{8}{20}$

2. What are the lengths of a triangle similar to $\triangle ABC$ using the scale factor 4 : 1?

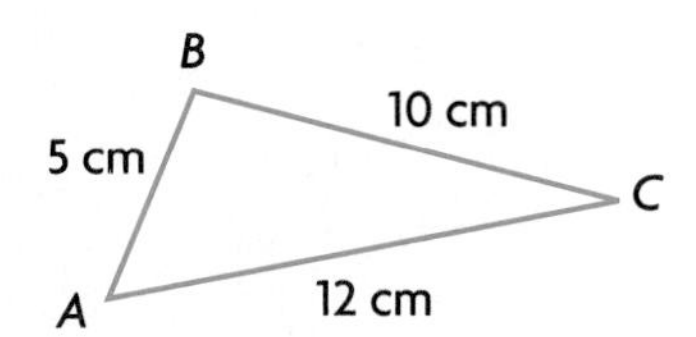

F $\frac{5}{4}$ cm, $\frac{5}{2}$ cm, $\frac{3}{2}$ cm
G 9 cm, 14 cm, 16 cm
H 10 cm, 20 cm, 24 cm
J 20 cm, 40 cm, 48 cm

3. What is the measure of the central angle representing 45% of a circle graph?

A 45°
B 81°
C 162°
D 198°

4. $12\frac{3}{4} \div 2\frac{1}{2} =$

F $\frac{10}{51}$

G $5\frac{1}{10}$

H $5\frac{1}{5}$

J $31\frac{7}{8}$

5. $^{-}432 \div 12 =$

A $^{-}36$
B $^{-}28$
C 28
D 36

6. What is the solution of the equation $r + 3(r - 4) = 42$?

F $r = 21.5$
G $r = 15.5$
H $r = 11.5$
J $r = 7.5$
K Not Here

7. A drawing of an amusement park ride is made using the scale 1 inch : 2 feet. If the height of the ride is 50 feet, what is the height of the drawing?

A 10 in. **B** 20 in.
C 25 in. **D** 100 in.

8. The first three triangular numbers are given. What is the fifth triangular number?

F 10 **G** 12
H 15 **J** 24

9. Three out of four parents attended the science fair. Which is a reasonable conclusion?

A Less than half of the parents attended the fair.
B 75% of the parents attended the fair.
C Over $\frac{9}{10}$ of the parents attended the fair.
D More parents attended the science fair than the art fair.

CHAPTER

19 NUMBER PATTERNS

LOOK AHEAD

In this chapter you will solve problems that involve

- decimals
- rational numbers
- sequences
- exponents

SOCIAL STUDIES **LINK**

The most active stocks on the New York Stock Exchange in 1996 included Micron Technology, Inc.; AT&T; PepsiCo, Inc.; IBM; and Wal-Mart Stores. The table shows the stock prices for these companies as of October 31, 1997.

STOCK PRICES AS OF OCTOBER 31, 1997	
Company	**Stock Price**
Micron Technology, Inc.	$26\frac{7}{8}$
AT&T	$48\frac{7}{8}$
PepsiCo, Inc.	$36\frac{7}{8}$
IBM	$98\frac{1}{2}$
Wal-Mart Stores	35

- Write each stock price as a decimal.
- What would have been the cost of 20 shares of AT&T stock?
- What would have been the cost of 15 shares of IBM stock?

Problem-Solving Project

You're the Stock Expert

Look at the stock pages of a newspaper. Choose 5 stocks to buy. "Buy" at least 10 shares of one stock, and spend no more than $500.00 in all. Change the prices to dollars and cents, and record your purchases. For example, if the price is $57\frac{1}{4}$, write $57.25. Check your stocks in a week to see if you made or lost money.

COMPANY	CLOSING PRICE OF 1 SHARE
CrLand (CereaLand)	$37\frac{3}{8}$
SportFt (Sportfoot)	$43\frac{1}{2}$
Compte (Compute)	$15\frac{5}{8}$
Bnktr (Banktrust)	$21\frac{3}{4}$
Ryl Htl (Royal Hotels)	$45\frac{7}{8}$
BargnSt (Bargain Stop)	$48\frac{1}{4}$

PROJECT CHECKLIST

- ✓ Did you change prices on the stock page to dollars and cents?
- ✓ Did you choose stocks totaling $500.00 or less?
- ✓ Did you record your purchases?
- ✓ Did you check your stocks after one week?

LESSON 19.1

Exploring Patterns in Decimals

What You'll Learn
How to recognize a pattern of repeating decimals

Why Learn This?
To recognize and write these patterns when you use a calculator

VOCABULARY
repeating decimal

When you take coins from your pocket, what patterns do you use to group them?

Look at the money amounts below.

1 quarter = \$0.25	3 quarters = \$0.75
2 quarters = \$0.50	4 quarters = \$1.00

- What pattern do you notice?
- What would 7 quarters equal?

You can show the same relationship in equivalent fractions and decimals.

$\frac{1}{4} = 0.25$ $\frac{2}{4} = 0.50$ $\frac{3}{4} = 0.75$ $\frac{4}{4} = 1.00$

The decimals in the examples above are called terminating decimals. All rational numbers can be expressed as ratios. When you divide to change a fraction to a decimal, if the remainder is zero, then the decimal is terminating.

REMEMBER:
You can change a fraction to a decimal by dividing the numerator by the denominator. **See page H9, Key Skill 16.**

$\frac{1}{4} \rightarrow 4\overline{)1.00}$

When you continue to divide and the remainder is never zero, the quotient is called a **repeating decimal**.

EXAMPLE 1 Rename $\frac{1}{3}$ as a decimal.

$$\begin{array}{r} 0.333 \\ 3\overline{)1.000} \\ -\ 9 \\ \hline 10 \\ -\ 9 \\ \hline 10 \\ -\ 9 \\ \hline 1 \end{array}$$

Divide.

Look for a pattern in the quotient.

If you continue to add zeros and divide, the 3 in the quotient will repeat endlessly.

$\frac{1}{3} = 0.\overline{3}$ *Draw a bar over the digit or digits that repeat.*

- **CRITICAL THINKING** Since $\frac{1}{3} = 0.\overline{3}$, what decimal represents $\frac{2}{3}$? What decimal represents $\frac{4}{3}$? What decimal represents $\frac{5}{3}$?

EXAMPLE 2 Rename $\frac{1}{11}$ as a decimal.

1 [÷] 11 [=] 0.0909090

Notice the pattern. The 0 and 9 repeat.

So, $\frac{1}{11} = 0.\overline{09}$.

- Rename $\frac{2}{11}$ as a decimal. Use mental math to rename $\frac{3}{11}$, $\frac{4}{11}$, and $\frac{5}{11}$ as decimals.

EXAMPLE 3 Rename $\frac{1}{12}$ as a decimal.

1 [÷] 12 [=] 0.083333333

In this pattern, the 3 repeats. So, $\frac{1}{12} = 0.08\overline{3}$.

CULTURAL LINK

In England a person's weight is measured in stone. One stone is equal to 14 pounds. For example, an adult who weighs $10\frac{2}{3}$ stone weighs $10\frac{2}{3} \times 14$, or $149\frac{1}{3}$, pounds. Write $10\frac{2}{3}$ stone as a decimal.

Talk About It

- In Example 2, what pattern can you use to find multiples of $\frac{1}{11}$, such as $\frac{3}{11}$ and $\frac{4}{11}$?
- Use a calculator to rename $\frac{5}{9}$ as a decimal. Does the calculator show 0.555555555 or 0.555555556? Why do some calculators show 0.555555556?
- Use a calculator to change $\frac{1}{7}$ to a decimal. What do you think the repeating pattern is? How could you make sure?

When changing fractions to decimals with calculators, you must be careful that you don't misinterpret the displays that appear.

Compare the calculator displays when these fractions are changed to decimals.

$\frac{9}{100} \rightarrow$ 9 [÷] 100 [=] 0.09

$\frac{909}{10,000} \rightarrow$ 909 [÷] 10000 [=] 0.0909

$\frac{1}{11} \rightarrow$ 1 [÷] 11 [=] 0.09090909

Even though the displays look similar, only $\frac{1}{11}$ is a repeating decimal. The other two fractions are terminating decimals.

GUIDED PRACTICE

Rename each fraction as a decimal. Use a bar to indicate repeating digits.

1. $\frac{4}{8}$ **2.** $\frac{7}{8}$ **3.** $\frac{7}{3}$ **4.** $\frac{5}{12}$

5. $\frac{2}{9}$ **6.** $\frac{3}{4}$ **7.** $\frac{1}{6}$ **8.** $\frac{2}{5}$

INDEPENDENT PRACTICE

For Exercises 1–5, choose the equivalent decimal from the box.

0.5	0.15	$1.\overline{27}$	$1.1\overline{6}$	$0.2\overline{6}$

1. $\frac{3}{20}$ **2.** $\frac{4}{15}$ **3.** $\frac{1}{2}$ **4.** $\frac{14}{11}$ **5.** $\frac{7}{6}$

Write *R* if the fraction can be renamed as a repeating decimal and *T* if the fraction can be renamed as a terminating decimal. Write the decimal equivalent for each, using a bar for a repeating decimal.

6. $\frac{3}{5}$ **7.** $\frac{1}{6}$ **8.** $\frac{7}{9}$ **9.** $\frac{3}{8}$ **10.** $\frac{5}{6}$

11. $\frac{9}{12}$ **12.** $\frac{33}{16}$ **13.** $\frac{13}{12}$ **14.** $\frac{6}{11}$ **15.** $\frac{8}{7}$

Rewrite the fraction as a decimal. Do not divide. Use the values $\frac{1}{9} = 0.\overline{1}$, $\frac{1}{8} = 0.125$, and $\frac{1}{3} = 0.\overline{3}$.

16. $\frac{2}{9}$ **17.** $\frac{3}{8}$ **18.** $\frac{2}{3}$ **19.** $\frac{8}{9}$ **20.** $\frac{7}{3}$

21. $\frac{10}{9}$ **22.** $\frac{5}{8}$ **23.** $\frac{13}{8}$ **24.** $\frac{7}{8}$ **25.** $\frac{23}{8}$

Doug's Discount Dollar Store sells all merchandise for less than a dollar. However, all prices are written as fractions. Convert each price to a decimal. Round to the nearest cent.

26. $\frac{3}{4}$ **27.** $\frac{5}{8}$ **28.** $\frac{5}{6}$ **29.** $\frac{8}{9}$ **30.** $\frac{7}{11}$

Problem-Solving Applications

31. Recently, the Acme Company stock was $12\frac{5}{8}$ per share. Find the dollars-and-cents equivalent for that price per share.

32. **BUSINESS** Bob's Bargain Barn is holding a storewide sale. Everything is marked $\frac{2}{3}$ off. Find the decimal value of $\frac{2}{3}$.

33. **NUMBER SENSE** Fred's gas tank holds 20 gal of gas. The gas gauge needle is halfway between $\frac{1}{4}$ and $\frac{1}{2}$. How many gallons of gas are needed to fill the tank? Write your answer as a decimal.

34. **DISTANCE** To get to the gym, Sheila must drive $6\frac{5}{11}$ mi north on Park Avenue. How can this be written as a decimal? About how many miles will register on her odometer, which shows tenths of a mile?

35. **WRITE ABOUT IT** How can you determine whether a fraction converts to a terminating or repeating decimal?

MORE PRACTICE Lesson 19.1, page H69

ALGEBRA CONNECTION

Patterns in Rational Numbers

LESSON 19.2

What You'll Learn
To use patterns to find a rational number between two rational numbers

Why Learn This?
To find the distance halfway between two points, as in the game of football

VOCABULARY
Density Property

Joel likes to shoot baskets after school. His first shot is 6 m away from the basket. He moves $\frac{1}{2}$ the distance to the basket for the second shot. If he continues this pattern, will he ever reach the basket?

Notice the pattern as he moves toward the basket.

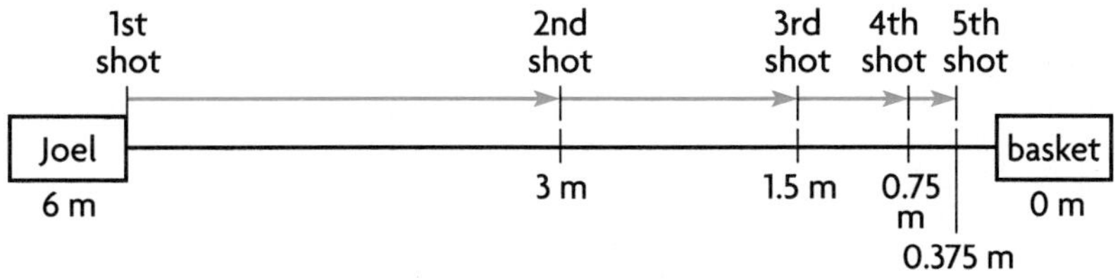

Joel gets closer and closer to the basket with each shot. However, in theory, he will never reach it because the remaining distance can always be divided by 2.

- On a number line, how many numbers are between 6, where Joel began, and 0, where the basket is?

Between any two rational numbers, there is always another rational number. This is called the **Density Property**. One way to find a rational number between any two rational numbers is to find the mean of the two numbers.

EXAMPLE 1 Find a number halfway between 1.24 and 1.25.

$$\begin{array}{r} 1.24 \\ +\ 1.25 \\ \hline 2.49 \end{array}$$

Find the sum of the numbers.

2.49 ÷ 2 = 1.245 *Divide the sum by 2.*

So, 1.245 is halfway between 1.24 and 1.25.

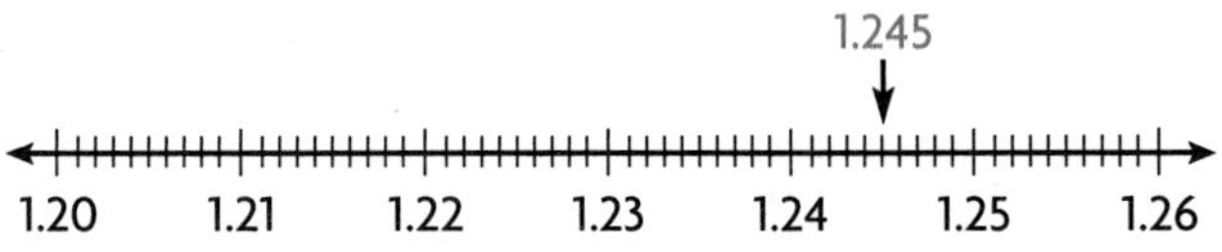

- Find the number halfway between 3.24 and 3.25.
- CRITICAL THINKING Find the number halfway between 1.24 and 1.245.

ANOTHER METHOD You can also use the method of adding zeros to find more numbers between numbers.

EXAMPLE 2 Find a rational number between $^-4.2$ and $^-4.3$.

$^-4.2 = {}^-4.20$

$^-4.3 = {}^-4.30$

Add zeros to each decimal so that both have the same number of decimal places.

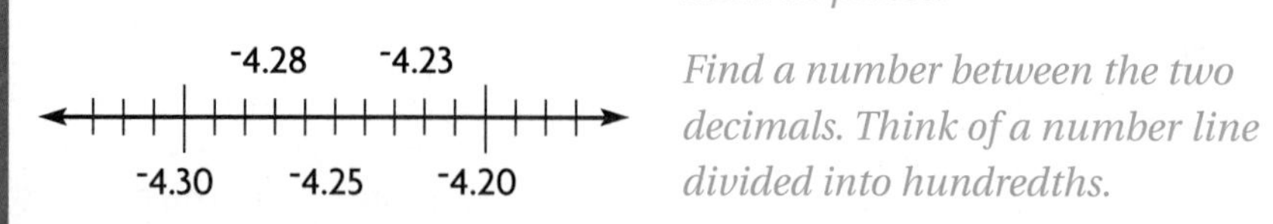

Find a number between the two decimals. Think of a number line divided into hundredths.

So, $^-4.23$, $^-4.25$, and $^-4.28$ are all between $^-4.2$ and $^-4.3$.

You can also find rational numbers between any two fractions.

EXAMPLE 3 Find a rational number between $\frac{4}{5}$ and $\frac{7}{8}$.

$\frac{4}{5} = \frac{32}{40}$

$\frac{7}{8} = \frac{35}{40}$

Use the least common multiple (LCM) to write equivalent fractions.

$\frac{33}{40}$ is one rational number between $\frac{32}{40}$ and $\frac{35}{40}$.

Find a rational number between the two fractions.

So, $\frac{33}{40}$ is between $\frac{4}{5}$ and $\frac{7}{8}$.

- How can you find a rational number between $\frac{1}{4}$ and 0.5?

TEEN TIMES

When a football team is penalized near its own goal line, the penalty is often "half the distance to the goal." For example, if the ball is on the 4-yd line, the penalty moves the ball to the 2-yd line. These half-the-distance penalties keep the other team from scoring points on a penalty.

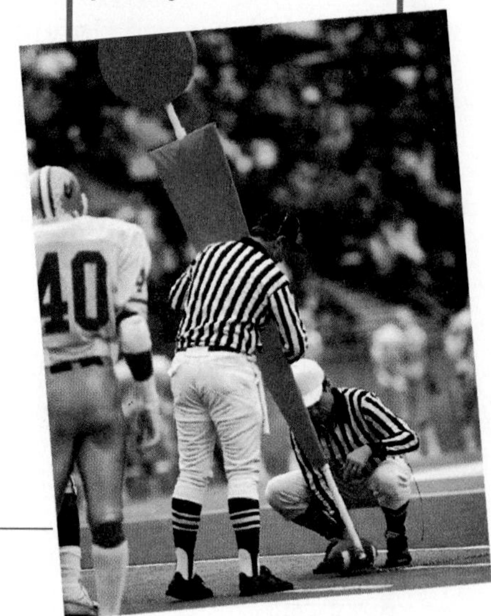

GUIDED PRACTICE

Find a number between the two rational numbers.

1. 1.55 and 1.56 **2.** 3.2 and 3.3 **3.** 0.1 and 0.3

4. 4.8 and 4.9 **5.** $\frac{1}{5}$ and $\frac{2}{5}$ **6.** $\frac{3}{5}$ and 0.7

7. $^-3.6$ and $^-3.7$ **8.** $\frac{1}{5}$ and $\frac{3}{8}$ **9.** 0.3 and $\frac{1}{3}$

INDEPENDENT PRACTICE

Name a rational number for the given point on the number line.

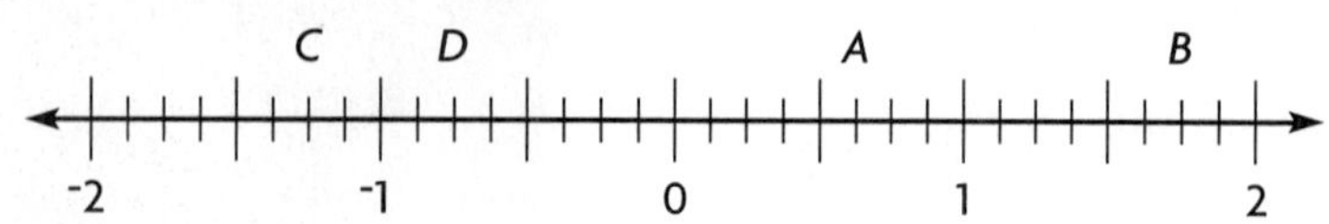

1. point A **2.** point B **3.** point C **4.** point D

Name a rational number between the two numbers.

5. 1.55 and 1.57 **6.** 1.63 and 1.64 **7.** $\frac{5}{8}$ and $\frac{7}{8}$ **8.** $\frac{1}{4}$ and $\frac{3}{4}$

9. $^{-}3$ and $^{-}4$ **10.** 1.600 and 1.650 **11.** 0.85 and 0.86 **12.** $\frac{1}{2}$ and 0.6

13. 100.01 and 100.1 **14.** 2.01 and 2.02 **15.** $1\frac{5}{8}$ and 1.7 **16.** 1.94 and 1.95

Problem-Solving Applications

17. DISTANCE The distance from Dallas to Houston is 242 mi and from Houston to New Orleans is 359 mi. The distance from Dallas to New Orleans is 498 mi. On a trip from Dallas to New Orleans through Houston, Teri wanted to stop halfway between Houston and New Orleans. How many miles from Dallas would she stop?

18. ESTIMATION Janiqua, Karyn, and Marty are selling cookies for a school club. Janiqua sold $\frac{1}{4}$ case of cookies. Karyn sold $\frac{3}{5}$ case. Marty sold more than Janiqua but less than Karyn. Estimate how much Marty sold.

19. TEMPERATURE Terrance recorded temperatures of $^{-}6$°C at 8:00 A.M. and $^{-}2$°C at 10:00 A.M. He recorded a temperature of 2°C at 11:00 A.M. Find and use a pattern to predict a reasonable temperature for 9:00 A.M.

20. WRITE ABOUT IT Explain how to find a rational number between $\frac{1}{2}$ and $\frac{4}{5}$.

Technology Link

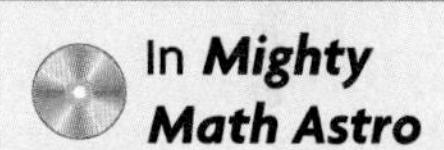

In ***Mighty Math Astro Algebra,*** you can go to the *Number Line* for more practice locating rational numbers as you explore *The Wonky Controls IV.* Use Grow Slide Level Red R.

Mixed Review and Test Prep

Write a rule for the pattern. Find the next term in the sequence.

21. 2, 6, 18, . . . **22.** 125, 25, 5, . . . **23.** 23, 29, 35, . . .

Tell whether the numbers *converge* or *diverge*.

24. 4, 8, 16, 32, . . . **25.** 12, 6, 3, 1.5, . . . **26.** 2, 1, $\frac{1}{2}$, $\frac{1}{4}$, . . .

27. CHOOSE A STRATEGY Katrina is 3 times as old as Ned and 4 years older than Paul. Paul is twice as old as Ned. What are the ages of the three people?

A 2, 4, and 6 **B** 4, 8, and 12
C 5, 10, and 15 **D** 6, 12, and 18

28. NUMBER SENSE The square root of which number is closest to 12?

F 24 **G** 60 **H** 96 **J** 150

MORE PRACTICE Lesson 19.2, page H69

ACTIVITY

What You'll Explore
Using a calculator to understand irrational numbers

What You'll Need
calculator

VOCABULARY
irrational numbers

Exploring Irrational Numbers

Recall that any rational number can be written as a ratio and can be changed to either a terminating or a repeating decimal. There are some numbers that cannot be written as terminating or repeating decimals.

Explore

- Use a calculator with a $\sqrt{\ }$ key. What is $\sqrt{1.96}$?
- Check your result by multiplying it by itself. Is the product 1.96? Is your result the exact square root of 1.96, or is it an approximation? How do you know?
- Is the square root of 1.96 a repeating or a terminating decimal?
- Is $\sqrt{1.96}$ a rational number? Explain.
- Now find $\sqrt{8}$, $\sqrt{2.5}$, and $\sqrt{426}$. Record your results in a table.

Think and Discuss

- Is each square root in your table the exact square root or an approximation? How do you know?
- Is each square root in your table a whole number? a terminating decimal? a repeating decimal?
- Are any of the square roots in your table rational numbers? Why or why not?

Numbers that cannot be written as whole numbers or terminating or repeating decimals are called **irrational numbers**.

- Is $\sqrt{13}$ rational or irrational? Explain.
- Is $\sqrt{64}$ rational or irrational? Explain?

Technology Link

You can analyze patterns of square roots by using E-Lab, Activity 19. Available on CD-ROM and on the Internet at **www.hbschool.com/elab**

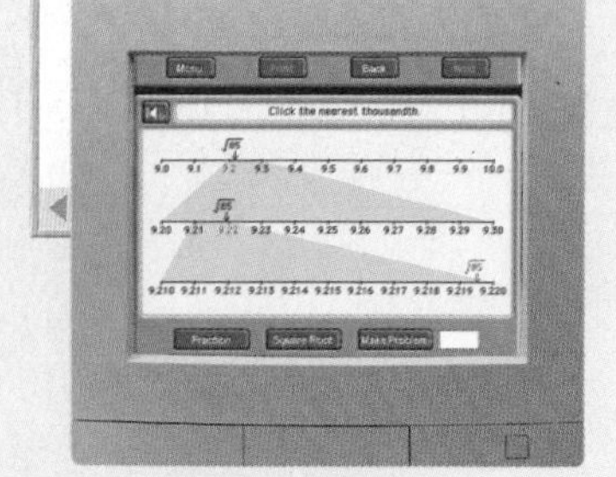

Try This

Tell whether each number is *rational* or *irrational.*

1. $\sqrt{49}$ **2.** $\sqrt{14}$ **3.** $\sqrt{0.09}$ **4.** $\sqrt{101}$

5. $\sqrt{97}$ **6.** $\sqrt{144}$ **7.** $\sqrt{225}$ **8.** $\sqrt{1.7}$

Patterns in Sequences

LESSON 19.3

What You'll Learn
To recognize and use patterns found in sequences

Why Learn This?
To recognize if sequences are arithmetic, geometric, or neither and find some of the continuing terms

VOCABULARY
Fibonacci sequence
geometric sequence
common ratio

A famous number pattern is the **Fibonacci sequence**.

Fibonacci sequence → 1, 1, 2, 3, 5, 8, 13, . . .

To find the pattern in the Fibonacci sequence, you can study the sequence, look for a relationship between the terms, and use the relationship to describe the pattern.

$1 + 1$	$1 + 2$	$2 + 3$	$3 + 5$	$5 + 8$
2	3	5	8	13

- What pattern do you see?
- Use the pattern to write the next four terms.

The Fibonacci sequence is related to real-life situations.

EXAMPLE 1 A token machine at the arcade accepts only quarters and half dollars. Each token costs $0.25. The table shows the ways to insert coins into the machine to buy tokens. In the table, Q stands for quarters and H stands for a half dollar. How many ways are there to buy 5 tokens?

Number of tokens	Order of coins	Number of ways
1	Q	1
2	QQ H	2
3	QQQ QH HQ	3
4	QQQQ QQH QHQ HQQ HH	5

Notice the pattern in the third column. Beginning with the third term, each term is the sum of the two terms before it.

If this pattern continues, it appears that there are $3 + 5 = 8$ ways to insert coins to buy 5 tokens.

This listing supports the conjecture that there are 8 ways.

QQQQQ	QQHQ	HQQQ	HQH
QQQH	QHQQ	QHH	HHQ

- Extend the pattern for buying 6 tokens. Support your conjecture with a listing.

So, there are 13 ways to insert coins to buy 6 tokens.

REMEMBER:

An **arithmetic sequence** is formed by a repeating addition or subtraction pattern. **See page 134.**

2, 7, 12, 17, 22, . . .

SCIENCE LINK

On DNA strands, there are four chemical units, abbreviated as A, C, G, and T. An A unit on one strand always pairs up with a T unit on the opposite strand, while a C unit always pairs up with a G unit. If the sequence of chemical units on one strand of DNA is A, A, C, G, T, C, T, A, what is the sequence of chemical units on the opposite strand?

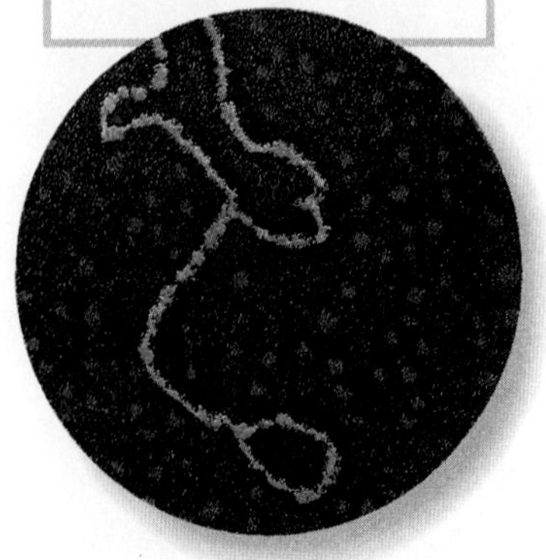

Sequences can have different types of patterns. Recall that in an arithmetic sequence, the difference between any term and the one after it is always the same. This is the common difference.

When the pattern in a sequence is made by multiplying by the same number, the sequence is called a **geometric sequence**. The number used to multiply each term to produce the next is called the **common ratio**.

The common ratio for these sequences is $\frac{1}{2}$, or 0.5.

$$100, 50, 25, \frac{25}{2}, \frac{25}{4}, \frac{25}{8}, \ldots$$

$$100, 50, 25, 12.5, 6.25, 3.125, \ldots$$

EXAMPLE 2 Look at the geometric sequence below. Find the common ratio. Then find the next term in the sequence.

$3, ^-6, 12, ^-24, \ldots$

$\frac{\text{second term}}{\text{first term}} \rightarrow \frac{^-6}{3} = {^-2}$ *Starting with the second term, write a ratio that compares a term to the term before it.*

$\frac{\text{third term}}{\text{second term}} \rightarrow \frac{12}{^-6} = {^-2}$

$\frac{\text{fourth term}}{\text{third term}} \rightarrow \frac{^-24}{12} = {^-2}$

The common ratio is $^-2$.

$^-24 \times {^-2} = 48$ *Multiply the last given term by the common ratio.*

The next term in the sequence is 48.

- Use the common ratio to find the next three terms after 48.

- **CRITICAL THINKING** Is the Fibonacci sequence an arithmetic sequence? Why or why not?
- Is the Fibonacci sequence a geometric sequence? Why or why not?

GUIDED PRACTICE

Look for a pattern in each sequence. Write *geometric, arithmetic,* or *neither*. Then find the next three terms.

1. 2, 6, 10, 14, . . .

2. 2, 2, 4, 6, 10, . . .

3. 1.2, 3.6, 10.8, . . .

4. 5, $^-2.5$, 1.25, . . .

5. 1, 3, 9, 27, . . .

6. 1, 2, 6, 24, . . .

INDEPENDENT PRACTICE

Look for the pattern in each sequence. Write *geometric, arithmetic,* or *neither.*

1. 0, 4, 8, 12, . . .

2. 9, 3, $^{-}3$, $^{-}9$, . . .

3. 2, 4, 8, 16, . . .

4. 3, 13, 23, 33, . . .

5. 1, 4, 9, 16, . . .

6. 2, 2.2, 2.4, 2.6, . . .

Write the next two terms in the sequence.

7. 1, 6, 11, 16, 21, 26, . . .

8. 3, 9, 27, 81, . . .

9. 2, 4, 7, 11, 16, 22, . . .

10. 1, 2, 4, 8, 16, 32, . . .

11. 3, 4, 6, 9, 13, 18, . . .

12. 56, 49, 42, 35, . . .

13. 0.1, 0.01, 0.001, . . .

14. 417.3, 391.6, 365.9, . . .

15. 120, 24, 4.8, 0.96, . . .

16. 1, 1, 2, 6, 24, 120, . . .

Problem-Solving Applications

17. **BUDGET** A computer software company is preparing its yearly budget. Over the last four years, the budget has been $8.4 million, $9 million, $10.2 million, and $12.6 million. If this pattern continues, what will be the budget for this year?

18. **CONSUMER MATH** Micah has a credit limit of $5,000 on his charge card. This month he has charged $200, $500, and then $1,250. If the pattern continues, what will be the amount of his next charge? How will the total charges compare with his limit?

19. Joey sells birdhouses to make money. In the first six months of his business, he sold 2, 2, 4, 6, 10, and 16 birdhouses. Following this pattern, how many birdhouses should he expect to sell in the eighth month?

20. **WRITE ABOUT IT** Describe the steps needed to find the next term in a sequence.

Mixed Review and Test Prep

Find the value.

21. 10^3 **22.** 10^6 **23.** 3^4 **24.** 7^3 **25.** 8^2 **26.** 5^3

Find the first four powers of the given number.

27. 4 **28.** 11 **29.** $\frac{1}{2}$ **30.** 2.3

31. **LOGICAL REASONING** Trees cost $123.45 each. Jacki has $2,215.00 to spend on trees. How many trees can she buy?

A 17 **B** 18
C 19 **D** 20

32. **BANKING** Maria had $118.00. She put 25% of it in the bank. She spent the rest. How much did she put in the bank?

F $18.00 **G** $25.00
H $29.50 **J** $88.50

MORE PRACTICE Lesson 19.3, page H69

LESSON 19.4

What You'll Learn
To recognize and use patterns involving positive and negative exponents

Why Learn This?
To use exponents to write very large or very small numbers such as those found in science

ALGEBRA CONNECTION

Patterns in Exponents

You can find patterns with positive and negative exponents.

The exponents you have used so far have been positive integers. You can also use negative integers as exponents.

EXAMPLE 1 Complete the pattern.

$10^3 = 10 \times 10 \times 10 = 1{,}000$
$10^2 = 10 \times 10 = 100$
$10^1 = 10$
$10^0 = 1$

Pattern: As the value of the exponent decreases, each number is $\frac{1}{10}$ as great as the previous number.

$10^{-1} = 0.1 = \frac{1}{10}$, or $\frac{1}{10^1}$

$10^{-2} = ■ = ■$ $\qquad 10^{-2} = 0.01 = \frac{1}{100}$, or $\frac{1}{10^2}$

$10^{-3} = ■ = ■$ $\qquad 10^{-3} = 0.001 = \frac{1}{1{,}000}$, or $\frac{1}{10^3}$

- For powers of 10, how is the negative exponent related to the number of decimal places?

The pattern also shows that an expression with a negative exponent can be written as a fraction, with 1 as the numerator and the expression with the corresponding positive exponent as the denominator.

$10^{-2} = \frac{1}{10^2}$ $\qquad 10^{-3} = \frac{1}{10^3}$

EXAMPLE 2 Write 2^{-3} and 5^{-6} as fractions.

$2^{-3} = \frac{1}{2^3} = \frac{1}{8}$ $\qquad 5^{-6} = \frac{1}{5^6} = \frac{1}{15{,}625}$

- Write 3^{-2} as a fraction.

SCIENCE LINK

The diameter of an influenza virus is about 0.000001 m. How is the number written as an expression with a negative exponent?

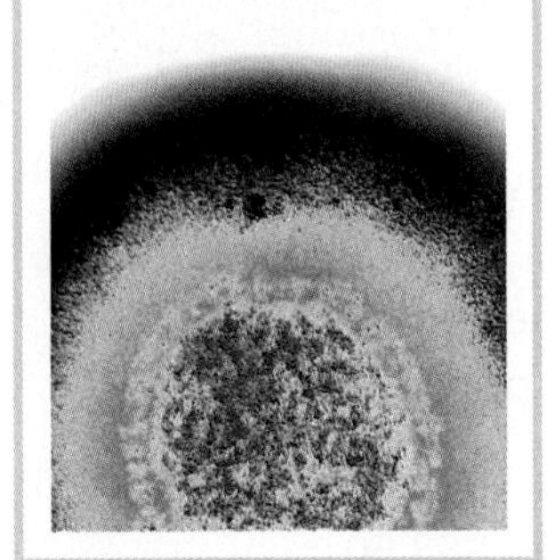

Talk About It CRITICAL THINKING

- Explain how you would rewrite the fraction $\frac{1}{25}$ as an expression with a negative exponent.
- When you write the expression $\left(\frac{1}{5}\right)^{-2}$ with a positive exponent, it becomes $\frac{1}{\left(\frac{1}{5}\right)^2}$. Is the value of this expression less than 1? Explain.
- Is the value of an expression with a negative exponent sometimes, always, or never less than 1? Explain.

GUIDED PRACTICE

Write each expression as a fraction.

1. 10^{-4} **2.** 4^{-5} **3.** 8^{-2} **4.** 3^{-4} **5.** 5^{-2}

6. 3^{-6} **7.** 10^{-6} **8.** 6^{-5} **9.** 4^{-2} **10.** 12^{-3}

INDEPENDENT PRACTICE

Write each expression using a positive exponent.

1. 10^{-8} **2.** 10^{-5} **3.** 7^{-3} **4.** 4^{-5}

5. 6^{-3} **6.** 2^{-4} **7.** 3^{-2} **8.** 8^{-4}

9. 2^{-3} **10.** 4^{-3} **11.** 2^{-2} **12.** 7^{-4}

Write each expression using a negative exponent.

13. $\frac{1}{10^1}$ **14.** $\frac{1}{10^6}$ **15.** $\frac{1}{4^2}$ **16.** $\frac{1}{3^3}$

17. $\frac{1}{6^4}$ **18.** $\frac{1}{5^7}$ **19.** $\frac{1}{7^3}$ **20.** $\frac{1}{4^5}$

21. $\frac{1}{10^7}$ **22.** $\frac{1}{2^3}$ **23.** $\frac{1}{100{,}000}$ **24.** $\frac{1}{2 \times 2 \times 2}$

25. $\frac{1}{5 \times 5}$ **26.** $\frac{1}{16}$ **27.** $\frac{1}{81}$ **28.** $\frac{1}{10 \times 10 \times 10}$

Problem-Solving Applications

For Problems 29–31, write *positive exponent* or *negative exponent* to tell how you would express the given number.

29. **MEASUREMENT** The diameter of a hydrogen atom is 0.0000000106 cm.

30. **MEASUREMENT** The weight of Earth is 6,600,000,000,000,000,000,000 T.

31. **MEASUREMENT** The weight of a dust particle is about 0.0000001 g.

32. **MEASUREMENT** The weight of a blue whale is about 200,000,000,000 mg.

33. **NUMBER SENSE** Eric wanted to see how much he grew in a year. He measured himself once a month and found he had grown an average of 2^{-2} in. each month. Express the average amount Eric grew each month as a fraction. What was his total growth for the year?

34. Brooke and Krista ran a race. Krista's time was 10.495 sec. It was $\frac{1}{1{,}000}$ sec faster than Brooke's time. Write the difference in their times by using an exponent. What was Brooke's time for the race?

35. **SCIENCE** A helium atom has a diameter of 2.2×10^{-8} cm. Write the power of 10 using a positive exponent.

36. **WRITE ABOUT IT** Explain which is greater, 2^{-3} or 3^{-2}.

MORE PRACTICE Lesson 19.4, page H70

CHAPTER 19 Review/Test

Rename the fraction as a decimal and identify it as terminating or repeating. (pages 372–374)

1. $\frac{5}{9}$ **2.** $\frac{3}{8}$ **3.** $\frac{9}{5}$ **4.** $\frac{5}{3}$

5. $\frac{9}{16}$ **6.** $\frac{9}{11}$ **7.** $\frac{5}{6}$ **8.** $\frac{1}{5}$

9. $\frac{3}{4}$ **10.** $\frac{7}{12}$ **11.** $\frac{1}{2}$ **12.** $\frac{5}{8}$

Find a rational number between the two numbers. (pages 375–377)

13. 2.56 and 2.57 **14.** $\frac{5}{8}$ and $\frac{7}{8}$ **15.** $\frac{1}{2}$ and 0.6

16. $^-4$ and $^-3$ **17.** $1\frac{5}{8}$ and 1.7 **18.** 1.3 and $\frac{7}{5}$

19. 2.7 and 2.8 **20.** $1\frac{3}{5}$ and 1.7 **21.** $^-1.38$ and $^-1.35$

22. $1\frac{2}{3}$ and 1.75 **23.** 3.6 and 3.7 **24.** $^-0.6$ and $^-0.5$

25. VOCABULARY When the pattern in a sequence is made by multiplying by the same number, the sequence is called a(n) __?__. (page 380)

Write the next two numbers in the sequence. (pages 379–381)

26. 1, 3, 5, 7, . . . **27.** 12.5, 12, 11.5, 11, . . . **28.** 18, 6, 2, $\frac{2}{3}$, . . . **29.** $\frac{1}{2}, \frac{1}{4}, \frac{1}{8}, \frac{1}{16}, \ldots$

30. 6, 12, 24, 48, . . . **31.** 0.3, 0.6, 1.2, 2.4, . . . **32.** $\frac{1}{3}, \frac{1}{9}, \frac{1}{27}, \frac{1}{81}, \ldots$ **33.** 6.1, 5.7, 5.3, 4.9, . . .

34. VOCABULARY The number used to multiply each term to produce the next is called the __?__. (page 380)

Write each expression using positive exponents. (pages 382–383)

35. 10^{-4} **36.** 4^{-4} **37.** 3^{-3} **38.** 2^{-2}

39. 5^{-2} **40.** 7^{-6} **41.** 8^{-3} **42.** 9^{-4}

Write each expression using a negative exponent. (pages 382–383)

43. $\frac{1}{2^6}$ **44.** $\frac{1}{4^2}$ **45.** $\frac{1}{3^7}$ **46.** $\frac{1}{49}$

47. $\frac{1}{25}$ **48.** $\frac{1}{9^3}$ **49.** $\frac{1}{12^5}$ **50.** $\frac{1}{6^3}$

Test Prep

CUMULATIVE CHAPTERS 1–19

1. Which is **NOT** a terminating decimal?

A $\frac{3}{4}$
B $\frac{7}{8}$
C $\frac{4}{3}$
D $\frac{18}{9}$

2. The scale on a map is 1 inch : 50 miles. If the map distance is 8.5 inches, what is the actual distance?

F 42.5 mi
G 400 mi
H 425 mi
J 850 mi

3. Which figure can be formed by the net?

A pentagonal pyramid
B cone
C hexagonal pyramid
D pentagonal prism

4. What is the value of the expression $x + 2(x - 5) + 7$ when $x = 3$?

F 6
G 10
H 11
J 28

5. Which rational number is between 3.8 and 3.9?

A 3.93
B 3.87
C 3.78
D 3.09

6. Natalie is reading a 352-page book. On the first day she read $\frac{1}{8}$ of the book. On the second day she read $\frac{1}{4}$ of the remaining pages. How many more pages does she have to read?

F 308
G 231
H 77
J 44

7. How many times must 4 be doubled to exceed 2,500?

A 8
B 9
C 10
D 11

8. A company's year-end profit was $59,728. Which is the best estimate of the company's average monthly profit?

F $5,000
G $6,000
H $7,000
J $8,000

9. The figures below are similar. What is the value of x?

A 5 cm
B 7.2 cm
C 8 cm
D 10 cm
E Not Here

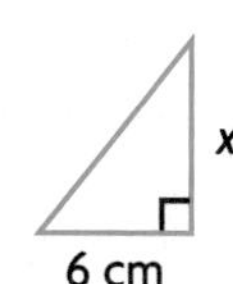

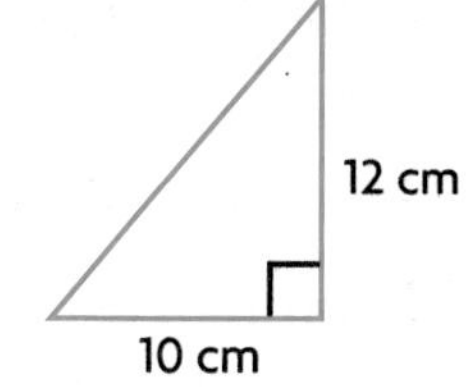

10. What is the seventh term in the sequence 48, 24, 12, 6, . . . ?

F 1.5
G 0.75
H 0.5
J 0.375

CHAPTERS 18–19

MATH FUN!

"I'M NOT MAKING A MESS."

PURPOSE To practice finding a rule for a divergent process (pages 362–363)
YOU WILL NEED a piece of paper, scissors

- Cut a piece of paper into five equal pieces.
- Cut any one of those pieces into five equal pieces, and so on.
- Make a table showing the number of times you cut and the number of pieces of paper you have after each cut.
- Can you think of a general rule or formula for the number of pieces you have after the nth time you complete the process?

DO ALL PATHS LEAD TO 1?

PURPOSE To practice following a repeating process (pages 365–367)

Start with any number in the diagram and you will get 1. Try with several different numbers.

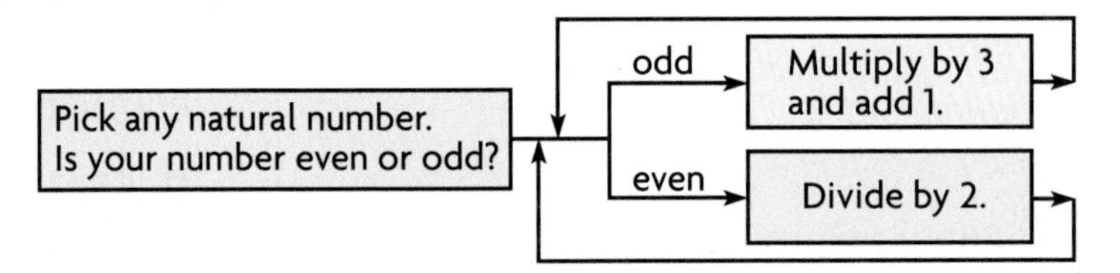

- Do you always get 1?
- Can you think of another pattern that will always lead to 1?

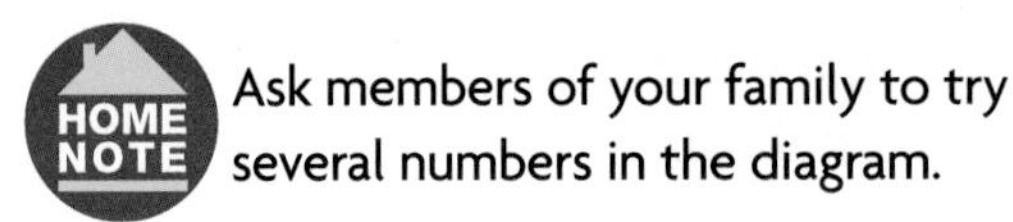

Ask members of your family to try several numbers in the diagram.

HARMONIC TRIANGLE

PURPOSE To practice identifying patterns in rational numbers (pages 375–377)

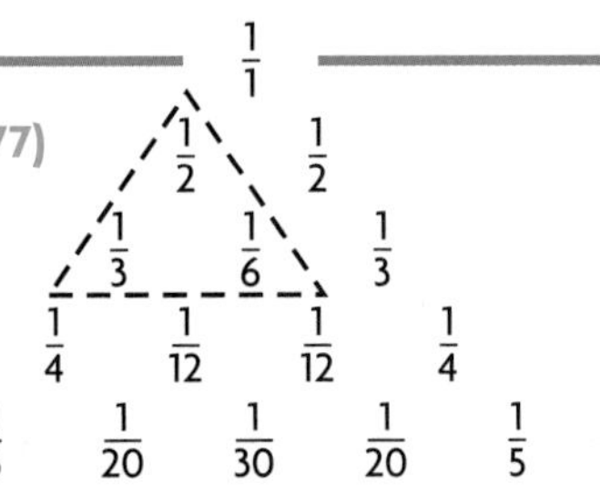

Gottfried Wilhelm Leibniz, a German mathematician, is known for the harmonic triangle. Each row in the triangle reads the same from left to right as from right to left.

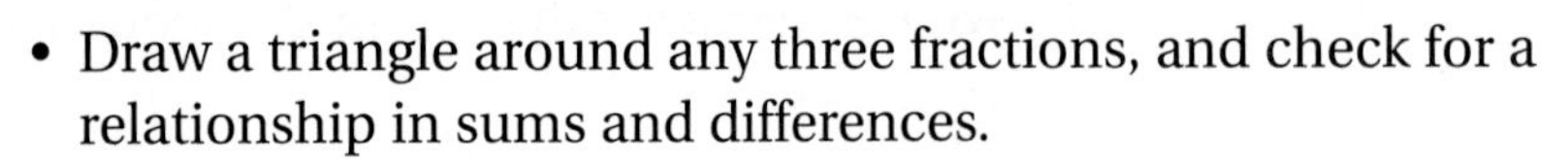

- Draw a triangle around any three fractions, and check for a relationship in sums and differences.

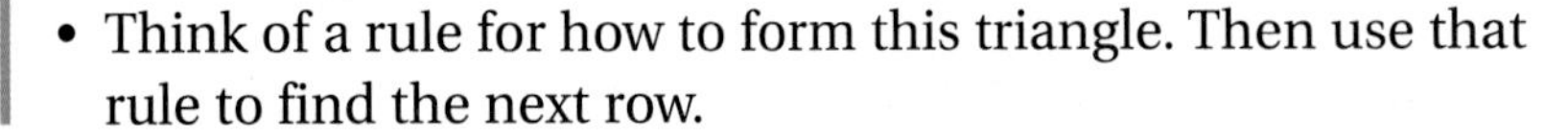

- Think of a rule for how to form this triangle. Then use that rule to find the next row.

Graphing Exponential Equations

You can generate the graph of powers of any number, n, by graphing an equation in the form of $y = n^x$. This type of equation is called an **exponential equation**. Use a *TI-82* graphing calculator to graph $y = 2^x$ and $y = 4^x$.

Enter the equation $y = 2^x$.

Y1=2^X
Y2=
Y3=
Y4=
Y5=
Y6=
Y7=
Y8=

Graph the equation.

GRAPH

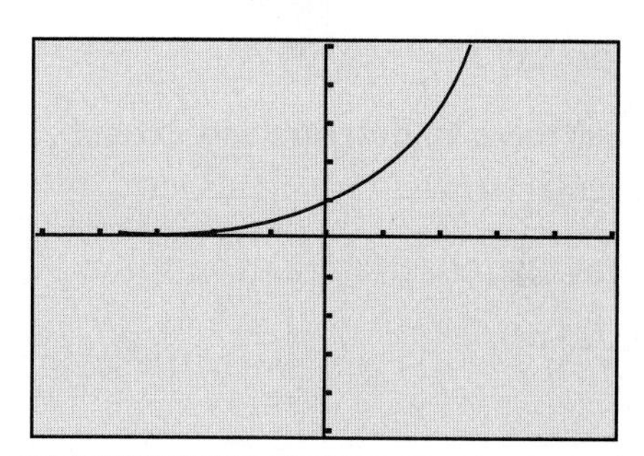

Enter the equation $y = 4^x$.

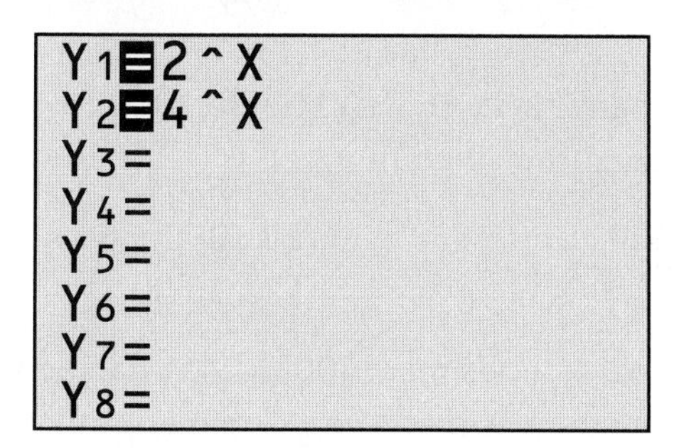

Graph the equation.

GRAPH

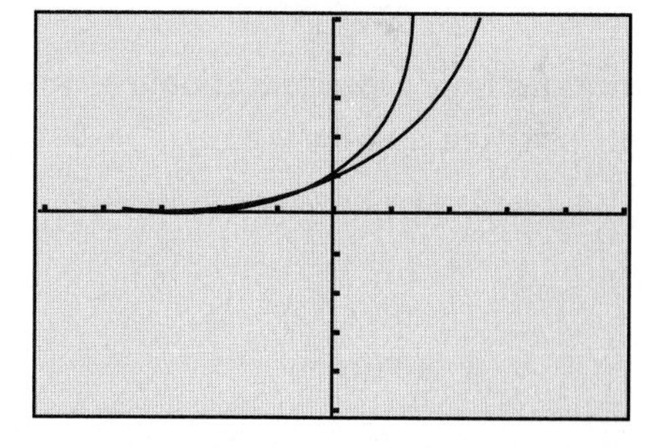

1. What does the x represent in each of the equations?

2. What does the ^ represent in each of the equations?

3. How would you graph the equation $y = 6^x$ using the graphing calculator?

4. Where do the graphs of $y = 2^x$ and $y = 4^x$ intersect?

USING THE GRAPHING CALCULATOR

Use a graphing calculator to graph the exponential equations.

5. $y = 3^x$ **6.** $y = 5^x$ **7.** $y = 6^x$ **8.** $y = 2.5^x$ **9.** $y = 0.5^x$ **10.** $y = 0.1^x$

11. Where do all of these graphs intersect?

12. What is $y = n^0$ for any value of n?

CHAPTERS 18–19

Study Guide and Review

Vocabulary Check

1. When you keep doubling a positive number, you can make it grow beyond any given number. We say the doubles _?_. (page 362)

2. When you divide to change a fraction to a decimal, and the remainder is not zero, the quotient is a(n) _?_ decimal. (page 372)

3. When the pattern in a sequence is found by multiplying the same number, the sequence is called a(n) _?_ sequence. (page 380)

EXAMPLES

- **Use patterns to describe and extend triangular arrays.** (pages 356–359)

Find the fortieth triangular number.

$\frac{n(n+1)}{2}$ *Write the formula.*

$\frac{40(41)}{2}$ *Replace n with 40.*

$\frac{1{,}640}{2} = 820$ ← fortieth number: 820

EXERCISES

Find the triangular number.

4. eighth **5.** seventeenth
6. thirty-ninth **7.** sixtieth
8. What will be the eighth row in this array?

1 ← Row 1
1 2 ← Row 2
1 2 3 ← Row 3
1 2 3 4 ← Row 4

EXAMPLES

- **Understand how repeated doubling or halving affects positive numbers.** (pages 362–363)

How many times must 8 be doubled to reach or exceed 50?

$8 \times 2 = 16$ *Double 1 time.*
$16 \times 2 = 32$ *Double 2 times.*
$32 \times 2 = 64$ *Double 3 times.*

So, 8 must be doubled at least 3 times.

EXERCISES

How many times must 10 be doubled to reach or exceed the given number?

9. 160 **10.** 300
11. 500 **12.** 10,000

How many times must 100,000 be halved to reach or be less than the given number?

13. 20,000 **14.** 6,250
15. 1,000 **16.** 50

EXAMPLES

- **See patterns in powers of numbers.** (pages 365–367)

Find the first four powers of 4.

Start with 1. → Multiply by 4. (repeat)

$4^1 = 4$
$4^2 = 4 \times 4 = 16$
$4^3 = 4 \times 4 \times 4 = 64$
$4^4 = 4 \times 4 \times 4 \times 4 = 256$

EXERCISES

Find the first four powers of each.

17. 2 **18.** $\frac{3}{4}$
19. $\frac{2}{3}$ **20.** 8
21. 5 **22.** $\frac{1}{2}$
23. $\frac{5}{6}$ **24.** 7

- **Recognize and use patterns in decimals.** (pages 372–374)

Rename the fraction as a decimal and identify it as terminating or repeating.

$\frac{1}{3} = 0.333\ldots$ or $0.\overline{3}$; repeating

$\frac{3}{8} = 0.375$; terminating

Rename the fraction as a decimal, and identify it as terminating or repeating.

25. $\frac{3}{4}$ **26.** $\frac{2}{3}$

27. $\frac{5}{12}$ **28.** $\frac{3}{8}$

29. $\frac{3}{10}$ **30.** $\frac{7}{15}$

- **Use patterns to find a rational number between two rational numbers.** (pages 375–377)

Find a rational number between 3.7 and 3.8.

3.7 = 3.70 *Add zeros to both decimals.*
3.8 = 3.80 3.70 and 3.80
Possible answers include 3.73 and 3.75.

Find a rational number between the two numbers.

31. 3.45 and 3.46 **32.** $\frac{3}{8}$ and $\frac{9}{16}$

33. $^-5$ and $^-6$ **34.** $\frac{2}{5}$ and $\frac{3}{5}$

35. $^-8.3$ and $^-8.5$ **36.** $\frac{-2}{3}$ and $\frac{-3}{4}$

- **Recognize and use patterns involving exponents.** (pages 382–383)

Write each expression. Use a positive or negative exponent.

$2^{-5} = \frac{1}{2^5}$ $\frac{1}{4^2} = 4^{-2}$

Write using a positive exponent.

37. 10^{-5} **38.** 2^{-3}

Write using a negative exponent.

39. $\frac{1}{6^7}$ **40.** $\frac{1}{64}$

PROBLEM-SOLVING APPLICATIONS

Solve. Explain your method.

41. At the chili festival, you can put cheese, onions, and chips on the chili. How many different kinds of chili can you make with 0, 1, 2, or 3 toppings? (pages 360–361)

42. At a closeout sale, everything is marked $\frac{1}{4}$ off. What decimal could you use to find the amount of savings? (pages 372–374)

43. Desmond started a job at \$6.00 per hour. After six months, he made \$6.35 per hour. After a year, he made \$6.70 per hour, and after a year and a half, he made \$7.05 per hour. If this trend continues, how much will he make per hour after two years? (pages 379–381)

44. The Jewelry Center ships friendship bracelets in boxes. In the first 6 weeks of business, it shipped 3, 3, 6, 9, 15, and 24 boxes of bracelets. How many boxes should the Jewelry Center expect to ship in the eighth week? (pages 379–381)

CHAPTERS 18–19

Performance Assessment

Tasks: Show What You Know

1. Explain each step as you determine how many times 3 must be doubled to reach or exceed 100. (pages 362–363)

2. Explain how you would use a positive exponent to write 4^{-5}, and how you would use a negative exponent to write $\frac{1}{7^3}$. (pages 382–383)

Problem Solving

Solve. Explain your method.

CHOOSE a strategy and a tool.

- **Find a Pattern**
- **Make a Model**
- **Write a Number Sentence**
- **Act It Out**
- **Make a Table**

Paper/Pencil

Calculator
Hands-On

Mental Math

3. Phil and Phoebe are planting flowers in pots to decorate the front of the school. The flowers are red, pink, white, yellow, orange, and purple. How many different combinations of 0, 1, 2, 3, 4, 5, or 6 flowers can they plant in the pots? (pages 360–361)

4. The students in Mrs. Garza's class want to collect 250 aluminum cans to raise money. The table below shows how many cans they collected each week in the first 6 weeks. If this pattern continues, how many cans will they collect in Week 9? In which week will the class reach its goal? (pages 379–381)

Week 1	8 cans
Week 2	8 cans
Week 3	16 cans
Week 4	24 cans
Week 5	40 cans
Week 6	64 cans

Cumulative Review

CHAPTERS 1–19

Solve the problem. Then write the letter of the correct answer.

1. What is the value of 70^2? (pages 36–39)

   A. 72 **B.** 140
   C. 702 **D.** 4,900

2. Subtract. Write the answer in simplest form. (pages 80–81)
   $\frac{4}{5} - \frac{3}{10}$

   A. $\frac{1}{5}$ **B.** $\frac{7}{15}$
   C. $\frac{1}{2}$ **D.** $\frac{1}{10}$

3. Find the product. (pages 106–108)
   $^-20 \times {^-10}$

   A. 200 **B.** 2
   C. $^-2$ **D.** $^-200$

4. What is the eighth term in the sequence? (pages 134–137)
   6, 11, 16, 21, . . .

   A. 26 **B.** 36
   C. 41 **D.** not here

5. Solve the proportion. (pages 152–155)
   $\frac{42.2}{16} = \frac{x}{12}$

   A. 4.55 **B.** 31.65
   C. 38.2 **D.** 506.4

6. The math test has 5 less than twice as many problems as the science test. The math test has 25 problems. How many problems are on the science test? (pages 162–163)

   A. 15 **B.** 20
   C. 30 **D.** not here

7. In the word VIDEO, which letter has line symmetry but not rotational symmetry? (pages 203–205)

   A. I **B.** E
   C. O **D.** not here

8. Name the figure you would see in the back view. (pages 246–249)

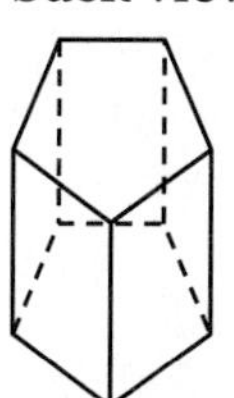

   A. prism **B.** rectangle
   C. square **D.** triangle

9. Find the unit price if 6 cans of soda cost \$2.58. (pages 280–283)

   A. \$0.43 **B.** \$3.42
   C. \$15.48 **D.** not here

10. What percent of 80 is 4? (pages 301–303)

    A. 0.05% **B.** 5%
    C. 20% **D.** 320%

11. What scale factor relates the volumes of the larger cube and the smaller cube? (pages 323–325)

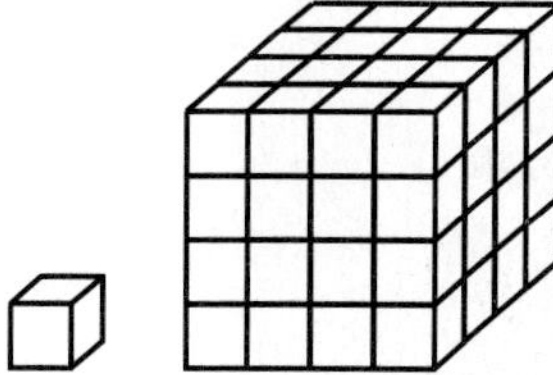

    A. 4 **B.** 3
    C. 16 **D.** 64

12. Rename $\frac{7}{3}$ as a decimal. (pages 372–374)

    A. $0.\overline{428571}$ **B.** $0.\overline{73}$
    C. $2.\overline{3}$ **D.** $4.\overline{124}$

CHAPTER

20 COLLECTING DATA: SAMPLING

LOOK AHEAD

In this chapter you will solve problems that involve

- choosing an appropriate sample
- determining whether a sample is biased
- writing survey questions and conducting a survey
- organizing the data from a survey

VOTE

SOCIAL STUDIES LINK

One of the major responsibilities of a political convention is to nominate candidates for presidential elections. Since 1856, the Democrats have nominated 9 winning candidates, who served a total of 15 terms. The Republicans have nominated 15 winning candidates for a total of 21 terms.

- In the 1996 election, about 49% of all Americans of voting age actually voted. If there were approximately 197,700,000 Americans of voting age, about how many voted?

Problem-Solving Project

Opinion Polls

Suppose you want to know what typical seventh graders prefer for music, snacks, movies, when to have a party, or other questions. Design a survey. Choose one question. Survey all the girls in your class. Survey all the boys in your class. Write a paragraph comparing the results from your two samples.

PROJECT CHECKLIST

- ✓ Did you design a survey?
- ✓ Did you survey two different samples?
- ✓ Did you write about your findings?

LESSON 20.1

Choosing a Sample

What You'll Learn
How to identify and use different types of samples

Why Learn This?
To understand what kind of sample to use when taking a poll or a survey

VOCABULARY
- **population**
- **sample**
- **random sample**
- **systematic sample**
- **stratified sample**

How can you find out which car is most popular among teenagers?

You can survey a whole group, or **population**, by taking a part, or a **sample** of the group. The sample must be representative of the population. The population can be a group of people or a group of objects.

There are many types of sampling methods. Three methods are random sampling, systematic sampling, and stratified sampling.

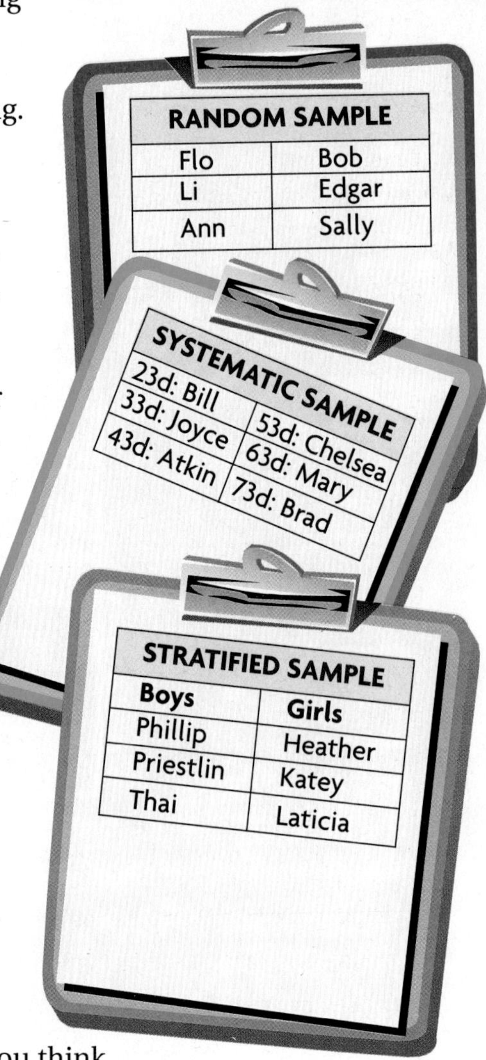

RANDOM SAMPLE
Flo
Bob
Li
Edgar
Ann
Sally
SYSTEMATIC SAMPLE
23d: Bill
53d: Chelsea
33d: Joyce
63d: Mary
43d: Atkin
73d: Brad
STRATIFIED SAMPLE
Boys
Girls
Phillip
Heather
Priestlin
Katey
Thai
Laticia

For a **random sample**, every individual or object in a given population has an equal chance of being selected for the sample.

For a **systematic sample**, you randomly select an individual or object and then follow a pattern to select others in the sample. For example, you could choose an individual or object and then choose every third, fifth, or *n*th individual or object.

For a **stratified sample**, a population is divided into subgroups, called strata, that contain similar individuals or objects. For example, one stratum may be girls and another stratum boys. A few individuals are then randomly selected from each stratum.

- CRITICAL THINKING Why do you think a sample is used rather than a whole population when surveying?

Before you collect data, you need to decide which type of sample to use.

EXAMPLE 1 The Mathematics Department was asked to conduct a survey to find which group of students uses calculators most often. They surveyed 25 elementary school students, 25 middle school students, 25 high school students, and 25 college students. Which sampling method did they use?

They used stratified sampling by dividing the student population into four strata: elementary school, middle school, high school, and college.

- Suppose you want to know the favorite model of calculator of students in Grade 6, Grade 7, and Grade 8. What type of sampling could you use? Explain.

SOCIAL STUDIES LINK

During any political campaign, but especially during a presidential campaign, many surveys are conducted to determine which candidate voters favor. Surveys for newspapers or TV are usually of a random sample of voters, but occasionally a stratified sample is used. What strata of American voters might a presidential candidate want to sample? Why?

EXAMPLE 2 Which of the following is an example of a systematic sampling procedure that a quality-checker might use on an assembly line?

a. Check the first 50 items that come off the assembly line.

b. Randomly check items from the assembly line.

c. Check every twentieth item off the assembly line.

Both **a** and **c** are examples of systematic sampling. In Choice **a**, the pattern is to select every item in the first fifty. In Choice **c**, the pattern is to select every twentieth item that comes off the assembly line.

- What other sampling method might be appropriate for checking the quality of items?

GUIDED PRACTICE

Determine the type of sample.

1. A survey crew randomly chose 200 motorists and asked them which route they take to the airport.

2. A survey is conducted to determine how many snacks boys eat and girls eat in a day.

3. Workers on an assembly line check every tenth tire in a bicycle-tire manufacturing plant.

4. A fitness center conducts a survey to find out how many men and how many women use its equipment.

INDEPENDENT PRACTICE

1. George is conducting a survey to find out how many people own pets. How can he get a systematic sample?

2. In a survey of pet owners, what are some possible strata, or subgroups, for a stratified sample?

3. Maria is conducting a survey to find out how many people own cars. How can she get a random sample?

4. The following table shows the results when people were randomly selected to name their favorite sport. Show how the results might look for a stratified sample. Do the same for a systematic sample.

RANDOM SAMPLE		
Tennis	Swimming	Soccer
Softball	Baseball	Bicycling

Problem-Solving Applications

Indicate the type of sample.

5. **ENTERTAINMENT** Out of 50 movie theater patrons, every fifth person is asked to complete a survey.

6. A group of 20 boys and 20 girls are asked if they prefer to go to a concert or a sports event.

7. **CAREER** One hundred mechanics are randomly chosen from a list of certified mechanics to find out which make and model of automobile needs the most repairs.

8. **WRITE ABOUT IT** Describe the differences between a random sample, a systematic sample, and a stratified sample.

Mixed Review and Test Prep

Tell whether each sample could represent your school population.

9. 100 boys

10. 100 boys and girls

11. 100 seventh graders

Give the next term in the sequence.

12. 0.75, 0.90, 1.05, . . .

13. $10^1, 10^2, 10^4, \ldots$

14. $^-2, 4, ^-8, 16, \ldots$

15. **RATIOS** Alicia is on a trip. A map's scale is 1 inch equals 52 miles. If Alicia covers a map distance of $6\frac{1}{2}$ inches, how far does she travel?

   A 520 mi **B** 364 mi
   C 338 mi **D** 312 mi

16. **RATES** Which is the best buy for a can of mushrooms?

   F 8-oz can for $1.29
   G 12-oz can for $1.69
   H 16-oz can for $2.29
   J 24-oz can for $3.59

MORE PRACTICE Lesson 20.1, page H70

Bias in Samples

LESSON 20.2

What You'll Learn
How to determine whether a sample is biased

Why Learn This?
To understand what is a good sample for a poll or survey

VOCABULARY
biased

When choosing a sample, you need to make sure the sample is not biased. A sample is **biased** when every feature of the population is not proportionately represented by the sample.

PERCENT WHO EXERCISE DAILY		
Grade	Sample	Percent
6	20 students	20
7	20 athletes	60
8	20 students	25

• Do you think the news flash shown on the television screen is right? Explain.

EXAMPLE Suppose the marketing department of a radio station wants to determine what times of day people under the age of 20 listen to the radio. Which of the following sampling approaches would be biased?

a. randomly surveying 100 listeners that are girls

b. randomly surveying 100 listeners under the age of 20

c. randomly surveying 100 listeners under the age of 16

d. randomly surveying 100 listeners

Choice **b** is the only sample that is probably not biased. Choice **a** leaves out boys, choice **c** leaves out the age-group 17–19, and choice **d** could include listeners who are 20 or older.

Sometimes the sample used is not biased but the questions used to gather the data for the sample are biased. Survey questions are biased if the questions lead to a specific response.

LANGUAGE LINK

The word *bias* is from a French word meaning "slope" or "slant." In English, *bias* can also mean "prejudice." Why is it important for a sample not to be biased toward one person or position?

GUIDED PRACTICE

1. Determine whether the following question is biased. Do you agree with all other teens that aerobics is a great way to stay in shape?

2. To identify the most popular style of shoes, a shoe store includes a questionnaire in every tenth shoe box that is sold. Do you think the results will be biased? Explain.

INDEPENDENT PRACTICE

Answer the following questions.

1. Is a survey about favorite toys of 2-year-olds biased if it includes 3-year-olds? Explain.

2. Is a survey of favorite restaurants biased if it names one restaurant as an example? Explain.

3. How do you determine if a sample is biased or not?

4. Give an example of a biased question.

A publishing company does a survey to find out when children aged 7–12 start reading paperback books. Tell whether the given sample is biased. If it is, tell why.

5. A random survey of 250 children

6. A random survey of 250 children aged 10–12

7. A random survey of 250 boys aged 7–12

8. A random survey of 250 children aged 7–12

An automobile dealer surveys 500 adults about the type of car they like. Tell whether the given sample is biased. If it is, tell why.

9. A random survey of 500 people who own Toyotas

10. A random survey of 500 women

11. A random survey of 500 adults

12. A random survey of 300 men and 200 women

Problem-Solving Applications

Determine whether the question is biased.

13. Do you agree with the president of the company that memos should be typed, not handwritten?

14. **CONSUMER MATH** Do you feel that the brand of sports watch worn by Olympic competitors is better than other brands?

15. **ENTERTAINMENT** What radio station do you listen to?

16. **ENTERTAINMENT** What is your favorite movie?

17. **FITNESS** Do you agree with your hometown basketball team that the best way to stay in shape is by exercising?

18. **HEALTH** Do you think your school cafeteria serves enough low-fat meals?

19. What book did you most enjoy reading this year?

20. **WRITE ABOUT IT** If you ask 12 boys in your class for their opinions, will your results be representative of your class? Explain.

MORE PRACTICE Lesson 20.2, page H70

Writing Survey Questions

LESSON 20.3

What You'll Learn
How to write survey questions

Why Learn This?
To write better questions to get useful data

Surveys are often used to gather data from a sample. Surveys are usually made up of questions or other items that require responses.

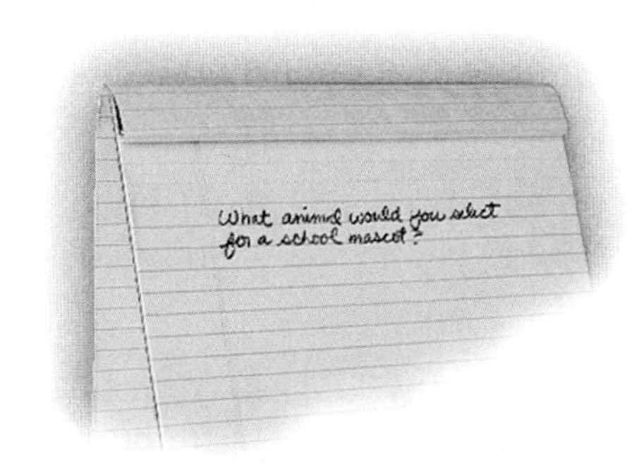

What animal would you select for a school mascot?

You can write survey questions in different formats to get different types of responses.

multiple-choice	fill-in-the-blank
numerical	short answer

Suppose Bob wants to determine the number of students who watch television programs about nature. He wrote one of his survey questions in different formats.

Do you watch programs about nature?

On a scale of 1 to 5, how often do you watch programs about nature?

Which program do you prefer?
a. nature **b.** music
c. art **d.** other

When you watch programs, you prefer them to be about __?__.

- Identify the format used in each of the questions above about television programs.
- CRITICAL THINKING Why would you choose one question format rather than another?

When writing survey questions, make sure they are concise, have only one response per question, and use words that have the same meaning to all persons.

ACTIVITY

- Choose one of the following topics: where students ride bikes, amount of time spent on homework by students involved in after-school activities, or number of students who buy their lunch versus bring their lunch.
- Write four or five survey questions for your topic. Trade survey questions with a classmate to check whether each is concise, requires one response, and means the same to everyone.

TEEN TIMES

Have you ever been asked questions for a survey? Many teens have. Some surveys are conducted in schools. Also, in many shopping malls, market research firms survey consumers for their opinions about various products. If you would like to take part in one of these surveys, see if there is a market research firm in a mall in your area, and then stop in and volunteer.

GUIDED PRACTICE

For Exercises 1–6, name the format of the survey question.

1. When ordering a pizza, your choice of topping is usually __?__.

2. What is your favorite topping on a pizza?

3. Which pizza topping do you prefer?
a. pepperoni **b.** mushrooms
c. peppers **d.** other

4. Using a scale of 1 to 3, how would you rate pizza with anchovy topping?

5. What kind of movie do you prefer to rent from a video store?

6. Your favorite kind of movie to rent from a video store is __?__.

INDEPENDENT PRACTICE

For Exercises 1–6, name the format of the survey question.

1. What is your favorite color for a car?

2. Your favorite video game is __?__.

3. What is your favorite subject?
a. math **b.** science
c. English **d.** other

4. What type of museum do you prefer?

5. From 1 to 5, how would you rate your school's volleyball team?

6. What is the primary language you speak at home?

Tell whether the question would be a good survey question.
Write *yes* or *no*. If you write *no*, explain.

7. Are the long hours in band practice fun?

8. What is your favorite fruit?

9. Is your favorite type of music jazz or classical?

10. Which season do you like best, and why?

Susan wrote these questions for a survey. Determine whether the questions are biased.

11. Do you prefer listening to that relaxing classical music or that loud rock music?

12. When listening to music, what type of music do you prefer?

Problem-Solving Applications

Write an appropriate question.

13. Tasha is conducting a survey to find out which advertisements are noticed the most. Write a question she could use.

14. **ENTERTAINMENT** Write a numerical-response survey question about a recent movie.

15. **CRITICAL THINKING** What is a good survey question to ask bicycle-shop owners before buying a bike?

16. **WRITE ABOUT IT** Describe the qualities of a good survey question.

MORE PRACTICE Lesson 20.3, page H71

Conducting a Survey

What You'll Explore
How to use what you have learned about samples, bias, and survey questions to conduct a survey

You can use what you have learned about samples, bias, and survey questions to conduct your own survey.

Explore

- Select one of the following topics for a survey.
  - **a.** Favorite television shows
  - **b.** Favorite fast-food restaurants
  - **c.** Favorite video games
- Prepare three multiple-choice questions for your survey.
- Survey 25 students. Select the students by random sampling, stratified sampling, or systematic sampling.
- Make a recording sheet for your data. Here is a sample recording sheet for collecting data from a stratified sample.

BOYS		
Questions		
1	2	3

GIRLS		
Questions		
1	2	3

Technology Link
You can collect and analyze data by using E-Lab, Activity 20. Available on CD-ROM and on the Internet at
www.hbschool.com/elab

Think and Discuss CRITICAL THINKING

- What other types of questions could you have written for your survey?
- Compare your survey results with those of other students who chose the same topic but used a different sampling method. Do your results show the same favorite television show, fast-food restaurant, or video game?

Try This

Write a paragraph describing how effective your questions were. Did the students you sampled understand the questions?

LESSON 20.4

Organizing and Displaying Results

What You'll Learn
How to organize and display data from a survey

Why Learn This?
To present collected data from a survey as a table or graph

Fifty teens were surveyed about the overall quality of a minibackpack. The results were organized in a cumulative frequency table. The table shows that 28 of 50 teens thought that the minibackpack had good or very good quality.

QUALITY OF MINIBACKPACK			
Quality	**Tally**	**Frequency**	**Cumulative Frequency**
Very good	HHT HHT HHT III	18	18
Good	HHT HHT	10	28
Fair	HHT III	8	36
Poor	HHT HHT IIII	14	50

- How many of the 50 teens surveyed rated the minibackpack's quality as fair or better?

Categories in frequency tables can be equal intervals, such as different age-groups.

EXAMPLE 1 Use the data to make a cumulative frequency table. Use age intervals of 7–10, 11–14, 15–18, and 19–22.

Age of Students Who Read Garfield				
8	12	16	20	22
15	7	8	11	13
14	9	14	8	10
21	18	11	13	9

Make a tally for each age in the appropriate interval. In the frequency column, record the total for each interval. To find the cumulative frequency, find the sum of the given frequency and all frequencies listed above it.

STUDENTS WHO READ GARFIELD				
Age Group	**Tally**	**Frequency**	**Cumulative Frequency**	
7–10	HHT II	7	7	
11–14	HHT II	7	14	← 7 + 7
15–18	III	3	17	← 14 + 3
19–22	III	3	20	← 17 + 3

Comics have gone high-tech. Some of the most popular sites on the Internet are those that feature cartoons and comics. Net comics receiving many hits include *Dilbert, The Far Side, BC,* and *Peanuts.* What's your favorite comic? Chances are, it has a home page on the World Wide Web. Check it out next time you're surfing the Net.

A line plot can be used to record as you collect data or to organize after you have collected data.

EXAMPLE 2 Eight different radio stations were surveyed about the average length of time they play music without a commercial interruption. Use the data to make a line plot.

Music Time on Radio Stations	
22 min	31 min
30 min	39 min
40 min	30 min
34 min	20 min

Step 1: Draw a horizontal line.

Step 2: Put a scale of numbers on this line in equal intervals, using vertical tick marks. Since the shortest time of music at a radio station is 20 min and the longest is 40 min, the scale could run from 15 to 45.

Step 3: Plot the data.

Each • represents the length of time that one radio station plays music without a commercial interruption.

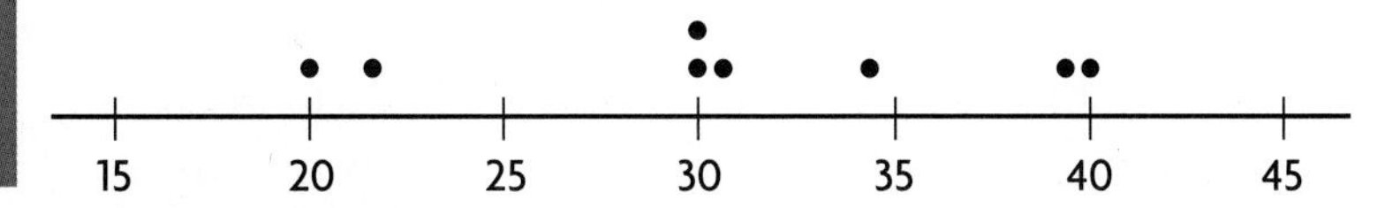

Technology Link
In Data ToolKit you can practice making line plots to record and organize data.
HARCOURT BRACE
Data ToolKit

- Ask ten people in your class to estimate how many minutes it takes them to get from home to school each day.
- Record the data in a cumulative frequency table.
- Make a line plot of your data.

GUIDED PRACTICE

The table shows how many hours three grades volunteered to help clean up the schoolyard. Copy and complete.

	VOLUNTEER HOURS			
	Grade	**Tally**	**Frequency**	**Cumulative Frequency**
1.	6th	𝍸 𝍸 𝍸 𝍸	?	20
2.	7th	𝍸 𝍸 𝍸 𝍸 ||||	24	?
3.	8th	𝍸 𝍸 𝍸 |	?	60

Stem-and-Leaf Plots

You can use a stem-and-leaf plot to display data. A stem-and-leaf plot is made up of leaves, which are the right-hand digits of each number, and stems, which are the remaining digits to the left.

Student Heights (in cm)		
167	152	130
140	158	136

Stem	Leaves
13	0 6
14	0
15	2 8
16	7

13 | 0 means 130.

EXAMPLE 3 Make a stem-and-leaf plot of the data in the table about speeds of different animals.

HOW FAST CAN THEY GO?	
Animal	**Speed (in mph)**
Lion	50
Cape hunting dog	45
Zebra	40
Rabbit	35
Reindeer	32
Grizzly bear	30
Cat (domestic)	30
Elephant	25

Stem	Leaves
2	
3	
4	
5	

Write the stems by listing the tens digits in order from least to greatest, vertically with a line to the right.

Stem	Leaves
2	5
3	0 0 2 5
4	0 5
5	0

Then write the corresponding leaves by listing the ones digits next to each stem, in order.

- What are the intervals in the stem-and-leaf plot in Example 3?
- What value is shown by the second leaf on the third stem?
- What value occurs twice?

INDEPENDENT PRACTICE

1. After totaling tally marks to find frequencies, how do you get cumulative frequencies?

2. The football team played 5 games in 5 weeks. List the team's scores shown in this line plot.

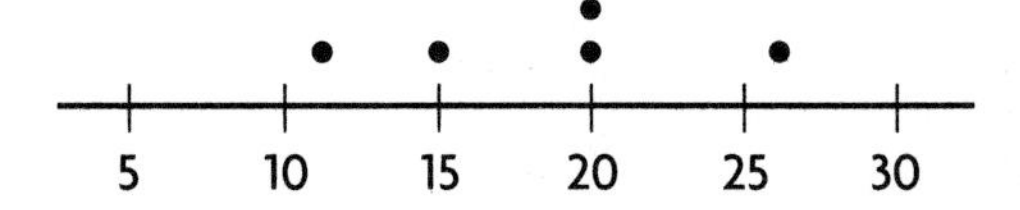

3. Name the intervals in the stem-and-leaf plot.

Stem	Leaves
1	1
2	0 0 1 6
3	2 7
4	0 8

4. Name the intervals in the stem-and-leaf plot.

Stem	Leaves
21	0 5
22	5 5 7 8
23	2 4 7
24	3

5. Make a stem-and-leaf plot for the following math scores: 72, 70, 75, 81, 73, 77, 80, 98, 85, 82, 77, 89, 93, 96, 92, 100, 90, 100, 88, 91, 75, 85, 77, 84.

6. Record this data in a line plot.

Miles Jogged Every Day						
S	M	T	W	T	F	S
3	2	3	4	4	6	8

Problem-Solving Applications

Seventh graders were asked about their favorite game shows. The results are in the table.

Game Show	Tally	Frequency	Cumulative Frequency
Name Songs	𝍸 ||||	9	9
Tell Truths	𝍸 |||	8	17
Eureka	𝍸 𝍸 |	11	28
Money Madness	𝍸 𝍸	10	38

7. COMPARE Which show was the most popular among seventh graders? How many seventh graders liked it?

8. Why is 38 the cumulative frequency for Money Madness?

9. SPORTS Make a cumulative frequency table to show that in Mrs. Webster's PE class, 15 students like basketball best, 10 like baseball, 5 like soccer, and 3 like hockey. What is the cumulative frequency for all the sports? What is the cumulative frequency for baseball and soccer?

10. WRITE ABOUT IT When would you use a stem-and-leaf plot instead of a line plot?

Mixed Review and Test Prep

Find the range of the temperatures.

11. 60°, 55°, 63°, 70°, 64°, 71°, 75°

12. 13°, 2°, 8°, 72°, 17°, 94°, 56°

Rename the fraction as a terminating or repeating decimal.

13. $\frac{1}{3}$ **14.** $\frac{1}{11}$ **15.** $\frac{1}{12}$ **16.** $\frac{3}{4}$ **17.** $\frac{2}{5}$ **18.** $\frac{5}{8}$

19. LOGICAL REASONING The Hungry Time sandwich shop changes its luncheon special once every two weeks. How many specials does it offer in one year?

A 24 **B** 25 **C** 26 **D** 52

20. ALGEBRA If you multiply the digits in a two-digit number and add 28, you get 48. What is the number?

F 10 **G** 12
H 20 **J** 45

MORE PRACTICE Lesson 20.4, page H71

CHAPTER 20 Review/Test

1. **VOCABULARY** A group of people or items chosen to represent a population is a(n) __?__. (page 394)

Determine which sampling method is used. (pages 394–396)

2. With an equal chance of being selected, 50 companies are chosen from a list of the Fortune 500 companies.
3. Every twentieth student is surveyed about after-school activities.
4. A park employee surveys 25 people from each of four age groups.
5. A supermarket surveys every fifth customer about cereal preferences.
6. Five students are surveyed from each of six grade levels.
7. One hundred employees are chosen at random from a list of all employees.

Determine whether the survey is biased. (pages 397–398)

8. A car dealer checks the quality of her service department by interviewing people after their cars have been serviced.
9. After customers have had their cars serviced, a car dealer asks, "Wouldn't you agree that we give friendly service?"
10. To evaluate students' use of the library, a school librarian randomly surveys 500 students in the school.
11. To learn people's favorite car color, a car manufacturer surveys 100 people who own white cars.

Identify the question format. (pages 399–400)

12. Are you between the ages of 12 and 15?
13. If you were to participate in a sport, you would choose _______.
14. How would you rate the safety of riding a bike *and* wearing a helmet, on a scale from 1 to 5?
15. Which is your favorite month?
    a. June **b.** December
    c. March **d.** September
16. Rewrite the question in Exercise 12 as a multiple-choice question.
17. Rewrite the question in Exercise 15 as a fill-in-the-blank question.

Use the data at the top right for Exercises 18 and 19. (pages 402–405)

18. Make a line plot.
19. Make a stem-and-leaf plot.
20. Use the data at the bottom right to make a line plot and a stem-and-leaf plot. (pages 402–405)

Heights of Ten Students (in inches)				
62	60	58	70	60
56	61	60	68	56

Numbers of Students in Homerooms					
37	35	35	34	24	27
32	29	27	35	28	21

Test Prep

1. Which set of data is represented by the line plot?

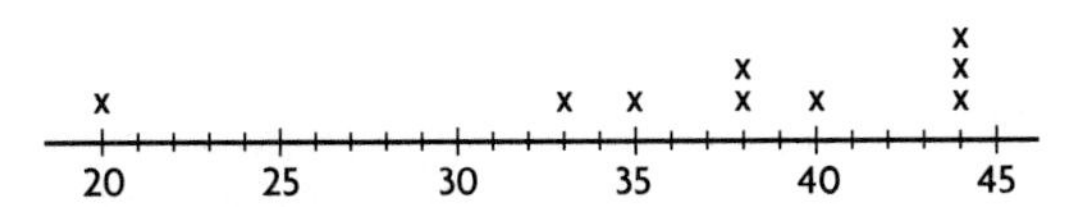

A 30, 34, 35, 37, 37, 40, 44
B 30, 33, 35, 38, 40, 44
C 30, 33, 35, 35, 37, 40, 44, 44
D 20, 33, 35, 38, 38, 40, 44, 44, 44

2. Which fraction can be written as a terminating decimal?

F $\frac{7}{9}$　　**G** $\frac{5}{6}$

H $\frac{3}{5}$　　**J** $\frac{1}{3}$

3. Which is less than the fourth power of $\frac{2}{5}$?

A $\left(\frac{3}{4}\right)^3$

B $\left(\frac{2}{3}\right)^2$

C $\left(\frac{1}{4}\right)^5$

D $\left(\frac{5}{6}\right)^1$

4. The scale factor for the areas of two similar triangles is 9:36. What is the scale factor for the lengths of the sides?

F 1:2
G 1:4
H 4.5:9
J 4.5:18

5. What is the solution of the equation $10n - 12 + 5n = 78$?

A $n = 4$
B $n = 6$
C $n = 11$
D $n = 18$

6. Triangle XYZ has coordinates $X(0,0)$, $Y(0,5)$, and $Z(4,0)$. What are the coordinates of the image of triangle XYZ translated 5 units left and 2 units down?

F $X'(^-5,^-2)$, $Y'(^-5,3)$, $Z'(^-1,^-2)$
G $X'(^-2,^-5)$, $Y'(^-2,0)$, $Z'(2,^-5)$
H $X'(2,5)$, $Y'(2,10)$, $Z'(6,5)$
J $X'(5,2)$, $Y'(5,7)$, $Z'(9,2)$

7. Two angles are complementary. One angle is 15° more than twice the other. What are the angle measures?

A 20°, 70°
B 25°, 65°
C 30°, 150°
D 35°, 145°

8. The table shows the number of words Lou can type in a certain amount of time. If the pattern continues, how many words will he type in 5 minutes?

Time	1 min	2 min	3 min
Number of Words	55	110	165

F 330
G 275
H 250
J 220

9. Kevin is making phone calls for a fund-raiser. He can make an average of 12 calls in 1 hour. About how many calls can he make in 3 hours?

A 24
B 36
C 48
D 60
E Not Here

CHAPTER

21 ANALYZING DATA

LOOK AHEAD

In this chapter you will solve problems that involve

- histograms, stem-and-leaf plots, and box-and-whisker graphs
- measures of central tendency
- appropriate uses of graphs
- analyzing misleading graphs

SOCIAL STUDIES LINK

In 1996, 98% of U.S. households, or 97 million homes, had at least one television. Of those homes, 99% had color televisions, 36% had two televisions, 38% had three or more televisions, 82% had a VCR, 66% had basic cable, and 33% had premium cable.

- About how many homes had three or more televisions?
- About how many homes had a VCR?

Problem-Solving Project

The Typical Seventh Grader

Conduct a survey to describe the typical seventh grader. Choose survey questions such as "What snack do you prefer?" or "How do you get to school?" Survey all the students in your class and graph the data. Analyze your results to find what is true of the typical seventh grader in your class. Share your results with the class. Use all the results to write a description of the typical seventh grader for the class.

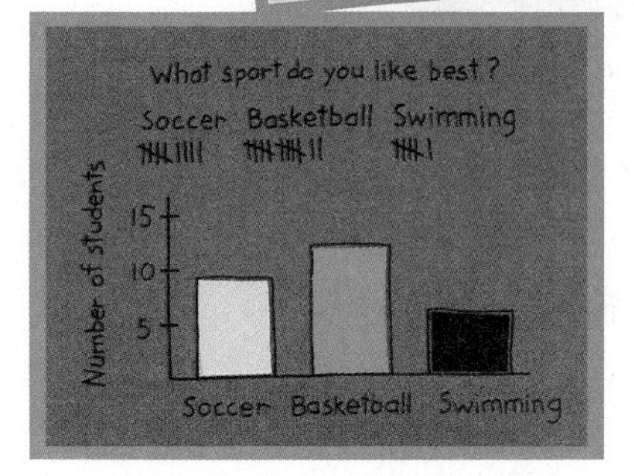

PROJECT CHECKLIST

- ✓ Did you choose survey questions?
- ✓ Did you survey the class and graph the data?
- ✓ Did you analyze the results?
- ✓ Did you use every student's data to write a description of the typical seventh grader for your class?

LESSON 21.1

How Do Your Data Shape Up?

What You'll Learn
How to show the distribution of data

Why Learn This?
To analyze data you have collected, such as for a science class experiment

People collect data to answer questions, make predictions, and solve problems.

To solve problems, you need to analyze the data that is collected. How are the data distributed? Are they spread out or clumped together?

There is more than one way to show the distribution of data.

ACTIVITY A science class did an aeronautics experiment. Students made paper airplanes, and then tested them to see which would fly the farthest. The results of the experiment are in the table.

DISTANCES FLOWN BY PAPER AIRPLANES (IN INCHES)				
Team 1	**Team 2**	**Team 3**	**Team 4**	**Team 5**
251	239	197	231	284
178	210	318	189	245
183	213	172	276	229
164	301	193	194	261
270	263	148	258	201
228	258	247	230	235

- To see how the class data are distributed, copy and complete this frequency table, using the results given above.

FREQUENCY OF DISTANCES FLOWN BY PAPER AIRPLANES		
Distance (in inches)	**Tally**	**Frequency**
141–170	||	2
171–200	?	?
201–230	?	?
231–260	?	?
261–290	?	5
291–320	?	?

- In what interval of distances did the most planes fly?
- When the data are grouped in equal intervals as in the frequency table, can you find the range? Explain.

REMEMBER:

The **range** is the difference between the greatest and the least values in a set of data. **See page H26.**

What is the range of the following data?

12 7 4 31 19 2 25

range → 31 − 2 = 29

To show the distribution of the class data, Julie made a histogram using the equal intervals shown in the frequency table.

- What does the histogram show you about the distribution of the data?
- Describe a histogram for someone who does not know what one is.

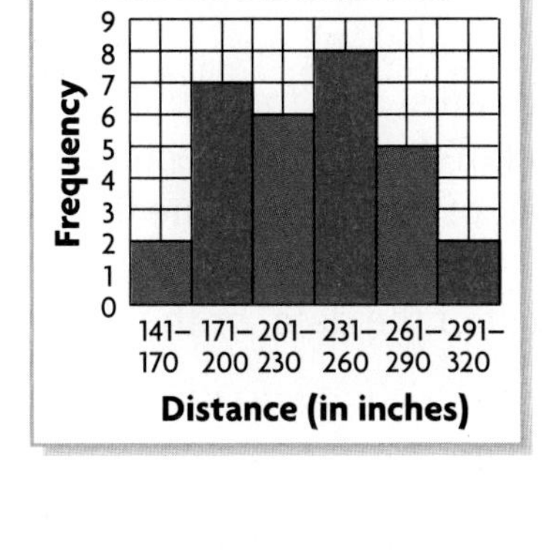

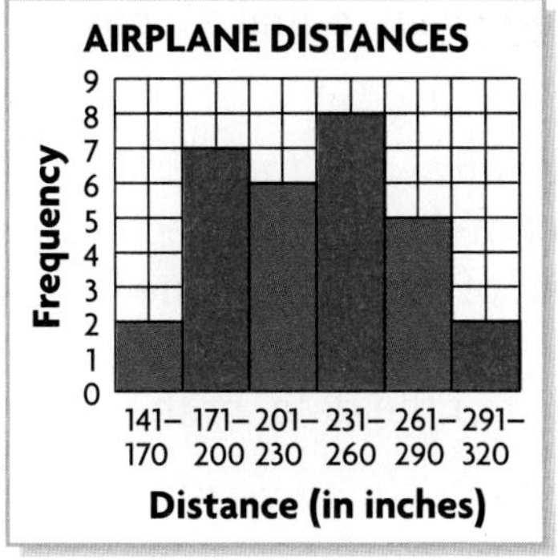

Andrew also grouped the data into equal intervals. However, he used a stem-and-leaf plot to display the data.

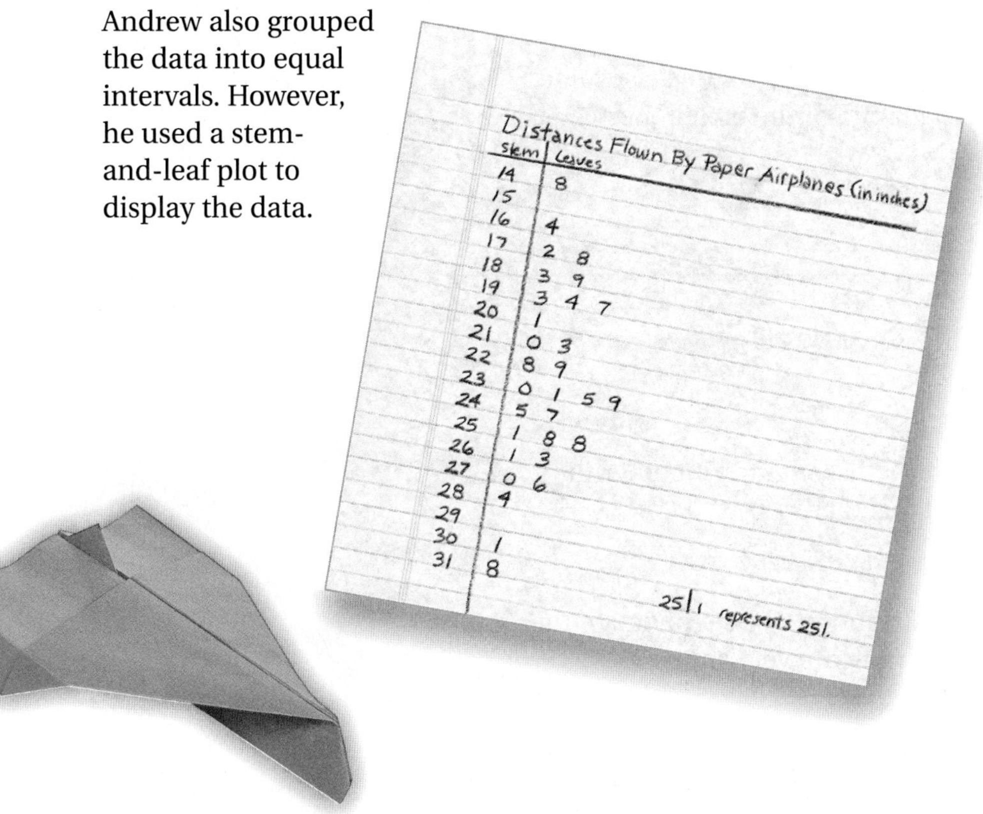

Distances Flown By Paper Airplanes (in inches)

Stem	Leaves
14	8
15	
16	4
17	2 8
18	3 9
19	3 4 7
20	1
21	0 3
22	8 9
23	0 1 5 9
24	5 7
25	1 8 8
26	1 3
27	0 6
28	4
29	
30	1
31	8

25|1 represents 251.

SCIENCE LINK

How can heavy airplanes defy gravity and stay in the air? Air traveling across a surface reduces the air pressure on that surface. This is the Bernoulli Principle. Wings are curved so the air above the wing travels faster than air below the wing. This results in lower air pressure on top of the wing than beneath the wing, and the airplane is pushed upward. This is called lift. How do you think an airplane's speed is related to lift?

GUIDED PRACTICE

For Exercises 1–4, compare the stem-and-leaf plot shown above with the histogram shown above.

1. Are the intervals the same? Explain.

2. Why is the stem-and-leaf plot better for finding the range of the data?

3. What is the range of the distances flown?

4. Which graph do you prefer for showing the distribution of the distances flown by the airplanes? Explain.

Reba and Paulo used a software program to make a box-and-whisker graph. The program

1. orders the data from least to greatest and then finds
   a. the median of the whole set of data, or the second quartile;
   b. the median of the lower half of the data, or the first quartile; and
   c. the median of the upper half of the data, or the third quartile;
2. finds the range to make a scale for the data;
3. draws a rectangular box above the scale to show the second and third quartiles;
4. draws whiskers from the left end of the box to the least value in the data set and from the right end of the box to the greatest value.

REMEMBER:

For an ordered data set with an even number of numbers, the **median** is the average, or mean, of the two middle numbers. **See page H25.**

27 35 38 42 47 56

↑

average of the two middle numbers

$(38 + 42) \div 2 = 40$

The median is 40.

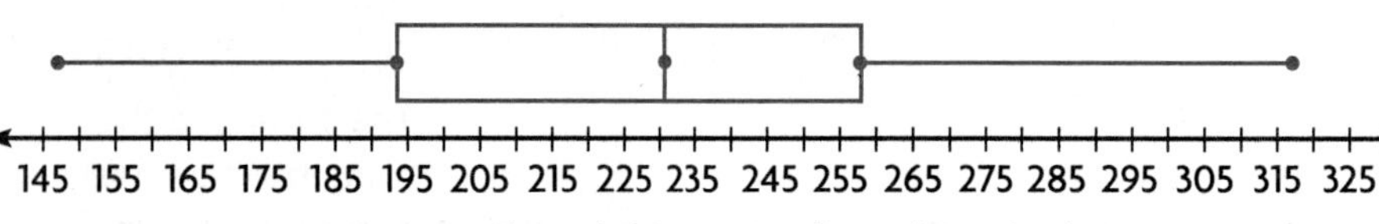

Distances Flown by Paper Airplanes (in inches)

Talk About It

- How can you tell from a box-and-whisker graph whether the data are spread out or clumped together?
- What part of the data is shown inside the box?
- What do you know about the distribution of a set of data if the whiskers on a box-and-whisker graph are very short?

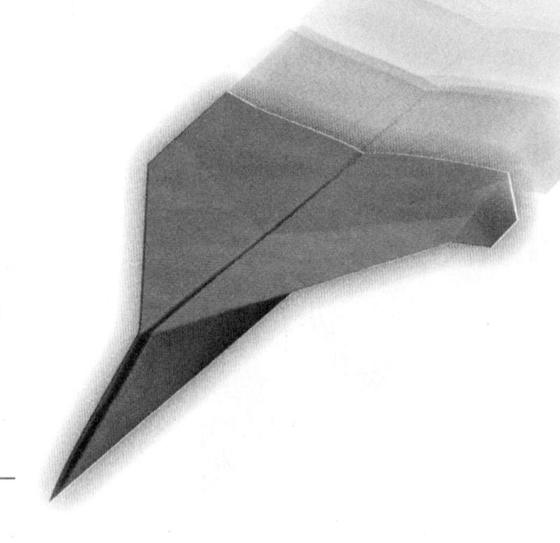

INDEPENDENT PRACTICE

For Exercises 1–6, use the stem-and-leaf plot shown below.

1. What is the lowest temperature?

2. What is the highest temperature?

3. What is the range of temperatures?

4. In what interval, shown as a stem, do most of the temperatures occur?

5. Were there more noon temperatures in the thirties or in the fifties?

6. Did more than half the days have a noon temperature less than 45°F? Explain.

NOVEMBER TEMPERATURES AT NOON (IN °F)

Stem	Leaves
3	6 8 8 8 9 9 9
4	0 0 1 1 2 2 2 3 3 4 5 5 6 7 9
5	0 2 2 4 5 9
6	0 1

For Exercises 7–10, use the histogram at right.

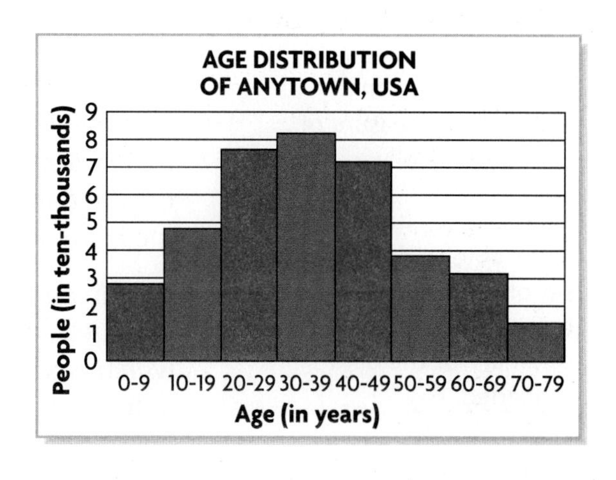

7. What does the histogram show you about the age distribution of Anytown?

8. Which age group has the least number of people? the greatest number of people?

9. What is the greatest possible age shown?

10. How many 30-year-olds are in the population?

For Exercises 11–12, use the box-and-whisker graph below, which shows the distribution of test scores.

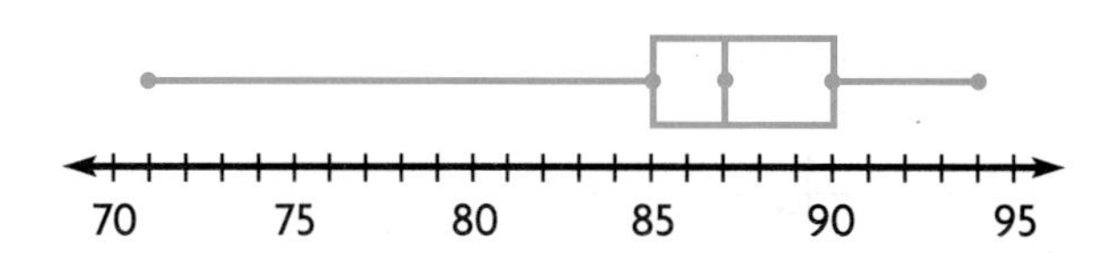

11. What is the median test score? What is the range of scores?

12. Did most of the class do well? Explain.

Problem-Solving Applications

Use the data below for Problems 13–14.

Pieces of Pizza Consumed in a Year by 13-Year-Olds
87 90 88 113 77 96 105 106 119 85 77 76 92 91 117 104 83 84 88 52 110 89 92

13. **STATISTICS** Make a frequency table, using intervals of 10 to organize the data.

14. **STATISTICS** Construct a stem-and-leaf plot and a histogram for the data.

15. **WRITE ABOUT IT** Which gives you more complete information about the distribution of a set of data, a histogram or a stem-and-leaf plot? Why?

Mixed Review and Test Prep

Find the average.

16. 90, 70

17. 65, 74, 98, 79

18. 64, 99, 90, 75, 82

19. 75, 85, 92

Tell whether the following random samples would be biased or not biased for a survey of people over 21 years of age.

20. 50 people at the mall

21. 50 people older than 21

22. 50 women older than 21

23. **NUMBER SENSE** To buy 8 videos for $1.99, you must first buy 6 videos at the regular price of $19.99 each. What is your average cost per video for the 14 videos?

A about $8.49 **B** about $9.42
C about $9.70 **D** about $12.56

24. **LOGICAL REASONING** Ted, Tom, Tim, and Kal sit at a square table. Tom is not opposite Ted, and Kal is on Ted's right. Who is sitting on Tim's left?

F Kal **G** Ted
H Tom **J** either Ted or Tom

MORE PRACTICE Lesson 21.1, page H71

LESSON 21.2 Central Tendencies

What You'll Learn
How to choose an appropriate measure of central tendency

Why Learn This?
To be able to describe a set of data with one number when a summary of the data is needed

VOCABULARY
central tendency
bimodal

How can you summarize a whole set of data? One way is to make a display of the distribution. Another way is to find a single number that represents "the middle of" the data. The number is called a measure of **central tendency**.

The mean, median, or mode can be used as a measure of central tendency. To decide which is the most appropriate, you can look at the distribution of the data. It is also helpful to know the intended use for this measure.

Suppose you are the manager of a boot store. Your cash registers record data about each sale. You can use the data in different ways.

EXAMPLE 1 You are to prepare a six-month sales report, using the data below. Which measure of central tendency can you use to summarize the set of data?

SALES AMOUNTS FOR JULY THROUGH DECEMBER

All	A	B	C	D	E	F	G	H
1		Jul	Aug	Sept	Oct	Nov	Dec	Total
2	Women's	$3,847	$5,675	$13,243	$3,504	$3,293	$15,015	$44,577
3	Men's	$3,352	$5,388	$14,913	$4,003	$2,894	$12,425	$42,975
4	Total	$7,199	$11,063	$28,156	$7,507	$6,187	$27,440	$87,552
5								

Find the mean, median, and mode.

mean:
$87,552 ÷ 6 = $14,592 — *Divide the sum of the totals by 6.*

median:
($7,507 + $11,063) ÷ 2 = $9,285 — *Arrange monthly totals in order from least to greatest. Divide the sum of the two middle numbers by 2.*

mode: none

Since the mean is distorted by two very high sales amounts, it is not the best measure of central tendency.

So, the median is the better measure of central tendency since it is more representative of the monthly sales amounts.

- **CRITICAL THINKING** Why is a measure of central tendency for monthly sales important to know?

REMEMBER:

The **mode** is the number that occurs most frequently. **See page H26.**
Example:
5 8 4 3 8 2 9 12
9 2 8 10 14 6 5
The mode is 8.

Calculator Activities, page H38

EXAMPLE 2 Samantha used the stem-and-leaf plot below to organize her data. What measure of central tendency can she use to represent the salaries of all 50 governors?

1995 Governors' Salaries
(in thousands, rounded)

Stem	Leaves
5	9
6	0 5
7	0 0 0 0 0 3 5 5 7 7 7 8
8	0 0 0 1 2 3 5 5 5 6 6 8
9	0 0 1 5 5 5 5 5 9 9
10	1 2 5 5
11	0 2 5 6 9
12	0 0 1
13	0

12 | 0 represents $120,000.

Find the median, mode, and mean.
The median salary is $86,000.

The modes are $70,000 and $95,000, values that appear five times each. The data are **bimodal** because there are two modes.

The mean salary is $89,740.

The median and mean are both representative of the salaries. There are 23 salaries greater than the mean and 24 salaries greater than the median.

So, both the mean and median are good measures of central tendency to represent this set of data.

LANGUAGE LINK

The word *average* is often used in the news instead of the word *mean*. Example: "The average advertising and promotion cost for a hit film is about $12 million." What is the average amount you spend going to movies each year?

GUIDED PRACTICE

The table lists the number of touchdowns for NFL touchdown leaders of the 1995 season.

Name	TDs
Emmitt Smith	25
Chris Warren	15
Curtis Martin	14
Marshall Faulk	11
Barry Sanders	11
Ricky Watters	11
Errict Rhett	11
Derick Loville	10
Rodney Hampton	10

1. Find the mean, median, and mode.
2. What is the most extreme number of touchdowns?
3. How does the extreme number affect the mean?
4. Would the mean, median, or mode best describe the data? Why?

INDEPENDENT PRACTICE

Find the mean, median, and mode of the set of numbers.

1. 144, 168, 148, 161, 159, 148, 163, 165

2. 5, 30, 35, 20, 5, 25, 20

3. 14, 33, 26, 28, 14

4. 1.4, 4.5, 5.9, 7.6, 7.6

The table at the right shows the number of hits by Atlanta Braves players for the 1996 baseball season. Use the table to answer Exercises 5–9.

Player Name	Position	Hits
Blauser, Jeff	Shortstop	65
Dye, Jermaine	Outfield	82
Grissom, Marquis	Outfield	207
Jones, Chipper	Third base	185
Justice, David	Outfield	45
Klesko, Ryan	Outfield	149
Lemke, Mark	Second base	127
Lopez, Javier	Catcher	138
McGriff, Fred	First base	182
Smoltz, John	Pitcher	17

5. Find the mean number of hits.

6. Find the median number of hits.

7. Find the mode for the number of hits.

8. Which measure best describes the numbers of hits by Braves players? Why?

9. Whose hit total is extreme? Why?

For Exercises 10–13, use the table at the right.

10. Find the mean military salary.

11. Find the median military salary.

12. Find the mode for the military salaries.

13. Which measures best describe the monthly military salaries? Why?

MONTHLY MILITARY SALARIES (rounded to nearest hundred)	
Rank	**Pay**
Private	$ 800
Corporal	$1,000
Sergeant	$1,100
Warrant officer	$1,400
2nd lieutenant	$1,700
Captain	$2,100

Problem-Solving Applications

14. **TEMPERATURE** The average daily temperatures, in °F, for one week in Mytown were 74, 75, 79, 74, 74, 81, and 86. To make the climate seem as cool as possible, should you use the mean, median, or mode to describe the average temperature? Why?

15. **CRITICAL THINKING** Write a set of numbers for which the mean, median, and mode are the same.

16. **HEALTH** The mean of Jon's heights at three annual checkups is 62 in. At the first two checkups, he was 58 in. and 61 in. tall. Find his height at the third checkup.

17. **WRITE ABOUT IT** Measure the heights, in inches, of four of your classmates. Find the mean, median, and mode of the heights. Which best describes the heights of your classmates? Why?

MORE PRACTICE Lesson 21.2, page H72

Using Appropriate Graphs

LESSON 21.3

What You'll Learn
How to choose an appropriate graph

Why Learn This?
To display a set of data so it is easy to understand when the data are included in a report

VOCABULARY
stacked bar graph

To display data you have collected, you must decide what type of graph to use. You have learned about many kinds of graphs. How do you decide which is best for your data?

If the data are grouped into categories, such as makes of cars, clubs at school, or types of careers, it is called categorical data. A bar graph is a good choice for displaying categorical data.

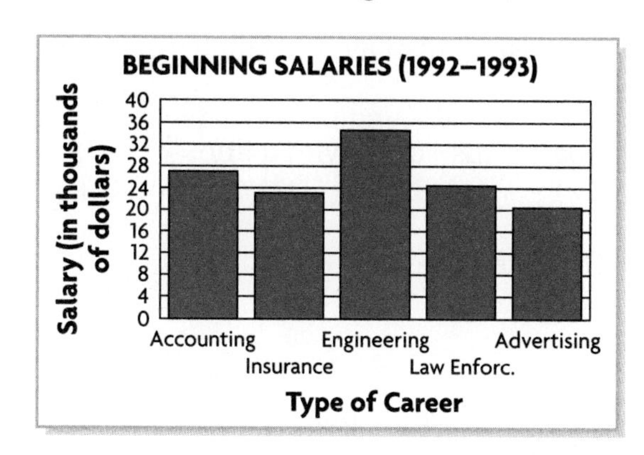

For a report on careers, Derrick is comparing average yearly salary offers made to beginning-level employees. He decided to use a bar graph to display the data.

- What does the graph show you about the beginning salaries?
- Which two careers have about the same beginning salaries?
- Which two careers have the greatest difference in beginning salaries?

When your data show changes over time, consider a line graph.

For her science fair experiment, Alisa compared plant growth in four different soils.

EXAMPLE 1 How can Alisa display the data for her experiment?

A line graph is appropriate since the data are plant heights recorded over time. Because there are four different soil types, the data are best displayed in a multiple-line graph as shown.

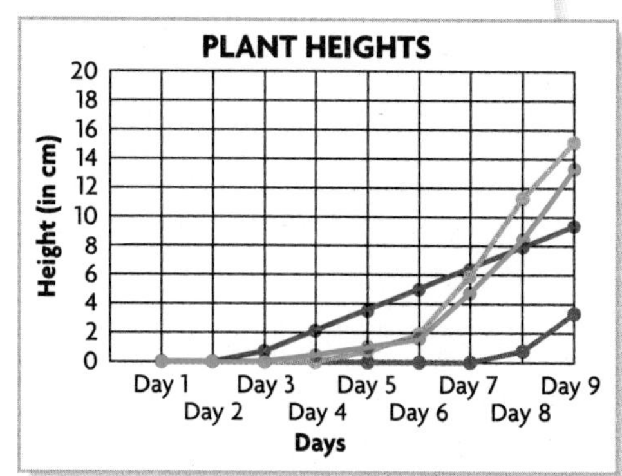

- What does the line graph show you about Alisa's results?

GUIDED PRACTICE

Use the data below to determine whether a line graph or bar graph is appropriate.

Favorite Colors of Seventh Graders at Kennedy Middle School				
Blue - 189	Red - 121	Green - 143	Yellow - 67	Purple - 96

1. What kind of data are displayed in the table?
2. What kind of graph should you use to display the data in the table?
3. What kind of data would be better displayed with a line graph?
4. Use the data above to make a bar graph.

Other Graphs

When you need to compare data sets, multiple box-and-whisker graphs can be excellent tools.

For his careers report, Delaño found the following data about the salaries of different occupations.

1992–1993 SALARIES (IN THOUSANDS OF DOLLARS)					
Career	Least	Greatest	First Quartile	Second Quartile	Third Quartile
Registered nurse	\$20.1	\$50.9	\$27.8	\$34.4	\$41.6
Public accountant	\$21.5	\$41.2	\$26.5	\$28.0	\$29.4
Maintenance electrician	\$16.5	\$46.5	\$27.2	\$34.7	\$40.9

Technology Link
In *Data ToolKit* you can practice making box-and-whisker graphs to compare data sets.
Data ToolKit

Delaño used the data in the table to make the box-and-whisker graphs below.

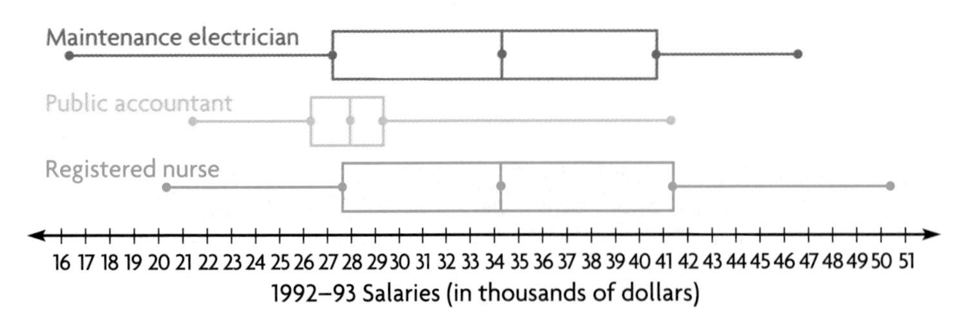

Talk About It

- What do the whiskers show?
- Compare the three graphs. Which career shows the greatest salary range? the smallest salary range?
- Compare the boxes on the three graphs. Which career has the highest median? the lowest median?
- The graph for the public accountant has the shortest box. What does this mean?
- What do the three graphs show you about the data?

You have probably used a circle graph to display data as percents. Another way to show the relationship between the parts and the whole is by using a **stacked bar graph**.

EXAMPLE 2 Trudy wants to show the following data about the percents of the Earth's ocean water.

Pacific, 46%	Atlantic, 23%	Indian, 20%
Arctic, 4%	Other, 7%	

She made this stacked bar graph to show her data.

- CRITICAL THINKING Do you think the stacked bar graph displays the data as well as a circle graph would? Explain.

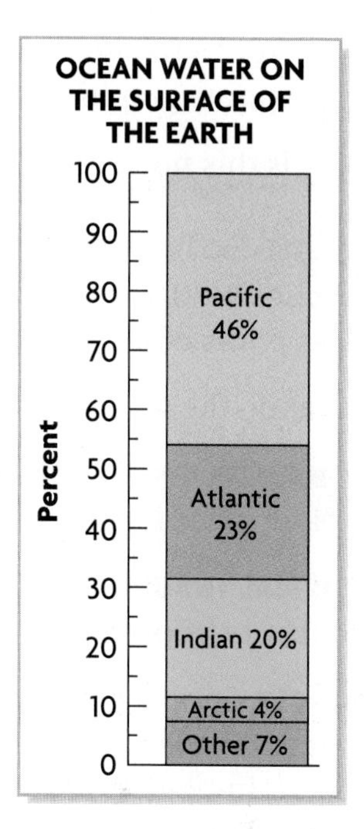

INDEPENDENT PRACTICE

For Exercises 1–2, make an appropriate line graph or bar graph with the given data. Explain your choice of graph.

1.

Seventh Graders' Favorite Sports			
Basketball	26	Football	12
Soccer	4	Baseball	17
Volleyball	8	Softball	16

2.

Customers at Emily's Eatery			
First hour	258	Fourth hour	173
Second hour	146	Fifth hour	120
Third hour	310	Sixth hour	246

3. The data in the table below show how people get to work. Sketch a stacked bar graph for the data.

HOW PEOPLE GET TO WORK			
Drive Alone	**Use Public Transportation**	**Walk, or Work at Home**	**Carpool**
75%	6%	6%	13%

For Exercises 4–7, use the following data. A recent survey of teenagers who used technology found that 96% used a VCR, 77% played video games, 66% watched cable TV, 46% used computers, 35% used cell phones, and 17% used the Internet. Teens could select more than one response, so the sum of the percents is greater than 100%.

4. Decide on an appropriate title for a graph.

5. Decide on appropriate labels for the axes.

6. Construct a bar graph with the data. Why is this an appropriate graph?

7. Why is this not a good set of data for a stacked bar graph?

Problem-Solving Applications

For Exercises 8–10, use the box-and-whisker graph below, which compares prices of in-line skates and skateboards.

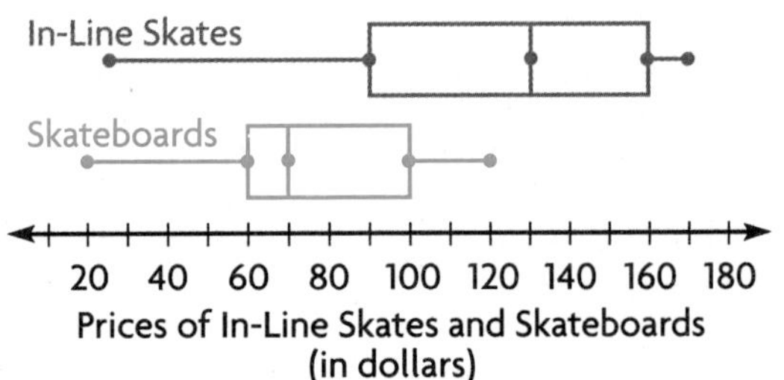

8. What do the whiskers show?

9. **CONSUMER MATH** Which item has the greater price range? the lower median?

10. **CRITICAL THINKING** What can you conclude from the graph?

11. **BUDGET** Suppose you received $100. What percent would you spend on entertainment, food, clothes, and other things? Answer with a graph.

12. **WRITE ABOUT IT** Consider the four types of graphs in this lesson. Find or make up a set of data that is appropriate for your favorite type of graph.

Mixed Review and Test Prep

Determine an appropriate scale for a graph of the given data.

13. $123, $57, $99, $213, $172, $146

14. 76°, 36°, 42°, 57°, 54°, 59°, 64°, 67°

15. 1,235 ft, 994 ft, 1,456 ft, 1,327 ft, 1,296 ft

16. 4.2 m, 8.6 m, 7.5 m, 5.7 m, 5.3 m

Determine if the following samples are stratified, random, or systematic.

17. Only part of a class is surveyed, but everyone has an equal chance of being chosen.

18. Every fourth person is surveyed.

19. **LOGICAL REASONING** Julio, Frank, Chris, Nino, and Tina are in the lunch line. Nino is two places ahead of Chris. Julio is not at the head of the line. Tina is in the middle. Who is last?

A Julio **B** Chris **C** Nino **D** Frank

20. **DECIMALS** Brooke ran the 100-yard dash. Her strides averaged 3.75 feet. How many steps did she take to run the 100-yard dash?

F 27 **G** 56
H 80 **J** 85

MORE PRACTICE Lesson 21.3, page H72

Contemporary Graphs

LAB ACTIVITY

What You'll Explore
How to make eye-catching graphs

What You'll Need
optional: graphs from newspapers and magazines

In this activity you will make graphs that combine drawings and data displays.

In many newspapers and magazines, you can find eye-catching graphs. They combine drawings with the display of data. This combination has become popular as computer software for both graphs and clip art has become readily accessible.

You can make graphs like these without a computer. You just provide your own ideas and drawings.

Explore

- Look at the graph at the right. What catches your eye?
- Make a new drawing and graph to represent the same data. Consider these things:
  - **a.** The type of graph to make
  - **b.** How to represent the population
  - **c.** How to show the two time periods

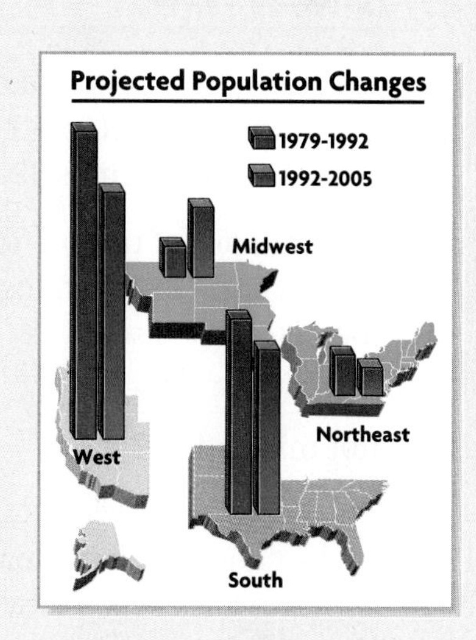

Think and Discuss

Compare your graph with your classmates' graphs.

- Which graphs catch your eye?
- Do they display all the data? Explain.
- Do they display the data appropriately? Explain.

Try This

Use the data set at the right to make a new graph that combines art and data displays.

Top Endorsement Earnings in 1995 (in millions of dollars)	
Michael Jordan	40
Shaquille O'Neal	17
Jack Nicklaus	14.5
Wayne Gretzky	6
Steffi Graf	5
Michael Chang	5
Steve Young	3
Hakeem Olajuwon	2

Technology Link

You can input data and make graphs by using E-Lab, Activity 21. Available on CD-ROM and on the Internet at **www.hbschool.com/elab**

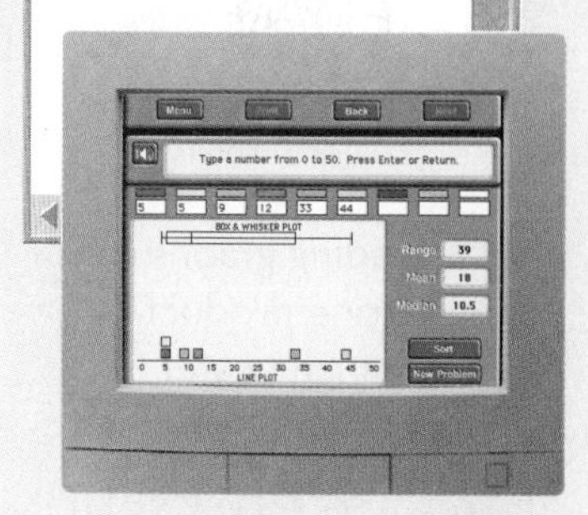

LESSON 21.4

Misleading Graphs

What You'll Learn
How to identify misleading graphs

Why Learn This?
To be able to recognize graphs that are intentionally made to mislead you

The way a set of data is displayed can influence how it is interpreted. Some graphs are made to show one point of view, and they can be misleading.

EXAMPLE 1 The members of the baseball team made the following graph to show the number of tickets sold for the school sports festival. How is the graph misleading?

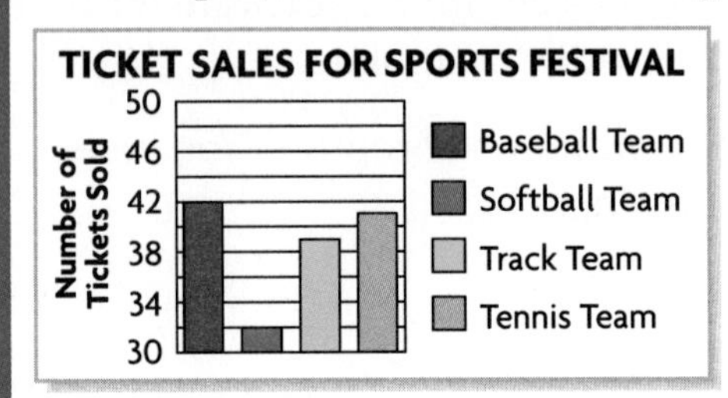

The lengths of the bars make it look as if the baseball team sold 6 times as many tickets as the softball team. This is misleading because 42 is not 6 times 32.

The bars are out of proportion because of the scale on the graph. The scale exaggerates the differences between the numbers of tickets sold.

- CRITICAL THINKING How can you change the graph so that it is not misleading?

CONSUMER LINK

PRICES OF NEW CARS

Car: Zoom, Snerd

$15,000 $15,500 $16,000

Cost (in dollars)

Misleading graphs can make one product look much better than another product. In this graph, which compares the prices of new cars, the Zoom seems much more expensive than the Snerd. What makes this graph misleading?

Line graphs can also be misleading. Like bar graphs, they must be analyzed to make sure they represent data accurately.

EXAMPLE 2 The weekly sales of a car dealer are shown. How are the graphs misleading?

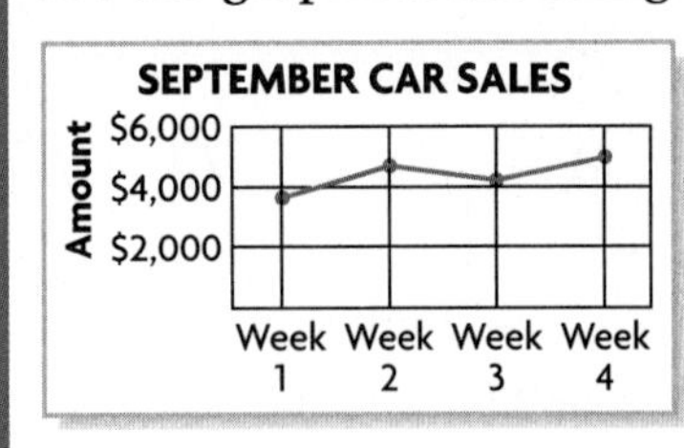

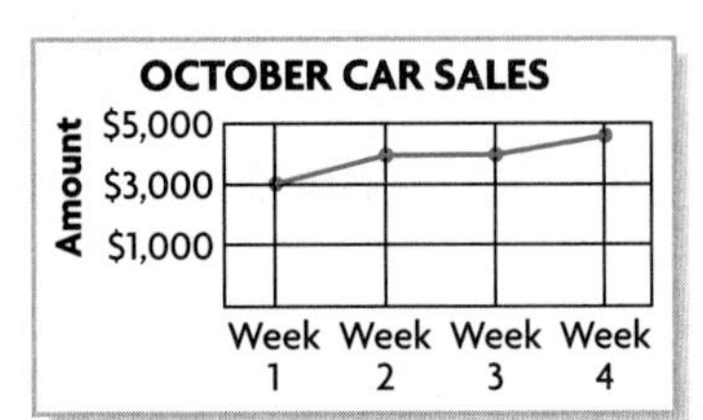

It appears there were better sales in October than in September. In fact, the sales were about the same or greater in September. The labels on the vertical scales make the October sales seem greater in Weeks 2, 3, and 4.

One way to avoid these problems is to make a double-line graph with one scale that starts at zero.

GUIDED PRACTICE

For Exercises 1–4, use the graph at the right.

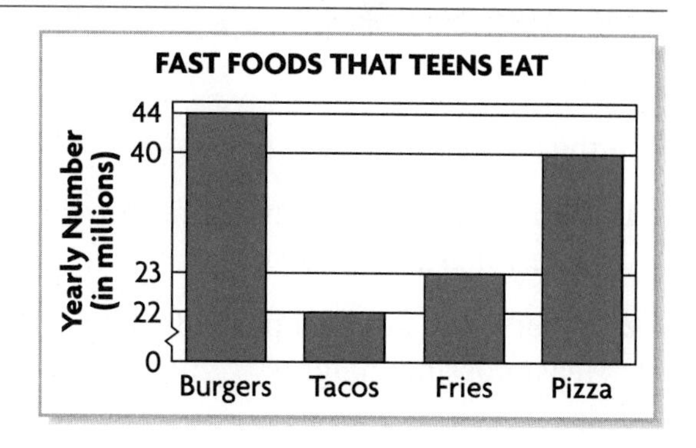

1. How many burgers are eaten by teens? How many tacos?
2. What is the ratio of burgers to tacos?
3. What ratio do the bars seem to show?
4. How can you change the graph so it is not misleading?

INDEPENDENT PRACTICE

For Exercises 1–4, use the graph at the right.

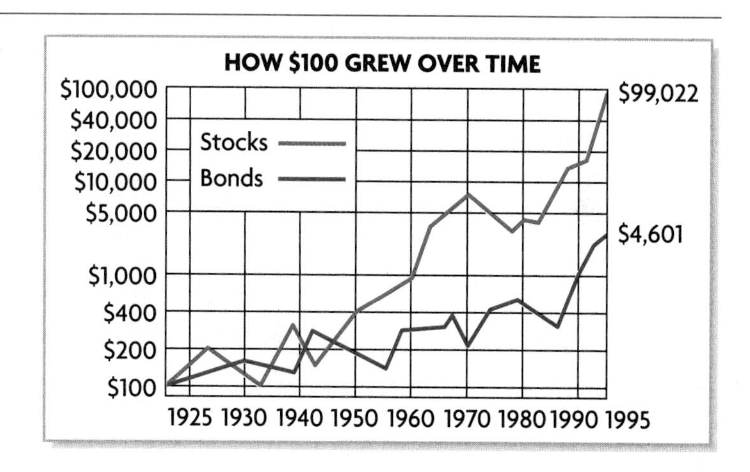

1. What was the 1995 value of the stocks? of the bonds?
2. What is the approximate ratio of this stock value to this bond value?
3. What ratio does the graph *seem* to show?
4. How can you change the graph so it is not misleading?

For Exercises 5–8, use the graphs below.

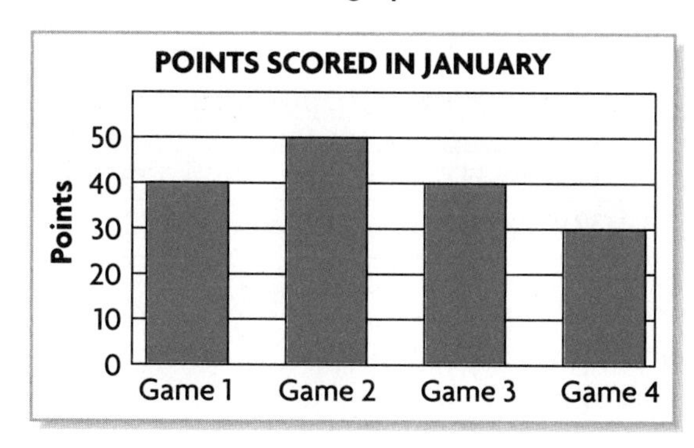

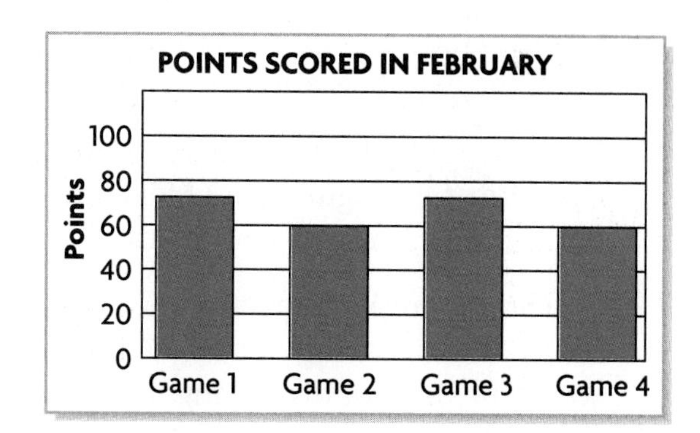

5. In which month did the team score more points?
6. In which month do the graphs make it look as if more points were scored?
7. Why are the graphs misleading?
8. How could this be corrected?

Problem-Solving Applications

9. **CRITICAL THINKING** Find a graph you think is misleading. Explain how it is misleading.
10. **WRITE ABOUT IT** How should you analyze a graph to make sure it is not misleading?

MORE PRACTICE Lesson 21.4, page H72

CHAPTER 21 Review/Test

Use the graph at the right. (pages 410–413)

HEIGHTS OF SEVENTH GRADERS

Number of Students: 0, 10, 20, 30, 40, 50, 60

Heights in Inches: 46-50, 51-55, 56-60, 61-65, 66-70

1. Which interval of heights has the most seventh graders? the least?

2. What is the greatest possible height? the least possible height?

Use the graph at the right. (pages 410–413)

WEIGHT OF FISH (in lb)

Stem	Leaves
0	6 6 7 7 8 8 8 9
1	0 0 0 0 1 2 5 5 5 7 8 8 9

3. What is the lowest fish weight? the highest?

4. What is the range of fish weights?

5. What is the most common fish weight?

6. **VOCABULARY** A single number that represents "the middle of" a set of data is called a measure of __?__. (page 414)

Find the mean, median, and mode. (pages 414–416)

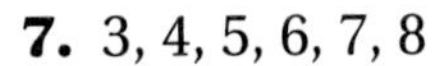

7. 3, 4, 5, 6, 7, 8

8. 80, 84, 76, 112

9. 25, 28, 32, 29, 35, 25

10. 92, 88, 65, 68, 76, 90, 84, 88, 93, 89

11. 54, 56, 58, 49, 52, 60, 59, 58

12. In Exercise 10, what is a good measure of central tendency?

13. In Exercise 11, what is a good measure of central tendency?

14. **VOCABULARY** A graph that uses bars to compare parts to a whole is a(n) __?__. (page 419)

15. What kind of graph should be used for the data at the right? Why? Make the appropriate graph. (pages 417–420)

Record Snowfall in 24 Hours		
Buffalo, NY	Valdez, AK	Yakutat, AK
37.9 in.	47.5 in.	32.4 in.

16. The Smith family budgets 45% of its income for bills, 25% for food, 20% for savings, and 10% for fun. What kind of graph would be best for displaying this budget? (pages 417–420)

Use the graph at the right. (pages 422–423)

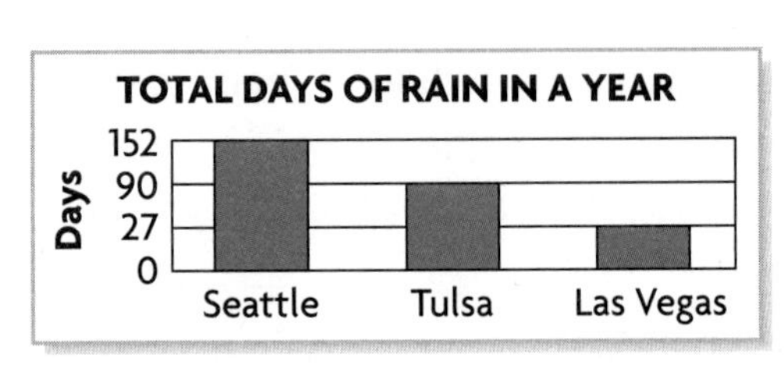

17. What is the ratio of days of rain in Seattle to days of rain in Las Vegas?

18. What ratio does the graph seem to show?

19. Why is the graph misleading?

20. Make a new graph for these data that is not misleading.

Test Prep

CUMULATIVE
CHAPTERS 1–21

1. What is the mean of the data?
85, 82, 76, 92, 78, 85, 83, 91

A 78
B 84
C 85
D 91

2. A triangle has side lengths 9 cm, 10 cm, and 15 cm. What are the lengths of a similar triangle with scale factor of $\frac{2}{3}$?

F 18 cm, 20 cm, 30 cm
G 13.5 cm, 15 cm, 22.5 cm
H 6 cm, 7 cm, 12 cm
J 6 cm, $6\frac{2}{3}$ cm, 10 cm

3. The ratio of teachers to students is 1:15. If there are 225 students, how many teachers are there?

A 25
B 15
C 10
D 8

4. What percent of 8 is 24?

F 25%
G $33\frac{1}{3}$%
H 250%
J 300%
K Not Here

5. The Carr family budgets 40% of its income for bills, 25% for food, 10% for savings, 10% for fun, and 15% for other expenses. Which display would be most appropriate to show the data?

A line plot
B stem-and-leaf plot
C circle graph
D line graph

6. Complete the pattern.

$4^2 = 16; 4^1 = 4; 4^0 = 1; 4^{-1} = \frac{1}{4}, 4^{-2} =$ __

F $\frac{-1}{16}$ **G** $\frac{1}{42}$
H $\frac{1}{16}$ **J** $\frac{1}{8}$

7. What is the tenth term in the sequence 800, 400, 200, 100, . . . ?

A 3.125
B 1.5625
C 1.5
D 0.15

8. A triangular pyramid has 6 edges, a rectangular pyramid has 8 edges, and a pentagonal pyramid has 10 edges. How many edges does a hexagonal pyramid have?

F 12 **G** 14
H 16 **J** 18

9. Two out of three students surveyed prefer having winter and spring vacations rather than a longer summer vacation. This is what percent of the students surveyed?

A 20% **B** 30%
C $33\frac{1}{3}$% **D** $66\frac{2}{3}$%

10. Which set of data is represented by the stem-and-leaf plot?

Stem	Leaves
3	2 4 5
4	0 1 2
5	1 1 3

F 23, 43, 5, 3, 4, 14, 24, 15, 15, 13
G 32, 34, 35, 41, 42, 51, 53
H 3,245; 4,012; 5,113
J 32, 34, 35, 40, 41, 42, 51, 51, 53

CHAPTER

22 DATA AND PROBABILITY

LOOK AHEAD

In this chapter you will solve problems by

- using tree diagrams and sample spaces
- finding the probability of simple events
- finding combinations and permutations

SOCIAL STUDIES LINK

Dominoes were brought from China to Italy in the fourteenth century. A standard set of dominoes consists of 28 pieces. Each piece has two halves that contain 0, 1, 2, 3, 4, 5, or 6 dots. Seven of the tiles contain halves with 0 dots.

- If you choose a tile at random from a standard set of dominoes, what is the probability that it contains a half with 0 dots?

Problem-Solving Project

Step Right Up

YOU WILL NEED: 2 number cubes, poster board

Suppose you are designing a game in which you earn points depending on the result of the roll of two number cubes. If certain sums are rolled, you earn a certain number of points. Find all the possible sums and the number of different ways each could be rolled. Make a plan for the game so the sums least likely to be rolled earn more points than the sums more likely to be rolled. In writing, describe the rules of your game. Include the probability of rolling each possible sum. Then, actually play your game. Record all results. Revise your plan if necessary. Make a poster and describe your final plan.

GAME TIME

Numbers Rolled	Sum	Points
1 1	2	30

PROJECT CHECKLIST

- ✓ Did you find all possible sums and ways to roll them?
- ✓ Did you describe the rules to your game?
- ✓ Did you play your game?
- ✓ Did you make a poster and describe your plan?

LESSON 22.1

Tree Diagrams and Sample Spaces

What You'll Learn
How to use tree diagrams and sample spaces to find possible outcomes

Why Learn This?
To solve real-life problems such as planning a meal

VOCABULARY

sample space

Fundamental Counting Principle

Do you eat a healthful diet? A balanced diet should include servings from each of the five basic food groups.

Before making a decision on what to include in a meal, you should look at all the choices, or possible outcomes. The set of all possible outcomes is called the **sample space**.

For dinner, Marsha can choose from 2 proteins (beef and fish), 4 vegetables (beans, broccoli, carrots, and corn), and 2 breads (rolls and biscuits). How many different protein-vegetable-bread selections can she make for dinner?

You can make a tree diagram to show the sample space.

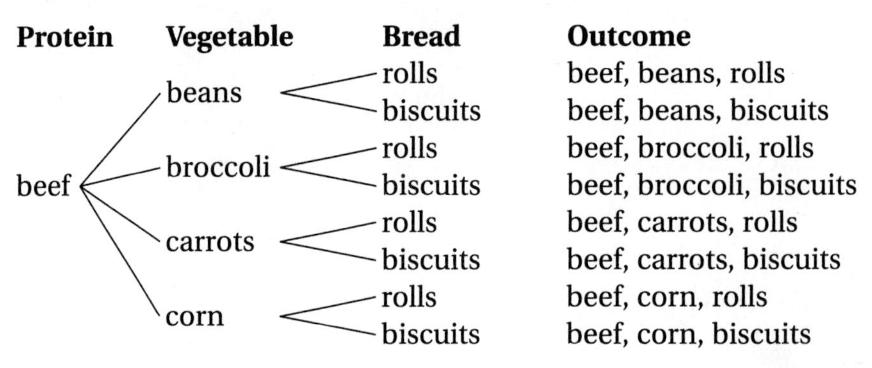

This shows only half of the tree diagram.

- Complete the tree diagram to show all protein-vegetable-bread selections. How many different outcomes are in the completed tree diagram?

ANOTHER METHOD To find the number of possible outcomes, you can use the **Fundamental Counting Principle**. It states that you multiply the number of different ways each choice can occur to find the total number of possible outcomes.

EXAMPLE Use the Fundamental Counting Principle to find the total number of protein-vegetable-bread selections Marsha can make for dinner.

Proteins		*Vegetables*		*Breads*	
2	×	4	×	2	= 16

So, Marsha can make 16 selections.

SCIENCE LINK

Biologists study characteristics of living things. For example, garden peas can be either green or yellow and either smooth or wrinkled. Name all the possible combinations of these characteristics.

GUIDED PRACTICE

Name the possible outcomes in the sample space. Tell the total number of possibilities.

1. rolling a number cube numbered from 1 to 6
2. spinning the pointer on this spinner
3. rolling the number cube and spinning the pointer
4. rolling two number cubes

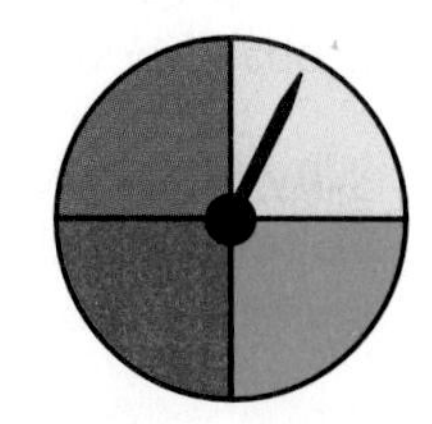

INDEPENDENT PRACTICE

For Exercises 1–4, use the information at the right. Make a tree diagram of the sample space. Tell the total number of possible outcomes.

1. One item is chosen from Group B and one from Group D.
2. One item is chosen from each of Groups A and B.
3. One item is chosen from each of Groups A, B, and C.
4. One item is chosen from each of Groups A, B, C, and D.

A	B
milk cheese yogurt	beef fish poultry
bread cereal	vegetables fruit
C	D

Problem-Solving Applications

For Problems 5–8, make a tree diagram of the sample space. Then solve.

5. **CONSUMER MATH** Sara sells barbecue-beef sandwiches, hamburgers, and hot dogs at a shop in the mall. She also sells orange drink, diet cola, and apple juice. How many choices of a sandwich and a drink are there?

6. Teri has to choose a blue, beige, green, or black T-shirt and a black, brown, or gray pair of shorts to wear to a cookout. How many choices of a shirt and a pair of shorts are there?
7. **HEALTH** Danny can eat pancakes, cereal, waffles, or eggs and drink orange juice, apple juice, pineapple juice, or milk. How many food-drink choices include pancakes?
8. **TRAVEL** There are 6 roads from Shook to Mexia and 4 roads from Mexia to West. How many different ways could you get from Shook to West when you pass through Mexia?
9. **WRITE ABOUT IT** How can you make sure you have included all possible outcomes in a sample space?

MORE PRACTICE Lesson 22.1, page H73

LESSON 22.2

Finding Probability

What You'll Learn
How to find the probability of an event

Why Learn This?
To find your chances of winning a prize

VOCABULARY
mathematical probability

Have you ever played a game based on chance?

The number used to describe the chance of an event's occurring is called the **mathematical probability**, P. To find the probability of an event's occurring, you can write this ratio.

$$P = \frac{\text{number of favorable outcomes}}{\text{number of possible outcomes}}$$

EXAMPLE 1 Corey hopes to win a CD in a drawing at the school carnival. He bought 4 tickets. There were 120 tickets sold. Find the probability of Corey's winning.

The number of favorable outcomes is the number of tickets Corey bought. The number of possible outcomes is the total number of tickets sold.

$$P(\text{Corey's winning}) = \frac{\text{number of tickets Corey bought}}{\text{total number of tickets sold}}$$ *Write the ratio.*

$$= \frac{4}{120} = \frac{1}{30}$$

So, the probability of Corey's winning is $\frac{1}{30}$, or 1 chance out of 30.

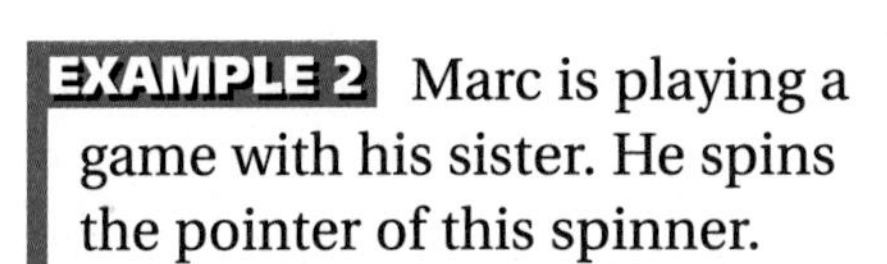

EXAMPLE 2 Marc is playing a game with his sister. He spins the pointer of this spinner.

Find these probabilities.

P(red) P(yellow) P(red or blue)

$P(\text{red}) = \frac{2}{4} = \frac{1}{2}$ $P(\text{yellow}) = \frac{0}{4} = 0$ $P(\text{red or blue}) = \frac{2+1}{4} = \frac{3}{4}$

Talk About It

- In Example 2, what is P(red, green, or blue)?
- Can a probability ever be greater than 1? Explain.
- Explain why P(yellow) = 0 in Example 2.
- **CRITICAL THINKING** Draw a spinner with 8 congruent sections, labeled as follows: 2 red, 2 blue, 1 green, 1 purple, and 2 orange. Write a problem like Example 2 that has an answer of $\frac{3}{4}$.

GUIDED PRACTICE

You roll a number cube numbered from 1 to 6. Find the probability.

1. P(4) **2.** P(7) **3.** P(3 or 5) **4.** P(1, 2, or 6) **5.** P(not 4)

6. There are 6 boys' names and 9 girls' names in a box. What is the probability of selecting a girl's name?

INDEPENDENT PRACTICE

You roll a number cube labeled with the numbers 2, 4, 6, 8, 10, and 12. Find the probability.

1. P(2 or 6) **2.** P(even number) **3.** P(odd number)

4. P(number less than 8) **5.** P(multiple of 6) **6.** P(factor of 24)

7. P(multiple of 2) **8.** P(4, 8, or 10) **9.** P(prime number)

When the probability of an event is close to 0, the event is unlikely to happen. When the probability is close to 1, the event is likely to happen. For Exercises 10–11, find the probability. Then tell whether the event is likely or unlikely to happen.

10. What is the probability that Myra will randomly choose a card with a composite number from a bag containing cards with the numbers 7–12?

11. What is the probability that Carin will guess the correct answer from the 3 choices in a multiple-choice question?

Problem-Solving Applications

12. Without looking, Marci will choose a math game from the storage box. It includes 12 fraction, 7 division, 4 percent, and 9 probability games. What is the probability that Marci will choose a fraction game?

13. **ENTERTAINMENT** Fran is playing a game at the carnival with a spinner that is divided into 8 congruent parts. There are 2 red, 4 yellow, and 2 white sections. What is the probability of the pointer's landing on a white or yellow section?

14. **NUMBER SENSE** Cristen has a 15% probability of winning a free meal at a fast-food restaurant. Her friend has a 0.125 probability of winning a free meal at the same restaurant. Which person has the better chance of winning the free meal? Explain.

15. **WRITE ABOUT IT** Suppose the probability of an event's happening is $\frac{3}{7}$. Explain what each number in the ratio represents.

MORE PRACTICE Lesson 22.2, page H73

ACTIVITY

What You'll Explore
The number of ways things can be combined

What You'll Need
6 index cards

VOCABULARY
combination

Technology Link
You can make combinations by using E-Lab, Activity 22. Available on CD-ROM and on the Internet at
www.hbschool.com/elab

Exploring Combinations

What are your favorite toppings on a pizza? Suppose your favorites are extra cheese, pepperoni, hamburger, sausage, black olives, and peppers. How many different ways can you order a pizza with 2 of these toppings?

Explore

- Label each index card with one of the 6 toppings.

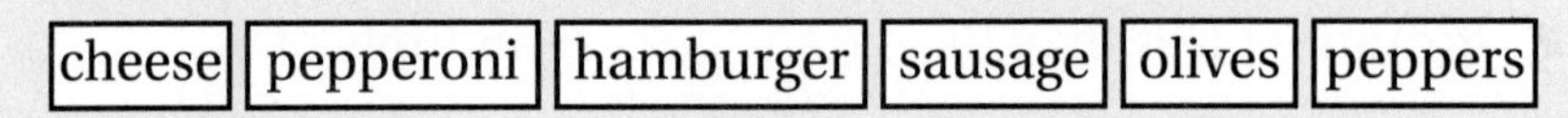

- Choose cheese as one topping.
- Record the other toppings you can choose with cheese.

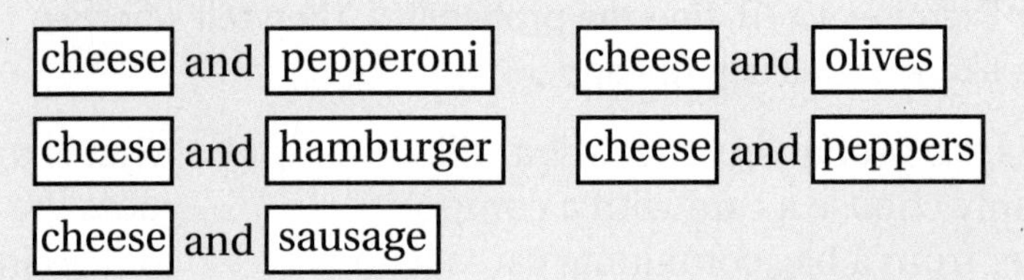

- Repeat this process with each of the other choices. Do not record any pair that is the reverse of a pair already recorded.

A **combination** of things or events is a selection of choices in which the order does not matter. The 15 pairs you recorded are all the possible combinations of 2 different toppings. There are 15 combinations for 6 things taken 2 at a time.

Think and Discuss

- Why is a pizza with cheese and pepperoni the same as one with pepperoni and cheese?
- When you use cheese for one topping, how many cards are left for the other toppings?
- How many of the 15 combinations contained olives or peppers?

Try This

- Find how many different combinations of 2 choices you can make from these 5 toppings: mushrooms, anchovies, cheese, olives, and sausage.

PROBLEM–SOLVING STRATEGY

LESSON 22.3

Account for All Possibilities

What You'll Learn
How to find the number of combinations and the probability of a combination

Why Learn This?
To find the different teams you can form from a group of players

You know that a combination of things or events is a selection in which the order does not matter. You can account for all possibilities to find the number of combinations or possible outcomes.

Dan, Mari, Kathy, and Lester play tennis together on the local middle school tennis team. Their coach wants to make teams of 2 players each. How many different teams can be formed from the group?

- **Understand**
- **Plan**
- **Solve**
- **Look Back**

UNDERSTAND What are you asked to find?

What facts are given?

PLAN What strategy will you use?

You can make a list of all combinations of 2 players to *account for all possibilities.*

SOLVE How will you complete the list?

Choose a person. Match him or her with each of the other players. Do not use any combination that reverses the pairs already listed. The team of Dan and Mari is the same as the team of Mari and Dan.

Dan and Mari	Mari and Kathy	Kathy and Lester
Dan and Kathy	Mari and Lester	
Dan and Lester		
3 combinations	+ 2 combinations	+ 1 combination

Since $3 + 2 + 1 = 6$, six different 2-member teams can be formed. There are 6 combinations for 4 players taken 2 at a time.

LOOK BACK Were any combinations used twice?

What if . . . there were 7 players instead of 4? How many different 2-member teams could be formed?

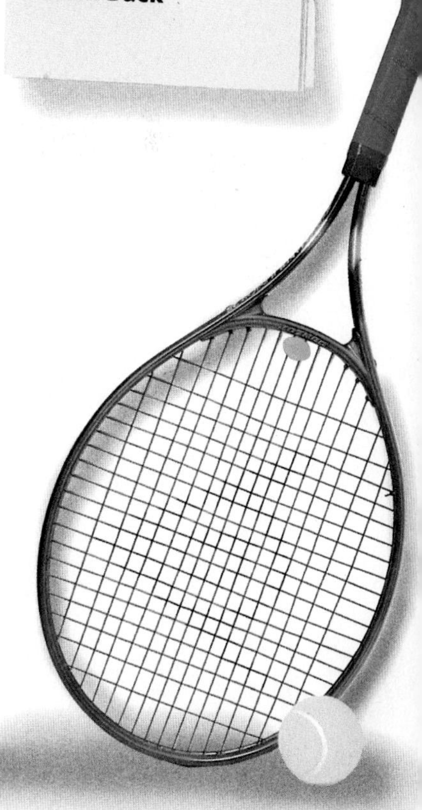

TEEN TIMES

More public schools are beginning to require school uniforms. Different combinations of shirts and pants or skirts are usually available to provide variety.

PRACTICE

Make a list to *account for all possibilities* and solve.

1. How many different ways can you have a hamburger with 2 of the following condiments: ketchup, mustard, mayonnaise, and relish?

2. Your class is taking a trip to Colorado. You can sightsee at Durango, Pikes Peak, Red Rocks Park, the United States Mint, and the Air Force Academy. Your group has time to visit 3 places. How many combinations of places could your group visit?

3. Karen has a sandwich, pudding, a pickle, chips, crackers, and a granola bar in her lunch bag. She is not very hungry at lunch today, so she decides to eat 4 of the items. How many combinations are possible?

Combinations and Probability

Remember that the number of combinations is also the number of possible outcomes. You can use the total number of outcomes to find probabilities.

EXAMPLE Dan and Lester want to be on the same team. Look at the possible team combinations on page 433. What is the probability that the coach will put Dan and Lester on the same team?

Let (D and L) represent the team of Dan and Lester.

Find P(D and L).

The team combinations are:

(D and M)	(D and K)	(D and L)
(M and K)	(M and L)	(K and L)

There are 6 different 2-member teams that can be formed. Dan and Lester form one of those teams.

$P(D \text{ and } L) = \frac{1}{6}$

Talk About It

- Dan would like to be on a team with Mari or Kathy. What is the probability of that?
- Is Dan more likely to be on a team with a girl than on a team with Lester? Explain.

MIXED APPLICATIONS

Solve.

CHOOSE a strategy and a tool.

- **Account for All Possibilities**
- **Draw a Diagram**
- **Use a Formula**
- **Guess and Check**
- **Work Backward**
- **Make a Table**

Paper/Pencil

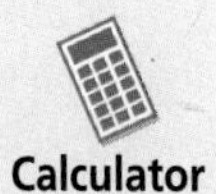
Calculator

Hands-On

Mental Math

1. At the school bus stop, there are 9 students waiting to get on the bus. There are only 2 seats available. How many combinations of 2 students can be made from 9 students?

2. The math club at the local middle school has 10 members. They want to elect 2 officers. How many combinations of 2 officers can be elected from the 10 members?

3. Find the different fractions less than 1 that can be made with the digits 1, 2, 4, and 8 without repeating digits in the same fraction. Use only 1 digit each for the numerator and denominator. What is the probability that 2 will not be used as the numerator?

4. As one of its projects, the student council decided to help repaint the school. Of the 7 members on the council, 5 must be selected to work in the afternoons. How many different selections of council members can be made?

5. Shannon and Tamara are sisters. Their ages add up to 21. Shannon is the oldest and is twice as old as Tamara. How old is each girl?

6. Kati's parents have saved $2,750 of the $5,000 required as a down payment on their new house. What percent of the down payment have they saved?

7. Mark, Joe, and 6 friends are going on a biking trip during spring break. They will ride in pairs. What is the probability that Mark and Joe will not ride together?

8. **WRITE ABOUT IT** Explain why Barry, Ann, and Aaron are the same combination as Aaron, Barry, and Ann in choosing these three from the class.

Mixed Review and Test Prep

Multiply.

9. $3 \times 2 \times 1$

10. $4 \times 3 \times 2 \times 1$

11. $5 \times 4 \times 3 \times 2 \times 1$

12. $6 \times 5 \times 4 \times 3 \times 2 \times 1$

Find the mean, median, mode, and range of the set of data.

13. 12, 5, 9, 7, 3

14. 83, 96, 72, 91, 83

15. 2.9, 8.6, 4.3, 8.6

16. **GEOMETRY** Draw the lines of symmetry for a rectangle, rhombus, isosceles triangle, and equilateral triangle. Which of the figures has the most lines of symmetry?

A rectangle
B rhombus
C isosceles triangle
D equilateral triangle

17. **RATES** A brand of cat food is sold in a 1-pound box for $1.95, a 3-pound box for $4.45, a 5-pound box for $6.50, and a 10-pound box for $12.50. Which is the best buy?

F 1-lb box
G 3-lb box
H 5-lb box
J 10-lb box

MORE PRACTICE Lesson 22.3, page H73

LESSON 22.4

Finding Permutations and Probability

What You'll Learn
How to find the number of permutations in a set of data

Why Learn This?
To find the different orders in which friends can sit in a row of seats at the movie theater

VOCABULARY
permutation

The inheritance of traits is not based on the assumption of equally likely outcomes. Certain traits occur with unequal probabilities. For example, color blindness occurs 10 times more often in males than in females. Also, there are no male calico cats, but $\frac{1}{4}$ of mixed-breed female cats are calico.

Suppose you go to a movie with 2 friends. How do you choose the order in which the 3 of you sit?

You have learned that a combination of things or events is a selection in which the order does not matter. But in some cases the order of things or events is important.

EXAMPLE 1 At the movie theater, there are 3 seats together in one row. In how many different orders can Ryan, Yoki, and Erin sit in the 3 seats?

Use a tree diagram to find the different orders the friends can sit in. This is the sample space of possible outcomes.

First Seat	Second Seat	Third Seat	Order
Ryan	Yoki	Erin	Ryan, Yoki, Erin
	Erin	Yoki	Ryan, Erin, Yoki
Yoki	Ryan	Erin	Yoki, Ryan, Erin
	Erin	Ryan	Yoki, Erin, Ryan
Erin	Ryan	Yoki	Erin, Ryan, Yoki
	Yoki	Ryan	Erin, Yoki, Ryan

So, there are 6 different orders.

When counting the arrangements, Ryan, Yoki, and Erin is different from Yoki, Ryan, and Erin.

- Make a tree diagram to find how many different orders there would be if there were 4 friends sitting together.

A **permutation** of items or events is an arrangement in which the order is important.

ANOTHER METHOD To find the number of permutations, you can think about how many choices there are for each position.

In Example 1, any of the 3 friends can sit in the first seat, so there are 3 choices. When the first seat is occupied, 2 choices remain for the second seat. When both the first seat and the second seats are occupied, only 1 choice remains for the third seat.

first seat	second seat	third seat
3 choices	2 choices	1 choice

Talk About It

- In Example 1 you saw that there are 6 orders in which Ryan, Erin, and Yoki can sit. Look at the numbers of choices. Explain how you can use the Fundamental Counting Principle to find the number of permutations.
- If there are 4 students to sit in 4 seats, there are 24 different orders. What multiplication expression can you write to find the number of permutations?

Sometimes there are more items than positions.

EXAMPLE 2 Sometimes there are 4 numbers in a street address, such as 4835 West Avenue. Using the digits 1–9, how many 4-digit addresses can there be if no digit is repeated?

There are 9 digits that can be used in the 4 positions of an address. Since each digit can be used only once, there are 9 choices for the first position, 8 for the second, 7 for the third, and 6 for the fourth.

position 1	position 2	position 3	position 4
9 digits	8 digits	7 digits	6 digits

$$9 \times 8 \times 7 \times 6 = 3{,}024$$

So, there can be 3,024 different 4-digit addresses with no digits repeated.

- Why aren't the digits 5, 4, 3, 2, and 1 part of the multiplication expression?
- Suppose you can repeat any of the digits. How many choices are there for each position? What multiplication expression can you write?

GUIDED PRACTICE

Solve by finding the number of permutations.

1. First, second, third, and fourth prizes will be awarded at a dog show. How many different ways can the awards be given to Bruno, Prissy, Fluffy, and Spot?

2. Cassy, Mary, Andrew, Chantel, and Scott are seated in a row of 5 seats. In how many orders can they be seated?

3. A baseball team has 9 players and 9 starting positions. How many lineups can be made assuming that the skills of the players are equal for each position?

Permutations and Probability

You can find the probability of a given permutation occurring.

The list at the right shows the permutations of 4 things taken 3 at a time. It is all the 3-digit numbers that can be made from the digits 1, 2, 3, and 4 without repeating a digit.

1 2 3	2 1 3	3 1 2	4 1 2
1 2 4	2 1 4	3 1 4	4 1 3
1 3 2	2 3 1	3 2 1	4 2 1
1 3 4	2 3 4	3 2 4	4 2 3
1 4 2	2 4 1	3 4 1	4 3 1
1 4 3	2 4 3	3 4 2	4 3 2

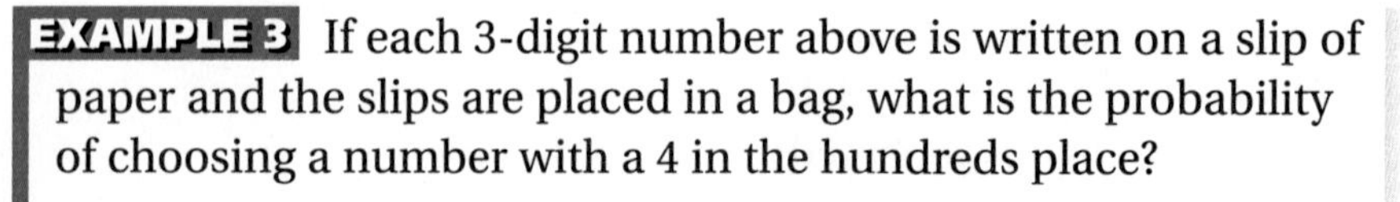

EXAMPLE 3 If each 3-digit number above is written on a slip of paper and the slips are placed in a bag, what is the probability of choosing a number with a 4 in the hundreds place?

$$P(\text{4 in hundreds place}) = \frac{\text{number of favorable outcomes}}{\text{number of possible outcomes}}$$

$$P(\text{4 in hundreds place}) = \frac{6}{24} = \frac{1}{4}$$

So, the probability of choosing a number with a 4 in the hundreds place is $\frac{1}{4}$.

- **CRITICAL THINKING** What is the probability of choosing a number with a 3 in the tens place? with a 3 in the tens or ones place?

INDEPENDENT PRACTICE

Aaron, Bart, Mark, and Ben are at a football game. They find 4 seats together in one row.

1. Draw a tree diagram to show the different orders in which Aaron and his friends can sit.

2. How many of the 24 permutations show Aaron in the first seat and Mark in the second seat?

3. How many permutations show Ben in the last seat?

4. How many permutations show this order: Bart, Mark, Aaron, and Ben?

Write a multiplication equation to find the number of permutations.

5. John is the pitcher for his baseball team. He can throw a fastball, a curveball, and a slider. Find the number of possible orders in which he can throw 3 different pitches.

6. Shelby bowls twice a week with 7 other people. Her job is to make a list of the order in which everyone will bowl. Help her find the number of possible orders for the 8 people.

Find the probability.

7. Todd's CD has 6 songs. The player has a shuffle feature, which randomly scrambles the order of the songs. What is the probability that the shuffle feature will arrange the songs in order from Todd's favorite to the one he likes least?

8. As you ride the bus to school, a gust of wind blows the 5-page report you wrote onto the floor. What is the probability that the papers will be in the correct order when you randomly pick them up?

Problem-Solving Applications

9. **TRAVEL** The Garzas want to visit Texas, Colorado, Florida, Pennsylvania, and Nevada. In how many orders can they visit 3 of these places in the next 3 summers?

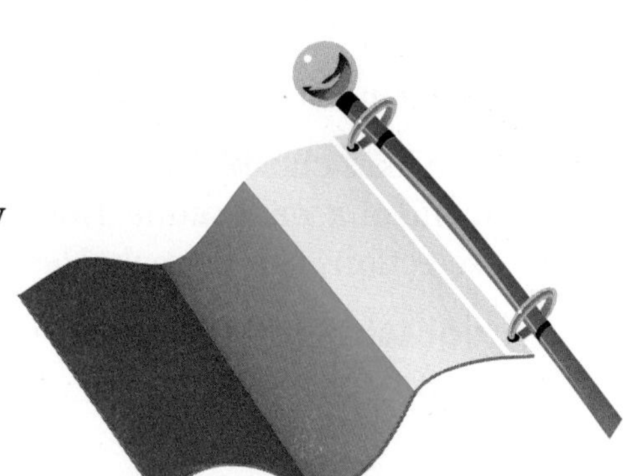

10. **ART** A flag will be divided into sections as shown. How many different designs can be made with red, green, and white if each color is used only once?

11. **NUMBER SENSE** Most ZIP codes contain 5 digits. Using the digits 1–9, how many different ZIP codes could you make without repeating digits within a ZIP code?

12. The Spanish Club rented a bus to go on a field trip. Richard, Melba, Sean, and Ricki have reserved a row of 4 seats. What is the probability that Sean will sit in the first seat?

13. **WRITE ABOUT IT** What is the difference between a combination and a permutation?

Mixed Review and Test Prep

Write each ratio as a fraction.

14. 4:7 **15.** 5:6 **16.** three to eight **17.** nine to five

Use the data at the right for Exercises 18–20.

10	22	14	32	13
24	28	13	28	20

18. These scores were recorded for the local basketball team. Make a stem-and-leaf plot for the scores.

19. What was the highest score?

20. What is the range of scores?

21. **SCALE DRAWINGS** On a map, Wink and Shook are $4\frac{1}{4}$ inches apart. The map scale is 1 inch:25 miles. What is the actual distance between Wink and Shook?

A 100 mi **B** $106\frac{1}{4}$ mi
C $112\frac{1}{2}$ mi **D** 125 mi

22. **SPORTS** Timmy ran 90 feet from first base to second base. Each of his strides was $3\frac{3}{4}$ feet. How many strides did Timmy take?

F 22 **G** 23
H 24 **J** 25

MORE PRACTICE Lesson 22.4, page H74

CHAPTER 22 Review/Test

1. **VOCABULARY** The set of all possible outcomes is called the __?__. (page 428)

For Exercises 2–5, make a tree diagram to show the sample space. Give the total number of possible outcomes. (pages 428–429)

A: sedan, station wagon, van **B:** green, blue, white, red **C:** two-door, four-door

2. one choice each from A and B
3. one choice each from A, B, and C
4. one choice each from B and C
5. one choice each from A and C
6. Jim likes chocolate, strawberry, or vanilla ice cream in a sugar cone or a waffle cone. How many different ice cream cone selections can he make? (pages 428–429)
7. **VOCABULARY** The number used to describe the chance of an event's occurring is the __?__. (page 430)

For Exercises 8–14, use the spinner to find the probability. (pages 430–431)

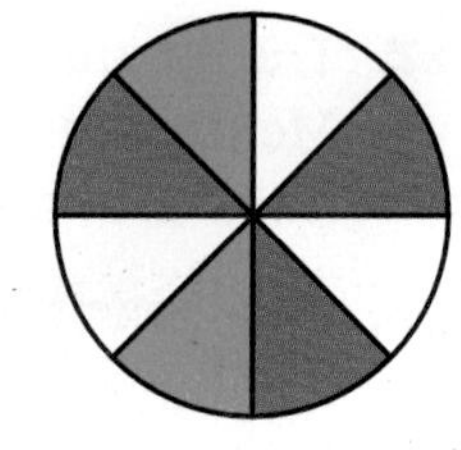

8. P(blue)
9. P(green)
10. P(green or blue)
11. P(white or blue)
12. P(white)
13. P(white or green)
14. P(white, green, or blue)

For Exercises 15–20, you roll a number cube numbered 1 to 6. Find the probability. (pages 430–431)

15. P(3 or 4)
16. P(even)
17. P(greater than 4)
18. P(7)
19. P(less than 4)
20. P(odd)
21. Dan ordered chicken, french fries, beans, cole slaw, cake, and a drink. He only wants 3 items. How many different combinations can he make? (pages 433–435)
22. Mike, Randy, and 5 friends are forming 2-member teams. What is the probability that Mike and Randy will be on the same team? (pages 433–435)
23. **VOCABULARY** An arrangement in which the order is important is a(n) __?__. (page 436)

Adam, Ben, Jim, David, and Evan found 5 seats together in the same row.

24. Find the number of different orders in which the 5 can sit. (pages 436–439)
25. What is the probability that Evan will sit in the second seat? (pages 436–439)

Test Prep

1. What is the probability that the spinner will land on green and 1?

A 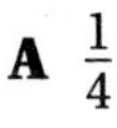 $\frac{1}{4}$

B 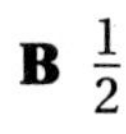 $\frac{1}{2}$

C 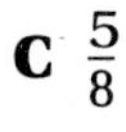 $\frac{5}{8}$

D 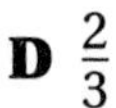 $\frac{2}{3}$

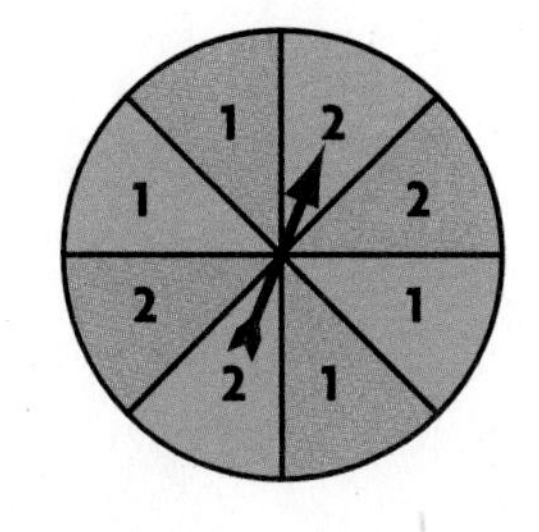

2. What are the next two terms in the sequence 6, 18, 54, 162, . . . ?

F 216, 374
G 314, 628
H 486, 1,458
J 548, 2,192

3. Enrique has to paint sections of a fence. He has enough paint to cover 500 square feet. Each section requires 12 square feet of paint per coat. To how many sections of the fence can he apply 2 coats?

A 21
B 22
C 25
D 41
E Not Here

4. What is the mean of the data?

5.5, 5.3, 5.1, 5.4, 5.6, 5.9, 5.0, 5.6

F 5.4 **G** 5.425
H 5.5 **J** 5.6

5. Which is a reasonable conclusion you can make about the sequence 3, 3, 6, 9, 15, . . . ?

A It is an arithmetic sequence.
B It is a geometric sequence.
C The next term is 24.
D The next term is 21.

6. A painting has a width of 28 inches and is a Golden Rectangle. Which could be its length?

F 17 in. **G** 45 in. **H** 56 in. **J** 81 in.

7. Which measure of central tendency best represents the data?

2, 35, 36, 37, 38, 40, 45

A mean **B** median
C mode **D** range

8. A rectangular lot is 20 feet long and 15 feet wide. Joe draws a scale drawing of the lot using the scale 1 inch : 5 feet. What is the area of the scale drawing?

F 300 in.^{2} **G** 70 in.^{2} **H** 25 in.^{2} **J** 12 in.^{2}

9. Which problem situation can be represented by the equation $2x + 5 = 7$?

A 5 less than twice Ann's age is 7.
B 2 more than five times Ann's age is 7.
C 2 less than five times Ann's age is 7.
D 5 more than twice Ann's age is 7.

10. From the graph, which statement can you conclude is true when the side length doubles?

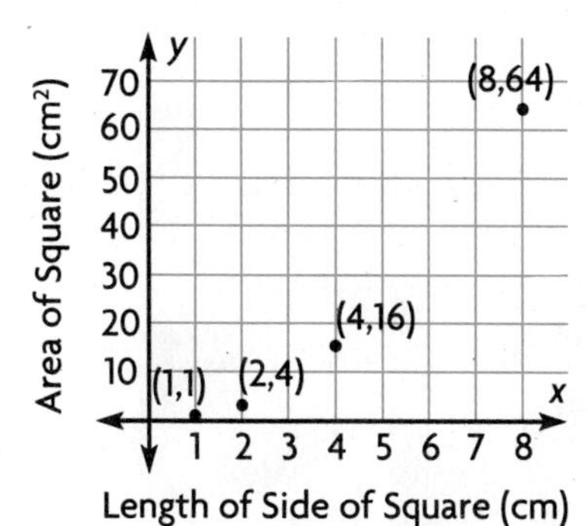

F The area doubles.
G The area is multiplied by 4.
H The area is multiplied by 3.
J The area stays the same.

CHAPTER

23 EXPERIMENTS WITH PROBABILITY

LOOK AHEAD

In this chapter you will solve problems that involve

- experimental probability
- random numbers
- simulations
- geometric probability

SCIENCE LINK

One way scientists estimate wildlife populations is with a tagging procedure. The table shows types of animals whose populations are decreasing in the United States.

- What percent of the species in the table are fish?
- Which group in the table has the largest percentage?

GROUP	NUMBER OF ENDANGERED SPECIES
Fishes	67
Mammals	57
Birds	75
Reptiles	14
Amphibians	9
Snails	15
Clams	56
Crustaceans	15
Insects	24
Arachnids	5

Problem-Solving Project

Counting Fish Populations

YOU WILL NEED: 2 lb dry lima beans, marker, large paper bag

You can simulate the way a scientist estimates the fish population of a lake by using dry lima beans. Pour the beans into a bag to represent the fish population. Estimate the number. Count out and mark 100 beans. Return them to the bag, shaking the bag to mix the beans. Draw 50 beans from the bag. Count the number of marked and unmarked beans. Record your findings. Use a proportion to estimate the total number of beans. Write up the results.

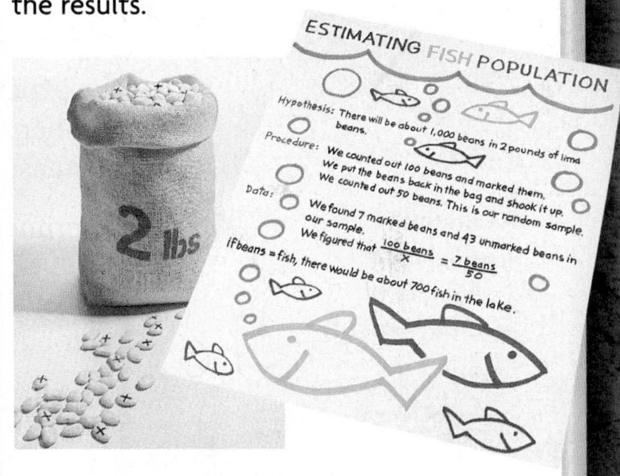

2 lbs
ESTIMATING FISH POPULATION
Hypothesis: There will be about 1,000 beans in 2 pounds of lima beans.
Procedure: We counted out 100 beans and marked them. We put the beans back in the bag and shook it up. We counted out 50 beans. This is our random sample.
Data: We found 7 marked beans and 43 unmarked beans in our sample.
We figured that $\frac{100 \text{ beans}}{x} = \frac{7 \text{ beans}}{50}$
If beans = fish, there would be about 700 fish in the lake.

PROJECT CHECKLIST

- ✓ Did you count and mark 100 beans?
- ✓ Did you draw a random sample of 50 beans?
- ✓ Did you use a proportion to estimate the total number of beans?
- ✓ Did you write up the results of your experiment?

LESSON 23.1

Experimental Probability

What You'll Learn
How to find the experimental probability of an event

Why Learn This?
To find probabilities of real-world events, such as rolling the number you need during a game

VOCABULARY

experimental probability

Tasha has a number cube with faces marked 1–6. She knows that when this number cube is rolled, the mathematical probability of its landing with a particular number up is $\frac{1}{6}$. Before playing a game with the number cube, Tasha wanted to see whether each number did indeed come up about $\frac{1}{6}$ of the times. So, she rolled the cube 100 times and recorded her results in this table and graph.

Number	1	2	3	4	5	6
Times rolled	15	14	7	33	15	16

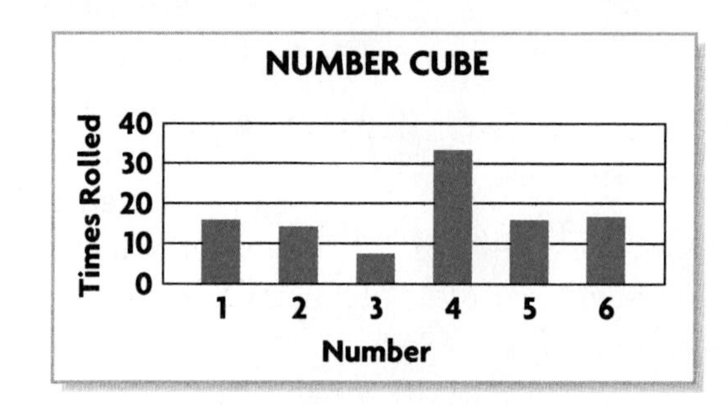

To find the **mathematical probability** of an event occurring, write this ratio:

$\frac{\text{number of favorable outcomes}}{\text{number of possible outcomes}}$

On a number cube with faces numbered 1–6, the mathematical probability of rolling a 5 is $\frac{1}{6}$.

See page 430.

The **experimental probability** of an event is the ratio of the number of times the event occurs to the total number of trials, or times you do the activity.

$$\text{experimental probability} = \frac{\text{number of times event occurs}}{\text{total number of trials}}$$

EXAMPLE 1 Use Tasha's results to find the experimental probability of rolling each number, 1–6, on a number cube.

The total number of trials is 100.

experimental probability of rolling a 1 $= \frac{15}{100}$, or $\frac{3}{20}$

experimental probability of rolling a 2 $= \frac{14}{100}$, or $\frac{7}{50}$

experimental probability of rolling a 3 $= \frac{7}{100}$

experimental probability of rolling a 4 $= \frac{33}{100}$

experimental probability of rolling a 5 $= \frac{15}{100}$, or $\frac{3}{20}$

experimental probability of rolling a 6 $= \frac{16}{100}$, or $\frac{4}{25}$

- If you rolled Tasha's number cube 100 times, do you think your results would be the same as hers? Explain.

GUIDED PRACTICE

1. Tasha decides to roll the number cube 100 more times. Her results are shown in the table below. Find the experimental probabilities of rolling the numbers 1–6, using these results.

Number	1	2	3	4	5	6
Times rolled	19	15	21	12	13	20

2. Tasha has now rolled the number cube a total of 200 times. Copy the table below. Then use the data on page 444 and in Exercise 1 to complete the table to show the combined results of the 200 rolls.

Number	1	2	3	4	5	6
Times rolled	34	?	?	?	?	?

3. Find the experimental probabilities of rolling the numbers 1–6, using the results of all 200 rolls.

4. As a group, are the probabilities you found in Exercise 3 closer to $\frac{1}{6}$ than the probabilities given in Example 1? Explain. (HINT: $\frac{1}{6}$ is about $\frac{17}{100}$ and about $\frac{33}{200}$.)

Technology Link

In ***Data ToolKit*** you can make different graphs to display your data.

Probabilities can be used to predict the likelihood, or chances, that possible future events will in fact occur.

EXAMPLE 2 On his first turn using this spinner, Ben got red on 14 of his 20 spins. On his second turn, he got red on 2 of 4 spins. Using Ben's results, what is the experimental probability that he will get red on his next spin?

Red Blue

To this point in the game, Ben has spun the pointer 20 + 4, or 24, times and has gotten red on 14 + 2, or 16, of them.

Experimental probability of red: $\frac{16}{24}$, or $\frac{2}{3}$

Since the spinner has equal areas for red and blue, the mathematical probability of getting red on any spin is $\frac{1}{2}$.

Talk About It CRITICAL THINKING

- If Ben continues to play the game, will the experimental probability change or stay the same?
- Will the mathematical probability change as he plays the game or stay the same?

INDEPENDENT PRACTICE

The game piece shown at the right has just four faces, numbered 1–4. In Exercises 1–4, each table shows the results of rolling the game piece 50 times. Find the experimental probability of rolling each number.

1.

Number	1	2	3	4
Times rolled	13	15	10	12

2.

Number	1	2	3	4
Times rolled	11	11	14	14

3.

Number	1	2	3	4
Times rolled	10	20	8	12

4.

Number	1	2	3	4
Times rolled	13	12	14	11

5. When you flip a coin, the mathematical probability of its landing heads up is $\frac{1}{2}$ and the mathematical probability of its landing tails up is also $\frac{1}{2}$. Flip a coin 20 times and keep track of the results. What is your experimental probability of flipping heads? of flipping tails?

6. Anders flips a coin 50 times and gets 8 tails. Why is this surprising?

Use the spinner at the right for Exercises 7–9.

7. The spinner has eight spaces of equal size. What is the mathematical probability of the pointer's stopping in the space marked 1? If you spin the pointer 40 times, how many times would you expect it to stop on 1?

8. Hilary spins the pointer 60 times. It stops on an even number 15 times. Why is this surprising?

9. Jimmy spins the pointer 80 times. It stops on the 3 space 10 times. Is this surprising? Explain.

Problem-Solving Applications

10. **SPORTS** A baseball player hit the ball 42 times out of the last 150 times at bat. What is the player's experimental probability of getting a hit the next time at bat?

11. **SPORTS** A professional baseball player had 48 hits in his first 196 at-bats. In the 20 games since then, he has had 28 hits in 64 at-bats. What is the experimental probability that he will get a hit in his next official at-bat?

12. **WRITE ABOUT IT** How is an experimental probability different from a mathematical probability?

MORE PRACTICE Lesson 23.1, page H74

Random Numbers

What You'll Explore
How to generate a list of random numbers

What You'll Need
number cube, a calculator with a random number function

Repeatedly rolling a cube numbered 1–6 and writing down the results generates a random sequence of ones, twos, threes, fours, fives, and sixes. Many of today's calculators have a built-in random function for generating random numbers.

On one calculator, entering 1 [2ND] [RAND] 6 [=] generates a random number from 1 to 6, just as rolling a number cube does. Repeatedly entering this key sequence generates a list of random numbers from 1 to 6. By entering 100 instead of 6, you can generate a random number from 1 to 100.

Explore

- The sequence 1, 5, 6, 6, 3, 2, 3, 5, 4, 4 was generated by rolling a number cube numbered from 1 to 6 a total of 10 times. Roll a number cube to generate a sequence of 20 more numbers.
- You can generate a sequence of two-digit numbers by rolling a number cube and recording pairs of consecutive rolls as a single number. Use a number cube to produce 20 two-digit numbers. What two-digit numbers cannot be produced by this method?
- With a calculator, generate 30 random numbers from 1 to 100.

Technology Link
You can explore random numbers by using E-Lab, Activity 23. Available on CD-ROM and on the Internet at www.hbschool.com/elab
6

Think and Discuss

- From what group are random numbers generated on a calculator by the key sequence 1 [2ND] [RAND] 10 [=]? by the key sequence 1 [2ND] [RAND] 50 [=]?
- The key sequence 101 [2ND] [RAND] 200 [=] produces a random number from 101 to 200. What key sequence will produce a random number from 201 to 300?

Try This

- Write a key sequence for a calculator that will generate a random number from 1 to 200. Then generate 20 random numbers from 1 to 200.

LESSON 23.2

What You'll Learn
How to use random numbers to act out a probability experiment

Why Learn This?
To model situations

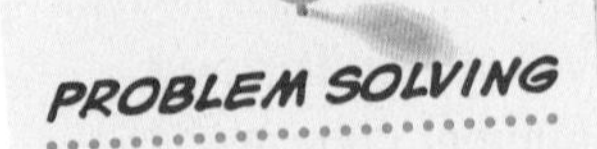

PROBLEM SOLVING
- Understand
- Plan
- Solve
- Look Back

Even though it seems that the world is full of random numbers, many of the important numbers in your life, such as credit card numbers and social security numbers, are assigned for specific reasons. Some of the truly random numbers you might come in contact with are those generated by computers for things such as phone surveys or lottery jackpots.

PROBLEM-SOLVING STRATEGY

Acting It Out by Using Random Numbers

To win a cereal company's contest, you have to collect five different puzzle pieces. The same number of each puzzle piece is produced, and one puzzle piece is placed in each box of cereal. About how many boxes will you have to buy ?

UNDERSTAND What are you asked to find?

What facts are given?

PLAN How can you solve the problem?

You can do an experiment, or *act it out,* by using random numbers to represent the puzzle pieces.

SOLVE The table shows 50 random numbers from 1 to 5.

2	4	2	3	2	2	2	2	2	1
4	2	4	3	1	1	1	1	3	3
5	2	3	3	1	3	3	2	5	3
1	2	2	3	4	3	4	4	3	4
4	4	4	4	1	2	5	5	4	1

Choose any starting point in the table and count how many numbers it takes before you get all the numbers from 1 to 5. Do this two times. Then find the average of the results.

3, 3, 3, 3, 4, 2, 1, 1, 4, 1, 2, 1, 3, 3, 2, 2, 1, 3, 4, 5

Start with 3 at the top of the fourth column. Read down each column, left to right.

Trial 1: 20 boxes

4, 5, 5, 2, 1, 4, 4, 4, 4, 4, 3

Start with 4 at the bottom of the ninth column and read across the rows, right to left.

Trial 2: 11 boxes

$\frac{20 + 11}{2} = 15.5$

Find the average number of boxes.

So, a good estimate would be to buy about 16 boxes.

LOOK BACK What other ways can you read the table to solve the problem?

What if . . . you performed the experiment one more time? How would the average change?

Calculator Activities, page H39

PRACTICE

A computer-generated list of random numbers from 1 to 8 is shown at the right. Use the table for Problems 1–3.

2	5	1	7	1	1
1	2	7	1	6	1
6	4	2	1	3	5
5	6	7	8	5	3
6	6	1	4	7	7
6	6	7	6	3	4
3	6	2	6	6	3
7	4	7	3	7	6

1. You are playing a game with a spinner that has 8 congruent sections labeled 1–8. Estimate the number of spins it will take before you get all the numbers 1 through 8.

2. A student randomly guesses the answers to 10 true-false questions. How many questions is the student probably going to answer as *true*? For each trial, count only 10 numbers, and let an even number mean *true* and an odd number mean *false.*

3. At a restaurant, 2 of every 8 drink glasses have a winning game piece glued to them. Let the numbers 5 and 6 in the random number table represent winning game pieces. Estimate the number of drinks you would have to buy to win.

MIXED APPLICATIONS

Solve.

CHOOSE a strategy and a tool.

- **Draw a Diagram**
- **Use a Formula**
- **Act It Out**
- **Write an Equation**
- **Find a Pattern**
- **Work Backward**

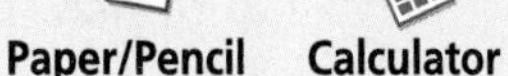

Paper/Pencil **Calculator** **Hands-On** **Mental Math**

4. You enter a hotel elevator while on vacation. You go up 6 floors, down 7 floors, and up 20 floors. You are now on the top floor. Then you go down 10 floors, up 3 floors, and down 15 floors. You are now on the first floor. On which floor did you enter the elevator?

5. Steve is putting a fence around a circular garden. The diameter of the garden is 10 ft. Use the formula $C = \pi d$ to find how much fencing he will need for the garden. Use 3.14 for π.

6. The low temperature in February was 15°F. This was 23° higher than the low temperature in January. What was the low temperature in January?

7. Tasha bought paint and wallpaper. She paid $3 more for a gallon of paint than for the wallpaper. She paid $41 for both. How much did she pay for the wallpaper?

8. Mr. Wilmoth needs to catch a flight that leaves at 6:00 P.M. It takes 45 min to get to the airport, and he wants to be there 1 hr 15 min early. At what time should Mr. Wilmoth leave home?

9. Vinnie and Matthew Johnson are brothers. When you add 5 to twice Vinnie's age, you get Matthew's age. If Matthew is 21 years old, how old is Vinnie?

10. **WRITE ABOUT IT** Write a problem that you would solve by using a random number table.

MORE PRACTICE Lesson 23.2, page H74

LESSON 23.3

ALGEBRA CONNECTION

Designing a Simulation

What You'll Learn
How to use a simulation to model an experiment

Why Learn This?
To predict the outcomes of various probability situations, such as sporting events

VOCABULARY
simulation

As you discovered in Lesson 23.2, you can use random numbers to conduct probability experiments. Generating random numbers is only one way to conduct a simulation.

A **simulation** is a model of an experiment that would be too difficult or time-consuming to actually perform.

EXAMPLE 1 The Iowa Department of Natural Resources (DNR) wants a reasonable estimate of the number of fish in Blackhawk Lake. Since it is impossible to catch every fish in the lake, workers catch and tag 100 fish and then release them into the lake. The next day the workers catch 50 fish, 12 of which have tags from the previous day. About how many fish are in the lake?

Use this proportion:

$$\frac{\text{tagged fish caught on 2nd day}}{\text{total tagged fish}} = \frac{\text{total fish caught on 2nd day}}{\text{total fish in lake}}$$

Let x be the total number of fish in the lake.

$\frac{12}{100} = \frac{50}{x}$ *Cross multiply.*

$12x = 5{,}000$ *Solve for x.*

$x \approx 417$

So, the experiment shows that there are about 417 fish in Blackhawk Lake.

- **CRITICAL THINKING** Suppose the DNR workers are back one month later and catch 50 fish, 4 of which have tags. Why do you think the number of tagged fish is lower than last month?

- The workers tag all 50 fish with a new color and remove the old tags before releasing the fish. Suppose that 7 of the 50 fish they catch the next day have the new tags. About how many fish are in the lake?

CULTURAL LINK

The Great Barrier Reef, located along the northeast coast of Australia, is home to about 1,500 species of fish. The people of Australia are proud of the reef and have made most of it a national park. Suppose a worker caught, tagged, and released 200 tuna. Later, the worker caught 100, and 9 were tagged. Estimate the tuna population in the area.

EXAMPLE 2 During the past three seasons, one professional football team has averaged 5 games per season that were won or lost by its field goal kicker in the final minute of the game. Their current kicker makes 70% of his field goal attempts. Design and conduct a simulation to model the number of game-winning field goals he will make in 5 attempts this season.

Here is one possible simulation.

Since the kicker makes 70% of the field goals he attempts, or 7 out of 10, make a spinner with 10 congruent sections and label 7 of the sections *made* and the other 3 sections *missed*. One spin of the pointer will then model a field goal attempt.

The spinner shown at the right was used 5 times to simulate 5 last-minute game-deciding field goals. The results of those spins are shown in the table below.

Spin Number	1	2	3	4	5
Spin Result	made	made	missed	made	missed

According to the results of this simulation, the team would win 3 of the 5 games and lose the other 2.

- If you conducted this simulation again, the results could be different. Which result do you think is more likely, all 5 field goals made or all 5 field goals missed? Explain.

GUIDED PRACTICE

The Iowa Department of Natural Resources is conducting fish counts at other lakes in the state, using the method described in Example 1.

1. At Lake Panorama, 100 fish are caught and tagged. Of 100 fish caught the next day, 10 have tags. Approximately how many fish are there in Lake Panorama?

2. At Rathbun Lake, 200 fish are caught and tagged. Of 200 fish caught the next day, 25 have tags. About how many fish are there in Rathbun Lake?

3. A basketball player makes 60% of her free throws. To simulate how many she will make in her next 6 attempts, you can use a 10-section spinner. How many sections of the spinner should be labeled *missed*?

4. In Problem 3, suppose you used a spinner with 5 sections for the simulation. How many sections would be labeled *missed*?

INDEPENDENT PRACTICE

For Problems 1–4, design a simulation in which a spinner, number cube, or coin is used to model each situation.

1. One of four class officers is to be selected to represent your class on the principal's new School Improvement Committee.

2. A basketball player who makes 2 of every 3 free throws he attempts is shooting a free throw to win the game.

3. Each day a teacher sends 1 of 6 rows of students to the board to show some of their homework problems.

4. A volleyball player who is successful with 50% of her spikes is set for the winning spike at the end of a game.

Problem-Solving Applications

5. **BUSINESS** Last year about 4 out of every 6 of Mr. Dandridge's customers made purchases over $10. He estimates that about 11 of his first 15 customers today will make purchases over $10. Design a simulation to check his estimate.

6. **PREDICTION** Suppose your math teacher gives your class a 10-question true-false quiz every Friday. You decide to simulate taking last week's quiz by flipping a coin 10 times, letting heads mean *true* and tails mean *false*. On last week's quiz, the first five answers were *true* and the last five were *false*. Conduct the simulation several times. If a passing score is 7 of 10 answers correct, is flipping a coin a good way to take these quizzes? Explain.

7. **WRITE ABOUT IT** Write a problem similar to Example 2 on page 451. Exchange with a classmate and solve.

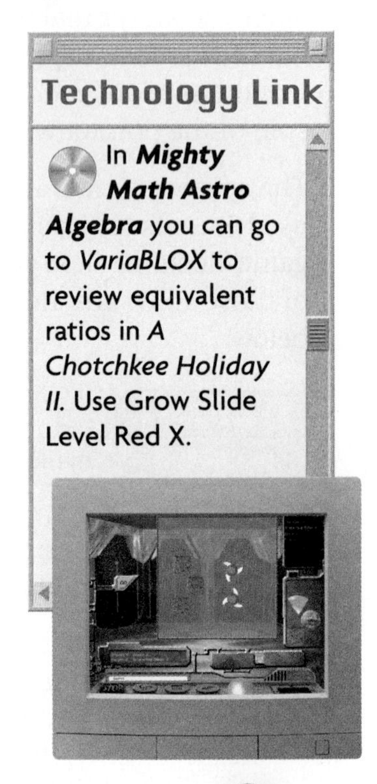

Technology Link
In ***Mighty Math Astro Algebra*** you can go to *VariaBLOX* to review equivalent ratios in *A Chotchkee Holiday II.* Use Grow Slide Level Red X.

Mixed Review and Test Prep

Find the area of each figure.

8.

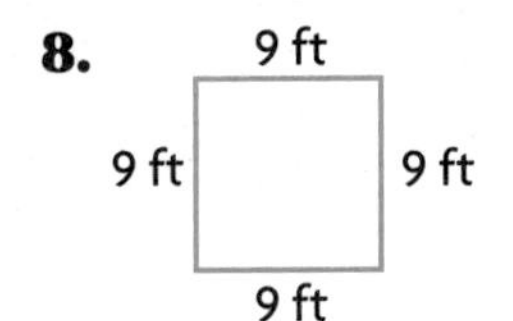

9. 20 ft, 30 ft

10. 5.5 m, 2 m

There are 20 pieces of candy in a bag. Of the 20 pieces, 4 are butterscotch-flavored, 6 are cherry-flavored, and 10 are grape-flavored. Find each probability.

11. P(grape) **12.** P(butterscotch) **13.** P(cherry) **14.** P(cherry or grape)

15. **WORK BACKWARD** Georgianna sells a red silk dress for 3 times her cost plus $15. The dress sells for $75. What is her cost?

A $15 **B** $20 **C** $30 **D** $60

16. **PATTERNS** What is the next number in the sequence 96, 24, 6, 1.5, . . . ?

F 3.75 **G** 0.75
H 0.5 **J** 0.375

MORE PRACTICE Lesson 23.3, page H75

Geometric Probability

LESSON 23.4

What You'll Learn
How to find probabilities related to area

Why Learn This?
To find the probability that an object will land in a certain region, such as a dart randomly hitting the bull's-eye of a dartboard

VOCABULARY
geometric probability

A probability you calculate by comparing the area of a specific part to that of a total region it is in is called a **geometric probability**.

EXAMPLE 1 A farmer's cornfield is shown in the diagram below. An electrical storm is passing over the farmer's land, and he is worried about lightning striking his field. Assuming that lightning strikes his field somewhere at random, what is the probability that it hits the part of the field on the left side of the road?

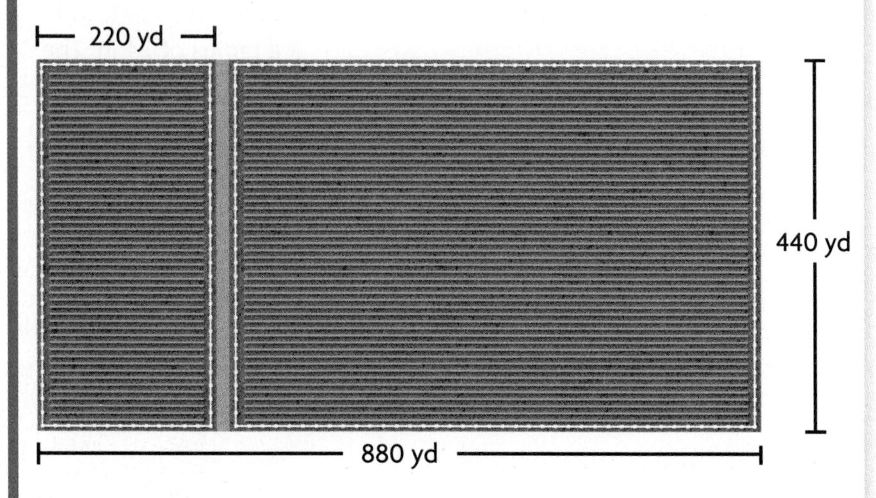

The probability that a lightning bolt that strikes will hit the left field is given by this ratio:

$$\frac{\text{area of left field}}{\text{total area of the farmer's field}}$$

$$\frac{220 \times 440}{880 \times 440} =$$ *Compute the areas.*

$$\frac{96{,}800}{387{,}200} =$$

96800   387200   *Use a calculator to find the probability.*

So, the probability is 25%, or $\frac{1}{4}$.

- What is the probability that lightning will strike the field on the right side of the road?
- Suppose 1,000 bolts of lightning hit the cornfield. About how many would hit the left field?

Many games, such as archery and darts, involve aiming at a target. If you assume all parts on the target are equally likely to be hit, you can estimate the probability of hitting a particular part of the target.

EXAMPLE 2 The bull's-eye of a certain dartboard has a diameter of 1 in. The diameter of the entire dartboard is 12 in. Find the geometric probability that a dart that hits the dartboard will land in the bull's-eye.

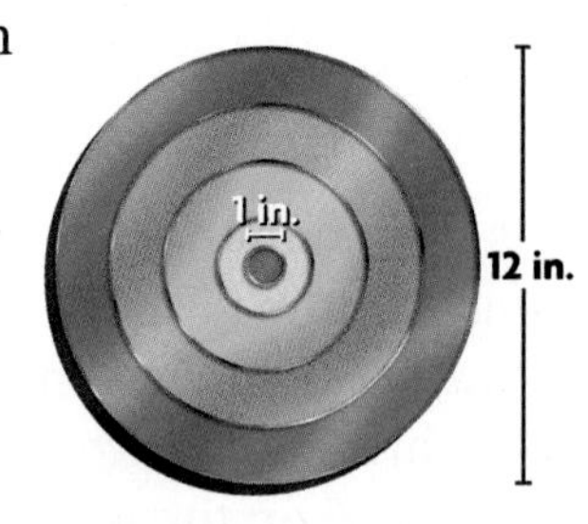

The geometric probability that a dart that hits the dartboard will land in the bull's-eye is given by this ratio:

$$\frac{\text{area of bull's-eye}}{\text{area of entire dartboard}} =$$

$$\frac{\pi(0.5)^2}{\pi(6)^2} = \quad \textit{Use the formula } A = \pi r^2.$$

$$\frac{\pi(0.25)}{\pi(36)} = \frac{1}{144}$$

The probability that a dart hitting the dartboard will land on the bull's-eye is $\frac{1}{144}$, or about 0.7%.

- What is the probability that a dart that hits the dartboard will not land in the bull's-eye?

SPORTS LINK

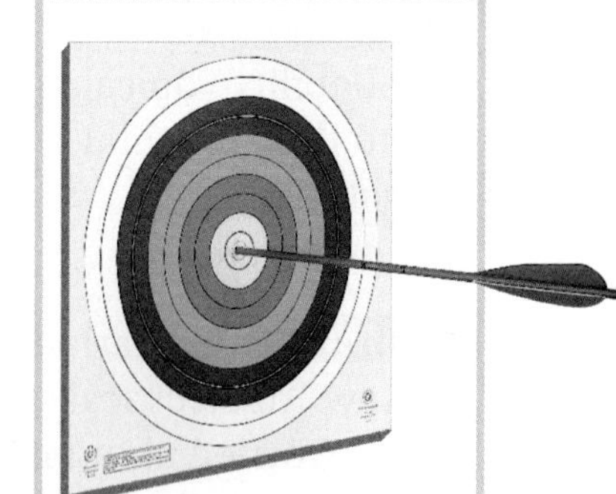

Archery is one of the oldest known sports. In target archery, the target is a circle with a radius of 24 in. The bull's-eye, or center circle, has a radius of 2 in. Assuming the target is hit, what is the probability that an archer will hit the bull's-eye?

GUIDED PRACTICE

Find the probability that a dart that hits the target will land in the shaded area. Assume all points are equally likely to be hit.

1.

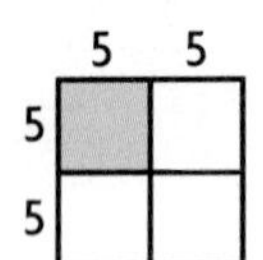

2.

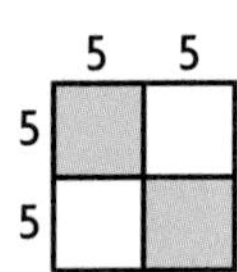

3.

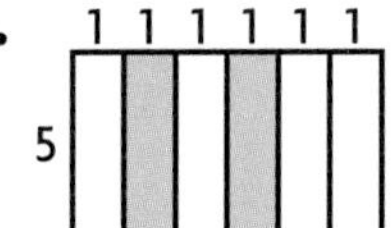

4.

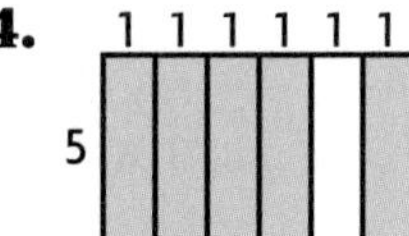

INDEPENDENT PRACTICE

Find the probability that a dart that hits the target will land in the shaded area. All measurements are in inches. Assume all points are equally likely to be hit.

1.

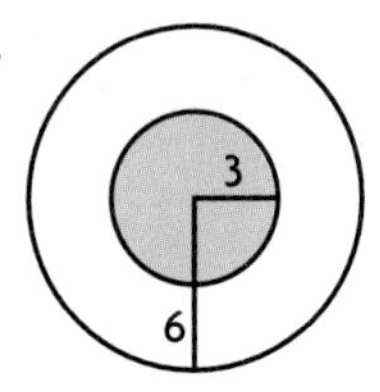

2.

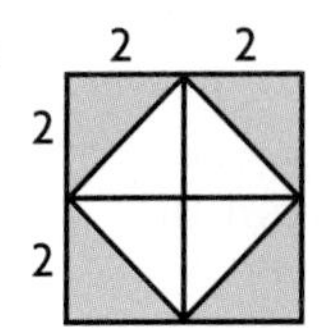

3.

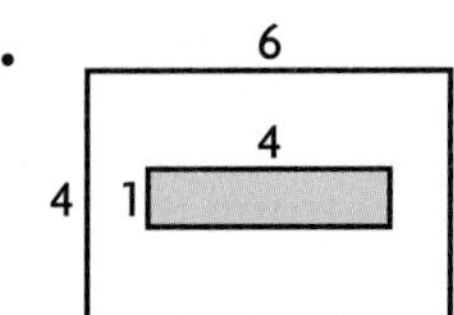

4.

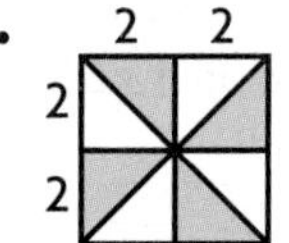

Suppose a meteor lands somewhere at random in the 48 states of the United States mainland, which has an area of about 3,120,000 mi^2. Find the probability that the meteor will land in the given state. Give your answers as percents to the nearest tenth.

5. Texas (about 268,600 mi^2)

6. Indiana (about 83,600 mi^2)

7. Virginia (about 42,800 mi^2)

8. Oregon (about 98,400 mi^2)

9. Arizona (about 114,000 mi^2)

10. New York (about 54,500 mi^2)

Problem-Solving Applications

11. Jake is on a baseball team. During a game he hits a high pop-up in the infield, somewhere within the 90-ft square formed by the bases. What is the probability that the ball will come down inside the 18-ft diameter circle marking the pitcher's mound?

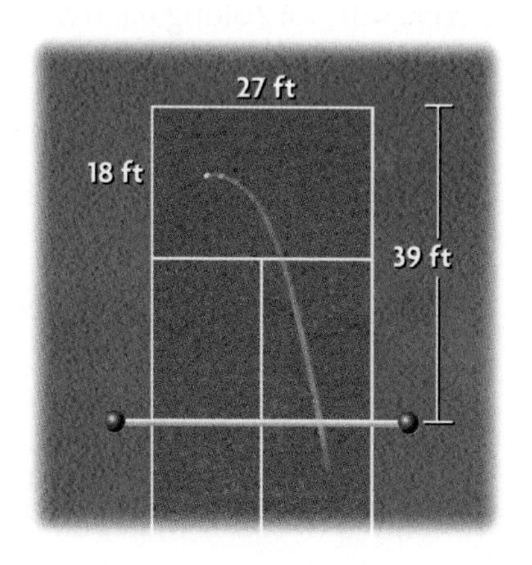

12. **SPORTS** During a tennis match, one player hits a lob (a high-arcing shot) that lands somewhere on the opponent's side of the court. If the opponent's side of the court is 27 ft by 39 ft, what is the probability that the ball will land in the back court, a 27-ft by 18-ft part of the opponent's side?

13. **WRITE ABOUT IT** Look back at Exercise 1. Explain in your own words and with a diagram how you found the probability.

Mixed Review and Test Prep

Which unit of measurement is smaller?

14. inch or foot

15. mile or yard

16. centimeter or meter

17. meter or kilometer

18. gram or kilogram

19. decimeter or meter

20. dekaliter or deciliter

21. milligram or centigram

Find the number of permutations.

22. James, Wanda, and Susie are seated in a row of 3 seats. In how many orders can they be seated?

23. In how many ways can a baseball coach choose the first, second, and third batters for a team of 9 players?

24. **POPULATION** The population at a school has increased by 30 students each year for the past 4 years. For every 40 students, the school hired a new teacher. How many more teachers are there now than 4 years ago?

A 3 **B** 4 **C** 5 **D** 6

25. **ESTIMATION** Jackie works as a waitress. Her customer has a bill of $48.00. About how much will Jackie receive as a tip if the customer leaves about 15% of the total bill?

F $10.00 **G** $7.50
H $6.00 **J** $4.00

MORE PRACTICE Lesson 23.4, page H75

CHAPTER 23 Review/Test

For Exercises 1–6, use the table below to find the experimental probability of rolling each number or type of number. (pages 444–446)

1. 2 **2.** 3 **3.** 4

4. 5 **5.** 6 **6.** even

Number	1	2	3	4	5	6
Times rolled	8	5	9	10	12	6

For Exercises 7–12, use the table below to find the experimental probability of rolling each number or type of number. (pages 444–446)

7. 5 **8.** 6 **9.** odd

10. 2 or 3 **11.** 2 **12.** not 1

Number	1	2	3	4	5	6
Times rolled	7	6	3	8	10	6

Use the random number list at the right for Exercises 13–14. (pages 448–449)

13. In a game, you roll a 12-sided die numbered 1–12. How many times will you have to roll it to get all the numbers 1–12?

14. One of every 6 boxes of a certain cereal contains a coupon for a free box of a new cereal. Let 6 and 12 represent the boxes with coupons. How many boxes would you have to buy to get a coupon?

11	5	11	1	12	9	4	7
12	1	7	8	12	7	3	8
8	10	1	8	3	12	5	4
5	2	6	5	11	3	4	10
1	2	3	10	8	8	11	5

Solve. (pages 450–452)

15. Design a simulation using a spinner, number cube, or coin to model the probability of the next pitch for a pitcher who throws a strike 60% of the time.

16. One of three class officers is to be selected each week to report concerns to the principal. Design a simulation for this activity.

17. **VOCABULARY** A probability you calculate by comparing the area of a specific part to that of a total region it is in is called a(n) __?__. (page 453)

Find the probability that a dart that falls at random somewhere on each target lands in the shaded area. (pages 453–455)

18.

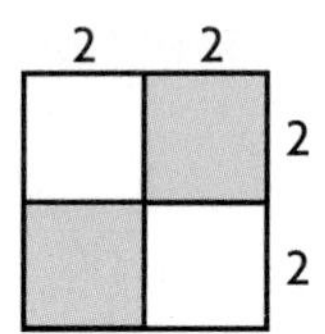

19.

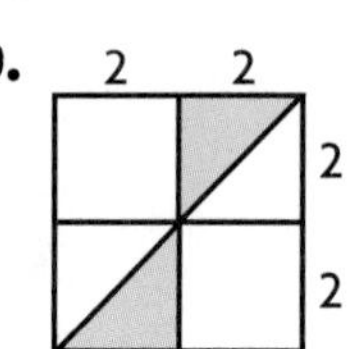

20.

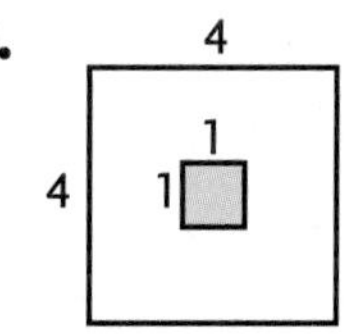

Test Prep

CUMULATIVE
CHAPTERS 1–23

1. What is the probability that a dart that hits the target will land in the shaded area?

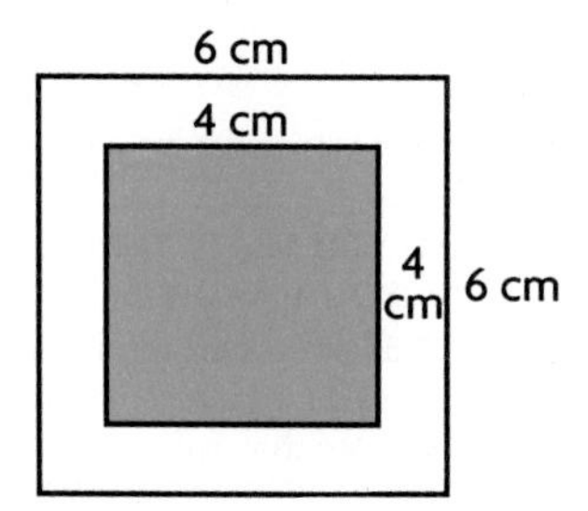

A $\frac{1}{4}$ B $\frac{4}{9}$ C $\frac{5}{9}$ D $\frac{2}{3}$

2. Jacki, Kim, and Marti find 3 seats together. In how many different orders can they sit?

F 2
G 3
H 6
J 9

3. Which interval of ages placed the most take-out orders?

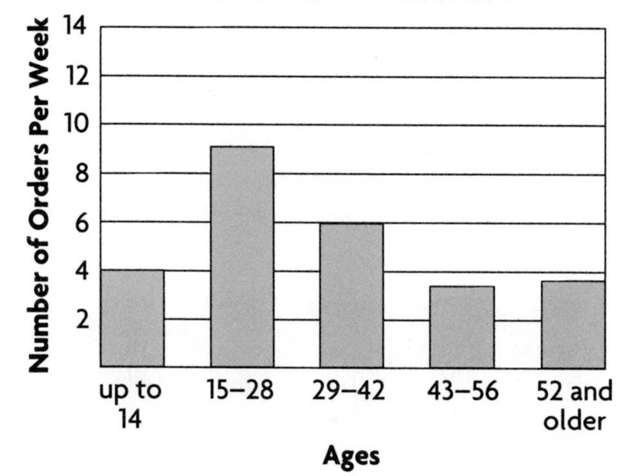

A Up to 14
B 15–28
C 29–42
D 43–56
E 57 and older

4. Rectangle *ABCD* has a length of 9 centimeters and a width of 5 centimeters. Which are the dimensions of a rectangle similar to *ABCD*?

F $l = 3$ cm, $w = 2$ cm
G $l = 13.5$ cm, $w = 7.5$ cm
H $l = 18$ cm, $w = 15$ cm
J $l = 27$ cm, $w = 10$ cm

5. $^{-}432 \div {}^{-}6 =$

A 72
B 64
C $^{-}36$
D $^{-}72$

6. 92% of what number is 266.8?

F 225
G 245.5
H 290
J 312
K Not Here

7. What figures are used to make the tessellation?

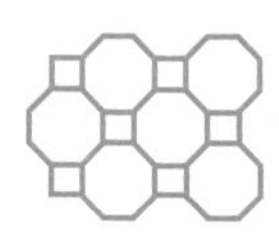

A hexagons and squares
B pentagons and squares
C octagons and pentagons
D octagons and squares

8. The Cortez family spent 35% of its vacation at the beach, 30% at amusement parks, 20% traveling, and 15% eating. What are the measures of the central angles of a circle graph representing the data?

F 140°, 120°, 70°, 30°
G 126°, 108°, 72°, 54°
H 63°, 36°, 54°, 18°
J 35°, 30°, 20°, 15°

CHAPTERS 20–23

MATH FUN!

SURVEY SUPERSTARS

PURPOSE To rewrite survey questions (pages 399–400)

Study the results of the survey. What format is the survey question? Is the survey biased?

Describe a population that would give you biased results.

Share this activity with family members. How would the members of your family respond to this survey?

WHY DID YOU SELECT THE MUSIC YOU BOUGHT?

Americans aged 12-54 bought an average of 12 music CDs, tapes, or records during a recent 6-month period. Here are their reasons:

Heard on radio	85%
On Top 50 List	48%
Fan loyalty	41%
Store display	33%
Watched TV concert	29%
On sale	28%
Read review, saw ad (tie)	20%
Attended concert	18%

Note: May name more than one reason

FLAG FUN

PURPOSE To practice finding permutations and probability (pages 436–439)

The South Korean flag has 4 trigrams, including this one, which means “fire.” A trigram is made of 3 parallel bars. Each bar is either a long bar or 2 short bars. How many different trigrams are there? What are 2 different methods you can use to find the answer?

Draw all the different trigrams.

What is the probability of picking one of the 4 trigrams from the South Korean flag out of all the possible trigrams?

RED, WHITE, AND BLUE

PURPOSE To find probabilities related to area (pages 453–455)

The object of this board game is to toss a coin on the board and earn points when the coin lands on a particular color. You earn 1 point for red, 2 points for blue, and 3 points for white. Each square has sides of length 2 in. Make the game board and play the game with a partner. What is the geometric probability that a randomly tossed coin will land on red? on blue? on white?

red = 1 pt   blue = 2 pts   white = 3 pts

Using a Spreadsheet to Display Data

A spreadsheet can be used to quickly display data by using different kinds of graphs. Use a spreadsheet to display the Kennedy Middle School Student Council budget shown in the table at the right. You can use the graph icons shown below to immediately display your data in a graph.

Student Council Budget	
Spring Festival	$412
Dances	$587
School Assemblies	$275
Awards Banquet	$384
Other	$250

B A C

Enter and highlight the data.

untitled

All	A	B
1		
2	Spring Festival	$412
3	Dances	$587
4	School Assemblies	$275
5	Awards Banquet	$384
6	Other	$250

Click icon A for a circle graph.

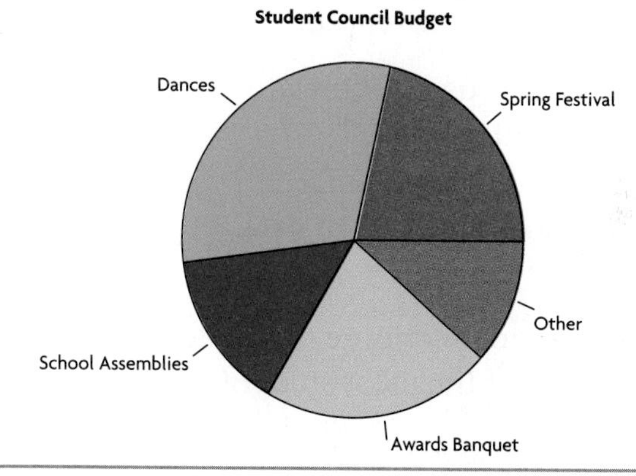

Click icon B for a bar graph.

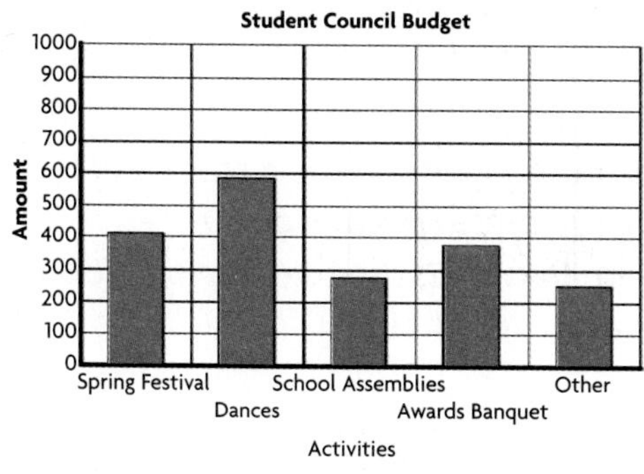

Click icon C for a line graph.

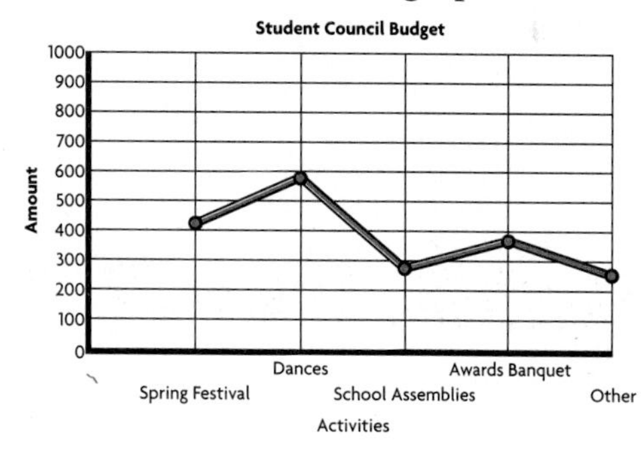

1. How would you display the data in a histogram?
2. Which graph best displays the Student Council budget?
3. Why is a line graph not a good choice to display the data?

USING THE SPREADSHEET

4. Find a table of data. Enter the data in a spreadsheet and display it with different kinds of graphs.

CHAPTERS 20–23

Study Guide and Review

Vocabulary Check

1. The number used to describe the chance of an event's occurring is the _?_. (page 430)

2. An arrangement of items or events in which the order is important is a(n) _?_. (page 436)

EXAMPLES

- **Identify and use different types of samples.** (pages 394–396)

Determine the sampling method used if 20 men and 20 women are surveyed.

Stratified sampling is used. There are subgroups: men and women.

- **Show the distribution of a set of data.** (pages 410–413)

Use the histogram to determine the interval that has the scores of the most students.

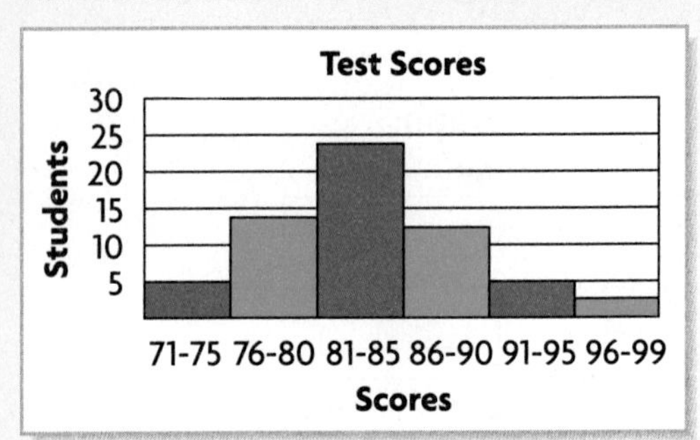

The greatest number of students, 24, have scores in the interval 81–85.

- **Choose an appropriate measure of central tendency.** (pages 414–416)

What is the best measure of central tendency for the heights of students below? Why?

60 in., 62 in., 58 in., 64 in., 59 in., 65 in., 63 in.

The mean, 61.6, and median, 62, are both central values.

EXERCISES

Determine the sampling method used.

3. From a computer list of students, each with an equal chance of being selected, 100 students are chosen.

4. Every tenth person walking down the street is surveyed about the President.

For Exercises 5–8, use the stem-and-leaf plot.

August Temperatures at Noon (in °F)

Stem	Leaves
7	6 8 8 8 9 9 9
8	0 0 1 1 2 2 2 3 3 4 5 5 6 7 9
9	0 2 2 4 5 5 7 7 9

5. What was the highest noon temperature in August?

6. What is the range?

7. In what interval, shown as a stem, do most of the temperatures occur?

8. Did more than half the days have a noon temperature less than 85°F?

Find the mean, median, and mode.

9. 20, 24, 29, 32, 35 **10.** 44, 68, 48, 48, 63

11. What is a good measure of central tendency for these scores? Explain.
91, 88, 91, 75, 82, 95, 80

- **Use tree diagrams and sample spaces to find possible outcomes.** (pages 428–429)

Jennifer has a choice of chicken or steak with beans, carrots, or squash. How many total selections does she have?

Meat	Vegetable	Outcome
chicken	beans	chicken, beans
	carrots	chicken, carrots
	squash	chicken, squash
steak	beans	steak, beans
	carrots	steak, carrots
	squash	steak, squash

6 selections

Make a tree diagram to show the sample space. Find the total number of outcomes.

Shirt: purple, yellow, red, green
Slacks: brown, gray, blue
Socks: black, white

12. Choose one shirt and one pair of slacks.

13. Choose one shirt, one pair of slacks, and one pair of socks.

14. George has a choice of whole wheat, rye, or white bread with tuna, roast beef, or cheese filling. How many selections of sandwiches does he have?

- **Find the experimental probability of an event.** (pages 444–446)

The results of 40 rolls of a number cube are in the table. Find the experimental probability of rolling a 3.

Number	1	2	3	4	5	6
Times Rolled	6	5	4	9	10	6

$\frac{4}{40}$, or $\frac{1}{10}$

For Exercises 15–20, use the table to find the experimental probability of rolling the number.

Number	1	2	3	4	5	6
Times Rolled	8	6	7	10	5	14

15. 1 **16.** 2 **17.** 3

18. 4 or 5 **19.** 5 or 6 **20.** 2 or 6

Problem-Solving Applications

Solve. Explain your methods.

21. One of every 8 soda bottles has a prize under the cap. Let 5 represent the bottle with a prize. Use the random number list to estimate how many bottles you have to buy to get a prize. (pages 448–449)

6	1	5	8	4	5	4	6	1
3	7	6	4	2	1	7	2	3
4	5	3	5	1	4	2	7	8

22. A target has a bull's-eye with an area of 12 in.^{2} The entire target circle has an area of 1,728 in.^{2} What is the probability that an arrow that randomly hits the target will hit the bull's-eye? (pages 453–455)

CHAPTERS 20–23

Performance Assessment

Tasks: Show What You Know

1. Is the following survey biased? Explain your thinking.
A manufacturer of backpacks wants to find out what color of backpack children ages 7–12 like best. The company randomly surveys 250 boys ages 7–12. (pages 397–398)

2. Explain each step as you find the mean, median, and mode for this set of test scores: 95, 62, 72, 88, 94, 85. Then explain which is a good measure of central tendency to represent the data.
(pages 414–416)

3. Suppose you roll a number cube labeled 1, 3, 5, 7, 9, and 11. Find P(a multiple of 3). Explain your method. (pages 430–431)

4. Look at the table of random numbers. Explain how you could use the number 1 in the table to solve the problem.

2	4	2	3	2	3	5	1
4	2	1	1	2	4	3	4
5	2	3	3	5	2	2	4

One out of every 5 tickets has a winning number. Estimate how many tickets you have to buy to get two winning tickets.
(pages 448–449)

Problem Solving

Solve. Explain your method.

CHOOSE a strategy and a tool.

- Find a Pattern
- Act It Out
- Make a Model
- Make a Table
- Write a Number Sentence

Paper/Pencil

Calculator

Hands-On

Mental Math

5. Sean wanted to know which radio stations were popular with teenagers, so he asked five of his friends on the football team. Was Sean's plan a good one? Explain. Suggest a better way for Sean to collect his data.
(pages 397–398)

6. The Oakhill Middle School basketball players are 67 in., 66 in., 72 in., 69 in., 74 in., 68 in., 68 in., 77 in., 73 in., 69 in., 68 in., and 72 in. tall. Make a graph to show the data. Explain how to interpret the data. What are the range, mean, median, and mode? (pages 417–420)

7. Len took one picture each of the Alamo, Sea World, the River Walk, Market Square, and the Witte Museum. He puts 2 of the 5 photos on each page of an album. How many combinations of photos can he make on a page? If he could put 3 photos on a page, would the number of combinations change? If so, how?
(pages 433–435)

8. At the batting cage, Manuel hit 15 out of 50 tries at bat. On his next 50 tries at bat, he had 23 hits. What is the experimental probability that he will get a hit his next time at bat? (pages 444–446)

Cumulative Review

CHAPTERS 1–23

Solve the problem. Then write the letter of the correct answer.

1. Which decimal is equivalent to 10%? (pages 26–29)

A. 0.01 **B.** 0.10
C. 1.0 **D.** 10.0

2. What is $\sqrt{625}$? (pages 43–45)

A. 25 **B.** 312.5
C. 1,250 **D.** not here

3. Find the quotient. (pages 70–72)

$140.4 \div 6.5$

A. 2.16 **B.** 21.6
C. 216 **D.** 912.6

4. Find the sum. (pages 99–101)

$^{-}14 + {}^{-}8$

A. $^{-}22$ **B.** $^{-}6$
C. 6 **D.** 22

5. Evaluate the expression for $x = 10$. (pages 126–129)

$3x - 6x - 3$

A. $^{-}33$ **B.** $^{-}27$
C. 27 **D.** 33

6. Solve $x + 1.25 < 4.75$. (pages 170–171)

A. $x < 6$ **B.** $x > 3.5$
C. $x > 6$ **D.** not here

7. Which ordered pair is a solution of $y = 3x - 4$? (pages 185–187)

A. (1,1) **B.** $(0,{}^{-}1)$
C. (2,2) **D.** $({}^{-}1,1)$

8. Name the figure. (pages 236–237)

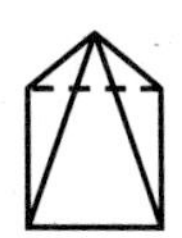

A. square prism
B. square pyramid
C. triangular prism
D. triangular pyramid

9. A triangular prism has 5 faces and 6 vertices. How many edges does it have? (pages 238–240)

A. 5 **B.** 6
C. 9 **D.** 11

10. 24 is 60% of what number? (pages 304–307)

A. 4 **B.** 14.4
C. 40 **D.** not here

11. How many times must 100 be halved to reach or be less than 5? (pages 362–363)

A. 2 times **B.** 3 times
C. 4 times **D.** 5 times

For Exercises 12–13, use the stem-and-leaf plot below. (pages 410–413)

Test Scores

Stem	Leaves
7	0 3 4 4 4 6 8 9
8	2 5 5 6 7 8
9	1 3 4 6 6 7 8

12. What is the highest test score?

A. 98 **B.** 70
C. 9 **D.** 8

13. What is the range?

A. 8 **B.** 28
C. 74 **D.** not here

CHAPTER

24 MEASURING LENGTH AND AREA

LOOK AHEAD

In this chapter you will solve problems that involve

- using appropriate units and precision
- measuring lengths in networks
- using the Pythagorean Property

CONSUMER LINK

The table below shows the U.S. newspapers with the largest circulations as of March 1997.

U.S. NEWSPAPERS WITH GREATEST AVERAGE DAILY CIRCULATIONS	
Paper	Circulation (to the nearest hundred thousand)
Wall Street Journal	1,800,000
USA Today	1,700,000
New York Times	1,100,000
Los Angeles Times	1,100,000
Washington Post	800,000
New York Daily News	700,000
Chicago Tribune	700,000
Long Island Newsday	600,000
Houston Chronicle	500,000
San Francisco Chronicle/Examiner	500,000

- Make a box-and-whisker graph for the data.
- Write one conclusion you can make from the data shown in your graph.

Problem-Solving Project

Bad News/ Good News

Read two newspapers and decide which front-page articles are about "good," "bad," and "neutral" news. Find the areas of all these articles. Measure to the nearest $\frac{1}{2}$ inch the heights of headlines for articles conveying good, bad, and neutral news. Make a table showing your results. Write a report about your conclusions.

Bad News/Good News

NEWSPAPER 1

Good			Bad			Neutral		
Length	Width	Area	Length	Width	Area	Length	Width	Area
5 in.	3 in.	15 in.^{2}	15 in.	3 in.	45 in.^{2}	10 in.	2 in.	20 in.^{2}
20 in.	3 in.	60 in.^{2}	2 in.	$2\frac{1}{2}$ in.	5 in.^{2}	5 in.	3 in.	15 in.^{2}
Total: 75 in.^{2}			Total: 50 in.^{2}			Total: 35 in.^{2}		

NEWSPAPER 2

Good			Bad			Neutral		
Length	Width	Area	Length	Width	Area	Length	Width	Area
6 in.	3 in.	18 in.^{2}	$10\frac{1}{2}$ in.	3 in.	$31\frac{1}{2}$ in.^{2}	5 in.	2 in.	10 in.^{2}
12 in.	3 in.	36 in.^{2}	18 in.	3 in.	54 in.^{2}	$2\frac{1}{2}$ in.	3 in.	$7\frac{1}{2}$ in.^{2}
Total: 54 in.^{2}			Total: $85\frac{1}{2}$ in.^{2}			Total: $17\frac{1}{2}$ in.^{2}		

PROJECT CHECKLIST

- ✓ Did you decide which articles are good, bad, and neutral?
- ✓ Did you measure the area of each article?
- ✓ Did you measure the height of each headline?
- ✓ Did you write about your conclusions?

LESSON 24.1

Measuring and Estimating Lengths

What You'll Learn
How to compare the precision of measurements and how to estimate lengths

Why Learn This?
To recognize whether a measurement is as precise as needed for the situation

VOCABULARY
precision
greatest possible error

Suppose you are in charge of buying fabric for the pep banners at school. Each banner is to be 32 in. long, and you have to make 30 banners. When you go to the store, what unit of measure will you use to describe how much fabric you need?

You will probably buy fabric in yards, not in inches. However, when you cut the fabric for each banner, you will want your measurement to be more precise.

The **precision** of a measurement is related to the unit of measure you choose. An object measured to the nearest $\frac{1}{2}$ in. has a precision of $\frac{1}{2}$ in. The smaller the unit of measure used, the more precise the measurement. A measurement of 36 in. is more precise than a measurement of 1 yd.

EXAMPLE 1 For each pair of measurements, tell which is more precise.

37 in. or 3 ft

Since an inch is a smaller unit than a foot, 37 in. is more precise.

5 km or 5,235 m

Since a meter is a smaller unit than a kilometer, 5,235 m is more precise.

- What is the precision of a measurement of 37 in.? 5,235 m?
- Which is more precise, feet or yards? Explain.

REMEMBER:
When measuring length, you can use metric or customary units. **See page H23.**

Metric
millimeter, centimeter, decimeter, meter, dekameter, hectometer, kilometer

Customary
inch, foot, yard, mile

No matter what unit of measure you use, the measurement is approximate. A certain amount of error is always possible. The **greatest possible error**, or GPE, of any measurement is half of the unit used in the measurement.

To find the possible actual lengths for a recorded measurement of 5 cm, add and subtract the greatest possible error from the measurement. The greatest possible error is half of 1 cm, or 0.5 cm. So, the actual length can be from 4.5 cm to 5.5 cm.

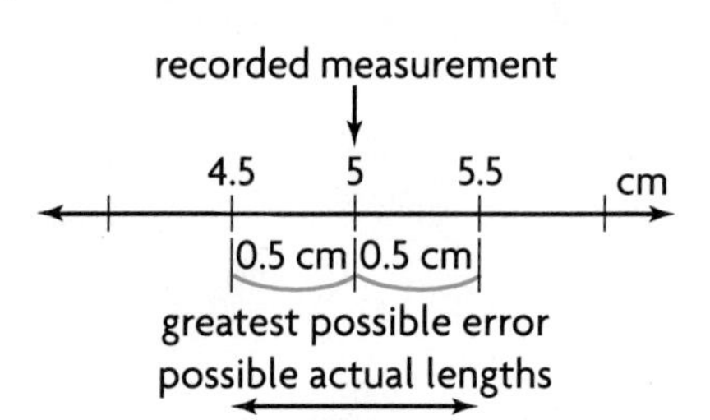

EXAMPLE 2 Mark measured a fish he caught using a foot as the unit. He said the fish measured 2 ft. What is the range of possible actual lengths of his fish?

Since the unit used is a foot, the greatest possible error is half of that, or $\frac{1}{2}$ ft.

To find the possible actual lengths for the measurement 2 ft, subtract and add the greatest possible error.

least length	greatest length
$2\text{ ft} - \frac{1}{2}\text{ ft} = 1\frac{1}{2}\text{ ft}$	$2\text{ ft} + \frac{1}{2}\text{ ft} = 2\frac{1}{2}\text{ ft}$

So, the actual length of the fish may be any length from $1\frac{1}{2}$ ft to $2\frac{1}{2}$ ft.

Talk About It CRITICAL THINKING

- Mark measured his fish again, this time in inches. He found it to be 22 in. long instead of 2 ft long. Which measurement is more precise? Find the greatest possible error for each measurement. Which is greater?
- When you measure to the nearest inch, the greatest possible error is $\frac{1}{2}$ in. What is the greatest possible error when you measure to the nearest $\frac{1}{2}$ in.? to the nearest $\frac{1}{4}$ in.?
- When you measure to the nearest centimeter, the greatest possible error is 0.5 cm. What is the greatest possible error when you measure to the nearest 0.1 cm? to the nearest 0.01 cm?

CAREER LINK

When manufacturers produce a large quantity of an item, they don't expect every one to be perfect. They define **tolerance** to be the amount by which each piece is allowed to vary from the standard. The hex nut below is supposed to be 1.5 cm wide, with a tolerance of ±1 mm. Measure the width. Is it within the given tolerance? Explain.

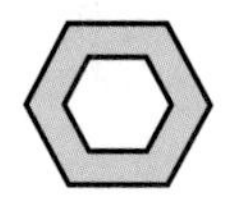

GUIDED PRACTICE

1. Would you measure the thickness of a coin to the nearest millimeter, centimeter, or meter?

2. Would you measure your height to the nearest inch, foot, yard, or mile?

Which measurement is more precise?

3. 19 in. or $2\frac{1}{2}$ ft
4. 1 km or 1,100 m
5. 20 mm or 2 cm
6. 10 ft or 3.5 yd
7. 98 cm or 1 m
8. 5 yd or 182 in.

Find the greatest possible error (GPE) for each measurement.

9. 9 cm
10. 62 mm
11. 0.5 cm
12. 3 ft
13. 18.5 in.
14. 27 km

Estimating Length

Sometimes it is necessary to have a precise measurement. At other times, an estimate is sufficient. A jeweler measuring a diamond wants a precise measurement. But, on a family trip, an estimate of the distance between two cities may be fine. When you estimate a length, it is helpful to have pictures of different units in your mind. For example, you can visualize the centimeter as the width of your little finger.

EXAMPLE 3 Joyce is cutting ribbon. One of the cut pieces looks like this:

About how many millimeters long is the ribbon?

Use your little finger to estimate the length.

There are about 5 cm of ribbon.
1 cm = 10 mm
5 cm = 5 × 10 mm = 50 mm

So, a reasonable estimate is about 50 mm.

CONSUMER LINK

In the United States, we use customary units, such as the foot, for everyday measurements of length. In almost every other country, metric units, such as the meter, are used to measure length. Which is longer, a foot or a meter?

Sometimes measurements are given in units different than you need. You can generate a formula to convert between units.

EXAMPLE 4 Write a formula to convert yards to feet. (1 yd = 3 ft)

Make a table.

Yards (Y)	1	2	3	4
Feet (F)	3	6	9	12

Use the relationship shown in the table to write a conversion formula.

$F = 3Y$

INDEPENDENT PRACTICE

Give the precision of each measurement.

1. 8 km **2.** $14\frac{1}{2}$ ft **3.** $4\frac{1}{3}$ mi **4.** 7 mi **5.** 6 in.

Find the greatest possible error (GPE) for each measurement.

6. 20 yd **7.** 14 in. **8.** 15 dm **9.** 8.6 km **10.** $4\frac{1}{3}$ mi

For the given measurement, give the smallest and largest possible actual lengths.

11. 52 mi **12.** 60 mm **13.** 82.7 km **14.** $11\frac{1}{4}$ yd

Tell whether a *precise measurement* is necessary or an *estimate* is sufficient.

15. the width of a new oven to be installed between two cabinets

16. the distance left on a trip using a map scale to measure length

17. the length of your math book

Choose the best estimate of length.

18.

a. 3 mm
b. 3 cm
c. 3 dm

19.

a. 2 in.
b. 3 in.
c. 12 in.

Problem-Solving Applications

20. **MONEY** Would you estimate the length of a dollar bill as 6 in. or as 16 in.?

21. **ESTIMATION** Would you estimate the length of a desk as 1 ft or as 1 m?

22. Would you estimate the height of a classroom as 15 ft or as 15 yd?

23. **MEASUREMENT** Steven measured the length of a newspaper headline as 2 in. Marta measured the same length as $1\frac{7}{8}$ in. Which measurement is more precise? Explain.

Extra! Extra! Extra! Complete news coverage delivered daily!
The Daily News
BIG NEWS!

24. **CONVERSIONS** Write a formula to convert feet to inches. Use F = ft and I = in. (1 ft = 12 in.)

25. **CONVERSIONS** Write a formula to convert inches to centimeters. Use C = cm and I = in. (1 in = 2.54 cm)

26. **WRITE ABOUT IT** How do you know when to estimate a length and when to find a precise measurement?

Mixed Review and Test Prep

Find the perimeter of each figure.

27.

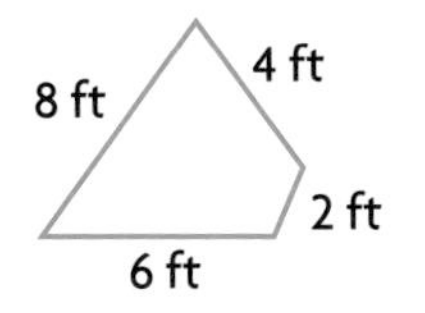

28.

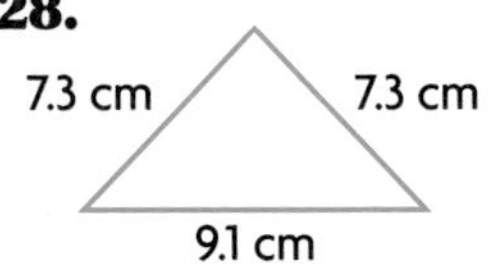

29.

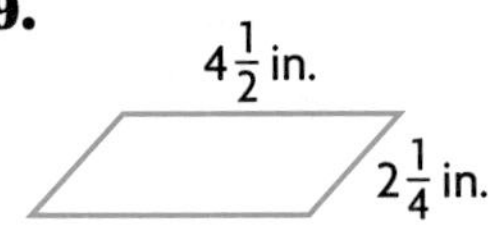

30. **CRITICAL THINKING** A bicycle wheel has a diameter of 26 inches. About how many revolutions does the wheel make during a 10-mile race?

A 64
B 646
C 6,467
D 7,760

31. **ESTIMATION** About how many pennies placed side by side would measure 1 meter in length?

F 40
G 50
H 60
J 100

LESSON 24.2 Networks

What You'll Learn
How to use a network to find all possible routes and to find the shortest route

Why Learn This?
To find the shortest route for a trip

VOCABULARY

network

The Diaz family is looking for the shortest route through four South American cities. One way they can show the distances between the cities is to draw a network. A **network** is a graph with vertices and edges. In the network below, the vertices are different South American cities, and the connecting edges are the roads between them. The estimated distances between the four cities are given in miles.

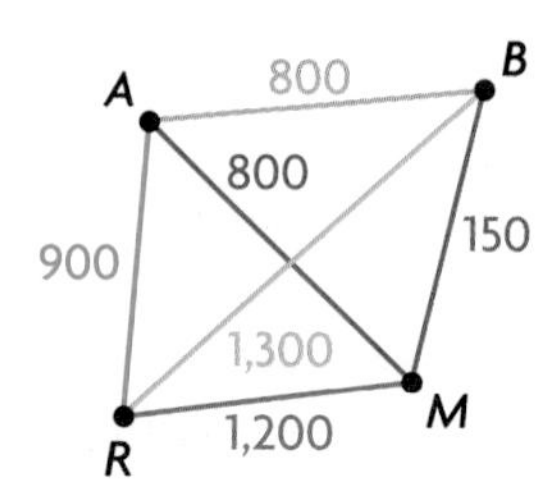

A – Asunción, Paraguay

B – Buenos Aires, Argentina

M – Montevideo, Uruguay

R – Rio de Janeiro, Brazil

You can use a network to help you find the shortest route.

EXAMPLE 1 Starting from Buenos Aires, find the shortest route that includes all the cities.

Find all possible routes, and determine the distance for each route.

BAMR	800 + 800 + 1,200 = 2,800
BMAR	150 + 800 + 900 = 1,850
BRAM	1,300 + 900 + 800 = 3,000
BARM	800 + 900 + 1,200 = 2,900
BMRA	150 + 1,200 + 900 = 2,250
BRMA	1,300 + 1,200 + 800 = 3,300

The shortest route, *BMAR*, is 1,850 mi.

EXAMPLE 2 What is the shortest route from Buenos Aires to the other three cities and back to Buenos Aires?

Find all possible routes.	*Determine the distance for each route.*
BAMRB	800 + 800 + 1,200 + 1,300 = 4,100
BMARB	150 + 800 + 900 + 1,300 = 3,150
BRAMB	1,300 + 900 + 800 + 150 = 3,150
BARMB	800 + 900 + 1,200 + 150 = 3,050
BMRAB	150 + 1,200 + 900 + 800 = 3,050
BRMAB	1,300 + 1,200 + 800 + 800 = 4,100

The shortest routes are *BARMB* and *BMRAB*.

Networks are a part of everyday life. Your school or community may have a network of bus routes providing transportation. Most local TV stations belong to a major network, allowing viewers in different cities to watch a program at the same time. The Internet is a network that connects computers all over the world.

GUIDED PRACTICE

Each vertex represents a city. Starting from *A*, find all the possible routes that include each of the cities only once.

1. 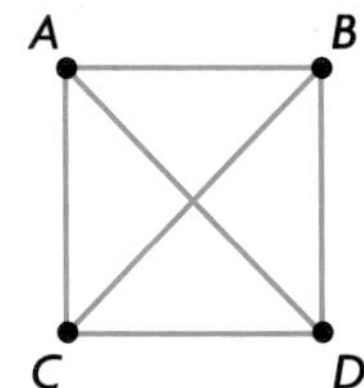

2. 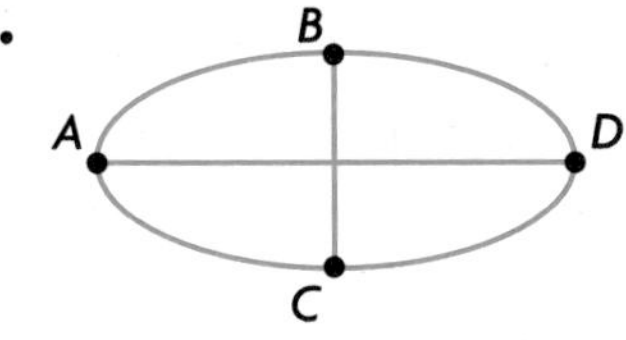

3. 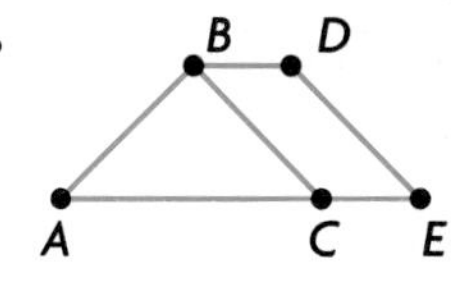

INDEPENDENT PRACTICE

Use the network at the right to determine the distance for the route.

1. *ABCD* **2.** *ACBD* **3.** *DBC*

4. *DACB* **5.** *CBA* **6.** *AC*

7. *DC* **8.** *ACDB* **9.** *ACD*

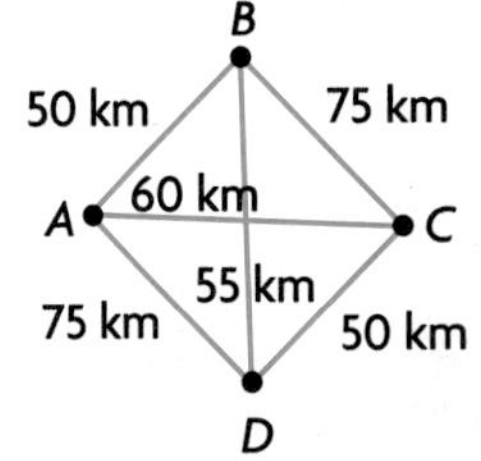

Starting from *A*, find all the possible routes that include every vertex. Find the distance for each. Distances are in miles.

10. 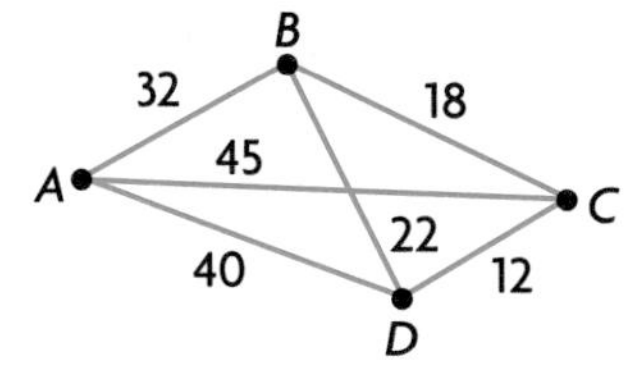

11. 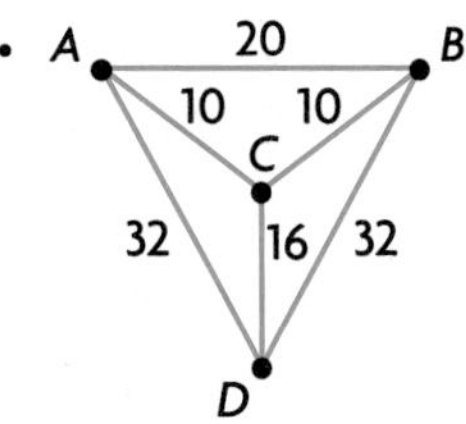

12. In Exercises 10 and 11, what is the shortest route? the longest route?

Problem-Solving Applications

13. **DISTANCE** José is late to band practice, and his mother is late to an important business meeting. What is the shortest route José's mother can take from home to get her son to band practice and then go to her business meeting?

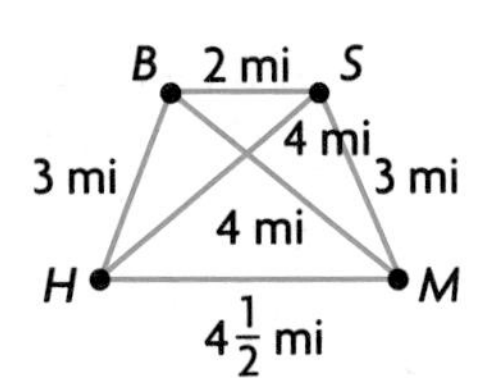

B – Band Practice
H – House
M – Meeting
S – Scenic View

14. **BUSINESS** One airline flies to six cities in the southeastern United States. It offers nonstop flights on some of its routes. Use the network at the right to determine which routes have nonstop flights.

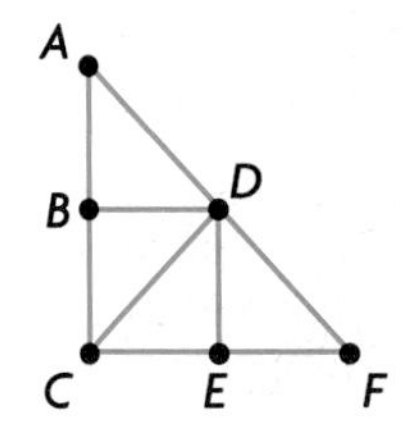

15. **WRITE ABOUT IT** Describe how you can use a network to find the shortest route.

ACTIVITY

What You'll Explore
How to find the shortest distance between two points

What You'll Need
centimeter graph paper, metric ruler

ALGEBRA CONNECTION

Finding the Shortest Distance

As you just learned, there often is more than one way to get from one point to another.

ACTIVITY 1

Explore

On the grid, the horizontal and vertical lines are streets, labeled at the left and at the bottom. The blocks shaded in are a city park.

J K L M N
6th 7th 8th 9th 10th

- Find all possible routes along the streets from 7th and M to 9th and K. How long is each route?

- Suppose you could travel in a straight line that went diagonally through the park. Estimate the length, in blocks, of the diagonal path through the park.

Technology Link

You can find the shortest route between points by using E-Lab, Activity 24. Available on CD-ROM and on the Internet at **www.hbschool.com/elab**

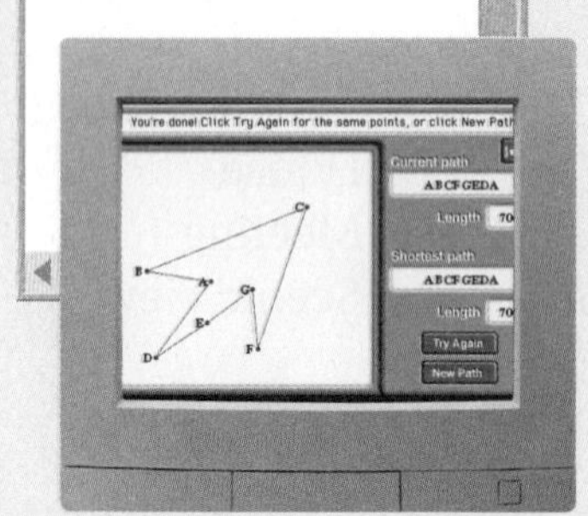

Think and Discuss

- How is the route through the park different from the routes along the streets?
- Do you think straight paths are always shorter than paths with turns? Explain your thinking.

Try This

- Find all possible routes along the streets from 1st and A to 57th and H. How long is each route?

- Estimate the number of blocks in the diagonal path through the park.

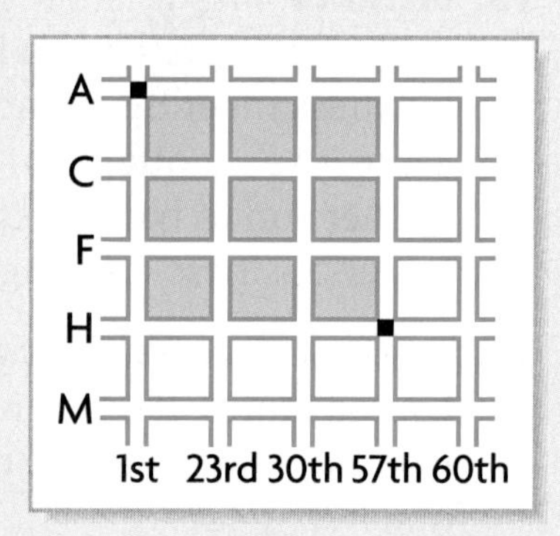

ACTIVITY 2

Explore

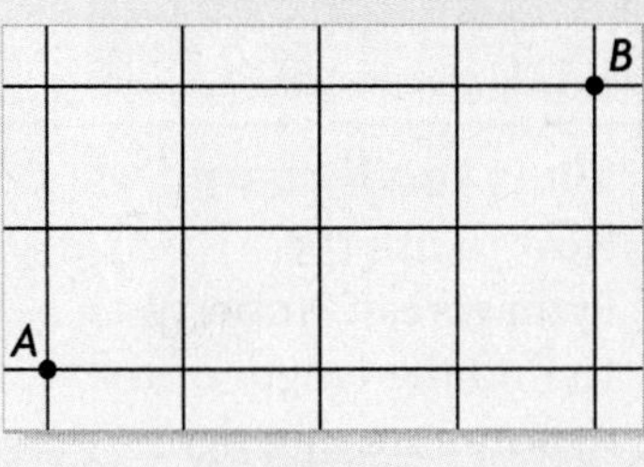

Figure 1

- Copy Figure 1 on centimeter graph paper.
- Imagine that you can go from A to B only by moving horizontally and vertically. What is the shortest distance from A to B?

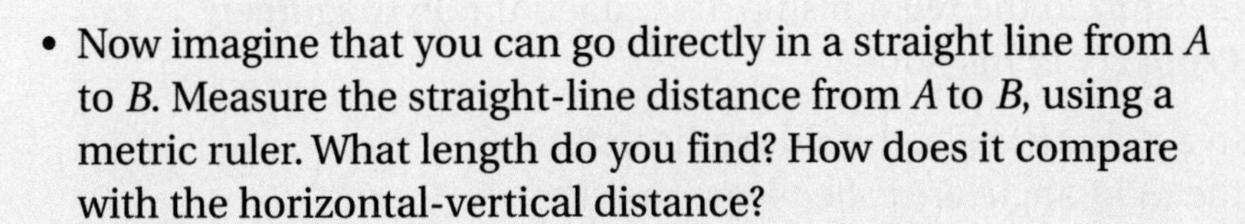

- Now imagine that you can go directly in a straight line from A to B. Measure the straight-line distance from A to B, using a metric ruler. What length do you find? How does it compare with the horizontal-vertical distance?

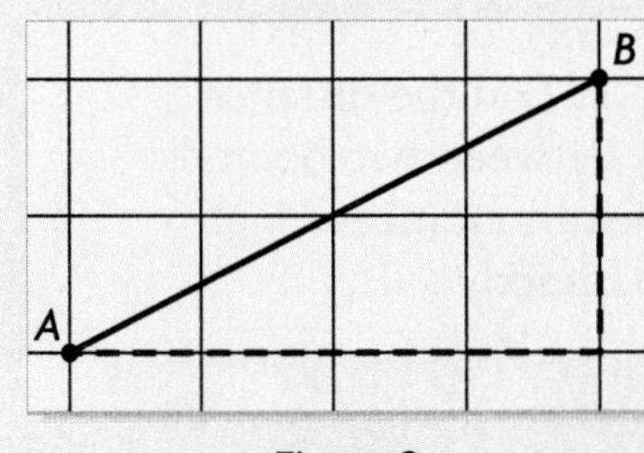

Figure 2

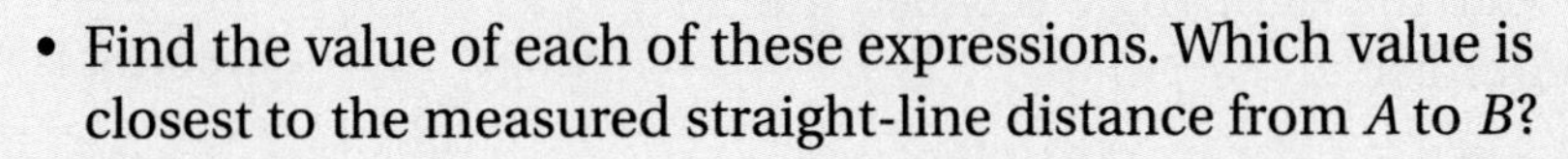

- Find the value of each of these expressions. Which value is closest to the measured straight-line distance from A to B?

a. $4 + 2$ **b.** $4^2 + 2^2$

c. $\sqrt{4 + 2}$ **d.** $\sqrt{4^2 + 2^2}$

Surprisingly, you can find the shortest distance from A to B from the units on the graph, without using a ruler. Square the 4 and 2, the horizontal and vertical distances, and then take the square root of their sum.

$4^2 + 2^2 = 16 + 4 = 20$ $\sqrt{20} \approx 4.47$

The straight-line distance from A to B is about 4.47 cm.

Think and Discuss

- Look at Figure 2. What type of triangle is formed by the horizontal, vertical, and straight-line paths?

Try This

- Look at the right triangle in Figure 3. What expression could you use to find the shortest distance from C to D?
- In Figure 3, calculate the straight-line distance from C to D. Then use a metric ruler to measure the same distance. How do the distances compare?
- Locate a new pair of points on your graph paper. Write an expression to find the shortest distance between the two points.

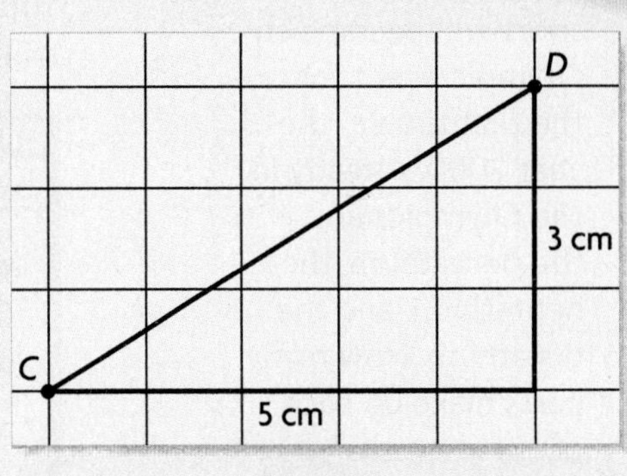

Figure 3

LESSON 24.3

ALGEBRA CONNECTION

Pythagorean Property

What You'll Learn
How to use the Pythagorean Property to find the length of the hypotenuse of a right triangle

Why Learn This?
To find the distance between two points without measuring directly

VOCABULARY

Pythagorean Property
leg
hypotenuse

The relationship among the sides of a right triangle has been used for thousands of years by carpenters and builders to make right angles. The ancient Greek mathematician Pythagoras recognized the relationship. It is called the **Pythagorean Property** in his honor.

In a right triangle, the sides adjacent to the right angle are called **legs**. The side opposite the right angle is called the **hypotenuse**.

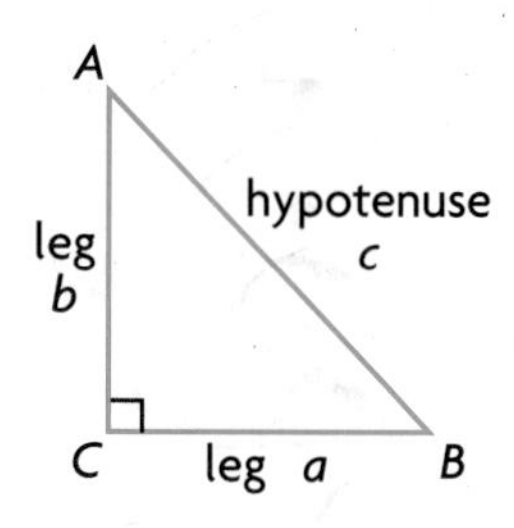

The Pythagorean Property states that if a and b are the lengths of the legs of a right triangle and c is the length of the hypotenuse, then $a^2 + b^2 = c^2$.

When you know the lengths of two sides of a right triangle, you can use the Pythagorean Property to find the third length.

EXAMPLE 1 Phillip is training for a triathlon. He swims, runs, and bikes. The course is shaped like a right triangle. Find the distance Phillip bikes.

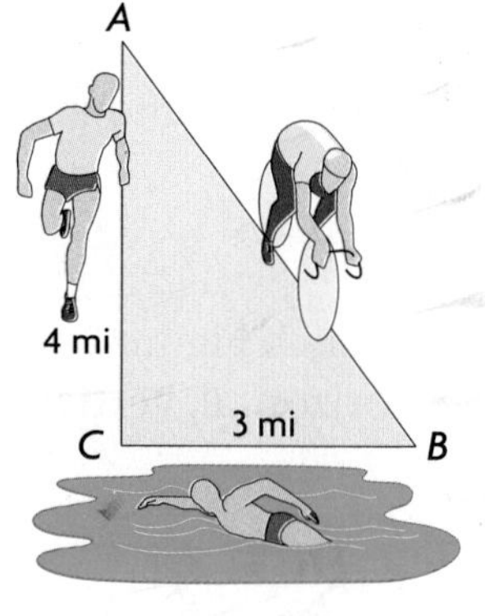

$a^2 + b^2 = c^2$ *Replace the variables*
$3^2 + 4^2 = c^2$ *with the known lengths.*

$9 + 16 = c^2$ *Solve for c.*
$25 = c^2$
$\sqrt{25} = c$
$5 = c$ So, Phillip bikes 5 mi.

You can use the Pythagorean Property to decide whether or not a triangle is a right triangle.

EXAMPLE 2 Use the Pythagorean Property to determine whether $\triangle DEF$ is a right triangle.

D, 8 in., 10 in., F, 6 in., E

$a^2 + b^2 = c^2$ *Replace the variables*
$6^2 + 8^2 \stackrel{?}{=} 10^2$ *with the lengths.*
$36 + 64 \stackrel{?}{=} 100$ *Perform the*
$100 = 100$ ✓ *operations.*

Since $6^2 + 8^2 = 100$ and $10^2 = 100$, $\triangle DEF$ is a right triangle.

SPORTS **LINK**

The triathlon consists of three parts: swimming, running, and bicycling. This sport will become an Olympic event for the first time in the year 2000. Already in the Olympics are the pentathlon, the heptathlon, and the decathlon. How many parts make up each of these events?

GUIDED PRACTICE

Name the legs and the hypotenuse of each right triangle.

1.

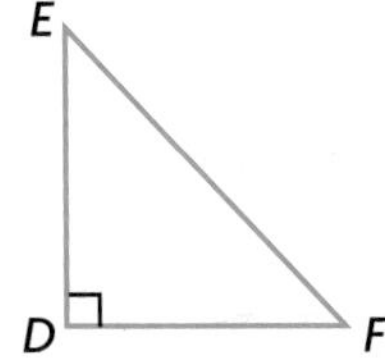

2.

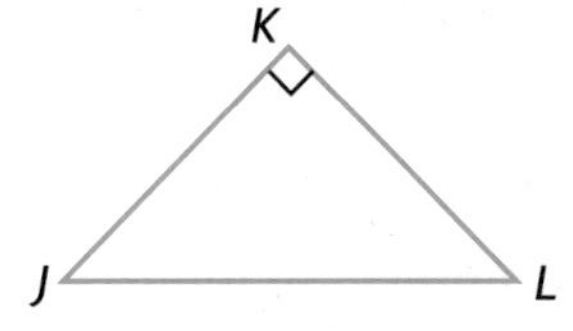

3.

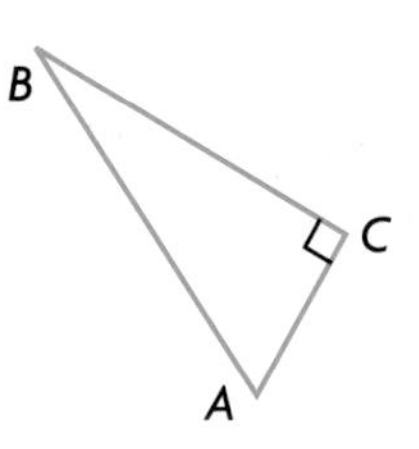

INDEPENDENT PRACTICE

Tell whether the three sides form a right triangle. Write *yes* or *no*.

1. 17 cm, 20 cm, 25 cm

2. 16 m, 30 m, 34 m

3. 11 in., 60 in., 61 in.

4. 8 cm, 11 cm, 15 cm

5. 12 mi, 13 mi, 14 mi

6. 2 mm, 5.7 mm, 6 mm

Find the length of the hypotenuse for each right triangle.

7.

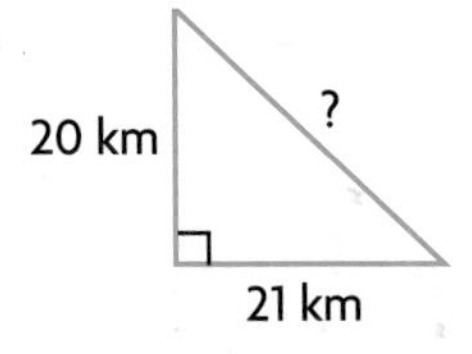

8.

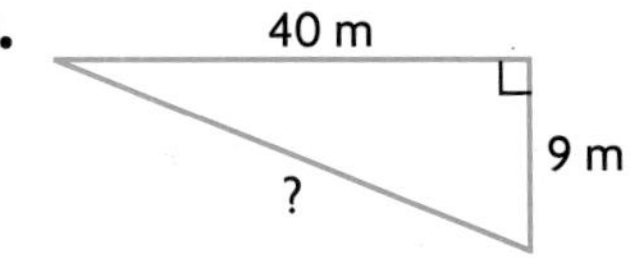

9.

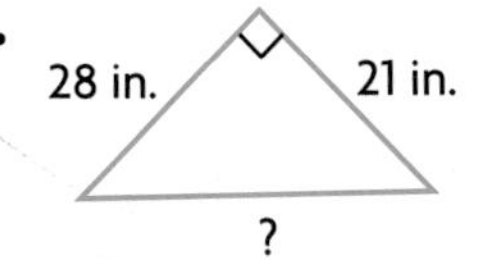

Find the length of the hypotenuse, *c*, of the right triangle with legs of lengths *a* and *b*. Round to the nearest tenth when necessary.

10. $a = 8$ m
$b = 6$ m
$c = \underline{?}$

11. $a = 5$ ft
$b = 12$ ft
$c = \underline{?}$

12. $a = 1$ mm
$b = 2$ mm
$c = \underline{?}$

13. $a = 33.5$ cm
$b = 20$ cm
$c = \underline{?}$

Problem-Solving Applications

14. Find the distance across the pond.

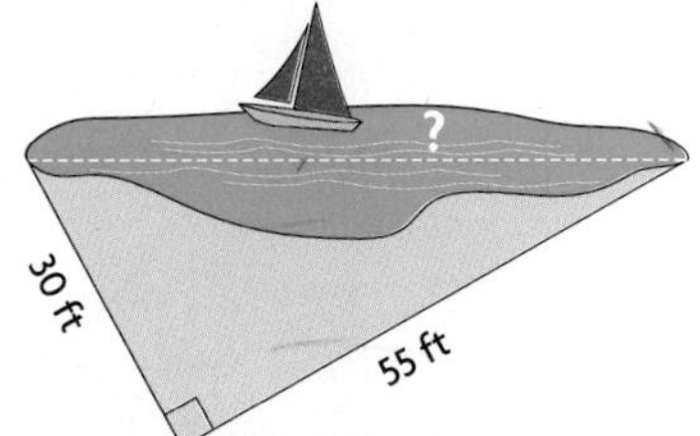

15. **DISTANCE** Tina walked 90 m up Oak Street, turned 90° left, and then walked another 50 m. Wanda left from the same place but took a diagonal path across a park to meet Tina. To the nearest meter, how far did Wanda walk?

16. **CRITICAL THINKING** Use the Pythagorean Property to find *b*.

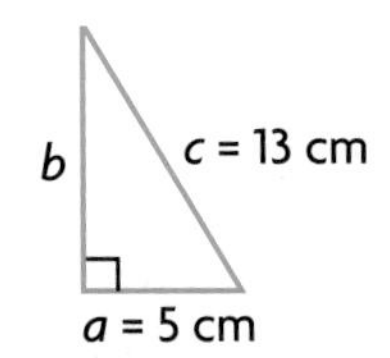

17. **HOBBIES** Jeff's kite is 45 ft above the ground. A tree is directly under the kite. Jeff is standing 12 ft from the tree. How long is the kite string?

18. **WRITE ABOUT IT** Explain the Pythagorean Property.

MORE PRACTICE Lesson 24.3, page H76

LESSON 24.4

PROBLEM-SOLVING STRATEGY

Using a Formula to Find the Area

What You'll Learn
How to use formulas to find the areas of a parallelogram, triangle, and circle

Why Learn This?
To find the amount of paint or carpet you would need to cover an area

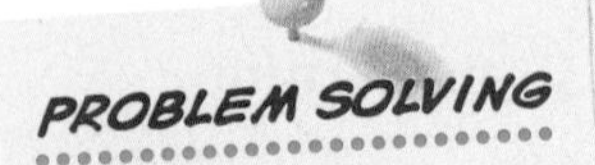

PROBLEM SOLVING

- **Understand**
- **Plan**
- **Solve**
- **Look Back**

When you measure length, you measure one dimension. Area is found by multiplying two dimensions. Area is expressed in square units because two dimensions are measured.

One of the CIT buildings in Herndon, Virginia, is shaped like a parallelogram. The front of this building has a base of 106.5 ft and a height of 35.5 ft and is covered with glass. Suppose the glass costs $12 per square foot. Find the area of the front of the building and the cost of the glass for the front of the building.

UNDERSTAND What are you asked to find?

What facts are given?

PLAN What strategy will you use?

You can *use a formula* to find the area of the front of the building. Then multiply the area by the cost of glass per square foot.

SOLVE What formula will you use to find the area of a parallelogram?

The formula for the area of a parallelogram is $A = bh$, where b is the base and h is the height.

h = 35.5 ft
b = 106.5 ft

$A = bh$ *Replace b with 106.5 and h with 35.5.*
$A = 106.5 \times 35.5$
$A = 3{,}780.75$

So, the area is 3,780.75 ft^2.

$3{,}780.75 \times \$12 = \$45{,}369$ *To find the cost of the glass, multiply 3,780.75 by $12.*

So, the cost of the glass is $45,369.

LOOK BACK Does $45,369 seem to be a reasonable cost? Explain.

What if . . . the front of the building were rectangular in shape with a base of 106.5 ft and a height of 35.5 ft? Would the cost of the glass be more, less, or the same?

PRACTICE

Use a formula to solve.

1. Howard made a fishnet in the shape of a parallelogram. His net has a height of 5 ft and a base of $5\frac{1}{2}$ ft. What is the area of the fishnet?

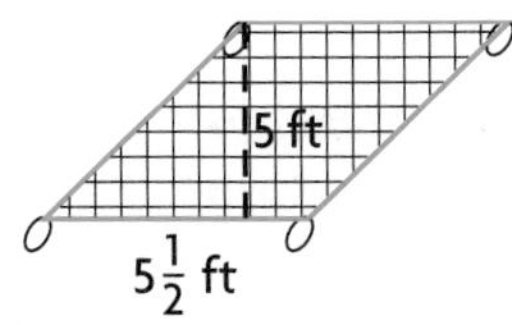

2. Mrs. Mathers wants to have her hardwood floor refinished. The rectangular floor is 16 ft × 14 ft. The carpenter charges $0.90 a square foot. How much should Mrs. Mathers expect to pay?

3. A sign for a museum is shaped like a parallelogram. The base of the sign is 20 ft, and the height is 25 ft. What is the area of the sign?

Finding Areas of Triangles and Circles

You can use formulas to find the areas of other geometric figures.

> The formula for the area of a triangle is $A = \frac{1}{2}bh$, where b is the length of the base and h is the length of the height.

EXAMPLE 1 Find the area of the triangle shown.

3 cm
5 cm

Area $= \frac{1}{2} \cdot \text{base} \cdot \text{height}$

$A = \frac{1}{2}bh$

$A = \frac{1}{2}(5 \cdot 3)$

$A = 7.5 \text{ cm}^2$

- Find the area of a triangle with base 9 cm and height 9 cm.

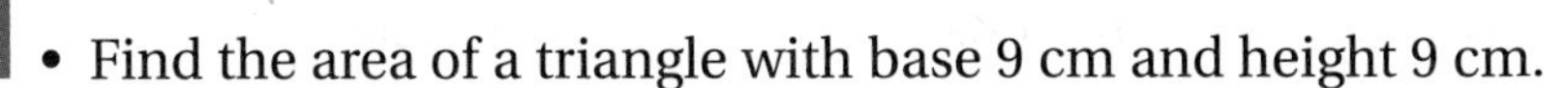

> The formula for the area of a circle is $A = \pi r^2$, where $\pi \approx 3.14$ and r is the length of the radius.

EXAMPLE 2 Scott's father works for an irrigation company. He is installing a sprinkler that sprays in a circle. The sprinkler sprays a distance of 15 ft. How large is the area covered by the sprinkler?

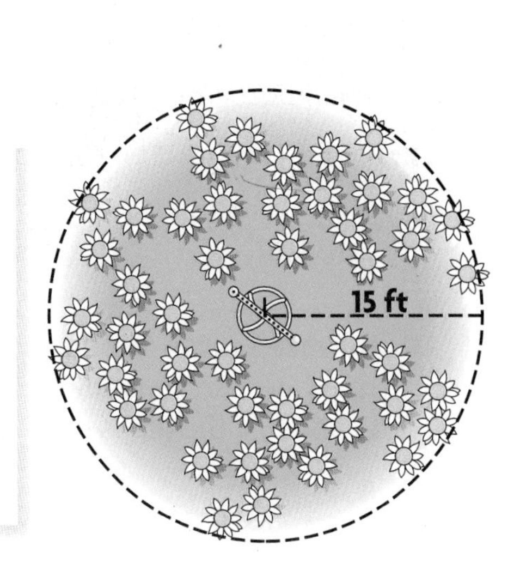

Area $= \pi r^2$, where $\pi \approx 3.14$ and r is the radius.

$A \approx 3.14 \cdot 15^2$

$A \approx 706.5$

So, the sprinkler covers an area of about 706.5 ft^2.

MIXED APPLICATIONS

Solve.

CHOOSE a strategy and a tool.

- **Use a Formula**
- **Draw a Diagram**
- **Guess and Check**
- **Write an Equation**
- **Look for a Pattern**
- **Solve a Simpler Problem**

Paper/Pencil

Calculator

Hands-On

Mental Math

1. The Pines Neighborhood has a pool in the shape of a circle. The radius is 20 ft. The community wants to protect the pool with a cover in the winter. What is the area of the pool cover they need to buy? Use $\pi = 3.14$.

2. Eric and his father want to make a triangular sail for their boat. The height of the sail will be 23 ft, and the base will be 18 ft. What will be the area of the sail in square feet?

3. Parallelogram *A* has a base and height of 1 cm and an area of 1 cm^2. Parallelogram *B* has twice the base and height, 2 cm, and the area is 4 cm^2. Parallelogram *C*'s base and height are doubled to measure 4 cm. What is the area of parallelogram *C*?

4. Ms. Hooper challenged one of her students with the following problem: The area of a parallelogram is 84 cm^2. The height is 6 cm. The base is 2 cm more than twice the height. What is the length of the base?

5. A 5-gal can of asphalt sealant covers about 250 ft^2. How many cans of sealant are needed to cover a tennis court that is 78 ft $\times$ 27 ft?

6. Kay has a garden in the shape of a circle, with a diameter of 8 ft. What is the area of her garden? Use $\pi = 3.14$.

7. **WRITE ABOUT IT** Write a problem that involves finding the area of a parallelogram, circle, or triangle. Exchange with a classmate and solve.

Mixed Review and Test Prep

Use the order of operations to evaluate each expression.

8. $\frac{1}{2}(21 + 9)$

9. $2(3.2 + 5.3)$

10. $\frac{1}{2}(19.7 + 2.6)$

11. $\frac{1}{2}(20 - 10.4)$

Find the probability of hitting the target in the shaded area.

12. 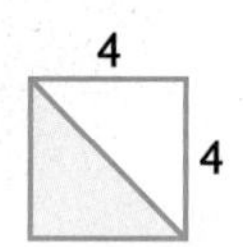

13. 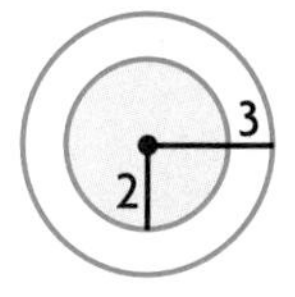

14. 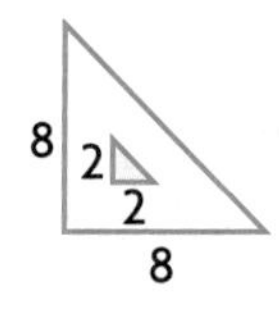

15. 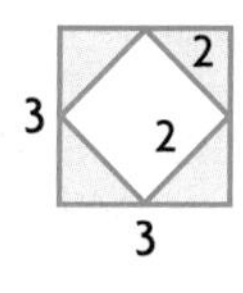

16. **NUMBER SENSE** How many different 3-digit numbers can be made using the digits 1, 2, and 3, if the digits can be repeated?

    A 9 **B** 18
    C 27 **D** 35

17. **GEOMETRY** Two equilateral triangles are placed together to form a quadrilateral. What kind of quadrilateral is formed?

    F square **G** rhombus
    H trapezoid **J** rectangle

MORE PRACTICE Lesson 24.4, page H76

ALGEBRA CONNECTION

LESSON 24.5

Area of a Trapezoid

What You'll Learn
How to use a formula to find the area of a trapezoid

Why Learn This?
To find the area of a figure shaped like a trapezoid, such as the side of a tent

A trapezoid is a quadrilateral with exactly two parallel sides, called bases. These bases are labeled b_1 and b_2. The height of a trapezoid, h, is the distance between the two bases.

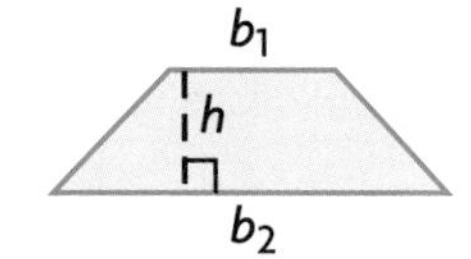

- How does the shape of a trapezoid compare with the shape of a parallelogram?

ACTIVITY **WHAT YOU'LL NEED:** scissors, centimeter graph paper, metric ruler

You can use the formula for the area of a parallelogram to find the area of a trapezoid.

2 cm
1 cm
4 cm

- Draw the trapezoid at the right on centimeter graph paper.
- Cut out the trapezoid, and fold it in half from base 1 to base 2.

base 1
base 2

- Cut the trapezoid along the fold line. Then use the pieces to form a parallelogram.

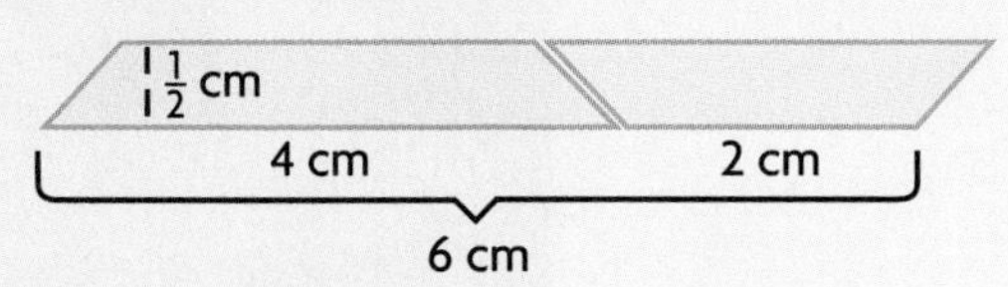

- Find the area of the parallelogram.

Talk About It

- What is the area of the trapezoid?
- Write an expression to show how the height of the parallelogram compares with the height of the trapezoid.
- Write an expression to show how the base, b, of the parallelogram compares with the two bases, b_1 and b_2, of the trapezoid.
- Write a formula for the area of a trapezoid, using what you know about the heights and bases of a trapezoid and a parallelogram.

You can use this formula to find the area of any trapezoid:

$$A = \frac{1}{2}h(b_1 + b_2)$$

EXAMPLE 1 Find the area of the trapezoid.

$A = \frac{1}{2}h(b_1 + b_2)$, where $h = 1.2$, $b_1 = 2.0$, and $b_2 = 2.8$.

$A = \frac{1}{2}(1.2)(2.0 + 2.8)$

$A = \frac{1}{2}(1.2)(4.8)$

$A = \frac{1}{2}(5.76)$

$A = 2.88$

So, the area is 2.88 m^2.

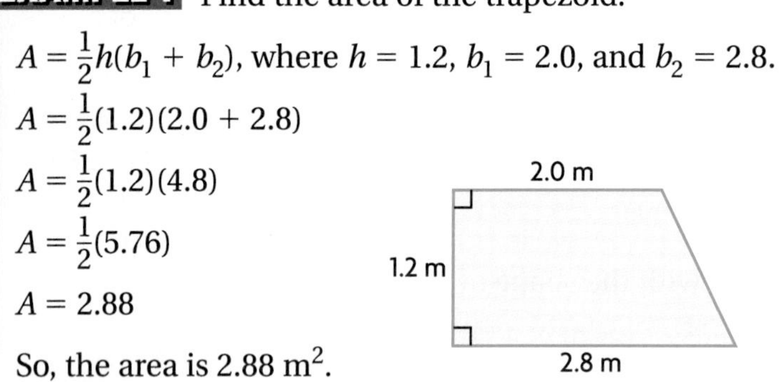

Sometimes you need to find the area of a trapezoid to solve a problem.

EXAMPLE 2 The Shivers are on a camping trip. They want to spray a water sealant on a side of the tent that is leaking. The side is shaped like a trapezoid. They have enough sealant to cover 52 ft^2. Do they have enough sealant for the side of the tent?

Find the area of the side of the tent.

$A = \frac{1}{2}h(b_1 + b_2)$

$A = \frac{1}{2} \cdot 5(8 + 12)$

$A = \frac{1}{2} \cdot 100$

$A = 50$

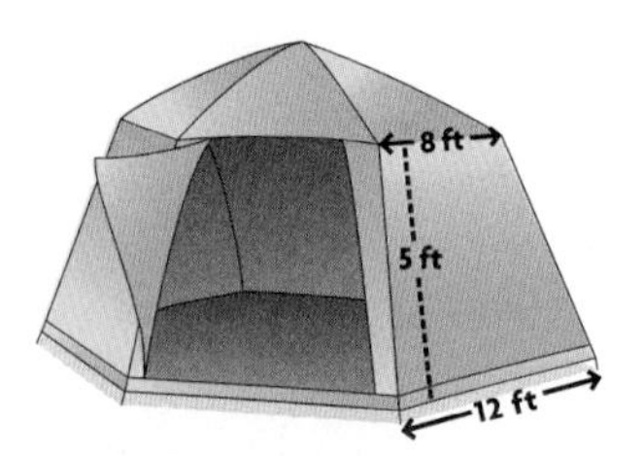

Since the area is only 50 ft^2, they do have enough sealant.

Have you ever wondered how umbrellas, raincoats, and tents shed water? Some fabrics, such as nylon, are naturally waterproof. Tents are usually made from heavier fabrics, such as canvas. One way to waterproof fabric is with liquid paraffin—wax. In an emergency, you can even waterproof a patched tent by rubbing a candle over the patch.

GUIDED PRACTICE

1. A parallelogram and a trapezoid have equal areas. The parallelogram's base is equivalent to the sum of the bases of the trapezoid. If the height of the parallelogram is 5 cm, what is the height of the trapezoid?

Select the correct answer for the area of the trapezoid.

a. 40 cm^2	**b.** 18.4 cm^2	**c.** $6\frac{1}{2}$ cm^2	**d.** $8\frac{1}{4}$ cm^2

2. $b_1 = 4$ cm, $b_2 = 5.2$ cm, $h = 4$ cm

3. $b_1 = 2$ cm, $b_2 = 3\frac{1}{2}$ cm, $h = 3$ cm

4. $b_1 = 2\frac{1}{2}$ cm, $b_2 = 4$ cm, $h = 2$ cm

5. $b_1 = 3$ cm, $b_2 = 5$ cm, $h = 10$ cm

INDEPENDENT PRACTICE

Find the area.

1. 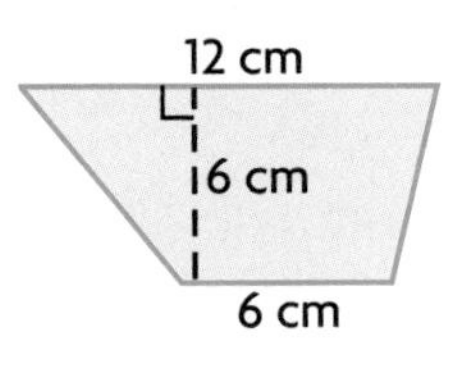

2. 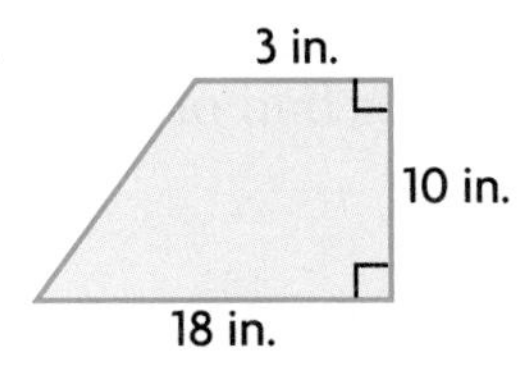

3. 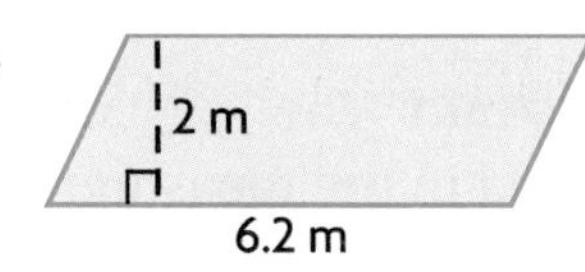

4. 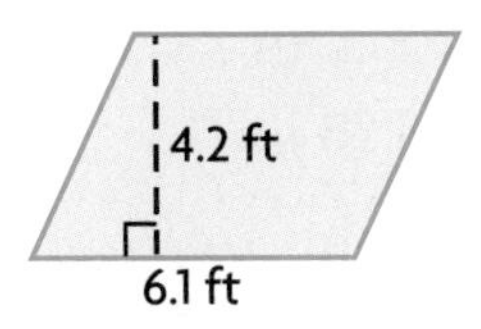

5. 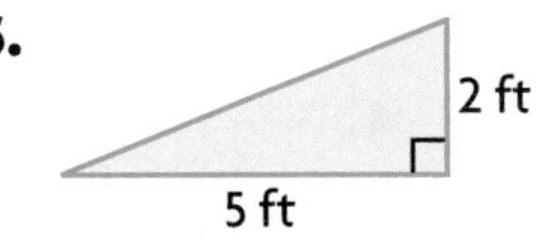

6. 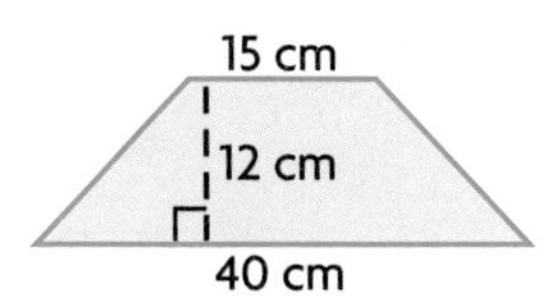

Find the area of the trapezoid.

7. $b_1 = 4$ m
$b_2 = 6$ m
$h = 5$ m

8. $b_1 = 23$ in.
$b_2 = 20$ in.
$h = 25$ in.

9. $b_1 = 6.7$ mm
$b_2 = 5.5$ mm
$h = 4.2$ mm

10. $b_1 = 20$ in.
$b_2 = 32$ in.
$h = 24$ in.

11. $b_1 = 5\frac{1}{2}$ yd
$b_2 = 2$ yd
$h = 1\frac{1}{2}$ yd

12. $b_1 = 12$ mm
$b_2 = 7.5$ mm
$h = 5.2$ mm

13. $b_1 = 3\frac{1}{4}$ ft
$b_2 = 4\frac{1}{2}$ ft
$h = 1\frac{1}{3}$ ft

14. $b_1 = 4$ ft
$b_2 = 2\frac{1}{2}$ ft
$h = \frac{1}{2}$ ft

Problem-Solving Applications

15. **GEOMETRY** A plaque is shaped like a trapezoid with a height of 6 in. and bases that measure 3.5 in. and 9.5 in. What is the area of the plaque?

16. **GEOMETRY** The wall of a building is in the shape of a trapezoid. Its bases are 12 m and 14 m. The height of the building is 10 m. What is the area of the wall?

17. **CRITICAL THINKING** The Lees want to carpet a patio that is in the shape of a trapezoid. The height is 2 yd. The bases are 3 yd and 4 yd. Each square yard of outdoor carpet costs $5.99. How much will it cost the Lees to carpet their patio?

18. Find the height of a trapezoid with an area of 20 ft^2 and bases 4 ft and 6 ft.

19. **WRITE ABOUT IT** Explain how to find the area of a trapezoid.

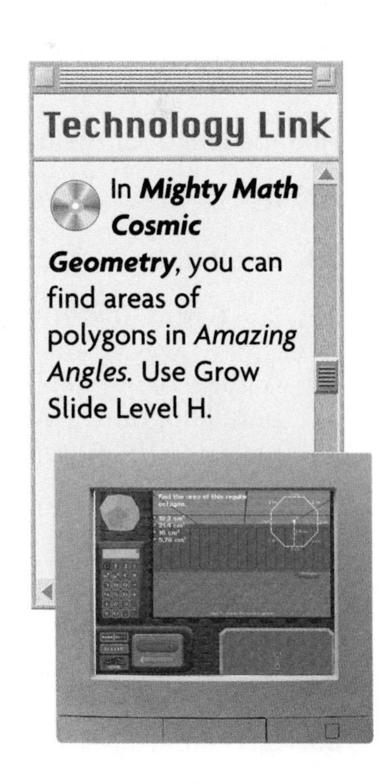
Technology Link

In ***Mighty Math Cosmic Geometry***, you can find areas of polygons in *Amazing Angles*. Use Grow Slide Level H.

MORE PRACTICE Lesson 24.5, page H77

CHAPTER 24 Review/Test

1. **VOCABULARY** The __?__ of any measurement is half of the unit used in the measurement. (page 466)

For the given measurement, tell how small and how large the actual length may be. (pages 466–469)

2. 19.4 m
3. 22 km
4. $12\frac{1}{2}$ ft
5. 5.35 in.
6. 4 cm
7. 56.3 m
8. 48 km
9. $9\frac{1}{2}$ in.

10. **VOCABULARY** A graph with vertices and edges is a(n) __?__. (page 470)

Use the diagram at the right to determine the distance for the route. (pages 470–471)

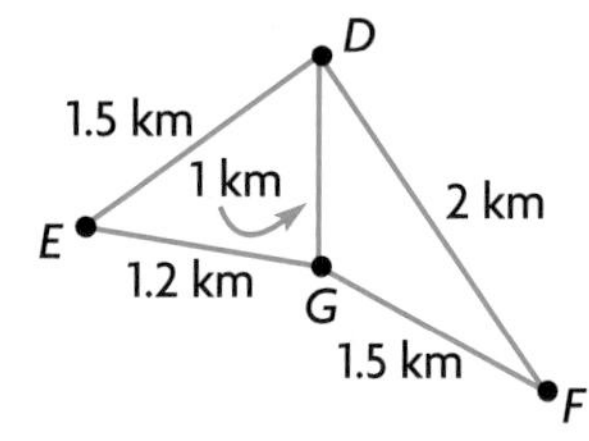

11. *DFG*
12. *EG*
13. *DEG*
14. *EDGF*
15. *DG*
16. *GFDE*
17. *EGF*
18. *GDF*

Use the diagram at the right to determine the distance for the route. (pages 470–471)

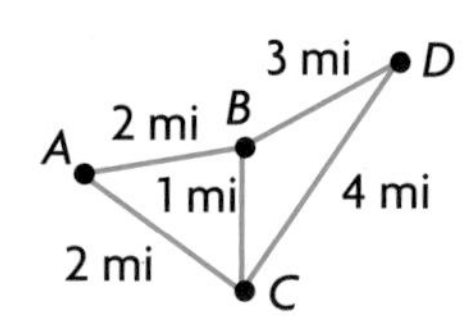

19. *ABD*
20. *ABC*
21. *ABCD*
22. *DCB*
23. *ACD*
24. *BACD*
25. *ACBD*
26. *CBAC*

Find the length of the hypotenuse. Round to the nearest tenth. (pages 474–475)

27. $a = 24$ in., $b = 4$ in., $c = ?$
28. $a = 15$ cm, $b = 15$ cm, $c = ?$
29. $a = 9$ ft, $b = 3$ ft, $c = ?$
30. $a = 7.5$ cm, $b = 10$ cm, $c = ?$
31. $a = 6$ mm, $b = 10$ mm, $c = ?$
32. $a = 8$ in., $b = 15$ in., $c = ?$

33. A piece of land is in the shape of a parallelogram. The base is 75 ft and the height is 125 ft. What is the area? (pages 476–478)

34. One end of a tent is a triangle. The height is 1.5 m and the base is 2.5 m. What is the area? (pages 476–478)

Find the area of each trapezoid. (pages 479–481)

35. $b_1 = 9$ in., $b_2 = 10$ in., $h = 8$ in.
36. $b_1 = 10.5$ cm, $b_2 = 12.2$ cm, $h = 8$ cm
37. $b_1 = 6$ mm, $b_2 = 7$ mm, $h = 9$ mm
38. $b_1 = 8$ cm, $b_2 = 10$ cm, $h = 5$ cm
39. $b_1 = 4$ in., $b_2 = 9$ in., $h = 5$ in.
40. $b_1 = 12$ cm, $b_2 = 15$ cm, $h = 10$ cm

Test Prep

CUMULATIVE
CHAPTERS 1–24

1. What is the area of the trapezoid?

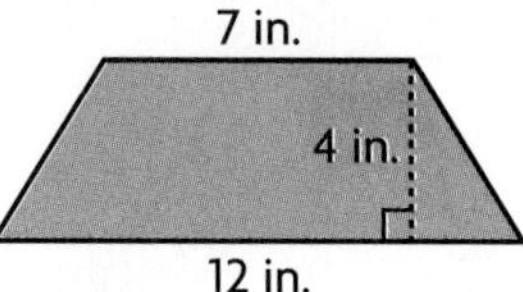

A 132 $in.^2$
B 112 $in.^2$
C 76 $in.^2$
D 38 $in.^2$

2. What is the probability that a dart that hits the target will land in the shaded area?

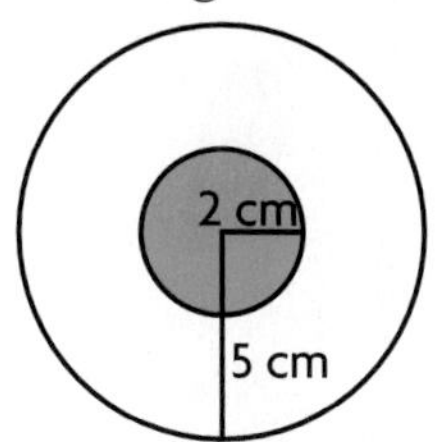

F $\frac{21}{25}$ **G** $\frac{2}{3}$ **H** $\frac{2}{5}$ **J** $\frac{4}{25}$

3. A deli serves roast beef, turkey, and ham on rye, white, or wheat bread. How many different combinations of one meat and one bread are there?

A 6
B 8
C 9
D 27

4. Use the stem-and-leaf plot below.

Test	Grades
6	9
7	1 2 5 6 6 9
8	2 4 4 5 7
9	3 5 6 8 8

What is the range of the grades?

F 29
G 69
H 98
J 167
K Not Here

5. Which is the best estimate of the length?

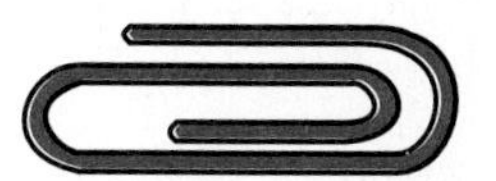

A 3 mm
B 3 cm
C 3 in.
D 3 m

6. A triangular prism has 5 faces, a rectangular prism has 6 faces, and a pentagonal prism has 7 faces. How many faces does an octagonal prism have?

F 8
G 9
H 11
J 12
K Not Here

7. Ms. Boule drove 73.1 miles on Monday, 85.6 miles on Tuesday, 58.6 miles on Wednesday, 96.5 miles on Thursday, and 47.4 miles on Friday. Which is the best estimate of how many miles she drove in all?

A 300 mi
B 330 mi
C 370 mi
D 400 mi

8. What are the first four powers of $\frac{1}{4}$?

F $\frac{1}{16}, \frac{1}{64}, \frac{1}{256}, \frac{1}{1{,}024}$

G $\frac{1}{4}, \frac{1}{8}, \frac{1}{16}, \frac{1}{32}$

H $\frac{1}{4}, \frac{1}{16}, \frac{1}{64}, \frac{1}{256}$

J $\frac{1}{4}, \frac{2}{4}, \frac{3}{4}, \frac{4}{4}$

9. Jamil measures the length of a building as $19\frac{1}{2}$ feet long. What is the greatest possible error?

A $\frac{1}{4}$ ft **B** $\frac{1}{2}$ ft **C** 1 ft **D** 20 ft

CHAPTER

25

SURFACE AREA AND VOLUME

LOOK AHEAD

In this chapter you will solve problems that involve finding

- the surface areas of prisms, pyramids, and cylinders
- the volumes of prisms, pyramids, cylinders, and cones

SCIENCE LINK

The Vehicle Assembly Building (VAB) at John F. Kennedy Space Center is one of the world's largest buildings. It is roughly the shape of a rectangular prism and houses space vehicles. Some dimensions of the VAB are given in the table below.

VEHICLE ASSEMBLY BUILDING	
Overall Length	716 feet 6 inches
Overall Width	518 feet
Height	525 feet 10 inches

- Estimate the volume of the VAB.
- The actual volume of the VAB is 129,428,000 ft^3. Why do you think your estimate is greater?

Problem-Solving Project

Volume of a Fist

YOU WILL NEED: large can, pan (or box lined with a plastic garbage bag), milk carton with the top cut off, ruler marked in millimeters

You can use a scientific method to find the volume of an irregularly shaped object, such as your fist. Fill a can to the top with water, and put it in a pan or lined box. Submerge your fist in the can, letting the water overflow. Use the available tools to estimate the volume of your fist. Write a description of your strategy for finding the volume. Include your results. Describe two or three other strategies for finding the volume.

PROJECT CHECKLIST

- ✓ Did you perform the experiment?
- ✓ Did you use tools to estimate the volume of your fist?
- ✓ Did you write about your strategy and other possible strategies?

LESSON 25.1

What You'll Learn
How to find the surface areas of prisms and pyramids

Why Learn This?
To solve real-life problems such as deciding how much paint or wrapping paper to buy

VOCABULARY
surface area

ALGEBRA CONNECTION

Surface Areas of Prisms and Pyramids

Amy is making a three-dimensional scale model of the local county courthouse. The courthouse is built in the shape of a rectangular prism. Amy chooses the scale 1 in. : 10 ft.

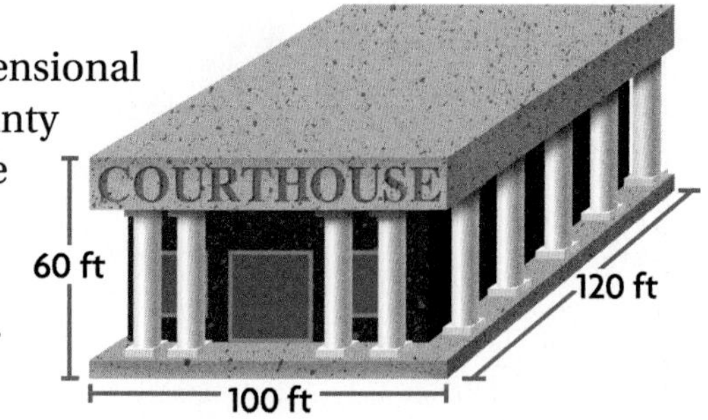

Can Amy make her model with one 28-in. × 22-in. piece of posterboard?

Amy can use a formula to find the area of the posterboard: $A = lw$.

$A = lw = 28 \times 22 = 616$ in.^{2} She can compare the surface area of her model with the area of the posterboard.

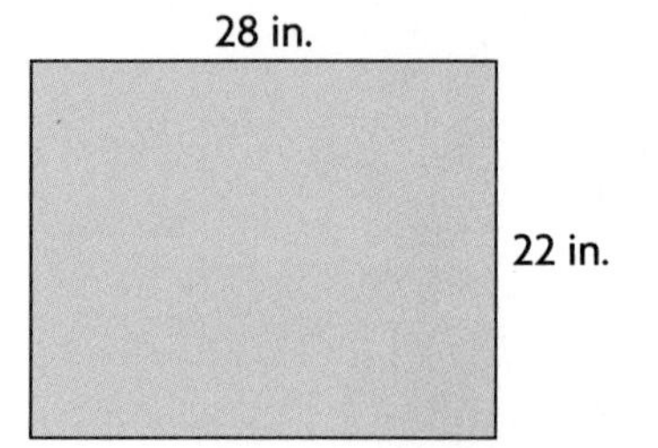

The **surface area** is the sum of the areas of all the surfaces of a solid.

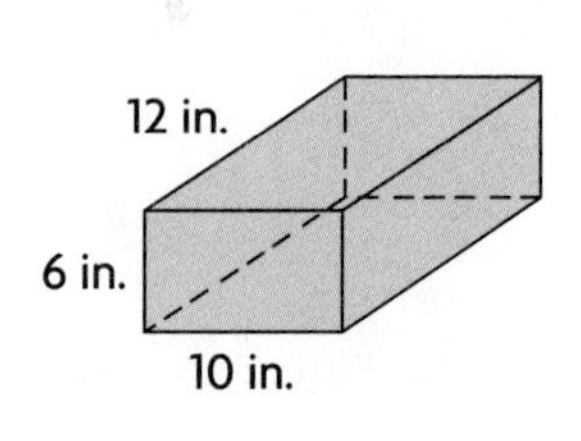

		top 12 x 10	
left 12 x 6	front 10 x 6	right 12 x 6	back 10 x 6
		bottom 12 x 10	

area of left and right sides $2(12 \times 6) = 144$
area of front and back $2(10 \times 6) = 120$
area of top and bottom $2(12 \times 10) = 240$
$S = 144 + 120 + 240 = 504$
So, the surface area of her model is 504 in.^{2}

Since 504 in.^{2} is less than 616 in.^{2}, Amy has enough area with one piece of posterboard if she arranges the six pieces carefully.

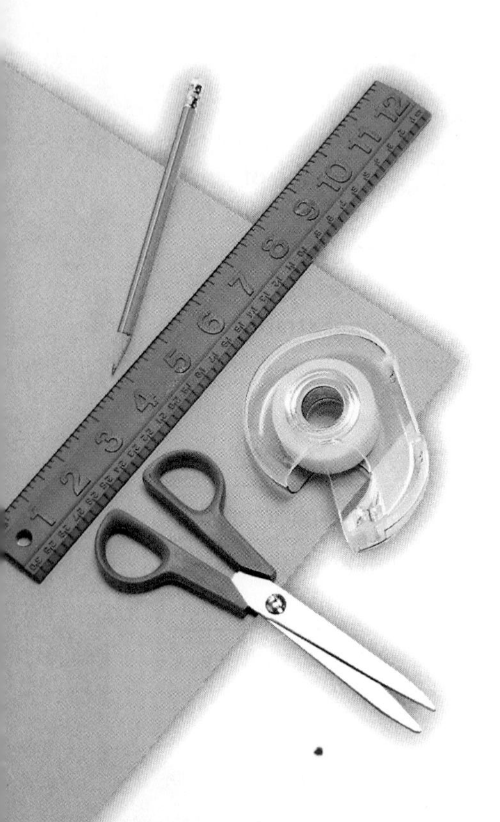

CRITICAL THINKING Draw a sketch to show how the six pieces can be cut from one 28-in. × 22-in. piece of posterboard.

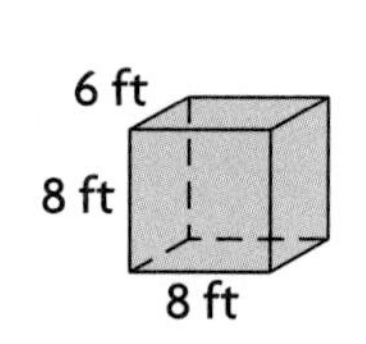

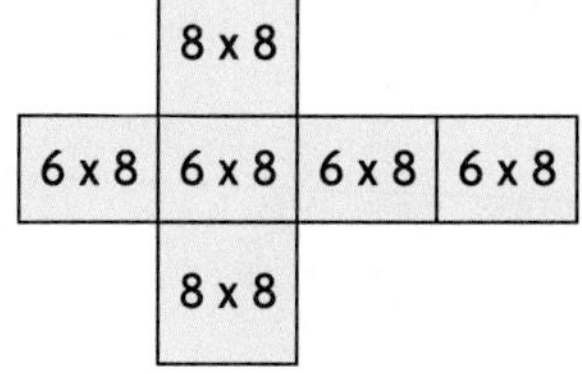

You can find the surface area of a triangular prism.

EXAMPLE 1 Matt is going camping and wants to waterproof all the outer surfaces of his pup tent, including the floor. One can of waterproofing covers 100 ft^2 of fabric. How many cans of waterproofing will he need?

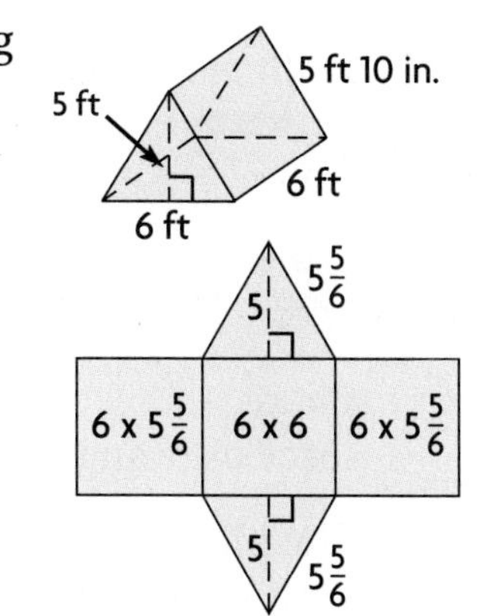

Find the surface area of the triangular prism.

S = area of 2 triangular faces + area of 2 rectangular faces + area of 1 square face

$S = 2(\frac{1}{2}bh) + 2(lw) + s^2$

$S = 2(\frac{1}{2} \times 6 \times 5) + 2(6 \times 5\frac{5}{6}) + 6^2 \leftarrow$ **Think:** 5 ft 10 in. $= 5\frac{5}{6}$ ft

$S = 2(15) + 2(35) + 36$

$S = 30 + 70 + 36$

$S = 136 \leftarrow$ The surface area is 136 ft^2.

Since 136 ft^2 is more than 100 ft^2, Matt needs 2 cans of waterproofing.

- Suppose Matt's tent did not have a floor. How many cans of waterproofing would he need? How do you know?

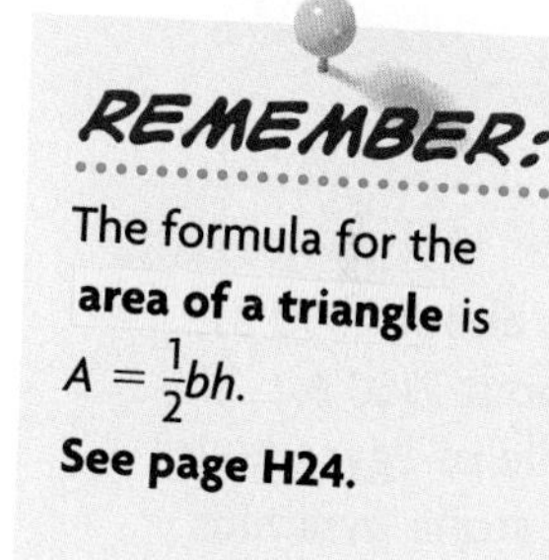

REMEMBER:

The formula for the **area of a triangle** is $A = \frac{1}{2}bh$.

See page H24.

GUIDED PRACTICE

For Exercises 1–4, use the prism at the right.

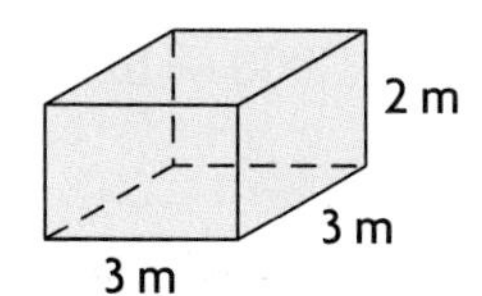

1. How many faces does the prism have?

2. What polygons are the faces?

3. Find the area of each face.

4. Find the total surface area of the prism.

Find the surface area of each figure.

5. 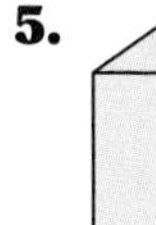 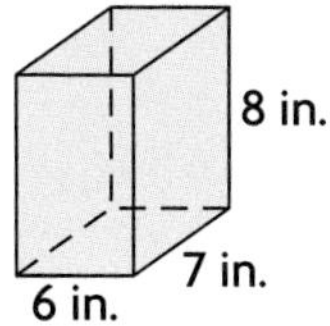

6. 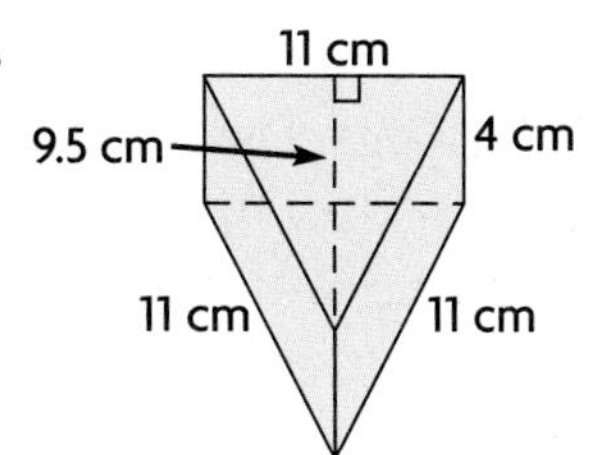

You can find the surface area of a pyramid by making a net.

ACTIVITY

WHAT YOU'LL NEED: 1-cm graph paper, ruler, protractor, scissors, transparent tape

- Cut these pieces from centimeter graph paper:

  1 square
  4 isosceles triangles

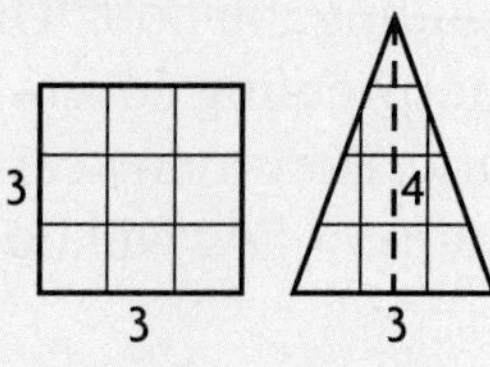

- Arrange the pieces to form a net for a square pyramid. Tape them together, and assemble the pyramid.
- Estimate the area of each face by counting the square centimeters.
- Estimate the total surface area of the square pyramid by adding your estimates of the areas of the faces.

HISTORY LINK

From about 2650 B.C. to about 2150 B.C., the people of Egypt built huge stone pyramids for their rulers. As many as 100,000 workers spent 20 years building the Great Pyramid of Giza. They moved more than 2,000,000 blocks of stone, each weighing about 5,000 lb. The Great Pyramid is about 480 ft high, and its square base covers about 13 acres. There are 43,560 ft^2 in an acre. About how long is each side of the base of the Great Pyramid?

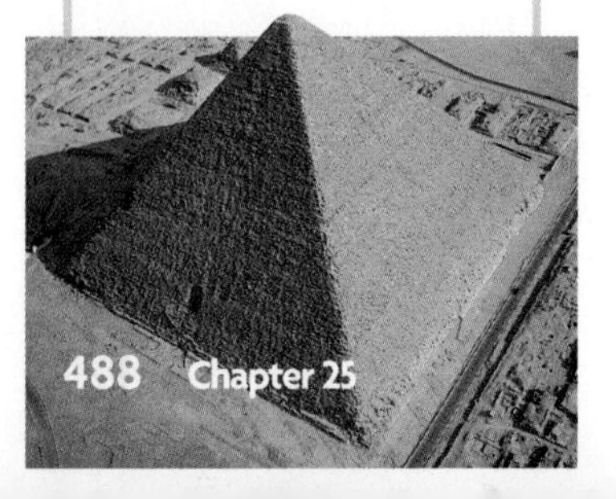

You can also find the surface area of a pyramid by using a formula to find the sum of the areas of the faces.

EXAMPLE 2 Find the surface area of the square pyramid shown at the right.

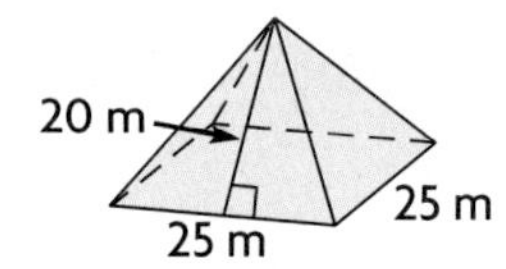

S = area of 4 triangular faces + area of 1 square face

$S = 4(\frac{1}{2}bh) + s^2$

$S = 4(\frac{1}{2} \times 25 \times 20) + 25^2$

$S = 4(250) + 625$

$S = 1{,}000 + 625$

$S = 1{,}625$

So, the surface area is 1,625 m^2.

- How would you find the surface area of a rectangular pyramid?

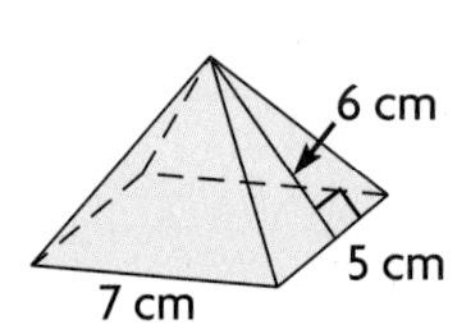

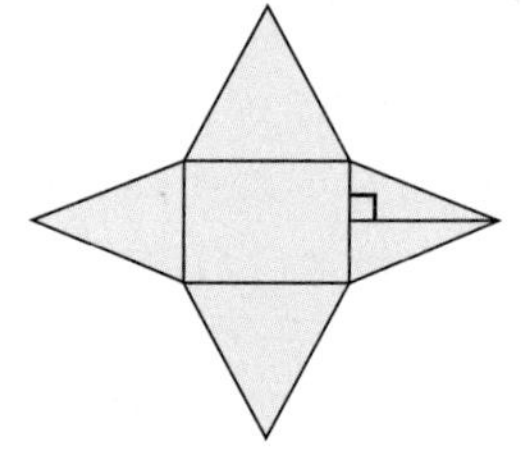

INDEPENDENT PRACTICE

Find the surface area of each figure.

1.

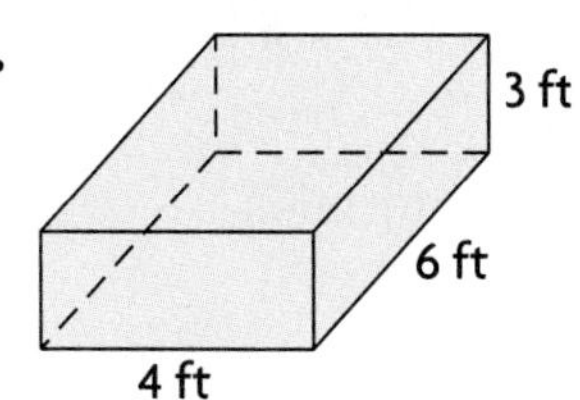

2.

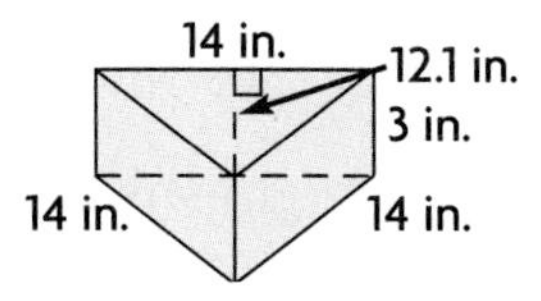

3.

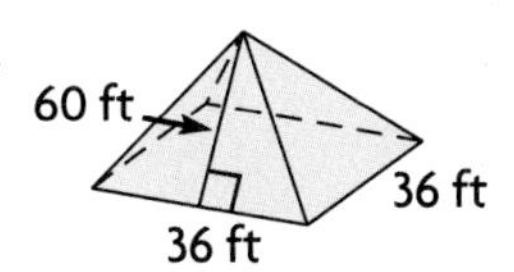

4.

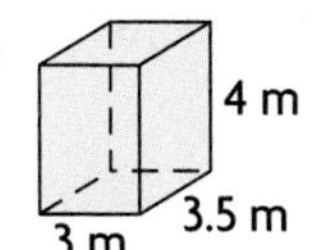

5.

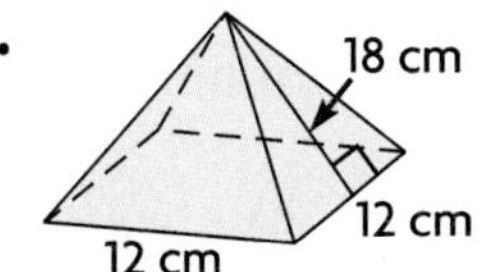

6.

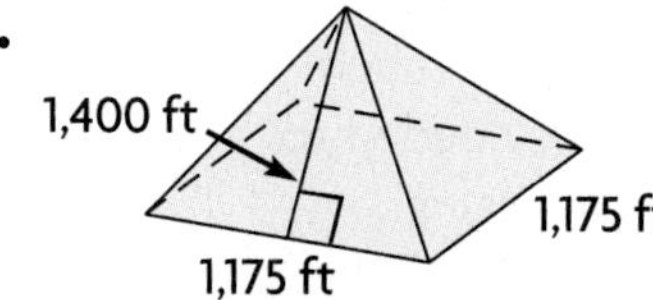

For Exercises 7–12, use the rectangular prism below. Six cubes, each with sides of length 1 in., are arranged to form the rectangular prism.

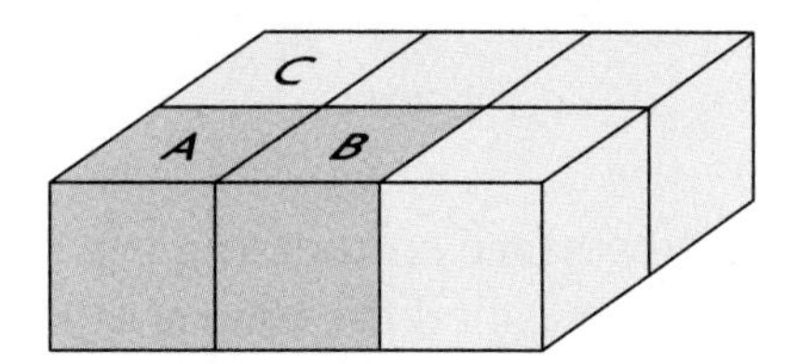

7. What is the total surface area of the four outside faces of cube *A*?

8. What is the total surface area of the rectangular prism?

9. Suppose only cube *A* is removed. What is the surface area of the new figure?

10. Suppose only cube *B* is removed. What is the surface area of the new figure?

11. Suppose cubes *A* and *B* are removed. What is the surface area of the new figure?

12. Suppose cubes *A* and *C* are removed. What is the surface area of the new figure?

Problem-Solving Applications

13. **GEOMETRY** Chen wants to paint the four walls of a rectangular room that is 12 ft long, 10 ft wide, and 8 ft tall. The room has one square window with sides of length 3 ft. How many square feet need to be painted? Chen will not paint the ceiling, floor, and window.

14. **HOBBIES** Lena made a model of a square pyramid with a base that is 30 cm long. Each triangular face has a base of 30 cm and a height of 25 cm. What is the surface area of her model?

15. **WRITE ABOUT IT** Cut the four pieces shown at the right from 1-cm graph paper. Arrange the pieces to form a net for a triangular pyramid. What is the surface area of the pyramid, to the nearest square centimeter?

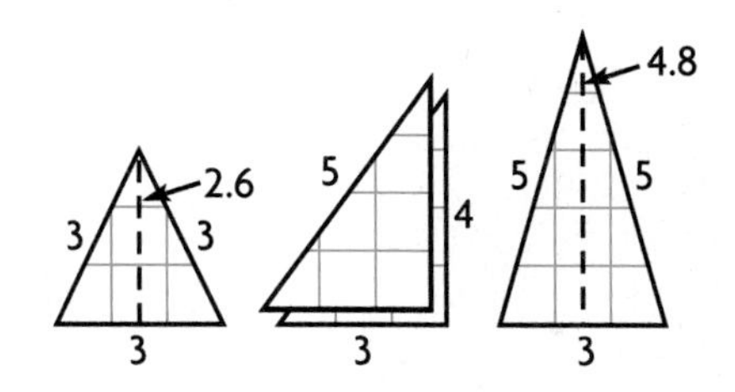

MORE PRACTICE Lesson 25.1, page H77

LESSON 25.2

ALGEBRA CONNECTION

Surface Areas of Cylinders

What You'll Learn
How to find the surface area of a cylinder

Why Learn This?
To solve real-life problems such as deciding how much material is needed to make packaging

VOCABULARY
lateral surface

How do product engineers find how much material is needed to make a cylindrical container?

Product designers choose the shape and size of the container. Then product engineers make detailed drawings of the assembled container and its parts.

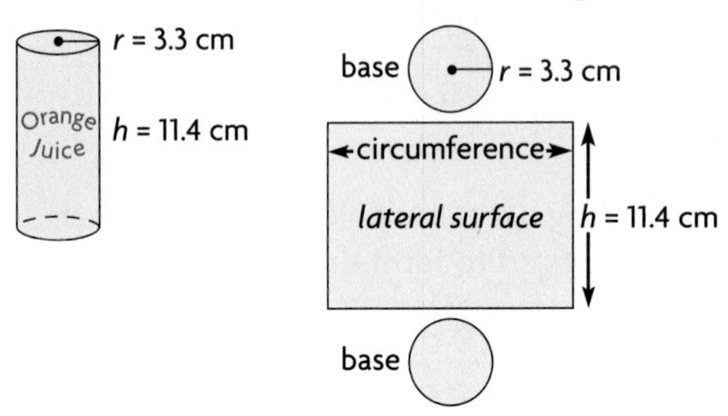

The curved surface connecting the circular bases of a cylinder is called the **lateral surface**.

Talk About It

- When the cylinder is taken apart and laid flat, what shape is the lateral surface?
- The height of the cylinder represents which dimension of the rectangle? The circumference of the circular base represents which dimension of the rectangle?

EXAMPLE 1 Suppose the product engineers use plastic to make the orange juice container shown above. To the nearest square centimeter, how much plastic is needed?

Find the amount of plastic by finding the surface area.

S = areas of bases + area of lateral surface
S = 2(area of circle) + area of rectangle
↑ circumference × height = $2\pi r \cdot h$

$S = 2(\pi r^2) + (2\pi r \cdot h)$

2 × π × 3.3 x^2 + 2 × π × 3.3 × 11.4 = 304.7973193

So, about 305 cm^2 of plastic is needed.

CAREER LINK

Citrus farmers truck their crops to a processing plant, where the juice from oranges is made into concentrate and packed in cans of various sizes. Suppose concentrate is packed in a cylindrical can with a radius of 4 cm and height of 11 cm. What is the surface area of the can?

Calculator Activities, page H35

You can apply the formula for surface area to any cylinder.

EXAMPLE 2 Find the surface area of a can with a $10\frac{1}{2}$-in. height and a 4-in. radius.

Think: $r = 4$, $h = 10\frac{1}{2}$, and $\pi \approx \frac{22}{7}$.

$S = 2(\pi r^2) + (2\pi r \cdot h)$

$S \approx 2(\frac{22}{7} \cdot 4^2) + (2 \cdot \frac{22}{7} \cdot 4 \cdot 10\frac{1}{2})$

$S \approx 2(50\frac{2}{7}) + 264$

$S \approx 100\frac{4}{7} + 264$

$S \approx 364\frac{4}{7}$

So, the surface area of the can is about $364\frac{4}{7}$ in.^{2}

- Why is $364\frac{4}{7}$ in.^{2} an approximation for the surface area of the cylinder?
- **CRITICAL THINKING** Suppose the height of the can is doubled. Is the surface area doubled? Explain.

TEEN TIMES

Most beverage cans used in the United States are aluminum. Aluminum is made from a mineral called bauxite, which is becoming scarce. Aluminum is one of the easiest and cheapest metals to recycle. Making a can from recycled aluminum instead of from bauxite not only saves the mineral but also uses 95% less energy.

GUIDED PRACTICE

For Exercises 1–6, use the figures shown at the right. Use 3.14 for π.

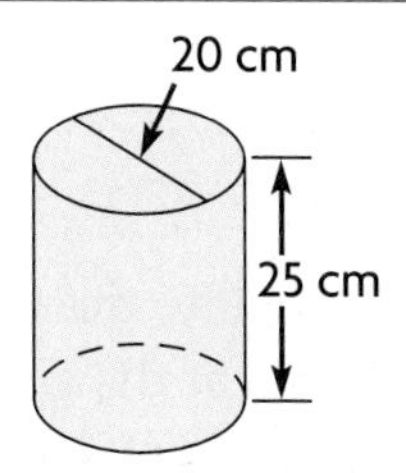

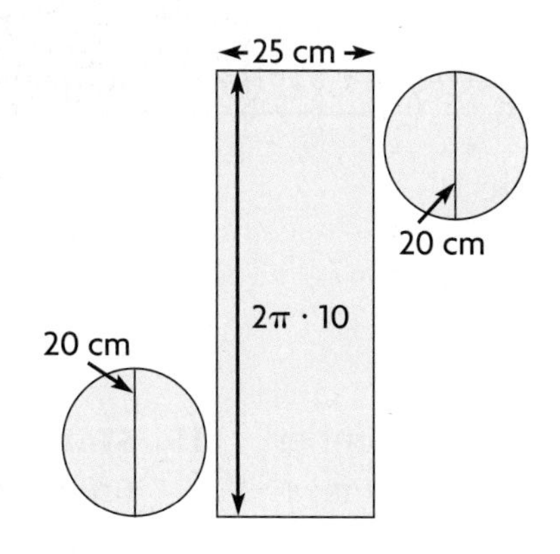

1. What is the radius of the cylinder?
2. What is the area of one base? of both bases?
3. What is the width of the lateral surface? the length of the lateral surface (circumference)?
4. What is the area of the lateral surface?
5. What is the surface area of the cylinder?
6. Suppose the diameter is 40 cm. What would be the area of one base? the length of the lateral surface? the area of the lateral surface?

INDEPENDENT PRACTICE

Find the surface area of each figure. Use 3.14 for π. Round your answer to the nearest tenth.

1. 2 m

10 m

2. 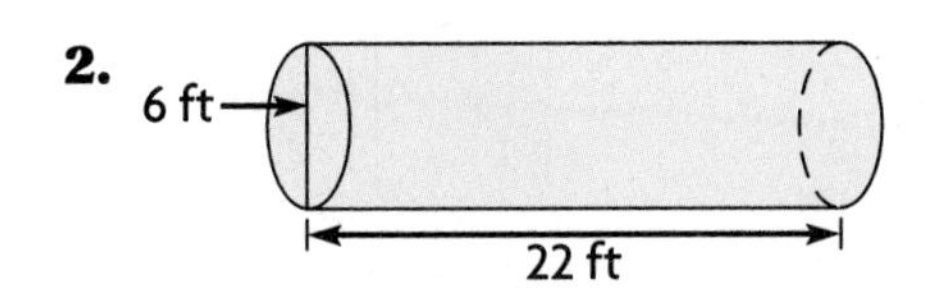

3. 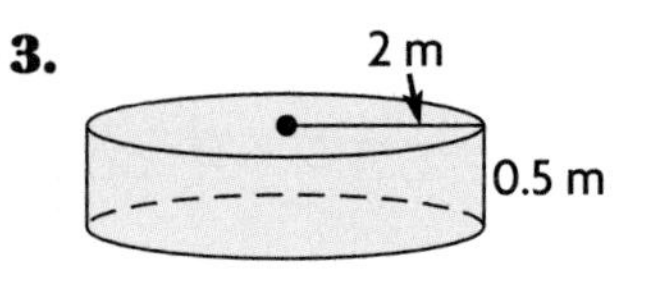

4. 13.5 ft

30.5 ft

5. 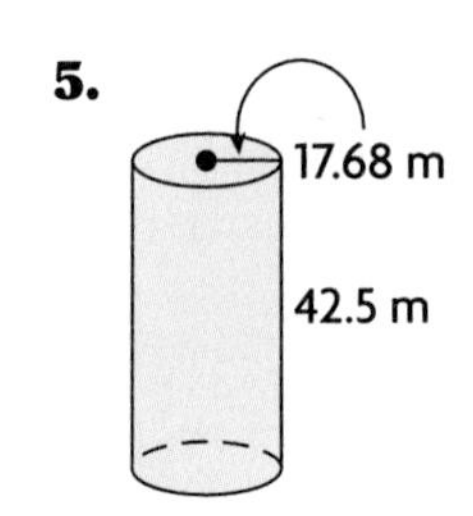

6. 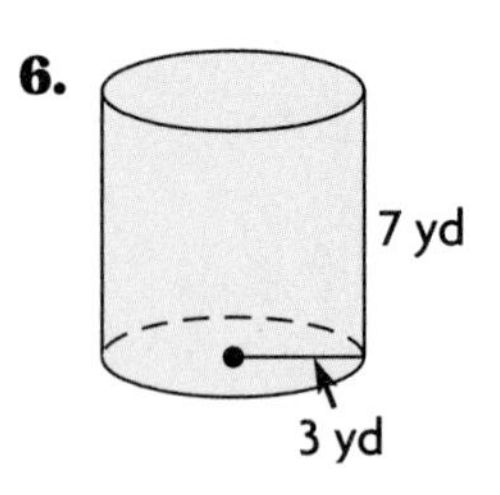

Problem-Solving Applications

7. **SCIENCE** Termites are found in a cylindrical building with a diameter of 16 yd and a height of 20 yd. The building must be covered and chemically treated. To the nearest square yard, how much fabric is needed to cover the building?

8. **BUSINESS** A company wants to sell potato chips in a cylindrical container with a height of 22 cm and a radius of 4 cm. How much area will be available on the lateral surface for a label? What is the total surface area of the container?

9. **WRITE ABOUT IT** How do you find the surface area of a cylinder?

Mixed Review and Test Prep

For Exercises 10–13, use the iteration diagram. Complete the iteration process three times. Give the perimeter and the area at the given stage.

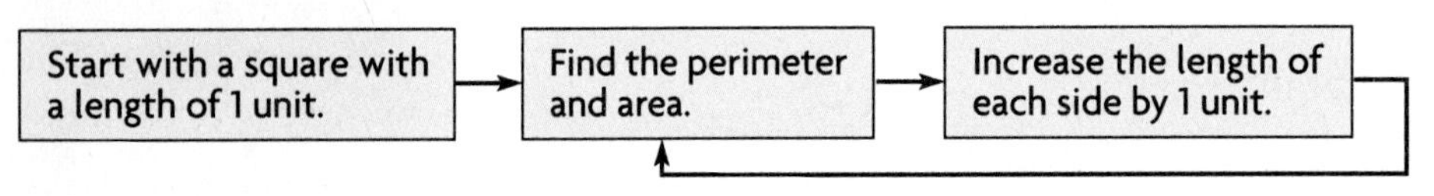

10. Stage 0 **11.** Stage 1 **12.** Stage 2 **13.** Stage 3

Give the precision of each measurement.

14. 15 mi **15.** $6\frac{1}{4}$ in. **16.** 12.1 km **17.** 255 cm

18. **NUMBER SENSE** The sum of 6 and a number is equal to 7 minus the number. What is the number?

A 0.5 **B** 1
C 1.5 **D** 2

19. **STATISTICS** Julio scored 86, 98, 94, and 99 on his first four tests. What must he score on the fifth test to have an average of 90?

F 81 **G** 75
H 73 **J** 70

MORE PRACTICE Lesson 25.2, page H77

Comparing Volumes of Prisms and Pyramids

LAB ACTIVITY

What You'll Explore
How to compare the volume of a prism with that of a pyramid

What You'll Need
scissors, prism-and-pyramid patterns, tape, unpopped popcorn

VOCABULARY
volume

The **volume** of a three-dimensional object is the number of cubic units needed to fill the space it occupies.

You can discover a special relationship between the volumes of prisms and the volumes of pyramids.

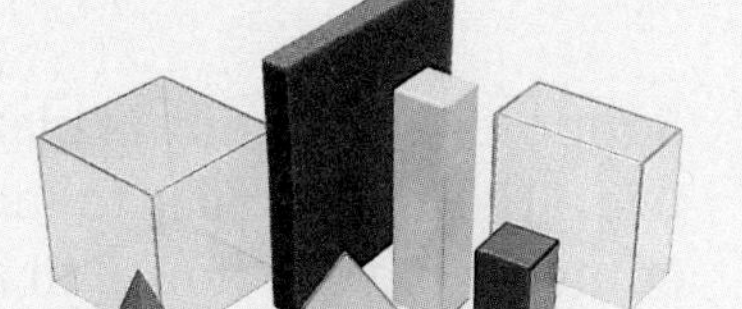

Explore

You can make a prism with no top and a pyramid with no base.

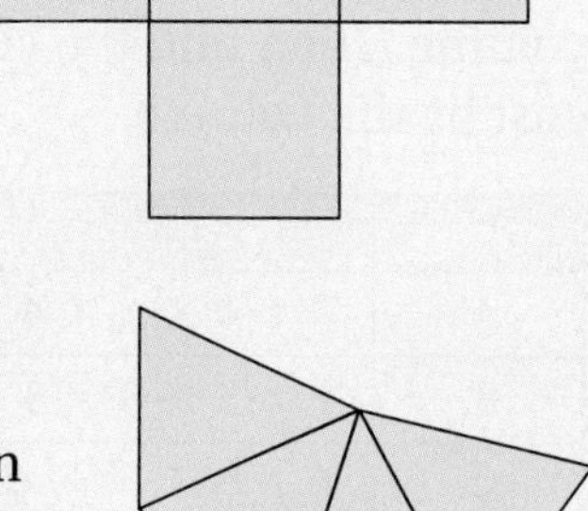

- Cut out the nets for a prism and a pyramid like the ones shown. Assemble each figure.
- How does the height of the prism compare with the height of the pyramid? How does the base of the prism compare with the base of the pyramid?
- Fill the pyramid with popcorn, and then pour the popcorn into the prism. Repeat until the prism is full. How many times did you have to fill the pyramid and pour the popcorn into the prism to fill the prism?

Think and Discuss CRITICAL THINKING

- What is the relationship between the volume of the pyramid and the volume of the prism?
- Suppose a prism has a volume of 72 in.^{3} Predict the volume of a pyramid with the same base and height.

Try This

- Suppose a pyramid has a volume of n. What is the volume of a prism with the same base and height?

Technology Link

You can explore the volumes of pyramids and prisms by using E-Lab, Activity 25. Available on CD-ROM and on the Internet at **www.hbschool.com/elab**

LESSON 25.3

ALGEBRA CONNECTION

Volumes of Prisms and Pyramids

What You'll Learn
How to find the volumes of prisms and pyramids

Why Learn This?
To be able to compare the space available in containers in the shapes of prisms and pyramids

Suppose your family is planning to use a U-Haul® trailer to move the contents of your house to an adjacent town. How can you find out which trailer is the best value?

Rent U-Haul® Trailers

Trailer A	*4 ft × 6 ft × 4 ft*	*\$6.95*
Trailer B	*5 ft × 8 ft × 5 ft*	*\$12.95*
Trailer C	*6 ft × 12 ft × 6 ft*	*\$18.95*

To find the best value, you can compare the costs and the volumes. Since each trailer is a rectangular prism, use the formula $V = lwh$ to find each volume. Then find the cost per cubic foot by dividing the total cost by the volume.

Trailer	Volume (in ft³)	Cost	Cost per ft³
A	$V = 4 \times 6 \times 4 = 96$	\$6.95	\$6.95 ÷ 96 = \$0.072
B	$V = 5 \times 8 \times 5 = 200$	\$12.95	\$12.95 ÷ 200 = \$0.065
C	$V = 6 \times 12 \times 6 = 432$	\$18.95	\$18.95 ÷ 432 = \$0.044

Talk About It

- How can you decide which trailer is the best buy?
- Which trailer is the best buy? Explain.

Have you moved recently? If you have, you're not alone. Nearly 20% of Americans moved in the past year. If you've moved recently, talk to someone about your feelings. Keep in touch with your old friends, and look for ways to make new friends.

You can also use the formula $V = Bh$ to find the volume of a prism. In this formula, B is the area of the base of the prism, and h is the height of the prism.

EXAMPLE 1 Find the volume.

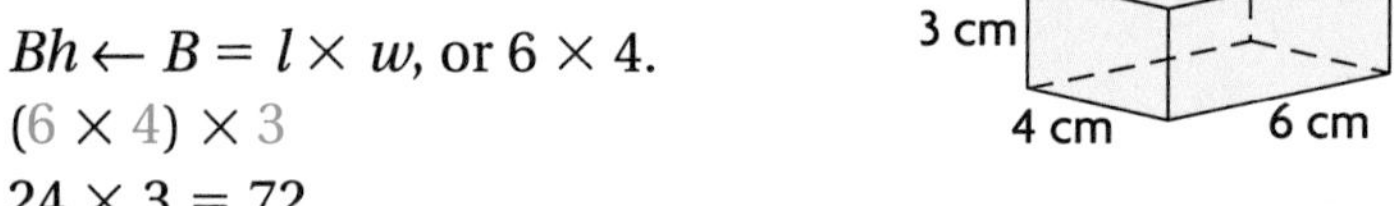

$V = Bh \leftarrow B = l \times w$, or 6×4.
$V = (6 \times 4) \times 3$
$V = 24 \times 3 = 72$

So, the volume is 72 cm³.

- Suppose you are given the volume, the length, and the width of a rectangular prism. How would you find the height?

The bases of a triangular prism are congruent triangles. To find the volume of a triangular prism, you need to find B, the area of a base. Use $\frac{1}{2}bh$, the formula for the area of a triangle.

EXAMPLE 2 Find the volume of the triangular prism shown at the right.

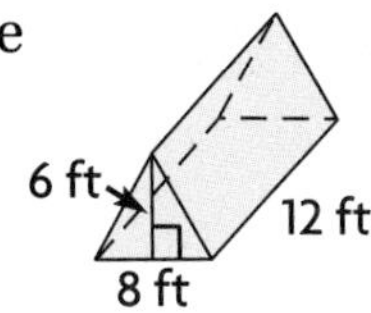

$B = \frac{1}{2} \times b \times h$

$B = \frac{1}{2} \times 8 \times 6 = 24$

$V = Bh$
$V = 24 \times 12$
$V = 288$

So, the volume of the triangular prism is 288 ft^3.

In the Lab Activity, you discovered that the pyramid held $\frac{1}{3}$ as much popcorn as the prism. This means that a pyramid has $\frac{1}{3}$ the volume of a prism with the same base and height.

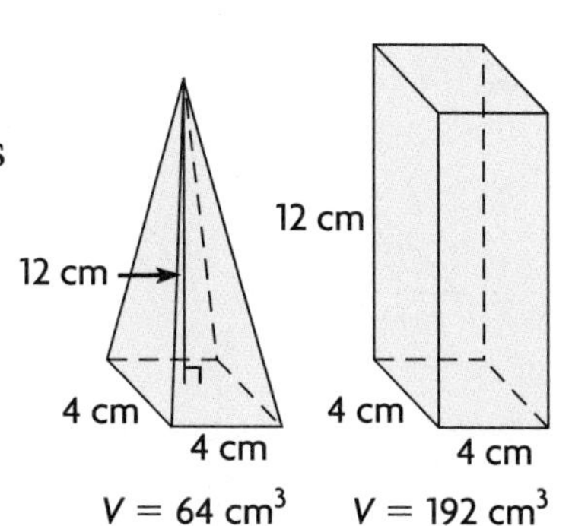

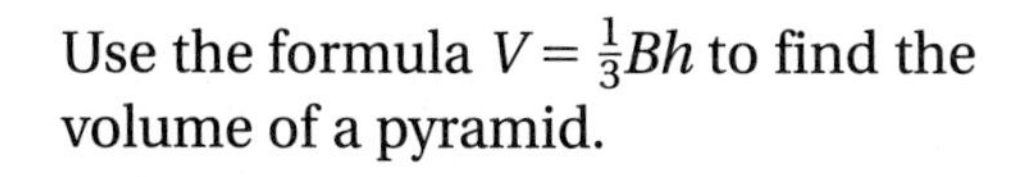

Use the formula $V = \frac{1}{3}Bh$ to find the volume of a pyramid.

EXAMPLE 3 Find the volume of the pyramid shown at the right.

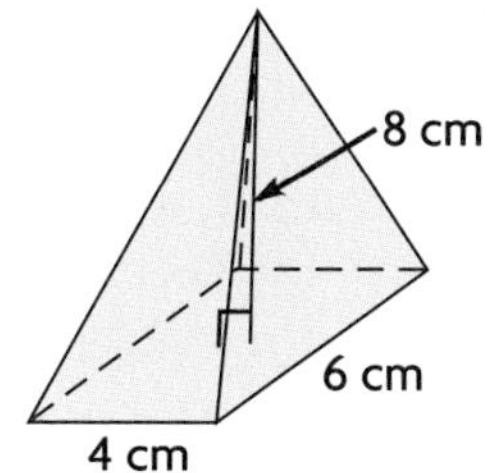

Think: The base of the pyramid is a rectangle.

$B = lw$
$B = 6 \times 4 = 24$

$V = \frac{1}{3} Bh$

$V = \frac{1}{3} \times 24 \times 8$

$V = 64$

So, the volume of the pyramid is 64 cm^3.

- Suppose the height of the pyramid doubles to 16 cm. What happens to the volume?

CULTURAL LINK

Blocks of ice and ice cubes are prisms. The Chinese cut and stored blocks of ice as long ago as 1000 B.C. The U.S. ice industry started in the northern states. Three-foot-square blocks of ice were cut from frozen lakes and stored in icehouses. Suppose a block of ice is 3 ft long, 3 ft wide, and 3 ft high. What is its volume?

GUIDED PRACTICE

Find the volume of each figure to the nearest whole number.

1.

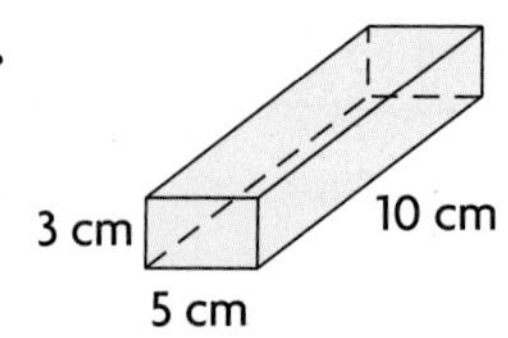

2.

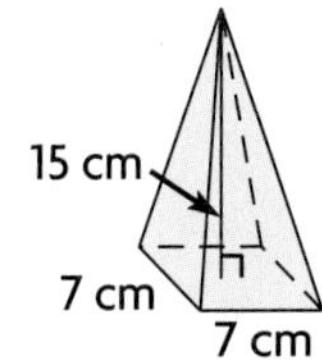

3.

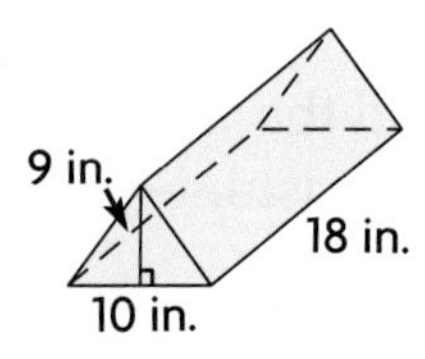

INDEPENDENT PRACTICE

Find the volume of each figure to the nearest whole number.

1.

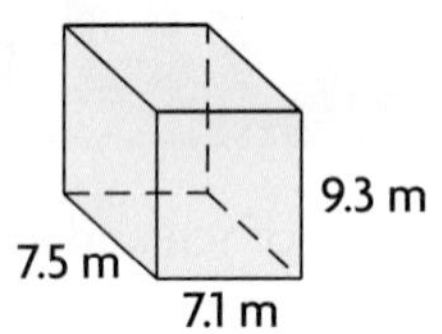

2.

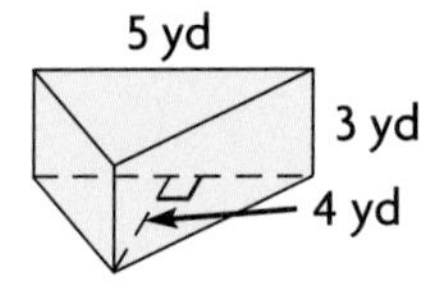

3.

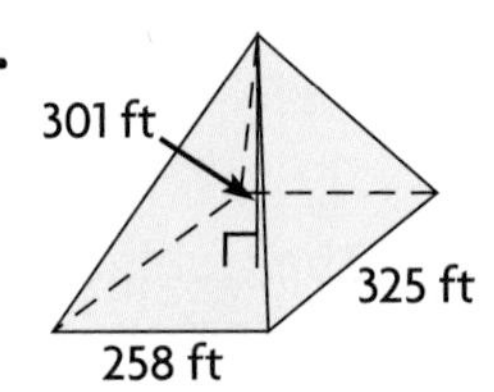

4.

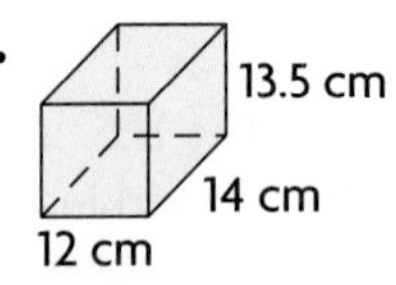

5.

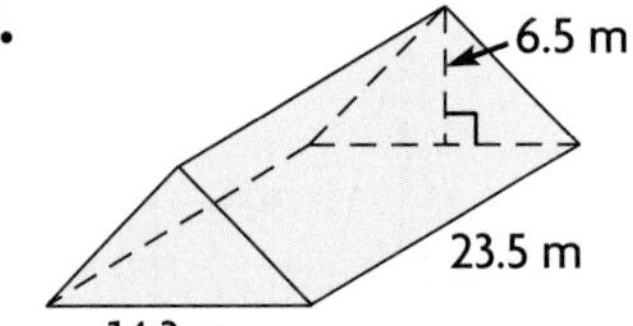

6.

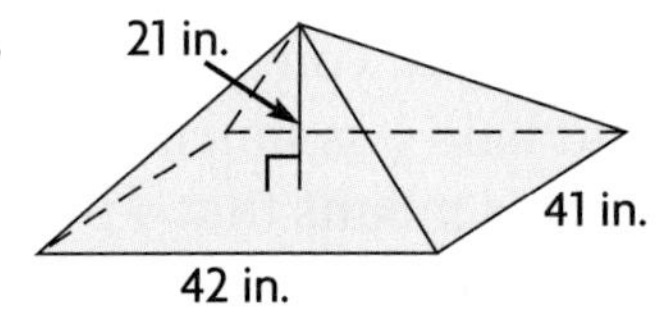

For Exercises 7–8, the volume and two dimensions are given for each rectangular prism. Find the missing dimension of the rectangular prism.

7.

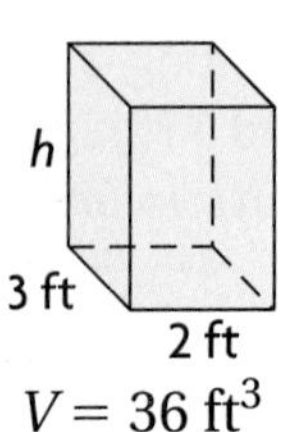

$V = 36\text{ ft}^3$

8.

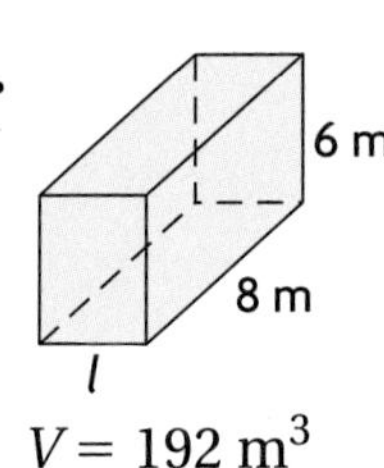

$V = 192\text{ m}^3$

Problem-Solving Applications

9. **ENTERTAINMENT** A compact-disc case is 14 cm long, 12.5 cm wide, and 1 cm tall. What is the volume of the disc case?

10. It takes 3 in.^{3} of cheese to make a sandwich. How many sandwiches can be made from the piece of cheese shown at the right?

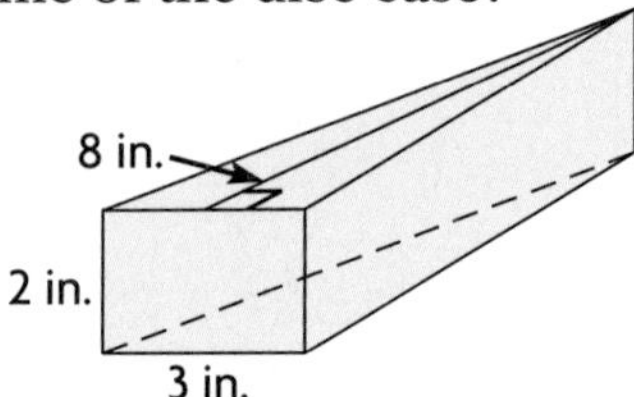

11. **WRITE ABOUT IT** How are the formulas for the volume of a prism and the volume of a pyramid alike? How are they different?

Technology Link

In ***Mighty Math Cosmic Geometry*** you can go to *Geometry Academy* to test your knowledge of volume and surface area. Use Grow Slide Level L.

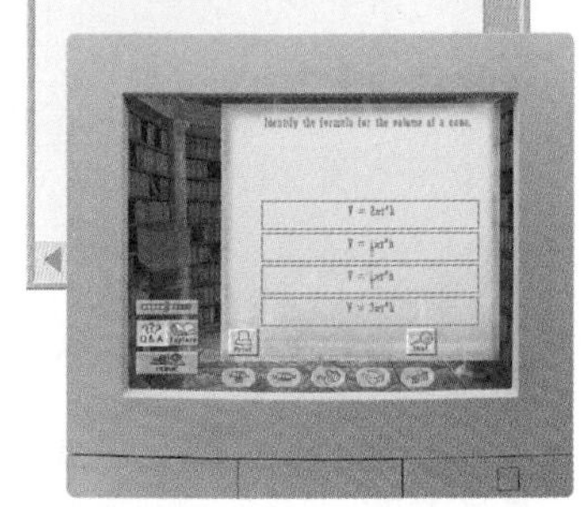

MORE PRACTICE Lesson 25.3, page H78

ALGEBRA CONNECTION

Volumes of Cylinders and Cones

What You'll Learn
How to find the volumes of cylinders and cones

Why Learn This?
To solve real-life packaging problems, such as determining how much a container can hold

Which container would hold more?

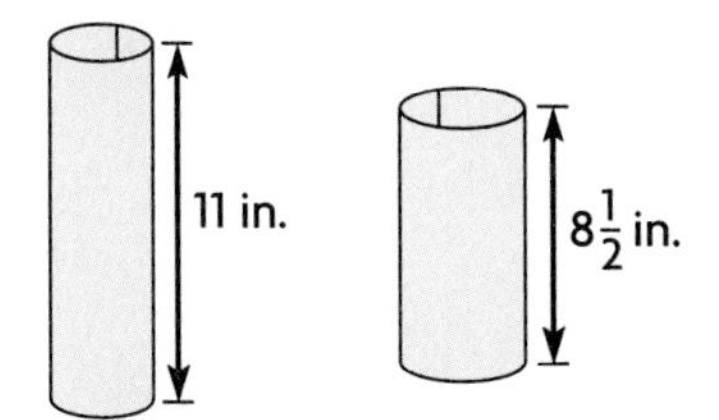

ACTIVITY 1 **WHAT YOU'LL NEED:** $8\frac{1}{2}$-in. × 11-in. piece of posterboard, transparent tape, unpopped popcorn

- Roll the posterboard the tall way. Then roll it the short way. Predict which would hold more popcorn.
- Roll the posterboard the tall way, without overlapping the edges. Tape it. Stand it on a flat surface. Fill it with popcorn. Remove the cylinder, and keep the popcorn in a pile.
- Roll the posterboard the short way, without overlapping the edges. Tape it. Stand it up on a flat surface. Fill the short cylinder with the popcorn from the tall cylinder. Does the popcorn fill the short cylinder?
- Which cylinder holds more popcorn? How do you know? Was your prediction correct?
- Which cylinder has the greater volume? Explain.

When you need to know the volume of a cylinder, multiply the area of the base by the height.

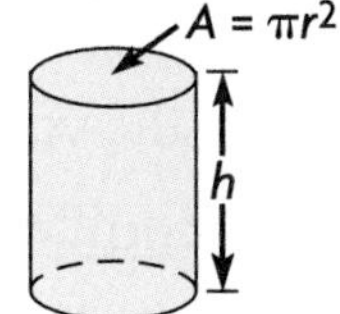

$V = Bh$

EXAMPLE 1 Find the volume of the cylinder. Use $\pi = 3.14$.

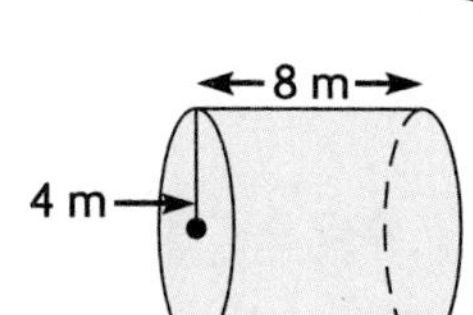

$V = \pi r^2 h$
$V \approx 3.14 \times 4^2 \times 8$
$V \approx 3.14 \times 16 \times 8$
$V \approx 401.92$
So, the volume is about 401.92 m^3.

ACTIVITY 2 **WHAT YOU'LL NEED:** scissors, cylinder-and-cone patterns, transparent tape, unpopped popcorn

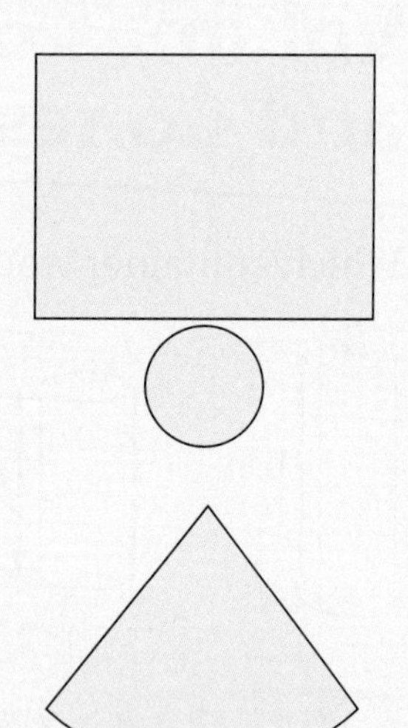

- Cut out the patterns for a cylinder with one base and an open cone. Assemble each figure.
- Place the figures side by side. How does the height of the cylinder compare with the height of the cone? How does the base of the cylinder compare with the base of the cone?
- Fill the cone with popcorn, and pour the popcorn into the cylinder. Repeat until the cylinder is full. How many times did you have to fill the cone and pour the popcorn into the cylinder to fill the cylinder?
- How does the volume of a cone compare with the volume of a cylinder that has the same height and base?

CONSUMER LINK

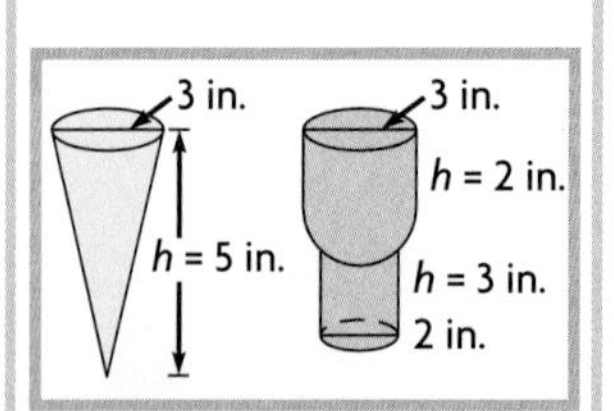

Which holds more frozen yogurt, a sugar cone or a cylinder-shaped cake cup? The cone and the cup are the same height, and the openings are the same size. The cake cup is actually two cylinders stacked together. What is the volume of each? Which holds more?

To find the volume of a cone, V, use the formula $V = \frac{1}{3}\pi r^2 h$.

EXAMPLE 2 Find the volume of the cone shown at the right. Use $\pi = 3.14$.

15 ft

10 ft

$V = \frac{1}{3}\pi r^2 h$

$V \approx \frac{1}{3} \times 3.14 \times 10^2 \times 15$

$V \approx \frac{1}{3} \times 3.14 \times 100 \times 15$

$V \approx 1{,}570$

So, the volume of the cone is about 1,570 ft^3.

- **CRITICAL THINKING** What is the volume of a cylinder with the same radius and height as the cone above? Explain.

GUIDED PRACTICE

Find the volume of the figure with the given dimensions.

1. cylinder: $r = 5$ cm, $h = 10$ cm

2. cylinder: $r = 2.6$ m, $h = 12.8$ m

3. cone: $r = 5$ cm, $h = 10$ cm

4. cone: $r = 2.6$ m, $h = 12.8$ m

INDEPENDENT PRACTICE

Find the volume. Use $\pi = 3.14$, and round to the nearest whole number.

1. 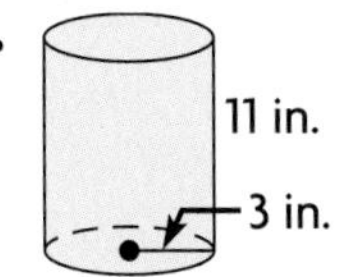

2. 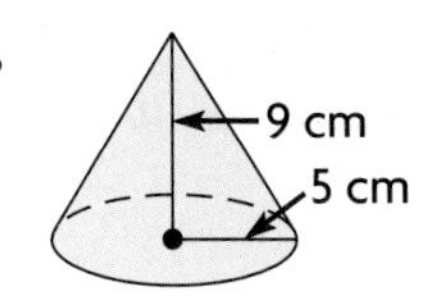

3. 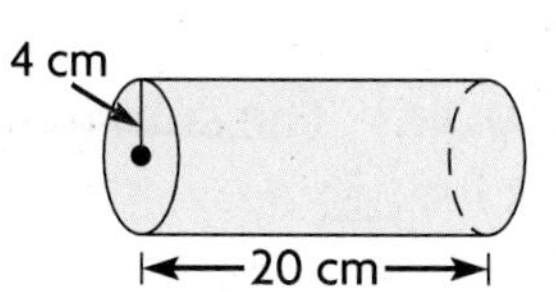

4. 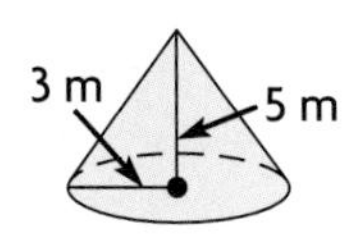

5. 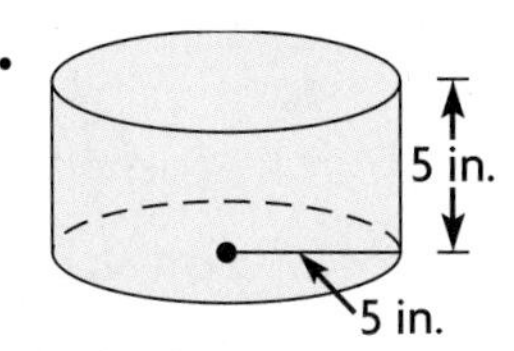

6. 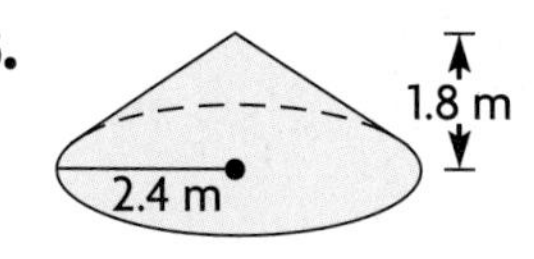

7. 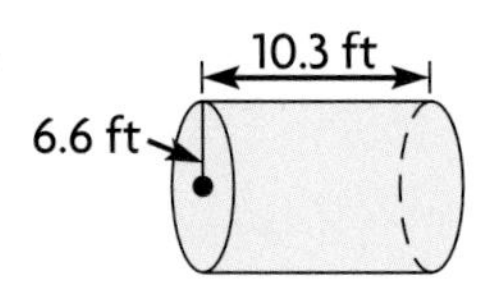

8. 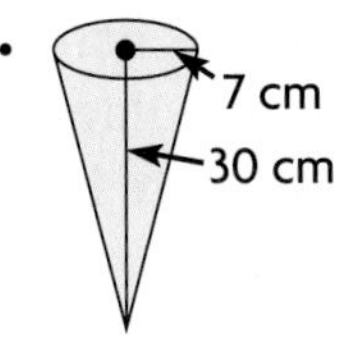

9. 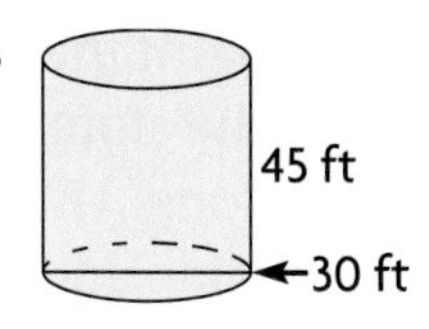

Problem-Solving Applications

10. **BUSINESS** An oil-storage tank shaped like a cylinder has a radius of 25 m and a height of 20 m. What is the volume of the tank?

11. **CRITICAL THINKING** To find the volume of your fist, suppose you use a cylinder that has a radius of about 4 in. and a height of about 11 in. Estimate the volume of the can.

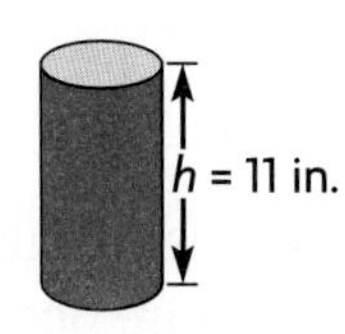

12. **WRITE ABOUT IT** How are the formulas alike for the volumes of cylinders and cones? How are they different?

Mixed Review and Test Prep

Give two different possible lengths and widths for each given perimeter of a rectangle.

13. 10 ft **14.** 60 in. **15.** 12 m **16.** 23 mi

Tell whether the following are lengths of sides of a right triangle.

17. 6, 8, 10 **18.** 5, 12, 13 **19.** 7, 10, 12 **20.** 14, 48, 50

21. **MONEY** You get a penny on day 1, 2 pennies on day 2, 4 pennies on day 3, 8 pennies on day 4, and so on. How much money will you get on day 30?

A \$465.00 **B** \$1,912.00
C \$2,684,354.56 **D** \$5,368,709.12

22. **AVERAGE** Jacob went on a hiking trip. He hiked 1.2 miles, 3.7 miles, 2.8 miles, and 1.9 miles on 4 days. What was his average daily hiking distance.

F 1.9 mi **G** 2.4 mi
H 5.8 mi **J** 9.6 mi

MORE PRACTICE Lesson 25.4, page H78

CHAPTER 25 Review/Test

1. **VOCABULARY** The sum of the areas of all the surfaces of a solid is its __?__ (page 486)

Find the surface area of each figure. (pages 486–489)

2. 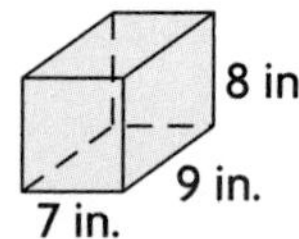

3. 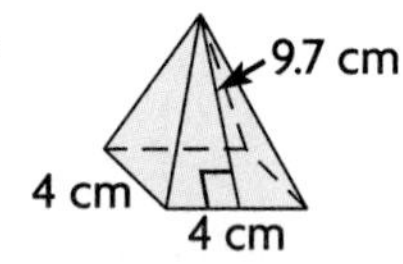

4. 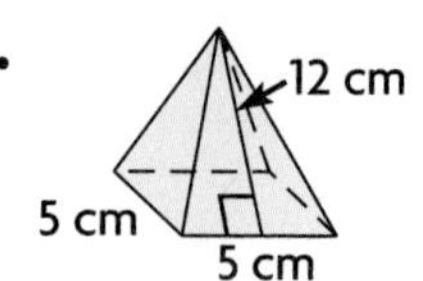

5. 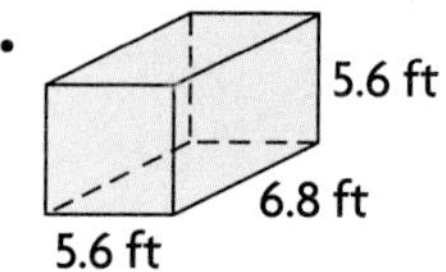

6. Andrew wants to paint the 4 walls of the outside of his fish and tackle store. The store is in the shape of a rectangular prism and is 18 ft long, 12 ft wide, and 9 ft tall. The store has a door that is 3 ft wide and 7 ft tall and will not be painted. How many square feet need to be painted? (pages 486–489)

Find the surface area of each figure. Use 3.14 for π. Round to the nearest whole number. (pages 490–492)

7. 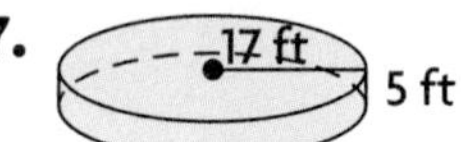

8. 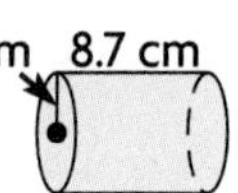

9. 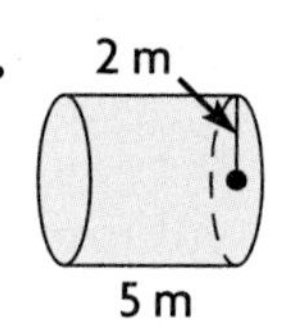

10. 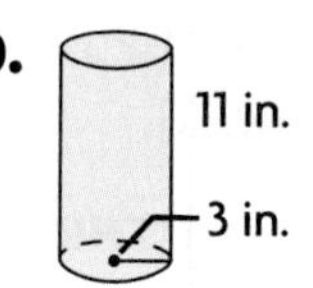

11. **VOCABULARY** The number of cubic units needed to fill the space a solid figure occupies is its __?__ (page 493)

Find the volume of each figure. (pages 494–496)

12. 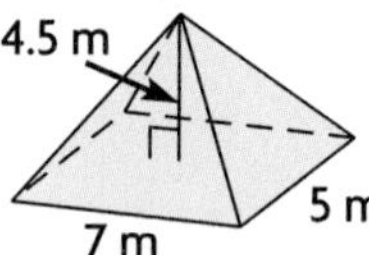

13. 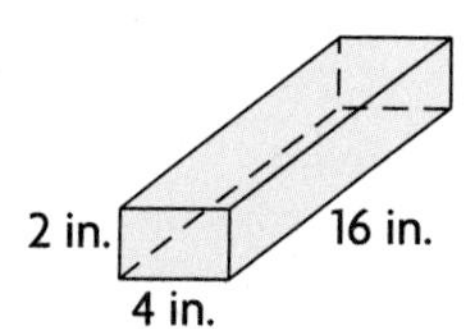

14. 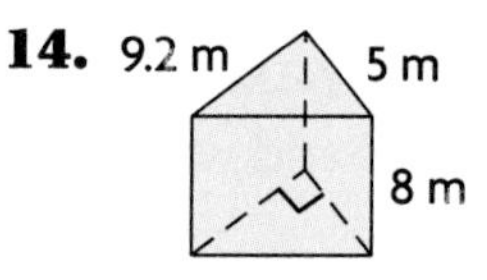

15. 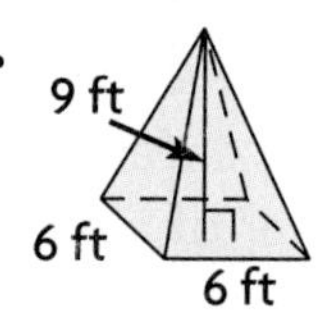

Find the volume. Use 3.14 for π. Round to the nearest whole number. (pages 497–499)

16. 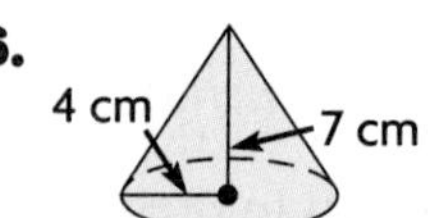

17. 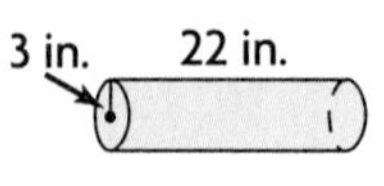

18. 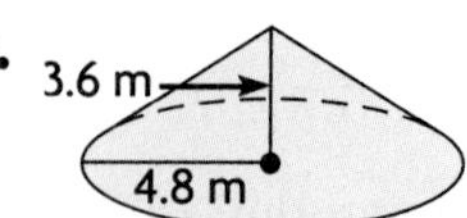

19. 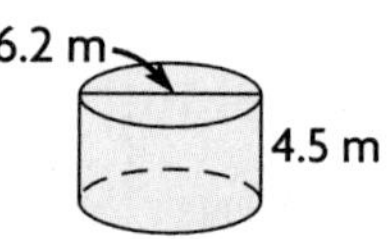

20. Mr. Lenz has a cylindrical building on his farm to store grain. The cylindrical building has a diameter of 10 ft and a height of 30 ft. This season, Mr. Lenz harvested 2,317 ft^3 of grain. Does the cylindrical building have enough room to store the grain? Explain. (pages 497–499)

Test Prep

CUMULATIVE
CHAPTERS 1–25

1. Which formula can be used to find the volume of a rectangular pyramid?

A $V = lwh$
B $V = lw + wh + lh$
C $V = \frac{1}{2}lwh$
D $V = l = w + h$
E Not Here

2. A sweatshirt is discounted $5 from its original price of $40. What percent of the original price is $5?

F 8%
G 12.5%
H 20%
J 80%

3. Karen made 54 free throws last season. That was 15 more than Brenda made. How many free throws did Brenda make?

A 39
B 45
C 69
D 72

4. Which is the best name for the figure shown below?

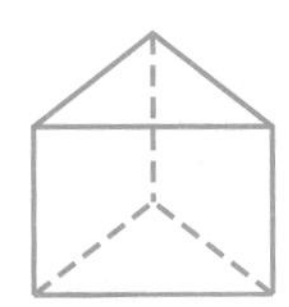

F triangular pyramid
G rectangular prism
H triangular prism
J rectangular pyramid
K Not Here

5. Which sequence is a geometric sequence?

A 14, 17, 21, 24, . . .
B 1, 4, 9, 25, . . .
C 3, 6, 12, 24, . . .
D 20, 18, 16, 14, . . .

6. What is the next row in the triangular array?

1
2 1
3 2 1
4 3 2 1

F 6 5 4 3 2 1
G 1 2 3 4 5
H 5 4 3 2 1
J 2 4 6 8 10

7. Mrs. Katsis is buying a new minivan. She has a choice of a white, gold, or red exterior. She can choose a black, tan, or gray interior. She can choose the 4-door or 5-door model. How many different ways can Mrs. Katsis choose an exterior color, an interior color, and a model?

A 8 **B** 14 **C** 18 **D** 27

8. The table below shows the results of rolling a number cube 40 times.

Number	1	2	3	4	5	6
Times rolled	6	8	5	4	6	11

What is the experimental probability of rolling an odd number greater than 3?

F $\frac{1}{8}$

G $\frac{3}{20}$

H $\frac{3}{8}$

J $\frac{21}{40}$

9. What is the surface area of a cylinder with radius 4 inches and height 10 inches? Use 3.14 for π.

A 502.65 in.^{2}
B 351.68 in.^{2}
C 251.2 in.^{2}
D 100.53 in.^{2}

CHAPTER

26 CHANGING DIMENSIONS

LOOK AHEAD

In this chapter you will solve problems that involve

- lengths and widths
- areas when the perimeter is fixed
- dimensions with scale factors
- surface areas and volumes

CONSUMER LINK

The world's largest jar of jelly beans was unveiled on October 14, 1992. The jar stood 96 inches high, contained 378,000 jelly beans, and weighed 2,910 pounds.

- Explain how you would find the number of jelly beans in a pound.
- Describe strategies you would use to determine the number of jelly beans in a jar.

Problem-Solving Project

Designing Containers

Suppose you design packages for jelly beans. Use no more than two sheets of $8\frac{1}{2}$-in. × 11-in. paper to make two closed containers. Predict which container will hold more jelly beans. Then, measure the volume of each container to verify your prediction. Record your findings. Show your containers to the class, telling their volumes and how you made them.

PROJECT CHECKLIST

- ✓ Did you make two closed containers?
- ✓ Did you predict which one would hold more jelly beans?
- ✓ Did you verify your prediction by measuring the volume?
- ✓ Did you describe your containers to the class?

ACTIVITY

What You'll Explore
How to model changing relationships in rectangles

What You'll Need
11-peg × 11-peg geoboard, or square dot paper

Technology Link

You can explore dimensions and area of rectangles by using E-Lab, Activity 26. Available on CD-ROM and on the Internet at **www.hbschool.com/elab**

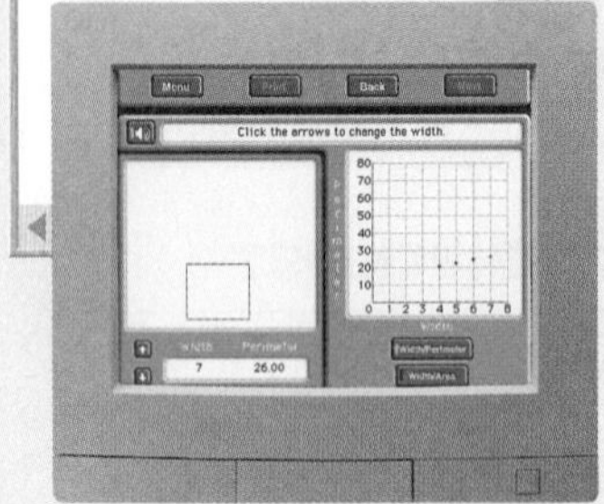

Changing Rectangles

The perimeter and area of a rectangle are related to the length and width. If one or both dimensions change, the perimeter and area can change. However, it is possible to keep the perimeter of the rectangle fixed, or the same, as you change the length and width.

Explore

- Make all the possible rectangles with a perimeter of 24 units, using an 11-peg × 11-peg geoboard or an 11-dot × 11-dot grid on dot paper. Let the horizontal or vertical distance between two pegs or dots be 1 unit.
- As you make each new rectangle, record the following data in a table: length, width, area, and perimeter. In your table, order the lengths from shortest to longest.

Think and Discuss

- What pattern do you see in your table?
- When the perimeter is fixed, is the area also fixed? Explain.
- How is this graph related to the data in your table?
- What pattern do you see in the graph?
- What conclusion can you make about the relationship between the lengths and widths of the possible rectangles with a fixed perimeter?

Dimensions of Rectangles
width: 0 1 2 3 4 5 6 7 8 9 10 11
length: 1 2 3 4 5 6 7 8 9 10 11

Try This

- What if you use the geoboard or dot paper to model rectangles with a fixed perimeter of 30 units? Predict how the length and width of these rectangles will be related.
- Verify your prediction by modeling the rectangles and making a table and graph.

ALGEBRA CONNECTION

LESSON 26.1

Changing Areas

What You'll Learn
How the area of a rectangle can change when the perimeter is fixed

Why Learn This?
To estimate the maximum area of a rectangle with a fixed perimeter

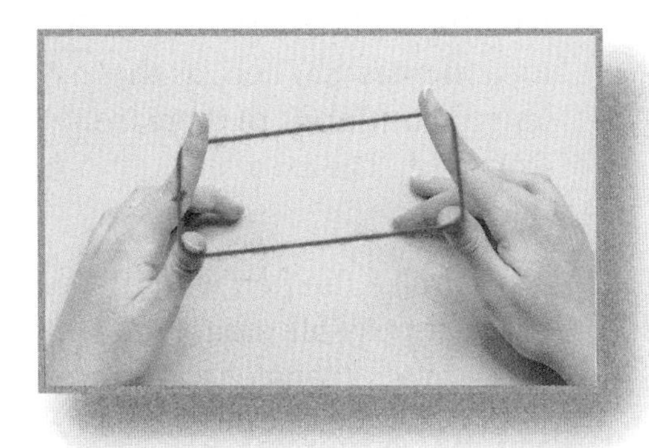

In the Lab Activity, you saw that the area of a rectangle can change when the perimeter is fixed.

Suppose you have an 18-in. loop of string.

Think about stretching the string tight and moving your fingers closer together or farther apart to make rectangles.

- As the shape changes, does the area change? the perimeter?
- What is a reasonable estimate of the greatest possible area for a rectangle with a fixed perimeter of 18 in.?

To find the greatest, or maximum, area possible, you may have to use a length that is not a whole number.

EXAMPLE Fran has 18 ft of fencing for a pen for her puppies. She wants to enclose as big a rectangular area as possible. What size rectangle should she make?

You can make a table and graph to find the rectangle with a perimeter of 18 ft that has the greatest area.

Length (in ft)	$\frac{1}{2}$	1	$1\frac{1}{2}$	2	$2\frac{1}{2}$	3	$3\frac{1}{2}$	4	$4\frac{1}{2}$	5	$5\frac{1}{2}$
Width (in ft)	$8\frac{1}{2}$	8	$7\frac{1}{2}$	7	$6\frac{1}{2}$	6	$5\frac{1}{2}$	5	$4\frac{1}{2}$	4	$3\frac{1}{2}$
Area (in ft^2)	$4\frac{1}{4}$	8	$11\frac{1}{4}$	14	$16\frac{1}{4}$	18	$19\frac{1}{4}$	20	$20\frac{1}{4}$	20	$19\frac{1}{4}$

The table shows the relationship of length, width, and area for rectangles with a perimeter of 18 ft.

- **CRITICAL THINKING** If you extend the table to include lengths through $8\frac{1}{2}$ ft, what pattern do you see?
- What do you think a graph relating the lengths and areas of the rectangles in the table would look like?

Each point on this graph relates the length and area of a rectangle with a perimeter of 18 ft.

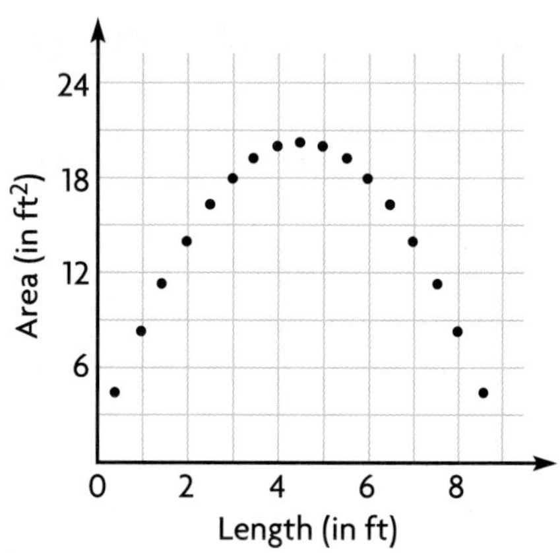

The graph shows that as the length increases up to $4\frac{1}{2}$ ft, the area increases. Then, as the length continues to increase from $4\frac{1}{2}$ ft, the area decreases.

So, to make the pen with the greatest possible area, Fran should fence in a rectangle that is a square, $4\frac{1}{2}$ ft long and $4\frac{1}{2}$ ft wide.

GUIDED PRACTICE

1. Suppose you need to make a rectangular pen with 30 ft of fencing. What whole-number lengths and widths can you use?

For Exercises 2 and 3, use the given rectangles.

a.

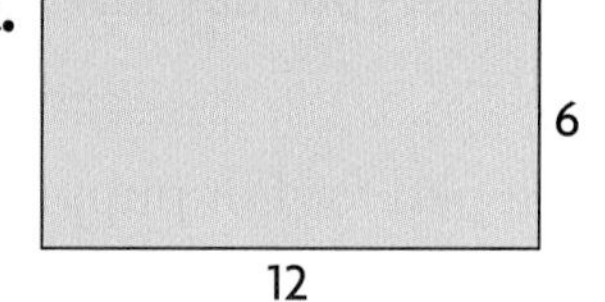

b.

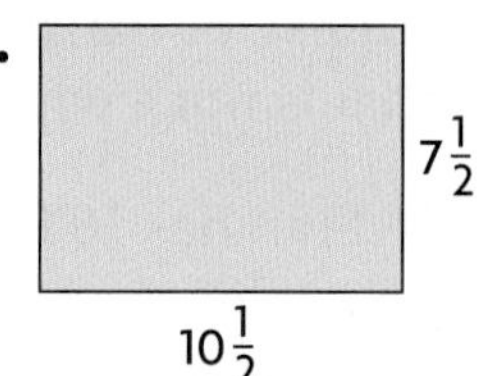

c.

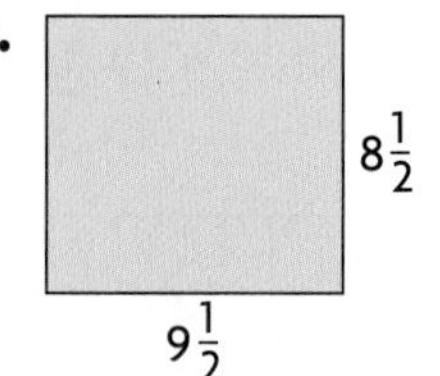

d.

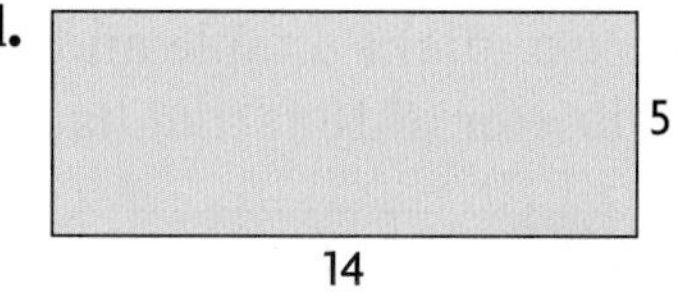

2. Which rectangles have the same perimeter?

3. Which rectangle has the greatest area? Support your answer.

4. Copy and complete the table for a rectangle with a perimeter of 20 ft.

Length (in ft)	1	2	3	4	5	6	7	8	9
Width (in ft)	?	?	7	?	?	?	?	2	?
Area (in ft²)	?	16	?	?	?	?	21	?	?

In ***Data ToolKit*** you can make a coordinate plane graph to compare the length and area of rectangles with fixed perimeters.

INDEPENDENT PRACTICE

For Exercises 1–3, use a rectangle with a perimeter of 12 m.

1. Copy and complete the table.

Length (in m)	0.5	1	1.5	2	2.5	3	3.5	4	4.5	5	5.5
Width (in m)	?	?	?	?	?	?	?	?	?	?	?
Area (in m^2)	?	?	?	?	?	?	?	?	?	?	?

2. Sketch a graph showing how the lengths and areas are related.

3. Sketch a graph showing how the lengths and widths are related.

In Exercises 4–9, the perimeter of a rectangle is given. Using dimensions to the nearest 0.5 unit, find the length and width that will give the rectangle the largest possible area.

4. 40 ft **5.** 50 yd **6.** 76 mi **7.** 100 in. **8.** 250 m **9.** 330 km

10. What do you notice about the dimensions you found for Exercises 4–9? What can you conclude from this information?

Problem-Solving Applications

11. **HOBBIES** A rectangular garden has an area of 28 m^2. What are some possible perimeters for this garden?

12. What is the area of 2 sheets of $8\frac{1}{2}$-in. × 11-in. paper?

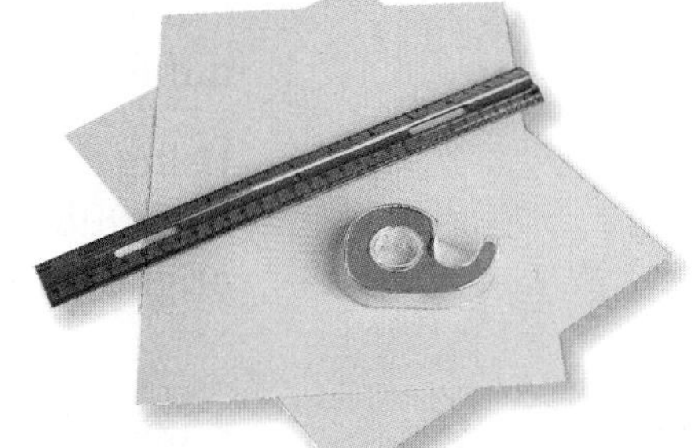

13. **WRITE ABOUT IT** As the length of a rectangle with a fixed perimeter increases, what happens to the area?

Mixed Review and Test Prep

Find the value.

14. 75% of 200 **15.** 25% of 8 **16.** 125% of 12 **17.** 150% of 16

Find the volume of the figure with the given dimensions. Round to the nearest cubic foot.

18. rectangular prism: $l = 5$ ft, $w = 4$ ft, $h = 7$ ft

19. rectangular pyramid: $l = 5$ ft, $w = 4$ ft, $h = 7$ ft

20. cylinder: $r = 4$ ft, $h = 8$ ft

21. **NUMBER SENSE** A bottling plant produced a batch of bottles that could be divided evenly into groups of 6 or 8. What is the smallest number of bottles that could have been produced?

A 16 **B** 18
C 24 **D** 32

22. **CONSUMER MATH** Suppose you work part-time and are offered a choice for a pay raise. The choices are listed below. Which is the best raise?

F 10% of \$4.00 **G** 6% of \$5.50
H \$0.25 **J** 110% of \$0.20

MORE PRACTICE Lesson 26.1, page H78

LESSON 26.2

Making Changes with Scaling

What You'll Learn
How to use scaling to change figures

Why Learn This?
To know how to enlarge or reduce drawings made with computer programs

Do you know how to change the size of your drawings on a computer?

Many software packages that contain a word processor also contain a draw program. One of the menus in a draw program lets you stretch and shrink figures by scaling.

Scaling at 100% keeps the original dimension.

original ————
100% ————

Scaling above 100% stretches the given dimension.

For example, using a scale factor of 125% means the linear dimension becomes 125% of the original. The dimension stretches 25%.

100% ————
125% —————
25% more

Scaling below 100% shrinks the given dimension.

Using a scale factor of 75% means the linear dimension becomes 75% of the original. The dimension shrinks 25%.

100% ————
75% ———
25% less

- Look at the original image of the house. Decide which scaled image matches the scale selections.

  length, 50%; height, 75%
  length, 100%; height, 50%
  length, 75%; height, 125%

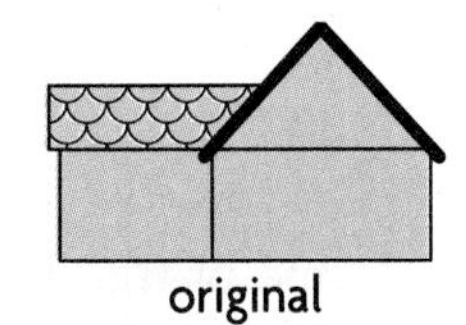
original

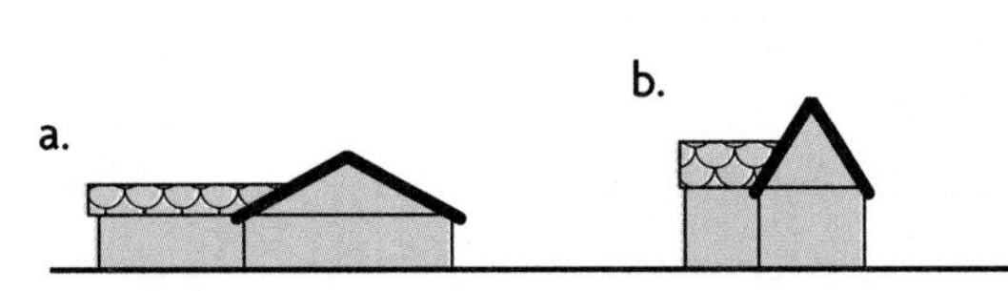

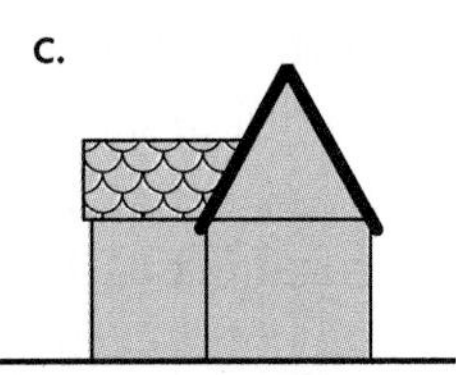

- Describe how the original image would look if both the length and the height were scaled 200%.

EXAMPLE 1 A rectangular diagram measures 6 in. long and 4 in. high on the screen. Find the new dimensions after these scale selections.

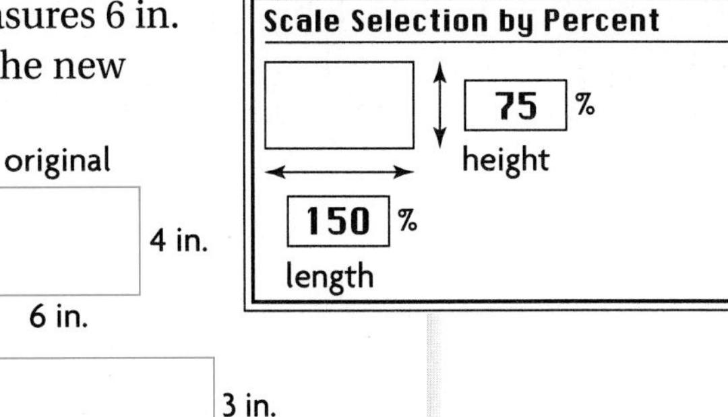

The length stretches to 150%.
150% = 1.50, and 1.50 × 6 = 9
So, the new length is 9 in.

The height shrinks to 75%.
75% = 0.75, and 0.75 × 4 = 3
So, the new height is 3 in.

3 in.
9 in.

Talk About It

- Compare the new rectangle in Example 1 with the original rectangle. Which looks larger to you?
- Suppose the length is x and the height is y. What formulas could you write to find the new length and height?

Suppose you want to use your computer to draw a series of different-size model houses. You can draw one pattern and create different sizes of the houses by changing the scale for the length and height.

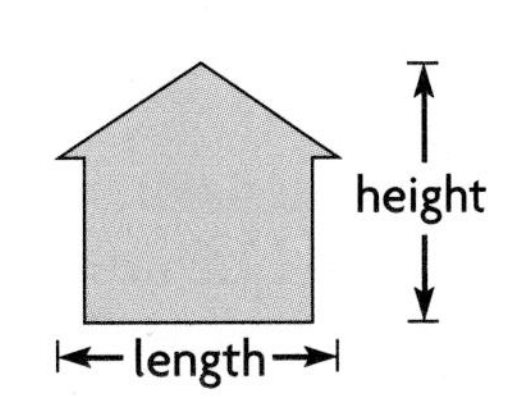

EXAMPLE 2 The image of a house measures 4 in. long and $3\frac{1}{2}$ in. high. Find the size of the new image after applying each of these scale selections. Give the dimensions to the nearest eighth of an inch.

A.

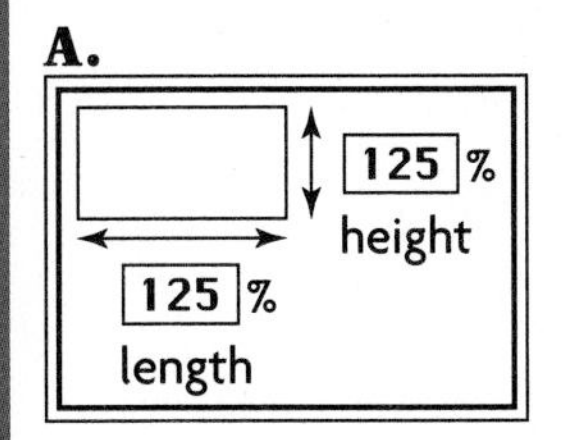

B.

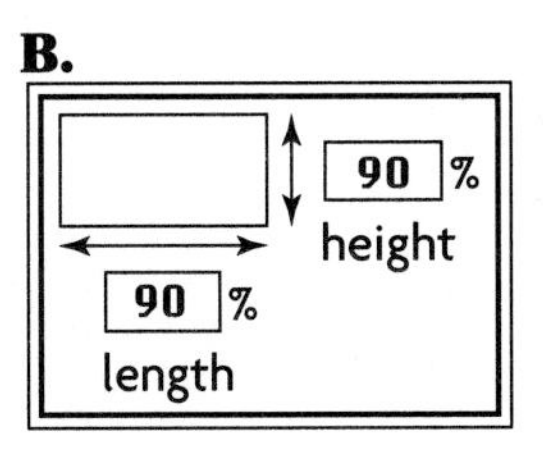

C.

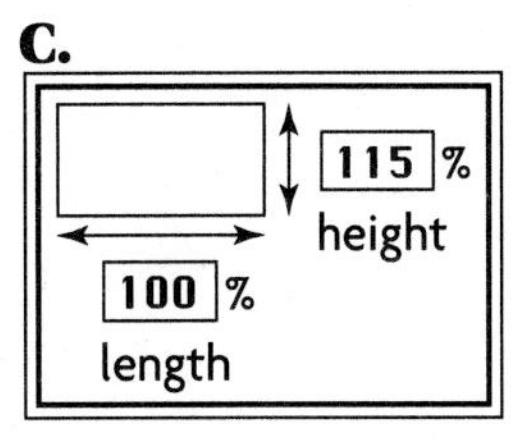

A. length: 1.25 × 4 in. = 5 in.
height: 1.25 × 3.5 in. = 4.375 in., or $4\frac{3}{8}$ in.

B. length: 0.9 × 4 in. = 3.6 in.
height: 0.9 × 3.5 in. = 3.15 in., or about $3\frac{1}{8}$ in.

C. length: 1.00 × 4 in. = 4 in.
height: 1.15 × 3.5 in. = 4.025 in., or about 4 in.

Scaling can be done not only with draw programs but also with copy machines. Many copy machines can scale each dimension of original documents from about 50% to 200%. Even greater scaling can be done by reducing or enlarging an already scaled copy of an original document.

EXAMPLE 3 A rectangle is 36 in. long and 24 in. wide. Its length is shrunk 25%, and its width is stretched 25%. Does the area increase, decrease, or stay the same? Does the perimeter increase, decrease, or stay the same?

36 in.

24 in.

New length: 75% of 36 in. = 0.75×36 in. = 27 in.

New width: 125% of 24 in. = 1.25×24 in. = 30 in.

Original Area	**New Area**
$A = lw$	$A = lw$
$A = 36 \times 24$	$A = 27 \text{ in.} \times 30 \text{ in.}$
$A = 864$	$A = 810$
Original area is 864 in.^{2}	New area is 810 in.^{2}
So, the area decreases.	

Original Perimeter	**New Perimeter**
$P = 2(l + w)$	$P = 2(l + w)$
$P = 2(36 + 24)$	$P = 2(27 + 30)$
$P = 2(60) = 120$	$P = 2(57) = 114$
The perimeter is 120 in.	New perimeter is 114 in.
So, the perimeter decreases.	

- **CRITICAL THINKING** Suppose the initial dimensions are 35 in. and 25 in. With the same scaling, does the area change or remain the same? Explain.

GUIDED PRACTICE

In Exercises 1–3, compare the drawing with the original, shown at the right. Estimate the percent of scaling for the length and height. Use a ruler if necessary.

1.

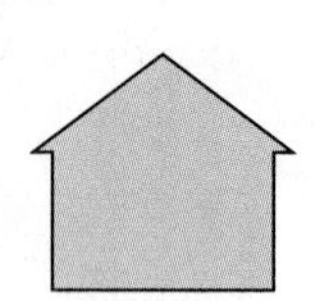

2.

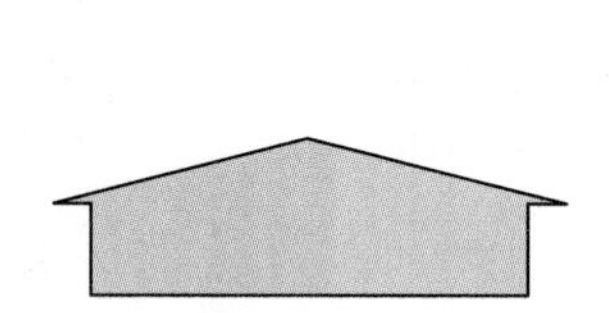

3.

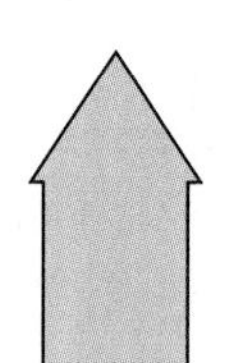

original

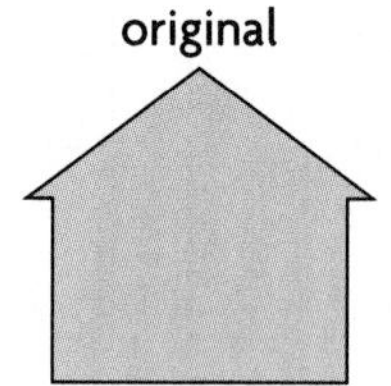

For Exercises 4–5, use the given scale selections. The scale is 80% for the length and 120% for the width.

4. Describe what these scale selections do to the length and width of a drawing.

5. Draw the new figure that results when you use these scale selections to change a square with a side of 2.5 in.

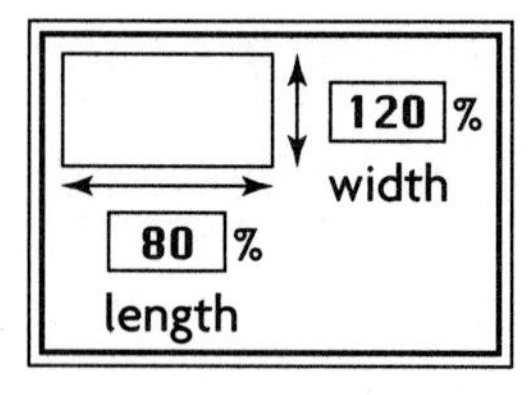

INDEPENDENT PRACTICE

For Exercises 1–4, use the given scale selections to find the new length and width of each rectangle. Round to the nearest half inch.

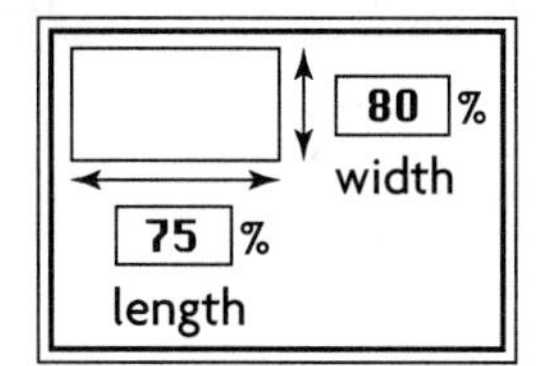

1. original length: 8 in.
original width: 12 in.

2. original length: 52 in.
original width: 20 in.

3. original length: 28 in.
original width: 35 in.

4. original length: 36 in.
original width: 30 in.

For Exercises 5–7, use the dimensions of the given rectangle and scale selections.

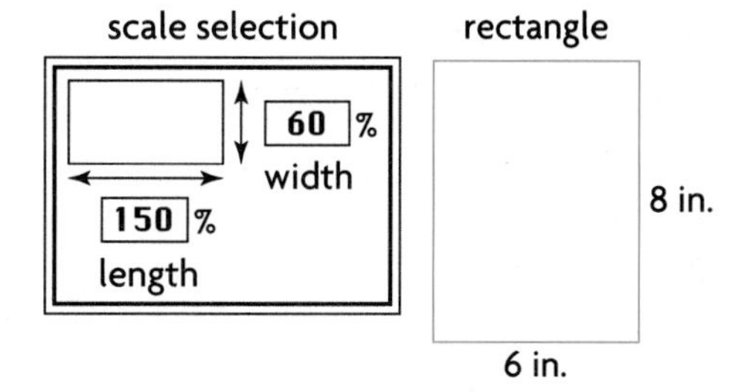

5. What are the new length and width?

6. Find the perimeter and area of the new rectangle.

7. Find the increase or decrease from the rectangle's original perimeter.

For Exercises 8–10, use the given scale selections.

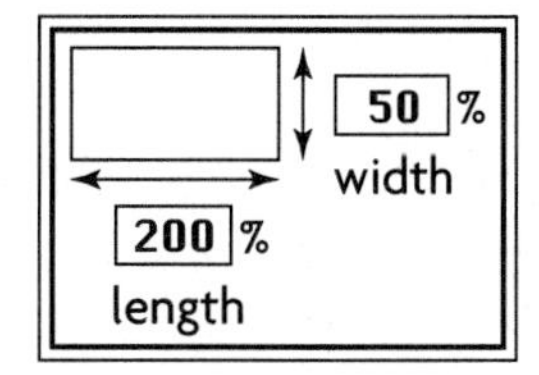

8. When these scale selections are applied to a rectangle 10 in. × 5 in., what happens to the area?

9. Give the length and width of another rectangle that shows this same area relationship.

10. Give the length and width of a rectangle that does not show this area relationship.

Problem-Solving Applications

11. **CRITICAL THINKING** A rectangle 5 in. long and 7 in. wide has its width scaled to 150%. What scale setting for the length will make the perimeter of the new rectangle the same as the perimeter of the original rectangle?

12. **PHOTOGRAPHY** A rectangular photograph is 3.5 in. long and 5 in. wide. The length is scaled to 40%. What scale selection for the width will make the area of the new photograph the same as the area of the original?

13. **WRITE ABOUT IT** For each change in a rectangle, write *area decreases, area remains the same*, or *area increases.* Give an example to support your choice.

a. Stretch the length.

b. Double the length and halve the width.

c. Shrink both the length and width.

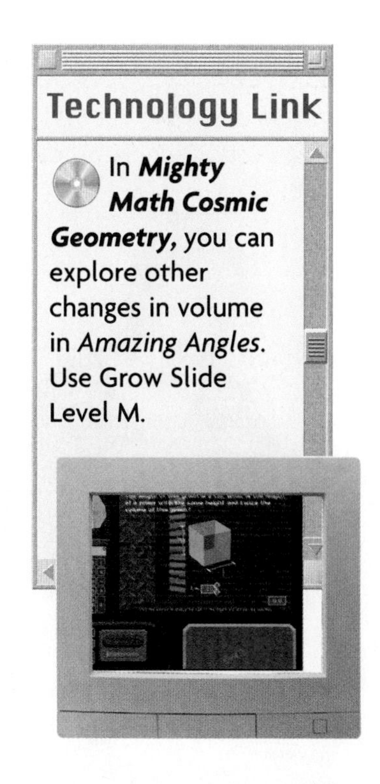

MORE PRACTICE Lesson 26.2, page H79

LESSON 26.3

PROBLEM-SOLVING STRATEGY

Making a Model: Volume and Surface Area

What You'll Learn
How to make models to compare volumes and surface areas

Why Learn This?
To compare the volumes and surface areas of storage containers

When you double the length, width, and height of a box, do you get a box that holds twice as much?

The size of a rectangular prism is determined by the dimensions of length, width, and height. When any of the three dimensions change, both the volume and the surface area can change.

The math class needs to make open storage boxes (boxes without lids) to store compasses and protractors. Compare the dimensions of Box A with those of Box B. How many of Box A will it take to hold the same amount as one of Box B?

Box	Length	Width	Height
A	11	11	10
B	22	22	20

- Understand
- Plan
- Solve
- Look Back

UNDERSTAND What are you asked to find?

PLAN What strategy will you use?

You can make models to solve the problem.

SOLVE How can you make a model of each box?

You can use graph paper to model each box. Cut out rectangles like those shown.

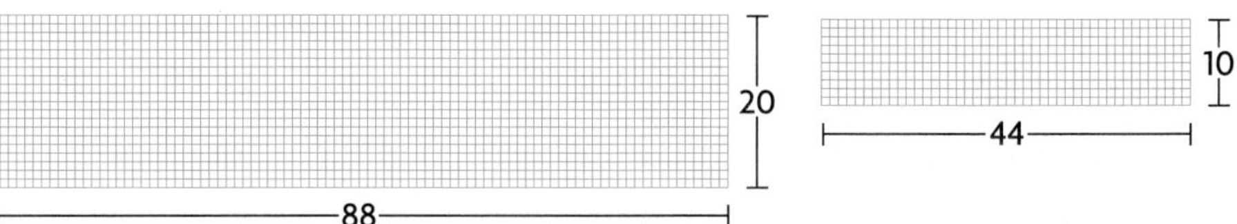

Fold the length of each rectangle into quarters, and make a model of a square prism as shown below.

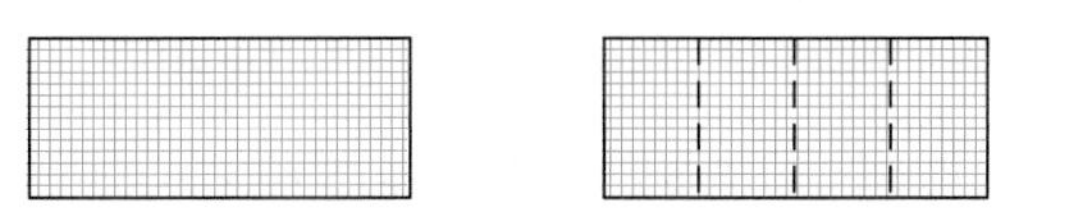

When you make and compare the two models, you can see that eight of the Box A models fit inside the Box B model. The volume of Box B is 8 times the volume of Box A.

LOOK BACK What other strategy could you use to compare the volumes of the boxes?

What if . . . the height of Box B is the same as the height of Box A? How many of Box A would it take to hold the same amount as Box B?

EXAMPLE The class knows that they will need eight Box A's to hold the same amount as one Box B. Which will use less cardboard to make?

The amount of cardboard used is the surface area of the box. You can use graph paper to make nets of Box A and Box B and then compare the surface areas. You could count the number of graph paper squares or use formulas to find the surface areas. On the nets below, measures are shown in inches.

Box B

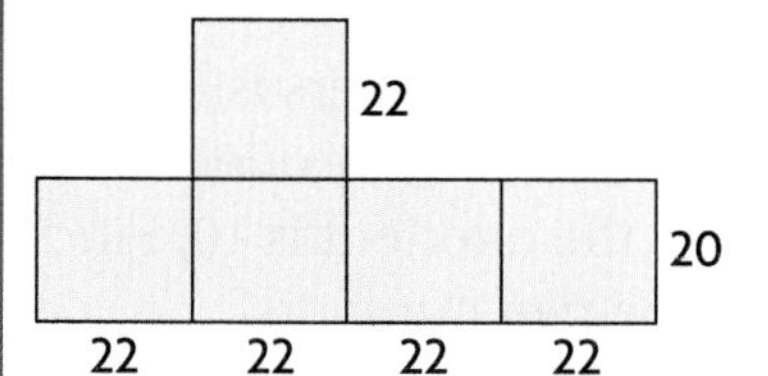

Box A

11
10
11 11 11 11

Surface Areas
Box B: 2,244 in.^{2}
Box A: 561 in.^{2}
8 Box A's:
8×561 in.$^2 = 4{,}488$ in.^{2}
So, it takes less cardboard to make one Box B.

PRACTICE

Make models to solve.

1. A baker uses rectangular boxes for cookies. The box she uses now has a length of 10 in., a width of 6 in., and a height of 4 in. She wants to change to a box that has the same height, but a width of 8 in. and a length of 8 in. Which box will hold the greater volume of cookies?

2. Charlie's Crunches come in a cylindrical can with diameter 4 in. and height 10 in. Charlie suggests a new container with diameter 6 in. and height 8 in. If the cost of making the containers is $1\frac{1}{4}$ cents per square inch, how much more will it cost the company to make the new container?

The **surface area** of an open box is the area of the bottom of the box plus the areas of all four sides. **See page 486.**

SCIENCE LINK

Do you know why organisms are made up of tiny cells, not big ones? Food and oxygen enter a cell through its surface, and waste products leave the same way. The larger a cell is, the more surface area it needs. But, larger cells have less surface area per unit of volume. Example: A 1-mm cube-shaped cell has a surface area of 6 mm^2 and a volume of 1 mm^3. Its surface-to-volume ratio is 6 : 1. What is the ratio of a 2-mm cube?

MIXED APPLICATIONS

Solve.

CHOOSE a strategy and a tool.

- Make a Model
- Use a Formula
- Draw a Diagram
- Make a Table
- Write an Equation
- Guess and Check

Paper/Pencil

Calculator

Hands-On

Mental Math

1. A new basketball usually comes in a rectangular box 12 in. wide, 12 in. long, and 12 in. tall. How many of these boxes can fit in a box that is 4 ft wide, 5 ft long, and 4 ft tall?

2. In the town of Centerville, there are 275 mi of roadway. All of the roads are 50 ft wide. How many square feet of land do the roads cover in Centerville? HINT: 1 mi = 5,280 ft.

3. Harry's Horn Company requires that at least 90% of the horns produce a honk on the first try. If 450 horns are randomly tested and 413 of them honk, has the company met its requirement? Explain.

4. Turner wants to save $120 in 5 months so he can buy a bike. After 2 months, he has saved $45. At this rate, will Turner be able to reach his goal? How far above or below his goal will he be?

5. A machine can fill 2,000 12-oz cans of soda per hour. If the machine runs 8 hr a day, 365 days a year, how many gallons of soda will it use in a year? HINT: 1 gal = 128 oz.

6. The difference of two numbers is 45. When the larger number is divided by the smaller number, the quotient is 10. Find the product of the two numbers.

7. Jake, Joan, John, and Jill ate a whole bowl of Jell-O™ at school today. Jake had $\frac{1}{3}$ of the Jell-O™ in the bowl, Joan had $\frac{1}{4}$, and John had $\frac{1}{6}$. How much of the Jell-O™ did Jill have?

8. **WRITE ABOUT IT** Write a problem for which you can use one of the problem-solving strategies listed above. Share your problem with the class.

Mixed Review and Test Prep

Solve the proportion.

9. $\frac{1}{3} = \frac{5}{d}$ **10.** $\frac{2}{5} = \frac{16}{d}$ **11.** $\frac{3}{4} = \frac{d}{20}$ **12.** $\frac{12}{d} = \frac{7}{14}$

Find the volume of a cylinder with the given dimensions.

13. radius: 12 in.
height: 10 in.

14. radius: 21.2 ft
height: 4 ft

15. diameter: 12 in.
height: 17 in.

16. diameter: 5.5 m
height: 13 m

17. **SCALE DRAWINGS** You are making a scale drawing of a blue whale that is 108 feet long. Using the scale 1 inch : 10 feet, how long is your drawing?

A 9.25 in. **B** 10 in.
C 10.8 in. **D** 11 in.

18. **MEASUREMENT** Dad's recipe for banana nut bread makes 6 loaves. It requires $10\frac{1}{3}$ cups of flour. How much flour is needed for 3 loaves?

F $20\frac{2}{3}$ c **G** $5\frac{1}{3}$ c **H** $5\frac{1}{6}$ c **J** $3\frac{4}{9}$ c

MORE PRACTICE Lesson 26.3, page H79

ALGEBRA CONNECTION

Volumes of Changing Cylinders

LESSON 26.4

What You'll Learn
How changing the dimensions of cylinders affects the volume

Why Learn This?
To compare volumes of cylinders

How does the volume of a popcorn tub change when the radius is reduced?

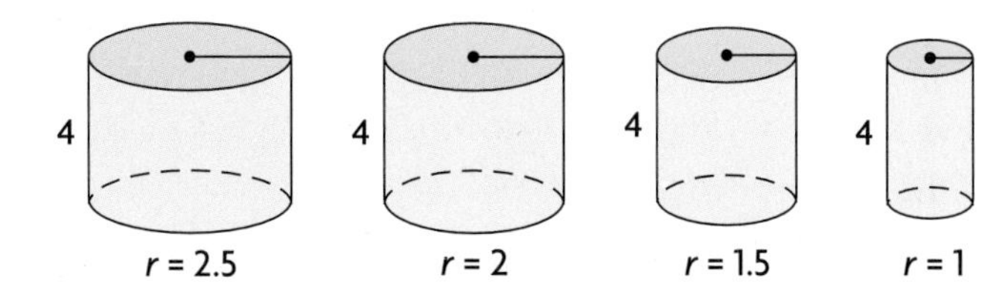

You can make a table and graph to show how the volume of the cylinder changes as the radius is reduced.

Radius (in cm)	2.5	2	1.5	1
Height (in cm)	4	4	4	4
Volume (in cm^3)	78.50	50.24	28.26	12.56

Both the table and the graph show that when the height stays the same and the radius is reduced, the volume of a cylinder decreases.

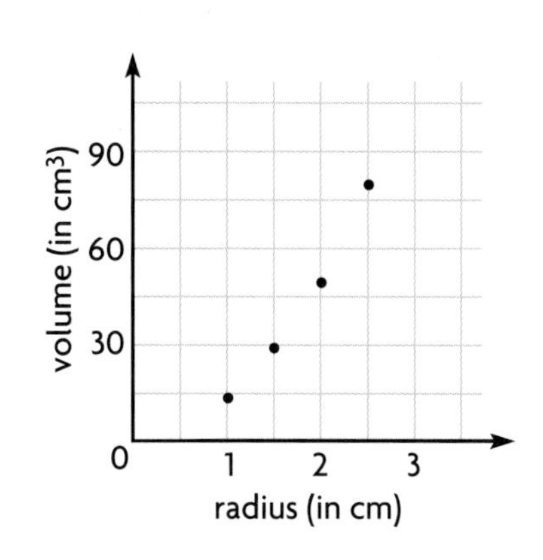

When you use a scale factor to change both the radius and the height of a cylinder, the volume also changes.

Talk About It

- What if you make a model of a cylinder, using a scale factor of $\frac{2}{3}$? Will the model be smaller than, the same size as, or larger than the original cylinder?
- What if you make a model of a cylinder, using a scale factor of $1\frac{2}{3}$? Will the model be smaller than, the same size as, or larger than the original cylinder?
- What conclusion can you draw about the scale factor if you want to make a model that is larger than the original object?

CONSUMER LINK

Many farmers store silage—winter animal feed—in large, cylindrical structures called silos. If a farmer has a silo 12 ft in diameter and about 30 ft high, the silo holds almost 3,400 ft^3 of silage. Suppose this silo is damaged in a storm and must be replaced, but a new county zoning law restricts silos to heights of 22 ft or less. What diameter must the new silo have in order to hold about as much silage as the old silo?

EXAMPLE A model of a cylinder was made with a scale factor for diameter and height of $\frac{2}{3}$. The model has a diameter of 5 in. and a height of 4 in. Find the radius and height of the original cylinder. Find the volumes of both cylinders.

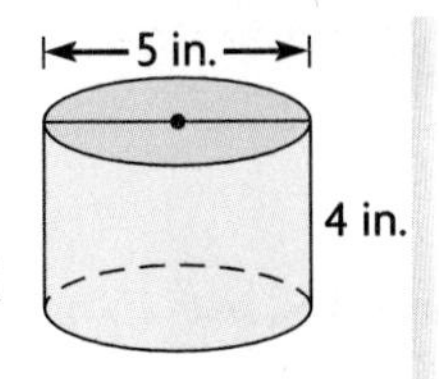

Use proportions to find the dimensions of the original cylinder.

Diameter

$$\frac{2}{3} = \frac{5}{d}$$
$$2 \times d = 5 \times 3$$
$$2d = 15$$
$$d = 7\frac{1}{2}$$

Height

$$\frac{2}{3} = \frac{4}{h}$$
$$2 \times h = 4 \times 3$$
$$2h = 12$$
$$h = 6$$

So, the original cylinder has a radius of $7\frac{1}{2}$ in. $\div$ 2, or $3\frac{3}{4}$ in., and a height of 6 in.

Volume of Model

$$V = \pi r^2 h$$
$$= 3.14 \times (2.5)^2 \times 4$$
$$= 3.14 \times 6.25 \times 4$$
$$= 78.5$$

Volume of Original

$$V = \pi r^2 h$$
$$= 3.14 \times (3.75)^2 \times 6$$
$$= 3.14 \times 14.0625 \times 6$$
$$= 264.9375$$
$$\approx 265$$

So, the volume of the model is 78.5 in.^{3}, and the volume of the original cylinder is about 265 in.^{3}

You can find the volume of a cylinder by using the formula $V = \pi r^2 h$, where r is the radius and h is the height. **See page 497.**

GUIDED PRACTICE

1. Compare the volume of the model with the volume of the original cylinder in a ratio. Use a calculator to find a decimal value for the ratio.
2. Find the cube of the scale factor, $\frac{2}{3}$. Use a calculator to write the scale factor as a decimal value.
3. What conclusion can you make about the relationship between the scale factor used to change the radius and height of the cylinder, and the ratio of the volumes?

INDEPENDENT PRACTICE

For Exercises 1–9, use the model of a cylinder shown here.

For Exercises 1–6, the given scale factor for diameter and height was used to create the model. Find the radius, height, and volume of the original cylinder. HINT: To find the radius, use the equation, scale factor $\times$ original radius = model radius.

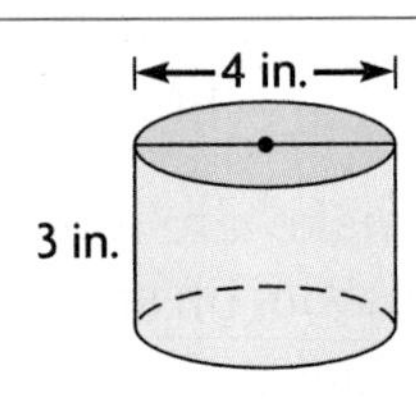

1. $\frac{1}{2}$
2. $\frac{2}{3}$
3. $\frac{1}{4}$
4. $\frac{1}{5}$
5. $\frac{4}{3}$
6. $\frac{5}{3}$

7. In which exercises did the scale factor decrease the volume of the original cylinder?

8. In which exercises did the scale factor increase the volume of the original cylinder?

9. Use a calculator to compare the volume of the model with the volume of the original cylinder in Exercise 6. How does the ratio compare with the scale factor?

Using the cylinders below, copy and complete the table. Round volumes to the nearest cubic foot.

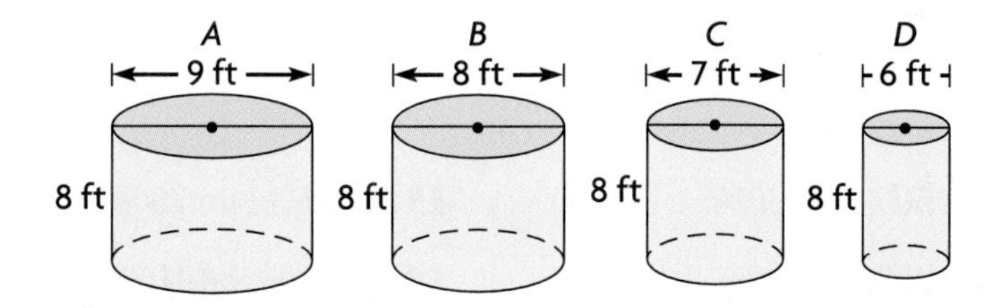

		Cylinder *A*	Cylinder *B*	Cylinder *C*	Cylinder *D*
10.	Radius (in ft)	?	?	?	?
11.	Height (in ft)	?	?	?	?
12.	Volume (in ft^3)	?	?	?	?

13. For all of the cylinders above, sketch a graph relating the radius and the volume.

14. Based on your graphs and your table, what are your conclusions?

Problem-Solving Applications

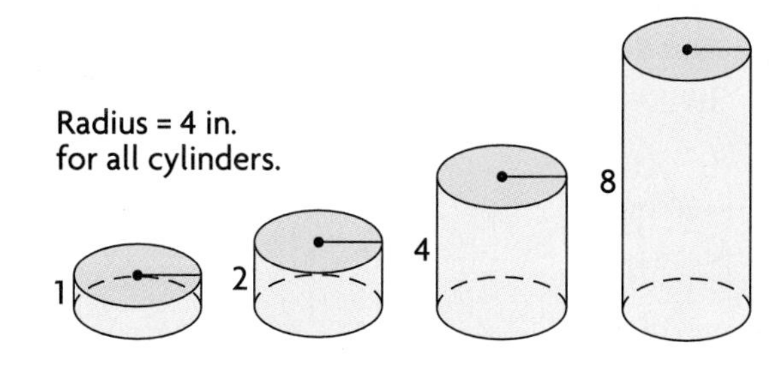

Heights are in inches.

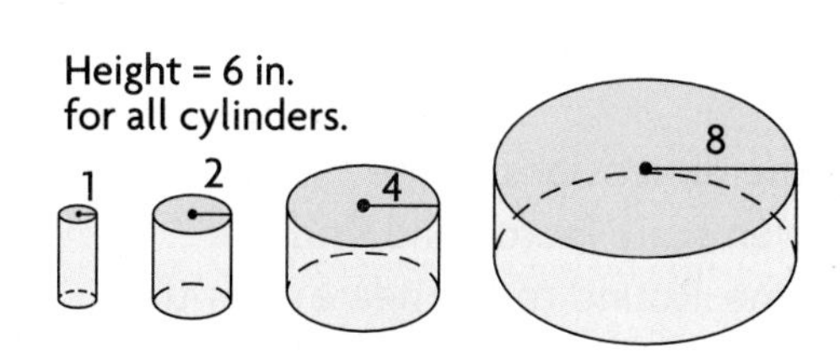

Radii are in inches.

15. **PATTERNS** Compute the volume of each cylinder. Sketch a graph to relate the heights and volumes, using the coordinates (h,V). What are your conclusions?

16. **PATTERNS** Compute the volume of each cylinder. Sketch a graph to relate the radii and volumes, using the coordinates (r,V). What are your conclusions?

17. **WRITE ABOUT IT** Explain how changing one dimension of a cylinder while keeping the other dimension the same affects its volume.

MORE PRACTICE Lesson 26.4, page H79

CHAPTER 26 Review/Test

Find the dimensions of a rectangle with the greatest possible area for the perimeter given. (pages 505–507)

1. 36 in. **2.** 26 ft **3.** 12 mi **4.** 120 km

5. 62 m **6.** 1,200 cm **7.** 20 ft **8.** 40 mm

A rectangle is 20 in. long and 12 in. wide. Determine whether the perimeter and area increase or decrease as a result of the given scale changes. (pages 508–511)

9. l: 60%, w: 150% **10.** l: 150%, w: 60% **11.** l: 75%, w: 75%

12. l: 110%, w: 110% **13.** l: 125%, w: 70% **14.** l: 98%, w: 103%

15. l: 130%, w: 50% **16.** l: 70%, w: 110% **17.** l: 150%, w: 150%

18. Complete. Scaling above 100% __?__ the dimension. (pages 508–511)

19. Complete. Scaling below 100% __?__ the dimension. (pages 508–511)

For Exercises 20–23, make a model to solve.

20. How many 0.5-in. sugar cubes will fit in a box 4 in. × 3 in. × 2 in.? (pages 512–514)

21. How many 2-in. cubes will fit in a box 6 in. × 8 in. × 10 in.? (pages 512–514)

22. A rectangular prism is 8 m wide × 4 m long × 6 m high. If you double the length and height, how many times as large will the surface area be? the volume? (pages 512–514)

23. A rectangular prism is 8 ft long × 8 ft wide × 10 ft high. If you double the length and width, how many times as large will the surface area be? the volume? (pages 512–514)

Change the dimensions of the cylinder by the given scale factor, and find the new volume. Round to the nearest tenth. (pages 515–517)

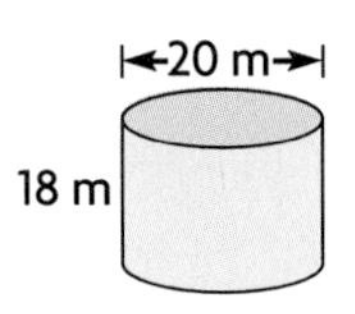

24. 50% **25.** 75% **26.** 125% **27.** 200%

28. 60% **29.** 120% **30.** 25% **31.** 500%

32. Use the cylinder above to sketch a graph relating the heights and volumes of the cylinders when the radius is changed to 9 m and 11 m. (pages 515–517)

33. A cylinder has a height of 5 cm and a radius of 4 cm. Make a table to show how decreasing the radius by 1, 2, 3, and 4 cm affects the volume. (pages 515–517)

Test Prep

CUMULATIVE CHAPTERS 1–26

1. A rectangle has a perimeter of 52 meters. What is its greatest possible area?

A 144 m^2
B 168 m^2
C 169 m^2
D 196 m^2

2. What is the surface area of a cube with sides of length 7.2 feet?

F 373.248 ft^2
G 311.04 ft^2
H 172.8 ft^2
J 51.84 ft^2
K Not Here

3. A moving truck traveled 832 miles in 16 hours. What was the truck's average rate of speed?

A 42 mph
B 48 mph
C 52 mph
D 56 mph

4. Fredo has guitar lessons every 7 days. His last lesson was on September 29. On which of the following dates did he have a lesson?

F September 5
G September 9
H September 15
J September 21

5. When the ratio of length to width of a rectangle is about 1.61, the rectangle is a Golden Rectangle. Which are dimensions of a Golden Rectangle?

A length = 29 ft, width = 16 ft
B length = 35 ft, width = 20 ft
C length = 8 ft, width = 5 ft
D length = 41 ft, width = 36 ft

6. The radius of a cylinder is 4 cm and its height is 10 cm. If the radius and height are decreased by 50%, what is the new volume?

F about 1,256 cm^3
G about 502.4 cm^3
H about 157 cm^3
J about 62.8 cm^3

7. Which is the mode of the data?

75, 80, 84, 91, 88, 79, 84, 93

A 18 **B** 84 **C** 84.5 **D** 86

8. What is the area of the triangle shown below?

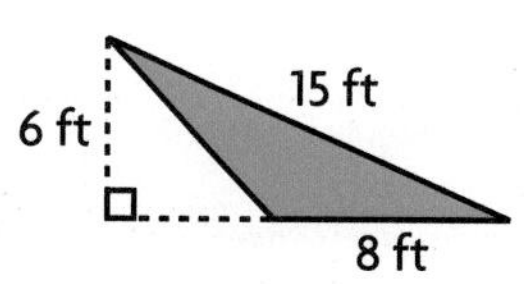

F 60 ft^2 **G** 48 ft^2 **H** 45 ft^2 **J** 24 ft^2

9. Use the tally table below.

Which choice was the least popular?

A broccoli
B carrots
C beans
D squash

Favorite Vegetable	Number
Broccoli	||||
Carrots	~~||||~~ |
Beans	~~||||~~ ~~||||~~
Squash	~~||||~~ |||

10. Jasmine ate $\frac{1}{2}$ bag of jelly beans. She gave $\frac{2}{3}$ of the remaining jelly beans to her friend Omar. Which expression represents the amount Omar received?

F $\frac{1}{2} \times \frac{2}{3}$ **G** $\frac{1}{2} \div \frac{2}{3}$

H $\frac{1}{2} + \frac{2}{3}$ **J** $\frac{1}{2} - \frac{2}{3}$

MATH FUN!

Nesting Prisms

PURPOSE To compare surface areas of prisms (pages 486–489)
YOU WILL NEED old newspaper, tape, and a ruler

Start with two rectangles, each measuring 12 in. × 8 in.

- Fold one of the rectangles into quarters along the 12-in. side. Tape the edges together to make an open-ended square prism.
- Cut the other rectangle into halves. Using one of the halves, make an open-ended square prism that will fit inside your first prism.
- Cut the other half into halves, and repeat the process.
- Continue the process of cutting the rectangle in half to make the next prism. How many prisms can you make?

Smashing Cans

PURPOSE To compare volumes of cylinders (pages 515–517)
YOU WILL NEED a few empty aluminum soda cans, a mm ruler

- Measure the height and diameter of a soda can, and use these measurements to find the volume.
- Smash the can to form a shorter cylinder.
- Measure the height, and find the new volume.
- Compare the two volumes. How much space can you save in a storage bin by smashing each can you save?

Challenge your family to see who can collect and smash the most cans to fill a grocery bag.

Pattern Block Area

PURPOSE To practice finding area (pages 476–481)
YOU WILL NEED pattern block triangles

- Suppose the area of the triangle is 3 square units. What is the area of the trapezoid? Use the pattern block triangles to make a triangle with an area of 75 square units and a trapezoid with an area of 48 square units.
- Make up your own figures with the triangles. Find the area and then challenge a classmate to make the figures.

Investigating Changing Areas

In this activity you will see how to investigate the changing area of a rectangle by using a drawing program.

Draw rectangle *ABCD* with length 1.5 in. and width 0.75 in.

AB = 1.5 inches BC = 0.75 inches

Use the Construct menu to construct the interior of the rectangle.

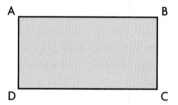

AB = 1.5 inches BC = 0.75 inches

Use the Measure menu to measure the perimeter and area of the rectangle.

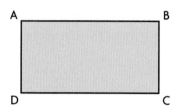

AB = 1.5 inches BC = 0.75 inches

Perimeter ABCD = 4.5 inches

Area ABCD = 1.125 square inches

Use your cursor to drag a vertex of the rectangle so it has length 3 in. and width 1.5 in.

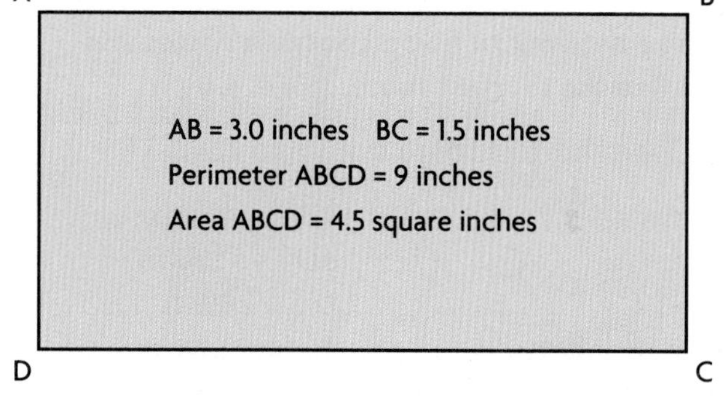

1. How does the perimeter of the larger rectangle compare to the perimeter of the original rectangle?

2. How does the area of the larger rectangle compare to the area of the original rectangle?

3. How would you triple the length and width of the rectangle?

4. How would you measure the perimeter and area of the new rectangle?

USING THE DRAWING TOOL

5. Draw a rectangle with a length of 4 in. and a width of 3 in. Measure the perimeter and area. Triple the dimensions and measure the perimeter and area. Compare the original perimeter and area to the new perimeter and area. What are your findings?

CHAPTERS 24–26

Study Guide and Review

Vocabulary Check

1. The GPE, or __?__, of any measurement is half of the unit used in the measurement. (page 466)

2. A graph with vertices and edges is a(n) __?__. (page 470)

3. The sum of the areas of all the surfaces of a solid is the __?__. (page 486)

EXAMPLES

- **Determine the precision and greatest possible error of a measurement, and estimate length.** (pages 466–469)

Tell what the least and greatest lengths measured as 3.5 m may be.

$0.1 \text{ m} \times 0.5 = 0.05 \text{ m}$ ← GPE for unit 0.1 m

$3.5 \text{ m} - 0.05 \text{ m} = 3.45 \text{ m}$ *least length*

$3.5 \text{ m} + 0.05 \text{ m} = 3.55 \text{ m}$ *greatest length*

EXERCISES

For the given measurement, tell the least and greatest lengths the actual length may be.

4. $10\frac{1}{2}$ in.

5. 21.3 km

6. 24 ft

7. 100.8 m

8. $7\frac{1}{3}$ cm

9. $6\frac{1}{4}$ mm

- **Use a network to find all possible routes and to find the shortest route.** (pages 470–471)

Find the shortest route from *A* to *C*.

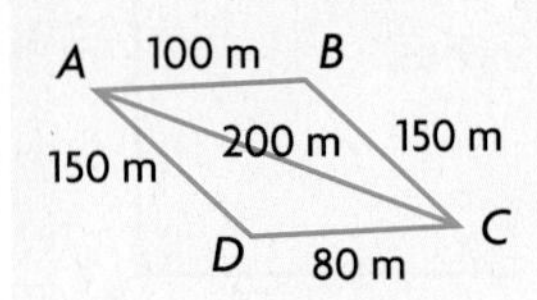

$ABC \rightarrow 250$ m
$ADC \rightarrow 230$ m
$AC \rightarrow 200$ m
AC is shortest.

Determine the distances for the route.

10. *ABD*

11. *ABCD*

12. *AED*

13. *AD*

14. Which route from *A* to *D* is shortest?

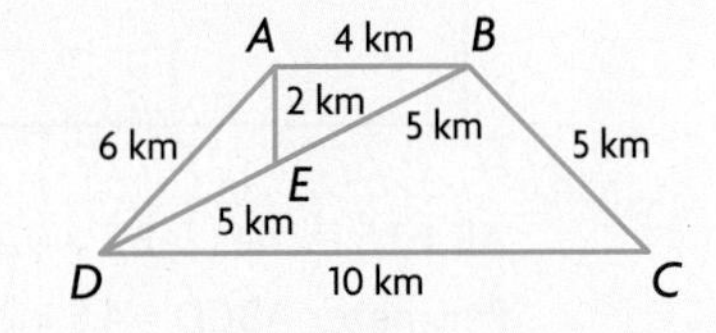

- **Use the Pythagorean Property to find the length of the hypotenuse.** (pages 474–475)

Find the length of the hypotenuse.

$8^2 + 15^2 = c^2$ ← $a^2 + b^2 = c^2$

$64 + 225 = c^2$

$\sqrt{289} = c$

$17 = c$

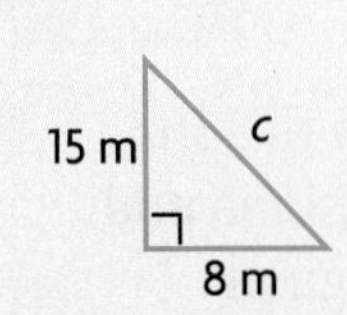

The length is 17 m.

Let *a* and *b* represent the legs of a right triangle and *c* represent the hypotenuse. Find the length of the hypotenuse.

15. $a = 6$ ft $\quad b = 8$ ft $\quad c = ?$

16. $a = 9$ mm $\quad b = 12$ mm $\quad c = ?$

17. $a = 30$ in. $\quad b = 40$ in. $\quad c = ?$

18. $a = 5$ m $\quad b = 12$ m $\quad c = ?$

19. $a = 16$ yd $\quad b = 30$ yd $\quad c = ?$

- **Find the volumes of cylinders and cones.** (pages 497–499)

Find the volume. Use $\pi = 3.14$.

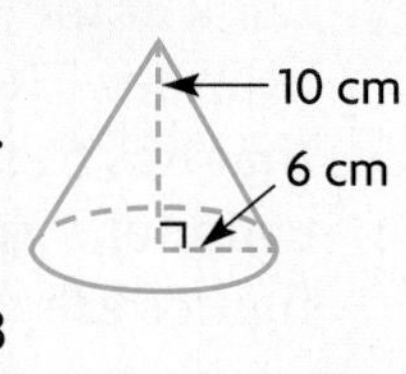

cone: $V = \frac{1}{3}Bh \quad \leftarrow \quad B = \pi r^2$

$V \approx \frac{1}{3} \times 3.14 \times 6^2 \times 10 \approx 376.8$

The volume is about 377 cm^3.

Find the volume. Use $\pi = 3.14$, and round to the nearest whole number.

20.

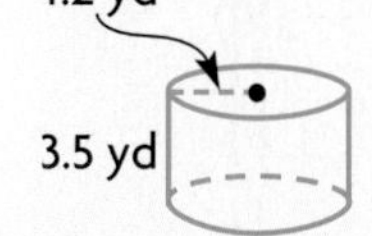

21.

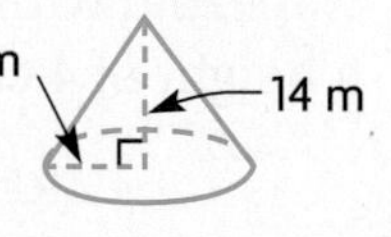

- **Use scaling to change figures.** (pages 508–511)

A rectangle 20 ft long and 15 ft wide is changed by the scale selection below. Find the new dimensions.

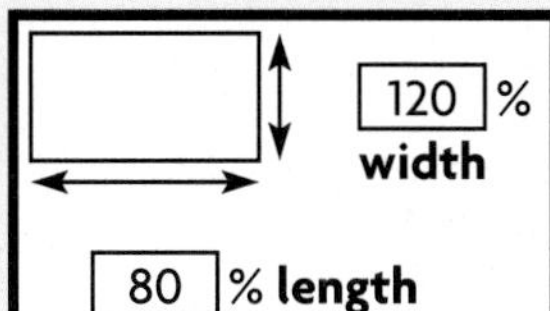

new length:
$20 \times 0.80 = 16$ ft
new width:
$15 \times 1.20 = 18$ ft

A rectangle is 40 in. long and 10 in. wide. Determine whether the perimeter and area increase or decrease as a result of the given scale changes.

22. L: 120%, W: 90% **23.** L: 75%, W: 160% **24.** L: 150%, W: 60%

- **Determine how changing the dimensions of cylinders affects the volume.** (pages 515–517)

A cylinder has a height of 12 m and a radius of 3 m. Show how decreasing the radius by 1 m affects the volume. $V = \pi r^2 h$

original: $(3.14) \bullet 9 \bullet 12 = 339.12$ m^3
new: $(3.14) \bullet 4 \bullet 12 = 150.72$ m^3
The volume decreases.

Change the dimensions of the cylinder by the given scale factor, and find the new volume. Round to the nearest tenth.

25. 30% **26.** 80%
27. 150% **28.** 200%
29. 50% **30.** 250%

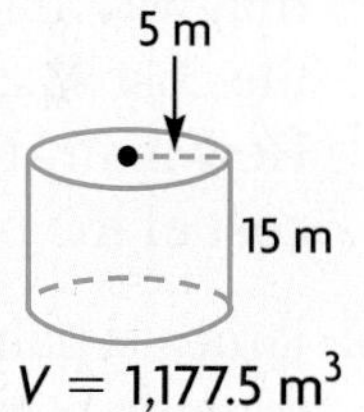

$V = 1{,}177.5$ m^3

Problem-Solving Applications

Solve. Explain your method.

31. Joseph is making a pennant in the shape of a triangle. The base is 30 cm and the height is 50 cm. What is the area? (pages 476–478)

32. A rectangle has a fixed perimeter of 60 ft. What dimensions will give the rectangle the greatest possible area? (pages 505–507)

33. How do the volume and surface area change when the dimensions of a rectangular prism are doubled? (pages 512–514)

34. A model of a cylinder was made with a scale factor for diameter and height of $\frac{2}{3}$. The model has a radius of 6 m and a height of 8 m. Find the volume of the original cylinder. (pages 515–517)

CHAPTERS 24–26

Performance Assessment

Tasks: Show What You Know

1. Explain each step as you find the area of a trapezoid with bases of 8 cm and 6 cm and a height of 4 cm. (pages 479–481)

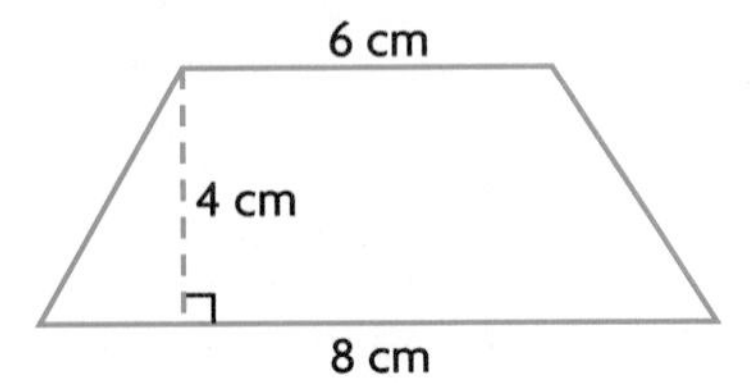

2. Look at the figure. Find the volume of the cylinder. Then find the volume of a cone that has the same base and height as the cylinder. Explain how the volumes of these figures are related. (pages 497–499)

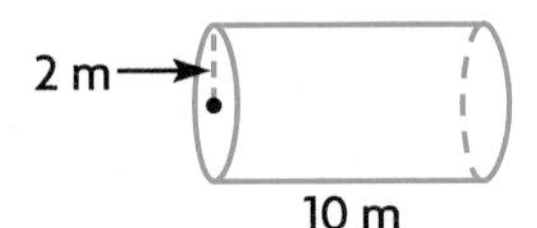

3. Find the greatest possible area for a rectangle with a perimeter of 16 ft. Explain your thinking. (pages 505–507)

Problem Solving

Solve. Explain your method.

CHOOSE a strategy and a tool.

- Find a Pattern
- Make a Model
- Act it Out
- Make a Table
- Write an Equation
- Use a Formula

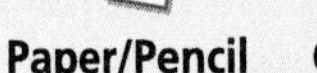
Paper/Pencil

Calculator

Hands-On
Mental Math

4. Lucas built a rectangular patio 12 ft × 7.5 ft that was made of 18-in. square tiles. Each tile cost $2.25. What is the area of the patio? How many tiles were used? What was the cost of the patio? (pages 476–478)

5. James is painting his bedroom walls. The room is 14 ft long, 12 ft wide, and 8 ft high. The door is 7 ft × 4 ft. Each of 2 windows is 4 ft × 3 ft. One gallon of paint covers 200 ft^2. How many gallons of paint does James need? Explain. (pages 486–489)

6. At a school football game, popcorn is sold in two sizes of boxes.
blue box 10 in. × 4 in. × 8 in.
green box 8 in. × 6 in. × 7 in.
Which box has the greater volume? Explain.
(pages 512–514)

Cumulative Review

CHAPTERS 1–26

Solve the problem. Then write the letter of the correct answer.

1. Which percent is equivalent to $\frac{1}{2}$? (pages 26–29)

   A. 0.5% B. 2%
   C. 12% D. 50%

2. What is 25,000,000 written in scientific notation? (pages 36–39)

   A. 2.5×0^6
   B. 2.5×10^6
   C. 2.5×10^7
   D. 2.5×10^8

3. $1\frac{2}{5} \times 5\frac{5}{7}$ (pages 88–91)

   A. $\frac{49}{200}$ B. $5\frac{2}{7}$
   C. 8 D. $8\frac{4}{7}$

4. $^-0.42 - 1.87$ (pages 109–111)

   A. $^-2.29$ B. $^-1.45$
   C. 1.45 D. 2.29

5. Solve the proportion. $\frac{x}{35.5} = \frac{3}{5}$ (pages 152–155)

   A. $x = 21.3$ B. $x = 33.5$
   C. $x = 59.17$ D. not here

6. Use the coordinate plane below. (pages 176–177)

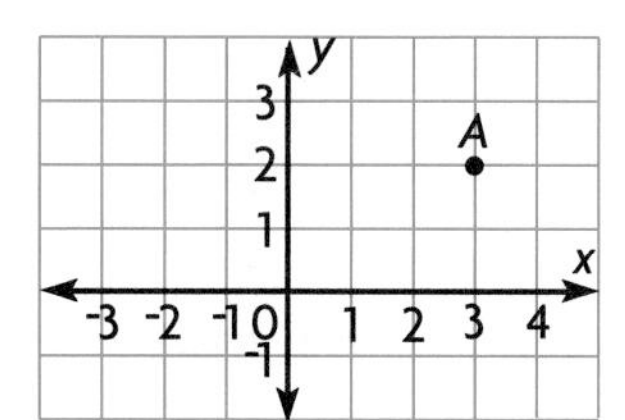

   What is the location of point A?

   A. (2,0) B. (2,3)
   C. (3,0) D. (3,2)

7. Use the figure below. What is the measure of $\angle A$? (pages 199–202)

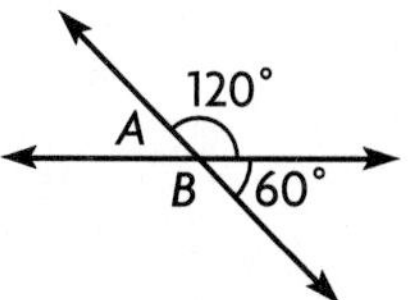

   A. 30° B. 60°
   C. 120° D. not here

8. Write the ratio 5:8 as a percent. (pages 294–296)

   A. 0.625% B. 40%
   C. 62.5% D. 160%

9. Write the expression 10^{-4} using a positive exponent. (pages 382–383)

   A. $\frac{1}{10^4}$ B. $\frac{14}{10}$
   C. 4^{10} D. 10^4

10. Every fifth person leaving the polls is asked who he or she voted for. Which sampling method is being used? (pages 394–396)

    A. biased B. random
    C. stratified D. systematic

11. What is the mode? 24, 60, 38, 70, 55, 38, 44. (pages 414–416)

    A. 38 B. 44
    C. 47 D. 55

12. Find the length of the hypotenuse. (pages 474–475)

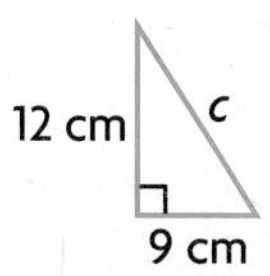

    A. 32 cm B. 15 cm
    C. 18 cm D. not here

CHAPTER

27 PERCENT: SPENDING AND SAVING

LOOK AHEAD

In this chapter you will solve problems that involve

- the three types of percent problems
- sales tax, discounts, and markups
- simple interest
- buying on credit

CONSUMER LINK

The bar graph below shows the annual sales for the top five retail stores in 1996.

- About how much more are the sales for Wal-Mart than the sales for Dayton Hudson?
- Write a sentence comparing the annual sales for Wal-Mart to the annual sales for the other four retail stores.

Problem-Solving Project

Spend $200

YOU WILL NEED: newspapers

Suppose you are given $200 to spend on books, hobbies, clothing, cassettes, CDs, videos, or computer software. Select 3 advertisements for each item you would like. Copy, draw, or cut out the ads. Attach them to a sheet of paper. Make a shopping list. Include the price and sales tax for each item. Write a report that compares prices from two or three stores. Tell which store has the best price for each item. Discuss whether the store with the lowest price is always the best choice.

BACKPACK
Yukon-tough backpack. Fashionable and affordable.
$19.95

CORDLESS PHONE
28 channels, 10-number memory. Handset volume control.
$49.00

BOOM BOX
CD player with AM/FM stereo and cassette. Remote included.
$109.99

MOUNTAIN BIKE
26-in. man's or woman's 18-speed bike for rough terrain.
$169.99

PROJECT CHECKLIST

- ✓ Did you select 3 ads for each item?
- ✓ Did you select items whose total cost is less than or equal to $200?
- ✓ Did you write a report?

LESSON 27.1

Percent and Sales Tax

What You'll Learn
How to find sales tax and total cost

Why Learn This?
To find the cost of your purchases, including sales tax, to know if you have enough money

VOCABULARY
sales tax

When you buy something at the store, why is the total amount you pay more than the price shown?

Most states raise money by charging a **sales tax** on purchases. For example, if the sales tax rate is 7%, you must pay the state $0.07 for every $1.00 that you spend.

Suppose you wanted to find the sales tax on a pair of shoes priced at $79.50 when the sales tax rate is 7%.

First, multiply by the sales tax rate. Write the percent as a decimal.

$$\begin{array}{rl} \$79.50 & \textit{Price} \\ \times\ 0.07 & \textit{7\% Sales tax rate} \\ \hline \$5.565 & \textit{Tax} \end{array}$$

Then, round the tax to the nearest cent and add the tax to the price.

$$\begin{array}{rl} \$79.50 & \textit{Price} \\ +\ 5.57 & \textit{Tax} \\ \hline \$85.07 & \textit{Total cost} \end{array}$$

ANOTHER METHOD There is another way to find the total cost. Think of the price as 100%. Add the 7% sales tax. The total cost is 107% of the price.

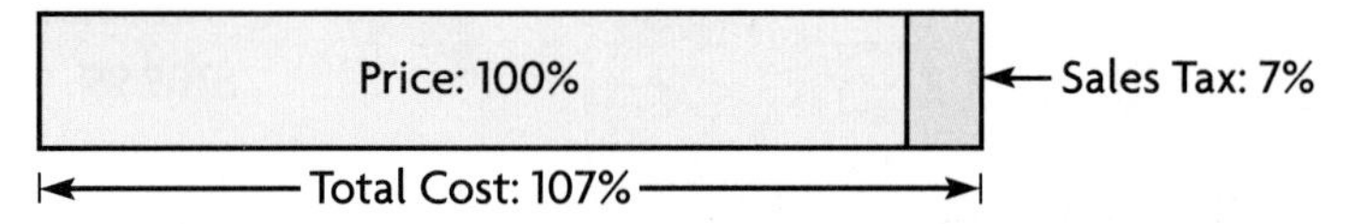

EXAMPLE 1 How can you find the total cost of the $79.50 shoes directly, using only one calculation?

$c = 107\% \times \$79.50$ *Write an equation. Let c represent the total cost. Multiply the price by 107%.*

$c = 1.07 \times \$79.50$

$c = \$85.065$, or $85.07 *Solve.*

The total cost is $85.07.

- Suppose the sales tax rate is $6\frac{1}{2}\%$, or 6.5%. Write an equation to find the cost directly. Then use the equation to find the total cost.
- What equation would you write to find the cost directly if the sales tax rate was 8.25%?

REMEMBER:

You can also find percent of a number by using a proportion. **See page 299.**

6% of 25 is what number?

$\frac{6}{100} = \frac{n}{25}$

$100n = 150$

$n = 1.5$

So, 6% of 25 equals 1.5.

GUIDED PRACTICE

Find the amount of sales tax. Round to the nearest cent.

1. 6% on $16.00 **2.** 8% on $24.95 **3.** $7\frac{1}{2}$% on $39.50

Find the total cost directly, using only one calculation.

4. 7% on $1.80 **5.** 4% on $11.99 **6.** $3\frac{1}{2}$% on $169.00

Solve.

7. The price of a pair of hiking boots is $65.00. The sales tax rate is 6%. What is the total price of the boots?

8. The price of a computer is $1,477.00. The sales tax rate is 5.5%. What is the total cost?

9. You have $3.15. You want to buy a sandwich for $2.09 and a soda for $0.89. The sales tax rate is 7%. Do you have enough money? Explain.

If you live in Alaska, Delaware, Montana, New Hampshire, Oregon, or Puerto Rico, you don't have to pay sales tax on anything that you buy!

You can find the price of an item if you know the total cost and the rate of sales tax.

EXAMPLE 2 Suppose you remember that you paid $29.82 for a backpack, but you don't have the sales receipt that shows the price. You know there is a $6\frac{1}{2}$% sales tax included in the total. How can you find the price of the backpack?

Since you multiplied to find the total cost, you can use the inverse, division, to find the price.

Divide the total cost by $106\frac{1}{2}$%, or 1.065.

Let p represent the price.

$p = \frac{\$29.82}{1.065}$ 29.82 ÷ 1.065 = 28.

$p = \$28.00$

The price of the backpack is $28.00.

- Find the price when the total cost is $15.75 and the sales tax rate is 5%.

You can also find the number when the percent is known by using a proportion. **See page 306.**

5% of what number is 3?

$\frac{5}{100} = \frac{3}{n}$

$5n = 300$

$n = 60$

So, 5% of 60 equals 3.

You can find the sales tax rate when you know the price and the amount of sales tax.

EXAMPLE 3 While on a family vacation to another state, you bought a sweatshirt priced at $24.00. The receipt shows the price, the amount of tax, and the total cost. What was the sales tax rate?

rate $= \frac{\$1.32}{\$24.00} \leftarrow \frac{\text{tax}}{\text{price}}$ *To find the sales tax rate, divide the tax by the price.*

rate $= 0.055 = 5.5\%$ *Write the rate as a percent.*

The sales tax rate was 5.5%.

- The price of another shirt you decide to buy is $17.40. The total cost is $19.14. Find the amount of sales tax and the sales tax rate.

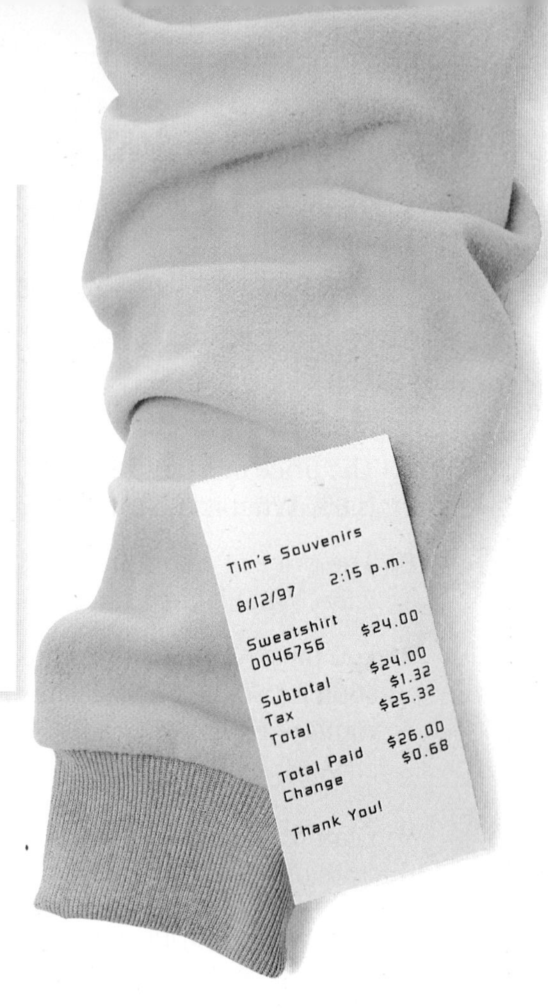

Tim's Souvenirs
8/12/97 2:15 p.m.
Sweatshirt $24.00
0046756
Subtotal $24.00
Tax $1.32
Total $25.32
Total Paid $26.00
Change $0.68
Thank You!

Talk About It CRITICAL THINKING

- If you know the sales tax rate and the price, how can you find the amount of sales tax?
- If you know the sales tax and the total cost, how can you find the price?
- If you know the price and the amount of sales tax, how can you find the sales tax rate?

INDEPENDENT PRACTICE

Find the sales tax and the total cost. Describe how you can do the computation mentally.

1. 7% on $30.00 **2.** 9% on $200.00 **3.** $6\frac{1}{2}$ % on $10.00 **4.** 8% on $25.00

Find the total cost directly. Round to the nearest cent when necessary.

5. 4% on $18.88 **6.** 9% on $33.75 **7.** $5\frac{1}{2}$ % on $49.95 **8.** 8.5% on $125.00

Find the price. Round to the nearest cent when necessary.

9. 5% sales tax
$12.18 total cost

10. 9% sales tax
$71.40 total cost

11. $6\frac{3}{4}$ % sales tax
$125.11 total cost

12. $4\frac{1}{2}$% sales tax
$104.50 total cost

Tell the number you would divide by to find the price directly from the total cost.

13. 9% sales tax **14.** 4% sales tax **15.** 10% sales tax **16.** $6\frac{3}{4}$% sales tax

Find the sales tax rate for the given price and amount of sales tax. Round to the nearest tenth of a percent.

17. price: $32.00
sales tax: $2.24

18. price: $125.99
sales tax: $10.71

19. price: $7.50
sales tax: $0.38

20. price: $72.00
sales tax: $4.32

Problem-Solving Applications

21. **CONSUMER MATH** The total cost of a soccer ball is $18.55. Find the price if the sales tax rate is 6%.

22. **BUSINESS** The price of a sports watch is $23.50. The total cost is $24.91. Find the amount of sales tax and the sales tax rate.

23. **CRITICAL THINKING** Merchandise is sold with a 6% sales tax rate. Is the sales tax 6% of the price or 6% of the total cost?

24. **CRITICAL THINKING** When the sales tax rate is 6%, is the total cost 106% of the price or is the price 106% of the total cost?

Many cities and counties charge an additional sales tax beyond the state sales tax. Suppose a customer pays a total of $260.40 for a TV. Of the $8\frac{1}{2}$ % sales tax charged, 5% goes to the state. The remainder goes to the city.

25. Find the price of the TV.

26. How much is the sales tax?

27. How much is the state sales tax?

28. How much does the city receive on the sale?

29. **WRITE ABOUT IT** Explain how to find the total cost of an item if you know the price and the sales tax rate.

Mixed Review and Test Prep

Write as a decimal.

30. 35%

31. 7%

32. 8.5%

33. $\frac{1}{2}$

34. $\frac{2}{5}$

35. $1\frac{1}{8}$

Use a proportion to find the unit price.

36. 4 pencils for $0.96

37. 12 brownies for $5.76

38. 3 hot dogs for $2.91

39. 8 magazines for $16.32

40. **PERCENT** Amy is a manager of a clothing store in a mall. She spends $\frac{1}{4}$ of her time with customers and $\frac{1}{2}$ of her time with employees. What percent of her time is left?

A 20% **B** 25% **C** 40% **D** 50%

41. **LOGICAL REASONING** If 2 days before yesterday was Friday, what is 2 days after tomorrow?

F Monday **G** Sunday **H** Tuesday **J** Thursday

CONSUMER LINK

Sales tax rates vary in the United States. In Houston, TX, the rate is 8.25%. What is the difference between Houston's sales tax rate and the rate where you live?

MORE PRACTICE Lesson 27.1, page H80

LESSON 27.2 Percent and Discount

What You'll Learn
How to find discount and sale price

Why Learn This?
To figure out how much you will save or pay if a sign says 20% off the ticketed price

VOCABULARY
discount
sale price

Have you ever waited for a sale to buy something you really wanted?

30%

You wait for a sale because the price is reduced. The amount the price is reduced, or marked down, is the **discount**.

With a 30% discount, you save \$0.30 on a dollar.

What is the discount on the Civilization video game?

$30\% \times \$40.00$ *Write 30% as a decimal.*

$0.30 \times \$40.00 = \$12.00$ *Multiply to find the discount.*

The discount on the game is \$12.00.

- What if the video game was marked $\frac{1}{4}$ off? What would the discount be?

When the price is reduced by the discount, the new price is the **sale price**. You can find the sale price directly by using a percent.

EXAMPLE 1 The discount on a jacket is 25%. The regular price is \$58.00. What percent is the sale price? Use the percent to find the sale price directly.

$100\% - 25\% = 75\%$ *Subtract to find the sale price percent.*

$75\% \times \$58.00 = 0.75 \times \$58.00$

$= \$43.50$ *Multiply to find the sale price.*

So, the sale price is \$43.50.

- Explain how you can find the amount of the discount for the jacket.
- Some game software is on sale for 40% off. The regular price is \$39.99. What percent is the sale price? What is the sale price?

CULTURAL LINK

Approximately $\frac{1}{2}$ of all clothing sold in the U.S. is made in other countries such as India and Pakistan. Some countries pay their workers less than $\frac{1}{4}$ of the wages earned in the U.S. Suppose a clothing factory worker in the U.S. makes \$10 per hour. How much would a worker in one of these other countries earn?

After you find the discount, you still need to add the sales tax in order to find the total cost. The discount reduces the price, and the sales tax adds to the cost.

EXAMPLE 2 A pair of in-line skates that regularly costs $79.00 are on sale at a discount of 30%. If the sales tax is 6%, what will the total cost of the in-line skates be?

$\$79.00 \times 70\% = \$79.00 \times 0.7$ — *Multiply the regular price by 70% to find the sale price.*
$= \$55.30$

$\$55.30 \times 106\% = \$55.30 \times 1.06$ — *Find the total cost. Multiply the sale price by 106%.*
$= \$58.618$
$\approx \$58.62$

The total cost of the in-line skates will be $58.62.

- CRITICAL THINKING Suppose you find the discount after you find the sales tax. Is your answer $58.62? Explain.

TEEN TIMES

Replacement wheels for in-line skates are very expensive. One way to make your wheels last longer is to rotate them. Move the wheel in position 1 to position 2, 2 to 3, 3 to 4, and 4 to 1.

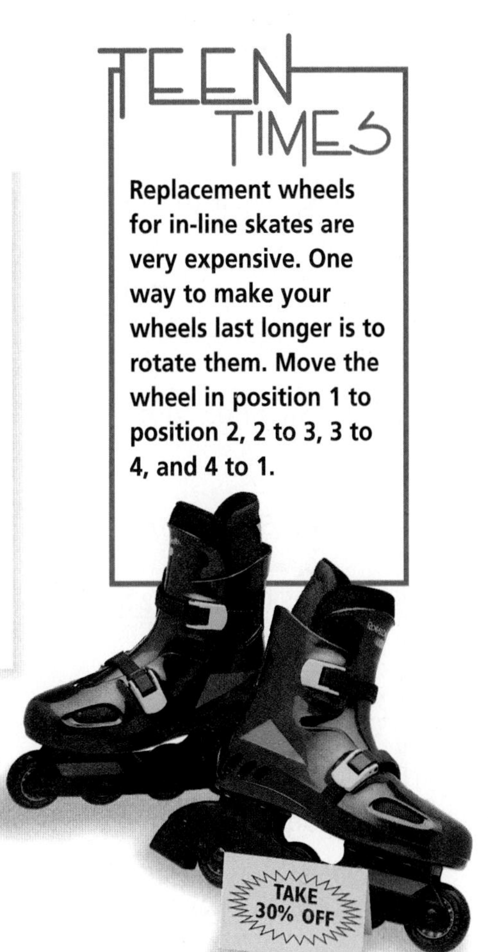

GUIDED PRACTICE

1. The regular price of a radio is $52.00. It is on sale at 30% off. Find the sale price.
2. The regular price of a music CD is $15.00. It is on sale for $11.25. What is the amount of discount?
3. The sales tax on the CD in Exercise 2 is 7%. Find the total cost of the CD.

The sale price of this soccer ball is 75% of the regular price. This equation shows the relationship between the regular price of the ball (p), the sale price, and 75%.

$$75\% \times p = \$18.30$$

4. Solve the equation to show that the regular price is $24.40. Then find the amount of the discount.
5. Copy the diagram. Insert the words "Regular Price" and "Sale Price" to show how regular price, discount, and sale price are related.

?	Discount

← ? →

Finding Rate of Discount and Regular Price

EXAMPLE 3 Suppose you saw the two advertisements at the right for the same model cassette player. Which has the better discount rate? Which has the lower sale price?

Advertisement 1

$\$35.95 - \$28.76 = \$7.19$ *Subtract to find the discount.*

$\frac{7.19}{35.95} = 0.20$, or 20% *Find the rate of discount. Divide the discount by the regular price.*

The rate of discount is 20% and the regular price is \$35.95.

Advertisement 2

$100\% - 30\% = 70\%$ *Find what percent the sale price is of the regular price.*

$\frac{\$32.55}{70\%} = \frac{\$32.55}{0.7}$ *Find the regular price. Divide the sale price by 70%.*

$= \$46.50$

The rate of discount is 30% and the regular price is \$46.50.

Advertisement 2 has the better discount rate. Advertisement 1 has the lower sale price.

- Does a greater discount rate always mean that the item is the best buy? Explain.

You can also use a proportion to find the percent. **See page 302.**

What percent of 20 is 8?

$\frac{n}{100} = \frac{8}{20}$

$20n = 800$

$n = 40$

So, 40% of 20 is 8.

INDEPENDENT PRACTICE

Find the sale price.

1. regular price: \$36.00

2. regular price: \$27.00

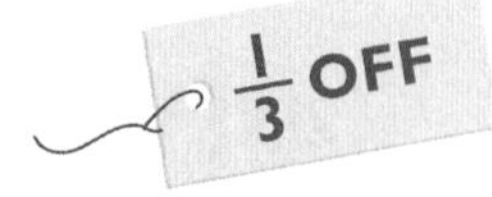

3. regular price: \$119.00

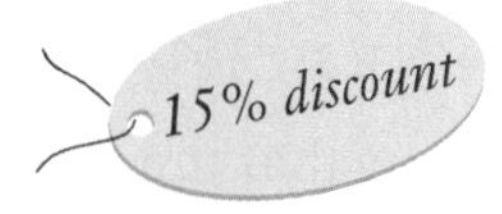

4. regular price: \$6.50

Find the regular price to the nearest cent.

5. sale price: \$99.00

6. sale price: \$18.00

7. sale price: \$64.00

8. sale price: \$3.75

Find the rate of discount.

9. Regular price: \$36.00
Sale price: \$28.80

10. Regular price: \$90.00
Sale price: \$67.50

11. Regular price: \$7.50
Sale price: \$3.75

12. Regular price: \$49.90
Sale price: \$44.91

13. Regular price: \$51.00
Sale price: \$35.70

14. Regular price: \$19.00
Sale price: \$12.35

Find the total cost of each item. The sales tax rate is 7%.

15. Regular price: \$160.00
Now 10% off

16. Regular price: \$8.88
Now 25% off

17. Regular price: \$25.60
Now 30% off

18. Regular price: \$49.50
Now 18% off

19. Regular price: \$50.50
Now 50% off

20. Regular price: \$8.75
Now 40% off

Problem-Solving Applications

21. **ESTIMATION** Suppose you want to buy a \$19.95 shirt that is discounted 40%. How can you use 50% to quickly estimate the sale price?

22. **MENTAL MATH** Suppose you want to buy a \$30.00 radio that is discounted 15%. Explain how you would mentally find the discount.

23. Stacy bought a CD with a regular price of \$15.00. The discount was 30%. She paid a total of \$11.13, which included a 6% sales tax. What was the sale price of the CD?

24. **CONSUMER MATH** Angela wants to buy a pair of jeans. The discount on the pair of jeans she likes is 40%. The regular price is \$56.00. What is the sale price?

25. **WRITE ABOUT IT** In your own words, explain what a discount does to the price of an item.

Mixed Review and Test Prep

Write as a fraction in simplest form.

26. 25% **27.** 35% **28.** 0.75 **29.** 0.06 **30.** 125% **31.** 1.6

Find the product.

32. 0.5×20 **33.** $\frac{1}{3} \times 36$ **34.** 2.35×60 **35.** $2^2 \times 2^2$

Solve.

36. **SEQUENCES** What are the next two numbers in the sequence?

1, 3, 5, 7, 9, 11, 13, 15, 17, . . .

A 18, 19 **B** 19, 20 **C** 19, 21 **D** 21, 23

37. **MENTAL MATH** Tom has 125 baseball cards. This is 30 more than Michael has. How many cards does Michael have?

F 85 **G** 95 **H** 135 **J** 155

Technology Link

In ***Mighty Math Astro Algebra,*** go to the *Cargo Bay* to find out-of-this world discounts in *The Great Galactic Garage Sale.* Use Grow Slide Level Green Q.

LESSON 27.3

Percent and Markup

What You'll Learn
How to find the markup and retail price

Why Learn This?
To understand what people mean when they talk about wholesale price, retail price, and markup

VOCABULARY

wholesale price
retail price
markup

Often, the prices of merchandise change. Stores buy large quantities of merchandise at **wholesale prices**. To make money, the stores sell the merchandise for a greater amount, called the **retail price**.

The difference between the wholesale price and the retail price is called the **markup**.

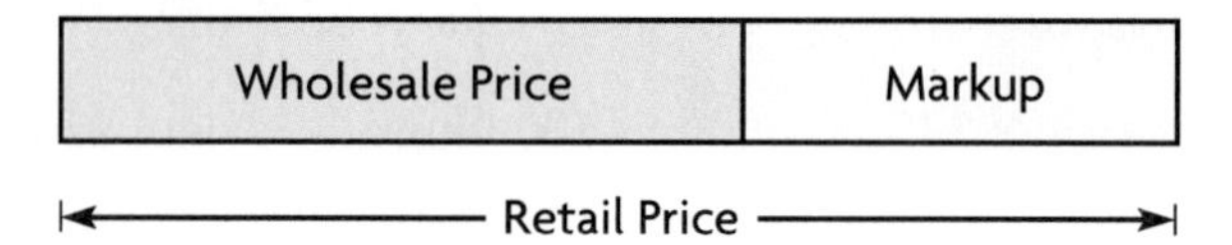

EXAMPLE 1 The diagram shows how the wholesale price, markup, and retail price are related.

A manufacturer sells skateboards at a wholesale price of \$50.50 each. A store sells the skateboards at a retail price of \$120.19 each. What is the value of the markup?

Markup = Retail price − Wholesale price

$m = \$120.19 - \$50.50$ *Let m represent the markup. Subtract to solve.*

$m = \$69.69$

The markup is \$69.69.

- The wholesale price for a video is \$9.00. The retail price is \$18.95. What is the value of the markup?
- Suppose the wholesale price of a case of soda is \$3.00 and the markup is \$2.40. Explain how to find the retail price.

CONSUMER LINK

The wholesale price for a can of soda is about \$0.15. What is the markup for a \$0.60 soda?

Businesses usually use a percent to determine the value of a markup.

EXAMPLE 2 A store's markup on bicycles is 50% of the wholesale price. The wholesale price of one bicycle is \$93.00. Find the retail price.

50% of $\$93.00 = 0.5 \times \$93.00$ — *Multiply by the percent to find the markup.*

$= \$46.50$

$\$46.50 + \$93.00 = \$139.50$ — *Add the markup to the wholesale price to find the retail price.*

- What percent can you use to find the retail price of the bicycle directly?

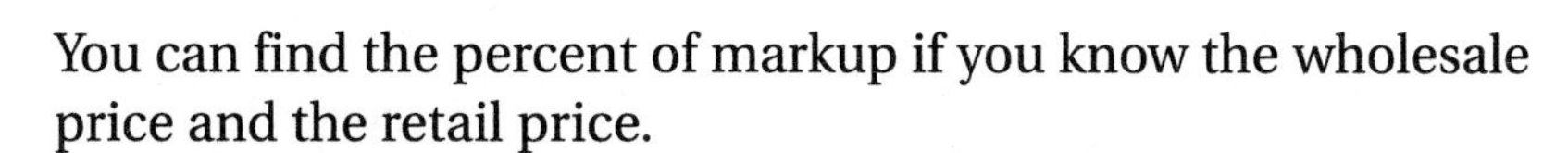

You can find the percent of markup if you know the wholesale price and the retail price.

EXAMPLE 3 The wholesale price of a music CD is \$10.00, and the retail price is \$20.00. What percent of the wholesale price is the markup?

$\$20.00 - \$10.00 = \$10.00$ — *Find the markup.*

$$\frac{\text{markup}}{\text{wholesale price}} = \frac{\$10}{\$10} = \frac{1}{1}$$ *Write a ratio to find the percent.*

$$\frac{1}{1} = \frac{100}{100} = 100\%$$

The markup is 100% of the wholesale price.

CONSUMER LINK

It costs \$0.10 to \$0.15 to make a music CD. The plastic box and paper wrapper costs about \$0.30 to \$0.35. Find the price of your favorite CD and calculate the markup.

GUIDED PRACTICE

Find the value of the markup.

1. wholesale price: \$32.45
   retail price: \$64.90
2. wholesale price: \$102.45
   retail price: \$184.41

Find the value of the markup and the retail price.

3. wholesale price: \$58.00
   markup percent: 50%
4. wholesale price: \$100.00
   markup percent: 75%

Find what percent the markup is of the wholesale price.

5. wholesale price: \$14.00
   retail price: \$28.00
6. wholesale price: \$30.00
   retail price: \$52.50

INDEPENDENT PRACTICE

Find the value of the markup.

1. wholesale price: $25.50
   retail price: $51.00
2. wholesale price: $122.00
   retail price: $213.50
3. wholesale price: $0.75
   retail price: $1.87
4. wholesale price: $32.00
   retail price: $40.00
5. wholesale price: $119.25
   retail price: $147.55
6. wholesale price: $5.72
   retail price: $17.29

You buy bicycles at a wholesale price of $49.50 each. Find the value of your markup and the retail price if you sell the bikes with these markups.

7. 100% markup
8. 125% markup
9. 150% markup
10. 110% markup
11. 175% markup
12. 200% markup

A store uses a markup of 40% of the wholesale price on all items. Use the given wholesale price to find the retail price.

13. wholesale price: $12.00
    retail price: ?
14. wholesale price: $279.45
    retail price: ?
15. wholesale price: $42.50
    retail price: ?
16. Look at Exercises 17–20. Identify the exercises in which the markup is at least 100% of the wholesale price. Explain your reasoning.

Find the amount and percent of each markup.

17. wholesale price: $15
    retail price: $36
18. wholesale price: $10
    retail price: $24
19. wholesale price: $6
    retail price: $16
20. wholesale price: $120
    retail price: $260

Problem-Solving Applications

A store's wholesale price for basketballs was $5,400.00 for 1,200 basketballs. The retail price was $13.75 each.

21. **BUSINESS** What did the store pay for each basketball?
22. **BUSINESS** What was the markup on each basketball?
23. Express the markup as a percent of the wholesale price.
24. Write a ratio to compare the store's retail price to its wholesale price.
25. What does the ratio tell you?
26. **WRITE ABOUT IT** Write a word problem that involves wholesale price, markup, and retail price. Share your problem with the class.

MORE PRACTICE Lesson 27.3, page H80

Growth from Interest

This activity will simulate how interest can be used to increase an amount.

What You'll Explore
How to model the relationship between percent and interest

What You'll Need
50 counters or centimeter cubes for each group

Explore

- Use 50 counters or centimeter cubes.
- Make a group of 20 counters to represent \$20. Then make another group of counters to represent 5% interest on \$20.
- Repeat putting down 5% of \$20 until you have \$20 in the second group, or a total of \$40.
- Make a table similar to the one below to record your results.

Number of Times We Found 5%	Amount of Interest	Total Amount
1	?	?
2	?	?

- Repeat the activity by finding 10% of \$20 until you have a total of \$40. Make a table to record your results.

Think and Discuss

- How many times did you have to find 5% to get a total of \$40?
- How many times did you have to find 10% to get a total of \$40?
- Suppose you earned 15% interest each year on \$20. Predict how many years it would take to double your money. Then use counters to check your prediction.
- As you increase the percent, does it take more time or less time to double your money?

Try This

Use the counters to determine what percent you would need to double \$50 to \$100 in 10 years.

Technology Link

You can explore interest earned on investments by using E-Lab, Activity 27. Available on CD-ROM and on the Internet at **www.hbschool.com/elab**

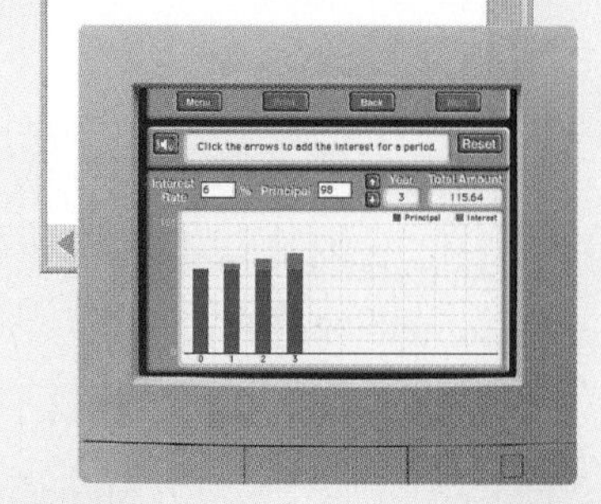

LESSON 27.4

ALGEBRA CONNECTION

Earning Simple Interest

What You'll Learn
How simple interest affects earnings on money saved

Why Learn This?
To figure out how much interest you might earn on money you save

VOCABULARY

simple interest
principal
total amount

Banks pay interest on your money. One type of interest that is paid on money is called **simple interest**. The amount you earn depends on how much you deposit, or the **principal**, and is computed only on the amount you deposit.

EXAMPLE 1 Suppose you deposit a principal of $100.00 in a bank that pays 5% simple interest. How much interest will you earn in 1 year?

Use the formula $I = prt$ where I = Interest earned, p = principal, r = interest rate, and t = time.

$I = prt$ *p = $100.00, r = 5%, t = 1 year*

$I = 100 \times 0.05 \times 1$ *Multiply.*

$I = 5$

So, you will earn $5.00.

- What if the interest rate was 8%? How much interest would you earn in 1 year on $100.00?

At 5% simple interest, your $100.00 principal earns $5.00 interest. At the end of the first year, the account has grown in value to $100.00 + $5.00, or $105.00.

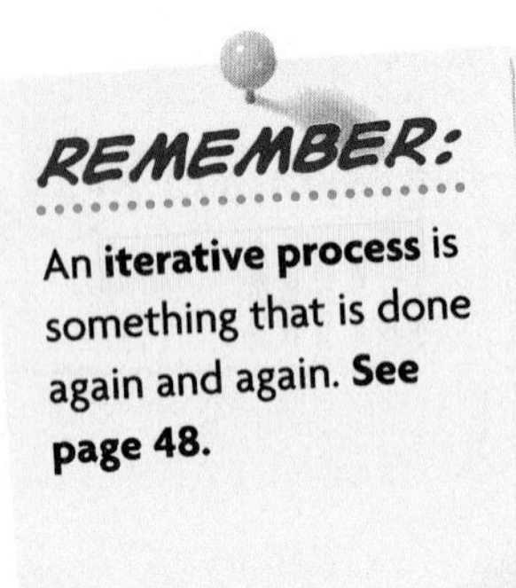

REMEMBER:
An **iterative process** is something that is done again and again. **See page 48.**

Think of the earnings on the principal as the result of an iterative process. For each year the $100.00 is invested, you continue to add 5 dollars.

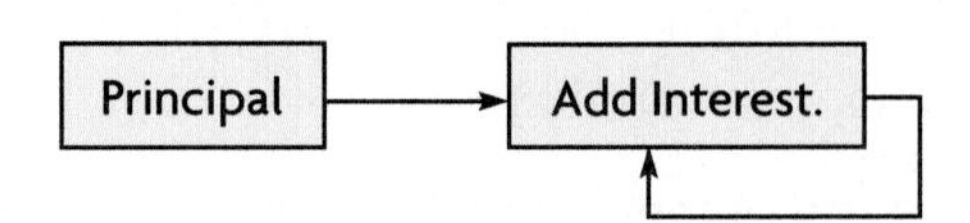

It may not seem like much at first, but over time it does add up.

In 10 years, the $100.00 grows to a value of $150.00.
$100.00 + (10)($5.00) = $100.00 + $50.00
= $150.00

In 20 years, the $100.00 grows to a value of $200.00.
$100.00 + (20)($5.00) = $100.00 + $100.00
= $200.00

At 5% simple interest, an amount doubles itself after 20 years.

EXAMPLE 2 Suppose you start with an investment of $500.00 at 8% simple interest. What amount does this investment grow to in 6 years? in 13 years?

You can use the formula $I = prt$ and the formula $A = p + I$ where A is the **total amount**.

6 years

$I = prt$
$I = \$500 \times 0.08 \times 6$
$I = \$240$

$A = p + I$
$A = \$500 + \$240 = \$740$

In 6 years, the $500.00 grows to $740.00.

13 years

$I = prt$
$I = \$500 \times 0.08 \times 13$
$I = \$520$

$A = p + I$
$A = \$500 + \$520 = \$1{,}020$

In 13 years, the $500.00 grows to $1,020.00.

- When do you think the total amount of the investment would be exactly doubled, or $1,000.00?

GUIDED PRACTICE

Find the interest earned on $100.00 at these simple interest rates and for these lengths of time.

1. 8% for 3 years

2. 6% for 15 years

3. $7\frac{1}{2}$% for 7 years

4. 5.5% for 8 years

5. 9.25% for 5 years

6. 12.75% for 8 years

7. If money doubles in 20 years, what is the simple interest rate being paid? (HINT: Work backward.)

8. At 10% simple interest, how many years will it take money to double itself?

TEEN TIMES

In Canada, many banks have accounts for teenagers 13–18 years old. The teenagers can earn interest, write checks, and use ATM cards.

INDEPENDENT PRACTICE

For Exercises 1–8, assume $250.00 is deposited at 7% simple interest.

Copy and complete the tables to show growth over a seven-year period.

	Year	Interest	Amount
	Start		$250.00
	1	$17.50	$267.50
1.	2	$17.50	?
2.	3	?	?

	Year	Interest	Amount
3.	4	?	?
4.	5	?	?
5.	6	?	?
6.	7	?	?

7. When the $250.00 is deposited for t years, you can compute the interest earned with the expression $\$250(0.07)t$. Write an expression for the total amount at the end of t years.

8. Suppose you decide you would like to invest $250 for $2\frac{1}{2}$ years at 7% simple interest. Use the expression from Exercise 7 to find the interest and total amount when $t = 2\frac{1}{2}$ years.

Use your calculator to find the interest.

9. $7\frac{1}{2}\%$ simple interest for 4 years on a principal of $350.00

10. $6\frac{3}{4}\%$ simple interest for 5 years on a principal of $4,500.00

11. 10.75% simple interest for 10 years on a principal of $4,000.00

12. 4.24% simple interest for 3 years on a principal of $1,200.00

13. $8\frac{1}{4}\%$ simple interest for 8 years on a principal of $900.00.

14. 15.9% simple interest for 5 years on a principal of $3,200.00.

Find the amount the investment will grow to for the given information.

15. $5\frac{1}{4}\%$ simple interest for 10 years on a principal of $500.00.

16. 3% simple interest for 3 years on a principal of $4,000.00.

17. 8% simple interest for 12 years on a principal of $750.00

18. $7\frac{1}{2}\%$ simple interest for 2 years on a principal of $875.00.

19. $17\frac{3}{4}\%$ simple interest for 8 years on a principal of $1,000.00.

20. 12.7% simple interest for 6 years on a principal of $2,500.00.

Problem-Solving Applications

21. **MONEY** Jim invested $527.00 for 5 years in an account that earned 4% simple interest. How much did he earn?

22. Kate invests $478.00 at 6% simple interest. What amount does this investment grow to in 8 years?

23. **BANKING** Alicia Jones keeps $1,000.00 in an account that earns 5% simple interest. How many years will it be before the total amount is $1,350.00?

24. **ESTIMATION** What is a reasonable estimate of the amount of money you will earn on $620.00 invested at 9% simple interest for 3 years?

25. **BANKING** You have $500.00 in an account that earns 5% simple interest annually. At the end of every year, you add the interest you earned to the principal and earn interest on both the next year. How much will you have in the account after 10 years? after 15 years?

26. **LOGICAL REASONING** Explain whether you would earn more simple interest if you used Plan A or Plan B.

Plan A: $1,500 for 7 years at 8%
Plan B: $1,500 for 8 years at 7%

27. **WRITE ABOUT IT** Write and solve a problem involving simple interest.

MORE PRACTICE Lesson 27.4, page H81

PROBLEM-SOLVING STRATEGY

Making a Table to Find Interest

What You'll Learn
How to make a table to find the effect interest has on the amount of money you owe

Why Learn This?
To understand minimum payments and the interest charged when you buy on credit

VOCABULARY
finance charge

When you buy an item with a credit card, you can pay the full amount when the bill comes or you can make payments. If you make payments, interest called a **finance charge** will be added to the new balance.

With the credit card that Joel's family has, the finance charge is 18% annually, or 1.5% monthly. Joel wants to charge \$65.00 for concert tickets on the credit card. If he makes the minimum payment of \$20.00 each month, how much interest will he pay? What will be the total amount he will pay?

PROBLEM SOLVING
- **Understand**
- **Plan**
- **Solve**
- **Look Back**

UNDERSTAND What are you asked to find?

What facts are given?

PLAN What strategy will you use?

You can *make a table* to show the interest charged, the balance, the payment, and the new balance for each month.

SOLVE How can you complete the table?

The computation for the second month is shown. Interest is rounded up to the next cent.

Interest: \$45.00 × 0.015 = \$0.68 *new balance × 1.5%*
Balance: \$45.00 + \$0.68 = \$45.68 *new balance + interest*
New Balance: \$45.68 − \$20.00 = \$25.68 *balance − payment*

Month	Interest	Balance	Payment	New Balance
1	\$0.00	\$65.00	\$20.00	\$45.00
2	\$0.68	\$45.68	\$20.00	\$25.68
3	\$0.39	\$26.07	\$20.00	\$6.07
4	\$0.10	\$6.17	\$6.17	\$0.00
Total	\$1.17		\$66.17	

Joel will pay \$1.17 in interest and a total amount of \$66.17.

LOOK BACK Is \$1.17 in interest reasonable? Explain.

What if . . . Joel's minimum payment is \$10.00? Will he pay more than \$1.17 in interest or less?

You could do a lot of shopping at the Mall of America in Bloomington, MN, the largest mall in the United States. It has an area of 4.2 million square feet and is large enough to have an amusement park in the center!

PRACTICE

Make a table and solve.

1. Amy Thomas charged $75.50 for a new keyboard. The interest rate is 18% annually, or 1.5% monthly. She will make a $20.00 payment each month. How much interest will she pay?

2. Roberto bought a $132.50 CD player with the family credit card. The interest rate is 21% annually, or 1.75% monthly. He will make minimum payments of $25.00 each month. What is the total amount he will pay? How many months will it take him to pay the total amount?

3. Mr. Chacko got a credit card that charges 12% interest annually, or 1% monthly. He charges $250.00 and sends a payment for half of that amount on his first bill. How much interest will he be charged the second month? How much will the new balance be?

Spreadsheets

A spreadsheet is a useful tool for organizing, computing, and analyzing interest data. Notice that the spreadsheet below is similar to the table on page 543. The advantage of using a spreadsheet on a computer is that you can use formulas and have the computer calculate the amounts for you.

EXAMPLE Tasha made a spreadsheet to calculate how much interest she would owe on a credit-card purchase of $100.00. What formula is used to find the amount in cell C3?

	A	B	C	D	E
1	**Month**	**Interest (1.5%)**	**Balance**	**Payment**	**New Balance**
2	January	$0	$100.00	$20.00	$80.00
3	February	$1.20	$81.20	$20.00	$61.20
4	March	$0.92	$62.12	$20.00	$42.12
5	April	$0.64	$42.76	$20.00	$22.76
6	May	$0.35	$23.11	$20.00	$3.11
7	June	$0.05	$3.16	$3.16	$0
8	Total	$3.16		$103.16	

The amount in cell C3 is the sum of the new balance for January and the interest for February. So, the formula for cell C3 is E2 + B3.

- What is the formula for cell E5?

Technology Link

In ***Data ToolKit*** you can learn about the cells of spreadsheets.

MIXED APPLICATIONS

Solve.

CHOOSE a strategy and a tool.

- **Make a Table**
- **Guess and Check**
- **Write an Equation**
- **Account for All Possibilities**
- **Use a Formula**
- **Work Backward**

Paper/Pencil

Calculator

Hands-On

Mental Math

1. Nola Walters spent $78.00 for merchandise to sell in her store. She bought pens for $4.00 each and wallets for $9.00 each. If she bought the same number of pens as wallets, how many of each did she buy?

2. Stan Thomas charged $208.95 for a quad-speed CD-ROM drive. If he makes a payment of $30.00 each month, how many months will it take him to pay the bill? The finance charge is 1.5% monthly.

3. Carley and her family walked around town from noon until 4:00 P.M. They walked at a rate of 3 kilometers per hour. How far did they walk?

4. There are 12 players in a tournament. If each player plays one game with every other player, how many games will be played in all?

5. Ben spent $6.00 for school supplies. He spent $3.00 for a notebook and $1.75 for a pen. How much did he spend for other supplies?

6. Jackie Wilson invests $1,200.00 for 2 years. The bank pays 8% simple interest annually. How much interest will she earn?

7. Taylor and Erik delivered 200 newspapers in all. Erik delivered 40 more newspapers than Taylor. How many did each deliver?

8. Annette has a vegetable garden in the shape of a circle with a diameter of 8 ft. How many square feet is the garden?

9. **WRITE ABOUT IT** Write a problem about charging an item on a credit card, making minimum payments, and paying interest. Share your problem with the class.

Mixed Review and Test Prep

Write as a fraction in simplest form.

10. 0.25 **11.** 6 to 8 **12.** 5:10 **13.** 15% **14.** 0.60

Write *always, sometimes,* or *never*.

15. Vertical angles are complementary.

16. A rectangle is a square.

17. A parallelogram is a quadrilateral.

18. A circle is a polygon.

19. **LOGICAL REASONING** There are 40 students trying out for a team. There are 16 more boys than girls. How many boys are there?

A 30 **B** 28
C 24 **D** 18

20. **WEATHER** In the Alaskan Arctic, the temperatures range from an average of $^-24$°C in January to 8°C in July. What is the difference between the temperatures?

F 32°C **G** 16°C **H** 8°C **J** $^-8$°C

MORE PRACTICE Lesson 27.5, page H81

CHAPTER 27 Review/Test

Find the sales tax and total cost. (pages 528–531)

1. 5% on a $14.00 CD
2. 6.5% on a $65.60 jacket
3. 7% on a $25.00 game
4. 7% on a $29.90 video

Find the sales tax rate. (pages 528–531)

5. price of TV: $299.00; sales tax: $17.94
6. price of book: $6.80; sales tax: $0.34
7. price of basketball: $24.50; sales tax: $1.96
8. price of skates: $42.00; sales tax: $2.94
9. **VOCABULARY** The amount that the price of an item is marked down is the __?__. (page 532)
10. regular price: $48.00; sale price: $40.80 Find the percent of discount. (pages 532–535)
11. regular price: $28.50; discount: 40% Find the sale price. (pages 532–535)
12. regular price: $28.40; sale price: $21.30 Find the percent of discount. (pages 532–535)
13. regular price: $8.95; discount: 20% Find the sale price. (pages 532–535)
14. **VOCABULARY** Add the markup to the wholesale price to find the __?__. (page 536)
15. wholesale price: $16.00; retail price: $24.00. Find the amount and percent of markup. (pages 536–538)
16. wholesale price: $8.00; markup: 100% Find the retail price. (pages 536–538)
17. wholesale price: $4.20; retail price $5.46 Find the amount and percent of markup. (pages 536–538)
18. wholesale price: $79.00; markup: 80% Find the retail price. (pages 536–538)
19. **VOCABULARY** The amount deposited in an interest-earning bank account is called the __?__. (page 540)

Find the simple interest. (pages 540–542)

20. $1,000 for 6 yr at 7% per year
21. $12,000 for 12 yr at 8.5% per year
22. You deposit $400.00 at 5.5% simple interest. What will be the total amount after 10 yr? (pages 540–542)
23. You deposit $500.00 at 6% simple interest. What will be the total after 5 yr? (pages 540–542)
24. Mr. Jones charged $125.50 for a video game. The interest rate is 1.5% monthly. He will pay $20.00 each month. How much interest will he pay? (pages 543–545)
25. Sue charged $75.20 for hockey tickets. The interest rate is 1.6% monthly. She will pay $15.00 each month. How long will it take her to pay the total? (pages 543–545)

Test Prep

CUMULATIVE
CHAPTERS 1–27

1. How much simple interest will you earn on $150 invested for 3 years at an 8% interest rate?

A $12
B $36
C $54
D $186

2. A rectangle is 12 inches long and 8 inches wide. The length is changed by a scale of 120%, and the width is changed by a scale of 60%. What are the dimensions of the new rectangle?

F $l = 7.2$ in., $w = 4.8$ in.

G $l = 10$ in., $w = 13\frac{1}{3}$ in.

H $l = 14.4$ in., $w = 4.8$ in.

J $l = 14.4$ in., $w = 9.6$ in.

3. What is the length of the kite string shown in the diagram below?

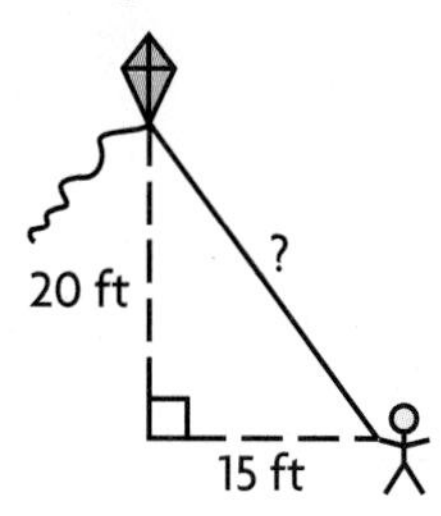

A 35 ft **B** 30 ft **C** 25 ft **D** 17 ft

4. What is the probability that a dart that lands on the target will land in the shaded area?

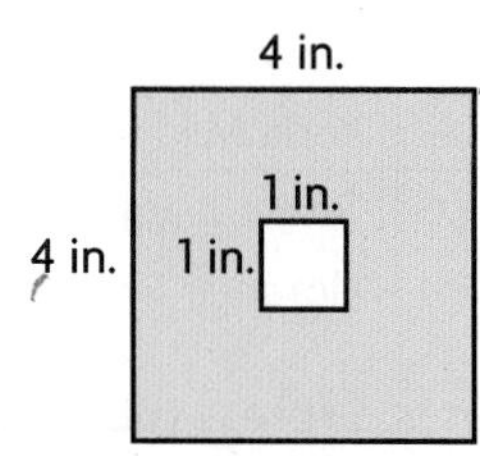

F $\frac{1}{16}$ **G** $\frac{1}{4}$ **H** $\frac{3}{4}$ **J** $\frac{15}{16}$

5. A bicycle costs $129.50. You pay $7.77 in sales tax. What is the sales tax rate?

A 16%
B 11%
C 6%
D 5%

6. Which measure of central tendency best represents the data?

3.4, 5.6, 7.1, 27.8, 5.4, 3.4

F mean
G median
H mode
J range

7. Which two angle measures are complementary?

A 72°, 18° **B** 54°, 126°
C 35°, 65° **D** 45°, 55°

8. Which point is in Quadrant III on the coordinate plane?

F (⁻2,3) **G** (⁻4,⁻5)
H (4,⁻1) **J** (5,4)

9. What is 72% of 350?

A 98 **B** 150
C 245 **D** 252

10. Terence plans to buy three shirts that range in price from $19.99 to $25.99. Which is the most reasonable estimate of the total cost of the three shirts, before tax is added?

F More than $80
G Between $60 and $80
H Between $50 and $80
J Between $40 and $50
K Less than $40

CHAPTER

28 SHOWING RELATIONSHIPS

LOOK AHEAD

In this chapter you will solve problems that involve

- pictures and words
- graphs and scatterplots

SPORTS LINK

The table below shows the fastest times ever for men and women wheelchair marathon racers.

BEST MARATHON TIMES IN WHEELCHAIR RACES			
Men		Women	
Name	Time	Name	Time
Christopher Philpott	1:54:02	Mary Thompson	2:26:38
Christopher Etzlstorfer	1:54:24	Mary Thompson	2:29:07
Theo Duijvestijn	1:54:31	Yoda Miki	2:41:43
Johann Kastner	1:54:35	Tatino Namiko	2:43:12
Christopher Etzlstorfer	1:54:47	Florence Gossiaux	2:45:33

- Express the men's time in minutes. Express the women's time in minutes.

Problem-Solving Project

Write a Sports Commentary

Distance In Meters	Time in Seconds Runner A	Time in Seconds Runner B
25	8	5
50	13	9
75	18	14
100	23	20
125	29	27
150	35	35
175	41	50
200	47	59

Two contestants ran a 1,000-m race. The table shows their times for parts of the race. The graph shows the whole race. Your job is to write a sports commentary describing the race from start to finish. Decide how the data in the table relate to the lines on the graph. Write a story each line in the graph might tell. Use your imagination to communicate the excitement of the race. Present your commentary to the class.

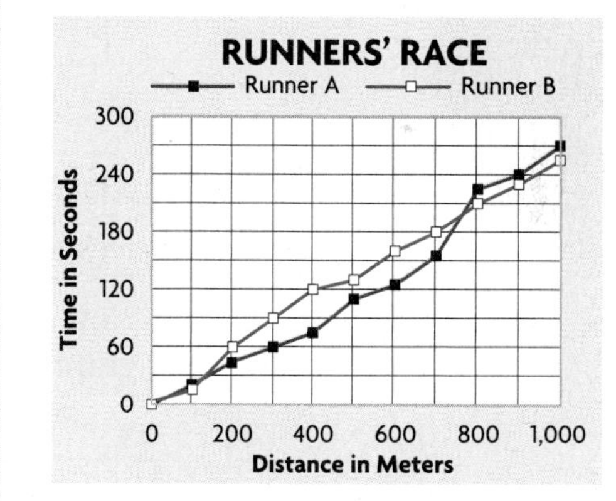

PROJECT CHECKLIST

- ✓ Did you decide how each line in the graph relates to the data in the table?
- ✓ Did you write an exciting sports commentary?
- ✓ Did you present your commentary to the class?

LESSON 28.1

ALGEBRA CONNECTION

Graphs and Pictures

What You'll Learn
How to represent a picture as a graph

Why Learn This?
To understand how relationships shown on graphs are related to pictures

Like a picture, a graph has a story to tell. A picture and a graph can tell the same story, but sometimes in different ways.

The picture at the right shows the path of a golf ball. On a graph you can represent the ball's path by showing the relationship between speed and time or between distance and time. *Be careful:* the picture and the graphs may not look the same.

This graph shows the relationship between the speed of the golf ball and time.

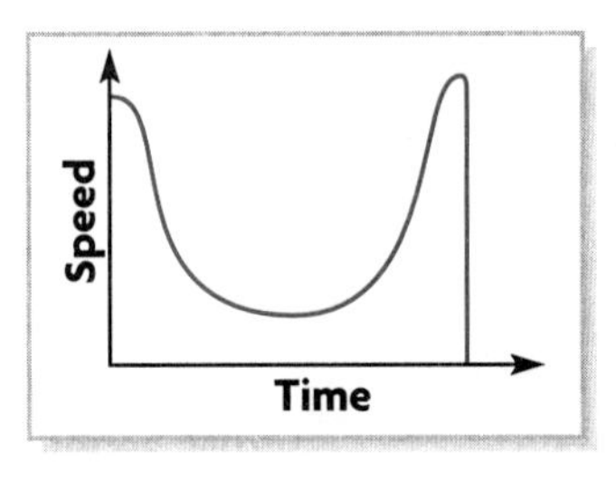

This graph shows the relationship between the distance the golf ball travels and time.

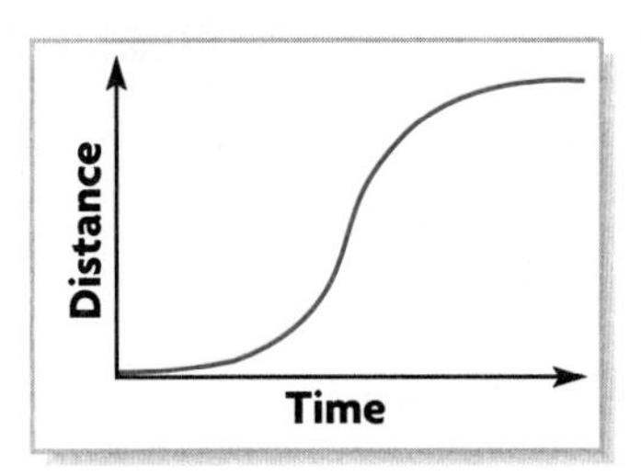

Talk About It

- Describe how the speed of the ball changes.
- How is the picture of the golf ball's path different from the graph that shows the relationship between speed and time?

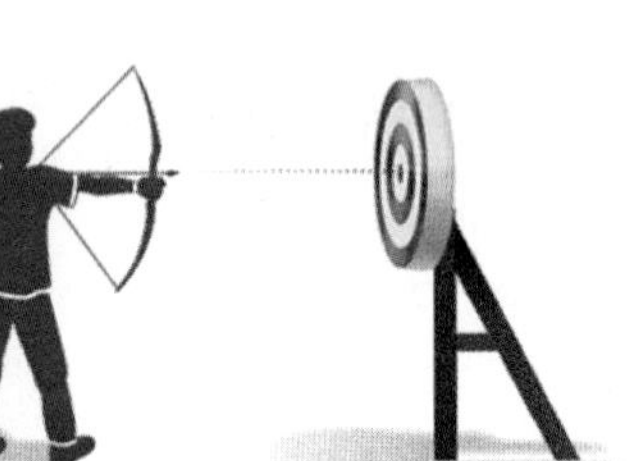

EXAMPLE Which graph illustrates the relationship between the distance traveled by the arrow and time, as shown in the picture at the left? Explain.

a.

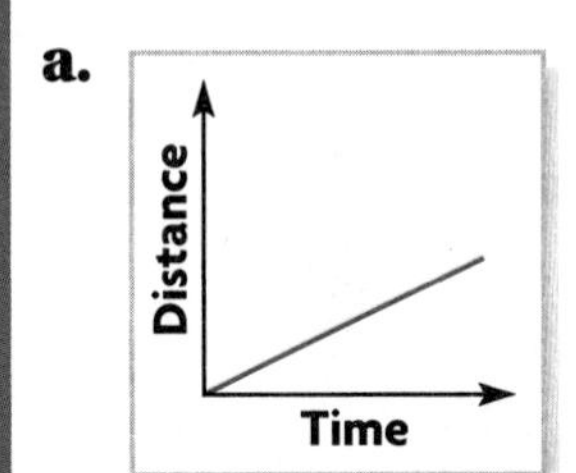

b.

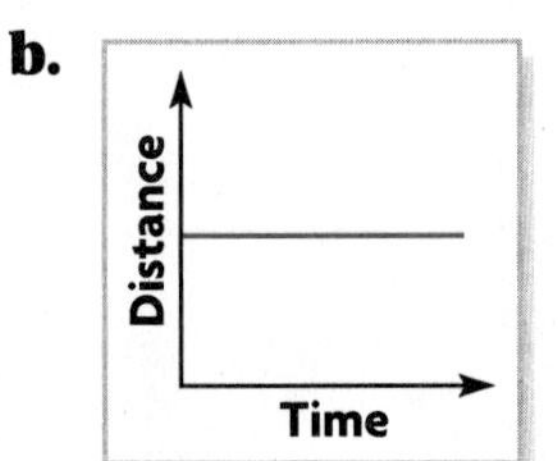

c.

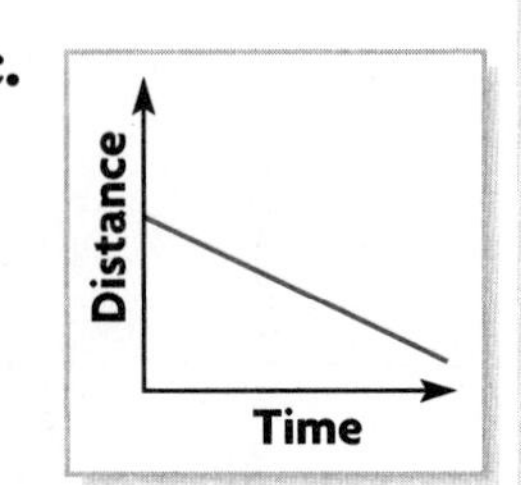

Graph **a** is the correct graph of the relationship. This graph shows that as the time increases, the distance increases.

GUIDED PRACTICE

The picture at the right shows the path of a skateboarder. Use this picture for Exercises 1–2.

1. Which graph shows the relationship between time and the speed of the skateboarder?

a. 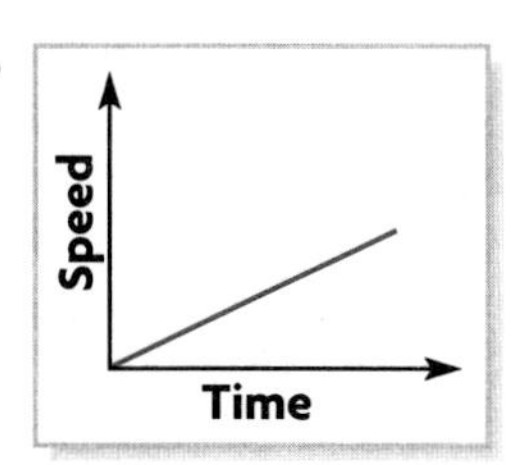

b. 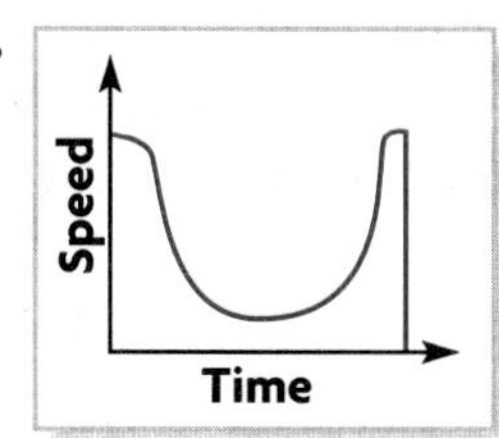

c. 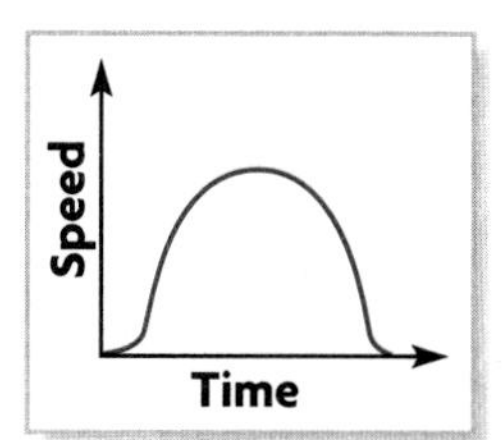

2. Draw a graph that shows the relationship between time and the distance the skateboarder travels.

INDEPENDENT PRACTICE

Use the graphs to find the relationship.

1. **CRITICAL THINKING** Which graph illustrates the relationship between time and the distance traveled by the wire-controlled model airplane shown in the picture at the right? Explain.

a. 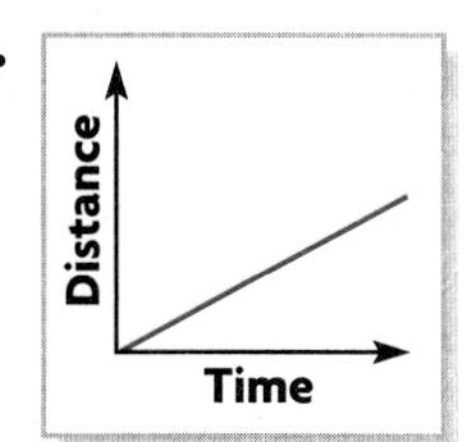

b. 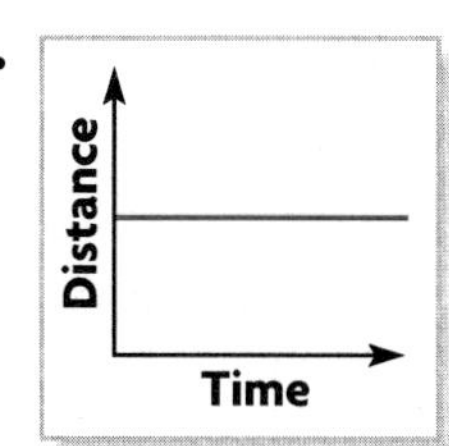

c. 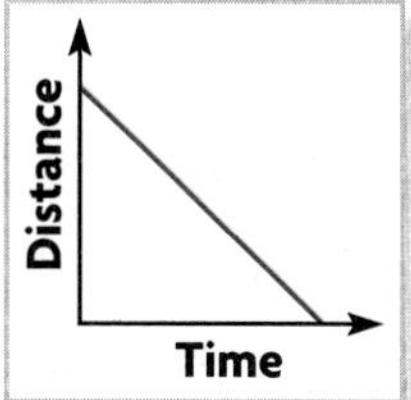

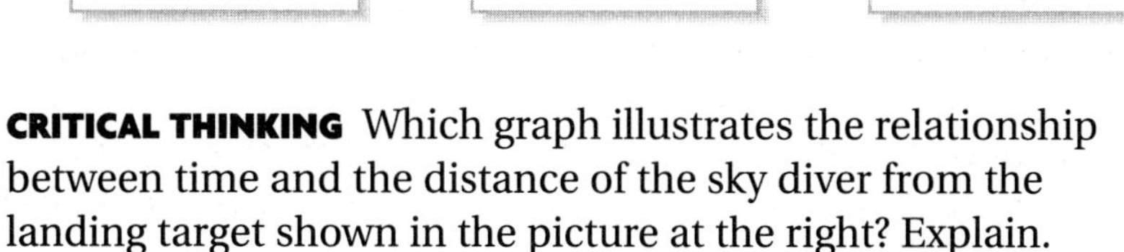

2. **CRITICAL THINKING** Which graph illustrates the relationship between time and the distance of the sky diver from the landing target shown in the picture at the right? Explain.

a. 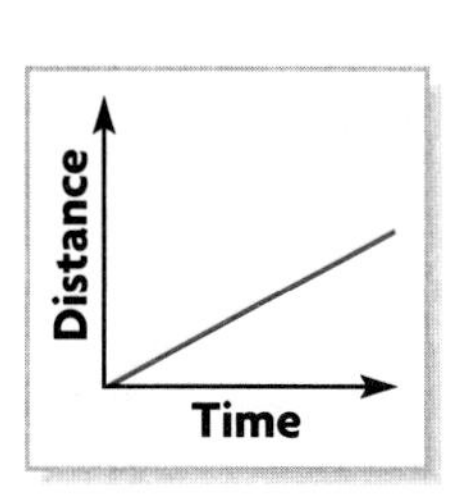

b. 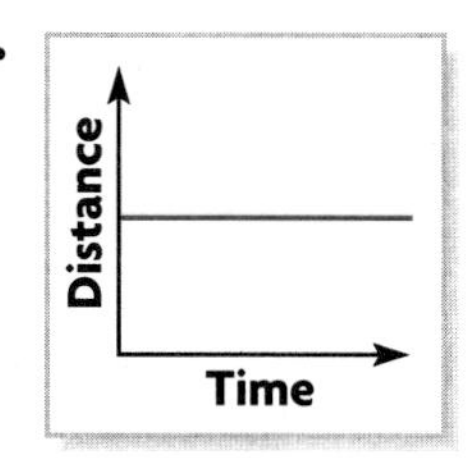

c. 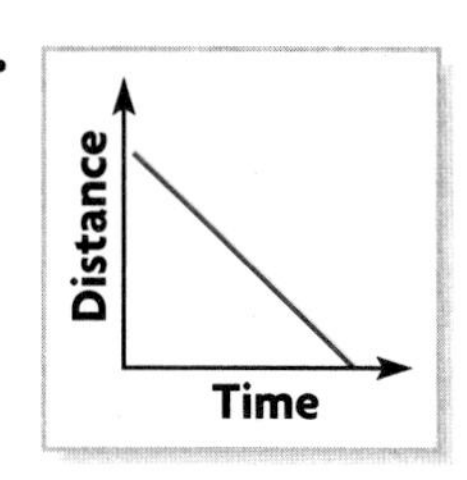

3. **WRITE ABOUT IT** Draw a picture that shows the relationship of distance and time as illustrated by graph **a** in Exercise 2 above.

MORE PRACTICE Lesson 28.1, page H81

LESSON 28.2

ALGEBRA CONNECTION

Relationships in Graphs

What You'll Learn
How to describe relationships shown in a graph

Why Learn This?
To understand graphs that show relationships between variables such as time and distance

An old saying is "A picture is worth 1,000 words." What do you think this saying means?

The graph below tells the story of the amount of water flowing from a faucet after it was first turned on full, then allowed to run, and finally turned down but not off.

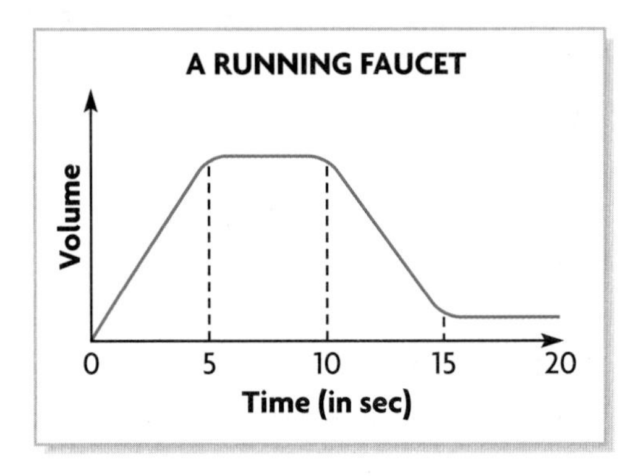

Talk About It

- What time interval represents turning the faucet on?
- During what interval was the faucet running at its maximum flow?
- After 15 sec the faucet continued to run at a slow but steady rate. How would the graph appear if the faucet had been turned all the way off during this period?

When you analyze a graph, look at the places where the graph changes. This will help you describe the relationship between such variables as time and speed.

EXAMPLE 1 Look at the graph. Describe how the speed changes as the time increases in each interval.

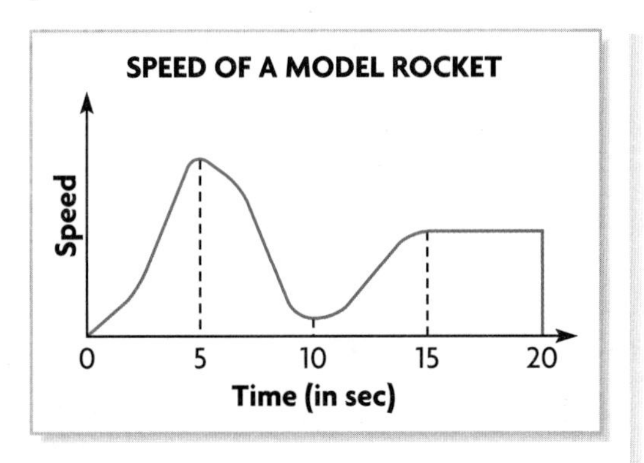

0 to 5 sec: increase

5 to 10 sec: decrease

10 to 15 sec: increase

15 to 20 sec: constant

At 20 sec the rocket's speed is zero.

You can also use the changes in the graph to help you write a story about the graph.

EXAMPLE 2 Use the information in the graph to tell a story about the bicycle racer's trip, using distance and time.

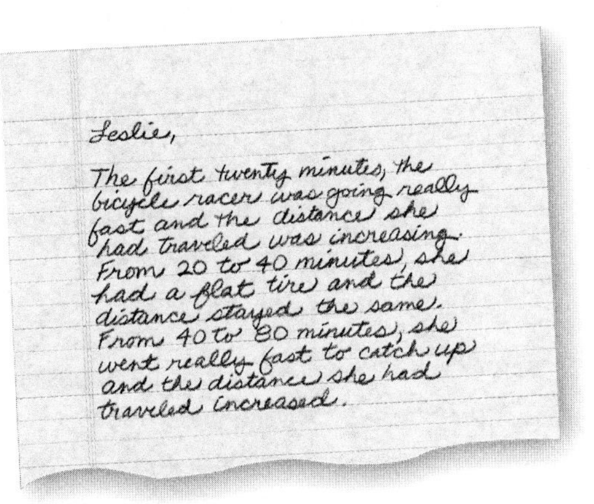
Leslie,

The first twenty minutes, the bicycle racer was going really fast and the distance she had traveled was increasing. From 20 to 40 minutes, she had a flat tire and the distance stayed the same. From 40 to 80 minutes, she went really fast to catch up and the distance she had traveled increased.

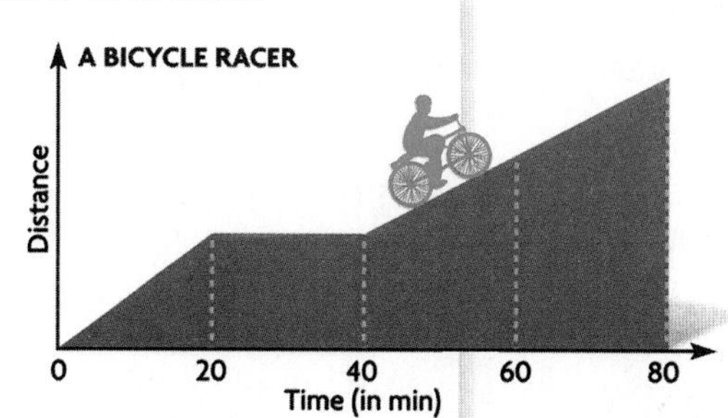

- Do you agree with the story shown above? Explain.
- **CRITICAL THINKING** Suppose that after the bicycle racer rode for 75 min, the chain on the bike broke. It took 20 min to replace the chain and continue with the race. How would the graph and the story change?

Technology Link

In ***Data ToolKit*** you can display data relating variables such as time and distance.

GUIDED PRACTICE

For each graph, choose the correct description. Write *a, b,* or *c*.

1.

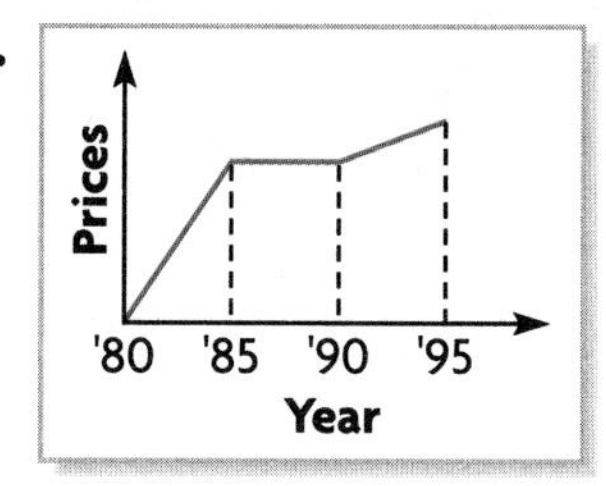

a. From 1980 to 1985, prices increased.
b. From 1980 to 1985, prices decreased.
c. From 1990 to 1995, prices decreased.

2.

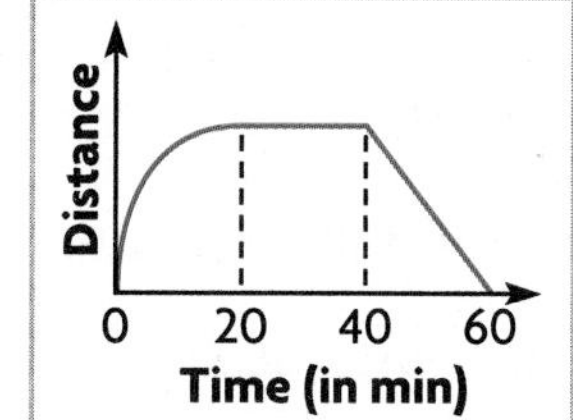

a. From 0 to 20 min, the distance stayed constant.
b. From 40 to 60 min, the distance decreased.
c. From 20 to 40 min, the distance increased.

3. In Exercise 1, between which years did prices stay constant? Between which years did prices increase to their highest level?

4. In Exercise 2, in which interval did the distance increase? stay constant?

Other Relationships

A graph often changes if you use different variables. In Example 2 the variables *distance* and *time* are used. When you use the variables *speed* and *time,* the graph looks different.

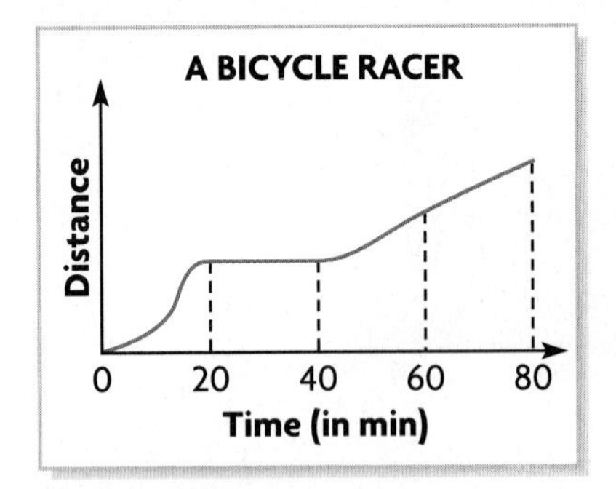

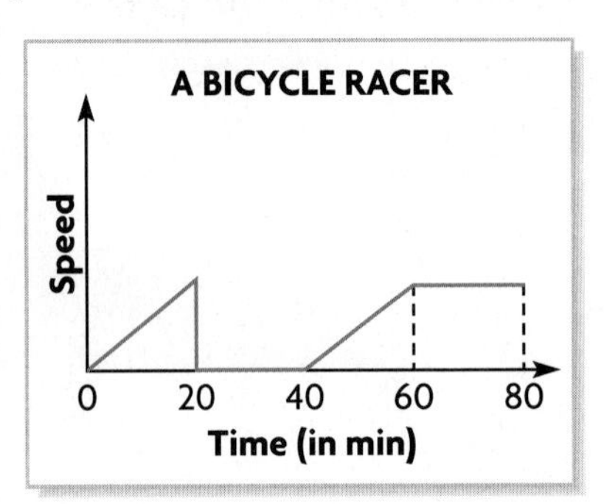

The graph on the left shows the bike stopped during the interval of 20 to 40 min. The graph on the right shows the bike stopped during that interval, because the speed dropped to zero.

EXAMPLE 3 From the graphs, what can you say about the distance and speed of the school bus over 20 min?

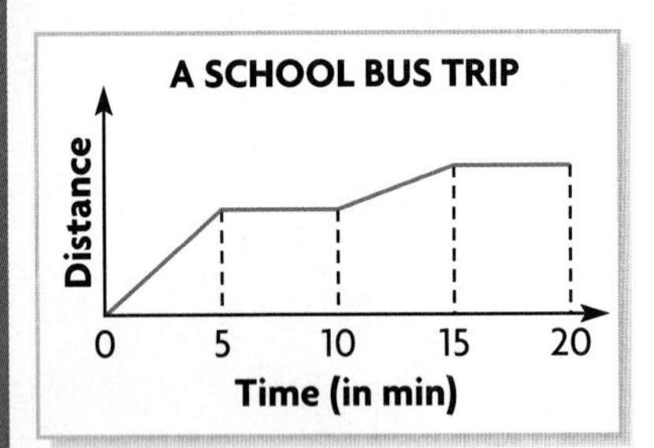

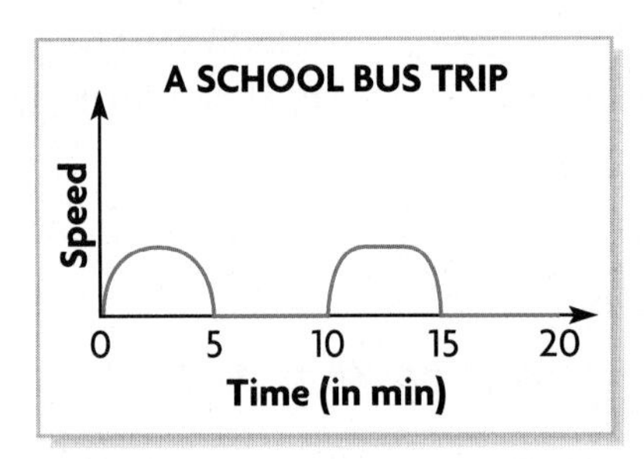

The distance increased, stayed the same, increased, and stayed the same.

The speed increased, decreased, and then stayed at zero. It did this two times.

- What story do the two graphs tell you about the school bus?

TEEN TIMES

In 1994 the U.S. Congress passed the Children's Bicycle Safety Act. This encouraged states and cities to pass laws requiring children under the age of 16 to wear approved bicycle helmets. Many states and cities have passed such laws. Today's helmets are light and look good.

INDEPENDENT PRACTICE

1. Look at the graph at the right. Describe how the air temperature inside the freezer changed as the time increased in each interval.

2. Use the information in the graph to tell a story about the changes in the air temperature inside the freezer.

3. After 25 min the temperature stayed constant. How would the temperature have changed during this period if the door had been opened?

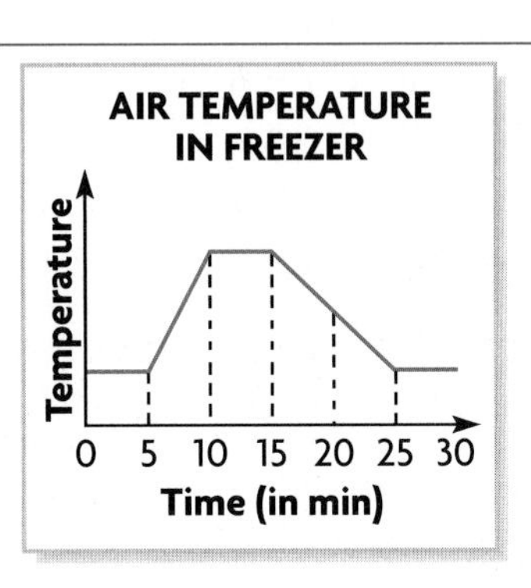

4. The graph at the right shows the relationship of speed and time for a car during its first lap on an oval track. Tell a story about the first lap.

5. Which parts of the graph represent the car traveling around the curves on the track?

6. Which parts of the graph represent the car traveling on the straightaways?

Problem-Solving Applications

7. **CRITICAL THINKING** The graphs below are of a car trip. What can you say about the distance and speed of the car?

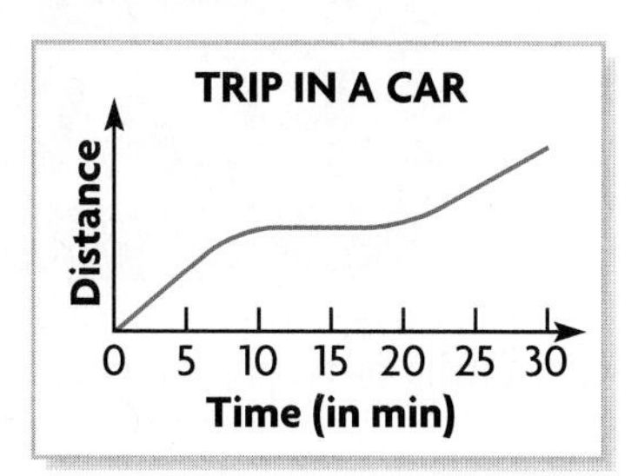

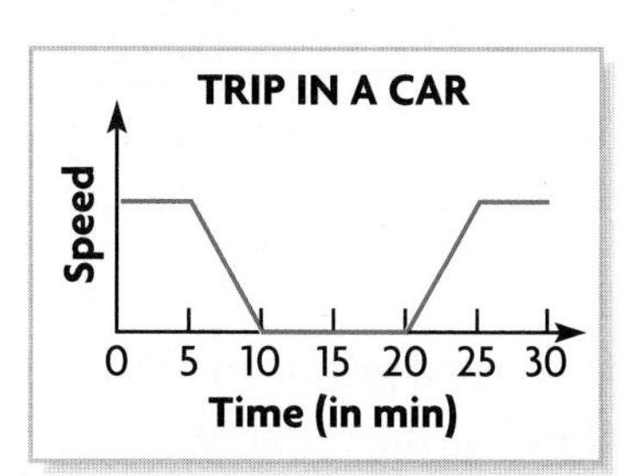

8. **TRANSPORTATION** Refer to the graphs in Problem 7. What story do the two graphs tell you about the car trip?

9. **RATES** For which interval do both graphs for a trip in a car show a constant rate?

10. **WRITE ABOUT IT** What three words can you use to describe the changes in a graph?

Mixed Review and Test Prep

11. Use the table to make a line graph.

Fund-Raiser Sales	
March	220
April	350
May	360
June	300
July	250
August	200
September	180
October	100

12. During which period did the fund-raiser sales decrease the most?

13. During which period did the fund-raiser sales increase the most?

Find the sales tax and total cost with a sales tax rate of 6%.

14. \$35.00
15. \$50
16. \$79.50
17. \$19.95

18. **CRITICAL THINKING** Hector was fishing at a lake. He saw his reflection in the water. He moved to the right. Which way did his reflection move?

A right **B** left **C** up **D** down

19. **NUMBER SENSE** Which combination of + and − signs makes a true sentence?

$5.25 \bullet 3.3 \bullet 14.72 \bullet 13.25 \bullet 3.0 = 6.42$

F −, +, +, −
G +, +, +, −
H −, +, −, +
J −, +, +, +

MORE PRACTICE Lesson 28.2, page H82

LESSON 28.3

ALGEBRA CONNECTION

Graphing Relationships

What You'll Learn
How to show the relationship between two variables on a graph

Why Learn This?
To understand how to show a relationship on a graph such as distance and time

Sometimes advertisements use graphs. Why do you think they use graphs to show relationships?

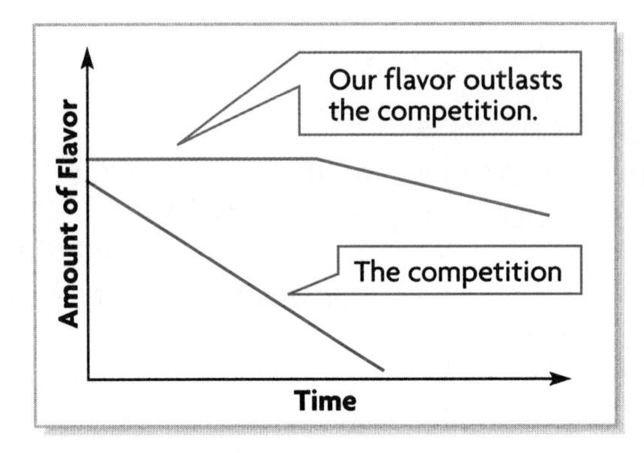

You can use a graph to show the relationship between two variables without using a lot of words.

Before you can sketch a graph of a relationship, you must identify the variables used in the relationship. Then the graph will show an increase, a decrease, or remain constant.

EXAMPLE Sketch a graph of the relationship in the following story. Label the axes.

At an amusement park, Phillip and his sister, Laticia, rode a roller coaster. After the ride Phillip commented, "My sister can really scream. The faster the roller coaster was moving, the louder she screamed."

Identify the variables in the relationship. Label the graph with the variables.

The variables used in this relationship are *speed* and *noise level.*

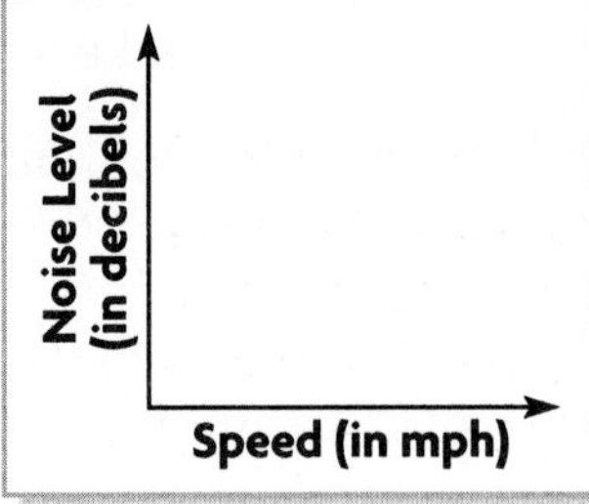

Sketch the graph. Determine whether the graph is increasing, decreasing, or constant.

Since the noise increases as the speed increases, this relationship is increasing.

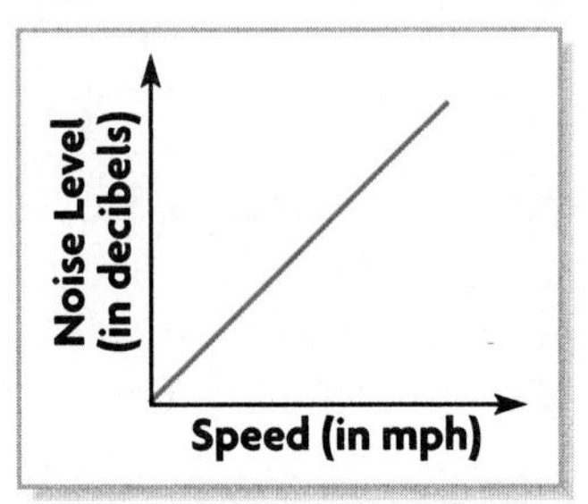

TEEN TIMES

The Mean Streak, a roller coaster at Cedar Point in Sandusky, Ohio, reaches a speed of 65 mph at the bottom of a 155-ft drop. Cedar Point has 11 other roller coasters, including looping coasters, inverted coasters, racing coasters, and a stand-up coaster.

GUIDED PRACTICE

Identify the variables you would use to graph the relationship.

1. The larger the crowd became, the higher the noise level became.
2. The heavier the bag of potatoes, the more it costs.
3. The smaller the boxes, the more boxes we can fit in the moving truck.
4. The higher the climb in a roller coaster, the faster the roller coaster will travel down.

INDEPENDENT PRACTICE

Copy and complete the graph.

1. The larger the circumference of the pizza, the more dough we will need.

Amount of Dough
Circumference

2. The diameter of a balloon decreases as air is released from the balloon.

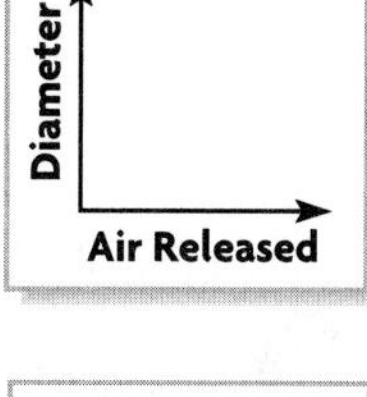

3. Since the product was first introduced, its price has not changed.

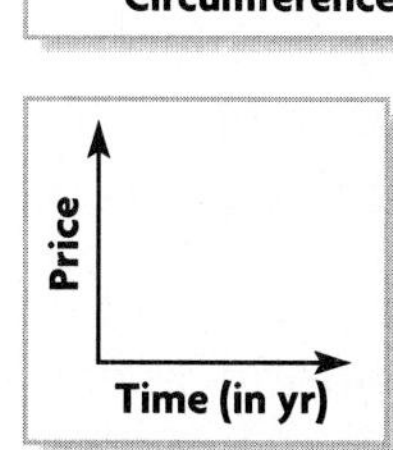

4. The larger the diamond, the more the diamond costs.

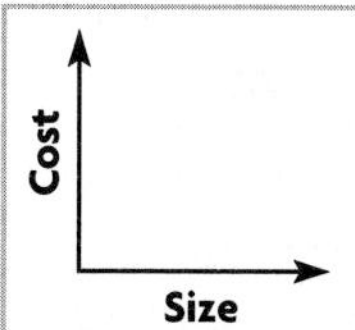

Sketch a graph of the relationship.

5. From summer to winter, the number of daylight hours decreases.
6. As the speed in miles per hour increases, the speed in kilometers per hour increases.
7. The greater the number of square feet of glass, the more it costs to replace the window.
8. The more money that you spend, the less money you save.

Problem-Solving Applications

9. **CRITICAL THINKING** Sheila is saving coupons for products she buys. She told her friend that the more coupons you use, the more money you save. Sheila showed her friend this graph. What is wrong with her graph? Draw your own graph of the relationship.

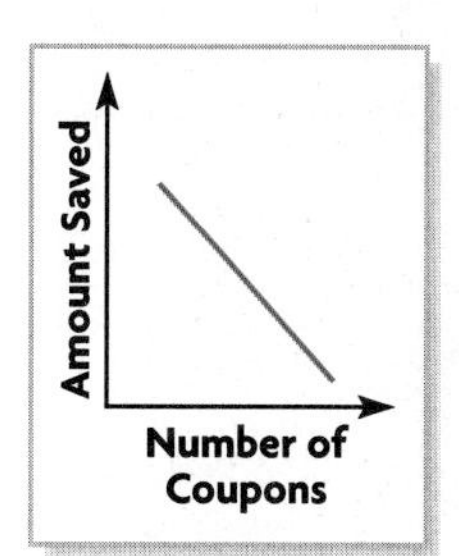

10. **ADVERTISING** A car company wants to run a new ad campaign. Its new slogan is "Practice makes perfect, and we have been making automobiles for 42 years." Sketch a graph that the company can use with the slogan.
11. **WRITE ABOUT IT** Write an example of a relationship like the ones in Exercises 5–8. Then draw a graph for the relationship.

MORE PRACTICE Lesson 28.3, page H82

ACTIVITY

What You'll Explore
How to plot data as ordered pairs and how to look for a relationship

What You'll Need
graph paper

Technology Link

You can make and analyze scatterplots by using E-Lab, Activity 28. Available on CD-ROM and on the Internet at **www.hbschool.com/elab**

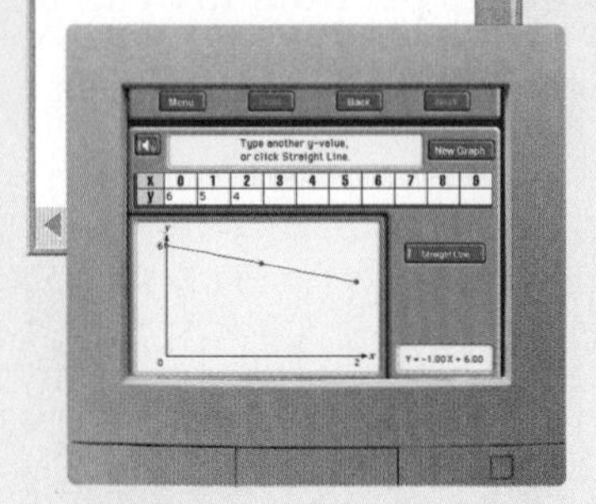

ALGEBRA CONNECTION

Exploring Scatterplots

Look at the graph. Do you think your shoe size has anything to do with your age? In this activity, you will explore data that may or may not have a relationship.

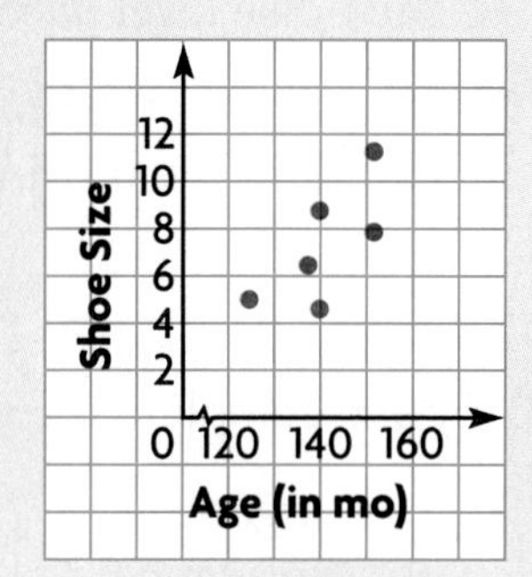

Explore

On a piece of graph paper, draw the horizontal and vertical axes for a graph.

- Select two variables from the list below.

shoe size	length of forearm
height	month of birth
age in months	last two digits of phone number

- Survey at least six people for information about these two variables. Write the information you get from each person as an ordered pair. For example, (shoe size, last two digits of phone number) could be (7,31).
- Label the axes of your graph with the variables. Then plot the data you gathered as points on the graph.

Think and Discuss

- Do the points on your graph form any kind of pattern? Explain.
- Do you have any point that does not fit your pattern? If so, how does this point compare with the other points?
- Do the points appear to be almost in a straight line? If so, describe the line.

Try This

Graph the following ordered pairs.

(1,2), (2,2), (2,3), (3,4), (4,3), (4,5), (5,5), (6,4), (7,6), (7,8), (8,7)

- How is the pattern in this graph similar to or different from the pattern formed in the graph you made above?

Using Scatterplots

What You'll Learn
How to show two variables in a data set on a scatterplot and how to identify their correlation

Why Learn This?
To compare two variables to decide if there is or is not a relationship

VOCABULARY
scatterplot
positive correlation
negative correlation
no correlation

Sometimes you want to know whether there is a relationship between two variables in a data set. If there is a relationship, you want to know what it is. To find out, you can graph the two variables on a graph called a **scatterplot**.

- Do you think a person's shoe size is related to his or her score on a math test?

(math score, shoe size)

(92,8) (90,5)
(78,9) (58,7)
(58,4) (34,10)
(34,5) (22,6)
(17,8)

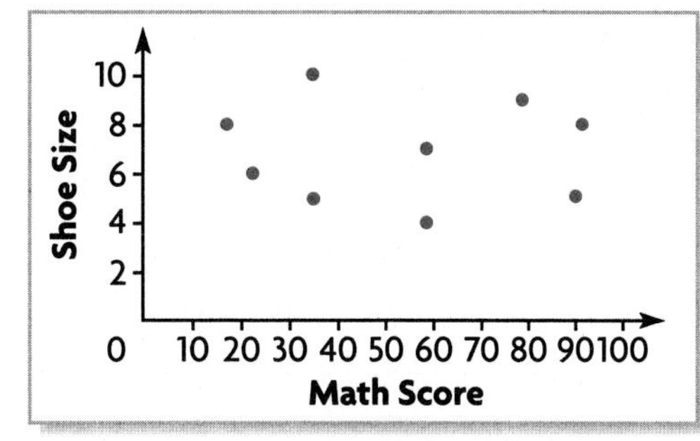

There are three ways to describe the data that is displayed in a scatterplot.

When the values of both variables increase or decrease together, there is a **positive correlation**. The points form a pattern that slants up in a straight line.

When the values of one variable increase and the other values decrease, there is a **negative correlation**. The points form a pattern that slants downward in a straight line.

When the data points are scattered and no pattern can be formed from the points, there is **no correlation**. In the example above, there appears to be no correlation between shoe size and math score.

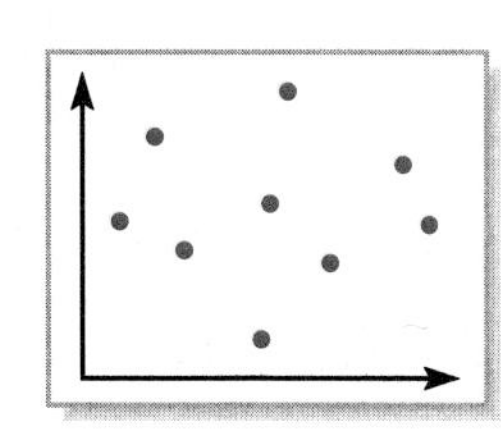

- CRITICAL THINKING What is an example of a relationship between two variables that show a positive correlation? a negative correlation? no correlation?

EXAMPLE 1 The graph at the right shows data for the number of hours worked and the amount of money earned. Identify the type of correlation shown in the graph.

The graph shows that as the number of hours worked increases, the amount of money earned increases.

So, this graph shows a positive correlation.

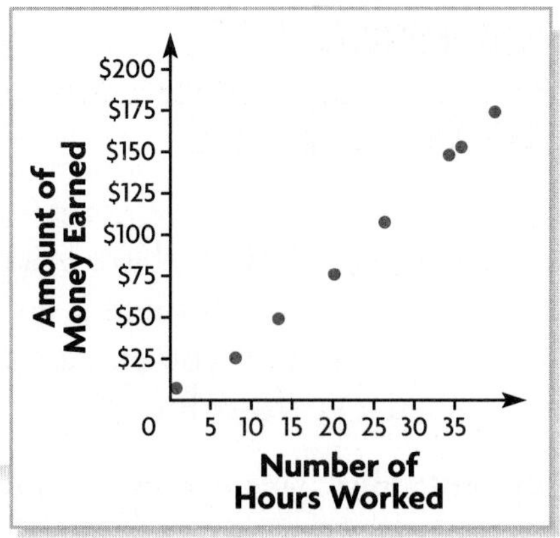

Suppose a toy company wants to determine whether advertising helps the sale of its products. It keeps track of the amount of money spent on advertising and the amount earned in sales.

Advertising Cost (in thousands of dollars)	47	56	45	59	35	75	65	25
Weekly Sales (in thousands of dollars)	495	501	502	506	490	520	515	475

EXAMPLE 2 Use the data above to make a scatterplot. Does advertising cost appear to be related to sales?

Make a scatterplot. From the graph, you can see that, as the amount spent on advertising increases the weekly sales increase. The graph shows a positive correlation.

So, it appears that advertising cost is related to sales.

- About how much do you think the company would sell if it spent $90,000 on advertising?

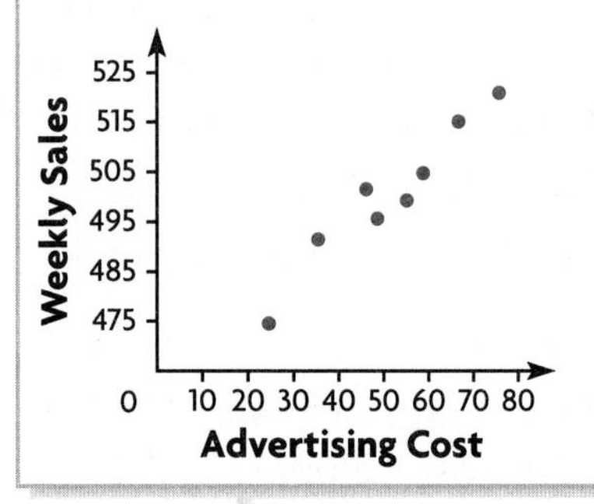

GUIDED PRACTICE

Write *positive, negative,* or *no correlation* to describe the relationship shown in the graph.

1.

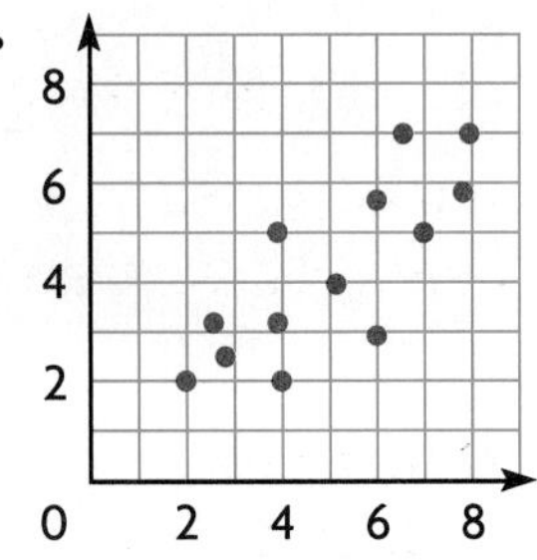

2.

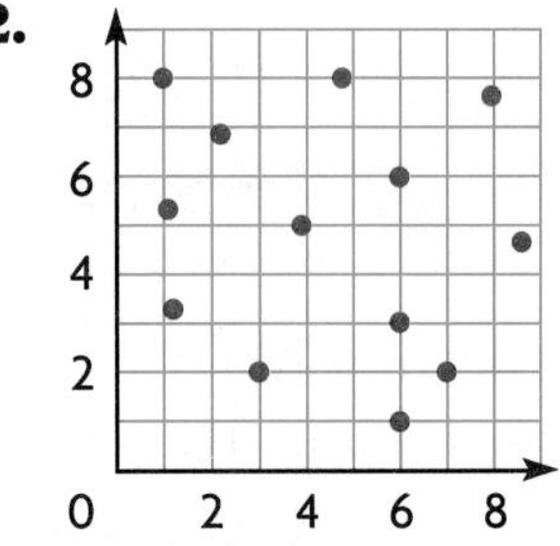

3.

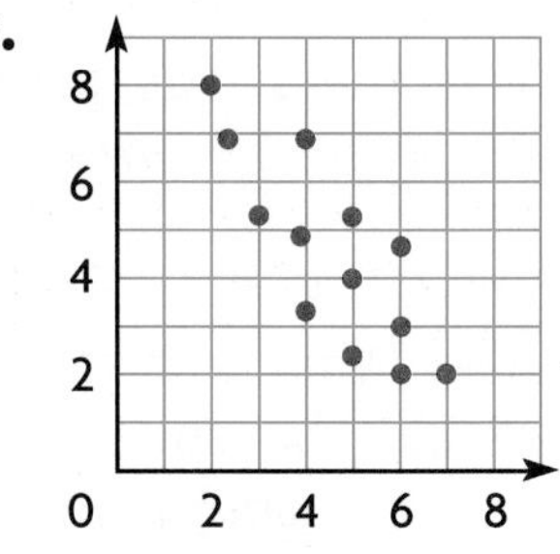

Calculator Activities, page H40

INDEPENDENT PRACTICE

Write *positive, negative,* or *no correlation* to describe the relationship between the two variables.

1. number of students in a school; number of school buses

2. amount of driver training; number of accidents

3. amount of traffic; number of traffic lights

Draw a scatterplot to represent the set of data. Write *positive, negative,* or *no correlation* to describe the relationship.

4.

ENERGY	U.S.	RUSSIA	CHINA	CANADA	GREAT BRITAIN	INDIA
Energy Produced (in quadrillion Btu)	66.68	45.66	30.18	14.36	9.23	6.94
Energy Used (in quadrillion Btu)	82.19	32.72	29.22	10.97	9.68	8.51

5.

Phone Number's Last Digit	0	6	2	7	4	1
Person's Weight (in lb)	90	100	120	75	110	160

Problem-Solving Applications

A scatterplot of the games won and the injuries for eight teams during a basketball season is shown at the right.

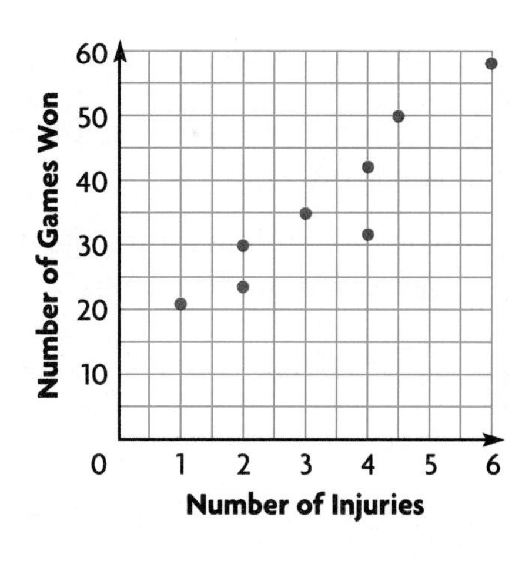

6. What is the relationship between the number of games won and the number of injuries?

7. **SPORTS** Suppose you added data for eight teams that have a high number of wins and a low number of injuries. How would these data affect the correlation shown in the scatterplot?

8. **WRITE ABOUT IT** What three possible relationships between two variables can be identified in a scatterplot?

Mixed Review and Test Prep

Find the simple interest earned on $1,500 for the given rate and time.

9. 6% for 5 years

10. 12% for 3 years

11. 8.75% for 4 years

12. 3.5% for 8.5 years

13. **RATES** It takes Nick 30 minutes to paint $\frac{3}{4}$ of a wall. At this rate, how long will it take him to paint 6 walls?

A 280 min
B 4 hr
C 180 min
D 2 hr

14. **NUMBER SENSE** The product of two numbers is 156. The sum is 25. What are the two numbers?

F 9 and 10
G 10 and 15
H 11 and 14
J 12 and 13

MORE PRACTICE Lesson 28.4, page H82

CHAPTER 28 Review/Test

1. Which graph shows the relationship between time and the distance the golf ball traveled? (pages 550–551)

a.
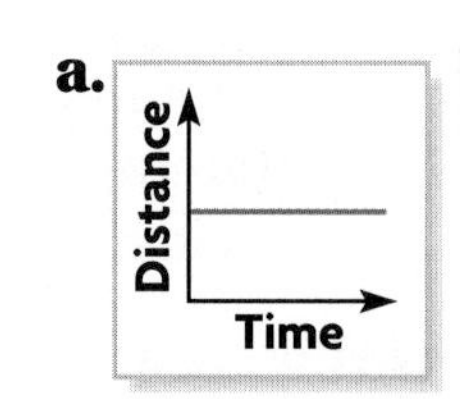

b.
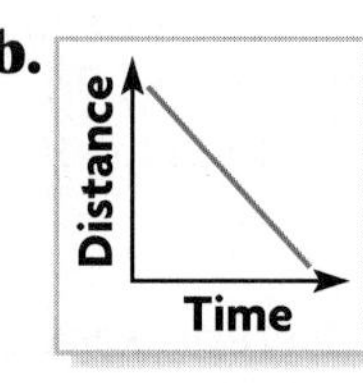

c.
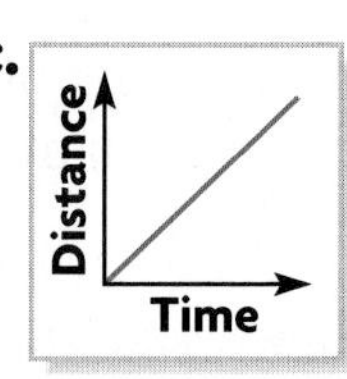

2. Describe the relationship shown in graph **b** in Exercise 1. (pages 550–551)

3. Which graph shows the relationship between altitude and time? (pages 550–551)

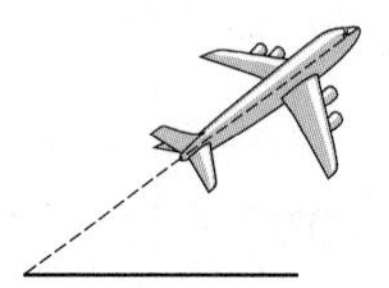

a.
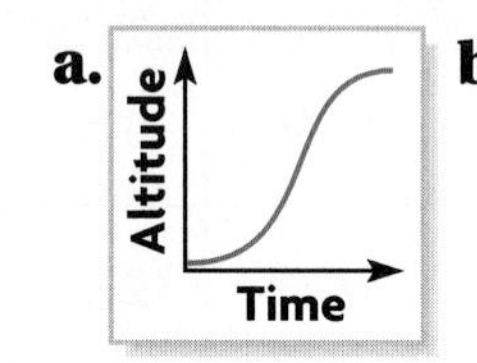

b.
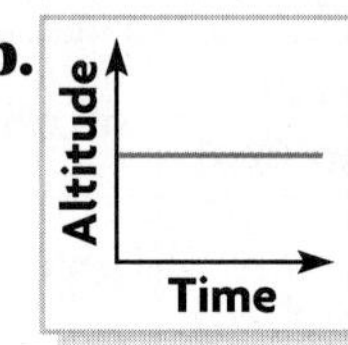

c.
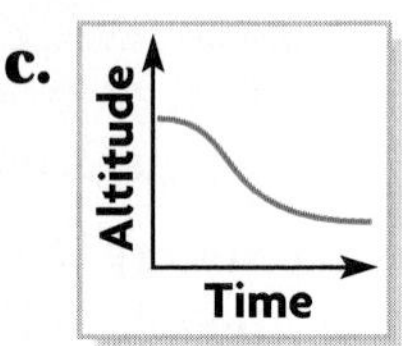

4. Describe the relationship shown in graph **b** in Exercise 3. (pages 550–551)

For Exercises 5–7, use the graph. (pages 552–555)

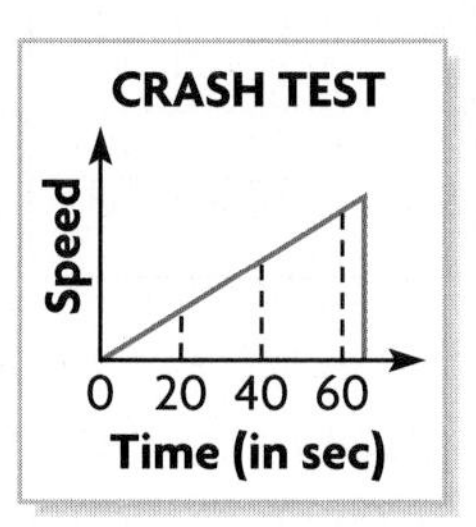

5. How does the speed change from 0 to 60 sec?

6. How does the speed change after 60 sec?

7. Write a story about the graph.

Sketch the graph for the relationship. (pages 556–557)

8. The more you exercise, the more calories you burn.

9. A car is driven at a constant speed for 1 hr.

10. The record time for the 100-m run has decreased over the years.

11. The larger the airplane, the more passengers it can carry.

Write *positive, negative,* or *no correlation* to describe each relationship. (pages 559–561)

12. speed and driving time for a 200-mi trip

13. size of hand and typing speed

14. the number of people invited to dinner and the number of plates needed

15. the number of students and the number of last names

16. height of a dropped object and time

17. number of sunny days and number of stars

18. **VOCABULARY** A graph of two sets of variables is a(n) __?__. (page 559)

19. Draw a scatterplot of the data below. (pages 559–561)

Time (in sec)	44.5	42.8	42.55	41.65
Year	1960	1968	1976	1984

20. Draw a scatterplot of the data below. (pages 559–561)

Number of Donuts	1	2	3	4	5	6
Cost	\$0.55	\$1.10	\$1.50	\$2.05	\$2.60	\$3.00

Test Prep

1. The graph shows the relationship between the diameter of a circle and its circumference. Which is a reasonable conclusion?

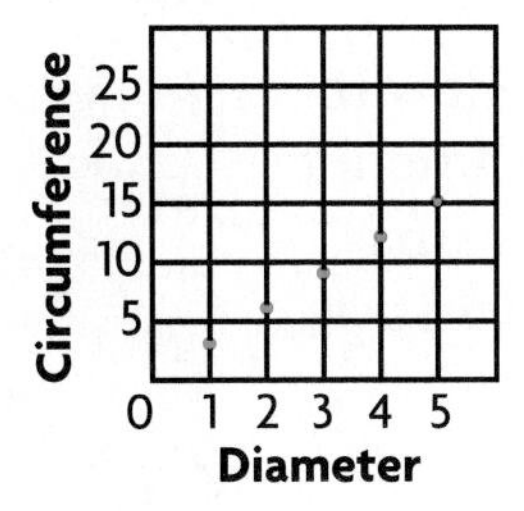

A Circumference increases as diameter decreases.
B As diameter increases by 1, circumference increases by 1.
C There is no relationship between diameter and circumference.
D Circumference increases as diameter increases.

2. Triangle *ABC* and triangle *XYZ* are similar. What is the value of x?

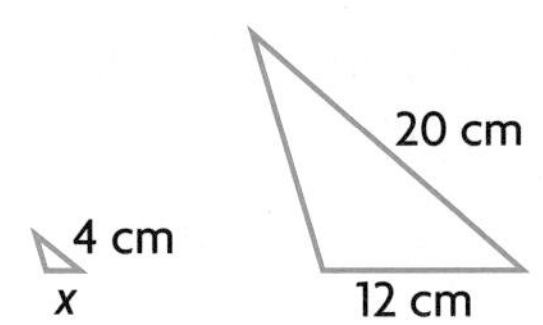

F 2.4 cm **G** 2.8 cm **H** 4 cm **J** 8 cm

3. A florist buys plants for $1.50 each and sells them for $3.75 each. What is the percent of markup?

A 250% **B** 150% **C** 60% **D** 40%

4. What is the correlation between your shoe size and your golf score?

F positive correlation
G negative correlation
H no correlation
J linear correlation

5. The length of a side of a cube is doubled. How is the surface area changed?

A It doubles.
B It is multiplied by 4.
C It is multiplied by 6.
D It is multiplied by 8.

6. Which is the best estimate of the length of the toothpick?

F 6 mm **G** 6 cm
H 6 m **J** 6 km

7. You want to make a graph to show the population of students at your school over the past 10 years. Which is the most appropriate graph?

A line plot
B line graph
C bar graph
D circle graph

8. Which fraction can be written as a terminating decimal?

F $\frac{1}{3}$ **G** $\frac{1}{9}$
H $\frac{1}{16}$ **J** $\frac{1}{24}$

9. Which figure has the following top, front, and side views?

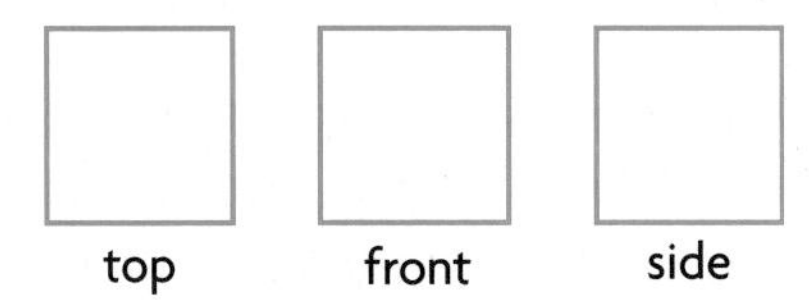

A rectangular pyramid
B square
C cube
D parallelogram

CHAPTERS 27–28

MATH FUN!

DISCOUNT DERBY

PURPOSE To practice finding amount of discount (pages 532–535)
YOU WILL NEED newspapers, scissors

Each player has 2 minutes to search through a newspaper to find the advertisement with the greatest amount of discount. The player with the advertisement with the greatest amount of discount earns 1 point. The first player to earn 5 points is the winner.

FLAVOR FEST

PURPOSE To practice making graphs that tell a story (pages 556–557)
YOU WILL NEED chewing gum, timepiece with a second hand

Every 10 sec, from the time you put your chewing gum in your mouth until 60 seconds are up, rate its flavor. Use a scale of 10 to 0 with 10 having the greatest flavor. Make a graph to show how the flavor changes. Label both axes. Write a story to match your graph.

Show the graph to family members. Challenge them to explain what it shows.

SURVEYS TO SCATTERPLOTS

PURPOSE To practice showing two variables on a scatterplot and describing their relationship (pages 558–561)
YOU WILL NEED graph paper

Survey 10–20 of your classmates. Choose topics below or two of your own:

- number of soft drinks per week you drink; number of fillings in your teeth
- number of pets you own; how much you like animals on a scale of 1 to 10

Make a scatterplot. Label both axes. Describe the relationship between the variables.

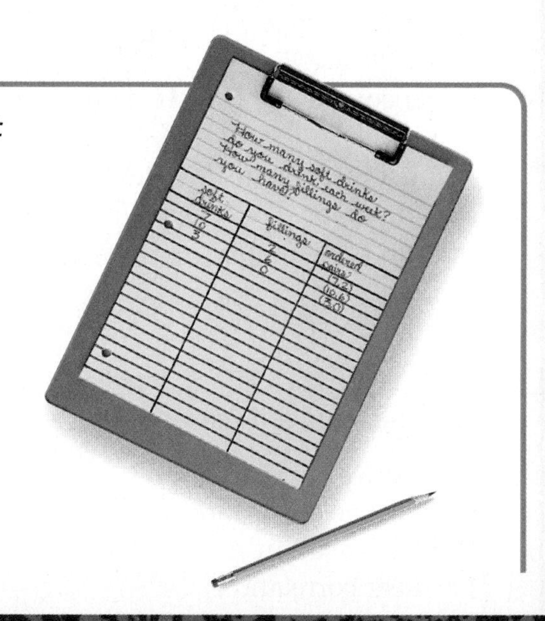

Compound and Simple Interest

You can earn interest on previously earned interest using **compound interest**. Suppose you have $500 to invest. You can invest $500 for 4 years at 8% simple interest or 8% compound interest compounded annually. Use a spreadsheet to decide.

Simple Interest

Enter the years and the principal. Then enter the formula to find the total amount of your investment for 1 year using simple interest.

untitled

All	A	B
1	Year	Amount
2	0	$500
3	1	=500+500*.08*A3
4	2	
5	3	
6	4	

Use the Fill Down command to find the total amount of your investment for 2–4 years.

untitled

All	A	B
1	Year	Amount
2	0	$500.00
3	1	$540.00
4	2	$580.00
5	3	$620.00
6	4	$660.00

Compound Interest

Enter the years and the principal. Then enter the formula to find the total amount of your investment for 1 year of compound interest.

untitled

All	A	B
2	0	$500.00
3	1	=B2*.08+B2
4	2	
5	3	
6	4	

Use the Fill Down Command to find the total amount of your investment for 2–4 years.

untitled

All	A	B
2	0	$500.00
3	1	$540.00
4	2	$583.20
5	3	$629.86
6	4	$660.24

1. Should you invest your money using simple or compound interest? Explain.

2. What does the formula =B2*.08+B2 in cell B3 represent?

USING THE SPREADSHEET

3. Use a spreadsheet to compare an investment of $2,750 for 10 years at 6.5% simple and compound interest.

CHAPTERS 27–28

Study Guide and Review

Vocabulary Check

1. The amount that an item is marked down is the __?__. (page 532)

2. Add the markup to the wholesale price to find the __?__ price. (page 536)

EXAMPLES

• Find sales tax and total cost. (pages 528–531)

Find the total cost.

Price of jacket: $70.00 ← 100%
Sales tax rate: 6% ← + 6%

$\$70.00 \times 1.06 = \$74.20$ *Multiply the price by 106%.*

EXERCISES

Find the sales tax and total cost.

3. 8% on a $28.50 game
4. 6.5% on a $22.00 shirt

Find the sales tax rate.

5. price of CD: $14.80; sales tax $0.74
6. price of stereo: $399.00; sales tax $23.94

EXAMPLES

• Find discount and sale price. (pages 532–535)

The regular price of a pair of shoes is $79.95. The discount is 40%. Find the sale price.

$100\% - 40\% = 60\%$ *Find the sale price percent.*

$\$79.95 \times 60\% = \$79.95 \times 0.6$ *Multiply by 60%.*
$= \$47.97$

EXERCISES

Find the sale price.

7. regular price: $45.50; discount: 50%
8. regular price: $24.00; discount: 20%

Find the percent of discount.

9. regular price: $125.00; sale price: $93.75
10. regular price: $48.00; sale price: $31.20

EXAMPLES

• Find markup and total price. (pages 536–538)

The markup on a pair of in-line skates is 60%. The wholesale price is $55. Find the retail price.

$60\% \text{ of } \$55.00 = 0.6 \times \$55.00$ *Multiply to find the markup.*
$= \$33.00$

$\$33.00 + \$55.00 = \$88.00$ *Add to find the retail price.*

EXERCISES

Find the retail price.

11. wholesale price: $65.00; markup: 40%
12. wholesale price: $24.98; markup: 100%

Find the percent of markup.

13. wholesale price: $10.00; retail price: $15.00
14. wholesale price: $45.00; retail price: $81.00

EXAMPLES

• Find simple interest. (pages 540–542)

Find the simple interest earned on $250.00 at 7% for 5 years.

$I = prt$
$I = \$250.00 \times 0.07 \times 5$
$I = \$87.50$

EXERCISES

Find the simple interest and the total amount.

15. $p = \$500.00$, $r = 7.5\%$, $t = 10$ yr

16. $p = \$1{,}000.00$, $r = 6\%$, $t = 4$ yr

- **Represent a picture as a graph.** (pages 550–551)

Which graph shows the relationship between time and the distance the ball has traveled?

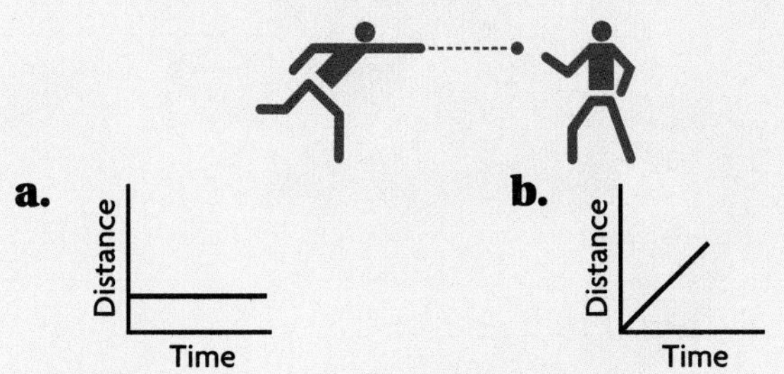

Graph **b** shows the relationship, because distance increases as time increases.

Which graph shows the relationship between time and the altitude of the basketball?

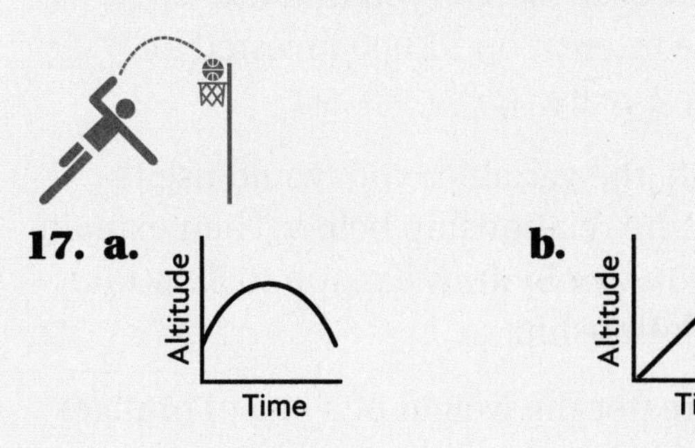

- **Show a relationship as a graph.** (pages 556–557)

Sketch a graph of the relationship: The larger the bus, the more passengers it can hold.

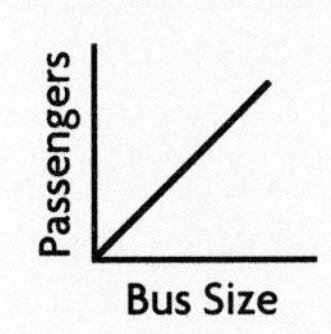

Sketch a graph of the relationship.

18. The larger the box of detergent you buy, the lower the unit cost.

19. The number of hours spent playing tennis is the same every week.

Problem-Solving Applications

Solve. Explain your method.

20. Jacques put $125.00 in a bank that paid a simple interest rate of 3%. How much did he have in his account at the end of two years? (pages 540–542)

21. Ms. Peterson charged a dress that cost $50.00. The interest rate is 1.2% monthly. She will pay $10.00 each month. How much interest will she pay? (pages 543–545)

22. From the graph below, what can you say about the distance a truck traveled? (pages 552–555)

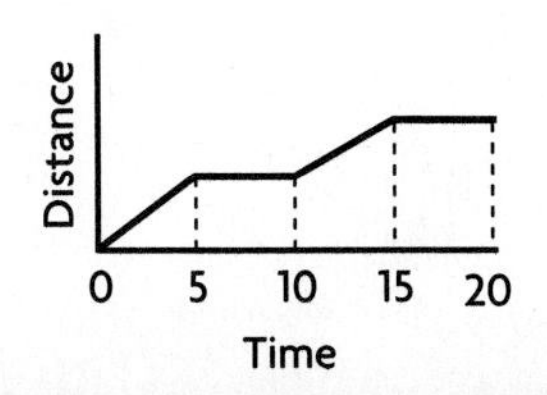

23. Draw a scatterplot from the data in the table below. (pages 559–561)

Age	11	12	13	14	15	16
Shoe Size	6	7	6	8	12	9

CHAPTERS 27–28

Performance Assessment

Tasks: Show What You Know

1. Explain each step as you find the simple interest on $1,000 invested at 8% for 2 years. (pages 540–542)

2. Identify the variables you would use to graph the relationship below. Then explain how you would draw a graph to illustrate the relationship.

   The greater the weight of a bag of oranges, the more it costs. (pages 556–557)

Problem Solving

Solve. Explain your method.

CHOOSE a strategy and a tool.

- Find a Pattern
- Make a Model
- Act It Out
- Make a Table
- Write a Number Sentence

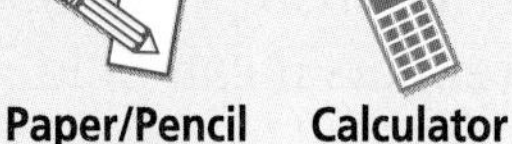
Paper/Pencil
Calculator

Hands-On

Mental Math

3. Craig put $125.00 in a savings account at a local bank. The account will earn 6% simple interest. After 4 years, will he have enough in the account to buy a $152.95 computer program? Explain your reasoning. (pages 540–542)

4. Juan plays chess on the computer every day after school. He finds that the more computer games he plays, the less he watches television. Make a graph of this relationship. Label the graph, and tell whether the graph is increasing, decreasing, or constant. (pages 556–557)

Cumulative Review

Solve the problem. Then write the letter of the correct answer.

1. Which of the following is a rational number between $^{-}6.3$ and $^{-}6.31$? (pages 20–21)

A. $^{-}6.32$ **B.** $^{-}6.305$
C. $^{-}6.2$ **D.** 6.304

---

2. What is the value of 60^3? (pages 36–39)

A. 180 **B.** 603
C. 3,600 **D.** not here

---

3. Subtract. Write the answer in simplest form. (pages 82–83)

$5\frac{7}{12} - 3\frac{3}{4}$

A. $1\frac{8}{12} = 1\frac{2}{3}$ **B.** $1\frac{5}{6}$
C. $2\frac{4}{8} = 2\frac{1}{2}$ **D.** $2\frac{10}{12}$

---

4. Find the product. (pages 106–108)

$48 \times {}^{-}8$

A. $^{-}384$ **B.** $^{-}6$
C. 6 **D.** not here

---

5. Solve $x + 3x - 5 = {}^{-}29$. (pages 164–166)

A. $x = {}^{-}8$ **B.** $x = {}^{-}6$
C. $x = 6$ **D.** $x = 8$

---

6. How are the following triangles shown to be congruent? (pages 224–227)

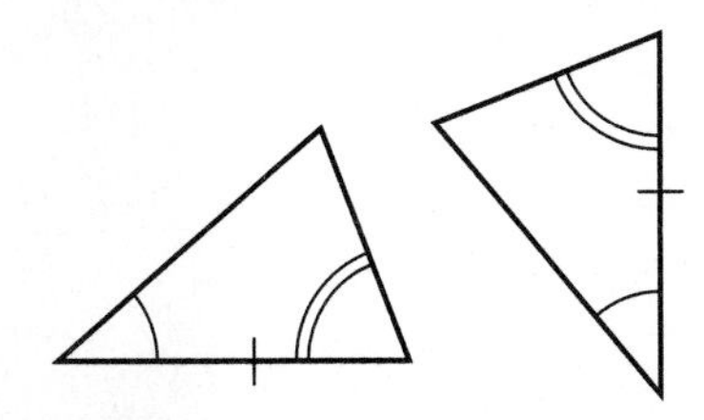

A. AAA **B.** ASA
C. SAS **D.** SSS

---

7. What is 150% of 50? (pages 298–300)

A. 0.75 **B.** 3
C. 75 **D.** not here

---

8. How many times must 10 be doubled to reach or exceed 300? (pages 362–363)

A. 2 times **B.** 3 times
C. 4 times **D.** 5 times

---

9. Rename $\frac{1}{3}$ as a decimal. (pages 372–374)

A. $^{-}3.0$ **B.** 0.13
C. 0.30 **D.** $0.\overline{3}$

For Exercises 10–11, use these data: 26, 38, 38, 44, 58, 69, 70 (pages 414–416)

10. What is the median?

A. 38 **B.** 44
C. 49 **D.** 70

---

11. What is the mean?

A. 38 **B.** 44
C. 49 **D.** not here

---

12. Tom, Matt, Rachel, Liz, and Sarah found 5 seats together in the same row. Find the number of different orders in which the 5 can sit. (pages 436–439)

A. 20 orders **B.** 26 orders
C. 100 orders **D.** 120 orders

---

13. Find the area of the trapezoid. Use the formula $A = \frac{1}{2}h(b_1 + b_2)$. (pages 479–481)

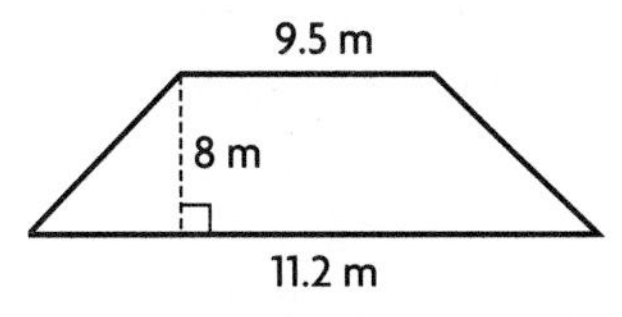

A. 28.7 m^2 **B.** 82.8 m^2
C. 165.6 m^2 **D.** 582.4 m^2

If you've forgotten how to do something in math, this list of Key Skills can help you. Use it to find the exact skill to review.

1 Place Value
2 Rules for Rounding
3 Compatible Numbers
4 Overestimates and Underestimates
5 Squares and Square Roots
6 Exponents
7 Order of Operations
8 Ways to Show Multiplication
9 Properties
10 Adding and Subtracting Decimals
11 Multiplying and Dividing by Powers of 10
12 Multiplying Decimals
13 Dividing Decimals
14 Writing Decimals as Fractions
15 Writing Decimals as Percents
16 Terminating and Repeating Decimals
17 Multiples
18 Factors
19 Divisibility Rules
20 Prime and Composite Numbers
21 Prime Factorization
22 Greatest Common Factor
23 Least Common Multiple
24 Equivalent Fractions
25 Simplest Form of Fractions
26 Mixed Numbers and Fractions
27 Adding and Subtracting Fractions
28 Multiplying and Dividing Fractions
29 Writing Fractions as Decimals
30 Writing Fractions as Percents
31 Ratios
32 Equivalent Ratios
33 Proportions
34 Solving a Proportion
35 Representing Percent
36 Writing Percents as Fractions and Decimals
37 Finding the Percent of a Number
38 Geometric Figures
39 Types of Angles
40 Measuring Angles
41 Customary Measures
42 Metric Measures
43 Perimeter and Area
44 Types of Polygons
45 Solid Figures
46 Mean and Median
47 Mode and Range
48 Integers and Their Opposites
49 Absolute Value
50 Modeling Integers
51 Adding Integers
52 Subtracting Integers
53 Multiplying Integers
54 Dividing Integers
55 Types of Triangles
56 Angles in a Triangle

1 PLACE VALUE

A place-value chart can help you read and write numbers. The number 345,012,678,912.5784 is shown.

Billions	Millions	Thousands	Ones	Tenths	Hundredths	Thousandths	Ten-Thousandths
345,	012,	678,	912 .	5	7	8	4

Example Use the number above to name the place value of the digit.

A. the 7 in the thousands period
7 → ten-thousands place

B. the 0 in the millions period
0 → hundred-millions place

C. the 5 in the billions period
5 → one billion, or billions place

D. the 5 to the right of the decimal
5 → tenths

PRACTICE Name the place value of the underlined digit.

1. 123,<u>4</u>56,789,123.0594

2. 1<u>2</u>3,456,789,123.0594

3. 123,456,789,123.05<u>9</u>4

4. 123,456,789,12<u>3</u>.0594

5. 123,456,789,123.<u>0</u>594

6. 123,45<u>6</u>,789,123.0594

2 RULES FOR ROUNDING

To round to a certain place, follow these steps.

- Locate the digit in that place, and consider the next digit to the right.
- If the digit to the right is 5 or greater, round up. If the digit to the right is 4 or less, round down.
- Change each digit to the right of the rounding place to zero.

Examples

A. Round 125,439.378 to the nearest thousand.

Locate digit.
↓
12<u>5</u>,439.378
↑
The digit to the right is less than 5, so the digit in the rounding location stays the same.
↓
125,000

B. Round 125,439.378 to the nearest tenth.

Locate digit.
↓
125,439.<u>3</u>78
↑
The digit to the right is greater than 5, so the digit in the rounding location increases by 1.
↓
125,439.4

PRACTICE Round 259,345.278 to the place indicated.

1. hundred thousand

2. ten thousand

3. thousand

4. hundred

5. hundredth

6. tenth

7. one

8. ten

3 COMPATIBLE NUMBERS

Use compatible numbers to estimate quotients. Compatible numbers divide without a remainder, are close to the actual numbers, and are easy to compute mentally.

Examples

A. Use compatible numbers to estimate the quotient. 6,134 ÷ 35

6,134 ÷ 35
6,000 ÷ 30 = 200 ← *estimate*
↑ ↑
compatible numbers

B. Use compatible numbers to estimate the quotient. 647 ÷ 7

647 ÷ 7
630 ÷ 7 = 90 ← *estimate*
↑ ↑
compatible numbers

PRACTICE Estimate the quotient by using compatible numbers.

1. 345 ÷ 5
2. 5,474 ÷ 23
3. 46,170 ÷ 18
4. 749 ÷ 7
5. 861 ÷ 41
6. 1,225 ÷ 2
7. 968 ÷ 47
8. 3,456 ÷ 432
9. 5,765 ÷ 26
10. 25,012 ÷ 64

4 OVERESTIMATES AND UNDERESTIMATES

When an estimate is greater than the actual answer, it is an **overestimate**.

When an estimate is less than the actual answer, it is an **underestimate**.

Overestimate Examples

Give an overestimate for 124 + 371.
124 + 371 → 130 + 380 = 510

Give an overestimate for 28 × 8.
28 × 8 → 30 × 10 = 300

Give an overestimate for 64 − 12.
64 − 12 → 70 − 10 = 60

Give an overestimate for 316 ÷ 12.
316 ÷ 12 → 320 ÷ 10 = 32

Underestimate Examples

Give an underestimate for 124 + 371.
124 + 371 → 120 + 370 = 490

Give an underestimate for 28 × 8.
28 × 8 → 25 × 8 = 200

Give an underestimate for 64 − 12.
64 − 12 → 60 − 15 = 45

Give an underestimate for 316 ÷ 12.
316 ÷ 12 → 300 ÷ 15 = 20

PRACTICE Give an overestimate and underestimate for each.

1. 124 + 345
2. 647 + 136
3. 453 − 107
4. 1,240 − 235
5. 12 × 16
6. 9 × 35
7. 345 ÷ 12
8. 75 ÷ 26

5 SQUARES AND SQUARE ROOTS

To find the square of a number, multiply the number by itself. The square root of a number is one of the two identical factors of the number. The symbol for n squared is n^2. The symbol for the positive square root of n is $\sqrt{n}$.

Examples Find the square.

A. 5^2

$5^2 = 5 \times 5 = 25$

B. 2.7^2

$2.7^2 = 2.7 \times 2.7 = 7.29$

Examples Find the square root.

A. $\sqrt{25}$

Since $5 \times 5 = 25$, $\sqrt{25} = 5$.

NOTE: Although $^-5 \times {}^-5 = 25$, $\sqrt{n}$ stands for the positive square root of n. Therefore, $\sqrt{25} \neq {}^-5$.

B. $\sqrt{7.29}$

Since $2.7 \times 2.7 = 7.29$, $\sqrt{7.29} = 2.7$.

PRACTICE Find the square or square root. Use a calculator if necessary.

1. 7^2 **2.** 10^2 **3.** 9^2 **4.** 15^2 **5.** 3.9^2 **6.** 6.25^2

7. $\sqrt{49}$ **8.** $\sqrt{100}$ **9.** $\sqrt{81}$ **10.** $\sqrt{225}$ **11.** $\sqrt{15.21}$ **12.** $\sqrt{39.0625}$

6 EXPONENTS

Exponents are used to represent repeated multiplication of the same number.

Example Write $7 \times 7 \times 7 \times 7 \times 7$ by using an exponent.

$7 \times 7 \times 7 \times 7 \times 7 = 7^5$ ← *exponent*

↑ *factors* ↑ *base*

The exponent equals the number of times the base is used as a factor.

Example Find the values of 3^6, 3^0, and 3^1.

$3^6 = 3 \times 3 \times 3 \times 3 \times 3 \times 3 = 729$

Any number $n^0 = 1$, $n \neq 0$. Any number $n^1 = n$.

$3^0 = 1$ $3^1 = 3$

PRACTICE Write by using an exponent.

1. $4 \times 4 \times 4 \times 4 \times 4$ **2.** $2 \times 2 \times 2 \times 2 \times 2 \times 2$ **3.** $8 \times 8 \times 8$ **4.** $14 \times 14 \times 14 \times 14$

Find the value.

5. 2^6 **6.** 4^3 **7.** 3^4 **8.** 5^3 **9.** 248^0 **10.** 15^1

7 ORDER OF OPERATIONS

Always follow this order to find the value of an expression.

1. Operate inside parentheses.
2. Clear exponents.
3. Multiply and divide from left to right.
4. Add and subtract from left to right.

Examples

A. Find the value.

$10 \div 2 + 8 \times 2^3 - 4$

$10 \div 2 + 8 \times 2^3 - 4$ *Clear exponent.*

$10 \div 2 + 8 \times 8 - 4$ *Multiply and divide.*

$5 + 64 - 4$ *Add and subtract.*

65

B. Find the value.

$10 \div (2 + 8) \times 2^3 - 4$

$10 \div (2 + 8) \times 2^3 - 4$ *Add inside parentheses.*

$10 \div 10 \times 2^3 - 4$ *Clear exponent.*

$10 \div 10 \times 8 - 4$ *Multiply and divide.*

$8 - 4$ *Subtract.*

4

PRACTICE Find the value.

1. $45 - 15 \div 3$
2. $(45 - 15) \div 3$
3. $10 \div 2 + 8 \times 2$
4. $4 \times 12 - (4 + 8) \div 2$
5. $3^2 - 10 \div 2 + 4 \times 2$
6. $4 \div 2 + 8 \times 2^3 - 4$
7. $(3 + 7) \times (5 - 1)^3$
8. $(30 + 22) \div (9 - 7) - 3^2$

8 WAYS TO SHOW MULTIPLICATION

Multiplication can be shown in several ways.

7×8 $7 \cdot 8$ $7(8)$ $(7)(8)$

When a variable is used in an expression with multiplication, the multiplication sign is usually omitted. An expression such as $5 \times n$ is written as $5n$.

PRACTICE Write the expression in two other ways.

1. 4×8
2. 9×10
3. $3 \cdot 15$
4. $2 \cdot 11$
5. $(9)(2)(5)$
6. $3 \times b$
7. $7 \cdot n$
8. $5(k)$
9. $2 \times a \times b$
10. $4(c)$

9 PROPERTIES

The following are basic properties of addition and multiplication.

Addition	
Commutative:	$a + b = b + a$
Associative:	$(a + b) + c = a + (b + c)$
Identity Property of Zero:	$a + 0 = a$ and $0 + a = a$

Multiplication	
Commutative:	$a \times b = b \times a$
Associative:	$(a \times b) \times c = a \times (b \times c)$
Identity Property of One:	$a \times 1 = a$ and $1 \times a = a$
Property of Zero:	$a \times 0 = 0$ and $0 \times a = 0$
Distributive:	$a \times (b + c) = ab + ac$

PRACTICE Name the property illustrated.

1. $4 + 0 = 4$

2. $(6 + 3) + 1 = 6 + (3 + 1)$

3. $7 \times 51 = 51 \times 7$

4. $5 \times 456 = 456 \times 5$

5. $17 \times (1 + 3) = 17 \times 1 + 17 \times 3$

6. $1 \times 5 = 5$

7. $(8 \times 2) \times 5 = 8 \times (2 \times 5)$

8. $72 + 1{,}234 = 1{,}234 + 72$

9. $0 \times 12 = 0$

10 ADDING AND SUBTRACTING DECIMALS

When adding and subtracting decimals, you must remember to line up the decimal points vertically. You may add zeros to the right of the decimal point as placeholders. Adding zeros to the right of the last digit after the decimal point doesn't change the value of the number.

Examples

A. Find the sum. 3.54 + 1.7 + 22 + 13.409

$$\begin{array}{r} 3.540 \\ 1.700 \\ 22.000 \\ +\ 13.409 \\ \hline 40.649 \end{array}$$

3.540 is equivalent to 3.54.

B. Find the difference. 636.2 − 28.538

$$\begin{array}{r} 636.200 \\ -28.538 \\ \hline 607.662 \end{array}$$

636.200 is equivalent to 636.2.

PRACTICE Find the sum or difference.

1. 0.687 + 0.9 + 27.25

2. 87.34 − 6.8

3. 65 + 0.0004 + 2.57

4. 17 − 0.095

5. 263.7 − 102.08

6. 27 + 3.24 + 0.256 + 0.3689

7. 29.23 − 19.9984

8. 34.2 + 196.79 + 5.825

9. 1,929.842 − 27.68

11 MULTIPLYING AND DIVIDING DECIMALS BY POWERS OF 10

Notice the pattern below.

$0.24 \times 10 = 2.4$ $\quad 10 = 10^1$
$0.24 \times 100 = 24$ $\quad 100 = 10^2$
$0.24 \times 1{,}000 = 240$ $\quad 1{,}000 = 10^3$
$0.24 \times 10{,}000 = 2{,}400$ $\quad 10{,}000 = 10^4$

Think: *When multiplying decimals by powers of 10, move the decimal point one place to the* right *for each power of 10, or for each zero.*

Notice the pattern below.

$0.24 \div 10 = 0.024$
$0.24 \div 100 = 0.0024$
$0.24 \div 1{,}000 = 0.00024$
$0.24 \div 10{,}000 = 0.000024$

Think: *When dividing decimals by powers of 10, move the decimal point one place to the* left *for each power of 10, or for each zero.*

PRACTICE Find the product or quotient.

1. 10×9.26 **2.** 0.642×100 **3.** $10^3 \times 84.2$ **4.** 0.44×10^4 **5.** $69.7 \times 1{,}000$

6. $11.32 \div 10$ **7.** $1.276 \div 1{,}000$ **8.** $536.5 \div 10^2$ **9.** $5.92 \div 10^3$ **10.** $25 \div 10{,}000$

11. 100×0.2 **12.** 3.79×10^5 **13.** $18.2 \div 10$ **14.** $117.6 \div 10^6$ **15.** 192.07×10^3

12 MULTIPLYING DECIMALS

When multiplying decimals, multiply as you would with whole numbers. The sum of the decimal places in the factors equals the number of decimal places in the product.

Examples Find the product.

A. 81.2×6.547

```
     6.547 ← 3 decimal places
    × 81.2 ← 1 decimal place
     13094
     65470
  + 5237600
  531.6164 ← 4 decimal places
```

B. 0.376×0.12

```
   0.376 ← 3 decimal places
  × 0.12 ← 2 decimal places
     752
  + 3760
 0.04512 ← 5 decimal places
```

PRACTICE Find the product.

1. 6.8×3.4 **2.** 2.56×4.6 **3.** 6.787×7.6 **4.** 0.98×4.6 **5.** 0.97×0.76

6. 0.5×3.761 **7.** 42×17.654 **8.** 7.005×32.1 **9.** 9.76×16.254 **10.** 296.5×2.4

11. 8.9×3.24 **12.** 19.992×3.1 **13.** 15.094×12 **14.** 84.76×0.23 **15.** $3{,}942.7 \times 11.1$

13 DIVIDING DECIMALS

When dividing with decimals, set up the division as you would with whole numbers. Pay attention to the decimal places, as shown below.

Examples

A. Division by a whole number: $3.4 \div 4$

Place decimal point ↓

$$\begin{array}{r} 0.85 \\ 4\overline{)3.40} \\ -\,3\,2 \\ \hline 20 \\ -\,20 \\ \hline 0 \end{array}$$

← *Insert zeros if necessary.*

B. Division by a decimal: $89.6 \div 0.16$

Think: *Multiply both the divisor and the dividend by* a power of 10.

$$\begin{array}{r} 560. \\ 016.\overline{)8960.} \\ -\,80 \\ \hline 96 \\ -\,96 \\ \hline 0 \end{array}$$

← *Place decimal point.* ← *Insert zeros if necessary.*

PRACTICE Find the quotient.

1. $242.76 \div 68$ **2.** $40.5 \div 18$ **3.** $121.03 \div 98$ **4.** $3.6 \div 4$ **5.** $1.58 \div 5$

6. $0.2835 \div 2.7$ **7.** $8.1 \div 0.09$ **8.** $0.42 \div 0.28$ **9.** $15.12 \div 0.063$ **10.** $480.48 \div 7.7$

11. $319.6 \div 68$ **12.** $4.617 \div 2.43$ **13.** $0.152 \div 3.8$ **14.** $81.6 \div 24$ **15.** $98.45 \div 35.8$

14 WRITING DECIMALS AS FRACTIONS

Using place value, you can write decimals as fractions.

Examples

A. Write 0.35 as a fraction in simplest form.

The last digit is in the hundredths place. ↓

$$0.35 = \frac{35}{100} = \frac{7}{20}$$

↑ *The denominator is the same as the place value of the last digit.*

B. Write 0.018 as a fraction in simplest form.

The last digit is in the thousandths place. ↓

$$0.018 = \frac{18}{1{,}000} = \frac{9}{500}$$

↑ *The denominator is the same as the place value of the last digit.*

PRACTICE Write as a fraction in simplest form.

1. 0.5 **2.** 0.09 **3.** 0.10 **4.** 0.15 **5.** 0.25 **6.** 0.025

7. 0.8 **8.** 0.04 **9.** 0.01 **10.** 0.046 **11.** 0.75 **12.** 0.87

13. 0.2 **14.** 0.42 **15.** 0.003 **16.** 0.29 **17.** 0.35 **18.** 0.002

15 WRITING DECIMALS AS PERCENTS

Percent means "per hundred." For example, 27% is 27 per hundred or $\frac{27}{100}$.

Examples Write 0.27, 0.78, and 0.05 as percents.

$0.27 = \frac{27}{100} = 27\%$ $\downarrow$ $0.27 = 27\%$

$0.78 = \frac{78}{100} = 78\%$ $\downarrow$ $0.78 = 78\%$

$0.05 = \frac{5}{100} = 5\%$ $\downarrow$ $0.05 = 5\%$

Think: *To change a decimal to a percent, move the decimal point two places to the right and add the percent symbol. This will work for any decimal number.*

Examples Write 1.25, 0.056, and 0.4 as percents.

$1.25 = 125\%$ $0.056 = 5.6\%$ $0.4 = 40\%$

PRACTICE Write each decimal as a percent.

1. 0.37 **2.** 0.21 **3.** 0.03 **4.** 0.7 **5.** 2.44 **6.** 1.45

7. 0.245 **8.** 0.507 **9.** 0.8 **10.** 0.75 **11.** 0.007 **12.** 9.456

16 TERMINATING AND REPEATING DECIMALS

You can change a fraction to a decimal by dividing the numerator by the denominator. When the division produces a remainder of zero, the resulting decimal is said to be **terminating.** When the remainder repeats over and over, the resulting decimal is said to be **repeating.**

Example Write $\frac{4}{5}$ and $\frac{2}{3}$ as decimals. Are the decimals terminating or repeating?

$\frac{4}{5} = 4 \div 5$ $\quad 5\overline{)4.0} = 0.8,\ 4.0 - 4\,0 = 0 \quad \rightarrow \quad \frac{4}{5} = 0.8$

$\frac{2}{3} = 2 \div 3$ $\quad 3\overline{)2.000} = 0.666,\ 2.0 - 1\,8 = 20 \quad \rightarrow \quad \frac{2}{3} = 0.666\ldots$

20 ← *This pattern will repeat.*

The number 0.8 is a terminating decimal.

The number 0.666. . . is a repeating decimal. It can also be written as $0.\overline{6}$. The bar is placed over the digit or digits that repeat.

PRACTICE Write as a decimal. Is the decimal terminating or repeating? Write *T* or *R*.

1. $\frac{1}{5}$ **2.** $\frac{1}{3}$ **3.** $\frac{3}{11}$ **4.** $\frac{3}{8}$ **5.** $\frac{7}{9}$ **6.** $\frac{7}{15}$

7. $\frac{3}{4}$ **8.** $\frac{5}{6}$ **9.** $\frac{4}{11}$ **10.** $\frac{5}{10}$ **11.** $\frac{1}{9}$ **12.** $\frac{11}{12}$

17 MULTIPLES

Multiples of a number can be found by multiplying the number by 1, 2, 3, 4, and so on.

Example Find the first five multiples of 3.

$3 \times 1 = 3$

$3 \times 2 = 6$

$3 \times 3 = 9$ → *The numbers 3, 6, 9, 12, and 15 are the first five multiples of 3.*

$3 \times 4 = 12$

$3 \times 5 = 15$

PRACTICE Write the first five multiples of each number.

1. 4 **2.** 2 **3.** 5 **4.** 7 **5.** 8 **6.** 12

7. 9 **8.** 10 **9.** 20 **10.** 15 **11.** 50 **12.** 18

18 FACTORS

When two numbers are multiplied to form a third, the two numbers are said to be **factors** of the third number.

$4 \times 8 = 32$
↑ ↑
factors

Example List all the factors of 32.

Think: *The only possibilities for factors of 32 are whole numbers from 1 to 32. Begin with 1, since every number has 1 and itself as factors.*

$1 \times 32 = 32$ ← *The numbers 1 and 32 are factors of 32.*

$2 \times 16 = 32$ ← *The numbers 2 and 16 are factors of 32.*

$3 \times \ ? \ = 32$ ← *No whole number times 3 equals 32, so 3 is not a factor of 32.*

$4 \times 8 = 32$ ← *The numbers 4 and 8 are factors of 32.*

Think: *The only remaining possibilities must be between 4 and 8. Since no whole number multiplied by 5, 6, or 7 equals 32, they are not factors of 32.*

The factors of 32 are 1, 2, 4, 8, 16, and 32.

PRACTICE List all the factors of each number.

1. 8 **2.** 20 **3.** 9 **4.** 51 **5.** 16 **6.** 27

7. 18 **8.** 63 **9.** 50 **10.** 17 **11.** 76 **12.** 23

19 DIVISIBILITY RULES

A number is divisible by another number when the division results in a remainder of 0. You can determine divisibility by some numbers with divisibility rules.

A number is divisible by		Divisible	Not Divisible
2	if the last digit is an even number.	11,994	2,175
3	if the sum of the digits is divisible by 3.	216	79
4	if the last two digits form a number divisible by 4.	1,024	621
5	if the last digit is 0 or 5.	15,195	10,007
6	if the number is divisible by 2 and 3.	1,332	44
9	if the sum of the digits is divisible by 9.	144	33
10	if the last digit is 0.	2,790	9,325

PRACTICE Determine whether each number is divisible by 2, 3, 4, 5, 6, 9, or 10.

1. 56 **2.** 200 **3.** 75 **4.** 324

5. 42 **6.** 812 **7.** 784 **8.** 501

9. 2,345 **10.** 555,555 **11.** 3,009 **12.** 2,001

20 PRIME AND COMPOSITE NUMBERS

A **prime number** has exactly two factors, 1 and the number itself. A **composite number** has more than two factors.

Primes ↓		*Composites* ↓	
2	Factors are 1 and 2.	4	Factors are 1, 2, and 4.
11	Factors are 1 and 11.	12	Factors are 1, 2, 3, 4, 6, and 12.
23	Factors are 1 and 23.	25	Factors are 1, 5, and 25.
47	Factors are 1 and 47.	63	Factors are 1, 3, 7, 9, 21, and 63.

Examples Determine whether the number is prime or composite.

A. 17

factors
1, 17 → prime

B. 16

factors
1, 2, 4, 8, 16 → composite

C. 51

factors
1, 3, 17, 51 → composite

PRACTICE Write *P* or *C* to tell whether the number is prime or composite.

1. 5 **2.** 14 **3.** 18 **4.** 2

5. 23 **6.** 27 **7.** 13 **8.** 39

9. 72 **10.** 49 **11.** 9 **12.** 89

21 PRIME FACTORIZATION

A composite number can be expressed as a product of prime numbers. This is the **prime factorization** of the number. To find the prime factorization of a number, you can use a factor tree.

Example Find the prime factorization of 24 by using a factor tree.

Think: *Use 2 × 12, 3 × 8, or 4 × 6.*

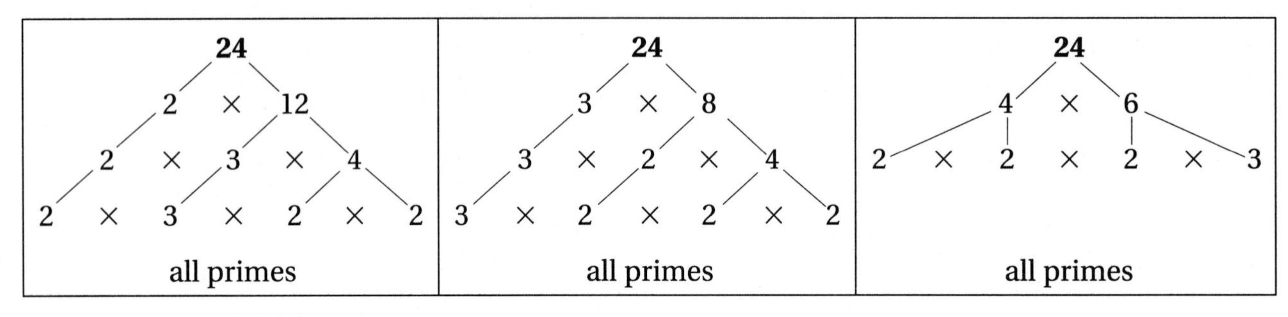

The prime factorization of 24 is $2 \times 2 \times 2 \times 3$, or $2^3 \times 3$.

PRACTICE Find the prime factorization by using a factor tree.

1. 25	**2.** 16	**3.** 56	**4.** 18	**5.** 72	**6.** 40
7. 12	**8.** 20	**9.** 30	**10.** 14	**11.** 8	**12.** 24

22 GREATEST COMMON FACTOR

The **greatest common factor (GCF)** of two whole numbers is the greatest factor the numbers have in common.

Example Find the GCF of 24 and 32.

Method 1
List all the factors for both numbers. Find all the common factors.

24: 1, 2, 3, 4, 6, 8, 12, 24

32: 1, 2, 4, 8, 16, 32

The common factors are 1, 2, 4, and 8.

So, the GCF is 8.

Method 2
Find the prime factorizations. Then find the common prime factors.

24: $2 \times 2 \times 2 \times 3$

32: $2 \times 2 \times 2 \times 2 \times 2$

The common prime factors are 2, 2, and 2. The product of these is the GCF.

So, the GCF is $2 \times 2 \times 2 = 8$.

PRACTICE Find the GCF of each pair of numbers by either method.

1. 9, 15	**2.** 25, 75	**3.** 18, 30	**4.** 4, 10	**5.** 12, 17	**6.** 30, 96
7. 54, 72	**8.** 15, 20	**9.** 40, 60	**10.** 40, 50	**11.** 14, 21	**12.** 14, 28

23 LEAST COMMON MULTIPLE

The **least common multiple (LCM)** of two numbers is the smallest common multiple the numbers share.

Example Find the least common multiple of 8 and 10.

Method 1
List multiples of both numbers.

8: 8, 16, 24, 32, 40, 48, 56, 64, 72, 80
10: 10, 20, 30, 40, 50, 60, 70, 80, 90

The smallest common multiple is 40.

So, the LCM is 40.

Method 2
Find the prime factorizations.

8: $2 \times 2 \times 2$
10: 2×5

The LCM is found by finding a product of factors.

$2 \times 2 \times 2 \times 5 = 40.$ So, the LCM is 40.

PRACTICE Find the LCM of each pair of numbers by either method.

1. 2, 4 **2.** 3, 15 **3.** 10, 25 **4.** 10, 15 **5.** 3, 7 **6.** 18, 27

24 EQUIVALENT FRACTIONS

Equivalent fractions are fractions that name the same amount.

Examples

A. Write two equivalent fractions for $\frac{15}{30}$.

Method 1 Multiply both the numerator and the denominator by a whole number.

$$\frac{15 \times 2}{30 \times 2} = \frac{30}{60}$$

Method 2 Divide by a common factor of the numerator and denominator.

$$\frac{15 \div 15}{30 \div 15} = \frac{1}{2}$$

The fractions $\frac{30}{60}$ and $\frac{1}{2}$ are equivalent to $\frac{15}{30}$.

B. Are $\frac{4}{6}$ and $\frac{12}{18}$ equivalent?

Method 1 Write the fractions in simplest form and compare.

$$\frac{4 \div 2}{6 \div 2} = \frac{2}{3} \qquad \frac{12 \div 6}{18 \div 6} = \frac{2}{3}$$

The fractions are equivalent.

Method 2 Cross multiply and compare.

$$4 \times 18 = 72 \qquad \frac{4}{6} \stackrel{?}{=} \frac{12}{18} \qquad 6 \times 12 = 72$$

The fractions are equivalent since the cross products both equal 72.

PRACTICE Tell whether the fractions are equivalent. Write *yes* or *no*. Then write two equivalent fractions for each.

1. $\frac{6}{10}, \frac{12}{20}$ **2.** $\frac{3}{18}, \frac{1}{3}$ **3.** $\frac{3}{4}, \frac{9}{12}$ **4.** $\frac{1}{2}, \frac{5}{10}$ **5.** $\frac{4}{16}, \frac{12}{18}$ **6.** $\frac{12}{21}, \frac{4}{7}$

25 SIMPLEST FORM OF FRACTIONS

A fraction is in simplest form when the numerator and denominator have no common factor other than 1.

Example Find the simplest form of $\frac{32}{40}$.

Method 1

Divide the numerator and denominator by common factors until the only common factor is 1.

$$\frac{32 \div 2}{40 \div 2} = \frac{16}{20} \qquad \frac{16 \div 4}{20 \div 4} = \frac{4}{5}$$

The simplest form of $\frac{32}{40}$ is $\frac{4}{5}$.

Method 2

Find the GCF of 32 and 40. Divide both the numerator and the denominator by the GCF.

$$\frac{32 \div 8}{40 \div 8} = \frac{4}{5} \quad \leftarrow \text{GCF: } 8$$

The simplest form of $\frac{32}{40}$ is $\frac{4}{5}$.

PRACTICE Write in simplest form.

1. $\frac{20}{24}$ **2.** $\frac{4}{12}$ **3.** $\frac{14}{49}$ **4.** $\frac{60}{72}$ **5.** $\frac{40}{75}$ **6.** $\frac{12}{12}$

7. $\frac{18}{24}$ **8.** $\frac{5}{10}$ **9.** $\frac{15}{45}$ **10.** $\frac{17}{51}$ **11.** $\frac{6}{32}$ **12.** $\frac{26}{39}$

26 MIXED NUMBERS AND FRACTIONS

Mixed numbers can be written as fractions greater than 1, and fractions greater than 1 can be written as mixed numbers.

Examples

A. Write $\frac{23}{5}$ as a mixed number.

$\frac{23}{5}$ *Divide the numerator by the denominator.*

$$\begin{array}{r} 4 \\ 5\overline{)23} \\ -20 \\ \hline 3 \end{array} \rightarrow 4\frac{3}{5}$$

Write the remainder as the numerator of a fraction.

B. Write $6\frac{2}{7}$ as a fraction.

$7 \times 6 = 42$ *Multiply the denominator by the whole number.*

$42 + 2 = 44$ *Add the product to the numerator.*

$\frac{44}{7}$ *Write the sum over the denominator.*

PRACTICE Write each mixed number as a fraction. Write each fraction as a mixed number.

1. $\frac{22}{5}$ **2.** $9\frac{1}{7}$ **3.** $\frac{41}{8}$ **4.** $5\frac{7}{9}$ **5.** $\frac{7}{3}$ **6.** $4\frac{9}{11}$

7. $\frac{47}{16}$ **8.** $3\frac{3}{8}$ **9.** $\frac{31}{9}$ **10.** $8\frac{2}{3}$ **11.** $\frac{33}{5}$ **12.** $12\frac{1}{9}$

27 ADDING AND SUBTRACTING FRACTIONS

When you add or subtract fractions, each fraction must have the same denominator.

Examples Add or subtract as indicated.

A. $\frac{1}{12} + \frac{3}{8}$

STEP 1 *Use the LCD to rename the fractions.*

$$\begin{array}{rl} \frac{1}{12} = \frac{1 \times 2}{12 \times 2} = \frac{2}{24} & \\ + \frac{3}{8} = \frac{3 \times 3}{8 \times 3} = \frac{9}{24} & \end{array} \leftarrow \text{LCD: } 24$$

STEP 2 *Add. Write in simplest form.*

$$\frac{2}{24} + \frac{9}{24} = \frac{11}{24}$$

B. $\frac{3}{4} - \frac{1}{12}$

STEP 1 *Use the LCD to rename the fractions.*

$$\begin{array}{rl} \frac{3}{4} = \frac{3 \times 3}{4 \times 3} = \frac{9}{12} & \\ - \frac{1}{12} = \frac{1 \times 1}{12 \times 1} = \frac{1}{12} & \end{array} \leftarrow \text{LCD: } 12$$

STEP 2 *Subtract. Write in simplest form.*

$$\frac{9}{12} - \frac{1}{12} = \frac{8}{12} = \frac{8 \div 4}{12 \div 4} = \frac{2}{3}$$

C. $2\frac{2}{3} + 1\frac{1}{2}$

STEP 1 *Use the LCD to rename the fractions.*

$$\begin{array}{rl} 2\frac{2}{3} = 2\frac{2 \times 2}{3 \times 2} = 2\frac{4}{6} & \\ + 1\frac{1}{2} = 1\frac{1 \times 3}{2 \times 3} = 1\frac{3}{6} & \end{array} \leftarrow \text{LCD: } 6$$

STEP 2 *Add the whole numbers, and then add the fractions.*

$$\begin{array}{r} 2\frac{4}{6} \\ + 1\frac{3}{6} \\ \hline 3\frac{7}{6} = 3 + 1\frac{1}{6} = 4\frac{1}{6} \end{array}$$

D. $4\frac{2}{3} - 2\frac{8}{9}$

STEP 1 *Use the LCD to rename the fractions.*

$$\begin{array}{rl} 4\frac{2}{3} = 4\frac{2 \times 3}{3 \times 3} = 4\frac{6}{9} & \\ - 2\frac{8}{9} = 2\frac{8 \times 1}{9 \times 1} = 2\frac{8}{9} & \end{array} \leftarrow \text{LCD: } 9$$

STEP 2 *Rename the mixed number if necessary. Subtract the whole numbers, and then subtract the fractions.*

$$\begin{array}{r} 4\frac{6}{9} = 3\frac{15}{9} \\ - 2\frac{8}{9} = 2\frac{8}{9} \\ \hline 1\frac{7}{9} \end{array} \leftarrow \text{Borrow 1 or } \frac{9}{9} \text{ from 4.}$$

PRACTICE Add or subtract. Write the fractions in simplest form.

1. $\frac{3}{4} + \frac{1}{6}$ **2.** $\frac{5}{6} + \frac{2}{3}$ **3.** $1\frac{1}{2} + 2\frac{3}{5}$ **4.** $3\frac{3}{8} + 5\frac{3}{4}$ **5.** $4\frac{5}{8} + 7\frac{3}{5}$

6. $\frac{7}{9} - \frac{1}{3}$ **7.** $\frac{2}{3} - \frac{2}{5}$ **8.** $7\frac{4}{9} - 3\frac{1}{2}$ **9.** $6\frac{2}{3} - 2\frac{1}{8}$ **10.** $20\frac{4}{5} - 6\frac{5}{6}$

11. $\frac{3}{5} + \frac{4}{7}$ **12.** $\frac{9}{11} + \frac{2}{3}$ **13.** $8\frac{3}{4} + 1\frac{5}{9}$ **14.** $\frac{9}{13} - \frac{3}{8}$ **15.** $5\frac{1}{3} - 3\frac{4}{5}$

28 MULTIPLYING AND DIVIDING FRACTIONS

When multiplying fractions, multiply numerator by numerator and denominator by denominator. Simplify the product if possible.

Examples Find the product.

A. $\frac{5}{6} \times \frac{2}{3}$

$\frac{5}{6} \times \frac{2}{3} = \frac{5 \times 2}{6 \times 3}$ *Multiply.*

$= \frac{10}{18}$ *Write in simplest form.*

$= \frac{5}{9}$

B. $4\frac{2}{3} \times 2\frac{1}{4}$

Write as fractions.

$4\frac{2}{3} \times 2\frac{1}{4} = \frac{14}{3} \times \frac{9}{4} = \frac{14 \times 9}{3 \times 4}$ *Multiply.*

$= \frac{126}{12}$ *Write in simplest form.*

$= \frac{21}{2}$, or $10\frac{1}{2}$

Two numbers whose product is 1 are called reciprocals.

$$\frac{3}{2} \times \frac{2}{3} = \frac{6}{6} = 1$$

So, $\frac{3}{2}$ and $\frac{2}{3}$ are reciprocals.

When dividing fractions, use the reciprocal of the divisor to write a multiplication problem.

Examples Find the quotient.

A. $\frac{5}{6} \div \frac{2}{3}$

$\frac{5}{6} \div \frac{2}{3} = \frac{5}{6} \times \frac{3}{2}$ *Use reciprocal of divisor.*

$= \frac{5 \times 3}{6 \times 2} = \frac{15}{12}$ *Multiply.*

$= \frac{5}{4}$, or $1\frac{1}{4}$ *Write in simplest form.*

B. $4\frac{2}{3} \div 2\frac{1}{4}$

$4\frac{2}{3} \div 2\frac{1}{4} = \frac{14}{3} \div \frac{9}{4}$ *Write as fractions.*

$= \frac{14}{3} \times \frac{4}{9}$ *Use reciprocal of divisor.*

$= \frac{56}{27}$, or $2\frac{2}{27}$

PRACTICE Multiply or divide as indicated. Write the fractions in simplest form.

1. $\frac{4}{9} \times \frac{7}{12}$ **2.** $\frac{1}{6} \times \frac{2}{3}$ **3.** $\frac{3}{8} \times \frac{4}{7}$ **4.** $6\frac{1}{4} \times 5\frac{3}{5}$

5. $3\frac{1}{3} \times 2\frac{1}{7}$ **6.** $4\frac{2}{5} \times 10$ **7.** $\frac{3}{4} \div \frac{1}{3}$ **8.** $\frac{1}{10} \div \frac{5}{6}$

9. $\frac{2}{5} \div \frac{1}{6}$ **10.** $1\frac{1}{6} \div 5\frac{1}{4}$ **11.** $4\frac{2}{4} \div 2\frac{2}{6}$ **12.** $5\frac{2}{3} \div 12$

29 WRITING FRACTIONS AS DECIMALS

Two methods of changing fractions to decimals are shown below.

Examples

Method 1
If the denominator is a factor of 10 or 100, multiply to make the denominator 10 or 100.

A. $\frac{3}{5} \times \frac{2}{2} = \frac{6}{10} = 0.6$

B. $\frac{43}{50} \times \frac{2}{2} = \frac{86}{100} = 0.86$

C. $\frac{12}{25} \times \frac{4}{4} = \frac{48}{100} = 0.48$

Method 2
If the denominator is not a factor of 10 or 100, divide the numerator by the denominator.

A. $\frac{5}{8} = 5 \div 8 = 0.625$

B. $\frac{6}{11} = 6 \div 11 = 0.\overline{54}$

NOTE: Method 2 will work for any fraction.

PRACTICE Write each fraction as a decimal.

1. $\frac{1}{4}$ **2.** $\frac{1}{8}$ **3.** $\frac{17}{50}$ **4.** $\frac{7}{20}$ **5.** $\frac{2}{9}$ **6.** $\frac{4}{11}$

7. $\frac{2}{5}$ **8.** $\frac{7}{8}$ **9.** $\frac{7}{25}$ **10.** $\frac{1}{3}$ **11.** $\frac{5}{6}$ **12.** $\frac{7}{22}$

30 WRITING FRACTIONS AS PERCENTS

You can write fractions as percents by first writing them as equivalent decimals. Then write the equivalent decimals as percents.

Examples

A. Write $\frac{1}{4}$ as a percent.

STEP 1 *Write $\frac{1}{4}$ as a decimal.*

$$\frac{1}{4} = \frac{1 \times 25}{4 \times 25} = \frac{25}{100} = 0.25$$

STEP 2 *Write 0.25 as a percent.*

$$0.25 = 25\%$$
$$\frac{1}{4} = 25\%$$

B. Write $2\frac{1}{3}$ as a percent.

STEP 1 *Write $2\frac{1}{3}$ as a decimal.*

$$2\frac{1}{3} = \frac{7}{3} = 7 \div 3 = 2.\overline{3}$$

STEP 2 *Write $2.\overline{3}$ as a percent.*

$$2.\overline{3} = 233.\overline{3}\%, \text{ or } 233\frac{1}{3}\%$$
$$2\frac{1}{3} = 233.\overline{3}\%, \text{ or } 233\frac{1}{3}\%$$

PRACTICE Write each fraction or mixed number as a percent.

1. $\frac{3}{4}$ **2.** $\frac{7}{20}$ **3.** $\frac{3}{10}$ **4.** $\frac{5}{8}$ **5.** $\frac{2}{3}$ **6.** $\frac{7}{11}$

7. $\frac{5}{6}$ **8.** $\frac{5}{9}$ **9.** $\frac{1}{2}$ **10.** $3\frac{1}{4}$ **11.** $5\frac{3}{4}$ **12.** $4\frac{5}{11}$

31 RATIOS

A **ratio** is a comparison of two numbers. There are three different ways to write ratios.

Example In a parking garage, there are 24 green cars and 78 red cars. Write the ratio of green cars to red cars.

Ratio: 24 to 78, or 24:78, or $\frac{24}{78}$

Each of these is read as "twenty-four to seventy-eight."

Ratios can be simplified in the same way as fractions.

$$\frac{24}{78} = \frac{24 \div 6}{78 \div 6} = \frac{4}{13}$$

So, for every 4 green cars in the parking garage there are 13 red cars.

PRACTICE Let $A = 12$, $B = 20$, and $C = 27$. Write each ratio in three different ways. Write the ratios in simplest form.

1. A to B **2.** A to C **3.** B to A **4.** B to C **5.** C to A

6. $A: (B + C)$ **7.** $B: (A + C)$ **8.** $C: (A + B)$ **9.** $(B + C): A$ **10.** $(A + C): B$

32 EQUIVALENT RATIOS

You can find an equivalent ratio by multiplying or dividing the ratio by a common factor.

Examples

A. Find two equivalent ratios for 5:15.

Multiply. $\frac{5}{15} = \frac{5 \times 2}{15 \times 2} = \frac{10}{30}$

Divide. $\frac{5}{15} = \frac{5 \div 5}{15 \div 5} = \frac{1}{3}$

$\frac{5}{15} = \frac{10}{30} = \frac{1}{3}$, or 5:15 = 10:30 = 1:3

B. Tell whether the ratios $\frac{27}{63}$ and $\frac{9}{21}$ are equivalent.

$\frac{27}{63} = \frac{27 \div 9}{63 \div 9} = \frac{3}{7}$ $\frac{9}{21} = \frac{9 \div 3}{21 \div 3} = \frac{3}{7}$

$\frac{27}{63}$ is equivalent to $\frac{9}{21}$ since both equal $\frac{3}{7}$.

PRACTICE Find two equivalent ratios for the given ratio.

1. 2:3 **2.** 6:11 **3.** 12:16 **4.** 6 to 8 **5.** 7 to 14 **6.** 10 to 12

Tell whether the ratios are equivalent. Write *yes* or *no*.

7. $\frac{2}{1}; \frac{8}{4}$ **8.** $\frac{2}{5}; \frac{6}{12}$ **9.** $\frac{2}{6}; \frac{7}{21}$ **10.** $\frac{8}{10}; \frac{16}{25}$ **11.** $\frac{20}{45}; \frac{12}{27}$ **12.** $\frac{18}{48}; \frac{12}{32}$

33 PROPORTIONS

A **proportion** is an equation that shows that two ratios are equal. Two ratios are equal if they can be simplified to the same ratio or if their cross products are equal.

Examples Determine whether the ratios form a proportion.

Method 1 Write the ratios in simplest form.

Ratios: $\frac{6}{8}, \frac{9}{12}$

$\frac{6}{8} = \frac{6 \div 2}{8 \div 2} = \frac{3}{4}$ $\quad \frac{9}{12} = \frac{9 \div 3}{12 \div 3} = \frac{3}{4}$

Since both ratios equal $\frac{3}{4}$, they form a proportion.

Method 2 Find the cross products.

Ratios: $\frac{4}{6}, \frac{5}{10}$

$\frac{4}{6} \stackrel{?}{=} \frac{5}{10}$

$4 \times 10 \neq 6 \times 5$

$40 \neq 30$

$\frac{4}{6} \neq \frac{5}{10}$

The ratios do not form a proportion.

PRACTICE Tell whether the ratios form a proportion. Write *yes* or *no*.

1. 5:6, 11:18 **2.** 8:6, 4:5 **3.** 9:4, 27:12 **4.** 4:10, 2:5 **5.** 6:9, 10:15

6. 15:8, 30:15 **7.** 5:8, 15:32 **8.** 18:4, 9:2 **9.** 22:4, 44:12 **10.** 18:6, 6:3

34 SOLVING A PROPORTION

To solve a proportion, write the cross products and solve the resulting equation.

Example Solve $\frac{6}{8} = \frac{n}{12}$.

STEP 1 Write the cross products.

$$\frac{6}{8} = \frac{n}{12}$$

$$6 \times 12 = 8 \times n$$

$$72 = 8n$$

STEP 2 Solve the equation.

$$72 = 8n$$

$$\frac{72}{8} = \frac{8n}{8}$$

$$9 = n$$

So, $\frac{6}{8} = \frac{9}{12}$.

PRACTICE Solve the proportion.

1. $\frac{9}{15} = \frac{a}{10}$ **2.** $\frac{3}{9} = \frac{b}{21}$ **3.** $\frac{t}{12} = \frac{12}{9}$ **4.** $\frac{20}{15} = \frac{16}{x}$ **5.** $\frac{12}{d} = \frac{4}{14}$ **6.** $\frac{a}{6} = \frac{2}{3}$

7. $\frac{2}{5} = \frac{x}{20}$ **8.** $\frac{4}{b} = \frac{12}{27}$ **9.** $\frac{n}{7} = \frac{4}{28}$ **10.** $\frac{5}{7} = \frac{25}{k}$ **11.** $\frac{3}{2} = \frac{x}{12}$ **12.** $\frac{8}{5} = \frac{24}{m}$

35 REPRESENTING PERCENT

Percent means "per one hundred." Percents can be represented on a 10×10 grid.

Examples

A. Represent 75% on the grid.

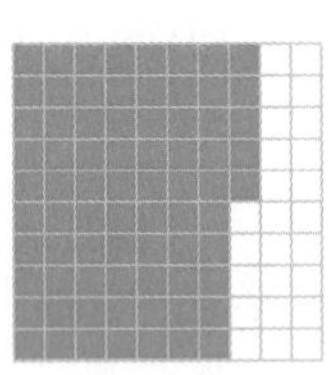

Shade 75 squares to represent 75 out of 100 or 75%.

B. Represent 9% on the grid.

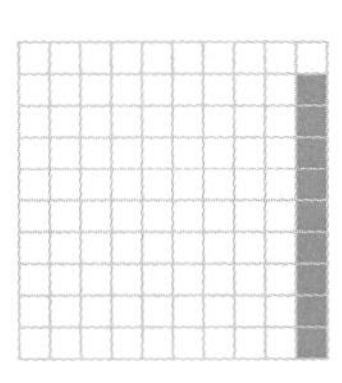

Shade 9 squares to represent 9 out of 100 or 9%.

PRACTICE Represent each percent on a 10×10 grid.

1. 12%	**2.** 92%	**3.** 24%	**4.** 47%	**5.** 76%	**6.** 39%
7. 50%	**8.** 66%	**9.** 83%	**10.** 19%	**11.** 7%	**12.** 0.5%

36 WRITING PERCENTS AS FRACTIONS AND DECIMALS

Recall that *percent* means "per hundred."

Examples

A. Write 75%, 0.06%, and 125% as fractions. Write the fractions in simplest form.

$$75\% = \frac{75}{100} = \frac{75 \div 25}{100 \div 25} = \frac{3}{4}$$

$$0.06\% = \frac{0.06}{100} = \frac{0.06 \times 100}{100 \times 100} = \frac{6}{10{,}000}$$

$$= \frac{6 \div 2}{10{,}000 \div 2} = \frac{3}{5{,}000}$$

$$125\% = \frac{125}{100} = \frac{125 \div 25}{100 \div 25} = \frac{5}{4} = 1\frac{1}{4}$$

So, $75\% = \frac{3}{4}$, $0.06\% = \frac{3}{5{,}000}$, and $125\% = 1\frac{1}{4}$.

B. Write 75%, 0.06%, and 125% as decimals. Look for a pattern.

$$75\% = \frac{75}{100} = 75 \div 100 = 0.75$$

$$0.06\% = \frac{0.06}{100} = 0.06 \div 100 = 0.0006$$

$$125\% = \frac{125}{100} = 125 \div 100 = 1.25$$

Think: *To change a percent to a decimal, move the decimal point two places to the left.*

PRACTICE Write each percent as a fraction and decimal. Write fractions in simplest form.

1. 36%	**2.** 79%	**3.** 136%	**4.** 159%	**5.** 0.07%	**6.** 0.18%
7. 29%	**8.** 42%	**9.** 4%	**10.** 125%	**11.** 210%	**12.** 0.5%

37 FINDING THE PERCENT OF A NUMBER

You can find the percent of a number by multiplying the number by the fraction or decimal equivalent of the percent.

Example What is 30% of 75?

Method 1

STEP 1 Write the percent as a fraction.

$$30\% = \frac{30}{100} = \frac{3}{10}$$

STEP 2 Multiply by the fraction.

$$\frac{3}{10} \times 75 = \frac{225}{10} = 22\frac{1}{2}$$

So, 30% of 75 = $22\frac{1}{2}$.

Method 2

STEP 1 Write the percent as a decimal.

$$30\% = 0.30 = 0.3$$

STEP 2 Multiply by the decimal.

$$0.3 \times 75 = 22.5$$

So, 30% of 75 = 22.5.

PRACTICE Find the percent of the number by either method.

1. 30% of 60 **2.** 50% of 40 **3.** 40% of 100 **4.** 25% of 44 **5.** 12% of 65

38 GEOMETRIC FIGURES

Definition	Example	Symbol/Read
A **point** is an exact location.	. A	none / point A
A **plane** is a set of points extending infinitely in all directions on the same surface.	P	none / plane P
A **ray** has one endpoint and extends infinitely in one direction.	X Y	$\overrightarrow{XY}$ / ray XY
A **line** is a set of points in a straight path extending infinitely in two directions.	X Y	$\overleftrightarrow{XY}$ / line XY
A **line segment** is part of a line or ray and consists of two endpoints and all points between those endpoints.	X Y	$\overline{XY}$ / line segment XY

PRACTICE

1. Name four points.

2. Name a plane.

3. Name five rays.

4. Name four line segments.

5. Name a line.

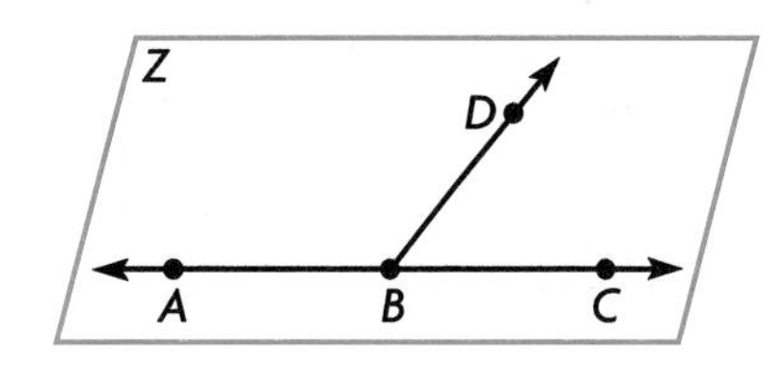

39 TYPES OF ANGLES

A circle is divided into 360 sections, each one of which is a degree. The degree is also the unit of measure for angles. An angle is acute, obtuse, right, or straight depending on its measure.

An **acute angle** measures between 0° and 90°.

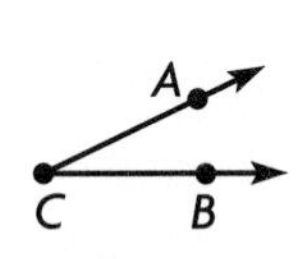

An **obtuse angle** measures between 90° and 180°.

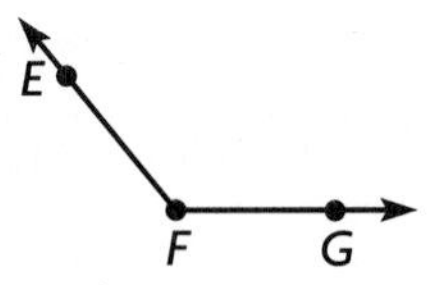

A **right angle** measures 90°.

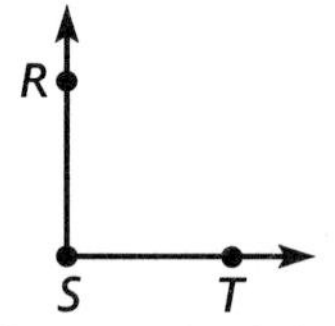

A **straight angle** measures 180°.

X Y Z

PRACTICE Classify the angle as acute, obtuse, right, or straight.

1.

A B C

2.

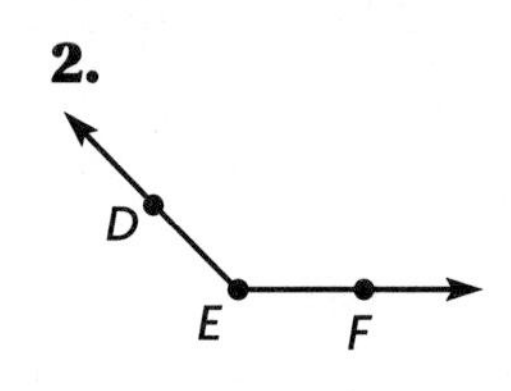

3.

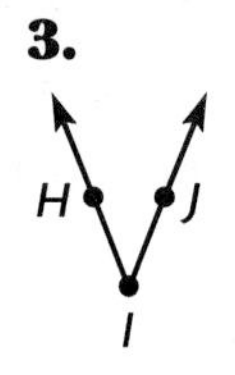

4.

5. **6.**

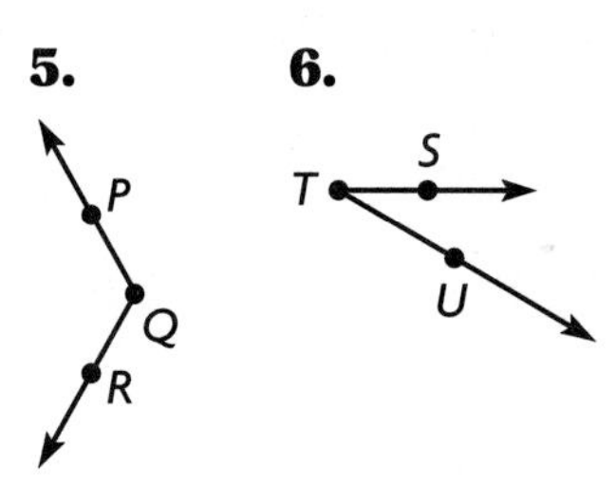

40 MEASURING ANGLES

You can use a protractor to measure angles. To measure an angle, place the base of the protractor on one of the rays of the angle and center it on the vertex. Look at the protractor scale that has zero on the first ray. Read the scale where the second ray crosses it. Extend the rays if necessary.

Examples

A. Measure ∠ *ABC.*

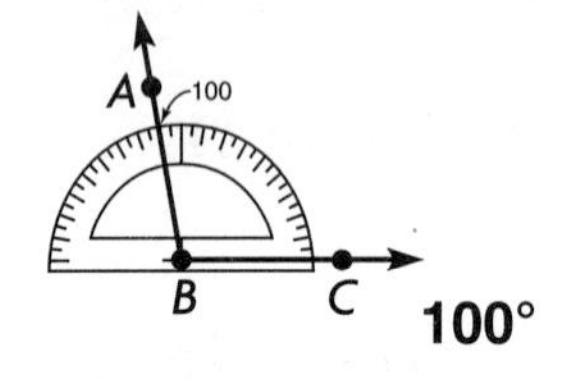

100°

B. Measure ∠ *ABC.*

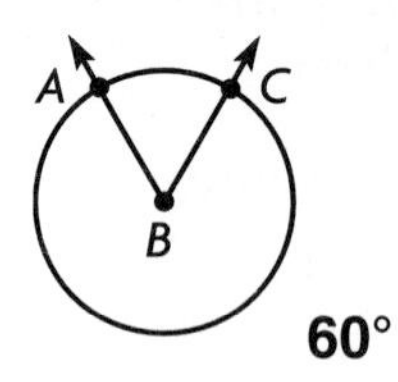

60°

∠ *ABC* is a central angle because it is formed by rays with a common vertex at the center of a circle.

PRACTICE Use a protractor to measure the angle.

1.

2.

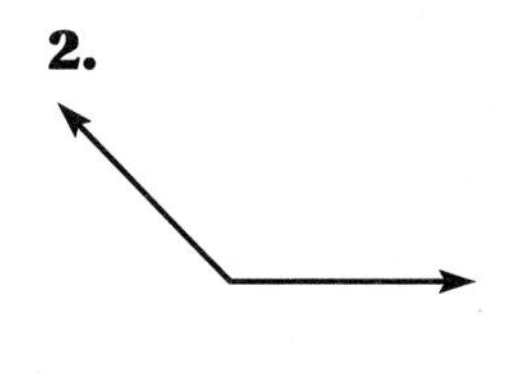

3.

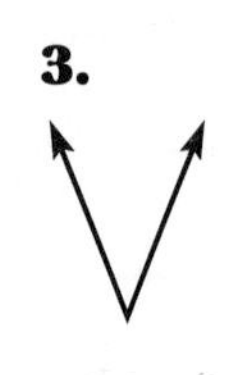

4.

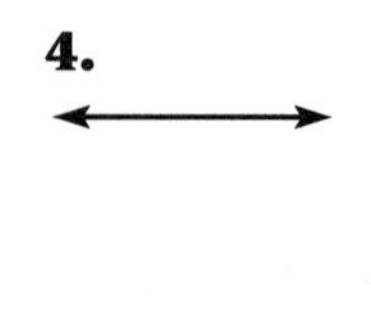

5. **6.**

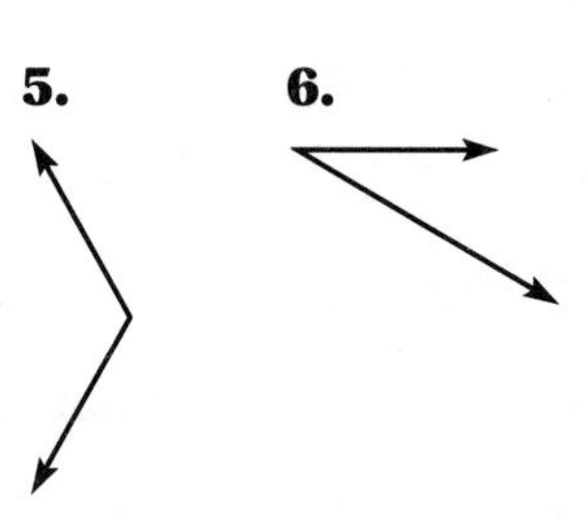

41 CUSTOMARY MEASURES

To convert a measurement from one unit to another, you multiply or divide.

Customary Units of Length

12 inches (in.) = 1 foot (ft)
36 inches (in.) = 1 yard (yd)
3 feet (ft) = 1 yard (yd)
5,280 feet (ft) = 1 mile (mi)
1,760 yards (yd) = 1 mile (mi)

Customary Units of Capacity and Weight

8 fluid ounces (fl oz) = 1 cup (c)
2 cups (c) = 1 pint (pt)
2 pints (pt) = 1 quart (qt)
4 quarts (qt) = 1 gallon (gal)
16 ounces (oz) = 1 pound (lb)
2,000 pounds (lb) = 1 ton (T)

Examples

A. 4 feet = __?__ inches

4 ft × 12 in. per ft = 48 in.

B. 78 fluid ounces = __?__ cups

78 fl oz ÷ 8 fl oz per c = $9\frac{3}{4}$ c

PRACTICE Convert the measure to the given unit.

1. 3 ft = __?__ in. **2.** 3 mi = __?__ ft **3.** 72 ft = __?__ yd **4.** 18 yd = __?__ ft

5. 55 gal = __?__ qt **6.** 19 c = __?__ fl oz **7.** 54 qt = __?__ gal **8.** 64 oz = __?__ lb

42 METRIC MEASURES

The metric system is based on the decimal system. When you move from left to right on the chart below, you multiply by powers of 10. When you move from right to left, you divide by powers of 10.

kilometer	hectometer	dekameter	meter	decimeter	centimeter	millimeter
1 km	1 hm	1 dam	1 m	1 dm	1 cm	1 mm
=	=	=	=	=	=	=
1,000 m	100 m	10 m	1 m	0.1 m	0.01 m	0.001 m

Examples

A. 4.5 m = __?__ mm

Think: *You move from left to right 3 places, so multiply by 1,000 or move the decimal point 3 places to the right.*

4.5 m = 4,500 mm

B. 4.5 m = __?__ hm

Think: *You move from right to left 2 places, so divide by 100 or move the decimal point 2 places to the left.*

4.5 m = 0.045 hm

PRACTICE Convert the measure to the given unit.

1. 4.5 m = __?__ cm **2.** 7.9 m = __?__ km **3.** 0.09 dm = __?__ m **4.** 0.15 m = __?__ hm

5. 12 m = __?__ mm **6.** 86 dam = __?__ m **7.** 0.34 km = __?__ m **8.** 480 cm = __?__ m

43 PERIMETER AND AREA

Perimeter is the distance around a figure. Area is the number of square units needed to cover a given surface.

Examples

Perimeter

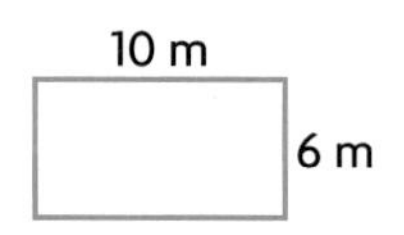

$P = 2(l + w)$
$P = 2(10 + 6)$
$P = 32 \rightarrow 32$ m

2 ft, 5 ft, 3 ft, 1 ft, 6 ft

$P = a + b + c + d + e$
$P = 3 + 2 + 5 + 1 + 6$
$P = 17 \rightarrow 17$ ft

Area

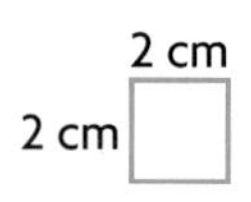

$A = l \times w$
$A = 2 \times 2$
$A = 4 \rightarrow 4 \text{ cm}^2$

6 in., 15 in.

$A = \frac{1}{2}(b \times h)$

$A = \frac{1}{2}(15 \times 6)$

$A = 45 \rightarrow 45 \text{ in.}^2$

PRACTICE Find the perimeter or area.

1. 8 m, 12 m, 11 m, 13 m

$P =$ ___?___

2. 22 ft, 10 ft

$A =$ ___?___

3.

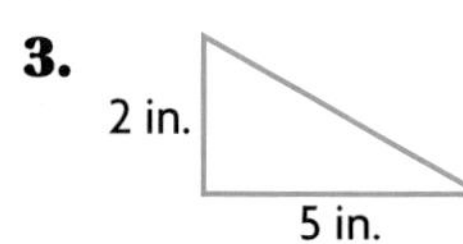

$A =$ ___?___

4. 6 cm, 6 cm, 6 cm, 6 cm, 6 cm, 6 cm

$P =$ ___?___

44 TYPES OF POLYGONS

A polygon is a closed plane figure with at least three sides. Polygons are classified by number of sides and angles.

triangle	**quadrilateral**	**pentagon**	**hexagon**	**octagon**

3 sides, 3 angles	4 sides, 4 angles	5 sides, 5 angles	6 sides, 6 angles	8 sides, 8 angles

parallelogram	**rectangle**	**rhombus**	**square**	**trapezoid**
	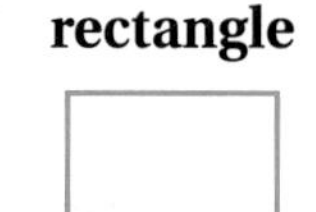			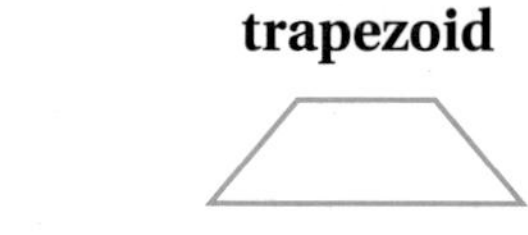
opposite sides parallel and congruent	parallelogram with 4 right angles	parallelogram with 4 congruent sides	rectangle with 4 congruent sides	quadrilateral with exactly 2 parallel sides

PRACTICE Name the polygon.

1. 

2. 

3. 

4. 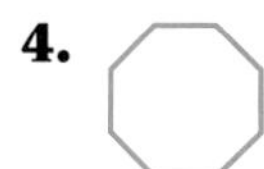

5. 

45 SOLID FIGURES

Five types of solid figures are shown below.

rectangular prism	square pyramid	cylinder	cone	sphere
		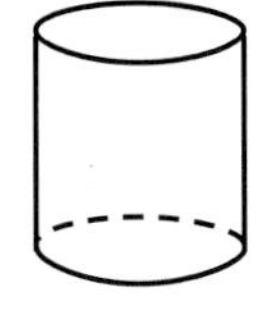	 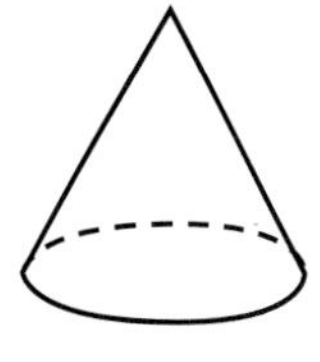	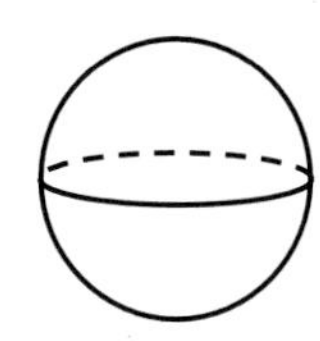
The base is a rectangle.	The base is a square.	The base is a circle.	The base is a circle.	

PRACTICE Name the figure.

1.  **2.**  **3.** 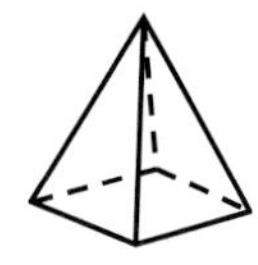 **4.** 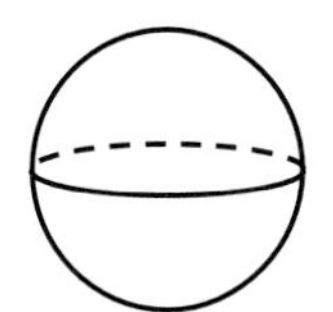 **5.** 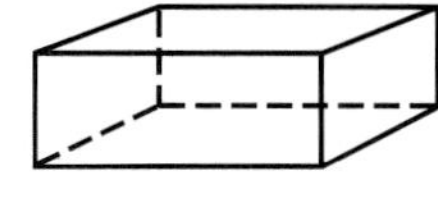

46 MEAN AND MEDIAN

The **mean** is the average of a set of numbers. To find the mean, add the numbers and divide the sum by the number of addends.

The **median** is the middle number of a set of numbers in numerical order. If there are two middle numbers, the median is the mean of those two numbers.

Examples

A. Find the mean of 36, 74, 43, 36, and 41.

STEP 1 Find the sum of the numbers.

$$36 + 74 + 43 + 36 + 41 = 230$$

STEP 2 Divide the sum by the number of addends.

$$230 \div 5 = 46$$

So, the mean is 46.

B. Find the median: 10, 6, 42, 18, 33, 64.

STEP 1 Put numbers in numerical order.

6, 10, 18, 33, 42, 64

STEP 2 Find the middle number.

There are two middle numbers, 18 and 33. Their mean is the median.

$\frac{18 + 33}{2} = 25.5 \rightarrow 25.5$ is the median.

PRACTICE Find the mean and the median.

1. 32, 87, 45, 63, 73 **2.** 17, 44, 33, 10 **3.** 6, 52, 41, 21, 36, 48 **4.** 126, 99, 234.3

5. 12, 9, 8, 6, 10 **6.** 18, 46, 40, 38 **7.** 3, 17, 7, 8, 8, 4, 2 **8.** 142, 146, 525

47 MODE AND RANGE

The **mode** of a set of numbers is the most commonly occurring number in the set. There may be more than one mode, or there may be no mode at all. The **range** is the distance between extremes in a set of numbers. You can find the range by finding the difference between the greatest number and the least number.

Examples

A. Find the mode and the range of 4, 25, 72, 4, 36, 4, 2, 25, 25, and 98.

Mode: Since both 4 and 25 occur three times, 4 and 25 are the modes.

Range: Greatest: 98 Least: 2

$98 - 2 = 96 \rightarrow 96$ is the range.

B. Find the mode and the range of 4, 25, 72, 36, 41, $^{-}2$, and 98.

Mode: Since no number in the set occurs more than once, there is no mode.

Range: Greatest: 98 Least: $^{-}2$

$98 - {}^{-}2 = 100 \rightarrow 100$ is the range.

PRACTICE Find the mode and the range.

1. 2, 1, 2, 5, 7, 9

2. 42, 8, 54, 192, 8, 0, 44, 16

3. $^{-}12$, 44, 324, 17, 41

4. 0, 77, 125, 77, 2, 2, 3, 5, 3

5. $^{-}5$, 0, 15, 25, $^{-}5$, $^{-}23$, 1

6. 297, 7, 12, 18, 5, 21, 17

48 INTEGERS AND THEIR OPPOSITES

Integers include all whole numbers and their opposites. Zero is neither positive nor negative so it does not have an opposite.

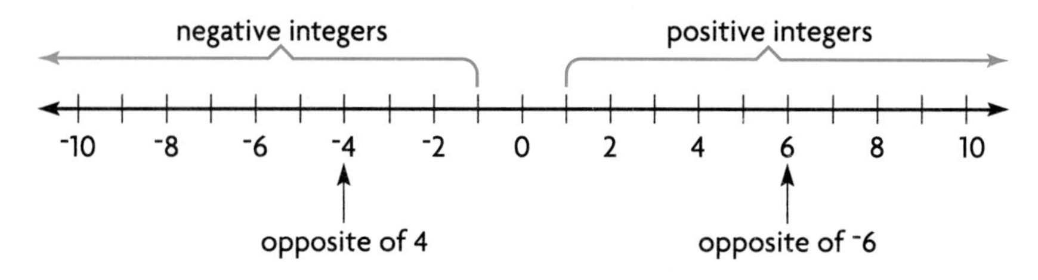

Examples

A. Graph $^{-}7$ on a number line.

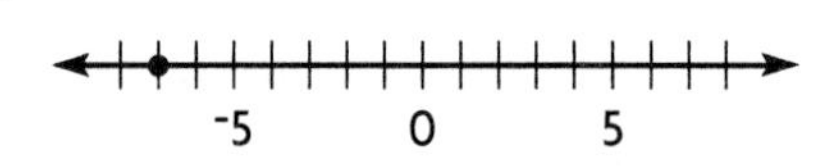

$^{-}7$ is 7 places to the left of 0.

B. Name the opposite of 24.

The opposite of 24 is $^{-}24$.

C. Name the opposite of $^{-}3$.

The opposite of $^{-}3$ is 3.

PRACTICE Graph the integer on a number line.

1. $^{-}5$ **2.** $^{-}2$ **3.** $^{-}9$ **4.** $^{-}12$ **5.** $^{-}34$ **6.** 0

Name the opposite of each integer.

7. 13 **8.** 9 **9.** $^{-}28$ **10.** $^{-}54$ **11.** 85 **12.** 1

49 ABSOLUTE VALUE

The **absolute value** of a number is the distance the number is from zero on a number line. The symbol for absolute value is $|\ \ |$.

Examples

A. Find $|5|$.

$^-5$ 0 5

5 is 5 units from 0.

$|5| = 5$

B. Find $|^-8|$.

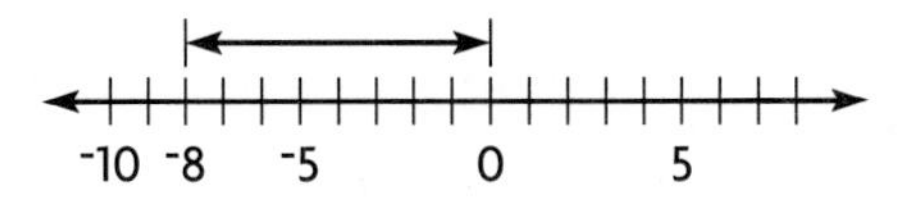

$^-8$ is 8 units from 0.

$|^-8| = 8$

PRACTICE Find the absolute value.

1. $|^-6|$ **2.** $|^-12|$ **3.** $|2.5|$ **4.** $|18|$ **5.** $|^-120|$ **6.** $|^-4.4|$ **7.** $|\frac{3}{4}|$

8. $|19|$ **9.** $|^-42|$ **10.** $|^-\frac{1}{8}|$ **11.** $|17.9|$ **12.** $|^-58.6|$ **13.** $|1{,}924|$ **14.** $|^-365|$

50 MODELING INTEGERS

You can show integers on the number line as shown in Key Skill 48 and you can model integers with counters. Let a yellow counter represent 1 and a red counter represent $^-1$. A yellow counter and red counter together represent 0.

Examples Model 5 and $^-6$.

Two models for 5

Model 1

Model 2

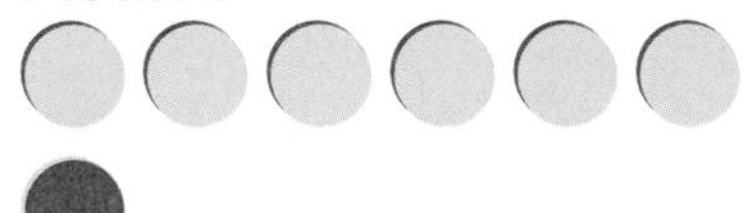

Two models for $^-6$

Model 1

Model 2

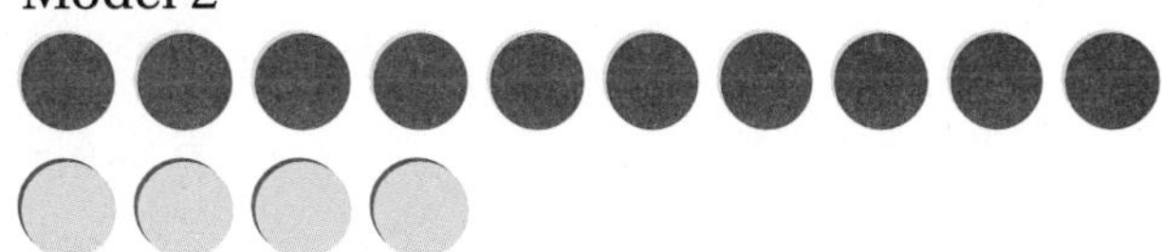

PRACTICE Use counters to model each integer two different ways.

1. 3 **2.** 8 **3.** $^-4$ **4.** $^-9$ **5.** 10 **6.** $^-6$

7. 0 **8.** $^-5$ **9.** $^-3$ **10.** 1 **11.** 3 **12.** $^-1$

51 ADDING INTEGERS

When adding integers, consider the absolute values of the addends.

Examples

A. Find the sum. $^-4 + {}^-1$

STEP 1 When the signs of the integers are the same, add the absolute values of the integers.

$$|{}^-4| + |{}^-1| = 4 + 1 = 5$$

STEP 2 Use the sign of the addends.

$$^-4 + {}^-1 = {}^-5$$

B. Find the sum. $7 + {}^-3$

STEP 1 When the signs of the integers are different, find the difference of their absolute values.

$$|7| - |{}^-3| = 7 - 3 = 4$$

STEP 2 Use the sign of the addend with the greater absolute value.

$$|7| > |{}^-3| \rightarrow 7 + {}^-3 = 4$$

PRACTICE Find the sum.

1. $5 + 8$ **2.** $^-8 + {}^-9$ **3.** $^-6 + 8$ **4.** $^-12 + {}^-2$ **5.** $8 + {}^-19$ **6.** $^-1 + {}^-24$

7. $19 + {}^-17$ **8.** $^-12 + {}^-10$ **9.** $^-25 + 7$ **10.** $^-24 + {}^-10$ **11.** $^-42 + 10$ **12.** $14 + {}^-10$

52 SUBTRACTING INTEGERS

To subtract an integer, add its opposite. Then use the rules for addition of integers to complete the problem.

Examples

A. $^-3 - 8$

STEP 1 Rewrite the sentence as an addition problem.

$$^-3 - 8 = {}^-3 + {}^-8$$

STEP 2 Use the rules of addition to complete the problem.

$$^-3 + {}^-8 \rightarrow |{}^-3| + |{}^-8| = 3 + 8 = 11$$

Both addends are negative. $\rightarrow {}^-3 - 8 = {}^-11$

B. $^-6 - {}^-4$

STEP 1 Rewrite the sentence as an addition problem.

$$^-6 - {}^-4 = {}^-6 + {}^+4 = {}^-6 + 4$$

STEP 2 Use the rules of addition to complete the problem.

$$^-6 + 4 \rightarrow |{}^-6| - |4| = 6 - 4 = 2$$

$$|{}^-6| > |4| \rightarrow {}^-6 - {}^-4 = {}^-2$$

PRACTICE Find the difference.

1. $^-4 - 9$ **2.** $12 - 28$ **3.** $^-10 - {}^-18$ **4.** $11 - {}^-11$ **5.** $^-6 - 2$ **6.** $^-10 - 12$

7. $16 - 20$ **8.** $24 - {}^-12$ **9.** $^-24 - {}^-12$ **10.** $^-14 - 10$ **11.** $90 - 98$ **12.** $^-17 - {}^-8$

53 MULTIPLYING INTEGERS

Look at the patterns below to discover rules for multiplying integers.

	$3 \times 3 = 9$			$3 \times {}^{-}3 = {}^{-}9$	
	$2 \times 3 = 6$			$2 \times {}^{-}3 = {}^{-}6$	
factors	$1 \times 3 = 3$	*products*	*factors*	$1 \times {}^{-}3 = {}^{-}3$	*products*
decreasing →	$0 \times 3 = 0$	← *decreasing*	*decreasing* →	$0 \times {}^{-}3 = 0$	← *increasing*
by 1	${}^{-}1 \times 3 = {}^{-}3$	*by 3*	*by 1*	${}^{-}1 \times {}^{-}3 = 3$	*by 3*
	${}^{-}2 \times 3 = {}^{-}6$			${}^{-}2 \times {}^{-}3 = 6$	
	${}^{-}3 \times 3 = {}^{-}9$			${}^{-}3 \times {}^{-}3 = 9$	

Think: *When the signs of the factors are the same, the product is positive.*
When the signs of the factors are different, the product is negative.

Examples Find the products ${}^{-}2 \times 4$, $2 \times {}^{-}4$, ${}^{-}2 \times {}^{-}4$, and 2×4.

${}^{-}2 \times 4 = {}^{-}8$ $\quad$ $2 \times {}^{-}4 = {}^{-}8$ $\quad$ ${}^{-}2 \times {}^{-}4 = 8$ $\quad$ $2 \times 4 = 8$

PRACTICE Find the product.

1. ${}^{-}3 \times 5$ **2.** $8 \times {}^{-}2$ **3.** ${}^{-}9 \times {}^{-}7$ **4.** 6×5 **5.** ${}^{-}12 \times 4$ **6.** $6 \times {}^{-}11$

7. $8 \times {}^{-}7$ **8.** ${}^{-}12 \times {}^{-}2$ **9.** ${}^{-}12 \times 10$ **10.** ${}^{-}6 \times {}^{-}3$ **11.** 19×4 **12.** ${}^{-}4 \times {}^{-}9$

54 DIVIDING INTEGERS

Look at the patterns below to discover rules for dividing integers.

	$9 \div 3 = 3$			$9 \div {}^{-}3 = {}^{-}3$	
	$6 \div 3 = 2$			$6 \div {}^{-}3 = {}^{-}2$	
dividend	$3 \div 3 = 1$	*quotients*	*dividend*	$3 \div {}^{-}3 = {}^{-}1$	*quotients*
decreasing →	$0 \div 3 = 0$	← *decreasing*	*decreasing* →	$0 \div {}^{-}3 = 0$	← *increasing*
by 3	${}^{-}3 \div 3 = {}^{-}1$	*by 1*	*by 3*	${}^{-}3 \div {}^{-}3 = 1$	*by 1*
	${}^{-}6 \div 3 = {}^{-}2$			${}^{-}6 \div {}^{-}3 = 2$	
	${}^{-}9 \div 3 = {}^{-}3$			${}^{-}9 \div {}^{-}3 = 3$	

Think: *When the signs of the dividend and divisor are the same, the quotient is positive.*
When the signs of the dividend and divisor are different, the quotient is negative.

Examples Find the quotients ${}^{-}20 \div 4$, $20 \div {}^{-}4$, ${}^{-}20 \div {}^{-}4$, and $20 \div 4$.

${}^{-}20 \div 4 = {}^{-}5$ $\quad$ $20 \div {}^{-}4 = {}^{-}5$ $\quad$ ${}^{-}20 \div {}^{-}4 = 5$ $\quad$ $20 \div 4 = 5$

PRACTICE Find the quotient.

1. ${}^{-}20 \div 5$ **2.** $8 \div {}^{-}2$ **3.** ${}^{-}12 \div {}^{-}3$ **4.** $25 \div 5$ **5.** ${}^{-}12 \div 4$ **6.** $77 \div {}^{-}11$

7. ${}^{-}28 \div 7$ **8.** $42 \div {}^{-}6$ **9.** ${}^{-}18 \div {}^{-}3$ **10.** ${}^{-}56 \div 8$ **11.** $108 \div 9$ **12.** ${}^{-}84 \div {}^{-}2$

55 TYPES OF TRIANGLES

Triangles are classified by the lengths of their sides and the measures of their angles.

acute triangle

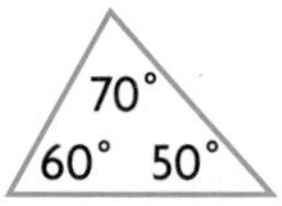

all angles $< 90°$

obtuse triangle

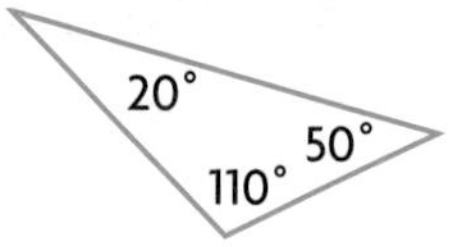

one angle > 90

right triangle

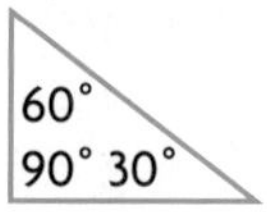

one angle $= 90°$

scalene triangle

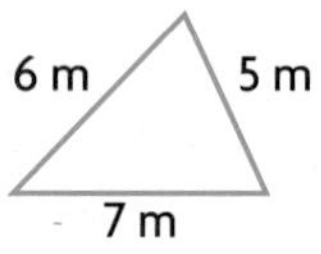

All sides have different lengths.

equilateral triangle

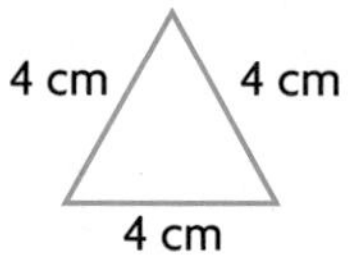

All sides have the same length.

isosceles triangle

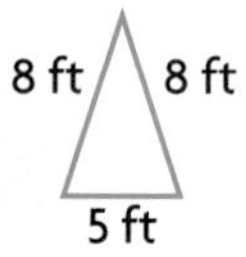

Two sides have the same length.

PRACTICE Classify the triangles by using the given information.

1.

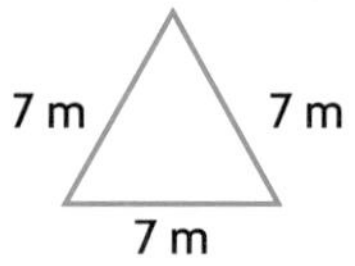

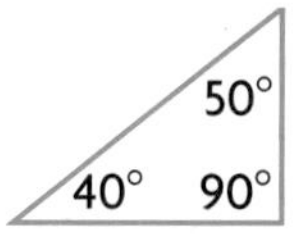

3.

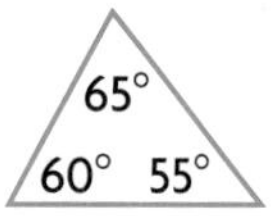

4.

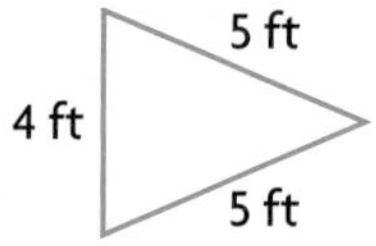

5.

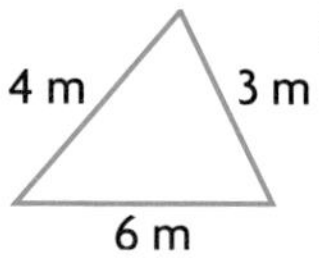

6.

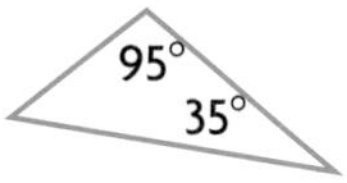

56 ANGLES IN A TRIANGLE

The sum of the measures of the three angles in any triangle is 180°. If you know the measure of two of the angles in a triangle, you can find the measure of the third.

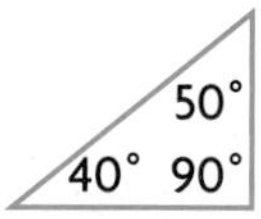

$40° + 50° + 90° = 180°$

Examples Find the measure of $\angle C$.

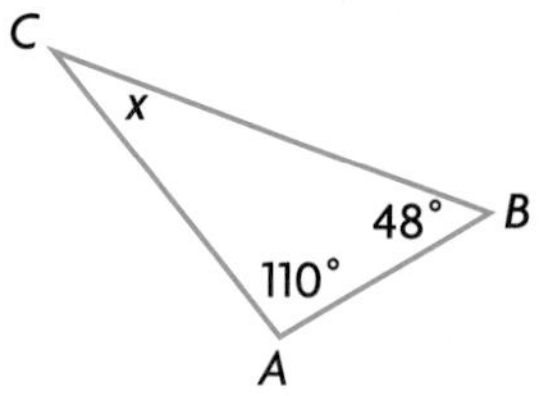

$$110° + 48° + x = 180°$$
$$158° + x = 180°$$
$$x = 180° - 158°$$
$$x = 22°$$

PRACTICE For each triangle, find the unknown angle measure.

1.

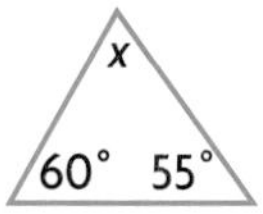

2.

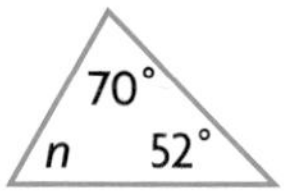

3.

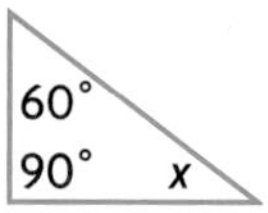

4.

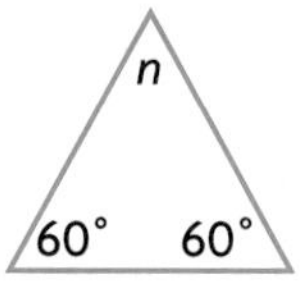

CALCULATOR Activities

HIP TO BE SQUARE

Squares and Square Roots

Look closely. Figure out the pattern for each group of numbers.

2, 4, 2, 8, 16, 32

3, 9, 3, 27, 81, 243

Start with 4. Using the same pattern, find the first six numbers. Use your calculator to help you.

A square root is one of the two equal factors of a number.

$\sqrt{25} = 5$ because $5^2 = 25$.

Using the Calculator

To find the first six numbers by using the *Casio fx-65,* enter the following:

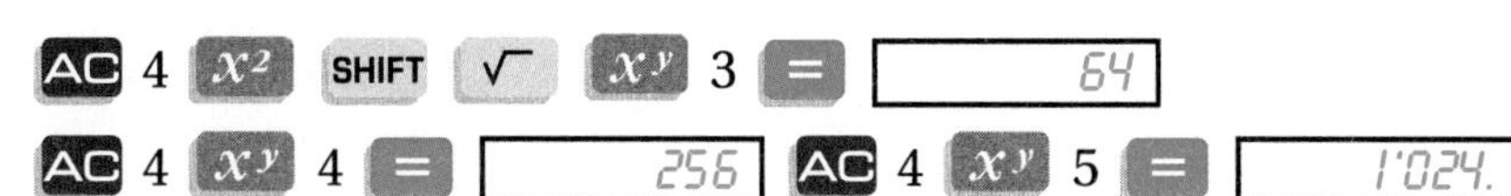

To find the first six numbers by using the *TI Explorer Plus,* enter the following:

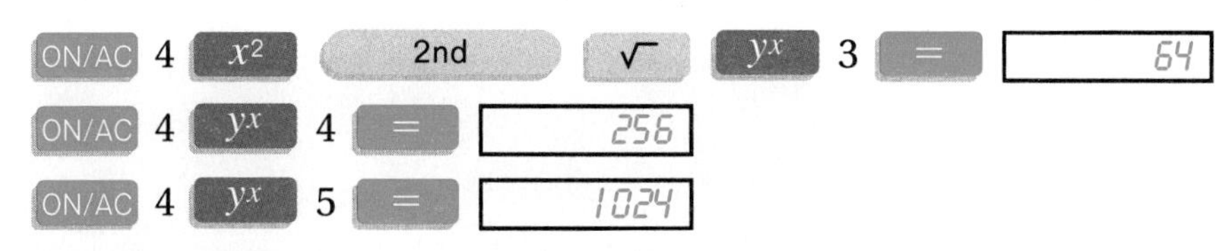

The first six numbers in the pattern are 4, 16, 4, 64, 256, 1,024.

PRACTICE

Use your calculator.

1. Find the next three numbers. 5, 25, 5, 125, ?, ?, ?

2. Find the square root of your answers for Exercise 1.

Solve for *x*.

3. $x^2 = 3{,}721$ **4.** $x^2 - 17 = 32$ **5.** $x^2 + 10 = 266$

6. Is $8 \times 12 = 8^{12}$?

7. What is 7^2?

8. What other number, besides 7, can you square to get 49?

MEMORIES

Patterns, Solve Problems

The following problems form a pattern. Find each product. Then find the total of the products. What pattern do you notice?

$12 \times 9 = ?$ $\quad 123 \times 9 = ?$ $\quad 1{,}234 \times 9 = ?$ $\quad 12{,}345 \times 9 = ?$

Total of products: ?

The multiples of 9 follow a pattern:

9, 18, 27, 36, 45, 54, 63, . . .

The sum of the digits of each multiple is always 9.

Using the Calculator

Here's how to solve by using the memory of the *Casio fx-65*.

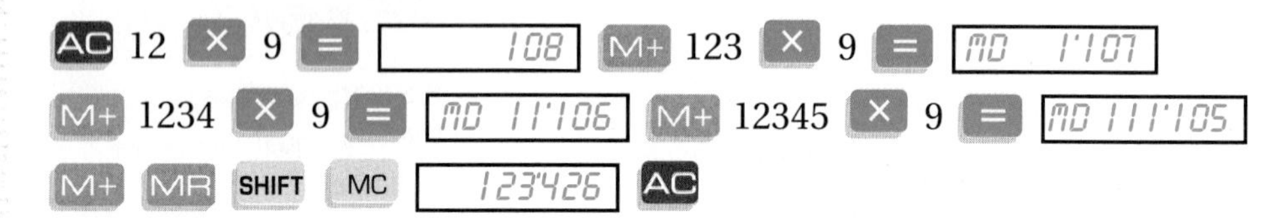

Here's how to solve by using the memory of the *TI Explorer Plus*:

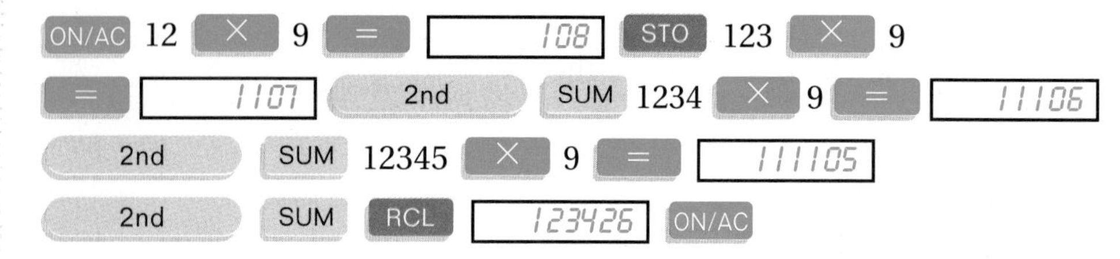

The products are 108; 1,107; 11,106; and 111,105. The total of the products is 123,426. The digits of the products always add up to 9. And the digits of the total of the products add up to 18, whose digits then add up to 9.

PRACTICE

Copy and complete the table. Use your calculator.

	Factors	Product
1.	23×9	?
2.	234×9	?
3.	$2{,}345 \times 9$	?
4.	$23{,}456 \times 9$	?
5.	Total of products	?

6. There are 9 days in a week on the planet Ninonus. If 234,567 Ninotians each eat an apple a day, how many apples will be eaten in a Ninotian week? Guess first! Then use your calculator to check.

7. Suppose there are 2,345,678 Ninotians on the planet Ninonus. How many apples will be eaten in a Ninotian week? Guess first! Then use your calculator to check.

CHILDREN FROM WHERE?

Equivalent Fractions, Mixed Numbers, and Decimals

The WOUDS (We Only Use Decimals) Science Group has discovered that the planets Zanobia and Claribia have many children. WOUDS has Zanobian $\left(\frac{11}{5}\right)$ and Claribian $\left(\frac{66}{30}\right)$ census data giving the number of children per household on these planets.

The group members want to figure out which planet has more children per household but since they work only in decimals, they are confused about the data. They could use calculators to work this out.

REMEMBER:

There are many ways to express the same amount.

$$1\frac{1}{5} = \frac{6}{5}$$
$$= \frac{12}{10} = 1\frac{2}{10}$$
$$= 1.2$$

Using the Calculator

Here's how to solve the problem by using the *Casio fx-65.*

AC 11 b/c 5 SHIFT ab/c↔d/c F↔D [2.2] AC

66 b/c 30 SHIFT ab/c↔d/c F↔D [2.2]

Here's how to solve the problem by using the *TI Explorer Plus*:

ON/AC 11 / 5 Ab/c F↔D [2.2]

ON/AC 66 / 30 Ab/c F↔D [2.2]

Zanobia and Claribia both average 2.2 children per household.

PRACTICE

Copy and complete the table. Use your calculator.

	Fraction	Mixed Number	Decimal
1.	$\frac{165}{4}$		
2.		$3\frac{329}{500}$	
3.		$7\frac{5}{8}$	
4.		$2\frac{123}{250}$	
5.		$2\frac{1}{2}$	
6.		$6\frac{3}{4}$	

Solve for x. Then convert the fractions to decimals.

7. $\frac{9}{54} = \frac{x}{6}$

8. $\frac{x}{6} = \frac{2}{3}$

9. $\frac{4}{5} = \frac{5}{x}$

10. $\frac{9}{x} = \frac{20}{37}$

MIRROR IMAGE

Reciprocals

Look at the map. Lyle lives the same distance from Joseph as he does from Rosa. How far does Lyle live from Joseph or from Rosa?

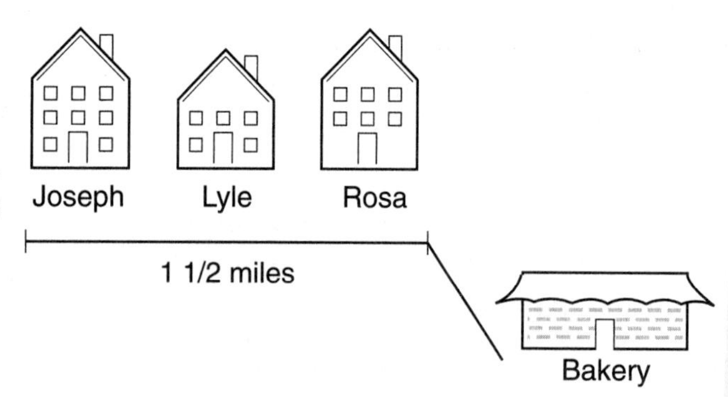

Solve the problem using division. Then solve the problem using multiplication and a reciprocal. Are your answers the same?

REMEMBER:

Reciprocals are two numbers whose product is 1.

$\frac{1}{2} \times \frac{2}{1} = 1$

To divide fractions, multiply by the reciprocal of the divisor.

$\frac{3}{4} \div \frac{2}{3} = \frac{3}{4} \times \frac{3}{2}$

$= \frac{9}{8}$, or $1\frac{1}{8}$

Using the Calculator

Here's how to solve by using the *Casio fx-65.*

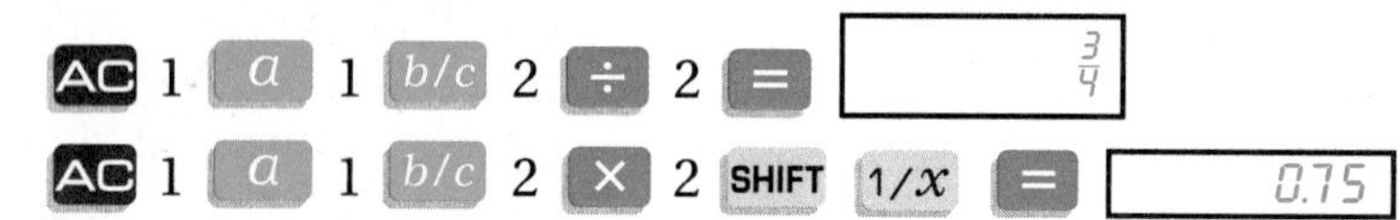

Here's how to solve by using the *TI Explorer Plus*:

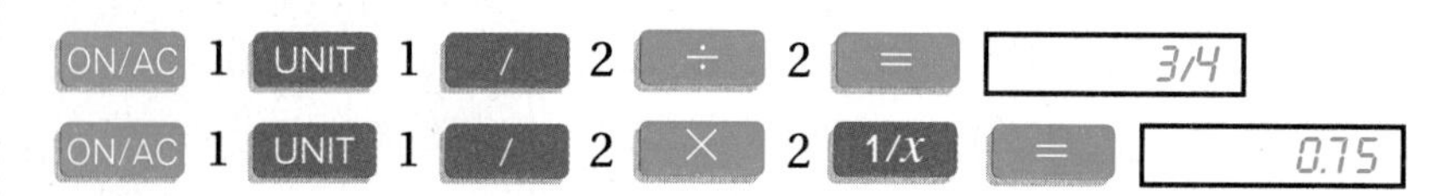

Lyle lives $\frac{3}{4}$ mi from both Joseph and Rosa. The answers are the same because $\frac{3}{4} = 0.75$.

PRACTICE

Use your calculator to solve.

1. The distance from Rosa's house to the bakery is one third the distance from her house to Lyle's house. How far does Rosa live from the bakery?
2. What's the reciprocal of 0.001?
3. What happens when you try to take the reciprocal of 0? Explain.
4. At the bakery, Rosa buys 6 pastries. On the way home she eats half of a pastry. She then divides the remaining $5\frac{1}{2}$ pastries evenly among Joseph, Lyle, and herself. Find each person's share.
5. Joseph, Lyle, and Rosa decide to jog after eating their pastries. Rosa and Joseph jog $3\frac{1}{2}$ mi. Lyle jogs $\frac{2}{3}$ as far as Rosa and Joseph. How far does Lyle jog?

RUNNING IN CIRCLES

Area and Circumference of Circles

Merion Elementary School just finished building a circular track with a playing field in the middle. To celebrate, the school is holding field events. Each teacher must participate in a "One Lap for the Teachers" sprint and a "Superstar Teacher" touch-football game.

Mrs. Garvey, a math teacher, decided she needed to know exactly how much running she should be prepared for. She measured from the center of the field to the track. This was 210 ft.

What is the distance of the sprint (rounded to the nearest whole number)? How much space is available for the football game (rounded to the nearest hundredth)?

REMEMBER:

To find the circumference of a circle, use the formula $C = \pi d$.

To find the area of a circle, use the formula $A = \pi r^2$.

Using the Calculator

To solve this problem by using the *Casio fx-65*, do the following:

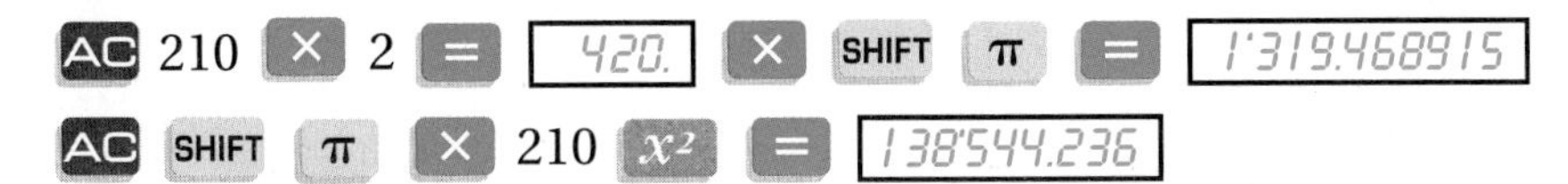

To solve this problem by using the *TI Explorer Plus*, do the following:

The distance of the "One Lap for the Teachers" sprint is 1,319 ft.

The area for the football game is 138,544.24 ft^2.

PRACTICE

Use your calculator. Round to the nearest hundredth.

1. The diameter of a circle is 8 cm. Find the circumference and the area.

2. If the radius of a circle is 1.2 in., find the circumference and the area.

3. The distance around the equator is 24,901 mi. How far is it from any point on the equator to the center of Earth?

4. The world's largest omelet was cooked in Belgium in a frying pan with a diameter of 41 ft 1 in. What was the surface area of the omelet, assuming that it was as big as the pan?

5. Ken and Tina are tossing a round disc to their dog Max. The disc has a diameter of 10 in. Find the circumference of the disc.

6. Mr. Ownby is planning to make a circular garden with a diameter of 14 ft in his backyard. Find the surface area of the garden.

HOW BIG IS BIG, HOW SMALL IS SMALL?

Scientific Notation

You know that the moon is a very large sphere. But did you know how large? The volume of the moon is 5.28×10^6 mi^3. How would you write the moon's volume in standard form?

Using the Calculator

Using the *TI Explorer Plus*, you can press the following:

ON/AC 5 . 28 EE 6 2nd ◄EE 5280000

The volume of the moon is 5,280,000 mi^3.

How do you go back to scientific notation on the *TI Explorer Plus?*

5280000 EE 5.28 06

REMEMBER:

Scientific notation consists of two factors. The first factor is a number greater than or equal to 1 and less than 10. The second factor is a power of 10.

$327{,}000 = 3.27 \times 10^5$

PRACTICE

Use your calculator.

1. The volume of Earth is 2.59×10^{11} mi^3. What is Earth's volume in standard form?
2. What is 0.00000005 in scientific notation?
3. Explain why the expression 36.7×10^{10} is not in scientific notation.

Convert these animal speeds to standard form. Then order them from slowest to fastest.

	Animal	Speed (in km/hr)
4.	giant tortoise	2.7×10^{-1}
5.	snail	4.8×10^{-2}
6.	sloth	2.4×10^{-1}
7.	sea horse	2.7×10^{-6}

Convert the number of eggs each state produced in 1995 to scientific notation.

	State	Number of Eggs Produced in 1995
8.	Indiana	5,496,000,000
9.	Wyoming	2,400,000
10.	Kansas	325,000,000
11.	Rhode Island	34,000,000

TWO STEPS FORWARD, THREE STEPS BACK

Integer Operations

Michael and Kay were playing a new version of Mother May I. Their rules were that the "mother" could both refuse to let a player take steps forward and instruct the player to take steps back. Michael has just taken his first three steps forward.

This is what Kay allowed Michael to do for his next three requests:

9 steps forward
5 steps back
3 steps back

How many steps from the beginning is Michael at this point in the game?

Subtracting a positive number from a negative number is the same as adding two negative numbers.

$^-4 - 2 = {^-4} + (^-2) = {^-6}$

Using the Calculator

To solve this problem by using the *Casio fx-65,* do the following:

AC 3 + 9 + 5 +/− + 3 +/− = | 4.

To solve this problem by using the *TI Explorer Plus,* do the following:

ON/AC 3 + 9 + 5 (+⟲−) + 3 (+⟲−) = | 4

Michael is 4 steps from the beginning.

PRACTICE

Use your calculator to solve.

1. $^-7 - 2 + 6 - 7 + 3$

2. $^-3.02 + 5.91 + 7.34 - (^-5.5) - 8.06$

3. $^-9 - 10 - (^-8) + 17 - 12$

4. $^-5.7 - (^-8.2) + 9.4 - (^-10.6)$

5. On a winter's day the temperature was $^-14$°C at 8:00 A.M. By 1:30 P.M., the temperature had increased by 5°C. What was the temperature at 1:30 P.M.?

6. A scuba diver went 30 ft below sea level. She then went down another 40 ft. How many feet below sea level is she?

7. During an experiment, the temperature of a liquid changed from 5°C to $^-27$°C. How many degrees did the temperature drop during the experiment?

8. A spelunker entered a cave 5 m above sea level. She traveled down 17 m, up 12 m, down 6 m, and up 2 m. How far below sea level is she now?

9. In the Arctic circle, the temperature was $^-8$°F. Twelve hours later the temperature had decreased 17°F. What was the new temperature?

10. A roller coaster starts 536 ft above sea level. It drops 400 ft, rises 157 ft, and drops 291 ft. At this point, how far above sea level is the roller coaster?

NOT YOUR AVERAGE BEAR

Summation, Mean

What would it be like to take a 3-hr test? Thousands of college-bound high school students take one every year. It is called the SAT (Scholastic Aptitude Test). A student's scores are sent to the colleges that he or she applies to. The SAT is divided into a math section and a verbal section, each of which is graded on a scale from 200 to 800.

The table below shows the mean math and verbal scores for each year from 1987 through 1992. What is the mean of the mean verbal scores for all six years, to the nearest tenth?

Year	Math	Verbal
1987	430	475
1988	428	476
1989	427	476
1990	424	476
1991	422	474
1992	423	476

The mean of a set of numbers is the sum of the numbers divided by the total number of addends.

$7 + 2 + 6 = 15$

$15 \div 3 = 5$

The mean of 7, 2, and 6 is 5.

Using the Calculator

The *TI Explorer Plus* can help you get the answer. Press the following keys:

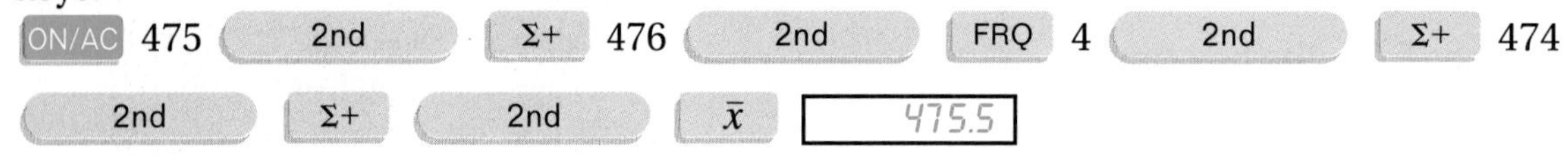

The mean verbal score for the SAT from 1987 through 1992 was 475.5.

PRACTICE

Use your calculator.

1. Use the table below to calculate the mean high temperature for the four months.

Month	Temperature
December	57°F
January	56°F
February	59°F
March	60°F

2. What is the mean for the last four math tests you have taken?

3. Can you determine your class's favorite music video by calculating a mean? Explain.

CHANCES ARE

Random Number Generator, Factorials

At the Bridgewater County Fair, the RANDECHOO (Random Decimal Chooser) is quite popular. The contestant picks ten numbers between 0 and 0.999. The contestant wins if he or she guesses at least one decimal that the chooser lands on.

REMEMBER:

The product $6 \times 5 \times 4 \times 3 \times 2 \times 1$ can be written as 6! and is called 6 factorial.

Using the Calculator

Play the RANDECHOO game. Write down ten numbers between 0 and 0.999.

Using a *Casio fx-65* as a RANDECHOO, do the following:

←Displays will vary.

Repeat this sequence nine more times. Did you win?

Radnor High School received ten free movie passes as thanks for community service provided by the 100 members of the senior class. Each student was given a number from 1 to 100. The class president used a calculator to choose the ten winning numbers. Imagine you are the class president. Use your calculator to find ten winning numbers.

Using the Calculator

Using a *TI Explorer Plus,* press the following keys:

←Displays will vary.

Do this sequence nine more times. Which numbers did your calculator choose?

To find the value of a factorial, such as 4!, you can use these keys on a *TI Explorer Plus:*

ON/AC 4 2nd x! [24]

To find the value of a factorial, such as 4!, you can use these keys on a *Casio fx-65:*

AC 4 SHIFT x! [24]

PRACTICE

Find the value. Use your calculator.

1. 10!

2. 12!

3. 69!

4. 42!

HI-TECH CALCULATOR 1

Scatterplots and Line Graphs

The table below shows the height of a baseball at different times after it was hit. Display the data in a scatterplot and a line graph.

Time (in sec)	Height (in ft)	Time (in sec)	Height (in ft)
0.5	10	3.0	50
1.0	25	3.5	46
1.5	38	4.0	32
2.0	48	4.5	20
2.5	52	5.0	6

You can use a scatterplot to see if there is a relationship between two variables. A line graph shows change over time.

Using the Calculator

Use the following keys on a *TI-82 Graphing Calculator* to make a scatterplot and then change it to a line graph.

Clear the memory and brighten screen.

[2nd] [MEM] 3 2 [2nd] [▲] (*hold down*) [ENTER]

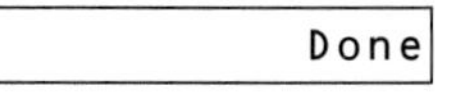

Enter the data from the list above. Let L1 be time and L2 be height.

[STAT] 1 0.5 [ENTER] 1.0 [ENTER] 1.5 [ENTER] 2.0 [ENTER] 2.5 [ENTER] 3.0 [ENTER] 3.5 [ENTER] 4.0 [ENTER] 4.5 [ENTER] 5.0

[▶] 10 [ENTER] 25 [ENTER] 38 [ENTER] 48 [ENTER] 52 [ENTER] 50 [ENTER] 46 [ENTER] 32 [ENTER] 20 [ENTER] 6

L1	L2	L3
2.5	52	
3	50	
3.5	46	
4	32	
4.5	20	
5	6	

L2(11)=

Next to type, select the scatterplot.

[2nd] [STAT PLOT] 1 [ENTER] [▼] [ENTER]

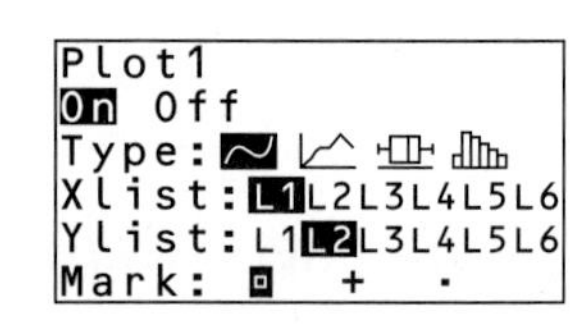

Display the scatterplot.

[2nd] [QUIT] [ZOOM] 9

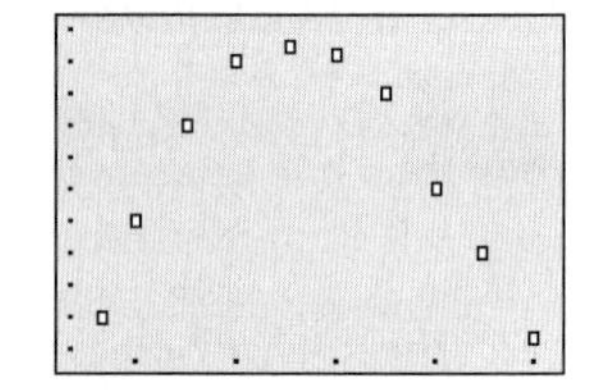

Change the scatterplot to a line graph.

[2nd] [STAT PLOT] 1 [▼] [▶] [ENTER] [2nd] [QUIT] [ZOOM] 9

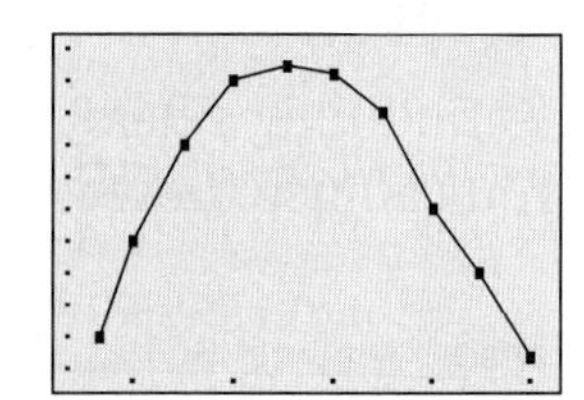

PRACTICE

Make a scatterplot of the data about the height of a golf ball at different times after it was hit. Then change it to a line graph.

Time (in sec)	0.5	1.0	1.5	2.0	2.5	3.0	3.5	4.0
Height (in ft)	4	18	28	35	34	24	11	0

HI-TECH CALCULATOR 2

Explore Functions and Relations

You can use the *TI-82 Graphing Calculator* to display a table of values for the equation $y = x + 2$, show the graph of the equation, and save the graph for future reference.

> **REMEMBER:**
> You can graph an equation by making a table of values. Solve the equation for y. Choose values for x and solve for y. Use the x and y values to write an ordered pair.

Using the Calculator

Use the following keys on the *TI-82 Graphing Calculator.*

Clear the memory and brighten screen. Hold ▲ *until the display reappears.*

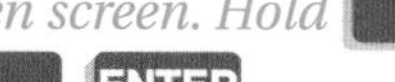

2nd MEM 3 2 2nd ▲ ENTER

```
Done
```

Enter the equation.

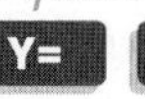

CLEAR Y= X,T,Θ + 2

```
Y1=X+2
Y2=
Y3=
```

Use the arrow keys to explore the table of values for $y = x + 2$.

2nd TABLE ▲ ▼

X	Y1
-3	-1
-2	0
-1	1
0	2
1	3
2	4
3	5

X=0

Change Xmin to $^-3$, Xmax to 1, Ymin to $^-1$, and Ymax to 3. This changes the view of the graph.

WINDOW ▼ (−) 3 ENTER 1 ENTER ENTER (−) 1 ENTER 3 ENTER

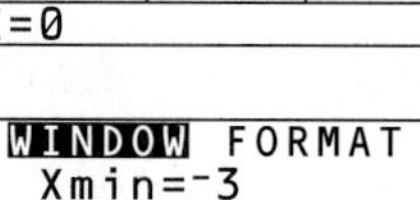

```
WINDOW FORMAT
 Xmin=-3
 Xmax=1
 Xscl=1
 Ymin=-1
 Ymax=3
 Yscl=1
```

Graph the equation.

GRAPH

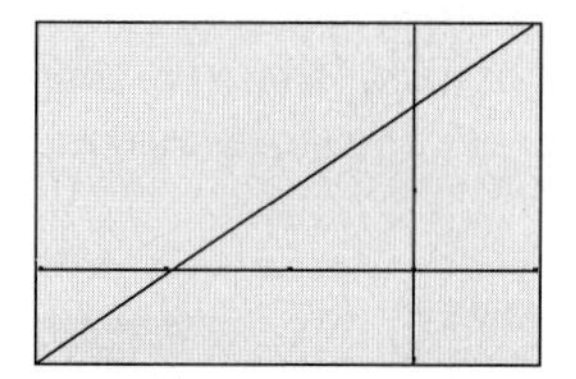

Store the graph.

2nd DRAW ▶ ▶ 1 VARS 4 1 ENTER CLEAR

```
StorePic Pic1
```

Recall and display the graph.

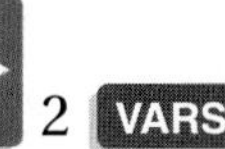

2nd DRAW ▶ ▶ 2 VARS 4 1 ENTER

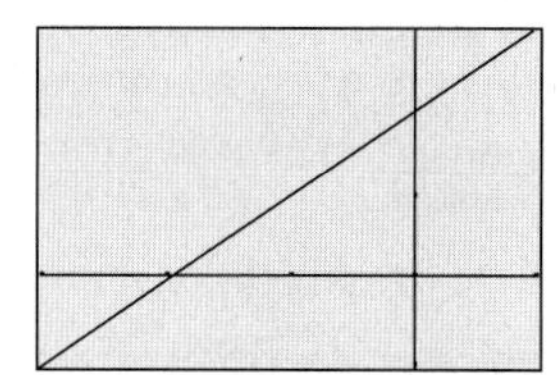

PRACTICE

Create a table of values for the equation. Graph, save, and recall the graph. Change the view of the graph as necessary.

1. $y = x - 2$ **2.** $y = x$ **3.** $y = x + 4$ **4.** $y = x - 4$

5. $y = x + 8$ **6.** $y = x - 8$ **7.** $y = x + 6$ **8.** $y = x - 6$

HI-TECH CALCULATOR 3

Showing Figures on the Coordinate Plane

Draw a triangle with vertices (⁻8,⁻4), (1,7), and (6,⁻5).

Using the Calculator

Use the following keys on the *TI-82 Graphing Calculator* to draw a triangle.

Clear the memory and brighten screen. Hold ▲ *until the display reappears.*

2nd MEM 3 2 2nd ▲ ENTER

```
Done
```

Ready to draw a line segment.

CLEAR 2nd DRAW 2

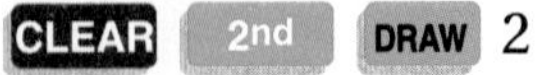

```
Line(
```

Enter ordered pairs for the line segment from (⁻8,⁻4) to (1,7).

(–) 8 , (–) 4 ,

1 , 7)

ENTER

```
Line(-8, -4, 1, 7)
```

CLEAR 2nd ENTRY

```
Line(-8, -4, 1, 7)
Line(-8, -4, 1, 7)
```

Use arrow keys to move cursor. Enter ordered pairs for the line segment from (1,7) to (6,⁻5). Use delete key as needed.

ENTER

```
Line(-8, -4, 1, 7)
Line(1, 7, 6, -5)
```

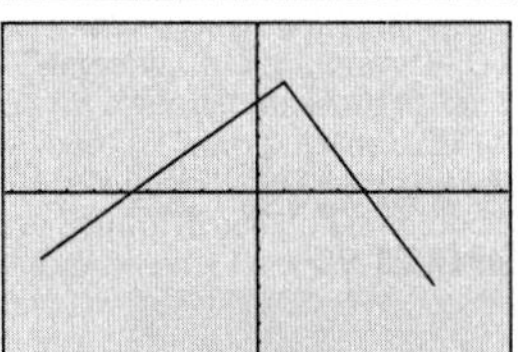

CLEAR 2nd ENTRY

```
Line(-8, -4, 1, 7)
Line(1, 7, 6, -5)
Line(1, 7, 6, -5)
```

Use arrow keys to move cursor and enter ordered pairs for the line segment from (6,⁻5) to (⁻8,⁻4).

ENTER

```
Line(-8, -4, 1, 7)
Line(1, 7, 6, -5)
Line(6, -5, -8, -4)
```

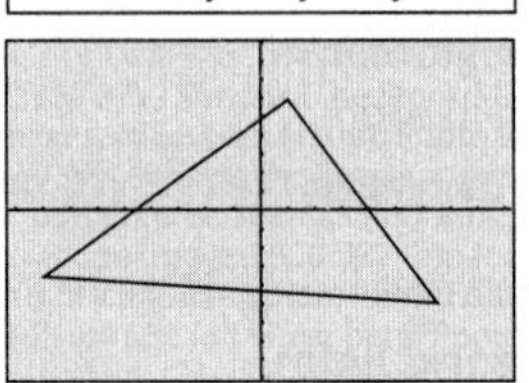

When writing ordered pairs, the *x*-value is written first and the *y*-value is written second. When graphing a point written as an ordered pair, the *x*-value represents the horizontal movement and the *y*-value represents the vertical movement. To graph the point (4,9) on the coordinate plane, move 4 units to the right of the origin. Then move 9 units up.

PRACTICE

Use your calculator to draw a triangle with the given vertices.

1. (1,9), (2,1), (7,8) **2.** (⁻2,3), (4,3), (4,⁻8) **3.** (0,0), (⁻5,⁻7), (7,⁻9)

More Practice

CHAPTER 1

Lesson 1.1

Classify the numbers as counting numbers, whole numbers, integers, or rational numbers.

1. $^-0.2, 37, \frac{^-2}{3}, 3.7, 4\frac{1}{4}$

2. $^-3\frac{5}{9}, ^-7, 14, 8.2, 375$

3. $0, 17, ^-0.23, 3\frac{1}{7}, ^-4.6$

4. $\frac{^-4}{7}, 0.038, 42, \frac{^-17}{4}, 0.7$

5. $\frac{2}{3}, ^-1, 5.4, 17, ^-2.6$

6. $5, ^-9, 3.6, \frac{1}{4}, ^-7.2$

Lesson 1.2

Give at least three other names for each rational number.

1. 7

2. $^-4$

3. 2.6

4. 4.1

5. $\frac{7}{10}$

6. 13

7. $^-1$

8. 1.1

9. $\frac{9}{10}$

10. 9

11. $^-8$

12. $\frac{1}{4}$

For Exercises 13-16, graph the rational numbers on the same number line.

13. $1.6, 1\frac{1}{2}, \frac{7}{4}$

14. $1.5, ^-1.5, 1\frac{3}{4}$

15. $^-2, 0.5, ^-1\frac{1}{2}$

16. $3.25, ^-1\frac{1}{4}, ^-2\frac{1}{2}$

Lesson 1.3

Write percents for the area covered by the small unshaded parts and for the area covered by the small shaded ones.

1. 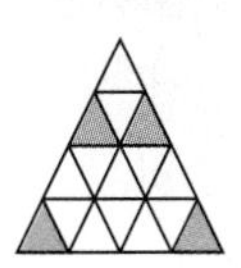

2. 

3. 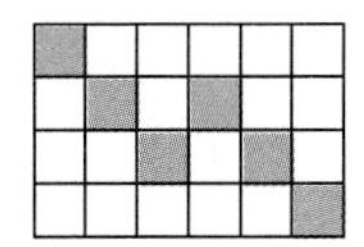

4. 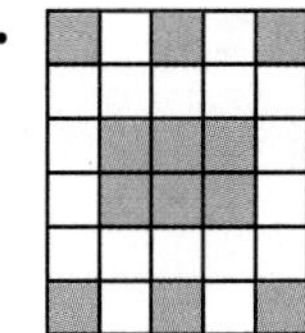

Suppose a 3 inch by 4 inch rectangular piece of paper gets folded and unfolded as shown.

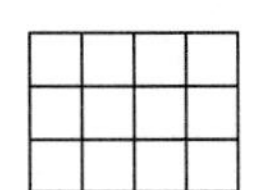

5. How many 1 in. × 1 in. squares are formed?

6. How many 1 in. × 2 in. rectangles are formed? 1 in. × 3 in. rectangles?

Lesson 1.4

Write as a percent.

1. $\frac{7}{10}$ **2.** $\frac{3}{1}$ **3.** $\frac{9}{12}$ **4.** 3 of 8

5. $2\frac{3}{25}$ **6.** 0.73 **7.** 0.08 **8.** $\frac{8}{1}$

9. 3.14 **10.** 0.001 **11.** 12 of 200 **12.** $4\frac{3}{4}$

Write each percent as a fraction in simplest form.

13. 12% **14.** 35% **15.** 18% **16.** 300%

17. 55% **18.** 2% **19.** 50% **20.** 75%

Write each percent as a decimal.

21. 3% **22.** 4.0% **23.** 11% **24.** 3.8%

25. 78% **26.** 300% **27.** 121% **28.** 9%

Lesson 1.5

Copy and complete the table to find the central angle measures for a circle graph of the results.

	MUSIC SHAWN LISTENS TO		
		Percent	Angle Measure
1.	Celtic	40%	
2.	Reggae	35%	
3.	Jazz	25%	

	7TH GRADERS' FAVORITE FAST FOODS		
		Percent	Angle Measure
4.	Pizza	60%	
5.	Burgers	22%	
6.	Tacos	18%	

CHAPTER 2

Lesson 2.1

Find the value.

1. 6^5 **2.** 86^2 **3.** 5^7 **4.** 2^{14} **5.** 10^5

6. 236^1 **7.** 4^9 **8.** 18^0 **9.** 0.14^2 **10.** 3.1^3

11. $\left(\frac{2}{3}\right)^4$ **12.** $\left(\frac{1}{4}\right)^3$ **13.** $\left(\frac{2}{5}\right)^3$ **14.** $\left(\frac{2}{7}\right)^2$ **15.** $\left(\frac{3}{4}\right)^3$

Write in scientific notation.

16. 2,100 **17.** 27,500 **18.** 305,000,000 **19.** 9,900,000,000

Write in standard form.

20. 2.8×10^4 **21.** 1.53×10^6 **22.** 1.5×10^{10} **23.** 1.04×10^5

Lesson 2.2

Use expanded form to write each binary number as a decimal number.

1. 1001_{two} **2.** 10001_{two} **3.** 11110_{two}

4. 10010001_{two} **5.** 1100001_{two} **6.** 1010_{two}

7. 1000011_{two} **8.** 10001100_{two} **9.** 11111_{two}

10. 101001_{two} **11.** 10010000_{two} **12.** 1100000_{two}

13. 1011_{two} **14.** 11100_{two} **15.** 10001101_{two}

Lesson 2.3

Tell how many counters you need to make a square array with the given number of counters on one side.

1. 5 **2.** 3 **3.** 10 **4.** 13 **5.** 25

Find the square.

6. 9^2 **7.** 15^2 **8.** 22^2 **9.** 1.6^2 **10.** 0.7^2

Find the square root.

11. $\sqrt{81}$ **12.** $\sqrt{196}$ **13.** $\sqrt{225}$ **14.** $\sqrt{900}$ **15.** $\sqrt{1{,}225}$

16. $\sqrt{2{,}500}$ **17.** $\sqrt{4{,}900}$ **18.** $\sqrt{1.44}$ **19.** $\sqrt{3.24}$ **20.** $\sqrt{0.0361}$

Locate each square root between two integers.

21. $\sqrt{13}$ **22.** $\sqrt{88}$ **23.** $\sqrt{72}$ **24.** $\sqrt{23}$ **25.** $\sqrt{48}$

26. $\sqrt{125}$ **27.** $\sqrt{147}$ **28.** $\sqrt{162}$ **29.** $\sqrt{191}$ **30.** $\sqrt{206}$

Lesson 2.4

Use the *guess and check* strategy to solve.

1. Jennifer wants to plant wild flowers in a square plot of land in her backyard. The area of the plot of land is 120 sq meters. What is the length of one side of that plot to the nearest tenth of a meter?

2. Larry wants to paint one wall of his living room. The wall is square in shape and has an area of 540 sq ft. What is the length of one side of the wall to the nearest tenth of a foot?

3. Art Jones spent a total of $96 for tickets to a play. The tickets cost $12 for each adult and $8 for each child. Find the number of adult tickets bought.

4. Herby gave Tim $4.20 in quarters and dimes to buy film. Herby gave Tim a total of 21 coins. How many of each coin did Herby give Tim?

Lesson 2.5

For Exercises 1–6, use the iteration process shown below. Write the results of the first six iterations.

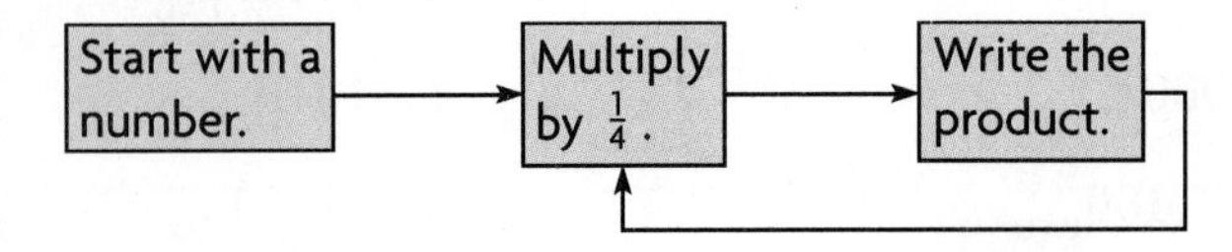

1. Start with 40.

2. Start with 400.

3. Start with $\frac{1}{3}$.

4. Start with 80.

5. Start with 800.

6. Start with $\frac{1}{2}$.

CHAPTER 3

Lesson 3.1

In the table below are the foods Ramone ate yesterday. The amount of calcium for each is given.

Breakfast:	3 pancakes	140 mg
	1 orange	56 mg
Lunch:	$1\frac{1}{3}$ cup of lentil soup	54 mg
	lettuce and tomato salad; 1 cup	24 mg
	English muffin	92 mg
Dinner:	vegetarian baked beans; 1 cup	128 mg
	broccoli; 1 cup	178 mg
	cornbread; 2 oz	133 mg

1. Find a range for an estimate of the amount of calcium he had at each meal.

2. Estimate the total calcium he had at each meal using rounding.

3. Use clustering to estimate the total amount of vitamin C in the following foods: a cup of broccoli, 98 mg; a cup of brussels sprouts, 96 mg; a medium grapefruit, 94 mg; and a cup of strawberries, 85 mg.

Lesson 3.2

Copy the problem. Place the decimal point in the product. Add zeros as needed.

1. $2.8 \times 34 = 952$

2. $83 \times 0.003 = 249$

3. $30.1 \times 0.04 = 1204$

4. $1.7 \times 2.5 = 425$

Find the product.

5. 4.3×5

6. 2.3×4.26

7. 3.93×23.02

8. 8.06×0.3

Lesson 3.3

Find the quotient.

1. $259.2 \div 2.4$ **2.** $6.075 \div 3$ **3.** $8.7 \div 2.9$

4. $10.78 \div 0.07$ **5.** $297.6 \div 0.24$ **6.** $3 \div 0.003$

7. $7.7 \div 2.5$ **8.** $427.692 \div 1.2$ **9.** $43.2 \div 32$

Find the speed in miles per hour by dividing the distance (*d*) by the time (*t*).

10. $d = 77.04$ $t = 1.2$ **11.** $d = 50.995$ $t = 1.55$

12. $d = 304.32$ $t = 3.2$ **13.** $d = 52.976$ $t = 17.2$

Estimate the quotient by using compatible numbers.

14. $9.26 \div 2.8$ **15.** $47.8 \div 5.91$ **16.** $10.38 \div 1.87$

17. $302.7 \div 2.01$ **18.** $81{,}480 \div 27.16$ **19.** $8.19 \div 3.775$

Lesson 3.4

Give the correct order of operations for finding the value.

1. $(24 - 6) \div 3$ **2.** $(20 - 16.2) \times 2.2$ **3.** $8 - 8 \div (5 + 3)$

4. $3^4 - (4 + 6.24 \div 2)$ **5.** $3 \times 8.3 + 1.8 \times 33$ **6.** $6 \div 2 \times 3 - 1$

Find the value by using a calculator.

7. $6 + 9 \times 4 - 3$ **8.** $63 \div (6 + 3) \times 2$ **9.** $9 - 4 \div 4 + 1$

10. $(72 - 2 \times 4 + 12) \div 5$ **11.** $28.37 - 3.6 \times 6.21$ **12.** $5 - 2^2 + 1 \times 8$

13. $(25 - 8) \times 3 + 42$ **14.** $19.72 + 5.6 \times 2.5$ **15.** $4^3 \div 16 \times 2^2$

CHAPTER 4

Lesson 4.1

Add. Write the answer in simplest form.

1. $\frac{1}{3} + \frac{1}{9}$ **2.** $\frac{1}{3} + \frac{3}{4}$ **3.** $\frac{1}{4} + \frac{3}{5}$ **4.** $\frac{2}{3} + \frac{1}{8} + \frac{1}{4}$

5. $\frac{5}{8} + \frac{2}{3} + \frac{1}{6}$ **6.** $\frac{7}{10} + \frac{1}{8} + \frac{3}{5}$ **7.** $\frac{2}{3} + \frac{1}{6} + \frac{1}{2} + \frac{7}{12}$ **8.** $\frac{3}{8} + \frac{5}{12}$

Subtract. Write the answer in simplest form.

9. $\frac{8}{9} - \frac{4}{9}$ **10.** $\frac{3}{5} - \frac{2}{10}$ **11.** $\frac{15}{18} - \frac{3}{12}$ **12.** $\frac{13}{24} - \frac{3}{8}$

13. $\frac{2}{3} - \frac{3}{7}$ **14.** $\frac{19}{20} - \frac{1}{2}$ **15.** $\frac{7}{12} - \frac{1}{4}$ **16.** $\frac{25}{27} - \frac{39}{81}$

Lesson 4.2

Add. Write the answer in simplest form.

1. $3\frac{1}{10} + 1\frac{1}{2}$ **2.** $2\frac{3}{8} + 5\frac{1}{3}$ **3.** $3\frac{5}{12} + 1\frac{3}{4}$ **4.** $4\frac{1}{4} + 2\frac{5}{6}$

5. $2\frac{5}{9} + 3\frac{1}{6}$ **6.** $8\frac{2}{7} + 7\frac{1}{2}$ **7.** $5\frac{1}{5} + 7\frac{1}{7}$ **8.** $1\frac{9}{14} + 3\frac{4}{21}$

Subtract. Write the answer in simplest form.

9. $9\frac{1}{8} - 3\frac{1}{4}$ **10.** $6\frac{2}{3} - 1\frac{3}{7}$ **11.** $8\frac{1}{2} - 6\frac{3}{4}$ **12.** $4\frac{1}{6} - 2\frac{5}{8}$

13. $2\frac{3}{4} - 1\frac{1}{6}$ **14.** $12\frac{1}{4} - 1\frac{1}{3}$ **15.** $4\frac{2}{3} - 3\frac{1}{12}$ **16.** $6\frac{5}{8} - 1\frac{1}{2}$

Lesson 4.3

Round each fraction to 0, $\frac{1}{2}$, or 1.

1. $\frac{4}{7}$ **2.** $\frac{5}{9}$ **3.** $\frac{8}{9}$ **4.** $\frac{2}{10}$ **5.** $\frac{5}{8}$ **6.** $\frac{5}{12}$

7. $\frac{3}{5}$ **8.** $\frac{1}{7}$ **9.** $\frac{3}{8}$ **10.** $\frac{4}{5}$ **11.** $\frac{2}{15}$ **12.** $\frac{14}{17}$

Estimate the sum or difference.

13. $9\frac{1}{7} - 3\frac{3}{4}$ **14.** $3\frac{7}{8} + 2\frac{1}{9}$ **15.** $\frac{3}{4} + \frac{1}{9} + \frac{7}{8}$ **16.** $\frac{7}{10} - \frac{1}{5}$

17. $\frac{1}{10} + \frac{5}{8}$ **18.** $3\frac{7}{8} + 4\frac{1}{8} + 1\frac{9}{10}$ **19.** $\frac{11}{12} - \frac{4}{7}$ **20.** $3\frac{1}{8} + 5\frac{9}{10}$

Lesson 4.4

Multiply. Write the answer in simplest form.

1. $\frac{5}{7} \times \frac{3}{9}$ **2.** $\frac{7}{18} \times \frac{2}{5}$ **3.** $\frac{1}{5} \times \frac{1}{4}$ **4.** $\frac{4}{5} \times \frac{3}{4}$

5. $\frac{3}{9} \times \frac{7}{8}$ **6.** $\frac{1}{15} \times \frac{3}{16}$ **7.** $1\frac{1}{8} \times 3\frac{3}{5}$ **8.** $1\frac{1}{6} \times \frac{3}{14}$

Write the related multiplication problem.

9. $\frac{1}{3} \div 8 = \frac{1}{24}$ **10.** $4 \div \frac{2}{7} = 14$ **11.** $\frac{2}{3} \div 4 = \frac{1}{6}$ **12.** $\frac{3}{4} \div \frac{5}{7} = 1\frac{1}{20}$

Write the reciprocal of each number.

13. 3 **14.** $\frac{2}{9}$ **15.** $2\frac{2}{3}$ **16.** $3\frac{4}{7}$ **17.** 5 **18.** $4\frac{1}{8}$

Divide. Write the answer in simplest form.

19. $3\frac{1}{2} \div 3\frac{1}{5}$ **20.** $20 \div \frac{1}{4}$ **21.** $\frac{5}{8} \div 5$ **22.** $4\frac{1}{5} \div 1\frac{2}{5}$

23. $\frac{3}{7} \div 12$ **24.** $1\frac{1}{3} \div \frac{4}{5}$ **25.** $3\frac{3}{8} \div 2\frac{1}{4}$ **26.** $\frac{3}{8} \div \frac{3}{4}$

Lesson 4.5

Solve a simpler problem.

1. Jasmine earned \$4,000 from her business. She gave $\frac{1}{5}$ of it to her daughter and her husband as a gift. She invested $\frac{1}{2}$ of the remaining amount. How much did she have left?

2. Yolanda invested \$1,500 in the stock market on January 1. She lost $\frac{1}{3}$ of it by the end of January and $\frac{2}{5}$ of the remaining amount by the end of February. How much did she have left?

3. Greg, a Canadian, traveled to the U.S. for vacation. He took 200 Canadian dollars with him. He lost $\frac{1}{5}$ of it by converting to American dollars. He spent $\frac{3}{4}$ of it on vacation. How many American dollars did he have left?

4. Armand set up a fund for contributions to charity. He began with \$2,000 in it. He gave $\frac{3}{5}$ of it to the American Red Cross. The remaining amount he gave to a local homeless shelter. How much did the shelter receive?

CHAPTER 5

Lesson 5.1

Write the addition equation modeled on the number line.

1.

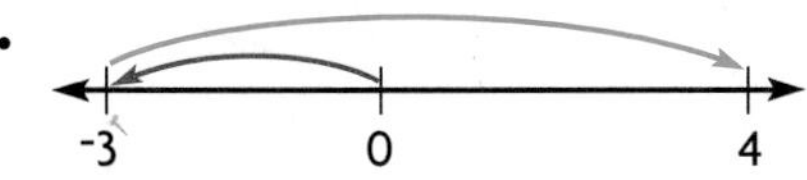

2.

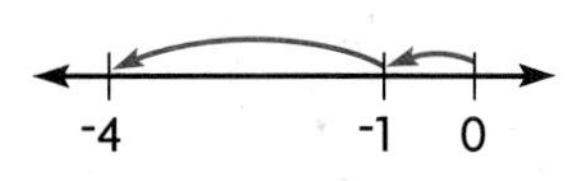

3.

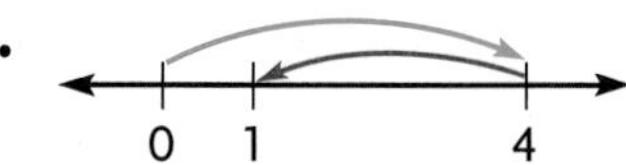

Draw a number line to find the sum.

4. $^-10 + 4$　**5.** $7 + {}^-15$　**6.** $5 + {}^-4$　**7.** $^-3 + 5$

Give the value of each.

8. $|^-7|$　**9.** $|12|$　**10.** $|^-64|$　**11.** $|^-71|$

Find the sum by using the absolute values.

12. $^-8 + {}^-9$　**13.** $18 + 21$　**14.** $^-17 + 18$　**15.** $3 + {}^-5 + {}^-2$

Lesson 5.2

Write an addition equation and a solution for each of the following.

1. $5 - {}^-8 = n$　**2.** $8 - {}^-2 = n$　**3.** $^-5 - {}^-3 = n$

4. $^-7 - 2 = n$　**5.** $8 - {}^-12 = n$　**6.** $^-10 - 2 = x$

Find the difference.

7. $^-3 - 2$　**8.** $^-1 - 7$　**9.** $^-3 - {}^-7$　**10.** $^-14 - 6$

11. $13 - {}^-13$　**12.** $^-17 - 17$　**13.** $8 - {}^-2$　**14.** $^-3 - 17$

Lesson 5.3

Find the product.

1. ${}^{-}3 \times {}^{-}7$

2. $7 \times {}^{-}4$

3. ${}^{-}5 \times {}^{-}21$

4. ${}^{-}2 \times {}^{-}13$

5. $4 \times {}^{-}17$

6. $25 \times {}^{-}20$

7. $6 \times {}^{-}15$

8. $20 \times {}^{-}17$

9. $5 \times {}^{-}82$

10. ${}^{-}73 \times {}^{-}5$

11. $13 \times {}^{-}14$

12. ${}^{-}2 \times {}^{-}13 \times {}^{-}21$

Find the quotient.

13. $91 \div 7$

14. ${}^{-}126 \div 6$

15. $68 \div {}^{-}4$

16. ${}^{-}272 \div {}^{-}17$

17. ${}^{-}38 \div 19$

18. ${}^{-}48 \div {}^{-}6$

19. $108 \div {}^{-}12$

20. $144 \div 8$

Lesson 5.4

Use the rules for adding rational numbers to tell whether the sum is positive or negative. Do not add.

1. ${}^{-}13.7 + {}^{-}2.67$

2. $27.6 + {}^{-}62.9$

3. ${}^{-}3\frac{1}{3} + 3\frac{1}{4}$

4. ${}^{-}1.067 + 1.10$

5. ${}^{-}18\frac{7}{8} + 18\frac{2}{7}$

6. ${}^{-}5.4 + {}^{-}4.5$

Find the sum or difference.

7. ${}^{-}3.1 + {}^{-}6.8$

8. ${}^{-}21.6 + 4.7$

9. $0 + {}^{-}3\frac{2}{3}$

10. $38.6 - 21.4$

11. $21\frac{1}{3} - 36\frac{3}{4}$

12. $27.4 - 61.8$

13. ${}^{-}12.8 - 5.2$

14. ${}^{-}17\frac{2}{3} - 3\frac{3}{4}$

15. $87.3 - 12.6$

Lesson 5.5

Find the product or quotient.

1. 14×7

2. ${}^{-}147 \div 7$

3. ${}^{-}168 \div 14$

4. ${}^{-}21 \times {}^{-}16$

5. 13.25×16

6. $3\frac{2}{3} \times {}^{-}3\frac{3}{4}$

7. ${}^{-}40.32 \div {}^{-}3.2$

8. $\frac{6}{7} \div \frac{{}^{-}1}{3}$

9. $3.4 \times {}^{-}1.6$

Find the quotient and tell what two integers the quotient is between.

10. $1225 \div 120$

11. $1{,}575 \div 150$

12. ${}^{-}26{,}150 \div {}^{-}220$

13. ${}^{-}41{,}470 \div 220$

14. ${}^{-}40{,}460 \div 320$

15. ${}^{-}52{,}500 \div {}^{-}840$

16. ${}^{-}250{,}500 \div {}^{-}3{,}200$

17. $\frac{3}{4} \div \frac{1}{2}$

18. $\frac{3}{4} \div \frac{{}^{-}2}{3}$

19. $\frac{{}^{-}4}{5} \div \frac{1}{8}$

CHAPTER 6

Lesson 6.1

Write an algebraic expression for each word expression.

1. the number of candles, c, decreased by 6

2. the sum of a number, n, and 5 squared

Write a word expression for each numerical expression.

3. $16 \div 4$

4. $^-3 + 36$

5. $8 \times {}^-7$

6. $^-7 - 5$

Write an algebraic expression for each word expression.

7. the sum of 7.6 and a number, a

8. three times the length, l

Write a word expression for each algebraic expression.

9. $n + 6$

10. $22 + 3v$

11. $\frac{17}{x}$

12. $k - 6$

Lesson 6.2

Evaluate each expression.

1. $32 - 3 \times 4$

2. $3 \times (12 \div 3)$

3. $\frac{1}{2} \times 8 - 5$

4. $8.6 + 3.7 - 4$

Evaluate the expression $8 - \frac{n}{4}$ for each value of n.

5. $n = 12$

6. $n = 20$

7. $n = 6$

8. $n = 4$

9. $n = {}^-8$

10. $n = 16$

Evaluate each expression for the given values of the variable.

11. $3x - 2y + 18$; $x = 2$ and $y = 4$

12. $\frac{x}{3} + y^3$; $x = 12$ and $y = 2$

Lesson 6.3

Identify the like terms in each list of terms.

1. $3m, 4q, 8, m$

2. $3x, 3y, 3w$

3. $8, 2x, 5w, {}^-3$

4. $x, {}^-4, {}^-x$

5. $9, 4y, 17$

6. $4x, {}^-3y, x$

Combine like terms.

7. $2w + 5w - 3$

8. $18z - 8 + 5z$

9. $13a + 9a - 7a$

10. $5x + 5y + 3x - 2y$

11. $7r - 3s + 10r - 7s$

12. $3a - 7b + 2.6a + 21b$

13. $3(5 - 2x) + x$

14. $3(4w - 3) - w$

Lesson 6.4

Tell whether the sequence is an arithmetic sequence. If it is, find the common difference.

1. 18, 22, 26, 30, 34, . . .
2. 3, 5, 8, 10, 13, 15, . . .
3. 2, 3, 5, 8, 13, 21, . . .
4. 1, 4, 7, 10, 13, 16, . . .
5. 1, 5, 9, 13, 17, 21, . . .
6. 5, 7, 9, 11, 13, 15, . . .
7. 20, 17, 14, 11, 8, . . .
8. 50, 45, 40, 35, 30, . . .
9. 160, 80, 40, 20, 10, 5, . . .

Write the next three terms in each sequence.

10. 20, 35, 50, 65, . . .
11. 10, 5, 0, $^-5$, $^-10$, . . .
12. 2, 5, 8, 11, 14, . . .
13. 0, 7, 14, 21, 28, . . .
14. $^-12$, $^-6$, 0, 6, 12, . . .
15. 26, 22, 18, 14, 10, . . .

Write an expression to describe each sequence.

16. 1, 5, 9, 13, 17, . . .
17. 2, 9, 16, 23, 30, . . .
18. 4, 7, 10, 13, 16, . . .

CHAPTER 7

Lesson 7.1

First, choose a variable and tell what it represents. Then, write an equation for each word sentence.

1. Four times the distance traveled is 4,000 miles
2. The quotient of $600 and a number of payments is $50
3. The total number of vehicles sold last year increased by 2,500 is 4,000
4. Three thousand degrees less than the temperature of the sun is 7,000°

Lesson 7.2

Tell whether the given value is the solution to the equation. Answer *yes* or *no*.

1. $x - 18 = 10$; $x = 28$
2. $p + 4 = 19$; $p = 15$
3. $d + 7 = 12$; $d = 19$
4. $n - 4 = 7$; $n = {}^-3$
5. $n - 3 = 81$; $n = 84$
6. $72 = k + 8$; $k = 80$

Tell whether you would add or subtract to solve.

7. $y - 2\frac{2}{3} = 1\frac{1}{4}$
8. $18.7 + d = 18.1$
9. $x + \frac{3}{8} = \frac{5}{8}$

Solve and check.

10. $x - 18 = 34$
11. $83 = k - 147$
12. $x + 5 = 4$
13. $r + 0.06 = 0.48$
14. $1.6 + p = {}^-6.1$
15. $n - 1.3 = {}^-1.1$
16. $18\frac{1}{2} = g - 5\frac{1}{2}$
17. $8 + m = {}^-5$
18. $5 = 7 + s$

Lesson 7.3

Tell whether the given value is the solution to the equation. Write *yes* or *no*.

1. $8b = 24;\ b = 3$

2. $12 = \frac{j}{13};\ j = 150$

3. $^{-}14 = 7x;\ x = 2$

4. $\frac{h}{2.5} = {}^{-}3,\ h = {}^{-}7.5$

5. $\frac{m}{26} = 14;\ m = 360$

6. $^{-}4 = \frac{n}{^{-}1.5};\ n = 6$

Solve and check.

7. $3x = 15$

8. $6n = 48$

9. $4.5 = {}^{-}5m$

10. $8n = 24$

11. $12k = 144$

12. $\frac{x}{^{-}4} = 1$

13. $6j = {}^{-}42$

14. $^{-}36 = {}^{-}6c$

15. $\frac{n}{1.5} = {}^{-}3$

For each word sentence, choose a variable and write an equation. Then find the value of the variable.

16. Grandmother Jacobs gives an amount of money to her seven grandchildren. Each one receives $8.50.

17. The members of a science club buy a telescope. Each pays $20, or $300 total.

Lesson 7.4

Use the *work backward* strategy to solve each problem.

1. Ali was reviewing his family video. The tape totaled 2 hours and 37 minutes. Video of his children totaled 72 minutes. How much of the video was not of his children?

2. Deana gave her younger sister $5.48 to buy some candy. Her sister returned the change, $2.84. How much did her sister spend on candy?

3. Nathan bought 500 mums and 300 tulips for his garden. After he planted his garden he had 82 mums and 61 tulips left over. How many plants did he put in the garden?

4. Cassandra saved $85.25 to buy a car stereo. The day she bought it, it was on sale. She had $9.73 left over. How much did she spend on the stereo?

Lesson 7.5

Solve each proportion.

1. $3 : 5 = 6 : n$

2. $\frac{c}{8} = \frac{5}{8}$

3. $\frac{7}{9} = \frac{a}{13.5}$

4. $\frac{18}{k} = \frac{9}{5}$

5. $\frac{2.3}{8.4} = \frac{3.45}{x}$

6. $\frac{9}{4} = \frac{m}{12}$

7. $b : 10 = 6 : 3$

8. $1.5 : j = 30 : 5$

9. $\frac{4}{5} = \frac{n}{9}$

Solve each proportion for *d*. Let $a = 3$, $b = 7$, and $c = 21$.

10. $\frac{a}{b} = \frac{c}{d}$

11. $\frac{18}{b} = \frac{3d}{2b}$

12. $\frac{3}{14} = \frac{21}{d}$

CHAPTER 8

Lesson 8.1

Write an equation and solve.

1. The length of a painting is 4 inches longer than twice its width. The length is 40 inches. How wide is it?

2. Jason saved $20 less than three times what he saved last year. This year he saved $110. How much did he save last year?

3. On Friday, Niles sold $3.25 more than twice what she sold on Thursday. She sold $20.25 Friday. How much did she sell on Thursday?

4. Amanda composed two songs. The longer song is 126 seconds less than twice the length of the short song. The longer song lasts 286 seconds. How long is the shorter song?

Lesson 8.2

Tell whether the given value is a solution to the equation. Write *yes* or *no*.

1. $3p + 6 = 12,\ p = 2$

2. $51d - 12 = 18;\ d = 5$

3. $5x - 4 + 3x = 10,\ x = 2$

4. $5j + 5(7 - j) = 35;\ j = 5$

5. $12y - 3y + 6 = 15,\ y = 2$

6. $3b + 12b - 6 = 54,\ b = 4$

Solve and check.

7. $7c - 8 - 6c = {}^{-}11$

8. $2(x - 3) - x + 8 = 8.5$

9. $8y - 16 + 5y = {}^{-}29$

10. $5(3d + 3) = {}^{-}15$

11. $2g + 8g - 4g = 48$

12. $3(f + 8) + 3f = 54$

13. $5r + 32 - r = 40$

14. $2(3d - 3) - 5 = {}^{-}23$

Lesson 8.3

Tell whether x is a solution to the inequality. Write *yes* or *no*.

1. $x + 2 \leq 6;\ x = 3$

2. $73x > 72;\ x = {}^{-}1$

3. $x - 7 < 0;\ x = 5$

4. $x - 5 \neq 8;\ x = 2$

5. $3x < 2^3;\ x = 3$

6. $x \leq \frac{2}{5} + \frac{4}{5};\ x = 1$

7. $x + 6.1 \geq 0.3;\ x = {}^{-}5.8$

8. $2x + 0.5 > 1.4;\ x = 0.5$

Write an inequality for each graph.

9. 0 3

10. -2 0

11. $-\frac{3}{2}$ 0

12. 0

Lesson 8.4

Tell what operation and number you would use to solve each inequality.

1. $x - 3 > 61$
2. $\frac{x}{37} \geq 1$
3. $5 + m \leq 7$
4. $n + 6 < 4$
5. $v - 8 \geq 110$
6. $6w \leq {}^-48$

Solve the equation or inequality.

7. $x - 2 < 6$
8. $\frac{w}{3} < 9$
9. $3y - 4 = 23$
10. $5m \geq {}^-10$
11. $j + 9 = 80$
12. $c - 4 > 1$
13. ${}^-2b = 12$
14. $\frac{s}{10} > {}^-1$

CHAPTER 9

Lesson 9.1

For Exercises 1–12, use the graph to the right. Write the ordered pair for each point.

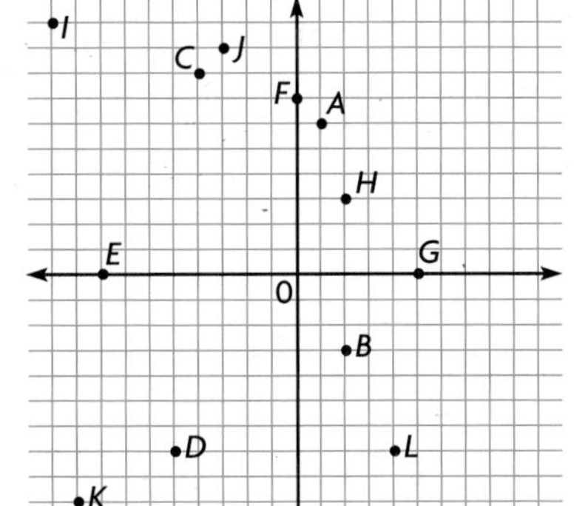

1. A
2. B
3. C
4. D
5. E
6. F

Write the letter for each ordered pair.

7. (2, 3)
8. (4, ⁻7)
9. (5, 0)
10. (⁻9, ⁻9)
11. (⁻10, 10)
12. (⁻3, 9)

Lesson 9.2

Use the relation {(⁻4, ⁻6), (⁻2, ⁻5), (0, 8), (1, 1), (2, 5)} for Exercises 1-3.

1. What is the domain of the relation?

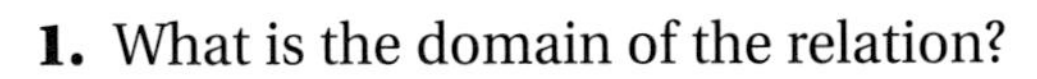

2. What is the range of the relation?
3. Make a table to show the relation.
4. Use the figure at the right to write the ordered pairs for the relation.

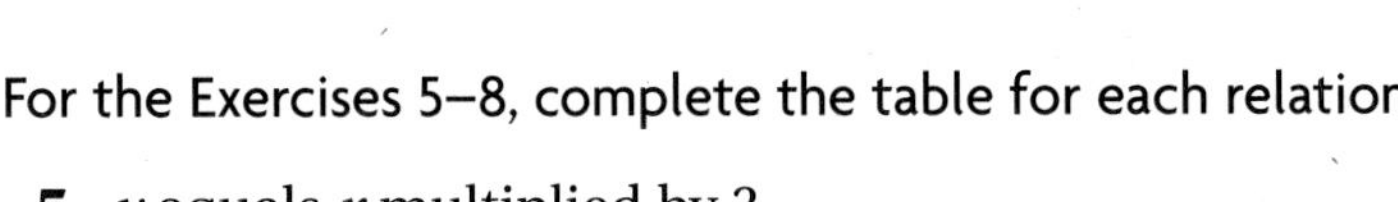
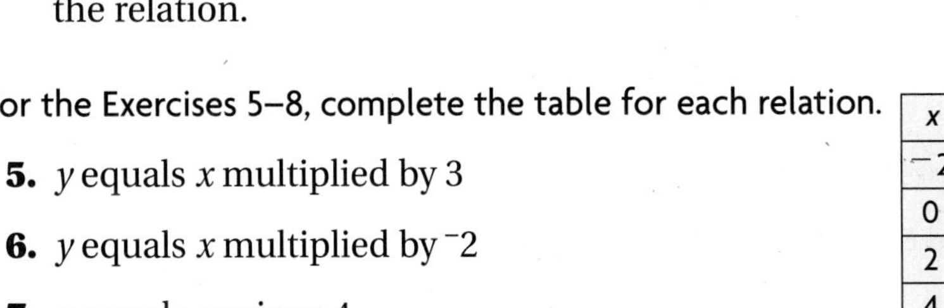
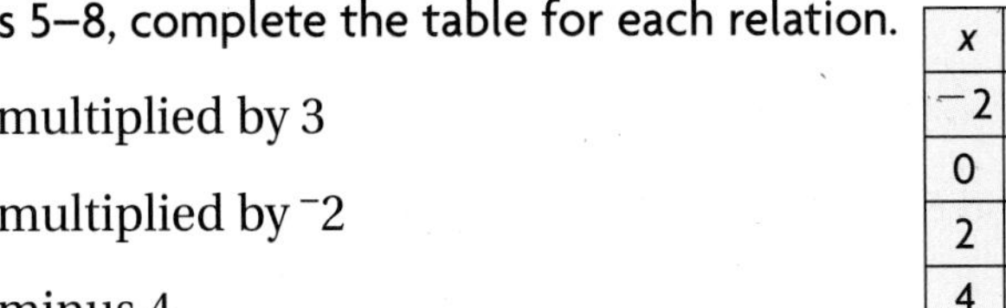
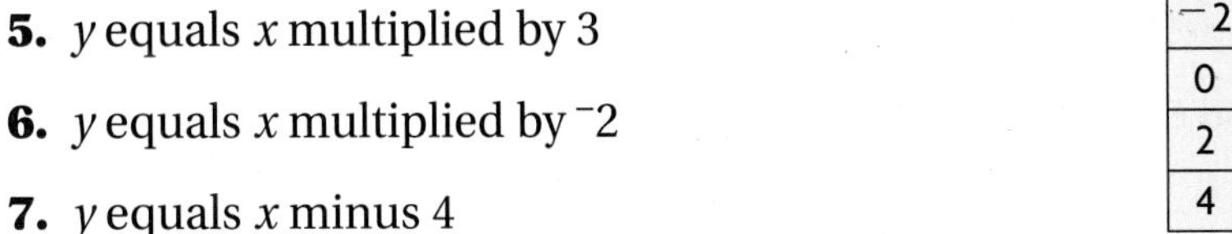

For the Exercises 5–8, complete the table for each relation.

x	y
⁻2	
0	
2	
4	

5. y equals x multiplied by 3
6. y equals x multiplied by ⁻2
7. y equals x minus 4
8. y equals x divided by ⁻2

Lesson 9.3

Is the relation a function? Write *yes* or *no*.

1. 

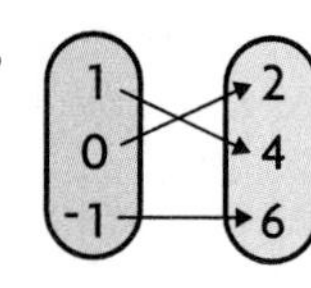

2.

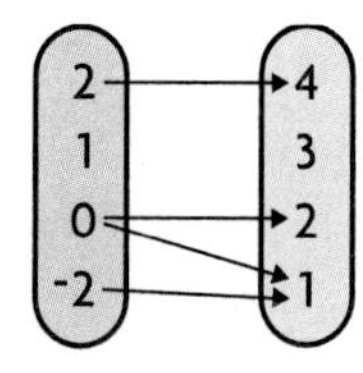

3.

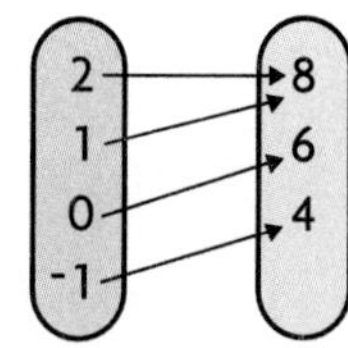

4. {(1, 2) (3, 6) (4, 8) (5, 2)}

5. {(0, 0) (2, 2) (0, 3) (4, 2)}

6. {(3, 9) (0, 4) (4, 0)}

7.

x	*y*
2	2
2	4
3	6
4	4
5	2

8.

x	*y*
1	0
2	2
3	4
4	6
4	0

9.

x	*y*
1	2
2	6
3	8
4	10
5	12

10.

x	*y*
2	5
3	14
10	9
17	8
19	12

Lesson 9.4

For each equation, replace *x* with 3. Write the solution as an ordered pair.

1. $y = x + 2$

2. $x - 3 = y$

3. $y = 4x$

4. $y = {}^{-}4x$

5. $y = \frac{x}{5}$

6. $y = x + 5$

7. $y = {}^{-}2x$

8. $y = 9x$

Write the equation for each table of values.

9.

x	*y*
1	2
2	4
3	6

10.

x	*y*
2	0
4	2
6	4

11.

x	*y*
2	1
4	5
6	9

12.

x	*y*
1	4
2	8
3	12

CHAPTER 10

Lesson 10.1

$\angle APB$ is congruent to $\angle BPC$ and $\angle CPD$. Find the measure of each angle.

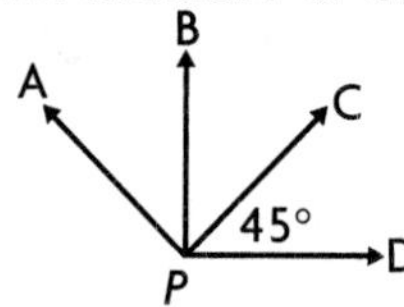

1. $\angle APB$

2. $\angle APC$

3. $\angle BPD$

4. $\angle APD$

Use the figure at right for Exercises 5 and 6.

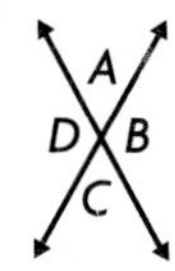

5. Which are vertical angles?

6. Which are adjacent angles?

Lesson 10.2

Write *line, rotational,* or *none* to describe the symmetry of each figure.

1. 

2. 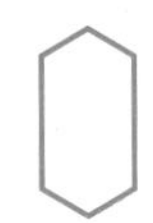

3. 

4. 

5. 

6. 

Lesson 10.3

Use the word shown at the right for Exercises 1–6.
Draw the image that is described.

MATH

1. Reflect the first letter horizontally.

2. Reflect the second letter vertically.

3. Rotate the third letter 180 degrees.

4. Rotate the fourth letter 90 degrees.

5. Rotate the third letter 270 degrees.

6. Reflect the second letter horizontally.

Identify the type of reflection. Write *vertical, horizontal,* or *diagonal.*

7. 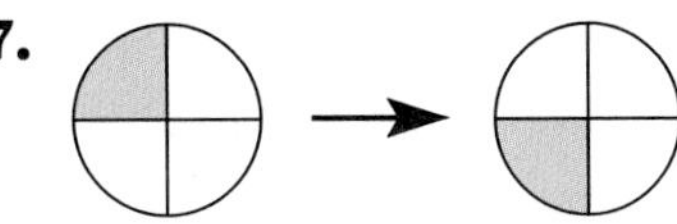

8. 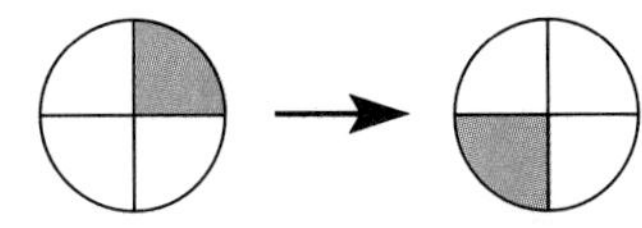

9. 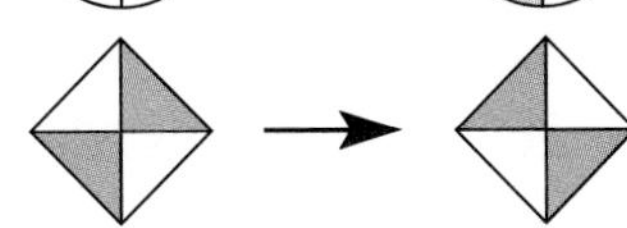

10. 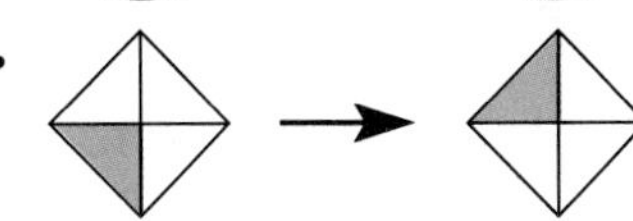

Lesson 10.4

Use figure *ABCD* to answer Exercises 1–5. Give coordinates of the image after the transformation given.

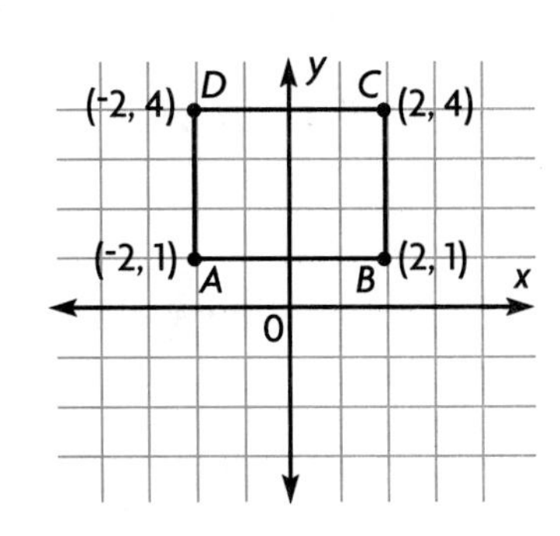

1. Reflect about the x-axis.

2. Translate 2 units left.

3. Rotate clockwise 90° about vertex A.

4. Translate 2 units up and 3 units left.

5. Rotate 180° about A.

CHAPTER 11

Lesson 11.1

Trace the angle. Use your tracing to construct a congruent angle.

1. 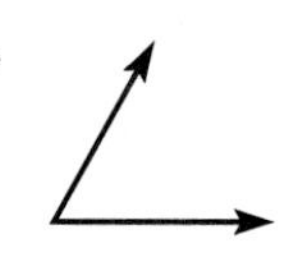

2. 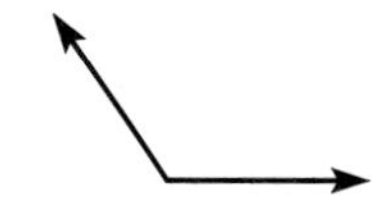

3. 

4. 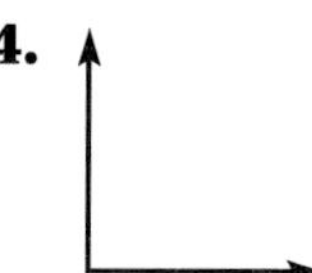

Trace the figure. Then bisect it.

5. 

6. 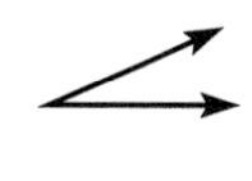

7. 

8. 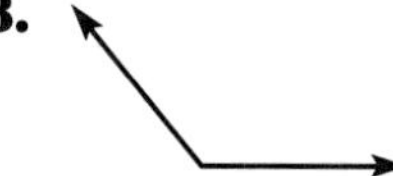

Lesson 11.2

Draw the lines and point shown.

1. Construct a line through point Q parallel to line JM.

2. Construct a line perpendicular to line AB.

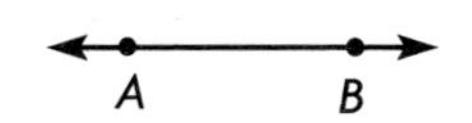

Lesson 11.3

Classify each triangle according to the lengths of its sides.

1. 4 in., 6 in., 4 in.

2. 3 cm, 3 cm, 3 cm

3. 45 in., 30 in., 22.5 in.

4. 8 cm, 10 cm, 8 cm

5. 5 in., 5 in., 5 in.

6. 7 in., 3 in., 7 in.

Classify each triangle according to the measures of its angles.

7. $40^\circ, 90^\circ, 50^\circ$

8. $20^\circ, 110^\circ, 50^\circ$

9. $35^\circ, 90^\circ, 55^\circ$

10. $60^\circ, 60^\circ, 60^\circ$

11. $30^\circ, 70^\circ, 80^\circ$

12. $40^\circ, 120^\circ, 20^\circ$

Determine whether the triangles are congruent by SSS, SAS, or ASA.

13. 

14. 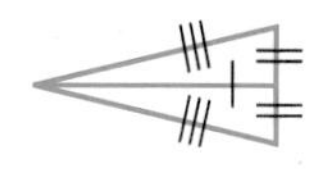

15. 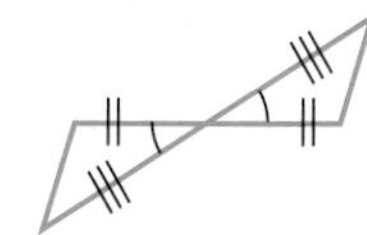

Lesson 11.4

Trace the triangle. Use the indicated rule to construct a congruent triangle.

1. SAS 

2. ASA 

3. SSS 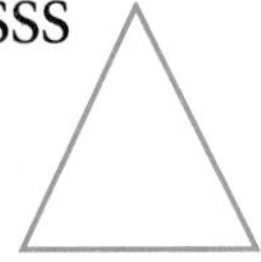

CHAPTER 12

Lesson 12.1

In Exercises 1–4, identify which are polyhedron and which are not. Then, for each solid figure, name the figure that is the base of that solid figure.

1. 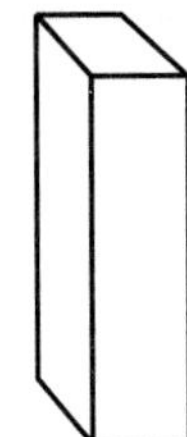

2. 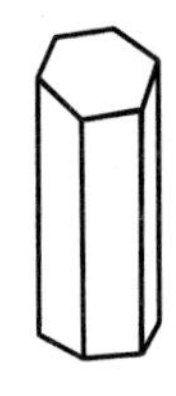

3. 

4. 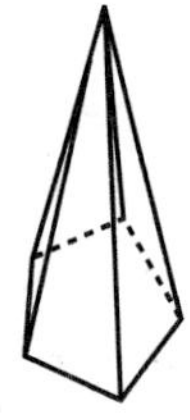

5. 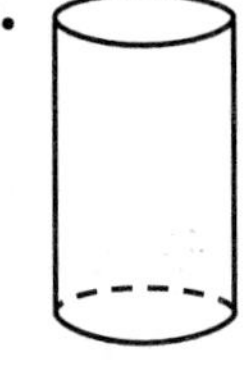

Write *true* or *false*. If *false,* give a possible explanation why.

6. All polyhedrons are prisms.

7. Some polyhedrons are polygons.

8. Some polyhedrons are cylinders.

9. A prism could have a triangle as a base.

10. Some cones are polyhedrons.

Lesson 12.2

For Exercises 1–2, use a pattern. For Exercise 3, find a pattern.

1. A pentagonal pyramid has 6 faces and 6 vertices. How many edges does it have?

2. To build a hexagonal pyramid, 7 vertices are needed and 12 edges. How many faces?

3. A triangular prism has 5 faces; a rectangular prism has 6 faces; a pentagonal prism has 7 faces. How many faces would an octagonal prism have? Make a sketch to check your guess.

4. A triangular prism has 4 faces and 4 vertices. How many edges does it have?

Lesson 12.3

Name the prism or pyramid that can be formed from the net.

1. 

2. 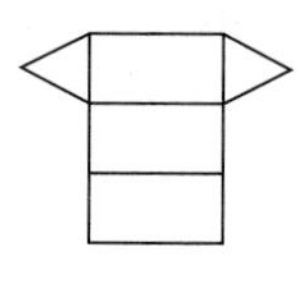

3. 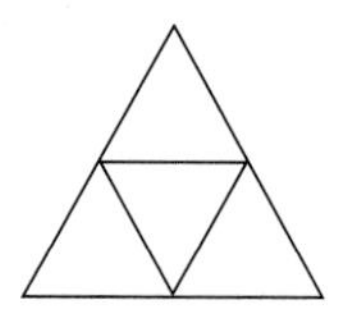

Tell whether each arrangement of squares will make a cube.

4. 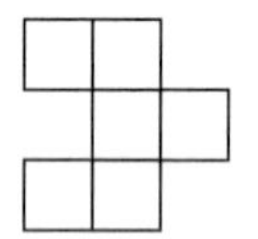

5. 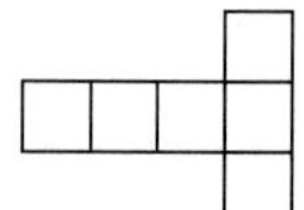

6. 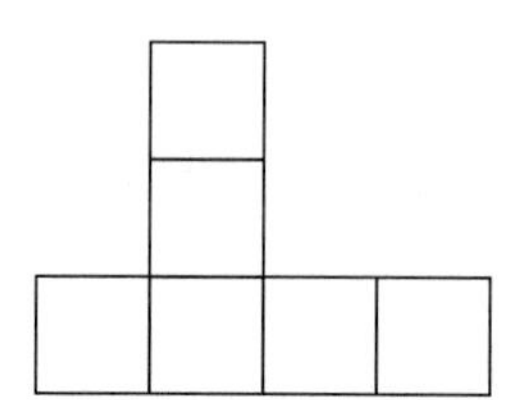

In Exercises 7–8, use this pentagonal prism. The prism has pentagons as its bases.

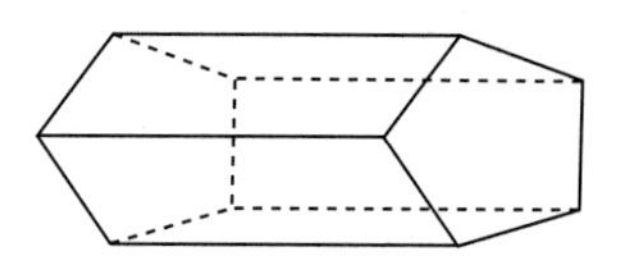

7. How many faces does the prism have? What type of polygons are the faces?

8. How many total edges are in the prism? How many are visible?

Lesson 12.4

1. A pentagonal prism has two bases that are pentagons and faces that are rectangles. For a pentagonal prism, how many faces are there? how many edges? how many vertices?

2. Draw a pentagonal prism so only 2 faces are in view. Use dotted lines to show hidden edges.

3. Is it possible to draw a pentagonal prism with only one face in view? Try drawing several!

4. Draw a net for a pentagonal prism.

CHAPTER 13

Lesson 13.1

Use the figure(s) to try to make at least two rows of a tessellation. Write *yes* or *no* to tell whether a tessellation can be made.

1. regular hexagon

2. scalene triangle

3. any quadrilateral

4. squares and isosceles triangles

5. square and regular pentagon

6. equilateral triangle

7. rectangle and right triangle

8. regular octagon and a square

Lesson 13.2

For Exercises 1–6, rotate the given triangle 120° clockwise. Complete the iteration process six times. Draw the figure at each stage.

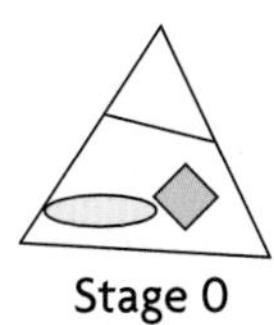
Stage 0

1. Stage 1 **2.** Stage 2 **3.** Stage 3 **4.** Stage 4 **5.** Stage 5 **6.** Stage 6

7. At what stage does the figure appear the same again as in Stage 0?

Lesson 13.3

Each of these drawings shows a stage in an iteration process.
For Exercises 1–3, refer to the drawings.

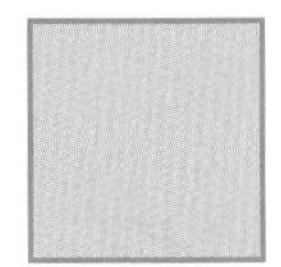
Stage 0

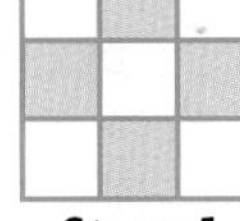
Stage 1

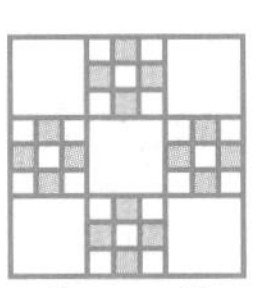
Stage 2

1. What geometric figure or figures are used?

2. How many reduced copies of Stage 2 will be in Stage 3?

3. Is the process generating a self-similar figure? Explain.

Lesson 13.4

For Exercises 1–4, use the figures shown at the right.

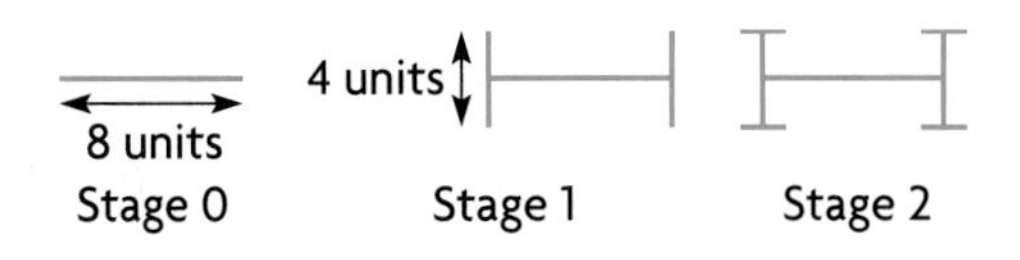

1. How many new segments do you see at Stage 1? at Stage 2?

2. How does the number of new segments change from Stage 0 to Stage 1? from Stage 1 to Stage 2?

3. If the pattern continues, predict how many new segments you would see at Stage 3; Stage 4; Stage n.

4. What is the length of each new segment at Stage 2?

5. Make a fractal spiral. Draw a line segment. Turn left 90°, and draw a segment with a length reduced by one-third. Repeat the process four times.

CHAPTER 14

Lesson 14.1

1. Two neon lights at a restaurant blink at different rates. One blinks every 3 seconds; the other blinks every 5 seconds. How often do they blink together?

2. Two race cars are speeding around the race track at different speeds. One goes around the track in 2 minutes; the other goes around the track in $1\frac{1}{2}$ minutes. How often does the faster car pass the slower one?

Lesson 14.2

Use the given rate of pay and the time worked to find how much is earned.

1. $7.20 per hour for 25 hr
2. $10 per hour for $6\frac{1}{2}$ hr
3. $4.50 per hour for 30 hr
4. $3.25 per hour for 15 hr
5. $9.20 per hour for 5.5 hr
6. $9.80 per hour for 13 hr

Find the unit rate.

7. 8 for $36, or _?_ each
8. $11.25 for 5 hr, or _?_ per hr
9. 175 mi in 5 hr, or _?_ mi per hr
10. 1,275 words in 15 min, or _?_ words per min
11. 110 rocks in 5 bags, or _?_ in each bag
12. 486 squares in 9 quilts, or _?_ squares per quilt

Lesson 14.3

1. The table shows increases in the price of a gallon of gasoline for the last three years. Compare the prices for any two years by making a ratio. Use the ratio to find the pattern. If the pattern continues, what will the cost of a gallon of gasoline be one year from now? two years from now?

GASOLINE PRICES				
Year	0	1	2	3
Price	$1.12	$1.34	$1.61	$1.94

2. The table shows how long it took stock cars at a 100-mile race to travel certain distances. If the cars continued at the same average speed, about how long did it take to complete the race?

CAR RACE	
20 mi	12 min
40 mi	24 min
60 mi	36 min

3. About how long did it take the stock cars to travel 70 mi? 80 mi? 90 mi?

4. A plug is left open on a 5-gallon container of water. The table at the right shows the amount of water remaining in the container at certain times after the plug was left open. At this rate, how long will it be before the container is empty?

Time	Remaining Water
7 sec	4.8 gal
14 sec	4.6 gal
21 sec	4.4 gal

Lesson 14.4

A rectangle with dimensions of the Golden Ratio has the given width. Find its length. Round to the nearest unit.

1. 12 in. **2.** 8 cm **3.** 5 ft **4.** 18 mm **5.** 25 m

6. Where would you cut a 20-ft log to make a Golden Cut?

7. Point B divides $\overline{AC}$ so that $AB = 42$ cm and $BC = 26$ cm. Does B come close to making a Golden Cut? Support your answer.

CHAPTER 15

Lesson 15.1

Write each ratio as a percent.

1. 16:25 **2.** 8 to 20 **3.** 9 to 1,500

4. 33:20 **5.** $\frac{9}{20}$ **6.** $\frac{13}{20}$

7. 24:25,000 **8.** $\frac{21}{5}$ **9.** 7 to 20

Use a proportion to write each ratio as a percent.

10. $\frac{34}{51}$ **11.** 17 to 40 **12.** 24 to 300

13. $\frac{1}{3}$ **14.** 15:500 **15.** $\frac{12}{20}$

16. 18:30 **17.** $\frac{3}{8}$ **18.** 24 to 96

Lesson 15.2

Find the percent of each number.

1. 3.30% of 103 **2.** 120% of 2,500 **3.** 75% of 60

4. 14% of 200 **5.** 7% of 15 **6.** 145% of 160

7. 100% of 76 **8.** 40% of 30 **9.** 0.5% of 145

10. 2.2% of 36 **11.** 7.19% of 150 **12.** 110% of 2,700

Use mental math to find the percent of each number.

13. 45% of 80 **14.** 145% of 300 **15.** 5% of 80

16. 15% of 40 **17.** 25% of 60 **18.** 75% of 200

19. 70% of 80 **20.** 30% of 250 **21.** 85% of 200

Lesson 15.3

Draw a diagram. Then solve.

1. What percent of 30 is 6?
2. What percent of 30 is 15?

Write a proportion. Then solve.

3. 16 is what percent of 25?
4. What percent of 72 is 18?

Write an equation. Then solve.

5. What percent of 50 is 20?
6. What percent of 32 is 8?

Solve. Use any of the methods you have studied.

7. What percent of 50 is 200?
8. What percent of 20 is 9?
9. What percent of 25 is 6?
10. What percent of 28 is 7?
11. What percent of 63 is 63?
12. 17 is what percent of 20?
13. What percent of 5 is 3?
14. 28 is what percent of 4?
15. What percent of 60 is 27?
16. 18 is what percent of 6?
17. 14 is what percent of 40?
18. What percent of 6 is 3?

Lesson 15.4

Solve.

1. 95% of what number is 25.27?
2. 6.5 is 52% of what number?
3. 960 is 6% of what number?
4. 104 is 160% of what number?
5. 94 is 400% of what number?
6. 18 is 5% of what number?
7. 60% of what number is 27?
8. 14 is 20% of what number?
9. 70% of what number is 210?
10. 34 is 40% of what number?
11. 60 is 25% of what number?
12. 40% of what number is 18?

CHAPTER 16

Lesson 16.1

Determine whether the figures are similar. Write *yes* or *no*, and support your answer.

1.

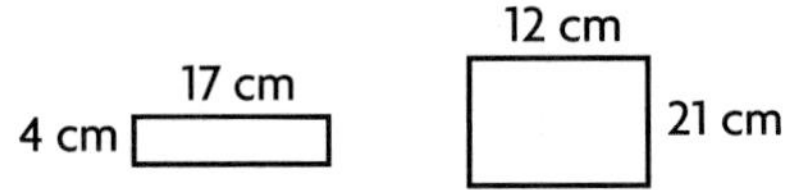

2.

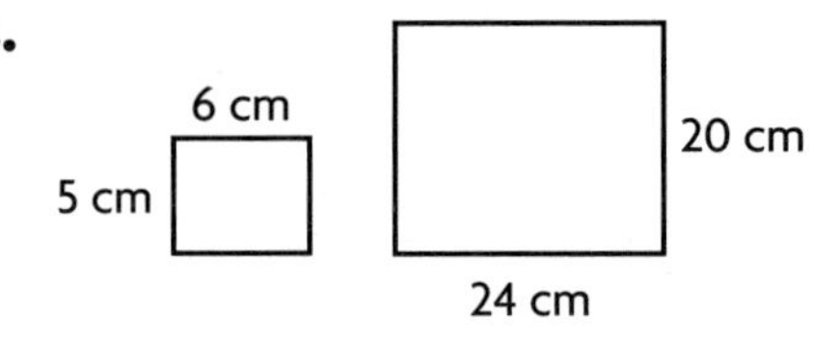

Lesson 16.2

Copy and complete the tables, using a scale factor of 3:1 for the enlarged model.

	Real Object		Model
1.	Length	16 in.	?
2.	Width	9 in.	?
3.	Height	4 in.	?

	Real Object		Model
4.	Length	14.5 cm	?
5.	Width	4.6 cm	?
6.	Height	7.1 cm	?

Lesson 16.3

Write a ratio to relate the area of the similar enlargement to the area of the original rectangle. The widths (*w*) and lengths (*l*) are given.

1. original rectangle: $w = 5$ cm, $l = 9$ cm
enlargement: $w = 10$ cm, $l = 18$ cm

2. original rectangle: $w = 4$ ft, $l = 8$ ft
enlargement: $w = 12$ ft, $l = 24$ ft

3. original rectangle: $w = 1.2$ m, $l = 3.7$ m
enlargement: $w = 3$ m, $l = 9.25$ m

4. original rectangle: $w = 6$ ft, $l = 8$ ft
enlargement: $w = 9$ ft, $l = 12$ ft

The scale factor for the sides of two similar polygons is given. Find the scale factor for their areas.

5. 5:2 **6.** $\frac{4}{5}$ **7.** 2:3

8. 4:1 **9.** $\frac{7}{5}$ **10.** 5:6

Lesson 16.4

Tell the dimensions of a similar enlarged figure, made with a scale factor of 3.5 for the sides.

1.

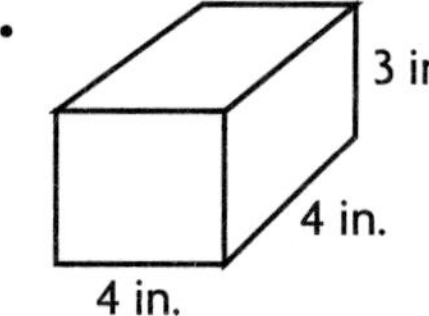

2.

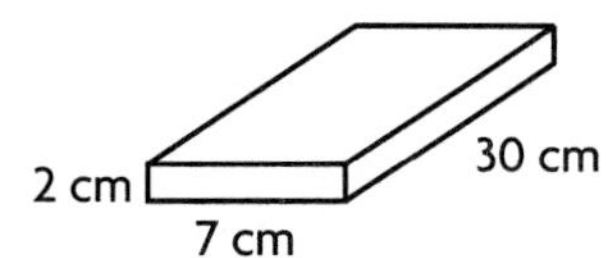

3.

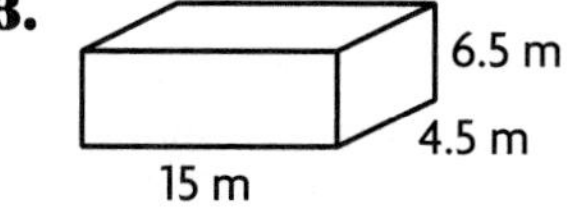

Write a scale factor for the volumes, relating the larger cube to the smaller cube.

4.

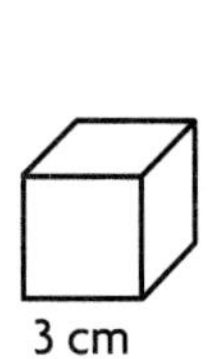

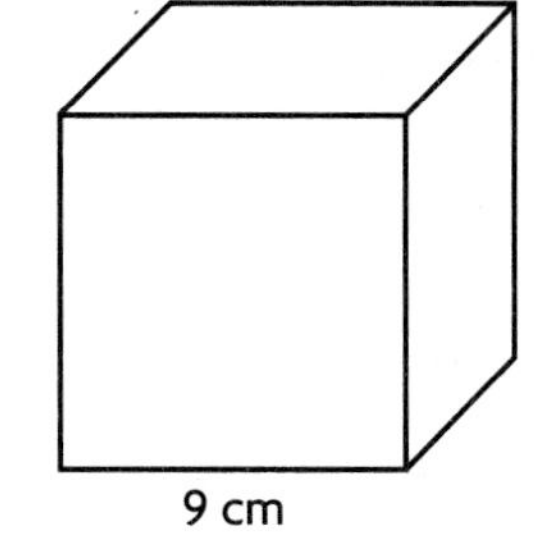

5.

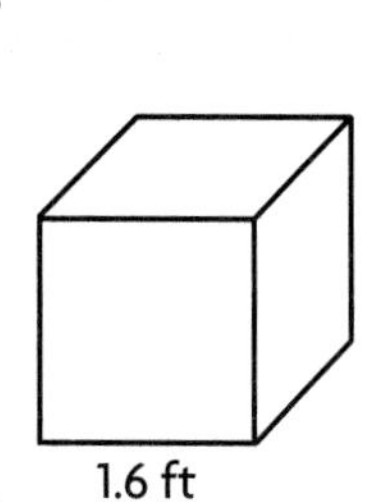

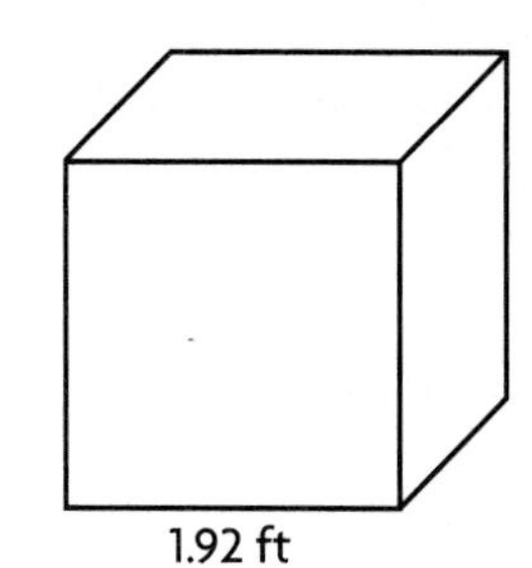

CHAPTER 17

Lesson 17.1

Use the scale factor to draw a triangle that is similar to the triangle at the right.

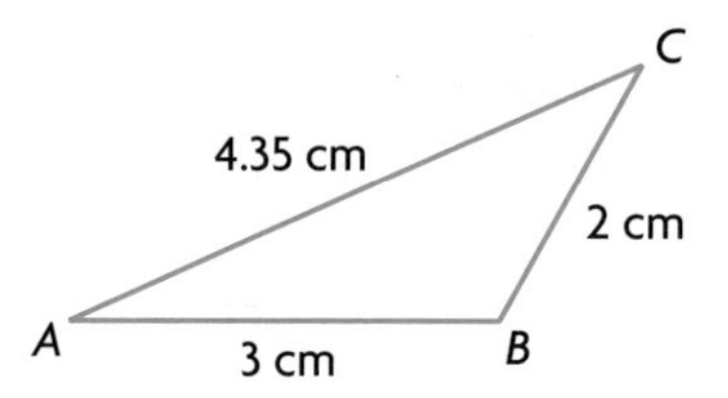

1. scale factor: $\frac{1}{5}$
2. scale factor: 2.5

Use the scale factor to draw a parallelogram that is similar to the parallelogram at the right.

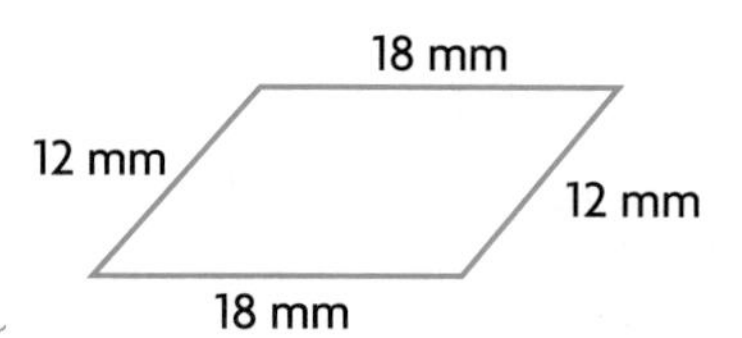

3. scale factor: $\frac{1}{2}$
4. scale factor: 1.5

Use the scale factor to draw a pentagon that is similar to the pentagon at the right.

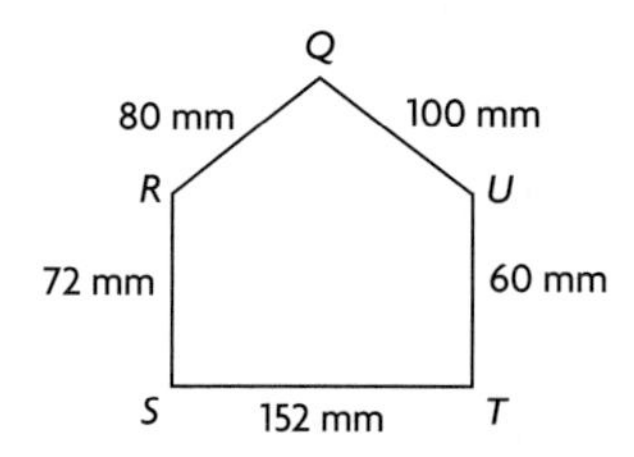

5. scale factor: $\frac{1}{4}$
6. scale factor: 3

Lesson 17.2

Use the scale of 1 cm : 12 cm to find the missing dimension. The first measure in the scale is for the scale drawing and the second measure is for the actual object.

1. Drawing: 9 cm, actual: __?__ cm
2. Drawing: __?__ cm, actual: 96 cm
3. Drawing: 16.5 cm, actual: __?__ cm
4. Drawing: __?__ cm, actual: 60 cm

Use the scale of 12 cm : 1 cm to find the missing dimension. The first measure in the scale is for the scale drawing and the second measure is for the actual object.

5. Drawing: 42 cm, actual: __?__ cm
6. Drawing: __?__ cm, actual: 8 cm
7. Drawing: 30 cm, actual: __?__ cm
8. Drawing: __?__ cm, actual: 0.7 cm

Lesson 17.3

Write and solve a proportion to find the actual distance using a map scale of 1 in. : 6 mi.

1. map distance: 18 in.
2. map distance: $\frac{1}{3}$ in.
3. map distance: $2\frac{1}{2}$ in.
4. map distance: 6 in.
5. map distance: $3\frac{1}{4}$ in.
6. map distance: $3\frac{3}{4}$ in.

Lesson 17.4

The lengths of the sides of two triangles are given. Tell which pairs of triangles are similar triangles. Write *yes* or *no*.

1. 8, 9, 15; 24, 27, 45

2. 3, 4, 5; 15, 19, 26

3. 6, 12, 13; 9, 18, 19.5

4. 4, 10, 12; 20, 50, 60

5. 10.5, 14, 17.5; 21, 28, 35

6. 12, 16, 20; 24, 18, 32

7. 12, 21, 27; 4, 7, 9

8. 3, 4, 5; 9, 17, 25

Lesson 17.5

The dimensions of several rectangles are given below. Tell which are Golden Rectangles. Write *yes* or *no*.

1. 12, 19.2

2. 20, 32.24

3. 16, 24

4. 75, 111

5. 120, 210

6. 38, 61

7. 17, 27.37

8. 325, 624

9. 45, 72

10. 16, 10

11. 47, 52

12. 82, 104

CHAPTER 18

Lesson 18.1

Find the triangular number.

1. tenth

2. fiftieth

3. fourteenth

4. seventeenth

5. thousandth

6. twentieth

Study the triangular array to the right to answer Exercises 7–12.

```
          1       ← Row 1
         1 1      ← Row 2
        1 3 1     ← Row 3
       1 3 3 1    ← Row 4
      1 3 5 3 1   ← Row 5
     1 3 5 5 3 1  ← Row 6
```

7. How is this triangular array different from the triangular array in Example 2 on page 358?

8. What will be the seventh row in the triangular array?

9. What will be the thirteenth row?

10. How many numbers are in the eighth row?

11. What is the sum of each of the first five rows? Explain how to find the sum of the seventh row.

12. What would be the middle number of the twenty-first row?

Lesson 18.2

For Exercises 1–4, use Pascal's triangle found on page 360.

1. The 56 in row 8 is the sum of what two numbers above it in row 7?
2. Write the numbers that should be in row ten.
3. How many entries are in row twelve?
4. True or False: The middle entry in each even numbered row will always be an even number.

Lesson 18.3

Determine how many times 3 must be doubled to reach or exceed the given number.

1. 29
2. 100
3. 48
4. 180

Determine how many times 512 must be halved to reach or be less than the given number.

5. 200
6. 100
7. zero
8. 1

As the pattern continues, tell whether the numbers diverge or converge.

9. 1, 1, 2, 3, 5, 8, 13, 21, . . .
10. one half, one third, one fourth, one fifth, one sixth, . . .

Write an equation to relate the first number (r) in each pair (r, s) to the second number(s).

11. (3, 1), (6, 2), (9, 3), (30, 10), (666, 222)
12. (2, 8), (5, 20), (8, 32), (13, 52), (15, 60)
13. (1, 5), (2, 6), (3, 7), (99, 103)
14. (17, 25), (22, 30), (28, 36), (40, 48), (52, 60)

Lesson 18.4

Find the first five powers.

1. Start with 1, then multiply by 5.
2. Start with 1, then multiply by 3.
3. Start with 1, then multiply by 0.3.
4. Start with 1, then multiply by 0.4.

For Exercises 5–8, find the first four powers of the given number.

5. 9
6. 20
7. $\frac{1}{2}$
8. 2

Find the values. Then show the sequence as an orbit of a point.

9. $1^0, 1^1, 1^2, 1^3$
10. $13^0, 13^1, 13^2, 13^3$

CHAPTER 19

Lesson 19.1

Write an equivalent decimal.

1. $\frac{1}{8}$ **2.** $\frac{3}{2}$ **3.** $\frac{6}{5}$ **4.** $\frac{8}{3}$

5. $\frac{7}{20}$ **6.** $\frac{1}{6}$ **7.** $\frac{5}{11}$ **8.** $\frac{4}{5}$

9. $\frac{17}{11}$ **10.** $\frac{5}{9}$ **11.** $\frac{5}{4}$ **12.** $\frac{11}{6}$

13. $\frac{10}{12}$ **14.** $\frac{5}{8}$ **15.** $\frac{11}{8}$ **16.** $\frac{3}{20}$

17. $\frac{7}{12}$ **18.** $\frac{4}{11}$ **19.** $\frac{13}{9}$ **20.** $\frac{1}{15}$

21. $\frac{1}{3}$ **22.** $\frac{7}{3}$ **23.** $\frac{8}{5}$ **24.** $\frac{21}{20}$

Lesson 19.2

Name a rational number between the two numbers.

1. 2.5 and 2.6 **2.** 0.31 and 0.33 **3.** $\frac{1}{8}$ and $\frac{3}{8}$

4. $\frac{1}{3}$ and 0.4 **5.** 2.005 and 2.1 **6.** $^-2$ and $^-3$

7. $^-5.6$ and $^-5.7$ **8.** 0.25 and 0.26 **9.** $\frac{1}{4}$ and $\frac{1}{2}$

10. Roger ran 4.5 mi and Julie ran 4.6 mi. Leslie ran farther than Roger but not as far as Julie. Estimate how far Leslie ran.

Lesson 19.3

Look for the pattern in each sequence. Write *geometric, arithmetic,* or *neither.*

1. 1, 3, 4, 16, . . . **2.** 3, 9, 27, 81, . . . **3.** 2, 4, 7, 11, 16, . . .

4. 5, 5.2, 5.4, 5.6, . . . **5.** 16, 4, $^-4$, $^-16$, . . . **6.** 2, 4, 6, 8, 10, . . .

7. 2, 12, 22, 32, . . . **8.** 0, 3, 6, 9, . . . **9.** 1, 2, 4, 8, 16, . . .

Write the next two terms in the sequence.

10. 3, 6, 12, 24, 48, 96, . . . **11.** 5, 7, 10, 14, . . .

12. 200, 50, 12.5, . . . **13.** 80, 74, 68, 62, 56, . . .

14. 4, 16, 64, 256, . . . **15.** 1, 7, 13, 19, 25, 31, . . .

16. 3; 9; 36; 180; 1,080; . . . **17.** 2, 4, 8, 14, 22, 32, . . .

18. 1, 0.5, 0.25, . . . **19.** 82.5, 74.8, 67.1, 59.4, . . .

Lesson 19.4

Write each expression using a positive exponent.

1. 3^{-7} **2.** 6^{-3} **3.** 3^{-2} **4.** 8^{-7}

5. 10^{-6} **6.** 5^{-2} **7.** 8^{-7} **8.** 3^{-5}

9. 9^{-4} **10.** 4^{-4} **11.** 7^{-3} **12.** 4^{-5}

Write each expression using a negative exponent.

13. $\frac{1}{3^2}$ **14.** $\frac{1}{6^5}$ **15.** $\frac{1}{20^1}$ **16.** $\frac{1}{5^5}$

17. $\frac{1}{9^3}$ **18.** $\frac{1}{5^4}$ **19.** $\frac{1}{10^3}$ **20.** $\frac{1}{5^2}$

21. $\frac{1}{27}$ **22.** $\frac{1}{3 \times 3 \times 3}$ **23.** $\frac{1}{1,000,000}$ **24.** $\frac{1}{10 \times 10 \times 10}$

25. $\frac{1}{64}$ **26.** $\frac{1}{10^3}$ **27.** $\frac{1}{6 \times 6 \times 6}$ **28.** $\frac{1}{3^4}$

CHAPTER 20

Lesson 20.1

1. Beth is conducting a survey to find out what is the favorite fast food of seventh graders. For her to get a stratified sample, what would be some possible strata, or subgroups?

2. Ms. Carter is the sponsor of the school newspaper. How could Ms. Carter select a random sample of students from her class to interview for the school paper?

3. Explain how to get a systematic sampling of all the people who rode bus #34 to school.

4. Every tenth person walking into the mall is surveyed. What kind of sampling method is being used?

5. Mr. Kohn randomly selected 8 students from his class to survey. What kind of sampling method is being used?

6. People in age groups from 20–25, 26–30, and 31–35 were surveyed about music. What kind of sampling method was used?

Lesson 20.2

1. Janine asked all her girlfriends what their favorite movie was. Is there any possibility of bias in her survey?

2. Give an example of a biased question you could ask when surveying adults about sports.

3. People who are really "cool" prefer the color green. What is your favorite color? Explain why the above might bias a survey about color.

4. In a survey of senior citizens regarding an increased school tax levy, Brian conducted a survey by talking to every 10th person to enter the library. Do you think this was a representative survey? Why or why not?

Lesson 20.3

For Exercises 1–5 name the format of the survey question.

1. Which sport is your favorite?
2. What is your favorite fast food? (a) hot dog (b) hamburger (c) french fries (d) salad
3. My favorite cartoon character is _?_.
4. Using a scale of 1 to 7, how many days do you watch the news?
5. What is your favorite season of the year?

Tell whether the question would be a good survey question. Write *yes* or *no*. If you write *no,* explain.

6. Are the exercises in gym class too difficult?
7. Why do you like broccoli?

Lesson 20.4

1. To make a line plot of these minutes of piano practice (35, 25, 34, 12, 56, 30, 48), the lowest tick mark could be at _?_ minutes, the highest tick mark could be at _?_ minutes, and the intervals could be every _?_ minutes.
2. In a cumulative frequency, several numbers in the cumulative frequency column could be less than the actual frequencies. Do you agree or disagree? Why or why not?
3. Several of the scores in a stem-and-leaf plot were 34, 59, 76, 74, 82, 78, and 52. Are the leaves the ones digits or the tens digits?
4. Make a stem-and leaf plot for the following test scores: 90, 87, 86, 72, 54, 99, 78, 83, 84, 86, 92, 92, 68, 67, 84, 91.

CHAPTER 21

Lesson 21.1

Karl has planted 25 plants in his garden, of varying heights. The heights are given in the table to the right.

HEIGHTS OF PLANTS (inches)				
34	39	36	32	34
11	19	10	17	17
22	29	24	23	22
30	31	35	35	35
12	18	15	15	18

1. What is the height of the tallest plant?
2. What is the height of the shortest plant?
3. What is the range of heights?
4. Are there more plants with heights in the twenties or thirties?
5. Which plant height is the most common?

Lesson 21.2

Find the mean, median, and mode of the set of numbers.

1. 6, 29, 38, 10, 8, 20, 29
2. 19, 25, 112, 419, 230, 3, 18, 20, 25, 82, 49
3. 4, 9, 16, 25, 36, 49, 64, 81, 100, 121, 144, 169, 196
4. 12.8, 10.7, 1.6, 10.7, 13.4, 8.7, 9.2, 9.2, 9.8, 10.7, 8.6, 12.5
5. 17.5, 18.3, 24.9, 121.7, 132.4, 7.6, 42.5, 18.3, 24.9, 96.4
6. 82, 94, 96, 112, 82, 76, 82, 90, 102, 117, 89, 91, 91, 84

Lesson 21.3

During a mountain climb, explorers recorded temperatures at different altitudes above the mountain base. The results are given in the table to the right.

ALTITUDE	TEMPERATURE
0 ft	90° F
1,000 ft	86° F
1,500 ft	80° F
2,000 ft	72° F
2,500 ft	66° F
3,000 ft	60° F
3,500 ft	54° F
4,000 ft	49° F
4,500 ft	46° F
5,000 ft	40° F

1. Would you use a line graph or a bar graph to represent the data? Explain your choice.
2. What values would you list on the horizontal axis, and what range of values would you give?
3. What range of values would you list along the vertical axis?
4. What title would you give for the graph?
5. Sketch your graph.

Lesson 21.4

Jessica, a music major, studied the sheet music for one of her favorite songs. She wanted to know how often each F and G note occurred. Her results are given in the bar graph to the right.

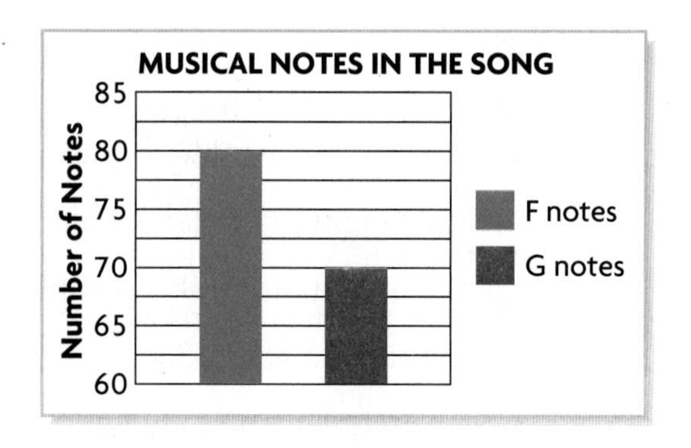

1. How many F notes are there? How many G notes are there?
2. What is the ratio of F notes to G notes?
3. What ratio do the bars on the graph reflect?
4. So that the graph is not misleading, would you change the scale on the vertical or horizontal axis?

CHAPTER 22

Lesson 22.1

For Exercises 1–3, use the following information. Student representatives from sixth grade are {Chic, Eli, Tom, Kay}; from seventh grade the representatives are {Bart, Jane}, and from eighth grade the representatives are {Manuel, Sally, Will}.

1. If one person is chosen from each grade, how many total possible outcomes are there?

2. If one person is chosen from sixth grade and only one from eighth grade, how many total possible outcomes are there?

3. If one person is chosen from grade seven and one from grade eight, how many total possible outcomes are there?

Lesson 22.2

A cube is labeled with the symbols 2, 3, 6, J, K, and *. Find the probability.

1. P(a number)

2. P(a letter)

3. P(a number less than 3)

4. P(a prime number)

5. P(a number greater than 9)

6. P(a number less than 5)

7. P(*)

8. P(J, K, or 6)

9. P(even number)

The probability of something happening for certain is 1; the probability of something not happening is 0. Tell whether these events are likely or unlikely to happen, and why.

10. The weather lady said the probability of rain tomorrow is 0.9.

11. I lost my keys in one of five possible places. The probability of my guessing the correct place on my first try would be ?.

Lesson 22. 3

Make a list and solve.

1. You are to write a report on three of the following TV topics: sports, movies, news, weather. How many selections of three topics are possible?

2. Jane, Beth, Marco, Sam, and Ed all want to be co-captains. How many different "pairs" would be possible for co-captains?

3. For lunch, possibilities are fish sandwich, hamburger, salad, pudding, soup, raisins, and chips. If you decided to pick four different items, how many combinations are possible?

Lesson 22.4

1. Monograms are three letters that could represent a person's first, middle and last initials. If the only letters you were allowed to use were B, C and D, how many possible permutations are there? Show all the possibilities.

2. To schedule three classes, Math, History, and Art, how many different orders have History as the last class in the day?

CHAPTER 23

Lesson 23.1

In Exercises 1–4 a cube is rolled. On each side is one of the following symbols: # & * @ % !. Find the experimental probability of rolling each "symbol" for each of the four separate lines of the table. On every line, the cube is rolled 60 times.

	Symbol	#	&	*	@	%	!
1.	Times rolled	10	15	10	15	5	5
2.	Times rolled	12	15	8	10	0	15
3.	Times rolled	17	13	10	4	1	15
4.	Times rolled	12	8	10	11	9	10

1. Find the probability of rolling each symbol using line 1.

2. Find the probability of rolling each symbol using line 2.

3. Find the probability of rolling each symbol using line 3.

4. Find the probability of rolling each symbol using line 4.

Lesson 23.2

For Exercises 1–2, a computer generated list of numbers 1–4 is given. Use this table of numbers, starting in the upper left corner, going from left to right in each row, to answer these questions.

Table of randomly generated numbers 1 to 4									
4	2	3	2	1	1	2	4	3
3	2	1	3	4	2	1	2	1
3	4	2	1	2	3	2	4	1
3	2	4	2	1	1	3	4	4

1. Suppose a spinner could land on one of four directions: North, East, South, or West. Further, suppose a 1 represents North, a 2 represents East, a 3 represents South, and a 4 represents West. How many spins before the spinner lands on North? In 18 spins, how many times was North obtained? In 36 spins how many times was North obtained?

2. Suppose a student randomly guessed on a 10 item multiple choice test, where the possible choices for each question were (1), (2), (3), and (4). Suppose on the answer key, the correct choices for the 10 questions were: 1 3 4 2 1 1 2 1 3 4. How many would the student have correct?

Lesson 23.3

For Exercises 1–3, design a simulation in which a spinner, cube, or coin is used to model each situation.

1. A major league player gets a hit 25% of the time he is at bat.

2. A student usually gets 80% (four out of every five) correct on all quizzes.

3. The chance of rain in a midwestern city is 50%.

Lesson 23.4

1. Draw a square with each side being 4 inches. Inside the square, draw a rectangle with a width of 2 inches and a length of 3 inches. If a dart was thrown, and it landed somewhere inside the square, what is the probability that the dart would have landed inside the rectangle?

Suppose before your next vacation, you decided to randomly throw a dart at a map of the United States, which has an area of about 3,120,000 square miles. Find the probability that the dart would land in the given state. Give your answer as percents to the nearest tenth, if possible.

2. Ohio (about 40,975 miles^2)

3. Rhode Island (about 1,049 miles^2)

4. Colorado (about 103,766 miles^2)

5. Florida (about 54,090 miles^2)

CHAPTER 24

Lesson 24.1

Give the precision of each measurement.

1. 12 ft

2. 6 mi

3. 12 km

4. 12.5 in

5. 6.5 mi

6. 250 mi

7. 527 ft

8. 12 in

9. 19 km

Find the greatest possible error (GPE) for each measurement.

10. 17 in

11. 12 dm

12. 4.3 cm

13. 26 ft

14. 19.7 km

15. $6\frac{1}{2}$ m

For the given measurement, give the smallest and largest possible actual lengths.

16. 27 mm

17. 21.6 km

18. $5\frac{1}{2}$ m

Lesson 24.2

Use the network at the right to determine the distance for the route.

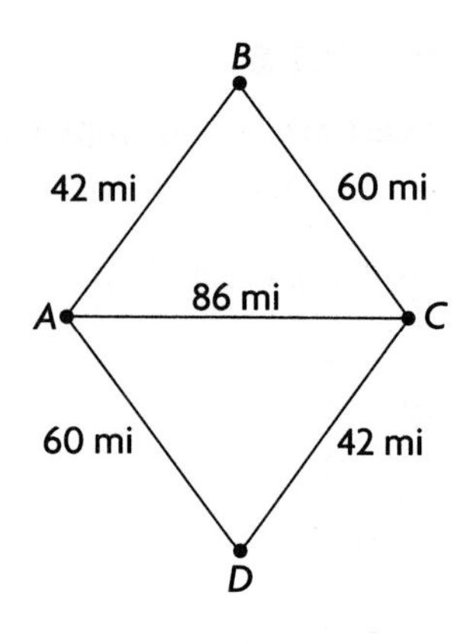

1. *ABCD*
2. *AB*
3. *BC*
4. *ABC*
5. *ACD*
6. *ACBA*
7. *CDA*
8. *DAB*
9. *BCA*

Lesson 24.3

Tell whether the three sides form a right triangle. Write *yes* or *no.*

1. 30 ft, 40 ft, 50 ft
2. 20 in., 30 in., 40 in.
3. 5 cm, 11 cm, 12 cm
4. 8 yd, 8 yd, 16 yd
5. 8 ft, 15 ft, 17 ft
6. 0.4 mi, 0.2 mi, 0.6 mi
7. 20 in., 4.5 in., 20.5 in.
8. 5 yd, 15 yd, 18 yd
9. 5.5 km, 30 km, 30.5 km
10. 4 mi, 0.9 mi, 4.1 mi
11. 2 mm, 2.2 mm, 3.1 mm
12. 2.5 cm, 6 cm, 6.5 cm

Find the length of the hypotenuse for each right triangle. Round to the nearest tenth when necessary.

13. $a = 3.5$ ft, $b = 2.6$ ft, $c = \underline{?}$
14. $a = 4.4$ yd, $b = 5.9$ yd, $c = \underline{?}$
15. $a = 10$ in., $b = 24$ in., $c = \underline{?}$
16. $a = 4$ m, $b = 7$ m, $c = \underline{?}$
17. $a = 33.3$ m, $b = 10$ m, $c = \underline{?}$
18. $a = 17.6$ cm, $b = 8$ cm, $c = \underline{?}$
19. $a = 6.1$ in., $b = 9.6$ in., $c = \underline{?}$
20. $a = 5.8$ ft, $b = 8.3$ ft, $c = \underline{?}$

Lesson 24.4

1. For the enjoyment of planes flying overhead, a farmer planted his corn field in the shape of a parallelogram. Its base is 2 mi and its height is 1.4 mi. What is the area of the corn field?
2. Jenny wants to paint a wall in her home. The wall is triangular shaped, with a base of 25 ft and a height of 18 ft. The paint costs 50 cents per square foot. How much will it cost to paint the wall?
3. A triangular counter has a base and height of 4 ft. A circle with a radius of 1 ft is cut out of the counter in order to put in a sink. How much area of the counter is left? Use 3.14 for π.
4. Emilio's dart board is in the shape of a circle. The diameter of the dart board is 22 in. What is the area of the dart board? Use 3.14 for π.

Lesson 24.5

Find the area of the trapezoid.

1. $b_1 = 1.5$ in.
   $b_2 = 6$ in.
   $h = 3$ in.
2. $b_1 = 2.0$ yd
   $b_2 = 2.5$ yd
   $h = 2.3$ yd
3. $b_1 = 27$ m
   $b_2 = 16$ m
   $h = 2.5$ m
4. $b_1 = 5.4$ cm
   $b_2 = 10$ cm
   $h = 4$ cm
5. $b_1 = 2.6$ ft
   $b_2 = 4.1$ ft
   $h = 9$ ft
6. $b_1 = 4$ mm
   $b_2 = 5$ mm
   $h = 10$ mm
7. $b_1 = 3$ yd
   $b_2 = 12$ yd
   $h = 8$ yd
8. $b_1 = 9.5$ in.
   $b_2 = 7$ in.
   $h = 11$ in.
9. $b_1 = 2.3$ cm
   $b_2 = 6$ cm
   $h = 4.5$ cm

CHAPTER 25

Lesson 25.1

Find the surface area of each figure.

1.
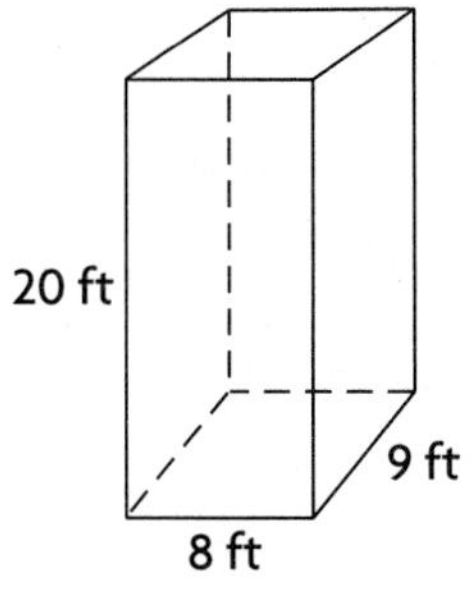

2.
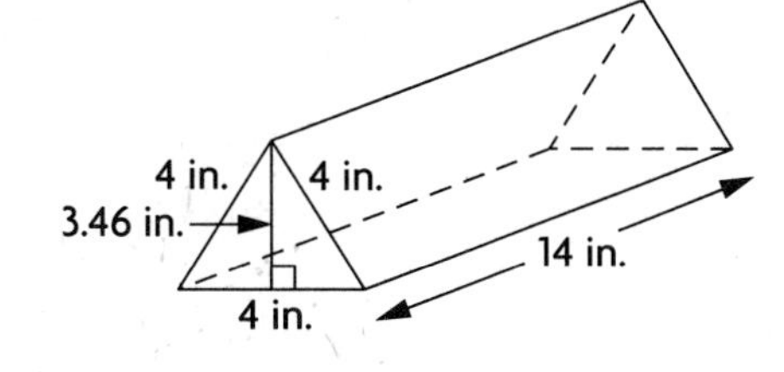

3.
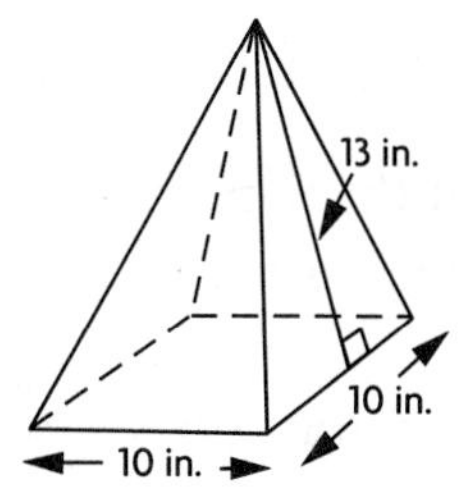

For Exercises 4–5, use the figure at the right. The figure is made of 12 cubes each with 2-inch sides.

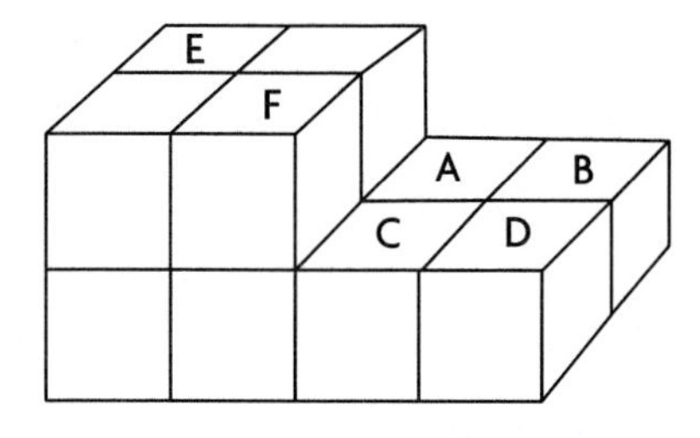

4. What is the total surface area of this figure?
5. What would be the new total surface area if the cubes labeled A, B, C, and D were removed?

Lesson 25.2

Find the surface area of the cylinders with the following dimensions. Use 3.14 for pi.

1. radius 8 in.; height 20 in.
2. radius 6 mm; height 12 mm
3. radius 3 ft; height 22 ft
4. radius 7 ft; height 9 ft
5. diameter 4 m; height 6 m
6. diameter 10 cm; height 8 cm
7. diameter 4.67 in.; height 24.3 in.
8. diameter 12 m; height 15 m

Lesson 25.3

Find the volume of each figure. Round your answer to the nearest whole number.

1.

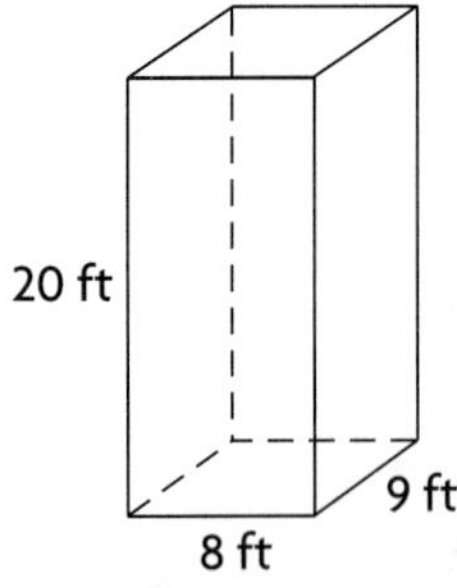

2.

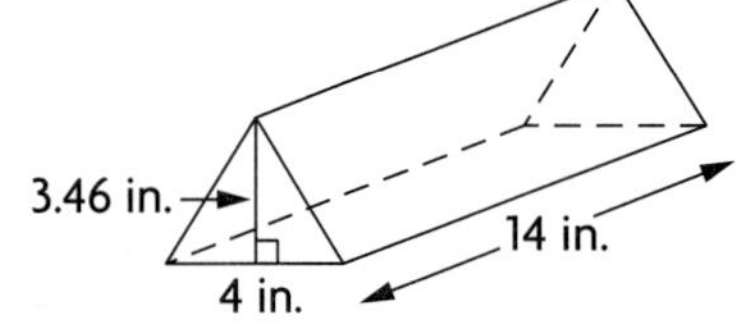

3.

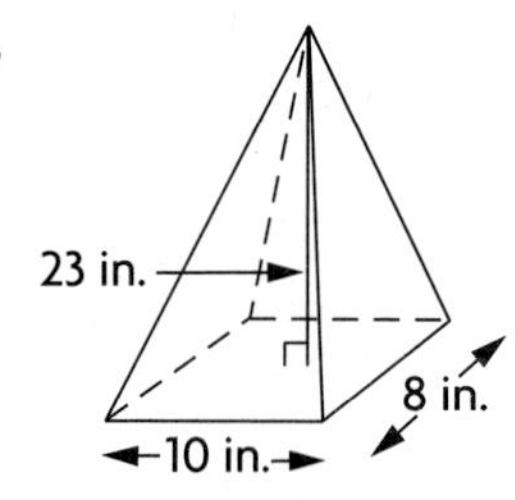

4. The volume of a rectangular prism is 144 in.^{3}, and two of the dimensions are 6 in. and 8 in. Find the missing dimension. (A sketch may help!)

Lesson 25.4

Find the volume of the cylinders with the following dimensions. Use 3.14 for pi and round to the nearest whole number.

1. radius 3 in.; height 22 in.

2. radius 5 m; height 12 m

3. diameter 10 ft; height 5 ft

4. diameter 12 mm; height 20 mm

5. radius 4 cm; height 80 cm

6. diameter 11 yd; height 10 yd

Find the volume of the cones with the following dimensions. Use 3.14 for pi and round to the nearest whole number.

7. radius 3 in.; height 20 in.

8. radius 5 cm; height 24 cm

9. radius 10 ft; height 5 ft

10. radius 12 m; height 30 m

11. radius 4 cm; height 80 cm

12. diameter 4 ft; height 6 ft

13. diameter 10 m; height 27 m

14. diameter 20 mm; height 60 mm

CHAPTER 26

Lesson 26.1

The perimeter of a rectangle is given. Using dimensions to the nearest 0.5 unit, find the length and width that will give the rectangle the largest possible area.

1. 130 yd

2. 64 in.

3. 74 ft

4. 8.8 cm

5. 18.8 m

6. 52 mm

7. 108 mi

8. 126 ft

9. 25.2 km

Lesson 26.2

Use the given scale selection, length = 50%, width = 65%, to find the new length and width of each rectangle. Round to the nearest half inch.

1. Original length: 10 in.
Original width: 5 in.

2. Original length: 14 in.
Original width: 16 in.

3. Original length: 23 in.
Original width: 30 in.

4. Original length: 47 in.
Original width: 52 in.

5. Original length: 16 in.
Original width: 25 in.

6. Original length: 70 in.
Original width: 90 in.

Use the dimensions of the given rectangle and scale selections.

7. rectangle: 12 in. × 16 in., scale: length = 225%, width = 90%

a. What are the new length and width?

b. Find the perimeter and area of the new rectangle.

c. Find the increase or decrease from the original perimeter.

8. rectangle: 5 in. × 7 in., scale: length = 150%, width = 75%

a. What are the new length and width?

b. Find the perimeter and area of the new rectangle.

c. Find the increase or decrease from the original perimeter.

Lesson 26.3

1. How many 2 ft × 2 ft × 2 ft boxes can fit inside a storage area that is 7 ft long, 5 ft wide, and 11 ft high?

2. How many 5 in. × 5 in. × 5 in. jewelry boxes will fit inside a drawer that is 2 ft wide, 17 in. deep, and 7 in. tall?

3. How many 2 cm × 2 cm × 2 cm boxes can fit inside a drawer that is 24 cm wide, 28 cm deep, and 4 cm high?

Lesson 26.4

The given scale factor was used to create a new cylinder with diameter = 6 cm and height = 9 cm. Find the radius (r), height (h), and volume (v) of the original cylinder.

1. $\frac{1}{3}$ **2.** $\frac{7}{9}$ **3.** $\frac{3}{2}$ **4.** $\frac{4}{3}$ **5.** $\frac{1}{6}$ **6.** $\frac{1}{9}$

CHAPTER 27

Lesson 27.1

Find sales tax. Describe how to do the computation mentally.

1. 5.5% on $40.00

2. 10% on $350.00

3. 3% on $50.00

Find the total cost directly. Round to the nearest cent when necessary.

4. 5% on $19.99

5. 7% on $23.65

6. 4.5% on $108.00

Find the price. Round to the nearest cent when necessary.

7. 7% sales tax
$13.77 total cost

8. $8\frac{1}{4}$ % sales tax
$44.62 total cost

9. 2.5% sales tax
$36.79 total cost

Lesson 27.2

Find the sale price.

1. Regular price: $50.00
60% off

2. Regular price: $17.00
10% off

3. Regular price: $102.50
30% off

Find the regular price.

4. Sale price: $99.50
50% off

5. Sale price: $60.75
25% off

6. Sale price: $62.40
35% off

Find the rate of discount.

7. Regular price: $72.00
Sale price: $61.20

8. Regular price: $15.50
Sale price: $10.33

9. Regular price: $9.00
Sale price: $2.70

Lesson 27.3

Find the value of the markup.

1. wholesale price: $66.66
retail price: $99.99

2. wholesale price: $400.00
retail price: $432.00

3. wholesale price: $0.45
retail price: $1.44

You buy videos at a wholesale price of $19.00 each. Find the amount of your markup and the retail price if you sell the videos at the markup.

4. 105% markup

5. 175% markup

6. 250% markup

Find the amount and percent of each markup.

7. wholesale price: $20
retail price: $35

8. wholesale price: $12
retail price: $48

9. wholesale price: $0.15
retail price: $0.33

Lesson 27.4

Use your calculator to find the interest.

1. 5% simple interest for 3 years on a principal of $425.00
2. 3.3% simple interest for 12 years on a principal of $93.00
3. 8.5% simple interest for 7 years on a principal of $5,600.00
4. 11.75% simple interest for 1 year on a principal of $2,100
5. 11% simple interest for 15 years on a principal of $22,000.00
6. 9% simple interest for 6 years on a principal of $300.00
7. 2% simple interest for 3 years on a principal of $13,200.00
8. 6.75% simple interest for 20 years on a principal of $85.00
9. 5.25% simple interest for 15 years on a principal of $89,000.00
10. 4% simple interest for 10 years on a principal of $2,000.00

Lesson 27.5

1. Adrienne bought a cassette recorder for $55 and put it on her charge card. The interest rate is 12% annually, or 1% monthly. She made monthly payments of $15 until she paid off her debt. How much interest did she pay?
2. Thomas bought a printer for his computer. It was priced at $623.54. He put it on the store charge at an interest rate of 24% annually, or 2% monthly. He made monthly payments of $200 to pay it off quickly. How much interest did he pay?

CHAPTER 28

Lesson 28.1

1. Draw a graph, comparing the speed to the time, of a school bus braking for a stoplight.
2. The rocket club launches toy rockets after school every week. Draw a graph, comparing the speed to the time, of a toy rocket launched upward.
3. Draw a graph that shows the relationship between the temperature in a hot cup of coffee, compared to time, after an ice cube was put into the coffee.
4. You just bought a ticket for a ride on a merry-go-round at the state fair. Draw a graph, comparing the speed to the time, of your ride on the merry-go-round.

Lesson 28.2

Answer Exercises 1–3 by using the given graphs.

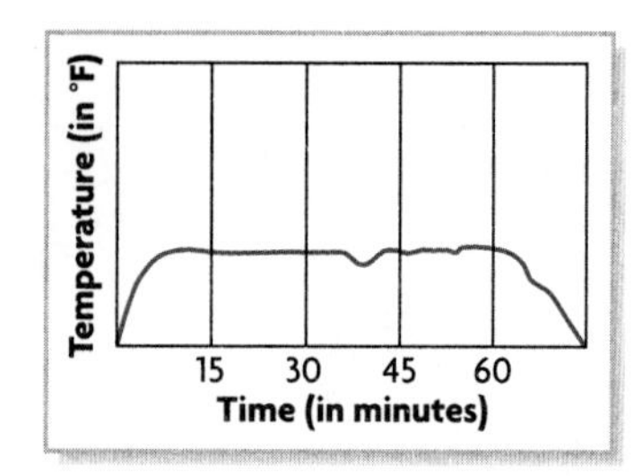

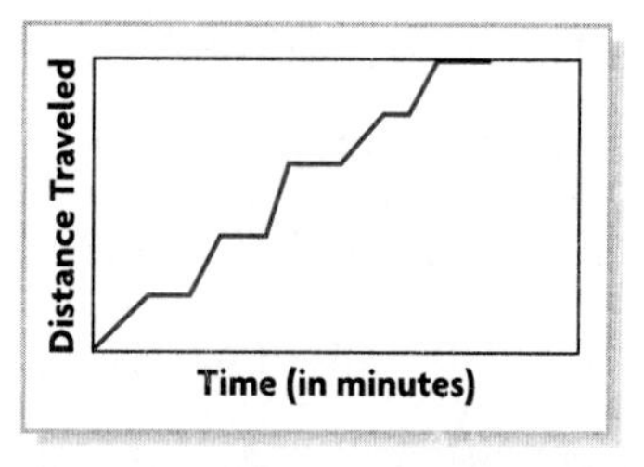

1. Look at the temperature vs. time graph above. Describe how the temperature in the oven changed as a meatloaf was being cooked.

2. What could have happened just before 45 minutes?

3. Study the distance vs. time graph above. This might be the graph of a U.S. mail carrier in a postal truck. Explain what seems to be happening. (Remember to think about distance traveled.)

Lesson 28.3

Identify the variables you would use to graph the relationship.

1. The hotter the day, the more crowded the swimming pool.
2. The smaller the sentence, the more sentences that will fit on a page.
3. The more people in a family, the higher the grocery bill.
4. The longer the race, the more time it takes to complete.
5. The taller the building, the more windows in it.
6. The more papers sold, the greater the profit.

Lesson 28.4

Write *positive, negative,* or *no correlation* to describe the relationship between the two sets of data.

1. the height of a person; the weight of a person
2. number of hours studying for a test; grade on the test
3. weight of a car; car's gas mileage
4. size of a person's shoe; money in the person's checking account
5. highest temperature on a given day; number of glasses of water consumed per day
6. outdoors temperature; time needed to dry clothing outdoors

Be a Good

A test is one way you show what you have learned. Almost every day in math class you answer questions, use manipulatives, or solve problems on paper. All of these activities are not very different from the tests you will take. So, you are getting ready for tests every day.

Some tests are used to give you a grade. Some are used to see how much you have learned over a long period of time. Some require that you choose from several possible answers. Some require that you explain how you got an answer.

THE TIPS ON THESE PAGES WILL HELP YOU BECOME A BETTER TEST TAKER.

GETTING READY FOR A TEST

What you do at home the night before the test and the morning of the test is very important. Studying hard at the last minute can make you so tired on the day of the test that you will not be able to do your best. But spending some time thinking over the topics and reminding yourself of what you have learned are important. Follow these tips:

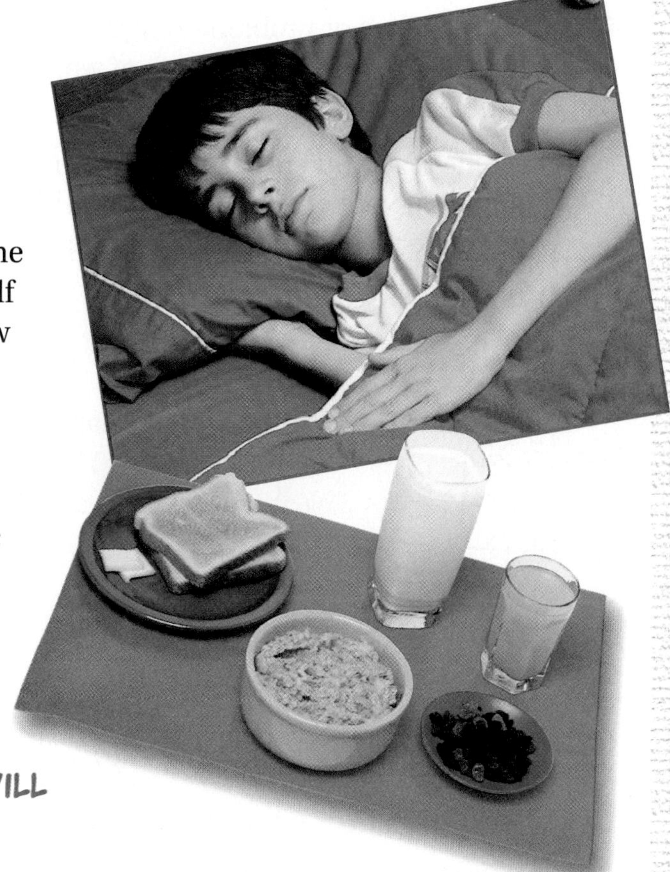

- RELAX AND GET A GOOD NIGHT'S SLEEP.
- EAT A GOOD BREAKFAST ON THE MORNING OF THE TEST.
- TELL YOURSELF THAT YOU WILL DO THE VERY BEST YOU CAN DURING THE TEST.
- PROMISE YOURSELF THAT YOU WILL NOT WORRY AND GET UPSET.

TAKING THE TEST

Understand the Directions

If your teacher gives directions orally, look at him or her and pay attention. Ask yourself these questions:

- Can I write on the test itself?
- How many items are on the test?
- How long can I work on the test?

If you don't understand printed directions, reread them. Follow all test directions carefully.

Answer the Questions

Read each question slowly. Be sure that you understand what you are asked to do. Read the question a second time if necessary.

If you are stopped by an unfamiliar word, try reading on to the end of the sentence or problem to figure it out. Or, try using the first part of the word as a clue, and think of what makes sense in the sentence or problem.

On some tests you are asked to explain your thinking. The questions require that you write an explanation of how you got an answer or why your answer is reasonable. Organize your thoughts before you write!

Choose the Correct Answer

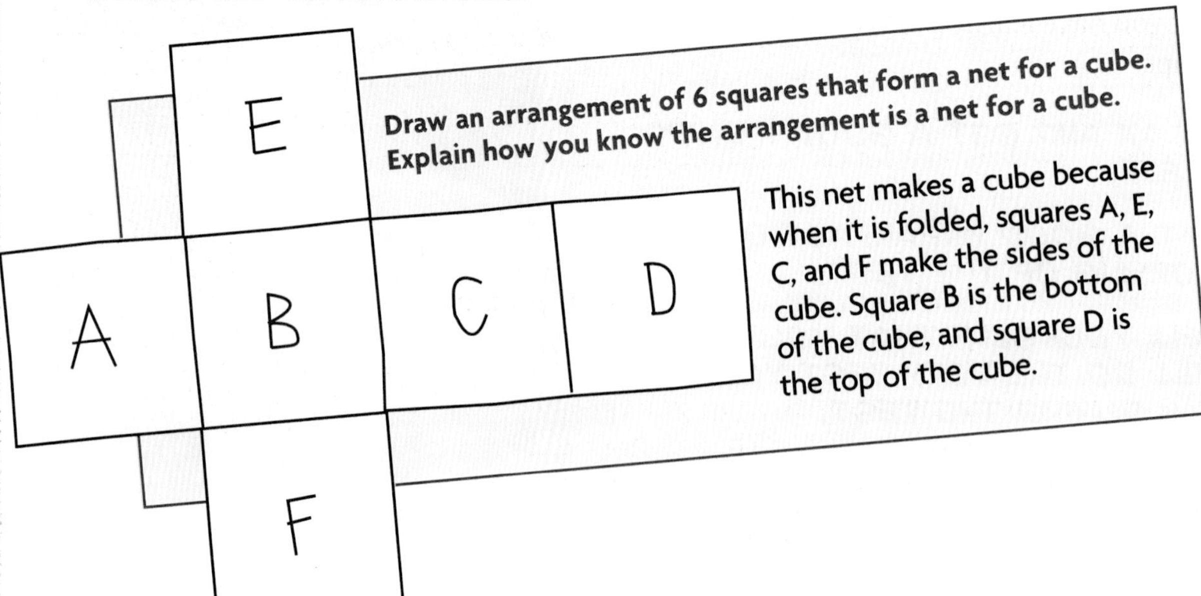

Draw an arrangement of 6 squares that form a net for a cube. Explain how you know the arrangement is a net for a cube.
E
A
B
C
D
F
This net makes a cube because when it is folded, squares A, E, C, and F make the sides of the cube. Square B is the bottom of the cube, and square D is the top of the cube.

Multiple-choice questions have answer choices. Look at each choice carefully.

- Eliminate the ones that look wrong to you. Sometimes estimating can help you eliminate unreasonable choices.
- Then concentrate on the ones that look like reasonable answers.
- If you are still not sure which choice is right, make your best guess.
- Skip the question if all the choices seem correct. Come back to the question later if you have time.
- Some multiple-choice questions give you the answer choice of *None* or *Not Here.* Before you choose one of these or any other answer, reread the problem and recheck your work to be sure your choice is correct.

1. Write an algebraic expression for the following.

6 less than the product of x and 5.

A $6 - x(5)$ **B** $6 - x + 5$

C $5x - 6$ **D** $6 < x5$

Think: I need to subtract 6 from the product of x and 5.

- Answer A can't be correct because the product is being subtracted from 6.
- Answer B can't be correct because 5 is being added to x.
- Answer C is correct because 6 is being subtracted from $5x$.

Mark Your Answers

Sometimes you will do all your work and show your answers on a piece of notebook paper. At other times you will use a separate answer sheet that may be scored by a machine. A machine can't tell the difference between your answers and other stray marks, so you need to mark carefully.

Study the answer sheet before you begin. Find out which way the numbers go. On some answer sheets you only have to mark the letter of the answer you choose. On other answer sheets you might have to make a mark for each digit of your answer in the right order.

Keep your place on the answer sheet. Make sure you mark the answer for each question on a choice for the right question number.

If you need to change an answer on an answer sheet, erase your mark cleanly. The machine will score an answer that was not erased cleanly as a wrong answer.

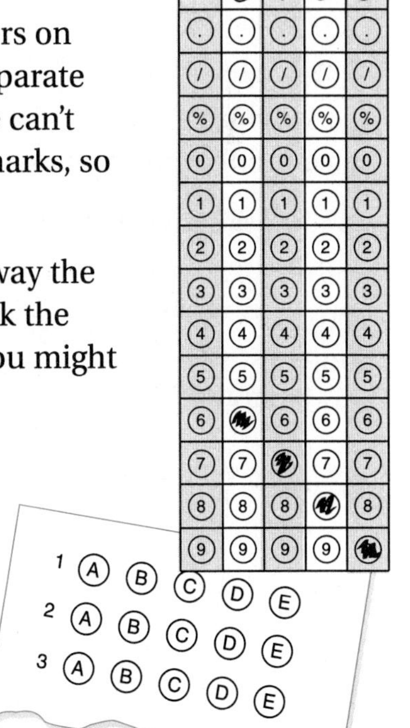

Keep Track of Time

If you have a set amount of time to complete a test or a section of a test, look at the clock to find out how much time you have left. Sometimes, your teacher will write on the chalkboard the number of minutes remaining. Glance quickly at the clock or the chalkboard to keep track of the time.

Don't waste a single minute while you are working. Move quickly from one question to another. But don't work so fast that you make careless mistakes.

If you are running out of time and still have many questions to do, try to work faster. If you have only a minute or two left, glance at the remaining questions to find the easiest ones. Answer those and skip the rest.

EVALUATING HOW YOU DID

When you finish the test, look over your answer sheet. Erase any stray marks you see. Use any time you have left to check your answers and be sure that you have recorded each answer in the correct place on the answer sheet.

If your graded test is returned to you, look carefully at the questions you missed. Try to determine what errors you made. Rework the problems if you can. Don't hesitate to ask your teacher for help in understanding what you did wrong.

YOU CAN BE A **GOOD TEST TAKER**. THE KEY TO SUCCESS IS DEVELOPING AND USING GOOD TEST-TAKING STRATEGIES.

METRIC UNITS	CUSTOMARY UNITS
Length	
1 millimeter (mm) = 0.001 meter (m)	1 foot (ft) = 12 inches (in.)
1 centimeter (cm) = 0.01 meter	1 yard (yd) = 36 inches
1 decimeter (dm) = 0.1 meter	1 yard = 3 feet
1 kilometer (km) = 1,000 meters	1 mile (mi) = 5,280 feet
	1 mile = 1,760 yards
	1 nautical mile = 6,076.115 feet
Capacity	
1 milliliter (mL) = 0.001 liter (L)	1 teaspoon (tsp) = $\frac{1}{6}$ fluid ounce (fl oz)
1 centiliter (cL) = 0.01 liter	1 tablespoon (tbsp) = $\frac{1}{2}$ fluid ounce
1 deciliter (dL) = 0.1 liter	1 cup (c) = 8 fluid ounces
1 kiloliter (kL) = 1,000 liters	1 pint (pt) = 2 cups
	1 quart (qt) = 2 pints
	1 quart = 4 cups
	1 gallon (gal) = 4 quarts
Mass/Weight	
1 milligram (mg) = 0.001 gram (g)	1 pound (lb) = 16 ounces (oz)
1 centigram (cg) = 0.01 gram	1 ton (T) = 2,000 pounds
1 decigram (dg) = 0.1 gram	
1 kilogram (kg) = 1,000 grams	
1 metric ton (t) = 1,000 kilograms	

Volume/Capacity/Mass for Water

1 cubic centimeter (cm^3) $\rightarrow$ 1 milliliter $\rightarrow$ 1 gram

1,000 cubic centimeters $\rightarrow$ 1 liter $\rightarrow$ 1 kilogram

TIME

1 minute (min) = 60 seconds (sec)	1 year (yr) = 12 months (mo)
1 hour (hr) = 60 minutes	1 year = 52 weeks
1 day = 24 hours	1 year = 365 days
1 week (wk) = 7 days	

FORMULAS

Perimeter

Polygon	$P =$ sum of the lengths of the sides
Rectangle	$P = 2(l + w)$
Square	$P = 4s$

Circumference

Circle	$C = 2\pi r$, or $C = \pi d$

Area

Circle	$A = \pi r^2$
Parallelogram	$A = bh$
Rectangle	$A = lw$
Square	$A = s^2$
Trapezoid	$A = \frac{1}{2}h(b_1 + b_2)$
Triangle	$A = \frac{1}{2}bh$

Surface Area

Cylinder	$S = 2(\pi r^2) + (2\pi rh)$
Rectangular Prism	$S = 2(lh + lw + wh)$

Volume

Cone	$V = \frac{1}{3}Bh$, or $V = \frac{1}{3}\pi r^2 h$
Cube	$V = e^3$
Cylinder	$V = Bh$, or $V = \pi r^2 h$
Prism	$V = Bh$
Pyramid	$V = \frac{1}{3}Bh$

Other

Diameter	$d = 2r$
Pythagorean Property	$c^2 = a^2 + b^2$

Consumer

Distance traveled	$d = rt$
Interest (simple)	$I = prt$

SYMBOLS

$<$	is less than
$>$	is greater than
$\leq$	is less than or equal to
$\geq$	is greater than or equal to
$\neq$	is not equal to
2^3	the third power of 2
3^{-5}	the negative fifth power of 3
$0.\overline{16}$	repeating decimal 0.161616 . . .
7	positive 7
$^-7$	negative 7
$\lvert ^-4 \rvert$	absolute value of negative 4
$\sqrt{}$	positive square root
$^-\sqrt{}$	negative square root
(4,7)	the ordered pair 4,7
\$5/hr	the rate \$5 per hour
1:2	ratio of 1 to 2
%	percent
$\perp$	is perpendicular to
$\parallel$	is parallel to
$\cong$	is congruent to
$\sim$	is similar to
$\approx$	is approximately equal to
$\overleftrightarrow{AB}$	line AB
$\overrightarrow{AB}$	ray AB
$\overline{AB}$	line segment AB
$\angle ABC$	angle ABC
$m\angle A$	measure of $\angle A$
$\triangle ABC$	triangle ABC
$\overset{\frown}{AB}$	arc AB
$^\circ$	degree (angle or temperature)
π	pi (about 3.14)
5!	factorial $5 \cdot 4 \cdot 3 \cdot 2 \cdot 1$
P(4)	the probability of the outcome 4

GLOSSARY

A

absolute value The distance from a point on the number line to zero *(page 100)*
Examples: $|{}^{-}3| = 3$; $|3| = 3$

acute angle An angle whose measure is greater than 0° but less than 90° *(page H22)*
Example:

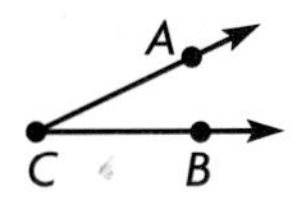

acute triangle A triangle in which all three angles are acute *(page H30)*
Example:

Addition Property of Opposites The property which states that the sum of a number and its opposite is zero *(page 98)*
Examples:
$5 + {}^{-}5 = 0$ $\quad$ ${}^{-}15 + 15 = 0$

adjacent angles Angles that share a common side, have the same vertex, and do not overlap *(page 200)*
Example:

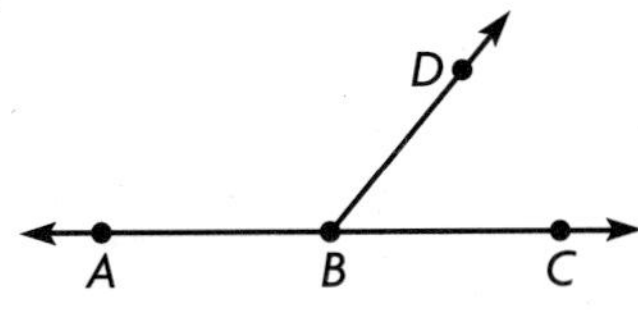

$\angle ABD$ is adjacent to $\angle DBC$.

algebraic expression An expression that is written using one or more variables *(page 124)*
Examples: $x - 4$; $2a + 5$; $a + b$

algebraic operating system (AOS) A system used by scientific calculators which automatically follows the order of operations *(page 74)*

angle A geometric figure formed by two rays that have a common endpoint *(page H22)*
Examples:

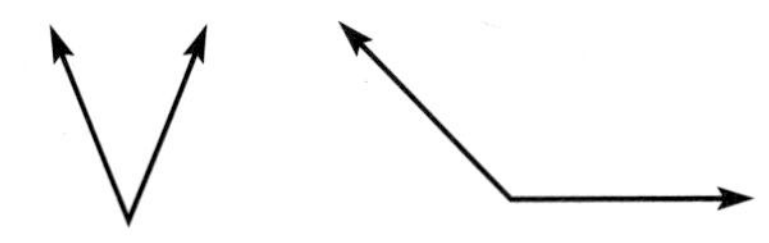

Angle-Side-Angle (ASA) A triangle congruence rule stating that when two angles and the included side of one triangle are congruent to two angles and the included side of another triangle, the two triangles are congruent *(page 226)*
Example:

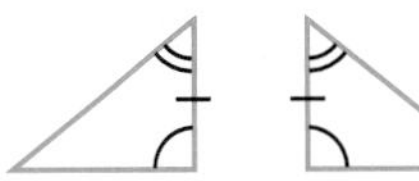

area The number of square units needed to cover a given surface *(page H24)*

arithmetic sequence An ordered list of numbers in which the difference of any term and the one after it is always the same *(page 134)*
Example:
5, 9, 13, 17, 21, . . . The common difference is 4.

Associative Property of Addition The property which states that for all real numbers *a, b,* and *c,* their sum is always the same, regardless of their grouping: $(a + b) + c = a + (b + c)$ *(page H6)*
Example:
$(2 + 3) + 4 = 2 + (3 + 4)$

Associative Property of Multiplication The property which states that for all real numbers *a, b,* and *c,* their product is always the same, regardless of their grouping:
$(a \bullet b) \bullet c = a \bullet (b \bullet c)$ *(page H6)*
Example:
$(5 \bullet 6) \bullet 7 = 5 \bullet (6 \bullet 7)$

average See *mean.*

axes Two perpendicular lines that intersect to form the coordinate plane *(page 176)*
Example:

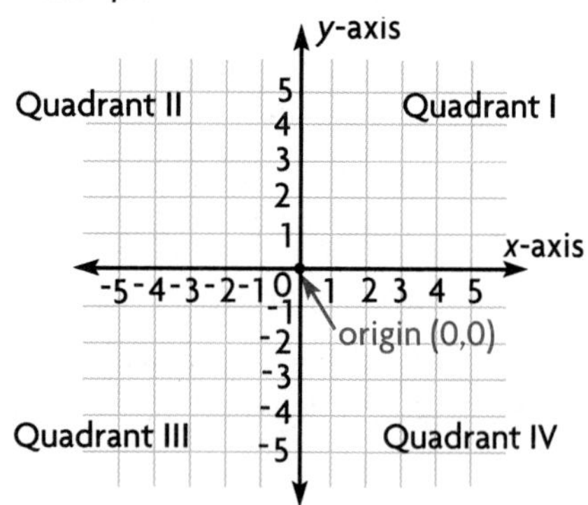

B

base The number that is used as a repeated factor *(page 36)*
Example: $4^3 = 4 \times 4 \times 4$
4 is the base; 3 is the exponent.

base A side of a polygon or a face of a solid figure by which the figure is measured or named *(page H25)*

basic unit In a tessellation, a figure that is repeated to make a pattern *(page 257)*

biased sample A sample that does not fairly represent the population *(page 397)*

bimodal Having two modes in a set of data *(page 415)*
Example: 12, 19, 34, 12, 21, 19, 17, 42
The set of data is bimodal since there are two modes, 12 and 19.

binary number system A number system in which all numbers are expressed using only two digits, 0 and 1 *(page 40)*
Example: The number 42 in our decimal number system is 101010_{two}.

bisect To divide into two congruent parts *(page 218)*
Example:

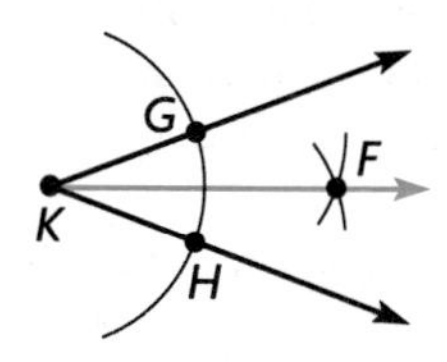

$\overrightarrow{KF}$ bisects $\angle GKH$.

box-and-whisker graph A graph that shows how far apart and how evenly the data are distributed; includes the lower and upper extreme values of data, the first and third quartiles of the data, and the median, or second quartile of the data *(page 412)*
Example:

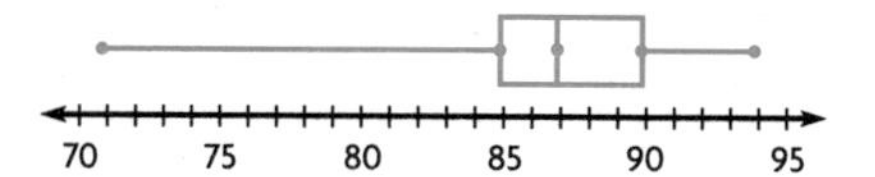

C

capacity The amount a container can hold when filled *(page H23)*

cell In a spreadsheet, a block area in which data or formulas can be entered; the cell is located by an address consisting of a letter and a number *(page 544)*

central angle An angle formed by two rays with a common vertex at the center of a circle *(page H22)*
Example:

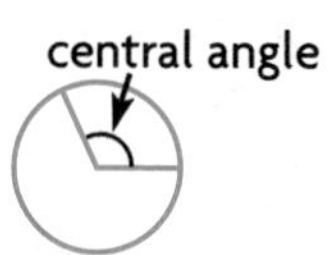

central tendency Any of three measures (mean, median, mode) that represent a type of average of a set of data *(page 414)*

circle A closed curve with all points on the curve an equal distance from a given point called the center of the circle

circle graph A graph used to compare the relationship of the parts to the whole *(page 30)*
Example:

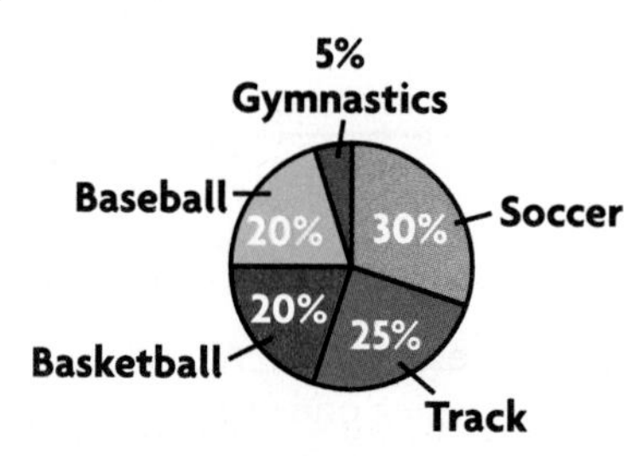

circumference The distance around a circle; $C = \pi d$ *(page 490)*

combination An arrangement of items or events in which order does not matter *(page 432)*

common difference The difference between any two successive terms in an arithmetic sequence *(page 134)*
Example: 3, 7, 11, 15, 19, . . .
The common difference in the arithmetic sequence is 7 − 3, or 4.

common ratio The ratio used to multiply each term to produce the next term in a geometric sequence *(page 380)*
Example: 1, 3, 9, 27, 81, . . .
The common ratio in the geometric sequence is $\frac{3}{1}$, or 3.

Commutative Property of Addition The property which states that two or more addends can be added in any order without changing the sum *(page H6)*
Examples: $a + 4 = 4 + a$
$(2 + 5) + r = r + (2 + 5)$

Commutative Property of Multiplication The property which states that two or more factors can be multiplied in any order without changing the product *(page H6)*
Examples: $3 \bullet a = a \bullet 3$
$4 \bullet 5 \bullet y = 5 \bullet 4 \bullet y$

compatible numbers Numbers that are close to a dividend and divisor and divide evenly, with no remainder *(page 71)*

complementary angles Two angles whose measures have a sum of 90° *(page 200)*
Example:

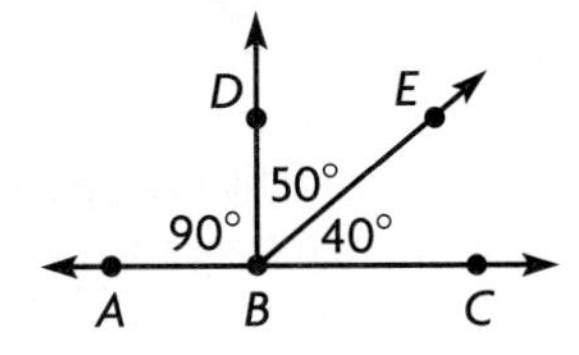

$\angle DBE$ and $\angle EBC$ are complementary.

composite number A whole number that has more than two whole-number factors *(page H11)*

compound interest Interest earned on principal and previously earned interest *(page 565)*

cone A solid figure with one vertex and one circular base *(page H25)*
Example:

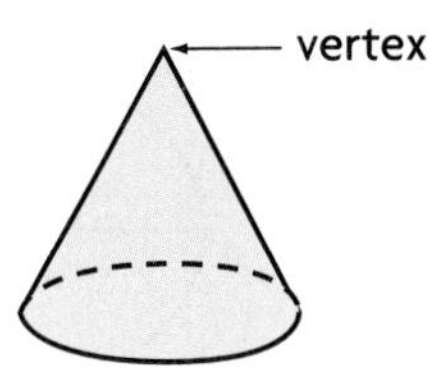

congruent Having the same size and shape *(page 198)*

converge To approach some fixed value *(page 362)*

coordinate plane A plane formed by two perpendicular number lines called axes; every point on the plane can be named by an ordered pair of numbers. *(page 176)*

counting numbers See *natural numbers.*

cube A rectangular prism with six congruent square faces *(page 236)*
Example:

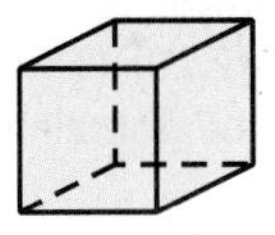

cylinder A solid figure with two parallel, congruent circular bases connected by a curved surface *(page H25)*
Example:

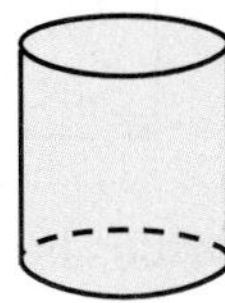

degree The unit of measure for angles or temperature *(pages 117 and H22)*

Density Property The property which states that between any two rational numbers, there is always another rational number *(page 375)*

diameter A line segment that passes through the center of a circle, with endpoints on the circle *(page 516)*
Example:

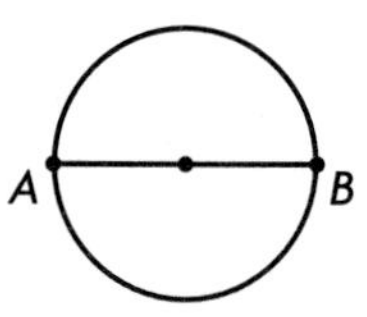

$\overline{AB}$ is a diameter of the circle.

dilation A transformation that enlarges or reduces a figure *(page 332)*

discount The amount by which the original price is reduced *(page 532)*

Distributive Property of Multiplication over Addition The property which states that multiplying a sum by a number gives the same result as multiplying each addend by the number and then adding the products *(page H6)*
Examples: $3(4 + 5) = 3 \times 4 + 3 \times 5$
$3(a + b) = 3a + 3b$

diverge To get larger without bound *(page 362)*

domain The set of the first elements of a relation; see *range*. *(page 179)*
Example: In the relation {(2,20), (3,30), (4,40), (5,50)}, the domain is {2, 3, 4, 5}.

edge The line segment along which two faces of a polyhedron intersect *(page 238)*
Example:

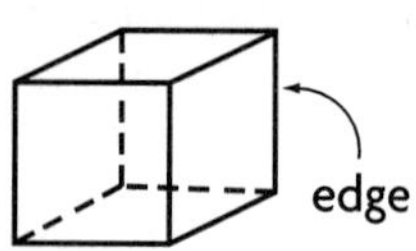

edge A connection between vertices in a network *(page 470)*
Example: The path from *A* to *B* is one edge of this network.

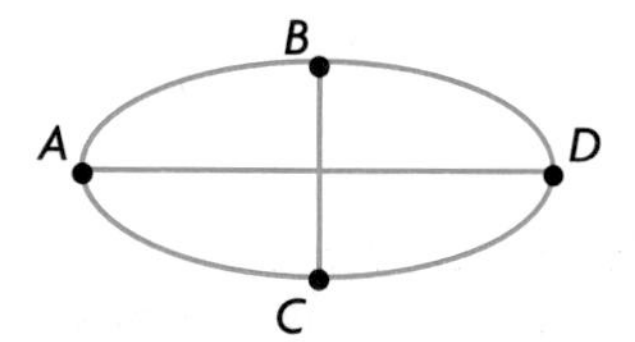

elements The words, numbers, or objects in a set *(page 178)*

equation A mathematical sentence that shows two expressions are equivalent *(page 142)*
Example: $x + 3 = 12$

equiangular triangle A triangle with three congruent angles and three congruent sides *(page 201)*
Example:

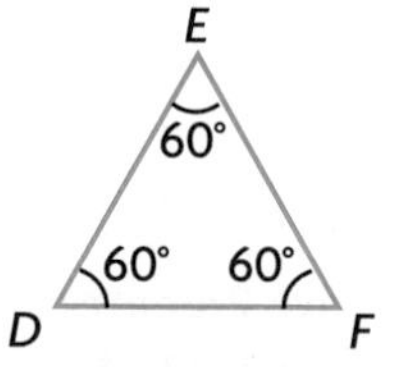

Triangle *DEF* is equiangular.

equilateral triangle A triangle with three congruent sides and three congruent angles *(pages 201 and H30)*
Example:

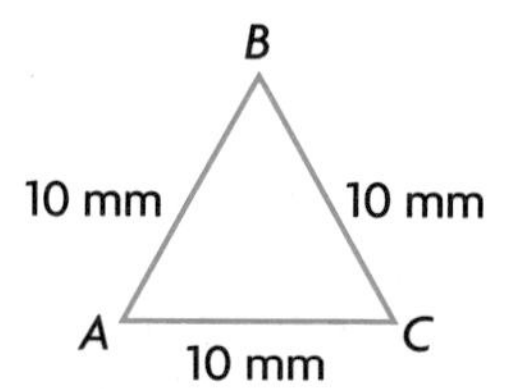

Triangle *ABC* is equilateral.

equivalent fractions Fractions that name the same number *(page H13)*
Example: $\frac{3}{4} = \frac{6}{8} = \frac{75}{100}$

equivalent ratios Ratios that make the same comparison *(page H18)*

estimate An answer that is close to the exact answer and is found by rounding, by using front-end digits, by clustering, or by using compatible numbers to compute *(pages H2 and H3)*

evaluating The process of putting an expression into its simplest numerical form, as a single number *(page 126)*

experimental probability The ratio of the number of times the event occurs to the total number of trials, or times the activity is performed *(page 444)*

exponent The number that indicates how many times the base is used as a factor; see *base.* *(page 36)*
Example: $4^3 = 4 \times 4 \times 4$
4 is the base; 3 is the exponent.

expression A mathematical phrase that combines operations, numerals, and/or variables to name a number *(page 124)*

face A flat surface of a polyhedron *(page 247)*

factor A number that is multiplied by another number to get a product *(page H10)*
Example: $2 \times 3 = 6$
2 and 3 are factors of 6.

Fibonacci sequence The infinite sequence of numbers formed by adding two previous numbers to get the next number *(page 379)*
Example: 1, 1, 2, 3, 5, 8, 13, 21, . . .

figurate number A number that can be represented by a geometric figure *(page 43)*

finance charge The interest charged when you pay a debt over time in payments *(page 543)*

first quartile The median of the lower half of a set of data *(page 412)*

formula A rule that is expressed using symbols *(page 476)*
Example: The area and the circumference of a circle can be computed by using the following formulas:
$A = \pi r^2$ $C = 2\pi r$

fractal A structure with repeating patterns containing shapes that are like the whole but of different sizes throughout *(page 264)*

frequency distribution table A table used to organize a collection of data *(page 402)*

function A relation in which each element in the domain is matched with only one element of the range *(page 181)*
Example:

Function	**Not a Function**
{(1,5), (2,6), (3,7), (4,8)}	{(1,5), (1,6), (2,7), (3,8)} 1 is matched with 5 and 6.

Fundamental Counting Principle The principle which states that all possible outcomes in a sample space can be found by multiplying the number of ways each event can occur *(page 428)*

geometric probability A probability calculated by comparing the area of a specific part to that of a total region *(page 453)*

geometric sequence An ordered list of numbers that has a common ratio between consecutive terms *(page 380)*
Example: 2, 6, 18, 54, . . .

Golden Cut The division of a segment into parts in the ratio of 1.61 to 1 *(page 286)*
Example:

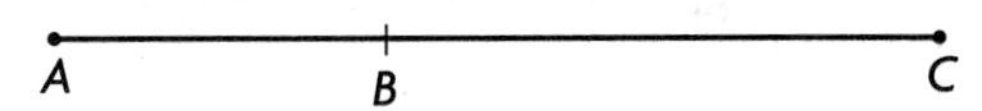

Golden Ratio A ratio that is approximately equal to 1.61 *(pages 286 and 344)*

Golden Rectangle Any rectangle with a length-to-width ratio of $\frac{1+\sqrt{5}}{2}$, or approximately 1.61 to 1 *(page 344)*

Golden Section See *Golden Cut.*

greatest common factor (GCF) The largest common factor of two or more given numbers *(page H12)*

greatest possible error (GPE) Half of the unit used in the measurement *(page 466)*

hexagon A six-sided polygon *(page H24)*
Example:

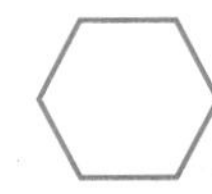

histogram A bar graph that shows the frequency of data within equal intervals *(page 411)*

hypotenuse In a right triangle, the side opposite the right angle *(page 474)*
Example:

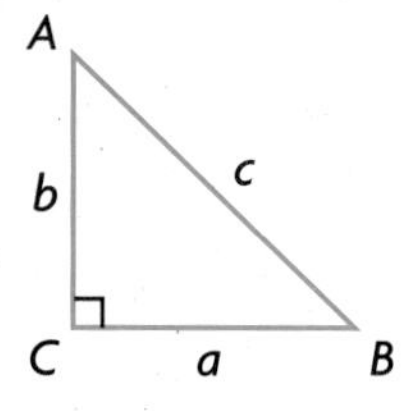

c is the hypotenuse of triangle ABC.

Identity Property of One The property which states that multiplying a number by 1 does not change the number's value *(page H6)*
Examples: $6 \times 1 = 6$; $1 \bullet a = a$

Identity Property of Zero The property which states that adding zero to a number does not change the number's value *(page H6)*
Examples: $3 + 0 = 3$; $0 + y = y$

image The figure in a new position or location as the result of a transformation *(page 207)*
Example:

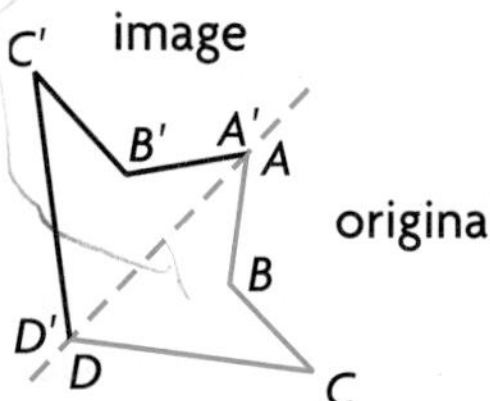

$A'B'C'D'$ is the image of $ABCD$.

indirect measurement A method of measuring distances by solving a proportion *(page 341)*

inequality A mathematical sentence that shows the relationship between quantities that are not equivalent, using $<$, $>$, $\leq$, $\geq$, or $\neq$ *(page 167)*

integer One of the set of whole numbers and their opposites *(page 17)*
Example:

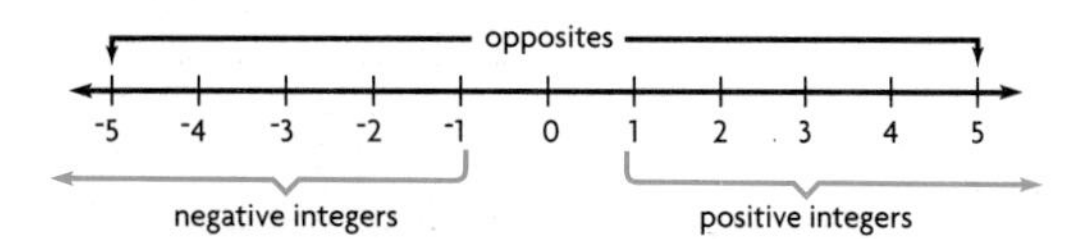

interest The amount of money paid for borrowing or using money *(page 540)*

intersecting lines Lines that cross at exactly one point *(page 221)*
Example:

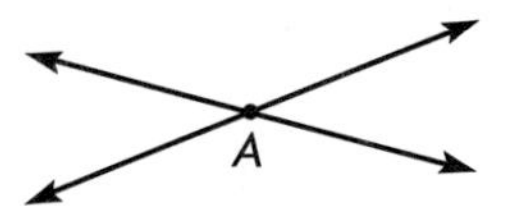

inverse operations Operations that undo each other *(page 145)*
Examples: $20 - 5 = 15$ and $15 + 5 = 20$
$20 \div 5 = 4$ and $4 \bullet 5 = 20$

irrational number A number that cannot be expressed as a repeating or terminating decimal *(page 378)*

isosceles triangle A triangle with two congruent sides *(page H30)*
Example:

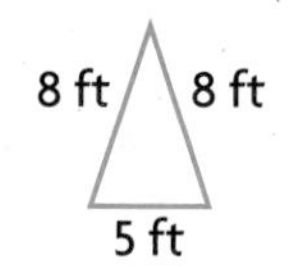

isosceles triangle

iteration A step in the process of repeating something over and over again *(pages 48 and 259)*

iteration diagram A picture showing the steps of an iterating process *(page 48)*

lateral face In a prism or a pyramid, a face that is not a base *(page 247)*

lateral surface In a cylinder, the curved surface connecting the circular bases *(page 490)*

least common denominator (LCD) The smallest common multiple of two or more denominators *(page H15)*
Example: The LCD of $\frac{2}{3}$ and $\frac{4}{5}$ is 15.

least common multiple (LCM) The smallest number, other than zero, that is a multiple of two or more given numbers *(page H13)*
Example: The LCM of 8 and 10 is 40.

leg In a right triangle, either of the two sides that intersect to form the right angle; in an isosceles triangle, one of the two congruent sides *(page 474)*
Example:

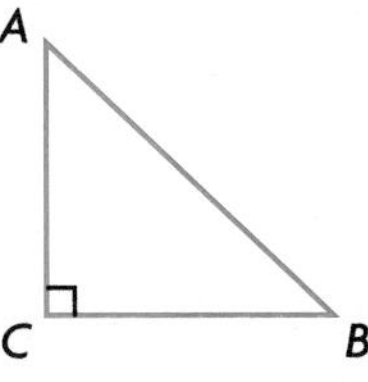

$\overline{AC}$ and $\overline{CB}$ are legs of triangle *ABC*.

like terms Two or more terms that have the same variable raised to the same power *(page 130)*
Example: $8y$, $-4y$, $9.1y$

line A set of points that extends without end in opposite directions *(page H21)*
Example:

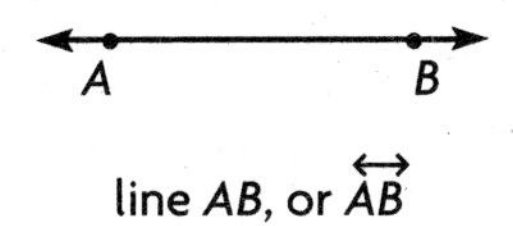

line *AB*, or $\overleftrightarrow{AB}$

line plot A number line with marks or dots to show frequency *(page 403)*

line segment A part of a line or ray, consisting of two endpoints and all points between those endpoints. *(page H21)*
Example:

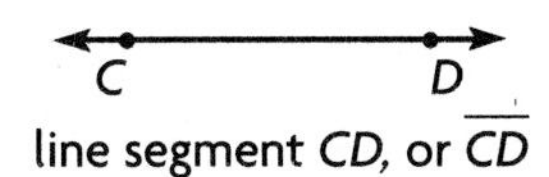

line segment *CD*, or $\overline{CD}$

line symmetry A figure has line symmetry if a line can separate the figure into two congruent parts. *(page 203)*

linear equation An equation that can be represented by a line on the coordinate plane *(page 185)*

lower quartile See *first quartile.*

markup The difference between the retail price and the wholesale price *(page 536)*

mathematical probability The ratio of the number of favorable outcomes to the number of all possible outcomes *(page 430)*

mean (average) The sum of a set of numbers divided by the number of addends *(page H25)*

measure of central tendency A measure used to describe data; the mean, median, and mode are measures of central tendency *(page 414)*

median The middle number or the average of the two middle numbers in an ordered set of data *(page H25)*

midpoint The point that divides a line segment into two congruent line segments *(page 219)*
Example:

3 3
A M B

M is the midpoint of $\overline{AB}$.

mode The number or numbers that occur most frequently in a set of data *(page H26)*

Multiplication Property of Zero The property which states that for all real numbers a, $a \times 0 = 0$ and $0 \times a = 0$ *(page H6)*
Example: $5 \times 0 = 0$ and $0 \times 5 = 0$

natural numbers The set of numbers {1, 2, 3, . . .} used for counting separate objects *(page 16)*

negative correlation In a scatterplot, a pattern formed from data points shows the values of one variable increase as the values of the other variable decrease. *(page 559)*
Example:

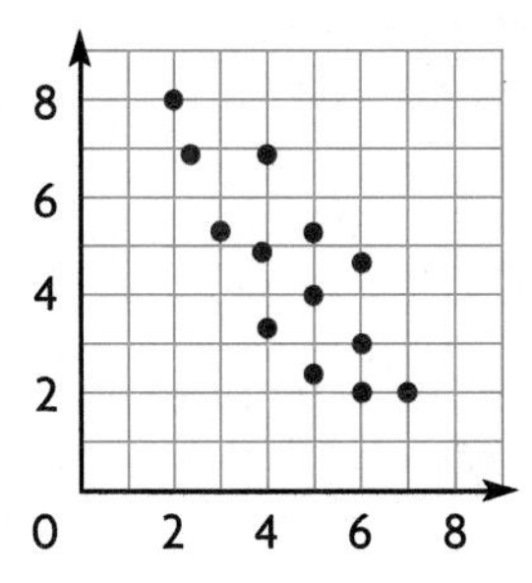

negative integer An integer less than zero *(page 17)*

net A connected arrangement of polygons in a plane that can be folded up to form a polyhedron *(page 243)*
Example:

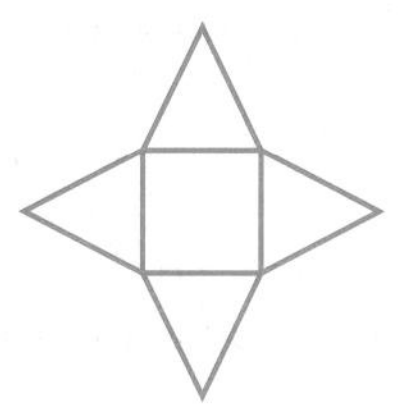

net for a square pyramid

network A figure made up of vertices and edges that show how objects are connected *(page 470)*
Example:

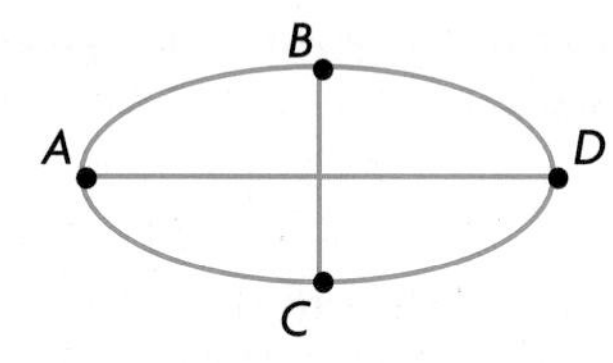

no correlation In a scatterplot, data points are scattered, and no pattern can be formed from the points. *(page 559)*

numerical expression An expression that contains only numbers and operations *(page 124)*

obtuse angle An angle whose measure is greater than 90° but less than 180° *(page H22)*
Example:

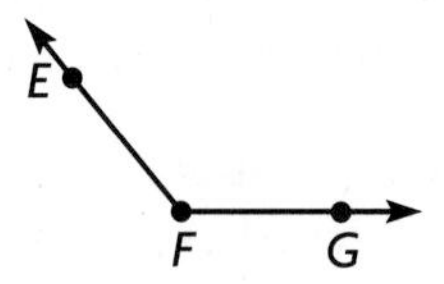

obtuse triangle A triangle containing one obtuse angle *(page H30)*
Example:

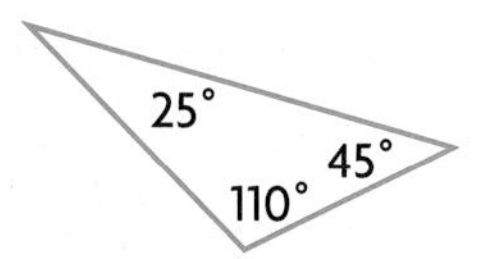

octagon An eight-sided polygon *(page H24)*
Example:

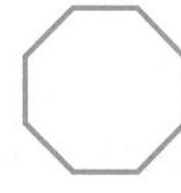

opposites Two numbers represented by points on the number line that are the same distance from zero but are on opposite sides of zero *(page 17)*

order of operations The order in which the operations are done within an expression *(pages 73 and H5)*

ordered pair A pair of numbers that can be used to locate a point on the coordinate plane *(page 176)*

origin The point on a coordinate plane where the x-axis and y-axis intersect (0,0) *(page 176)*

overestimate An estimate that is greater than the actual answer *(page H3)*

parallel lines Lines in a plane that do not intersect *(page 221)*
Example:

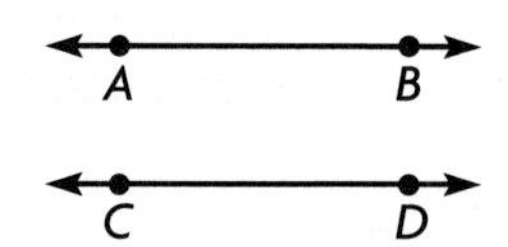

$\overleftrightarrow{AB} \parallel \overleftrightarrow{CD}$, *or* $\overleftrightarrow{AB}$ *is parallel to* $\overleftrightarrow{CD}$.

parallelogram A quadrilateral in which opposite sides are congruent and parallel *(page H24)*
Example:

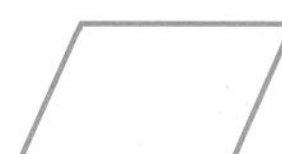

Pascal's triangle A triangular arrangement of numbers in which each row starts and ends with 1, and each other number is the sum of the two numbers above it *(page 360)*

pentagon A five-sided polygon *(page H24)*
Example:

percent Ratio of a number to 100; *percent* means per hundred *(page 22)*
Example: $25\% = \frac{25}{100}$

perfect square A number that has an integer as its square root *(page 43)*
Example: 16 is a perfect square.

perimeter The distance around a polygon *(page H24)*

permutation An arrangement of items or events in which order is important *(page 436)*

perpendicular bisector A line that intersects a line segment at its midpoint *(page 222)*
Example:

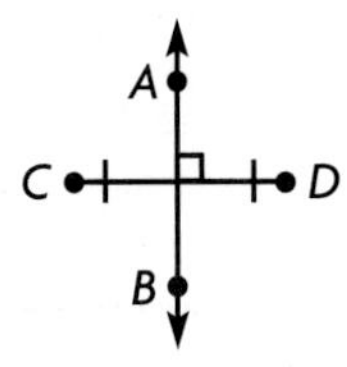

perpendicular lines Lines that intersect to form right angles *(page 221)*

pi (π) The ratio of the circumference of a circle to the length of its diameter; $\pi \approx 3.14$, or $\frac{22}{7}$ *(page 289)*

plane A set of points forming a flat surface that extends without end in all directions *(page H21)*

plane figure A figure which lies in a plane *(page H24)*

point An exact location *(page H21)*

point of rotation The point about which a rotation is centered *(page 203)*
Example:

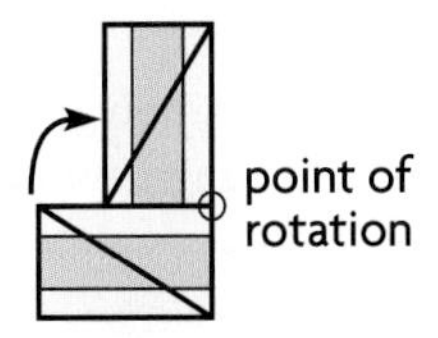

polygon A closed plane figure formed by three or more line segments *(page H24)*

polyhedron A solid figure in which all the surfaces, or faces, are polygons *(page 236)*
Example:

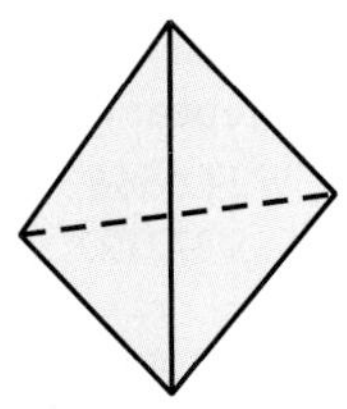

population The total or entire group to be studied *(page 394)*

positive correlation When values of two sets of data increase or decrease together *(page 559)*
Example:

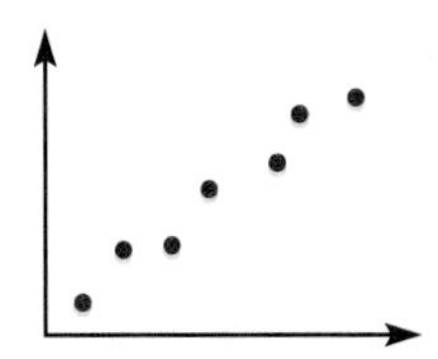

power The value of a number represented by a base and an exponent. *(page 36)*
Example: $4^3 = 4 \times 4 \times 4 = 64$
4 is the base; 3 is the exponent; 64 is the power.

precision A property of measurement that is related to the unit of measure used; the smaller the unit of measure used, the more precise the measurement is. *(page 466)*
Example: 27 mm is more precise than 3 cm.

prime factorization A number written as the product of its prime factors *(page H12)*
Example: $98 = 2 \times 7 \times 7 = 2 \times 7^2$

prime number A whole number greater than 1 that has exactly two factors, itself and 1 *(page H11)*

principal The amount of money borrowed or saved *(page 540)*

prism A polyhedron whose two bases are congruent, parallel polygons in parallel planes and whose lateral faces are parallelograms *(page H25)*
Example:

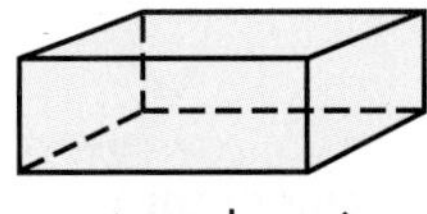

rectangular prism

probability The number used to describe the chance of an event occurring *(page 444)*

proportion An equation which states that two ratios are equivalent *(pages 152 and 317)*
Example: $\frac{5}{10} = \frac{1}{2}$, or $5:10 = 1:2$

proportional Two ratios that are equivalent are proportional *(page 313)*

pyramid A polyhedron with one base that is a polygon and with lateral faces that are triangles which share a common vertex *(page H25)*
Example:

square pyramid

Pythagorean Property In any right triangle, if a and b are the lengths of the legs and c is the length of the hypotenuse, then $a^2 + b^2 = c^2$ *(page 474)*

quadrant One of the four regions of the coordinate plane *(page 176)*
Example:

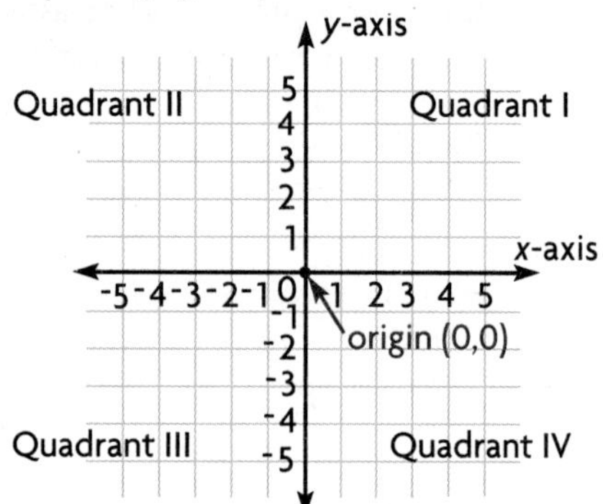

quadrilateral A four-sided polygon *(page H24)*

radius A line segment with one endpoint at the center of the circle and the other endpoint on the circle *(page 490)*
Example:

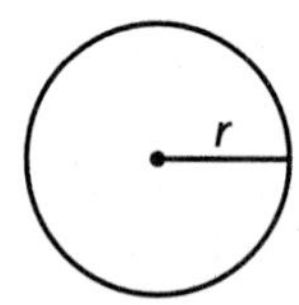

r is the radius of the circle.

random sample A population sample for which every individual in the population had an equal chance of being chosen *(page 394)*

range The difference between the greatest number and the least number in a set of data *(page H26)*

range The set of the second elements of a relation; see *domain.* *(page 179)*
Example: In the relation {(2,20), (3,30), (4,40), (5,50)}, the range is {20, 30, 40, 50}.

rate A ratio that compares quantities of different units, such as miles per hour, price per pound, students per class *(page 280)*

ratio A comparison of two numbers *(page H18)*
Example: 6 to 7, or 6:7, or $\frac{6}{7}$

rational number Any number that can be expressed as a ratio $\frac{a}{b}$ where a and b are integers and $b \neq 0$ *(page 17)*

ray A part of a line, having one endpoint and extending in one direction without end *(page H21)*
Example:

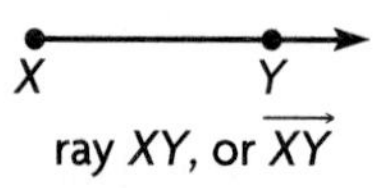

ray XY, or $\overrightarrow{XY}$

reciprocal One of two numbers whose product is 1 *(page 89)*

rectangle A parallelogram with four right angles *(page H24)*

reflection (flip) The figure formed by flipping a geometric figure about a line to obtain a mirror image *(page 206)*
Example:

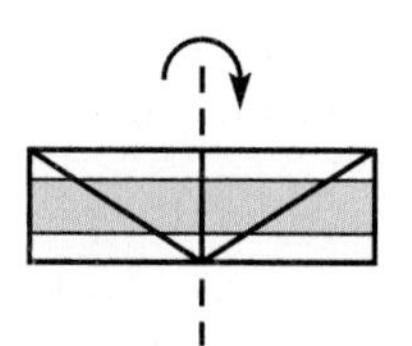

regular polygon A polygon in which all sides and all angles are congruent *(page 204)*
Example:

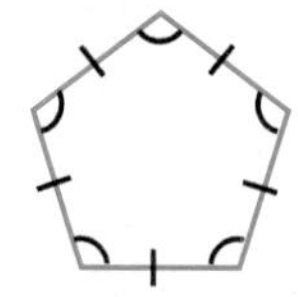

relation A set of ordered pairs *(page 178)*

repeating decimal A decimal in which one or more digits repeat indefinitely *(page H9)*
Examples: 24.6666 . . . or $24.\overline{6}$
5.272727 . . . or $5.\overline{27}$

retail price The sum of the wholesale price and markup *(page 536)*
Example: wholesale + markup = retail
\$15 + \$5 = \$20

rhombus A parallelogram whose four sides are congruent and whose opposite angles are congruent *(page H24)*
Example:

right angle An angle whose measure is 90° *(page H22)*
Example:

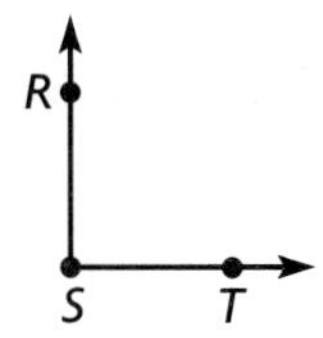

$\angle RST$ is a right angle.

right triangle A triangle containing exactly one right angle *(page H30)*
Example:

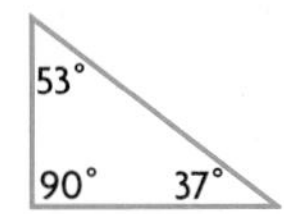

rotation A type of transformation, or movement, that results when a geometric figure is turned about a fixed point *(page 206)*
Example:

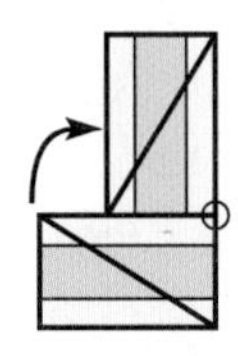

rotational symmetry When a figure can be rotated less than 360° about a central point and be made to match or coincide with the original figure *(page 203)*
Example:

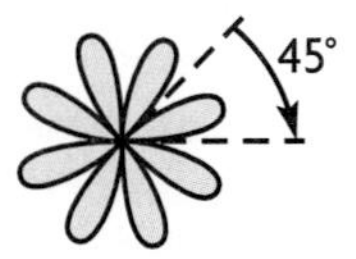

S

sale price The price of a product after the discount has been subtracted from the original price *(page 532)*
Example: original − discount = sale price
$25 − $5 = $20

sales tax An amount equal to a percent of purchase price, that is charged by states to raise money *(page 528)*

sample A smaller group of people or objects chosen from a larger group, or population *(page 394)*

sample space All possible outcomes in a given situation *(page 428)*
Example: The sample space for tossing 2 coins is (H,H), (H,T), (T,H), (T,T).

scale drawing A drawing that has its dimensions related by a scale factor to the dimensions of the object it represents *(page 334)*

scale factor The common ratio for pairs of corresponding sides of similar figures *(page 314)*

scalene triangle A triangle with no congruent sides *(page H30)*
Example:

scatterplot A graph with points plotted that attempt to show a relationship between two variables *(page 559)*
Example:

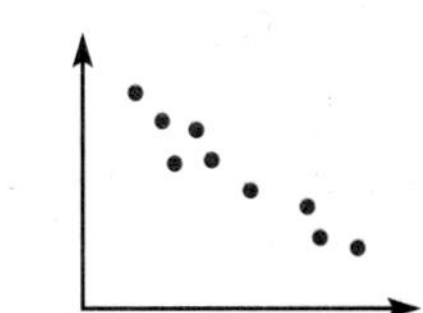

scientific notation A method of writing very large or very small numbers by using powers of 10 *(page 38)*
Example: $1{,}200{,}000 = 1.2 \times 10^6$

second quartile The median of a set of data *(page 412)*

self-similarity A figure has self-similarity if it contains a repeating pattern of smaller and smaller parts that are like the whole, but different in size *(page 261)*
Example:

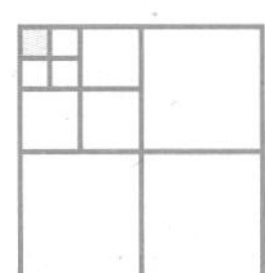

sequence An ordered list of numbers *(page 134)*

Side-Angle-Side (SAS) A triangle congruence rule stating that two sides and the included angle of one triangle match two sides and the included angle of another triangle *(page 226)*
Example:

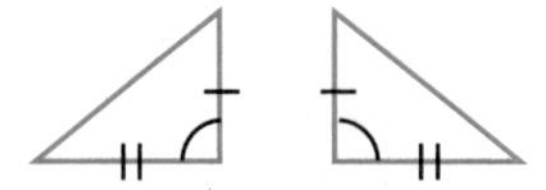

Side-Side-Side (SSS) A triangle congruence rule stating that three sides of one triangle match three sides of another *(page 226)*
Example:

similar figures Figures with the same shape but not necessarily the same size *(page 313)*
Example:

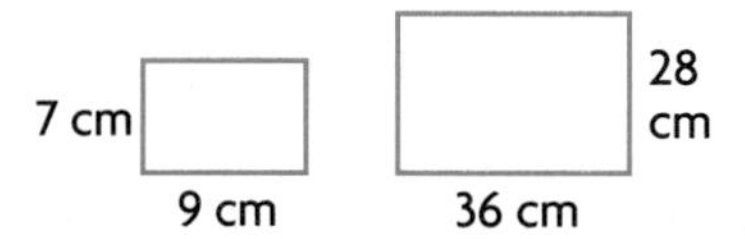

simple interest The amount obtained by multiplying the principal by the rate by the time; $I = prt$ *(page 540)*

simplest form A fraction is in simplest form when the numerator and denominator have no common factors other than 1. *(page 28)*
Example: $\frac{6}{8}$ written in simplest form is $\frac{3}{4}$.

simplest form The result of combining like terms in an expression *(page 131)*
Example: $4x + 3x + 2 = 7x + 2$

simulation A model of an experiment that would be too difficult or too time-consuming to actually perform *(page 450)*

solid figure A three-dimensional figure *(page 236)*

solution The value that makes two sides of an equation equal *(page 144)*

solve To find the correct value of the variable in an equation *(page 144)*

space figure See *solid figure.*

sphere A solid figure with all points the same distance from the center *(page H25)*
Example:

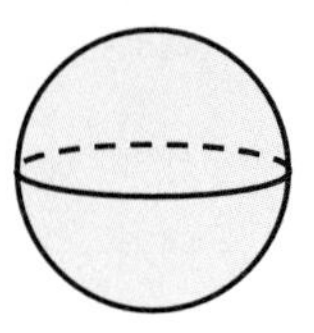

spreadsheet A computer program that organizes information in rows and columns and does calculations with numbers and formulas *(page 55)*

square A rectangle with four congruent sides *(page H24)*
Example:

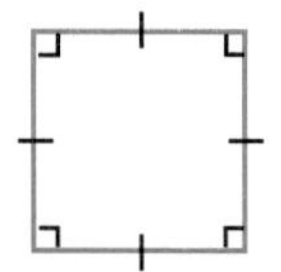

square The product of a number and itself *(page H4)*
Example: 25 is the square of 5 because $5^2 = 5 \times 5 = 25$.

square number A number that can be represented with a square array *(page 43)*
Example:

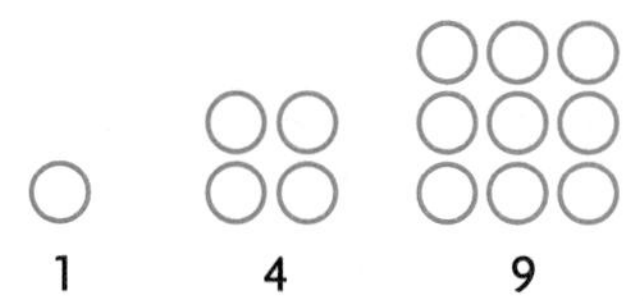

square root One of the two equal factors of a number *(page H4)*
Example: 6 is the square root of 36 because $6^2 = 36$.

stacked bar graph A graph used to compare the parts to the whole *(page 419)*

stem-and-leaf plot A method of organizing intervals or groups of data *(page 404)*
Example: Set of Data
140, 130, 136, 158, 152, 167

Stem	Leaves
13	0 6
14	0
15	2 8
16	7

straight angle An angle whose measure is 180° *(page H22)*

Example:

∠*XYZ* is a straight angle.

stratified sample A sample of a population that has been divided into subgroups *(page 394)*

supplementary angles Two angles whose sum equals 180° *(page 200)*

Example:

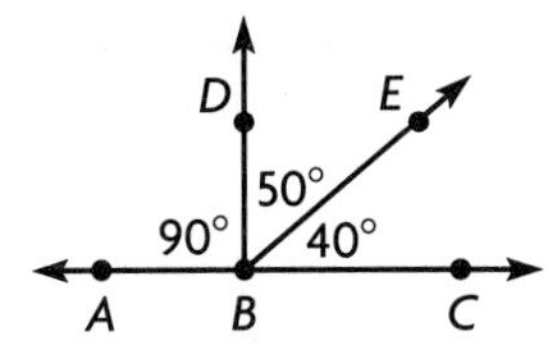

∠*ABD* and ∠*DBC* are supplementary.

surface area The sum of the areas of the faces, or surfaces, of a solid figure *(page 486)*

survey A method of gathering information about a population *(page 394)*

systematic sample A sample of a population that has been selected using a pattern *(page 394)*

term The parts of an expression that are separated by the + or − symbol *(page 130)*

term An element or number in a sequence *(page 134)*

terminating decimal A decimal that ends; a decimal for which the division operation results in a remainder of zero *(page H9)*

Examples: $\frac{1}{2} = 0.5$ and $\frac{5}{8} = 0.625$

tessellation A repeating pattern of congruent plane figures that completely cover a plane with no gaps or overlapping *(page 256)*

Example:

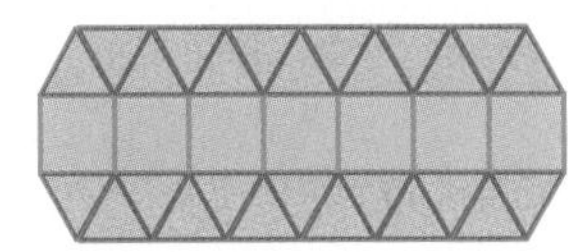

third quartile The median of the upper half of a set of data *(page 412)*

total amount In the formula $A = p + I$, A is the sum of the principal and the interest. *(page 541)*

transformation A change in a figure that results in a different position, shape, size, and/or orientation *(page 206)*

translation (slide) A movement of a geometric figure to a new position without turning or flipping it *(page 206)*

Example:

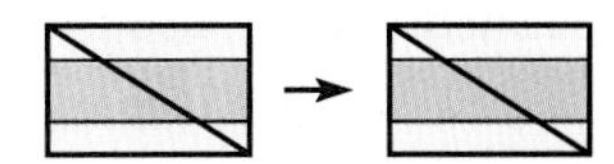

trapezoid A quadrilateral with only one pair of parallel sides *(page H24)*

Example:

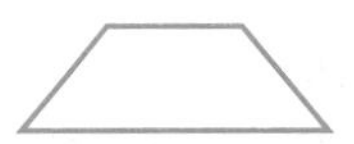

tree diagram A branching diagram which shows all possible combinations or outcomes *(page 428)*

triangle A three-sided polygon *(page H24)*

triangular numbers A sequence of numbers, 1, 3, 6, 10, 15, . . ., that can be shown geometrically with triangular arrays *(page 356)*

Example: 6 is a triangular number.

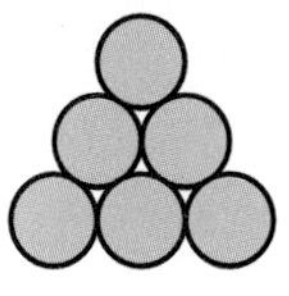

turn symmetry See *rotational symmetry*.

underestimate An estimate that is less than the actual answer *(page H3)*

unit price A unit rate used to compare prices *(page 282)*

unit rate A rate in which the second term is 1 *(page 281)*

upper quartile See *third quartile.*

variable A letter used to represent one or more numbers in an expression, equation, or inequality *(page 124)*
Examples: $5a$; $2x = 8$; $3y + 4 \neq 10$

Venn diagram A diagram that is used to show relationships between sets *(page 16)*

vertex A point where two or more rays meet, where sides of a polygon meet, or where edges of a polyhedron meet; also the top point of a cone or a pyramid *(page H22)*

vertical angles A pair of opposite congruent angles formed by intersecting lines *(page 200)*
Examples:

vertical angles

$\angle 1$ and $\angle 3$
$\angle 2$ and $\angle 4$

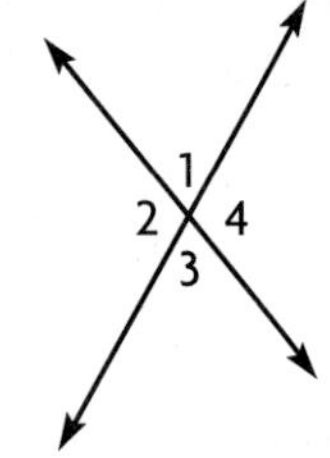

vertical line test A test to determine whether or not a relation is a function *(page 182)*

volume The number of cubic units needed to occupy a given space *(page 493)*

whole numbers The set of natural numbers and 0, {0, 1, 2, 3, . . .} *(page 16)*

wholesale price The price paid when large quantities of products are purchased *(page 536)*

***x*-axis** The horizontal axis on a coordinate plane *(page 176)*

***x*-coordinate** The first number in an ordered pair; tells whether to move right or left along the *x*-axis of the coordinate plane *(page 176)*

***y*-axis** The vertical axis on a coordinate plane *(page 176)*

***y*-coordinate** The second number in an ordered pair; tells whether to move up or down along the *y*-axis of the coordinate plane *(page 176)*

Answers to Selected Exercises

Chapter 1

Pages 18–19

1. No even number is odd.
3. All counting numbers are integers.
7. R; I, R; C, W, I, R; R; C, W, I, R **9.** false
11. true **13.** none **15.** 9, 15, 21, 25, 27
17. 1 **19.** 2; 6 **21.** $^{-}45$ **23.** $^{+}3$ **25.** F

Page 21

1. $\frac{5}{8}$ **3.** $^{-}1.25$ **5.** $\frac{^{-}12}{1}, \frac{^{-}24}{2}, ^{-}12.00$
7. $\frac{90}{100}$, 0.9, 0.90 **9.** $^{-}2.10, \frac{^{-}21}{10}, ^{-}2.100$
11. $\frac{15}{1}, \frac{30}{2}$, 15.0 **13.** $^{-}3\frac{4}{10}, ^{-}3.4, \frac{^{-}17}{5}$
23. $^{-}3 < ^{-}1 < 2\frac{3}{4}$ **25.** $^{-}8 < ^{-}5 < 6\frac{2}{7}$
27. 0.290 **29.** at least 9 free throws

Page 25

1. u: 75%; s: 25% **3.** u: 50%; s: 50%
5. 13; 6 **7.** 8 **9.** 25% **11.** 20 pieces

Pages 28–29

1. 90% **3.** 75% **5.** 98% **7.** 250%
9. 4% **11.** $\frac{2}{25}$ **13.** $\frac{4}{25}$ **15.** $\frac{1}{100}$ **17.** $\frac{9}{20}$
19. $\frac{1}{2}$ **21.** 0.02 **23.** 0.10 **25.** 8.00
27. 0.04 **29.** 0.48 **31.** 0.25; 25%
33. $\frac{39}{100}$; 39% **35.** $\frac{87}{100}$; 87% **37.** $15\% = \frac{3}{20}$
39. 10 **41.** 40 **43.** 26 **45.** 10.51 **47.** 17
49. J

Page 31

1. 144° **3.** 32° **5.** 11° **7.** 18° **9.** Graphs will vary. **11.** by reducing other categories a total of 11% of income **13.** For greater percents, the areas are greater. **15.** Tables and graphs will vary.

Page 33

1. C **3.** B **5.** C **7.** C **9.** B

Chapter 2

Pages 38–39

1. 6; 2 **3.** 6; 3 **5.** $512^1; 8^3; 2^9$ **7.** $2{,}401^1; 49^2; 7^4$ **9.** 512 **11.** 15,625 **13.** 10,000,000
15. 65,536 **17.** 1 **19.** 32.768 **21.** 16,384
23. $\frac{4}{25}$ **25.** 4.53×10^4 **27.** 1.802×10^9
29. 176,000 **31.** 67,000,000,000
33. about 100,000,000 years **35.** Possible answers: 741,100,000 L; 7.411×10^8 L
37. 1.010 **39.** 0.77 **41.** $^{-}10.5$ **43.** G

Page 42

1. 6 **3.** 4 **5.** 11 **7.** 33 **9.** 64 **11.** 75
13. 50; 2 **15.** 37; % **17.** Mr.: 42; Mrs.: 41

Page 45

1. 49 **3.** 121 **5.** 400 **7.** 116 pennies
9. n^2 pennies **11.** Since $A = s^2$, $s = \sqrt{A}$. So, $s = \sqrt{144} = 12$. **13.** 100 **15.** 1.44
17. 10 **19.** 40 **21.** 60 **23.** 1.3 **25.** 4.5
27. 0.6 **29.** 0.3 **31.** 80 **33.** 100 **35.** 900
37. 3 and 4 **39.** 8 and 9 **41.** 6 and 7
43. 10 and 11 **45.** 11 and 12 **47.** 0 or 2
49. 100 mi

Page 47

1. 8.6 m **3.** 20 ft **5.** 0.35 cm **7.** Amy, Bill, Molly, Juan; Amy, Juan, Molly, Bill; Molly, Bill, Amy, Juan; Molly, Juan, Amy, Bill **9.** about 159 km **11.** 9 years old **13.** 40 posts

Page 50

1. 10, 5, 2.5, 1.25, 0.625, 0.3125
3. $\frac{3}{4}, \frac{3}{8}, \frac{3}{16}, \frac{3}{32}, \frac{3}{64}, \frac{3}{128}$
5. 6.2, 3.1, 1.55, 0.775, 0.3875, 0.19375
7. stage 5 **9.** 43,046,721; Possible answer: start with 3 and square the result 4 times.
11. Answers will vary. **13.** 862; 860; 900
15. 955; 960; 1,000 **17.** 0.54 **19.** 0.0005
21. 0.074 **23.** H

Page 53
1. A **3.** C **5.** B **7.** C

Page 55

1. 36.87% 3. Highlight those flavors only and check the circle graph icon.

Pages 56–57
1. integers **3.** binary
5. Possible answer: $^{-}0.25, \frac{-2}{8}$
7. Possible answer: $0.75, \frac{3}{4}$
9. Possible answer: 0.25 **11.** S = 25%, U = 75% **13.** 0.05 **15.** 0.64 **17.** 60%
19. 216° **21.** 54° **23.** 343
25. 64 **27.** 5.52×10^4 **29.** 156,000
31. 81 **33.** 400 **35.** 7 **37.** 9
39. Possible answer: $\frac{367}{1{,}000}$, 0.3670
41. 1.0×10^9

Page 59
1. C **3.** D **5.** C **7.** D **9.** B **11.** C

Chapter 3
Pages 64–65
1. 100g **3.** 180g **5.** $26; rounding
7. 240; clustering **9.** 65 to 70 points
11. 67 to 72 points **13.** No; cost is about $29.00; rounding. **15.** Yes; cost is about $22.00; rounding. **17.** 7 **19.** 160
21. 7,600 **23.** 3 **25.** No. The total cost is about $114.00. **27.** Yes. Clustering gives an estimate of 30 points. **29.** 1 decimal place
31. 4 decimal places **33.** 16 **35.** 125
37. 216 **39.** B

Page 68
1. 3.0 **3.** 0.28 **5.** 0.06 **7.** 0.02 **9.** 107.4
11. 0.00006 **13.** 10.32 **15.** 0.00444
17. 47.2 **19.** 26.4 **21.** 86.172
23. 112.2576 **25.** 69.92 **27.** 2.25
29. 0.04416 **31.** 85.1432 **33.** 0.2848
35. 7.106 **37.** 0.0405 **39.** 0.042
41. No. It should be about $1,000.
43. $174.57 **45.** Neither; both equal 0.8.

Page 72
1. 12.5 **3.** 6.2 **5.** 6.02 **7.** 6 **9.** 25.4
11. 0.325 **13.** 80.1 m **15.** 5.785 m
17. 16.4 mph **19.** 85.2 mph **21.** about 4
23. about 4 **25.** 24.5 sec per lap; yes
27. No. The payment is $373.79.

Page 75
1. −, ÷ **3.** ÷, +, exponent, − **5.** ×, −
7. 79 **9.** ÷, exponent, ×, +, −; 79
11. −, exponent, ÷, +; 54.16
13. +, −, exponent, −; 8 **15.** 9 **17.** 6
19. 21.18 **21.** 6 dimes and 4 nickels
23. 15 **25.** 12 **27.** 4 **29.** 19
31. B

Page 77
1. C **3.** C **5.** B **7.** C **9.** B

Chapter 4
Page 81
1. $\frac{1}{4}$ **3.** $\frac{19}{12}$, or $1\frac{7}{12}$ **5.** $\frac{31}{40}$ **7.** $\frac{9}{8}$, or $1\frac{1}{8}$
9. $\frac{1}{3}$ **11.** $\frac{1}{24}$ **13.** $\frac{19}{36}$ **15.** $\frac{1}{6}$ **17.** $\frac{2}{63}$
19. $\frac{1}{30}$ **21.** $\frac{13}{28}$ **23.** $\frac{1}{6}$ **25.** $\frac{5}{8}$ lb

Page 83
1. $6\frac{4}{5}$ **3.** $13\frac{5}{6}$ **5.** $15\frac{8}{15}$ **7.** $15\frac{1}{40}$
9. $10\frac{1}{24}$ **11.** $16\frac{19}{24}$ **13.** $4\frac{8}{21}$ **15.** $2\frac{5}{8}$
17. $8\frac{1}{4}$ **19.** $\frac{7}{10}$ **21.** $4\frac{1}{4}$ hr
23. $10\frac{5}{12}$ c; $4\frac{7}{12}$ c
25. Possible answer: $4\frac{1}{3} - 1\frac{5}{6}$

Page 85
1. 1 or $\frac{1}{2}$ **3.** 4 **5.** 10 **7.** $\frac{1}{2}$ **9.** $\frac{1}{2}$
11. $\frac{1}{2}$ **13.** about 9 lb **15.** about $17\frac{1}{2}$ hr
17. $\frac{5}{2}$ **19.** $\frac{25}{7}$ **21.** $1\frac{1}{3}$ **23.** 300 **25.** 50,000
27. D

Pages 90–91

1. $\frac{3}{10}$ **3.** $\frac{17}{30}$ **5.** $\frac{16}{21}$ **7.** $\frac{5}{7}$ **9.** $4\frac{1}{21}$ **11.** $\frac{3}{28}$
13. $\frac{32}{3}$, or $10\frac{2}{3}$ **15.** $\frac{132}{35}$, or $3\frac{27}{35}$ **17.** $8\frac{1}{3}$
19. $7\frac{7}{8}$ **21.** $15 \times \frac{1}{5} = 3$ **23.** $\frac{2}{3} \times \frac{5}{3} = 1\frac{1}{9}$
25. $\frac{1}{5}$ **27.** $\frac{9}{2}$ **29.** $\frac{4}{13}$ **31.** $\frac{10}{9}$, or $1\frac{1}{9}$
33. $\frac{3}{2}$, or $1\frac{1}{2}$ **35.** $\frac{22}{1}$, or 22 **37.** $\frac{1}{7}$
39. $\frac{9}{2}$, or $4\frac{1}{2}$ **41.** $\frac{68}{33}$, or $2\frac{2}{33}$ **43.** $\frac{4}{3}$, or $1\frac{1}{3}$
45. $\frac{11}{14}$ **47.** 45 in.
49. Yes. The numerator is always less than the denominator. **51.** Multiply the denominator by the whole number, add the product to the numerator, and place the sum over the denominator. **53.** 3,000 **55.** 6
57. 0.0885 **59.** 2 **61.** F

Page 93

1. 1,500 CDs **3.** 400 mi **5.** 16 years old
7. April 29 **9.** 840 magazines **11.** 3,000 kits

Page 95

1. B **3.** A **5.** C **7.** D

Chapter 5

Page 101

9. 8 **11.** 100 **13.** $^{-}21$ **15.** 60 **17.** 70
19. $^{-}7$ **21.** $^{-}47°$ **23.** $^{-}24$; Mark owes $24.
25. a, b **27.** a, c **29.** $1\frac{7}{10}$ **31.** $6\frac{5}{12}$
33. G

Page 105

1. $3 + 9 = n$; $n = 12$ **3.** $^{-}3 + 4 = n$; $n = 1$
5. $^{-}3$ **7.** $^{-}8$ **9.** $^{-}6$ **11.** 4 **13.** 22 **15.** 0
17. 10 **19.** $^{-}17$ **21.** $^{-}55$ **23.** $^{-}188$
25. 19 yards **27.** $^{-}7$; Rani dove 7 feet deeper than Sue. **29.** $^{-}18$ **31.** $^{-}10$ **33.** $\frac{9}{14}$
35. $\frac{7}{12}$ **37.** J

Page 108

1. $^{-}8$ **3.** 24 **5.** $^{-}24$ **7.** 240 **9.** $^{-}45$
11. $^{-}450$ **13.** $^{-}48$ **15.** $^{-}360$ **17.** $^{-}6{,}000$
19. $^{-}275$ **21.** 0 **23.** $^{-}425$ **25.** 4,125
27. $^{-}2{,}856$ **29.** $^{-}4$; $^{-}4$ **31.** $^{-}27$ **33.** 0
35. $^{-}6$ **37.** $^{-}25$ **39.** negative
41. Possible answer: The rules for the signs for multiplication and for division are the same.

Page 111

1. $^{-}12.0$ **3.** $^{-}19.3$ **5.** 6.0 **7.** $^{-}8\frac{1}{4}$
9. $^{-}21.6$ **11.** $^{-}1\frac{7}{8}$ **13.** $^{-}56.7$ **15.** $25\frac{7}{8}$
19. about $4 \times \$8 = \$32$ **21.** Possible answer: The rules are the same. Rational numbers include integers.

Page 113

5. 135 **7.** $^{-}13$ **9.** 183 **11.** $^{-}13\frac{1}{3}$
13. 11.733... **15.** $^{-}3.255$ **17.** 46.98
19. $\frac{^{-}5}{21}$ **21.** $9.1\overline{6}$; between 9 and 10
23. $^{-}202.1$; between $^{-}202$ and $^{-}203$ **25.** $^{-}8.63$; $^{-}8$ and $^{-}9$ **27.** $^{-}28.45$; $^{-}28$ and $^{-}29$
29. $633.00 **31.** $85\frac{3}{4}$ oz **33.** positive: $+ \times +$, $- \times -$, $+ \div +$, $- \div -$; negative: $+ \times -$, $- \times +$, $+ \div -$, $- \div +$

Page 115

1. A **3.** C **5.** E **7.** B **9.** B

Page 117

1. / **3.** °F is positive, °C is negative.
5. 50°F **7.** 14°F **9.** $^{-}22$°F

Pages 118–119

1. 15 to 18 **3.** 40 **5.** 30 **7.** 8 **9.** 61
11. 89.30 **13.** 6.1 **15.** 4.592 **17.** 28.1
19. 6.183 **21.** 8.6 **23.** 3.864 **25.** 24
27. 175 **29.** 19 **31.** $\frac{1}{12}$ **33.** $11\frac{13}{24}$ **35.** $2\frac{1}{3}$
37. $2\frac{7}{9}$ **39.** $15\frac{27}{40}$ **41.** $21\frac{5}{6}$ **43.** $\frac{1}{36}$ **45.** $11\frac{1}{5}$
47. $1\frac{3}{5}$ **49.** 12 **51.** $32\frac{1}{7}$ **53.** $^{-}14$ **55.** 55
57. 27 **59.** 27.1 **61.** $1\frac{1}{6}$, or $\frac{7}{6}$ **63.** 7
65. $^{-}2\frac{1}{6}$ **67.** 300 prizes **69.** 2,100 cards

Page 121
1. B **3.** C **5.** D **7.** A **9.** D **11.** D **13.** B **15.** B

Chapter 6

Page 125
1. $7 + n$ **3.** $n + 7^3$ **5.** $\frac{20}{4} + 6$ **7.** the sum of 78 and $^-7$ **9.** the sum of 59 and 4^2 **11.** t decreased by 19 **13.** 4^2 added to w times 8 **15.** $100x$ **17.** $6 - r$ **19.** $2.5y$ **21.** $r -$ \$3.25 **23.** An algebraic expression includes variables.

Pages 128–129
1. division **3.** addition **5.** 6 **7.** $^-4$ **9.** 12 **11.** 27 **13.** 3 **15.** 4 **17.** $^-11$ **19.** $\frac{^-1}{2}$ **21.** 248 **23.** $^-159$ **25.** 1,000 **27.** 109 **29.** 103 **31.** \$5.45 **33.** The value of $3 + 2$ is 5. The value of $x + 2$ varies, depending on the value of x. **35.** 7; Distributive **37.** $^-2$ **39.** $^-26$ **41.** $^-33$ **43.** $^-41$ **45.** D

Pages 132–133
1. $23r + 32s$ **3.** $^-3c - 2d$ **5.** $26.5a + 8b$ **7.** $3x + 20$ **9.** $t + 15$ **11.** $r + {}^-24$ **13.** $c + 5$ **15.** 0 **17.** $a + 2b$ **19.** $4x + 5.5$ **21.** $^-11m - n$ **23.** $^-0.14r + 9.6s$ **25.** $2n + 3n + 2.5n$; $7.5n$; \$28.50 **29.** $1\frac{2}{3}$, 2, $2\frac{1}{3}$ **31.** $2\frac{1}{2}$, 3, $3\frac{1}{2}$ **33.** 22 **35.** $^-18$ **37.** $^-7$ **39.** G

Pages 136–137
1. No; there is no common difference. **3.** 5 **5.** $^-2$ **7.** 175, 210, 245 **9.** 1, 4, 7 **11.** $9 + 4 \times 12 = 57$ **13.** $12 + 3 \times (n - 1)$; 45 **15.** $0.5 + 1 \times (n - 1)$; 11.5 **17.** 4, 2, 0 **19.** $\frac{1}{4} + \frac{1}{4} \times (n - 1)$; the sixteenth day **21.** No, there is not a common difference. **23.** 5 **25.** 1 **27.** 4 **29.** B

Page 139
1. A **3.** C **5.** E **7.** C **9.** D

Chapter 7

Page 143
1. h = number of hours worked; $h + 6 = 45$
3. c = total number of cars; $c - 39 = 29$
5. p = number of payments; $570 \div p = 47.50$
11. $x + 13 = 62$ **13.** $x \div 4 = 5.25$
15. $x - 63 = 312$

Page 147
1. $x = 58$ **3.** $n = 22$ **5.** $c = 24$ **7.** $r = 0.19$ **9.** $x = 5.0$ **11.** $n = 2$ **13.** $r = \frac{3}{6}$, or $\frac{1}{2}$ **15.** $n = {}^-5$ **17.** p = points; $p + 15 = 82$; $p = 67$ **19.** p = pounds; $p - 35.6 = 125.6$; $p = 161.2$ **21.** 67°, 113° **23.** $s =$ \$8,800 **25.** 6 **27.** 24 **29.** 7.7 **31.** 38 **33.** C

Page 149
1. $t = 3$ **3.** $n = 3$ **5.** $y = 9$ **7.** $t = 63$ **9.** $w = 82$ **11.** $n = 3$ **13.** $x = 27.6$ **15.** $h = 0.4$ **17.** $k = 243$ **19.** $n = {}^-8$ **21.** $30x = 120$; $x = 4$ **23.** $\frac{x}{6} = 7.80$; $x = 46.80$ **25.** $1{,}100 = 440t$, $t = 2.5$; $2\frac{1}{2}$ hours **27.** $\frac{s}{8} = 3\frac{1}{2}$, $s = 28$; 28 slices

Page 151
1. 3 shelves **3.** 11:45 A.M. **5.** 15 lb, 9 lb **7.** 173 women **9.** \$2.39

Pages 154–155
1. $n = 12$ **3.** $n = 21$ **7.** $8x = 40 \cdot 5$ **9.** $25t = 3 \cdot 50$ **11.** $5a = 0.75 \cdot 1.25$ **13.** $n = 10$ **15.** $p = 18$ **17.** $c = 9$ **19.** $x = 75$ **21.** $z = 0.25$ **23.** $t = 1.875$ **25.** $n = 2$ **27.** $a = 5.665$ **29.** $d = 20$ **31.** 50.25 seconds **33.** 180 hamburgers **35.** $2a + 8c$; 32.06 **37.** $a + 6c$; 23.03 **39.** add 7; 67, 74, 81 **41.** A

Page 157
1. C **3.** D **5.** B **7.** B **9.** B

Chapter 8

Page 163

1. $2x - 10 = 35$; $x = 22.5$; 22.5 ft
3. $3x + 1.75 = 22.75$; $x = 7$; \$7.00
5. about 8 cans **7.** soccer **9.** 28 members

Page 166

1. yes **3.** no **5.** no **7.** $m = 5$ **9.** $x = 12.5$
11. $f = {}^{-}1.8$ **13.** $p = {}^{-}2$ **15.** $x = 0.6$
17. $d = 2$ **19.** $i + i - 10.11 = \$58.33$; \$24.11
21. $r + r + r + r + 2 = 44$; $r = 10.5$;
$r + 2 = 12.5$; 12.5 ft, 10.5 ft, 10.5 ft, 10.5 ft
23. In the equation, replace the variable with the solution and perform the operations.
25. true **27.** true **29.** $n = {}^{-}3$ **31.** $n = 24$
33. H

Page 169

1. yes **3.** no **5.** yes **7.** no **9.** yes
11. $x \leq 4$ **13.** $x \neq 0$ **15.** $x = {}^{-}1$
17. $b + 30 < 52$ **21.** $x - 12 = 5$
23. A

Page 171

1. $n < 4$; 0, 1, 2, 3 **3.** $n > 4$; 5, 6, 7
5. $c \leq {}^{-}5$ **7.** $z \neq 3$ **9.** $c > 5$ **11.** $n \geq 3$
13. $x = 1$ **15.** $e = 7$ **17.** $y \neq 7$ **19.** $p \leq {}^{-}1$
21. $r \neq 3\frac{1}{2}$ **23.** $n < 80$; fewer than 80 in April; fewer than 40 in May **25.** $s > 93$; 94

Page 173

1. B **3.** A **5.** B **7.** C **9.** A

Chapter 9

Page 177

5. triangle; Quadrants I and IV **7.** Quadrant III; Quadrant I **9.** (P,34) or (34,P) **11.** (4,2)

Page 180

1. $\{{}^{-}2, {}^{-}1, 0, 1, 2, 3\}$; $\{{}^{-}4, {}^{-}2, 0, 2, 4, 6\}$
5. $\{(12,10), (14,8), (16,6), (18,4), (20,2)\}$
7. ${}^{-}8$, 0, 2, 6 **9.** ${}^{-}5$, ${}^{-}1$, 0, 2 **11.** $y = 125x$
13. (3,4), (3,2) **15.** $m = 5$ **17.** $z = {}^{-}2$
19. C

Page 183

1. no **3.** no **5.** $(1,{}^{-}1)$, (1,0), (1,1), (1,2), (1,3); not a function **7.** yes; possible pairs: (0,32), (10,50), (20,68) **15.** equation **17.** C

Page 187

1. (4,3) **3.** (4,24) **5.** (4,6) **7.** $(4,{}^{-}12)$
9. (1,7), (2,8), (3,9) **11.** (1,3), (2,6), (3,9)
13. (1,7), (2,9), (3,11) **15.** (1,7), (2,11), (3,15)
17. $y = 3x$ **19.** $y = \frac{1}{2}x$
21. $({}^{-}1,{}^{-}1)$, (0,0), (1,1) **23.** $({}^{-}1,1)$, $(0,{}^{-}1)$, $(1,{}^{-}3)$
25. (0,2), (1,3), (2,4) **27.** (0,2), (1,6), (2,10)
29. (0,20), (1,22), (2,24), (3,26), (4,28), (5,30); $y = 20 + 2x$ **31.** infinite number

Page 189

1. C **3.** B **5.** A **7.** E **9.** B

Page 191

1. (0,0)
3. The lines are parallel; they cross the y-axis at different points.
5. The lines are at the same angle.
7. Possible equation: $y = 2x - 5$

Pages 192–193

1. like terms **3.** inequality
5. $15 + 4 \times (n - 1)$; 39
7. $8 + 2 \times (n - 1)$; 20 **9.** $8 + {}^{-}2 \times (n - 1)$; ${}^{-}4$
11. $7.5 + {}^{-}2.5 \times (n - 1)$; ${}^{-}7.5$ **13.** $z = 3.6$
15. $a = 24.5$ **17.** $y = 3.9$ **19.** $x = 3$
21. $e = 1.5$ **23.** $x \leq 8$ **25.** $z \neq 5$
27. $m \geq {}^{-}3$ **29.** Possible answers: (2,8), (3,10), (4,12) **33.** $3x - 5 = 25$; $x = 10$; 10 books **35.** 40 min

Page 195

1. C **3.** D **5.** B **7.** B **9.** A **11.** A
13. D

Chapter 10

Pages 201–202

1. 10° **3.** 50° **5.** Yes. They both have a measure of 50°. **7.** $\angle 1$ and $\angle 3$, $\angle 2$ and $\angle 4$ **9.** 30° **11.** always **13.** always **15.** never **17.** No. Two angles must have the same measure. **19.** scalene **21.** isosceles **23.** $(0,{}^{-}1)$, $(2,1)$, $(4,3)$ **25.** $({}^{-}2,3)$, $({}^{-}1,4)$, $(0,5)$ **27.** B

Pages 204–205

1. always **3.** sometimes **5.** none **7.** line, rotational **9.** line **11.** $\frac{1}{2}$ turn, or 180° **13.** $\frac{1}{5}$ turn, or 72° **15.** square **17.** regular hexagon **19.** Possible answers: A, H, I, M, O, T, U, V, W, X, Y **21.** Possible answers: H, I, O, X **23.** Possible answers: H, I, O, X **25.** Answers will vary. **27.** Yes. Yes. Yes. Explanations will vary.

Pages 208–209

7. vertical reflection **9.** 90° clockwise rotation **13.** horizontal **15.** vertical **19.** reflection **21.** (horizontal) reflection **23.** a translation; a reflection or a rotation **25.** 4; 4 **31.** H

Page 211

1. translation **3.** reflection **5.** $A'({}^{-}3,5)$, $B'({}^{-}1,3)$, $C'({}^{-}1,0)$, $D'({}^{-}5,0)$, $E'({}^{-}5,3)$ **7.** $A'({}^{-}2,{}^{-}3)$, $B'({}^{-}1,3)$, $C'(2,1)$, $D'(2,{}^{-}3)$ **9.** $A'(4,0)$, $B'(3,{}^{-}6)$, $C'(0,{}^{-}4)$, $D'(0,0)$

Page 213

1. B **3.** A **5.** C **7.** D **9.** A

Chapter 11

Page 220

11. 11.25° **13.** parallel lines **15.** neither **17.** 8 **19.** 4 **21.** D

Page 223

5. Answers will vary **7.** No. A line goes on forever in two directions, so you cannot divide it into two congruent parts. **9.** a square **11.** Use a protractor to show that the lines form 90° angles.

Pages 226–227

1. scalene **3.** equilateral or isosceles **5.** right **7.** $\overline{UQ} \cong \overline{VZ}$, $\overline{UM} \cong \overline{VR}$, $\overline{MQ} \cong \overline{RZ}$; $\angle U \cong \angle V$, $\angle M \cong \angle R$, $\angle Q \cong \angle Z$ **9.** ASA **11.** SAS **13.** not enough information **15.** no; possible exception: an equilateral triangle **17.** Vertical angles are congruent. **19.** SSS: three sides match; SAS: two sides and included angle match; ASA: two angles and included side match

Page 231

11. Exercise 9; the three line segments did not form a triangle. **13.** The SSS, SAS, and ASA rules tell what sets of three parts you can use for the construction. **15.** pyramid **17.** rotation **19.** translation **21.** G

Page 233

1. C **3.** E **5.** B **7.** B **9.** B

Chapter 12

Page 237

1. triangle **3.** circle **5.** true **7.** False; no cylinders are polyhedrons. **9.** False; no polygons are polyhedrons. **11.** The areas for pyramids and prisms should not overlap. **13.** Yes; it is a solid in which all faces are polygons.

Page 240

1. 12 km **3.** 43 red shirts **5.** 28 games **9.** triangles **11.** triangles, square **13.** acute **15.** obtuse **17.** H

Pages 244–245

1. rectangular prism **3.** triangular prism **5.** no **7.** no **11.** 5 faces; 2 right triangles and 3 rectangles **13.** face F **15.** face A **17.** four colors

Pages 248–249
1. 3 faces **5.** 6 edges, 5 vertices visible; 3 edges, 1 vertex hidden **7.** c, e **9.** d **11.** pentagon **13.** triangle **21.** rectangle **23.** triangle **25.** SSS **27.** SAS **29.** J

Page 253
1. C **3.** B. **5.** B **7.** A **9.** C

Chapter 13
Page 258
1. yes **3.** no **5.** no **11.** 360° **13.** yes **17.** 8 **19.** 24 **21.** G

Page 260
7. red: 4; blue: 2 **9.** red: 6; blue: 4 **11.** 8 **13.** 2 **15.** 6 **17.** 8 **19.** 6 times

Page 263
1. triangle **3.** 216 **5.** Reduce the sides of the square by $\frac{1}{2}$. Replicate it 4 times. Rebuild by shading 3 of the squares. **7.** Answers will vary. **9.** 50, 25, 12.5, 6.25 **11.** 25, 12.5, 6.25, 3.125 **17.** F

Page 266
1. 2 branches; 4 branches **3.** 8 branches; 16 branches; 2^n branches **5.** decreases by 0.5 **7.** decreases by $\frac{1}{2}$ **9.** 8 squares **11.** The number of shaded squares doubles.
13. Possible fractals: fern leaf, cloud, tree
15. Answers will vary.

Page 269
1. C **3.** E **5.** C **7.** B

Page 271
1. $\angle B$ **3.** $\angle X'$

Pages 272–273
1. vertical angles **3.** perpendicular bisector **5.** 110° **7.** 70° **9.** Possible answers: $\angle A$ and $\angle C$, $\angle B$ and $\angle D$ **11.** $A'(^-3,^-2)$, $B'(^-3,0)$, $C'(^-1,0)$ **17.** SSS **21.** 24 edges **23.** 5 faces

Page 275
1. A **3.** B **5.** A **7.** A **9.** B **11.** A **13.** D

Chapter 14
Page 279
1. at the end of 6, 12, 18, and 24 min
3. 1 time **5.** $12\frac{1}{2}$ mi, 8 mi, $11\frac{1}{2}$ mi
7. $50 **9.** 2 times (at the end of Lisa's laps 12 and 24) **11.** Possible explanation: by drawing a number line to find the common multiples of 2 and 3

Pages 282–283
1. $132.00 **3.** $114.00 **5.** 38 students **7.** $0.99; $0.85; 10-lb box **9.** two pairs for $43.00 **13.** about $30,000 **15.** Answers will vary. **21.** G

Page 285
1. $3.52 to $3.20 is 1.1 to 1; pattern: multiply by 1.1 **3.** $1.60; $0.20 **5.** no; first mi = $3.00; second mi = $1.60; total for 2 mi = $4.60 **7.** $17.40

Page 288
1. *C* marked at about 4.5 or about 7.5
3. yes; $\frac{MT}{TN} = \frac{24}{15} = 1.6$ **5.** The intersection of any two diagonals makes a Golden Cut on each of those diagonals. **9.** $\frac{40}{100}$ **11.** $\frac{60}{100}$ **13.** $\frac{450}{100}$ **15.** $\frac{425}{100}$ **17.** yes **19.** yes **21.** H

Page 291
1. B **3.** C **5.** A **7.** C **9.** B

Chapter 15
Page 296
1. 20% **3.** 0.8% **5.** 0.12% **7.** 38% **9.** 15% **11.** 62.5% **13.** 3% **15.** 7%
17. A: 50%, B: 25%, C: $12\frac{1}{2}$%, D: $6\frac{1}{4}$%, E: $6\frac{1}{4}$%
21. 6 **23.** 117 **25.** yes **27.** yes **29.** B

Page 300
1. 6 **3.** 4.5 **5.** 11.75 **7.** 5,125 **9.** 8 **11.** 12 **13.** $0.26; $5.51 per hour
17. Possible answer: 10% of 10 is 1. **19.** 4
21. $\frac{3}{4}$ **23.** $\frac{1}{3}$ **25.** J

Page 303

1. 20% **3.** $p \cdot 36 = 9$; $p = 0.25$, or 25%
5. $\frac{18}{36} = \frac{n}{100}$; $n = 50$; 50% **7.** 25% **9.** 80%
11. 125% **13.** No; 10 is $66\frac{2}{3}$% of 15, and $66\frac{2}{3}\% < 75\%$. **15.** about 4% **17.** The proportion expresses that 2 is to 5 as n is to 100; the ratio "n to 100" is n%, the solution to the problem.

Pages 306–307

1. 60 **3.** 36 **5.** 10.5 **7.** 420 **9.** 70
11. 20 **13.** 100 **15.** 20 **17.** 34 **19.** 550
21. 60 students **23.** 940 students
25. Answers will vary. Problem should be appropriate for the following question: 35 is 20% of what number? **27.** yes **29.** no
31. G

Page 309

1. C **3.** D **5.** D **7.** A **9.** C

Chapter 16

Pages 314–315

1. yes; angles congruent and $\frac{7}{28} = \frac{9}{36}$
3. yes; angles congruent and $\frac{4.5}{22.5} = \frac{4.5}{22.5}$
5. 37.5 cm, 42.5 cm, 20 cm **7.** 4 in. × 6 in., 16 in. × 24 in., 20 in. × 30 in. **11.** $n = 12$
13. $y = 3$ **15.** 1.6 **17.** 41.5
19. B

Page 319

1. $x = 7\frac{1}{2}$ **3.** $n = 12$ ft **5.** 15 in.
7. 4 in. **9.** 23.2 cm
11. $l = 7.5$ cm, $w = 3$ cm, $h = 10.5$ cm
13. $l = 15$ ft, $w = 15$ ft, $h = 18$ ft
15. 1.5 ft × 1.5 ft × 1 ft

Page 322

1. 2.25 cm^2; 9 cm^2; 4 **3.** 15 m^2; 135 m^2; 9
5. No. They would need 15,552 $in.^2$
7. 12 m^3 **9.** 24 m^3 **11.** 50% **13.** G

Page 325

1. 7.5 in.; 7.5 in.; 5 in. **3.** 30 m; 13.75 m; 21.25 m **5.** $V_{small} = 2$ $units^3$; $V_{large} = 128$ $units^3$; 64 **7.** 3.375 **9.** 8-oz size; $\frac{16}{8} = 2$ and $2 \times \$1.25 = \$2.50$, $\frac{32}{8} = 4$ and $4 \times \$1.25 = \$5.00$ **11.** 2.5^3, or 15.625

Page 327

1. D **3.** B **5.** D **7.** A **9.** C

Chapter 17

Page 331

1. 8 mm, 12 mm, 8 mm, 12 mm **3.** 30 mm, 45 mm, 30 mm, 45 mm **5.** 10 mm, 9 mm, 19 mm, 7.5 mm, 12.5 mm **7.** 40 mm, 36 mm, 76 mm, 30 mm, 50 mm
11. 4.5 in. × 3 in.

Pages 336–337

1. 45 **3.** 4 **5.** 1.4 **7.** 2.4 **9.** 3.2 **11.** 15
13. 10 in.:20 ft, or 1 in.:2 ft
15. 10 in.:1,250 ft, or 1 in.:125 ft **17.** 82.5 ft, 30 ft **19.** 5 ft, 5 ft **21.** $x = 2$ **23.** $n = 17.6$
25. 3 cm **27.** 5 mm **29.** G

Page 340

1. 48 mi **3.** 2 mi **5.** 11 mi **7.** 36 mi
9. 3 mi **11.** 45 mi **13.** about 4.5 mi
15. 35 mi **17.** Find the straight-line distance between two points on a map. Use the map scale to write and solve a proportion and find the actual distance.

Page 343

1. $x = 21$ mm **3.** $x = 39$ mm **5.** $x = 4$ cm
7. 16 m **11.** 1.25 **13.** 0.625 **15.** 9:1
17. 49:16 **19.** 81:16 **21.** F

Page 345
1. Yes. Ratio of length to width is near 1.61. **3.** No. Ratio of length to width is 1.25 rather than 1.61. **5.** yes; $\frac{4}{2.5} = 1.6$ **7.** no; $\frac{12.5}{6.5} = 1.923$ **9.** no; $\frac{1.5}{0.75} = 2$ **17.** no; $\frac{7}{3} = 2.\overline{3}$

Page 347
1. D **3.** D **5.** B **7.** D **9.** D

Page 349
1. values for x, x', and y
3. You could use the fill down command.
5. $y' = 3.75$

Pages 350–351
1. unit **3.** proportional **5.** 415 **7.** about $0.98 **9.** 150% **11.** 24% **13.** 500% **15.** 25% **17.** 740 **19.** 22.5 **21.** $n = 9$ ft **23.** 128 cm^3; 1,024 cm^3; 8 **25.** 3.1 **27.** $93\frac{3}{4}$ mi **29.** $0.13; $6.63 **31.** 36 ft

Page 353
1. B **3.** C **5.** B **7.** C **9.** B **11.** C

Chapter 18

Pages 358–359
1. 45 **3.** 820 **5.** All entries in a given row are alike; it uses circles instead of numbers. **9.** 1, 2, 3, 4, 5, 6, 7; 15; n **11.** 1 2 3 4 5 6 7 6 5 4 3 2 1; put the next counting number in the middle, and count up to it and then down. **13.** 1, 3, 5; 12 + 11, or 23; $2n - 1$ **15.** 10 boxes **19.** $^-2$ **21.** $^-9$ **23.** $\frac{2.5}{5} = \frac{3}{6}$; yes **25.** G

Page 361
3. 1, 2, 4, 8, 16, 32; each is twice the sum for the previous row; 64 **5.** 1, 2, 3, 4, 5, 6, 7, 8, 9; 51; $n + 1$ **7.** Odd entries are shaded, but even entries are not. **9.** 10 ways

Page 363
1. diverge **3.** converge **5.** diverge **7.** August **9.** 960 lb **11.** No, you get $\frac{1}{16{,}000}$, because there is always a smaller number between the previous one and zero.

Page 367
1. They diverge. **3.** $\left(\frac{1}{6}\right)^0, \left(\frac{1}{6}\right)^1, \left(\frac{1}{6}\right)^2, \left(\frac{1}{6}\right)^3$
5. $1, \frac{1}{12}, \frac{1}{144}$ **7.** 1; 11; 121; 1,331 **9.** 3
11. 0 **13.** $\frac{1}{27}$ **15.** 0.25 **17.** 0.1 **19.** 0.375
21. $x = 30$ mm **23.** G

Page 369
1. B **3.** C **5.** A **7.** C **9.** B

Chapter 19

Page 374
1. 0.15 **3.** 0.5 **5.** $1.1\overline{6}$ **7.** R; $0.1\overline{6}$ **9.** T; 0.375 **11.** T; 0.75 **13.** R; $1.08\overline{3}$ **15.** R; $1.\overline{142857}$ **17.** 0.375 **19.** $0.\overline{8}$ **21.** $1.\overline{1}$ **23.** 1.625 **25.** 2.875 **27.** 0.625 = $0.63 **29.** $0.\overline{8}$ = $0.89 **31.** $12.63 per share **33.** 12.5 gal **35.** by dividing the numerator by the denominator and observing the pattern of the resulting decimal

Pages 376–377
1. $\frac{5}{8}$ **3.** $^-1\frac{1}{4}$ **5.** Possible answer: 1.56
7. Possible answer: $\frac{6}{8}$ **9.** Possible answer: $^-3\frac{1}{2}$
11. Possible answer: 0.855
13. Possible answer: 100.05
15. Possible answer: 1.65 **17.** 421.5 mi
19. Possible answer: $^-4$°C **21.** multiply by 3; 54 **23.** add 6; 41 **25.** converge **27.** B

Page 381
1. arithmetic **3.** geometric **5.** neither **7.** 31, 36 **9.** 29, 37 **11.** 24, 31 **13.** 0.0001, 0.00001 **15.** 0.192, 0.0384 **17.** $17.4 million **19.** 42 **21.** 1,000 **23.** 81 **25.** 64 **27.** 4; 16; 64; 256 **29.** $\frac{1}{2}, \frac{1}{4}, \frac{1}{8}, \frac{1}{16}$ **31.** A

Page 383

1. $\frac{1}{10^8}$ **3.** $\frac{1}{7^3}$ **5.** $\frac{1}{6^3}$ **7.** $\frac{1}{3^2}$ **9.** $\frac{1}{2^3}$ **11.** $\frac{1}{2^2}$
13. 10^{-1} **15.** 4^{-2} **17.** 6^{-4} **19.** 7^{-3}
21. 10^{-7} **23.** 10^{-5} **25.** 5^{-2} **27.** 9^{-2}, or 3^{-4}
29. negative exponent **31.** negative exponent **33.** $\frac{1}{4}$; 3 in. **35.** $\frac{1}{10^8}$

Page 385

1. C **3.** A **5.** B **7.** C **9.** B

Page 387

1. It represents the exponent. **3.** Enter $y = 6^\wedge x$ and then enter GRAPH. **11.** 1

Pages 388–389

1. diverge **3.** geometric **5.** 183 **7.** 1,830
9. 4 **11.** 6 **13.** 3 **15.** 7 **17.** 16
19. $\frac{2}{3}, \frac{4}{9}, \frac{8}{27}, \frac{16}{81}$ **21.** $\frac{1}{2}, \frac{1}{4}, \frac{1}{8}, \frac{1}{16}$
23. $\frac{5}{6}, \frac{25}{36}, \frac{125}{216}, \frac{625}{1,296}$ **25.** 0.75; terminating
27. $0.41\overline{6}$; repeating **29.** 0.3; terminating
31. 3.455 **33.** $^{-}5.5$ **35.** $^{-}8.4$ **37.** $\frac{1}{10^5}$
39. 6^{-7} **41.** 8 kinds **43.** $7.40 per hr

Page 391

1. D **3.** A **5.** B **7.** B **9.** A **11.** D

Chapter 20

Page 396

1. Possible answer: by surveying every tenth person **3.** giving every person in the population an equal chance **5.** systematic sample **7.** random sample **13.** 10^8
15. C

Page 398

1. Yes; 3-year-olds are not in the given population. **3.** by determining if the given population is represented **5.** biased because it includes children under 7 and over 12
7. biased because no girls are included
9. biased; they all selected the same brand
11. probably not biased **13.** biased
15. not biased **17.** biased **19.** not biased

Page 400

1. short answer **3.** multiple choice
5. numerical **7.** No; it is biased. **9.** No; it is biased. **11.** biased **13.** Answers will vary. **15.** Answers will vary.

Pages 404–405

1. Add the frequency in each interval to those above it. **3.** 10–19, 20–29, 30–39, 40–49
7. Eureka; 11 **9.** 33; 15 **11.** 20° **13.** $0.\overline{3}$
15. $0.08\overline{3}$ **17.** 0.4 **19.** C

Page 407

1. D **3.** C **5.** B **7.** B **9.** B

Chapter 21

Pages 412–413

1. 36°F **3.** 25°F **5.** thirties
7. Possible answer: There are more than twice as many people in the 20–29 interval than in the 0–9 interval. **9.** 79 yr **11.** 87; 23
15. Possible answer: Stem-and-leaf plot; you see all of the data set. **17.** 79 **19.** 84
21. not biased **23.** C

Page 416

1. mean: 157; median: 160; mode: 148
3. mean: 23; median: 26; mode: 14 **5.** 119.7
7. none **9.** Smoltz's; not near any other hit total **11.** $1,250
13. Mean or median; both are central values.
15. Answers will vary.
17. Answers will vary.

Pages 419–420

1. bar graph; categorical data **5.** Possible labels: horizontal, Items used; vertical, Percent
7. The sum of the percents is greater than 100%. **9.** in-line skates; skateboards
13. intervals of $50, starting at $0
15. intervals of 500 ft, starting at 0 ft
17. random **19.** A

Page 423

1. $99,022; $4,601 **3.** about 2 to 1
5. February **7.** The scales are different.

Page 425

1. B **3.** B **5.** C **7.** B **9.** D

Chapter 22

Page 429

1. $3 \times 2 = 6$; 6 outcomes **3.** $3 \times 3 \times 2 = 18$; 18 outcomes **5.** 19 choices **7.** 4 choices **9.** by using the Fundamental Counting Principle

Page 431

1. $\frac{1}{3}$ **3.** 0 **5.** $\frac{1}{3}$ **7.** 1 **9.** $\frac{1}{6}$ **11.** $\frac{1}{3}$; unlikely **13.** $\frac{3}{4}$ **15.** 3 is the number of favorable outcomes; 7 is the total number of possible outcomes.

Page 435

1. 36 combinations **3.** $\frac{2}{3}$ **5.** Shannon is 14 and Tamara is 7. **7.** $\frac{27}{28}$ **9.** 6 **11.** 120 **13.** 7.2; 7; none; 9 **15.** 6.1; 6.45; 8.6; 5.7 **17.** J

Pages 438–439

3. 6 permutations **5.** $3 \times 2 \times 1 = 6$ **7.** $\frac{1}{720}$ **9.** $5 \times 4 \times 3 = 60$ orders **11.** $9 \times 8 \times 7 \times 6 \times 5 = 15{,}120$ different ZIP codes **13.** In a combination, the order is not important; in a permutation, the order is important. **15.** $\frac{5}{6}$ **17.** $\frac{9}{5}$ **19.** 32 **21.** B

Page 441

1. A **3.** E **5.** C **7.** B **9.** D

Chapter 23

Page 446

1. 1: $\frac{13}{50}$, 2: $\frac{3}{10}$, 3: $\frac{1}{5}$, 4: $\frac{6}{25}$ **3.** 1: $\frac{1}{5}$, 2: $\frac{2}{5}$, 3: $\frac{4}{25}$, 4: $\frac{6}{25}$ **5.** Answers will vary. **7.** $\frac{1}{8}$; 5 times **9.** No. The mathematical probability is $\frac{1}{8}$. **11.** $\frac{19}{65}$

Page 449

1. Answers vary according to starting point and movement in the table. **3.** Answers vary according to starting point and movement in the table. **5.** 31.4 ft **7.** \$19 **9.** 8 years old

Page 452

1. a spinner with four equal sections **3.** a number cube or a spinner with 6 equal sections **5.** Use a number cube, with 3–6 meaning "over \$10." **9.** 600 ft^2 **11.** $\frac{1}{2}$ **13.** $\frac{3}{10}$ **15.** B

Pages 454–455

1. $\frac{1}{4}$ **3.** $\frac{1}{6}$ **5.** about 8.6% **7.** about 1.4% **9.** about 3.7% **11.** $\frac{\pi}{100}$, or about 3.1% **13.** Possible answer: found the area of each circle; wrote the ratio of shaded area to area of larger circle **15.** yard **17.** meter **19.** decimeter **21.** milligram **23.** $9 \times 8 \times 7 = 504$ ways **25.** G

Page 457

1. B **3.** B **5.** A **7.** D

Page 459

1. Click the icon representing a histogram. **3.** The data do not show change over time.

Pages 460–461

1. mathematical probability **3.** random sampling **5.** 99°F **7.** 80–89°F **9.** 28; 29; none **11.** The mean, 86, and median, 88, are both middle values. **13.** 24 outcomes **15.** $\frac{8}{50}$, or $\frac{4}{25}$ **17.** $\frac{7}{50}$ **19.** $\frac{19}{50}$ **21.** Answers will vary.

Page 463

1. B **3.** B **5.** A **7.** C **9.** C **11.** D **13.** B

Chapter 24

Pages 468–469

1. 1 km **3.** $\frac{1}{3}$ mi **5.** 1 in. **7.** $\frac{1}{2}$ in. **9.** 0.05 km **11.** $51\frac{1}{2}$ mi; $52\frac{1}{2}$ mi **13.** 82.65 km; 82.75 km **17.** estimate **19.** a **21.** 1 m **23.** $1\frac{7}{8}$ in.; the smaller the unit of measure, the more precise the measurement. **25.** 20 ft **27.** $13\frac{1}{2}$ in. **29.** 5 times **31.** G

Page 471

1. 175 km **3.** 130 km **5.** 125 km **7.** 50 km **9.** 110 km **11.** *ABCD,* 46 mi; *ADCB,* 58 mi; *ACBD,* 52 mi; *ACDB,* 58 mi; *ABDC,* 68 mi; *ADBC,* 74 mi **13.** *HBM,* 7 mi **15.** Determine all the possible routes, find the distance of each route, and identify the shortest route.

Page 475

1. no **3.** yes **5.** no **7.** 29 km **9.** 35 in. **11.** 13 ft **13.** 39 cm **15.** 103 m **17.** about 46.6 ft

Page 478

1. about 1,256 ft^3 **3.** 16 cm^3 **5.** 9 cans **9.** 17 **11.** 4.8 **13.** $\frac{4}{9}$ **15.** $\frac{5}{9}$ **17.** G

Page 481

1. 54 cm^2 **3.** 12.4 m^2 **5.** 5 ft^2 **7.** 25 m^2 **9.** 25.62 mm^2 **11.** $5\frac{5}{8}$ yd^2 **13.** $5\frac{1}{6}$ ft^2 **15.** 39 $in.^2$ **17.** $41.93

Page 483

1. D **3.** C **5.** B **7.** C **9.** A

Chapter 25

Page 489

1. 108 ft^2 **3.** 5,616 ft^2 **5.** 576 cm^2 **7.** 4 $in.^2$ **9.** 20 $in.^2$ **11.** 18 $in.^2$ **13.** 343 ft^2 **15.** 23 cm^2

Page 492

1. 150.7 m^2 **3.** 31.4 m^2 **5.** 6,681.8 m^2 **7.** 1,206 yd^2 **9.** by adding the areas of the bases and the area of the lateral surface **11.** 8 units; 4 square units **13.** 16 units; 16 square units **15.** $\frac{1}{4}$ in. **17.** 1 cm **19.** H

Page 496

1. 495 m^3 **3.** 8,412,950 ft^3 **5.** 1,092 m^3 **7.** $h = 6$ ft **9.** 175 cm^3 **11.** Both include the area of the base times the height; prism: $V = Bh$; pyramid: $V = \frac{1}{3}Bh$.

Page 499

1. 311 $in.^3$ **3.** 1,005 cm^3 **5.** 393 $in.^3$ **7.** 1,409 ft^3 **9.** 31,793 ft^3 **11.** about 550 $in.^3$ **13.** 2 ft × 3 ft, 1 ft × 4 ft **15.** 2 m × 4 m, 1 m × 5 m **17.** yes **19.** no **21.** D

Page 501

1. E **3.** A **5.** C **7.** C **9.** B

Chapter 26

Page 507

1. *w*: 5.5, 5, 4.5, 4, 3.5, 3, 2.5, 2, 1.5, 1, 0.5; *A*: 2.75, 5, 6.75, 8, 8.75, 9, 8.75, 8, 6.75, 5, 2.75 **5.** 12.5 yd × 12.5 yd **7.** 25 in. × 25 in. **9.** 82.5 km × 82.5 km **11.** Possible answers: 58 m, 32 m, 22 m **13.** It increases to a maximum and then decreases. **15.** 2 **17.** 24 **19.** about 47 ft^3 **21.** C

Page 511

1. length = 6 in.; width ≈ $9\frac{1}{2}$ in. **3.** length = 21 in.; width = 28 in. **5.** length 9 in., width 4.8 in. **7.** decrease of 0.4 in. **9.** any rectangle with any length or width **11.** 30% **13. a.** area increases **b.** area remains the same **c.** area decreases

Page 514
1. 80 boxes **3.** yes; $0.90 \times 450 = 405$
5. 547,500 gal **7.** $\frac{1}{4}$ **9.** $d = 15$ **11.** $d = 15$
13. about 4,522 in.^{3} **15.** about 1,922 in.^{3}
17. C

Pages 516–517
1. $r = 4$ in.; $h = 6$ in.; $V \approx 301$ in.^{3}
3. $r = 8$ in.; $h = 12$ in.; $V \approx 2{,}412$ in.^{3}
5. $r = 1.5$ in.; $h = 2.25$ in.; $V \approx 16$ in.^{3}
7. 1, 2, 3, and 4 **9.** The ratio is approximately equal to the scale factor cubed.
11. 8 ft, 8 ft, 8 ft, 8 ft **15.** Volume increases as height increases. **17.** The volume increases or decreases as the changing dimension increases or decreases.

Page 519
1. C **3.** C **5.** C **7.** B **9.** A

Page 521
1. The perimeter is twice as long. **3.** Drag the rectangle to a length of 4.5 in. and a width of 2.25 in. **5.** The perimeter is 3 times as long. The area is 9 times as large.

Pages 522–523
1. greatest possible error **3.** surface area
5. 21.25 km, 21.35 km **7.** 100.75 m, 100.85 m **9.** $6\frac{1}{8}$ mm, $6\frac{3}{8}$ mm **11.** 19 km
13. 6 km **15.** 10 ft **17.** 50 in. **19.** 34 yd
21. 938 m^3 **23.** P: dec; A: inc. **25.** 31.8 m^3
27. 3,974.1 m^3 **29.** 147.2 m^3
31. 750 cm^2 **33.** $V = 8$ times as large; $S = 4$ times as large

Page 525
1. D **3.** C **5.** A **7.** B **9.** A **11.** A

Chapter 27

Pages 530–531
1. \$2.10; \$32.10 **3.** \$0.65; \$10.65 **5.** \$19.64
7. \$52.70 **9.** \$11.60 **11.** \$117.20 **13.** 1.09
15. 1.10 **17.** 7% **19.** 5.1% **21.** \$17.50
23. 6% of the price **25.** \$240.00 **27.** \$12.00
29. Possible answer: Multiply the price by the sales tax rate. Add the tax to the price.
31. 0.07 **33.** 0.5 **35.** 1.125 **37.** \$0.48
39. \$2.04 **41.** J

Pages 534–535
1. \$27.00 **3.** \$101.15 **5.** \$116.47
7. \$80.00 **9.** 20% **11.** 50% **13.** 30%
15. \$154.08 **17.** \$19.17 **19.** \$27.02
21. Possible answer: 50% of \$20 = \$10
23. \$10.50 **25.** Possible response: A discount lowers the price. **27.** $\frac{7}{20}$ **29.** $\frac{3}{50}$
31. $\frac{8}{5}$ **33.** 12 **35.** 16 **37.** G

Page 538
1. \$25.50 **3.** \$1.12 **5.** \$28.30
7. \$49.50; \$99.00 **9.** \$74.25; \$123.75
11. \$86.63; \$136.13 **13.** \$16.80 **15.** \$59.50
17. \$21; 140% **19.** \$10; about 167%
21. \$4.50 **23.** about 206% **25.** The retail price is about 3 times the wholesale price.

Pages 541–542
1. \$285.00 **3.** \$17.50; \$320.00 **5.** \$17.50; \$355.00 **7.** $\$250 + \$250(0.07)t$ **9.** \$105.00
11. \$4,300.00 **13.** \$594.00 **15.** \$762.50
17. \$1,470.00 **19.** \$2,420.00 **21.** \$105.40
23. 7 years **25.** \$814.45; \$1,039.47

Page 545
1. 6 of each **3.** $d = rt$, $d = 3 \times 4 = 12$; 12 km
5. \$1.25 **7.** Taylor: 80 newspapers; Erik: 120 newspapers **11.** $\frac{3}{4}$ **13.** $\frac{3}{20}$ **15.** sometimes
17. always **19.** B

Page 547
1. B **3.** C **5.** C **7.** A **9.** D

Chapter 28

Page 551

1. a; as time increases, the distance increases.
3. Pictures should show an event where distance increases as time increases.

Pages 554–555

1. The temperature stayed the same, increased, stayed the same, decreased, and stayed the same. **3.** The temperature would have increased. **5.** the decreasing parts
7. The distance increased, became constant, and increased again. The speed was constant, decreased to zero, became constant, increased, and became constant again.
9. 0–5 min, or 25–30 min **13.** from March to April **15.** $3; $53 **17.** $1.20; $21.15
19. H

Page 557

9. Sheila's graph shows that the more coupons you use, the less you save.

Page 561

1. positive **3.** positive **5.** no correlation
7. The scatterplot would show no correlation.
9. $450 **11.** $525 **13.** B

Page 563

1. D **3.** B **5.** B **7.** B **9.** C

Page 565

1. Compound; it is worth more.
3. $4,537.50, $5,162.13

Pages 566–567

1. discount **3.** $2.28, $30.78 **5.** 5%
7. $22.75 **9.** 25% **11.** $91.00 **13.** 50%
15. $375.00; $875.00 **17.** a **21.** $1.24

Page 569

1. B **3.** B **5.** B **7.** C **9.** D **11.** C
13. B

A

B

C

D

M

N

O

P

Q

R

S

T

W

X

Y

Z

PHOTO CREDITS *Page Placement Key:* (t)-top (c)-center (b)-bottom (l)-left (r)-right (fg)-foreground (bg)-background (i)-inset

Harcourt Brace & Company: Page: iv (l) Weronica Ankarorn; iv (r) Eric Camden; v, vi (l) Weronica Ankarorn; vi (r) Sheri O'Neal; vii (l), vii (t) Harcourt Brace & Company; vii (br) Weronica Ankarorn; viii Harcourt Brace & Company; ix Weronica Ankarorn; x (l) Harcourt Brace & Company; x (t) Terry Sinclair; x (r) Weronica Ankarorn; xi (t) Richard Hutchings; xi (b), xii (t) Weronica Ankarorn; xii (b) Harcourt Brace & Company; xiii Victoria Bowen; xiv (l) Joe Brooks; xiv (r), xv (t) Harcourt Brace & Company; xv (b) Weronica Ankarorn; xvi (l) Sheri O'Neal; xvi (t) Harcourt Brace & Company; xvi (b) Ed McDonald; xvii Victoria Bowen; xviii Britt Runion; xviii (tr) Sheri O'Neal; xix (br) Harcourt Brace & Company; xix (l) Weronica Ankarorn; xx (l) Sheri O'Neal; xx (r) Harcourt Brace & Company; xxi (t) Ed McDonald; xxi (b) Weronica Ankarorn; 3, 4 Sheri O'Neal; 5,6 Harcourt Brace & Company; 11 (t) Victoria Bowen; 11 (b) Harcourt Brace & Company; 14 (li) Harcourt Brace & Company; 15 (ri), 24 Weronica Ankarorn; 25 Eric Camden; 27 Weronica Ankarorn; 35 (i) Eric Camden; 37 Britt Runion; 39, 40 Sheri O'Neal; 43 Weronica Ankarorn; 45 Harcourt Brace & Company; 46 Eric Camden; 47, 49 Weronica Ankarorn; 54 (c), 54 (b) Sheri O'Neal; 58 Eric Camden; 60 (i) Harcourt Brace & Company; 63 (t) Victoria Bowen; 63 (b) Eric Camden; 64 Sheri O'Neal; 66 Don Couch; 67 Sheri O'Neal; 68, 69, 70 Weronica Ankarorn; 71 Victoria Bowen; 73 (t) Sheri O'Neal; 74 (t) Weronica Ankarorn; 78-79 (bg), 78 (i), 79 (i) Harcourt Brace & Company; 80, 82 Victoria Bowen; 83 Sheri O'Neal; 85 Victoria Bowen; 86, 87 Weronica Ankarorn; 89, 90, 91, 92, 93 Victoria Bowen; 97 (i), 98 Weronica Ankarorn; 102 Sheri O'Neal; 103, 104 (t) Weronica Ankarorn; 104 (r) Victoria Bowen; 104 (l) Weronica Ankarorn; 106 Victoria Bowen; 107 Weronica Ankarorn; 109 Victoria Bowen; 111 Weronica Ankarorn; 112, 116, 120 (t) Victoria Bowen; 125 Weronica Ankarorn; 129 Sheri O'Neal; 130, 131 Weronica Ankarorn; 137 Sheri O'Neal; 140 (li) Ed McDonald; 142 Sheri O'Neal; 144 Weronica Ankarorn; 146, 149 Sheri O'Neal; 150 Harcourt Brace & Company; 151, 152, 155 Sheri O'Neal; 160 Weronica Ankarorn; 162 (t) Eric Camden; 163 Weronica Ankarorn; 166, 167, 168, 170, 171 Eric Camden; 175 (ri) Harcourt Brace & Company; 176 Terry Sinclair; 177 Weronica Ankarorn; 178 Charlie Burton; 183 Harcourt Brace & Company; 190 Eric Camden; 194 Harcourt Brace & Company; 196 (i) Ed McDonald; 200 Sheri O'Neal; 207 Harcourt Brace & Company; 210, 215 (ri), 216 Weronica Ankarorn; 218 (c) Eric Camden; 218 (b) Weronica Ankarorn; 228 Eric Camden; 234 (i) Harcourt Brace & Company; 238 Richard Hutchings; 241 (t) Weronica Ankarorn; 241 (c), 241 (bl) Don Couch; 241 (br) Weronica Ankarorn; 242 (t), 242 (c) Don Couch; 242 (b), 243, 246 Sheri O'Neal; 250 Weronica Ankarorn; 251 Don Couch; 254 (i) Eric Camden; 255 (ri) Victoria Bowen; 264 (tb), 270, 277 (ri) Weronica Ankarorn; 278, 279 Victoria Bowen; 280 Weronica Ankarorn; 281 (t) Don Couch; 281 (b) Victoria Bowen; 287 (l) Harcourt Brace & Company; 289, 292-293 (bg), 292 (i) Weronica Ankarorn; 294 Ed McDonald; 296 Sheri O'Neal; 298, 299, 301 Ed McDonald; 302 (l) Sheri O'Neal; 302 (r) Ed McDonald; 304 (l) Sheri O'Neal; 304 (r) Ed McDonald; 305 (l) Maria Paraskevas; 306 (c) Ed McDonald; 314 Victoria Bowen; 315 (t), 316 Weronica Ankarorn; 317, 320, 323 (t), 323 (b) Victoria Bowen; 323 (bg) Weronica Ankarorn; 330 Victoria Bowen; 332, 333 Weronica Ankarorn; 334 Victoria Bowen; 335 (t) Eric Camden; 336 Victoria Bowen; 342 Weronica Ankarorn; 343 Sheri O'Neal; 355 (i) Weronica Ankarorn; 356 (b) Eric Camden; 360 Weronica Ankarorn; 361 Sheri O'Neal; 363 Weronica Ankarorn; 366 Eric Camden; 372, 373 (t) Weronica Ankarorn; 373 (b) Eric Camden; 375 Ed McDonald; 377 Eric Camden; 379 Britt Runion; 380 (t) Sheri O'Neal; 381, 383 Ed McDonald; 386, 390 Eric Camden; 395, 398 (t) Victoria Bowen; 398 (b) Harcourt Brace & Company; 399 (t) Victoria Bowen; 399 (b) Eric Camden; 405 Don Couch; 409 (ti), 409 (bi) Weronica Ankarorn; 411 (b), 412, 414, 415, 417, 420, 421 Victoria Bowen; 422 Britt Runion; 427 (i), 428 Weronica Ankarorn; 429, 430 Eric Camden; 433 Weronica Ankarorn; 434 (r) Eric Camden; 438 (t) Weronica Ankarorn; 443 (li) Harcourt Brace & Company; 443 (ri) Weronica Ankarorn; 444 Don Couch; 445 Victoria Bowen; 448 Don Couch; 451 (t) Sheri O'Neal; 452, 454 Don Couch; 465 (ri), 466, 468 (l) Weronica Ankarorn; 470 Richard Hutchings; 473 Weronica Ankarorn; 475 Earl Kogler; 477 Don Couch; 479 Victoria Bowen; 480 Don Couch; 486, 487 Weronica Ankarorn; 488 (t) Victoria Bowen; 491 Britt Runion; 492 Weronica Ankarorn; 493 Eric Camden; 494 (t) Ed McDonald; 494 (b), 497, 498 Britt Runion; 502 (i) Sheri O'Neal; 505 (t) Weronica Ankarorn; 505 (b), 506 Ed McDonald; 507 Victoria Bowen; 508 Sheri O'Neal; 509, 512 Ed McDonald; 513 (t) Weronica Ankarorn; 524 Harcourt Brace & Company; 528 Sheri O'Neal; 529 (t) Harcourt Brace & Company; 529 (b) Sheri O'Neal; 530 Victoria Bowen; 532 (t) Harcourt Brace & Company; 532 (c) Sheri O'Neal; 532 (b), 533 (t) Allan Landau; 533 (b), 536 (l) Victoria Bowen; 537 (b) Allan Landau; 538 Victoria Bowen; 539 Allan Landau; 545, 548 (bi) Victoria Bowen; 550 Weronica Ankarorn; 553, 554 Eric Camden; 556 (t) Sheri O'Neal; 558, 564 (t) Weronica Ankarorn; 564 (c), 564 (b) Sheri O'Neal; 568 Harcourt Brace & Company; Facing H1 (l) Sheri O'Neal; Facing H1 (r), H1 (tl) Victoria Bowen; H1 (tr) Weronica Ankarorn; H1 (b) Eric Camden; H31, H33, H34, H35, H38, H39, H42 Harcourt Brace & Company; H83 (t) Beverly Brosius; H83 (b), H86 Sheri O'Neal.

Other: Cover: D. Boone/Westlight. Page: 14-15 (bg) Lori Adamski/Tony Stone Images; 14 (ri) The Image Bank; 15 (li) Andre Gallant/The Image Bank; 18 Wyatt McSpadden/McSpadden Photography; 20 Glenn James/NBA Photo; 23 Christoph Burki/Tony Stone Images; 26 Alfred Pasieka/SPL/Photo Researchers; 28 Focus on Sports; 34-35 (bg) The Stock Market; 34 (i) Index Stock Photography; 44 Superstock; 60-61 (bg) Wide World Photos; 61 (i) Kevin Hatt/The Image Bank; 73 (c) Tony Garcia/Tony Stone Images; 74 (b) Myrleen Ferguson/PhotoEdit; 84 David Young-Wolff/PhotoEdit; 88 Kevin Morris/Tony Stone Images; 96-97 (bg), 96 (li), 96 (ri) William R. Sallaz/Duomo; 99 Richard Laird/FPG International; 122-123 (bg) Alex Bartel/SPL/Photo Researchers; 122 (li) Walter Bibikow/The Image Bank; 122 (ri) Michael Keller/FPG International; 127 Tony Freeman/PhotoEdit; 134 Peter Garfield/The Stock Market; 135 The Granger Collection, New York; 140-141 (bg) Lou Jones/The Image Bank; 140 (ri) P&G Bowater/The Image Bank; 141 (i) Michael Goldman/FPG International; 145 (c) Frank Lawrence Stevens/Nawrocki Stock Photo; 145 (b) William Nawrocki; 148 John Kelly/The Image Bank; 154 Damian Strohmeyer/Sports Illustrated; 158-159 (bg) Chris Trotman/Duomo; 162 (b) Mike Dobel/Masterfile; 165 Didier Dorval/Explorer/Photo Researchers; 174-175 (bg) Jim Cummins/FPG International; 174 (i) Superstock; 175 (li) Scott Markewitz/FPG International; 179 The Granger Collection, New York; 181 Jay Freis/The Image Bank; 186 Ward Burton/Focus on Sports; 196-197 (bg) David Sutherland/Tony Stone Images; 196-197 (bg) Stuart McClymont/Tony Stone Images; 202 Kay Chernush/The Image Bank; 204 Patti Murray/Animals Animals; 214-215 (bg) Paul Steel/The Stock Market; 214 (i) Kunio Owaki/The Stock Market; 215 (ti) Richard Berenholtz/The Stock Market; 215 (bi) Kunio Owaki/The Stock Market; 222 Tony Freeman/PhotoEdit; 224, 224 (i) Leo De Wys, Inc./Steve Vidler; 225 Michele Burgess/The Stock Market; 229 Photri; 234-235 (bg) Michael A. Keller/The Stock Market; 235 (i) Marcus Matzel/FotoArchive/Black Star; 236 Telegraph Colour Library/FPG International; 239 The Granger Collection, New York; 254-255 (bg) The Lowe Art Museum, The University of Miami/Superstock; 255 (ti) National Museum of Art, Washington, DC/Art Resource, NY; 255 (bi) Christie's Images/Superstock; 256 Jim Harrison/Stock, Boston; 257 (tr) Adam Woolfitt/Woodfin Camp & Assoc.; 257 (c) M.C. Escher's "Symmetry Drawing E 56" ©1997 Cordon Art-Baarn-Holland. All rights reserved.; 257 (b) The Granger Collection, New York; 259 (t) Deborah Davis/PhotoEdit; 259 (b) Scott Berner/Photri; 261 Rich Iwasaki/Tony Stone Images; 262 Steven Needham/Envision; 264 (tl) Steve Solum/Bruce Coleman, Inc.; 264 (tr) Rod Planck/Tony Stone Images; 264 (cl) Eric Crichton/Bruce Coleman, Inc.; 267 Larry West/Bruce Coleman. Inc.; 276-277 (bg) Romilly Lockyer/The Image Bank; 276 (i) Tim Davis/Photo Researchers; 277 (li) Bruce Forster/Tony Stone Images; 282 Bob Daemmrich/Stock, Boston; 284 Eric Draper/Wide World Photos; 286 The Museum of Modern Art, New York; 287 (r) Erich Lessing/Art Resource; 305 (r) NASA/Media Services Corp.; 306 (tr) Patti McConville/The Image Bank; 310-311 (bg) Alex Bartel/FPG International; 310 (i) Murray & Associates/Picturesque Stock Photo; 312 David Ball/The Stock Market; 315 (b) M & E Bernheim/Woodfin Camp & Assoc.; 321, 321 (i) SteveElmore/The Stock Market; 328-329 (bg) Rainer Grosskopf/Tony Stone Images; 328 (i) Thomas Brase/Tony Stone Images; 329 (i) Rainer Grosskopf/Tony Stone Images; 335 (b) Tektoff-Meriux, CNRI/SPL/Photo Researchers; 337 Superstock; 338 The Granger Collection, New York; 344 (c) Vic Thomasson/Tony Stone Images; 344 (l) Ed Carlin/Archive Photos; 345 Lori Adamski Peek/Tony Stone Images; 354-355 (bg) Rex A. Butcher/Tony Stone Images; 354 (i) Bruce Byers/FPG International; 356 (t) David Young-Wolff/PhotoEdit; 357 The Granger Collection, New York; 358 John Feingersh/Superstock; 359 Chip Henderson/Tony Stone Images; 362 Superstock; 370-371 (bg) Harald Sund/The Image Bank; 376 Kevin Morris/Tony Stone Images; 380 (b) Professor Stanley Cohen/SPL/Photo Researchers; 382 NIBSC/SPL/Photo Researchers; 392-393 (bg) Cynthia Johnson/Gamma Liaison; 392 (li) William Whitehurst/The Stock Market; 392 (ri) Jonathon Nourok/Tony Stone Images; 393 (i) Elderfield/Liaison; 394 Ford Motor Company/FPG International; 396 Walter Chandoha; 397 Don Smetzer/Tony Stone Images; 403 James Levin/FPG International; 404 (t) Stephen J. Krasemann/DRK; 404 (b) Renee Lynn/Photo Researchers; 408-409 (bg) Jeff Zaruba/Tony Stone Images; 408 (i) Hans Peter Merten/Tony Stone Images; 410 NASA/Peter Arnold, Inc.; 411 (t) P&G Bowater/The Image Bank; 426-427 (bg) Mark Tomalty/Masterfile; 426 (i) Bokelberg/The Image Bank; 431 Roy Morsch/The Stock Market; 434 (l) Ian Shaw/Tony Stone Images; 436 G. Robert Bishop/Tony Stone Images; 437 John Eastcott/YVA Momatiuk/Woodfin Camp & Assoc.; 438 (b) Bo Zaunders/The Stock Market; 442-443 (bg) Ted Levin/Animals Animals; 442 (ti) Michio Hoshino/Minden Pictures; 442 (bi) Frans Lanting/Minden Pictures; 446 Frank Cezus/FPG International; 449 Dale Rosene/Bruce Coleman, Inc.; 450 (l) Jeff Hunter/The Image Bank; 450 (r) Jeff Foott/Bruce Coleman, Inc.; 451 (b) Richard Mackson/FPG International; 453 A & J Verkaik/The Stock Market; 464-465 (bg) JP Williams/Tony Stone Images; 464 (i) G K & Vikki Hart/The Image Bank; 465 (li) Randy Wells/Tony Stone Images; 468 Aaron Haupt/Photo Researchers; 474 Thomas Zimmerman/Tony Stone Images; 476 Timothy Hursley/The Arkansas Office; 484-485 (bg) NASA; 485 (i) NASA/Photo Researchers; 488 (b) Will & Deni McIntyre/Photo Researchers; 490 (t) Alan L. Detrick/Photo Researchers; 490 (b) Superstock; 495 David Brownell Photography; 502-503 (bg) Amy Reichman/Envision; 503 (i) Daryl J. Solomon/Envision; 513 (b) Andrew Syred/SPL/Photo Researchers; 515 Don Spiro/Tony Stone Images; 526-527 (bg) Joachim Messerschmidt/FPG International; 526 (i) Chuck Savage/The Stock Market; 536 (r) David Young-Wolff/PhotoEdit; 537 (t) Michael Newman/PhotoEdit; 544 Cleo/PhotoEdit; 548-549 (bg) Walter Iooss/Sports Illustrated; 548 (ti) Kaz Mori/The Image Bank; 549 (i) David Madison; 552 Jeff Greenberg/PhotoEdit; 556 (b) Superstock.

ART CREDITS

Joanne Burger 2, 12, 340, 467; Karen Dunaitis-Blaise 254; GeoSystems 338, 339; Daphne Hewett 110, 133; Darrin Johnston 17; Dave Jonason 38, 40, 48, 247; Calos LaTorre 4, 7, 159, 237, 244, 352, 397, 458, 469, 524, 534, 541, 567; Tom Powers 287, 288; The Quarasan Group, Inc 197, 531; Rob Schuster 24, 219, 224, 341, 342, 446, 453-455, 469, 486, 550, 551, 553, 562; Geoffrey Smith 41, 48, 62, 294, 348, 394,420, 439, 455; Steven Stankiewicz 100, 227, 339, 340, 342, 345, 421, 474, 475, 477, 480, 562; Blake Thornton 23, 37, 124, 153, 282, 285, 318, 520; Tim West 123, 293, 374, 527.

$m\angle ABC = 45^\circ$; $12\% \times n = 75$; 1,

$7x + 2x + 5 = 9x + 5$; $-1.2 + {}^{-}3.45$;

$c + 2.8 = 4.1$; $y = 2x + 4$; $A = \pi r^2$

$7^3 = 343$; $7x + 2x + 5 = 9x + 5$

$c + 2.8 = 4.1$; $12\% \times n = 75$; 1, 1, 2, 3, 5, 8,

$7x + 2x + 5 = 9x + 5$; $-1.2 + {}^{-}3.45$; $\frac{n}{100} = \frac{81}{300}$

$c + 2.8 = 4.1$; $12\% \times n = 75$; 1, 1, 2, 3, 5,

$m\angle ABC = 45^\circ$; $y = 2x + 4$;

$c + 2.8 = 4.1$; $12\% \times n$